Java™ Power Tools

John Ferguson Smart

Beijing • Cambridge • Farnham • Köln • Paris • Sebastopol • Taipei • Tokyo

Java™ Power Tools
by John Ferguson Smart

Printed in the United States of America.

Published by O'Reilly Media, Inc., 1005 Gravenstein Highway North, Sebastopol, CA 95472

O'Reilly books may be purchased for educational, business, or sales promotional use. Online editions are also available for most titles (*http://safari.oreilly.com*). For more information, contact our corporate/institutional sales department: (800) 998-9938 or *corporate@oreilly.com*.

Editor: Mike Loukides
Production Editor: Loranah Dimant
Production Services: GEX, Inc.
Cover Designer: Karen Montgomery
Interior Designer: David Futato
Illustrator: Robert Romano

Printing History:
April 2008: First Edition

ISBN: 978-0-596-52793-8

[C]

1207602808

This book is dedicated to my wonderful wife Chantal, and my two lovely boys, James and William, who are my constant source of inspiration, wonder, and joy.

Table of Contents

Part VII. Issue Management Tools

Part VIII. Technical Documentation Tools

Foreword

Designing, coding, and deploying working Java applications isn't easy. Doing it in a predictable manner rapidly with an acceptable level of quality is even harder. In addition to having to understand what stakeholders want or the varying skills of team members or even the myriad web, data access, and utility frameworks one can choose from, you've got to actually manage the development process itself!

The coding of requirements is challenging enough, but as anyone who's ever delivered a working application knows, in the grand scheme of things, that's one sliver of the development process—in fact, some may say that's the easiest part. Think about all the techniques and processes that aggregate up to produce a software application.

First, you've got to figure out how to deliver the working application in a predictable manner. At a high level, this means three things: tracking changes to source code assets, keeping up with any uncovered issues, defects, or feature requests, and assembling the application in a reliable and repeatable manner.

Next, you're going to want to actually ensure the application under development actually works—ideally *during* development. This means writing tests early. Of course, this process is easier said than done. Although arguably there are few standard testing frameworks from which to chose, there is a cornucopia of associated tools that accelerate writing developer tests by addressing specific challenges.

What's more, as the code base grows, you'll probably want to understand what's being coded and how well it's being developed. Although tests cancertainly verify code functionality, you may also want lighter-weight tools that can report on various metrics, such as complexity, coding standards, or even the coverage of tests.

Of course, if you've got a mechanism for assembling your application in a repeatable and reliable manner, it makes sense to augment this process by running tests and even analysis tools. What's more, given that you want to produce working code quickly, it makes sense to assemble the application *often*—in fact, assembling it continuously facilitates discovering issues as they arise.

Finally, you're going to want to enable easy maintenance of the code base so that features can be added often—in the same rapid and repeatable manner that the application was built.

John has assembled what I think is the "A" list of tools and techniques that will help you meet each and everyone of the challenges above. In fact, John presents multiple choices in some cases, giving you the opportunity to decide which tool works best for you. Whether you decide to use Ant or Maven for delivering a working application in a predictable manner, TestNG or JUnit for early developer testing, PMD or FindBugs for code analysis, or CruiseControl or Luntbuild for Continuous Integration, this book addresses the fundamental techniques for effectively employing these tools (and a multitude of others as well).

Rapid development of Java applications (which have an acceptable level of associated quality) is still hard as ever; however, after reading John's magnum opus on the tools and techniques that ultimately enable predictability, confident, and accelerated delivery in a software development process, you'll find that designing, coding, and deploying high-quality Java applications rapidly just got a whole lot easier.

—Andrew Glover, *President, Stelligent Incorporated*

Preface

> Here is Edward Bear[*] coming downstairs now, bump, bump, bump, on the back of his head, behind Christopher Robin. It is, as far as he knows, the only way of coming downstairs, but sometimes he feels that there really is another way, if only he could stop bumping for a moment and think of it.
>
> —"We are introduced to Winnie-the-Pooh and some bees, and the stories begin," *Winnie the Pooh*, A. A. Milne

Thus does A. A. Milne introduce that classic character of children's literature, Winnie the Pooh. As you can see, Winnie the Pooh seems to have some issues with the way he goes downstairs (we probably wouldn't be too far off if we were to speak of "pain points").

Software development sometimes feels like this. It is easy to get so bogged down in the details, under the pressure of tight deadlines and changing requirements, that you forget that there might just be a better way. A high number of bugs, a difficult integration process, long and painful builds, and poor project visibility become an accepted part of the developer's life.

The good news is that there are in fact many easy ways to improve your software development lifecycle.

A judicious use of tools can go a long way in boosting developer productivity. For example, many distributed development teams use nothing more sophisticated than a CVS or Subversion repository for storing application code and a mailing list for discussion. Imagine a system in which, whenever someone commits a change, issues are automatically closed or updated based on the commit comment. The issue management system then automatically notifies the issue owner of the change of status. Meanwhile, a dedicated build server detects the commit, builds and tests the system, and notifies the developer of any failures. In a few relatively simple steps, you've taken your development platform to a new level of reactivity and responsiveness.

[*] For nonnative English readers: Edward Bear is a round-about way of saying "Teddy Bear." In the original book, this text is accompanied by a drawing of Christopher Robin, a boy of about four years old, going down a flight of stairs dragging his teddy bear behind him.

This is just a first step. Soon you will be integrating automatically running unit and possibly integration tests, code coverage tools, style checking tools, and more to create a highly reactive, informative, finely tuned project infrastructure.

Tools are the key to making such an infrastructure work efficiently. Once you start to adopt a set of SDLC tools that suit your project and your organization, you will see a revolutionary shift in a groups development practices. Agile development authors such as Alistair Cockburn rightly point to optimal communication as being the cornerstone of productive development. Developing in a team without continuous integration is like rock climbing without a rope. In addition, developing in a team without collaboration and connective development infrastructure is like developing in a boring beige office space where everyone comes to work on time, enters a closed office, closes the door, and starts programming without ever stopping to have meetings. In other words, programming without a good set of SDLC tools is very much the equivalent of fighting a modern war with swords and armor—the adoption of SDLC tools is a generational shift, the programmers just coming into the workforce will never know an alternative, but the programmers who haven't experienced this shift are in danger of missing the trend altogether.

Now you shouldn't go thinking that SDLC tools are only for large teams or big organizations. They aren't. In fact, most SDLC tools are easy to setup, and almost all organizations can benefit, even a small outfit with only two or three developers.

Most of these tools and techniques are not particularly difficult to put into place, but they do require a minimum of effort, to step back and take a long, hard look at your current practices. Chances are, there are things that can be improved.

This book is part of the O'Reilly Power Tools series, which began with the illustrious Unix Power Tools back in 1993. It has no relation to the "Java Power Tools" library (*http://www.ccs.neu.edu/jpt/*), which is a software research project in the Java GUI field, conducted by College of Computer & Information Science at the Northeastern University, Boston, under the direction of Richard Rasala.

How This Book Is Organized

One of the most characteristic traits of the open source (*http://opensource.org*) Java world is choice. It seems that, for any given task, there are always at least two open source tools that can do the job. To reflect this, I have tried to give a representative survey of the available open source tools for each area of software development that we cover. The book does not try to "sell" any one tool, or even any one tool in each domain. On the contrary, we try to give readers enough information so that they can decide for themselves which tool is the most appropriate for their particular organization, and give enough practical information to get them up and running.

This book is organized into sections, with each section covering a particular aspect of the software development lifecycle (or SDLC). With each section, we look at a number of available tools that can be used to improve this aspect of the SDLC.

Build Tools

In the first section, we cover possibly the most fundamental tool of all (after the compiler and the IDE, that is): the build tool. Indeed, when used well, the build tool becomes the cornerstone of your SDLC process. It is this tool that coordinates, federates, and binds the other SDLC tools together into a single, coherent process. And the build tool helps to ensure that your project can be built on any machine, in any environment.

In the Java world, two tools dominate this area. The first is Ant, the traditional Java build tool, which uses a straightforward procedural approach and benefits from a very large user base and a rich set of extensions. The second is Maven 2, which uses a powerful, declarative approach to project build management and, as we will see, goes much further than being a simple build tool. We will look at each of them in some detail in this section.

Version Control Tools

The second section covers that other fundamental component of any software development infrastructure: a version control system not only provides critical backups of your source code, it also lets developers work together on the same project without getting in each other's way. Version control systems also allow you to identify versions and coordinate releases and (if necessary) rollbacks. Finally, as we will see in Part VIII, it is a cornerstone of any Continuous Integration environment.

In this section, we will look at the two most prominent open source version control tools on the market: CVS and Subversion.

Unit Testing

Unit testing is another important best practice of modern software development. Although testing is certainly not new in itself, unit testing, and practices such as Test-Driven Development, have been gaining popularity over recent years. Not only does proper unit testing help ensure that your code works; it also fosters cleaner, more modular, and better designed code. Automated unit testing takes this a step further. By simply integrating your unit tests into your standard build process, and running them automatically with every build, you can go a long way toward increasing the quality and reliability of your code.

Writing tests is good, but it is even better to be sure of what code you are actually testing. Test coverage tools help you check how much of your application is actually being executed during your unit tests. This in turn helps you identify untested code and improve the overall quality of your tests.

In this section, we will cover the latest tools in the unit testing domain, including JUnit 4 and TestNG, and see how these tests can be integrated smoothly into the build process. We also will look at how to verify test coverage with Cobertura, a powerful open source coverage tool.

Integration, Load, and Performance Testing

Unit testing is not the end of the story as far as testing goes. This section looks at other testing techniques such as integration, load and performance, and user interface testing. All of these are important, and all can benefit from being integrated into the build process.

In this section, we will see how to integrate performance tests into your unit tests, how to load-test your application, and how to automatically test web services, Swing interfaces, and web interfaces.

Quality Metrics Tools

It is important to be able to measure the quality of your code in objective terms. Code quality has a direct bearing on the number of bugs and the ease of maintenance later on. Code quality metrics can also be a good way to bring inexperienced developers up to speed with coding conventions and best practices. This section looks at a range of automated tools that measure different aspects of code quality, including CheckStyle, PMD, FindBugs, and Jupiter.

Technical Documentation Tools

A professional project needs professional documentation. A significant part of this documentation can (and should) be generated automatically, based on the source code and comments. This is the most reliable way to get consistently up-to-date technical documentation. This section describes tools that can help you generate good technical documentation without having to spend too much effort writing and maintaining it.

Issue Management Tools

We will look at that vital communication tool in the SDLC, the issue tracking system. Of course, issue tracking systems can be used by testers to raise bugs and by developers to document bug fixes. But they can also be used to help organize and document releases, to plan iterations, and to assign work tasks to team members.

There are literally hundreds of issue tracking systems out there, both open source and commercial. In this section, we will look at two of the more interesting open source solutions seen in the Java world. The first is Bugzilla, the original open source issue tracking system. The second is Trac, which excels by its excellent Subversion integration and its innovative project management and wiki features.

Continuous Integration Tools

Finally, we look at a tool to wrap it all up together under a single process. This is the proverbial "one tool to rule them all." This process is called continuous integration.

In software development, it is a common observation that the longer you wait to integrate your team's code, the harder it gets. Continuous Integration is based on the idea that you can greatly facilitate this process by committing small changes regularly, and then running automatic builds whenever code changes are committed. Whenever a developper commits new or modified code to the source code repository, the build server checks it out and runs a build. In the very least, this makes sure that the modifications compile correctly. However, why stop at simply checking that everything compiles? While you're at it, you might as well check that all the unit tests still run not forgetting, of course, the integration, performance, and user interface tests.

Indeed, virtually all of the tools and techniques that we have discussed above can benefit from being run automatically on a regular basis.

Although this sort of integration is certainly possible with a well-tailored shell script and a cron job, nowadays there are a lot of tools that can save you a great deal of time and effort in this area. In this section, we will be looking at some of the more interesting open source CI tools: Continuum, CruiseControl, LuntBuild, and Hudson.

Who Should Read This Book

This is, fundamentally, a techie book. It is a hands on tour of a wide range of tools, for people who like to get their hands dirty.

If you are a Java developer, these tools can help to improve your development practices, and make your life easier in the process. Lead developers, architects, and people interested in the wider picture will be able to glean from these pages some useful ideas about improving your project infrastructure and best practices. You will learn about the different build tools of the Java world. You will learn how to set up a version control server or a Continuous Integration server using open source tools. You will find tools to support your coding standards and design recommendations, and automatically generate high-quality technical documentation. You will find out how to get the most out of your unit and integration tests.

Readers are expected to have a basic knowledge of Java and XML. Many build servers run on Linux boxes, so there will be a mixture of Windows and Linux examples, when operating systems issues are discussed. No prior experience of any of the tools is required.

What This Book Doesn't Cover

This book cannot come close to covering all the good software tools on the market. Some aren't here for lack of space, or simply because I wasn't familiar enough with them to do them justice.

This book is limited to open source tools. This is not because there are not commercial tools in the software development lifecycle field: there are. Nor is it because these tools aren't worth considering for your project or organization; again, they may be. No, commercial tools are off limits for a simple question of scope (I did want to finish this book one day), and, to be fair to everyone, it would be hard to include one tool without including all the others.

Having said this, there are a few excellent commercial tools on the market which it would be a shame not to mention. These commercial tools are often of very high quality, with many innovative features. And, as in any field, competition is always an excellent driver for innovation.

Two organizations that deserve special mention in this area are Atlassian and JetBrains. Atlassian is behind the very popular JIRA issue tracking system. They also market Bamboo, an innovative Continuous Integration server, as well as a set of integrated tools such as Clover, a test coverage tool; FishEye, a tool that helps you to visualize the contents of your source code repository; and Crucible, a code review tool.

JetBrains is the author of the well-known and highly innovative Java IDE IntelliJ. Recently, JetBrains have also developed TeamCity, a next-generation Continuous Integration server that builds and tests code *before* it is committed to version control.

At the time of this writing, both of these companies offered free licencing arrangements for open source products.

Contributing Authors

This book was not written alone. Indeed, it has been a collaborative effort, with the direct and indirect participation of many people. The following are those who generously contributed their time and energy into providing valuable material for this book:

Brian Agnew

Brian Agnew is the founder and principal consultant with OOPS Consultancy Ltd, located in London, U.K. He holds a B.Eng. in Electrical and Electronic Engineering from Sheffield University. He advises and works with major financial houses and leading consultancies on a wide range of projects, including trading systems, network management infrastructures and grid-based architectures, working in Java mainly, C++ when he has to, and Perl when nothing else will do.

Brian contributed material on XMLTask, an Ant task that provides sophisticated XML manipulation.

Jettro Coenradie

Jettro Coenradie is a Java (enterprise) specialist living in the Netherlands. Jettro has been working in the ICT for about 10 years now. He likes to try out new frameworks that are focused on quality and productivity, so he is interested in tools like Luntbuild, Continuum and Maven. In addition, Jettro is a software architect focusing on the Spring framework. You can find more information about Jettro on his blog, *http://www.gridshore.nl/blog*.

Jettro contributed an article on integrating Maven with LuntBuild.

Keith Coughtrey

Keith gained a wealth of development experience at some of the U.K.'s largest companies before moving to New Zealand in 2004. He is currently leading development at First NZ Captial, New Zealand's largest stockbroker, where he is applying many of the tools and techniques espoused in this book.

Keith contributed material on Mylyn.

John Hurst

John Hurst is an experienced Java developer. an independent software developer, and a systems integrator working in the Wellington, New Zealand, area. John is an active member of the Java community, and plays a key role in the Wellington Java User Group.

John contributed the chapter on DBUnit.

Masoud Kalali

With more than eight years of experience, Masoud Kalali is a senior staff engineer at E-peyk. He is mostly responsible for the design and technology architecture of E-peyk enterprise framework, which is a service-oriented framework based on Java EE 5 and other open standards. Masoud's area of expertise are SOA and web services in addition to performance monitoring and management. Masoud is a contributor of several open source projects that are utilized in the E-peyk framework.

Masoud contributed material on SchemaSpy and on SoapUI.

Avneet Mangat

Avneet Mangat has six years' experience with Java/JEE. He is currently working as the Lead Developer at Active Health Partners, U.K. He is a Sun-certified programmer and web developer and is also Prince2-certified. He is also the lead developer of DBBrowser open source database browsing tool (*http://databasebrowser.sourceforge.net/*). Outside interests are photography and traveling.

Avneet contributed material on setting up a Maven repository with Artifactory.

Eric Redmond

Eric Redmond has been involved in the Maven community for over two years as a user, contributor, speaker, author, and patch provider, as well as a founder of two professional education and consulting companies surrounding Maven and other aspects of large-scale application lifecycle management. He is currently enjoying some downtime, meaning a simple life as a Ruby (and Rails) developer, yet keeping a keen eye on JRuby. He is the proprietor of Propellors Consulting and an active blogger at *http://blog.propellors.net*.

Eric contributed material on Maven 2 and Achiva.

Alex Ruiz
: Alex Ruiz is a Software Engineer in the development tools organization at Oracle (*http://www.oracle.com*). Alex enjoys reading anything related to Java, testing, OOP, AOP, and concurrency, and has programming as his first love. Alex has spoken at JavaOne, JavaPolis, Desktop Matters, and SD West. He also has publications with IEEE Software, Dev2Dev, JavaWorld and Objective View. Before joining Oracle, Alex was a consultant for ThoughtWorks. Alex maintains a blog at *http://www.jroller.com/page/alexRuiz*.

  Alex has contributed material on FEST.

Tim O'Brien also helped out with ideas for the introduction.

Technical Reviewers

The following people were brave enough to accept the task of formally reviewing the finished manuscript:

Nigel Charman
: Nigel is a Java consultant living in Wellington, New Zealand, with a special interest in developer testing and code quality. In his spare time, he's currently working on the JiBX/WS web services framework and helping to organize the Wellington Java User Group.

Paul Duvall
: Paul M. Duvall is the CTO of Stelligent Incorporated in Reston, VA—an Agile infrastructure consulting firm. He coauthored *Continuous Integration: Improving Software Quality and Reducing Risk* (Addison-Wesley, 2007), authors a series for IBM developer*Works* called "Automation for the People," and is a contributing author to the *No Fluff Just Stuff Anthology* (Pragmatic Programmers, 2007) and the "UML 2 Toolkit" (Wiley, 2003). He actively blogs on TestEarly.com and IntegrateButton.com.

Greg Ostravich
: Greg Ostravich works for the Colorado Department of Transportation in Denver, Colorado, where he leverages the knowledge from the local Denver Java User Group and books such as *Java Power Tools* to implement best practices in software development for the State of Colorado. In addition to being a technical editor for *Java Power Tools*, he is currently the President of the Denver Java User Group and did the technical editing for JBoss at Work, No Fluff Just Anthologies (2006 and 2007), and *GIS for Web Developers* (2007). He also wrote reviews for *Pragmatic Unit Testing in Java with JUnit* and *Pragmatic Project Automation*, which can be found on the Denver Java User Group and The Server Side web sites.

Many other people also reviewed individual chapters or sections, including Cédric Beust, Keith Coughtrey, Richard Hancock, Jimmy Kemp, Gregor Lawson, Andrew McDowell, Brett Porter, Bill Ross, and Martin White.

Conventions

Most of the conventions used in this book should be fairly self-explanatory. Literal text such as file names, class names, and so on, is represented using `a fixed width font`. Commands intended to be executed on the command line are written in ***`constant width italic`***. Code listings are written like this:

```
<settings>
    <servers>
        <server>
            <id>organisation-internal</id>
            <username>admin</username>
            <password>password</password>
        </server>
    </servers>
</settings>
```

Sometimes, for the sake of brevity, I will use three dots ("...") to indicate that I've left out some stuff, as shown here:

```
<config xmlns:xsi="http://www.w3.org/2001/XMLSchema-instance"
        xmlns="http://artifactory.jfrog.org/xsd/1.0.0"
        xsi:schemaLocation="http://artifactory.jfrog.org/xsd/1.0.0
        http://www.jfrog.org/xsd/artifactory-v1_0_0.xsd">
    ...
    <remoteRepositories>
      <remoteRepository>
          <key>ibiblio</key>
          <handleReleases>true</handleReleases>
          <handleSnapshots>false</handleSnapshots>
          <excludesPattern>org/artifactory/**,org/jfrog/**</excludesPattern>
          <url>http://repo1.maven.org/maven2</url>
          <proxyRef>proxy1</proxyRef>
      </remoteRepository>
    </remoteRepositories>
    <proxies>
        <proxy>
            <key>proxy1</key>
            <host>proxyhost</host>
            <port>8080</port>
            <username>proxy</username>
            <password>secret</password>
        </proxy>
    </proxies>
</config>
```

When giving examples of commands executed from the command line, I usually use the Unix-style "$" to indicate the command-line prompt (or "#" for root access). The

Windows equivalent would be something like "C:>." Commands that are typed by are written *like this*. System output is written in normal type:

```
$ mvn compile
[INFO] Scanning for projects...
Downloading: http://buildserver:8080/artifactory/repo/org/apache/maven/wagon/wagon-
ssh-external/1.0-alpha-5/wagon-ssh-external-1.0-alpha-5.pom
5K downloaded
...
```

The commands themselves are generally the same under Unix and Windows, with the exception of the usual things such as class pathes. You might also see the occasional *ls* rather than *dir* in some of the examples.

When a command is split over several lines for readability, I use the Unix convention of putting a "\" at the end of each line except the last one. In Windows, you will have to put everything on one line (excluding the trailing "\" characters):

```
$ mvn deploy:deploy-file -DrepositoryId=organisation-internal \
  -Durl=http://buildserver:8080/artifactory/private-internal-repository \
  DgroupId=test -DartifactId=test -Dversion=1.1 -Dpackaging=jar -Dfile=target
  /test-1.1.jar
```

In a book like this, there are many occasions where screenshots come in handy. To save space and avoid distraction, all of the browser screenshots have been cropped to remove the window header and navigation bars. On the rare occasion where this has not been done, the URL is usually relevent to the discussion. Application windows such as IDEs are shown in full or partially, depending on the context.

Source Code

There are a lot of practical examples throughout this book. You can download the source code for these examples from the publisher's web site, or from the Java Power Tools web site (*http://www.javapowertools.com*). In general, the code is designed to illustrate how to use the various tools, and to make it possible for you to experiment with the tools. As a rule, it is not of production code quality, as production quality code tends to be more complex and project-specific.

About the Title

This book is part of the O'Reilly Power Tools series, which began with the illustrious Unix Power Tools back in 1993. It has no relation with the "Java Power Tools" library (*http://www.ccs.neu.edu/jpt/*), which is a software research project in the Java GUI field, conducted by College of Computer & Information Science at the Northeastern University, Boston, under the direction of Richard Rasala.

Acknowledgments

First and foremost, I would like to deeply thank my wife, Chantal, and my two boys, James and William, whose great love, patience, and support over the last two years have made this book possible. Writing this book involved a seemingly unending stream of late night writing and grumpy mornings, as well as frequently delegating important tasks such as playing with the kids, putting them to bed and story-telling. Chantal nevertheless provided unrelenting support and love throughout the whole endeavor.

I would also like to thank the team at Equinox, New Zealand. Equinox provided invaluable time and resources for this book, as well as many challenging opportunities to research and work with the tools and techniques described in the book. First and foremost, a warm thanks to Roger Dalgleish and Paul Ramsay, without whose help this book would simply not have been possible. Also, thanks to all the Equinox staff members who took the time to read the (sometimes very) rough draft chapters and provide valued feedback, and to those who helped in all sorts of other ways: Willy Bartholomeusz, Keith Coughtrey, Candi Cunningham, Nev Flaws, Richard Hancock, Jimmy Kemp, Gregor Lawson, Brian Levy, Brendon Livingstone, Craig McLean, Andrew McDowell, Robin Newton, Bill Ross, Pete Tanesey, Kenneth Wells, Martin White, Yolanda van Dorrestein, and everyone else at Equinox.

A big thanks to all the contributors—Brian Agnew, Jettro Coenradie, Keith Coughtrey, John Hurst, Masoud Kalali, Avneet Mangat, Eric Redmond, and Alex Ruiz—without whose help this book would have been considerably poorer.

Thanks also to the reviewers who spent uncounted time and energy reading the draft manuscript and providing many valuable comments and suggestions: Nigel Charman, Paul Duvall, Greg Ostravich, and also Cédric Beust, Keith Coughtrey, Richard Hancock, Jimmy Kemp, Gregor Lawson, Andrew McDowell, Tim O'Brien, Bill Ross, and Martin White.

Warm thanks to Andy Glover, for his valued support and friendship. I am honored to have him as the author of the Foreword. Groovy, man!

I also want to thank the many organizations where I have been able to put these tools into practice during the writing of the book: notably, the staff of the National Library of New Zealand—in particular Jenny McDonald and Paul Curtis—and the staff at the Inland Revenue department of New Zealand, especially the members of the O2C2 team: Susanna McSweeny, Yujia Huang, Eduard Letifov, Leah Xu, Bryden Davenport, and Aijun Kang.

Thanks to my parents for their love and support, and for reading me *Winnie the Pooh* as a child.

And to Maryse and Emmanuel Consul, for their kindness and hospitality during all those years, and for letting their daughter depart for a far-off foreign land.

Thanks also to my "kiwi" family, Diana and Owen Lowe, and Yvonne and Cornelius Van Veen, for their warm welcome, permanent support, and for those many evenings during which wine, beer, and friendship rejuvenated my mind between chapters.

A book like this would not be possile without the vibrant Java open source community in existance today. Thanks to tool authors and contributors the Wellington Java Users Group and to other members of the Java community with whom I have exchanged words, emails, and ideas over the last few years: Cédric Beust, Mandy Chung, Scott Davis, Mohamad Easawy, Jeremy Flowers, Rob Harwood, John Hurst, Mik Kersten, Surjendu Kuila, Steve Loughran, Brett Porter, Cameron Purdy, Matt Raible, and Rob Williams.

Using Code Examples

This book is here to help you get your job done. In general, you may use the code in this book in your programs and documentation. You do not need to contact us for permission unless you're reproducing a significant portion of the code. For example, writing a program that uses several chunks of code from this book does not require permission. Selling or distributing a CD-ROM of examples from O'Reilly books does require permission. Answering a question by citing this book and quoting example code does not require permission. Incorporating a significant amount of example code from this book into your product's documentation does require permission.

We appreciate, but do not require, attribution. An attribution usually includes the title, author, publisher, and ISBN. For example: "*Java Power Tools* by John Ferguson Smart. Copyright 2008 John Ferguson Smart, 978-0-596-52793-8."

If you feel your use of code examples falls outside fair use or the permission given above, feel free to contact us at *permissions@oreilly.com*.

Safari® Enabled

When you see a Safari® Enabled icon on the cover of your favorite technology book, that means the book is available online through the O'Reilly Network Safari Bookshelf.

Safari offers a solution that's better than e-books. It's a virtual library that lets you easily search thousands of top tech books, cut and paste code samples, download chapters, and find quick answers when you need the most accurate, current information. Try it for free at http://safari.oreilly.com." (*http://safari.oreilly.com*)

How to Contact Us

Please address comments and questions concerning this book to the publisher:

O'Reilly Media, Inc.
1005 Gravenstein Highway North
Sebastopol, CA 95472
800-998-9938 (in the United States or Canada)
707-829-0515 (international or local)
707 829-0104 (fax)

We have a web page for this book, where we list errata, examples, and any additional information. You can access this page at:

http://www.oreilly.com/catalog/9780596527938

To comment or ask technical questions about this book, send email to:

bookquestions@oreilly.com

For more information about our books, conferences, Resource Centers, and the O'Reilly Network, see our web site at:

http://www.oreilly.com

Introduction

Since the dawn of time, people have been using tools to make their life easier. Tools let you solve a problem at hand more quickly and more efficiently, so that you can spend your time doing more interesting things. The stone axe, for example, enabled your prehistoric hunter to cut up meat more efficiently, thus leaving the tribe with time to do much more satisfying activities such as grilling mammoth steaks and painting on cave walls.

Of course, not all tools are equal, and tools have a tendency to evolve. If you go down to your local hardware store nowadays, you can probably find something even better to chop up your firewood or to chop down a tree. In all things, it is important to find the tool that is most appropriate for the job at hand.

The software industry is no exception in this regard. There are thousands of tools out there, and there is a good chance that some of these can help you work more efficiently. If you use them well, they will enable you to work better and smarter, producing higher quality software, and avoiding too much overtime on late software projects. The hardest thing is knowing what tools exist, and how you can put them to good use.

That's where this book can help. In a nutshell, this book is about software development tools that you can use to make your life easier. And, in particular, tools that can help you optimize your software development life cycle.

The Software Development Life Cycle (or SDLC) is basically the process you follow to produce working software. This naturally involves coding, but there is more to building an application than just cutting code.

You also need a build environment.

When I talk of a build environment, I am referring to everything that contributes to letting the developers get on with their job: coding. This can include things like a version control system (to store your source code) and an issue management system (to keep track of your bugs). It can also include integration, testing, and staging platforms, in which your application will be deployed at different stages. But the build environment also includes tools that make life easier for the developer. For example, build scripts that help you compile, package and deploy your application in a consistent and reproducible manner. Testing tools that make testing a less painful task, and therefore encourage developers to test their code. And much more.

Let's look at a concrete example. My picture of an efficient, productive build environment goes something along the following lines.

You build your application using a finely tuned build script. Your build script is clean, portable, and maintainable. It runs on any machine, and a new developer can simply check the project out of the version control system and be up and running immediately. It just works.

You store your code in a central source code repository. Whenever you commit your code, a build server detects the change to the code base, and automatically runs a full suite of unit, integration, and functional tests. If any problems crop up, you (and the rest of the team) are immediately notified. You have learned from experience that committing small, regular changes makes the integration process go a whole lot smoother, and you organize your work accordingly.

You use an issue tracking system to keep tabs on features to implement, bugs to fix, or any other jobs that need doing. When you commit changes to your source code repository, you mention the issues that this change addresses in the commit message. This message is automatically recorded against these issue in the issue management system. Furthermore, if you say "Fixes #101," the issue automatically will be closed.

Conversely, when you view an issue in the issue management system, you can also see not only the commit messages but also the exact modifications that were made in the source code. When you prepare a release, it is easy to compile a set of reliable release notes based on the issues that were reported as fixed in the issue tracking system since the last release.

Your team now writes unit tests as a matter of habit. It wasn't easy to start with, but over time, coaching and peer programming have convinced everyone of the merits of test-driven development. Automatic test coverage tools help them ensure that their unit tests aren't missing out on any important code. The extensive test suite, combined with the test coverage reports, gives them enough confidence to refactor their code as necessary. This, in turn, helps keep the code at a high level of reliability and flexibility.

Coding standards and best practices are actively encouraged. A battery of automatic code auditing tools checks for any violations of the agreed set of rules. These tools raise issues relating to coding standards as well as potential defects. They also note any code that is not sufficiently documented.

These statistics can be viewed at any time, but, each week, the code audit statistics are reviewed in a special team meeting. The developers can see how they are doing as a team, and how the statistics have changed since last week. This encourages the developers to incorporate coding standards and best practices into their daily work. Because collective code ownership is actively encouraged, and peer-programming is quite frequent, these statistics also helps to foster pride in the code they are writing.

Occasionally, some of the violations are reviewed in more detail during this meeting. This gives people the opportunity to discuss the relevence of such and such a rule in certain circumstances, or to learn about why, and how, this rule should be respected.

You can view up-to-date technical documentation about your project and your application at any time. This documentation is a combination of human-written high-level architecture and design guidelines, and low-level API documentation for your application, including graphical UML class diagrams and database schemas. The automatic code audits help to ensure that the code itself is adequately documented.

The cornerstone of this process is your Continuous Integration, or CI, server. This powerful tool binds the other tools into one coherent, efficient, process. It is this server that monitors your source code repository, and automatically builds and tests your application whenever a new set of changes are committed. The CI server also takes care of automatically running regular code audits and generating the project documentation. It automatically deploys your application to an integration server, for all to see and play around with at any time. It maintains a graphical dashboard, where team members and project sponsors can get a good idea of the general state of health of your appplication at a glance. And it keeps track of builds, making it easier to deploy a specific version into the test, staging, or production environments when the time comes.

None of the tools discussed in this book are the silver bullet that will miraculously solve all your team's productivity issues. To yield its full benefits, any tool needs to be used properly. And the proper use of many of these tools can entail significant changes in the way you work. For example, to benefit from automated testing, developers must get into the habit of writing unit tests for their code. For a continous integration system to provide maximum benefits, they will need to learn to commit frequent, small changes to the version control system, and to organize their work accordingly. And, if you want to generate half-decent technical documentation automatically, you will need to make sure that your code is well-commented in the first place.

You may need to change the way people work, which is never easy. This can involve training, coaching, peer-programming, mentoring, championing, bribing, menacing, or some combination of the above. But, in the long run, it's worth it.

PART I
Build Tools

> "It just shows what can be done by taking a little trouble," said Eeyore. "Do you see, Pooh? Do you see, Piglet? Brains first and then Hard Work. Look at it! *That's* the way to build a house."
>
> —"A House is Built at Pooh Corner for Eeyore," *The House at Pooh Corner*, A. A. Milne

Putting some thought and effort into planning your build process from the outset can pay off abundantly further on down the line, when the going gets tough and the pressure is on. This is where a well-designed build process and fine-tuned build tools show their worth.

Like many things, in IT and elsewhere, build tools are primarily the fruit of human laziness. Compiling C or C++ (or Java, for that matter) from the command line is a terribly tedious affair. And, in the Unix world, where scripts abound, the next step was natural: why not write a script to do it for you? A basic shell script written to compile a few C source code files was probably the oldest ancestor of our modern Java build tools such as Ant and Maven.

Shell scripts work fine for a small number of source code files, but this approach is difficult to scale to larger applications. This is where Make enters the scene. Make is the principal Unix build tool, and anyone familiar with linux or Unix will have come across it at some stage. A makefile (the name of the scripts run by Make) is basically a list of instructions used to compile your application. The idea is to automate the build process, by working out exactly what files need to be compiled, and in what order. You do this by defining dependency rules, which tell Make when it should compile a particular file, and how it should go about compiling it. A very simple makefile is shown here:

```
# top-level rule to create the program.
all: main

# compiling the source code.
main.o: main.c
	gcc -g -Wall -c main.c
```

```
# linking the compiled files.
main: main.o
	gcc -g main.o -o main

# Remove generated files
clean:
	/bin/rm -f main main.o
```

This makefile will compile and link the C program contained in the `main.c` source code file. Real-world makefiles can get much bigger and more complicated than this, and Make does a lot more than what can be gleaned here. Indeed, Make is a powerful tool: it is used regularly to build very large and complex C and C++ applications, including the Linux kernal itself. It marks an important step in the history of automating the build process. Make, along with Unix/Linux, also helped to promote the idea of a portable build: you should be able to build an application from the source code on any machine. Of course, the use of libraries in Linux and Unix makes this a bit more complicated then that, but the idea is there.

However, as we will see, nowadays there are build tools that are much better adapted to Java development: leave Make to the C and C++ programmers.

The history of builds in Windows environments is slightly different. In the days of yore, when Turbo Pascal was king, you usually would write, compile, and build your application directly from within the IDE. This remained the tendency for a very long time —builds would be performed on an individual developer's machine from within his IDE.

This approach is still used in many organizations. However, it is not a good idea for several reasons. A build process that relies on an IDE is likely to depend on how the IDE is installed. This in turn makes it dependent on the configuration of particular machines. If your build process depends on how a particular developer has configured his or her machine, you're in trouble.

A good build process has a certain number of characteristics, for example:

- Builds should be portable. A new developer should be able to check out the source code of a project, and run a build, independent of the IDE. Builds should also be portable between operating systems. Nowadays, it is common to develop on one OS and to build on another.
- You should be able to run a build without human intervention. This is one of the underlying principles of Continuous Integration, which we look at in Part VIII of this book. A build that needs human intervention reveals a very fragile and vunerable build process.
- A build tool should federate a set of tools and processes into a single, coherent build process. Building a software application can involve many steps—compiling the code, of course—but also other steps such as downloading dependencies, running unit, integration and functional tests, performing automatic code audits,

bundling the application into an executable package, possibly deploying the application into a test environment, and even generating technical documentation. As we will see throughout the rest of this book, the build tool is the underlying framework that ties all of these tools and processes together.

In Java, there are two main build tools: Ant and Maven. These two products are radically different in their approach and in the way they are used. Both tools have staunch partisans and opponents, and the choice of build tools is a subject that tends to evoke a lot of passion amongst Java developers. However, both are worthy of interest, and we will try to look at both with the diligence that they deserve.

Ant is a well-known and widely used build scripting tool based on a procedural, task-driven approach that gives you a very high degree of flexibiliy. Build scripts are written in XML, rather than the somewhat fickle syntax found in Make files. Ant comes with a rich set of built-in tasks, allowing you to automate virtually any part of the software development lifecycle, from compilation and unit tests to deployment over the network and notifications to team members by email.

Maven takes a higher-level, declarative approach, favoring convention over configuration, and relying on standards and conventions to take much of the grunt work out of the build process. Like Ant, Maven uses XML for its scripting language. However, rather than describing the steps required to build your project, a Maven script describes the project itself, in a very declarative manner. Maven provides built-in support for declarative dependency management, and is a powerful means of organizing your internal and external dependencies. Maven also benefits from a rich library of plug-ins that you can use to integrate extra features into your build process. And, if there isn't a plug-in, you can always use an embedded Ant script, or even write your own plug-in!

Which build tool is best for you? Build tools are subjective things, and your choice may be as influenced as much by your own personal background and experience as by technical matters. Personally, I would recommend Maven for any new project, even for small ones. Despite the higher initial learning curve, Maven actively encourages better programming habits and compliance to best practices, whereas Ant really leaves these matters to your own personal judgment and better nature. I find that Maven pays off in the long term with a more consistent, well-structured project organization.

On the other hand, I wouldn't rush off and convert my 10,000 lines of Ant build script to Maven without a good business justification. Such justifications do exist, but they need considered thought. As a rule, the bigger the Ant file, the more work will be involved migrating the project into a Maven structure. Ant is also a good choice if you really do need to do things a little "out-of-the box"—for instance, if you are writing a build script that doesn't really involve the classic build structure. There's no point trying to fit a round peg into a square hole, so to speak.

In the following chapters, we will look at both of these tools in some detail. In addition, throughout the rest of the book, you will find many examples of how to integrate the other tools that we discuss with Ant and Maven.

CHAPTER 1

Setting Up a Project Using Ant

1.1 Ant in the Build Process

Ant is a popular and widely used open source build tool, written in Java. Indeed, it is probably *the* most widely used build tool in the Java world. It is supported by virtually all modern IDEs, and (being a Java application) runs on almost any Java-friendly platform.

In a nutshell, Ant helps you transform the source code, libraries, and other files that make up your project into a deliverable software package. And, more importantly, it helps you do this in an orderly, repeatable manner. If you design your build script well, you can also ensure that it will behave the same way on any machine. This leads the way to automatic builds, which can be run on a remote machine with little or no human intervention. In Part III, we discuss how to use Continuous Integration tools to take this process even further.

Ant is a highly flexible tool—you can make it do pretty much anything you want. However, this flexibility can come at a cost of complexity. Good Ant build scripts are written in a way that will be easy to read and maintain in a year's time. In this chapter, I will try to show some best practices that should help make your scripts clean and readable.

1.2 Installing Ant

At the time of this writing, there were no graphical installers available, although Ant is now provided as a standard package for many Unix distributions. Nevertheless, you will often get a more complete installation if you download and install Ant manually.

Ant should run correctly on any Java-friendly platform. Ant is a pure Java tool, so it does require a (preferably recent) JDK installation to work.*

* The Ant team recommends Java 1.5 or later, mentioning that less tasks will work correctly with older versions of Java.

So, as a prerequisite for installation, you should check that your machine has a correctly installed JVM:

```
$ java -version
java version "1.6.0"
Java(TM) SE Runtime Environment (build 1.6.0-b105)
Java HotSpot(TM) Server VM (build 1.6.0-b105, mixed mode)
```

The following two sections will discuss how to install Ant on Unix and Windows environments.

Installing Ant on a Unix Machine

Download the latest stable binary release of Ant from the Ant web site,* and extract it into an appropriate directory. On my machine, I installed it into the `/usr/share` directory. I also created a convenient symbolic link to make later updates easier:

```
# cd /usr/share
# tar xvfz apache-ant-1.7.0-bin.tar.gz ant-1.7.0
# ln -s ant-1.7.0 Ant
```

Now, you should have a full Ant distribution installed on your machine:

```
# ls -al /usr/share/ant
lrwxrwxrwx 1 root root 9 2007-08-04 22:36 Ant -> ant-1.7.0
# ls /usr/share/ant
bin    fetch.xml   KEYS     LICENSE.dom     NOTICE
docs   get-m2.xml  lib      LICENSE.sax     README
etc    INSTALL     LICENSE  LICENSE.xerces  WHATSNEW
```

Once this is done, you need to set up some environment variables. Ant requires two to function. First, set the *ANT_HOME* variable to the directory where you have installed Ant. You also need to ensure that the *JAVA_HOME* variable is correctly defined, as the Ant startup script uses both of these variables. This usually goes in one of your environment initialization scripts (for example, if you are using Bash, you could place this configuration in the *~/.bashrc* file if you just need to set it up for your account, or in */etc/bashrc* if you want to set it up for all users on this machine):

```
ANT_HOME=/usr/share/ant
JAVA_HOME=/usr/lib/jvm/java
PATH=$PATH:$ANT_HOME/bin:$JAVA_HOME/bin
export PATH ANT_HOME JAVA_HOME
```

Now you should be able to run Ant from the command line. Make sure it works by running the following command:

```
$ ant -version
Apache Ant version 1.7.0 compiled on July 11 2007
```

* *http://ant.apache.org/*

Installing Ant on Windows

Installing Ant on Windows is, like for Unix, a largely manual process. Download the binary distribution from the Ant web site and unzip it to a convenient place on your disk. It is usually safer to install Ant into a short directory name, without spaces, such as `C:\ant`. Although in Windows you would usually do this using one of the many Windows graphical compression utilities, you can also do this using the Java *jar* tool if you need to, as shown in the following example:

```
> mkdir C:\tools
> cd C:\tools
> jar xvf apache-ant-1.7.0-bin.zip
inflated: apache-ant-1.7.0/bin/ant
inflated: apache-ant-1.7.0/bin/antRun
...
```

This will extract the Ant installation into a directory called `C:\tools\apache-ant-1.7.0-bin`. You may want to rename this to something a little more manageable, such as `C:\tools\ant`.

The next step involves adding the Ant `bin` directory (in this case, `C:\tools\ant\bin`) to your system path. In Windows, you do this in the "System Properties" screen, which is accessed from the control panel. From here, go to the "Advanced" tab and click "Environment Variables" (see "Installing Maven on a Windows Machine" in Section 2.3). Now just add your Ant `bin` directory to your system PATH variable, separated from the other values by a semicolon.

You also need to add the *ANT_HOME* environment variable (`C:\tools\ant` in this case) using the "New" button in the Environmen Variables screen. You also need to ensure that the *JAVA_HOME* environment variable is correctly set to the directory where your JDK is installed. Ant needs both of these variables to work correctly.

Once this is done, you should be able to run Ant from the command line:

```
> Ant -version
Apache Ant version 1.7.0 compiled on July 11 2007
```

ANT_OPTS and ANT_ARGS: Some Other Useful Environment Variables

In addition to *JAVA_HOME* and *ANT_HOME*, there are two other variables used by Ant that you may occasionally find useful: *ANT_OPTS* and *ANT_ARGS*.

As with any other Java application, when you run Ant it is sometimes nice to be able to tinker with the various JVM options. The *ANT_OPTS* variable lets you do just that, allowing you to fine-tune memory requirements or define proxy configurations. Although Ant itself is not particularly demanding in terms of memory, some third-party tasks such as code coverage tools may be, and you may need to increase the available heap size as shown here:

```
export ANT_OPTS=-Xmx512M
```

In many organizations, you will need to access the Internet via a proxy. Another common use of the *ANT_OPTS* variable is to define proxy configuration details for tasks that need to access the Internet. You can do this using the *http.proxyHost* and *http.proxyPort* variables:

```
export ANT_OPTS="-Dhttp.proxyHost=proxy.mycompany.com -Dhttp.proxyPort=8080"
```

The second variable, *ANT_ARGS*, lets you define command-line arguments that will be passed to Ant. For example, the following configuration (attributed to Erik Hatcher in a blog entry by Matt Raible) gives color-coded output when you run Ant (green for success, red for failures, blue for log messages, and so on):

```
export ANT_ARGS=-logger org.apache.tools.ant.listener.AnsiColorLogger
```

1.3 A Gentle Introduction to Ant

Now that you have installed Ant, we can take it through its paces. Ant is an extremely powerful tool, and experienced users can really make it sing. We will start off simply, going through how to set up a small Java project with Ant.

Basic Ant Concepts

Ant build files are written in XML, using a quite readable set of tags. The overall structure of an Ant file is relatively straightforward and intuitive. An Ant build file describes how to build one (and only one) *project*. A build project is made up of *targets* and *tasks*.

A *target* is a goal that you want your build process to achieve. Such a goal might be to compile your application code, run your tests, or prepare a production-ready release package. You can (and usually do) define several targets in your build file, which you may run on different occasions.

A target can also depend on other targets. This lets you ensure that certain targets are always executed before others. For example, you might want to ensure that your unit test's target is always run before you prepare a new release. You do this by declaring dependencies between your targets.

A *task* lets you define a piece of work you want done. This might be compiling some Java source code using *javac*, running a set of unit tests using JUnit, or generating a production-ready JAR file using the *jar* utility. This is where the work actually gets done. The task is the workhorse of the Ant build process and the source of a lot of its power and flexibility. Behind the scenes, Ant tasks are actually implemented as Java classes, which makes it fairly easy to extend Ant by writing new tasks. This is one of the reasons that the majority of Java tools, both open source and commercial, provide an Ant task library. Indeed, Ant comes with a rich library of built-in (or "core") and optional tasks. Core tasks are built into Ant, and need no special configuration. Optional tasks are maintained by the Ant team and delivered with Ant, but they rely on an external library. For example, the *junit* task, which runs JUnit test cases, is an optional task because it requires the JUnit library to be supplied separately. Ant 1.7.0 is delivered with almost 100 core tasks and around 50 optional ones.

There is also a third type of task, referred to as "third-party" tasks. These are written and maintained outside of the Ant project, and they often provide support for other Java or non-Java tools. For example, Subversion support in Ant (see Section 4.30) is provided by Tigris, the team that maintains Subversion. The number of third-party tasks is countless.

Finally, Ant allows you to define and use a set of properties. In Ant, a *property* can be used as a way to make your build script simpler and easier to understand, and also to access system-level properties such as *user.dir* (the current working directory) or *os.name* (the name of the operating system). We look at this in some detail in Section 1.5.

A Simple Ant Build File

Let's look at a simple Ant build file. This build file will be designed to help us build a small, very simple Java project. We will build a library designed to calculate various types of taxes. This project is designed to provide an API for other projects, in the form of a JAR file called `tax-calculator.jar`.

Ant imposes no particular directory structure for your projects: instead, you need to define your own. Depending on your viewpoint, this can be seen as a strength or a weakness. On the positive side, it gives you the maximum degree of flexibility in structuring your project. On the other hand, the lack of a standard directory structure may make the learning curve a little harder when you switch from one project to another.

Having said that Ant requires no particular structure, there *are* some practices that are more common than others. In this project, we will use a directory structure that is frequently seen in Ant-based projects (though details may vary). This directory structure places the application source code in a directory called `src`, and it places compiled classes in a directory called `build`. Production classes and unit tests are placed in separate, parallel directory structures (`src` and `test`, respectively). Compiled production classes are stored in the `build/classes` directory, whereas compiled unit tests are placed in `build/test-classes`.

Finally, any libraries required by the application are stored in a directory called `lib`.

This directory layout is summarized in Table 1-1.

Table 1-1. Directory structure for our project

Directory	Contents
`src`	Application source code
`test`	Unit test code
`lib`	Project dependencies
`build`	Any files generated by the build process
`build/classes`	Compiled Java classes
`build/test-classes`	Compiled unit tests
`dist`	Distribution files, such as bundled JAR or WAR files

Having a clean, well-defined directory structure is important for any project, and is particularly important if you are using a tool like Ant. A clear directory layout makes the build script easier to write and understand. Separating compiled classes from source code, for example, makes it easier to do a clean recompile simply by deleting the target directory, and makes it easier to place source code (and *only* source code) under version control.

Using a `lib` directory to store your dependencies is one commonly used approach in Ant projects, though it is not the only solution to this problem. If the libraries are simply stored here with no indication of their version, it can be difficult to keep track of the exact list of libraries required by your project. To address this issue, many teams are starting to identify the version of each library using a Maven 2-like naming convention (see "Project Context and Artifacts" in Section 2.4). For example, if you are using JUnit 4.4, the JAR in your lib directory would be called `junit-4.4.jar`. This makes it easier to know which versions of each library your application is currently using.

This is not the only way to store dependencies. Indeed, keeping them in the `lib` directory may mean that your JARs end up being stored in your version control system. This is not always ideal. Maven (see Chapter 2) uses a different approach, where JAR files are stored on a central repository, and dependencies are listed in the build file, instead of in one of the project directories. In Section 1.11, we look at how to declare dependencies using Maven 2-style repositories.

Maven uses a similar standardized directory structure (see Section 2.6), which can also be used for Ant projects.

For our first example, we will be working with a simple one-class application that displays some information about the installed JVM and operating system. This remarkably useful piece of code is shown here:

```
package com.javapowertools.taxcalculator;

public class Main {

    public static void main(String[] args) {
        String jvm = System.getProperty("java.version");
```

```
        String osName = System.getProperty("os.name");
        String osVersion = System.getProperty("os.version");

        System.out.println("Running Java " + jvm
                       + " on " + osName
                       + " (version " + osVersion + ")");
    }
}
```

Now let's see how you could use Ant to build this application. At this stage, we just want to compile our code and bundle up a JAR file containing the compiled classes. You could do this with a `build.xml` file, along the following lines:

```
<?xml version="1.0" ?>
<project name="tax-calculator" default="package">

  <target name="init">
    <mkdir dir="build/classes" />
    <mkdir dir="dist" />
  </target>

  <target name="compile" depends="init" description="Compile Java code">
    <javac srcdir="src" destdir="build/classes"/>
  </target>

  <target name="package" depends="compile" description="Generate JAR file">
    <jar destfile="dist/tax-calculator.jar" basedir="build/classes"/>
  </target>

  <target name="clean" description="Deletes generated directories">
    <delete dir="build" />
    <delete dir="dist" />
  </target>

</project>
```

Let's go through this build file, and see how it uses the basic concepts we discussed earlier. Like all Ant build scripts, the root element is called *<project>*. The main role of the *<project>* element is to act as a container for the other build elements such as properties, targets, and tasks. It also lets you define an (optional) default target. We will learn more about default targets later on.

Each target uses various built-in Ant tasks. The first thing we need to do in our build process is create any missing directories. You need to make sure these directories have been created before compiling your classes. So, the first target, called "init," simply creates the `build` and `dist` directories using the *mkdir* task:

```
  <target name="init">
    <mkdir dir="build/classes" />
    <mkdir dir="dist" />
  </target>
```

We don't need to create the "build" directory before the "build/classes" directory because Ant will do this automatically for us.

Next we need to compile our classes. The "compile" target uses *javac* (or, more precisely, the *javac* Ant task) to compile the source code in the `src` directory and place the compiled classes in the `build/classes` directory:

```
<target name="compile" depends="init" description="Compile Java code">
  <javac srcdir="src" destdir="build/classes"/>
</target>
```

The "package" target creates a JAR file in the `dist` directory containing all of the compiled classes in the `build/classes` directory:

```
<target name="package" depends="compile" description="Generate JAR file">
  <jar destfile="dist/tax-calculator.jar" basedir="build/classes"/>
</target>
```

Finally, the "clean" target simply deletes the generated directories using the *delete* task:

```
<target name="clean" depends="init" description="Deletes generated directories">
  <delete dir="build" />
  <delete dir="dist" />
</target>
```

Running Ant

We are now ready to run this build script. You can do so by running Ant in the root directory of your project. If you run Ant with no arguments, Ant will invoke the default target, which is "package" for this project:

```
$ ant
Buildfile: build.xml

init:
    [mkdir] Created dir: /home/wakaleo/projects/jpt-sample-code/ant-demo/build/classes
    [mkdir] Created dir: /home/wakaleo/projects/jpt-sample-code/ant-demo/dist

compile:
    [javac] Compiling 1 source file to /home/wakaleo/projects/jpt-sample-code/ant-demo
    /build/classes

package:
      [jar] Building jar: /home/wakaleo/projects/jpt-sample-code/ant-demo/dist
      /tax-calculator.jar

BUILD SUCCESSFUL
Total time: 1 second
```

Alternatively, you can specify the target you want to run, as shown here with the "clean" target:

```
$ ant clean
Buildfile: build.xml

init:

clean:
```

```
   [delete] Deleting directory /home/wakaleo/projects/jpt-sample-code/ant-demo/build
   [delete] Deleting directory /home/wakaleo/projects/jpt-sample-code/ant-demo/dist

BUILD SUCCESSFUL
Total time: 0 seconds
```

You can also run several targets at the same time, simply by listing them as arguments on the command line:

```
$ ant clean compile
Buildfile: build.xml

clean:
   [delete] Deleting directory /home/wakaleo/projects/jpt-sample-code/ant-demo/build
   [delete] Deleting directory /home/wakaleo/projects/jpt-sample-code/ant-demo/dist

init:
    [mkdir] Created dir: /home/wakaleo/projects/jpt-sample-code/ant-demo/build/classes
    [mkdir] Created dir: /home/wakaleo/projects/jpt-sample-code/ant-demo/dist

compile:
    [javac] Compiling 1 source file to /home/wakaleo/projects/jpt-sample-code/ant-demo
    /build/classes

BUILD SUCCESSFUL
Total time: 2 seconds
```

By convention, Ant files are called `build.xml`, but you can specify a different build script using the *-f* option:

```
$ ant -f my-special-buildfile.xml
```

Finally, like many tools, you can activate a verbose mode (using the *-v* command-line option) to display more details about what Ant is doing. This can be useful when debugging your build scripts:

```
$ ant -v
Apache Ant version 1.7.0 compiled on July 11 2007
Buildfile: build.xml
Detected Java version: 1.6 in: /usr/lib/jvm/java-6-sun-1.6.0.00/jre
Detected OS: Linux
parsing buildfile /home/wakaleo/projects/java-power-tools/sample-code/ch01/ant-demo
/build.xml with URI = file:/home/wakaleo/projects/java-power-tools/sample-code/ch01
/ant-demo/build.xml
Project base dir set to: /home/wakaleo/projects/java-power-tools/sample-code/ch01
/ant-demo
...
```

Ant also accepts many other command-line options, which can be used to fine-tune the behavior of your build script. We will look at a few of these options later on in this chapter.

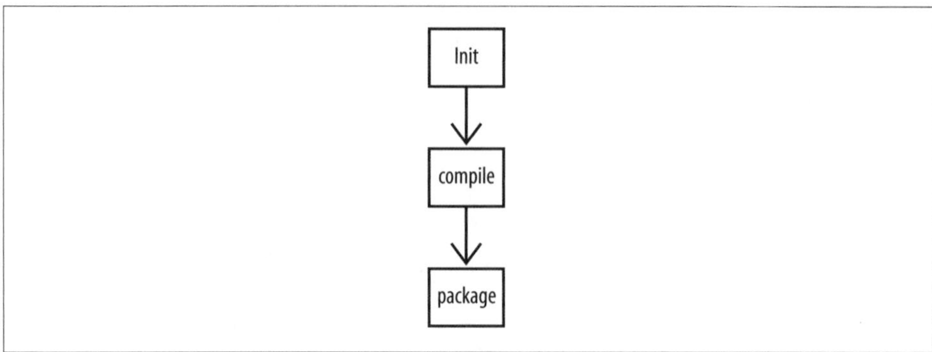

Figure 1-1. A dependency graph of Ant targets

Dependencies Between Targets

Most Ant targets are not designed to be run in isolation. Before compiling the Java source code, we need to create the target directories. And we obviously need to compile the latest version of the source code before we can generate a new version of the JAR file. In other words, there is a precise order in which the targets need to be executed. Certain targets depend on others.

In Ant, you use the *depends* attribute to declare a target's direct dependencies:

```
<target name="package" depends="compile" description="Generate JAR file">
<target name="compile" depends="init" description="Generate JAR file">
```

In this example, the "package" target depends on the "compile" target to compile the Java classes, which in turn depends on the "init" target to prepare the output directories. In fact, the "package" target *also* depends on "init," but we don't need to list "init" in the "package" target dependencies because it will automatically be called when the "compile" target is executed. These dependencies can be expressed as a dependency graph, as shown in Figure 1-1.

Some targets can have multiple dependencies. For example, in the following code the "test" target directly depends on both the "unit-test" and the "integration-test" targets.

```
<target name="test" depends="unit-test, integration-test" description=
"Generate JAR file">
```

Ant is fairly smart about how it handles dependencies. For example, if both the "unit-test" and the "integration-test" targets depend on the "compile" target, this target will only be executed once.

Documenting Your Project

Documenting build scripts is important, and Ant build files are no exception. Left unattended, they can quickly become a nightmare to understand, both for you and other developers later on.

In addition to traditional techniques such as XML comments, Ant comes with a few built-in features to help you document your build scripts. The *description* attribute lets you provide a short description for your targets, as shown here:

```
<target name="compile" depends="init" description="Compile Java code">
  <javac srcdir="src" destdir="build/classes"/>
</target>
```

It is a good idea to use the *description* attribute for the targets in your build script that are intended for external use. You can then use the *-projecthelp* command-line option to list the main build targets, complete with a brief description. With large build scripts (and Ant build scripts can become very large), this can be a valuable time-saver:

```
$ ant -projecthelp
Buildfile: build.xml

Main targets:

 compile  Compile Java code
 package  Generate JAR file
 clean    Deletes generated directories
Default target: package
```

1.4 Compiling Your Java Code in Ant

In Java development, one of the most fundamental things that any build script needs to do is compile your code. In Ant, the *<javac>* task provides a convenient one-stop shop for Java compilation.

Let's look at a simple use of the *<javac>* task. In the example given above, we use a simple form of this task to compile the Java classes in the `src/main` directory, and place the compiled classes in the build/classes directory:

```
<target name="compile" depends="init" description="Compile Java code">
  <javac srcdir="src" destdir="build/classes"/>
</target>
```

This is equivalent to executing the *javac* tool as shown here:

```
$ javac -nowarn -d build/classes src/main
```

Admittedly, you would rarely compile an application this simple in the real world. In most real applications, your application will require a set of libraries both to compile and to run. In Ant projects, these libraries are often stored (in the form of JAR files) in a directory called `lib`. When you compile your application, you need to tell Ant where to find these libraries.

Ant comes with some very powerful features to help you do this. Ant excels at defining and manipulating classpaths and other file path definitions. In Ant, these definitions are known as "path-like" structures, and they are used extensively in all but the most trivial build files. At its simplest, you can use the *<path>* tag to identify a particular library using the *location* attribute:

```
<path id="junit.classpath" location="lib/junit.jar"/>
```

This path could also be defined in the same way using the path attribute. However, in addition to defining single JAR files or directories, the *path* attribute lets you use a more path-like construction using a combination of directory paths and a JAR file, as shown here:

```
<path id="junit.classpath" path="build/classes:lib/junit.jar"/>
```

One of the nice things about the Ant path-handling features is that they are (like the underlying Java APIs) portable across different operating systems. Here, by convention, we use Unix-style paths containing forward slashes ("/"). For example, on a Windows machine, Ant will automatically translate the above path into "build\classes;lib \junit.jar."

Although this certainly makes for more readable build files, the real advantages of Ant's path-handling features come into play when you need to manipulate large sets of files. The following example creates a path definition including all the *.jar files in the `lib` directory:

```
<path id="compile.classpath">
  <fileset dir="lib" includes="*.jar" />
</path>
```

This sort of thing is exactly what you often need to define classpaths for real-world Java builds. You can use this classpath in the *<javac>* task using the *classpathref* attribute, as shown here:

```
<target name="compile" depends="init" description="Compile Java code">
  <javac srcdir="src"
         destdir="build/classes"
         classpathref="compile.classpath" />
</target>
```

Alternatively, if you don't think you will need this classpath elsewhere in your build file, you can embed the *<classpath>* element directly in the *<javac>* task:

```
<target name="compile" depends="init" description="Compile Java code">
  <javac srcdir="src" destdir="build/classes">
    <classpath>
      <fileset dir="lib" includes="*.jar"/>
    </classpath>
  </javac>
</target>
```

These paths actually use a shorthand notation for convenience. You can also use embedded tags for a more readable notation, which is useful when many separate classpath elements are required. This is also convenient if you want to reuse paths defined elsewhere in the build file. The *<pathelement>* tag lets you define a classpath element using either a JAR file, a directory, or even a reference to another classpath element:

```
<path id="test.classpath">
  <path refid="compile.classpath"/>
  <pathelement location="lib/junit.jar"/>
  <pathelement path="build/test-classes"/>
</path>
```

You can also use path-like expressions within the *<javac>* task itself to tell Ant what classes to include or which ones should be excluded from the compilation process, using the *includes* and *excludes* attributes. For example, to compile only the classes in the `com.mycompany.myapp.web` package (and below), you could do this:

```
<javac srcdir="src" destdir="build/classes" includes="com/mycompany/myapp/web/**" />
```

One frequent requirement when compiling Java code is to compile for a specific Java version. For example, you may use Java 6 on your development machine, but need to deploy to an environment where only Java 1.4 is supported. You can ensure that your Java code is compatible with Java 1.4, and that none of the nice Java 5 syntactic sugar is used, by setting the *source* attribute to "1.4." Similarly, you can tell Ant to generate byte-code compatible with a Java 1.4 JVM by specifying the *target* attribute as "1.4."

```
<javac srcdir="src" destdir="build/classes" source="1.4" target="1.4" />
```

You may also need to indicate if you want the source code compiled with debug information. By default, this is turned off, but it can come in handy when testing and debugging your code. To turn this option on, set the *debug* attribute to "on" (or "true"):

```
<javac srcdir="src" destdir="build/classes" debug="on" />
```

Despite its name, the *<javac>* task is not tied to the standard Sun Java compiler, also called *javac*. In fact, fans of alternative compilers like Jikes and GCJ can use these compilers, or a number of other more exotic choices, by specifying the *compiler* attribute:

```
<javac srcdir="src" destdir="build/classes" compiler="jikes"/>
```

You can also define this value for the entire build file by setting the *build.compiler* property (see Section 1.5).

As you can see, the *<javac>* task provides a powerful, flexible tool for Java compilation. Many of the techniques covered here are typical of many Ant tasks, and we will see more examples of these later on.

1.5 Customizing Your Build Script Using Properties

In development, people often speak of the DRY (Don't Repeat Yourself) principle. This is a general principle aimed at making code more readable and easier to maintain by avoiding the duplication of data. In a Java application, for example, key values that are used in several places, or that may need to be modified easily, are stored as constants or as parameters in a configuration file. This makes the code easier to read and understand, and makes maintenance less of a headache.

In Ant, you can do the same sort of thing by using the *<property>* tag, which lets you declare constant values that can be used throughout the rest of your build file. Declaring a property is straightforward; you just need to provide a *name* and *value* attribute, as shown here:

```
<property name="javac.debug" value="on"/>
```

If you are referring to a directory, you can use the *location* attribute instead of *value*:

```
<property name="build.dir" location="build"/>
```

This property value will be set to the absolute filename of the `build` directory.

To use a property elsewhere in the build file, you just quote the name of the property surrounded by *${...}*. For example, you can subsequently refer to this property anywhere in your build file as *${build.dir}*. You could use the *<echo>* task to display the property value to the screen, as shown here:

```
<target name="display-properties">
    <echo>Debug = ${javac.debug}</echo>
    <echo>Build directory (build.dir) = ${build.dir}</echo>
</target>
```

Calling this target would display the value of this property on the console. On my machine, it displays the following:

```
$ ant display-properties
Buildfile: build.xml

display-properties:
     [echo] Build directory (build.dir) = /home/john/projects/tax-calculator/build

BUILD SUCCESSFUL
Total time: 0 seconds
```

Another way to do this would be to use the *<echoproperties>* task, which, as the name suggests, lets you display all of the current property values to the console:

```
<target name="display-properties">
    <echoproperties />
</target>
```

Properties can also be used to take into account environment differences on each developer's machine. For example, you may need to store a path to a local server or to application directories, which may be different on different machines. To do this, you can store local properties in an ordinary Java properties file. The following directories would be different on Unix and Windows machines. On a Linux development box, you might have the following set of properties:

```
checkstyle.home = /usr/local/tools/checkstyle
pmd.home = /usr/local/tools/pmd
findbugs.home = /usr/local/tools/findbugs
cobertura.home = /usr/local/tools/cobertura
```

On a Windows machine, by contrast, you might have something like this:

```
checkstyle.home = C:\tools\checkstyle
pmd.home = C:\tools\pmd
findbugs.home = C:\tools\findbugs
cobertura.home = C:\tools\cobertura
```

Another common use of local properties files is to store user-specific and/or potentially sensitive details such as logins and passwords. This way, this sort of data doesn't end up in the version control system.

Ant also comes with a set of built-in properties, such as *${basedir}*, which is the absolute path of the project base directory, as well as Java system properties like *${java.home}*, *${java.version}*, and *${user.home}*. You can also define other properties based on these properties. This can limit the need to put a lot of variables in local properties files. For example, suppose you want to use the FindBugs (see Chapter 23) library in your build process. You could define a default FindBugs installation directory as a subdirectory of the user's home directory:

```
<property name="findbugs.home" value="${user.home}/.findbugs"/>
```

Using this definition, any user who has installed FindBugs into this directory would not need to configure their local properties file—the default property value would suffice.

One nice feature here is that you can also use properties that you define in a properties file to define *other* properties, as shown below:

```
test.server = jupiter.mycompany.com
test.server.port = 8080
test.server.url = http://${test.server}:${test.server.port}
test.server.manager.url = ${test.server.url}/manager
```

All team members need to be aware of where these properties should be defined. This is important, because by definition this is not something you can place under version control. One good approach is to agree on a properties file naming convention (say, use a file called `local.properties` in the project home directory) and to place a documented sample file under version control (called, for example, `sample.local.properties`). Another, possibly complementary, convention is to use a global properties file, stored in the user's home directory, which contains properties that are shared between several projects. This file is often called "`ant-global.properties`" or "`.ant-global.properties.`"

You can incorporate these properties into your build script by using the *file* attribute in the *<property>* tag:

```
<property file="${user.home}/ant-global.properties"/>
<property file="${basedir}/local.properties"/>

<echo>checkstyle.home = ${checkstyle.home}</echo>
<echo>pmd.home = ${pmd.home}</echo>
<echo>findbugs.home = ${findbugs.home}</echo>
<echo>cobertura.home = ${cobertura.home}</echo>
```

When you run this, the property values will be loaded and integrated into the build file:

```
$ ant compile
Buildfile: build.xml
     [echo] checkstyle.home = /usr/local/tools/checkstyle
     [echo] pmd.home = /usr/local/tools/pmd
     [echo] findbugs.home = /usr/local/tools/findbugs
     [echo] cobertura.home = /usr/local/tools/cobertura
     ...
```

You can make your build file more robust by setting up sensible default values for locally defined properties. One very powerful feature of Ant properties (which has caused a lot of confusion among inexperienced Ant users) is immutability. Once defined, Ant properties cannot be modified for the duration of the build, no matter how many *<property>* tags refer to them afterward. In other words, the first declaration of any property wins.

Let's look at a practical example. Suppose you define a property called *${javac.debug}* to indicate if you want to include debug information in your compiled classes. You could do this as follows:

```
<property name="javac.debug" value="off"/>
...
<target name="compile" depends="init" description="Compile Java code">
    <echo message="Debug: ${javac.debug}" />
    <javac srcdir="${src.dir}"
           destdir="${build.classes.dir}"
           classpathref="compile.classpath"
           debug="${javac.debug}"/>
</target>
```

When you run this, unsurprisingly, the *${javac.debug}* property is set to "off":

```
$ ant compile
Buildfile: build.xml
...
compile:
     [echo] Debug: off

BUILD SUCCESSFUL
Total time: 0 seconds
```

Now suppose you write a file called `local.properties` that you store in your project directory. This properties file contains your own personal preferences for build options such as debugging. In it, you stipulate that debugging should be on:

```
javac.debug = on
```

And now we incorporate this properties file into our build file (note that we include the properties file *before* the property declaration):

```
<property file="${basedir}/local.properties"/>
<property name="javac.debug" value="off"/>
<javac srcdir="src" destdir="build/classes" debug="${javac.debug}" />
```

When you run the build again, the first declaration of *${javac.debug}* (in the properties file) is considered definitive, and the second (in the build file) is ignored:

```
$ ant compile
Buildfile: build.xml
...
compile:
     [echo] Debug: on

BUILD SUCCESSFUL
Total time: 0 seconds
```

The story doesn't end there, however. You can override any property value from the command line, using the *-D* command-line option. For example, here we override the *${javac.debug}* property value to "off." This will take precedence over all other property declarations:

```
$ ant -Djavac.debug=off compile
Buildfile: build.xml

init:

compile:
     [echo] Debug: off

BUILD SUCCESSFUL
Total time: 0 seconds
```

1.6 Running Unit Tests in Ant

Unit testing is a fundamental part of Java development, and, applied correctly, can contribute substantially to the quality and reliability of your code. Modern coding techniques, such as test-driven development (TDD) and, more recently, behavior-driven development, rely heavily on unit testing to ensure that code is both well designed and well tested.

Unit testing is good, but automated unit testing is better. When your unit tests are integrated into your build process, you can run them automatically before each build or before committing code to your version control system. This helps to ensure that your latest changes haven't introduced any new errors. This is also known as regression testing. It makes refactoring your code safer and easier, as you can change code without having to worry about unknowingly breaking existing code—as long as you rerun the entire set of unit tests at frequent intervals.

Let's look at how to integrate JUnit tests into your Ant build process.

Using JUnit in Ant

JUnit (see Chapter 10) is probably the most well-known and widely used unit testing framework in the Java world. A groundbreaking piece of software in its time, JUnit 3 is still the basis of a very large range of unit testing libraries. The more recent JUnit 4 introduces annotation-based testing and some other more modern features.

You can run your JUnit tests in Ant using the *<junit>* task, which is what's known as an *optional task*. In Ant, optional tasks are tasks that generally depend on external libraries, such as the JUnit library in this case. Ant comes bundled with the task itself, but, if you want to use the task, you need to provide the external library yourself. This is as opposed to *core tasks*, which are fully integrated into Ant and need no external libraries.

Historically, Ant's JUnit integration has been a bit rough. In older versions of Ant (prior to Ant 1.7), you need to place your own copy of the `junit.jar` file into the `$ANT_HOME/lib` directory, alongside the `ant-junit.jar` file. As of Ant 1.7, things have improved, and you no longer need to modify your Ant installation just to run your unit tests. You still need to provide your own copy of the JUnit file (it is, after all, up to you what version of JUnit you use), but you can specify this library in the normal build classpaths, just as you would your other project dependencies.

Preparing Your Build for Automated Tests

The best way to explore how to use JUnit in Ant is to look at a practical example. In this chapter, we are going to test a simple domain class called TaxCalculator, which, rather surprisingly, calculates tax. In this particular case, we will be calculating income tax using a very simple (but nevertheless real) income tax system. The tax rates in this system are illustrated in Table 1-2.

Table 1-2. Income tax rates for our sample application

Taxable incomes	Tax rate for every $1 of taxable income
up to $38,000	19.5 cents
$38,001 to $60,000 inclusive	33 cents
$60,001 and over	39 cents

In Section 1.3, we discussed a recommended directory layout in which the application source code was separated from the unit tests. In this layout, the application classes are placed in the `src` directory, whereas the unit test classes go in the `test` directory. This practice will make your builds cleaner and easier to manage. The name of the directories is not particularly important (another option is to follow the Maven convention of a `src/main/java` directory for the Java application code, and `src/test/java` for Java unit tests)—the essential thing is to keep the unit tests away from the application code.

The first class we will implement for this calculator is a `TaxRate` class, which represents a single tax rate. It will also know how to calculate the income tax applicable for its own income bracket.

Methods such as TDD recommend writing unit tests *before* writing the code itself. This class is a good example of where TDD can be used effectively. So, before writing this class, let's start off with some unit tests to figure out how the class should behave. To test this class, we will test each income bracket using a varied set of values. Rather than testing every possible value, we test a selection of key values to check for boundary conditions. For example, for an initial test, you might test the first tax bracket against $0 and $10,000:

```
package com.javapowertools.taxcalculator.domain;

import static org.junit.Assert.*;
import org.junit.Test;

public class TaxRateTest {

    @Test
    public void testCalculateTaxBracket1() {
        TaxRate rate = new TaxRate(0, 38000, 0.195);
        assertEquals(rate.calculateTax(0), 0);
        assertEquals(rate.calculateTax(10000), 10000 * 0.195);
    }
}
```

You can now start to code. An initial class that passes these simple tests might look like this:

```
public class TaxRate {

    private double minimumRevenue;
    private double maxiumuRevenue;
    private double rate;

    public TaxRate(double minimumRevenue, double maxiumuRevenue, double rate) {
        super();
        this.minimumRevenue = minimumRevenue;
        this.maxiumuRevenue = maxiumuRevenue;
        this.rate = rate;
    }

    public double getMinimumRevenue() {
        return minimumRevenue;
    }

    public double getMaxiumuRevenue() {
        return maxiumuRevenue;
    }

    public double getRate() {
        return rate;
    }

    public double calculateTax(double totalRevenue) {
        return totalRevenue * rate;
```

```
    }
}
```

This is not enough, however, so we need to add some more test cases to check the other boundary conditions:

```
@Test
public void testCalculateTaxBracket1() {
    TaxRate rate = new TaxRate(0, 38000, 0.195);
    assertEquals(rate.calculateTax(0), 0);
    assertEquals(rate.calculateTax(10000), 10000 * 0.195);
    assertEquals(rate.calculateTax(38000), 38000 * 0.195);
    assertEquals( rate.calculateTax(50000), 38000 * 0.195);
}
```

Your class will now need some refactoring to take into account the maximum revenue. Once your class performs this correctly, you can progressively add new test cases to test other values, until the class does everything required of it. The full unit test class is shown here:

```
package com.javapowertools.taxcalculator.domain;

import static org.junit.Assert.*;
import org.junit.Test;

public class TaxRateTest {

    private static final double FIRST_TAX_BRACKET_RATE = 0.195;
    private static final double SECOND_TAX_BRACKET_RATE = 0.33;
    private static final double THIRD_TAX_BRACKET_RATE = 0.39;

    @Test
    public void testCalculateTaxBracket1() {
        TaxRate rate = new TaxRate(0, 38000, FIRST_TAX_BRACKET_RATE);
        assertEquals(0.0, rate.calculateTax(0), 0.0);
        assertEquals(10000 * FIRST_TAX_BRACKET_RATE,
                     rate.calculateTax(10000), 0.0);
        assertEquals(38000 * FIRST_TAX_BRACKET_RATE,
                     rate.calculateTax(38000), 0.0);
        assertEquals(38000 * FIRST_TAX_BRACKET_RATE,
                     rate.calculateTax(50000), 0.0);
    }

    @Test
    public void testCalculateTaxBracket2() {
        TaxRate rate = new TaxRate(38000, 60000, SECOND_TAX_BRACKET_RATE);
        assertEquals(0.0, rate.calculateTax(0), 0.0);
        assertEquals(0.0, rate.calculateTax(10000), 0.0);
        assertEquals(0.0, rate.calculateTax(38000), 0);
        assertEquals(2000 * SECOND_TAX_BRACKET_RATE,
                     rate.calculateTax(40000), 0);
        assertEquals(22000 * SECOND_TAX_BRACKET_RATE,
                     rate.calculateTax(60000), 0.0);
        assertEquals(22000 * SECOND_TAX_BRACKET_RATE,
                     rate.calculateTax(80000), 0.0);
```

```
    }

    @Test
    public void testCalculateTaxBracket3() {
        TaxRate rate = new TaxRate(60000, 60000, THIRD_TAX_BRACKET_RATE);
        assertEquals(0.0, rate.calculateTax(0), 0.0);
        assertEquals(0.0, rate.calculateTax(10000), 0.0);
        assertEquals(0.0, rate.calculateTax(38000), 0);
        assertEquals(0.0, rate.calculateTax(40000), 0);
        assertEquals(0.0, rate.calculateTax(60000), 0.0);
        assertEquals(20000 * THIRD_TAX_BRACKET_RATE,
                     rate.calculateTax(80000), 0.0);
        assertEquals(40000 * THIRD_TAX_BRACKET_RATE,
                     rate.calculateTax(100000), 0.0);
    }
}
```

Note that this is not necessarily how a tax application would be coded or tested in real life. For example, some tests are actually regrouped into a single test method for simplicity, and a real business application would probably use BigDecimals rather than doubles for more precision. However, these tests should be sufficient to verify that our class functions correctly for all the tax brackets. Let's fast-forward to the solution—the `TaxRate` class is shown in full here:

```
public class TaxRate {

    private double minimumRevenue;
    private double maxiumuRevenue;
    private double rate;

    public TaxRate(double minimumRevenue, double maxiumuRevenue, double rate) {
        super();
        this.minimumRevenue = minimumRevenue;
        this.maxiumuRevenue = maxiumuRevenue;
        this.rate = rate;
    }

    public double getMinimumRevenue() {
        return minimumRevenue;
    }

    public double getMaxiumuRevenue() {
        return maxiumuRevenue;
    }

    public double getRate() {
        return rate;
    }

    private double getApplicableAmount(double totalRevenue) {
        double applicableAmount = 0.0;
        if (totalRevenue >= minimumRevenue) {
            applicableAmount = totalRevenue - minimumRevenue;
```

```
            if (maxiumuRevenue > 0) {
                if (totalRevenue > maxiumuRevenue) {
                    applicableAmount = maxiumuRevenue - minimumRevenue;
                }
            }
        }
        return applicableAmount;
    }

    public double calculateTax(double totalRevenue) {
        return getApplicableAmount(totalRevenue) * rate;
    }
}
```

Now to the heart of the matter: running the unit tests. Before we get to the JUnit task itself, we need to do a little housekeeping. First, we define our directory structure, using property definitions for easier maintenance and clarity. As discussed, we place the application source code in the `src` directory (represented by the *$src.dir* property) and the unit tests in the `test` directory (the *$test.dir* property). Likewise, the application source code is compiled to the `build/classes` directory (*$build.classes.dir*), whereas the unit tests are compiled to `build/test-classes` (*$test.classes.dir*). The properties definitions are shown here:

```
<?xml version="1.0" ?>
<project name="tax-calculator" default="package">
    <property name="src.dir" location="src" />
    <property name="build.dir" location="build" />
    <property name="tests.dir" location="test" />
    <property name="build.classes.dir" location="${build.dir}/classes" />
    <property name="test.classes.dir" location="${build.dir}/test-classes" />
    <property name="lib" location="lib" />
    <property name="dist.dir" location="dist" />
```

Next, we need to define some paths. The first is the classpath used to compile the application classes. This simply contains all the JAR files in the lib directory:

```
    <path id="compile.classpath">
        <fileset dir="${lib}" includes="*.jar" />
    </path>
```

The second is the classpath that we will use when we compile the unit tests. Here, in addition to the libraries in the JAR file, we also need the compiled application classes that we are meant to test. To do this, we create a path with two elements: a *<path>* tag containing a reference to the compile classpath, and a *<pathelement>* tag containing the compiled application classes:

```
    <path id="test.compile.classpath">
      <path refid="compile.classpath"/>
      <pathelement location="${build.classes.dir}"/>
    </path>
```

We're not quite done with the paths just yet. We also need to define a classpath containing all of these classes, *plus* the compiled unit tests. We will be needing this one when we run our unit tests:

```
<path id="test.classpath">
  <path refid="test.compile.classpath"/>
  <pathelement path="${test.classes.dir}"/>
</path>
```

The next thing we need to provide in the build script is an initialization task to build the output directories, if necessary. This target simply uses the *<mkdir>* task to create the target directories. Note that there is no need to create the `build` directory before creating the `build/classes` directory; Ant will do that for us:

```
<target name="init">
    <mkdir dir="${build.classes.dir}" />
    <mkdir dir="${test.classes.dir}" />
    <mkdir dir="${dist.dir}" />
</target>
```

Now we can proceed to the compilation tasks. The *<javac>* task used to compile the application classes is straightforward, and simply compiles the application classes in the *${src.dir}* directory into the *${build.classes.dir}* directory:

```
<target name="compile" depends="init" description="Compile Java code">
    <javac srcdir="${src.dir}"
           destdir="${build.classes.dir}"
           classpathref="compile.classpath" />
</target>
```

Next we need to compile our test classes. It's always nicer to test against the latest version of your application classes, so we make this target depend on the "compile" target. This will ensure that the application classes are compiled or recompiled, if necessary, before the unit test classes are compiled. Then we simply compile the unit test classes in the *${tests.dir}* directory, using the *test.compile.classpath* classpath we defined above.

```
<target name="compile-tests" depends="compile" description="Compile Unit Tests">
    <javac srcdir="${tests.dir}"
           destdir="${test.classes.dir}">
           <classpath refid="test.compile.classpath"/>
    </javac>
</target>
```

Using the <junit> Task

We are now (finally) ready to run our unit tests from within Ant. Our application classes are up-to-date, and our unit tests are compiled and ready to go. Let's see how we run unit tests from within Ant.

```
<target name="test" depends="compile-tests" description="Run unit tests">
    <junit printsummary="true" haltonfailure="true">
        <classpath refid="test.classpath" />
```

```
            <test name="com.javapowertools.taxcalculator.domain.TaxRateTest" />
        </junit>
    </target>
```

This is a fairly minimal, but usable, *<junit>* task configuration. It runs the TaxRateTest test case, using the *test.classpath* classpath that we set up earlier. The *printsummary* attribute tells Ant to display a list of the unit test classes being executed. Otherwise, it will run the tests, but keep the results to itself unless any of the unit tests fail. The *haltonfailure* attribute tells Ant to stop the build if there are test failures. The default behavior is to continue the build even if there are test failures, so you might want to generate test reports afterward (see "Generating HTML Test Reports," later in this section). When you run this target, Ant will run the unit tests and display a brief summary of the test results:

```
$ ant test
Buildfile: build.xml

init:

compile:

compile-tests:

test:
    [junit] Running com.javapowertools.taxcalculator.domain.TaxRateTest
    [junit] Tests run: 3, Failures: 0, Errors: 0, Time elapsed: 0.033 sec

BUILD SUCCESSFUL
Total time: 0 seconds
```

If any of the tests fail, JUnit will indicate the number of failed tests and the build will fail:

```
$ ant test
Buildfile: build.xml

init:

compile:

compile-tests:

test:
    [junit] Running com.javapowertools.taxcalculator.domain.TaxRateTest
    [junit] Tests run: 3, Failures: 1, Errors: 0, Time elapsed: 0.048 sec

BUILD FAILED
/home/wakaleo/projects/jpt-sample-code/ant-demo/build.xml:46:
Test com.javapowertools.taxcalculator.domain.TaxRateTest failed
```

The only problem with this is that the error message is not particularly informative. Details of what went wrong are not provided, which makes it a bit hard to debug. As you might expect, JUnit (and Ant) can do much better than that. JUnit comes with a set of formatters that can be used to display the test results in a more usable form. You can use JUnit formatters in the *<junit>* task by adding nested *<formatter>* elements to the *<junit>* task.

The *<junit>* task comes with three types of formatter. The simplest formatter is the "brief" formatter, which just provides details for any test failures. The "plain" formatter provides information on the number of tests passed and failed, and also lists the tests that actually succeeded. The third type, the "xml" formatter, is mainly used for report generation. We look at how to generate HTML test reports later in this section in "Generating HTML Test Reports."

You can add a formatter using the *<formatter>* element as shown here:

```
<target name="test" depends="compile-tests" description="Run unit tests">
    <junit printsummary="true" haltonfailure="true">
        <classpath refid="test.classpath" />
        <formatter type="plain"/>
        <test name="com.javapowertools.taxcalculator.domain.TaxRateTest" />
    </junit>
</target>
```

This will generate a text report in the working directory with a little more information about the failure:

```
$ ant test
...
test:
    [junit] Running com.javapowertools.taxcalculator.domain.TaxRateTest
    [junit] Tests run: 3, Failures: 1, Errors: 0, Time elapsed: 0.048 sec

BUILD FAILED
/home/wakaleo/projects/jpt-sample-code/ant-demo/build.xml:46:
Test com.javapowertools.taxcalculator.domain.TaxRateTest failed

$ more TEST-com.javapowertools.taxcalculator.domain.TaxRateTest.txt
Testsuite: com.javapowertools.taxcalculator.domain.TaxRateTest
Tests run: 3, Failures: 1, Errors: 0, Time elapsed: 0.059 sec

Testcase: testCalculateTaxBracket1 took 0.016 sec
        FAILED
expected:<7410.0> but was:<5850.0>
junit.framework.AssertionFailedError: expected:<7410.0> but was:<5850.0>
        at com.javapowertools.taxcalculator.domain.TaxRateTest.
        testCalculateTaxBracket1(Unknown Source)

Testcase: testCalculateTaxBracket2 took 0.002 sec
Testcase: testCalculateTaxBracket3 took 0.008 sec
```

Writing test results to text files has a lot going for it, especially if you have many hundreds of unit tests. However, you may want a quick heads-up on your test failures, without having to sift through text files. A good way to do this is to have Ant write the test reports to the console instead of to a file, using the *usefile* attribute:

```
<formatter type="plain" usefile="false"/>
```

This will write the test results to the console, which has the advantage of making any errors stand out fairly clearly.

```
$ ant test
Buildfile: build.xml

init:

compile:

compile-tests:

test:
    [junit] Running com.javapowertools.taxcalculator.domain.TaxRateTest
    [junit] Testsuite: com.javapowertools.taxcalculator.domain.TaxRateTest
    [junit] Tests run: 3, Failures: 1, Errors: 0, Time elapsed: 0.062 sec
    [junit] Tests run: 3, Failures: 1, Errors: 0, Time elapsed: 0.062 sec
    [junit]
    [junit] Testcase: testCalculateTaxBracket1 took 0.028 sec
    [junit]     FAILED
    [junit] expected:<7410.0> but was:<5850.0>
    [junit] junit.framework.AssertionFailedError: expected:<7410.0> but was:<5850.0>
    [junit]     at com.javapowertools.taxcalculator.domain.TaxRateTest.testCalculate
                TaxBracket1(Unknown Source)
    [junit]
    [junit] Testcase: testCalculateTaxBracket2 took 0.001 sec
    [junit] Testcase: testCalculateTaxBracket3 took 0.006 sec

BUILD FAILED
/home/wakaleo/projects/jpt-sample-code/ant-demo/build.xml:46:
Test com.javapowertools.taxcalculator.domain.TaxRateTest failed

Total time: 0 seconds
```

Or you can have the best of both worlds, and write both to a file and to the console, by specifying two *formatter* elements:

```
<formatter type="plain"/>
<formatter type="plain" usefile="false"/>
```

Finally, if you find the "plain" formatter a bit verbose, you can always use the "brief" formatter, shown in the following example:

```
<formatter type="brief" usefile="false"/>
```

This formatter generates a more concise output that is well-suited to console output:

```
$ ant test
Buildfile: build.xml

init:

compile:

compile-tests:
```

```
test:
    [junit] Running com.javapowertools.taxcalculator.domain.TaxRateTest
    [junit] Testsuite: com.javapowertools.taxcalculator.domain.TaxRateTest
    [junit] Tests run: 3, Failures: 1, Errors: 0, Time elapsed: 0.062 sec
    [junit] Tests run: 3, Failures: 1, Errors: 0, Time elapsed: 0.062 sec
    [junit]
    [junit] Testcase: testCalculateTaxBracket1 took 0.028 sec
    [junit]     FAILED
    [junit] expected:<7410.0> but was:<5850.0>
    [junit] junit.framework.AssertionFailedError: expected:<7410.0> but was:<5850.0>
    [junit]     at com.javapowertools.taxcalculator.domain.TaxRateTest.
                testCalculateTaxBracket1(Unknown Source)
    [junit]
    [junit] Testcase: testCalculateTaxBracket2 took 0.001 sec
    [junit] Testcase: testCalculateTaxBracket3 took 0.006 sec

BUILD FAILED
/home/wakaleo/projects/jpt-sample-code/ant-demo/build.xml:46: Test com.javapowertools.
taxcalculator.domain.TaxRateTest failed

Total time: 0 seconds
```

Running Multiple Tests

Now that we are sure that the "TaxRateCalculator" works correctly, we can proceed to writing the `TaxCalculator` itself. We could test this class in a traditional, JUnit 3-style approach by writing test cases for a (hopefully representative) set of values, as shown here:

```
public class TaxCalculatorTest extends TestCase {

    private TaxCalculator calc = null;

    @Override
    protected void setUp() throws Exception {
        calc = new TaxCalculator();
    }
    public void testCalculation1() {
        assertEquals(calc.calculateIncomeTax(0), 0.0, 0.0);
    }
    public void testCalculation2() {
        assertEquals(calc.calculateIncomeTax(10000), 1950.00, 0.0);
    }
    public void testCalculation3() {
        assertEquals(calc.calculateIncomeTax(20000), 3900.00, 0.0);
    }
    public void testCalculation4() {
        assertEquals(calc.calculateIncomeTax(30000), 5850.00, 0.0);
    }
    public void testCalculation5() {
        assertEquals(calc.calculateIncomeTax(60000), 14670.00, 0.0);
    }
    public void testCalculation6() {
        assertEquals(calc.calculateIncomeTax(100000), 30270.00, 0.0);
    }
```

```
    public void testCalculation7() {
        assertEquals(calc.calculateIncomeTax(160000), 53670.00, 0.0);
    }
    public void testCalculation8() {
        assertEquals(calc.calculateIncomeTax(200000), 69270.00, 0.0);
    }
}
```

Alternatively, we could use a new JUnit 4 feature called parameterized tests (see Section 10.6) to write an arguably cleaner and more maintainable test case:

```
@RunWith(Parameterized.class)
public class TaxCalculatorTest {

    @Parameters
    public static Collection data() {
        return Arrays.asList(new Object[][]{
                /* Income      Tax  */
                {     0.00,     0.00},
                { 10000.00,  1950.00},
                { 20000.00,  3900.00},
                { 38000.00,  7410.00},
                { 38001.00,  7410.33},
                { 40000.00,  8070.00},
                { 60000.00, 14670.00},
                {100000.00, 30270.00},
                {160000.00, 53670.00},
                {200000.00, 69270.00},
        });
    }

    private double revenue;
    private double expectedTax;
    private TaxCalculator calculator = new TaxCalculator();

    public TaxCalculatorTest(double input, double expectedTax) {
        this.revenue = input;
        this.expectedTax = expectedTax;
    }

    @Test public void calculateTax() {
        assertEquals(expectedTax, calculator.calculateIncomeTax(revenue), 0.0);
    }
}
```

One of the nice things about the *<junit>* task in Ant 1.7 is that the testing method doesn't really matter—you can use JUnit 4 test cases, JUnit 3 test cases, or a mixture of the two, and the *<junit>* task will still run them all in a consistent manner. This is handy if you want to use the modern features of JUnit 4 where possible, while still using testing frameworks that rely on JUnit 3 for some of your tests.

Just for completeness, here is the `TaxCalculator` class itself:

```
public class TaxCalculator {
```

```
    public static final List<TaxRate> TAX_RATES
        = new ArrayList<TaxRate>();

    static {
        TAX_RATES.add(new TaxRate(0, 38000, 0.195));
        TAX_RATES.add(new TaxRate(38000, 60000, 0.33));
        TAX_RATES.add(new TaxRate(60000, 0, 0.39));
    }

    public TaxCalculator() {
    }

    public double calculateIncomeTax(double totalRevenue) {
        double totalTax = 0.0;
        for(TaxRate rate : TAX_RATES) {
            totalTax += rate.calculateTax(totalRevenue);
        }
        return totalTax;
    }
}
```

So, now we have several test classes to test. The *<test>* task is a fine example of an Ant task (as tasks go), and is an excellent way to get familiar with the features of JUnit in Ant. However, it is not always the most appropriate way to run tests in a real project. In a real project, you usually have more than one unit test. In fact, for a typical small- to medium-sized project, you may have hundreds. You shouldn't have to add a new *<test>* task to your build file for each new unit test class you write.

Indeed, there is a much better way. The *<batchtest>* element lets you run multiple unit tests in one go, using Ant *filesets* to tell Ant which tests to run. In the following example, we use *<batchtest>* to run all the test classes in the test classes directory whose names end with "Test." This naming convention is useful if you wish to include other utility or abstract classes alongside your test classes.

```
<junit printsummary="true" haltonfailure="true">
    <classpath refid="test.classpath" />
    <formatter type="plain" usefile="false" />
    <batchtest>
        <fileset dir="${test.classes.dir}" includes="**/*Test.class" />
    </batchtest>
</junit>
```

Of course, it is also useful to store the test results in the form of text files so that you can come back and analyze them later. However, it isn't very tidy to generate large numbers of test reports in the project root directory. It would be much tidier to place them in their own directory. This is easy to do using the *todir* attribute in the *<batchtest>* element. In the following listing, we place all the test reports in the `reports` directory.

```
<property name="reports.dir" location="reports" />
...
<target name="init">
    <mkdir dir="${build.classes.dir}" />
```

```
        <mkdir dir="${test.classes.dir}" />
        <mkdir dir="${dist.dir}" />
        <mkdir dir="${reports.dir}" />
    </target>
    ...
    <target name="test" depends="compile-tests" description="Run unit tests">
        <junit printsummary="true" haltonfailure="true">
            <classpath refid="test.classpath" />
            <formatter type="plain" usefile="false" />
            <formatter type="plain" />
            <batchtest>
                <fileset dir="${test.classes.dir}" includes="**/*Test.class" />
            </batchtest>
        </junit>
    </target>
```

Running Tests in a Separate JVM

By default, the *<junit>* task runs unit tests in the current JVM; however, there are times when it can be useful to run your tests in a separate JVM. You can do this using the *fork* attribute, which spawns a new process and runs your tests in a brand new JVM. Just set the *fork* attribute of your *<junit>* task to "true," as shown here:

```
<junit printsummary="true" fork="true">
    <classpath refid="test.classpath" />
    <formatter type="plain" />
    <batchtest>
        <fileset dir="${test.classes.dir}" includes="**/*Test.class" />
    </batchtest>
</junit>
```

You can also use the *forkmode* attribute to indicate if you want a new process for each test (using "perTest," which is the default value), for each *<batchtest>* ("perBatch"), or just one for all the tests ("once"). Creating a new JVM for each test is the cleanest way to separate your tests, but it is also the slowest.

Running your *<junit>* task as a forked process gives you much more control over your tests. You can use the *maxmemory* attribute to run your tests under specific memory constraints. You can specify a *timeout* value to force tests to fail if they run longer than a certain number of milliseconds. And it also means that your tests can fail dramatically (for example, with an `OutOfMemory` exception) without breaking your build process.

Generating HTML Test Reports

When your project has many hundreds of unit tests, the generated text files can get very large, and it can be hard to sift through them all to find out exactly what went wrong.

JUnit lets you generate your test results in XML form. Now, on the surface, an XML test report is even less readable than a plain text one. However, Ant comes with the *<junitreport>* task, which lets you turn this raw XML data into a quite presentable

HTML report. More precisely, the *<junitreport>* task regroups the XML test reports into a single XML document, and then applies an XSL stylesheet of your choice. The end result is much more readable and usable than the plain text equivalent, and you can easily publish your test results onto a project web site for all to see.

The first thing you need to do is generate some test results in XML format, using the "xml" *formatter* element. You could do this as follows:

```
<target name="test" depends="compile-tests" description="Run unit tests">
    <junit printsummary="true">
        <classpath refid="test.classpath" />
        <formatter type="plain" />
        <formatter type="xml" />
        <batchtest todir="${reports.data.dir}" >
            <fileset dir="${test.classes.dir}" includes="**/*Test.class" />
        </batchtest>
    </junit>
</target>
```

We have added some new directories here to make things a little tidier. The raw report data is placed in the **reports/xml** directory, whereas the final HTML report (which takes the form of a multipage web site) is stored in the **reports/html** directory. This makes it easier to clean up test data and to deploy your HTML reports.

```
<property name="reports.dir" location="reports" />
<property name="reports.data.dir" location="reports/xml" />
<property name="reports.html.dir" location="reports/html" />
```

Now that we have the data, we still need to generate the report itself. We can do this using the *<junitreport>* task as follows:

```
<target name="test.report" depends="test" description="Generate HTML unit
 test reports">
    <junitreport todir="${reports.data.dir}">
      <fileset dir="${reports.data.dir}">
        <include name="TEST-*.xml"/>
      </fileset>
      <report format="frames" todir="${reports.html.dir}"/>
    </junitreport>
</target>
```

This basically takes all the XML test reports in **reports/xml** and generates an HTML report using the frames-based format (the most commonly used) in the **reports/html** directory.

Both versions of the reports are dynamic—you can click on a package or test class for more details, and display the failed assertion and other useful details (see Figure 1-2).

This format is fine for most situations (see Figure 1-3), and is generated by the XSL stylesheet that comes bundled in the `ant-junit.jar` library. Alternatively, you may want to use the "noframes" stylesheet (just use *format="noframes"*) to generate the test results in a single (big) HTML page.

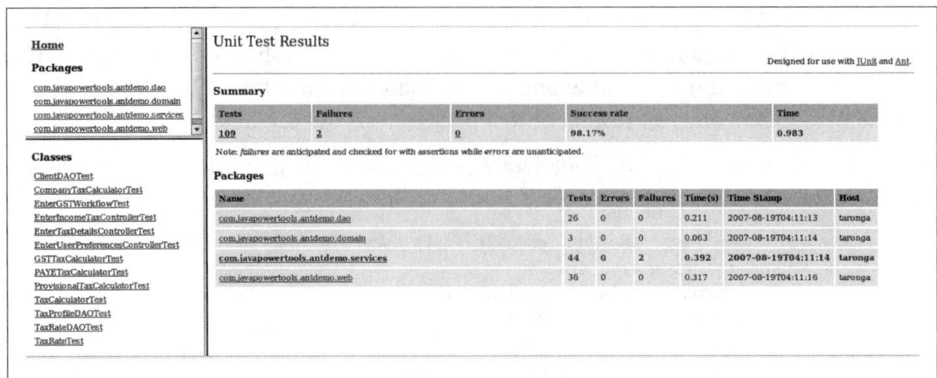

Figure 1-2. The report generated by <junitreport>

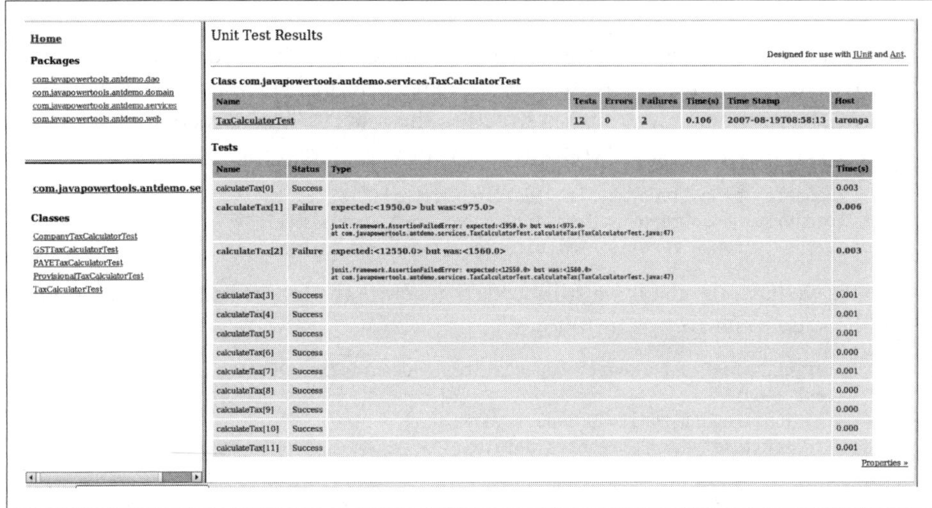

Figure 1-3. Displaying detailed results for a particular test case

In some cases, you might want to customize the stylesheets a little more. For example, you may want to add the company logo or change the color scheme to suite your project web site. You can do this without too much trouble by using the *styledir* attribute of the *<report>* element to override the default stylesheets. The first thing you need to do is copy the `junit-frames.xsl` and `junit-noframes.xsl` files into a directory of your own (`conf/css`, for example). You can get these files from the `ant-junit.jar` file, or from the `etc` directory in the Ant distribution (`$ANT_HOME/etc`). Don't change their names, as Ant will look for stylesheets with these names in the directory you provide, and won't accept any value other than "frames" or "noframes." You can now tailor these stylesheets to your heart's content. Then just specify the directory using the *styledir* attribute, as shown here:

```
<junitreport todir="${reports.data.dir}">
    <fileset dir="${reports.data.dir}">
        <include name="TEST-*.xml"/>
    </fileset>
    <report format="frames"
            todir="${reports.html.dir}"
            styledir="conf/css"/>
</junitreport>
```

As you would expect, you need to generate your test reports *after* your unit tests have finished. As far as the build process goes, this has some fairly major side effects. For one thing, it means that you cannot simply let the build stop if the tests fail, so setting the *haltonfailure* attribute to "true" (see "Using the <junit> Task," earlier in this section) is a really bad idea. On the other hand, it *is* a good idea for the build to fail if there are test failures. In fact, your continuous build system may rely on it. This puts us in somewhat of a dilemma.

Fortunately, there is a solution. The *<junit>* task has two special attributes, *failureproperty* and *errorproperty*. These attributes name properties that will be set to "true" if a failure (or error) occurs. In fact, *failureproperty* is usually sufficient, as errors are treated as failures as well. This lets you proceed with the build until you decide it is time to stop, and then (and only then) stop the build with an error message. You could do this as follows (the *haltonfailure* attribute is just here for clarity, as the default value for this attribute is "false"):

```
<target name="test" depends="compile-tests" description="Run unit tests">
    <junit printsummary="true" haltonfailure="false" failureproperty=
     "test.failures">
        <classpath refid="test.classpath" />
        <formatter type="plain" />
        <formatter type="xml" />
        <batchtest todir="${reports.data.dir}" >
            <fileset dir="${test.classes.dir}" includes="**/*Test.class" />
        </batchtest>
    </junit>
</target>
```

If any failures (or errors) occur, the *test.failures* property will be set to "true." Now, just after the *<junitreport>* task, we add a *<fail>* task. The *<fail>* task lets you force the build to fail if a particular condition is met.

```
<target name="test.report" depends="test"
        description="Generate HTML unit test reports">
    <junitreport todir="${reports.data.dir}">
      <fileset dir="${reports.data.dir}">
        <include name="TEST-*.xml"/>
      </fileset>
      <report format="noframes" todir="${reports.html.dir}"/>
    </junitreport>
    <fail if="test.failures" message="There were test failures." />
</target>
```

Now, when you run the test.report target, the tests will be executed, the report generated, and then the build will fail with an appropriate error message:

```
$ ant test.report
Buildfile: build.xml

init:
    [mkdir] Created dir: /home/wakaleo/projects/jpt-sample-code/ant-demo/build/classes
    [mkdir] Created dir: /home/wakaleo/projects/jpt-sample-code/ant-demo/build/test-classes
    [mkdir] Created dir: /home/wakaleo/projects/jpt-sample-code/ant-demo/dist
    [mkdir] Created dir: /home/wakaleo/projects/jpt-sample-code/ant-demo/reports/xml
    [mkdir] Created dir: /home/wakaleo/projects/jpt-sample-code/ant-demo/reports/html

compile:

compile-tests:

test:
    [junit] Running com.javapowertools.taxcalculator.services.TaxCalculatorTest
    [junit] Tests run: 12, Failures: 2, Errors: 0, Time elapsed: 0.108 sec
    ...

test.report:
[junitreport] Processing /home/wakaleo/projects/jpt-sample-code/ant-demo/reports/xml/
TESTS-TestSuites.xml to /home/wakaleo/projects/jpt-sample-code/ant-demo/reports/html/
junit-noframes.html
[junitreport] Loading stylesheet jar:file:/usr/share/ant/lib/ant-junit.jar!/org
/apache/tools/ant/taskdefs/optional/junit/xsl/junit-noframes.xsl
[junitreport] Transform time: 531ms

BUILD FAILED
/home/wakaleo/projects/jpt-sample-code/ant-demo/build.xml:74: There were test failures.
Total time: 7 seconds
```

Using Asserts in Your Test Cases

In many examples of JUnit 4 test cases (and also TestNG test cases), the *assert* keyword is used as a convenient way to test application code. The *assert* keyword is built-in to the language, and thus needs no particular imports or dependencies. It also has a quite readable syntax. A typical *assert* in this context is shown here:

```
double tax = rate.calculateTax(100000);
assert tax > 0 : "Tax should not be zero";
```

Asserts are not just used for test cases: they can also be placed within application code as a way of documenting the intended behavior of your classes, and the assumptions that you have made when coding a particular method. For example, here we indicate that we are never expecting to receive a negative value for the totalRevenue parameter:

```
    public double calculateIncomeTax(double totalRevenue) {
        assert totalRevenue >= 0 : "Revenue should not be negative";
        ...
```

The only problem with using this approach with JUnit is that, out-of-the-box, it won't work. Assertions can be expensive operations, and by default, they are disabled at runtime. To use them, you need to activate them explicitly.

You can do this fairly easily in Ant. First of all, you need to run JUnit in a forked process (by setting the *fork* attribute to "true"). Then you need to add an *<assertions>* element to your *<junit>* task, containing at least one *<enable>* element. The following task will activate assertions for all nonsystem classes:

```
<junit printsummary="true" haltonfailure="true" fork="true">
    <assertions>
        <enable/>
    </assertions>
    <classpath refid="test.classpath" />
    <formatter type="plain" />
    <batchtest todir="${reports.dir}" >
        <fileset dir="${test.classes.dir}" includes="**/*Test.class" />
    </batchtest>
</junit>
```

If need be, you can narrow this down to a particular package or class, using the *package* and class attributes, respectively. After all, you don't need to activate assertions for the whole JDK. Here we activate assertions uniquely for classes underneath the `com.javapowertools` package:

```
<assertions>
    <enable package="com.javapowertools" />
</assertions>
```

Now, when you run your tests, JUnit will integrate any failed assertions into the test results, albeit with a little less information in the details:

```
Testsuite: com.javapowertools.taxcalculator.domain.TaxRateTest
Tests run: 3, Failures: 1, Errors: 0, Time elapsed: 0.027 sec

Testcase: testCalculateTaxBracket1 took 0.005 sec
Testcase: testCalculateTaxBracket2 took 0.001 sec
Testcase: testCalculateTaxBracket3 took 0.002 sec
        FAILED
Tax should not be zero
junit.framework.AssertionFailedError: Tax should not be zero
        at com.javapowertools.taxcalculator.domain.TaxRateTest.testCalculateTaxBracket3
        (Unknown Source)
```

1.7 Generating Documentation with Javadoc

Technical documentation is an important part of any project, and Javadoc is one of the cornerstones of technical documentation in Java. Javadoc produces a quite decent, usable set of API documentation for your Java code, which can be a valuable aid as a communication tool, helping team members understand what other team members are doing. Of course, good Javadoc requires well-written and meaningful comments within the source code, and enforcing that is a tall order for any tool. And Javadoc documentation is by definition low-level reference material—it can be very useful for an application developer familiar with the application, but it will be of limited use for a new developer trying to learn the application architecture. Despite these reservations, Javadoc should be an integral part of any development project.

It is a good idea to generate Javadoc as part of your build process. Javadoc documentation should be generated and published alongside the compiled source code and the unit test results as part of the automatic build lifecycle. In Ant, you can do this using the *<javadoc>* task. This task has a lot of attributes and nested elements, but only a few are essential. Here is a simple example:

```
<target name="javadoc" depends="compile,init" description="Generate JavaDocs.">
     <javadoc sourcepath="${src.dir}"
              destdir="${reports.javadoc}"
              author="true"
              version="true"
              use="true"
              access="private"
              linksource="true"
              windowtitle="${ant.project.name} API">
       <classpath>
           <path refid="compile.classpath" />
           <pathelement path="${build.classes.dir}" />
       </classpath>
       <doctitle><![CDATA[<h1>${ant.project.name}</h1>]]></doctitle>
       <bottom><![CDATA[<i>Copyright &#169; 2007 All Rights Reserved.
       </i>]]></bottom>
     </javadoc>
</target>
```

This task will generate Javadoc documentation for all the classes in the `${src.dir}` directory. We needed to provide it with a classpath containing both the compiled classes and the application dependencies. We did this using an embedded *<classpath>* structure. We could also have defined this classpath elsewhere in the build file and referred to it using the *classpathref* attribute.

Most of the other attributes used here are fairly self-explanatory. The *listsource* attribute causes Ant to insert links in the Javadoc document to the source code in HTML form. This is similar to the Maven JXR plugin, although the formatting is less polished. The *access* property determines what parts of the classes should be documented. Here we document everything, from the *private* fields up. If you want a more succinct view, you might want to limit the javadoc to the *protected* or even to only the *public* fields and methods.

There are many other options for this task, far too many, in fact, to cover here. Most involve fine-tuning formatting details, and aren't particularly interesting. You can limit the classes being documented by providing a list of packages in the *packagenames* attribute, although if you separate your test classes from your application source code, the reasons for doing so are generally more rare.

Javadoc documentation is generated in the form of a self-contained web site. This makes it easy to deploy to your local project web site, or to bundle up with your library, as most open source projects do.

In Chapter 30, we look at other tools you can use to enhance your technical documentation, all of which can be easily integrated into an Ant build script.

1.8 Packaging Your Application

Once you have compiled and tested your application, the next step is to bundle up the compiled code into a deliverable application or library. This can take different forms, depending on your project: you may have to prepare a JAR file, a WAR file, or possibly a ZIP or TAR file containing the executable code plus other files such as documentation and source code. Ant has many powerful features that can help you prepare your application for delivery. In the following sections, we will look at a few of the more interesting ones.

Generating a JAR File

The most fundamental Java packaging mechanism is the JAR file. A JAR file is essentially a ZIP file containing a hierarchy of compiled Java classes, plus some metadata. WAR and EAR files are similar, with some extra constraints on their internal directory structure and content.

The basic usage of the *<jar>* task is simple. Here is an example from our sample application, where we bundle the compiled classes into a JAR file:

```
<property name="project.name" value="{ant.project.name}" />
<property name="project.version" value="1.0" />
...
<target name="package" depends="compile" description="Generate JAR file">
    <jar destfile="${dist.dir}/${project.name}-${project.version}.jar" basedir=
     "${build.classes.dir}"/>
</target>
```

Running this will (surprise, surprise!) generate a JAR file containing your compiled classes:

```
$ ant clean package
Buildfile: build.xml

clean:
   [delete] Deleting directory /home/wakaleo/projects/jpt-sample-code/ant-demo/dist
   [delete] Deleting directory /home/wakaleo/projects/jpt-sample-code/ant-demo/reports

init:
    [mkdir] Created dir: /home/wakaleo/projects/jpt-sample-code/ant-demo/dist
    [mkdir] Created dir: /home/wakaleo/projects/jpt-sample-code/ant-demo/reports/xml
    [mkdir] Created dir: /home/wakaleo/projects/jpt-sample-code/ant-demo/reports/html

compile:
```

```
package:
      [jar] Building jar: /home/wakaleo/projects/jpt-sample-code/ant-demo/dist/
      tax-calculator-1.0.jar

BUILD SUCCESSFUL
Total time: 0 seconds
```

We use the Maven convention for naming JAR files here, which is to add the version number to the end of the filename. This makes it easier to identify file versions at a glance. The project name comes from the *ant.project.name* property, which is defined in the <project> root element. Using a different property means that developers are free to change the name of the generated JAR file by overriding this variable.*

If you need to deploy files from several different directories, you can use *<fileset>* elements to define which files to include. For example, if you also want to include files from the `src/resources` directory, you could do the following:

```
<property name="project.name" value="{ant.project.name}" />
<property name="project.version" value="1.0" />
...
<target name="package" depends="compile" description="Generate JAR file">
    <jar destfile="${dist.dir}/${project.name}-${project.version}.jar">
        <fileset dir="${build.classes.dir}"/>
        <fileset dir="src/resources"/>
    </jar>
</target>
```

If we have a look inside the JAR file generated by this task, we might notice the extra META-INF directory, which contains a file called MANIFEST.MF. This is where metadata about the version of the file is stored, along with other details such as the product and vendor names:

```
$ jar -tf dist/tax-calculator-1.0.jar
META-INF/
META-INF/MANIFEST.MF
com/
com/javapowertools/
com/javapowertools/antdemo/
com/javapowertools/antdemo/domain/
com/javapowertools/antdemo/web/
com/javapowertools/antdemo/Main.class
com/javapowertools/antdemo/domain/Customer.class
com/javapowertools/antdemo/domain/TaxCalculator.class
com/javapowertools/antdemo/domain/TaxRate.class
com/javapowertools/antdemo/web/TaxCalculatorController.clas
...
```

By default, the MANIFEST.MF file contains very little. A sample is shown here:

* I first came across this technique in the excellent *Ant In Action* (Manning Publications), by Steve Loughran and Erik Hatcher.

```
Manifest-Version: 1.0
Ant-Version: Apache Ant 1.7.0
Created-By: 1.6.0-b105 (Sun Microsystems Inc.)
```

However, this file is a great place to put version and build numbers and/or timestamps. Putting a version number and a build number (or timestamp) into your deployed packages is a good habit to get into—you never know when you need to work out exactly which build has just been deployed into production. In Ant, you can add extra details into the MANIFEST.MF file using the *<manifest>* element in the *<jar>* task:

```
<target name="package" depends="compile" description="Generate JAR file">
    <tstamp>
        <format property="build.date" pattern="EEEE, d MMMM yyyy"/>
        <format property="build.time" pattern="hh:mm a"/>
    </tstamp>
    <jar destfile="${dist.dir}/${project.name}-${project.version}.jar"
     basedir="${build.classes.dir}" >
          <manifest>
            <attribute name="Built-By" value="${user.name}"/>
              <attribute name="Specification-Title" value="${project.name}"/>
            <attribute name="Specification-Version" value="${project.version}"/>
            <attribute name="Specification-Vendor" value="ACME Incorporated"/>
            <attribute name="Implementation-Title" value="common"/>
            <attribute name="Implementation-Version" value="${project.version}
             - built at ${build.time} on ${build.date} "/>
            <attribute name="Implementation-Vendor" value="ACME Incorporated"/>
          </manifest>
    </jar>
</target>
```

Here we use the *<tstamp>* task to generate a timestamp corresponding to the current time. This task automatically sets three properties: *DSTAMP*, *TSTAMP*, and *TODAY*. The first two (*DSTAMP* and *TSTAMP*) are set to the current date and time, respectively, in a fairly machine-friendly (but not particularly readable) format (e.g., "20070820" and "2024," respectively). The *TODAY* value is more readable (e.g., "August 20 2007"), but for a build date, we want something a little more precise. So, we use the nested *<format>* element to set some properties of our own. The deployed MANIFEST.MF file will now look something like this:

```
Manifest-Version: 1.0
Ant-Version: Apache Ant 1.7.0
Created-By: 1.6.0-b105 (Sun Microsystems Inc.)
Built-By: wakaleo
Specification-Title: tax-calculator
Specification-Version: 1.0
Specification-Vendor: ACME Incorporated
Implementation-Title: common
Implementation-Version: 1.0 - built at 10:26 PM on Monday, 20 August
Implementation-Vendor: ACME Incorporated
```

Generating a WAR File or an EAR File

Web applications are usually distributed in the form of a WAR file. WAR files can (usually) be deployed to any Java web server using a very simple deployment procedure. The exact procedure will vary from one application server to another, but it is usually something that can be done by a system administrator without a detailed understanding of the application.

A WAR file is simply a JAR file with a few extra requirements. In particular, a WAR file needs a special directory called `WEB-INF`, which contains application classes, libraries, and configuration files. Files placed under this directory cannot be accessed directly on the deployed web application, so this is a convenient place to put compiled classes, libraries, configuration files, and JSP pages. The basic directory structure of a WAR file is illustrated in Table 1-3.

Table 1-3. A typical WAR directory structure

Directory	Description
/	Publicly accessible web pages
WEB-INF/	Configuration files, not visible from the web site
WEB-INF/classes	Compiled classes
WEB-INF/lib	Application libraries

The *<war>* task is an extension of the *<jar>* task that takes into account the special structure of a WAR file. You use special nested elements to define the files to go into the `WEB-INF/classes`, `WEB-INF/lib` or `WEB-INF` directories.

Suppose you need to generate a WAR file for a JSP-based web application. The JSP files are stored in a directory called `web`. This directory also contains the WEB-INF subdirectory, where we store the `web.xml` file and any other configuration files we need. However, the application libraries and compiled classes will be obtained from other project directories.

You can create a WAR file from this directory structure using the *<war>* task, as shown here:

```
<property name="web.dir" location="web" />
<property name="dist.dir" location="dist" />

<target name="war" depends="compile" description="Generate WAR file">
  <war destfile="${dist.dir}/${project.name}-${project.version}.war"
   webxml="${web.dir}/WEB-INF/web.xml">
      <fileset dir="${web.dir}" />
      <classes dir="${build.classes.dir}"/>
      <lib dir="${lib}">
          <include name="*.jar" />
      </lib>
  </war>
</target>
```

The usage of this task is similar to the *<jar>* task we saw previously (see "Generating a JAR File," earlier in this section), with a few additions. The most important configuration file in the `WEB-INF` directory is the `web.xml` file. As can be seen here, you use the *webxml* attribute to specify the location of this file.

As with the *<jar>* task, you can use one or more *<fileset>* elements to define the files you want to deploy in the root directory. In addition, the *<classes>* element defines the files that will be placed in the `WEB-INF/classes` directory. And the *<lib>* element defines the application libraries to be deployed in the `WEB-INF/lib` directory.

Like the *<jar>* task, the *<war>* task will generate a `MANIFEST.MF` file in the `META-INF` directory. And like the *<jar>* task, you can use the *<manifest>* element to add extra information into this file.

For more complex applications, a WAR file will not be enough. If you are developing an EJB-based application, you may need to deploy your application as an EAR file. An EAR file, like a WAR file, is an extension of the JAR file format. Instead of a `web.xml` file, every EAR file contains an `application.xml` file. The *<ear>* task, another extension of the *<jar>* task, is fairly easy to use. You simply specify the location of your application.xml file using the appxml attribute, and then use one or more *<fileset>* elements to indicate what files need to be bundled. For example, if you wanted to deploy the previous WAR file, plus a few particular JAR files (stored in a directory specified by the *${ear.lib}* property), you could do the following:

```
<target name="ear" depends="war" description="Generate EAR file">
  <ear destfile="${dist.dir}/${project.name}-${project.version}.ear"
       appxml="src/metadata/application.xml">
    <fileset file="${dist.dir}/${project.name}-${project.version}.war" />
    <fileset dir="${ear.lib}">
      <include name="*.jar" />
    </fileset>
  </ear>
</target>
```

1.9 Deploying Your Application

Once you have generated a packaged version of your application, you will certainly want to deploy it. For example, if you are developing a web application, you may want to deploy it to a web server on your own machine, or to a remote server for testing. Or, if you are developing a shared library, you may copy your latest version to a local web server, where other users can consult the documentation and download the API.

Copying Files

The simplest way to deploy an application is to copy the packaged file to the target server. Of course, this will only work if the target server is hosted on the development machine or if the target server has a shared drive that can be mapped to from the development/build machine, and the current user has write access to these directories.

Because this is generally the case for a local development machine, this approach is often a simple, pragmatic way to deploy (and redeploy) a web application to a locally running application server. You can copy a file to another directory by using the *<copy>* task, as shown here:

```
<property name="tomcat.install.dir" location="${user.home}/servers/tomcat
 /apache-tomcat-5.5.23" />

<target name="local.deploy" depends="war" description="Deploy to local
Tomcat instance">
    <copy file="${dist.dir}/${project.name}-${project.version}.war"
          todir="${tomcat.install.dir}/webapps" />
</target>
```

In this example, we simply defined a property pointing to a local Tomcat installation, and used the *<copy>* task to copy the generated WAR file to the Tomcat webapps directory, where Tomcat will be able to pick it up and deploy it automatically. Many application servers work in the same way.

Of course, you may want to rename the WAR file on the way. Typically, you may want to strip off the version number when you deploy the web application so that users can simply access the application using the project name. You can do this using the *tofile* attribute instead of *todir*:

```
<property name="tomcat.install.dir" location="${user.home}/servers/tomcat
 /apache-tomcat-5.5.23" />

<target name="local.deploy" depends="war" description="Deploy to local
 Tomcat instance">
    <copy file="${dist.dir}/${project.name}-${project.version}.war"
          tofile="${tomcat.install.dir}/webapps/${project.name}.war" />
</target>
```

As you might expect, you aren't limited to copying a single file. You can also use the *<copy>* task to copy sets of files, using the usual Ant path-like tags. For example, you might want to deploy the latest Javadoc to a local Apache web server. Suppose your Apache server's web directory is `/var/www/public_html`, with a special subdirectory for each project. The Javadoc needs to be deployed to a directory called **javadoc** directly underneath the project directory. If you are running Ant on the same machine as the Apache server, you could deploy your Javadoc simply using the *<copy>* task, as shown here:

```
<property name="web.dir" location="/var/www/public_html" />

<target name="local.documentation" depends="javadoc"
 description="Deploy documentation to local web server">
    <copy todir="${web.dir}/${project.name}/javadoc">
        <fileset dir="${reports.javadoc"/>
    </copy>
</target>
```

The *<copy>* task is a powerful, flexible tool for file manipulation, and here we only cover its main features. Check out the Ant documentation for more details about what it can do.

Other Deployment Techniques

Ant provides many other ways to deploy your application. For example, the *<ftp>* task lets you deploy to an FTP server. And the *<scp>* task lets you deploy files using the widely used (Secure Copy) SCP protocol. A simple example of the *<scp>* task is shown here:

```
<target name="remote.deploy" depends="war"
 description="Deploy to a remote integration server using SCP">
    <scp file="${dist.dir}/${project.name}-${project.version}.war"
         todir="user@testserver:/home/integration/tomcatbase/webapps"
         password="password"/>
</target>
```

There are also many third-party libraries that can help you here. One tool worth investigating is Cargo,* from Codehaus. This powerful tool lets you deploy to (and manipulate in other ways) a wide range of application servers in a uniform manner. For example, using Cargo's Ant integration, you can deploy your application to Tomcat, JBoss, Jetty, or a number of other servers with little or no modification to your build script.

1.10 Bootstrapping Your Build Scripts

As a rule, your build scripts should be as portable as possible. In an ideal world, a new user with a vanilla installation of Ant should be able to check out the project source code and use the build scripts immediately, as-is. No extra configuration should be required—no deploying JAR files in strange places, no setting up exotic configuration files, and so on.

Of course, in real-world projects, things often aren't quite this simple. Your build file will often use nonstandard tasks that need to be installed. It is a tiresome task to hunt down and install the dozen or more Ant extensions that a real-world Ant build file will typically need, and issues may arise if different users have different versions of the extension libraries. This is clearly a good place to automate things.

One useful technique for doing this is writing bootstrap build files that download and install extra libraries that your project needs. This is fairly easy to do using standard Ant tasks such as *<get>*, *<unzip>*, and *<available>*. An example of a typical bootstrap script (called `bootstrap-findbugs.xml`), which downloads and installs the Findbugs package, is shown here:

* *http://cargo.codehaus.org/*

```
<project name="FindBugs Bootstrap script" default="bootstrap" basedir="." >

  <!-- Define the environment-specific variable "findbugs.home" in this file. -->
  <property file="${user.home}/ant-global.properties"/>
  <!-- This default values used if no properties file is present -->
  <property name="findbugs.home" value="${user.home}/.findbugs"/>
  <property name="findbugs.version" value="1.2.0"/>

  <echo>Installing FindBugs into ${findbugs.home}</echo>
  <property name="sourceforge.mirror"
          value="http://optusnet.dl.sourceforge.net/sourceforge" />

  <available file="${findbugs.home}/findbugs.zip" property="findbugs.installed"/>

  <echo>Bootstrap FindBugs</echo>
  <target name="bootstrap" unless="findbugs.installed">
    <echo>Installing FindBugs</echo>
    <mkdir dir="${findbugs.home}" />
    <get src="${sourceforge.mirror}/findbugs/findbugs-${findbugs.version}.zip"
         dest="${findbugs.home}/findbugs.zip" usetimestamp="true"/>
    <unzip src="${findbugs.home}/findbugs.zip"
           dest="${findbugs.home}"/>
    <move todir="${findbugs.home}">
        <fileset dir="${findbugs.home}/findbugs-${findbugs.version}">
          <include name="**/*"/>
        </fileset>
    </move>
    <delete dir="${findbugs.home}/findbugs-${findbugs.version}"/>
  </target>

</project>
```

This script will download and install the FindBugs library (see Chapter 23). Note how we load system-wide property values defined in the **ant-global.properties** file. We also use the *<property>* task to declare a default value for the *${svnant.home}* property, in case no value has been defined in the global properties file.

Downloading files can be a long process, so we use the *<available>* task and the *unless* attribute to ensure that if the library has already been installed, the script will do nothing.

You now have a reusable bootstrap script that will download and install the FindBugs library. To use it, you call the bootstrap target in your main build script using the *<ant>* tag:

```
<ant antfile="bootstrap-findbugs.xml"/>
```

Next, you need to define the FindBugs task using the *<taskdef>* tag:

```
<taskdef name="findbugs" classname="edu.umd.cs.findbugs.anttask.FindBugsTask" >
    <classpath>
        <fileset dir="${findbugs.home}/lib">
          <include name="**/*.jar"/>
        </fileset>
```

```
        </classpath>
    </taskdef>
```

The exact implementation of a bootstrap script will obviously vary from library to library. Another real-world example of this technique is discussed in "Using QALab in Ant.

You may run into difficulties with this approach if your build file is running behind a proxy server. There is some discussion of the options in the Ant documentation (see *http://ant.apache.org/manual/proxy.html*). The *<setproxy>* task is the most reliable, but needs the username and password to be set as propertites. If this is an issue, along with the limitations of the other options, it may be best to manually download a copy of the bootstrap files and install it on an HTTP or file server within the domain to remove the need to get through the proxy server.

1.11 Using Maven Dependencies in Ant with the Maven Tasks

One of the key features of Maven (see Chapter 2) is its use of a central repository to store dependencies and identify the libraries needed by an application. Maven 2 also supports transitive dependencies, a powerful concept that lets you limit the dependencies you need to declare to the strict minimum.

When you bundle and deploy an application, you not only need to include the libraries that *your* application requires, but you also need to include the additional libraries required by these libraries to work. So, if your application uses Hibernate, you will also need all of the libraries required by Hibernate. In real-world projects, this can amount to quite a list.

If your build framework supports transitive dependency management, you need only to declare the libraries that your application uses directly. The build tool will take care of the others. So, if your application uses Hibernate, you only need to state the exact version of Hibernate you are using, and not the other libraries that Hibernate needs. This makes your project dependencies simpler and easier to understand.

Ant does not support dependency management "out-of-the-box." In Ant projects, all the libraries needed by an application are typically placed in a project directory—sometimes stored in the version control system, sometimes not (opinions vary on this point). This can create a number of problems because it is hard to know exactly which versions of libraries are required or currently being used. When libraries are stored in the version control system, projects can take up a lot of space (particularly if CVS is used), and they can take a long time to download. By contrast, if they are not stored in the version control system, some convention needs to be established to work out where to obtain the libraries needed for a given project.

A much better approach is to use one of several Ant extensions to manage dependencies declaratively. In this chapter, we will discuss the Maven 2.0 Ant tasks.

An alternative approach to dependency management in Ant is to use Ivy. Ivy is a powerful and flexible dependency management tool that integrates well into Ant projects, and it provides some interesting features as well as some nice reporting capabilities (*http://incubator.apache.org/ivy/*). Ivy can also leverage the rich public Maven repositories such as Ibiblio and Codehaus. Although we don't have space to look at Ivy in this book, it may be worth a look if you are evaluating dependency management tools for Ant.

The Maven 2.0 Ant Tasks

One of the more powerful features of Maven is its ability to manage transitive dependencies (see "Managing Transitive Dependencies). The Maven 2.0 project provides a library of Ant tasks that lets you take advantage of the powerful transitive dependency management features of Maven 2.0, along with the Maven 2.0 repositories, all from within your Ant project. It also lets you create Ant build files that integrate more smoothly with Maven projects, by enabling you to read a Maven 2.0 product object model (POM) file (see Section 2.4) directly from within your Ant build file.

Installing the Maven Ant Tasks

The Maven Ant Tasks come bundled as a simple JAR file, which you can download from the Maven web site. There are two main ways to install the tasks. The simplest way is to just place the JAR file into the Ant `lib` directory. Then, you simply add the appropriate namespace declaration to the Ant project file, as shown here:

```
<project ... xmlns:artifact="antlib:org.apache.maven.artifact.ant">
```

A more platform-independent way of installing the Ant tasks is to use a *typedef* declaration. This is useful if you don't have access to the Ant installation, or if you don't want to force your developers to install the Maven antlib manually onto each of their machines. You still need to have the Maven Ant Tasks jar file available somewhere, but you can now place it in some commonly available location, such as in your version control system. In the following code sample, we assume that the Maven Ant Tasks JAR file is stored in the project `lib` directory:

```
<project name="tax-calculator" default="package" xmlns:artifact="urn:maven-
artifact-ant">
   ...
   <property name="maven.antlib.version" value="2.0.7" />
   <path id="maven-ant-tasks.classpath" path="lib/maven-ant-tasks-
    ${maven.antlib.version}.jar" />
   <typedef resource="org/apache/maven/artifact/ant/antlib.xml" uri=
    "urn:maven-artifact-ant"
           classpathref="maven-ant-tasks.classpath" />
```

Declaring and Using Maven Dependencies in Ant

Once you have declared the `antlib` library, you can declare your project dependencies as you would in a Maven project. A typical list of dependencies might look like this:

```
<artifact:dependencies pathId="compile.classpath">
    <dependency groupId="commons-logging" artifactId="commons-logging" version="1.1"/>
    <dependency groupId="log4j" artifactId="log4j" version="1.2.9" />
    <dependency groupId="junit" artifactId="junit" version= />
    ...
</artifact:dependencies>
```

For Maven users, the dependencies will look very familiar. The *groupId*, *artifactId*, and *version* attributes uniquely identify each dependency within a Maven repository. As with Maven, dependencies are downloaded as required and stored in the user's home directory, under `${user.home}/.m2/repository`.

You use the *pathId* attribute to refer to the dependencies in other Ant tasks. For example, you could refer to these libraries in the Java compiler task as follows:

```
<target name="compile" depends="init" description="Compile Java code">
    <echo message="Debug: ${javac.debug}" />
    <javac srcdir="${src.dir}"
           destdir="${build.classes.dir}"
           classpathref="compile.classpath"
           debug="${javac.debug}"/>
</target>
```

Or, of course, you can include the dependencies within another broader classpath variable:

```
<path id="java.classpath">
    <path refid="compile.classpath" />
    <pathelement location="${java.classes}" />
    <pathelement location="${java.resources}" />
</path>
```

Packaging the Dependencies

When you deliver your application, you generally need to bundle it up into a deployable package. This may take the form of a WAR file, an EAR file, a ZIP file, or some other kind of format. Whatever the format, you will probably want to include the project dependencies.

The Maven Ant tasks let you do this fairly easily, using the *filesetId* attribute. When you specify a *filesetId* for your dependency list, you will be able to refer to the dependency list as an ordinary fileset. The following listing shows how you can copy the project dependencies into the `WEB-INF/lib` directory:

```
    <artifact:dependencies pathId="dependency.classpath" filesetId="dependency.
fileset" useScope="runtime">
      <dependency groupId="commons-logging" artifactId="commons-logging"
       version="1.1"/>
      <dependency groupId="javax.persistence" artifactId="persistence-api"
       version="1.0"/>
      <dependency groupId="log4j" artifactId="log4j" version="1.2.9" />
      <dependency groupId="junit" artifactId="junit" version="3.8.1"
            scope="test" />
      <dependency groupId="javax.servlet" artifactId="servlet-api" version="2.4"
```

```
    scope="provided" />
  ...
</artifact:dependencies>
...
<target name="package">
    <mkdir dir="${build.dir}/WEB-INF/lib" />
    <copy todir="${build.dir}/WEB-INF/lib">
        <fileset refid="dependency.fileset" />
        <mapper type="flatten" />
    </copy>
</target>
```

The *useScope* attribute lets you limit the jars you want to deploy to the strict minimum. In Maven, the notion of scope lets you define which dependencies should be used at different stages in the build lifecycle (compile, test, deploy, and so on—see "Dependency Scope). For example, in the listing shown here, the `junit` jars will not be necessary in the production environment, and the Servlet API libraries will already be provided by the application server. By declaring this dependency list to use the *runtime* scope, we can avoid having to bundle the `junit` jars (which are scoped to *test*) and the servlet-api jars (scoped to *provided*).

One limitation of this approach is that a given dependency list can only have one *useScope* qualifier.

Choosing Your Repositories

By default, the Maven Ant task will use the standard Maven 2 repository to resolve your project's dependencies (*http://repo1.maven.org/maven2*). But you may want to use different, or additional, repositories. For example, you may want to first look in your local company Maven 2 repository. To do this, just declare a remote repository in your dependency list using the *<artifact:remoteRepository>* tag:

```
<artifact:dependencies>
  ...
  <artifact:remoteRepository id="remote.repository"
   url="http://repository.mycompany.com/" />
</artifact:dependencies>
```

Using an Existing Maven POM File

The Maven Ant Tasks also let you lever an existing Maven POM file from within Ant. This can be useful if you need to store information, such as project and artifact names and versions in a central place (the POM file), or if you want to use the Maven build directories in the Ant build file.

You can set up a reference to your POM file using the *<artifact:pom>* tag, as shown here:

```
<artifact:pom id="maven.project" file="pom.xml" />
```

From then on, you can refer to objects and fields in the Maven project structure using a JSTL-style expression language:

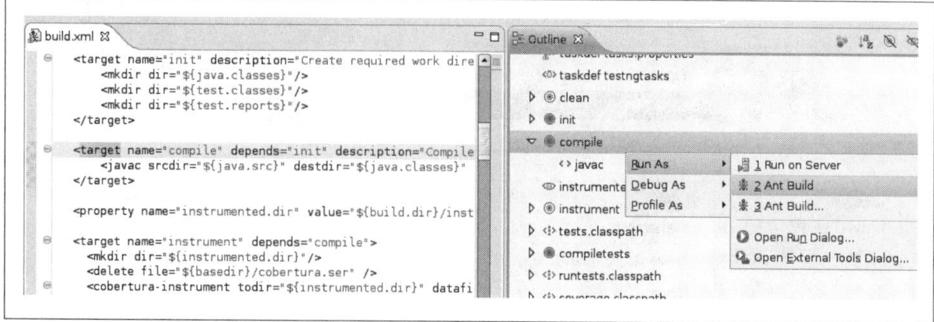

Figure 1-4. Using Ant in Eclipse

```
<echo>Building project ${maven.project.name} version ${maven.project.version}
</echo>
<echo>Application classes directory: ${maven.project.build.outputDirectory}
</echo>
<echo>Test classes directory: ${maven.project.build.testOutputDirectory}
</echo>
```

This would produce something along the following lines:

```
[echo] Building project planestore-core version 1.0-SNAPSHOT
[echo] Application classes directory: /home/john/projects/jpt-sample-code
      /planestore/planestore-core/target/classes
[echo] Test classes directory: /home/john/projects/jpt-sample-code
      /planestore/planestore-core/target/test-classes
```

1.12 Using Ant in Eclipse

Ant is well-supported in virtually all modern Java IDEs, and Eclipse is no exception. Eclipse allows you to create a new Eclipse project using an existing Ant file, and recognizes the structure of Ant build files. The Outline view gives you a structured vision of your build file. In addition, you can execute any target directly from within Eclipse using the contextual menu (see Figure 1-4).

1.13 Using Ant in NetBeans

Ant integrates smoothly into NetBeans. Indeed, by default, NetBeans uses Ant internally to organize your project, even if you don't ask it to. NetBeans automatically recognizes Ant build files and displays the build file targets. As in Eclipse, you can execute targets directly using the contextual menu (see Figure 1-5).

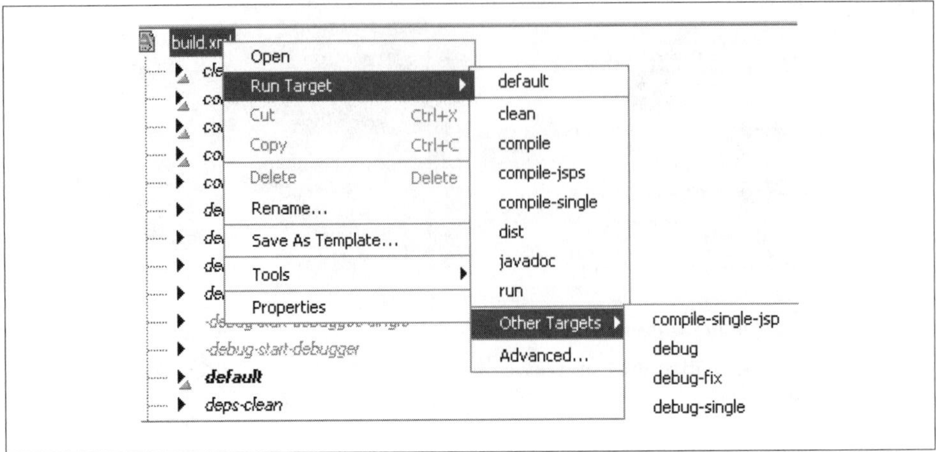

Figure 1-5. Using Ant in NetBeans

1.14 Manipulating XML with XMLTask

Contributed by: Brian Agnew

For simple text search and replace operations, the Ant *<replace>* task is sufficient. But in modern Java frameworks, you are more likely to need powerful XML manipulation capabilities to modify servlet descriptors, Spring configurations, and the like.

XMLTask is an Ant external task that provides powerful XML editing tools focused on creating and changing XML files as part of a build/deployment process.

What are the advantages of using XMLTask?

- Unlike the Ant task, *<replace>* XMLTask gives you the ability to identify parts of an XML document using XPath, and to insert, remove and copy XML at these locations. You can use XPath to simply identify an XML element, or use more complex logic with predicates ("find me the element called 'X' with an attribute of 'Y'...").
- XMLTask is "XML-aware." This means that you can't create an XML document that isn't well-formed. XMLTask will handle character-encoding issues, whereas *<replace>* has no knowledge of the encoding requirements of your XML documents. For example, *<replace>* will allow you to insert the characters "<," ">," and "&" into an XML document without using the corresponding entities ("<" ">" and "&"), and thus possibly break the "well-formedness" of your document.
- XMLTask doesn't require you to learn or use XSLT to perform XML manipulations. It uses intuitive instructions such as *insert*, *replace*, and *remove*.

XMLTask is easy to use. Take a look at the XMLTask home page,* or download from Sourceforge.† You don't need to be knowledgeable about XPath to use XMLTask, but if you need an introduction, take a look at the tutorial on *http://www.zvon.org*.‡

Examples

Let's look at a simple example. Imagine you have a Spring configuration that you want to modify. For instance, you may be making changes for development, test, and release versions, and want to perform insertions, replacements, and removals.

A simple XMLTask is shown below:

```
<project name="xmltask-demo" default="main">
  <!--xmltask.jar should be referenced via lib, or in the ${ant.home}/lib or similar
   --> <taskdef  name="xmltask" classname="com.oopsconsultancy.xmltask.ant.XmlTask"/>

  <!-- you may need to reference a local copy of the DTD here if your XML
         documents specify one. See below for more info -->
  <xmlcatalog id="dtd">
     <dtd
        publicId="-//SPRING//DTD BEAN//EN"
        location="./spring-1.0.dtd"/>
  </xmlcatalog>

  <target name="main">
    <xmltask source="spring-template.xml" dest="spring.xml" preserveType="true">
      <xmlcatalog refid="dtd"/>
      <insert path="/beans" position="under">
          <![CDATA[
            <bean id="bean-to-insert" class="com.oopsconsultancy.example.Bean1">
                <constructor-arg index="0">
                  .....
                </constructor-arg>
            </bean>
          ]]>
      </insert>
    </xmltask>
  </target>
</project>
```

You reference the XMLTask task as you would any external task, using *<taskdef>*.

In the *<xmltask>* task, you specify a source XML file and a destination XML file. XMLTask will read from the source XML, apply any instructions you've configured XMLTask with, and then write the XML to the destination file.

Each instruction identifies a set of matching XML elements (using XPath) and performs an action on each of these. For example, an *<insert>* instruction will perform an insert

* *http://www.oopsconsultancy.com/software/xmltask*

† *http://sourceforge.net/project/showfiles.php?group_id=27398*

‡ *http://www.zvon.org/xxl/XPathTutorial/General/examples.html*

on all matching XML elements specified by its XPath (using XPath you can restrict this to the first match, the last match, and so on).

Sets of instructions are applied sequentially. So, you can specify inserts followed by replacements, followed by removals, etc.

The above example inserts a Spring bean definition under the *<beans>* root element in the spring-template.xml file, and writes it out to `spring.xml`. Suppose your spring-template.xml is an empty configuration like the following:

```
<?xml version="1.0" encoding="UTF-8"?>
<!DOCTYPE beans PUBLIC "-//SPRING//DTD BEAN//EN" "http://www.springframework.org/dtd
/spring-beans.dtd">
<beans>
</beans>
```

After running the *<xmltask>* task listed above, your `spring.xml` will look like this:

```
<?xml version="1.0" encoding="UTF-8"?>
<!DOCTYPE beans PUBLIC "-//SPRING//DTD BEAN//EN" "http://www.springframework.org/dtd
 /spring-beans.dtd">
<beans>
   <bean id=”bean-to-insert” class=”com.oopsconsultany.example.Bean1”
    dependency-check="default"
    lazy-init="default" singleton="true">
        <constructor-arg index=”0”>
          ......
        </constructor-arg>
   </bean>
</beans>
```

Note that attributes specified in the DTD with default values will be generated and inserted in the output XML (with their defaults appropriately set—e.g., “dependency-check,” “lazy-init,” “singleton”).

You don’t have to specify your XML in the Ant build. You can reference it from a file. For example, you can store the bean definition in a file called `development-bean.xml` and use the code below:

```
<insert path="/beans" position="under" file="development-bean.xml">
```

to insert the contents of development-bean.xml into your Spring configuration.

So far this is relatively straightforward, but you can perform more complex manipulations. For example, if you want to modify the login details for a Spring-configured data source bean that looks like:

```
<bean id="ExampleDataSource" class="org.apache.commons.dbcp.BasicDataSource"
destroy-method="close">
    <property name="driverClassName" ref="db-driver-name"/>
    <property name="url" value="...."/>
    <property name="username" value=""/>
    <property name="password" value=""/>
</bean>
```

You can use <replace> operations to insert the username and password from properties *${dev.username}* and *${dev.password}*:

```
<xmltask source="spring-template.xml" dest="spring.xml" preserveType="true">
  <replace path="/beans/bean[@id='ExampleDataSource']/property[@name='username']/@value"
   withText="${dev.username}"/>
  <replace path="/beans/bean[@id='ExampleDataSource']/property[@name='password']/@value"
   withText="${dev.password}"/>
</xmltask>
```

Note that in this example you're using XPath to specify which bean to change (ExampleDataSource) by using a predicate. The XPath expression says "find the bean with a given id, and find the property under that with a given name," allowing you to change attributes for particular elements.

You can remove XML as well. For instance, you may want to remove all your test beans:

```
<remove path="/beans/bean[contains(@id, 'Test')]"/>
```

This removes all beans that have "Test" in their id from your Spring configuration.

DTDs and XMLTask

In the above example we've specified that a local version of the DTD. XMLTask needs access to a DTD, if specified in the source document, to perform entity replacements. If you have a direct connection to the Internet then XMLTask (and other tools) may get the DTD transparently. However, if you don't have a direct connection to the Internet, or if speed is an issue, you'll need to specify a local copy (or tell XMLTask that one isn't available).

This is straightforward. Simply specify an Ant *<xmlcatalog>*. For example, the code below specifies a Servlet DTD and a local copy:

```
<xmlcatalog id="dtd">
   <dtd publicId="-//Sun Microsystems, Inc.//DTD Web Application 2.3//EN"
      location="./servlet-2.3.dtd"
   />
</xmlcatalog>
```

which specifies a local copy of the DTD (servlet-2.3.dtd) with the given public ID.

And then reference this within the *<xmltask>* invocation:

```
<xmltask
   source="src/web.xml" dest="target/web.xml"
   preserveType="true">
  <xmlcatalog refid="dtd"/>
   .....
```

What DTD should your output document use? This depends on how you're manipulating your source document. In most cases, the target document will match the source document's DTD. In this scenario, you can tell XMLTask to generate a DTD instruction in your target document that matches that of your source document:

```
<xmltask
   source="src/web.xml" dest="target/web.xml"
   preserveType="true">
```

In other scenarios (you may be creating a document from scratch or heavily changing the source document), you'll want to specify the DTD public and system identifiers:

```
<!-- we're creating a 2.3 web.xml document from scratch -->
<xmltask
   source="src/web.xml" dest="target/web.xml"
   public="-//Sun Microsystems, Inc.//DTD Web Application 2.3//EN"
   system="http://java.sun.com/dtd/web-app_2_3.dtd">
```

Driving Ant via XMLTask

You can use XMLTask to read an XML file, and use this to call different Ant targets for each occurrence of a specified XML element. Thus, you can drive parts of your build via an external configuration file. This file could represent (for example) environments that you want to build, classes that you need to test, cataloges of files you need to process, etc.

For instance, imagine you have a set of test classes that you need to run. These are encapsulated in one configuration XML:

```
<environments>
   <env name="Test Scenario 1" enabled="true">
     <class>com.oopsconsultancy.example.TestScenario1</class>
     <db>database1</db>
    <results>development/test/scenario1.txt</results>
   </env>
   <env name="Test Scenario 2" enabled="true">
     <class>com.oopsconsultancy.example.TestScenario2</class>
     <db>database2</db>
    <results>development/test/test_data_2.txt</results>
   </env>
</environments>
```

Each environment has a test class, a test database, and a results text file.

You can use XMLTask to iterate over this file, and execute each test class to perform the appropriate tests:

```
<!-- XMLTask only needs a source here, since it's only reading -->
<xmltask source="environments.xml">
   <call path="/environments/env[@enabled='true']" target="execute-tests">
      <param name="class" path="class/text()"/>
      <param name="db" path="db/text()" default="devDb"/>
      <param name="results" path="results/text()"/>
   </call>
</xmltask>

<target name="execute-tests">
   <echo>Running ${class} against ${db}, results in ${results}</echo>
   <!-- run the appropriate tests -->
</target>
```

For each XML element identified by /environments/env (where enabled is "true"), XMLTask will call the Ant target "execute-tests". Properties are set for each Ant target called using the contents of the XML file being read. Each time it calls "execute-tests," it will set the ${class} property to the class specified for that XML element, the ${db} property to the database specified for that element, and the ${results} property to the results file required.

If you run the above, you'll see:

```
Running com.oopsconsultancy.example.TestScenario1 against database1, results in
 development/test/scenario1.txt
Running com.oopsconsultancy.example.TestScenario2 against database2, results in
 development/test/test_data_2.txt
```

Other Tricks

Changing encodings

You can trivially change the character encoding of an XML file:

```
<xmltask source="windows-encoded.xml" dest="16bit-unicode-encoded.xml"
encoding="UnicodeBig"/>
```

(UnicodeBig is the encoding code for 16-bit Unicode encoding (big-endian). See *http://java.sun.com/j2se/1.5.0/docs/guide/intl/encoding.doc.html* for supported encodings). This will convert your XML document to a 16-bit Unicode-encoded document on output. Note that you don't have to define any instructions, since XMLTask is simply reading the document in and writing it out.

Maintaining documents with comments

You can use XMLTask to uncomment sections of your XML files. This means you can maintain one configuration file with multiple commented sections, and simply uncomment the section you require at deployment time. For example:

```
<configurations>
  <!--
  <configuration env="dev">
  ....
  </configuration>
  -->
  <!--
  <configuration env="test">
  ....
  </configuration>
  -->
  <!--
  <configuration env="prod">
  ....
  </configuration>
  -->
</configurations>
```

```
<!--
<xmltask source="source.xml" dest="dest.xml" >
  <uncomment path="/configurations/comment()[2]"/>
  ...
</xmltask>
```

This enables the second commented block (beware: XPath indexes elements from element one on, not zero!). So each of your deployed documents will have the same sections present, but only one needs to be uncommented. This can make your life a lot easier when you have to compare different deployed versions and the differences between them.

1.15 Conclusion

Using XMLTask, you can maintain, create, and modify XML files with a tool that is much more powerful than the standard *<replace>* or file creation tasks, and yet not have to worry about using XSLT. We've not covered many of its functions here. See the home page (*http://www.oopsconsultancy.com/software/xmltask*) for more information and examples. A mailing list (subscription only) is also available (*https://lists.sourceforge.net/lists/listinfo/xmltask-users*).

CHAPTER 2

Setting Up a Project Using Maven 2

2.1 Maven and the Development Build Process

In this chapter, we look at the second major player in the Java build tools arena: Maven.* Maven is an increasingly popular open source build management tool for enterprise Java projects, designed to take much of the hard work out of the build process. Maven uses a declarative approach, in which the project structure and contents are described, rather then the task-based approach used in Ant or in traditional Make files or shell scripts. Maven also strongly promotes the use of standard directory structures and a well-defined build lifecycle. This helps enforce company-wide development standards and reduces the time needed to write and maintain build scripts.

Maven's authors describe Maven as a "project management framework," and it is indeed much more than just a simple build scripting tool. Maven's declarative, standards-based approach to project build management simplifies many aspects of the project lifecycle. As well as catering for compiling, building, testing, and deploying your application with a minimum of effort, Maven offers a number of other key advantages:

- Project dependencies are declared and managed in a clean, transparent way, which reduces the risk of dependency-related errors and makes for better documentation.
- Maven lets you easily generate useful, high-quality, technical documentation and reports about the current state of the project and project team members. Note that we aren't taking about a good user manual, which is an altogether different issue, but, rather, about technical documentation, written by developers for developers. In many technical projects, decent technical documentation is woefully inadequate. It is nevertheless a vital part of modern software development, especially when dislocated teams are involved.
- Maven proposes a clear standard directory layout for source code, project resources and configuration files, generated output, and project documentation. This makes

* In this book, we will be focusing exclusively on the most recent version of Maven, Maven 2, which is radically different from its predecessor, Maven 1.

it easier to understand new Maven projects, and also makes the Maven build scripts cleaner and simpler.

- Maven integrates smoothly with source code repositories, continuous integration servers, and issue tracking systems.
- The Maven build cycle is flexible: it is easy to integrate additional build tasks, using existing Maven plug-ins or by writing Ant scriptlets.

All of these points make Maven an invaluable tool for Java development teams. Indeed, Maven touches so many parts of the SDLC that this book contains two distinct chapters on the subject. In this chapter, we will look at the basics of using Maven in the real world. In Chapter 29, we will focus on how to generate a technical web site for your project using Maven.

2.2 Maven and Ant

Without a doubt, the most popular and most well-known build tool in the Java sphere is Ant. Ant (see Chapter 1) is a fine tool and a hugely successful open source project. Millions of Java developers are familiar with it. And, as we will see throughout the rest of the book, there is hardly a Java tool in existence that doesn't integrate with Ant.

However, when you write a lot of Ant build scripts, you find yourself asking yourself (and other teamg members) the same questions over and over again: Where will the source code go? What about the unit tests? How do we handle dependencies? How will we bundle up the deliverable application? What shall we call the main targets? Individually, Ant lets you deal with each of these tasks with a high degree of flexibility and power. However, you still have to write the tasks from scratch or duplicate and modify an Ant script from a previous project. And when you move to a new project or company, you need to ask these questions once again to (begin to) understand the build process in place.

Many (although not all) projects do follow fairly common and well-known patterns. A lot of what you need to configure in your build process is pretty much run-of-the-mill. It always seems a shame to redo the work again for each new project.

Maven can help you here. Maven takes a lot of the grunt work out of the build process, and tries to lever the combined experience and best practice of a large community of developers. By adhering to a certain number of conventions and best practices, Maven lets you remove the drudgery of all the low-level tasks in your build scripts. In the rest of this chapter, we will see how.

2.3 Installing Maven

In this chapter, we will go through how to install Maven 2 on various platforms. The basic installation process is straightforward, and is the same for all platforms. Maven is a pure Java tool, so first of all you need to ensure that there is a recent version of Java (1.4 or later) on your machine. Then, download the latest distribution from the Maven download site* and extract it into an appropriate directory. Finally, just add the bin subdirectory to the system path.

If you are familiar with installing Java tools, this should be enough to get you started. In the rest of this chapter, we discuss some more detailed environment-specific considerations.

Installing Maven on a Unix Machine

In this chapter, we run through how to install Maven into a Unix environment.

Installing Maven in a Unix-based environment is a relatively simple task. Download the latest version in the format of your choice, and extract it to an appropriate directory. Conventions vary greatly from one system to another, and from one system administrator to another: I generally place the maven installation in a nonuser-specific directory such as /usr/local, as shown here:

```
# cd /usr/local
# tar xvfz maven-2.0.7-bin.tar.gz
# ls
```

This will extract the maven installation in a directory called `maven-2.0.7`. For convenience, on a Unix system, I generally create a symbolic link to this directory to make upgrades easier to manage:

```
# ln -s maven-2.0.7 maven
# ls -al
total 16
drwxr-xr-x  3 root root 4096 2006-08-06 13:18 .
drwxr-xr-x 53 root root 4096 2006-07-20 21:32 ..
lrwxrwxrwx  1 root root   11 2006-08-06 13:17 maven -> maven-2.0.7
drwxr-xr-x  6 root root 4096 2006-08-06 13:17 maven-2.0.7
```

Now just add the `maven/bin` directory to your environment path. Typically, you will set this up in one of your environment initialization scripts (for example, if you are using Bash, you could place this configuration in the `~/.bashrc` file if you just need to set it up for your account, or in /etc/bashrc if you want to set it up for all users on this machine). Don't forget to make sure that the `JAVA_HOME` environment variable is defined as well. Here is a typical example:

```
PATH=$PATH:/usr/local/maven/bin
JAVA_HOME=/usr/lib/jvm/java
export PATH JAVA_HOME
```

Now check that it works by running the *maven* command from the command line:

```
# mvn --version
Maven version: 2.0.7
```

* *http://maven.apache.org/download.html*

Installing Maven on a Windows Machine

Installing Maven on a Windows machine is also relatively straightforward, although the application still lacks the graphical installation package familiar to Windows users. First, download and unzip the Maven distribution into an appropriate directory. Most Windows machines will have a graphical compression utility that you can use to extract the ZIP file, although if you are stuck, you can always use the Java jar command-line tool, as shown here:

```
C:> jar -xf maven-2.0.4-bin.zip
```

In Figure 2-1, Maven has been installed in the `P:\tools\maven\maven-2.0.4` directory, although of course you can install it anywhere that suits your particular needs. A more conventional choice might be something like `C:\Program Files\Apache Software Foundation\maven-2.0.4`. Because it is a Java application, Maven also expects the `JAVA_HOME` environment variable to be correctly defined.

Next add the Maven bin directory to your PATH user variable (Figure 2-1). You will need to open a new console window to see the new path taken into account.

Now, check that Maven is correctly installed by running *mvn --version*:

```
C:\>mvn --version
Maven version: 2.0.4
```

Now you should have a working Maven environment ready to go!

2.4 Declarative Builds and the Maven Project Object Model

An Introduction to Declarative Build Management

Before we look at how to create and work with projects in Maven, we need to discuss some of the basics. The most fundamental of these is the Maven Project Object Model, or POM, which we will look at in this chapter. In the process, we also will cover some important basic principles of Maven development, as well as a lot of the key features of Maven. As many, if not most, new Maven users are already familiar with Ant, we will look at how the Maven approach differs from the one used by Ant, and how this can help simplify your builds.

For Ant users, the Maven philosophy can take a little getting use to. Unlike Ant, which is very much task-oriented, Maven uses a highly declarative approach to project builds. In Ant, for example, you list the tasks that must be performed to compile, test, and deliver your product. In Maven, by contrast, you *describe* your project and your build process, relying on conventions and sensible default values to do much of the grunt work. The heart of a Maven 2 project, the POM, describes your project, its structure, and its dependencies. It contains a detailed description of your project, including information about versioning and configuration management, dependencies, application and testing resources, team members and structure, and much more. The POM takes

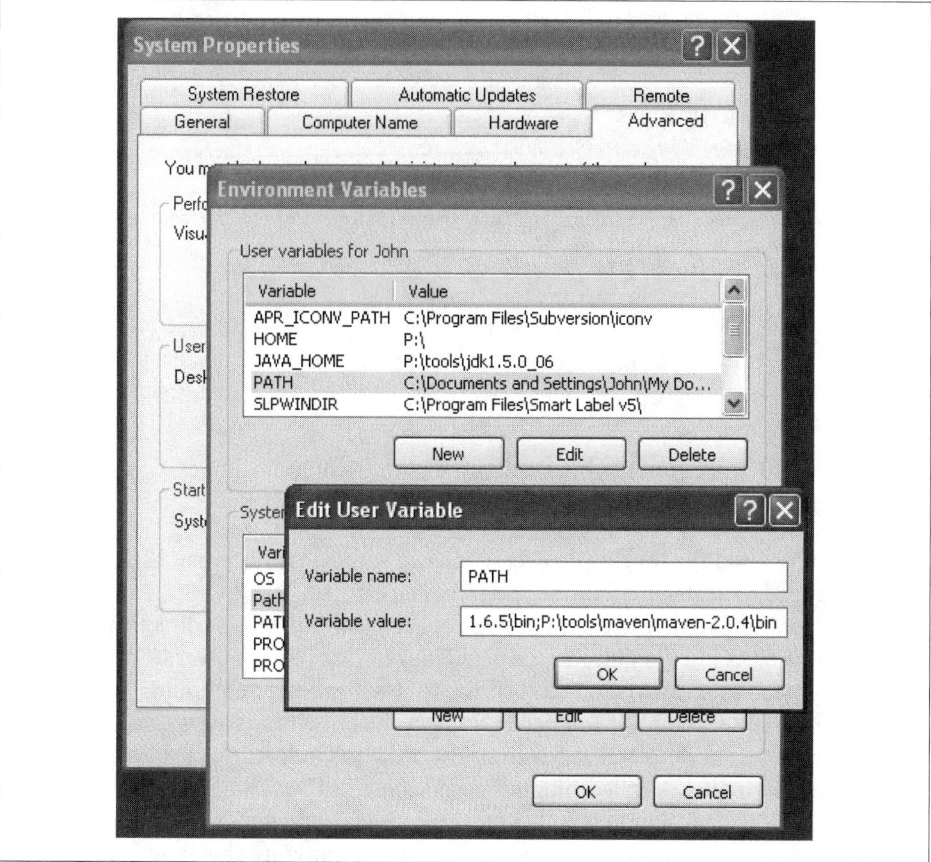

Figure 2-1. Adding the Maven bin directory to the PATH environment variable

the form of an XML file (called **pom.xml** by default), which is placed in your project home directory.

Let's look at a practical example. One of the most fundamental parts of any Java build process involves compiling your Java classes. In a typical Ant build, you would use the *<javac>* task (see Section 1.4) to compile your classes. This involves defining the directory or directories containing your Java source code, the directory into which the compiled classes will be placed, and creating a classpath that contains any dependencies needed to compile your classes. Before invoking the compiler, you need to be sure to create the target directory. The corresponding Ant script might look something like this:

```
<project name="killer-app">
    ...
    <property name="src.dir" location="src/main/java"/>
    <property name="target.dir" location="target/classes"/>
    ...
    <path id="compile.classpath">
        <fileset dir="lib">
```

```
            <include name="**/*.jar"/>
        </fileset>
    </path>
    ...
    <target name="init">
        <mkdir directory="${target.dir}"/>
    </target>

    <target name="compile" depends="init" description="Compile the application classes">
        <javac srcdir="${src.dir}"
               destdir="${target.dir}"
               classpathref="compile.classpath"
               source="1.5"
               target="1.5"
        />
    </target>
</project>
```

To compile your application, you would invoke the "compile" target:

```
$ ant compile
```

In Maven, the build file for this project would be somewhat different. First of all, you would not need to declare the source and target directories. If you do not say otherwise, Maven will assume that you intend to respect the standard Maven directory structure (see Section 2.6), using the well-known principle of "Convention Over Configuration." Nor do you need to create the target directory manually before compiling your code—Maven will do this for you automatically. In fact, the only thing that we need to specify is that our project code is written using Java 5 language features, for a Java 5 JVM. Maven uses components called plug-ins to do most of the serious work. The plug-in that handles Java compilation is called *maven-compiler-plugin*. So, to set up Java compilation in our Maven script, all we need to do is to configure this plug-in, which we do as follows:

```
<project...>
    ...
    <build>
        <plug-ins>
            <!-- Using Java 5 -->
            <plugin>
                <artifactId>maven-compiler-plugin</artifactId>
                <configuration>
                    <source>1.5</source>
                    <target>1.5</target>
                </configuration>
            </plugin>
        </plug-ins>
    </build>
    ...
</project>
```

Note that had we been using the default *javac* source and target values, even this configuration would not have been needed.

The one thing that we glossed over here is the Maven equivalent of the `lib` directory. In Ant, the libraries required by a project are stored in a local project directory, often called `lib`. In the above example, we defined a classpath called *compile.classpath*, which included all the JAR files in this directory.

Maven uses a totally different approach. In Maven, JAR files are rarely, if ever, stored in the project directory structure. Instead, dependencies are declared within the build script itself.

An extract from a list of Maven dependencies is shown here:

```
<project...>
    ...
    <!-- PROJECT DEPENDENCIES -->
    <dependencies>
        <!-- Hibernate -->
        <dependency>
            <groupId>org.hibernate</groupId>
            <artifactId>hibernate</artifactId>
            <version>3.2.4.</version>
        </dependency>
        <!-- Log4j -->
        <dependency>
            <groupId>log4j</groupId>
            <artifactId>log4j</artifactId>
            <version>1.2.14</version>
        </dependency>
        ...
    </dependencies>
</project>
```

Dependency management is a major feature of Maven 2, and we look at it in much more detail in "Managing Transitive Dependencies" in ch02-dependency-management.

The third part of our POM file contains information that is largely irrelevant for the task at hand (compiling our Java class), but will come in handy later on. At the start of each Maven POM file, you will find a list of descriptive elements describing things like the project name, version number, how it is to be packaged, and so on. This is shown here:

```
<project...>
    <!-- PROJECT DESCRIPTION -->
    <modelVersion>4.0.0</modelVersion>
    <groupId>com.mycompany</groupId>
    <artifactId>myapp</artifactId>
    <packaging>jar</packaging>
    <name>Killer application</name>
    <version>1.0</version>
    <description>My new killer app</description>
    ...
</project>
```

Here is the complete corresponding Maven build file:

```
<?xml version="1.0" encoding="UTF-8"?>
<project xmlns="http://maven.apache.org/POM/4.0.0"
    xmlns:xsi="http://www.w3.org/2001/XMLSchema-instance"
    xsi:schemaLocation="http://maven.apache.org/POM/4.0.0 http://maven.apache.org
    /maven-v4_0_0.xsd">

    <!-- PROJECT DESCRIPTION -->
    <modelVersion>4.0.0</modelVersion>
    <groupId>com.mycompany</groupId>
    <artifactId>myapp</artifactId>
    <packaging>war</packaging>
    <name>Killer application</name>
    <version>1.0</version>
    <description>My new killer app</description>

    <!-- BUILD CONFIGURATION -->
    <build>
        <plug-ins>
           <plugin>
                <artifactId>maven-compiler-plugin</artifactId>
                <configuration>
                    <source>1.5</source>
                    <target>1.5</target>
                </configuration>
            </plugin>
        </plug-ins>
    </build>

    <!-- PROJECT DEPENDENCIES -->
    <dependencies>
        <!-- Hibernate -->
        <dependency>
            <groupId>org.hibernate</groupId>
            <artifactId>hibernate</artifactId>
            <version>3.2.4.</version>
        </dependency>
        <!-- Log4j -->
        <dependency>
            <groupId>log4j</groupId>
            <artifactId>log4j</artifactId>
            <version>1.2.14</version>
        </dependency>
        ...
    </dependencies>
</project>
```

So a Maven build file is not necessarily any shorter than an Ant build file for an equivalent project. But the nature of the information it contains is very different. Ant users will notice that there is no sign of any target-like structures, or any indication of what goals can be run:*

```
$ mvn compile
```

In a similar manner, this same build file can be used to run the application's unit tests, stored by convention in the `src/test/java` directory, by invoking the "test" goal:

```
$ mvn test
```

And this same build file can be used to bundle up a JAR file containing the compiled classes, via the "package" goal:

```
$ mvn package
```

There are many other goals. We will cover the main ones in the remainder of this chapter, and in the other Maven-related chapters of this book.

This illustrates another of Maven's strong points: all of these goals are standard Maven goals and will work in a similar way on any Maven project.

As can be gleaned here, one of the guiding principles of Maven is to use sensible default values wherever possible. This is where the Maven conventions play an important role. Maven projects are expected to respect a certain number of conventions, such as placing your main source code in the `src/main/java` directory and your test code in the `src/main/test` directory (see Section 2.6). These conventions are largely defined in a special POM file, the so-called Super POM, from which every POM is extended. In practice, this means that if you respect the standard Maven conventions, you can get away with surprisingly little in your POM file.

Even so, a typical real-world POM file can get pretty complex. In the remainder of this chapter, we will go through the main areas of the POM file, in order of appearance. This approach is intentionally superficial: because of the central nature of the POM file in all Maven projects, we will be coming back to various sections in much more detail as we look at other topics later on.

Project Context and Artifacts

The first part of a POM file basically introduces the project and its context, including the group and artifact IDs that uniquely identify this project in the Maven world, as well as how the artifact is packaged (jar, war, ear...), and the current version number. This is a small but crucial part of the Maven POM file, in which you define many key aspects of your project. A typical example is shown here:

* For Windows users: following a common Unix convention, I am using the "$" symbol to represent the command-line prompt. On a Windows machine, you might have something like "C:\projects\myproject> mvn compile."

```
<project xmlns="http://maven.apache.org/POM/4.0.0"
  xmlns:xsi="http://www.w3.org/2001/XMLSchema-instance"
  xsi:schemaLocation="http://maven.apache.org/POM/4.0.0
  http://maven.apache.org/maven-v4_0_0.xsd">
   <modelVersion>4.0.0</modelVersion>
   <groupId>com.mycompany.accounting</groupId>
   <artifactId>accounting-core</artifactId>
   <packaging>jar</packaging>
   <version>1.1</version>
   ...
```

The information in this section is used to identify the project uniquely and, in particular, the artifact that it produces. This is one of the hallmarks of Maven, and it is what enables you to define very precisely your projects dependencies (see "Managing Transitive Dependencies," in Section 2.8). Indeed, the information in this section allows Maven to derive a unique path to the artifact generated by this project. For example, in this case, the unique path to this artifact is illustrated in Figure 2-2.

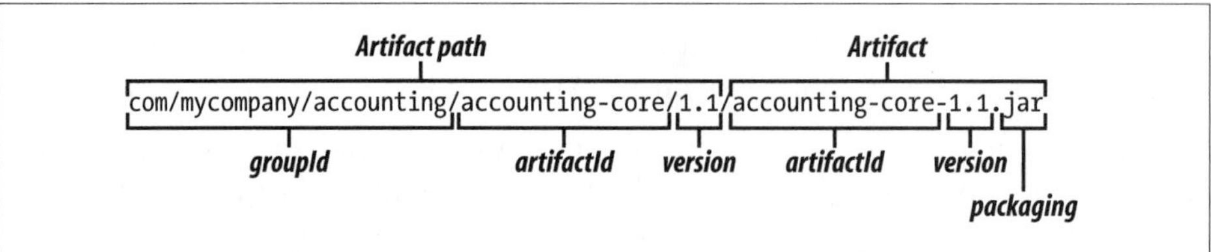

Figure 2-2. The Maven 2 artifact

Let's look at how Maven does this in a little more detail.

The *<groupId>* element is supposed to identify a particular project or set of libraries within a company or organization. By convention, it often corresponds to the initial part of the Java package used for the application classes (e.g., "org.apache.maven" for Maven projects, "org.springframework" for the Spring libraries, and so on), although this is not always the case. When the artifact is deployed to a Maven repository, the *groupId* is split out into a matching directory structure on the repository.

The *artifactId* represents the actual name of the project. This, combined with the *groupId*, should uniquely identify the project.

Every project also has a *<version>* element, which indicates the current version number. This number usually refers to major releases ("Hibernate 3.2.4," "Spring 2.0.5," and so on), as opposed to specific build numbers, which are different for each build. Each version has its own directory on the Maven repository, which is a subdirectory of the project directory.

So, in the above example, the generated artifact would be stored on the Maven repository in a directory called `com/mycompany/accounting/accounting-core/1.1`.

When it comes to finally generating a deliverable package, Maven supports many different file formats. At the time of this writing, supported package types included pom, jar, maven-plugin, ejb, war, ear, rar, and par. As the name suggests, you use the *<packaging>* element to indicate the packaging type. For example, in this listing, Maven will generate a file called `accounting-core-1.1.jar`. The "jar" extension comes from the *<packaging>* element. Maven saves you the hassle of knowing exactly what files need to go into the delivered package and what files were delivered. All you need to do is provide the type and Maven will do the rest.

Finally, there is an optional element called *<classifier>* that can be used to distinguish different distributions of the same version of a product. For example, you might have a distribution for Java 1.4, and a different distribution for Java 5. The TestNG unit testing library does just this. The project description for the Java 5 version of this product might contain something like this:

```
<groupId>org.testng</groupId>
<artifactId>testng</artifactId>
<packaging>jar</packaging>
<version>5.5</version>
<classifier>jdk15</classifier>
```

This would produce a file called `testng-5.1-jdk15.jar`. The equivalent version for Java 1.4 would be `testng-5.1-jdk14.jar`.

A Human-Readable Project Description

The next section of the POM file is largely for human consumption, and contains information that is primarily used to generate the Maven project web site. It can contain details such as the name of the project, the URL of the project home page (if one exists), details on the issue tracking system, the Continuous Integration system, and/or the SCM system, as well as details such as the year of inception and the development team:

```
...
<name>Accounting Core API</name>
<url>http://myproject.mycompany.com</url>
<scm>
   <connection>scm:svn:http://devserver.mycompany.com/svn/accounting
    /accounting-core/trunk/accounting-core</connection>
   <developerConnection>scm:svn:http://devserver.mycompany.com/
    svn/accounting/accounting-core/trunk/accounting-core</developerConnection>
   <url>http://devserver.mycompany.com/trac/accounting-core/browser
    /accounting/accounting-core/trunk/accounting-core</url>
</scm>
<issueManagement>
   <system>trac</system>
   <url>http://devserver.mycompany.com/trac/accounting-core</url>
</issueManagement>
<inceptionYear>2006</inceptionYear>
...
```

Most of this information is project documentation, and it is a recommended practice to make it as complete as possible. Some of it, such as the Issue Tracking and CI system details, may be used by Maven to generate appropriate links in the Maven site. For common version control systems such as CVS and Subversion, Maven uses the SCM section to generate a page of instructions on how to check out the project, which is very useful for new team members. Also, Continuous Integration servers such as Continuum (see Chapter 5) can read the SCM and CI details when you import the project onto the Continuous Integration server.

Declaring your Continuous Integration Server

If your project uses a continuous integration tool of some sort, such as Continuum (see Chapter 5) CruiseControl (see Chapter 6), you can tell people about it in the *<ciManagement>* tag, as shown in the code below. (If your project does not using such a tool, consider using one!)

```
<ciManagement>
    <system>Continuum</system>
    <url>http://integrationserver.wakaleo.com/continuum</url>
    <notifiers>
      <notifier>
        <type>mail</type>
        <address>duke@wakaleo.com</address>
      </notifier>
    </notifiers>
 </ciManagement>
```

Maven 2 integrates well with Continuum: you can install a Maven 2 project onto a Continuum server just by providing the `pom.xml` file (see Section 5.7). Notifiers declare ways that particular users can be sent notification of build results on the CI server. In Continuum, they can be set up both from the Continuum administration web site (Section 5.12) or from within the Maven POM file.

Defining the Development Team

People like to know who they are working with, especially these days, when a project team can be spread across organizations and continents. In the developers section, you list details about your project team members. The time zone field is useful for international teams; this field is offset from Greenwich Mean Time (GMT), or London time, and lets people see what time it is wherever the team member is located. For example, –5 is for New York time, +1 is for Paris, and +10 is for Sydney.

A typical developer definition is shown here:

```
...
<developers>
  <developer>
    <id>smartj</id>
    <name>John Smart</name>
    <email>john.smart@acme.co.nz</email>
    <roles>
      <role>Developer</role>
    </roles>
    <organization>ACME NZ</organization>
```

```
        <timezone>+12</timezone>
      </developer>
      ...
    </developers>
    ...
```

Although totally optional, listing your development team in your POM file can be worthwhile for several reasons. This information will be used to create a team directory page on the Maven generated site. The Maven SCM plug-ins can use the developer id to map changes made in the source code repository against developer names. And, if you are using the Continuum Continuous Integration server (see Chapter 5), Continuum can pick up the developer email addresses and use them for email notifications.

Managing Dependencies

One of the most powerful Maven features is the way it handles dependencies. A typical medium-size Java project can require dozens, or even hundreds, of JAR files. Without a strict dependency management strategy, this can quickly become out of control. It can rapidly become difficult to know exactly what library versions a particular project is using, and conflicting dependency requirements can trigger hard-to-find errors. Maven addresses these issues using a two-pronged approach, based on the notions of declarative dependencies and a central repository of JAR files.

In Maven, a project's dependencies are declared in the *pom.xml* file. The *<dependencies>* section, shown here, lets you list the libraries that your application needs to compile, be tested, and be run. Dependencies are defined using the Maven artifact naming schema (see "Project Context and Artifacts," earlier in this section), which allows you to precisely identify the exact version of each library you need. In addition, you usually only need to list the libraries you need directly to compile your code: with a feature called Transitive Dependencies (see "Managing Transitive Dependencies" in Section 2.8) Maven 2 will discover and retrieve any additional libraries that *those* libraries need to work.

Here is a simple example of the dependencies section in a POM file:

```
...
<dependencies>
  <dependency>
    <groupId>org.hibernate</groupId>
    <artifactId>hibernate</artifactId>
    <version>3.1</version>
  </dependency>
  <dependency>
     <groupId>junit</groupId>
     <artifactId>junit</artifactId>
     <version>3.8.1</version>
     <scope>test</scope>
  </dependency>
</dependencies>
...
```

We are saying that our application requires Hibernate 3.1 (and, implicitly, all the other libraries that this version of Hibernate requires). And, to run our unit tests, we need JUnit 3.8.1.

This section is not only used in the build lifecycle; it also can be used to generate reports listing the project dependencies (see "Setting Up Reporting," later in this section). We will look at dependencies in Maven in more detail in "Managing Transitive Dependencies," in Section 2.8.

Customizing Your Build Process

Although optional, the *<build>* section is a key part of any but the simplest of POM files. This section is where you tailor your Maven project build process to your exact needs, defining various plug-in configurations and setting up additional tasks that need to be performed at various points in the build lifecycle.

The Maven build process is very flexible, and it is easy to integrate new tasks by using plug-ins. Plug-ins are a powerful way to encapsulate build logic into reusable components, for use in future projects. You may use plug-ins to generate source code from a WSDL file or from Hibernate mappings, for example. Many plug-ins are available, both from the Maven web site and from other third-party providers such as Codehaus.*

Because they are used extensively in the standard Maven build lifecycle tasks, you also can use plug-ins to customize existing aspects of the Maven lifecycle. A common example of this type of configuration, shown in the example below, is to configure the *maven-compiler-plugin*, which compiles the project source code for use with Java 5 (by default, the Maven compiler generates code compatible with JDK 1.3).

The *<build>* section is also where resource directories are defined. You also can define resources that will be bundled into the final package produced by the project, and resources that need to be on the classpath during unit tests. By default, any files placed in the `src/main/resources` will be packaged into the generated project artifact. Any files in `src/test/resources` will be made available on the project classpath during unit tests.

You also can add additional resource directories. In the following example, we set up an additional resource directory for Hibernate mapping files. At build-time, these files automatically will be bundled into the resulting project artifact, along with the compiled classes and other resource files.

The following listing illustrates a typical build section, illustrating these examples:

```
...
<build>
  <plug-ins>
      <plugin>
          <groupId>org.apache.maven.plug-ins</groupId>
          <artifactId>maven-compiler-plugin</artifactId>
```

* *http://mojo.codehaus.org*

```
            <configuration>
                <source>1.5</source>
                <target>1.5</target>
            </configuration>
        </plugin>
    </plug-ins>
    <resources>
        <resource>
            <directory>src/main/hibernate</directory>
        </resource>
    </resources>
</build>
...
```

Setting Up Reporting

An important part of any project is internal communication. Although it is not a silver bullet, a centralized technical project web site can go a long way toward improving visibility within the team, especially with large or geographically dispersed teams. The site generation functionality in Maven 2 lets you set up a professional-quality project web site with little effort.

You use the *<reporting>* section to configure options for Maven site generation. In the absence of any reporting section, Maven will generate a simple site with information about the project derived from the information provided in the POM file. The *<reporting>* section lets you add many other additional reports, such as javadoc, unit test results, Checkstyle or PMD reports, and so on.

In this example, we add Checkstyle reporting to the generated site:

```
<reporting>
  <plug-ins>
    <plugin>
      <artifactId>maven-checkstyle-plugin</artifactId>
      <configuration>
        <configLocation>config/company-checks.xml</configLocation>
        <enableRulesSummary>false</enableRulesSummary>
        <failsOnError>true</failsOnError>
      </configuration>
    </plugin>
</reporting>
```

Defining Build Profiles

The final major section of the POM file is the *<profiles>* section. Profiles are a useful way to customize the build lifecycle for different environments. They let you define properties that change depending on your target environment, such as database connections or filepaths. At compile time, these properties can be inserted into your project configuration files. For example, you may need to configure different database connections for different platforms. Suppose JDBC configuration details are stored in a file called `jdbc.properties`, stored in the `src/main/resources` directory. In this file, you would use a variable expression in the place of the property value, as shown here:

```
jdbc.connection.url=${jdbc.connection.url}
```

In this case, we will define two profiles: one for a development database, and one for a test database. The *<profiles>* section of the POM file would look like this:

```
<profiles>
   <!-- Development environment -->
   <profile>
      <id>development</id>
      <activation>
         <activeByDefault>true</activeByDefault>
     </activation>
     <properties>
        <!-- The development database -->
        <jdbc.connection.url>jdbc:mysql://localhost/devdb</jdbc.connection.url>
     </properties>
   </profile>
   <!-- Test environment -->
   <profile>
     <id>test</id>
     <properties>
        <!-- The test database -->
        <jdbc.connection.url>jdbc:mysql://localhost/testdb</jdbc.connection.url>
     </properties>
   </profile>
  </profiles>
```

Each profile has an identifier (*<id>*) that lets you invoke the profile by name, and a list of property values to be used for variable substitution (in the *<properties>* section). For variable substitution to work correctly, Maven needs to know which files are likely to contain variables. You do this by activating filtering on resource directories in the *<build>* section (see "Customizing Your Build Process," earlier in this section). To do this in our case, we need to activate filtering on the resource directory entry in the build section (see "Customizing Your Build Process"), as shown here:

```
    ...
    <build>
       <resources>
          <resource>
              <directory>src/main/resources</directory>
              <filtering>true</filtering>
          </resource>
       </resources>
    </build>
    ...
```

Profiles can be activated in several ways. In this case, we use the *activeByDefault* property to define the development profile as the default profile. Therefore, running a standard Maven compile with no profiling options will use this profile:

```
$ mvn compile
```

In this case, the generated jdbc.properties file in the target/classes directory will look like this:

```
jdbc.connection.url=jdbc:mysql://localhost/devdb
```

To activate the test profile, you need to name it explicitly, using the *-P* command line option as shown here:

```
$ mvn compile -Ptest
```

Now, the generated jdbc.properties file, in the target/classes directory, will be configured for the test database:

```
jdbc.connection.url=jdbc:mysql://localhost/testdb
```

We look at how to use profiles in more detail in "Defining Build Profiles.

2.5 Understanding the Maven 2 Lifecycle

Project lifecycles are central to Maven 2. Most developers are familiar with the notion of build phases such as compile, test, and deploy. Ant build scripts typically have targets with names like these. In Maven 2, this notion is standardized into a set of well-known and well-defined lifecycle phases (see Figure 2-3). Instead of invoking tasks or targets, the Maven 2 developer invokes a lifecycle phase. For example, to compile the application source code, you invoke the "compile" lifecycle phase:

```
$ mvn compile
```

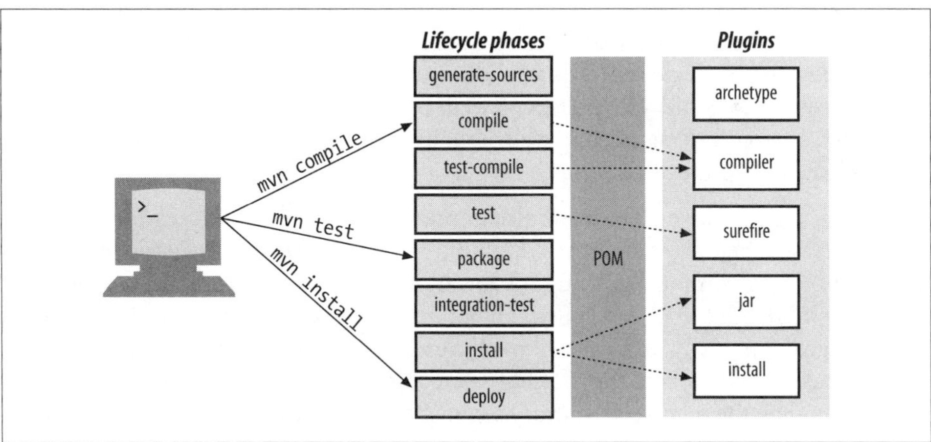

Figure 2-3. Maven 2 lifecycle phases

Some of the more useful Maven 2 lifecycle phases are the following (see Figure 2-3):

generate-sources
: Generates any extra source code needed for the application, which is generally accomplished using the appropriate plug-ins.

compile
: Compiles the project source code.

test-compile
: Compiles the project unit tests.

test
: Runs the unit tests (typically using JUnit) in the `src/test` directory. If any tests fail, the build will stop. In all cases, Maven generates a set of test reports in text and XML test reports in the `target/surefire-reports` directory (see Section 2.13).

package
: Packages the compiled code in its distributable format (JAR, WAR, etc.).

integration-test
: Processes and deploys the package if necessary into an environment in which integration tests can be run.

install
: Installs the package into the local repository for use as a dependency in other projects on your local machine.

deploy
: In an integration or release environment, this copies the final package to the remote repository for sharing with other developers and projects.

The full list is much longer than this, and can be found on the Maven web site.*

These phases illustrate the benefits of the recommended practices encouraged by Maven 2: once a developer is familiar with the main Maven lifecycle phases, he or she should feel at ease with the lifecycle phases of any Maven project. The lifecycle phase invokes the plug-ins it needs to do the job. Invoking a lifecycle phase automatically invokes any previous lifecycle phases as well. Because the lifecycle phases are limited in number, easy to understand, and well organized, becoming familiar with the lifecycle of a new Maven 2 project is easy.

Understanding the Maven lifecycle is also important when it comes to customizing your build process. When you customize your build process, you basically attach (or "bind," to use the Maven terminology) plug-ins to various phases in the project lifecycle. This may seem more rigid than Ant, in which you basically can define any tasks you want and arrange them in any order you like. However, once you are familiar with the basic Maven phases, customizing the build lifecycle in this way is easier to understand and to maintain than the relatively arbitrary sequences of tasks that you need to implement in an Ant build process.

* *http://maven.apache.org/guides/introduction/introduction-to-the-lifecycle.html*

2.6 The Maven Directory Structure

Much of Maven's power comes from the standard practices that it encourages. A developer who has previously worked on a Maven project immediately will feel familiar with the structure and organization of a new one. Time need not be wasted reinventing directory structures, conventions, and customized Ant build scripts for each project. Although you can override any particular directory location for your own specific ends, you really should respect the standard Maven 2 directory structure as much as possible, for several reasons:

- It makes your POM file smaller and simpler.
- It makes the project easier to understand and makes life easier for the poor guy who must maintain the project when you leave.
- It makes it easier to integrate plug-ins.

The standard Maven 2 directory structure is illustrated in Figure 2-4.

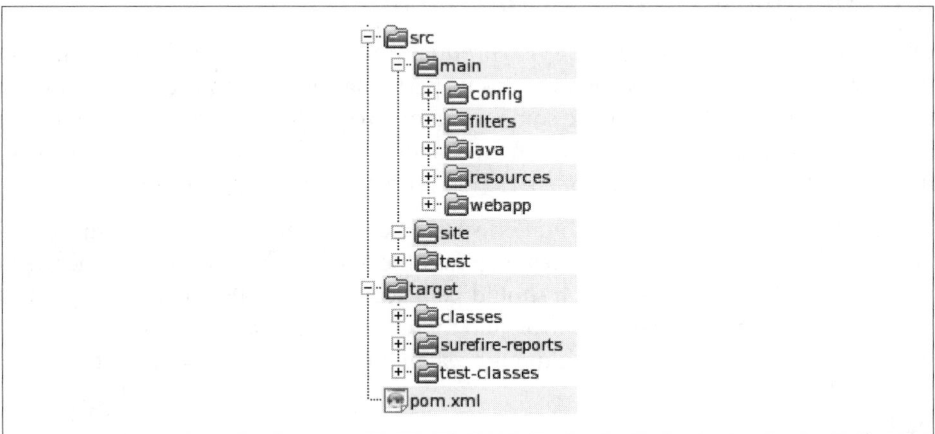

Figure 2-4. A typical Maven directory structure

The POM (`pom.xml`) and two subdirectories go into the project home directory: src for all source code and target for generated artifacts. The src directory has a number of subdirectories, each of which has a clearly defined purpose:

`src/main/java`
: Your Java source code goes here (strangely enough!)

`src/main/resources`
: Other resources your application needs

`src/main/filters`
: Resource filters, in the form of properties files, which may be used to define variables only known at runtime

`src/main/config`
: Configuration files

`src/main/webapp`
: The web application directory for a WAR project

`src/test/java`
: Source code for unit tests, by convention in a directory structure mirroring the one in your main source code directory

`src/test/resources`
: Resources to be used for unit tests, but that will not be deployed

`src/test/filters`
: Resources filters to be used for unit tests, but that will not be deployed

`src/site`
: Files used to generate the Maven project web site

2.7 Configuring Maven to Your Environment

One of the principal aims of Maven is to produce portable project build environments. Nevertheless, each work environment has its particularities, which need to be catered for. In this chapter, we investigate some common areas where you may need to tailor Maven to suit your particular work environment, such as configuring proxy servers, defining enterprise repositories, or specifying usernames and passwords.

When it comes to defining environment-specific configuration details, the most important tool at your disposal is the `settings.xml` file. Each user can have his or her own individual `settings.xml` file, which should be placed in the `$HOME/.m2` directory. This file is not placed under version control, and therefore can contain details such as usernames and passwords, which should not be shared in the source code repository.

Using a Proxy

If you are working in a company, you may well be accessing the Internet via a proxy. Maven relies heavily on accessing the Internet to download the libraries that it needs for your projects and for its own purposes. Therefore, if you are behind a proxy, you will need to tell Maven about it. Maven stores environment-specific parameters in a file called `$HOME/.m2/settings.xml`. You will have to create this file if it doesn't already exist. To define a proxy, just add a *<proxy>* element in this file, as follows:

```
<settings>
  <proxies>
   <proxy>
      <active>true</active>
      <protocol>http</protocol>
      <host>proxy.mycompany.com</host>
      <port>8080</port>
      <username>user</username>
```

```
        <password>password</password>
        <nonProxyHosts>*.mycompany.com</nonProxyHosts>
      </proxy>
    </proxies>
  </settings>
```

The *<nonProxyHosts>* element is useful to define servers that do not need proxy access, such as internal enterprise repositories.

Using a Local Mirror

Another common use of the `settings.xml` file is to configure mirror servers. This typically is done to configure an organization-wide repository. Many organizations use a local repository to store and share internal packages and to act as a proxy to external repositories. This solution is faster and more reliable than requiring users to go to the Internet whenever a new dependency is required.

The following example shows how to configure a Maven installation to use an Artifactory repository exclusively:

```
<settings>
  <mirrors>
      <mirror>
        <id>artifactory</id>
        <mirrorOf>*</mirrorOf>
        <url>http://buildserver.mycomany.org:8080/artifactory/repo</url>
        <name>Artifactory</name>
      </mirror>
  </mirrors>
</settings>
```

Changing Your Maven Cache Location

Maven stores downloaded JAR files in a local directory on your machine, known as the local repository. This directory generally is found at `$HOME/.m2/repository`. Over time, this directory can get pretty big. Although this usually is not an issue, it can be in some environments where your home directory is actually stored on a remote server and downloaded whenever you log on to a computer. In this case, if you prefer to keep your local repository on your machine, you can redefine the local repository directory by using the `<localRepository>` tag in your `$HOME/.m2/settings.xml` file:

```
<settings>
  <localRepository>C:/maven/repository</localRepository>
</settings>
```

Defining Arbitrary Environment-Specific Variables

The `settings.xml` file is also a good place to let users tailor their environment variables if they really need to. For example, you might need to specify the directory of some locally installed product, which may vary from machine to machine. You do this by defining a default profile in the `settings.xml` file. Any properties defined here will override property values in the POM file. Command-line tools like SchemaSpy (see Section 30.1) are a good example. This is a tool that needs to be downloaded and installed on each local machine. Of course, you can get the Maven build process to do this automatically. However, users who have already installed SchemaSpy, and may not want to duplicate installations, can override the SchemaSpy-related parameters by setting up properties in their local `settings.xml` file. In the following example, a user sets the installation directory (the *schemaspy.home* property) to `P:\tools\schemaspy`, which will override any property values defined in the main POM file:

```
<settings>
  ...
  <profiles>
   <profile>
      <id>development</id>
      <activation>
         <activeByDefault>true</activeByDefault>
     </activation>
     <properties>
        <schemaspy.home>P:\tools\schemaspy</schemaspy.home>
        <schemaspy.version>3.1.1</schemaspy.version>
     </properties>
   </profile>
  </profiles>
</settings>
```

Note that we still need to provide sensible default values in the POM file so that customizing your environment becomes optional, not mandatory. Users only need to modify their local file if they really want to (and, presumably, when they know what they are doing!). The best way to set up these default values is by using the *<properties>* element at the end of your POM file, as shown here:

```
<project>
  ...
  <properties>
        <schemaspy.home>${user.home}/.schemaspy</schemaspy.home>
        <schemaspy.version>3.1.1</schemaspy.version>
  </properties>
<project>
```

Don't be tempted to put these default values in a default profile element in your POM file; in this case, the profile in the POM file would override the profile in your local settings.

2.8 Dependency Management in Maven 2

Dependency management is one of the more powerful features of Maven 2. Dependencies are the libraries you need to compile, test, and run your application. In tools such as Ant, these libraries typically are stored in a special directory (often called `lib`), and are maintained either by hand or as project artifacts that are stored in the source code repository along with the source code. Maven, by contrast, uses a declarative approach. In a Maven project, you list the libraries your application needs, including the exact version number of each library. Using this information, Maven will do its best to find, retrieve, and assemble the libraries it needs during the different stages in the build lifecycle. In addition, using a powerful feature called Transitive Dependencies (see "Managing Transitive Dependencies," later in this section), it will include not only the libraries that you declare but also all the extra libraries that your declared libraries need to work correctly.

In this chapter, we will look at different aspects of how to handle dependencies in Maven 2.

Declaring Dependencies

One of the most powerful features of Maven 2 is its ability to handle dependencies in a consistent and reliable manner. In the *<dependencies>* section of the POM file, you declare the libraries that you need to compile, test, and run your application. Dependencies are retrieved from local or remote repositories, and cached locally on your development machine, in the `$HOME/.m2/repository` directory structure. If you use the same jar in two projects, it will only be downloaded (and stored) once, which saves time and disk space.

In Maven, dependencies are handled declaratively. Suppose that your project needs to use Hibernate, and that your unit tests are written in JUnit. In this case, the dependency section in your POM file might look something like the following:

```
...
<dependencies>
  <dependency>
    <groupId>org.hibernate</groupId>
    <artifactId>hibernate</artifactId>
    <version>3.1</version>
  </dependency>
  <dependency>
     <groupId>junit</groupId>
     <artifactId>junit</artifactId>
     <version>3.8.1</version>
     <scope>test</scope>
  </dependency>
</dependencies>
...
```

Each dependency is uniquely identified, using a Maven-style artifact reference (see "Project Context and Artifacts," in Section 2.4). Dependencies can refer both to other projects within your organization and to publicly available libraries on the public Maven repositories.

In some cases, libraries may have several different versions of a library with the same version number. The TestNG library, for example, has two versions for each release, one compiled for Java 1.4 and another compiled for Java 1.5:

```
testng-5.1-jdk14.jar        15-Aug-2006 08:55  817K
testng-5.1-jdk15.jar        15-Aug-2006 08:55  676K
```

When you declare your dependencies, Maven needs to know exactly which version you need. You do this by providing the *<classifier>* element, as shown here:

```
<dependency>
  <groupId>org.testng</groupId>
  <artifactId>testng</artifactId>
  <version>5.1</version>
  <classifier>jdk15</classifier>
  <scope>test</scope>
</dependency>
```

Dependencies declarations are not limited to precise version numbers. In fact, Maven is quite flexible about version numbers, and you can use a form of interval notation to define ranges of permissible version numbers. Interval notation comes from set theory, and is one of those things you probably learned at school or university and subsequently forgot. Here is a quick refresher. Interval notation is a flexible and succinct way of defining ranges of values using square brackets and parentheses to indicate boundary values. You use parentheses when the boundary value is not included in the set. For example, the following notation indicates a set of values greater than 1 (noninclusive) and less than 4 (noninclusive):

```
(1,4)
```

You use square brackets when the boundary values *are* included in the set. For example, the following notation indicates a set of values greater than *or equal to* 1 and less than *or equal to* 4:

```
[1,4]
```

You can combine different types of boundary values in the same expression. For example, this is how you would represent a set of values greater than or equal to 1, and strictly less than 4:

```
[1,4)
```

You can leave a value out to leave one side of the set unbounded. Here we include all values greater or equal to 2:

```
[2,)
```

You can even define a set made up of multiple intervals, simply by listing the intervals in a comma-separated list. The following example shows how you would define all the values between 1 and 10 inclusive, except for 5:

```
[1,5),(5,10]
```

Now that you have mastered the theory, let's see how it applies to dependency management. By using interval notation, you can give Maven more flexibility in its dependency management, which means that you spend less time chasing the latest API updates. Maven will use the highest available version within the range you provide. For example, the following dependency will use the latest available version of Hibernate, but requires at least Hibernate 3.0:

```
<dependency>
  <groupId>org.hibernate</groupId>
  <artifactId>hibernate</artifactId>
  <version>[3.0,)</version>
</dependency>
```

Or you may want to limit the versions of an API to a particular range. Using the following dependency, Maven will look for the highest version of the commons-collections in the 2.x series, but will exclude any versions from 3.0 onward:

```
<dependency>
  <groupId>commons-collections</groupId>
  <artifactId>commons-collections</artifactId>
  <version>[2.0,3.0)</version>
</dependency>
```

Managing Transitive Dependencies

Transitive Dependencies are arguably one of the most useful features of Maven 2. If you have ever used a tool like *urpmi* or *apt-get* on a Linux box, you will be familiar with the concept of Transitive Dependencies. Simply put, if you tell Maven 2 that your project needs a particular library, it will try to work out what other libraries this library needs, and retrieve them as well.

Let's look at how this works with a practical example. Suppose that our project uses Hibernate 3.1. We might declare this dependency as follows:

```
<dependency>
  <groupId>org.hibernate</groupId>
  <artifactId>hibernate</artifactId>
  <version>3.1</version>
</dependency>
```

Exactly where Maven looks for dependencies will depend on how your repositories are set up. The default Maven 2 repository is located at `http://repo1.maven.org/maven2` (if in doubt, this is actually defined in the Super POM file). In this case, Maven will look for the Hibernate JAR file in the following directory:

```
http://repo1.maven.org/maven2/org/hibernate/hibernate/3.1/
```

If you look in this directory, you will see a list of files similar to the following:

```
hibernate-3.1-sources.jar          10-Jan-2006 07:05  1.2M
hibernate-3.1-sources.jar.md5      10-Jan-2006 07:06  148
hibernate-3.1-sources.jar.sha1     10-Jan-2006 07:07  156
hibernate-3.1.jar                  15-Dec-2005 11:32  1.8M
hibernate-3.1.jar.md5              15-Dec-2005 11:32   32
hibernate-3.1.jar.sha1             15-Dec-2005 11:32   40
hibernate-3.1.pom                  26-Dec-2005 06:22  3.8K
```

```
hibernate-3.1.pom.md5          04-Jan-2006 07:33  138
hibernate-3.1.pom.sha1         04-Jan-2006 07:33  146
maven-metadata.xml             15-Dec-2005 11:32  119
maven-metadata.xml.md5         09-Jul-2006 08:41  130
maven-metadata.xml.sha1        09-Jul-2006 08:41  138
```

Note that there is much more than just the JAR file: there is also a POM file and (for good measure) digest files that let Maven verify the consistency of the files it downloads. The POM file here is the POM file for the Hibernate project. If your project needs to use Hibernate, it also needs to include all the Hibernate dependencies in its distribution. These secondary dependencies are listed in this POM file. Maven uses the dependencies in this POM to work out what other library it needs to retrieve.

This is the main weakness of Maven Transitive Dependency management: it relies on the accuracy and completeness of the POM files stored on the public repository. However, in some cases, the dependencies in the POM file may not be up-to-date, and, in other cases, the POM file may actually be just an empty POM file with no dependencies at all! In these cases, you will need to supply the dependencies explicitly in your own POM file.

Dependency management can be a complicated beast, and sometimes you will want to understand exactly which libraries Maven is using and why. One option is to use the *–X* command-line option with any Maven command to produce (among many other things) very detailed dependency information. This option generates a lot of text, so it is useful to redirect output into a text file and to view the file in a text editor, rather than to wrestle with the command line:

```
$ mvn -X test > out.txt
```

The resulting output file will contain lines like the following, detailing the resolved dependencies and the corresponding dependency graphs:

```
[DEBUG]   org.hibernate:hibernate:jar:3.1.3:compile (setting version to: 3.1.3
from range: [3.0,))
[DEBUG]   org.hibernate:hibernate:jar:3.1.3:compile (selected for compile)
[DEBUG]     javax.transaction:jta:jar:1.0.1B:compile (selected for compile)
[DEBUG]     dom4j:dom4j:jar:1.6.1:compile (selected for compile)
[DEBUG]     cglib:cglib:jar:2.1_3:compile (selected for compile)
[DEBUG]       asm:asm:jar:1.5.3:compile (selected for compile)
[DEBUG]     asm:asm-attrs:jar:1.5.3:compile (selected for compile)
[DEBUG]     asm:asm:jar:1.5.3:compile (selected for compile)
[DEBUG]     commons-collections:commons-collections:jar:2.1.1:compile (removed -
nearer found: 2.1)
[DEBUG]     antlr:antlr:jar:2.7.6rc1:compile (selected for compile)
```

This is a representation of the dependency tree: you can see exactly which library versions were requested, and which were retained for the final dependency list. It also indicates which libraries were removed because a nearer dependency was found (look at the "commons-collections" library in the above listing). This can give useful clues if a library is not behaving as expected.

The other useful tool in understanding your project's dependencies is the Dependency report. This report is generated by default when you generate the Maven site, and placed in the `target/dependencies.html` file:

```
$ mvn site
```

This report displays lists of direct and transitive dependencies for each dependency scope (see "Dependency Scope," later in this section), as well as the full dependency tree (see Figure 2-5).

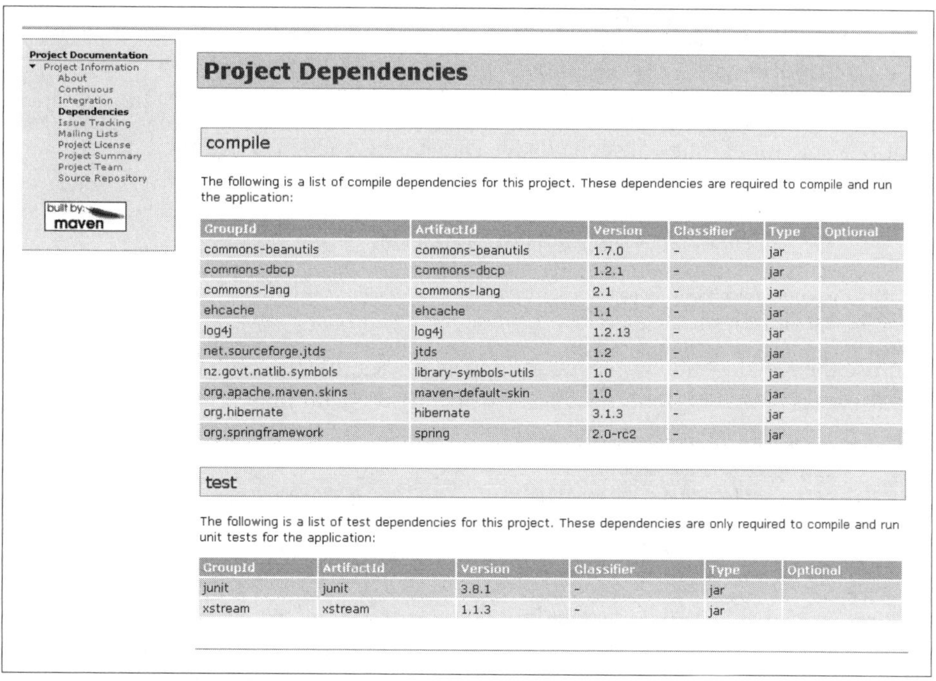

Project Documentation
- Project Information
  - About
  - Continuous Integration
  - **Dependencies**
  - Issue Tracking
  - Mailing Lists
  - Project License
  - Project Summary
  - Project Team
  - Source Repository

built by: maven

Project Dependencies

compile

The following is a list of compile dependencies for this project. These dependencies are required to compile and run the application:

GroupId	ArtifactId	Version	Classifier	Type	Optional
commons-beanutils	commons-beanutils	1.7.0	-	jar	
commons-dbcp	commons-dbcp	1.2.1	-	jar	
commons-lang	commons-lang	2.1	-	jar	
ehcache	ehcache	1.1	-	jar	
log4j	log4j	1.2.13	-	jar	
net.sourceforge.jtds	jtds	1.2	-	jar	
nz.govt.natlib.symbols	library-symbols-utils	1.0	-	jar	
org.apache.maven.skins	maven-default-skin	1.0	-	jar	
org.hibernate	hibernate	3.1.3	-	jar	
org.springframework	spring	2.0-rc2	-	jar	

test

The following is a list of test dependencies for this project. These dependencies are only required to compile and run unit tests for the application:

GroupId	ArtifactId	Version	Classifier	Type	Optional
junit	junit	3.8.1	-	jar	
xstream	xstream	1.1.3	-	jar	

Figure 2-5. Maven 2 dependency report

Dependency Scope

In a real-world enterprise application, you may not need to include all the dependencies in the deployed application. Some JARs are needed only for unit testing, while others will be provided at runtime by the application server. Using a technique called dependency scoping, Maven 2 lets you use certain JARs only when you really need them and excludes them from the classpath when you don't. Maven provides several dependency scopes.

The default scope is the *compile* scope. Compile-scope dependencies are available in all phases.

```
<dependency>
  <groupId>org.hibernate</groupId>
```

```
    <artifactId>hibernate</artifactId>
    <version>3.1</version>
  </dependency>
```

A *provided* dependency is used to compile the application but will not be deployed. You would use this scope when you expect the JDK or application server to provide the JAR. The servlet APIs are a good example:

```
  <dependency>
    <groupId>javax.servlet</groupId>
    <artifactId>servlet-api</artifactId>
    <version>2.4</version>
    <scope>provided</scope>
  </dependency>
```

The *runtime* dependency scope is used for dependencies that are not needed for compilation, only for execution, such as Java Database Connectivity (JDBC) drivers:

```
<dependency>
   <groupId>mysql</groupId>
   <artifactId>mysql-connector-java</artifactId>
   <version>3.1.13</version>
   <scope>runtime</scope>
</dependency>
```

You use the *test* dependency scope for dependencies that are only needed to compile and run tests, and that don't need to be distributed (JUnit or TestNG, for example):

```
<dependency>
   <groupId>junit</groupId>
   <artifactId>junit</artifactId>
   <version>3.8.1</version>
   <scope>test</scope>
</dependency>
```

In some special cases, you may need to use system dependencies, such as the *tools.jar* file provided with the Java SDK. For example, you may need to use the Sun *Apt* or *WSGen* tools within your build process. You can do this using the *system* dependency scope. In this case (and in this case only), you need to provide a *systemPath* value that indicates the absolute path to this file. This is illustrated in the following code extract:

```
<dependency>
    <groupId>com.sun</groupId>
    <artifactId>tools</artifactId>
    <version>1.5.0</version>
    <scope>system</scope>
    <systemPath>${java.home}/lib/tools.jar</systemPath>
</dependency>
```

Handling Proprietary Dependencies

For commercial and copyright reasons, not all of the commonly used libraries are available on the public Maven repositories. A common example is the Oracle JDBC Driver, which is available free-of-charge on the Oracle web site,* but it cannot be redistributed via a public Maven repository. Another frequently encountered example is the Java Transaction API (JTA), which is notably required by Hibernate. The JTA library is produced by Sun, which requires you to agree to a license agreement before you are able to download the JAR.

If you need to use a proprietary library like these in your Maven project, you will need to add it manually to your local repository. Let's see how this is done, using the Oracle driver as an example.

First, download the appropriate JAR file from the Oracle web site (for example, odbc14.jar). At the time of this writing, this corresponded to the "Oracle Database 10*g* Release 2 (10.2.0.2) JDBC Driver." It is important to note the exact version, as it is not visible from the name of the file. This version number will be used to identify the JAR file in our repository. The dependency declaration would look something like this:

```
<dependency>
    <groupId>oracle</groupId>
    <artifactId>oracle-jdbc</artifactId>
    <version>10.1.0.2.0</version>
    <scope>runtime</scope>
</dependency>
```

To get this to work, we need to copy the JAR into the correct place in our Maven repository. There are several ways to do this. You may first want to test on your development machine before installing the JAR onto the organization repository. You can install the jar into your local repository by using the *mvn install:install-file* command, as shown here:

```
mvn install:install-file -DgroupId=oracle \
     -DartifactId=oracle-jdbc \
     -Dpackaging=jar \
     -Dversion=10.1.0.2.0 \
     -DgeneratePom=true \
     -Dfile=ojdbc14.jar
```

Installing the JTA jar is similar: download it from the Sun site† and use the *mvn install* command as follows:

```
mvn install:install-file -DgroupId=javax.transaction \
     -DartifactId=jta \
     -Dpackaging=jar \
     -Dversion=1.0.1B \
```

* *http://www.oracle.com/technology/software/tech/java/sqlj_jdbc/index.html*

† *http://java.sun.com/products/jta/*

```
-DgeneratePom=true \
-Dfile=jta-1_0_1B-classes.zip
```

Now you can test the installation, typically by running some unit tests and seeing if Maven correctly finds the dependency.

When you are happy, you can either deploy the file to using the *mvn deploy:deploy-file* command, or simply copy the appropriate directory onto your company Maven repository. When this is done, this dependency can be seamlessly downloaded by all the team members in exactly the same way as any other new dependency.

Refactoring Your Dependencies Using Properties

In large projects, even with the benefits of transitive dependency management, you will often end up with a lot of dependencies. Sometimes, it is useful to declare key version numbers in a central place, making them easier to find and update if necessary. One good way to do this is by using properties.

We saw in "Defining Build Profiles" in Section 2.4 and Section 2.7 the ways in which you can define profile or environment-specific properties in a profile or in the settings.xml file. However, you also can declare properties directly at the root level in your `pom.xml` file. Like constants in a Java class, or Ant properties (see Section 1.5) in an Ant build script, this is a convenient way to define reusable values in an easy-to-maintain manner. The actual *<properties>* block can appear anywhere in the build file, but you may want to put it in an easy-to-find place such as near the start or right at the end.

Let's look at an example. Suppose that we are developing a web application using JSP and JSTL. In the following listing, we use two properties, somewhat unimaginatively named *servlet-api.version* and *jstl.version*, to identify what version of the Java Servlet and JSTL APIs we are using:

```
<project>
  ...
  <properties>
    ...
    <servlet-api.version>2.4</servlet-api.version>
    <jstl.version>1.1.2</jstl.version>
  </properties>
  ...
</project>
```

These properties can then be used to declare our dependencies in a more flexible manner. Now we can use these properties to declare our Servlet API and JSTL dependencies. Note that this makes it easier to ensure that the JSTL API and JSTL standard taglibs versions stay in sync:

```
<project>
  ...
  <properties>
    ...
    <servlet-api.version>2.4</servlet-api.version>
```

```
    <jstl.version>1.1.2</jstl.version>
  </properties>
  ...
  <dependencies>
    ...
    <dependency>
      <groupId>javax.servlet</groupId>
      <artifactId>servlet-api</artifactId>
      <version>${servlet-api.version}</version>
      <scope>provided</scope>
    </dependency>
    <dependency>
      <groupId>javax.servlet</groupId>
      <artifactId>jstl</artifactId>
      <version>${jstl.version}</version>
    </dependency>
    <dependency>
      <groupId>taglibs</groupId>
      <artifactId>standard</artifactId>
      <version>${jstl.version}</version>
    </dependency>
    ...
  </dependencies>
</project>
```

2.9 Looking for Dependencies with MvnRepository

When you are working with Maven, you often need to look up a particular dependency so that you can add it to your POM file. It can be quite tricky to remember and/or hunt down the precise group and artifact names and the latest version numbers for any but the most well-known artifacts. For example, do you remember the exact group and latest version of the Hibernate or Spring MVC libraries?

One useful resource that can help out here is the MvnRepository site* (see Figure 2-6). Using this site, you can search the central Maven repository for artifacts by name. When you find the version you are looking for, simply copy the displayed dependency block into your POM file. While you're there, you also can list the dependencies of a particular library, view the latest updates to the repository, or browse the overall structure of the repository.

2.10 Project Inheritance and Aggregation

Maven actively encourages you to write your projects as a set of small, flexible, modules rather than as a monolithic block of code. Dependencies are one way that you can create well-defined relationships between a set of modules to form an overall project. Project inheritance is another.

* *http://www.mvnrepository.com*

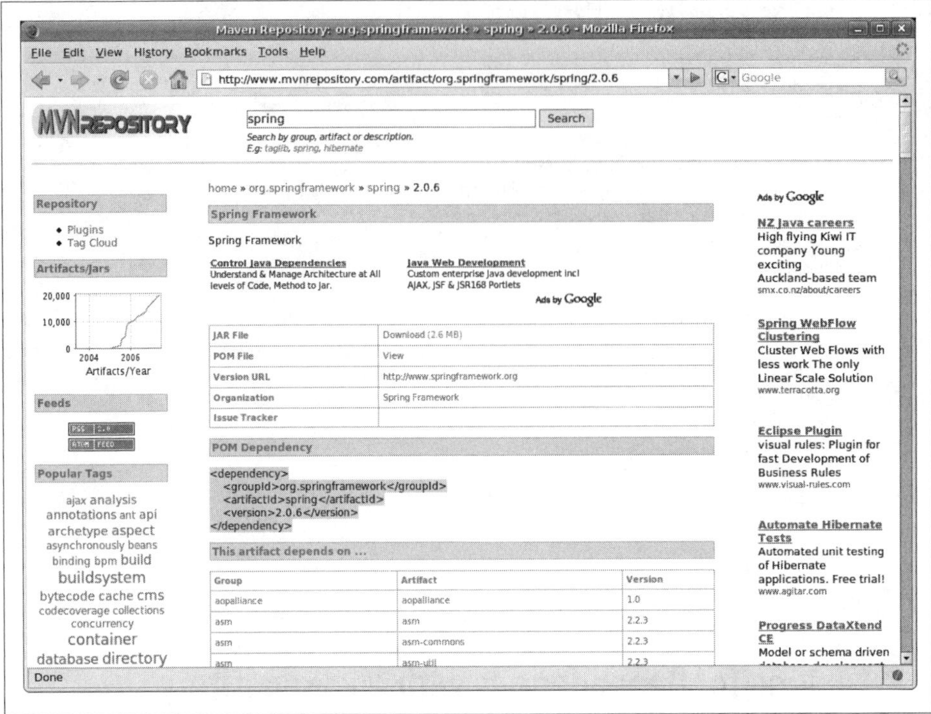

Figure 2-6. The MVN Repository web site

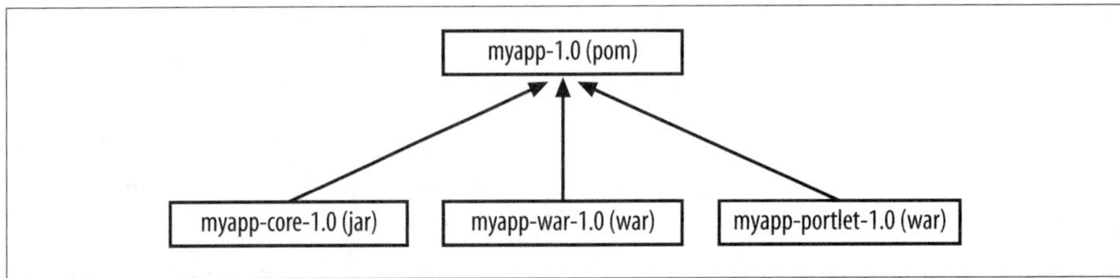

Figure 2-7. A multi-module Maven project structure

Project inheritance lets you define project-wide properties and values that will be inherited by all of the child projects. This is most easily understood by an example.

Suppose you are writing a simple web application, which will be deployed both as a traditional web application and as a portlet. One way that you might do this is to define three modules: a core module, containing the application business logic, and two user interface modules, one for each target platform. All three modules would have a common parent POM file, as illustrated in Figure 2-7.

Let's see how you would implement this project structure.

Parent POM files are very much like any other POM file. The following listing shows a very simple one:

```
<project>
  <modelVersion>4.0.0</modelVersion>
  <groupId>com.mycompany</groupId>
  <artifactId>myapp</artifactId>
  <packaging>pom</packaging>
  <name>Killer application</name>
  <version>1.0</version>
</project>
```

The main distinguishing factor is the *<packaging>* element, which is declared as a POM, rather than the WAR or JAR values that we have seen in previous examples. Indeed, all parent POM files must use the *pom* packaging type.

Then, within each child project, you need to declare a *<parent>* element that refers, suprisingly enough, to the parent POM file:

```
<project>
  <parent>
    <groupId>com.mycompany</groupId>
    <artifactId>myapp</artifactId>
    <version>1.0</version>
  </parent>
  <modelVersion>4.0.0</modelVersion>
  <artifactId>debtcalculator-core</artifactId>
  ...
</project>
```

Note that you don't need to define the version or groupId of the child project—these values are inherited from the parent.

The parent POM file is an excellent place to define project-wide properties or build configuration details. A typical use is to define the Java compile options in one central place. We can set the Java compiler to Java 1.5. This will be inherited by all the children projects, without any special configuration in their POM files:

```
<project>
  <modelVersion>4.0.0</modelVersion>
  <groupId>com.mycompany</groupId>
  <artifactId>myapp</artifactId>
  <packaging>pom</packaging>
  <name>Killer application</name>
  <version>1.0</version>
  <properties>
    <java-api.version>1.5</java-api.version>
  </properties>
  <build>
    <plugins>
      <plugin>
        <artifactId>maven-compiler-plugin</artifactId>
        <configuration>
          <source>${java-api.version}</source>
          <target>${java-api.version}</target>
```

```
        </configuration>
      </plugin>
    </plugins>
  </build>
</project>
```

In a similar way, you can define project-wide dependencies at this level:

```
<project>
  <modelVersion>4.0.0</modelVersion>
  <groupId>com.mycompany</groupId>
  <artifactId>myapp</artifactId>
  <packaging>pom</packaging>
  <name>Killer application</name>
  <version>1.0</version>
  <properties>
    <java-api.version>1.5</java-api.version>
    <junit.version>4.4</junit.version>
  </properties>
  ...
  <dependencies>
    <dependency>
      <groupId>junit</groupId>
      <artifactId>junit</artifactId>
      <version>${junit.version}</version>
      <scope>test</scope>
    </dependency>
  </dependencies>
</project>
```

All the children projects will now be able to use these dependencies without having to list them among their specific dependencies. This is also an excellent way to ensure that all of your children projects use the same versions of particular APIs.

The parent POM file is also an excellent place to set up reporting configurations. This way, you can define and configure the reports that you want generated for all the children projects in one central place.

```
<project>
  <modelVersion>4.0.0</modelVersion>
  <groupId>com.mycompany</groupId>
  <artifactId>myapp</artifactId>
  <packaging>pom</packaging>
  <name>Killer application</name>
  <version>1.0</version>
  ...
  <reporting>
    <plugins>
      <plugin>
        <artifactId>maven-surefire-report-plugin</artifactId>
      </plugin>
      <plugin>
        <artifactId>maven-checkstyle-plugin</artifactId>
      </plugin>
      ...
```

```
    </plugins>
  </reporting>
</project>
```

Although, at the time of this writing, multimodule reporting is still a bit dodgy, each child project will inherit the reporting configuration defined in the parent POM file, making these files simpler and easier to maintain.

You can also define the subprojects as modules. This is known as aggregation, and allows you to build all the child projects in one go from the parent directory.

```
<project>
  ...
  <modules>
    <module>myapp-core</module>
    <module>myapp-war</module>
    <module>myapp-portlet</module>
  </modules>
  ...
</project>
```

When you run mvn compile from the parent root directory, all of the child projects also would be compiled:

```
$ mvn compile
[INFO] Scanning for projects...
[INFO] Reactor build order:
[INFO]   Killer App
[INFO]   Killer App - Core
[INFO]   Killer App - Portlet
[INFO]   Killer App - Webapp
[INFO] ----------------------------------------------------------------------------
[INFO] Building Killer App
[INFO]    task-segment: [compile]
[INFO] ----------------------------------------------------------------------------
...
[INFO] ----------------------------------------------------------------------------
[INFO] Building Killer App - Core
[INFO]    task-segment: [compile]
[INFO] ----------------------------------------------------------------------------
...
[INFO] ----------------------------------------------------------------------------
[INFO] Building Killer App - Portlet
[INFO]    task-segment: [compile]
[INFO] ----------------------------------------------------------------------------
...
[INFO] ----------------------------------------------------------------------------
[INFO] Building Killer App - Webapp
[INFO]    task-segment: [compile]
[INFO] ----------------------------------------------------------------------------
...
[INFO] ------------------------------------------------------------------------
[INFO] Reactor Summary:
[INFO] ------------------------------------------------------------------------
[INFO] Killer App ............................................. SUCCESS [0.317s]
```

```
[INFO] Killer App - Core ..................................... SUCCESS [1.012s]
[INFO] Killer App - Portlet .................................. SUCCESS [0.602s]
[INFO] Killer App - Webapp ................................... SUCCESS [0.753s]
[INFO] ------------------------------------------------------------------------
[INFO] ------------------------------------------------------------------------
[INFO] BUILD SUCCESSFUL
[INFO] ------------------------------------------------------------------------
[INFO] Total time: 4 seconds
[INFO] Finished at: Sun Nov 18 02:54:32 GMT 2007
[INFO] Final Memory: 7M/80M
[INFO] ------------------------------------------------------------------------
```

2.11 Creating a Project Template with Archetypes

Even with a standardized directory structure, it is tiresome to have to create a full set of empty directories by hand whenever you start a new Maven project. To make life easier, Maven 2 provides the *archetype* plug-in, which builds an empty Maven 2—compatible project template, containing a standard directory structure as well as some sample files illustrating Maven conventions and best practices. This is an excellent way to get a basic project environment up and running quickly. The default archetype model will produce a JAR library project. Several other artifact types are available for other specific project types, including web applications, Maven plug-ins, and others.

Let's take a quick tour to see what you can do with Maven Archetypes. Suppose that we want to create an online store using Maven. Following Maven's recommendations, we will divide the project into several distinct modules. Our backend module will be called ShopCoreApi:

```
$ mvn archetype:create -DgroupId=com.acme.shop -DartifactId=ShopCoreApi
-Dpackagename=com.acme.shop
[INFO] Scanning for projects...
[INFO] Searching repository for plugin with prefix: 'archetype'.
[INFO] ---------------------------------------------------------------------------
[INFO] Building Maven Default Project
[INFO]    task-segment: [archetype:create] (aggregator-style)
[INFO] ---------------------------------------------------------------------------
...
[INFO] Archetype created in dir: /home/john/dev/projects/shop/ShopCoreApi
[INFO] ------------------------------------------------------------------------
[INFO] BUILD SUCCESSFUL
[INFO] ------------------------------------------------------------------------
[INFO] Total time: 2 seconds
[INFO] Finished at: Sun Oct 15 21:50:38 NZDT 2006
[INFO] Final Memory: 4M/8M
[INFO] ------------------------------------------------------------------------
```

This will create a complete, correctly structured, working, albeit minimalist, Maven project, including a simple POM file, a sample class, and a unit test. The POM file looks like this:

```
<project xmlns="http://maven.apache.org/POM/4.0.0" xmlns:xsi=
 "http://www.w3.org/2001/XMLSchema-instance"
```

```
  xsi:schemaLocation="http://maven.apache.org/POM/4.0.0
  http://maven.apache.org/maven-v4_0_0.xsd">
  <modelVersion>4.0.0</modelVersion>
  <groupId>com.acme.shop</groupId>
  <artifactId>ShopCoreApi</artifactId>
  <packaging>jar</packaging>
  <version>1.0-SNAPSHOT</version>
  <name>ShopCoreApi</name>
  <url>http://maven.apache.org</url>
  <dependencies>
    <dependency>
      <groupId>junit</groupId>
      <artifactId>junit</artifactId>
      <version>3.8.1</version>
      <scope>test</scope>
    </dependency>
  </dependencies>
</project>
```

The project will be created in a subdirectory with the same name of the artifact (in this case, "ShopCoreApi"). The *groupId* and the artifactId are used to identify the artifact produced by the project (see "Project Context and Artifacts" in Section 2.4). The *packagename* is the root package for your project. More often than not, the *packagename* option will be the same at the *groupId*: in this case, you can drop the *packagename* option.

This project is now ready to try out. Switch to this directory and build the project using *mvn package*:

```
$ ls
ShopCoreApi
$ cd ShopCoreApi
$ mvn package
[INFO] Scanning for projects...
[INFO] ------------------------------------------------------------------------
[INFO] Building Maven Quick Start Archetype
[INFO]    task-segment: [package]
[INFO] ------------------------------------------------------------------------
...
-------------------------------------------------------
 T E S T S
-------------------------------------------------------
Running com.acme.shop.AppTest
Tests run: 1, Failures: 0, Errors: 0, Skipped: 0, Time elapsed: 0.039 sec

Results :
Tests run: 1, Failures: 0, Errors: 0, Skipped: 0
[INFO] [jar:jar]
[INFO] Building jar: /home/john/dev/projects/shop/ShopCoreApi/target
/ShopCoreApi-1.0-SNAPSHOT.jar
[INFO] ----------------------------------------------------------------------
[INFO] BUILD SUCCESSFUL
[INFO] ----------------------------------------------------------------------
[INFO] Total time: 4 seconds
```

```
[INFO] Finished at: Sun Oct 15 21:52:22 NZDT 2006
[INFO] Final Memory: 4M/10M
[INFO] ------------------------------------------------------------------------
```

So, now you have a working Maven project template, generated in just a few minutes!

The default Archetype template (the `maven-archetype-quickstart` archetype) is designed to produce a JAR file. There are also several other archetypes that can be used to create templates for different types of projects. You can use a different archetype by using the *archetypeArtifactId* command-line option, as shown here:

```
$ mvn archetype:create -DgroupId=com.acme.shop -DartifactId=ShopWeb \
  -DarchetypeArtifactId=maven-archetype-webapp
```

This example uses the `maven-archetype-webapp` archetype, which creates (surprisingly enough!) an empty WAR project. Following Maven's recommendations about Separation of Concerns, the WAR project is expected to contain only dynamic web pages (JSPs), with the actual Java code being written in another project.

Another useful archetype is the `maven-archetype-site` archetype, which creates a template for a Maven web site for an existing project, including a full, multilingual (well, bilingual) site structure with sample XDoc, APT, and FAQs content. This archetype is the only one that you run on an existing project. Although it provides none of the source code-based reporting features, such as unit test reports, checkstyle reports, and so on (which need to be configured in the main POM file), it does provide a good starting point for manually added site content:

```
$ mvn archetype:create -DgroupId=com.acme.shop -DartifactId=ShopCoreApi \
  -DarchetypeArtifactId=maven-archetype-site
$ mvn site
[INFO] Scanning for projects...
[INFO] ----------------------------------------------------------------------------
[INFO] Building Maven Quick Start Archetype
[INFO]    task-segment: [site]
[INFO] ----------------------------------------------------------------------------
...
[INFO] Generate "Continuous Integration" report.
[INFO] Generate "Dependencies" report.
[INFO] Generate "Issue Tracking" report.
[INFO] Generate "Project License" report.
[INFO] Generate "Mailing Lists" report.
[INFO] Generate "Project Summary" report.
[INFO] Generate "Source Repository" report.
[INFO] Generate "Project Team" report.
[INFO] ------------------------------------------------------------------------
[INFO] BUILD SUCCESSFUL
[INFO] ------------------------------------------------------------------------
[INFO] Total time: 11 seconds
[INFO] Finished at: Sun Oct 15 22:47:04 NZDT 2006
[INFO] Final Memory: 11M/21M
[INFO] ------------------------------------------------------------------------
```

There is also an increasing number of third-party archetypes available for other types of web applications and web technology stacks, such as Struts, Spring, JSF, Hibernate, Ageci, and many more. A list of some of these can be found on the Codehaus web site.* Matt Raible's AppFuse project† provides a large number of archetypes that you can use to create working application templates based on a wide range of open source architectures and libraries, such as JSF, Spring, Spring MVC, Struts, Hibernate, and Tapestry. For example, the *appfuse-basic-spring* archetype, shown here, will create a very complete web application prototype based on Hibernate, Spring, and JSF:

```
$ mvn archetype:create -DgroupId=com.jpt -DartifactId=shopfront \
  -DarchetypeArtifactId=appfuse-basic-jsf -DarchetypeGroupId=org.appfuse.archetypes
...
[INFO] Archetype created in dir: /home/john/projects/shopfront
[INFO] ------------------------------------------------------------------------
[INFO] BUILD SUCCESSFUL
[INFO] ------------------------------------------------------------------------
[INFO] Total time: 1 minute 8 seconds
[INFO] Finished at: Wed Oct 10 20:46:27 GMT+12:00 2007
[INFO] Final Memory: 6M/65M
[INFO] ------------------------------------------------------------------------
```

This will create a executable web application, as well as a good example of a working, detailed POM file for a realBy default. It will try to connect to a local MySQL database (using the "root" user with no password). You can try it out by running the Jetty plug-in, as shown here:

```
$ cd shopfront
$ mvn jetty:run
...
 mvn jetty:run-war
[INFO] Scanning for projects...
[INFO] Searching repository for plugin with prefix: 'jetty'.
[INFO] ----------------------------------------------------------------------------
[INFO] Building AppFuse JSF Application
[INFO]    task-segment: [jetty:run-war]
[INFO] ----------------------------------------------------------------------------
...
2007-10-10 21:30:48.410::INFO:  Started SelectChannelConnector@0.0.0.0:8080
[INFO] Started Jetty Server
```

You can now view this application by going to *http://localhost:8080*. Log in using a username and password of "admin," and check it out (see Figure 2-8).

* *http://docs.codehaus.org/display/MAVENUSER/Archetypes+List*

† *http://appfuse.org/display/APF/Home*

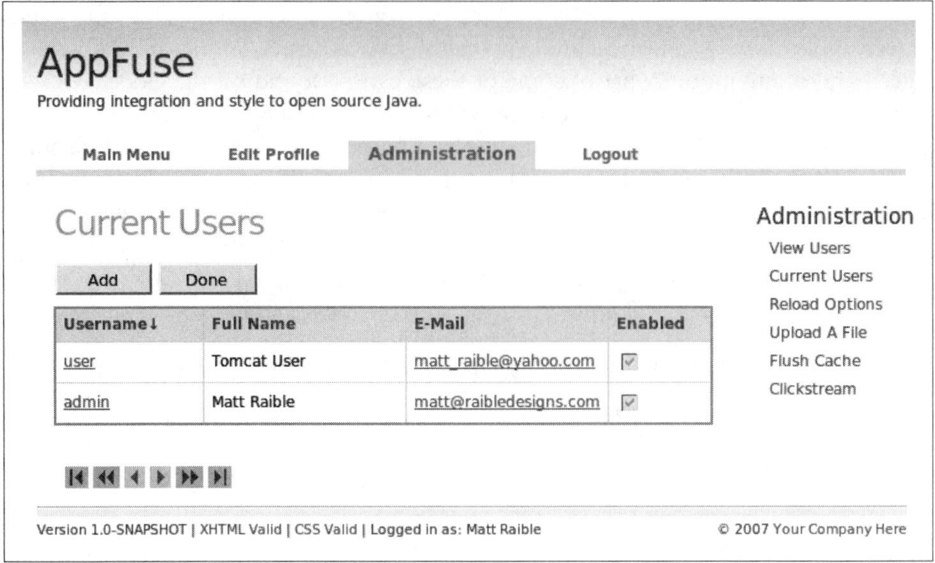

Figure 2-8. The running AppFuse application

You also can create your own archetypes, which can be useful if you want to encourage organization-wide project conventions, or to support particular types of projects that you use often. We will discuss how to do this in Section 2.22.

2.12 Compiling Code

A key part of any development lifecycle is compiling your source code. Compiling your project with Maven is easy—just run *mvn compile*:

```
$ mvn compile
```

Before compiling, Maven will check that all the project's dependencies have been downloaded, and will fetch any that it doesn't already have. It also will generate any source code or project resources that need to be generated and instantiate any variables in the resources and configuration files (see "Defining Build Profiles" in Section 2.4). One of the nice things about Maven is that these tasks are done automatically, as part of the normal Maven lifecycle, without needing any particular configuration.

To be sure that there are no stale objects remaining in the target directories, you can also call the clean plug-in, which, as the name indicates, empties the output directories in preparation for a clean build:

```
$ mvn clean compile
```

By default, Java compilation in Maven 2 supports backward compatibility to JDK 1.3, which means that your generated artifacts will work fine with pretty much any modern version of Java. This is a useful thing to do if you are generating JAR files for community use, or for multiple JDKs. However, if you compile your brand-new Java class full of generics, for example, you'll get a message like this:

```
[ERROR] BUILD FAILURE
[INFO] ------------------------------------------------------------------------
[INFO] Compilation failure

/Users/jfsmart/chapters/caching/app/hibernateCaching/src/main/java/com/wakaleo/
chapters/caching/businessobjects/Country.java:[41,18] generics are not supported
in -source 1.3
(try -source 1.5 to enable generics)
        public Set getAirports() {
```

To get your code to compile correctly using the new Java 5 features (generics and so forth), you need to configure the special *maven-compiler-plugin* in your *pom.xml* file. This allows you to define the *source* and *target* parameters for the Java compiler. For Java 5, you could do the following:

```
<project...>
  ...
  <build>
    <plugins>
        <plugin>
            <groupId>org.apache.maven.plug-ins</groupId>
            <artifactId>maven-compiler-plugin</artifactId>
            <configuration>
                <source>1.5</source>
                <target>1.5</target>
            </configuration>
         </plugin>
     </plugins>
  </build>
</project>
```

2.13 Testing Your Code

Unit tests are an important part of any modern development methodology, and they play a key role in the Maven development lifecycle. By default, Maven will not let you package or deploy your application unless all the unit tests succeed. Maven will recognize both JUnit 3.x, JUnit 4 (Section 10.9) and TestNG unit tests (see Chapter 11), as long as they are placed in the `src/test` directory structure.

Running unit tests from Maven is done using the *mvn test* command, as shown here:

```
$ mvn test
[INFO] Scanning for projects...
.
.
.
[INFO] [surefire:test]
[INFO] Surefire report directory: /home/john/projects/java-power-tools/...
/target/surefire-reports
```

```
-------------------------------------------------------
 T E S T S
-------------------------------------------------------
Running com.javapowertools.taxcalculator.services.TaxCalculatorTest
Tests run: 10, Failures: 0, Errors: 0, Skipped: 0, Time elapsed: 0.036 sec
Running com.javapowertools.taxcalculator.domain.TaxRateTest
Tests run: 3, Failures: 0, Errors: 0, Skipped: 0, Time elapsed: 0.009 sec

Results :

Tests run: 13, Failures: 0, Errors: 0, Skipped: 0
```

Maven will compile if necessary before running the application's unit tests. By default, Maven expects unit tests to be placed in the **src/test** directory, and will automatically pick up any test classes with names that start or end with "Test" or that end with "TestCase."

Detailed test results are produced in text and XML form in the target/surefire-reports directory. Alternatively, you can generate the test results in HTML form using the surefire reporting feature:

```
$ mvn surefire-report:report
```

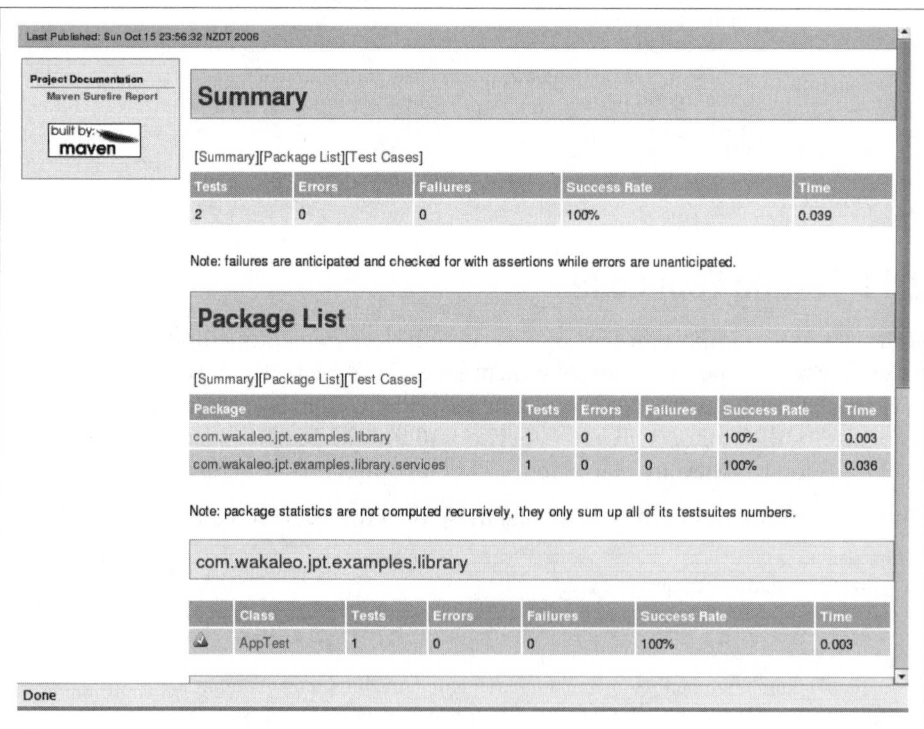

Figure 2-9. Unit test results in HTML form

The HTML report will be generated in a file called `target/site/surefire-report.html` (see Figure 2-9).

Another important aspect of unit testing is Test Coverage, which makes sure that a high proportion of your code is actually being exercised by your tests. Although high test coverage is not sufficient in itself to prove that your code is being well tested, the opposite is probably true—poor test coverage is usually a reliable sign of poorly tested code.

Cobertura (see Chapter 12) is an open source coverage tool that integrates well with Maven. You can measure test coverage with Cobertura without any additional configuration by simply invoking the *cobertura* plug-in, as shown here:

```
$ mvn cobertura:cobertura
[INFO] Scanning for projects...
[INFO] Searching repository for plugin with prefix: 'cobertura'.
[INFO] ------------------------------------------------------------------------
[INFO] Building Tax Calculator
[INFO]    task-segment: [cobertura:cobertura]
[INFO] ------------------------------------------------------------------------
[INFO] Preparing cobertura:cobertura
...
Report time: 178ms

[INFO] Cobertura Report generation was successful.
[INFO] ------------------------------------------------------------------------
[INFO] BUILD SUCCESSFUL
[INFO] ------------------------------------------------------------------------
[INFO] Total time: 17 seconds
[INFO] Finished at: Wed Nov 28 09:25:55 GMT 2007
[INFO] Final Memory: 6M/81M
[INFO] ------------------------------------------------------------------------
```

This will generate a detailed HTML coverage report, which can be found in `target/site/cobertura/index.html` (see Figure 2-10). Cobertura gives a high-level summary of code coverage across the whole project, and lets you drill down into a package to individual classes where you can see which lines of code have not been tested.

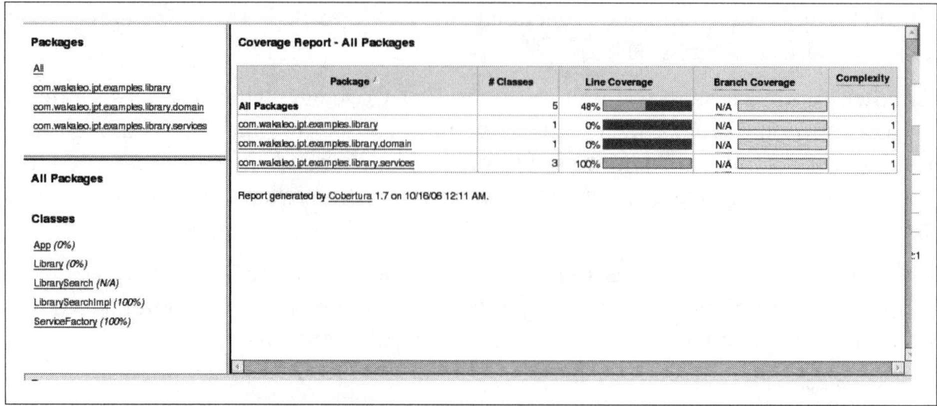

Figure 2-10. Unit test results in HTML form

Both of these reports also can be easily integrated into the Maven-generated project web site.

Actually, at the time of writing, there is one slight hitch, and this won't work as shown. In fact, you need to use version 2.0 or 2.2 of the Cobertura plug-in. You do this by overriding the standard Cobertura plug-in configuration in the *<build>* section of your *pom.xml* file, as shown here:

```
<!-- BUILD CONFIGURATION -->
<build>
    <plugins>
       ...
       <plugin>
            <groupId>org.codehaus.mojo</groupId>
            <artifactId>cobertura-maven-plugin</artifactId>
            <version>2.2</version>
        </plugin>
    </plugins>
</build>
```

This is discussed in more detail in Section 12.6.

During debugging, you often want to just run a single test. In Maven, you can do this using the *-Dtest* command-line option, specifying the name of your unit test class:

```
$ mvn -Dtest=ProductDAOTests test
```

Finally, if you need to, you can also skip tests entirely using the *-Dmaven.test.skip* option:

```
$ mvn -Dmaven.test.skip package
```

2.14 Packaging and Deploying Your Application

One of the fundamental principles of Maven is that each Maven project generates one, and only one, main artifact. The type of artifact generated by a Maven project is defined in the *<packaging>* section of the POM file. The main types of packaging are self-explanatory: *jar*, *war*, and *ear*. A typical example is shown here:

```
<project...>
   <modelVersion>4.0.0</modelVersion>
   <groupId>com.mycompany.accounting</groupId>
   <artifactId>accounting-webapp</artifactId>
   <packaging>war</packaging>
   <version>1.1</version>
   ...
```

The packaging type will determine exactly how your project is bundled together: compiled classes are placed at the root of a JAR file and in the `WEB-INF/classes` subdirectory in a WAR file, for example.

The next step is to install and/or deploy your application. The *install* command will generate and deploy your project artifact to the local repository on your local machine, where it will become available to other projects on your machine:

```
$ mvn install
```

The *deploy* command will generate and deploy your project artifact to a remote server via one of the supported protocols (SSH2, SFTP, FTP, and external SSH), or simply to a local filesystem:

```
$ mvn deploy
```

Your application will be deployed to the remote repository defined in the *<distributionManagement>* section in your POM file. If you are deploying to a *NIX machine, you will probably need to use one of the network copying protocols: SSH2, SFTP, FTP, or external SSH, as in this example:

```
<distributionManagement>
  <repository>
    <id>company.repository</id>
    <name>Enterprise Maven Repository</name>
    <url>scp://repo.acme.com/maven</url>
  </repository>
</distributionManagement>
```

If you are deploying to a local filesystem, or to a Windows shared drive, you can use the *file* URL protocol, as shown here:

```
<distributionManagement>
  <repository>
    <id>company.repository</id>
    <name>Enterprise Maven Repository</name>
    <url>file:///D:/maven/repo</url>
```

```
    </repository>
  </distributionManagement>
```

If you need to supply a username and password when you copy to the remote repository, you also will need to provide this information in your `settings.xml` file (see Section 2.7):

```
<settings>
  ...
  <servers>
    <server>
      <id>company.repository</id>
      <username>scott</username>
      <password>tiger</password>
    </server>
  </servers>
</settings>
```

Maven supports a variety of distribution protocols, including FTP, DAV, and SCP. However, not all protocols are supported out-of-the-box. You often will need to add an *<extension>* element to the *<build>* section in your `pom.xml` file. This is illustrated here, where we add support for FTP and deploy our application to an enterprise FTP server:

```
    </build>
        ...
        <extensions>
          <extension>
            <groupId>org.apache.maven.wagon</groupId>
             <artifactId>wagon-ftp</artifactId>
             <version>1.0-beta-2</version>
          </extension>
        </extensions>
    </build>
    ...
    <distributionManagement>
      <repository>
        <id>ftp.repository</id>
        <name>Remote FTP Repository</name>
        <url>ftp://www.mycompany.com/public_html/repos</url>
      </repository>
      <site>
        <id>web site</id>
        <url>ftp://www.mycompany.com/public_html</url>
      </site>
    </distributionManagement>
```

2.15 Deploying an Application Using Cargo

There are also many third-party tools and libraries that can help you deploy your application. One of the most versatile is Cargo.* Cargo is a powerful tool that allows you to deploy your application to a number of different application servers, including Tomcat, JBoss, Geronimo, and Weblogic. It integrates well with both Maven and Ant. We don't have room to explore all of its possibilities here. In this chapter, we will just look at how to configure Cargo to deploy a WAR application to a running remote Tomcat server.

Cargo provides a Maven plug-in that allows you to integrate Cargo functionalities smoothly into the Maven lifecycle. The configuration is a bit wordy, mainly as a result of the large degree of flexibity offered by the tool. The full plug-in configuration is shown here:

```
<plugin>
  <groupId>org.codehaus.cargo</groupId>
  <artifactId>cargo-maven2-plugin</artifactId>
  <executions>
    <execution>
      <id>verify-deploy</id>
      <phase>pre-integration-test</phase>
      <goals>
        <goal>deployer-redeploy</goal>
      </goals>
    </execution>
  </executions>
  <configuration>
    <container>
      <containerId>tomcat5x</containerId>
      <type>remote</type>
    </container>
    <configuration>
      <type>runtime</type>
      <properties>
        <cargo.tomcat.manager.url>${tomcat.manager}</cargo.tomcat.manager.url>
        <cargo.remote.username>${tomcat.manager.username}</cargo.remote.username>
        <cargo.remote.password>${tomcat.manager.password}</cargo.remote.password>
      </properties>
    </configuration>
    <deployer>
      <type>remote</type>
      <deployables>
        <deployable>
          <groupId>nz.govt.ird.egst</groupId>
          <artifactId>egst-web</artifactId>
          <type>war</type>
          <pingURL>http://${tomcat.host}:${tomcat.port}/${project.build.finalName}
           /welcome.do
          </pingURL>
```

* *http://cargo.codehaus.org/*

```
          </deployable>
        </deployables>
      </deployer>
    </configuration>
  </plugin>
```

Let's look at each section in more detail.

The first section simply declares the plug-in in the usual way:

```
<plugin>
  <groupId>org.codehaus.cargo</groupId>
  <artifactId>cargo-maven2-plugin</artifactId>
  ...
```

In this example, we automatically deploy the packaged WAR file just before the integration tests phase. This section is optional and is designed to make it easier to run automatic integration or functional tests against the latest version of the application. The *deployer-redeploy* goal will, as you would expect, redeploy the application on the targetted Tomcat server:

```
...
<executions>
  <execution>
    <id>verify-deploy</id>
    <phase>pre-integration-test</phase>
    <goals>
      <goal>deployer-redeploy</goal>
    </goals>
  </execution>
</executions>
...
```

The next section is the *<configuration>* element. We define the type of application server (in this case, a remote Tomcat 5 server), and provide some server-specific configuration details indicating how to deploy to this server. For Tomcat, this consists of the URL for the Tomcat Manager application, as well as a valid Tomcat username and password that will give us access to this server:

```
...
<configuration>
  <container>
    <containerId>tomcat5x</containerId>
    <type>remote</type>
  </container>
  <configuration>
    <type>runtime</type>
    <properties>
      <cargo.tomcat.manager.url>${tomcat.manager}</cargo.tomcat.manager.url>
      <cargo.remote.username>${tomcat.manager.username}</cargo.remote.username>
      <cargo.remote.password>${tomcat.manager.password}</cargo.remote.password>
    </properties>
  </configuration>
  ...
```

For this to work correctly, you need to have defined a Tomcat user with the "manager" role. This is not the case by default, so you may have to modify your Tomcat configuration manually. In a default installation, the simplest way is to add a user to the Tomcat `conf/tomcat-users.xml` file, as shown here:

```
<?xml version='1.0' encoding='utf-8'?>
<tomcat-users>
  <role rolename="tomcat"/>
  <role rolename="manager"/>
  <user username="tomcat" password="tomcat" roles="tomcat"/>
  <user username="admin" password="secret" roles="tomcat,manager"/>
</tomcat-users>
```

This example uses a number of properties, among them are th*tomcat.manager*, *tomcat.manager.username*, and *tomcat.manager.password*. These properties are typically by used both by Cargo and by functional testing tools such as Selenium (see Chapter 20). They allow you to tailor the build process to different environments without modifying the build script itself. Here, the *tomcat.manager* property indicates the URL pointing to the Tomcat manager application. Cargo uses this application to deploy the WAR file, so it needs to be installed and running on your Tomcat instance.

This URL is built using other more environment-specific properties. It can be placed at the end of the `pom.xml` file, in the *<properties>* element, as shown here:

```
<project>
  ...
  <properties>
    <tomcat.manager>http://${tomcat.host}:${tomcat.port}/manager</tomcat.manager>
  </properties>
</project>
```

The other properties will vary depending on the target environment. Probably the best way to set this up is to use Maven profiles (see "Defining Build Profiles" in Section 2.4).

Profiles can be placed either in the `pom.xml` file (where they will be available to all users), or in the `settings.xml` file (for profiles that contain sensitive information such as server passwords). You might place the development profile directly in the `pom.xml` file for convenience:

```
  ...
  <profiles>
    <!-- Local development environment -->
    <profile>
      <id>dev</id>
      <activation>
        <activeByDefault>true</activeByDefault>
      </activation>
      <properties>
        <tomcat.port>8080</tomcat.port>
        <tomcat.server>development</tomcat.server>
        <tomcat.host>localhost</tomcat.host>
        <tomcat.manager.username>admin</tomcat.manager.username>
        <tomcat.manager.password></tomcat.manager.password>
```

```
        </properties>
      </profile>
      ...
    <profiles>
    ...
</project>
```

A developer can then redeploy by using the *cargo:redeploy* goal:

```
$ mvn package cargo:redeploy
```

Cargo also comes with other similar goals, such as *cargo:deploy* and *cargo:undeploy*, which can be useful on occasions.

Deploying to the integration server, by contrast, requires a server password that you may not want to place under version control. In addition, you may not want developers deploying directly to the integration server from their own machines—they may have to do this on the build server or through a Continuous Integration tool. You can arrange this by defining an integration server profile in the `settings.xml` file on the machine (or machines) that will be deploying to this server (for example, on the build server):

```
<settings>
  ...
  <profiles>
    ...
    <!-- Integration environment on a remote build server -->
    <profile>
      <id>integration</id>
      <activation>
        <property>
          <name>env</name>
          <value>integration</value>
        </property>
      </activation>
      <properties>
        <tomcat.port>10001</tomcat.port>
        <tomcat.server>integration</tomcat.server>
        <tomcat.host>buildserver.mycompany.com</tomcat.host>
        <tomcat.manager.username>admin</tomcat.manager.username>
        <tomcat.manager.password>secret</tomcat.manager.password>
      </properties>
    </profile>
    ...
  <profiles>
</settings>
```

Now, from these machines, you can redeploy your application onto the integration server, as shown here:

```
$ mvn package cargo:redeploy -Denv=integration
```

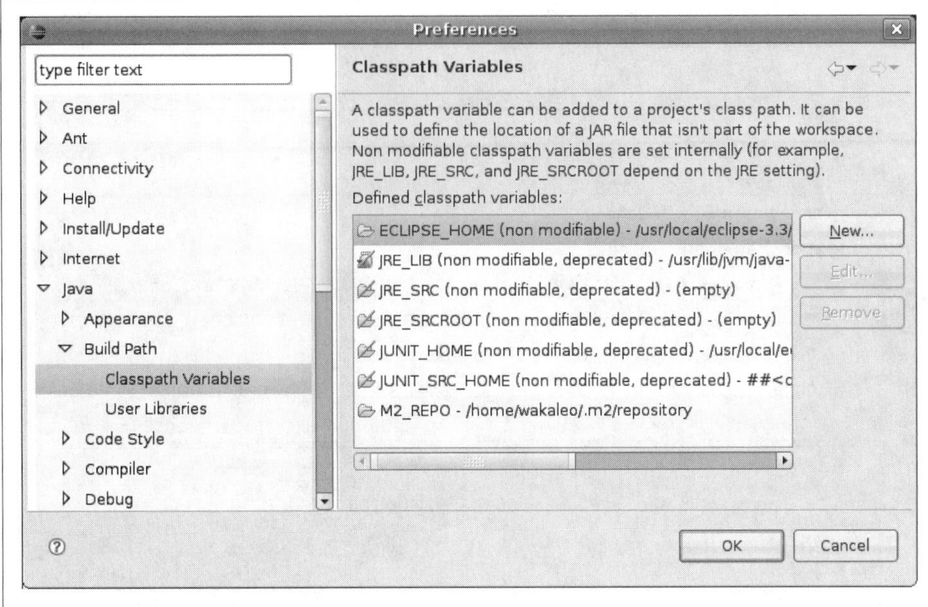

Figure 2-11. Configuring the M2_REPO variable in Eclipse

2.16 Using Maven in Eclipse

If you are using the Eclipse IDE, you can generate a new Eclipse project file (or synchronize an existing one) with a Maven project using the Maven Eclipse plug-in. The simplest approach is often to create a project skeleton using *mvn:archetype*, and then import this project into Eclipse as a simple Java project. However, Eclipse will not recognise the Maven dependencies without a bit of help. The main purpose of the Maven Eclipse plug-in is to synchronize the Eclipse build path with the dependencies defined in the Maven POM file. For this to work, Eclipse needs to use a classpath variable called *M2_REPO*, which points to your local Maven repository (see Figure 2-11). You can either set this up manually in Eclipse, or use the Maven plug-in to configure your workspace, using the *add-maven-repo* goal:

```
$ mvn -Declipse.workspace=/home/wakaleo/workspace eclipse:add-maven-repo
```

When you next open Eclipse, your classpath variables should be set correctly.

Next, you need to synchronize your Eclipse project dependencies with the ones defined in your Maven project. To do this, go to your project directory and run the *mvn eclipse* plug-in:

```
$ mvn eclipse:eclipse
```

This will update the Eclipse project file with your Maven project dependencies. All you need to do now is simply refresh your project in Eclipse, and the dependencies that you have defined in your Maven project will appear in Eclipse.

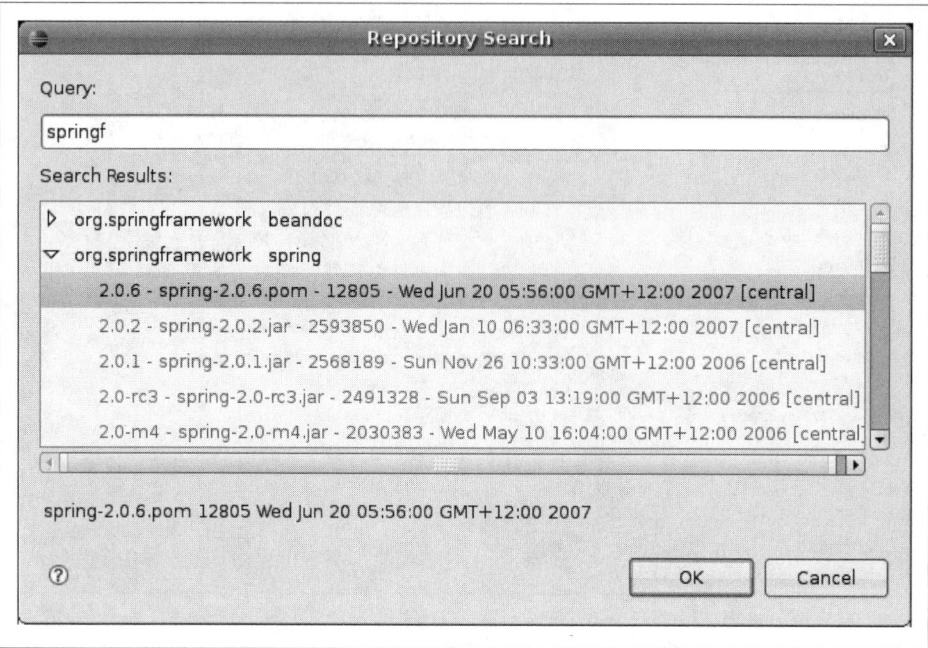

Figure 2-12. The MVN Repository web site

There is also a plug-in for Eclipse that provides excellent Maven support from within Eclipse itself. The Maven Integration for *Eclipse* plug-in* from Codehaus provides some very useful features in this area. You can install this plug-in using the following remote site:

http://m2eclipse.codehaus.org/update/

Once installed, you will need to activate Maven Support for the project. Click on the project and select "Maven→Enable Dependency Management." If a POM file doesn't already exist for this project, you will be able to create a new one. Otherwise, the existing POM file will be used.

Now, whenever you need to add a new dependency to your project, click on the project and select "Maven →Add Dependency" in the contextual menu. This will open a window (see Figure 2-12), allowing you to search for artifacts on all of the repositories declared in your POM file. Type the name of the dependency that you need, then select the version that you want to use. Eclipse will automatically add this dependency to your POM file.

This plug-in also has the advantage of integrating your Maven dependencies with your Eclipse project—any new dependencies you add will automatically be downloaded and made available to your eclipse project.

* *http://m2eclipse.codehaus.org/*

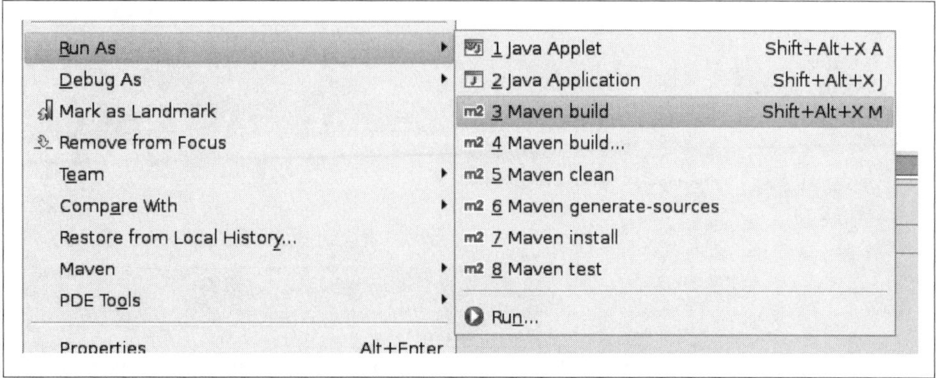

Figure 2-13. Executing a Maven goal from Eclipse.

The Maven Integration plug-in also lets you execute Maven goals from within Eclipse. On any Maven-enabled project, you can use the "Run As" contextual menu to execute Maven goals. This menu proposes several common Maven goals such as *mvn clean*, *mvn install*, and *mvn test* (see Figure 2-13), as well as the "Maven build" option, which can be configured to execute the goal of your choice.

You can configure the default Maven build by selecting "Run As→Maven build...") in the contextual menu. In a similar way, you can also configure more sophisticated Maven goals through the "External Tools..." menu (see Figure 2-14). In both cases, you can select the goal you want to execute, along with any required profiles, system variables, or command-line parameters.

2.17 Using Maven in NetBeans

For a long time, Maven support in NetBeans was very limited. However, from NetBeans 6.0 onward, NetBeans provided excellent built-in Maven support, and Maven can now be used as its underlying build tool in the same way as previous versions used Ant. In NetBeans 6, you can add an existing Maven project directly into the workspace or create a new one using one of several Maven archetypes (see Figure 2-15).

You also can add dependencies to your POM file using a graphical interface.

2.18 Using Plug-Ins to Customize the Build Process

Contributed by: Eric Redmond

If there has been one substantial improvement between Maven 1 and Maven 2, it is the simplicity and flexibility of extending the default execution set with custom plug-ins. One can even write plug-ins in other programming languages, such as JRuby, Groovy, or Ant. However, we will turn our focus to the most heavily used and supported default language: Java.

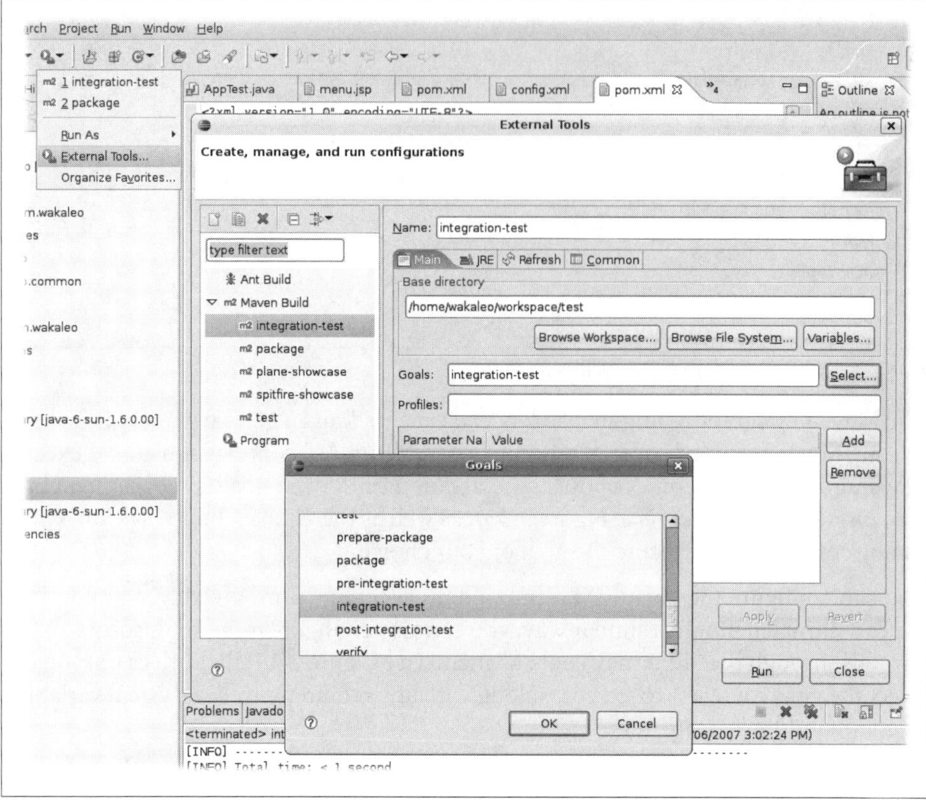

Figure 2-14. Executing a Maven goal from Eclipse.

A Maven plug-in is a collection of goals and, as mentioned in previous sections of this chapter, a goal is a unit of work in the Maven build lifecycle. Maven comes with tools allowing you to easily create and install your own goals. This allows you to extend the default build lifecycle in any way you can imagine—like Ant tasks if you are so inclined to draw the comparison—but with the benefits of the well-defined lifecycle and network portability of Maven.

Creating a Plug-In

In order to create a simple plug-in through the archetype, type the following in your command line:

```
$ mvn archetype:create
    -DgroupId=my.plugin
    -DartifactId=maven-my-plugin
    -DarchetypeGroupId=org.apache.maven.archetypes
    -DarchetypeArtifactId=maven-archetype-mojo
```

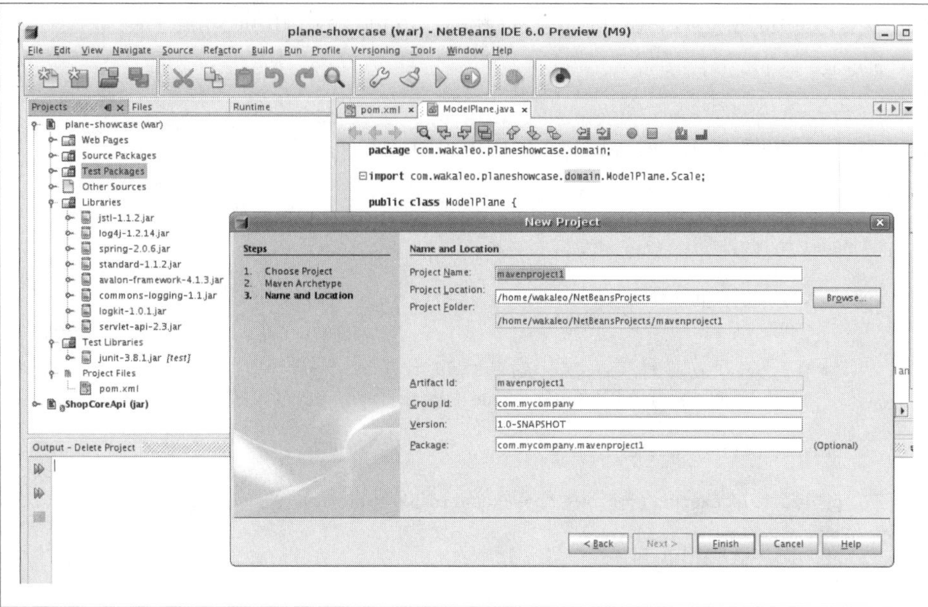

Figure 2-15. Maven 2 support in NetBeans

In Maven, the implementation of a goal is done in a Mojo—a play on words meaning Maven POJO (Plain Old Java Object) and, well, mojo. All Java Maven Mojos implement the `org.apache.maven.plug-ins.Mojo` interface. Without getting too detailed, it is good to understand that Maven is built on the inversion of control (IoC) container/dependency injection (DI) framework called Plexus. If you are familiar with Spring, you are close to understanding Plexus. Plexus is built around the concept that components each play a *role*, and each role has an implementation. The role name tends to be the fully qualified name of the interface. Like Spring, Plexus components (think Spring beans) are defined in an XML file. In Plexus, that XML file is named `components.xml` and lives in `META-INF/plexus`. The consumers of a component need not know the role's implementation, as that is managed by the Plexus DI framework. When you create your own Mojo implementation, you effectively are creating your own component that implements the `org.apache.maven.plug-ins.Mojo` role.

You may be thinking, what does this have to do with Maven goals? When you create a Mojo class, you annotate the class with certain values; those values are then used to generate a variant of the Plexus `components.xml` file named `plugin.xml` living under `META-INF/maven`. So, what translates those annotations to a `plugin.xml` file? Maven goals, of course! Your Maven plug-in packaging project's build lifecycle binds goals that generate the descriptor for you. In short, nonjargon speak: Maven does that work for you.

In the plug-in that you generated above, navigate to the **maven-my-plugin/src/main/java/my/plugin/MyMojo.java** file and set the contents to the following:

```
package my.plugin;

import org.apache.maven.plugin.AbstractMojo;
import org.apache.maven.plugin.MojoExecutionException;

/**
 * A simple Mojo.
 * @goal my-goal
 */
public class MyMojo extends AbstractMojo
{
    /**
     * This populates the message to print.
     * @parameter required default-value="No message set"
     */
    private String  message;

    public void execute()throws MojoExecutionException
    {
        getLog().info( message );
    }
}
```

Now install the plug-in via the normal Maven method. Type:

```
$ mvn install
```

The execute method is solely responsible for executing the goal. Any other methods that you encounter in a Mojo are just helper methods. Maven injects values into the Mojo object directly into the project's fields. In the example above, the **message** field is a valid Maven property and is printed out the logger returned by the **getLog()** method. Remember that Plexus is a *dependency injection* framework. Because we annotated the message field as a parameter, that parameter can now be populated by Maven (via Plexus). You can populate your goal in the same way as you do any goal, through the configuration element in the POM:

```
<project>
  ...
  <build>
    ...
    <plugins>
      <plugin>
        <groupId>my.plugin</groupId>
        <artifactId>maven-my-plugin</artifactId>
        <configuration>
          <message>Hello World!</message>
        </configuration>
      </plugin>
      ...
    </plugins>
    ...
```

```
  </build>
  ...
</project>
```

This sets the configuration for all goals under `maven-my-plugin`. Remember, a plug-in can contain multiple goals, one per Mojo in the project. If you wish to configure a specific goal: you can create an execution. An execution is a configured set of goals to be executed:

```
<project>
  ...
  <build>
    ...
    <plugins>
      <plugin>
        <groupId>my.plugin</groupId>
        <artifactId>maven-my-plugin</artifactId>
        <executions>
          <execution>
            <goals>
              <goal>my-goal</goal>
            </goals>
            <configuration>
              <message>Hello World!</message>
            </configuration>
          </execution>
        </executions>
      </plugin>
      ...
    </plugins>
    ...
  </build>
  ...
</project>
```

In either case, you execute the goal in the same way:

```
$ mvn my.plugin:maven-my-plugin:my-goal
Hello World!
```

You may wonder why we have to do so much typing when the create goal that we ran was only `archetype:create`? That's because the archetype goal has the groupId `org.apache.maven.plugins`, which is prepended as a possible prefix by default when none is provided. You can add more plug-in groups to your system by adding this to your `.m2/settings.xml` file:

```
<settings>
  ...
  <pluginGroups>
    <pluginGroup>my.plugin</pluginGroup>
  </pluginGroups>
</settings>
```

Furthermore, if your plug-in name is surrounded by `maven-*-plugin`, Maven will allow you to simply type the name represented by * in the middle. Because we have already done this, you can now just run the much simpler goal:

```
$ mvn my:my-goal
```

The final way to configure a goal is via a property. You can set an expression to populate the property rather than a direct value:

```
/**
 ...
 * @parameter expression="${my.message}"
 */
```

This gives you the flexibility to set the property within the POM, in the `settings.xml`, or even on the command line...anywhere that you can set a property in Maven.

```
$ mvn my:my-goal -Dmy.message=Hello
Hello
```

Manipulating the Build Lifecycle

Creating goals is great; however, that alone is hardly much better than just creating Ant tasks. To benefit from Maven's well-defined build lifecycle, it often makes sense to put your goal into the lifecycle somehow. In rare cases, your plug-in may need to create its own lifecycle definition.

There are two major ways in which to bind a goal to a lifecycle. The first is to just add the goal to an execution phase, defined in your running project's POM:

```
<project>
  ...
  <build>
    ...
    <plugins>
      <plugin>
        <groupId>my.plugin</groupId>
        <artifactId>maven-my-plugin</artifactId>
        <executions>
          <execution>
            <phase>validate</phase>
            <goals>
              <goal>my-goal</goal>
            </goals>
            <configuration>
              <message>I am validating</message>
            <configuration>
          </execution>
        </executions>
      </plugin>
      ...
    </plugins>
    ...
  </build>
```

```
  ...
</project>
```

Running `mvn validate` will print the configured message. Oftentimes, a goal will be created with a specific phase in mind. When creating your Mojo, you can define a phase that the goal will run in. Add the following annotation to the `my-goal` goal and install the plug-in via `mvn install`:

```
/**
 ...
 * @phase validate
 */
```

Now you need add only the plug-in to your POM configuration, and the `my:my-goal` goal will be bound to the validate phase for you:

```
<project>
  ...
  <build>
    ...
    <plugins>
      <plugin>
        <groupId>my.plugin</groupId>
        <artifactId>maven-my-plugin</artifactId>
      </plugin>
    </plugins>
    ...
  </build>
  ...
</project>
```

Another way to manipulate the build lifecycle is to create your own forked lifecycle. You can tell the Mojo to execute the forked lifecycle up to a given phase. If you do not set the lifecycle, then the default is used. However, if you do, you must provide a definition of that new lifecycle:

```
/**
 ...
 * @execute phase="validate" lifecycle="mycycle"
 */
```

You define the `mycycle` build lifecycle in a `META-INF/maven/lifecycle.xml` file. The following lifecycle executes the `my-goal` goal (only once, not recursively) in the `validate` phase:

```
<lifecycles>
  <lifecycle>
    <id>mycycle</id>
    <phases>
      <phase>
        <id>validate</id>
        <executions>
          <execution>
            <goals>
              <goal>my-goal</goal>
```

```
            </goals>
            <configuration>
              <message>I am forked</message>
            </configuration>
          </execution>
        </executions>
      </phase>
    </phases>
  </lifecycle>
</lifecycles>
```

When combined with the above POM configuration, it will execute two validate phases:

```
I am forked
No message set
```

Hooking into Maven

The simplest way to hook into the Maven runtime is to create parameters populated by Maven parameters. Some commonly used parameters are discussed in this section.

The current project (the POM data)
: This parameter lets you access data contained in the Maven POM file for your current project:

```
/**
 * @parameter expression="${project}"
 */
private org.apache.maven.project.MavenProject project;
```

The current project's version
: You can obtain the current version of the project (always handy for testing purposes!) as follows:

```
/**
 * @parameter expression="${project.version}"
 */
private String version;
```

A similar method may be used for getting simple properties from the POM, such as `project.groupId`, `project.artifactId` or `project.url`.

The project's build directory
: It is often useful for a plug-in to know where the project should be placing any generated files. You can obtain this directory as follows:

```
/**
 * @parameter expression="${project.build.directory}"
 */
private java.io.File outputDirectory;
```

The local repository
: You can find the local repository directory as follows:

```
/**
 * @parameter expression="${localRepository}"
 */
private org.apache.maven.artifact.repository.ArtifactRepository
localRepository;
```

More complex values can be acquired with the following parameter names of the following types, as shown in Table 2-1.

Table 2-1. Maven plug-in variables

Variable name	Class
project.build	org.apache.maven.model.Build
project.ciManagement	org.apache.maven.model.CiManagement
project.dependency	org.apache.maven.model.Dependency
project.dependencyManagement	org.apache.maven.model.DependencyManagement
project.distributionManagement	org.apache.maven.model.DistributionManagement
project.issueManagement	org.apache.maven.model.IssueManagement
project.license	org.apache.maven.model.License
project.mailingList	org.apache.maven.model.MailingList
project.organization	org.apache.maven.model.Organization
project.reporting	org.apache.maven.model.Reporting
project.scm	org.apache.maven.model.Scm

Using Plexus Components

As mentioned above, Maven is built on Plexus, which is an IoC container that manages components. There are components in Plexus that you may wish to use in your Mojos. For example, the following code would allow you to use the Plexus JarArchiver component in your plug-in:

```
/**
 * @parameter expression="${component.org.codehaus.plexus.archiver.Archiver#jar}"
 * @required
 */
private org.codehaus.plexus.archiver.jar.JarArchiver jarArchiver;
```

Just like other Maven expressions, these values can be injected from components when the parameter is prefixed with "component," followed by the Plexus role name. If the role can play varying roles, you can pinpoint that role via the role-hint, specified by "#jar," or "#zip," or whatever that role-hint may be.

Many plexus components exist in the Maven repository, and can be used in a similar way. For example, the following code illustrates the Plexus i18n component:

```
/**
 * @parameter expression="${component.org.codehaus.plexus.i18n.I18N}"
 * @required
```

```
     * @readonly
     */
    private org.codehaus.plexus.i18n.I18N i18n;
```

There is a full, up-to-date list of Plexus components in the Central Repository at *http://repo1.maven.org/maven2/org/codehaus/plexus/*.

Your goals can and probably will be more complicated than the examples shown, but you have been given the basic tools to start writing your own plug-ins, utilizing full control of Maven.

2.19 Setting Up an Enterprise Repository with Archiva

Contributed by: Eric Redmond

A large part of Maven's power comes from its use of remote repositories. When a project dependency is required or a plug-in is used, Maven's first task is to reach out to a set of remote repositories, defined in the POM file and/or in the `settings.xml`, and download required artifacts to its local repository. This local repository then acts as a local cache. Maven's Central Repository is a community-driven, open-source set of projects available for download and is accessible by any Maven installation with network access to it. You can browse the repository at *http://repo1.maven.org/maven2*. Sometimes your organization will wish to publish its own remote repository, either publicly to the rest of the Internet, or privately in-house. There are two major methods for setting up a repository: either through a dedicated repository manager—such as Archiva or Artifactory—or through a standard server such as Apache HTTP or an FTP server. The latter method is on the wane, so in the next couple of chapters, we will focus on Maven's recommended repository management tool, Archiva, and one promising contender, Artifactory. First, let's look at Archiva.

Installing Archiva

Download Archiva from *http://maven.apache.org/archiva*, and unpack the ZIP file to the desired installation location. This location need not have plenty of disk space, because you can set the local repositories to reside on different disks.

If you just wish to run the server, select the corresponding operating system directory and run the `run.bat` or `run.sh` script. If you are running Windows, you can install Plexus as a service via the `bin/windows-x86-32/InstallService.bat` script and find a new service installed in your Control Panel's Services list. For other operating systems, you can use the `run.sh` script as part of your server startup routine. Alternatively, with a little more effort, you can deploy Archiva onto another web application server such as Tomcat (see *http://maven.apache.org/archiva/guides/getting-started.html*).

Once you have the server installed and running, navigate your web browser of choice to *http://localhost:8080/archiva*. If this is the first time that you are running Archiva, you will be confronted with a screen requesting you to create an admin user (see Fig-

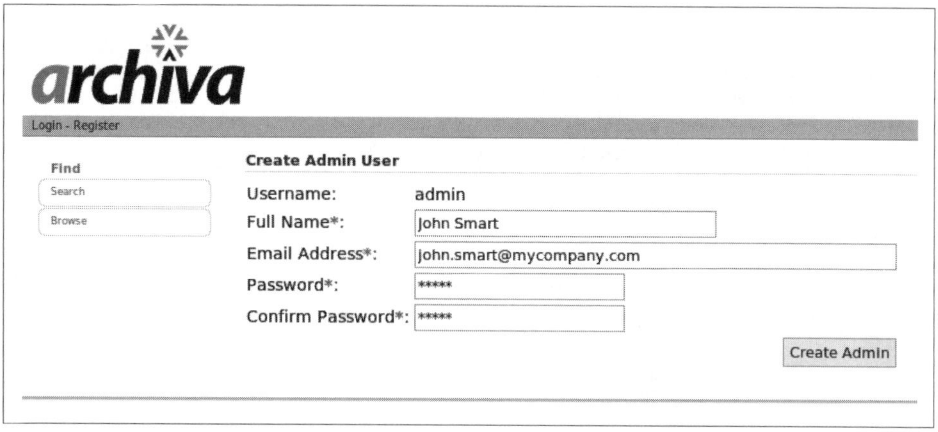

Figure 2-16. Adding an Archiva user

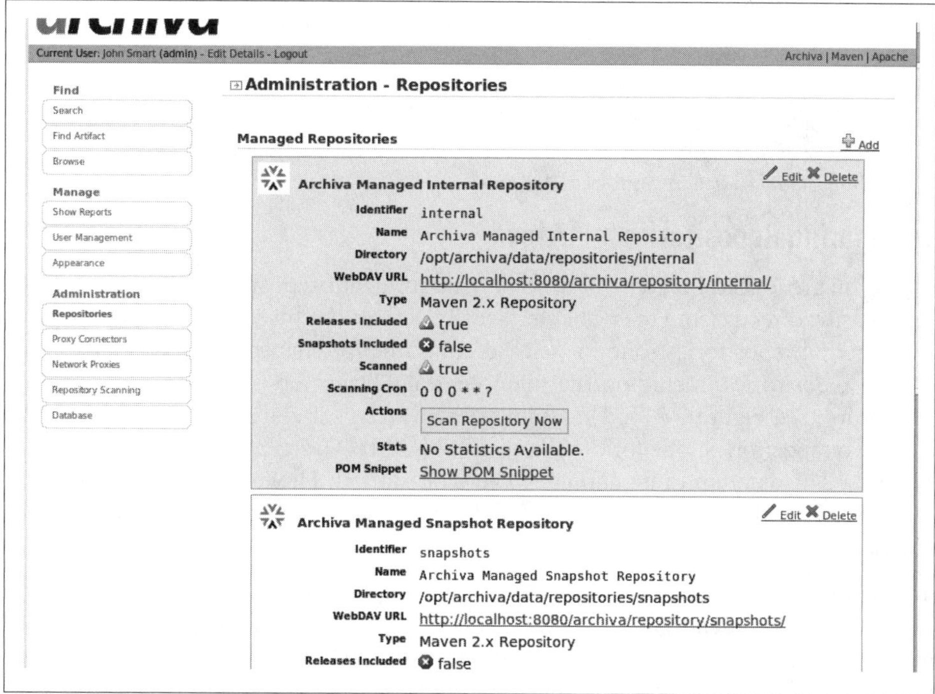

Figure 2-17. Archiva comes with a number of preinstalled repositories

ure 2-16). After submission, you can log in as an administrator using the account you just created.

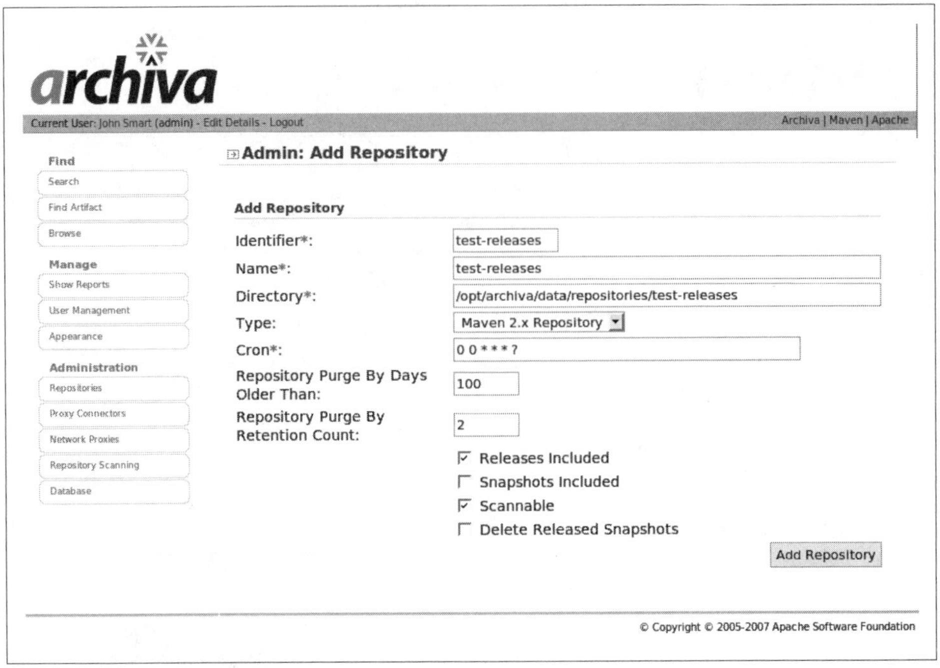

Figure 2-18. Adding a new repository in Archiva

Configuring Repositories in Archiva

Once you are logged in, you will need to configure your repositories. You can do this fairly easily, directly from the web interface. By default, Archiva comes configured with two internal repositories (one for releases, and one for snapshots), and some public Maven repositories, including the main central Maven repository and the Java.net repository (see Figure 2-17). This follows the Maven standard, which is to create at least two repositories, one for development SNAPSHOT artifacts, and one for release artifacts. This is often quite enough to get you started. However, if you need to use libraries from other sources (such as Codehaus), you will have to add new repositories yourself.

You can create as many repositories as you wish, for example, testing and staging releases. We recommend giving the URL extensions and identifiers the same value, to avoid confusion. Note that you are not limited to Maven 2 repositories; you also can manage Maven 1-style repositories (see Figure 2-18).

The Directory field refers to the OS-specific absolute path where this repository will place its artifacts. If you are installing on a Windows-based machine, note that because Windows has an upper limit on directory filenames, it is best to make the directory path fairly short. The "Snapshots Included" option does what you would expect; the repository will make snapshots available to end users.

In the "Repositories" entry in the LHS menu, you will be treated to the basic information about the repositories. A nice little feature is that if you select "Show POM Snippet," a div will expand, revealing the correct values for connecting to the specific repository, as well as information for deploying built artifacts to this repository via WebDAV, which Archiva manages for you (see Figure 2-19).

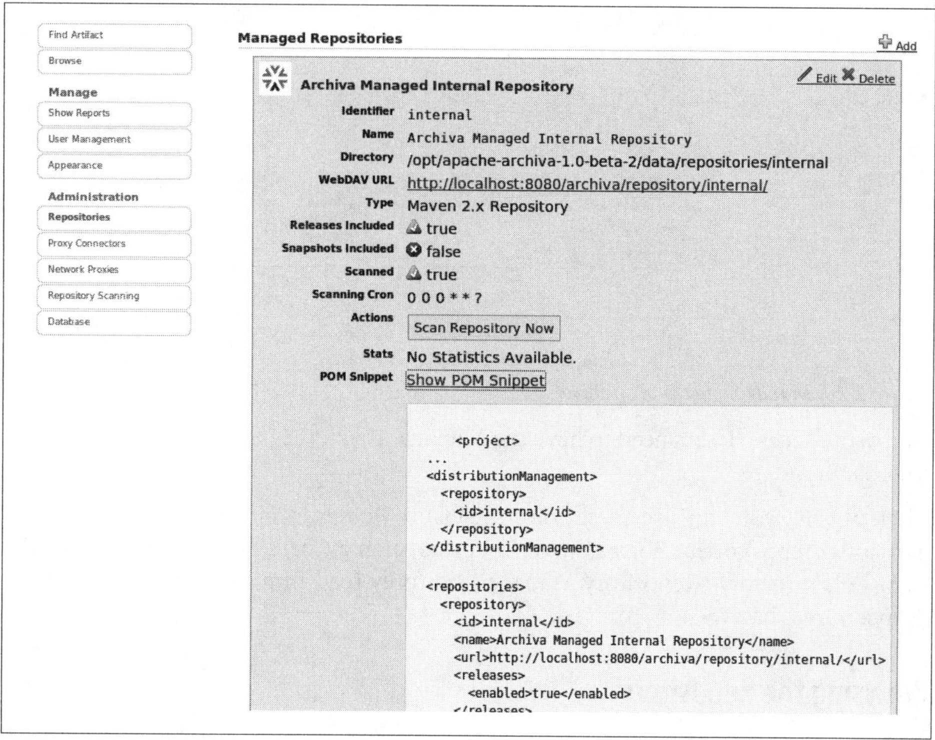

Figure 2-19. Displaying repository information

User Management

You also will need to set up your repository users. Archiva provides good support for user management, and you can set up access to your cached and proxied repositories to be as open or as restrictive as required. User accounts are managed from the User Management screen, shown in Figure 2-20, where you can display or search your user database in a variety of ways.

Archiva allows you to define fine-grained access rights for individual users, or simply allow all users to access the repository contents freely. If you want your repositories to be freely accessible to all users, you need to edit the "guest" user and provide them with at least the Global Repository Observer role (see Figure 2-21). The Observer role provides read-only access to a repository content, whereas the Manager role provides full

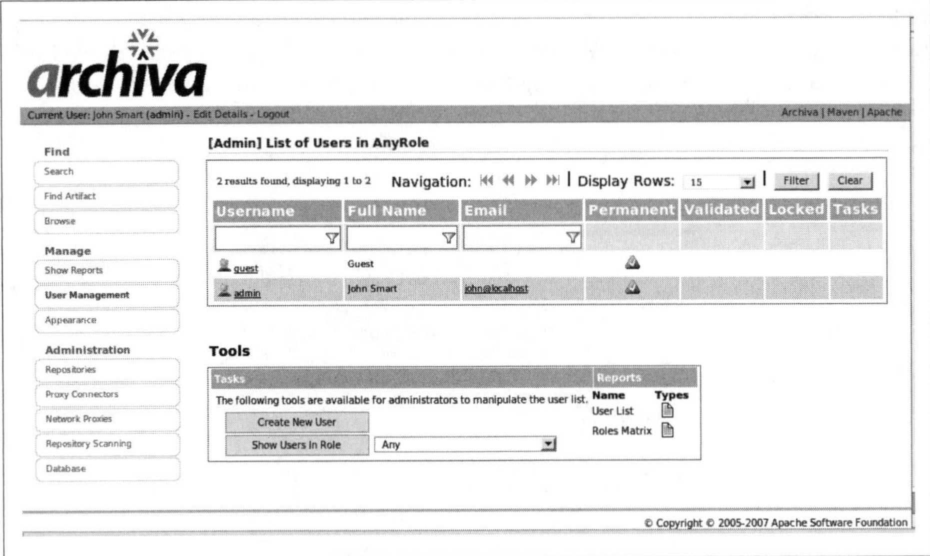

Figure 2-20. Managing users in Archiva

read-write access. Users need to have the Manager role if they are to deploy libraries to a repository.

Alternatively, you can use these roles to set up Observer and/or Manager roles for individual repositories. For example, a developer may be allowed to deploy to the snapshots directory (Repository Manager) but only read from the internal repository (Repository Observer).

Browsing the Repository

Archiva lets you search or browse the repository using the Search and Browse screens, respectively. This gives you a convenient way to check the contents of your repository, both on a high level to know what libraries are currently stored in the repository and also at a detailed level to find out specific information about a particular library (see Figure 2-22).

Running Archiva on Another Port

By default, Archiva runs on the 8080 port. To change this port, you need to modify the value of the *<port>* element in the `apps/archiva/conf/application.xml` file, as shown here:

```
<application>
  <services>
    <service>
      ...
      <configuration>
```

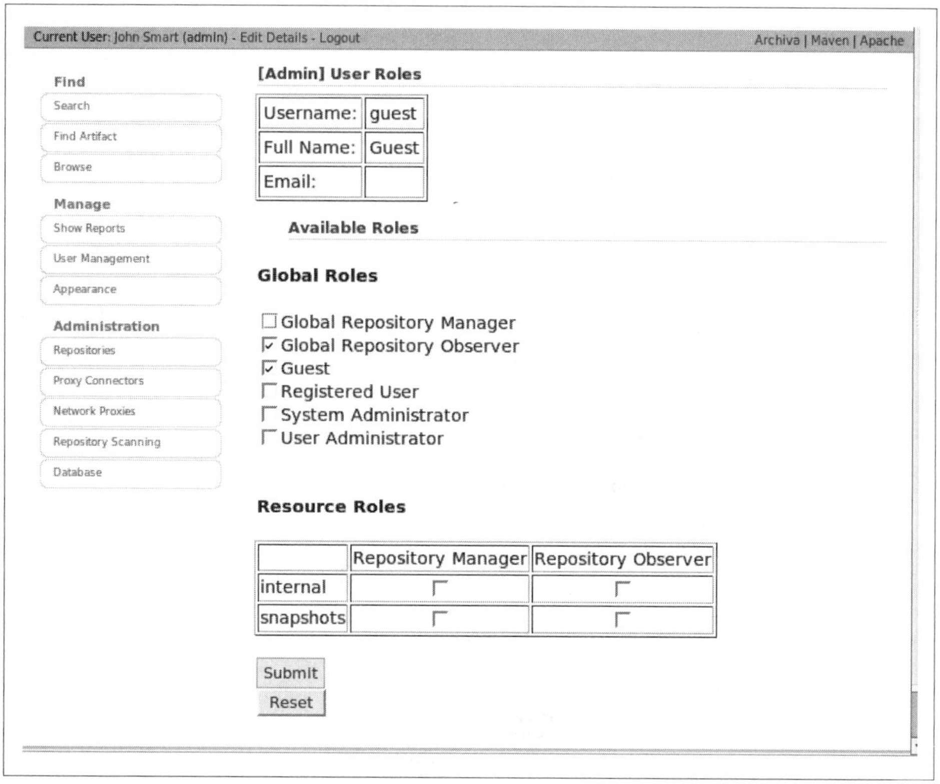

Figure 2-21. Managing user roles in Archiva

```
<webapps>
  <webapp>
    ...
    <listeners>
      <http-listener>
        <port>9090</port>
      </http-listener>
    ...
```

Archiva Proxy Connectors

In addition to caching repository JARs, you can configure Archiva to act as a proxy to Internet repositories. In an organizational context, this gives you better control over which external repositories can be accessed by project teams. In Archiva, you can manage repository proxies in the Proxy Connectors screen (see Figure 2-23). In the out-of-the-box configuration, the default internal repository acts as a proxy for the Ibiblio and Java.net repositories. In other words, whenever a user requests a publicly available library from the internal repository for the first time, Archiva will transparently download and cache the file from the Ibiblio or Java.net repositories. Note that

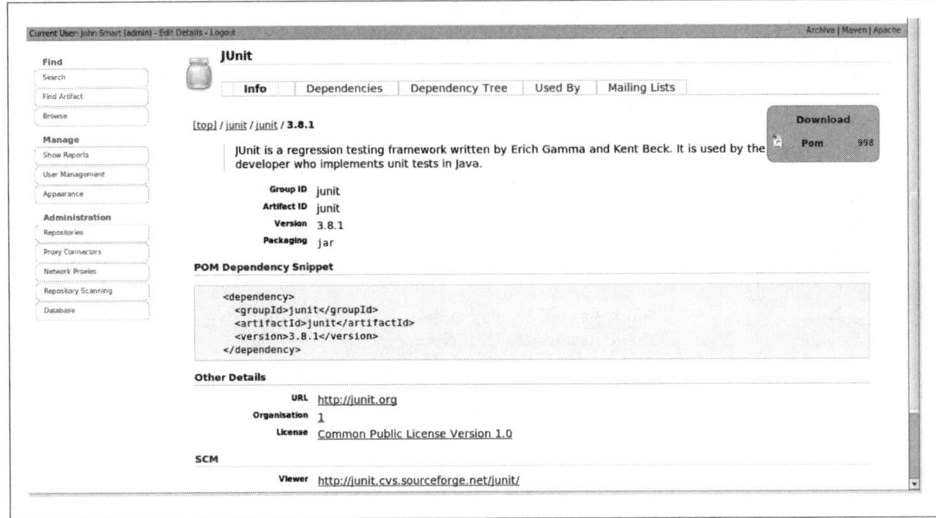

Figure 2-22. Viewing information about a particular library

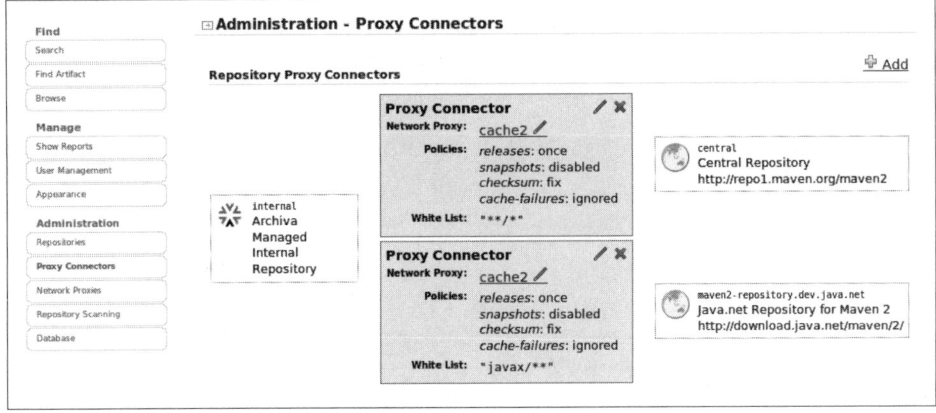

Figure 2-23. Managing repository proxies

you can modify the configuration of each connector, including details such as how often releases should be downloaded, whether snapshots should be allowed, and what to do if the checksum calculation is incorrect.

At the time of this writing, in certain environments the *cache-failures* policy option causes problems if it is set to anything except "ignore." Because this is not the default value, you sometimes have to configure it by hand.

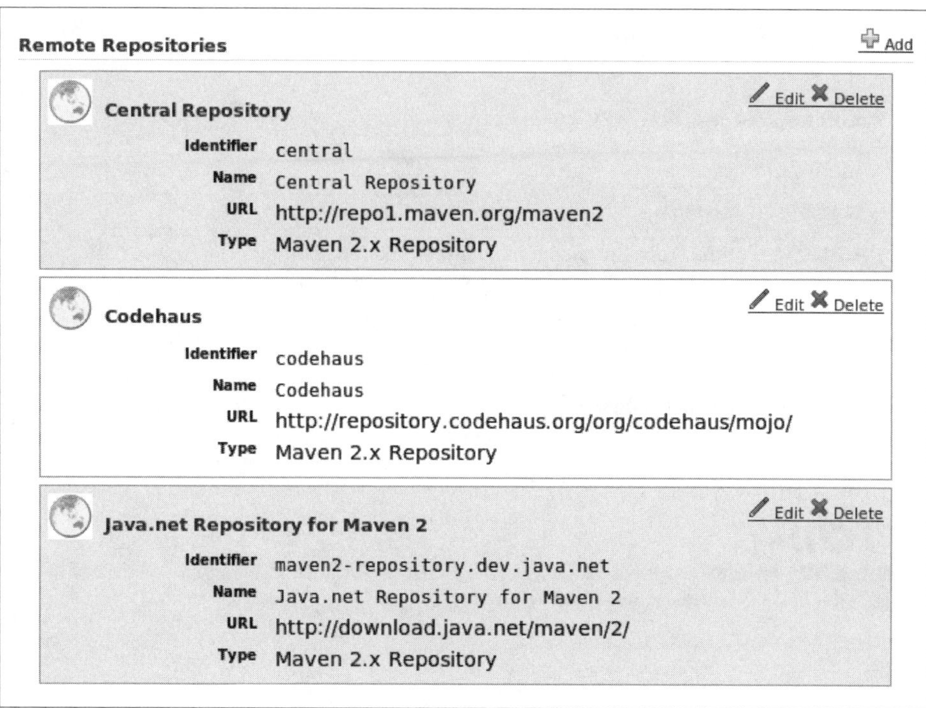

Figure 2-24. A list of proxied repositories: the more the merrier

Setting Up Remote Repositories

Once you have configured your local repositories, you can proxy any number of remote repositories, such as the Codehaus repository. By default, Archive comes configured with the standard Maven repository, but you can add as many as you like (see Figure 2-24).

The benefit of this practice is threefold. One, it allows your build manager to control network access to remote repositories locally. Two, it allows a convenient single-access point repository across an organization (you can add any number of proxied repositories, but your user's POMs need only point to the single managed repository). Three, if the proxied repositories are indexed, your builds are not bound to the remote repositories' network access in order to succeed. I am certain that there are more.

For example, you also may want to add some other remote repositories, such as the Codehaus repository. This is a simple task: just provide an appropriate name and the repository URL (see Figure 2-25).

If you are using Archiva as a proxy repository, after you have added a new remote repository you will need to add a new proxy connector to provide users with access to this repository (see Figure 2-26). In this example, we configure the proxy connector to

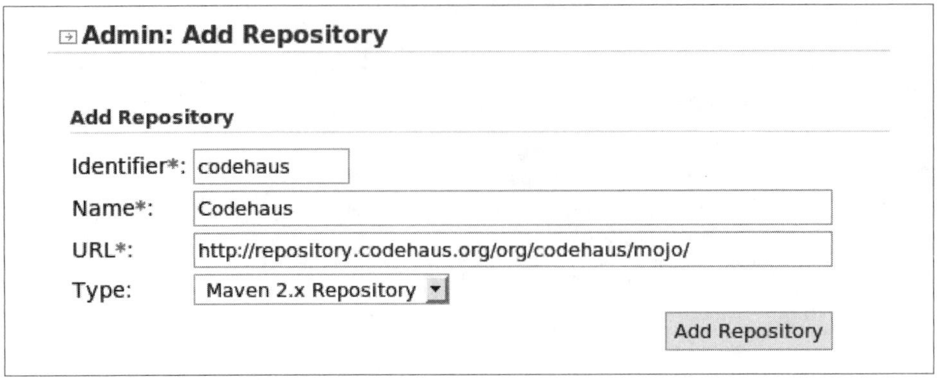

Figure 2-25. Adding a new remote repository

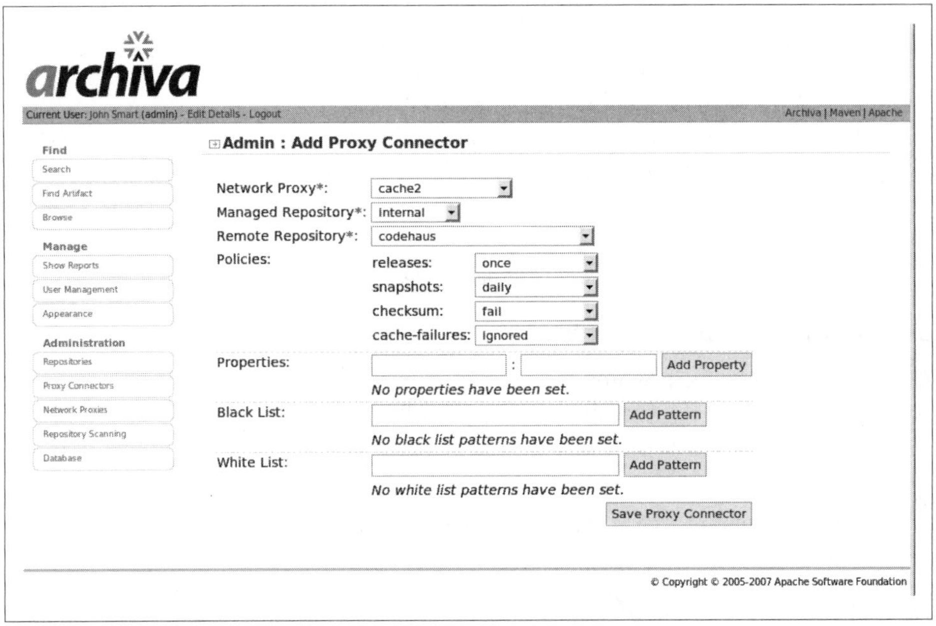

Figure 2-26. Adding a new proxy connector

allow users to download both releases and snapshots from the Codehaus repository via the standard internal Archiva repository.

Configuring Archiva Behind a Proxy

In an enterprise environment, you will often need to install Archiva behind a proxy. Proxies are easy to configure in Archiva. First, go to the Network Proxies screen and add a new Network Proxy. Here, you can define a proxy that Archiva will use to access repositories on the Internet (see Figure 2-27).

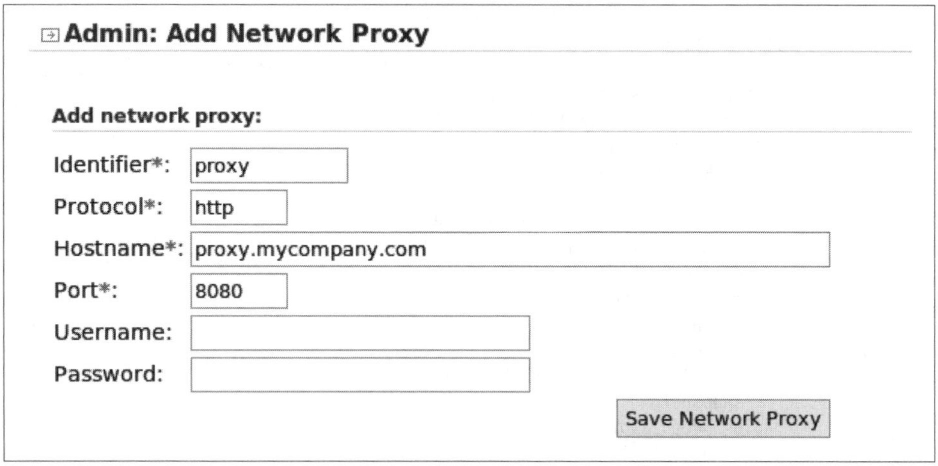

Figure 2-27. Managing repository proxies

Once you have set up a network proxy, you need to configure your proxy connectors to use this proxy. You can do this in the Proxy Connectors screen (see Figure 2-23). Here, you simply edit the proxy connector of your choice and select the proxy you just created in the Network Proxy field.

Using Maven with Archiva

Using an Archiva repository from within Maven can be done in several ways. Because a repository will usually be shared across several projects, the most common approach is to define this in the user's `settings.xml` file. The following *settings.xml* file defines a default profile that will access an Archiva repository running on a server called *taronga*:

```
<settings>
  <profiles>
    <profile>
      <id>Repository Proxy</id>
      <activation>
        <activeByDefault>true</activeByDefault>
      </activation>
      <!-- ******************************************************* -->
      <!-- repositories for jar artifacts -->
      <!-- ******************************************************* -->
      <repositories>
        <repository>
          <id>internal</id>
          <name>Archiva Managed Internal Repository</name>
          <url>http://taronga:8080/archiva/repository/internal/</url>
          <releases>
            <enabled>true</enabled>
          </releases>
          <snapshots>
            <enabled>false</enabled>
```

```
      </snapshots>
    </repository>
  </repositories>
  <!-- ******************************************************* -->
  <!-- repositories for maven plug-ins -->
  <!-- ******************************************************* -->
  <pluginRepositories>
    <pluginRepository>
      <id>internal</id>
      <name>Archiva Managed Internal Repository</name>
      <url>http://taronga:8080/archiva/repository/internal/</url>
      <releases>
        <enabled>true</enabled>
      </releases>
      <snapshots>
        <enabled>false</enabled>
      </snapshots>
    </pluginRepository>
  </pluginRepositories>
</profile>
</profiles>
</settings>
```

If you are using the Archiva server as the unique entry point to all internal and external Maven repositories, you don't need to explicitly declare the Archiva repositories. A simpler solution is to add a *<mirror>* element at the end of your `settings.xml` file. This will force Maven to go through the Archiva server for any artifact, no matter what repository it is stored in:

```
<settings>
  ...
  <mirrors>
    <mirror>
      <id>artifactory</id>
      <mirrorOf>*</mirrorOf>
      <url>http://taronga:8080/archiva/repository/internal</url>
      <name>Artifactory</name>
    </mirror>
  </mirrors>
</settings>
```

If you want to deploy your generated artifacts to this repository, you need to set up the *<distributionManagement>* section in your `pom.xml` file. For the server we described above, the corresponding *<distributionManagement>* section would look something like this:

```
<distributionManagement>
  <repository>
    <id>internal</id>
    <name>Internal Repository</name>
    <url>http://taronga:8080/archiva/repository/internal</url>
  </repository>
  <snapshotRepository>
    <id>snapshots</id>
```

```
      <name>Snapshots Repository</name>
      <url>http://taronga:8080/archiva/repository/snapshots</url>
    </snapshotRepository>
  </distributionManagement>
```

You can either allow all users to update the repository by giving the guest user full repository manager rights, or you can set up individual user accounts with repository manager rights for the users who will be updating the repository. If you do this, you will need to add a *<servers>* section to your `settings.xml` file containing your username and password for each server, as shown here:

```
<servers>
  <server>
    <id>internal</id>
    <username>john</username>
    <password>secret</password>
  </server>
  <server>
    <id>snapshots</id>
    <username>john</username>
    <password>secret</password>
  </server>
</servers>
```

Finally, because Archiva uses WebDAV to deploy artifacts, you need to add the Wagon WebDAV extension to your *pom.xml* file:

```
<build>
  ...
  <extensions>
    <extension>
      <groupId>org.apache.maven.wagon</groupId>
      <artifactId>wagon-webdav</artifactId>
      <version>1.0-beta-2</version>
    </extension>
  </extensions>
</build>
```

Now you can deploy to this repository simply by using the *mvn deploy* command:

```
$ mvn deploy
...
[INFO] Uploading repository metadata for: 'artifact com.acme.shop:ShopCoreApi'
[INFO] Retrieving previous metadata from snapshots
[INFO] Uploading project information for ShopCoreApi 1.0-20071008.122038-3
[INFO] ------------------------------------------------------------------------
[INFO] BUILD SUCCESSFUL
[INFO] ------------------------------------------------------------------------
[INFO] Total time: 3 seconds
[INFO] Finished at: Tue Oct 09 00:20:39 GMT+12:00 2007
[INFO] Final Memory: 9M/81M
[INFO] ------------------------------------------------------------------------
```

Manually Deploying a File to an Archiva Repository

Sometimes you need to manually deploy a file to your enterprise repository. For example, many Java applications and libraries require the Sun JTA library. The Spring framework is a common example of an open source library that requires this dependency to run. Unfortunately, for licensing reasons the JTA library cannot be published on the public Maven repositories such as Ibiblio. You need to download it from the Sun web site (*http://java.sun.com/products/jta/*) and deploy it manually to your enterprise repository.

You can do this in Archiva, although the process is somewhat cumbersome. First, download the JTA library from the Sun web site and place it in a temporary directory. Then, create a *pom.xml* file in this directory, as follows:

```
<project>
   <modelVersion>4.0.0</modelVersion>
   <groupId>com.mycompany</groupId>
   <artifactId>webdav-deploy</artifactId>
   <packaging>pom</packaging>
   <version>1</version>
   <name>Webdav Deployment POM</name>

   <build>
      <extensions>
         <extension>
            <groupId>org.apache.maven.wagon</groupId>
            <artifactId>wagon-webdav</artifactId>
            <version>1.0-beta-2</version>
         </extension>
      </extensions>
   </build>

</project>
```

We only need this *pom.xml* file to leverage the Maven WebDAV libraries; it won't be deployed to the enterprise repository. Now deploy the file using the *mvn deploy:deploy-file* command. You need to specify the file, the groupId, artifactId, and version number, and also the target repository URL. This is shown here:

```
$ mvn deploy:deploy-file \
    -Dfile=./jta-1_1-classes.zip \
    -DgroupId=javax.transaction \
    -DartifactId=jta  \
    -Dversion=1.1 \
    -Dpackaging=jar \
    -DrepositoryId=deployment.webdav \
    -Durl=dav:http://taronga:8080/archiva/repository/internal

[INFO] Scanning for projects...
...
[INFO] [deploy:deploy-file]
Uploading: http://taronga:8080/archiva/repository/internal/javax/transaction/jta/1.1*
/jta-1.1.jar
```

```
...
[INFO] Uploading project information for jta 1.1
...
[INFO] Uploading repository metadata for: 'artifact javax.transaction:jta'
[INFO] ------------------------------------------------------------------------
[INFO] BUILD SUCCESSFUL
[INFO] ------------------------------------------------------------------------
[INFO] Total time: 19 seconds
[INFO] Finished at: Wed Oct 10 16:20:01 NZDT 2007
[INFO] Final Memory: 3M/5M
[INFO] ------------------------------------------------------------------------
```

Now your users will be able to refer to this dependency in the usual way.

2.20 Setting Up an Enterprise Repository Using Artifactory

Contributed by: Avneet Mangat[*]

The second enterprise repository tool that we will look at is Artifactory. The main purpose of Artifactory is twofold:

- First, it acts as a proxy/cache for any dependencies that you download from repositories on the Internet. This is much faster and more reliable than having each developer download JARs directly from the Internet, and allows some control over which Internet repositories are used by projects in your organization.
- Second, it can be used to store your own enterprise dependencies, or third-party libraries that cannot be published on public repositories (such as JDBC drivers). This makes it much easier for developers to set up new projects, as they don't need to download and install any JARs manually.

Artifactory is a powerful, well-polished open source tool that provides a number of cool features, including:

- A nice AJAX-based web interface, where you can search and browse the repository
- The ability to perform bulk imports and exports of your repository
- Automatic backups of your repository

Let's take a closer look.

Setting Up the Maven Repository Using Artifactory

To install Artifactory, just download the latest version from the Artifactory web site[†] and extract it to a convenient place. In the following examples, we have installed Artifactory to the `/usr/local/artifactory` directory.

[*] This article is based on material originally published on TheServerSide in June 2007 (*http://www.theserverside.com/tt/articles/article.tss?l=SettingUpMavenRepository*).

[†] *http://www.jfrog.org/sites/artifactory/latest/*

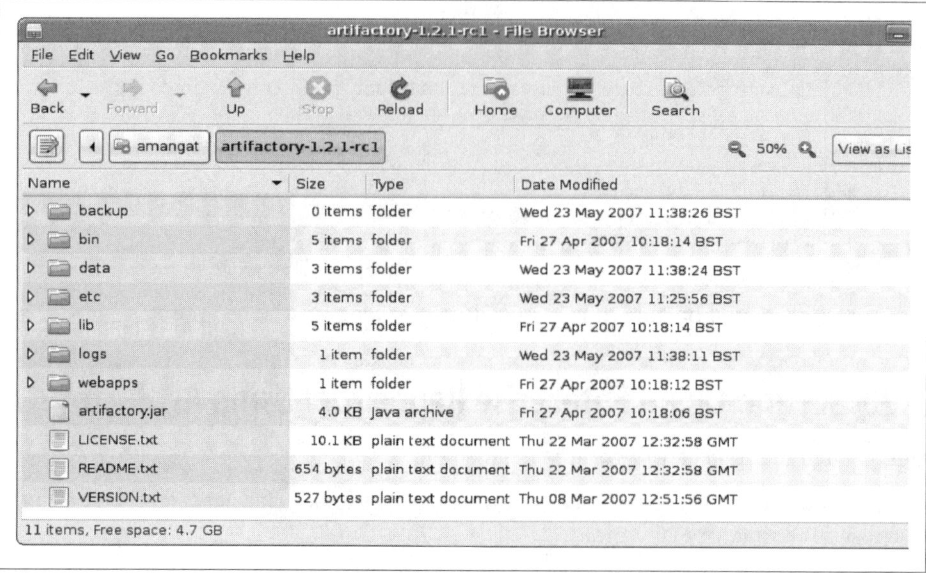

Figure 2-28. The Artifactory directory structure

Artifactory can be used out of box with little or no configuration. Artifactory comes bundled with a Jetty web server, with default settings that are sufficient for most users. To start Artifactory as a web application inside Jetty, run the batch file or Unix shell script. On Unix, you can use the `artifactoryctl` script to start and stop the server:

```
$ /usr/local/artifactory/bin/artifactoryctl start
```

On Windows, use the `artifactory.bat` script.

You may want to change the default configuration or run Artifactory on under a different server. For example, an organization might have an Apache/Tomcat that it has configured and optimized and that it is comfortable with. In such circumstances, it might be easier and quicker to deploy the artifactory web application directly on the Tomcat server. Another example is if you need to have greater control over subrepositories created in the repository. The rest of this section deals with setting up an Artifactory web application inside a Tomcat server and setting up subrepositories inside the repository.

The Artifactory directory structure

First, download and extract the latest Artifactory distribution. The directory structure is shown in Figure 2-28.

The folders are:

backup
: Repository backups are stored here. Backups are run at regular intervals, based on a cron expression that you set in the Artifactory configuration file.

bin
: Batch files used to run the embedded jetty web server.

data
: This directory contains the Derby database files. Artifactory uses an embedded Derby database to store artifacts. Everything in this folder can be deleted if you wish to start with a clean repository. In a new installation of artifactory, this folder is empty.

etc
: This directory contains the Artifactory configuration files, including "artifactory.config.xml" (the main configuration file), as well as "jetty.xml" and "log4j.properties."

lib
: Dependent JAR files.

logs
: Artifactory logfiles go here.

webapps
: This directory contains the entire Artifactory application bundled into a WAR file. This WAR file can be directly deployed to another Java web application server.

Deploy in Tomcat 6

To deploy Artifactory on to an existing Tomcat server, you need to copy the WAR file mentioned above into the Tomcat webapps directory. The Artifactory web application needs some external parameters to work correctly:

- The location of the database used to store the artifacts
- The location of the artifactory config xml file
- The location of backup folder

In fact, we only have to specify the location of the artifactory installation folder during Tomcat startup and artifactory will be able to work out the rest. An alternative to this approach is to set up a connection to the derby database using jdbc and configure artifactory in the web application (by including the `artifactory.config.xml` in the web application). However, this approach is simpler. The location of the artifactory installation folder can be specified as a environment variable. For Linux, for example, you can configure the location of the artifactory installation folder in your environment scripts as shown below:

```
$ export JAVA_OPTS = -Dartifactory.home=/usr/local/artifactory-1.2.1
```

For Windows, it can be added to Tomcat startup options as shown in Figure 2-29.

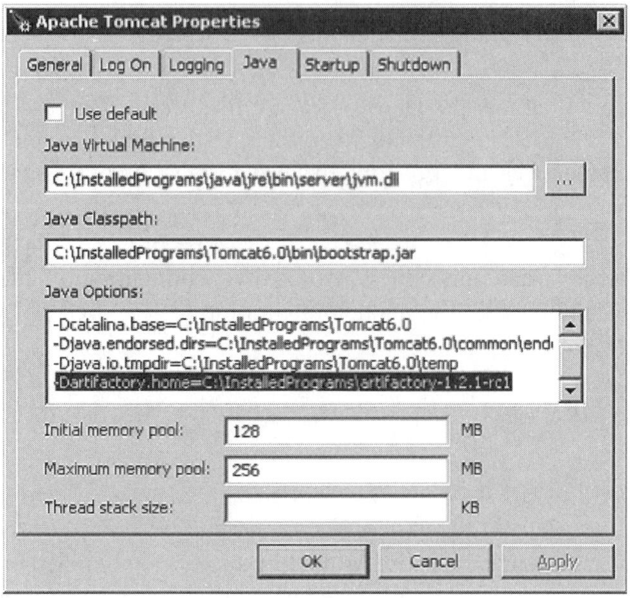

Figure 2-29. Running Artifactory in Tomcat

Set up the Maven repositories

There are many ways to organize your repositories. One suggested approach is to create three repositories (or subrepositories) in the maven repository. They are:

Private-internal repository
: This repository contains artifacts that are used only within the organization. These are manually uploaded by the development team. Because these artifacts are private to the organization, this repository does not need to synchronize with any remote repository such as ibiblio.

Third-party repository
: This repository contains artifacts that are publicly available, but not in the ibiblio repository. This could be the latest versions of libraries that are not yet available on ibiblio or proprietary jdbc drivers. This repository is not synchronized with ibiblio as ibiblio does not have these jars.

Ibiblio-cache
: This repository is synchronized with ibiblio repository and acts as a cache of the artifacts from ibiblio.

They are configured in the <ARTIFACTORY_INSTALLATION_FOLDER>/etc/artifactory.config.xml. The configuration to setup these three repositories is shown below:

```
<config xmlns:xsi="http://www.w3.org/2001/XMLSchema-instance"
        xmlns="http://artifactory.jfrog.org/xsd/1.0.0"
```

```
        xsi:schemaLocation="http://artifactory.jfrog.org/xsd/1.0.0
        http://www.jfrog.org/xsd/artifactory-v1_0_0.xsd">

    <localRepositories>
        <localRepository>
            <key>private-internal-repository</key>
            <description>Private internal repository</description>
            <handleReleases>true</handleReleases>
            <handleSnapshots>true</handleSnapshots>
        </localRepository>
        <localRepository>
            <key>3rd-party</key>
            <description>3rd party jars added manually</description>
            <handleReleases>true</handleReleases>
            <handleSnapshots>false</handleSnapshots>
        </localRepository>
    </localRepositories>

    <remoteRepositories>
        <remoteRepository>
            <key>ibiblio</key>
            <handleReleases>true</handleReleases>
            <handleSnapshots>false</handleSnapshots>
            <excludesPattern>org/artifactory/**,org/jfrog/**</excludesPattern>
            <url>http://repo1.maven.org/maven2</url>
        </remoteRepository>
    </remoteRepositories>

</config>
```

To see this in action, start Tomcat and navigate to *http://localhost:8080/artifactory*. The artifactory home page is shown in Figure 2-30.

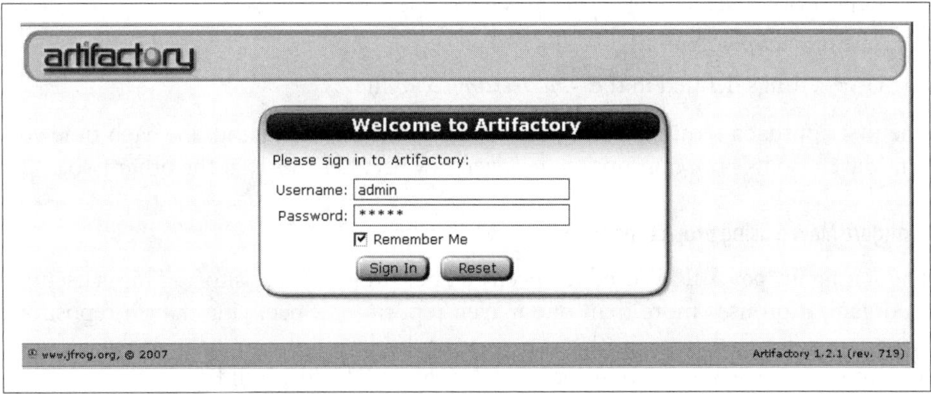

Figure 2-30. The Artifactory login page

Sign in using username "admin" and password "password." Click on the Browse repository link and you should be able to view the contents of the repository (see Figure 2-31).

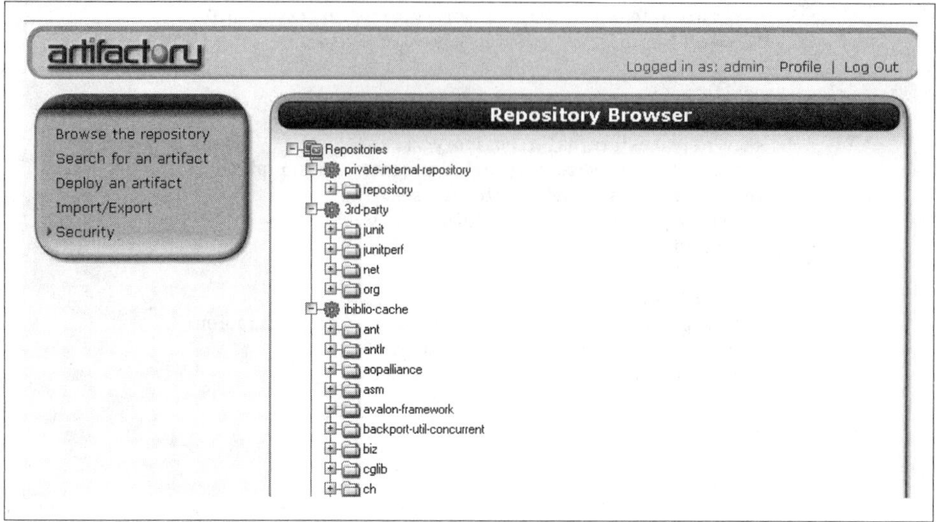

Figure 2-31. Browsing the Artifactory repositories

Configuring Maven to Use the New Repository

Once the maven repository is set up, we have to change Maven settings so that it downloads artifacts from our new internal repository rather than the public Maven repository. Maven looks for repository settings in three locations, in this order of precedence:

1. Repository specified using the command line
2. The project *pom.xml* file
3. User settings defined in the *~.m2/settings.xml* file

The first approach requires you to set properties at the command line each time you run Maven, so it is not appropriate for everyday use. Let's look at the other two.

Configure Maven using project "pom.xml"

The setting in "`pom.xml`" is used to specify a "per-project." repository. This is useful if an organization uses more than one maven repository. Specifying maven repository settings in `pom.xml` also means that, once a user checks out the code, he or she does not have to make any changes to his or her `settings.xml` to do a build.

A project setting also makes configuration easier with a continuous integration server such as Apache Continuum. With Continuum, all the user has to do is to specify the URL of the POM file in a version control system (e.g., SVN) and Continuum will build the project using the correct maven repository. If the project setting is not used, the user has to manually add the maven repository location to the `settings.xml` file.

A simple *pom.xml* is shown below, using an Artifactory repository running on a server called “buildserver”:

```
<project xmlns="http://maven.apache.org/POM/4.0.0"
    xmlns:xsi="http://www.w3.org/2001/XMLSchema-instance"
    xsi:schemaLocation="http://maven.apache.org/POM/4.0.0
    http://maven.apache.org/maven-v4_0_0.xsd">
    <modelVersion>4.0.0</modelVersion>
    <groupId>test</groupId>
    <artifactId>test</artifactId>
    <packaging>jar</packaging>
    <version>1.0-SNAPSHOT</version>
    <name>test</name>
    <url>http://maven.apache.org</url>

    <repositories>
        <repository>
            <id>central</id>
            <url>http://buildserver:8080/artifactory/repo</url>
            <snapshots>
                <enabled>false</enabled>
            </snapshots>
        </repository>
        <repository>
            <id>snapshots</id>
            <url>http://buildserver:8080/artifactory/repo</url>
            <releases>
                <enabled>false</enabled>
            </releases>
        </repository>
    </repositories>
    <pluginRepositories>
        <pluginRepository>
            <id>central</id>
            <url>http://buildserver:8080/artifactory/repo</url>
            <snapshots>
                <enabled>false</enabled>
            </snapshots>
        </pluginRepository>
        <pluginRepository>
            <id>snapshots</id>
            <url>http://buildserver:8080/artifactory/repo</url>
            <releases>
                <enabled>false</enabled>
            </releases>
        </pluginRepository>
    </pluginRepositories>

    <dependencies>
        <dependency>
            <groupId>junit</groupId>
            <artifactId>junit</artifactId>
            <version>3.8.1</version>
            <scope>test</scope>
        </dependency>
```

```
    </dependencies>
</project>
```

Configure Maven using settings.xml

This should be used if there is only one repository used by the developer. This repository will be used for every project and every build. This is sufficient for most developers.

Maven uses the settings.xml file located at "`~/.m2/settings.xml`" to get the location of maven repository. If no repository is specified, Maven uses the default repository, which is at ibiblio.org. The `settings.xml` file has to be changed to use the new repository. The settings are shown below:

```
<settings xmlns="http://maven.apache.org/POM/4.0.0"
    xmlns:xsi="http://www.w3.org/2001/XMLSchema-instance"
    xsi:schemaLocation="http://maven.apache.org/POM/4.0.0
                        http://maven.apache.org/xsd/settings-1.0.0.xsd">
    <profiles>
        <profile>
            <id>dev</id>
            <properties>
                <tomcat5x.home>C:/InstalledPrograms/apache-tomcat-5.5.20</tomcat5x.home>
            </properties>
            <repositories>
                <repository>
                    <id>central</id>
                    <url>http://buildserver:8080/artifactory/repo</url>
                    <snapshots>
                        <enabled>false</enabled>
                    </snapshots>
                </repository>
                <repository>
                    <id>snapshots</id>
                    <url>http://buildserver:8080/artifactory/repo</url>
                    <releases>
                        <enabled>false</enabled>
                    </releases>
                </repository>
            </repositories>
            <pluginRepositories>
                <pluginRepository>
                    <id>central</id>
                    <url>http://buildserver:8080/artifactory/repo</url>
                    <snapshots>
                        <enabled>false</enabled>
                    </snapshots>
                </pluginRepository>
                <pluginRepository>
                    <id>snapshots</id>
                    <url>http://buildserver:8080/artifactory/repo</url>
                    <releases>
                        <enabled>false</enabled>
                    </releases>
                </pluginRepository>
```

```
            </pluginRepositories>
        </profile>
    </profiles>
</settings>
```

Another approach is to use Artifactory as a mirror. Using a mirror is a convenient solution if you need to centralize access to the Internet repositories. This way, all downloaded artifacts will go through, and be cached on, the Artifactory server. Users do not need to set up proxy configurations for Maven on their individual machines. A simple mirror configuration is shown here:

```
<settings xmlns="http://maven.apache.org/POM/4.0.0"
    xmlns:xsi="http://www.w3.org/2001/XMLSchema-instance"
    xsi:schemaLocation="http://maven.apache.org/POM/4.0.0
                        http://maven.apache.org/xsd/settings-1.0.0.xsd">

    <mirrors>
        <mirror>
          <id>artifactory</id>
          <mirrorOf>*</mirrorOf>
          <url>http://buildserver:8080/artifactory/repo</url>
          <name>Artifactory</name>
        </mirror>
    </mirrors>
</settings>
```

Building using the new Maven repository

When building the Maven project, all of the repositories should be downloaded using the new repository. The console will show the server Maven uses, as shown below:

```
$ mvn compile
[INFO] Scanning for projects...
Downloading: http://buildserver:8080/artifactory/repo/org/apache/maven/wagon
/wagon-ssh-external/1.0-alpha-5/wagon-ssh-external-1.0-alpha-5.pom
5K downloaded
Downloading: http://buildserver:8080/artifactory/repo/org/codehaus/plexus
/plexus-utils/1.0.4/plexus-utils-1.0.4.pom
6K downloaded
Downloading: http://buildserver:8080/artifactory/repo/org/apache/maven
/wagon/wagon-provider-api/1.0-alpha-5/wagon-provider-api-1.0-alpha-5.pom
4K downloaded
Downloading: http://buildserver:8080/artifactory/repo/org/codehaus/plexus
/plexus-utils/1.1/plexus-utils-1.1.pom
767b downloaded
Downloading: http://buildserver:8080/artifactory/repo/org/codehaus/plexus
/plexus/1.0.4/plexus-1.0.4.pom
5K downloaded
...
```

Artifactory will automatically fetch any artifacts that are not already cached from the appropriate repository on the Internet. You can check this by browsing the repository using the Artifactory web console (see Figure 2-31).

Installing Artifacts to the Repository

Artifacts can be installed using the web UI or the Maven command line. Installation using the web UI is simple and faster and does not require any configuration changes. Installation using the command line requires some initial configuration changes in `settings.xml`.

Installing artifacts using the web UI

It is easy to manually install a new artifact to the Artifactory repository. First, upload the artifact to deploy (usually a "jar" or "POM" file) using the "Deploy an artifact" link on the Artifactory web console. Artifactory will upload the file, and detect the groupId, artifactID, and version details if they are available (see Figure 2-32). You can choose the repository that you want to store the artifact in, and provide any missing details. When you are done, Artifactory will deploy your artifact to the appropriate place in the enterprise repository, where it can be accessed by all other users.

Installing artifacts from Maven command line

When using the "mvn clean install" command, Maven only packages and installs the artifact to the local repository on your development machine. To install it to your enterprise repository, you need to add an additional *<server>* configuration section in your `settings.xml` file, where you specify the username and password required to access the Artifactory repository:

```
<settings>
    <servers>
        <server>
            <id>organization-internal</id>
            <username>admin</username>
            <password>password</password>
        </server>
    </servers>
</settings>
```

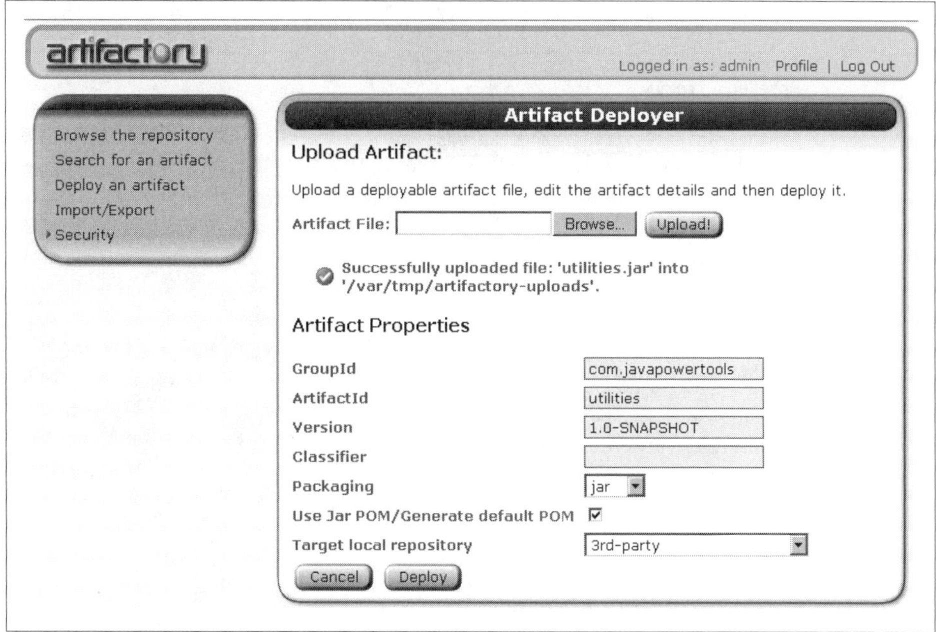

Figure 2-32. Deploying an artifact

Then, to install an artifact to internal Maven repository, you run the *mvn deploy* command as shown here:

```
$ mvn deploy:deploy-file -DrepositoryId=organization-internal \
  -Durl=http://buildserver:8080/artifactory/private-internal-repository \
  DgroupId=test -DartifactId=test -Dversion=1.1 -Dpackaging=jar
-Dfile=target/test-1.1.jar
```

The repository id should match the server id defined in the `settings.xml`. The URL should include the name of the repository into which the artifact is to be installed. Once deployed, the artifact will appear on the Artifactory repository and be available to other users.

Of course, if you want to save typing, you might want to configure your Continuous Build server to do this for you.

Running Artifactory Through a Proxy

Typically, in an enterprise environment, you will need to go though a proxy server to access the Internet. Artifactory needs to know how to do this to be able to fetch the JARs it needs from the Internet. You do this by defining a *<proxies>* section in your `artifactory.config.xml` file, as shown here:

```
<config xmlns:xsi="http://www.w3.org/2001/XMLSchema-instance"
        xmlns="http://artifactory.jfrog.org/xsd/1.0.0"
        xsi:schemaLocation="http://artifactory.jfrog.org/xsd/1.0.0
```

```
        http://www.jfrog.org/xsd/artifactory-v1_0_0.xsd">
    ...
    <remoteRepositories>
      <remoteRepository>
          <key>ibiblio</key>
          <handleReleases>true</handleReleases>
          <handleSnapshots>false</handleSnapshots>
          <excludesPattern>org/artifactory/**,org/jfrog/**</excludesPattern>
          <url>http://repo1.maven.org/maven2</url>
          <proxyRef>proxy1</proxyRef>
      </remoteRepository>
    </remoteRepositories>
    <proxies>
        <proxy>
            <key>proxy1</key>
            <host>proxyhost</host>
            <port>8080</port>
            <username>proxy</username>
            <password>secret</password>
        </proxy>
    </proxies>
</config>
```

Adding Other Remote Repositories

Artifactory comes by default configured to access the standard ibiblio repository, but you may well need to access other repositories, such as Codehaus. You do this by simply adding extra *<remoteRepository>* elements in the `artifactory.config.xml` file. If you are accessing the Internet via a proxy, don't forget the *<proxyRef>* tag as well:

```
<remoteRepositories>
  <remoteRepository>
      <key>ibiblio</key>
      <handleReleases>true</handleReleases>
      <handleSnapshots>false</handleSnapshots>
      <excludesPattern>org/artifactory/**,org/jfrog/**</excludesPattern>
      <url>http://repo1.maven.org/maven2</url>
      <proxyRef>proxy1</proxyRef>
  </remoteRepository>
  <remoteRepository>
      <key>codehaus</key>
      <handleReleases>true</handleReleases>
      <handleSnapshots>false</handleSnapshots>
      <url>http://repository.codehaus.org</url>
      <proxyRef>proxy1</proxyRef>
  </remoteRepository>
  <remoteRepository>
      <key>OpenQA</key>
      <handleReleases>true</handleReleases>
      <handleSnapshots>true</handleSnapshots>
      <url>http://maven.openqa.org</url>
      <proxyRef>proxy1</proxyRef>
  </remoteRepository>
  ...
<remoteRepositories>
```

Backing Up the Repository

Artifactory lets you program regular backups of your repository. Backup policy is specified in the **artifactory.config.xml**, using a "cron" expression. The backup configuration element is illustrated below:

```
<config xmlns:xsi="http://www.w3.org/2001/XMLSchema-instance"
        xmlns="http://artifactory.jfrog.org/xsd/1.0.0"
        xsi:schemaLocation="http://artifactory.jfrog.org/xsd/1.0.0
        http://www.jfrog.org/xsd/artifactory-v1_0_0.xsd">
    <!-- Backup every 12 hours -->
    <backupCronExp>0 0 /12 * * ?</backupCronExp>
    <localRepositories>
    ...
</config>
```

Backups are stored in "<ARTIFACTORY_INSTALLATION_FOLDER>/backups." The backups are in the standard maven repository format. This is the same format as the local repository on developers, machine. This makes it very easy to migrate the repository contents to another implementation of maven repository.

2.21 Using Ant in Maven

Contributed by: Eric Redmond

Ant has had a good run. The past decade has been good for the undisputed Java build tool, but it is time for it to turn in its crown. Ant scripts have a few glaring problems—lack of built-in network portability (you must manually download and install Ant task jars—or perhaps write a script to do it for you); it does not handle dependencies; Ant script size is related to build complexity—i.e., it is procedural, not declarative like Maven; nor does it have any standard concept of a project. Ant is effectively an XML scripting language—Maven would be better described as a comprehensive build scripting platform.

But many organizations that wish to convert to Maven have spent considerable resources on creating Ant scripts. Maven has accounted for this and created tools to allow organizations to move forward with Maven, while continuing to utilize their Ant investment. And, to show what good sports that they are, they also have created a toolkit allowing Ant users to utilize some of Maven's features, such as downloading from remote repositories.

Using Existing build.xml Files

The most straightforward way to move from Ant to Maven is to use the existing Ant scripts, wholesale. This can be done by adding the Maven-antrun-plug-in to the POM, and binding it to a phase. What you are actually doing here is embedding Ant code into the POM. However, for the sake of using an existing Ant file, you execute Ant's `Ant` task:

```
<tasks>
  <ant antfile="${basedir}/build.xml" dir="${basedir}" inheritRefs="true"
   target="jar">
    <property name="ant.proj.version" value="${project.version}" />
  </ant>
</tasks>
```

dir actually defaults to the project's basedir, antfile defaults to $basedir/build.xml, and target defaults to the project's default. inheritRefs defaults to false, but you may not require them. So if you stick to the defaults, you can get away with something simpler:

```
<tasks>
   <ant />
 </tasks>
```

Assuming that your build.xml file executes steps to building a complete project, you may be best served by setting the project packaging type as pom via the project's packaging element—this will stop Maven from attempting to generate its own JAR artifact. Then you can bind the Ant file to the package phase.

Embedding Ant Code in the POM

In addition to using an existing build.xml, you can embed other Ant code directly in the POM. Although this is not usually a great idea (it is better to use Maven proper and create a plug-in for any tasks you may need to execute), it can be useful to do a few odd tasks in a quick and simple way.

Execute external commands. For example, perhaps we wish to execute the command *java -version* during the verify phase:

```
<project>
  ...
  <build>
    ...
    <plugins>
      <plugin>
        <artifactId>maven-antrun-plugin</artifactId>
        <executions>
          <execution>
            <phase>verify</phase>
            <goals>
              <goal>run</goal>
            </goals>
            <configuration>
              <tasks>
                <exec executable="java" failonerror="true">
                  <arg line="-version" />
                </exec>
              </tasks>
            </configuration>
          </execution>
```

```
        </executions>
      </plugin>
    </plugins>
  </build>
</project>
```

Another useful task is for simple debugging. For example, viewing the values of properties, echo is a very useful command:

```
<tasks>
  <echo>Output will go to ${project.build.directory}</echo>
</tasks>
```

External Dependencies

You must add dependencies of the tasks that you plan to use—Maven makes such a demand. Just like adding dependencies to the project itself through the `dependencies` element, you also may add dependencies to a plug-in. For example, if you require the ant-optional jar, just add the dependencies under the plug-in declaration:

```
<project>
  ...
  <build>
    ...
    <plugins>
      <plugin>
        <artifactId>maven-antrun-plugin</artifactId>
        <configuration>
          <tasks>
            <ftp server="ftp.mycompany.com" userid="usr1" password="pass1" action="list"
             listing="${project.build.directory}/ftplist.txt">
              <fileset>
                <include name="*"/>
              </fileset>
            </ftp>
          </tasks>
        </configuration>
        <dependencies>
          <dependency>
            <groupId>ant</groupId>
            <artifactId>optional</artifactId>
            <version>1.5.4</version>
          </dependency>
          <dependency>
            <groupId>ant</groupId>
            <artifactId>ant-commons-net</artifactId>
            <version>1.6.5</version>
          </dependency>
          <dependency>
            <groupId>commons-net</groupId>
            <artifactId>commons-net</artifactId>
            <version>1.4.1</version>
          </dependency>
        </dependencies>
      </plugin>
```

```
    </plugins>
  </build>
</project>
```

Making Ant Plug-Ins

In addition to using existing Ant files to execute steps in Maven, you also can create plug-ins in Ant, using them just as any Java plug-in. Because Maven goals are defined through the concept of a *mojo*, any Ant script that you wish to convert to a goal must be mapped to the mojo concept. Your Ant build script must be named `<something><<.build.xml>>`, and the mojo is then defined through a corresponding `<something><<.mojos.xml>>` file.

Create a simple project directory with a POM and two files under `src/main/scripts`: `echo.build.xml` and `echo.mojos.xml`.

```
my-ant-plugin
|-- pom.xml
`-- src
    `-- main
        `-- scripts
            |-- echo.build.xml
            `-- echo.mojos.xml
```

The POM is a Maven plug-in like any other but slightly more complex than a Java-based Maven plug-in. It requires two pieces of information. First the `maven-plugin-plugin` (the plug-in responsible for creating plug-in descriptors) only defaults to Java. If you wish it to know how to handle alternate plug-in styles, you must add that alternate type as a dependency of the maven-plugin-plugin. Indeed, this will set the `org.apache.maven:maven-plugin-tools-ant` project into the descriptor generator's runtime. Second, once the plug-in is installed, it will not run without a mechanism for Maven to be able to interpret the Ant scripts as though they were regular Java-based mojos. So we add the dependency to our plug-in to require that mechanism in the form of the `org.apache.maven:maven-script-ant` project:

```
<project>
  <modelVersion>4.0.0</modelVersion>
  <groupId>com.mycompany</groupId>
  <artifactId>my-ant-plugin</artifactId>
  <version>1.0-SNAPSHOT</version>
  <packaging>maven-plugin</packaging>

  <build>
    <plugins>
      <plugin>
        <artifactId>maven-plugin-plugin</artifactId>
        <dependencies>
          <dependency>
            <groupId>org.apache.maven</groupId>
            <artifactId>maven-plugin-tools-ant</artifactId>
            <version>2.0.4</version>
          </dependency>
```

```
        </dependencies>
      </plugin>
    </plugins>
  </build>

  <dependencies>
    <dependency>
      <groupId>org.apache.maven</groupId>
      <artifactId>maven-script-ant</artifactId>
      <version>2.0.4</version>
    </dependency>
  </dependencies>
</project>
```

When you run the install phase later on, notice the lines:

```
[INFO] Applying extractor for language: Ant

[INFO] Extractor for language: Ant found 1 mojo descriptors.
```

This is the `maven-plugin-tools-ant` project at work.

Next, create a simple Ant build with a target named `echo.build.xml`. This is a plain old Ant script, nothing special:

```
<project>
  <target name="echotarget">
    <echo>${echo.value}</echo>
  </target>
</project>
```

Our plain old Ant script (or POAS, to coin a phrase) must be mapped to the Maven world, and this is done through the `echo.mojos.xml` file. Its fairly self-explanatory. `goal` is this mojo's goal name; `description` is a short blurb about the goal. `call` is the name of the target to execute when this goal is called:

```
<pluginMetadata>
  <mojos>
    <mojo>
      <goal>echo</goal>
      <description>Print out the echo.value property</description>
      <call>echotarget</call>
    </mojo>
  </mojos>
</pluginMetadata>
```

Now install this plug-in the normal way, via `mvn install` (if something does not work, try installing again with `mvn -U install`; the `-U` flag tells Maven to update its dependencies). After install, run the new `echo` goal, giving it a property value to print to the screen:

```
$ mvn com.mycompany:my-ant-plugin:echo -Decho.value=Hello
```

Out will print the value:

```
echotarget:

     [echo] Hello
```

Using Maven in Ant

To bring home the Maven-and-Ant dance, we will finish with how to use Maven within Ant. Although I always recommend using Maven, it is not always a possibility. In these circumstances, you can embed useful tools such as Maven repository management. It is downloadable as a jar from the Maven site. Just place it in your Ant installation's lib directory (or by any other method used to add tasks to Ant). The complete set of tasks can be found on the Maven site, but some of the more useful ones are described in this section.

One useful trick is letting Maven manage your dependencies via `artifact:dependencies`. It's a good idea to pass in a `filesetId` to keep a fileset reference for later use. You also can use a `pathId` attribute instead to get a classpath reference. A typical example is shown here:

```
<artifact:dependencies filesetId="dependency.fileset">
  <dependency groupId="commons-net" artifactId="commons-net" version="1.4.1"/>
</artifact:dependencies>
```

If you wish to use a repository other than the default Maven Central repository, add the repository, and set the remoteRepositories under the dependencies set:

```
<artifact:dependencies>
  ...
  <artifact:remoteRepository id="remote.repository"
   url="http://repository.mycompany.com/" />
</artifact:dependencies>
```

You also can install or deploy an Ant-built artifact just like any other Maven project, provided that you have a `pom.xml` file available:

```
<artifact:pom id="project" file="pom.xml" />
<artifact:install file="${project.build.directory}/my-artifact-1.0-SNAPSHOT.jar"
pomRefId="project" />
```

There are more tasks than these concerned with POM access and authentication, but we will stop here so as not to get off track. This topic is dealt with in a little more detail in the Ant chapter (see Section 1.11). Or check out the Maven web site documentation when you download the Ant lib.

Generating Ant Script from a POM

We began this chapter discussing the `maven-antrun-plugin`, which is used to bring Ant into Maven. We will end with the `maven-ant-plugin`, which is used to export Maven into Ant. The `ant:ant` goal is run within an existing Maven project and generates a `build.xml` file—an Ant representation of the Maven project. Begin by creating a simple project with the quickstart archetype:

```
$ mvn archetype:create -DgroupId=com.mycompany \
    -DartifactId=my-project \
    -Dversion=1.0-SNAPSHOT
```

In that base directory, run `mvn ant:ant`, which generates a fair-sized `build.xml` Ant file with a good cross-section of tasks to compile, test, and package the project. It even throws in clean, for good measure. You can test this by new script by executing `Ant` in the base directory, assuming that you have it installed. It may take a while, depending on the size of your repository, if the build classpath is set to your entire repository:

```
<property name="maven.repo.local" value="${user.home}/.m2/repository"/>
<path id="build.classpath">
  <fileset dir="${maven.repo.local}"/>
</path>
```

If this is the case, then you can change the fileset to be only the files you need. You can, it just makes more work for you.

2.22 Advanced Archetypes

Contributed by: Eric Redmond

Archetypes are a simple and useful way to bootstrap new development across your organization and urge your developers to follow a similar project pattern. Archetypes are a template of a Maven project used to generate skeleton layout for projects of any desired type in a consistent way.

The default archetype is called *quickstart*, and generates a simple project with some "Hello World" Java code and a unit test. Running the `archetype:create` goal as follows:

```
$ mvn archetype:create -DgroupId=com.mycompany -DartifactId=my-proj
```

will yield a project with the following project structure:

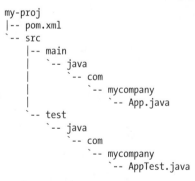

```
my-proj
|-- pom.xml
`-- src
    |-- main
    |   `-- java
    |       `-- com
    |           `-- mycompany
    |               `-- App.java
    `-- test
        `-- java
            `-- com
                `-- mycompany
                    `-- AppTest.java
```

The archetype that generates this simple project is outlined by two mechanisms: the `META-INF/maven/archetype.xml` resource definition file, and the archetype resources under the `src/main/resources/archetype-resources` directory.

```
maven-quickstart-archetype
|-- pom.xml
`-- src
    `-- main
        `-- resources
            |-- META-INF
            |   `-- maven
            |       `-- archetype.xml
            `-- archetype-resources
                |-- pom.xml
                `-- src
                    |-- main
                    |   `-- java
                    |       `-- App.java
                    `-- test
                        `-- java
                            `-- AppTest.java
```

There are other archetypes available by default from Maven Central Repository. Check out the list at *http://repo1.maven.org/maven2/org/apache/maven/archetypes*. At the time of this writing, the following archetypes are supported:

- maven-archetype-archetype
- maven-archetype-bundles
- maven-archetype-j2ee-simple
- maven-archetype-marmalade-mojo
- maven-archetype-mojo
- maven-archetype-plugin-site
- maven-archetype-plugin
- maven-archetype-portlet
- maven-archetype-profiles
- maven-archetype-quickstart
- maven-archetype-simple
- maven-archetype-site-simple
- maven-archetype-site
- maven-archetype-webapp

Creating Your Own Archetypes

`org.apache.maven.archetypes:maven-archetype-archetype` is the easiest way to start creating archetypes:

```
$ mvn archetype:create -DarchetypeGroupId=org.apache.maven.archetypes \
                       -DarchetypeArtifactId=maven-archetype-archetype \
                       -DarchetypeVersion=1.0 \
                       -DgroupId=com.mycompany \
                       -DartifactId=my-archetype
```

This will generate a simple archetype that is built to generate a simple project—similar to the `maven-quickstart-archetype` shown in the beginning of this chapter, under the directory of the artifactId defined.

By default, an archetype cannot overwrite a project. A useful construct for converting your existing non-Maven projects to Maven is to create a simple archetype with a POM construct of your design. Let's create a simple archetype that will be run over non-Maven projects to give them a *pom.xml* file with a custom MANIFEST.MF file.

Let's begin by removing the extraneous files under the `src/main/resources/archetype-resources/src` directory, leaving us just with a `pom.xml` and create a file `src/main/resources/archetype-resources/src/main/resources/META-INF/MANIFEST.MF`. This will leave the following project structure:

```
my-archetype
|-- pom.xml
`-- src
    `-- main
        `-- resources
            |-- META-INF
            |   `-- maven
            |       `-- archetype.xml
            `-- archetype-resources
                |-- pom.xml
                `-- src
                    `-- main
                        `-- resources
                            `-- META-INF
                                `-- MANIFEST.MF
```

Alter the `src/main/resources/archetype-resources/pom.xml` to be a project that contains a base MANIFEST.MF file to be packaged into a jar with extra entries. Because most—if not every—non-Maven project places its source code in a directory other than Maven's default `src/main/java`, we also set the `sourceDirectory` build element to another directory, `src`. Set this directory to whatever your legacy project structure requires:

```
<project xmlns="http://maven.apache.org/POM/4.0.0"
 xmlns:xsi="http://www.w3.org/2001/XMLSchema-instance"
  xsi:schemaLocation="http://maven.apache.org/POM/4.0.0
  http://maven.apache.org/maven-v4_0_0.xsd">
  <modelVersion>4.0.0</modelVersion>
  <groupId>${groupId}</groupId>
  <artifactId>${artifactId}</artifactId>
  <version>${version}</version>
  <name>Project - ${artifactId}</name>
  <url>http://mycompany.com</url>
  <build>
    <sourceDirectory>src</sourceDirectory>
    <resources>
      <resource>
        <directory>src/main/resources</directory>
        <excludes>
```

```
          <exclude>**/MANIFEST.MF</exclude>
        </excludes>
      </resource>
    </resources>
    <plugins>
      <plugin>
        <groupId>org.apache.maven.plug-ins</groupId>
        <artifactId>maven-jar-plugin</artifactId>
        <configuration>
          <archive>
            <manifestFile>src/main/resources/META-INF/MANIFEST.MF</manifestFile>
            <manifestEntries>
              <Built-By>${user.name}</Built-By>
              <Project-Name>${project.name}</Project-Name>
            </manifestEntries>
          </archive>
        </configuration>
      </plugin>
    </plugins>
  </build>

  <dependencies>
    <dependency>
      <groupId>junit</groupId>
      <artifactId>junit</artifactId>
      <version>3.8.1</version>
      <scope>test</scope>
    </dependency>
  </dependencies>
</project>
```

Fill the `src/main/resources/archetype-resources/src/main/resources/META-INF/MANIFEST.MF` file with whatever valid manifest values you wish. Mine contains the following:

```
Manifest-Version: 1.1
Created-By: Apache Maven 2
Company-Name: My Company
```

Now we need to set the `src/main/resources/META-INF/maven/archetype.xml` descriptor to bundle up our MANIFEST.MF file as a resource and to allow us to run our archetype over the top of an existing one via the `allowPartial` element. The `archetype:create` goal will not allow the creation of an archetype, by default, when a project with the same artifactId already exists in the current directory.

```
<archetype>
  <id>my-archetype</id>
  <allowPartial>true</allowPartial>
  <resources>
    <resource>src/main/resources/META-INF/MANIFEST.MF</resource>
  </resources>
</archetype>
```

As with any other Maven project, you can install it by running in the base directory:

```
$ mvn install
```

This builds and installs the archetype to your local repository. To test our new archetype, run the following command, which will generate a new project with the pom.xml and MANIFEST.MF files. If you run the same command again, it will work, only because we set `allowPartial` to `true`:

```
$ mvn archetype:create -DarchetypeGroupId=com.mycompany \
                      -DarchetypeArtifactId=my-archetype \
                      -DarchetypeVersion=1.0-SNAPSHOT \
                      -DgroupId=com.mycompany \
                      -DartifactId=my-project
```

Voilà! You can now outfit your legacy projects with a shiny new Maven 2 compliant version.

2.23 Using Assemblies

Contributed by: Eric Redmond

Creating Assemblies

Maven is built on the concept of conventions. It does so for a very good reason: if all Maven users follow the same conventions, then all Maven users can navigate and build other Maven-based projects without the need for further training. Tools such as Make and Ant can make no such boast. However, there are cases when the standard conventions cannot apply, for perhaps industrial or technological reasons. With this in mind, the Maven Assembly Plug-in was created.

Assemblies in Maven are a collection of files following a certain structure that are packaged for distribution as some artifact, for example, as a zip file. The "structure" is defined through an assembly descriptor xml file, which is pointed to through the project's POM plug-in configuration and possibly bound to a phase:

```
<project>
  ...
  <build>
    ...
    <plugins>
      <plugin>
        <artifactId>maven-assembly-plugin</artifactId>
        <configuration>
          <descriptor>src/main/assembly/src.xml</descriptor>
        </configuration>
        <executions>
          <execution>
            <id>package-source</id>
            <phase>package</phase>
            <goals>
              <goal>attached</goal>
            </goals>
          </execution>
        </executions>
```

```
    </plugin>
  </plugins>
</build>
```

The src/main/assembly/src.xml file is an assembly descriptor that packages up the source directory and other files into a zip file suffixed with an ID:

```
<assembly>
  <id>src</id>
  <formats>
    <format>zip</format>
  </formats>
  <fileSets>
    <fileSet>
      <includes>
        <include>README*</include>
        <include>LICENSE*</include>
        <include>NOTICE*</include>
        <include>pom.xml</include>
      </includes>
    </fileSet>
    <fileSet>
      <directory>src</directory>
    </fileSet>
  </fileSets>
</assembly>
```

The example above has an ID of `src`. When the package phase is run, it will still create the artifact of the packaging type, for example, the `target/artifactId-version.jar` file, but in addition will bundle up the source code into a `target/artifactId-version-src.zip` file. This assembly will generate all the formats defined above. The possible archive types are limited to the Plexus implementations of `component.org.codehaus.plexus.archiver.Archiver` role, in the `plexus-archiver` component. The list at the time of this writing is:

- bzip2
- dir
- ear
- gzip
- jar
- tar
- tar.gz
- tar.bz2
- tbz2
- war
- zip

Everything beyond the `id` and `formats` define which files to package up:

`includeBaseDirectory`
: Includes the base directory in the artifact if set to true (default), otherwise the directory will not be included as the root of the artifact.

`baseDirectory`
: The name of the base directory, if `includeBaseDirecctory` is set to true. Defaults to the POM's artifacctId.

`includeSiteDirectory`
: Set to true if you wish to assemble the project's site into the artifact. Default is false.

`moduleSets`
: Configure modules to assemble if this project is a `pom` multimodule project. Note that you must run the packaging phase for any added modules to succeed (`mvn package assembly:assembly`) because such modules must be packaged first.

`fileSets`
: A set of file sets (under directories) to include/exclude into the assembly, as well as other information, such as directory mode or output directory name.

`files`
: A set of specific files to include/exclude into the assembly, as well as other information, such as file mode or output filename.

`dependencySets`
: This section manages the inclusion/exclusion of the project's dependencies.

Built-in Descriptors

There are some descriptors that are so common that they were just built into the `maven-assembly-plugin` for convenience. They are:

bin
: Generates `zip`, `tar.gz`, and `tar.bz2` files packaged with `README*`, `LICENSE*`, and `NOTICE*` files in the project's base directory.

src
: Generates `zip`, `tar.gz`, and `tar.bz2` files packaged with `README*`, `LICENSE*`, `NOTICE*`, and the `pom.xml`, along with all files under the project's `src` directory.

jar-with-dependencies
: Explodes all dependencies of this project and packages the exploded forms into a `jar` along with the project's `outputDirectory`.

project
: Generates `zip`, `tar.gz`, and `tar.bz2` files packaged with all files in the project, sans the `target` directory. Note that your project must use the default build directory `target` for this to not package built files.

The above descriptors can be used on the command line with the given *descriptorId*:

```
$ mvn assembly:assembly -DdescriptorId=jar-with-dependencies
```

Or, as always, defined via plug-in configuration:

```
<project>
  ...
  <build>
    ...
    <plugins>
      <plugin>
        <artifactId>maven-assembly-plugin</artifactId>
        <configuration>
          <descriptorRefs>
            <descriptorRef>jar-with-dependencies</descriptorRef>
            <descriptorRef>bin</descriptorRef>
            <descriptorRef>src</descriptorRef>
          </descriptorRefs>
        </configuration>
      </plugin>
    </plugins>
  </build>
</project>
```

Assemblies are very useful for creating distributions for projects, be it by source or just binaries. The full assembly descriptor is a large beast, which you can find online with the maven assembly plug-in documentation at *http://maven.apache.org/plugins/maven-assembly-plugin/assembly.html*.

Assemblies with Profiles

A useful combination is assemblies that are chosen via profiles. Oftentimes, a distribution will be different, depending on the operating system run—especially if the project contains native code or is run by a script. For example, suppose we have a project that contains two scripts, `run.bat` for Windowss and `run.sh` for Linux:

```
my-native-project
|-- pom.xml
`-- src
    `-- main
        |-- assembly
        |   |-- windows.xml
        |   `-- linux.xml
        `-- scripts
            |-- run-windows.bat
            `-- run-linux.sh
```

In the project's POM, we have two profiles—one for Windows and one for Linux:

```
<project>
  ...
  <profiles>
    <profile>
      <activation>
        <os>
          <family>Windows</family>
        </os>
      </activation>
```

```
    <build>
      <plugins>
        <plugin>
          <artifactId>maven-assembly-plugin</artifactId>
          <configuration>
            <descriptors>
              <descriptor>src/main/assembly/windows.xml</descriptor>
            </descriptors>
          </configuration>
        </plugin>
      </plugins>
    </build>
  </profile>
  <profile>
    <activation>
      <os>
        <family>Linux</family>
      </os>
    </activation>
    <build>
      <plugins>
        <plugin>
          <artifactId>maven-assembly-plugin</artifactId>
          <configuration>
            <descriptors>
              <descriptor>src/main/assembly/linux.xml</descriptor>
            </descriptors>
          </configuration>
        </plugin>
      </plugins>
    </build>
  </profile>
</profiles>
</project>
```

The **windows.xml** assembly descriptor will package the **run-windows.bat** file as **bin/run.bat** in a **zip** artifact, filtering the batch script first:

```
<assembly>
  <id>windows</id>
  <formats>
    <format>zip</format>
  </formats>
  <files>
    <file>
      <source>src/main/scripts/run-windows.bat</source>
      <destName>run.bat</destName>
      <outputDirectory>bin</outputDirectory>
      <filtered>true</filtered>
    </file>
  </files>
</assembly>
```

The **linux.xml** assembly descriptor will, in turn, package the **bin/run.sh** file as a **tar.gz** artifact:

```
<assembly>
  <id>linux</id>
  <formats>
    <format>tar.gz</format>
  </formats>
  <files>
    <file>
      <source>src/main/scripts/run-linux.sh</source>
      <destName>run.sh</destName>
      <outputDirectory>bin</outputDirectory>
      <filtered>true</filtered>
    </file>
  </files>
</assembly>
```

Building the project with `mvn assembly:assembly` will generate the assembly artifact of the current operating system, Windows (`target/artifactId-version-windows.zip`) or Linux (`target/artifactId-version-linux.tar.gz`). Better yet, you can bind the `assembly:attached` goal to the `package` phase to execute as `mvn package`.

As the project grows in complexity, the project's POM will not need to change—just the assembly for the desired operating system supported. This is a contrived example for certain, but it is very useful for more complex scenarios, such as native code compilation and distribution.

PART II
Version Control Tools

> "You ought to see that bird from here," said Rabbit. "Unless it's a fish." "It isn't a fish, it's a bird," said Piglet. "So it is," said Rabbit. "Is it a starling or a blackbird?" said Pooh. "That's the whole question," said Rabbit. "Is it a blackbird or a starling?"
>
> —"Kanga and Baby Roo Come to the Forest," *Winnie the Pooh*, A. A. Milne

In all things, it is useful to know exactly what you are dealing with at any point in time. In software development, where source code is changing perpetually, this is particularly important. This is why version control systems play such a crucial role in modern software development environments. The advantages of using such a system are well known. A well-designed version control solution facilitates teamwork by allowing many developers to work on the same project (or even the same files) simultaneously without stepping on each other's toes. It provides a central place to store your application source code as well as a reliable history of the changes that have been made over the life of the project. It also allows developers to return to a previous stable version of the source code if need be. And it allows developers to identify (or "tag") a particular version of the source code, such as for a particular release. In modern development environments, version control systems are an essential building brick for more sophisticated techniques such as Continuous Integration (see Chapters 5, 6, and 7).

In Java projects, the two most prominent open source version control systems are, without a doubt, CVS and Subversion. The venerable open source tool CVS is widely used in many organizations. Subversion, its natural successor, is rapidly gaining ground in new Java projects because of its features, which are aguably better adapted to modern development practices than CVS.

CHAPTER 3

Setting Up Version Control Using CVS

3.1 An Introduction to CVS

CVS is a venerable open source version control system first released in the 1980s, one that has a long history in the open source community. Indeed, a great number of open source projects are still hosted under CVS. CVS uses a client-server architecture, with a source code repository residing on a central server. Users connect to the server to download (or "check out," to use CVS terminology) a copy of the project source code, modify it, and then submit (or "check in") their changes back to the repository. Several users can work simultaneously on the same file. CVS will attempt to merge the modifications of users as they check in their changes. If it cannot do so for some reason, the user has to resolve the conflict manually. And when the time comes to make a release, users can "tag" a version to be able to retrieve it reliably later on.

For some years now, CVS has been showing its age, and it has a number of deep-seated architectural flaws and missing features that make it poorly adapted to Java development projects and the more modern agile development practices in general. For example, it is very difficult to rename or move directories, which makes refactoring cumbersome and difficult. Directory structures in CVS are very rigid—once added, it is very hard to get rid of a directory in the repository. In addition, CVS was designed at a time when most applications consisted entirely of text files, so support for other formats, such as binary files, is limited. The important notion of atomic commits (see "Revision Numbers and Atomic Updates" in Section 4.1), present in virtually all other modern version control systems, is totally absent from CVS.

It should be noted that Subversion (see Chapter 4) was designed from the ground up to overcome many of the limitations of CVS, something that it has done rather successfully. Subversion is now stable, mature, and technically superior to CVS. If you are given a choice for a new project, it would be wise to consider Subversion seriously.

Nevertheless, CVS is still widely used in many organizations, on web sites, and in open source projects, and it is arguably still a tool with which you should be familiar. Thus, rather than being a detailed reference, this chapter is designed more along the lines of a survival guide for Java developers who need to use CVS.

3.2 Setting Up a CVS Repository

CVS is essentially a Unix application, although there is an independent fork for Windows called CVSNT. You can run the CVS client virtually anywhere, but the CVS server is most commonly seen in a Unix environment. The first step is to create a directory in which the CVS repository will be stored. In this example, we will place it in the `/usr/local/cvs` directory, although it can go anywhere you like. For security reasons, it is also a good idea to create a dedicated group for CVS users (say, "cvs"), and to make our new directory belong to this group. You generally need to set up a Unix user account on this machine for each developer that will be using the repository. To be able to check out source code from this repository, users need read access on these files. To be able to commit changes, users need write access.

To set up a new CVS repository, you need to run the *cvs init* command. A CVS repository is essentially stored as a collection of files. The *cvs init* command sets up the appropriate directory structure and administrative files, which are stored in a directory called CVSROOT, as shown here:

```
# cvs -d /usr/local/cvs init
# ls /usr/local/cvs/
CVSROOT
# ls /usr/local/cvs/CVSROOT/
checkoutlist    cvswrappers,v  notify        posttag,v     taginfo
checkoutlist,v  Emptydir       notify,v      postwatch     taginfo,v
commitinfo      history        postadmin     postwatch,v   val-tags
commitinfo,v    loginfo        postadmin,v   preproxy      verifymsg
config          loginfo,v      postproxy     preproxy,v    verifymsg,v
config,v        modules        postproxy,v   rcsinfo
cvswrappers     modules,v      posttag       rcsinfo,v
```

These are the raw CVS data files. Don't mess with them directly.

3.3 Creating a New Project in CVS

When you start work on a new project, you naturally will want to put it under version control quickly. Importing an empty directory structure or a skeleton project containing only text files into CVS is fairly easy. You may have created a skeleton directory structure manually using a Maven archetype (see Section 2.11).

First, you need to tell CVS where to look for your repository by defining the *CVSROOT* environment variable. This also will make things easier for the other CVS commands. This variable points to the default CVS repository to be used in all CVS commands. If your CVS repository has been set up on the local machine in `/usr/local/cvs`, for example, you might do something like this:

```
$ export CVSROOT=/usr/local/cvs
```

If you are accessing an organization-wide CVS server across the network, you will probably need to access the repository using the pserver protocol:

```
$ export CVSROOT=:pserver:john@cvs.mycompany.com:2401/usr/local/cvs
```

We will talk about the pserver protocol a bit more later in this chapter.

If this repository doesn't support anonymous access (which is usually the case with an enterprise repository, for example), you will need to login before you can go any further:

```
$ cvs login
```

If the server authorizes you to access the repository, your password will be stored locally so that you don't need to login each time.

Next, you import the directory structure using the *cvs import* command. The *import* command takes the following form:

```
$ cvs import -m "Initial message" project vendortag releasetag
```

The *project* field refers to the directory that you want to store in CVS.

You need to provide a text message describing the import. You can either do this using the *-m* option or let CVS prompt you for a message by opening the default system text editor.

You don't have to worry too much about what you put in the *vendortag* and *releasetag* fields, as they are very rarely used in practice.

Let's look at an example. Suppose that our project is a module of an online store called "ShopCoreApi." To import this project into CVS, just run this command from the project root directory, as illustrated here:

```
$ cd ~/projects/ShopCoreApi
$ cvs import -m "New Project" ShopCoreApi vendortag start
N ShopCoreApi/pom.xml
cvs import: Importing /usr/local/cvs/ShopCoreApi/src
cvs import: Importing /usr/local/cvs/ShopCoreApi/src/main
cvs import: Importing /usr/local/cvs/ShopCoreApi/src/main/java
cvs import: Importing /usr/local/cvs/ShopCoreApi/src/main/java/com
cvs import: Importing /usr/local/cvs/ShopCoreApi/src/main/java/com/acme
cvs import: Importing /usr/local/cvs/ShopCoreApi/src/main/java/com/acme/shop
N ShopCoreApi/src/main/java/com/acme/shop/App.java
cvs import: Importing /usr/local/cvs/ShopCoreApi/src/test
cvs import: Importing /usr/local/cvs/ShopCoreApi/src/test/java
cvs import: Importing /usr/local/cvs/ShopCoreApi/src/test/java/com
cvs import: Importing /usr/local/cvs/ShopCoreApi/src/test/java/com/acme
cvs import: Importing /usr/local/cvs/ShopCoreApi/src/test/java/com/acme/shop
N ShopCoreApi/src/test/java/com/acme/shop/AppTest.java

No conflicts created by this import

$ ls /usr/local/cvs/
CVSROOT  ShopCoreApi
```

You supply an appropriate log message using the *-m* option, followed by the directory to be imported into CVS. The following two parameters are the vendor name (for example, your company) and a tag for the initial version. Once you are done, there will be a new directory in the CVS repository, called `ShopCoreApi`, containing your project files in a CVS format:

```
$ ls /usr/local/cvs/
CVSROOT  ShopCoreApi
$ ls /usr/local/cvs/ShopCoreApi/
pom.xml,v  src
```

Now your project is safely stored away in CVS. You're not quite ready to use it, though. Importing a project into CVS does not alter the original project directory, and this original directory cannot be used as a working copy. It is a good idea to back up your original directory for safe keeping, and to put it somewhere out of the way. This is to avoid confusion later on—you don't want to accidentally update the unversioned files instead of the CVS ones. On a Unix system, for example, you could do something like this:

```
$ tar cfz ShopCoreApi-backup.tgz ShopCoreApi/
$ rm -Rf ShopCoreApi
```

Then, check out a new working copy of your project. We will look at how to do this in Section 3.4.

If you need to import an existing project into the repository, things can get a bit more complicated. If you are working on a project that contains only text files, the procedure described above will work fine. However, most modern software projects require a variety of different file formats. In addition to text files, you will may come across various other binary file formats such as images and JAR files. If you need to import an existing project containing binary files, you will need to do a little extra work. We will look at techniques for dealing with binary files in Section 3.8.

3.4 Checking Out a Project

Before you can make any changes to the repository, you need to download a local copy of the project source code to your machine. This process is referred to as "checking out" the source code. To do this, run the *cvs checkout* command (or its shorter version *cvs co*). Its simplest usable form is illustrated here:

```
$ cvs checkout -R ShopCoreApi
U ShopCoreApi/pom.xml
cvs checkout: Updating ShopCoreApi/src
cvs checkout: Updating ShopCoreApi/src/main
cvs checkout: Updating ShopCoreApi/src/main/java
cvs checkout: Updating ShopCoreApi/src/main/java/com
cvs checkout: Updating ShopCoreApi/src/main/java/com/acme
cvs checkout: Updating ShopCoreApi/src/main/java/com/acme/shop
U ShopCoreApi/src/main/java/com/acme/shop/App.java
cvs checkout: Updating ShopCoreApi/src/test
```

```
cvs checkout: Updating ShopCoreApi/src/test/java
cvs checkout: Updating ShopCoreApi/src/test/java/com
cvs checkout: Updating ShopCoreApi/src/test/java/com/acme
cvs checkout: Updating ShopCoreApi/src/test/java/com/acme/shop
U ShopCoreApi/src/test/java/com/acme/shop/AppTest.java
```

For less typing, you can also use *cvs co* instead.

By default, CVS will not check out any subdirectories. If you want to check out project subdirectories, as you usually will, you need to use the *-R* option shown above.

Like the *import* command described earlier, *cvs checkout* expects you to have correctly configured the *CVSROOT* environment variable. If you are working on the same machine as the CVS repository, you can simply refer to the physical directory path, as shown here:

```
$ export CVSROOT=/usr/local/cvs/
```

You can also provide the repository location on the command line using the *-d* option:

```
$ cvs -d /usr/local/cvs checkout ShopCoreApi
cvs checkout: Updating ShopCoreApi
U ShopCoreApi/pom.xml
cvs checkout: Updating ShopCoreApi/src
cvs checkout: Updating ShopCoreApi/src/config
U ShopCoreApi/src/config/hibernate.properties
cvs checkout: Updating ShopCoreApi/src/main
cvs checkout: Updating ShopCoreApi/src/main/java
...
```

It is more likely, however, that the CVS repository will be on another machine. CVS provides several remote access methods, the most common of which is *pserver*. The *pserver* protocol provides simple password-based access to a CVS repository hosted on a remote machine:

```
$ cvs -d :pserver:john@cvs.mycompany.com:/usr/local/cvs login
```

The repository path is long but not particularly complicated. You specify the protocol (in this case, "pserver"), surrounded by colons. This is followed by a username and host name, separated by a "@" character, indicating the machine on which the CVS repository is hosted, along with a valid user account with access to the CVS repository. Finally, you need to provide the path of the CVS repository on this machine.

In this example, we ran the *login* command, which makes sure you have sufficient rights to access a repository. When accessing a remote repository, you need to run this command before running any other command. You only need to do this once. However, CVS will store your password in a file called *.cvspass* in your home directory. Once you've done this, you can run other CVS commands against this repository (using the *-d* option or the *CVSROOT* environment variable to specify the repository, of course).

Let's look at a real-world example. At the time of this writing, the source code for the JUnit project (see Chapter 10) is stored in a CVS repository hosted by SourceForge.*

Because this is an open source project, you are free to download the JUnit source code using the *pserver* protocol with an anonymous login (just press Enter for the password):

```
$ cvs -d :pserver:anonymous@junit.cvs.sourceforge.net:/cvsroot/junit login
Logging in to :pserver:anonymous@junit.cvs.sourceforge.net:2401/cvsroot/junit
CVS password:
$ cvs -d:pserver:anonymous@junit.cvs.sourceforge.net:/cvsroot/junit co -R junit
cvs checkout: Updating junit
U junit/.classpath
U junit/.cvsignore
U junit/.project
U junit/README.html
U junit/acknowledgements.txt
U junit/build.xml
...
```

This will download your very own copy of the JUnit source code into a directory called `junit`.

3.5 Working with Your Files—Updating and Committing

In this section, we will take a guided tour of CVS in everyday life—well, the everyday life of a software developer, in any case. Typically, this will involve updating a local copy of the source code from the repository, doing some work, and, in the process, making some changes to the source code. Then, you will update the repository with the said changes. Let's look at this process in more detail.

Before starting a day's work on a project, you will usually need to update your local working copy. This allows you to download any modifications that other developers have committed since the last time you talked to the CVS repository. You do this by using the *cvs update* command. This is straightforward enough, although there are a few options that you should probably use systematically. The *-R* option processes subdirectories as well as the root directory, which is a must in any modern Java project. The *-d* option tells CVS to create any missing directories, and the *-P* option removes any (presumably redundant) empty directories in the directory structure. To update your project, go to the project root directory and run the *cvs update* command with these options:

```
$ cd ~/projects/ShopCoreApi
$ cvs update -RPd
cvs update: Updating .
cvs update: Updating src
cvs update: Updating src/main
cvs update: Updating src/main/java
cvs update: Updating src/main/java/com
cvs update: Updating src/main/java/com/acme
cvs update: Updating src/main/java/com/acme/shop
U src/main/java/com/acme/shop/App.java
```

* *http://sourceforge.net/cvs/?group_id=15278*

```
cvs update: Updating src/main/resources
U src/main/resources/log4j.properties
cvs update: Updating src/test
cvs update: Updating src/test/java
cvs update: Updating src/test/java/com
cvs update: Updating src/test/java/com/acme
cvs update: Updating src/test/java/com/acme/shop
```

Any new or modified files will be indicated by a "U." In this case, the `App.java` file has been modified, and the `log4j.properties` file has been added.

Once you have an updated copy of the source code, you can proceed to get some work done. After a while, presumably once you're coded a little and tested a little, you will be ready to commit your changes to the repository. By this time, someone else also may have updated the repository. To check this, run *cvs update* again to compare the status of your files against the repository and to download any modified files:

```
$ cvs update
cvs update: Updating .
cvs update: Updating src
cvs update: Updating src/main
cvs update: Updating src/main/java
cvs update: Updating src/main/java/com
cvs update: Updating src/main/java/com/acme
cvs update: Updating src/main/java/com/acme/shop
M src/main/java/com/acme/shop/App.java
cvs update: Updating src/main/resources
U src/main/resources/applicationContext.xml
M src/main/resources/log4j.properties
? src/main/resources/messages.properties
cvs update: Updating src/test
cvs update: Updating src/test/java
cvs update: Updating src/test/java/com
cvs update: Updating src/test/java/com/acme
cvs update: Updating src/test/java/com/acme/shop
```

This gives you a quick rundown on the status of your files compared to those on the server. The "M" next to `App.java` and `applicationContext.xml` files means that you've modified these files since the last check out. The "U" next to `applicationContext.xml` means that this file has been added or modified in the repository since the last time you updated your local working copy and that CVS has updated your local copy. The question mark next to `message.properties` lets you know that this is a file that is not currently under version control, and you will need to add it to the repository. To add files to the repository, you use the *cvs add* command:

```
$ cvs add src/main/resources/messages.properties
cvs add: scheduling file 'src/main/resources/messages.properties' for addition
cvs add: use 'cvs commit' to add this file permanently
```

You can also use *cvs add* to add a new directory to your project:

```
$ mkdir src/main/resources
$ cvs add src/main/resources
Directory /usr/local/cvs/ShopCoreApi/src/main/resources added to the repository
```

When you add a directory to CVS, however, you don't need to commit your changes. This is because CVS keeps no record of directory structure changes, only of file changes. Indeed, CVS keeps track of the modifications on each individual file but has no notion of the changes made to your project directory structure over time. Naturally, this can cause a certain number of problems when refactoring code. For example, if you check out an older version of your project, CVS will give you the older versions of your files but with the latest directory structure.

If you need to delete a file or directory, you use the *cvs rm* command. Note that, by default, *cvs rm* will schedule the file for removal from the repository but will not actually delete it from your local directory; you are expected to do this yourself. If you want CVS to remove your local copy at the same time, use the *-f* option, as shown here:

```
$ cvs rm -f src/test/java/com/acme/shop/RedundantClass.java
cvs remove: scheduling 'src/main/java/com/acme/shop/RedundantClass.java' for removal
cvs remove: use 'cvs commit' to remove this file permanently
```

To remove an entire directory, you need to use the *-R* option:

```
$ cvs rm -Rf src/test/java/com/acme/shop/redundantpackage
cvs remove: scheduling 'src/main/java/com/acme/shop/redundantpackage' for removal
cvs remove: use 'cvs commit' to remove this file permanently
```

When you're ready, simply commit using the *cvs commit* command. You need to provide a short log message (either using the *-m* option, or letting CVS prompt you with the system editor):

```
$ cvs commit -m "Made some changes"
cvs commit: Examining .
cvs commit: Examining src
cvs commit: Examining src/main
cvs commit: Examining src/main/java
cvs commit: Examining src/main/java/com
cvs commit: Examining src/main/java/com/acme
cvs commit: Examining src/main/java/com/acme/shop
cvs commit: Examining src/main/resources
cvs commit: Examining src/test
cvs commit: Examining src/test/java
cvs commit: Examining src/test/java/com
cvs commit: Examining src/test/java/com/acme
cvs commit: Examining src/test/java/com/acme/shop
/usr/local/cvs/ShopCoreApi/src/main/java/com/acme/shop/App.java,v
<--  src/main/java/com/acme/shop/App.java
new revision: delete; previous revision: 1.2
/usr/local/cvs/ShopCoreApi/src/main/resources/log4j.properties,v
<--  src/main/resources/log4j.properties
new revision: 1.2; previous revision: 1.1
/usr/local/cvs/ShopCoreApi/src/main/resources/messages.properties,v
<--  src/main/resources/messages.properties
initial revision: 1.1
```

As can be seen here, CVS indicates which files have been updated, along with their new revision numbers. Whenever a file is modified in CVS, it is given a new revision number.

Indeed, CVS keeps track of each file individually. If two files have the same revision number (say, 1.2), it does not mean that these particular versions of the files are related in any way. This is as opposed to products such as Subversion (see Chapter 4), which deal in terms of change sets, in which a revision number refers to a snapshot of the whole project directory and its contents. If this concept seems a little fuzzy, don't worry; it will become clearer when you read about Subversion in Chapter 4.

During the update process, CVS updates any out-of-date files that you have in your local copy with the latest and greatest versions from the repository. CVS, like Subversion and many other open source version control system, does not prevent two developers from simultaneously modifying the same file. When the changes are made in different areas of the source code, CVS will attempt to merge the modifications. If you have made any modifications in your local copy since your last update, CVS will try to merge your version with the repository version. In most cases, CVS does a good job of integrating changes make in text files (including Java source code, XML, and so on). However, it will occasionally find some changes that it can't merge correctly. In this case, it will display an error, indicating the conflicting files with a "C":

```
$ cvs update
cvs update: Updating .
RCS file: /usr/local/cvs/ShopCoreApi/pom.xml,v
retrieving revision 1.5
retrieving revision 1.6
Merging differences between 1.5 and 1.6 into pom.xml
rcsmerge: warning: conflicts during merge
cvs update: conflicts found in pom.xml
C pom.xml
cvs update: Updating src
cvs update: Updating src/main
```

CVS indicates conflicts in the fairly visible format shown here:

```
<project xmlns="http://maven.apache.org/POM/4.0.0"
  xmlns:xsi="http://www.w3.org/2001/XMLSchema-instance"
  xsi:schemaLocation="http://maven.apache.org/POM/4.0.0
  http://maven.apache.org/maven-v4_0_0.xsd">
    .
    .
    .
    <dependency>
      <groupId>org.springframework</groupId>
      <artifactId>spring</artifactId>
<<<<<<< pom.xml
      <version>2.0.5</version>
=======
      <version>2.0.6</version>
>>>>>>> 1.6
    </dependency>
  </dependencies>
</project>
```

In this example, we have modified the pom.xml file, upgrading the Spring dependency to 2.0.5. Our own take is indicated first, between the "<<<<<<<" and the "=======." Next comes the equivalent code on the server, between the "=======" and the ">>>>>>>." Resolving conflicts simply involves manually correcting the code and recommitting. Because it is fairly trusting, CVS doesn't actually care what you do to the file as long as you change it. Then, you can commit again normally.

3.6 Resolving a Locked Repository

When you commit a file, CVS will place a lock on the file to prevent another user updating the repository at the same time. If you commit your changes at *exactly* the same time as another user, you might get a message along the following lines:

```
$ cvs commit -m "Added a log4j.properties file"
cvs commit: [04:37:15] waiting for joe's lock in /usr/local/cvs/ShopCoreApi
cvs commit: [04:37:45] waiting for joe's lock in /usr/local/cvs/ShopCoreApi
...
```

This is theoretically normal behavior, and the lock should be removed after a short time. Occasionally, however, CVS will maintain the lock when it is no longer needed. If the message persists, check with the user mentioned in the error message (Joe, in this case) to see if the user isn't currently working with CVS. If he is not, you may need to tidy up the CVS repository manually. To do this, check the directory mentioned in the error message for files whose names start with "#cvs.pfl," "#cvs.rfl," "cvs.wfl," or "#cvs.lock." If they are present, this directory will be locked by CVS:

```
$ ls /usr/local/cvs/ShopCoreApi/
#cvs.pfl.taronga.14035 #cvs.rfl.taronga.14035  pom.xml,v  src  vs,v
```

If you think that this should not be the case, just remove these files. However, if your project has any subdirectories, you will need to remove similar files from those directories, too. For example, on a Unix server, you could do something along the following lines:

```
$ find /usr/local/cvs/ -name "#cvs.*" -exec rm {} \;
```

After that, your commit should work fine.

3.7 Working with Keyword Substitution

CVS provides a feature that lets you replace certain special keyword strings with data provided by CVS. This is often used in file headers, to provide information about the current state and version of the file in CVS. For example your Java files might all start with a header comment block along the following lines:

```
/*
 * ...
 * $Author$
 * $Revision$
```

```
 * Last Modified: $Date$
 */
```

At each commit, CVS will replace these fields with the appropriate values:

```
/*
 * $Id: TaxCalculator.java 1.5 2007/10/26 23:28:42 john Exp $
 * $Author: john$
 * $Revision: 1.5$
 * Last Modified: $Date: 2007/10/26 23:28:42$
 */
```

There are other keywords as well. The "*Id*" keyword wraps up all of this information into one line:

```
/*
 * $Id: TaxCalculator.java 1.5 2007/10/26 23:28:42 john Exp $
 */
```

Other common keywords are *$Source$*, which indicates the path to the file in the version control system, and *Log*, which lists the changes made to the file. The *Log* keyword is a good one to avoid, as it bloats your source code files with information that can easily be obtained directly from CVS, and can cause unnecessary conflicts during file merges.

Keyword substitution is frowned on in some other version control systems, for example, in Subversion. This is mainly because it duplicates information by placing data that should normally be the responsibility of the version control system in the source code files. Occasionally, however, there are valid reasons to do it. If necessary, you can configure Subversion to perform keyword substitution, in particular with the *Id* keyword. If you are considering a migration to Subversion and use keyword substitution for some mission-critical purpose, the *Id* keyword may be worth a look.

Keyword substitution is not a good idea with binary files, as it will almost certainly corrupt the binary files. We will look at how to deal with this issue in the next section.

3.8 Working with Binary Files

Traditionally, CVS handles binary file formats quite poorly. By default, it will assume that all of your files are text files. As a result, it will try to perform text operations on these files, such as keyword substitution and merging, which inevitably will corrupt your binary file. To avoid this, you need to tell CVS explicitly which of your files are binary.

When you add a binary file to an existing project, you can use the *-kb* option, as shown here:

```
$ cvs add -kb src/main/webapp/images/logo.png
cvs add: scheduling file 'src/main/webapp/images/logo.png' for addition
```

However, this is not a particularly practical solution, as you need to remember to do this individually for each binary file. In addition, the *cvs import* command does not provide this option. A more convenient approach is to use the "cvswrappers" file. This is a special file that lets you tell CVS which options to use for particular file types, based on their extensions.

The "cvswrappers" file lives under the CVSROOT project in the CVS repository. To modify this file, you first need to check it out using a standard *cvs checkout* command:

```
$ mkdir cvsroot
$ cd cvsroot
$ cvs co CVSROOT
cvs checkout: Updating CVSROOT
U CVSROOT/checkoutlist
U CVSROOT/commitinfo
U CVSROOT/config
U CVSROOT/cvswrappers
U CVSROOT/loginfo
U CVSROOT/modules
U CVSROOT/notify
U CVSROOT/postadmin
U CVSROOT/postproxy
U CVSROOT/posttag
U CVSROOT/postwatch
U CVSROOT/preproxy
U CVSROOT/rcsinfo
U CVSROOT/taginfo
U CVSROOT/verifymsg
```

Now edit the "cvswrappers" file with your favorite text editor. The file is a list of one-line entries. Each entry indicates how a particular file format should be handled in terms of keywork substitution and file merges. For binary files, the lines look something like this:

```
*.gif   -k 'b' -m 'COPY'
```

This tells CVS to treat all GIF files as binary files, with no keyword substitution and no file merging (the *-k* option refers to keyword substitution, and the *-m* option tells CVS to create a new copy of the file for each new version, rather than attempting to merge the new file with the previous one). A more complete example of this file is shown here:

```
# This file affects handling of files based on their names.
#
# The -m option specifies whether CVS attempts to merge files.
#
# The -k option specifies keyword expansion (e.g. -kb for binary).
#
# Format of wrapper file ($CVSROOT/CVSROOT/cvswrappers or .cvswrappers)
#
#  wildcard    [option value][option value]...
#
#  where option is one of
#  -f        from cvs filter        value: path to filter
#  -t        to cvs filter          value: path to filter
```

```
#  -m        update methodology      value: MERGE or COPY
#  -k        expansion mode          value: b, o, kkv, &c
#
#  and value is a single-quote delimited value.
# For example:
#*.gif -k 'b'
*.avi   -k 'b' -m 'COPY'
*.bin   -k 'b' -m 'COPY'
*.bz    -k 'b' -m 'COPY'
*.bz2   -k 'b' -m 'COPY'
*.class   -k 'b' -m 'COPY'
*.doc   -k 'b' -m 'COPY'
*.ear   -k 'b' -m 'COPY'
*.exe   -k 'b' -m 'COPY'
*.gif   -k 'b' -m 'COPY'
*.gz    -k 'b' -m 'COPY'
*.hqx   -k 'b' -m 'COPY'
*.jar   -k 'b' -m 'COPY'
*.jpeg  -k 'b' -m 'COPY'
*.jpg   -k 'b' -m 'COPY'
*.mov   -k 'b' -m 'COPY'
*.mp3   -k 'b' -m 'COPY'
*.mpg   -k 'b' -m 'COPY'
*.pdf   -k 'b' -m 'COPY'
*.png   -k 'b' -m 'COPY'
*.ppt   -k 'b' -m 'COPY'
*.rpm   -k 'b' -m 'COPY'
*.sit   -k 'b' -m 'COPY'
*.srpm  -k 'b' -m 'COPY'
*.swf   -k 'b' -m 'COPY'
*.tar   -k 'b' -m 'COPY'
*.tbz   -k 'b' -m 'COPY'
*.tgz   -k 'b' -m 'COPY'
*.tif   -k 'b' -m 'COPY'
*.tiff  -k 'b' -m 'COPY'
*.war   -k 'b' -m 'COPY'
*.xbm   -k 'b' -m 'COPY'
*.xls   -k 'b' -m 'COPY'
*.zip   -k 'b' -m 'COPY'
```

Once you have added a line for every file type you need to handle, just commit your changes as you would any other CVS changes:

```
$ cvs commit -m "Updated cvswrappers to handle binary file types"
cvs commit: Examining .
/usr/local/cvs/CVSROOT/cvswrappers,v  <--  cvswrappers
new revision: 1.2; previous revision: 1.1
cvs commit: Rebuilding administrative file database
```

Now any binary files of the types listed in the "cvswrapper" file automatically will be correctly treated as binary files.

3.9 Tags in CVS

One of the core features of a version control system is to identify particular versions of your application. You may want to identify a particular test or public release, or an end-of-iteration milestone, or you may want to identify nightly builds. This allows you to return to a known stable version at any time, and it makes it easier to reproduce and fix bugs found in a particular release.

In CVS, you use tags to identify a particular version of your application. You do this by running the *cvs tag* command. The following command, for example, will mark the files in the current working copy as "milestone-iteration-1":

```
$ cvs tag milestone-iteration-1
cvs tag: Tagging .
T pom.xml
cvs tag: Tagging src
cvs tag: Tagging src/main
cvs tag: Tagging src/main/java
cvs tag: Tagging src/main/java/com
cvs tag: Tagging src/main/java/com/acme
cvs tag: Tagging src/main/java/com/acme/shop
cvs tag: Tagging src/main/resources
T src/main/resources/applicationContext.xml
T src/main/resources/log4j.properties
T src/main/resources/messages.properties
cvs tag: Tagging src/test
cvs tag: Tagging src/test/java
cvs tag: Tagging src/test/java/com
cvs tag: Tagging src/test/java/com/acme
cvs tag: Tagging src/test/java/com/acme/shop
T src/test/java/com/acme/shop/AppTest.java
```

Note that the version that you are tagging here is the version currently in your working directory. This gives you a better control over what version you are actually tagging. If any files have been updated in the repository since you last updated your local copy, they won't be included in the version that you tag.

The syntax for tag labels is fairly strict. Basically, you are not allowed to have spaces, periods, colons, commas, or any other punctuation, with the exception of hyphens ("-") and underlines ("_"). One reason for this is to avoid confusion with revision numbers.

Another common use of tagging is to "promote" a version, putting a special label on a particular version. For example, after user acceptance testing, you might decide to label a particular release candidate as the official production release. You can do this by using the *-r* option to refer to the version that you wish to tag:

```
$ cvs tag -r version-1-0-release-candidate-3 production-release-1-0
```

Tags are applied individually to each file in your project, so the process can be *extremely* time-consuming for larger projects. I have seen builds take hours because of the tagging involved. Unfortunately, there's not a lot you can do about this, other than to make sure that your disks are fast.

3.10 Creating Branches in CVS

Branches are an important part of any version control system. In CVS, the main stream of development work is known as the *trunk*. By default, any changes that you make to the source code will go here. However, developers can create *branches*, where development is carried out in parallel. This is illustrated in Figure 3-1. Typical uses of branches include freezing a production release in one branch while the development team continues to work on the next release in a separate branch. Whenever a production release is made, a new branch is created at this point. If a bug is found in the production release, it can be identified and fixed and a new, stable production version can be released, without interfering with or being affected by the work on the unstable development version.

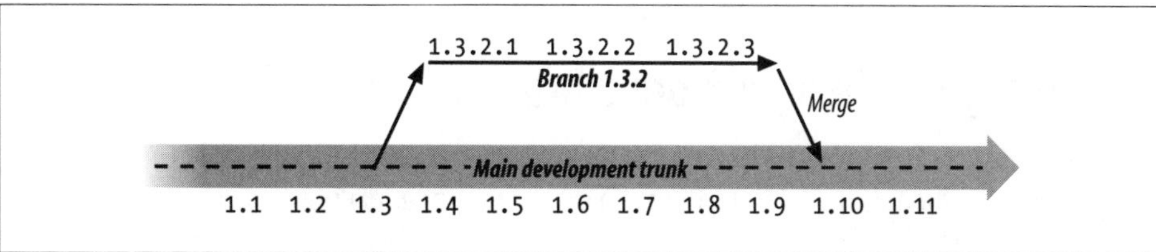

Figure 3-1. Branching in CVS

Branches are an integral part of the CVS architecture, and they are closely related to tagging (see Section 3.9). It is relatively straightforward to create new branches and to merge changes made in one branch into another. To create a new branch from the current working copy, you simply run the *cvs tag* command using the *-b* option:

```
$ cvs tag -b production-release-1-0-patches
```

It is also a good habit to tag the main trunk when you create a branch. This makes it easier to keep tabs on when branches were made just by looking at the main trunk.

From now on, you will be working on the "production-release-1-0-patches" branch, and your changes will not affect anyone who is not working on this branch. Until further notice, all of your commits will go to this branch.

Suppose that another developer needs to work on this branch. There are two ways to do this. You can either check out an entirely new working copy for this branch, or you can switch your current working copy to this branch.

Checking out a new working copy of the branch in a new directory is a good approach if you need to work on several branches at the same time. For example, you might need to fix bugs in a production release while continuing work on the next version on a separate branch. To do this, you run *cvs checkout* in a new directory, specifying the branch you want with the *-t* option:

```
$ mkdir production-release-branch
$ cd production-release-branch
$ cvs co -r production-release-1-0-patches ShopCoreApi
```

This approach also makes it easier later, when you need to merge the modifications made in your new branch into the main development trunk.

If the switch is a long-term change, you might prefer to switch your main working directory to the new branch. You can do this by using the *cvs update* command with the *-r* option:

```
$cvs update -r production-release-1-0-patches
```

This approach is not as tidy as the first one. One disadvantage of updating your current working directory is that if you have any uncommitted changes, CVS will try to merge your code with the branched release, possibly causing conflicts. In any case, it might not correctly reflect the contents of the repository version.

3.11 Merging Changes from a Branch

Suppose that you have fixed a bug in the production release branch, and you now want to incorporate this fix in the main trunk. You do this by *merging* your corrections back into the main trunk. CVS basically works out what has been modified in your branch since it left the trunk, and applies these changes to the most recent revision in the main trunk.

You can do this by updating your main trunk using the *-j* (for "join") option. You need an up-to-date working copy of the main development trunk. If you don't have one on hand, you will need to check out a copy into a new directory. Otherwise, you simply go to your main trunk directory and run *cvs update* to make sure that you have the latest version:

```
$ cd ../main_trunk/ShopCoreApi
$ cvs update
```

Once you have an updated working copy of the main development trunk, you need to run the *cvs update* command again, this time with the *-j* option. Specify the name of the branch that you want to integrate into the trunk, as shown here:

```
$ cvs update -j production-release-1-0-patches
cvs update: Updating ShopCoreApi
RCS file: /usr/local/cvs/ShopCoreApi/pom.xml,
retrieving revision 1.7
retrieving revision 1.7.2.3
Merging differences between 1.7 and 1.7.2.3 into pom.xml
cvs update: Updating ShopCoreApi/src
cvs update: Updating ShopCoreApi/src/main
```

```
cvs update: Updating ShopCoreApi/src/main/java
...
```

When you merge, you should also tag this point in the main trunk as well. This makes it easier to merge further modifications made in your branch in the future. For example, suppose we tag our branch at the point of the merge with a significantly named tag, like "production-release-1-0-patch-1-0," as shown here:

```
$ cd ../../production-release-branch
$ cvs tag production-release-1-0-patch-1-0
```

Then we continue to work on the production release 1.0 branch, applying the occasional bug fix. The next time that we want to integrate our changes, we only need the changes that have been made since the last merge. You can indicate that you are only interested in the changes that occured from a particular point onward by providing an additional *-j* parameter. The first *-j* parameter indicates the point from which the changes are to start and the second indicates the branch:

```
$ cd ../main_trunk/ShopCoreApi
$ cvs update -j production-release-1-0-patch-1-0 -j production-release-1-0-patches
```

3.12 Viewing Change History

It often can be useful to know what changes a file, or a project, has undergone over time. The *cvs log* command lets you review the log messages (which of course everyone has diligently completed) for a particular file or directory, along with useful information such as who made the modifications, when they were made, and so on. For example, we could inspect the changes made to the `log4j.properties` file as follows:

```
$ cvs log src/main/resources/log4j.properties
RCS file: /usr/local/cvs/ShopCoreApi/src/main/resources/log4j.properties,v
Working file: src/main/resources/log4j.properties
head: 1.2
branch:
locks: strict
access list:
symbolic names:
keyword substitution: kv
total revisions: 2;     selected revisions: 2
description:
----------------------------
revision 1.2
date: 2007-07-09 00:35:02 +1200;  author: wakaleo;  state: Exp;  lines: +4 -0;
commitid: BQCkVlCIqlpjKXos;
Made some changes
----------------------------
revision 1.1
date: 2007-07-08 23:19:41 +1200;  author: wakaleo;  state: Exp;
commitid: i5z7fsQ3cUMskXos;
Minor modifications
=============================================================================
```

There is a lot of information here, most of which you can safely skip over. The most useful information is contained between the lines of dashes at the end of the file.

You also can do the same operation on a directory, as shown here for the whole Java source code directory:

```
$ cvs log src/main/java
cvs log: Logging src/main/java
cvs log: Logging src/main/java/com
cvs log: Logging src/main/java/com/acme
cvs log: Logging src/main/java/com/acme/shop

RCS file: /usr/local/cvs/ShopCoreApi/src/main/java/com/acme/shop/Attic/App.java,v
Working file: src/main/java/com/acme/shop/App.java
head: 1.3
branch:
locks: strict
access list:
symbolic names:
        start: 1.1.1.1
        vendortag: 1.1.1
keyword substitution: kv
total revisions: 4;     selected revisions: 4
description:
----------------------------
revision 1.3
date: 2007-07-09 00:35:02 +1200;  author: wakaleo;  state: dead;  lines: +0 -0;
commitid: BQCkVlCIqlpjKXos;
Made some changes
----------------------------
revision 1.2
date: 2007-07-08 23:19:10 +1200;  author: wakaleo;  state: Exp;  lines: +0 -1;
commitid: 6mKyqOemuQLhkXos;
Minor modifications
----------------------------
revision 1.1
date: 2007-07-08 23:17:01 +1200;  author: wakaleo;  state: Exp;
commitid: 5lpTqvi8JXQxjXos;
branches:  1.1.1;
Initial revision
----------------------------
revision 1.1.1.1
date: 2007-07-08 23:17:01 +1200;  author: wakaleo;  state: Exp;  lines: +0 -0;
commitid: 5lpTqvi8JXQxjXos;
New Project
=============================================================================
```

On a real project, however, this may be a bit overwhelming. You might want to narrow things down a little, for example, by defining a particular revision or a range of dates. You can do this using the *-r* and *-d* options, respectively. In the best Unix tradition, these options are rich, powerful, and flexible, so I will just provide a few examples here:

- Show the log messages for the changes made to the `src/main/java` directory on July 10:

```
$ cvs log -d '10 July 2007' src/main/java
```

- Show the changes made to the `src/main/java` directory between July 1 and 15:

```
$ cvs log -d '01-jul<15-jul' src/main/java
```

- Show log messages for the changes made to the `src/main/java` directory since December 31, 2006 inclusive (note the "<"):

```
$ cvs log -d '2006-12-31<' src/main/java
```

- Show log messages for the changes made to the `src/main/java` directory over the last month:

```
$ cvs log -d 'last month<' src/main/java
```

- Show the changes made in revision 1.2 of the log4j.properties file:

```
$ cvs log -r 1.2 src/main/resources/log4j.properties
```

Another useful command is *cvs annotate*, which provides a detailed view of the modifications made to a particular file, including who last modified each line of the file and when she made the modification. The following is a real-world example taken from the build script of the JUnit project:

```
$ cvs annotate junit/build.xml

Annotations for junit/build.xml
***************
1.1          (egamma   09-Jan-01): <project name="junit" default="dist" basedir=".">
1.26         (dsaff    22-Mar-07):       <tstamp />
1.29         (dsaff    02-Jul-07):
1.8          (emeade   06-Feb-02):       <property file=
                                          "${user.home}/.junit.properties" />
1.19         (dsaff    21-Nov-06):       <property name="src" value="src" />
1.19         (dsaff    21-Nov-06):       <property name="bin" value="bin" />
1.26         (dsaff    22-Mar-07):       <property name="version"
                                          value="4.4-snapshot-${DSTAMP}-${TSTAMP}" />
1.7          (emeade   06-Feb-02):       <property name="dist"
                                          value="junit${version}" />
...
```

3.13 Reverting Changes

In the previous section, we saw how to examine the change history for a file or directory. But what happens if you realize that a change wasn't what you wanted? Once you realize that you have committed an incorrect version of a file, it is fairly easy to revert to a previous version. Let's look at a concrete example. Suppose that you have just committed a new version of the messages.properties file, as shown here:

```
$ cvs commit -m "Added an important message"
cvs commit: Examining .
cvs commit: Examining src
...
/usr/local/cvs/ShopCoreApi/src/main/resources/messages.properties,v  <--
```

```
src/main/resources/messages.properties
new revision: 1.5; previous revision: 1.4
```

However, you have a doubt—was this the right version? You can use the *cvs diff* command to check exactly what changes were made in your last commit as shown here (the *-c* option gives a slightly more readable output):

```
$ cvs diff -c -r 1.4 -r 1.5 src/main/resources/messages.properties
Index: src/main/resources/messages.properties
===================================================================
RCS file: /usr/local/cvs/ShopCoreApi/src/main/resources/messages.properties,v
retrieving revision 1.4
retrieving revision 1.5
diff -c -r1.4 -r1.5
*** src/main/resources/messages.properties      10 Jul 2007 12:36:14 -0000      1.4
--- src/main/resources/messages.properties      10 Jul 2007 12:36:37 -0000      1.5
***************
*** 1,6 ****
  # Messages
- hello.world=Hello, World!
  my.message=Welcome to our online shop
  shopping.cart=Shopping Cart


--- 1,6 ----
  # Messages
  my.message=Welcome to our online shop
+ my.new.message=Utter rubbish!
  shopping.cart=Shopping Cart
```

The *cvs diff* command arguably is not the most readable way to compare to files—and generally you are better off using a graphical tool such as the CVS plug-in for Eclipse—but it will do in a pinch. CVS is telling us that we have removed the `hello.world` message and added a new message (`my.new.message`), which is, apparently, utter rubbish. So, not wanting this to appear in today's production release, we need to revert to the previous revision.

Now, strictly speaking, we aren't reverting to revision 1.4. Much as we would like to erase all traces of our errors, a version control system is designed to keep track of versions, not delete them. So, we will actually be creating a new revision, revision number 1.6, which will be identical to revision 1.4.

Enough theory; let's see how to do it. The easiest way to revert is use the *cvs update* command, using the *-j* option. The *-j* stands for "join," and tells CVS that you want to merge a particular revision, either with the current version or, as here, with some other revision in the repository. The command in this case is shown here:

```
$ cvs update -j 1.5 -j 1.4 src/main/resources/messages.properties
RCS file: /usr/local/cvs/ShopCoreApi/src/main/resources/messages.properties,v
retrieving revision 1.5
retrieving revision 1.4
Merging differences between 1.5 and 1.4 into messages.properties
```

When you use two *-j* options in the same command, you are telling CVS to apply the difference between the first and second revisions to your current copy. Order is important, so, in this case, the difference effectively takes you back to the previous version, which is what we want.

Now you have your original version back again. Once you've checked that everything is as you want it, commit this reverted version to the repository using a standard *cvs commit* command:

```
$ cvs commit -m "Reverted to previous version"
cvs commit: Examining .
cvs commit: Examining src
cvs commit: Examining src/main
cvs commit: Examining src/main/java
cvs commit: Examining src/main/java/com
cvs commit: Examining src/main/java/com/acme
cvs commit: Examining src/main/java/com/acme/shop
cvs commit: Examining src/main/resources
cvs commit: Examining src/test
cvs commit: Examining src/test/java
cvs commit: Examining src/test/java/com
cvs commit: Examining src/test/java/com/acme
cvs commit: Examining src/test/java/com/acme/shop
/usr/local/cvs/ShopCoreApi/src/main/resources/messages.properties,v  <--
src/main/resources/messages.properties
new revision: 1.6; previous revision: 1.5
```

Now the new revision 1.6 contains a copy of the old revision 1.4.

3.14 Using CVS in Windows

There are several graphical clients that you can use to manage CVS in Windows. Probably the best of these is TortoiseCVS,* a graphical CVS client that integrates smoothly into Windows Explorer. TortoiseCVS comes bundled with a CVS client, so users don't need to install the CVS tool manually. Using TortoiseCVS, you can do pretty much everything you normally would do from the command line, but via a nice graphical interface. This includes checkout modules, updating folders, and committing changes, as well as more sophisticated operations such as tagging, branching, merging, and viewing the CVS logfiles (see Figure 3-2).

* *http://www.tortoisecvs.org*

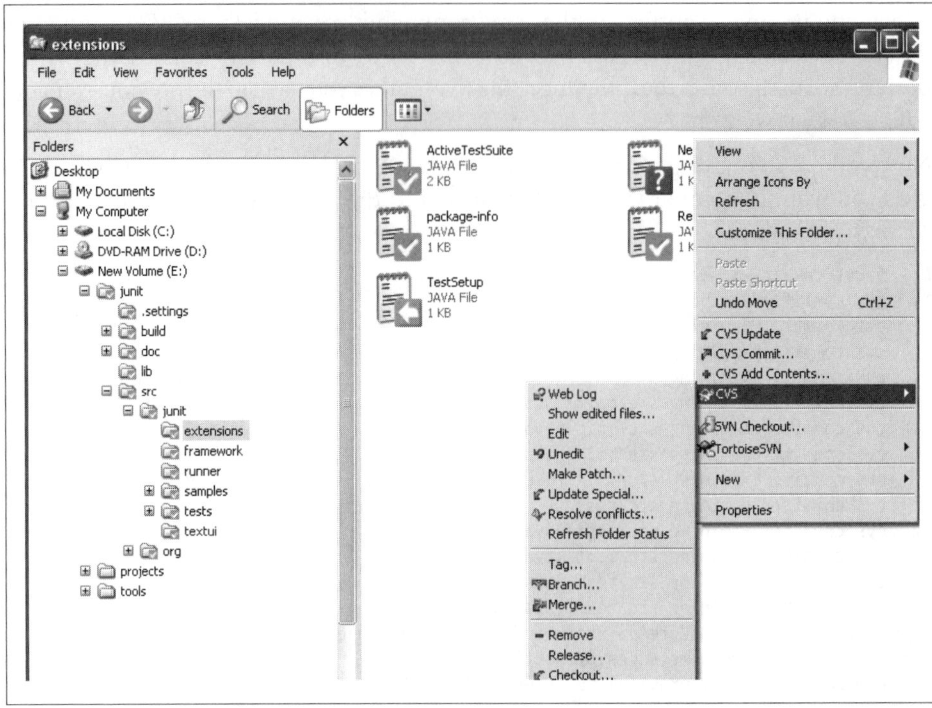

Figure 3-2. TortoiseCVS in action

CHAPTER 4

Setting Up Version Control Using Subversion

4.1 An Introduction to Subversion

When it comes to version control tools, you will often be stuck with whatever happens to be in use in your organization, be it an open source solution like CVS (see Chapter 3) or one of the many commercial products. However, if you are free to choose your open source version control system (or SCM), Subversion is probably one of the best choices around.

Subversion (pronounced "Sub-Version," for those who are interested in such details) is a relatively new product explicitly designed to overcome the historical shortfalls of CVS (see Chapter 3) and become the new standard in open source version control tools.* It is a superbly engineered piece of software, actively developed and maintained by paid staff from CollabNet. Although it does have a very CVS-ish feel to it, its underlying architecture is quite different, and it has a number of major improvements compared to its venerable predecessor.

In this section, we will run through some of the key improvements of Subversion when compared to CVS, and, in doing so, gain some insight into the Subversion architecture and philosophy.

Revision Numbers and Atomic Updates

Perhaps one of the most profound changes between CVS and Subversion is the way each system keeps track of changes.

CVS keeps track of individual file versions. In CVS, when you commit a set of changes, each modified file is updated separately. Tags can be used to identify a snapshot of the

* Version Control tools such as Subversion, CVS, ClearCase, and so forth are often referred to as SCM (Software Configuration Management) tools. Strictly speaking, most of these tools are actually Version Control tools. Configuration Management is a broader topic, including defect and change control and tracking, traceability, and so on.

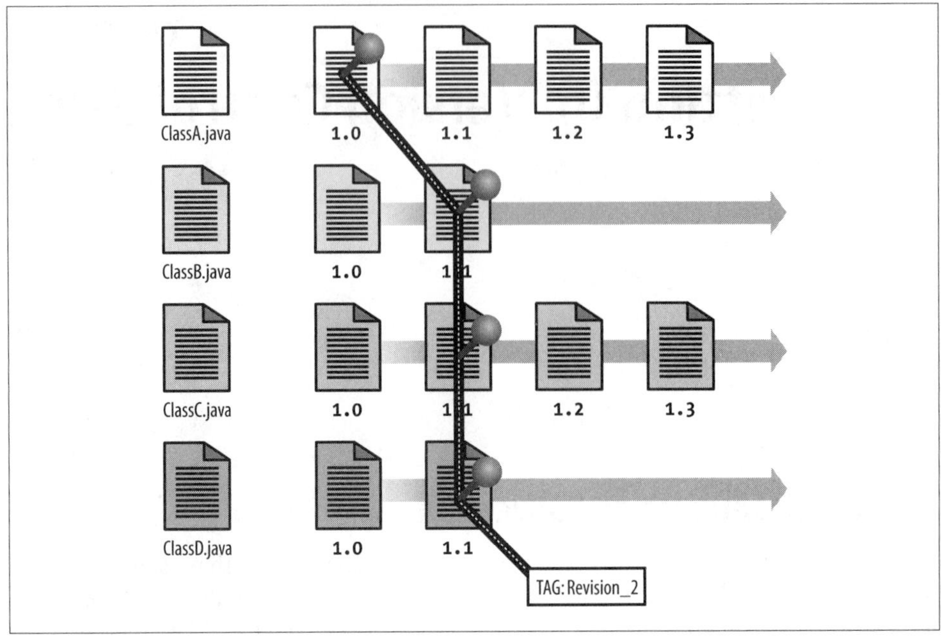

Figure 4-1. File versioning with CVS

repository at a particular point in time. This is illustrated in Figure 4-1. Here we have a set of four Java classes. When the developer adds these files to CVS, each will be attributed a version number (1.0). Now our developer makes some modifications to `ClassB`, `ClassC` and `ClassD`, and commits these changes to CVS. Each of these files will be updated on the server and assigned a new version number: 1.1. Our developer may now be so happy with this version that she adds a tag called (imaginatively) "Revision_2." Each file will be "tagged" with this label, making it easier to fetch from the repository at a later date or from another machine.

Now that we can visualize how CVS does things, let's look at one of the major weaknesses of this architecture. Suppose during a commit that someone else starts committing changes at the same time and a conflict occurs. In this case, some of the files will have been updated, but others will have been refused, which leaves the repository in an unstable state. If you kill the process, switch off your machine, or a street worker drills through your Internet connection, similar nasty things can occur. The CVS repository can be left in an unstable state until the street worker in question repairs the cable and lets you resolve any conflicts and complete your commit operation.

Subversion, by contrast, keeps track of *revisions*. A revision (or, more precisely, a revision tree) is a representation of the repository structure and contents at a given point in time. Revisions are the cornerstone of a powerful Subversion feature: *atomic updates*. Updating the Subversion repository is a bit like updating a relational database using transactions: when you commit a set of changes, you are guaranteed that either all of your changes have been integrated into the repository, or none at all have.

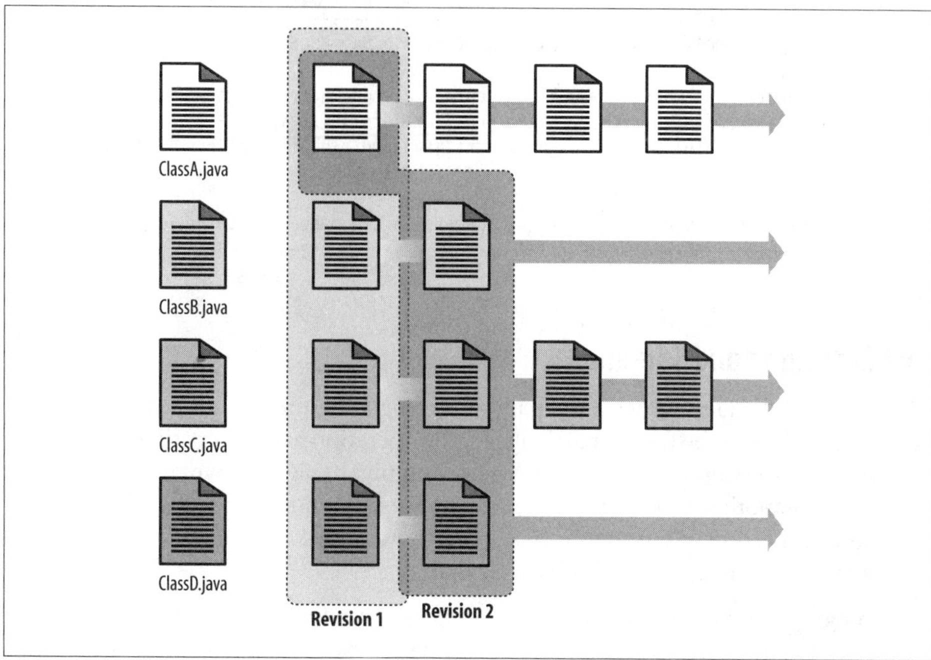

Figure 4-2. Subversion revisions

Behind the scenes, Subversion stores successive representations of the entire repository structure as a whole (see Figure 4-2). Each revision is identified by a unique number. When changes are committed, Subversion prepares a new repository structure incorporating the changes. If (and only if) every change is successfully integrated, a new repository tree will be created with a new revision number. So, in practice, either all of your changes are updated correctly in the repository, and you get a new revision number incorporating these changes, or none are, and you get to fix the problem and try again. An offshoot of this strategy is that a given set of changes can be viewed as a distinct bundle. This notion is frequent among commercial SCM solutions but painfully absent from CVS.

In CVS, you can (and should) provide a message indicating the type of modification that you have made. You might put, for example, "Fixed bug number 123" or "Added support for the XYWZ file type." This is all well and good, but you have no easy way of working out exactly which files were modified by this change, as the message is attached to each individual file.

Not so in Subversion. In Subversion, when you commit a set of changes, these changes are recorded for posterity as a single transaction, including (hopefully) an appropriate comment describing what they were for. The Subversion log function makes it easy to get a summary of the changes made in a particular revision, and why they were made, as shown here:

```
$ svn log -vr 5
------------------------------------------------------------------------
r5 | taronga | 2006-05-19 13:42:04 +1200 (Fri, 19 May 2006) | 1 line
Changed paths:
   M /trunk/src/main/java/com/wakaleo/jdpt/javalamp/CIServerPlugin.java
   M /trunk/src/main/java/com/wakaleo/jdpt/javalamp/JavaLamp.java
   M /trunk/src/main/java/com/wakaleo/jdpt/javalamp/plugins/ContinuumPlugin.java


New feature added: project status now appears in the menu for Continuum projects.
------------------------------------------------------------------------
```

Fast Branching and Tagging

CVS users will be familiar with the pain of tagging a big project under CVS. Because every single file must be individually tagged, the operation can be very time-consuming indeed. In Subversion, tagging a new version simply involves copying the current repository into another directory on the server. Subversion does not actually copy the whole directory content but simply makes a reference to the original version of the data. This is extremely fast, and takes very little disk space.

Branching is another important function in any version control system (see Section 4.12). In Subversion, creating a new branch uses exactly the same technique: when you create a new branch, Subversion simply copies the current repository into a special directory.

Lightweight Network Transactions

Subversion provides excellent network performance, even when dealing with large binary files. Subversion stores a local copy of the original repository files, and transmits only the difference between the original repository revision and the local changes. So, in Subversion, the quantity of data sent over the network is proportional to the size of your modifications, not to the size of your files.

This local copy also allows many operations, such as status, diff, and revert, to be done without accessing the server at all.

Handling Binary Files

CVS handles binary files very poorly. Not only are they sent over the network in their totality at each update, but each version is stored on the server in its complete form. This alone is enough to put you off storing big Word documents on a CVS server! Subversion, by contrast, was designed from the ground up to treat binary files with the same efficiency as text. Indeed, in Subversion, all files are internally stored as binary files, and only the binary differences between revisions are actually stored on the server. Subversion only distinguishes between binary and text files to avoid trying to merge binary files (see "Forcing the File Type with svn:mime-type" in Section 4.17).

4.2 Installing Subversion

With a bit of luck, you will be able to use a binary installation package adapted to your platform to install Subversion. This is the case with Windows, and also with many distributions of Linux. For Windows, you can download graphical installer packages for both Subversion and the Subversion Python bindings. You will need the Python bindings if you intend to install Trac (see Chapter 28) as well. Finally, if you intend to run Subversion with Apache on a Windows server, make sure that you use the installer package built against the version of Apache (2.0 or 2.2) that you are using.

For many distributions of Linux, there are prebundled installation packages available. On Ubuntu, for example, installing Subversion is as simple as running *apt-get install* with the appropriate packages:

```
$ sudo apt-get install subversion libapache2-svn
```

In some cases, you may need to build and install Subversion yourself. For example, if you want to install Trac on a Linux server, you might need to build Subversion with the correct Python bindings, or you may want to build and install the Apache modules so that you can use Subversion through your Apache server. Be warned that building Subversion from the source code is not always a simple task. The dependencies and configuration options are numerous and complex, and you can find detailed instructions regarding how to do this regarding the Subversion web site.* For example, the following listing gives some idea of the steps involved in installing Subversion 1.4.5 on a typical Linux box, with the Apache configuration and Python bindings configured correctly:

```
$ wget http://subversion.tigris.org/downloads/subversion-1.4.5.tar.gz
$ tar xvfz subversion-1.4.5.tar.gz
$ cd subversion-1.4.5
$ ./configure --prefix=/usr/local --enable-so --enable-rewrite \
  --with-susexec --enable-mods-shared=all  --with-apr=/usr/local/apache2 \
  --with-apr-util=/usr/local/apache2 --with-swig
$ make
$ make swig-py
$ sudo make install
$ sudo make install-swig-py
```

4.3 Subversion Repository Types

When you set up a new Subversion project, the first thing you need to decide is where to store the source code repository, and in what form.

* *http://svn.collab.net/repos/svn/trunk/INSTALL*

In fact, Subversion users have the choice of two quite different storage systems for their repositories: either in a Berkeley DB database, or as a set of flat files. The latter is known in Subversion circles as FSFS* because it is effectively a filesystem built on the native filesystem.

For the history buffs, this is how this choice came about. In the beginning, Subversion used the Berkeley DB database engine. Berkeley DB is a nice fast, robust, fully transactional open source database designed to be embedded within an application (that is, there is no separate Berkeley DB database to maintain and administer). For many years, all Subversion repositories were based on a Berkeley DB database.

The Berkeley DB solution does have a few problems, however.

First, it has some major portability and architectural issues. A Berkeley DB database is absolutely not portable from one OS to another: you can't simply duplicate a Subversion repository created under Linux and have it work under Windows, as you could do with CVS, for instance. Also, according to the Subversion authors, Berkeley DB database repositories don't work well on a shared network drive, and don't work at all under Windows 95/98. (OK, I've never heard of anyone nowadays setting up an SCM server on a Windows 95 box, but I thought you should know. Anyway...)

Second, it may get into trouble if the client suddenly crashes or is brutally cut off. If this happens, the Berkeley DB may end up stuck in an unstable and inaccessible state, and will have to be restored by a system administrator.

To get around these problems, the Subversion team released a new storage system in 2004, one based entirely on a flat file structure, and known as FSFS. In an FSFS repository, each revision tree (see "An Introduction to Subversion," earlier in this section) is stored in a single file, in a special directory dedicated to this purpose. All the revisions are stored in this directory, as shown here:

```
$ ls -al /data/svn/training/db/revs/
total 172
drwxr-sr-x  2 taronga users   4096 2006-04-29 12:27 .
drwxr-sr-x  5 taronga users   4096 2006-04-29 12:27 ..
-rw-r--r--  1 taronga users    115 2006-04-25 10:46 0
-rw-r--r--  1 taronga users 103967 2006-04-25 10:50 1
-rw-r--r--  1 taronga users  29881 2006-04-29 10:25 2
-rw-r--r--  1 taronga users  10344 2006-04-29 11:11 3
-rw-r--r--  1 taronga users   4827 2006-04-29 12:27 4
```

One interesting thing about this directory listing is that the files keep getting smaller. "Aha!" I hear astute readers say, "Subversion must use some cunning incremental storage strategy!" Indeed it does. Subversion updates are highly optimized both in terms of disk space (only the modifications are stored, and in compressed form at that), and in terms of time and network load (the less data you transfer, the less time it takes).

* Pronounced "Fuzz-Fuzz," according to people who should know.

Another interesting thing that Unix-literate readers will immediately note is that all the revision files are read-only, safe from anyone except a root administrator gone mad. Or a very clever hacker. Pretty safe, in any case. This can give some insight into Subversion's transactional updating strategy: as we mentioned earlier, a revision contains the entire state of the project at a given point in time. When new files are added, or existing files are deleted, or the project source code is modified in some way, the existing revisions are never modified. Instead, an entirely new directory structure is built in a temporary directory, using the most recent revision plus the proposed changes. Once all the changes are committed, and if (and only if) no conflicts occurred, a new revision file is built using the delta between the previous revision and the new directory structure. This is Subversion's way of guaranteeing atomic updates: either every modification you submit gets included in a new revision, or none do.

Another advantage of FSFS over Berkeley DB is that a user who simply requires read-only access to your repository-only has to have read access to the repository directory and files. If a Berkeley DB repository is used, *all* clients need physical read-write access to the repository. The security implications of this are quite major: with an FSFS repository, you can confidently provide anonymous access to your repository (see "Setting up a Subversion Server with svnserve" in Section 4.19) with no risk to your repository files.

Because FSFS files are just ordinary files, you can store them anywhere you like. You can also transfer them from one operating system to another without modification, and shared network drives do not bother FSFS in the slightest. And it is also reportedly much more resilient to client interruptions or disconnections.

FSFS repositories are now the default option when creating new repositories in Subversion, and should be the preferred option for any new work.

4.4 Setting Up a Subversion Repository

Creating a Subversion repository is easy. All you need to do is use the *svnadmin create* command:

```
$ svnadmin create /path/to/repos
```

By default, this will set up an FSFS repository (see Section 4.3) at the specified location. If you really need to, you can use the *--fs-type* option to specify a Berkeley Database backend:

```
$ svnadmin create --fs-type bdb /path/to/repos
```

To give a concrete example, here is how I set up the repository for development projects (called, appropriately enough, "*dev-repos*") on my home machine, in a dedicated directory called `/data/svn`:

```
$ svnadmin create /data/svn/dev-repos
```

Note that there is nothing fancy about the repository path: it's just a plain old OS-dependent file path. On a Windows server, you would do something like this (note the backslashes):

```
C:\> svnadmin create C:\data\svn\dev-repos
```

You do need to be on the server where your repository is to be stored since it won't work across a network connection.

You rarely have to delve into the details of the repository file structure. One exception is if you need to install some hook scripts, which are scripts triggered by certain repository events, such as creating a new revision. Nevertheless, it can be useful to know a little about how the repository directory is structured. The standard repository structure looks like this:

```
$ ls  /data/svn/dev-repos/
conf/  dav/  db/  format  hooks/  locks/  README.txt
```

Each directory serves a specific purpose:

conf
: This directory contains repository configuration files, such as the configuration files for svnserve (see Section 4.19), Subversion's custom repository server program.

dav
: This directory is reserved for use by Apache and mod_dav_svn, the Apache module which provides access to the repository using the WebDAV/DeltaV protocol.

db
: This directory is the real McCoy, the genuine article, the place where all your hours of slaving over a hot keyboard are stored for perpetuity—in other words, this is where the actual repository data is stored. The exact content will vary depending on the repository type, and you shouldn't have to delve into this directory, except by curiosity. If you have an FSFS (see Section 4.3) repository, for example, the revisions can be found in the form of numbered files in the db/revs directory, as illustrated here:

```
$ ls -al /data/svn/dev-repos/db/revs/
total 1100
drwxr-sr-x  2 taronga users   4096 2006-05-20 19:13 .
drwxr-sr-x  5 taronga users   4096 2006-05-20 19:13 ..
-rw-r--r--  1 taronga users    115 2006-05-11 19:51 0
-rw-r--r--  1 taronga users   6342 2006-05-11 22:23 1
-rw-r--r--  1 taronga users    696 2006-05-11 23:36 2
-rw-r--r--  1 taronga users   2591 2006-05-15 00:25 3
-rw-r--r--  1 taronga users 350309 2006-05-16 02:30 4
-rw-r--r--  1 taronga users 574211 2006-05-18 00:42 5
-rw-r--r--  1 taronga users  97501 2006-05-19 20:06 6
-rw-r--r--  1 taronga users  34294 2006-05-19 21:34 7
-rw-r--r--  1 taronga users   5434 2006-05-20 15:23 8
-rw-r--r--  1 taronga users    897 2006-05-20 15:24 9
```

format
: This is just a file containing the version number of the repository layout.

hooks
: This directory is where your hook scripts go. In a new repository installation, it will contain some useful script templates which can be used as the basis for your own scripts.

locks
: This directory is used by Subversion to keep track of locks of the versioned filesystem.

Although (or perhaps, because) creating repositories is so easy you should take some time to think about how you want to store your Subversion repository or repositories. Your friendly system administrator may have some thoughts on this question as well. You can create a single repository for all your projects, or a repository for each project or group of related projects. Creating a single company-wide project means that some metadata and repository configuration details (such as hook scripts) can be shared. From an administrator's point of view, having all the data in one place arguably simplifies maintenance.

By contrast, different projects may have different needs, such as different access rights or different mailing lists to be updated. This is much easier to manage using several distinct repositories. Another minor disadvantage of the first approach is that revisions are shared for all projects, so your revision number will go up whenever anyone changes a project anywhere in the company, which may get people confused.

4.5 Setting Up a New Subversion Project

In general, a Subversion repository will contain many related projects. In fact, once you have a repository (see Section 4.4), creating a project in Subversion is also an easy task. However, before starting, you should think about your directory structures.

Over time, Subversion users have come up with a number of conventions concerning Subversion directory structures. These conventions actually make good sense, though they may surprise CVS users at first. The key issue is knowing where to store tags and branches. In Subversion, branches and tags (see Section 4.12) are performed by simply copying the current revision into another directory. So, the recommended Subversion directory structure is to create three subdirectories in the project root directory, as follows:

```
$ ls
  trunk/  tags/  branches/
```

The convention involves using each subdirectory for a (fairly obvious) purpose:

trunk/
: The *trunk* directory is where the main development work is stored.

tags/
: The *tags* directory contains project repository snapshots, identified by human-readable names such as "Release 1.0."

branches/
: This directory contains named branches coming off the main development line.

However, this is just a convention, with the aim of making life simpler for the human users of the repository: Subversion will be happy with any directory structure.

The easiest way to create a new Subversion project is to create the empty directory structure in a temporary directory, and then to import this directory structure into the Subversion repository using the *svn import* command, as shown here.* Subversion naming conventions can be a bit surprising for the uninitiated, so let's go through the process step-by-step. I start off in my home directory, where I create a temporary directory that I will use to set up an initial empty directory structure:

```
$ pwd
/home/john
$ mkdir svn-tmp
$ cd svn-tmp
$ mkdir myproject
$ mkdir myproject/trunk
$ mkdir myproject/branches
$ mkdir myproject/tags
```

We are going to use the Subversion repository in the */data/svn/dev-repos* directory. This could be on a local disk or a remote drive. We refer to this directory using a Subversion URL (see Section 4.8). In this case the target directory is directly accessible, so we can use the *"file://"* URL prefix, followed by the path of the target directory. The *svn import* command "imports" files and/or directories from your local directory into the Subversion repository.

```
$ svn import . file:///data/svn/dev-repos -m "Initial repository structure"
Adding         myproject
Adding         myproject/trunk
Adding         myproject/branches
Adding         myproject/tags

Committed revision 1.
```

Windows users should note that the file path uses forward slashes, even if the repository is on a Windows server. Here we are using the standard URL-type path format that Subversion uses for almost all communication with the repository:

```
C:\> svn import . file:///c:/svn/dev-repos -m "Initial repository structure"
Adding         myproject
Adding         myproject\trunk
```

* I'll be using the Unix file syntax for the rest of the chapter. If you are working on a Windows machine, just replace "file:///data/svn/dev-repos" with "file:///c:/data/svn/dev-repos" (with forwardslashes, not backslashes).

```
Adding         myproject\branches
Adding         myproject\tags
```

For simplicity, these examples use the "file:" protocol. Naturally, if you already have a remote Subversion server running, you can use any of the other network-based protocols (see Section 4.8) to import your project into the repository. Here, for example, we import the project onto a remote server via HTTP:

```
C:\> svn import . http://myserver/svn/dev-repos  -m "Initial repository structure"
Adding         myproject
Adding         myproject\trunk
Adding         myproject\branches
Adding         myproject\tags
```

Once this is done, your project has been created in the Subversion repository. You don't need the temporary directory anymore, so you can safely delete it (although you might want to wait until you check out your working copy in the next article, just to be on the safe side). In the next section, we will look at how to obtain a working copy.

4.6 Checking Out Your Working Copy

Now that you have created your project in the Subversion repository, you need to obtain a working copy of the project. A common error for new Subversion users is to attempt to use the directory that they just imported as their working directory. This approach is natural, intuitive, and, unfortunately, wrong. Before you can actually use Subversion on your project, you need to obtain a working copy of your project, using the *svn checkout* command.

This is often the first thing you do when you start work on a new project that has been created by someone else, or when you check out the source code from an open source project.

First of all, you need to decide where your project is going to live on your disk. In this example, my projects are stored in a directory called projects, which is a subdirectory of my home directory:

```
$ mkdir ~/projects
```

Now you need to check out the actual project. Subversion is happy to let you check out any part of the repository you like. You can check out the whole project structure if you want, but you probably really only need one subdirectory: the main development branch (by convention called the trunk). Later on, you might want to create other directories for development branches, but for now, let's just set up a working copy of the main development branch. To do this, you need to use the *svn checkout* command:

```
$ svn checkout file:///data/svn/dev-repos/myproject/trunk myproject
Checked out revision 1.
$ ls
  myproject/
```

Subversion just created a directory called *myproject* in your working directory. Inside, if you look closely, you will see a lone ".svn" directory. This directory contains everything Subversion needs to do its magic, and notably a pristine copy of the revision you checked out, which it will use, for among other purposes, to calculate the changes you've made when you commit your modifications to the server:

```
$ ls -al myproject
drwxrwxr-x    3 taronga users 4096 2006-05-20 21:15 ./
drwxr-xr-x  125 taronga users 4096 2006-05-20 21:15 ../
drwxrwxr-x    7 taronga users 4096 2006-05-20 21:15 .svn/
```

Subversion gives you a fair bit of flexibility as to where you check things out to. If you leave out the target directory, Subversion will simply create the final directory in the repository path in your current working directory:

```
$ svn checkout file:///data/svn/dev-repos/myproject
Checked out revision 1.
$ ls myproject
  branches/
  tags/
  trunk/
```

Note that in this case the `branches` and `tags` directories are also downloaded, which isn't usually what we want.

You don't have to checkout the whole branch either. Imagine you're just working on the users' manual, which is stored in the *docs/users-manual* directory. You can simply check out the subdirectory that you need, as shown here:

```
$ svn checkout file:///data/svn/dev-repos/myproject/trunk/docs/users-manual
Checked out revision 1.
$ ls
  users-manual/
```

4.7 Importing Existing Files into Subversion

When you create a new Subversion repository, you may already have some files that you want to import into your project. This is easy. First, make sure your project directory contains *only* the files you want to store on Subversion: no compiled files, no temporary files, and so on. Copy this directory into your working folder.

Now the tricky thing is to import your new project into the right place in the repository. What you will typically want to do is to import your files into the *trunk* subdirectory of your new project directory in the repository. So, when you import the files, you have to provide the full path, including the *trunk* subdirectory. The idea is to do something like the following:

```
$ svn import newproject file:///data/svn/dev-repos/newproject/trunk -m
"Initial Import"

Committed revision 3.
```

Here's an example. In the following listing, I import a new project called *JavaLamp* into the subversion repository. Now I've already cleaned up the directory by removing the compiled classes, and copied the clean project directory into my working directory (*~/dev-repos*). The project already has some source code, so Subversion builds up the correct structure in the repository and adds all the project files recursively:

```
$ cd ~/dev-repos
$ svn import JavaLamp file:///data/svn/dev-repos/javalamp/trunk -m "Initial Import"
Adding         JavaLamp/src
Adding         JavaLamp/src/test
Adding         JavaLamp/src/test/java
Adding         JavaLamp/src/test/java/com
Adding         JavaLamp/src/test/java/com/wakaleo
Adding         JavaLamp/src/test/java/com/wakaleo/jdpt
Adding         JavaLamp/src/test/java/com/wakaleo/jdpt/javalamp
Adding         JavaLamp/src/test/java/com/wakaleo/jdpt/javalamp/JavaLampTest.java
...
Adding         JavaLamp/src/main/resources
Adding         JavaLamp/src/main/resources/META-INF
Adding         JavaLamp/src/main/resources/META-INF/MANIFEST.MF
Adding         JavaLamp/src/main/resources/images
Adding  (bin)  JavaLamp/src/main/resources/images/green-lavalamp.gif
Adding  (bin)  JavaLamp/src/main/resources/images/icon_success_sml.gif
Adding  (bin)  JavaLamp/src/main/resources/images/inqueue.gif
Adding  (bin)  JavaLamp/src/main/resources/images/continuum_logo_75.gif
Adding  (bin)  JavaLamp/src/main/resources/images/icon_error_sml.gif
Adding  (bin)  JavaLamp/src/main/resources/images/building.gif
Adding  (bin)  JavaLamp/src/main/resources/images/buildnow.gif
Adding  (bin)  JavaLamp/src/main/resources/images/checkingout.gif
...
Committed revision 4.
```

Astute readers will notice the "(bin)." This is just for information. Subversion basically detects which of your files are binary and which are text, based on their type. Subversion may attempt to merge conflicting text files but will never do so with binary files. Subversion does a pretty good job of detecting file types, but if you use some really obscure file formats, you may need to tell Subversion about it explicitly (see "Forcing the File Type with svn:mime-type" in Section 4.17).

We're not quite done yet. Now we have a trunk directory, but nothing else. If we want to follow the recommendations of the Subversion community, we also need a *branches* directory and a *tags* directory. (In fact, we can always do that later, but let's stick to the conventions for now.) You can checkout the contents of your repository using the *svn list* command:

```
$ svn list file:///data/svn/dev-repos/javalamp
trunk/
$ svn list file:///data/svn/dev-repos/myproject
```

```
branches/
tags/
trunk/
```

To add the missing directories, you just use the *svn mkdir* command, as follows:

```
$ svn mkdir file:///data/svn/dev-repos/javalamp/branches -m "Added branches"

Committed revision 5.

$ svn mkdir file:///data/svn/dev-repos/javalamp/tags -m "Added tags"

Committed revision 6.
```

This creates the two new directories directly on the server, without modifying anything on your local machine. Now, if you check the repository contents using the *svn list* command, you should get something like the following:

```
$ svn list file:///data/svn/dev-repos/javalamp
branches/
tags/
trunk/
```

4.8 Understanding Subversion Repository URLs

In Subversion, you use a special form of URLs to access repositories. Subversion repositories can be accessed through a variety of protocols, and it can come in handy to understand some of the finer points. This section describes the different protocols and how to use them.

The various types of Subversion URLs are listed in Table 4-1.

Table 4-1. Subversion URLs

URL Schema	Examples	Description
file:///	*file:///data/svn/dev-repos* or *file:///d:/svn/dev-repos*	Direct access to a repository on a local disk. This is the only form that varies depending on the underlying OS.
http://	*http://svn.mycompany.com:9834/repos*	Access to a repository over a standard HTTP connection using the WebDAV/DeltaV protocol. Behind the scenes you will find a →Subversion-friendly Apache server fitted out with a mod_dav_svn module (see Section 4.21). This protocol has obvious advantages when it comes to crossing corporate firewalls and so forth.
https://	*https://svn.mycompany.com:9834/repos*	Access to a repository over a secured HTTPS connection, also using a Subversion-friendly Apache server.
svn://	*svn://svn.mycompany.com:3690/dev-repos*	Access to a repository via the proprietary protocol used by svnserve server (see Section 4.19).

URL Schema	Examples	Description
svn+ssh://	*svn+ssh://svn.mycompany.com:3690/dev-repos*	Secured access to a repository via the proprietary protocol used by svnserve server, with SSH tunnelling.

The HTTP and svn-based URLs are pretty standard, and allow you to specify host names, and ports, as you would expect. Using the file:/// URLs is a bit more specific because you are dealing with a physical directory path on the local machine. You may have wondered why there are three slashes ("///") at the start instead of two, as is the case with the other URL forms. This is because you are actually allowed to put a hostname in the URL, as with the other URL forms (e.g., *file://localhost/data/svn/dev-repos*). However, the only authorised hostname is "localhost," so people tend to leave it out.

Also note that, because these are URLs, Windows paths use forward slashes rather than backslashes (*file:///d:/svn/dev-repos* and not *file:///d:\svn\dev*).

4.9 Working with Your Files

As with many tools, Subversion provides a rich set of functionalities. In practice, however, you can get by quite well if you only know a few key functions, which you will need on a daily basis. This article takes you through what you need to know to get by with Subversion in your everyday work.

Updating Your Work Directory

No man is an island, as someone once said.[*] Or, in this case, (almost) no developer works in isolation. If, like most of us, you work in a team, the first thing you will need to do before you start working is to update your local files with any changes made by your fellow developers. To do this, you run the *svn update* command:

```
$ svn update
U    src\main\java\com\wakaleo\jdpt\javalamp\plugins\ContinuumPlugin.java
D    src\main\resources\ApplicationResources.properties
A    src\main\resources\images\icon_success_sml.gif
A    src\main\resources\images\icon_error_sml.gif
A    src\main\resources\images\icon_warning_sml.gif
Updated to revision 7.
```

Subversion updates your local files, and gives you a summary of the modifications which it has performed. All of the files affected by changes in the repository are listed, each with a code indicating the type of modification. The main codes you will see, if all goes well, are the following:

[*] *It was John Donne, actually, but this is not particularly relevant for the subject under discussion.

A
: A new file has been added to the repository, and has been successfully transferred to your local working copy.

D
: A file has been deleted from the repository, and, as a result, from your local working copy.

U
: A file has been modified (updated) in the repository, and the modification has been correctly updated in your local working copy.

Updates do not always go according to plan, however. Suppose you do some work on your local copy, and then perform an update:

```
$ svn update
G    src\main\java\com\wakaleo\jdpt\javalamp\plugins\ContinuumPlugin.java
C    src\main\java\com\wakaleo\jdpt\javalamp\JavaLamp.java
Updated to revision 10.
```

There are some new codes here. Let's see what they mean:

G
: Subversion has detected some modifications to this file on the server. However, Subversion was able to merge (merGe) them together and update your local copy with the new modifications, so you should be all right. This new file exists only in your local copy at the moment; you'll need to commit it later to update the repository.

C
: Again, Subversion has detected some modifications on the server in a file that you have modified locally. However, this time there's a conflict: Subversion can't merge the two versions, so you'll have to resolve the conflict yourself. We'll see how to do this later on.

Working with Your Local Copy

Once you've updated your local directory, you can get on and do some work. You can work on existing files just as you would normally; Subversion will pick up the modifications when you decide to commit the files to the server. However, if you do any structural modifications—adding, moving, or deleting files or directories—Subversion will want to know about it.

svn add
: This command tells Subversion to add a new file or directory to the repository during the next commit. Adding a directory will also recursively add the directory contents (if need be, you can disable this function, and only add an empty directory

to the repository by using the *-N* option). Note that nothing will actually be added to the repository until you run *svn commit*, as shown here:

```
$ svn add README.txt
A         README.txt
$ svn commit -m "Added a README file"
Adding         README.txt
Transmitting file data ..
Committed revision 11.
```

svn copy
: Duplicates a file or directory (including its contents), with a complete record of its change history and metadata. As with *svn add*, the operation is scheduled for the next commit:

```
$ svn copy README.txt README2.txt
A         README2.txt
```

svn delete
: Schedules a file or directory to be deleted in the next commit. Files will also be immediately deleted from the local working copy. Directories will not be deleted until the commit operation:

```
$ svn delete OLD_FILE.txt
D         OLD_FILE.txt
```

svn move
: Moves a file or directory to another location, while maintaining its change history. This is equivalent to doing a *svn copy* followed by an *svn delete*. Here is an example in which we rename a directory called *lib* directory to *jars*:

```
$ svn move lib jars
A         jars
D         lib\continuum-core-1.0.3.jar
D         lib\continuum-api-1.0.3.jar
D         lib\continuum-notifier-irc-1.0.3.jar
D         lib\continuum-notifier-msn-1.0.3.jar
D         lib\continuum-store-1.0.3.jar
D         lib\continuum-web-1.0.3.jar
D         lib\continuum-model-1.0.3.jar
D         lib\continuum-rpc-client-1.0.3.jar
D         lib\continuum-notifier-jabber-1.0.3.jar
D         lib\continuum-xmlrpc-1.0.3.jar
D         lib\continuum-notifier-api-1.0.3.jar
D         lib
```

If you are using the Subversion plugin for Eclipse (see Section 4.26), most of these operations will be done for you automatically when you modify, move, or delete files or directories from within the IDE.

Committing Your Work

At some point (preferably fairly often), you will decide that you are ready to update the repository with your latest and greatest changes.

It can be handy to run the *svn status* (see Section 4.10) command just to check what is about to be sent to the server. This command lists all the currently scheduled changes. It might look something like this:

```
$ svn status
A       INSTALL.txt
D       README-bis.txt
M       README.txt
```

If you get any conflicts here (code "C"), you could be in trouble; check out the article on resolving conflicts (see Section 4.11) before proceeding. Otherwise, you are now ready to commit your changes by using the *svn commit* command:

```
$ svn commit -m "Added installation instructions and put a reference to
INSTALL.txt in README.txt"
Adding          INSTALL.txt
Deleting        README-bis.txt
Sending         README.txt
Transmitting file data ..
Committed revision 15.
```

It is a good habit to put a meaningful message to sum up the changes you are committing. Remember, one of the nice things about Subversion is that, when you commit a set of changes, they are recorded for posterity as a single atomic transaction. The changes are yours, and yours alone, so you might as well document them as they deserve!

If your comment is short and snappy, you can use the *-m* command-line option, as shown above. However, this should be reserved for small changes. If you take the time to write three or four lines of more detailed comments, it will pay itself off handsomely when you come back in a few months trying to refactor or fix obscure bugs.

If you don't use the *-m* option, Subversion will open your favorite text editor and let you write away to your heart's content. However, in some systems (such as Windows), no default editor is defined, so this won't work. You can define your preferred text editor in the SVN_EDITOR environment variable. In Windows, for example, you can use *notepad* as the default editor by setting the SVN_EDITOR environment variable to notepad (see Figure 4-3):

```
C:\> set SVN_EDITOR=notepad
```

Once you have committed your changes, it is a good practice to update your folders from Subversion, in order to avoid mixed revisions in your local working copy.

This is because of the way Subversion handles updates and commits. One of the underlying principles of Subversion is that when you commit your changes, you should

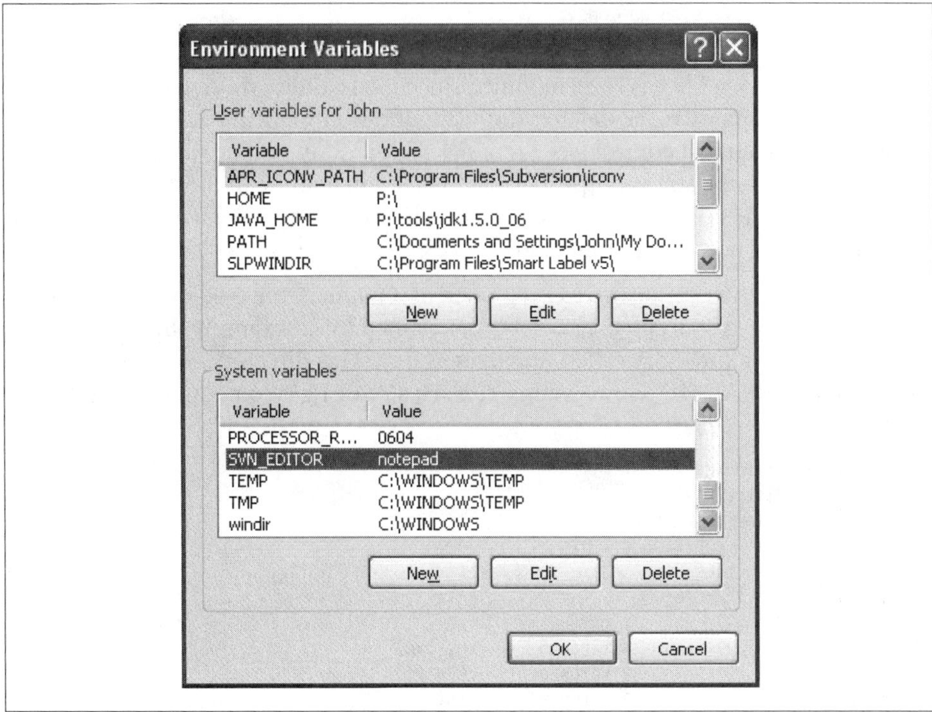

Figure 4-3. Setting up an editor for Subversion

not be obliged to update your local copy, and vice versa. This means that, at any point in time, it is possible to have a mixture of up-to-date, out-of-date, and modified files and directories. This is fine if you really know what you are doing, but it is easy to run into trouble if you're not paying attention. For example, when you commit, the revision of the file in your working copy is updated, but the versions of the parent folders of that file are not updated. If you subsequently try to commit changes to the parent folder(s) (such as deleted files or metadata changes), those commits will be rejected.

4.10 Seeing Where You're At: The Status Command

The *svn status* command is one of the more useful commands in the Subversion toolbox. In a nutshell, it lets you know what you've modified since the last time you synchronized your working copy with the latest version in the Subversion repository. This is a useful thing to do before committing your changes, since it gives you a quick summary of the work you've done, and it can help you to remember everything in the comment when you commit. A typical example is the following:

```
$ svn status
M      ch04.xml
A      figs/subversion-revisions.gif
```

```
D       figs/subversion-no-longer-used.gif
?       ch04.html
```

In this example, one file has been modified since the last file (M), one new file is to be added (A), and one is to be deleted (D). The question mark (?) indicates a file not currently under version control (see Section 4.17 for a way to hide files that you don't want to appear in the status output). This is what you will use in most situations, but in fact the *svn status* command can tell you much, much more. Try *svn status --help* for a detailed description of the command.

You can also use this command to keep track of renamed or moved directories, when you use *svn move* or *svn copy*. This is best explained by an example. In the following listing, I rename a directory called *resources* as *dist*. This directory contains two files, *INSTALL* and *README*. Now, when I run *svn status*, I get something along the following lines:

```
$ svn move resources/ dist
A         dist
D         resources/INSTALL
D         resources/README
D         resources
$ svn status -v
               27       27 taronga      .
               27       24 taronga      ch25.xml
               33       33 taronga      ch04.xml
A  +            -       33 taronga      dist
   +            -       33 taronga      dist/INSTALL
   +            -       33 taronga      dist/README
...
D              33       33 taronga      resources
D              33       33 taronga      resources/INSTALL
D              33       33 taronga      resources/README
...
```

Astute readers will notice several things here:

- The new directory is scheduled to be added (the "A" marker).
- The files, in their new directory, as well as the new directory itself, are marked with a "+." This shows that they are being added to the repository, but that they already have existing history data from their former life in another part of the repository.
- The files are scheduled to be deleted in their old location (the "D" marker).

The files scheduled to be added are marked with a "+" in the fourth column, to indicate that they are all being added within the one operation.

If all these codes don't make you dizzy, you can add the *-v* option (*--verbose*) to get more detailed information about every file in the project:

```
$ svn status -v
               27       27 taronga      .
               27       24 taronga      ch25.xml
M              31       31 taronga      ch04.xml
```

```
                27          24 taronga       bin
                27           5 koala         bin/count_words.sh
                27          24 koala         bin/book2html3
                27           5 taronga       bin/stripmarkup.xslt
                27          24 taronga       figs
                27          24 wombat        figs/continuum-build-history.gif
A               27          24 taronga       figs/subversion-revisions.gif
D               27          24 taronga       figs/subversion-no-longer-used.gif
...
```

So, what does all this mean? The first column contain the usual codes, which we saw earlier. The next column is the working revision, the revision your local file is based on. Then, we get the last revision in which a change was made to this file, and the user who made the last change.

One of the nice things about this command is that it doesn't need to access the network to work: it simply compares your working files with the original copies of the files you checked out, which it has safely tucked away behind the scenes. But sometimes you would actually *like* to touch base with the repository and see if any of your local files need updating. To do this, you use the *-u* (*--show-updates*) option:

```
$ svn status -u
       *        27   dev/JavaLamp/src/main/java/com/wakaleo/jdpt/javalamp/JavaLamp.java
M               31   ch04.xml
A               31   figs/subversion-revisions.gif
D               31   figs/subversion-no-longer-used.gif
```

The asterisk in the first line means that another user has modified *JavaLamp.java*, and our local copy is out-of-date. In this case, Subversion will not let us commit our modifications before we update our local copy and resolve any conflicts.

If you want to know exactly what you've changed since your last update, you can use the *svn diff* command. Running this command with no parameters will compare your local copy with the original revision you checked out:

```
$ svn diff
Index: src/main/java/com/wakaleo/jdpt/javalamp/plugins/ContinuumPlugin.java
===================================================================
--- src/main/java/com/wakaleo/jdpt/javalamp/plugins/ContinuumPlugin.java
(revision 35)
+++ src/main/java/com/wakaleo/jdpt/javalamp/plugins/ContinuumPlugin.java
(working copy)
@@ -123,7 +123,7 @@
                               case NEW_BUILD:
                               case ALT_NEW_BUILD:
                                    statusInfo.setStatusMessage("New Build");
-                                   statusInfo.setStatusIcon(IN_PROGRESS_ICON);
+                                   statusInfo.setStatusIcon(NEW_BUILD_ICON);
                                    break;

                               case SUCCESSFUL:
```

So, in this case, we've just replaced IN_PROGRESS_ICON with NEW_BUILD_ICON. But what if we realize that this was an error, and we didn't mean to touch this file at all? Just use the *svn revert* command, and you'll get your untouched original back, as good as new:

```
$ svn revert src/main/java/com/wakaleo/jdpt/javalamp/plugins/ContinuumPlugin.java
Reverted 'src/main/java/com/wakaleo/jdpt/javalamp/plugins/ContinuumPlugin.java'
$ svn diff
$
```

4.11 Resolving Conflicts

When two users modify the same file, Subversion will try to merge the changes together. This often works well enough if the modifications occur in different parts of the file. If the modifications affect the same lines of code, or if the file in question is a binary file, Subversion may well throw in the towel and let you sort it out (see Section 4.14 for more on how to use file locking to avoid conflicts with binary files). In this case, you're on your own. Well, not quite. Subversion does give you some tools to work with.

Let's work through an example. Suppose you want to update the INSTALL.txt file, to give it a sensible heading like the one shown here:

```
Installation instructions for the JavaLamp application
------------------------------------------------------
```

So you make the change to your local copy and commit. Often, this is the first warning of trouble you get: Subversion refuses your commit because someone else has already committed a more recent version since your last update:

```
$ svn commit -m "Added a nice new title for the installation instructions."
Sending        INSTALL.txt
svn: Commit failed (details follow):
svn: Out of date: '/trunk/INSTALL.txt' in transaction '21-1'
```

Fair enough, you might say, so let's update:

```
$ svn update
C    INSTALL.txt
G    src\main\java\com\wakaleo\jdpt\javalamp\plugins\ContinuumPlugin.java
Updated to revision 21.
```

At this stage, Subversion can often fix the problem on its own by merging the two versions. In this case, two modifications could have caused a conflict, but one was successfully merged ("G") by Subversion. The "C" next to INSTALL.txt, on the other hand, indicates an unresolved conflict. Now it's up to you to fix it. In the unlikely event that you forget to resolve the conflict, Subversion will just refuse to commit until you fix the problem:

```
$ svn commit
svn: Commit failed (details follow):
svn: Aborting commit: 'C:\dev\AnotherJavaLamp\INSTALL.txt' remains in conflict
```

So, now we need to take a look at the file:

```
<<<<<<< .mine
Installation instructions for the JavaLamp application
------------------------------------------------------
=======
JavaLamp Installation instructions
----------------------------------

>>>>>>> .r21
```

One of the nice things about the Subversion notation is the ".mine" label, which lets you know the code coming from your version, and the ".r21" (in this case) label, which indicates the code coming from the revision on the server. In CVS, I always have to think twice to know which code is which. The next step is just to resolve the conflict by manually editing the file.

If you're still not sure about the exact nature of the changes, Subversion provides a few files that may be of use:

```
$ ls INSTALL*
INSTALL.txt  INSTALL.txt.mine  INSTALL.txt.r20  INSTALL.txt.r21
```

The INSTALL.txt is the file we just looked at. The others are explained here:

INSTALL.txt.mine
: Your locally modified version (the one you tried to commit)

INSTALL.txt.r20
: The original version from your last update

INSTALL.txt.r21
: The latest version in the server repository

You need to make your corrections in the original file (INSTALL.txt); the other files are simply there to help you along the way. When you are happy with your corrections, you need to tell Subversion that you're done by using the *svn resolved* command. This will remove the temporary files and enable commits on this file again:

```
$ svn resolved INSTALL.txt
Resolved conflicted state of 'INSTALL.txt'
$ ls INSTALL*
INSTALL.txt
$ svn commit -m "My changes are now correctly integrated"
```

Now you can commit your file in the usual way. The new revision will include your corrected version of the file.

One last thing: remember that a correct merge does not guarantee correct code. Modifications in one part of a file may affect code in another part of the file. Therefore, it is a good idea to review any merged code and run the corresponding regression tests before committing.

4.12 Using Tags, Branches, and Merges

Branching and tagging are central concepts in Configuration Management theory. Branching allows us parallel development work to be done on a separate set of files, while allowing work to continue on the main development line without interference. This is typically done in software projects near a release date, where one part of the team will work on bug fixes and code stabilization on the main development branch (or "trunk," in Subversion terms), while another part of the team continues working on new modules, without putting the upcoming release version at risk. After the release, the new modules must be reintegrated (or "merged") back into the principal development line.

A tag is simply a way of assigning a human-readable label to a given version (or, in Subversion terms, "Revision") of a project. This is useful when you need to identify releases of your product for future reference.

Unlike most other SCM systems, Subversion has no distinct notion of branches or tags; for Subversion, both branches and tags are simply repository copies. As we will see, this has some advantages and some disadvantages.

Creating a new branch or tag is essentially the same operation in Subversion: you just copy the directory you want to branch or tag. And with Subversion, copying directories is fast and cheap, since you are essentially creating the Subversion equivalent of a symbolic link to the original revision.

In CVS, for example, each file must be individually tagged, one by one. Experienced CVS users will know the pain of tagging a big projects, where you can go off for a coffee, pizza, or even a four-course meal while waiting for the tagging to finish. In Subversion, by contrast, tagging is pretty much instantaneous. The most efficient way of doing this is copying the repositories on the server, as shown here:

```
$ svn copy -m "Tagging Release 1.0" file:///data/svn/dev-repos/javalamp/trunk
file:///data/svn/dev-repos/javalamp/tags/release-1.0

Committed revision 57.

$ svn list file:///data/svn/dev-repos/javalamp/tags
release-1.0/
```

You can also copy from the working copy, which is slightly different. When you copy from your working copy, you create a new revision, which includes all your current files in their current state, *even uncommitted work*. And just because you create a new revision doesn't mean Subversion will commit your files behind your back; after the copy, your files stay in their uncommitted state.

This will be clearer with an example. In the following listing, we add a new file (README) and then create a tag called "Release-1.1-alpha" by copying our working copy to a revision of this name. As a rule, when you create a tag, you want to tag the entire project directory. The easiest way to do this is from the project root directory, where we can use the dot notation (".") to refer to the current directory:

```
$ svn add README
A         README
$ svn status
A      README
$ svn copy -m "Tagging Release 1.1-alpha" . \
  file:///data/svn/dev-repos/javalamp/tags/release-1.1-alpha
Committed revision 58.
```

So, now we have a new revision called "release-1.1-alpha" in the tags directory, which (take my word for it) contains our new README file.

```
$ svn list file:///data/svn/dev-repos/javalamp/tags
release-1.0/
release-1.1-alpha/
```

And lo and behold! The status of our files has not changed!

```
$ svn status
A      README
```

Now, in Subversion, the only difference between branches and tags is that branches are intended to be modified, and tags aren't. A tag is just a copy of the repository at a given point in time. A branch is also a copy of the repository at a given point in time, but one that is used as the departure point for new development work. Suppose that we want to create a development branch for work on version 1.4 of our product. We just create a new copy in the *branches* directory on the server (of course, using the *branches* directory is just a convention, but it is one that makes good sense):

```
$ cd ~/projects/javalamp
$ svn copy . file:///data/svn/dev-repos/javalamp/branches/release-1.4-development  \
  -m "Creating Release 1.4 development branch"
```

Here we created a new branch of the whole project structure, working from the project root directory.

So, now we have just created a new development branch. We're not quite ready to use it yet, however. If we commit work straight away, it will go to the main branch (the "trunk"). We need to switch to the new development branch. We do this, appropriately enough, by using the *switch* command, as shown here:

```
$ svn switch file:///data/svn/dev-repos/javalamp/branches/release-1.4-development
U    README.txt
Updated to revision 11.
```

This will update any files it needs to switch this directory to the release-1.4-development branch. From now on, any commits will go to our new branch.

At any point you can switch back to the main development trunk or to another branch:

```
$ svn switch  file:///data/svn/dev-repos/javalamp/trunk
```

And if you're not sure what branch you're currently working with, running *svn info* can help:

```
$ svn info
Path: .
URL: file:///data/svn/svn-repository/dev-repos/javalamp/branches/release-
1.5-development
Repository Root: file:///data/svn/svn-repository/dev-repos
Repository UUID: 20b9c9b3-4814-0410-9739-d611b8f56fd3
Revision: 11
Node Kind: directory
Schedule: normal
Last Changed Author: taronga
Last Changed Rev: 10
Last Changed Date: 2006-06-06 21:28:21 +1200 (Tue, 06 Jun 2006)
```

Finally, you will probably want to merge your development branch back into the main trunk at some stage. You do this with the *svn merge* command, which, in its simplest form, will apply the differences between two branches to your current repository. Read that sentence again, because merging in Subversion is one of the less-intuitive functions.

First, switch to the development trunk, which is where we want our new code to be incorporated:

```
$ svn switch file:///data/svn/dev-repos/javalamp/trunk
```

Now, we need to work out exactly what we need to add to the main trunk. In fact, we need to add (merge) all the work done on the development branch from its creation up until now. In other words, you need to know where your development branch started and ended. One convenient way to do this is to use the svn log command on the development branch, using the *--stop-on-copy* option. This option will display log messages going back to the creation of the branch, which is exactly what we need:

```
$ svn log file:///data/svn/svn-repository/dev-repos/javalamp/branches
/release-1.5-development \
  --stop-on-copy

r16 | taronga | 2006-06-06 22:00:38 +1200 (Tue, 06 Jun 2006) | 1 line


------------------------------------------------------------------------
r15 | taronga | 2006-06-06 22:00:31 +1200 (Tue, 06 Jun 2006) | 1 line
.
.
.
r11 | taronga | 2006-06-06 21:59:08 +1200 (Tue, 06 Jun 2006) | 1 line

Creating development branch for version 1.4
------------------------------------------------------------------------
```

Looking at this, we can conclude that our branch went from revision 11 to revision 16. So, we need to apply the changes made between revisions 11 and 16 (the *-r* option) in the "release-1.4-development" branch to our current working copy. We run this command first using the *--dry-run* option: this simply lists the changes that would be applied by this merge so that we know what we're getting ourselves into. In this rather contrived case, only the README has changed:

```
$ svn merge --dry-run \
  -r 11:16 \
  file:///data/svn/svn-repository/dev-repos/javalamp/branches/release-1.4-development
G    README.txt
```

So, now we can commit the changes:

```
$ svn merge -r 11:16 \
  file:///data/svn/svn-repository/dev-repos/javalamp/branches/release-1.4-development
G    README.txt
$ svn commit -m "Merged branch release-1.4-development into trunk"
Sending        README.txt
Transmitting file data .
Committed revision 18.
```

One thing to be wary of is merging file or directory name changes. This is something that Subversion has trouble coping with. For example, suppose that Joe decides to rename a directory called "someDirectory" to "newDirectory:"

```
$ svn move someDirectory/ newDirectory
A         newDirectory
D         someDirectory/file1
D         someDirectory/file2
D         someDirectory/file3
D         someDirectory
$ svn status
D      someDirectory
D      someDirectory/file1
D      someDirectory/file2
D      someDirectory/file3
A  +   newDirectory
```

Meanwhile, on another machine, Jill decides to rename this same directory to "brandNewDirectory":

```
$ svn move someDirectory/ brandNewDirectory
A         brandNewDirectory
D         someDirectory/file1
D         someDirectory/file2
D         someDirectory/file3
D         someDirectory
$ svn status
D      someDirectory
D      someDirectory/file1
D      someDirectory/file2
D      someDirectory/file3
A  +   brandNewDirectory
```

Now Jill commits her changes:

```
$ svn commit -m "Rename someDirectory to brandNewDirectory"
Deleting       someDirectory
Adding         brandNewDirectory
```

Meanwhile, back at the ranch, Joe commits his changes. Somewhat suprisingly, Subversion does not object. It simply deletes the old directory and then puts it back under its new name:

```
$ svn commit -m "Rename someDirectory to newDirectory"
Deleting       someDirectory
Adding         newDirectory
```

Now, when you update, you will find two equivalent directories in the repository:

```
$ svn update
Adding         brandNewDirectory
Adding         brandNewDirectory/file1
Adding         brandNewDirectory/file2
Adding         brandNewDirectory/file3
$ ls
...
newDirectory
brandNewDirectory
```

This is because of the way that Subversion renames files and directories, and, unfortunately, there isn't really much you can do to avoid it.

4.13 Rolling Back to a Previous Revision

One important thing that you often need to do with a version control system is to undo changes by rolling back to a previous version. Suppose, for example, that you spend a few days working on your favorite project. You make some changes, add some files, and so on. You commit your changes into the code repository several times as you go. Then, in a flash of genius, you realize that you've got it all wrong, irreparably wrong. (As a rule, this flash of genius will arrive around 4 p.m. on a Friday, before a planned demonstration on Monday.) The only thing to do is to rollback your changes and return to a previous, stable version.

So how do you do this in Subversion? The simplest way is to use the *svn merge* command (see Section 4.12) to undo your changes. The trick is to merge backward, so that the older version takes precedence over the more recent (incorrect) changes.

Let's go through an example.

First, I add a class to a project, delete another, and modify yet another class. Here's what happens when I commit these changes:

```
$ svn commit -m "Changes we will regret later"
Sending        src\main\java\com\wakaleo\maven\plugin\schemaspy\SchemaSpyReport.java
Adding         src\main\java\com\wakaleo\maven\plugin\schemaspy\util\DatabaseHelper.
               java
Deleting       src\main\java\com\wakaleo\maven\plugin\schemaspy\util\JDBCHelper.java
```

```
Transmitting file data ..
Committed revision 11.
```

So far so good. However, some time (and several revisions) later, I decide that these changes are going nowhere. I want to go back to good old revision 10, and start over again. To do this, just merge backward, starting with revision 14, back to revision 10. In practice, this will undo each change done since revision 10, which, it so happens, is exactly what we want:

```
$ svn merge -r 14:10 https://wakaleo.devguard.com/svn/maven-plugins
/maven-schemaspy-plugin/trunk
U    src\main\java\com\wakaleo\maven\plugin\schemaspy\SchemaSpyReport.java
D    src\main\java\com\wakaleo\maven\plugin\schemaspy\util\DatabaseHelper.java
A    src\main\java\com\wakaleo\maven\plugin\schemaspy\util\JDBCHelper.java
```

At this stage, my local copy will be back to where it was in revision 10. Now I just commit the changes to the repository:

```
$ svn commit -m "Back to revision 10"
Sending        src\main\java\com\wakaleo\maven\plugin\schemaspy\SchemaSpyReport.java
Deleting       src\main\java\com\wakaleo\maven\plugin\schemaspy\util\DatabaseHelper
               .java
Adding         src\main\java\com\wakaleo\maven\plugin\schemaspy\util\JDBCHelper.java
Transmitting file data .
Committed revision 15.
```

Revision 15 will be identical to revision 10. Note that you will not have erased all traces of your erroneous commits; because it is a version control system, Subversion likes to keep track of all the versions, even the incorrect ones.

4.14 Using File Locking with Binary Files

In any development project of any size, there will be times when two people want to modify the same file at the same time. The risk is that one developer may overwrite the changes of the other, which has the potential to cause delays, lost code, and unnecessary bloodshed among irate team members. In the version control world, there are two schools as to how to deal with this.

Using file locking
: In this approach, only one person can modify a given file at any given time. When a user checks out a file, it becomes unmodifiable for all other users. This approach guarantees that your changes will not be overwritten inadvertently by another user, but potentially at the cost of slowing down development work by making it impossible for more than one developer to work on a given file at the same time. Indeed, there are many cases in which it is quite legitimate for several users to modify the same file simultaneously; for example, adding distinct localised messages into the same properties file. File locking can also create maintenance headaches, as files may become or remain locked unnecessarily, for instance, if a user goes on vacation without checking in his work.

Using file merging
: File merging is a more flexible approach. Any number of users can check out a local copy of a file in the repository, and modify it on their machine. The first user to complete his or her modifications updates the repository. When the next developer tries to commit his or her changes, they will be informed that the file has been updated on the repository, and needs to be updated (see Section 4.10). So, they update their local copy of the file. If the changes were in different parts of the code, Subversion can merge the two versions automatically. If the changes modify the same lines of code, it's up to the user to sort them out manually (see Section 4.11).

By default, Subversion uses the second approach. It is a tried-and-true approach that has worked well for many years in the open source world. It has only one major problem: although it works well with text files (in which conflicts are fairly easy to display and to resolve), it is poorly adapted to binary files. You can't merge two versions of an image or a sound recording, for example. So, if two people are working on the same image at the same time, someone is in for some lost work. In these cases, it would sometimes be nice to be able to lock a file so that other users don't waste their time trying to modify it themselves.

As of version 1.2 of Subversion, the *svn lock* command lets you do just that:

```
$ svn lock images/product-logo.gif
'product-logo.gif' locked by user 'taronga'.
```

Now if you run *svn status*, you will see a "K," which indicates that this file has been locked locally:

```
$ svn status
     K images/product-logo.gif
```

You can obtain more details by using *svn info*:

```
$ svn info images/product-logo.gif
Path: images/product-logo.gif
Name: images/product-logo.gif
URL: file:///data/svn/java-power-tools/trunk/images/product-logo
Repository UUID: 087d467d-7e13-0410-ab08-e4ad2953aa79
Revision: 35
Node Kind: file
Schedule: normal
Last Changed Author: taronga
Last Changed Rev: 24
Last Changed Date: 2006-05-21 19:39:59 +1200 (Sun, 21 May 2006)
Text Last Updated: 2006-05-22 19:14:31 +1200 (Mon, 22 May 2006)
Properties Last Updated: 2006-05-22 19:13:54 +1200 (Mon, 22 May 2006)
Checksum: 2152f30f8ec8a8d211f6c136cebd60fa
Lock Token: opaquelocktoken:31af1e64-8614-0410-9df7-cf255c995479
Lock Owner: taronga
Lock Created: 2006-05-24 22:42:24 +1200 (Wed, 24 May 2006)
Lock Comment (1 line):
This picture needs some nicer colors.
```

Notice the last five lines. This lets everyone know who has locked the file, when it was locked, and (because everyone *always* adds a message when they lock a file) why it was locked. If another user runs *svn status* (with the *-u* option to check with the server), they will get a line containing an "O," which means that another user has locked the file, as shown here:

```
$ svn -u status
     O          37   images/product-logo.gif
Status against revision:     37
```

If the user forgets to check the status, or insists on modifying or deleting the file, the operation will be politely refused when the user attempts to commit her modifications:

```
$  svn delete images/product-logo.gif
D          images/product-logo.gif
$  svn commit -m ""
svn: Commit failed (details follow):
svn: Can't create directory '/data/svn/java-power-tools/db/transactions/37-1.txn':
Permission denied
```

Once the developer has finished working on the image, they commit their changes. Committing automatically releases all current locks in the committed file set, even if the locked files were not modified. This is designed to promote good developing practices: it encourages developers to lock files only for short periods, as well as serving to limit the number of files a user locks at any one time.

You can also use *svn unlock* to release the file without committing, if you locked a file by mistake, for example:

```
$ svn unlock images/product-logo.gif
'product-logo.gif' unlocked.
```

4.15 Breaking and Stealing Locks

Administrators of course have absolute power over their repositories, and a minor measure such as locking files will not resist a determined administrator very long. There are occasionally times when a user forgets to commit their modifications before going on holidays. In situations such as this, the administrator may have to intervene and manually unlock the file.

The first step is to verify which files have been locked, and by whom. The *svnadmin lslocks* lists the active locks on a given repository:

```
$ svnadmin lslocks /data/svn/dev-repos
Path: /trunk/images/product-logo.gif
UUID Token: opaquelocktoken:f9366d36-8714-0410-8278-b1076b57a982
Owner: taronga
Created: 2006-05-24 23:41:13 +1200 (Wed, 24 May 2006)
Expires:
Comment (0 lines):
```

The administrator can use the *svnadmin rmlocks* command to manually remove any offending locks, as shown here:

```
$ svnadmin rmlocks /data/svn/dev-repos /trunk/images/product-logo.gif
Removed lock on '/trunk/images/product-logo.gif'.
```

The other way to get around an unwanted lock is to steal it. This is, of course, terribly unethical, and so should be used with caution. But if you really need to (say, your administrator went on vacation, too), here's how you do it.

Suppose that your boss just asked you to modify the product logo, as it needs a few more bright yellow stripes. You better lock the file before you do any work on it:

```
$ svn lock images/product-logo.gif
svn: Path '/trunk/images/product-logo.gif' is already locked by user
'bill' in filesystem '/data/svn/dev-repos/db'
```

Uh oh, looks like Bill's forgotten to commit his changes before he left for Fiji last week. OK, we'll just unlock it ourselves:

```
$ svn unlock file:///data/svn/java-power-tools/trunk/images/product-logo.gif
svn: User 'taronga' is trying to use a lock owned by 'bill'
in filesystem '/data/svn/dev-repos/db'
```

OK, no more Mister Nice Guy. If we use the *--force*, we can move just about anything (apologies to Yoda):

```
$ svn unlock --force file:///data/svn/java-power-tools/trunk/images/product-logo.gif
'product-logo.gif' unlocked.
```

And, indeed, this did the job. Now the file is unlocked, and we can lock it ourselves and get the job done.

When Bill gets back from Fiji, he is in for a surprise. As soon as he tries to commit, he will get a nasty error message (see below). He can find out more using *svn status -u*. If the lock has just been removed, Subversion will display the "B," or "broken," status code. If, in addition, another user has locked the file out, he will see the "T" (sTolen) code, indicating that his lock has been forcefully replaced by that of another user:

```
$ whoami
bill
$ svn images/product-logo.gif
Deleting       images/product-logo.gif
$ svn commit -m "Didn't want this file anyway"
svn: Commit failed (details follow):
svn: User root does not own lock on path '/trunk/figs/subversion-revisions.gif'
(currently locked by taronga)
$ svn status -u images/product-logo.gif
D    T         37   images/product-logo.gif
Status against revision:     39
```

Running *svn -u status* will simply let you know that another user has stolen your lock and possibly modified the file. To reestablish the situation, you need to run *svn update*. If you have also changed the file locally, you may end up with a conflict, as shown here (note the "C" flag):

```
$ svn update
C B        39   images/product-logo.gif
```

4.16 Making Locked Files Read-Only with the svn:needs-lock Property

Unlike more strict lock-based version control systems that physically prevent users from modifying a locked file, even on their own machines, the default Subversion approach to locking is not foolproof. If a user locks a file, she is guaranteed that it will remain untouched by other users (except perhaps for the occasional mad administrator...). However, there is still the risk that another user may work for three days to redo your product logo in a brilliant new shade of purple, only to discover that the file has been locked by the developer down the corridor. One way to avoid this is to convince users to check the status and to lock binary files before starting any work on them. If this practice is respected, the system is quite robust. However, it does require some discipline, and it may be difficult to enforce.

Another approach is to use a special property, *svn:needs-lock*. All you have to do is to assign this property to a file (any value will do), and it will become read-only. To make it read-write, a user needs to lock the file. When the lock is released, the file becomes read-only again:

```
$ cd ~john/projects/javalamp
$ svn propset svn:needs-lock 'true' images/product-logo.gif
property 'svn:needs-lock' set on 'images/product-logo.gif'
$ svn commit -m "This is a binary file which needs to be locked to modify."
Transmitting file data .
Committed revision 40.
$ svn update
At revision 40.
$ ls -al images/product-logo.gif
-r-xr-xr-x  1 taronga users 12943 2006-05-22 19:14 images/product-logo.gif
```

Here we have updated the property and committed the change to the repository. Note that when you set a property on a file, you refer to the local copy of the file. In the above example, we did this from the project root, but you can actually do it from any directory.

Once we update our local work copy; the file is placed in read-only mode. If we want to modify the file, we need to lock it first:

```
$ svn lock images/product-logo.gif
'product-logo.gif' locked by user 'taronga'.
```

```
$ ls -al images/product-logo.gif
-rwxr-xr-x  1 taronga users 12943 2006-05-22 19:14 images/product-logo.gif
```

Now, when we commit our modifications, the lock will be automatically released and the file will revert to read-only:

```
$ svn commit -m "Changed colours to suite new company look"
Sending        images/product-logo.gif
Transmitting file data .
Committed revision 41.
$ ls -al images/product-logo.gif
-r-xr-xr-x  1 taronga users 12943 2006-05-22 19:14 images/product-logo.gif
```

4.17 Using Properties

One of the more innovative aspects of Subversion is the ability to assign and version metadata that you associate with files or directories. This metadata can take the form of just about anything you want, from simple text values to binary objects. The possibilities are virtually unlimited, and you can have a great deal of fun building complicated (and sometimes incomprehensible) build scripts using custom properties.

However, without going this far, there is a lot of added value to be had simply by using standard out-of-the-box Subversion properties. In this section, we will look at some of the more useful built-in Subversion properties.

Preserving the Executable Flag using svn:executable

On Unix systems, you can define a file as an "executable," meaning it can be executed directly from the command line. The concept does not exist in other operating systems such as Windows. Subversion provides the *svn:executable* property to cater to this. If you assign a value (any value) to this property for a given file, Subversion will make this file executable whenever you check it out in a compatible operating system:

```
$ svn propset svn:executable "true" INSTALL
property 'svn:executable' set on 'INSTALL'
```

Forcing the File Type with svn:mime-type

The *svn:mime-type* property plays an important role in Subversion. Although Subversion stores all files internally as binary files for performance reasons, Subversion needs to distinguish between text files, which can be merged, and true binary files, which can't. When you add a file, Subversion will try to automatically detect any binary files you add. Subversion will assign the value "application/octet-stream" to the *svn:mime-type* property for these files. You can always use the *svn propget* command to verify their mime-type:

```
$ svn add *
Adding  (bin)  icon.jpg
```

```
Adding  (bin)  plan.mpp
Adding  (bin)  stakeholders.xls

$ svn propget svn:mime-type *
icon.jpg - application/octet-stream
plan.mpp - application/octet-stream
stakeholders.xls - application/octet-stream
```

There are two main uses for this property. First, Subversion will not attempt to merge changes in binary files. When you update your working copy, if there is a newer version of a binary file on the server, it will simply replace your current one. If you have modified the file locally, Subversion will generate three distinct files, and place the file in an unresolved status, as shown below. It is up to you to decide which copy is correct, and to resolve the conflict manually using *svn resolve*:

```
$ svn status -u
M      *        4   logo.jpg
$
$ ls -al
drwxrwxr-x    3 taronga users 118,775 2006-05-20 21:15 logo.jpg
drwxrwxr-x    3 taronga users  38,590 2006-05-20 21:15 logo.jpg.r5
drwxrwxr-x    3 taronga users  76,560 2006-05-20 21:15 logo.jpg.r6

$ svn resolved logo.jpg
```

Subversion will also use the mime-type property when it serves files out to WebDAV clients through Apache, using the "Content-type:" HTTP header attribute. This can help your browser know the best way to display the file.

Making Subversion Ignore Files with svn:ignore

In the real world, working directories tend to contain files that you don't want to place in the Subversion repository, such as temporary files, IDE project files, logfiles, or generated files. For example, when writing this book, I often generate HTML files from the docbook source code. In some places and projects, HTML files would be legitimate source code, but not here. Because Subversion has no way of knowing which files you don't need in the repository, and which you have forgotten to add, Subversion will nevertheless display all of these files with a "?" whenever you run *svn status*.

The *svn:ignore* property lets you get around this. It lets you specify a list of file patterns which will be ignored by Subversion projects. It takes a file containing a list of file patterns separated by new lines. Consider the following:

```
$ svn status -v
?                                       tomcat.log
?                                       ch01.html
?                                       ch02.html
?                                       ch03.html
?                                       ch01.xml.bak
                8         8 John        .
                9         9 John        .ignore
                8         3 John        ch01.xml
```

```
                    9        9 John          ch02.xml
                    8        5 John          ch03.xml
```

This directory contains logfiles, backup files, and html files that you don't want cluttering up your Subversion status reports. To get around this, you create a file (here it's called *.ignore*), which contains the file patterns that you want to exclude:

```
*.html
*.log
*~
*.bak
```

Now just set the *svn:ignore* property of this directory to the "*.ignore*" file:

```
$ svn propset svn:ignore -F .ignore .
property 'svn:ignore' set on '.'

$ svn status -v
 M              8        8 John          .
                9        9 John          .ignore
                8        3 John          ch01.xml
                9        9 John          ch02.xml
                8        5 John          ch03.xml
```

Note that you assigned this property to a directory, it is not recursive. If you want to apply this property to an entire directory tree, you need to use the *-R* option:

```
$ svn propset svn:ignore -RF .ignore .
property 'svn:ignore' set (recursively) on '.'
```

Handling OS-Specific End-of-Lines with svn:eol-style

By default, Subversion will not modify your file contents in any way, shape, or form, except when merging text files. So, if you commit a file created in Unix, and then check it out under Windows, you will end up with Unix end-of-lines (a single line feed character) in a Windows environment (where end of lines are represented by a carriage return followed by a line feed character), and vice versa. Some tools may react badly to this. Under Unix, you may see lots of "^M" characters if you edit a file under VI, for example.

You can make Subversion convert line feeds to the appropriate OS-specific value using the *svn:eol-style* property. The most useful value accepted by this property is "Native," which tells Subversion to adapt the end-of-line characters to the target OS. Three others, "CR," "LF," and "CRLF," force Subversion to always provide a certain type of end-of-line character, whatever the operating system.

4.18 Change History in Subversion: Logging and Blaming

Subversion has a couple of handy ways of checking the change history of a file or repository.

The *svn log* command can be used to obtain a short history of all changes ever done to the repository:

```
$ svn log
------------------------------------------------------------------------
r427 | john | 2007-04-11 16:42:09 +1200 (Wed, 11 Apr 2007) | 1 line

Added draft contributions for SchemaSpy material
------------------------------------------------------------------------
r426 | john | 2007-04-04 16:41:48 +1200 (Wed, 04 Apr 2007) | 1 line
...
```

If you add the "-v" (--verbose) option, you get a detailed summary of each commit, including the files modified in each commit:

```
$ svn log -v
------------------------------------------------------------------------
r427 | john | 2007-04-11 16:42:09 +1200 (Wed, 11 Apr 2007) | 1 line
Changed paths:
   A /java-power-tools/trunk/src/ch-XX-schemaspy.xml
   D /java-power-tools/trunk/src/contrib/kalali/SchemaSpy/image-1.png
   D /java-power-tools/trunk/src/contrib/kalali/SchemaSpy/image-2.png
   D /java-power-tools/trunk/src/contrib/kalali/SchemaSpy/image-3.png
   A /java-power-tools/trunk/src/contrib/kalali/SchemaSpy/schemaspy-image-1.png
   A /java-power-tools/trunk/src/contrib/kalali/SchemaSpy/schemaspy-image-2.png
   A /java-power-tools/trunk/src/contrib/kalali/SchemaSpy/schemaspy-image-3.png
...
```

And if you need to narrow the history to a single revision, or a small range of revisions, you can use the *-r* (--revision) option. Here are a few examples:

```
$ svn log -vr HEAD          # What was modified in the latest version on the server?*

$ svn log -vr {2006-05-25}  # What was modified in the last revision before
                     the 25th of May 2006?

$ svn log svn log -vr 10:15 # What was modified between revisions 10 and 15
```

If you run *svn log* from within a particular directory, it will only list the revisions in which a file in this directory (or one of its subdirectories) has been modified:

```
$ cd ~projects/java-power-tools/src/sample-code/spitfire
$ svn log
------------------------------------------------------------------------
r436 | john | 2007-05-07 12:47:23 +1200 (Mon, 07 May 2007) | 1 line
```

* In Subversion, HEAD indicates the latest (most recent) version on the server.

```
------------------------------------------------------------------------
r410 | john | 2007-03-24 13:14:55 +1200 (Sat, 24 Mar 2007) | 1 line


------------------------------------------------------------------------
r406 | john | 2007-03-19 07:36:14 +1200 (Mon, 19 Mar 2007) | 1 line
...
```

You can also display the history of a particular file, either by using the local copy or by providing a full repository path:

```
$ svn log README.TXT
------------------------------------------------------------------------
r438 | john | 2007-05-07 12:54:07 +1200 (Mon, 07 May 2007) | 1 line


------------------------------------------------------------------------
r437 | john | 2007-05-07 12:48:05 +1200 (Mon, 07 May 2007) | 1 line


------------------------------------------------------------------------
r436 | john | 2007-05-07 12:47:23 +1200 (Mon, 07 May 2007) | 1 line


------------------------------------------------------------------------
r344 | john | 2007-01-04 16:10:01 +1300 (Thu, 04 Jan 2007) | 1 line
```

Another command that can come in handy is the *svn blame* command (you can also use the synonyms *svn praise* or *svn annotate*, depending on how you feel at the time). This command displays the current contents of a file, with, to the side of each line, the last person to have modified this line and the revision in which the last modification was made:

```
$ svn blame INSTALL.txt
    22      taronga Installation instructions for the JavaLamp application
    22      taronga -------------------------------------------------------
    25      bill    Installing JavaLamp is a long and difficult task,
    28      toni    And writing the documentation involves many steps and many people.
```

4.19 Setting Up a Subversion Server with svnserve

Subversion also comes with a lightweight server called *svnserve*, which can be used to provide network access via the proprietary svn and svn+ssl protocols. *Svnserve* is easier to configure and offers higher performance than accessing Subversion via Apache. It works equally well in both Windows and *NIX environments.

You can start up the svnserve as a standalone server process from the command line, as follows:

```
$ svnserve --daemon --root /data/svn
```

The *--daemon* (or *-d*) option tells *svnserve* run as a background process. The *--root* (or *-r*) option lets you specify the repository root path. If provided, URL paths will be relative to this directory. Although optional, it is good practice to provide this path, because in this case the *svnserve* process cannot access anywhere outside this path.

The default port is 3690, but if you need to change this, you can use the *--listen-port* option. The *--listen-host* can be used to define the interface that svnserve listens on. You can use either a regular hostname or an IP address.

Logically enough, the *svnserve* process needs to have read/write access on this directory. One way of doing this is to create a user and a group, both called *svn*. This user should have ownership of the Subversion repository directory. You could do this, as root, as follows:

```
# chown -R svn:svn /data/svn
# chmod -R 775 /data/svn
```

Then execute *svnserve* as this user.

You can do a quick check to see if the server is functioning correctly by running *svn list* using a svn URL, as shown here:

```
$ svn list svn://localhost/dev-repos
branches/
trunk/
```

Of course, on a real server, you would typically set up the *svnserve* process to run as a service. This varies from system to system, and if you've gotten this far, you're probably big enough to work this out for yourself.

Now that *svnserve* is running, you can now check out a project:

```
$ svn co svn://localhost/dev-repos/javalamp/trunk  JavaLampRemote
A    remoteJavaLamp\INSTALL.txt
A    remoteJavaLamp\src
A    remoteJavaLamp\src\test
A    remoteJavaLamp\src\test\java
A    remoteJavaLamp\src\test\java\com
A    remoteJavaLamp\src\test\java\com\wakaleo
A    remoteJavaLamp\src\test\java\com\wakaleo\jdpt
...
```

By default, anyone can checkout a project from the repository, but only authorized users can submit modifications. If you try to modify something (say the README.txt file), your attempt will be refused:

```
$ svn commit -m "A remote update of README.txt"
svn: Commit failed (details follow):
svn: Authorization failed
```

Basic authorizations are managed individually for each repository. As of Subversion 1.3, you can also manage fine-grained path-orientated authorizations using the *authz-db* option, or you can just set up a repository for each project.

First of all, you need to configure the *svnserve* server. The server configuration for *svnserve* is stored in the conf/svnserve.conf file (so for our javalamp repository, you would find this file at */data/svn/javalamp/conf/svnserve.conf*). A typical configuration file might look like this:

```
[general]
anon-access = read
auth-access = write
password-db = passwd
realm = JavaLamp Repository
authz-db = authz
```

anon-access
: This field determines repository access for anonymous users. This can be *read*, *write*, or *none*.

auth-access
: This field determines repository access for authorised users. This can be *read*, *write*, or *none*, although the last option would be a bit silly.

password-db
: This indicates the file (as a relative path) where the user accounts are configured.

realm
: The realm is a human-readable name that describes the "authentication namespace" covered by this configuration. It appears when users are asked for their passwords, and is used to locally cache password values. I generally just give it a name related to the name of the repository.

authz-db
: If present, this field points to a configuration file that contains rules for path-based access control.

Next, you need to set up user accounts. You configure authorizations in the repository's *conf/passwd* file (so for our javalamp repository, you would find this file at */data/svn/javalamp/conf/passwd*). The format of this file is quite simple: it contains one section labeled *[users]*, which contains user accounts, one on each line, of the form *USERNAME = PASSWORD*.

```
[users]
taronga = secret1
bill = secret2
toni = secret3
```

Now, when you commit your modifications for the first time, Subversion will prompt you for a password. User credentials are cached on the local disk, so from then on, whenever you commit from this working copy using the username option, Subversion will recognize you automatically:

```
$ svn commit --username taronga -m "A remote update of README.txt"
Authentication realm: <svn://localhost:3690> JavaLamp Repository
Password for 'taronga': *******
```

```
Sending        README.txt
Transmitting file data .
Committed revision 23.
```

If you need fine-grained authentication rules, you can set up an authz-db file as well. This file format is compatible with the mod_authz_svn authorization files used for the Apache WebDAV configuration (see Section 4.21). The file contains an optional section labeled [groups], where user groups can be defined, followed by a list of repository path sections. Each section is labeled by a repository path, and contains a set of authorization rules. Each rule associates a user or group of users with an authorization level, which can be read-write ("w"), read-only ("r"), or no access at all ("").

In the following example, Bill has exclusive read-write access on the *bin* directory, and all other users are forbidden access. The *web_dev* group (Taronga and Toni) have read-write access on the src directory, whereas all other users have read-only access. The last rule is a general catch-all rule that states that if no other rule applies, all users (even anonymous users) have read-only access:

```
[groups]
web_dev = taronga, toni

[javalamp:/trunk/bin]
bill = rw
* =

[javalamp:/trunk/src]
@web_dev  = rw
* = r

[/]
* = r
```

Now let's see this in action. Suppose Toni tries to modify a file in the *bin* directory. According to the rules we just defined, only Bill can modify files here. So, when she tries to commit, she will get an error along the following lines:

```
$ svn commit --username toni -m "Updating bin scripts."
Authentication realm: <svn://localhost:3690> JavaLamp Repository
Password for 'toni': *******
Sending        bin\javalamp.bat
Transmitting file data .svn: Commit failed (details follow):
svn: Access denied
```

If Bill does the same thing, Subversion will offer no resistance because he has read-write access on this directory:

```
$ svn commit --username bill -m "Updating bin scripts."
Authentication realm: <svn://localhost:3690> JavaLamp Repository
Password for 'bill': *******
Sending        bin\javalamp.bat
Transmitting file data .
Committed revision 29.
```

Using a *svnserve* server can be a good option if you need to provide access to a Subversion repository over a secure network environment such as a company LAN or over a VPN network. It is fast and easy to install, and offers fairly low-effort maintenance, even when you take into account the fact that user accounts need to be maintained by hand.

4.20 Setting Up a Secure svnserve Server

The *svnserve* server is not a particularly security-oriented solution: in particular, file contents are sent over the network in unsecured form, and passwords are stored in unencrypted form on the server. As such, it is not well suited to publishing a repository over an unsecured network or over the Internet, for example. If security is an issue in your environment, it is worth knowing that *svnserve* supports SSH tunneling via the *svn+ssh* protocol.

To make *svnserve* use SSH tunneling, you simply use the "svn+ssh" from the client machine. No demon process needs to be running on the server: instead, an SSH tunnel is created for each server access and the *svnserve* command is run on the server machine through the SSH tunnel. When SSH tunneling is used, *svnserve* does not use the password database that we saw earlier (see Section 4.19). Instead, users need to have a physical account on the server, with authorization to login to the repository server using SSH.

User rights are determined by physical access to the repository directory: a user with read access to a repository directory on the server will only have read access to the repository, whereas a user with read-wight access to a repository directory will have read and write access to the repository. An easy (if rudimentary) way to do this is to define read-write access to the Subversion repository for the "svn" group. This way, members of the "svn" group have read and write access to the repository, whereas all other users have read-only access.

Whenever you access the server, you will be prompted for a password, as illustrated here:

```
$ svn list svn+ssh://svnserver.mycompany.com//data/svn/dev-repos/myproject
Password:
branches/
tags/
trunk/
```

Note that, by default, the full repository path must be provided (like when we used the "file:" protocol).

Accessing an *svnserve* server through SSH tunneling is pretty simple to set up, and is certainly secure. On the down side, it is not particularly flexible, and doesn't allow the fine-grained access rules you get with the other network access mechanisms. The ssh +svn tunneling mechanism also has an annoying habit of re-requesting passwords because they are not cached on the local machine, and a new ssh tunnel is created for each operation.

System administrators may prefer this approach, for example, if they do not want to have to manage a WebDAV access, and users already have system accounts on the server.

4.21 Setting Up a WebDAV/DeltaV Enabled Subversion Server

If you want to provide access to your Subversion repository via Internet, setting up WebDAV access may well be the solution of choice. WebDAV (Web-based Distributed Authoring and Versioning) is an extension of the HTTP protocol designed to allow users to collaboratively create and modify documents on a remote server. DeltaV is an extension of WebDAV, which provides versioning and version control services. WebDAV access has many things going for it: it is standard, widely used, well supported by many operating systems, and is based on the very ubiquitous HTTP/HTTPS protocol. It is widely supported by most modern operating systems (Figure 4-4, for example, shows a WebDAV access to the repository of one of the Apache projects under KDE in Linux).

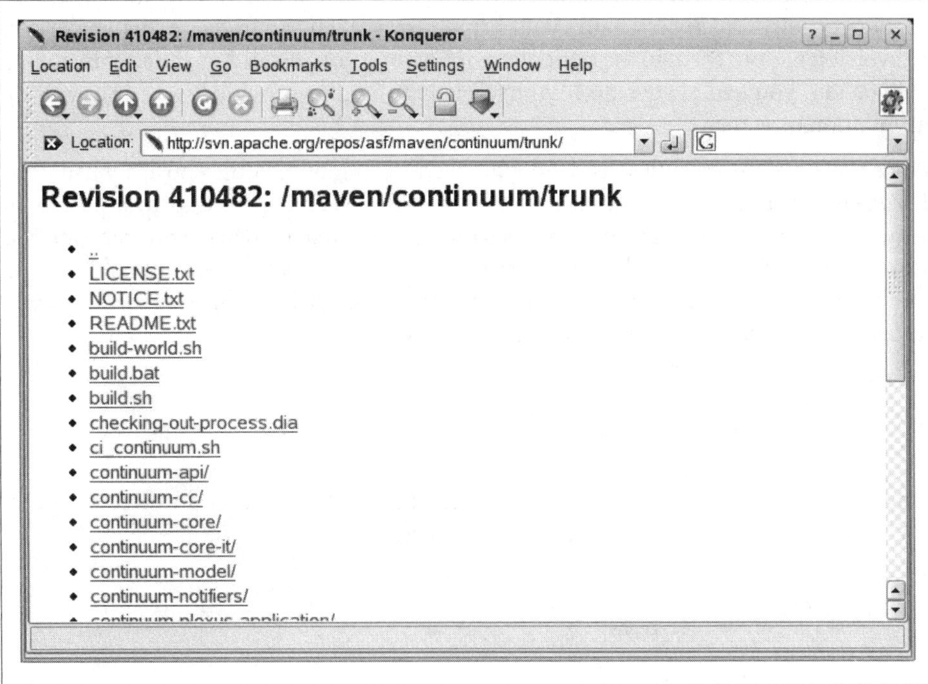

Figure 4-4. A WebDAV connection to the Apache Maven Continuum repository viewed from a Linux client

Subversion uses the robust Apache web server to provide repository access via WebDAV/DeltaV. Here, we'll see how to set up an Apache server to do this.

First, you will need an installation of Apache 2.0 or better, with the *mod_dav* module (*mod_dav* is included with most distributions of Apache nowadays; if not, you may have to compile and install Apache with the right configuration options yourself). You also need the *mod_dav_svn* module, which is Subversion's *mod_dav* plug-in. If Apache is already installed when you install Subversion, the Subversion installer will have a go at updating the Apache configuration files correctly. Still, it is wise to check. The Apache configuration file is called *httpd.conf*, and its exact location will vary depending on your OS and how Apache was installed. On Unix machines, it can often be found at */usr/local/apache2/conf/httpd.conf* or */etc/apache2/http.conf*. On Windows machines, you will usually find it in the Apache installation directory (something like *C:\Program Files\Apache Group\Apache2\conf*).

To access Subversion via Apache, you will need the mod_dav_svn and mod_authz_svn modules to be loaded with a *LoadModule* directive:

```
LoadModule dav_svn_module      /path/to/modules/dir/mod_dav_svn.so
LoadModule authz_svn_module    /path/to/modules/dir/modules/mod_authz_svn.so
```

Again, the path to the modules directory can vary depending on your Apache installation. Subversion provides these modules during the installation process and (with a bit of chance) will correctly configure your httpd.conf file if it can find one. Just make sure Subversion has put them in the right place. If not, or if you install Apache after installing Subversion, you can always do it yourself using the files provided in the Subversion installation directory.

Once you have the modules installed, you need to configure your repository using the *Location* directive. The *Location* directive provides WebDAV access to a particular Subversion repository or group of repositories. It tells Apache where your repository is stored, what URL it should be mapped to, and other such details. A minimal Location directive, which will give public access to your repository via WebDAV (and allow you to test your WebDAV installation) is shown here:

```
<Location /repos>
  DAV svn
  SVNPath /data/svn/dev-repos
</Location>
```

On a Windows machine, you just have to provide a Windows-friendly directory path, enclosed in double-quotes if there are any spaces:

```
<Location /repos>
  DAV svn
  SVNPath "c:/svn/dev-repos"
</Location>
```

You can also narrow access down to a particular project within your repository, as shown here, where access is limited to a particular project called "javalamp":

```
<Location /javalamp>
  DAV svn
  SVNPath /data/svn/dev-repos/javalamp
</Location>
```

This can be a good option. If you need to manage several different and unrelated projects. Simply add several <Location> entries like this one in your repository, one for each project. This makes it easier to set up separate Apache-based security configurations for each project.

Add this at the end of your Apache configuration file and restart the server. Now, you should be able to connect to your repository via a standard WebDAV client, using a URL like *http://myrepositoryserver.mycompany.com/repos*. Most modern operating systems integrate WebDAV interfaces nowadays (see Figure 4-5).

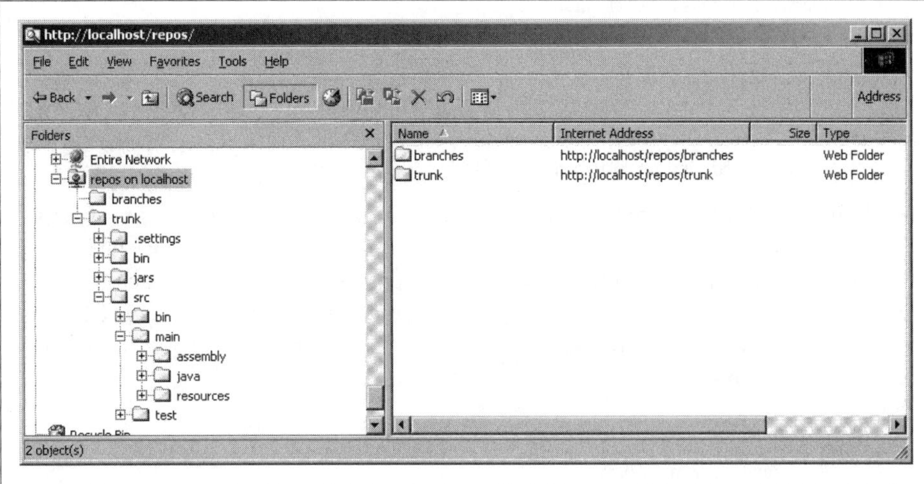

Figure 4-5. A Windows Web-DAV client accessing the JavaLamp project

But, of course, that is just icing on the cake. What we really want is to access our repository using an HTTP URL. Nothing could be easier! In the following example, we check out our project from the WebDAV repository, and, just for good measure, modify something in the README.txt file and commit it back:

```
C:\> svn co http://localhost/repos/trunk webdavProject
A    webdavProject\src
A    webdavProject\src\test
A    webdavProject\src\test\java
A    webdavProject\src\test\java\com
A    webdavProject\src\test\java\com\wakaleo
A    webdavProject\src\test\java\com\wakaleo\jdpt
...
Checked out revision 29.
...
C:\> svn commit -m "Updated a WebDAV project"
```

```
Sending        README.txt
Transmitting file data .
Committed revision 30.
```

Another useful trick if you have all your repositories in the same directory is to provide access to the root directory, using the SVNParentPath directive:

```
<Location /repos>
  DAV svn
  SVNParentPath /data/svn
</Location>
```

In this case, you use URLs that include the repository name as well, as shown here:

```
$ svn checkout http://localhost/repos/dev-repos/dev/javalamp/trunk webdavProject2
A    webdavProject\src
A    webdavProject\src\test
A    webdavProject\src\test\java
A    webdavProject\src\test\java\com
...
```

Note that here WebDAV access is provided to each individual repository (e.g., *http://localhost/repos/dev*) and not to the root directory (*http://localhost/repos*). If you try to access the root directory through a WebDAV client, your request will be rejected.

Now that we have the basic access working, we can start thinking about security issues. You probably don't want your repository to be modifiable by everyone on the Internet, or even everyone in your company. There are several ways of restricting access to your WebDAV-enabled repository. The simplest and most widely accepted is HTTP Basic authentication, where the browser prompts for a username and password before allowing access to the repository. You can set this up as follows:

```
<Location /repos>
    DAV svn
    SVNParentPath /data/svn
    AuthType Basic
    AuthName "Subversion repository"
    AuthUserFile "/data/svn/svn-auth-file"
    Require valid-user
</Location>
```

Let's look at the new options that we've added here:

AuthType
: The AuthType indicates the type of HTTP authentication, which can be either "Basic" or "Digest." Basic authentication works with most client browsers, but is, well, basic, as far as security goes. Digest authentication is accepted by fewer browsers (although most modern browsers will still work fine), but offers better security. More on this later.

AuthName
: AuthName is the (arbitrary) name of your authentication domain, which is typically used when prompting for passwords.

AuthUserFile
: User accounts are stored in a special file which is specified in the AuthUserFile directive.

Require
: This tells Apache when the authentication mechanism should be used.

You set up and manage user accounts using the *htpasswd* (or *htpasswd2*, depending on your distribution) tool delivered with the Apache server. This tool is pretty basic, but easy to use. The following listing shows how you would create two users. The *-c* option in the first line tells *htpasswd* to create a new file:

```
# htpasswd2 -cm /data/svn/svn-auth-file john
New password: ****
Re-type new password: ****
Adding password for user john
# htpasswd2 -m /data/svn/svn-auth-file mike
New password: **** R
e-type new password: ****
Adding password for user mike
```

If you want to specify the password in the command line, rather than prompting for it, you can use the *-b* option. This can come in handy if you need to write a script to create many users:

```
$ htpasswd2 -bm /data/svn/svn-auth-file jack secret
```

And, finally, if you need to delete a user, just use *-D*:

```
$ htpasswd2 -D /data/svn/svn-auth-file jack
```

Now you're ready to go. Users can still check out the project without restriction, but if they commit any modifications, they will be prompted for a username and password.

The *valid-user* parameter in the above example means that only authenticated users can access the repository in any way. Users need a proper account both to checkout code and to commit changes. This is a fairly strict policy, and does not always match your needs. Sometimes, for example, you would like to give all users read-only access, but only allow authenticated users to modify the code. One of the easiest ways to do this is to use the Apache *<LimitExcept>* directive to allow the read-only HTTP access methods (GET, PROPFIND, and so on) for nonauthenticated users, and require authentication for the read-write access methods such as POST. An example of such a configuration is shown here:

```
<Location /svn/repos>
    DAV svn
    SVNParentPath /data/svn
    AuthType Basic
    AuthName "Subversion repository"
    AuthUserFile "/data/svn/svn-auth-file"
    <LimitExcept GET PROPFIND OPTIONS REPORT>
        Require valid-user
```

```
    </LimitExcept>
</Location>
```

Actually, Basic HTTP authentication is not very secure, since passwords can be sniffed on the network without too much trouble. If your users have reasonably modern browsers and/or WebDAV client software, you should use Digest authentication, which is more secure. Using Digest authentication, passwords are never stored or transmitted in user-readable form but are transmitted using a one-way encryption technique (MD5, to be precise).

To use Digest authentication, you need to make sure that the *auth_digest_module* is activated in the Apache configuration file (in many installations it isn't by default). You should have something along the following lines in your Apache configuration file:

```
LoadModule auth_digest_module modules/mod_auth_digest.so
```

You need to change the *Location* directive in your Apache configuration file as follows:

```
<Location /repos>
    DAV svn
    SVNParentPath /data/svn
    AuthType Digest
    AuthName "Subversion repository"
    AuthDigestDomain /repos/
    AuthDigestFile /data/svn/svn-digest-auth-file
    Require valid-user
</Location>
```

The "AuthDigestDomain" indicates the URL path you want to protect, and "AuthDigestFile" indicates the user account file. Digest authentication does not use the same user account file as Basic authentication. You manage user accounts using the *htdigest* (or *htdigest2*) tool, as shown here:

```
# htdigest2 -c /data/svn/svn-digest-auth-file "Subversion repository" john
Adding password for john in realm Subversion repository.
New password: ****
Re-type new password: ****
```

Now just restart the Apache server. Clients won't notice any difference, but passwords will now be transmitted in MD5 form.

4.22 Setting Up a Secure WebDAV/DeltaV Server

Although Digest authentication provides a reasonable level of security, and is often quite sufficient for a secured enterprise network or VPN, for example. However, it will not resist the efforts of a determined hacker, and is not suitable if you need to communicate sensitive data across the Internet. True security in a web environment requires HTTPS encryption. Configuring Apache SSL configuration and managing SSL certificates is beyond the scope of this book, but is well documented elsewhere, such as on the Apache web site.

4.23 Customizing Subversion with Hook Scripts

Subversion is a very flexible tool, and it is easy to extend its features to suit your particular environment. For example, you might want to send a mail on each commit, update your issue tracking system, or even to force users to include a reference to a bug number in their commit message.

Subversion hooks allow you to do this sort of thing. Subversion hooks allow you to trigger arbitrary actions whenever a particular event (typically a commit) occurs in the repository. The hook scripts live in the *hooks* directory of your Subversion repository. When you install Subversion, there will be a number of sample scripts already provided, indicated by the ".tmpl" suffix:

```
# cd /data/svn/repos
# ls
conf  dav  db  format  hooks  locks  README.txt
# ls hooks
post-commit.tmpl  post-revprop-change.tmpl  pre-commit.tmpl  pre-revprop-change.tmpl
start-commit.tmpl
post-lock.tmpl    post-unlock.tmpl          pre-lock.tmpl    pre-unlock.tmpl
```

The events are fairly intuitive. For example, the *pre-commit* script is run just before a commit happens, and the *post-commit* just afterward. Subversion supports five hooks, which are each used for different purposes:

start-commit
: This script is run just before a commit transaction begins, and is typically used to prevent a commit from happening at all if some condition is not met. If this script returns a nonzero result, the commit will not take place.

pre-commit
: This script is run when the commit is ready to happen, but just before it actually takes place. You can use this script to enforce constraints; you might want to require that developers include a reference to an issue in your issue tracking system in the commit message, for example. If this script returns a nonzero result, the commit will be aborted.

post-commit
: This script is invoked after the transaction has been processed and once a new revision has been created. You would typically use this script to send notification messages or to update your issue tracking system, for example.

pre-revprop-change
: This script is executed just before a revision property is modified. Because revision properties are not versioned, this can be used if necessary to add some extra security checks.

post-revprop-change
: This script is run just after a revision property has been modified. Like the *post-commit* hook, this is typically used for notification purposes.

The simplest way to activate a script is simply to duplicate one of the template files and remove the ".tmpl" suffix. On a Unix machine, make sure the script is executable. And on Windows, you will need to add an executable extension such as ".bat."

You can write Subversion hook scripts in any language, although Python and plain old shell scripts seem to be popular options. There are also many useful scripts are available on the Internet (see, in particular, *http://svn.collab.net/repos/svn/trunk/tools/hook-scripts/* and *http://svn.collab.net/repos/svn/trunk/contrib/hook-scripts/*).

There are many practical applications for Subversion hook scripts. Some useful applications of hook scripts are described here:

Sending email nofitications
: One common notification technique is to send an email notification to all team members whenever someone commits code. This is a fairly commonly used approach for distributed projects. Actually, in most cases, you're probably better off letting a Continuous Build server take care of this kind of automation, and only send mail when a build fails.

Updating your issue management system
: This is a very useful integration techique. If developers include references to issue numbers, you can get Subversion to update the corresponding issues in your issue tracking system. We look at how to update a Trac issue in Section 28.11. For users of the popular JIRA issue management system, no script was available at the time of writing, but a JIRA plug-in is available that polls the Subversion logs and updates any issues accordingly (see *http://confluence.atlassian.com/display/JIRAEXT/JIRA+Subversion+plugin*).

Enforcing coding practices
: The *pre-commit* hook can be used to enforce particular coding or development practices. For example, you might want to make sure there are no tab characters in the source code files, or that every log message contains at least one reference to an issue in your issue management system. This is a more proactive (and aggressive!) approach than using static analysis tools such as Checkstyle (see Chapter 21).

4.24 Installing Subversion As a Windows Service

If you have to install Subversion on a Windows server, you'll probably want to install it as a service. Unfortunately, this feature doesn't come out of the box with the Windows Subversion installation package: you have to set it up yourself.

Magnus Norddahl* has written a small Windows service wrapper utility called SVNService, which can be used to install Subversion as a Windows service. Download the package, place the executable file (SVNService.exe) in the same directory as your subversion executable, and set up the service as follows:

```
C:\> SVNService -install -d -r d:\svn-repository
```

An alternative approach is to use the generic Windows *InstSrv* and *SrvAny* tools, which come with the Windows Server Resource Toolkits. First, you need to set up a new Windows service by running InstSrv. You need to provide the name of the service you want to create (say "svnserve," just to be original), and the full path of the *Srvany.exe*:

```
C:\>InstSrv svnserve "C:\Program Files\Windows Resource Kits\Tools\srvany.exe"
The service was successfuly added!

Make sure that you go into the Control Panel and use
the Services applet to change the Account Name and
Password that this newly installed service will use
for its Security Context.
```

Now you need to configure the service in the Windows registry (see Figure 4-6). Open the Registry Editor, go to *HKEY_LOCAL_MACHINE\SYSTEM\CurrentControlSet \Services\svnserve*, add a Parameters Key and two String Values:

- *Application*, which indicates the full path to your svnserve executable
- *AppParameters*, in which you place the command-line parameters you would normally pass to *svnserve* (such as "-d -r D:\svn\repository")

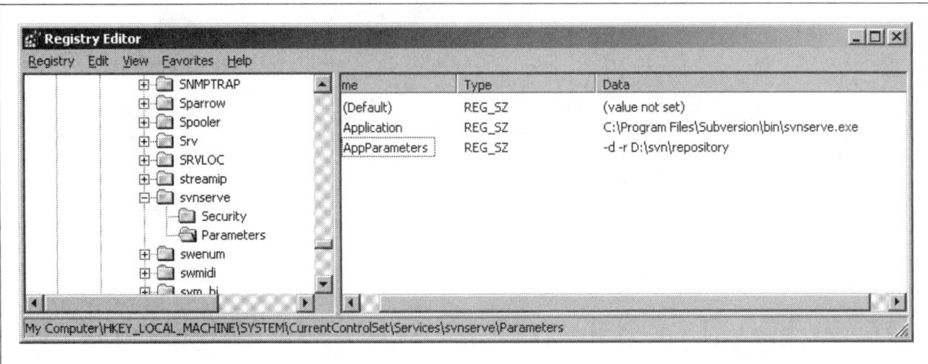

Figure 4-6. Setting up Subversion as a Windows service

Now you should have a new Windows service. By default, the service will start up automatically when you reboot the server. You can start (or stop) the service manually in the Services administration screen (see Figure 4-7) or using the *NET START* and *NET STOP* commands at the command line, as follows:

* *http://www.clanlib.org/~mbn/svnservice/*

```
C:\>net start svnserve
The svnserve service is starting.
The svnserve service was started successfully.

C:\>net stop svnserve

The svnserve service was stopped successfully.
```

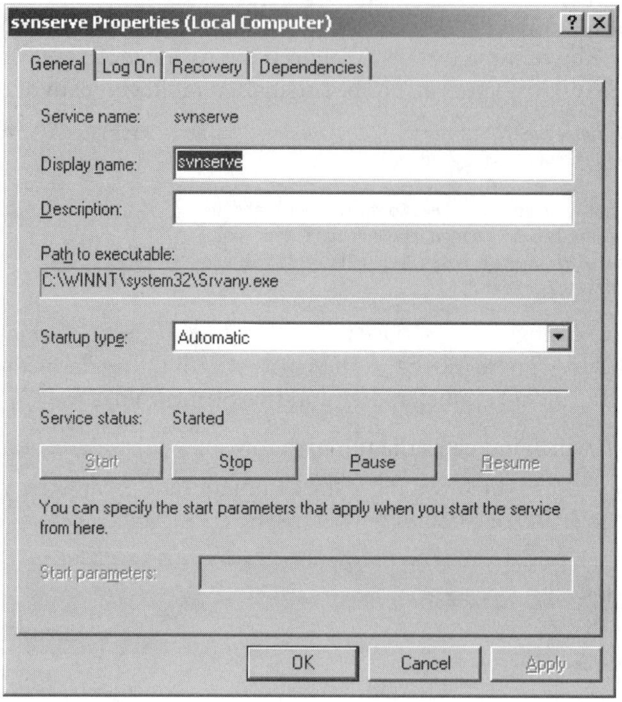

Figure 4-7. Subversion as a Windows service

4.25 Backing Up and Restoring a Subversion Repository

If you are in charge of administering a Subversion repository; it can come in handy to know how to back it up. The *svnadmin dump* command lets you do just that: it generates a portable (although not very readable) format that you can use to restore your precious repository if disaster strikes. This is also recommended procedure when upgrading to a new version of Subversion.

The following line will dump the whole repository into a file called *svn-backup*:

```
$ svnadmin dump /data/svn/dev-repos > svn-backup.
* Dumped revision 0.
```

```
* Dumped revision 1.
* Dumped revision 2.
...
* Dumped revision 30.
* Dumped revision 31.
```

Of course, you can gain some space (I gain around 25% on my repository) by compressing the backup format with a tool like *gzip*:

```
$ svnadmin dump /data/svn/dev-repos | gzip -9 > svn-backup.gz
```

To rebuild your repository after a disaster, or after an upgrade, you need to recreate your repository and then load the backed-up repository data using *svnadmin load*:

```
$ svnadmin create /data/svn/dev-repos svn-backup
$ svnadmin load /data/svn/dev-repos <
<<< Started new transaction, based on original revision 1
     * adding path : book.xml ... done.
     * adding path : ch04.xml ... done.
     * adding path : ch25.xml ... done.

------- Committed revision 1 >>>

<<< Started new transaction, based on original revision 2
...
```

If you compressed the backup file as shown above, you can also restore the repository directly from the compressed file as shown here:

```
$ gunzip -c svn-backup.gz | svnadmin load /data/svn/dev-repos
```

4.26 Using Subversion in Eclipse

Subversion integrates quite smoothly into the Eclipse IDE. There are currently two open source plug-ins available providing Subversion integration in Eclipse. It is worth noting that there is also an Eclipse project (in incubation at the time of writing) aiming at provided integrated Subversion support in Eclipse (see *http://www.eclipse.org/subversive/*). However, at the time of this writing, Subversive is younger and less mature than Subclipse, so we will focus on Subclipse.

Installing Subclipse

You install Subclipse from the Subclipse update site at *http://subclipse.tigris.org/update_1.2.x* for Eclipse 3.2 or higher, in the usual way via the Install/Update window (see Figure 4-8).

Depending on your OS, you may need to do some configuration in the Preferences screen (see Figure 4-9). The most important choice is the SVN Interface. Subclipse supports two ways of accessing the Subversion server: JavaSVN and JavaHL. The JavaSVN interface is a pure Java Subversion interface, which is reported to be faster than, and to support a few more features than JavaHL. At the time of writing, it did

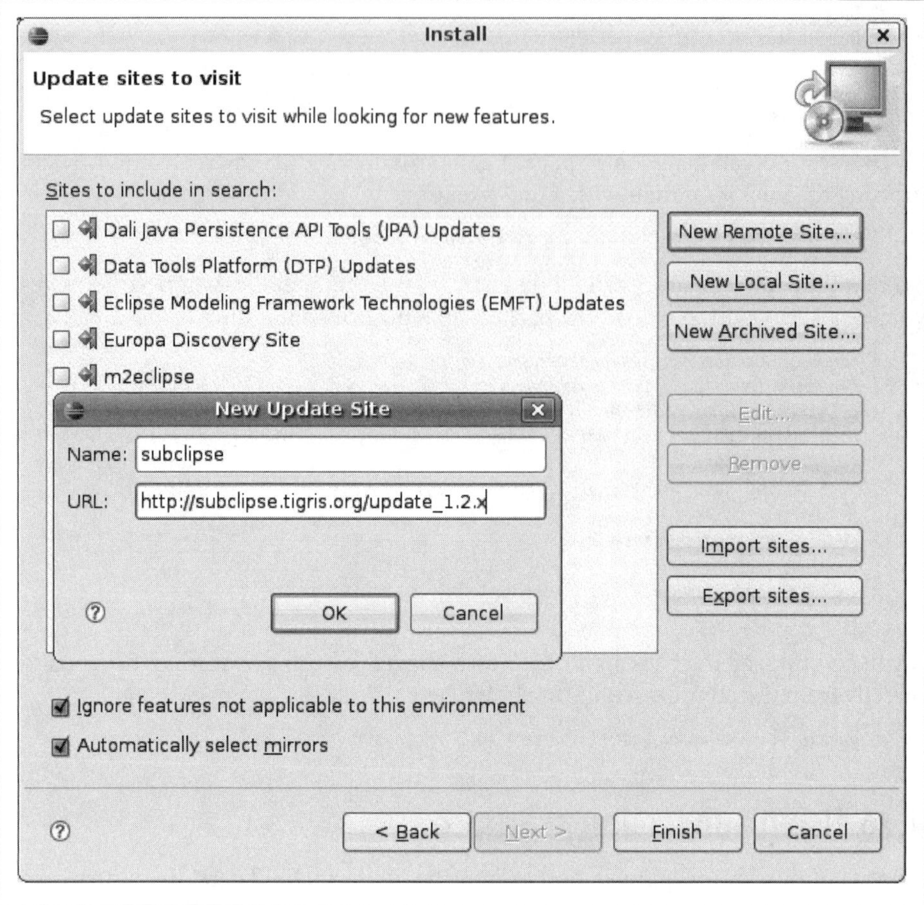

Figure 4-8. Installing Subclipse

not support *file://* protocol. The JavaHL Interface is a native library provided with the Windows installation of Subclipse, and which does support the *file://* protocol. However, on a non-Windows platform, you will have to find and compile JavaHL on your own. I guess you can't have your cake and eat it too...

Defining a Repository

The first thing you will need to do is set up some repositories in. Open the "SVN Repository" view, and select New→Repository Location in the contextual menu (see Figure 4-10). All you need to provide is the Subversion repository URL.

The "SVN Repository" view can be useful for other tasks as well (see Figure 4-11). Using the contextual menu, you can checkout project directories, import local direc-

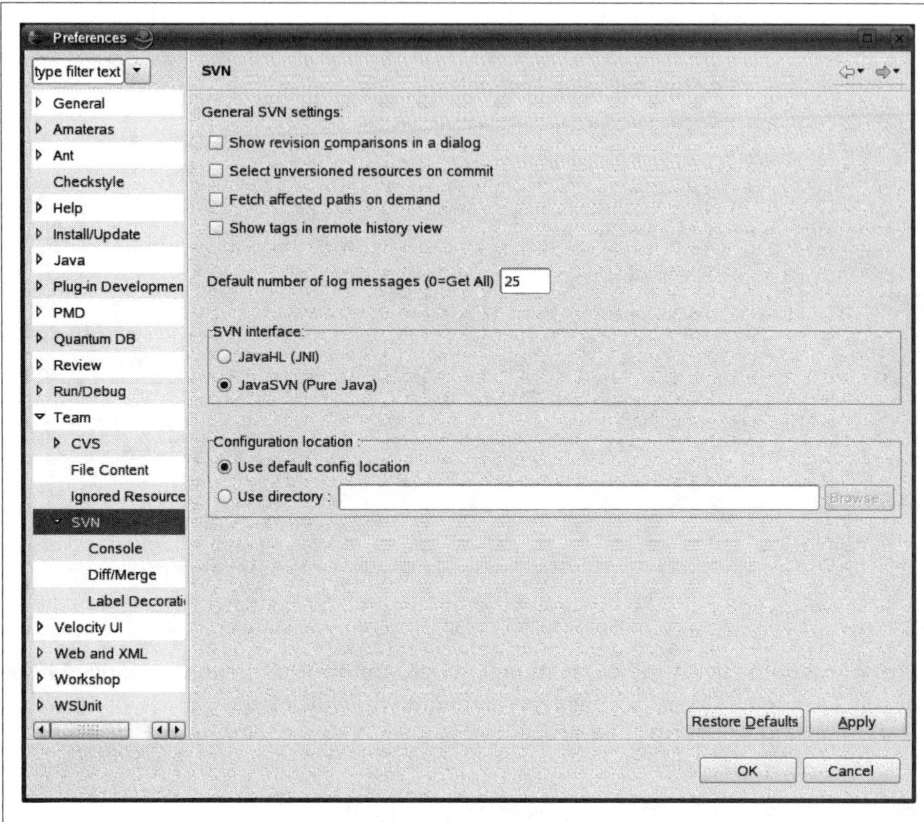

Figure 4-9. Configuring Subclipse

tories into the repository, or export them to your local machine, and even create branches or move directories.

Adding a New Project to the Repository

If your project is brand new, or if it hasn't been placed in the Subversion repository yet, you will need to import it into the repository. You just open the Share window (right click, Team, Share Project...) (see Figure 4-12). You will need to provide the URL of your Subversion repository, or use one of the existing repositories.

Once you have specified the repository and the project name, you indicate the files and directories you want to place in the repository and provide an initial comment (see Figure 4-13). This lets you easily create a Subversion repository project containing just the project source code, even if your project directory contains generated classes, temporary files, or other unnecessary artifacts.

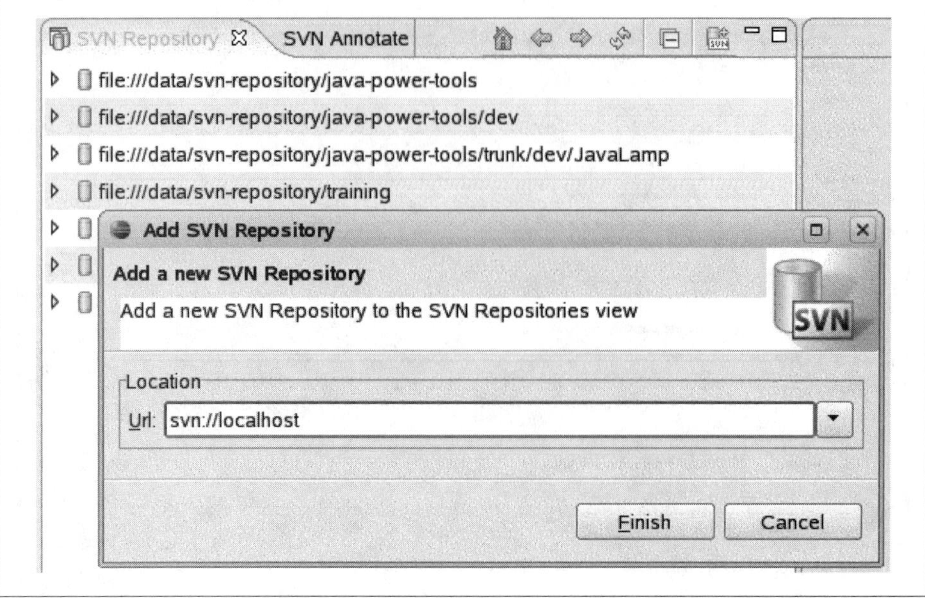

Figure 4-10. Adding a new Subversion repository

Now you should have a fully operational Subversion project up and running. Check out the Team menu now (see Figure 4-14), and you will see the a range of available Subversion commands.

Creating a Project from the Subversion Repository

Subclipse makes it easy to check out a Subversion project into your Eclipse workspace. In the New Project window (File→New→Project), open the Subversion menu entry and select "Checkout Projects from SVN" (see Figure 4-15).

You will need to provide the Subversion repository URL. Then Eclipse will list the projects stored in this repository (see Figure 4-16). Choose the directory you want to check out (typically, you will be creating a project from the main trunk of your project).

Once you have chosen the directory, you can either checkout the repository contents directly into your Eclipse workspace ("Check out as a project in the workspace") or you can create a new project using one of the other project types based on the repository contents ("Checkout as a project configured using the New Project Wizard"). The latter option is better for Java projects, because you can then use the Eclipse project template that you're used to. In both cases, you will still need to update the project build path, because Eclipse can't work out where the Java source code is before checking out the project source code.

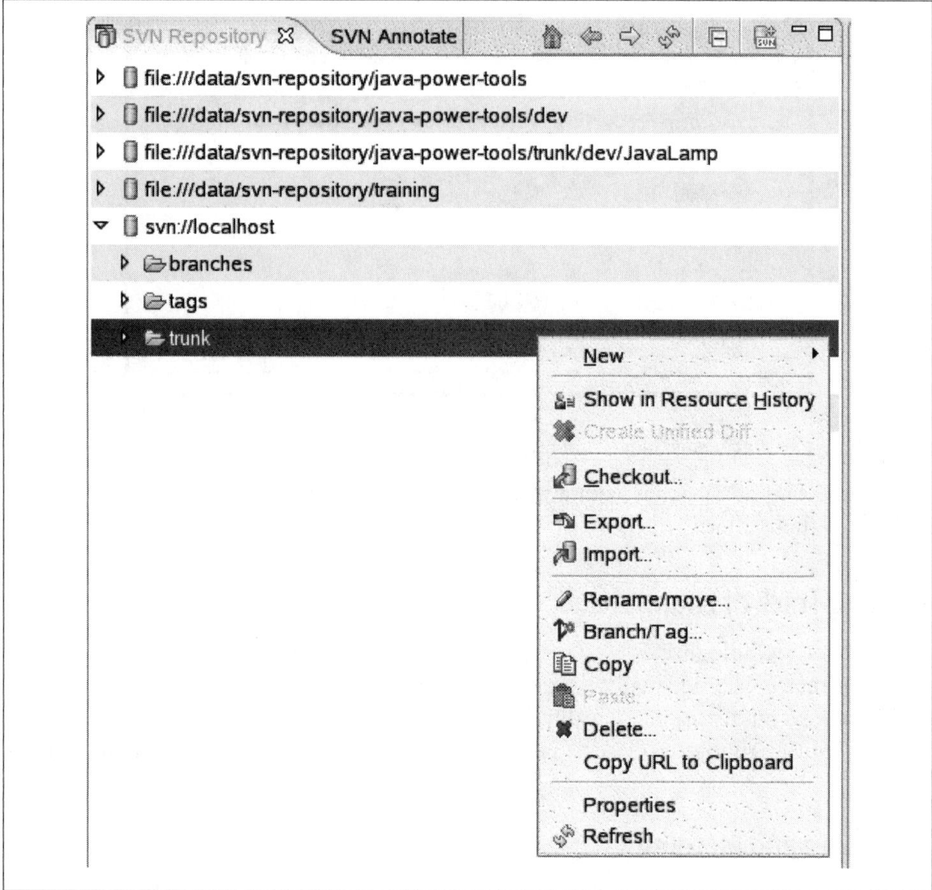

Figure 4-11. Working with the Subversion repository

If you have created an Eclipse project using a directory that has already been checked out of a Subversion repository, you can also use the "Team→Share Project" command in the contextual menu to enable Subversion features within Eclipse for this project.

Working with Files

Most of the main Subversion commands are available through the "Team" contextual menu (see Figure 4-14). From here, you can update your project and commit changes, along with more advanced functions such as branching and merging. The "Synchronize with Repository" option essentially lets you do an update and a commit at the same time, by comparing your local modifications with any changes in the repository (see Figure 4-17), and selectively incorporate the repository modifications into your local copy. When you are satisfied, you can safely update and commit your changes to the

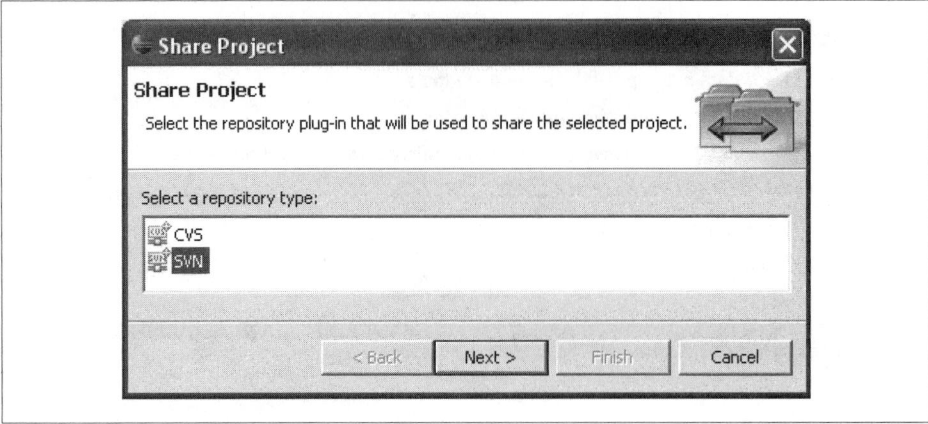

Figure 4-12. Creating a new Subversion project using the Share menu

repository. This approach is safer and more efficient than waiting for conflicts to occur and fixing them afterward.

Keeping Track of Changes

Locally modified files are easy to see in the Eclipse. Both modified files and their containing directories are visually flagged, making them easy to locate. You can list the modifications made to a file or group of files using the "Show History" option. You can also use "Show Annotation" to visualize what user made each modification in the file's history.

Branching and Merging

Subclipse provides good support for branching and merging operations. You can create a new branch or tag easily using the "Branch/Tag" menu option. Switching over to a different development tag or branch (see Section 4.12) is also fairly straightforward. Go to the project root directory and select "Team→Switch to another branch/tag" in the contextual menu. In both cases, a *Browse* button lets you select the branch or tag you need, without having to remember the exact spelling.

You can merge changes done in another branch using the "Merge" option (see Figure 4-18). This is not a particularly simple window, reflecting the fact the merges in Subversion are powerful but not especially intuitive. The most important thing to get right here is the initial revision number, which indicates the point in time from which changes in the branch will be included into your workspace. The "Show Log" button can help here.

To roll back to a previous revision (see Section 4.13), you simply start from the Head revision, and provide the revision number to which you want to return in the "To"

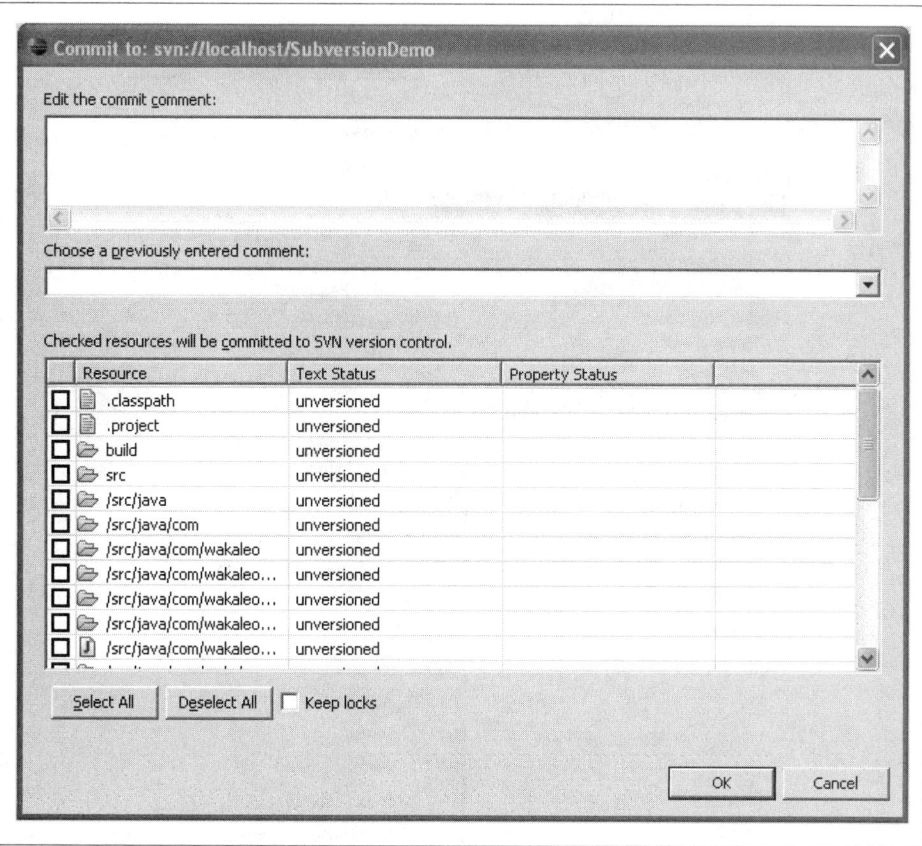

Figure 4-13. Creating a new Subversion project

field, (see Figure 4-19). Once the rollback is completed, you need to submit your new version to update the repository.

4.27 Using Subversion in NetBeans

NetBeans provides some excellent Subversion integration features, which we will look at here.

Installing Subversion Support

Subversion support is not installed in NetBeans 5.5 by default: you need to install it through the Update option. Open the "Tools→Update Center" and make sure the "NetBeans Update Center" option is ticked. Then, in the "NetBeans Update Center" choices, choose "Subversion" (see Figure 4-20). Step though the installation process.

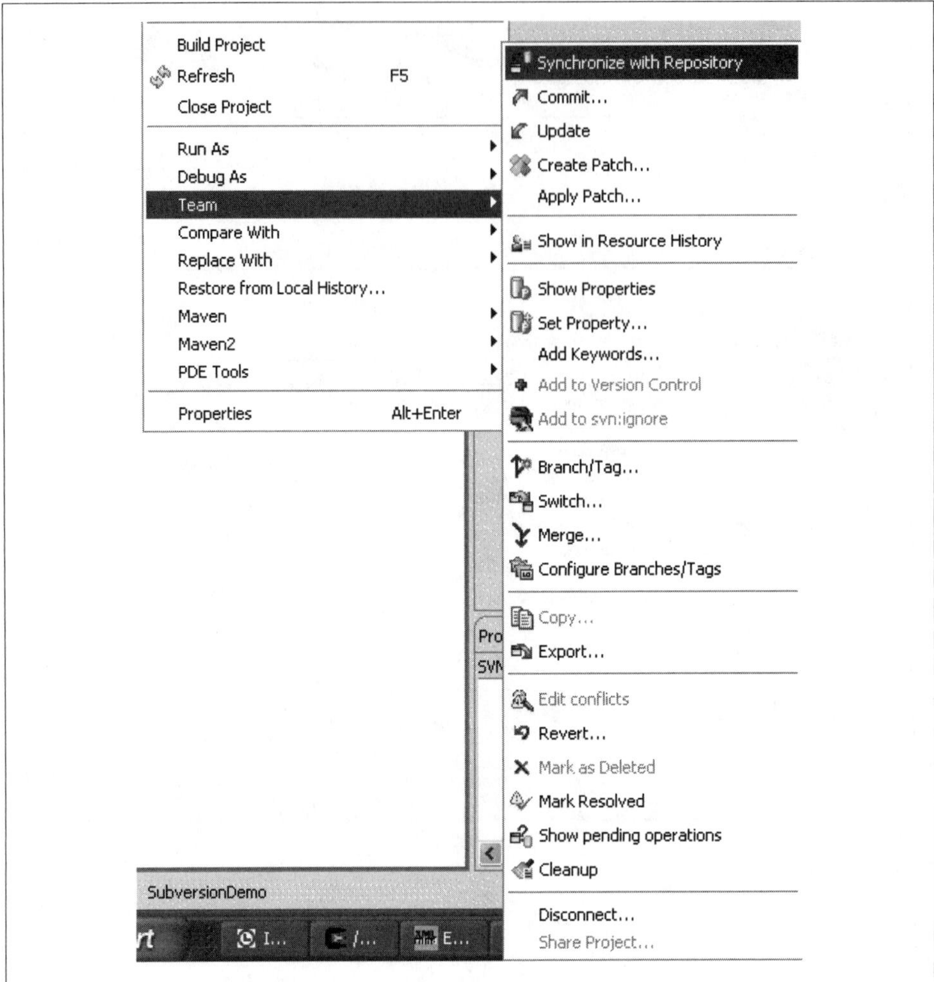

Figure 4-14. The Team menu for a Subversion project

When you're done, a new "Subversion" menu will appear in the main menu bar. Most of the principal Subversion commands are available, either from the main menu, or from the contextual menu for commands relating to a specific file or directory.

In NetBeans 6, both Subversion and CVS are supported out of the box in the "Versioning" menu. The rest of this section will look at the NetBeans 6 Subversion integration.

Creating a Subversion-Based Project

If you want to create a new project by downloading source code from a Subversion repository, NetBeans makes life very easy. Open the "Subversion→Checkout" menu

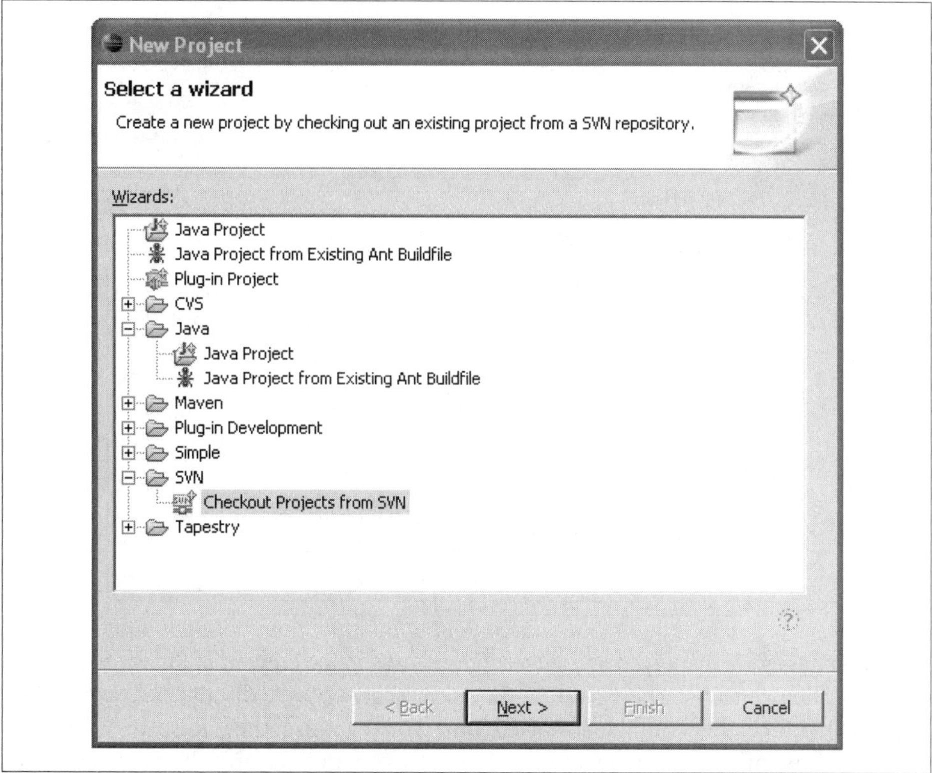

Figure 4-15. Creating a new project in Eclipse from a Subversion repository

(see Figure 4-21). Here, you provide the URL of the Subversion repository you need to checkout. Once you specify your local directory, NetBeans will proceed to download the entire project into the target directory and set up a corresponding NetBeans project in your workspace.

Once the source code has been downloaded, NetBeans will recognize and correctly configure a corresponding NetBeans project for both Ant and Maven-based projects (if you have the Maven extensions installed, that is). If it does not recognize the project structure, you can create a new project based on the new working directory using the normal Project Creation Wizard.

Working with Your Files

NetBeans does a good job of integrating Subversion into the everyday work environment of a NetBeans developer. Update and commit operations can be performed on files or directories using the contextual menu (see Figure 4-22). When you commit your changes, NetBeans will list modified files as well as any new files that you might have forgotten to add manually.

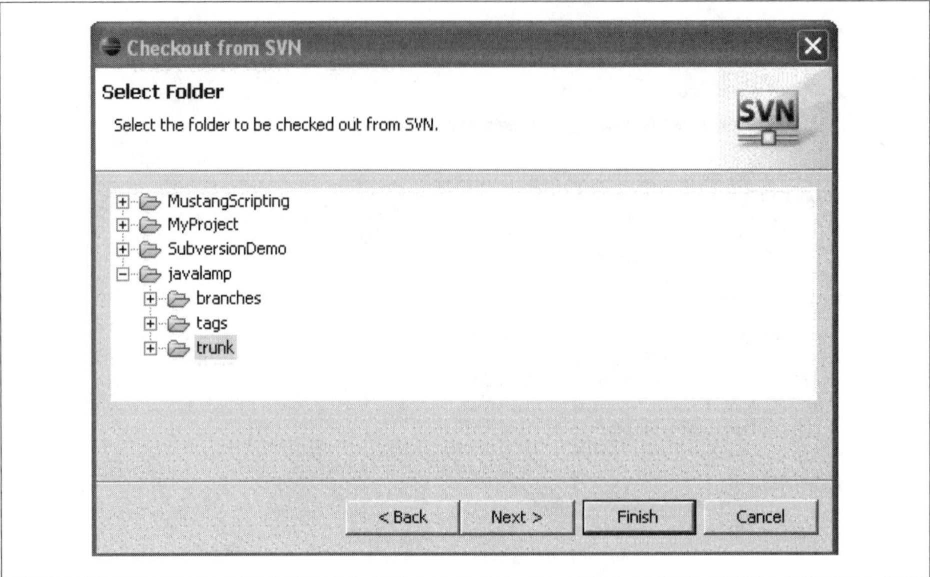

Figure 4-16. Checking out a Subversion project in Eclipse

Conflicting files are displayed in red (see Figure 4-23). One convenient way of resolving these conflicts is to use the visual "diff" editor that we will, discuss below (see Figure 4-24). Once the conflict is sorted out, you can use the "Resolve Conflicts" contextual menu option to declare the conflict fixed and commit the new version of the file.

Keeping Track of Changes

It is fairly easy to keep track of changes you have made in your local copy. Modified files are highlighted in blue and listed in the "Subversion" window, which you can open via the "Subversion→Show Changes" contextual menu, or by selecting the "Window→Versioning→Subversion" menu option. Like Eclipse and TortoiseSVN, the directories containing the modified files are flagged (a blue drum indicates modifications, whereas a red drum indicates conflicting files). You can compare versions in an interactive visual tool (see Figure 4-24). This view not only displays the differences between files but also allows you to selectively restore particular changes in the file (using the small arrow icons in the margin of the Base source code window).

There are also other ways of keeping track of changes. The "Show Annotations" menu option will run the *svn annotate* command, displaying when and by whom each line of a file has been modified. The "Search History" option, which has no native Subversion equivalent, lets you search the Subversion history for log messages containing a particular text and/or changes made by a particular user.

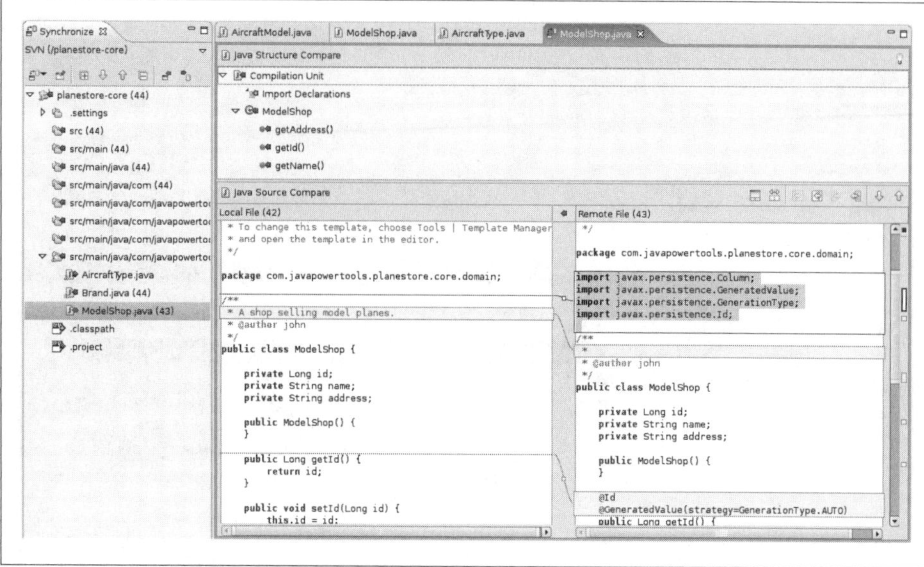

Figure 4-17. Synchronizing changes

Branching and Merging

As we have seen, branching and tagging in Subversion is essentially the same operation; a cheap directory copy (see Section 4.12). You can create new tags and branches in NetBeans using the "Copy To..." menu option. This opens a window where you can select the new branch or tag location by browsing the repository (see Figure 4-25). You also have the option of switching directly to the new copy, which is convenient if you are creating a new branch. Alternatively, you can switch to the new branch at any time using the "Switch To Copy..." menu option.

After you have worked on a separate development branch for a time, you will generally need to integrate your changes into the main development trunk. When it is time to merge your changes back into the main trunk, you can do this directly from within NetBeans. Switch to your main (target) branch (typically the trunk). This is the code base into which you want to incorporate your modifications. Then select "Merge Changes" in the Subversion menu. This will open a window where you select the branch containing your modifications. You can merge all the changes from a particular date or revision (using the "Merge From One Repository Folder" option), or, as shown in Figure 4-26, all the changes since the creation of the branch. This largely will depend on whether this is the first time you have merged code from this development branch.

Once you have merged your modifications into the main trunk in this way, you will still have to commit the changes to the repository.

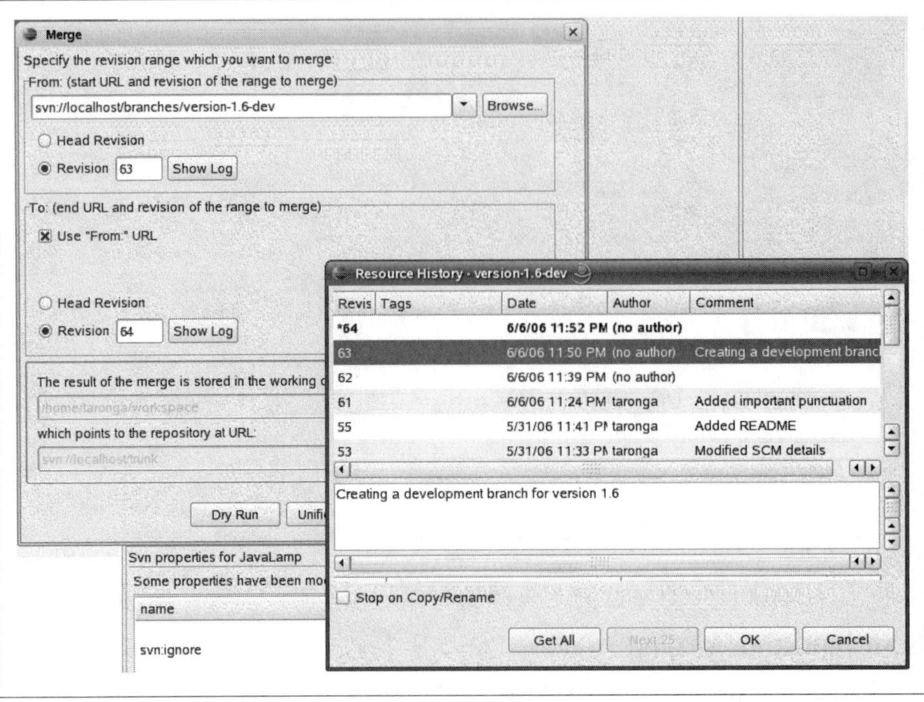

Figure 4-18. Merging branches in Eclipse

You can use this technique to roll back changes (see Section 4.13). Choose "One Repository Folder" in the "Merge From" drop-down list, and set the Ending Revision to the revision to which you want to roll back (see Figure 4-27). You can leave the Starting Revision field empty, as, in this case, the rollback process will start with the HEAD revision. Then, when you're done, you need to commit your changes to the repository.

4.28 Using Subversion in Windows

There are several Subversion clients for Windows, but one of the better ones is TortoiseSVN, a free open source tool from Tigris (*http://tortoisesvn.tigris.org/*). Using TortoiseSVN, Subversion integrates seamlessly into a Windows desktop environment. TortoiseSVN lets you access virtually all the Subversion commands via a graphical client interface, directly from within Windows Explorer (see Figure 4-28). In addition to a slick graphical interface, TortoiseSVN offers nice-to-have features such as spell checking and contextual help in the comments fields.

Like Subversion, TortoiseSVN is a very rich product, as can be gleaned by the number of commands available in the contextual menu (see Figure 4-28). Here, we will look at

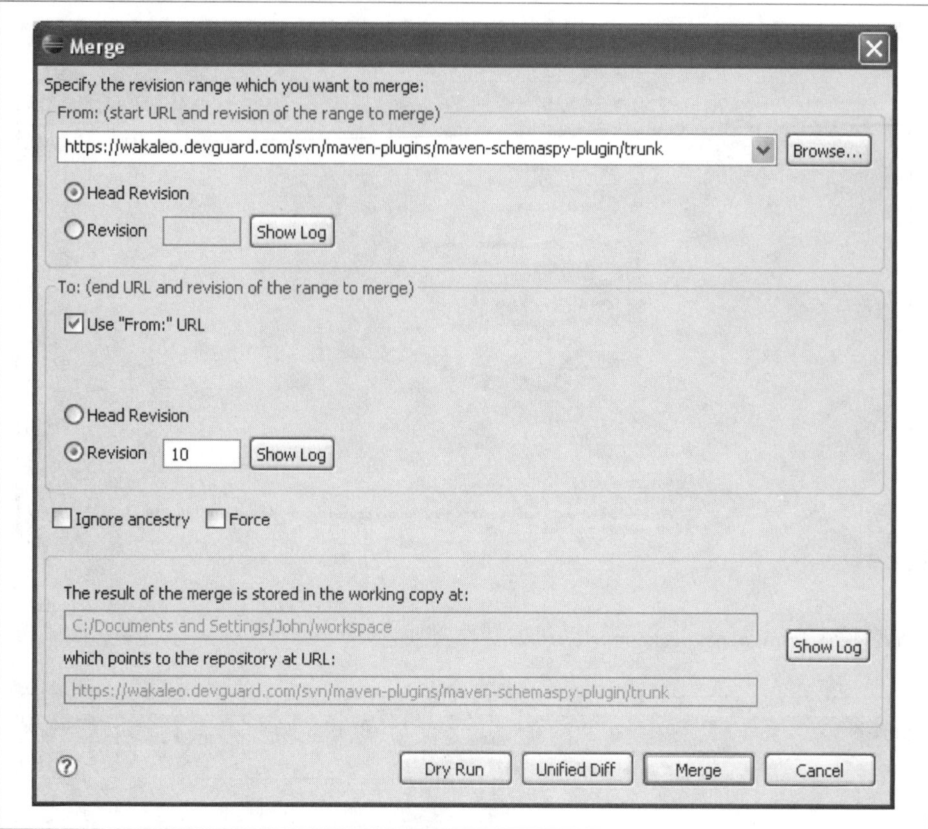

Figure 4-19. Merging branches in Eclipse

how TortoiseSVN can make life easier for Windows-based Subversion users, concentrating on a few of the most commonly used features.

Using TortoiseSVN in Windows Explorer

One of the key features of TortoiseSVN is its strong integration with Windows Explorer (see Figure 4-28). You don't have to run a client application: just open a Windows Explorer window.

Virtually all of the Subversion commands are available via the contextual menu, either directly for updates or commits, or in the "TortoiseSVN" submenu for everything else. TortoiseSVN uses intuitive icon overlays to let you see at a glance the status of each file: a green tick indicates an up-to-date file, a red exclamation mark indicates a modified file (or a directory containing a modified file), a red cross indicates an item scheduled for deletion, and so on.

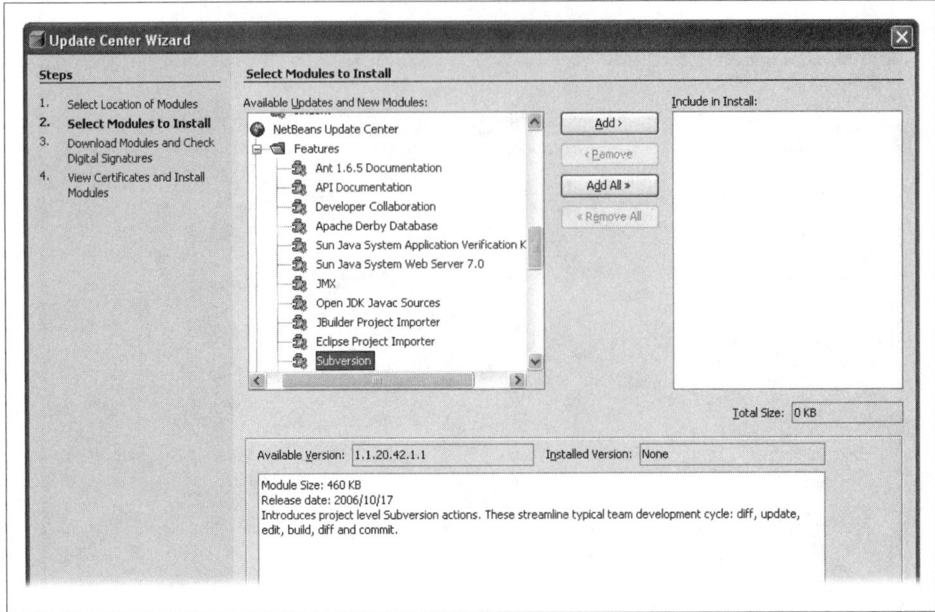

Figure 4-20. Installing Subversion in NetBeans

Checkout
Steps
1. Subversion Repository
2. Folders to Checkout
Subversion Repository
Specify the location of Subversion repository.
Repository URL: http://svn.apache.org/repos/asf/maven/continuum/trunk/
http://hostname/repository_path[@REV]
User: (leave blank for anonymous access)
Password:
Proxy Configuration...
< Back | Next > | Finish | Cancel | Help

Figure 4-21. Checking out a new project from Subversion

If your project is on a network drive or a removable drive (in fact, pretty much anything other than your standard built-in disk drives), you may not see the icon overlays at first. Open the "TortoiseSVN→Settings" dialog and go to "Look and Feel→Icon Overlays."

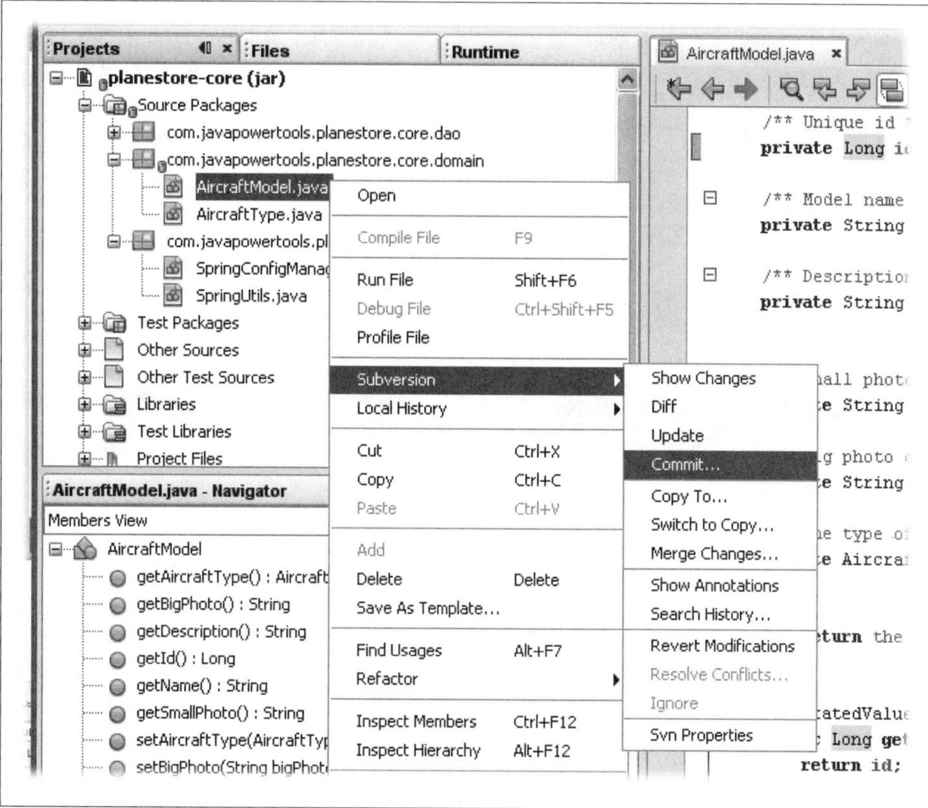

Figure 4-22. Most Subversion commands are accessible through the contextual menu

If you are working on a remote repository through a proxy server, you will need to configure this, too. You can set proxy settings in the "Network" entry of the "TortoiseSVN→Settings."

Importing a New Project into the Repository

When you create a new project using Subversion, one of the first things you need to do is to import the project into your Subversion repository (see Section 4.7). Doing this using TortoiseSVN is quite simple. Once you have set up your basic project directory structure, use the contextual menu in Windows Explorer (see Figure 4-29). You will need to specify the URL of your Subversion repository (or select one in the list of previously used repositories), and provide an (optional but recommended) comment.

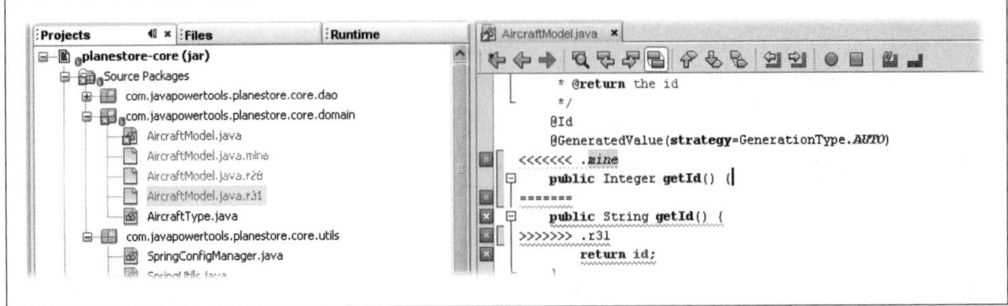

Figure 4-23. Most Subversion commands are accessible through the contextual menu

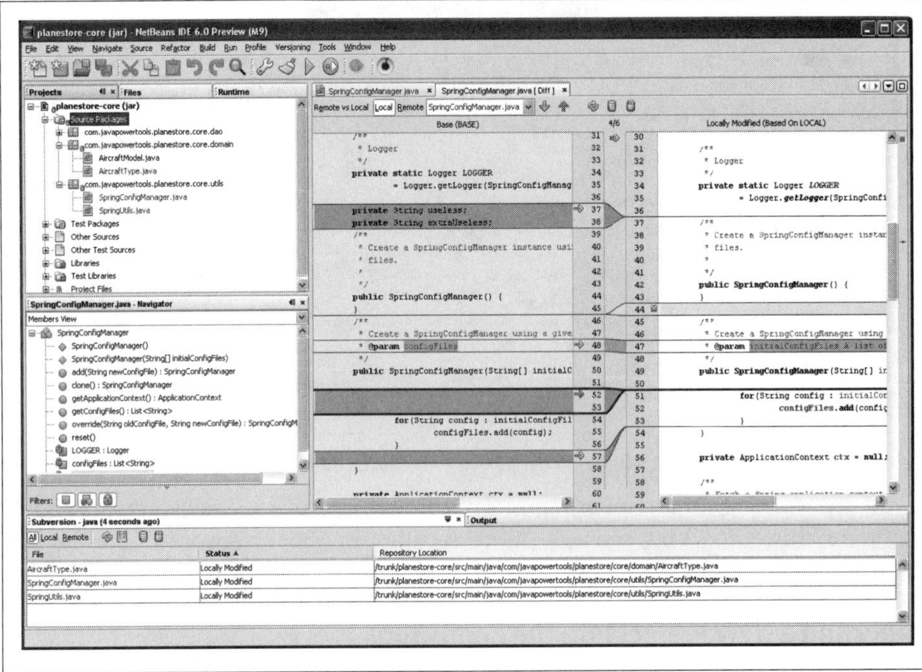

Figure 4-24. Seeing what files have been modified

Arguably, one of the quirks of Subversion is that, once you have imported the project, you still need to checkout a working copy of your project to actually be able to do anything useful.* This is also the case when you are using TortoiseSVN. We look at how to do this using TortoiseSVN next in "Obtaining a Working Copy."

* In fact, this is actually quite logical: you generally import your entire directory structure, branches, tags, and all, whereas your working copy is usually confined to the trunk directory.

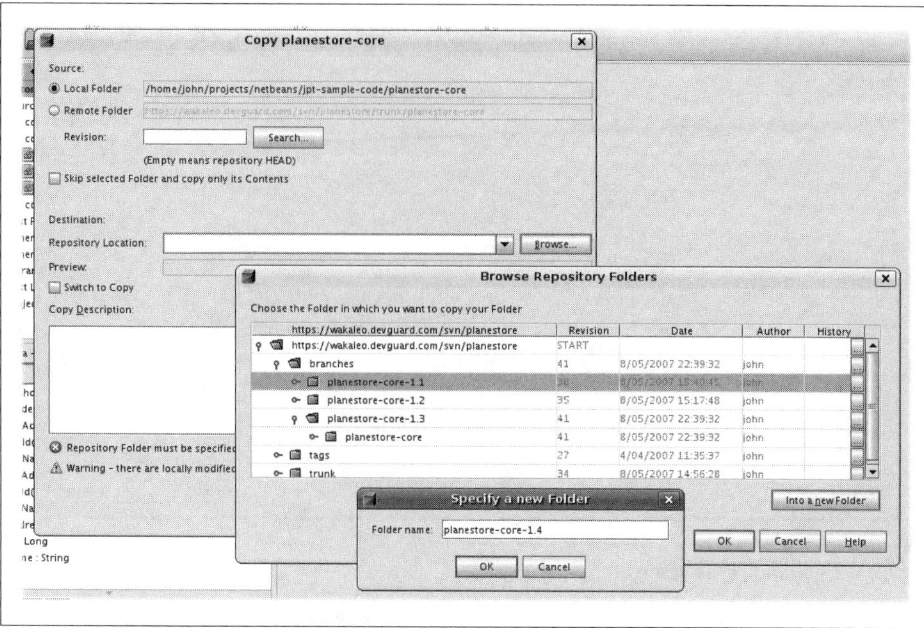

Figure 4-25. Creating a new tag or branch using the "Copy To..." option

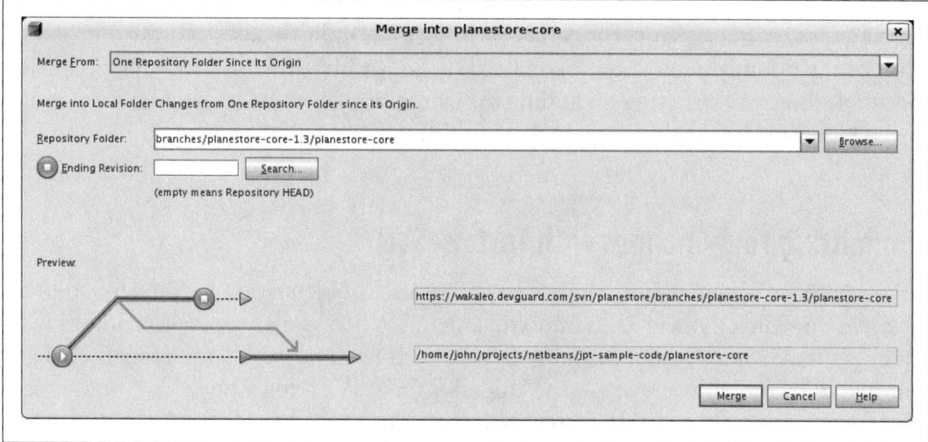

Figure 4-26. Merging a development branch back into the main trunk

Obtaining a Working Copy

Once your project is safely stored in the Subversion repository, you need to obtain a working copy on your local machine. You can do this using the "TortoiseSVN→Checkout" menu option in the contextual menu. First, specify the URL of the Subversion repository you want to checkout (see Figure 4-30).

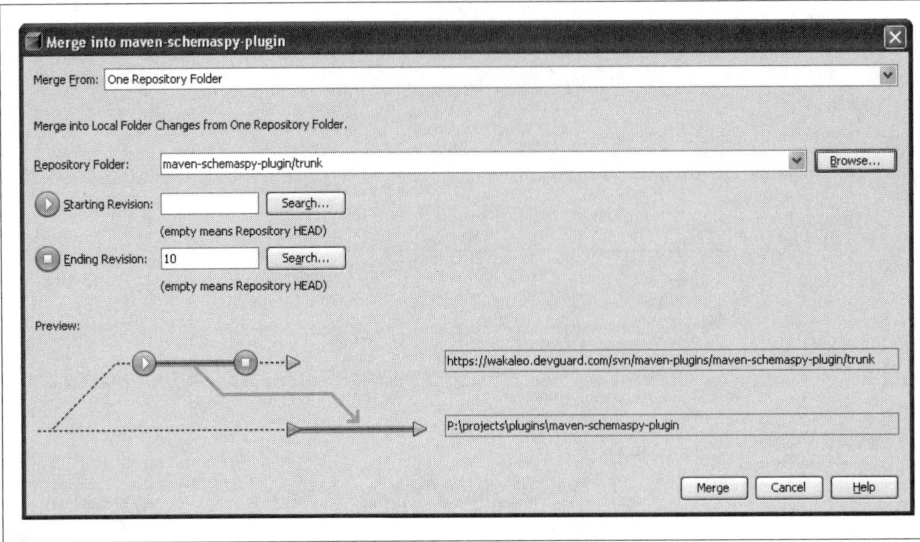

Figure 4-27. Rolling back changes

You need to specify the checkout directory, which is where the working copy will be created. This directory should be empty (or nonexistent). One common error is to try to check out into the directory that you just imported into Subversion. This is a bad idea for two reasons. First of all, it won't work. Subversion will refuse to overwrite your existing files with its own versioned copies. Second, in most cases, you will probably want your working directory to be confined to the "trunk" directory, rather than having the whole directory structure, including the trunk, branches, and tags. It is easy enough to switch to other branches or tags later on using the "switch" command.

Committing Your Changes with TortoiseSVN

Once you have obtained a working copy, TortoiseSVN lets you use Subversion in an intuitive way, directly from the contextual menu. When you are ready to commit your changes, make sure your working copy is up-to-date with any recent changes committed by other developers (see "Updating Your Working Copy," later in this section). Then select the project directory in Explorer and choose the "SVN Commit" option in the contextual menu.

Committing changes is one of the places where TortoiseSVN makes life a lot easier, and it can help you to avoid many a silly mistake or forgotten file. Indeed, forgetting to commit (or update) a file is a very effective way to annoy fellow developers and interrupt their work with inexplicable compilation errors.

The TortoiseSVN commit dialog (see Figure 4-31) lists any modified files (including added or deleted ones) as well as any unversioned ones. It is a good idea to run through

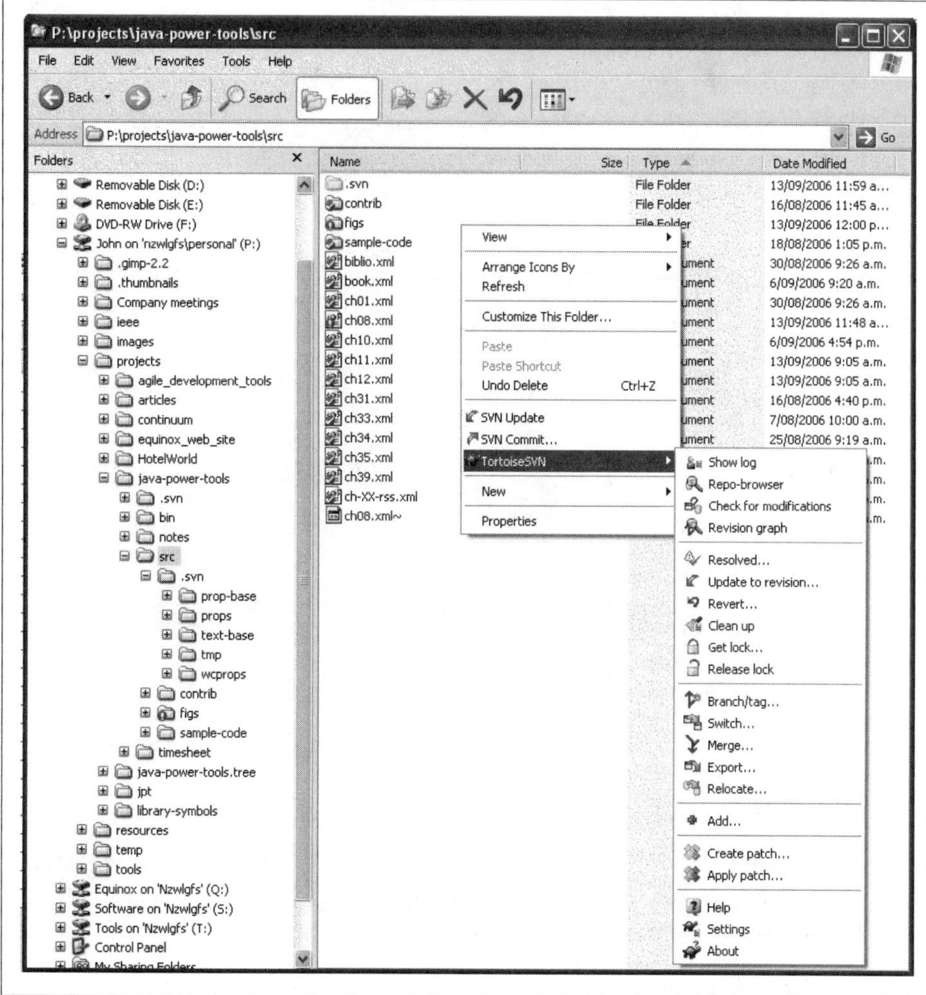

Figure 4-28. TortoiseSVN is a Subversion client that integrates seamlessly with Windows Explorer

the unversioned files carefully before committing your changes, since this can often reveal files that should have been added to Subversion. If you find you have forgotten to add a file, just check the file in the list and it will be added during the commit.

Sometimes you will be unsure why a particular file appears in the list of modified files. If you are unsure of the changes made to a file, you can visualise the changes done using the *Compare with base* command, or display the history of modifications made by using *Show log*. If you think this file has been modified by mistake, you can always *Revert* back to the repository version.

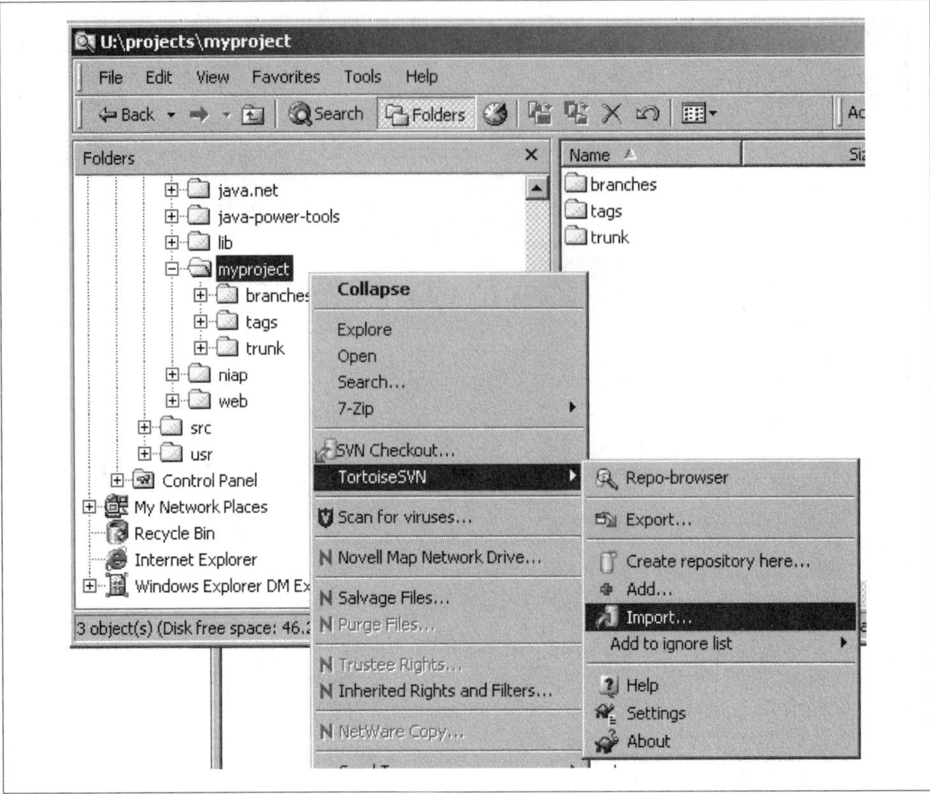

Figure 4-29. Importing a project structure into a Subversion repository

Finally, you should also include a (hopefully) meaningful message with your commit. TortoiseSVN provides a few nice features to help here, including a spellchecker and a list of previously used messages.

Updating Your Working Copy

Updating your working copy from the repository in TortoiseSVN is simple, just select the project directory in Explorer and select the "SVN Update" command in the contextual menu. Updated files are listed as they would be on the command line (see Section 4.9), but with color-coding to highlight the nature of the changes: black for normally updated files, green for merges, purple for newly added files, dark red for deleted files, and bright red for conflicts.

Exploring the Repository

One nice feature in TortoiseSVN is the Repository Browser. This lets you explore the repository structure directly on the Subversion server without needing to check out any files (see Figure 4-32).

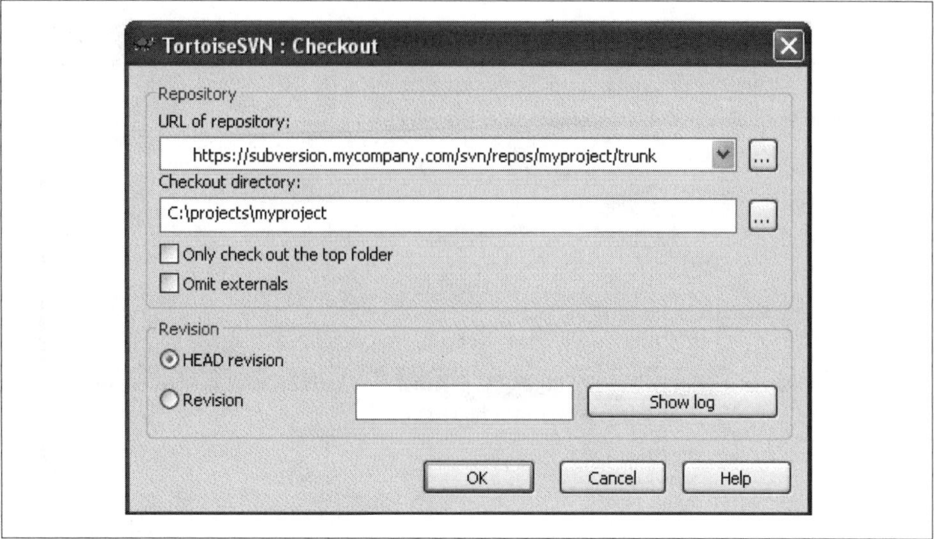

Figure 4-30. Checking out a project using TortoiseSVN

If you need to rename, create, or move directories, working directly on the Subversion server is considerably faster and easier than working with your local copy and committing your changes. The Repository Browser also lets you create new folders, delete or rename existing files or folders, or move files or folders using drag-and-drop.

One thing that Subversion is not particularly good at doing is keeping track of the relationship between tags, branches and versions. In TortoiseSVN, you can use the revision graph to display a visual treelike representation of this structure (see Figure 4-33). You can display a revision graph in the Repository Browser, or directly from Explorer using "TortoiseSVN→Revision Graph...." The graph shows when branches or tags where added to (green boxes) or deleted from (red boxes) the main trunk, and lets you display details about a revision (author, date, log messages, and so on). If you select two revisions in the graph, you can also compare them, which is useful for comparing branches or releases.

The only inconvenient thing with revision graphs is speed. A revision graph is a complicated thing to build, requiring a fair bit of analysis by TortoiseSVN to sort out the links, and it can take some time to build for nontrivial projects, especially over a slow Internet connection. Exact times will obviously vary depending on project size, network speed, lunar cycles, and various other factors, but a large, remotely hosted open source project with over 11,000 revisions takes 15 minutes or so to process on my machine.

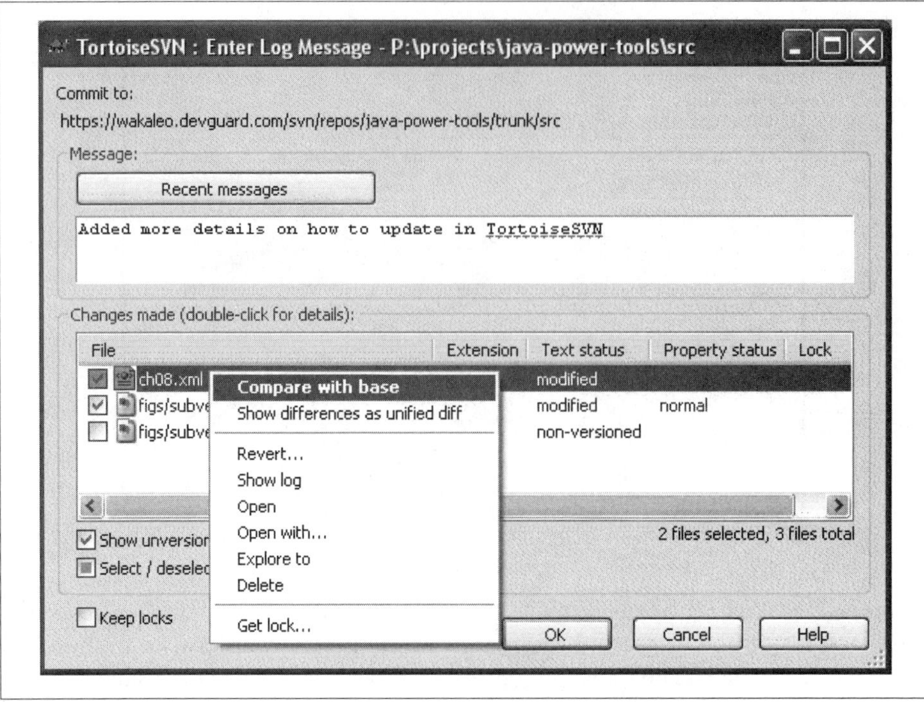

Figure 4-31. Commiting your changes

4.29 Defect Tracking and Change Control

Subversion, like many other similar tools, is often referred to as an SCM, or Software Configuration Management, tool. Strictly speaking, this is not the case. For people in the Configuration Management (CM) business, the term *Software Configuration Management* refers to solutions that provide, in addition to version control, features such as defect and change request tracking. These tools should be able to tell you which particular version of code fixed a particular bug (provided that the developers bother to mention this minor detail in their commit messages, of course).

Subversion has no built-in issue management solution as such. However, other issue management solutions do integrate well with Subversion. One good example is Trac (see Chapter 28), a wiki-like issue tracking system closely integrated with Subversion which lets you browse the Subversion repository, keep track of committed modifications, and create links to change sets or individual versions of files from within issues and project documentation.

Using Trac, you can browse the Subversion repository (see Figure 4-34), viewing not only the current version but also the revision history associated with each file or directory. You can also review at a glance the differences between different versions of a file.

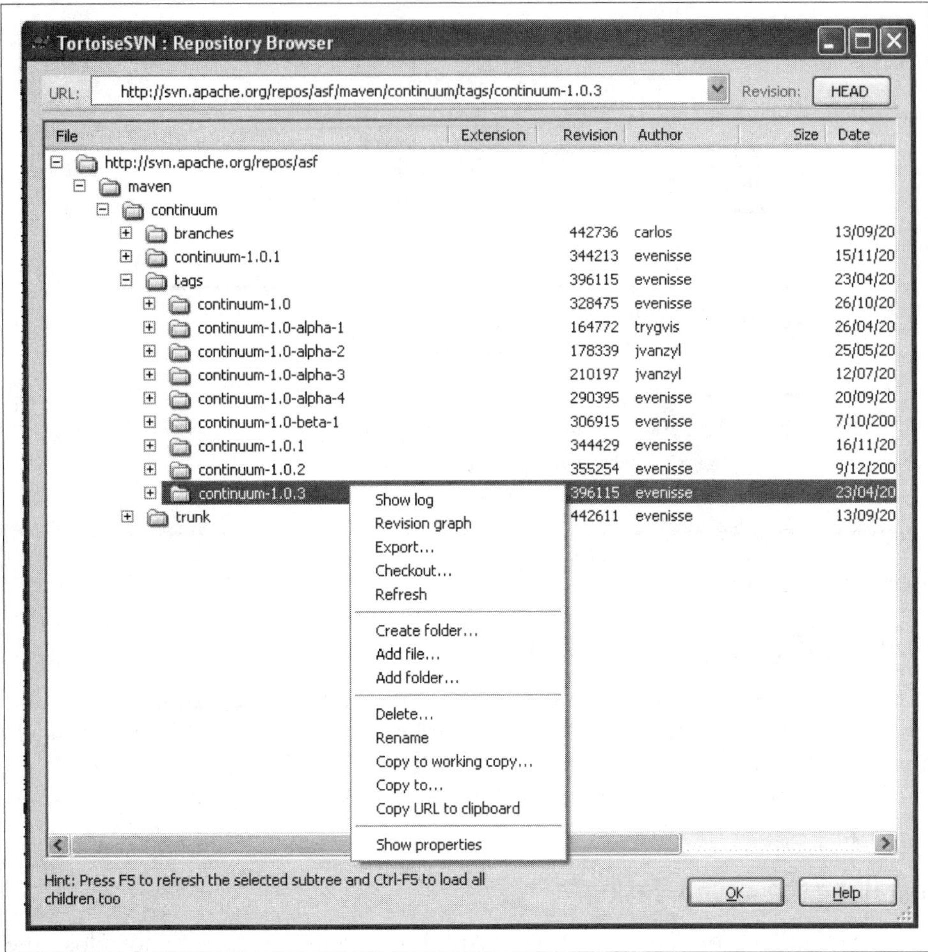

Figure 4-32. The TortoiseSVN Repository Browser

Intuitive hyperlinking makes navigating through the source code repository an easy task.

Issue tracking becomes a particularly powerful tool when you can associate tickets with version control change sets and with particular files in the version control system. For example, when a developer commits her corrections for a particular issue, she can record the corresponding change set and even links the affected files. Later on, when a QA staff member (or another developer) reviews this issue, she can easily visualize all the relevant information, included what version contains the corrected code, what were the developers comments, what files were affected, and even the exact changes made. All this information can be viewed from within the same web interface (see Figure 4-35).

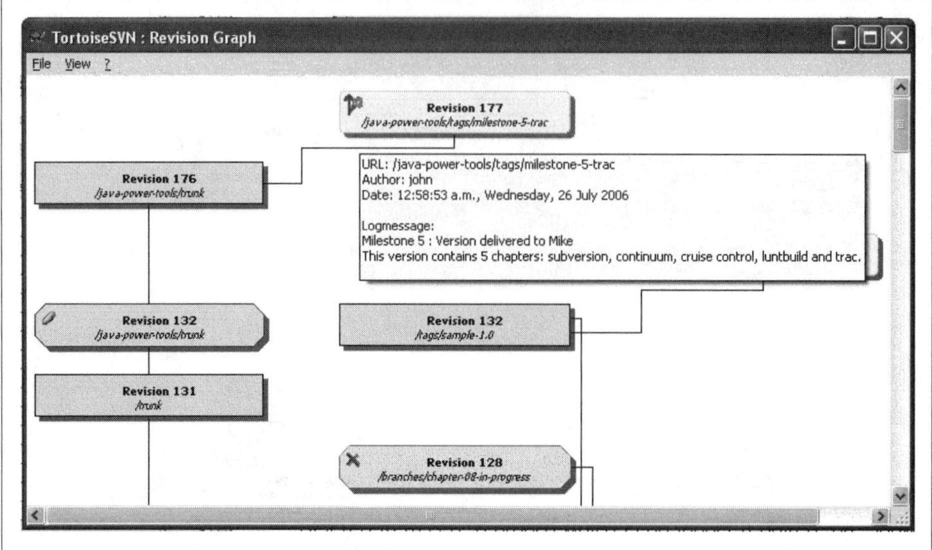

Figure 4-33. The TortoiseSVN Revision Graph

4.30 Using Subversion in Ant

There are times when you may want to access your Subversion repository from within your Ant script. For example, this can be useful when writing bootstrap scripts to set up a project environment. The *<svn>* task, developed by Tigris.org, allows you to do just that. So, without further ado, we will see how to install and use this plug-in in your Ant scripts.

Installing the <svn> Task

The *<svn>* task is not part of the default Ant distribution: you have to download the latest version from the Tigris.org web site.* Download and unzip the latest version. Now you need to declare the *<svn>* task in your build file, using the *<taskdef>* tag. For this to work, Ant will need the appropriate JAR files: you can either add the JAR files in the `lib` directory into your Ant lib directory, or refer directly to these jars in the *<taskdef>* classpath, as shown here:

```
<taskdef name="svn" classname="org.tigris.subversion.svnant.SvnTask" >
    <classpath>
        <fileset dir="${svnant.home}/lib">
          <include name="**/*.jar"/>
        </fileset>
    </classpath>
</taskdef>
```

* *http://subclipse.tigris.org/svnant.html*

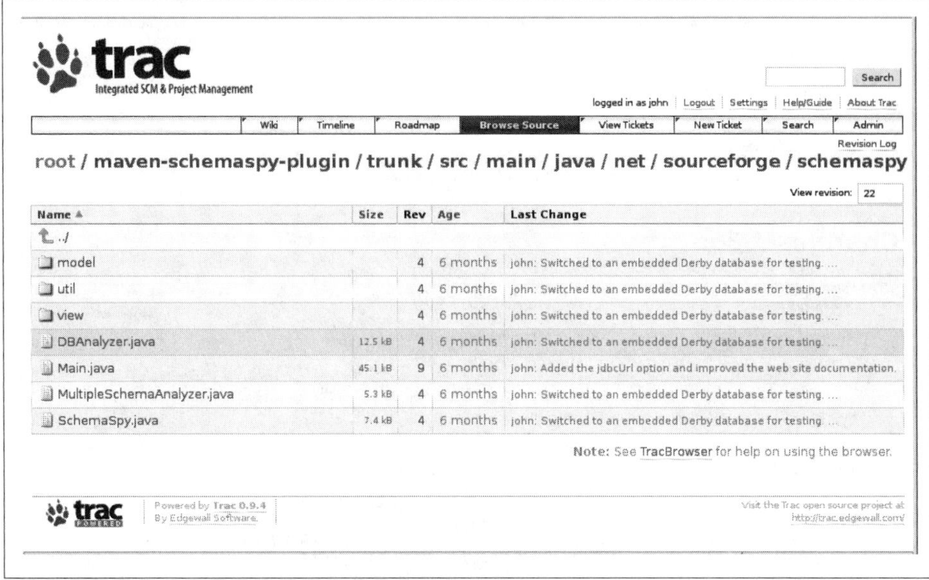

Figure 4-34. Browsing a Subversion repository in Trac

Note that the *<svn>* task requires Subversion to be installed on the local machine; it will use either a native JNI library called JavaHL if it can find one, or use the command line directly.

The *<svn>* task lets you do almost anything you could do with Subversion from the command line (with the notable exception of the *svn log* command, which was not implemented at the time of writing). In SvnAnt, subversion commands are implemented as nested elements of the *<svn>* task, in a fairly intuitive way. In the rest of this section, we will go though how to perform a few common Subversion tasks with this library.

Checking Out a Project

A common requirement is to be able to check out the full source code of a project using a bootstrap script. This can make it easier for users to set up the project, without having to remember the details of where the repository is stored, what branch to check out, and so on. You can checkout a project to a local directory using the *<checkout>* option, as shown here:

```
<svn username="${svn.username}" password="${svn.password}">
    <checkout url="http://svnserver.mycompany.com/svn/repos/myproject/trunk"
              revision="HEAD"
              destPath="myproject" />
</svn>
```

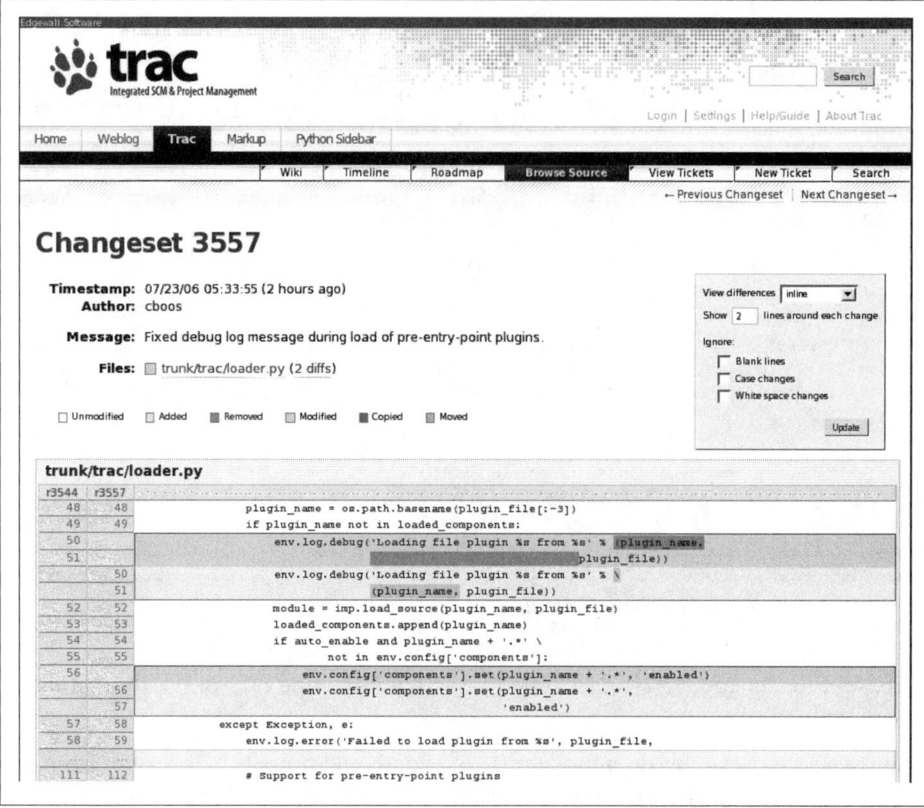

Figure 4-35. Visualising a Subversion Changeset in Trac

Updating Code from the Repository

In Subversion, the *svn update* command updates your local project to match the latest version on the server. You can do the same thing in Ant using the *<update>* tag:

```
<svn username="${svn.username}" password="${svn.password}">
    <update dir="${basedir}" />
</svn>
```

Exporting a Directory Structure

In Subversion, the *export* command lets you download a "clean" copy of the project file structure, devoid of all those unsightly ".svn" directories. This is useful when you are preparing a distribution containing source code, for example:

```
<svn username="${svn.username}" password="${svn.password}">
    <export srcUrl="http://svnserver.mycompany.com/svn/repos/myproject/trunk"
            revision="HEAD"
            destPath="export"/>
</svn>
```

You can also use the *srcPath* attribute instead of *srcUrl* to specify the physical directory path of the repository.

Creating a New Tag

In a build process, it is sometimes useful to be able to automate the process of building, deploying, and tagging a new release. In Subversion, tagging a particular revision essentially involves making a new lightweight copy of that revision (see Section 4.12). With SvnAnt, you can use the *<copy>* tag to do this directly from within the build process. In the following example, we create a new tag for a nightly snapshot, and then proceed to build and deploy this tag:

```
<target name="nightly-release">
    <!-- Tag current build -->
    <tstamp />
    <svn username="john" password="srr&amp;srb">
        <copy srcUrl="http://svnserver.mycompany.com/svn/repos/myproject/trunk"
              revision="HEAD"
              destUrl="http://svnserver.mycompany.com/svn/repos/myproject/tags
              /myproject-snapshot-${DSTAMP}-${TSTAMP}"
              message="Nightly build"/>
    </svn>
    <!-- Build and deploy nightly release using this tag -->
    ...
</target>
```

4.31 Conclusion

As far as open source version control solutions go, Subversion is an excellent choice. It is modern and efficient by design, and some of its features, such as atomic updates, and optimized network traffic, place it technically ahead of many well-known commercial solutions. It integrates well with both Eclipse and NetBeans. Subversion is well documented, particularly for an open source product. Subversion's main weakness lies in tracking branches and merges, which it does not handle by itself; you need to do this yourself by carefully tracking your merges in the log messages. This can be a downer for big projects and/or undisciplined developers.* Nevertheless, it *is* used by the open source community for many very large projects, and it is arguably one of the best, if not *the* best, open source version control tool.

* This is true of Subversion 1.4. The upcoming release, Subversion 1.5, comes with powerful support for merge tracking, which rectifies most if not all of these issues....

PART III
Continuous Integration

"I don't see much sense in that," said Rabbit. "No," said Pooh humbly, "there isn't. But there was going to be when I began it. It's just that something happened to it along the way."

—"Tigger is unbounced," *The House at Pooh Corner*, A.A. Milne.

One of the hardest things to do in any development project is keeping on track. Many software projects end up going off in unexpected directions, both from a technical perspective and from a business one. Modules built by different developers can be difficult to integrate. Lack of visibility of the application being coded often leads to an ever-widening gap between what the user expects and what the development team actually builds.

Continuous Integration can help your project in both regards, as it is a powerful technique that can be used to make your development process smoother, more visible, and less risky.

If there is one technique that can revolutionize your development process, it is Continuous Integration.

The underlying principle of Continuous Integration is simple: integrate early, and integrate often. Continuous Integration has been around for at least 10 years, although more recently it has been brought into the spotlight by Agile methodologies.

So what is Continuous Integration anyway? Continuous Integration is based on the observation that the longer you wait to integrate your team's code, the harder it gets. In many projects, a typical development lifecycle goes something like this. Initially, coding goes along just fine; there may even be unit tests to prove it! Then, at some point in time, the team leader decides (or reminds everyone) that a delivery is due in a couple of weeks. It may be just an alpha or a prototype, but it is a delivery nevertheless. So it's all hands on deck to get something working for the due deadline. The problem is, when I check out my code, it doesn't compile any more! Of course, I know that my code is OK, so it's probably some other developer's fault—maybe they forgot to commit a class, or changed one of my interfaces without asking my permission...oh, yeah, and some of the unit tests no longer work, but they belong to the DB team down the corridor, so I won't worry about them too much...and so on.

This widely observed phenomenon is known in Agile circles and elsewhere as "Integration Hell."

Continous Integration is the antidote to Integration Hell. It offers a powerful way to detect bugs and conflicts early so that they can be fixed quickly and easily and without too much bloodshed among team members. It basically involves automatically building and testing code at regular intervals. Team members commit their code to version control very frequently (at least on a daily basis). A central server regularly checks out the latest version of the project source code, and runs a complete build, including compilation and tests. The build process automatically notifies team members of any build failures, and (hopefully) the team member responsible for commiting faulty or conflicting code will immediately jump out of his chair (figuratively speaking) and rush off to fix the problem before anyone else notices!

This practice is first and foremost a risk-reduction strategy, ensuring that the application integrates correctly at all times and reducing the risk of integration issues appearing late in the project. Additional benefits include improving communication between team members and reducing the time needed to prepare a release. Indeed, in a project using Continuous Integration, you virtually always have a demonstratable, if not deliverable, version of the application running somewhere.

However, Continuous Integration goes much further than simply ensuring that your application builds correctly at all times. Continuous Integration means that you always (well, almost always) have a working version of your application to show to testers, users, and project sponsors. Don't underestimate the benefits that this can have on your project. This means that, at any point, you can demonstrate a particular feature, and get fast, early feedback from testers and end users. Users and sponsors get better visibility on the application's features and on the project's real progress, and potential issues are raised (and fixed) sooner rather than later.

Now, in practice, a Continuous Integration process can be automated to varying degrees. Some teams use a largely manual process; once developers have completed a task, they run an integration build using an automated build on a separate integration build machine. Other teams use a Continuous Integration tool such as CruiseControl to automate the process.

The most fundamental feature of any Continuous Integration tool is the automatic build cycle. The Continuous Integration tool, either at a scheduled point in time or whenever any changes are detected in the source code repository, fetches the source code's latest version and attempts to build and test the project. If the build fails, developers can be notified in any number of ways: e-mail, instant messaging, telepathy, courier pigeon, or through some other, more exotic, notification technique.

There are many Continuous Integration tools, both open source and commercial, on the market, and deciding which one would best suit your particular environment can prove difficult. Some Continuous Integration tools also boast additional SDLC features, such as release management and build artifact management, whereas others concentrate on core Continuous Integration functionalities. Some try to provide a wide range of notification methods and support virtually every version control system under the sun, whereas others concentrate on delivering a small, light, easy-to-understand product.

In this part, we will look at four of the more interesting open source Continous Integration tools: Continuum, CruiseControl, LuntBuild, and Hudson.

Continuum is a simple, lightweight, web-based Continuous Integration tool. It is easy to install and involves little initial configuration. On the downside, it is not as feature-rich as some of the other tools, and the user interface is a little clunky.

CruiseControl is a mature and robust Java Continuous Integration tool that enjoys a strong user base and a solid industry reputation. It supports virtually any type of project, be it Ant, Maven, Maven 2, make, or just a plain-old command line script, as well as a wide range of SCM (source configuration management) tools. Its notification techniques are second to none, and it can integrate easily with anything from a mail server to a Lava Lamp. It also benefits from a large number of third-party plug-ins. On the downside, it is much harder to set up, to configure, and to maintain than any of the other tools, and the user interface is somewhat unappealing.

Luntbuild is another open source Continuous Integration tool written in Java. It is fairly easy to install and configure, and, like Continuum, all server administration tasks are done via a (somewhat clunky) web-based administration console. Luntbuild is designed to do more than just manage the continuous integration process: it also lets you store and manage generated artifacts, label and promote versions, and manage dependencies between builds. It supports a wide range of version control tools, and notifications can be diffused via e-mail, IM, and even on a blog site.

The last product on our list, Hudson, is a relative newcomer to the Continuous Integration field, but it is one that is rapidly gaining a substantial following over the last year or so. Hudson is entirely web-based and has a pleasant and very functional user interface. Hudson supports fewer SCM products than the other tools we have seen, concentrating exclusively on Subversion and CVS-based projects. By contrast, it comes with many useful advanced features not seen on some of the other tools, such as parallel builds, inter-project dependencies, graphical build statistics, and the storage of build artifacts. Hudson also benefits from a large and increasing library of plug-ins, allowing integration with a wide variety of other tools, including static analysis data from Checkstyle, PMD and FindBugs, test coverage statistics using Cobertura or Emma, and issue management systems such as JIRA and Trac. To date, Hudson is probably one of the most innovative of the open source Continuous Integration tools.

Finally, although it is not in the scope of this book to discuss commercial products in any detail, some are worth a mention. Over the past few years, a number of high-quality commercial Continuous Integration tools have emerged, such as TeamCity (from JetBrains), Bamboo (from Atlassian), and Pulse (from Zutubi). These "next-generation" Continuous Integration tools propose slick user interfaces, integration with lots of other products, and interesting new features such as the ability to build and test an application *before* it is committed to the source code repository. This strategy preemptively prevents broken builds being ever placed in the source code repository.

For any readers interested in learning more about Continuous Integration as a process, I would recommend the excellent book *Continuous Integration* (Addison-Wesley), by Paul Duvall, Steve Matyas, and Andrew Glover.

Finally, in this section we will also look at Openfire, an open source Java instant messaging tool that can be a useful addition to your Continous Integration infrastructure.

CHAPTER 5

Setting Up a Continuous Integration Server with Continuum

5.1 An Introduction to Continuum

In this chapter, we look at Continuum (*http://maven.apache.org/continuum/*). Continuum* is a flexible, easy-to-use tool that can help you put Continuous Integration into action. It is fast, lightweight, and undemanding. It is also self-reliant. Like Maven, it is built on the Plexus component framework and comes bundled with its own Jetty application server. For its database needs, it uses Apache Derby, a 100 percent Java fully embedded database. As we will see, this makes Continuum particularly easy to install in almost any environment.

5.2 Installing a Continuum Server

Installing a Continuum server is easy. Make sure that you have a recent Java Development Kit (JDK) installed (and JAVA_HOME defined) and download the appropriate installation package from the Continuum web site. I used Java 5 for this chapter.

Continuum, like other Continuous Integration tools, uses locally installed tools to check out source code and build your project. So, if you are using Maven and Subversion on your projects, you will need to install these tools on your build machine.

Next, just extract the downloaded file into the directory where you want to install Continuum. Extracting the installation package is pretty much all you need to do to get a basic server up and running.

If you are installing Continuum onto an integration server, you will probably need to have Continuum starting automatically. Continuum comes with a useful wrapper program and an installation script in the *bin\win32* directory called *InstallService*:

* *http://maven.apache.org/continuum/*

```
D:\continuum\bin\win32>InstallService
wrapper  | continuum installed.
```

This will install a standard Windows service, which you can manage in the usual manner from the Services window (see Figure 5-1). By default, the service will run as the local system account and will be unable to access all of the resources that it needs to start up Continuum. To get around this, you will need to start the service as the same user account in which you installed Continuum. To do this, open the service properties window and change the account used to start the service in the tab "Log On."

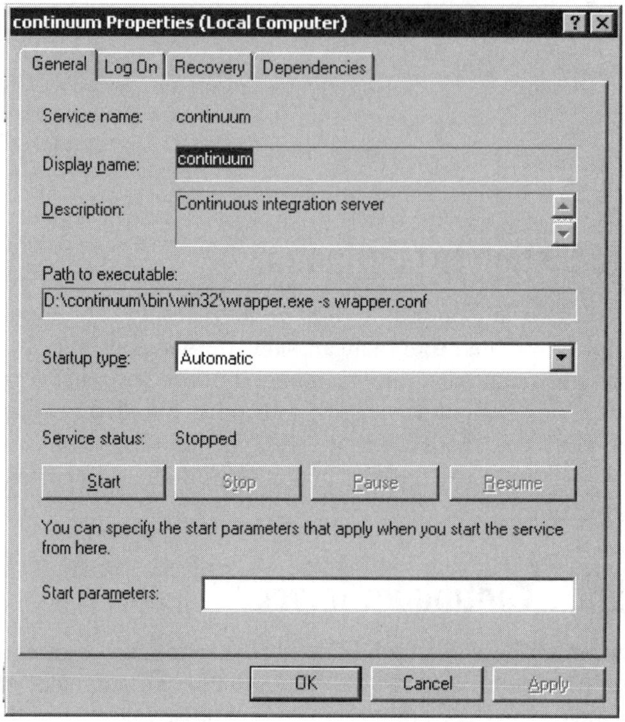

Figure 5-1. Continuum as a Windows service

For Debian-based Linux systems, you can do the following: first, extract Continuum into your `/usr/local/` directory. Then, for ease of maintenance, create a symbolic link to this directory called *continuum*:

```
# ln -s continuum-1.1/ continuum
# ls -dl continuum*
lrwxrwxrwx  1 root root   16 2006-04-29 10:10 continuum -> continuum-1.1/
drwxr-xr-x  9 root root 4096 2006-04-29 10:10 continuum-1.0.3
```

It just so happens that the Continuum Linux startup script takes the same arguments as the classic Linux boot scripts that we all know and love. So, all you need to do is to update a symbolic link to this script in your */etc/init.d* directory, as follows:

```
ln -s /usr/local/continuum/bin/Linux/run.sh /etc/init.d/continuum
```

Then, you will need to set up symbolic links in the appropriate */etc/init.d* subdirectories. Here's what it looks like on my Suse machine:

```
# ls -al /etc/init.d/*/*continuum
lrwxrwxrwx  1 root root 12 2006-05-16 01:07 /etc/init.d/rc2.d/K21continuum ->
../continuum
lrwxrwxrwx  1 root root 12 2006-05-16 01:07 /etc/init.d/rc2.d/S01continuum ->
../continuum
lrwxrwxrwx  1 root root 12 2006-05-16 01:07 /etc/init.d/rc3.d/K21continuum ->
../continuum
lrwxrwxrwx  1 root root 12 2006-05-16 01:07 /etc/init.d/rc3.d/S01continuum ->
../continuum
lrwxrwxrwx  1 root root 12 2006-05-16 01:07 /etc/init.d/rc5.d/K21continuum ->
../continuum
lrwxrwxrwx  1 root root 12 2006-05-16 01:07 /etc/init.d/rc5.d/S01continuum ->
../continuum
```

In fact I cheated—the Suse graphical control center (YasST) lets you set up all these links quickly and painlessly. Similar tools exist in other flavors of Linux as well.

Now that Continuum is correctly installed, you can display the Continuum web administration console at `http://localhost:8080/continuum`. The first time that you start Continuum, you will need to provide an admin account username and password (see Figure 5-2).

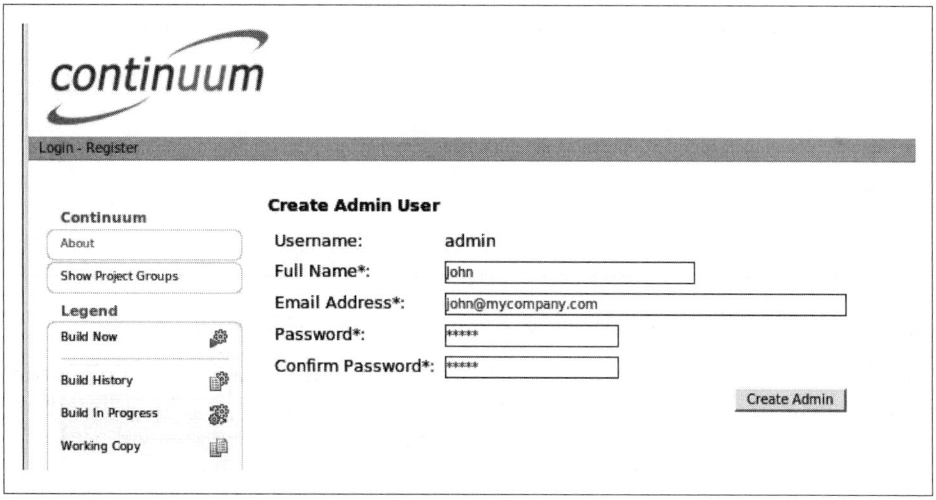

Figure 5-2. Continuum needs to be configured the first time you start it up

On the following screen, you can configure the application work directories (see Figure 5-3). Unless you are setting up a fairly sophisticated installation, you can leave the working directory and build output directory fields with their default values.

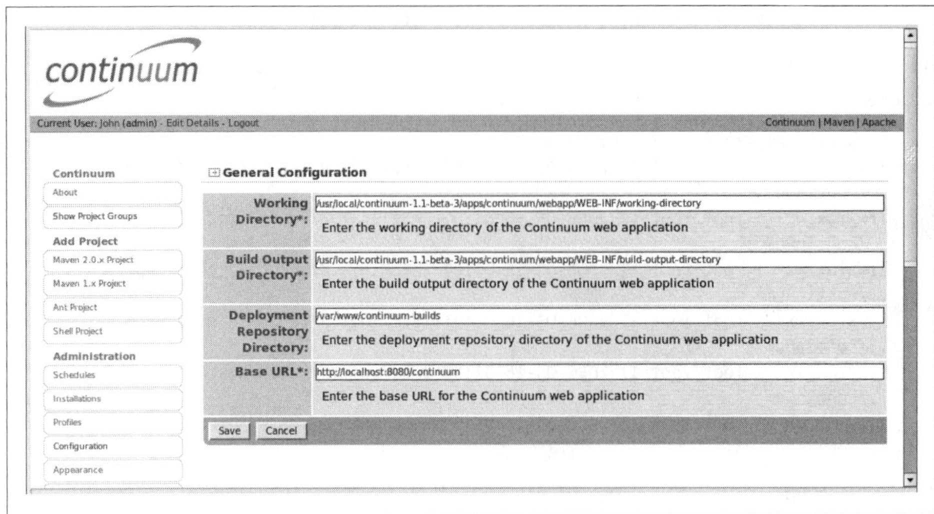

Figure 5-3. Continuum needs to be configured the first time you start it up

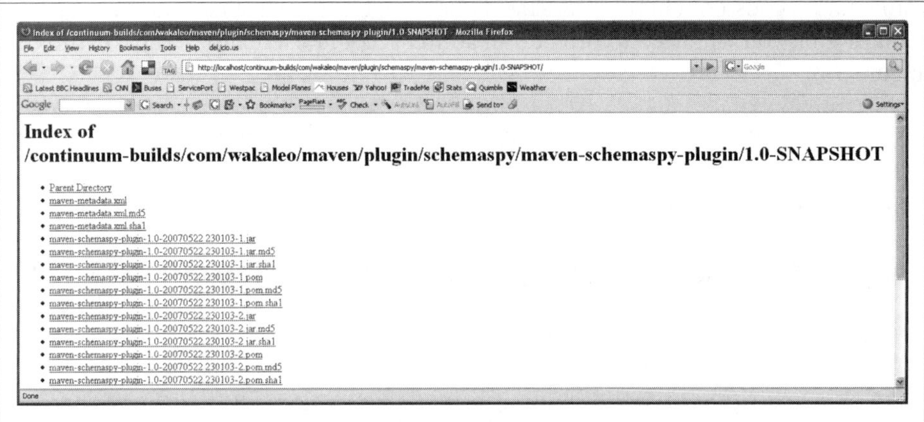

Figure 5-4. Continuum can automatically deploy snapshots to a local enterprise repository

The (optional) Deployment Repository Directory lets you set up a Maven repository where generated products will be deployed. This will typically be a local Enterprise repository (see Section 2.19), and can be a useful way to provide users with access to automatically deployed snapshot builds. Each snapshot will have a unique timestamp, making it easy to integrate and test particular snapshots in other projects (see Figure 5-4).

The base URL is the public URL that will be included in email notifications to encode links to build results. This is useful if Continuum is running behind a web server. This often defaults to a local host address, which is fairly useless for anything other than

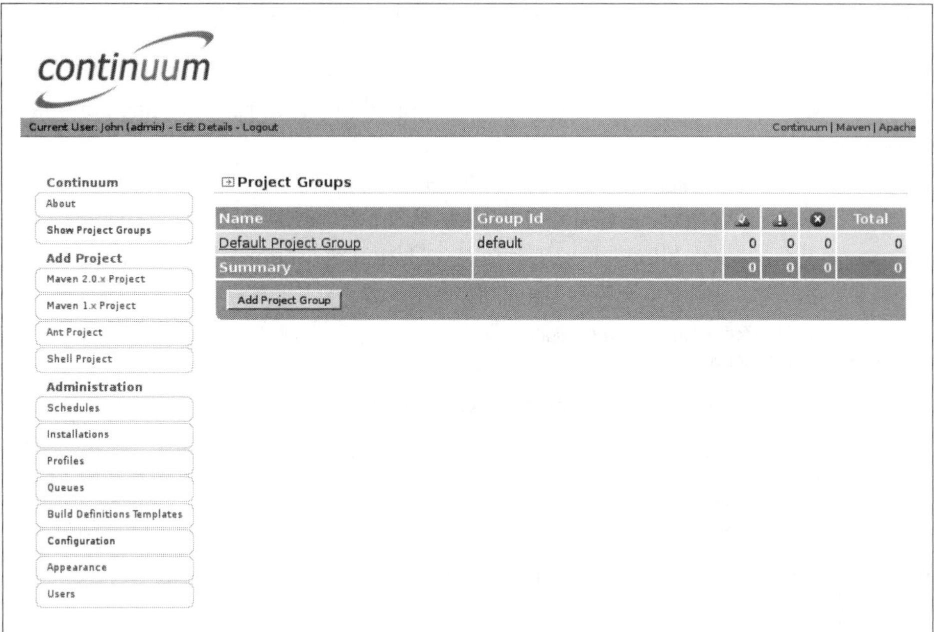

Figure 5-5. The Continuum administration home page

local testing, so make sure you change this field to something sensible for any live installations.

You can also tailor company-related information in the "Appearance" screen. This lets Continuum customize the web site somewhat by displaying your company logo in the top right corner of the screen.

Once you validate this data, all subsequent connections will go directly to the Continuum administration page (see Figure 5-5). All users can consult the standard view, which shows the build status of the different projects on the server. To do any configuration, such as adding or configuring projects or project groups, you need to log in using the administration login you provided earlier.

5.3 Manually Starting and Stopping the Server

There are basically two ways to start and stop the Continuum server manually.

First, you can start the server using one of the environment-specific start scripts. The basic way to start the server from the command line is as follows:

- For Linux boxes, use ${CONTINUUM_HOME}/bin/Linux/run.sh
- For Macintosh OS X systems, use ${CONTINUUM_HOME}/bin/macosx/run.sh

- On Solaris, use ${CONTINUUM_HOME}/bin/solaris/run.sh
- And on a Windows box, use $CONTINUUM_HOME\bin\win32\run.bat

The basic way to start the server from the command line is to run the *start* command as follows:

```
# /usr/local/continuum/bin/Linux/run.sh start
Starting continuum...
```

Of course, if you have followed the Linux installation procedure described above (see Section 5.2), you can also do the following:

```
# /etc/init.d/continuum start
Starting continuum...
```

You can also restart the server using the (wait for it!) *restart* command:

```
# /etc/init.d/continuum restart
Stopping continuum...
Stopped continuum.
Starting continuum...
```

And to stop the server, just use the *stop* command:

```
# /etc/init.d/continuum stop
Stopping continuum...
Stopped continuum.
```

5.4 Checking the Status of the Server

Operating systems being what they are, you may sometimes need to check if Continuum is running correctly. If the process seems to have hung, you can always use the *status* option to check if there is a process running, and, if so, what its Process Identification (PID) number is. The PID number can always come in handy if you need to kill the process at some point:

```
$ /usr/local/continuum/bin/Linux/run.sh status
continuum is running (16259).
```

This information is actually stored in a file called *continuum.pid*, in the same directory as the startup script. So, if you accidentally remove this file, the *status* option can get quite confused.

5.5 Running the Continuum Server in Verbose Mode

If you need to see more details about what the Continuum server is doing (usually to identify and fix a problem), you can always start the server in console mode:

```
# /etc/init.d/continuum console
Running continuum...
```

```
wrapper  | --> Wrapper Started as Console
wrapper  | Launching a JVM...
jvm 1    | Wrapper (Version 3.1.2) http://wrapper.tanukisoftware.org
jvm 1    |
jvm 1    | [INFO] Services will be deployed in: '../../services'.
jvm 1    | [INFO] Applications will be deployed in: '../../apps'.
jvm 1    | [INFO] The application server has been initialized.
...
```

This will display ample details of what the server is getting up to, and hopefully it will also show what is going wrong.

5.6 Adding a Project Group

Once the server is running, you can add some new projects to the Continuous Build system. If you're not logged on, you will need to do this first.

In Continuum, projects are organized into groups. The installation comes with a default group (called, rather unimaginatively, "Default Project Group"), but you can create as many of your own groups as you like, depending on your needs. Once you have created a group, you can then proceed to creating projects within this group (see Figure 5-6).

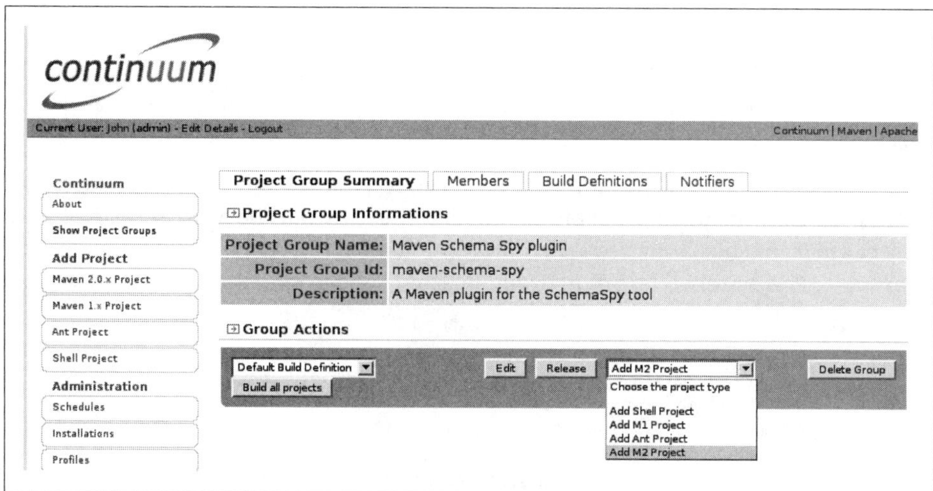

Figure 5-6. Adding a Maven 2 project

5.7 Adding a Maven Project

Now that we have a group, let's add a Maven 2 project. Because of the particularly close integration with Maven 2, this sort of project is easy to add. Continuum simply reads the *pom.xml* file and gets all the information it needs there (see Figure 5-7). You can either upload a POM file from your local machine, or specify a URL pointing to the

POM file on some accessible repository. If you want to follow along at home, you can go pick your favorite Maven-powered open source project, or use the following publicly available URL:

```
https://wakaleo.devguard.com/svn/jpt-sample-code/maven-schemaspy-plugin/trunk/pom.xml
```

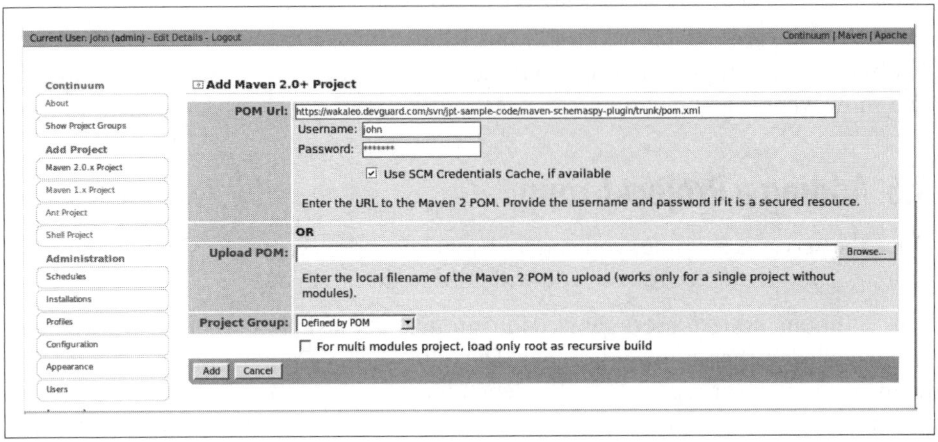

Figure 5-7. Adding a Maven 2 project

Not just any old Maven 2 project will do, however. Your Maven 2 project needs to provide a minimum of useful information to make Continuum happy, so you should check that your project file is correctly configured.

In fact, the only really essential information is the Software Configuration Management (SCM) details, which you probably already have. Check out the SCM section of your project's *pom.xml* file. You need the connection element to be correctly configured with your local SCM system. Here is an example using Subversion:

```
<scm>
  <connection>
    scm:svn:https://wakaleo.devguard.com/svn/maven-plugins
    /maven-schemaspy-plugin/trunk
  </connection>
  <developerConnection>
    scm:svn:https://wakaleo.devguard.com/svn/maven-plugins
    /maven-schemaspy-plugin/trunk
  </developerConnection>
  <url>
    https://wakaleo.devguard.com/svn/maven-plugins/maven-schemaspy-plugin/trunk
  </url>
</scm>
```

The syntax used is that of the Maven SCM project (see "A Human-Readable Project Description" in Section 2.4). The Maven SCM project (and therefore Continuum) currently support CVS, Subversion, ClearCase, Perforce, Starteam, and Bazaar, although support for other SCM tools such as PVCS, MKS, and Visual SourceSafe is planned.

One thing worth knowing is that Continuum expects your *pom.xml* file to be in the project root directory. Should this not be the case (for example, if you are checking out a from a higher-level directory in your source code repository), you need to provide a relative path to the *pom.xml* file in your build definitions.

Continuum will read other details if they are available. In Continuum, each project has a list of developers. Continuum can read the developer team details list from the *pom.xml* file, if this information is present. The list typically includes an entry for each developer, including (at least) their system login, name, and email. In the current version, this information is just for informative purposes. Future versions of Continuum might use this information directly for mail notifications. An example is shown here:

```
<developers>
  <developer>
    <id>duke</id>
    <name>Duke Java</name>
    <email>duke@java-developers.com</email>
    <role>Super developer</role>
  </developer>
  ...
</developers>
```

Finally, you can configure the `ciManagement` section, if it is not already done. This section contains the URL for the project Continuum site (so that a link can be displayed on the Maven-generated project web site) and a list of notifiers. The notifiers tell Continuum how to inform developers in the developer list about the build results. There are many different types of notifiers available, including email, and several types of Instant Messagers (IRC, Jabber, and MSN). In the current version of Continuum, you need to provide one (or more) individual notifier for each developer in your team:

```
<ciManagement>
  <system>continuum</system>
  <url>http://mybuildserver:8080/continuum</url>
  <notifiers>
      <notifier>
        <type>mail</type>
        <configuration>
          <address>duke</address>
        </configuration>
      </notifier>
      </notifier>
  </notifiers>
</ciManagement>
```

You can also add notifiers very easily directly from the Continuum web interface (see Section 5.12).

Once you have added your project, it will appear in the list of projects for this group (see Figure 5-8).

Maven 1 projects can be added in the same way, by simply providing the Maven 1 *project.xml* file.

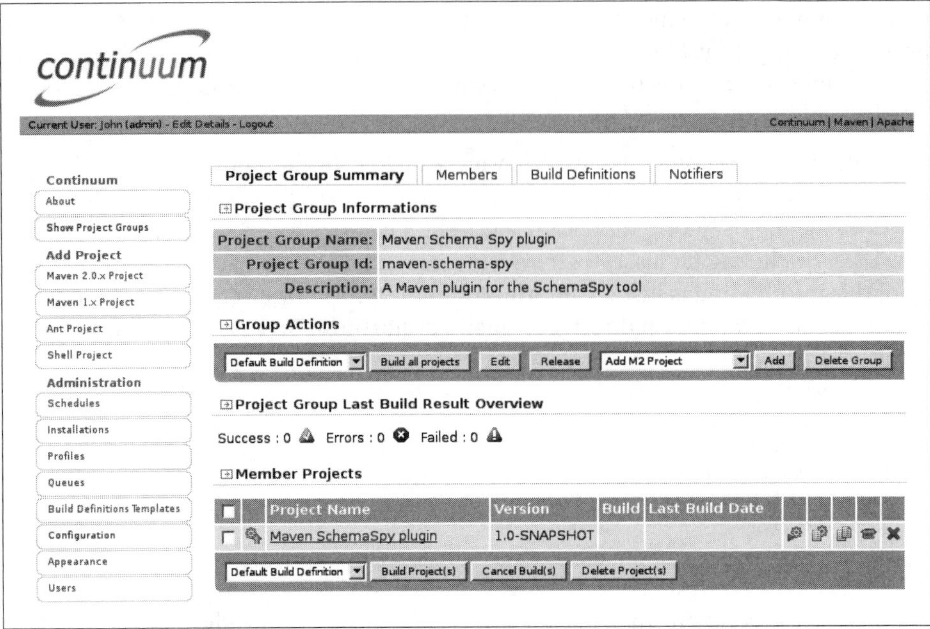

Figure 5-8. The new project appears in the project group list

5.8 Adding an Ant Project

If you want to add an Ant project to your Continuum server, you need to provide a little more detail, simply because this information isn't present (or at least not in an easy-to-find format) in the *build.xml* file. Just enter a project name and version (for display purposes), and the relevant SCM details (see Figure 5-9). Note that the SCM URL uses the Maven format for SCM URLs (see "The Source Repository). The SCM URL should point to the project's root directory.

Again, you can follow along at home by using the following URL:

```
https://wakaleo.devguard.com/svn/jpt-sample-code/jsfpetstore/trunk
```

By default, Continuum expects to find a file called *build.xml* in this directory. If your project is configured differently, you need to edit the build configuration once you have created the project (see Section 5.13).

5.9 Adding a Shell Project

You can even add a project that is built via an OS-specific script. I once worked on a project where we used a plain old Makefile to read environment-specific variables from a local configuration file, and then call Maven. Other examples could be when

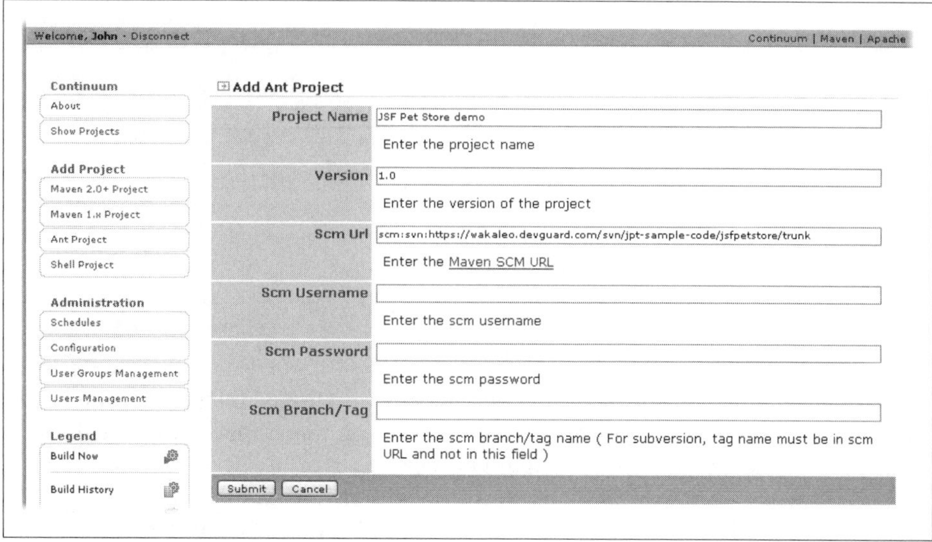

Figure 5-9. Adding an Ant project to Continuum

OS-specific initialization or cleanup tasks need to be done before or after the main build task.

The script must respect a few conditions: it should call Maven at some point, and it should return a result value of 0 for success and 1 for failure.

Setting up a script in Continuum is similar to setting up an Ant project (see Section 5.8). You just provide a name and version and appropriate SCM information.

5.10 Managing Your Project Builds

Continuum provides a convenient dashboard where you can see the status of all your projects at a glance (see Figure 5-10). Projects are organized in groups, which is convenient because, in practice, you will often have several build projects for a given development project.

Each project is listed with an icon indicating the current build status (1). See the following table.

Success—The last project build was an unqualified success.

Failure—Uh-oh. There is a problem of some kind, such as a compilation error or unit test failures. The build history screen will help isolate the exact problem.

Error—A major stuff-up has occurred. This is often a configuration error or a problem with obtaining the source code from the version control system. Checkout the build history for more details.

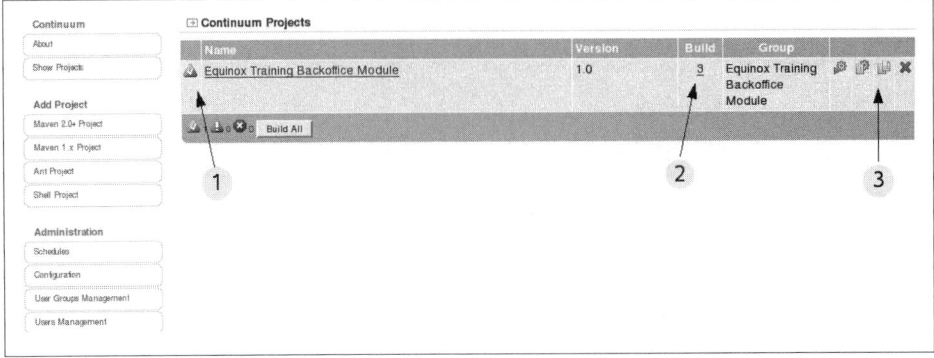

Figure 5-10. The Continuum project dashboard

In the Build column (2), you will find the number of attempted integration builds that have taken place since the project was added to Continuum. Special icons will sometimes appear here if a build is queued or in progress.

Further to the right (3), we have a set of useful little icons, which allow you (going from left to right) to force an immediate build (useful to verify whether the correction you just committed has fixed the integration problem detected by Continuum), to display the build history, and to display the working copy used by Continuum for its builds.

If you click on the project name, you can view and modify the build configuration details (see Figure 5-11). This is a useful screen where you can configure and schedule build targets, set up notifications, and (for Maven projects) display project dependencies and team details. We will look at this page in more detail later on.

The Build History page lets you consult a list of all builds for this project (see Figure 5-12).

You can also display detailed results for each build, including changes made to the source code repository and the appropriate build logs (see Figure 5-13). This is *very* useful for debugging an integration error.

Finally, the Working Copy page lets you browse through the version of the project source code that Continuum is currently using for its builds. This is useful to check whether Continuum is using the version you think it is. Don't forget, Continuum gets its source code from the version control repository, not from your machine, so there may be differences.

5.11 Managing Users

Continuum provides good support for user management. As you might expect, you add or delete users as required in the "Users" screen (see Figure 5-14). This screen also lets you define user roles for each user, either in terms of global roles that apply across

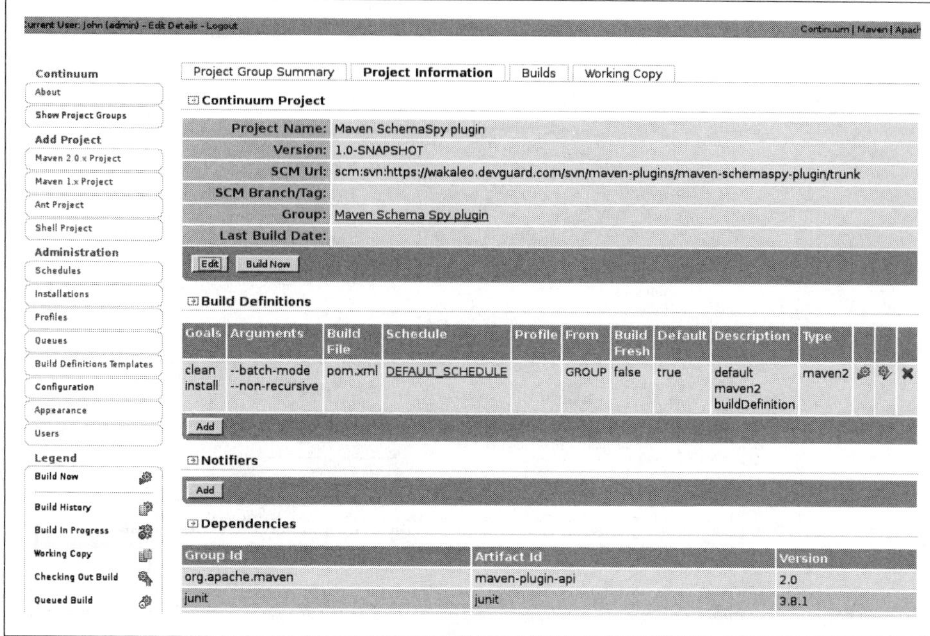

Figure 5-11. The Continuum Build Configuration details

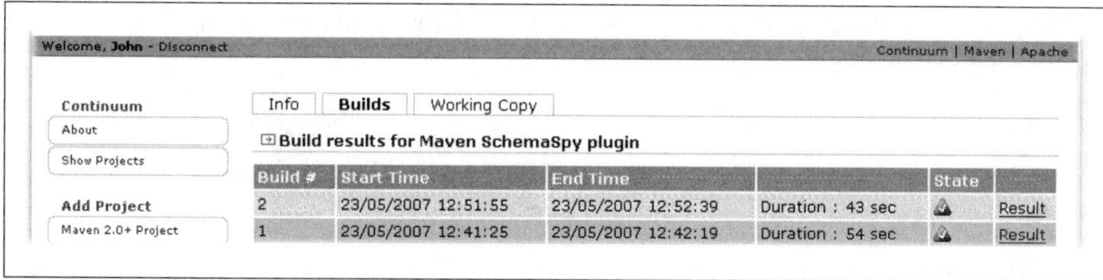

Figure 5-12. The Continuum Build History page

all projects (such as "System Administrator" or "Guest"), or, more specifically, for individual projects. For specific projects, you can define a user as being a Project Administrator (who can do pretty much anything within that particular project), a Project Developer (who can start builds), or a Project User (who can consult the build results).

5.12 Setting Up Notifiers

Receiving notification by mail is all very well, but sometimes mail is slow to arrive, or it can be ignored. Continuum provides for a few other notification mechanisms, such

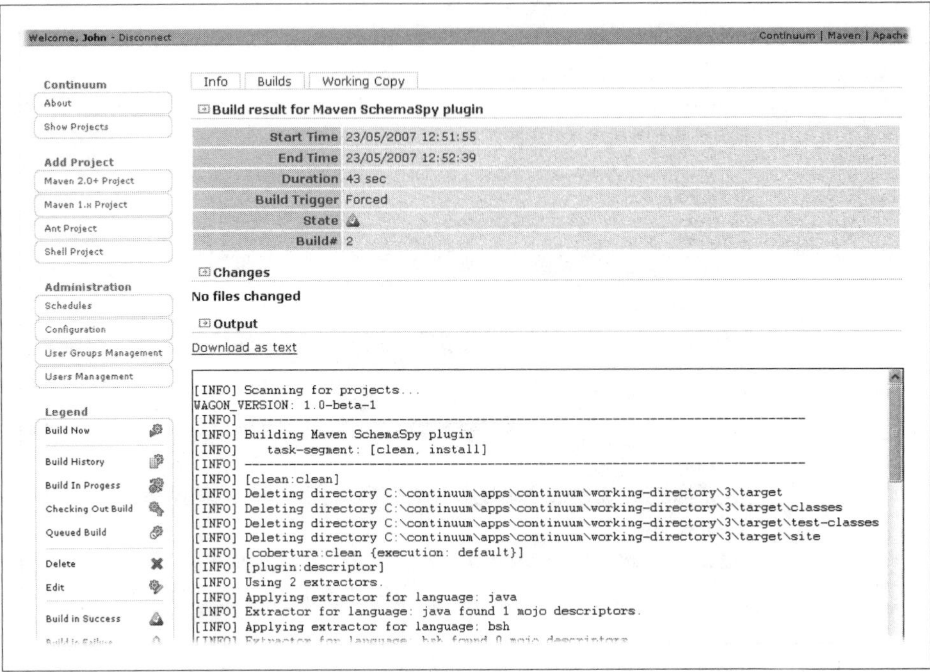

Figure 5-13. A Continuum build report

as various forms of chat and instant messaging. At the time of this writing, these current mechanisms were supported:

- IRC
- Jabber
- MSN

All of these are fairly easy to configure from the Continuum web console. When you configure instant messaging, you will need to set up a special account with your messaging service for the Continuum server. Most instant messaging services don't appreciate users being logged on simultaneously in several different places, so you can't use an account that is already being used by someone in the development team.

The main problem with Continuum notifications is that you need to set them up one-by-one for each project team member, even if the members are defined in the POM file.

There is no out-of-the-box support for RSS, although this is not hard to implement using the Continuum RCP Application Programming Interface (API).

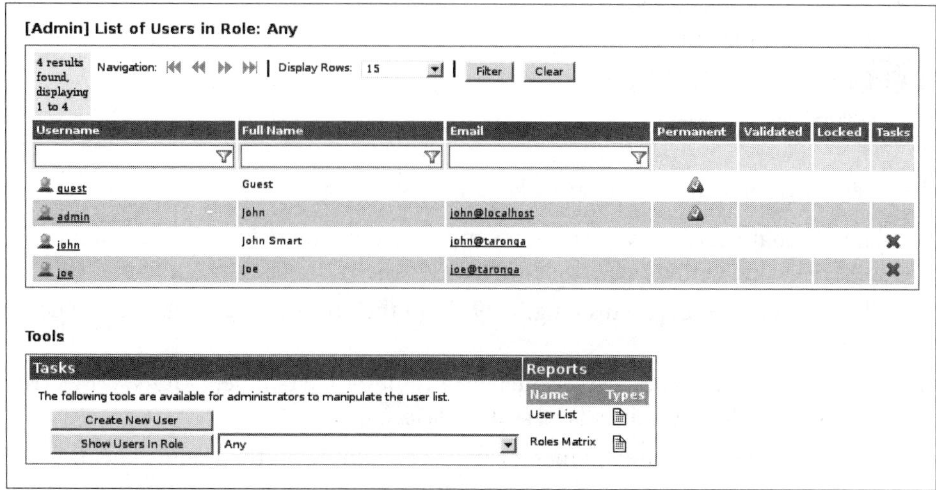

Figure 5-14. A Continuum build report

5.13 Configuring and Scheduling Builds

As far as builds are concerned, the term "Continuous Integration" is inexact: "Regular Automatic Integration" would be closer, but it probably doesn't sound as snappy. In any case, builds on a Continuous Integration server need to be scheduled carefully: too few, too far apart, and you lose in reaction time; too many, too close together, and your server may go down. And if you have several projects on the same server, it's advisable to schedule them in a way that avoids all the projects being built at the same time.

As you would expect, Continuum lets you set up build schedules for your projects (see Figure 5-15). You can define as many build schedules as you like, giving them (hopefully) meaningful names and planning the builds using the superbly powerful, if somewhat cryptic, Cron expression syntax. A detailed description of the Cron syntax can be readily found on the Internet, but we'll give a brief description here for clarity.

Cron expressions are a precise, concise, and flexible way of describing exactly when a task should be performed. In Continuum, a Cron expression is composed of seven fields, which represent seconds, minutes, hours, days of the month, months, days of the week, and years (see Table 5-2).

Table 5-1. CRON fields in Continuum

Field	Authorized values
Seconds	0-59
Minutes	0-59
Hours	0-23
Days of the month	1-31

Field	Authorized values
Months	1-12 or JAN-DEC
Days of the week	1-7 or SUN-SAT
Years (optional)	1970-2099

There are also some important special characters:

- The "*" character is a wildcard—it can be used in any field, to represent any authorized value in that field.
- The "-" character expresses ranges: "9–5" in the hours field means "All the hours from 9 to 5."
- The "," character expresses a sequence of values; for example, "MON,WED,FRI" means "Mondays, Wednesdays, and Fridays."
- The "/" character expresses increments; for example, in the minutes field, "0/5" means every 5 minutes, and "15/5" means every 5 minutes from a quarter past on.
- The "?" character is used in the "Days of the month" and "Days of the week" fields to tell Continuum to ignore this value and use the other.

Here are a few useful examples:

*0 * * * **
: Build every hour, on the hour.

*0 15,45 * * * **
: Build every 30 minutes, at a quarter past the hour, and at a quarter to the hour, every day of the year.

*0 0 6-18 ? * MON-FRI*
: Build every hour, on the hour, between 6 a.m. and 6 p.m., Monday to Friday.

*"0 0/10 9-17 * * ?"*
: Every 10 minutes from 9 a.m. to 5 p.m., every day of the week.

At the scheduled time, the source code repository will be queried for changes. If any changes are detected, then the build will be run.

Now, each project has a list of build definitions (see Figure 5-16). For Maven projects, it comes with a default one set to "mvn clean install," as you may not have noticed when you created your projects. For Ant, the default build definition will simply invoke default goal in the *build.xml* file at the project root.

You can, of course, modify these default build definitions for your project, and you can also add as many additional goals as you like (see Figure 5-16). For example, you might want an hourly continuous build schedule for integration tests and a nightly deployment of the Maven web site. In this case, you just create a "NIGHTLY BUILD" schedule, add a new build definition to your project with an appropriate goal (for

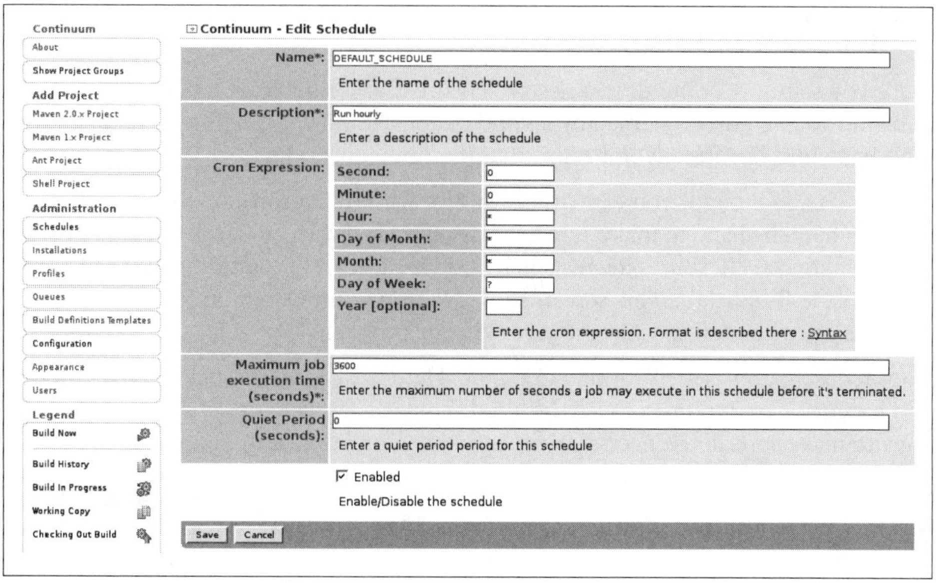

Figure 5-15. Adding a schedule in Continuum

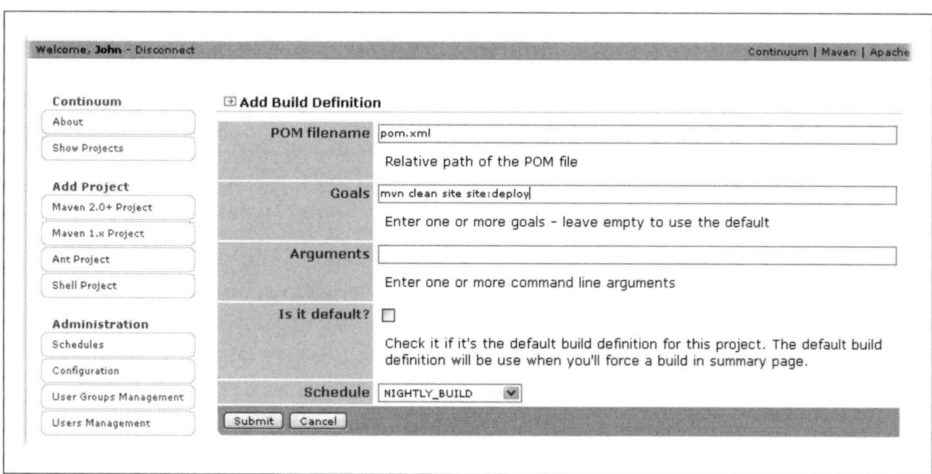

Figure 5-16. Adding a new build definition

example, "clean site site:deploy" for a Maven 2 project), and finally assign the "NIGHTLY BUILD" schedule to this build definition.

5.14 Debugging Your Builds

Once you set up your build, you need to ensure that it runs correctly. Otherwise, you may find yourself overwhelmed by a flood of abusive email from irate developers who have been told (incorrectly, for once) that their build is broken.

When you add a build, you can either wait for it to run automatically or, better still, trigger a build by hand to make sure it works. If it fails, you can check out exactly what happened in the "Result" screen, which you can access through the link of the same name in the Builds tab. This screen shows the raw output of your build execution, which is often enough to isolate and correct the problem.

Another useful tool is the Working Copy tab. Here you can view the directory structure and files that Continuum used for the build. You can compare this with your own local copy to make sure all the necessary files are there, and that their content is correct.

5.15 Configuring the Continuum Mail Server

The Continuum web site provides a good summary of the project build status, but developers cannot be expected to stay glued to the screens watching it—they have to write code from time to time, too! As we have seen (see Section 5.12), that's what notifiers are for.

By default, the mail notifier will attempt to use the mail service installed on the machine where Continuum has been installed. The default configuration expects to find a Simple Mail Transfer Protocol (SMTP) server on the local machine (local host) using the standard SMTP port (25): this will work fine for most Linux or Unix environments with a mail service installed.

However, you may need to configure the mail server for Continuum if you are not sending mail directly via a service on the server. To do this, you need to modify the application configuration file, which can be found at *apps/continuum/conf/applica tion.xml*. This is the Plexus framework configuration file for your Continuum server, and as such should be treated with due caution and respect. The bit you need to look for is the `MailSender` component: modify the values to suit your environment. Here is one possible configuration:

```
<component>
  <role>org.codehaus.plexus.mailsender.MailSender</role>
  <implementation>org.codehaus.plexus.mailsender.javamail.JavamailMailSender
  </implementation>
  <configuration>
    <smtp-host>smtp.mycompany.com</smtp-host>
    <smtp-port>25</smtp-port>
    <sslProvider>com.sun.net.ssl.internal.ssl.Provider</sslProvider>
    <username>mylogin</username>
    <password>mypassword</password>
    <sslMode>true</sslMode>
```

```
    </configuration>
  </component>
```

It's worth taking some time to think about how build results are going to be published. As a rule, for example, notifications for successful builds are of limited value to anyone except (possibly) the developer who just committed some changes. Failures, warnings, and errors, by contrast, should definitely be required reading for the whole team. Using a mailing list for noncritical messages is often a good compromise.

Continuum lets you configure notifiers to be sent on errors, warnings, failures, and/or successful builds, so you have a fair bit of flexibility at your disposal.

5.16 Configuring the Continuum Web Site Ports

By default, Continuum runs its web server on port 8080, and listens for XML-RPC requests on port 8000. Of course, this may not suit everyone. To change these ports, you need to modify the following configuration file:

```
apps/continuum/conf/application.xml
```

Edit this file and find the services section. In the following listing, the port is set to 8081 instead of the default 8080:

```
<services>
  <service>
    <id>jetty</id>
    <configuration>
      <webapps>
        <webapp>
          <file>${plexus.home}/lib/continuum-web-1.0.3.jar</file>
          <context>/continuum</context>
          <extraction-path>${plexus.home}/webapp</extraction-path>
          <listeners>
            <http-listener>
              <port>8081</port>
            </http-listener>
          </listeners>
        </webapp>
      </webapps>
    </configuration>
  </service>
  ...
```

Now just restart the Continuum server.

As of Continum 1.1, you can also configure the port in the conf/plexus.xml file, as shown here:

```
<plexus>
  ...
  <!-- START SNIPPET: jetty_port -->
  <component>
    <role>org.codehaus.plexus.contextualizer.Contextualizer</role>
```

```
      <role-hint>jettyConfiguration</role-hint>
      <implementation>org.codehaus.plexus.contextualizer.DefaultContextualizer
      </implementation>
      <configuration>
        <contextValues>
          <jetty.port>8081</jetty.port>
        </contextValues>
      </configuration>
    </component>
    ...
</plexus>
```

5.17 Automatically Generating a Maven Site with Continuum

One of the nice features of Maven is its built-in ability to generate a web site containing an abundance of technical information and reports about your project (see Chapter 29). One common use of Continuum is to automatically generate and publish this web site.

The standard way to build a Maven web site is to run the following command:

```
$ mvn site
```

This will generate a Maven site in the target directory. However, it is of limited use there. You generally want to copy it to a local web server, in order to publish your site to the world (or even just for your fellow workers). One simple (some would say "quick and dirty") way to do this is to use the *stagingDirectory* variable. The following code will generate a Maven site and publish it in the */var/www* directory:

```
$ mvn site -DstagingDirectory=/var/www
```

This will deploy your Maven web site to the */var/www* directory, in a directory with the same name as your project.

Typically, you run CI builds regularly. If the build fails, the build indicator goes red, notifications are sent, and the build stops. This is fine for detecting build failures, but is less satisfactory if you need to publish a web site to display, among other things, details of these build failures.

The conventional way to do this is to use two distinct build tasks: one to build the application and run the unit and integration tests, and another to publish the web site. The first should fail if there are any test failures, the second should not. To prevent a Maven target from stopping in the presence of unit test failures, use the *maven.test.testFailureIgnore* command-line option, as shown here:

```
$ mvn site -DstagingDirectory=/var/www -Dmaven.test.testFailureIgnore=true
```

This is illustrated in Figure 5-17, in which the Maven site is updated every hour, even if there are unit test failures.

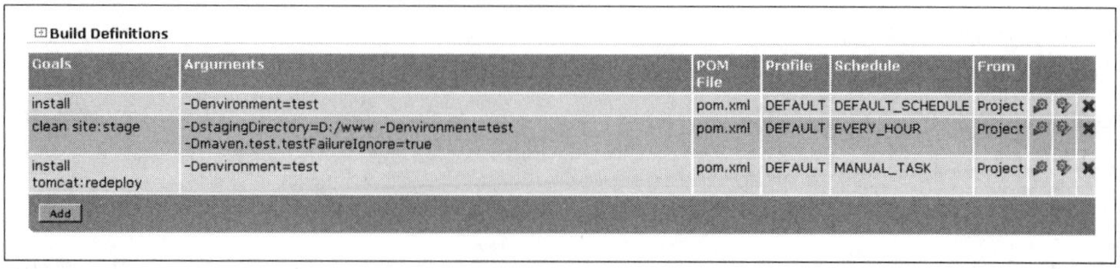

Build Definitions

Goals	Arguments	POM File	Profile	Schedule	From
install	-Denvironment=test	pom.xml	DEFAULT	DEFAULT_SCHEDULE	Project
clean site:stage	-DstagingDirectory=D:/www -Denvironment=test -Dmaven.test.testFailureIgnore=true	pom.xml	DEFAULT	EVERY_HOUR	Project
install tomcat:redeploy	-Denvironment=test	pom.xml	DEFAULT	MANUAL_TASK	Project

Add

Figure 5-17. Building the Maven site with hourly builds

Another approach, originally suggested by Max Cooper,[*] is to set up a profile in which test failures are ignored.

```
<!-- skip tests by default, but allow override on command line -->
<profile>
    <id>skiptests</id>
    <activation>
        <property>
            <name>!maven.test.skip</name>
        </property>
    </activation>
    <properties>
        <maven.test.skip>true</maven.test.skip>
    </properties>
</profile>
```

Then, just run your site generation normally:

```
$ mvn site:site
```

5.18 Configuring a Manual Build Task

Continuum is without doubt a useful tool for optimizing the build process. Developers will appreciate getting quick feedback on any new integration issues thanks to regular automatic builds. However, in real-world projects, not all builds are automatic. For example, in a test or staging environment, you generally want to decide yourself when a new version is to be released onto the test environment, rather than doing it automatically. Test releases need more coordination and communication efforts than regular automatic builds for developers: test teams appreciate being able to test on a stable, well-defined version, and not be confronted suddenly by the latest snapshot.

As we have seen, Continuum makes it easy to set up one or several automatic builds. You can also use Continuum to make your life easier when you build the release versions of your product. This way, releases can be done directly from the Continuum web interface, in a controlled environment, rather than on a developer's machine.

[*] *http://docs.codehaus.org/display/MAVENUSER/Surefire+Plugin*

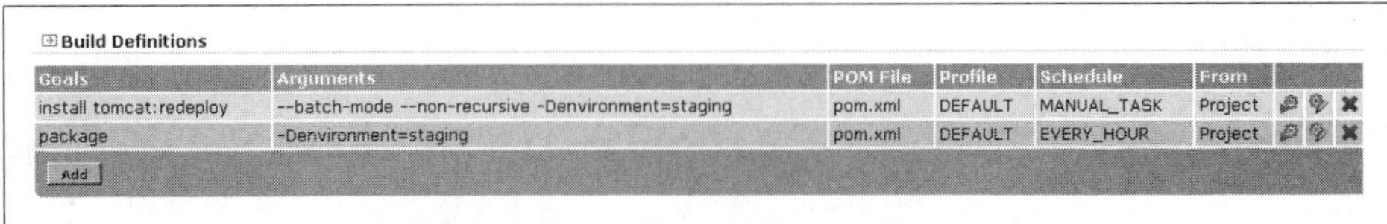

Figure 5-18. A project containing manual build definitions

To do this, you need to set up a schedule that is never actually run. We will use this special schedule to define tasks that are to be activated manually.

Create a new schedule, with a name like "MANUAL_TASK." You will need to provide a syntactically correct CRON expression, although you may want to give an impossible value such as a past date (e.g., "0 0 12 * * ? 1999") or one far in the future (e.g., "0 0 12 * * ? 2099") to make your intention clear. As we will see, this value will not actually be used. Just make sure that the schedule is disabled (uncheck the "Enabled" checkbox at the bottom of the screen) and save.

Now you need to create an additional build target for your manual build. This can be a separate project or an additional build target within the same project. In both cases, you will end up with a build definition like the second one in Figure 5-18.

Next, you need to distinguish the target environments, so that your manual task deploys to your staging environment. In Ant, you might do this using command-line property definitions or by calling a different target, for example. The above example is for a Maven 2 project. Maven profiles (see "Defining Build Profiles" in Section 2.4) are a good way to customize environment-specific deployment details. You can set up profiles for each target environment in your *pom.xml* or *profiles.xml* file, as shown here:

```
<!-- Staging environment profile -->
<profile>
    <id>env-staging</id>
    <activation>
        <property>
            <name>environment</name>
            <value>staging</value>
        </property>
    </activation>
    <properties>
        <appserver.autodeploy.dir>/appserver/staging/myapp/webapps
        </appserver.autodeploy.dir>
    </properties>
</profile>

<!-- Integration test profile -->
<profile>
    <id>env-test</id>
    <activation>
        <activeByDefault>true</activeByDefault>
        <property>
            <name>environment</name>
            <value>test</value>
```

```
        </property>
    </activation>
    <properties>
        <appserver.autodeploy.dir>/appserver/test/myapp/webapps
        </appserver.autodeploy.dir>
    </properties>
</profile>
```

Two profiles are defined: one for an integration test environment (identified by setting the "environment" variable to "test") and one for a staging environment (identified by setting the "environment" variable to "staging"). Each has its own definition of the *appserver.autodeploy.dir* property, which is used to indicate where to place the generated application (WAR).

Note that if you are using profiles in this way, it is wise to set up a separate Continuum project for each profile. This is because Continuum uses the same work directory for all the builds for a given project. So, if you use two different profiles in builds in the same Continuum project, you run the risk of overriding your generated artifacts with versions using the wrong profile. This feature is not particularly well supported in Continuum, as Maven 2 projects are listed by their project name in the list of Continuum projects. If you create multiple projects using the same POM file, they will appear as identical entries in this list.

The other main disadvantage of this approach is that you have less control over the exact version you are releasing. You cannot specify a particular Subversion or CVS tag to release, for example, without modifying the task goal to include the revision tag you need.

5.19 Conclusion

Continuum is still a relatively young product, with a lot of room for new and improved features. It has, nevertheless, made a lot of progress since it first appeared. It is easy to install and easy to use and will suffice in many situations. Its simplicity and its intuitive web administration console make it a good candidate for introducing continuous integration into organizations that have had no previous experience with the subject.

On the negative side, Continuum lacks some of the more advanced features found in other tools, although this has greatly improved since the release of Continuum 1.1.

CHAPTER 6

Setting Up a Continuous Integration Server with CruiseControl

6.1 An Introduction to CruiseControl

CruiseControl is a widely used and widely regarded open source continuous integration tool written in Java. CruiseControl is backed by ThoughtWorks, a leading proponent of agile methodologies and open source technologies. One of the first open source Continuous Integration tools, it benefits from a large user base and a number of third-party tools. ThoughtWorks now also offers CruiseControl Enterprise, a supported version of the product.

For those who skipped the introduction to this part of the book, Continuous Integration is a powerful technique used to keep development teams in phase and reduce the risks and complexities involved in combining code written by a number of individual developers into a unified working product. It basically involves automatically building and testing the latest source code at frequent intervals. At the same time, team members test and commit their changes frequently into the source code repository. It can considerably reduce the costs and risks traditionally involved in the integration phase of a project.

CruiseControl falls into the same category of tools as Continuum (Chapter 5), Lunt-Build (Chapter 7), and Hudson (Chapter 8). CruiseControl is the oldest of the three tools. Up until recently, configuration was still entirely done via an Extensible Markup Language (XML) configuration file. As of version 2.7, a basic administration console was added, similar to the ones found in the other tools we look at. CruiseControl supports an extensive range of software configuration management tools and notification mechanisms.

In this chapter, we will talk about CruiseControl 2.7.1, the latest release at the time of this writing.

CruiseControl runs as a process on the Continuous Integration server (known as the "Build Loop") that periodically checks for updates in the source code repository.

Whenever updates are detected in a project's source code, CruiseControl runs the corresponding build process and notifies a configurable list of listener modules. These listener modules let you notify team members about build results via email, IM, RSS, or using other methods.

CruiseControl also runs a web site containing a summary of build results and generated artifacts.

6.2 Installing CruiseControl

This section will show you how to get CruiseControl up and running on your machine.

I recommend creating a dedicated user account for CruiseControl. On a Linux machine, you can create a new user, as follows:

```
# useradd cruisecontrol
# su - cruisecontrol
cruisecontrol@linux-gxu0:~>
```

Now download the CruiseControl binaries from the CruiseControl web site (*http://cruisecontrol.sourceforge.net/download.html*). CruiseControl comes packaged as either a Windows executable installer or as a simple ZIP file. Here we will use the ZIP file, as this will work in any environment. If you are installing CruiseControl on a remote server, you can download the latest version from the CruiseControl web site using a command-line tool like *wget*, as shown here:

```
$ wget http://prdownloads.sourceforge.net/cruisecontrol/cruisecontrol
-bin-2.7.1.zip?download
...
13:46:56 (30.21 KB/s) - 'cruisecontrol-bin-2.7.1.zip?download' saved [14487]
```

Now unzip the package into the home directory:

```
$ unzip cruisecontrol-bin-2.7.1.zip
Archive:  ../cruisecontrol-bin-2.7.1.zip
   creating: cruisecontrol-bin-2.7.1/
   creating: cruisecontrol-bin-2.7.1/lib/
   creating: cruisecontrol-bin-2.7.1/logs/
   creating: cruisecontrol-bin-2.7.1/logs/connectfour/
  inflating: cruisecontrol-bin-2.7.1/cruisecontrol.bat
  inflating: cruisecontrol-bin-2.7.1/lib/commons-el.jar
  inflating: cruisecontrol-bin-2.7.1/lib/commons-logging.jar
  inflating: cruisecontrol-bin-2.7.1/lib/jasper-compiler.jar
  ...
$ cd cruisecontrol-bin-2.7.1
$ ls
apache-ant-1.7.0  cruisecontrol.bat  dashboard-config.xml  lib   projects
webapps
config.xml        cruisecontrol.sh   docs                  logs  README.txt
widgets.cfg
```

And that's it as far as installing things goes. Now we can test the installation. CruiseControl comes with its own bundled Jetty web server, so you don't have to worry about configuring (yet) another web server to monitor builds. Starting up CruiseControl is simple: just run the `cruisecontrol.sh` script (or `cruisecontrol.bat` for Windows installations):

```
$ cd ~/cruisecontrol-bin-2.7.1
$ ./cruisecontrol.sh
[cc]Sep-19 01:08:29 Main            - CruiseControl Version 2.7.1 Compiled on
                                      September 4 2007 1821
...
[cc]Jun-18 14:09:38 ontrollerAgent- Starting HttpAdaptor with CC-Stylesheets
[cc]Jun-18 14:09:38 ontrollerAgent- starting httpAdaptor
[cc]Jun-18 14:09:38 BuildQueue     - BuildQueue started
HttpAdaptor version 3.0.1 started on port 8000
[cc]Jun-18 14:09:38 Container      - Started org.mortbay.jetty.servlet.
                                      WebApplicationHandler@e2cb55
[cc]Jun-18 14:09:38 Container      - Started WebApplicationContext
                                      [/,CruiseControl Reporting App]
[cc]Jun-18 14:09:39 Container      - Started org.mortbay.jetty.servlet.
                                      WebApplicationHandler@29e357
[cc]Jun-18 14:09:39 Container      - Started WebApplicationContext[/cruisecontrol,
                                      CruiseControl Reporting App]
[cc]Jun-18 14:09:39 SocketListener- Started SocketListener on 0.0.0.0:8080
[cc]Jun-18 14:09:39 Container      - Started org.mortbay.jetty.Server@b4d3d5
```

This script initializes the continuous build process and starts up a Jetty web server.

By default, it will use port for the web site and port 8000 for Java Management Extensions (JMX) administration. As these are pretty common ports, you may need to modify them on your own server (especially if you are experimenting on a machine with other tools already installed). To do this, you provide `webport` and *webport* and *jmxport* command-line options, as follows:

```
$ ./cruisecontrol.sh -webport 8888 -jmxport 8880
```

CruiseControl comes with a small demonstration project you can use to make sure everything is running correctly. If you open *http://localhost:8080* (for a standard configuration) or *http://localhost:8888* (if you ran the above command), you will get the rather spartan console shown in Figure 6-1.

6.3 Configuring an Ant Project

Now that the server is installed, we'll look at how to add a simple project to CruiseControl. CruiseControl works best with Ant, so we'll look at this configuration first.

When it builds a project, CruiseControl uses a dedicated work directory for each project, where it checks out the source code and runs its builds. However, CruiseControl will not create this directory by itself, even if you tell it where to find the

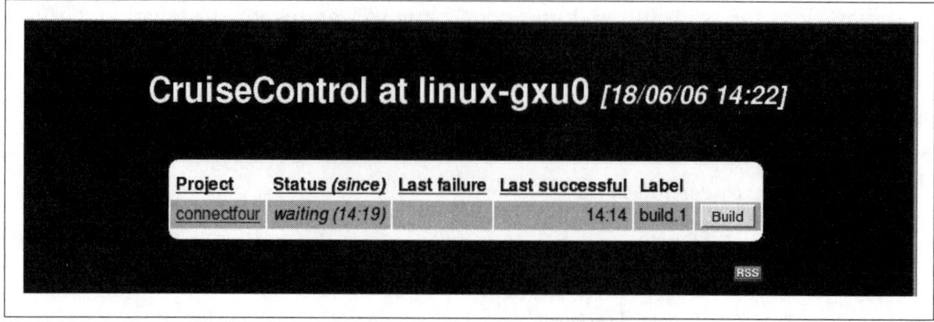

Figure 6-1. A CruiseControl web site

SCM tool. You have to do it yourself. So the first thing to do is to create a working directory for your project. These directories live (by convention) in the $CC_HOME/projects directory, where $CC_HOME is your CruiseControl installation directory. So before you start, you need to manually create the project and check out an initial copy of the source code. In this example, we will be working with a sample project called library-loans, an imaginary API designed to interface to a library loans database. First, we check out our project from the SCM repository into the projects directory (in this example, we use Subversion [Chapter 4], but CruiseControl supports a wide range of SCM tools):

```
$ su - cruisecontrol
Password:
$ cd cruisecontrol-bin-2.7.1/projects/
$ svn co svn://localhost/library-loans/trunk library-loans
A    library-loans/test
...
A    library-loans/build.xml
Checked out revision 31.
$ ls
connectfour/  library-loans/
```

It's also wise to verify that the build works properly in this environment. A lot of time-wasting errors come from badly configured Continuous Integration user accounts. In this sample project, we use some fairly standard *ant* targets: *clean*, to delete all generated artifacts; *compile*, to compile the main classes; *build*, to package the compiled classes into a jar called *library-loans.jar*; and *test*, to run the unit tests against this jar. Our continuous build process will go as far as running the unit tests:

```
$ cd library-loads
$ ant test
Buildfile: build.xml

init:
...
    [junit] Testcase: testSetName took 0.004 sec
    [junit] Testcase: testSetSymbol took 0 sec
```

```
BUILD SUCCESSFUL
Total time: 2 seconds
```

Now that we have a working project, we need to tell CruiseControl how to update the source code from the repository before each build. CruiseControl supports a large number of SCM tools, both open source and commercial. The current version (2.5) supports CVS, Subversion, BitKeeper, ClearCase, MKS, Perforce, PVCS, StarTeam, Visual SourceSafe, and more. However, there's a catch. When you configure CruiseControl to talk to a particular SCM tool, you are actually just telling it where to check for updates. If it detects updates, it will start a build. Period. It won't actually update your project source code from the repository before it does so: it leaves that minor detail to you.

As a rule, you don't usually integrate this task into your normal *build.xml* file. For one thing, your *build.xml* file is usually in the source code repository, so you have to update this file manually before updating the rest of the project through CruiseControl.

One common solution, of which several variations are described on the CruiseControl wiki, is to use a "wrapper" build file, which updates from the source code repository and then invokes the ordinary build file. This avoids cluttering up the ordinary build file with details about your source code repository. In our example, this file is simply called *build-cc.xml*, and it looks like this:

```
<project name="library-loans-cc">
    <target name="svn-update" description="Update from Subversion">
        <exec executable="svn">
            <arg line="update"/>
        </exec>
    </target>

    <target name="clean">
        <ant target="clean"/>
    </target>

    <target name="build" depends="svn-update">
        <ant target="build"/>
    </target>

    <target name="test" depends="build">
        <ant target="test"/>
    </target>

    <target name="load-tests" depends="build">
        <ant target="load-tests"/>
    </target>
</project>
```

So, now we can update the source code from the repository and build the project. Now you can add this project to the CruiseControl configuration file. Sure, CruiseControl has a web site where you can monitor builds, but all the serious configuration takes place in a file called *config.xml*. This makes CruiseControl less convenient to manage when compared to other similar tools such as Continuum (Chapter 5), LuntBuild (Chapter 7), and Hudson (Chapter 8). However, as we will see, the configuration file is relatively short and isn't too hard to master.

A basic CruiseControl configuration file goes something like this:

```
<cruisecontrol>
    <property name="build" value="projects/${project.name}/build"/>

    <project name="library-loans">

        <listeners>
            <currentbuildstatuslistener file="logs/${project.name}/status.txt"/>
        </listeners>

        <bootstrappers>
                <svnbootstrapper file="projects/${project.name}/build-cc.xml"
                                 localWorkingCopy="projects/${project.name}" />
        </bootstrappers>

        <modificationset quietperiod="0">
            <svn localWorkingCopy="projects/${project.name}"/>
        </modificationset>

        <schedule interval="600">
            <ant anthome="apache-ant-1.6.5"
                  buildfile="projects/${project.name}/build-cc.xml"
                  target="clean test"/>
            <ant anthome="apache-ant-1.6.5"
                  buildfile="projects/${project.name}/build-cc.xml"
                  time="0200"
                  target="clean load-tests"/>
        </schedule>

        <log>
             <merge dir="${build}/test-results"/>
        </log>

        <publishers>
            <onsuccess>
                <artifactspublisher dest="artifacts/${project.name}"
                                    file="${build}/${project.name}.jar"/>
            </onsuccess>
        </publishers>

    </project>

</cruisecontrol>
```

The CruiseControl configuration file contains a list of project entries. Properties like ${project.name} and ${build} are used to improve readability and reduce duplication. This is an example of how Ant-style properties can be used in CruiseControl configuration files. The ${project.name} property is automatically set by CruiseControl, but you can also define and use your own just as you would in an Ant build file, as shown here with the ${build} property.

You can configure each project using a number of elements, which are described briefly here. Some of the more interesting ones are treated in more detail in other articles.

<listeners>
: Listeners are used to perform actions when various project events occur. The *currentbuildstatuslistener* listener is the only one you really need from the word go, as it is used to display the build status of each project on the CruiseControl web site (see Figure 6-1).

<bootstrappers>
: Bootstrappers are tasks that are executed just before a build starts. One useful strategy, described by Lasse Koskela* is to use a bootstrapper task to update the cruise control build file (*build-cc.xml*) before performing the full build.

<modificationset>
: The modification set tells CruiseControl where and how to check for updates in the source repository. Here we are using Subversion, so we use the *<svn>* task. The *localWorkingCopy* attribute points to the local directory in which the Subversion project has been checked out: it is almost always the project directory. This task basically runs *svn log* to determine the modifications, which have occurred since the last build.

  We could also have used CVS, StarTeam, ClearCase, or one of the many other SCM tools supported by CruiseControl. We could even use a directory on the file system, using the *<filesystem>* element.

  If you are using an SCM tool, which doesn't support atomic commits, such as CVS, ClearCase, or Visual SourceSafe, you may need to use the *quietperiod* attribute. This value corresponds to the number of seconds that must have passed without any repository modifications. It is designed to avoid builds being started when someone is in the middle of committing her changes. You can set it to "0," as shown here, for SCM tools that support atomic commits and therefore don't need to wait until all the changes files have been committed.

  Another useful attribute is "*requiredmodification.*" Normally, CruiseControl will only start a build if it detects modifications in the source code repository. However, in some situations, you may want to run a build systematically, even if no modifications have been detected. For example, you may want a full nightly build to be run systematically at midnight every night; just set "*requiredmodification*" to "false."

<schedule>
: The schedule element is where you schedule your builds. CruiseControl supports two scheduling models. In the first approach, CruiseControl periodically polls the

* In "Driving On CruiseControl—Part 1," appearing on *http://www.javaranch.com* in September 2004.

source code repository for changes and runs a build whenever a change is detected. You define the number of seconds between these queries in the "interval" attribute. In the following example, the source code repository will be polled every 60 seconds. If any changes are detected, CruiseControl will run the build specified in the embedded build task:

```
<schedule interval="60">
    <ant anthome="apache-ant-1.6.5"
          buildfile="projects/${project.name}/build-cc.xml"
          target="test"/>
</schedule>
```

As shown here, you define the actual build tasks within the schedule element. CruiseControl 2.5 supports Ant, NAnt, Maven, and Maven 2 builds, via the *<ant>*, *<nant>*, *<maven>*, and *<maven2>* build tasks. The build task shown here runs the standard unit tests by invoking the *test* target in the *build-cc.xml* build file, which is the equivalent of the following:

```
$ cd projects/library-loans
$ ant -f build-cc.xml test
```

The second scheduling approach is to specify the actual times at which you want the builds to be run. This is useful if you want to set up a nightly integration build, for example. Suppose that you want to add a task to regularly run load tests. As load tests are expected to put the server under some stress, they are only performed once a day at 1 a.m. To run a task at a particular time, you use the *time* attribute, as shown in this example ("time="0100""). If you define a time for a build, the schedule frequency is ignored:

```
<schedule interval="60">
    <ant anthome="apache-ant-1.6.5"
          buildfile="projects/${project.name}/build-cc.xml"
          target="load-tests"
          time="0100"/>
</schedule>
```

A third scheduling possibility is to use the *multiple* attribute, which lets you run a task only every Nth build. For example, you may want to do incremental builds ("ant test") and do a full build ("ant clean test") only every 10th build. You could do this as follows:

```
<schedule interval="60">
    <ant anthome="apache-ant-1.6.5"
          buildfile="projects/${project.name}/build-cc.xml"
          multiple=10
          target="clean test"/>
</schedule>
```

In some cases, you need to stop build tasks over a certain period of time. Suppose your database goes down every night from 2 a.m. to 4 a.m. for backups. If you run any builds during this period, it will create unnecessary build failures. To get around this, you can temporarily suspend builds during a certain period using the *<pause>* element, as shown here:

```
<schedule interval="60">
    <ant anthome="apache-ant-1.6.5"
         buildfile="projects/${project.name}/build-cc.xml"
         target="test"/>
    <pause starttime="0200" endtime="0400"/>
</schedule>
```

<log>
: Here we merge the JUnit test results into the CruiseControl logfile. This lets CruiseControl correctly display the unit test results on the web site.

<publishers>
: Publisher entries are run at the end of each build, successful or not. They are typically used to notify developers of build results in some way, shape, or form. The most common method is old-fashioned email, but CruiseControl supports many other methods, and you can be quite imaginative if you put your mind to it. Another common use is to deploy generated files somewhere useful. In this example we place a copy of the generated JAR file into the *artifacts* directory, where it can be accessed from the CruiseControl web site. We look at publishers in more detail in Section 6.4.

Now restart CruiseControl and open the CruiseControl web site. You should see your new project, which has been added to the list of projects.

We saw earlier how the build status screen gives you an overview of all your projects. From this page, you can drill down to see the details for each project (see Figure 6-2). Here you will find the results of the last build and a list of the files modified since the previous successful build. The Test Results page provides a list of unit test results. There's also a "Metrics" page (see Figure 6-3), which gives you some nice graphs about the number of successful builds over time.

6.4 Keeping People Notified with Publishers

It's a good thing to have your builds running regularly, but it's even better to let everyone know how they're going. Developers will not, as a rule, spend their time glued to the CruiseControl web console waiting for the next build results to come up: they have better things to do with their time.

Publishing notification is one of the areas in which CruiseControl excels. Out-of-the-box, CruiseControl supports eMail, Jabber IM, RSS feeds, and even blogs. You can also perform various tasks such as ftp or scp file transfers, invoking an Ant target, running command-line tasks, or even using an X10 interface to hook up a lava lamp.

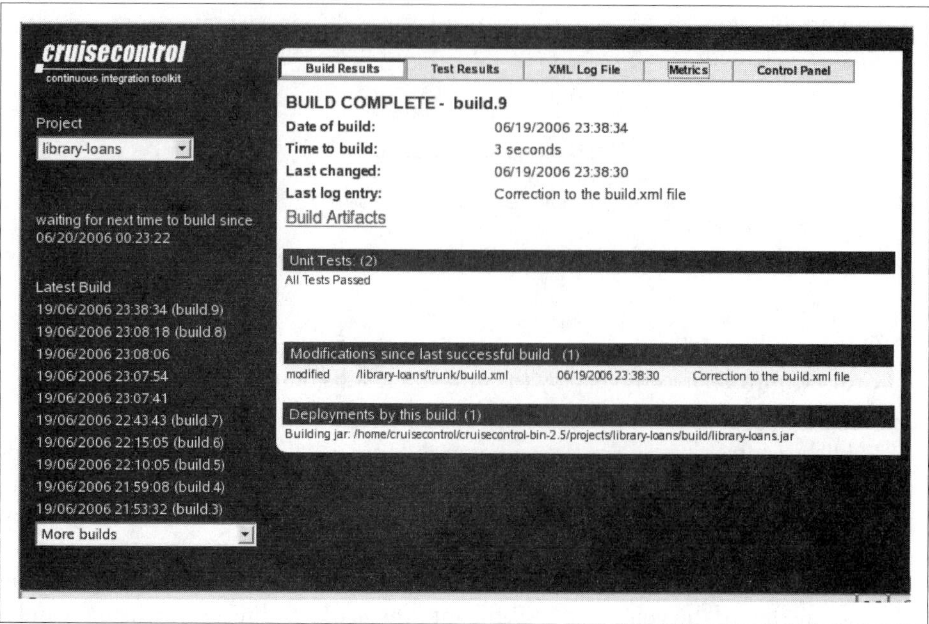

Figure 6-2. Build results for a project are displayed on the CruiseControl web site

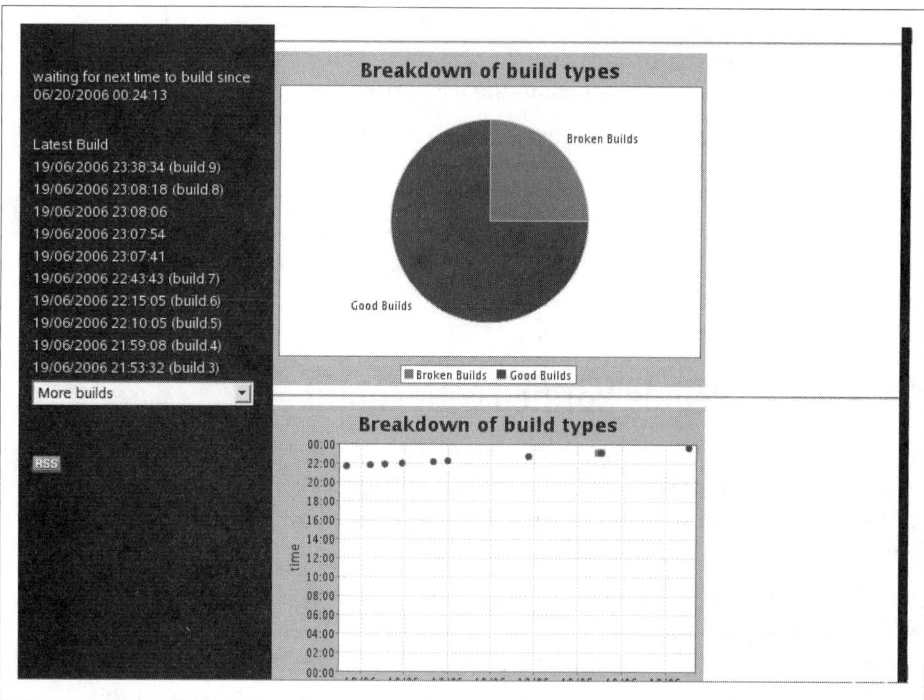

Figure 6-3. The CruiseControl web site displays metrics concerning build history for a project

Publishers are usually called after every build, whether the build succeeds or fails. If you need to run a publisher task only when a build succeeds or only when it fails, you can place it inside either a *<onsuccess>* or *<onfailure>* block, respectively. So, in the following example, the JAR file is deployed to the artifacts directory only if the build is successful:

```
<publishers>
    <onsuccess>
        <artifactspublisher dest="artifacts/${project.name}"
                            file="${build}/${project.name}.jar"/>
    </onsuccess>
</publishers>
```

The most common notification method is by email. CruiseControl supports both plain text email and HyperText Markup Language (HTML) email. The plain text email (*<email>*) simply sends a lightweight text message containing a link to the build results (see Figure 6-4). Configuring the email publisher is relatively straightforward. A typical example is shown here:

```
<property name="web.server.url" value="http://localhost:8080"/>
...
<publishers>
    ....
    <email mailhost="localhost"
           returnaddress="cruisecontrol"
           defaultsuffix="mycompany.com"
           subjectprefix="Build report:"
           reportsuccess="fixes"
           spamwhilebroken="false"
           buildresultsurl="${web.server.url}/buildresults/${project.name}">
        <always address="build-archives" />
        <failure address="developers" reportWhenFixed="true"/ />
        <map alias="john" address="john.smart@mycompany.com" />
        <map alias="mike" address="mikel@othercompany.com" />
        <map alias="developers" address="john, mike, harry" />
    </email>
    ....
</publishers>
```

Most of the attributes are fairly self-explanatory:

mailhost
: This attribute points to your mail server. If you're on a Unix machine, you can use the local machine, of course.

returnaddress
: The mail address to which errors are sent if the notification mail did not get through.

defaultsuffix
: This suffix is used to build email addresses. For instance, here, "build-archives" in the *<always>* element will map to "build-archives@mycompany.com."

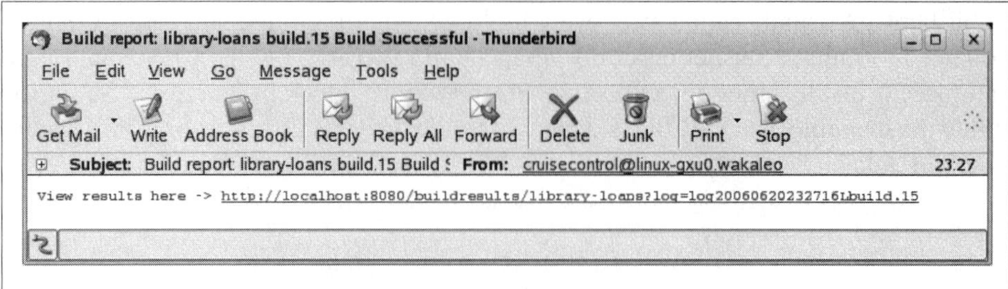

Figure 6-4. A plain-text email notification

subjectprefix
: The prefix added to the start of email titles.

reportsuccess
: This determines when mail is to be sent, and can be either "always," "fixes," or "failures." The first option sends mail for every successful build, whereas "fixes" only sends mail for the first successful build and the first successful build after a failure. The "failures" option only sends mail for failed builds.

spamwhilebroken
: If this is set to "true" (which is the default value), CruiseControl will send a mail each time the build fails, until the problem is fixed. If this seems overkill, set this attribute to "false" and CruiseControl will just send one message when the build breaks, and then another (if requested) when the problem is fixed.

buildresultsurl
: This is the base Uniform Resource Locator (URL) used to build the link to the build page. You shouldn't need to change this.

always
: This element contains an address, or an address list, to which a message is sent after each build, whatever its outcome.

failure
: This element contains an address, or an address list, to which a message is sent whenever a build fails. (There is also the *<success>* element, which does the opposite, but its utility is not particularly obvious.) A useful attribute of the *<failure>* element is the *reportWhenFixed* attribute: if this is set to "true," a message will be sent to report when the problem has been fixed.

map
: The *<map>* element defines aliases between SCM tool user accounts and email addresses. This is quite useful, as very often they don't match. You can also define lists of addresses, which in practice lets you set up team mailing lists.

The other way to send mail is as a self-contained HTML document. The HTML email task (*<htmlemail>*) sends a summary of the build in HTML (see Figure 6-5). It is very similar to the *<email>* element that we just looked at:

```
...
<htmlemail mailhost="localhost"
           returnaddress="cruisecontrol"
           defaultsuffix="mycompany.com"
           subjectprefix="Build report:"
           reportsuccess="fixes"
           spamwhilebroken="false"
           buildresultsurl="${web.server.url}/buildresults/${project.name}"
           css="webapps/cruisecontrol/css/cruisecontrol.css"
           xsldir="webapps/cruisecontrol/xsl"
           buildresultsurl="${web.server.url}/buildresults/${project.name}">
        <always address="build-archives" />
        <failure address="developers" reportWhenFixed="true"/ />
        <map alias="john" address="john.smart@mycompany.com" />
        <map alias="mike" address="mikel@othercompany.com" />
        <map alias="developers" address="john, mike, harry" />
</htmlemail>
...
```

In fact, it is identical, with a few extra attributes. None are mandatory, but in many cases CruiseControl will have a hard time finding the correct files if you don't give it a bit of a hand with the following two:

css
: The path to *cruisecontrol.css*, which is the stylesheet used to generate the mail. You could substitute your own, of course, if you really wanted to.

xsldir
: The path to the CruiseControl XSL directory, where CruiseControl keeps its XSL files (strangely enough).

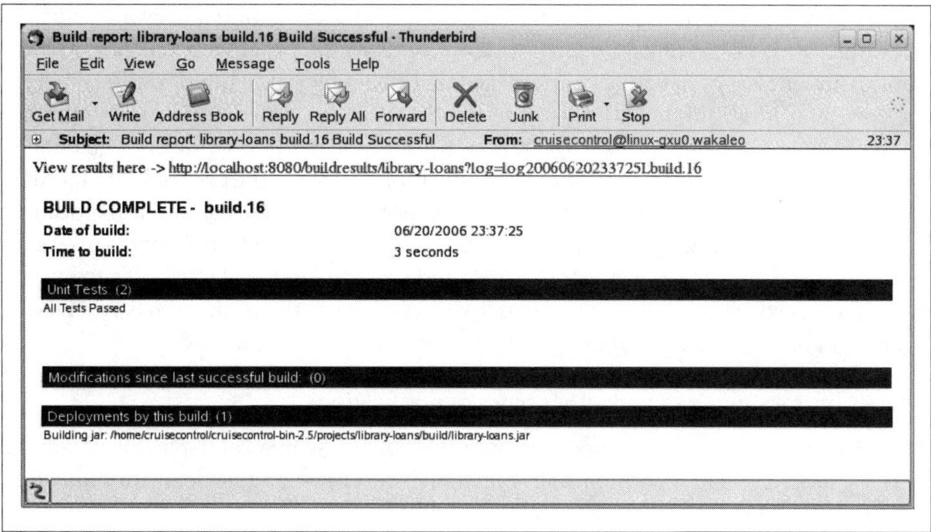

Figure 6-5. An HTML email notification

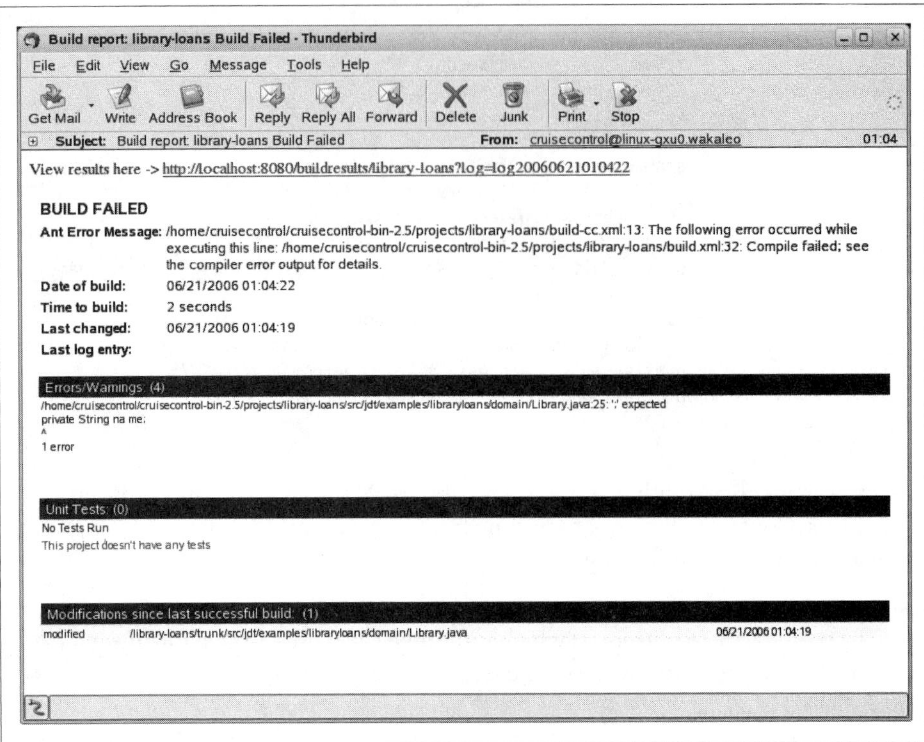

Figure 6-6. An HTML email notification for a failed build

Using the HTML mail format in this context can sometimes have some practical advantages. If the build server is an internal machine hidden behind a firewall (which is often the case), external users may not have access to the build web site. The HTML notification messages in CruiseControl contain full details of the build results, whereas the text mail just contains a link to the build server. So, for external users who are unable to access the build server, the text notification may not provide enough details. Developers often appreciate the HTML notification format in the case of build failures, since they can immediately see details of the error that has occurred and the modifications since the last build, without having to go to the build site (see Figure 6-6). As we have seen earlier, you can use *reportsuccess* and *reportWhenFixed* attributes to let you keep track of when integration errors are fixed. As soon as the problem has been fixed, a mail will be published to let everyone know about it (see Figure 6-7).

CruiseControl supports many other types of notification.

The *<jabber>* task lets you notify users via an IM client, which can have the advantage of being more eye-catching than a simple mail. The *<weblog>* task lets you publish to a weblog, and the *<rss>* to an RSS channel.

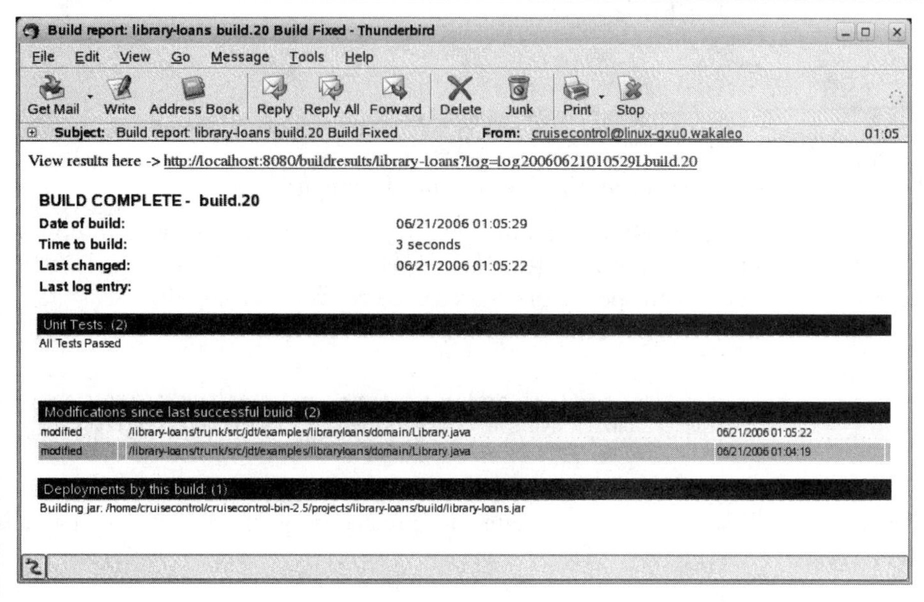

Figure 6-7. An HTML email notification for a fixed build

The *<x10>* task can be used to control lava lamps and other similar electronic devices. The principle of lava lamps is well known in Agile circles: you have two lava lamps hooked up to the build server, one green and one red. When the builds are successful, the green one bubbles. If a build fails, the red one bubbles. The nature of lava lamps is that the longer they stay on, the more agitated they get, so the longer the build stays broken, the more red bubbles you get. Another property of lava lamps is that they tend to take 10 to 15 minutes to warm up. If the developer is quick, she may be able to fix the failure before the lamp starts bubbling and the rest of the team notices.*

The *<socket>* task lets you write your build results directly to a socket. And if that isn't enough, the *<execute>* task lets you run an external program.

6.5 Setting Up a Maven 2 Project in CruiseControl

CruiseControl isn't as well integrated with Maven as it is with Ant. However, you can actually use the SCM features of Maven to make life easier. In this section, we'll go through the steps involved in configuring a Maven 2 project under CruiseControl.

For this example, we'll use a project called "tasker."

First of all, check out the source code in a working directory for CruiseControl:

* This technique is well documented on the CruiseControl wiki and also by Mike Clark (visit *http://www.pragmaticautomation.com/cgi-bin/pragauto.cgi/Monitor/Devices/BubbleBubbleBuildsInTrouble.rdoc**).

```
$ cd projects
$ svn co svn://localhost/tasker/trunk tasker
A    tasker/src
...
Checked out revision 24.
$ ls
connectfour  library-loans  tasker
```

Now add the Maven project to the CruiseControl configuration file.

Next you need to set up version control. In CruiseControl, this is easier to do for a Maven 2 project than for an Ant project, mainly because of Maven's integrated lifecycle support. In Maven 2, you specify the source code repository using the *<scm>* tag in your *pom.xml* file. A simple *<scm>* entry might look like this:

```
<scm>
    <connection>scm:svn:svn://subversion.mycompany.com/tasker/trunk</connection>
    <developerConnection>scm:svn:svn://subversion.mycompany.com/tasker/trunk
    </developerConnection>
</scm>
```

If this is correctly set up, you can update your project using the Maven *scm* plugin, as shown here:

```
$ mvn svn:update
```

In other words, you don't have to worry about the build wrapper we saw in the Ant project configuration. You just have to add the project to the CruiseControl configuration file. Here is an example:

```
<project name="tasker">

    <listeners>
        <currentbuildstatuslistener file="logs/${project.name}/status.txt"/>
    </listeners>

    <modificationset quietperiod="0">
        <svn localWorkingCopy="projects/${project.name}"/>
    </modificationset>

    <schedule interval="10">
        <maven2
            mvnscript="/usr/local/bin/mvn"
            pomfile="projects/${project.name}/pom.xml"
            goal="scm:update package"
        />
    </schedule>

    <log>
        <merge dir="projects/${project.name}/target/surefire-reports"/>
    </log>
    <publishers>
        <onsuccess>
            <artifactspublisher dest="artifacts/${project.name}"
                    file="projects/${project.name}/target/${project.name}-1.0.jar"/>
```

```
            </onsuccess>
        </publishers>

    </project>
```

The major change here is that we replaced the *<ant>* schedule task with a *<maven2>* task. The *<maven2>* task is relatively simple: you provide a *mvnscript* attribute (to tell CruiseControl where to find the *mvn* executable), the project *pom.xml*, and the goals to be executed. The first goal must be *scm:update*, which updates your project from the source repository. The next goal here is *package*, which compiles the source code, runs the unit tests, and generates a JAR file.

There are a few tricks that you should be aware of here. First of all, make sure you set the *<merge>* element in *<logs>* to point to your */target/surefire-reports* directory. This tells CruiseControl where to find Maven's unit test results.

Second, we have to tell CruiseControl about the generated artifact (the JAR file). For Maven users, one of the big weaknesses in CruiseControl is its poor support for Maven artifact versions. CruiseControl expects an artifact with a constant name, such as "tasker.jar." Maven, by contrast, generates versioned artifacts, such as "tasker-1.0.jar." And CruiseControl doesn't know how to talk to Maven to know what the current version is. So, the simplest solution is to make sure that the "file" attribute in the *<artifactspublisher>* tag matches the current version in Maven. Unfortunately, this requires you to manually update your CruiseControl script whenever you update your Maven artifact version number.

Now you're done! Your Maven 2 project is now correctly integrated into CruiseControl (see Figure 6-8).

6.6 The CruiseControl Dashboard

For a long time, the CruiseControl user interface was somewhat basic, to say the least. In the more recent releases, however, there is a new and revamped graphical dashboard that gives you a convenient overview of the status of your projects, as shown in Figure 6-9. This dashboard gives you a color-coded summary of the status of your builds: tones of green for success, tones of red for failure, yellow for a build in progress, and gray for inactive projects.

You can also drill down to view the details of a particular build, or view a summary of all the latest build results in the Builds tab. From here, you can also force a build to run manually. The dashboard also lets you add a project to the CruiseControl configuration file (although in general you still need to go and tailor the configuration file manually to suite your needs), and provides access to RSS feeds for server build results.

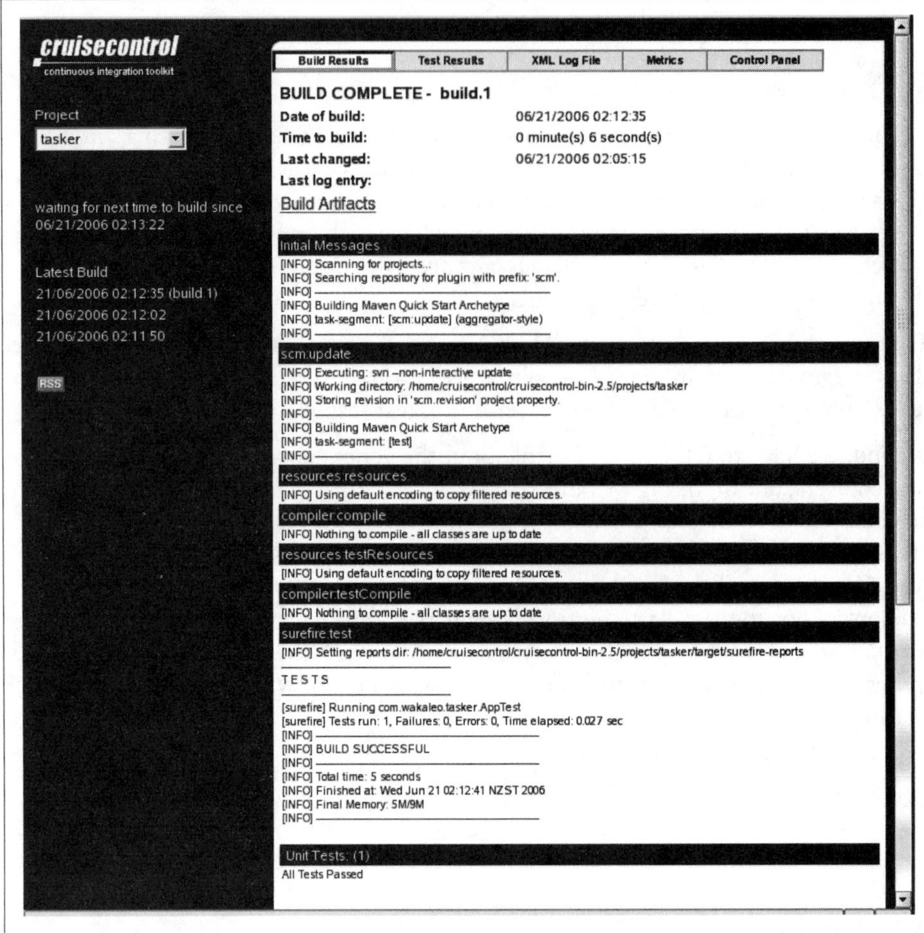

Figure 6-8. A Maven 2 build in CruiseControl

6.7 Third-Party Tools

CruiseControl boasts a rich collection of third-party tools. In this section, I describe a few of the more useful of them. Many, if not most, are listed on the CruiseControl wiki.

CruiseControl Configuration Tool

The CruiseControl Configuration UI* is a Java client application that can help you write and maintain CruiseControl configuration files using a Swing interface (see Figure 6-10). The CruiseControl configuration file is presented in the form of a tree, in which you can add, delete, or modify elements. One nice piece of functionality is the

* See *http://cc-config.sourceforge.net/*.

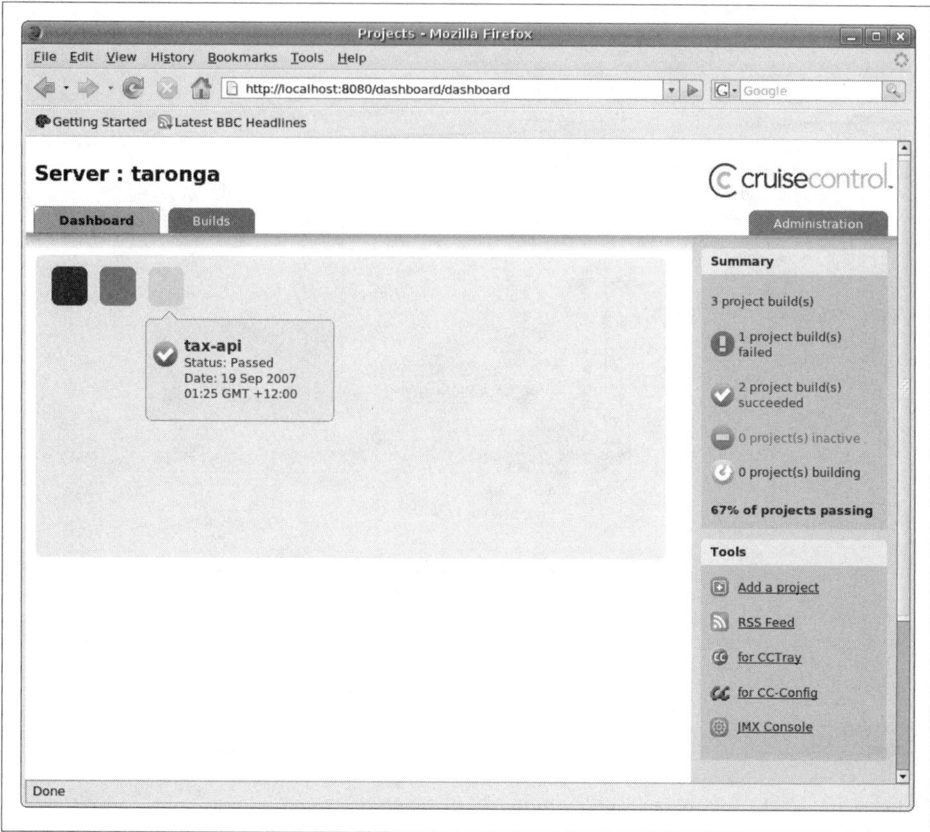

Figure 6-9. The CruiseControl dashboard

help panel, which displays contextual help for the current element and can be a useful learning aid or memory-jogger.

Firefox and Thunderbird Integration

Dmitri Maximovich* has written a neat little CruiseControl plug-in for Firefox and Thunderbird. You configure the plug-in by specifying a name and the JMX URL for the server (or servers) you want to monitor. CruiseControl runs JMX by default on port 8000, so your JMX URL will probably look like *http://cruisecontrol.mycompany.com:8000*. Once you've configured your server, you will see a panel in the lower right corner of the Firefox window, which summarizes the current build status (see Figure 6-11).

* See *http://www.md.pp.ru/mozilla/cc/*.

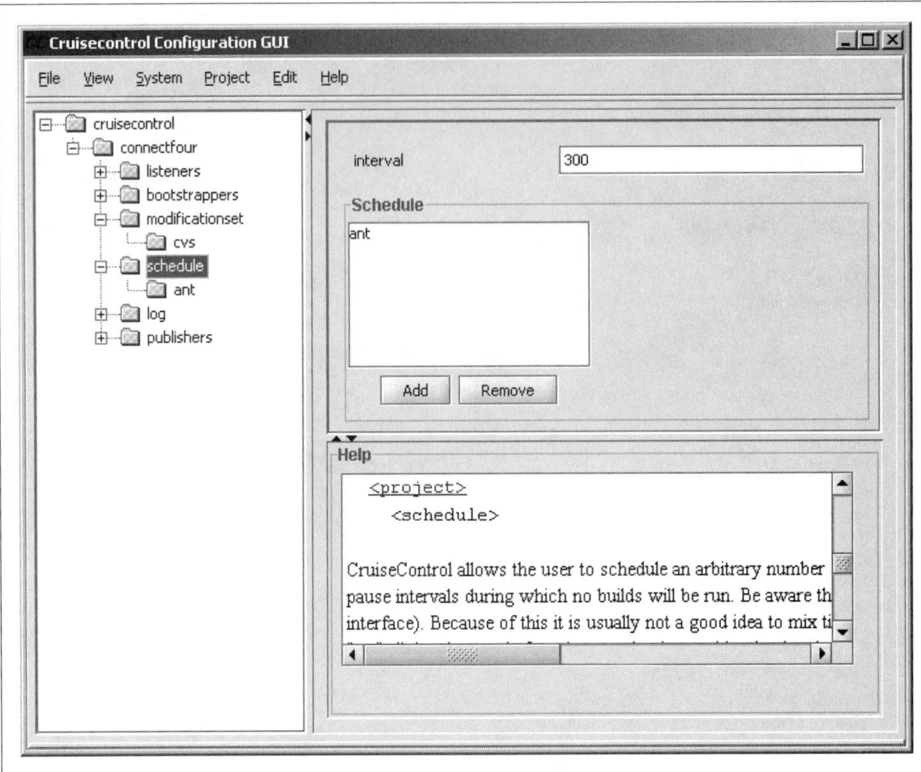

Figure 6-10. The CruiseControl Configuration UI in action

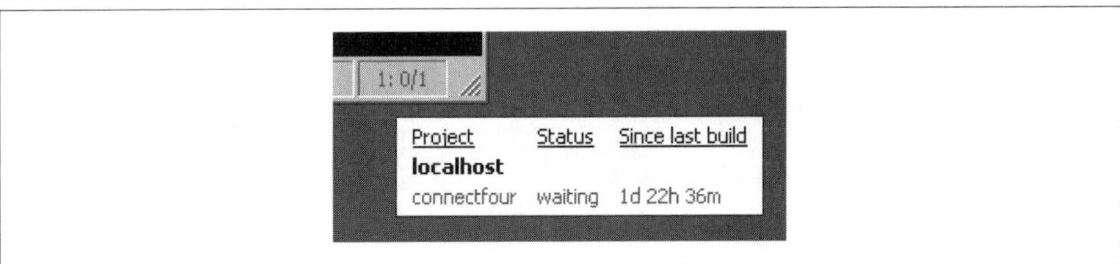

Figure 6-11. A CruiseControl plug-in for Firefox

6.8 Conclusion

CruiseControl is a powerful and flexible continuous integration tool, albeit with a nontrivial learning curve. It is a pure CI tool, with little in the way of interproject dependency or build artifact management. However, its flexibility and sophisticated notification techniques can make it an excellent choice for experienced Continuous Integration practitioners.

CHAPTER 7

LuntBuild—A Web-Based Continuous Integration Server

7.1 An Introduction to LuntBuild

LuntBuild* is another open source Continuous Integration tool written in Java. It is quite easy to install and configure, and all server administration tasks are done via a simple but convenient web-based administration console. In fact, LuntBuild is designed to do more than just managing the continuous integration process: it also lets you store and manage generated artifacts, label and promote versions, and manage dependencies between builds. It supports a wide range of version control tools, and notifications can be diffused via email, instant message (IM), and even on a blog site. Indeed, it is one of the most feature-rich of the open source Continuous Integration tools.

LuntBuild is produced and maintained by a company called PMEase.† The source code is hosted on JavaForge. LuntBuild also has a commercial cousin, called QuickBuild, which is marketed by the same company. Quickbuild is a commercial open source product (the source code is provided at a cost), with some extra features such as enhanced user and group management, and functionality aimed at larger organizations managing a large number of projects.

7.2 Installing LuntBuild

Installing and configuring LuntBuild is relatively simple, and you can have a server up and running in less than an hour. The installation package comes in the form of a self-installing jar file. Download it from the LuntBuild web site and run the graphical installation program as follows:

```
$ java -jar LuntBuild-1.5.2-installer.jar
```

* *http://luntbuild.javaforge.com/*

† *http://www.pmease.com/Home.page*

The installer takes you step-by-step through the installation process. LuntBuild is a very flexible tool, and can be configured to work with many external web servers and databases. It also works just fine all by itself as a standalone application. During the installation process, you can choose among various configuration options. If you leave the fields with their default values, LuntBuild will install and configure a fully functional standalone installation. For a production environment, you may want to modify some of the options, such as installing it on your own web application server or using your enterprise database. Some of the choices are described briefly here:

Customizing the web server
: LuntBuild is a web-based application. As such, you can either deploy it on your favorite Java web server (such as Apache Tomcat), or let LuntBuild run its own standalone web Jetty-based web server. If you want to deploy it onto your own J2EE-compliant application server, just specify the war deployment directory, and LuntBuild will do the rest.

Configuring the database
: LuntBuild uses a relational database to keep track of generated artifacts, build history, and so on. By default, LuntBuild uses an embedded HSQL DB database, but you can also configure it to use an external database such as MySQL, PostgreSQL, Oracle, or Microsoft SQL Server.

Configuring authentication
: If your company has an LDAP-based user directory, you can configure LuntBuild to use it for logins and passwords. LuntBuild supports some quite sophisticated options for LDAP integration: LuntBuild can import your LDAP users into the LuntBuild user directory where you can give them LuntBuild-specific access rights, you can give all the LDAP users read-only access to the site, you can reserve project administration rights to a selected few, you can map LuntBuild user IDs and email addresses to LDAP fields, and so on.

Once you've finished the installation, you can start the server. Go to the installation directory (here we have installed it in a directory called *LuntBuild* in our home directory) and run the *LuntBuild.sh* script:

```
$ cd /usr/local/luntbuild-1.5.2
$ bin/luntbuild.sh localhost 8080
bin/LuntBuild.sh localhost 8080
22:23:50.218 EVENT  Starting Jetty/4.2.23
22:23:50.726 EVENT  Started WebApplicationContext[/LuntBuild,LuntBuild]
LuntBuild : --> context initialization started
LuntBuild : --> context initialization finished
22:23:57.583 EVENT  Started SocketListener on 127.0.0.1:8080
22:23:57.583 EVENT  Started org.mortbay.jetty.Server@5ffb18
```

And to stop the server, just run the *stop-LuntBuild.sh* script, as shown here:

```
$ cd /usr/local/luntbuild-1.5.2
$ bin/stop-luntbuild.sh localhost 8889
```

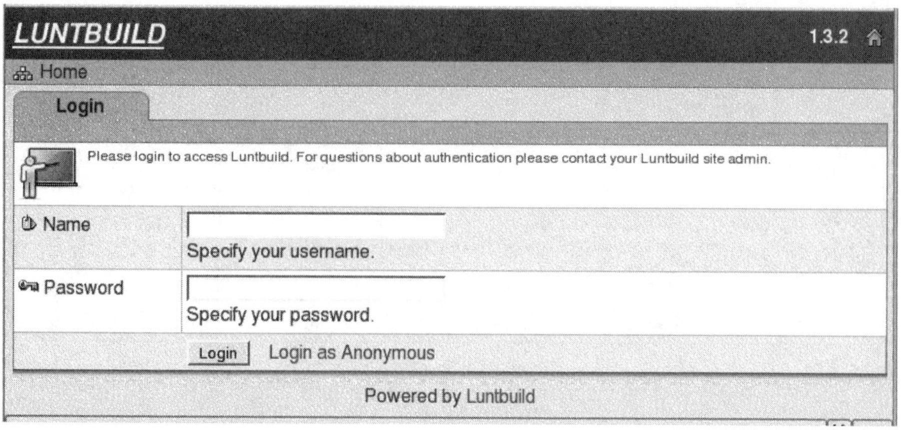

Figure 7-1. *Connecting to the LuntBuild administration console*

7.3 Configuring the LuntBuild Server

Once you have started the server, you manage everything via the web administration console (the URL will be something like *http://localhost:8080/LuntBuild*). Logically enough, LuntBuild requires you to identify yourself before you can do anything interesting (see Figure 7-1). When you first install LuntBuild, you can use "LuntBuild/LuntBuild" to connect as an administrator. Anonymous users are also allowed to view certain parts of the site, but cannot modify anything.

The LuntBuild administration web site lets you view and manage different aspects of your server and of the projects you manage (see Figure 7-2). Here, you can manage build projects and build history, user accounts, server configuration properties, and perform other administrative tasks such as backing up and restoring build and artifact history.

The first thing you need to do when you set up your server is to verify the server configuration properties. You do this in the "Properties" tab (see Figure 7-3). Many server configuration properties, such as the server URL and work directories, use sensible default values, which are well documented on the Properties page. Others, such as the SMTP server for mail notification, will need to be configured if you want to use these notification methods. LuntBuild supports a fairly limited range of notification methods, including SMTP email, MSN, Jabber, SameTime, and some blog sites. To use any one of these methods, you will need to provide information on the host server, as well as user account and password details.

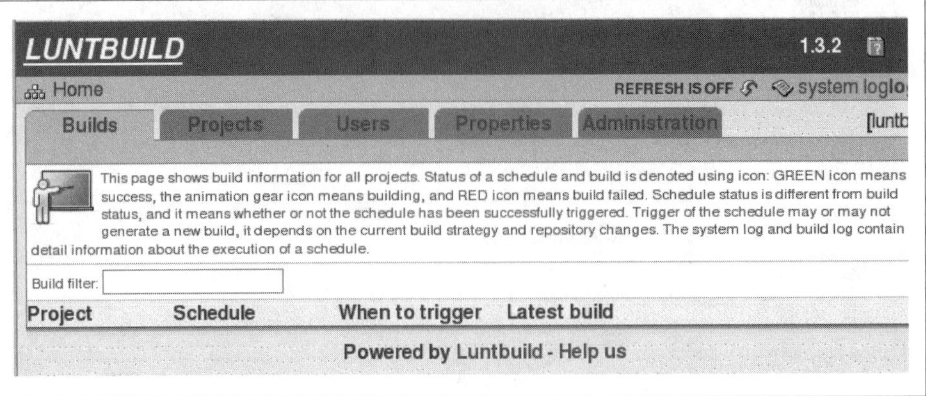

Figure 7-2. The LuntBuild home page

If configuring one of the IM notification types (MSN or Jabber), you will need to create a special account for the LuntBuild server (e.g., *LuntBuild.mycompany@hotmail.com*). Users will need to add this account to their list of contacts in their IM clients. Then users simply log on to their IM clients as usual.

To use blog notification, you will need to provide user account information, the URL of the blog web service, and also the type of blog. Several blog sites today let you submit posts via a web service interface. Unfortunately, there is no standard interface. At the time of this writing, LuntBuild supports the three main blogging application programming interfaces (API's): the Blogger API (the oldest standard, used for sites like *http://www.blogger.com*), the Metaweblog API (an extension of the Blogger API, used for sites like *http://www.jroller.com* and *http://wordpress.com*), and the LiveJournal API (used by the *http://www.livejournal.com* blog site).

When you are happy with your server configuration, you can set up some user accounts for your team members. You do this in the "Users" tab (see Figure 7-4). User account management at this level is not particularly sophisticated, and users are basically separated into two categories: those who can create projects, and those who can't. More detailed user-access rules are defined at the project level (see Section 7.4).

Configuring a LuntBuild server using the web administration site is simple and intuitive. Even if they wouldn't win any prizes for graphical design, the screens are functional and well documented. The next step is to add some projects. And the judicious use of default values and optional fields means that you can be operational in very little time indeed!

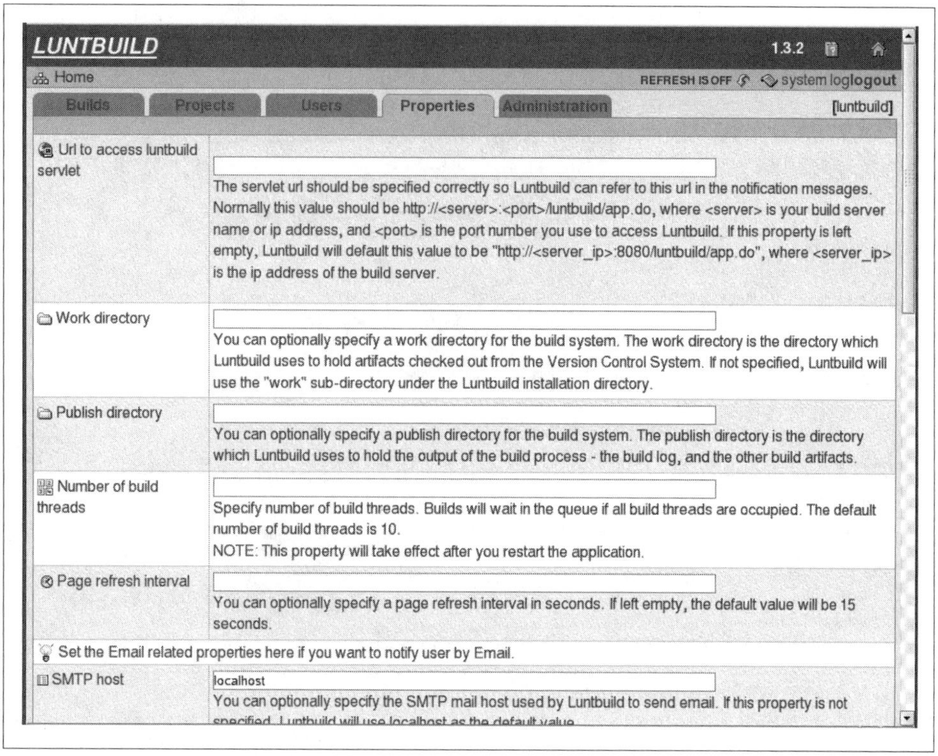

Figure 7-3. Server configuration properties

7.4 Adding a Project

In LuntBuild, build schedules are organized around projects. LuntBuild provides a rich set of functions for managing project builds.

You add a new project in the “Project” tab (see Figure 7-5) by clicking on the “New Project” icon. LuntBuild lets you configure a number of different aspects of your project (see Figure 7-6). Don’t let the number of screens put you off, though; the screens are intuitive and well documented, and you can get a simple project up and running in very little time.

In LuntBuild, project information and management activities are organized into five areas, each represented by a tab:

Basic
: This is where you define general project details, user access rights, and notification methods.

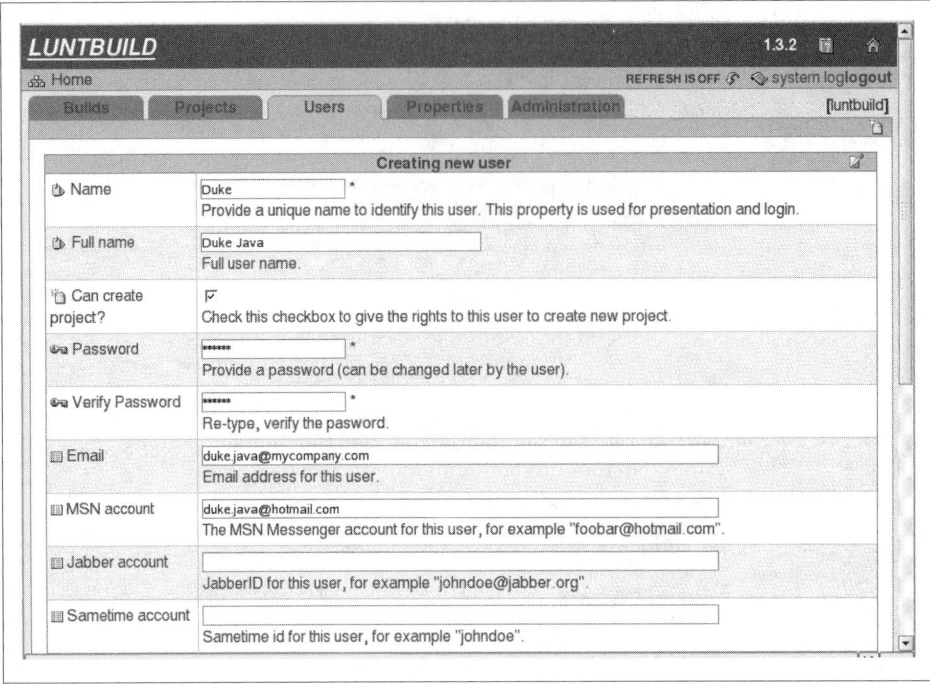

Figure 7-4. Setting up user accounts

VCS Adaptors
: Version control systems (also known as SCM, or Software Configuration Management, systems).

Builders
: The Builders page lets you configure one or more build scripts for this project.

Schedulers
: Schedulers let you specify *when* the build scripts will be run.

Login mapping
: This page lets you map your LuntBuild users to your VCS users.

In the remainder of this section, we will go through the steps involved in configuring a project in LuntBuild.

Configuring the Project Basics

The first thing to define are the general project details, user access rights, and notification methods, which are displayed in the "Basic" tab (see Figure 7-6). You will need to save this information before LuntBuild will let you proceed to the other screens.

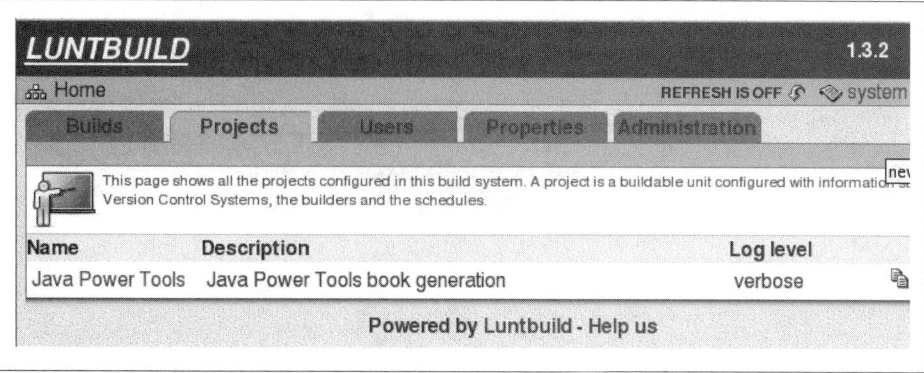

Figure 7-5. The Projects tab

An important part of this screen concerns user rights. In LuntBuild, you can assign different levels of access to different users for each project. There are three types of access:

Project Admins
: Project admins can manage all aspects of projects in LuntBuild, including project and SCM configuration, user management, and build management.

Project builders
: Project builders are restricted to build scheduling and build management activities.

Project viewers
: Project viewers can simply consult build results and download generated artifacts.

You also define notification methods here. LuntBuild supports several types of notification: Email, MSN Messager, Jabber, Sametime, and Blog sites. These notification types are configured in the server configuration pages (see Section 7.3): in the project screens, you simply indicate which notification methods should be used for this project.

You also indicate *who* must be notified. In addition to being able to specify users by name, you can also tell LuntBuild to notify users who have made recent updates to the source repository. For example, you may want to systematically notify the lead developer (specify by name), as well as any other users who have committed any recent changes: this avoids wasting time for developers who haven't made any updates, and therefore, who shouldn't be concerned by integration issues.

Finally, you can define project variables. Project variables can be used in ONGL expressions that can in turn be used to build the names of successive build versions. This approach can be used to build sophisticated version naming strategies (see Section 7.5).

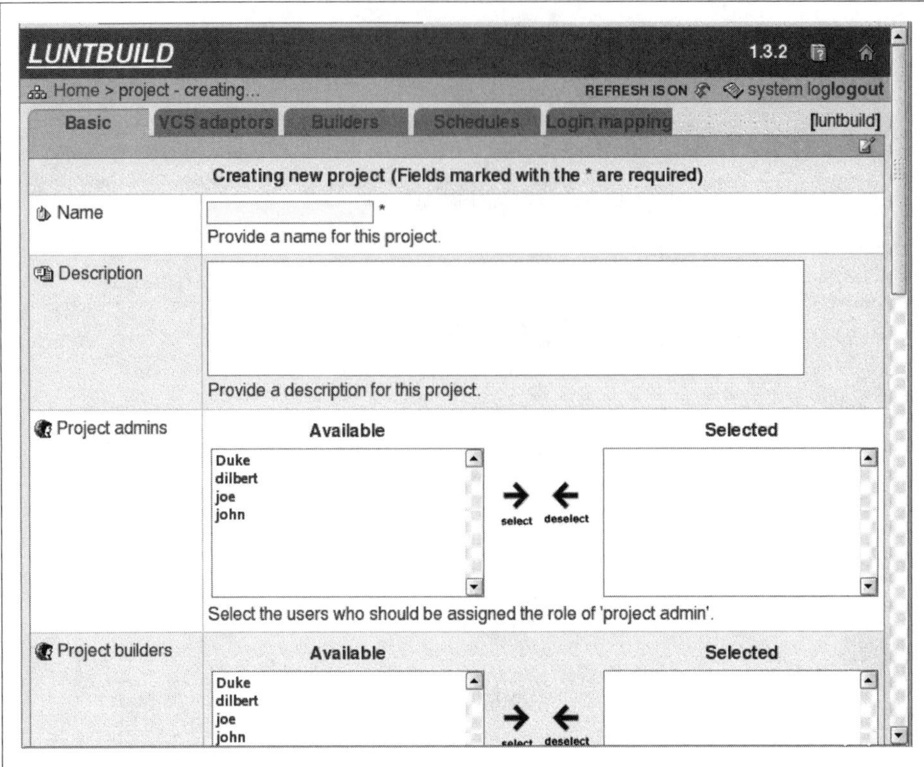

Figure 7-6. Adding a new project

VCS Adaptors

The next step involves configuring the VCS adaptors (see Figure 7-7). This is where you define where LuntBuild should look for the project source code. LuntBuild supports a wide range of VCS products, including CVS, Subversion, StarTeam, AccuRev, ClearCase, and even Visual SourceSafe. Since each VCS product has its own peculiarities, each VCS adaptor has its own specific configuration screen. The Subversion screen, for example, recognizes the Subversion convention of storing the main development trunk, separate branches, and revision tags in separate specific directories. If you are using a VCS product that does not support atomic commits, such as CVS, ClearCase, or Visual SourceSafe (just to name a few), you can also define a "quiet time." This forces LuntBuild to wait until the VCS has been inactive for a certain period of time before it starts to check out a new version. The idea is to make sure any in-progress commits have been finished before LuntBuild starts its build.

Once you have configured the VCS adaptor, you need to define some modules. Modules let you check out different parts of the project from different areas in your source code repository. Depending on what VCS you are using, and how your source code

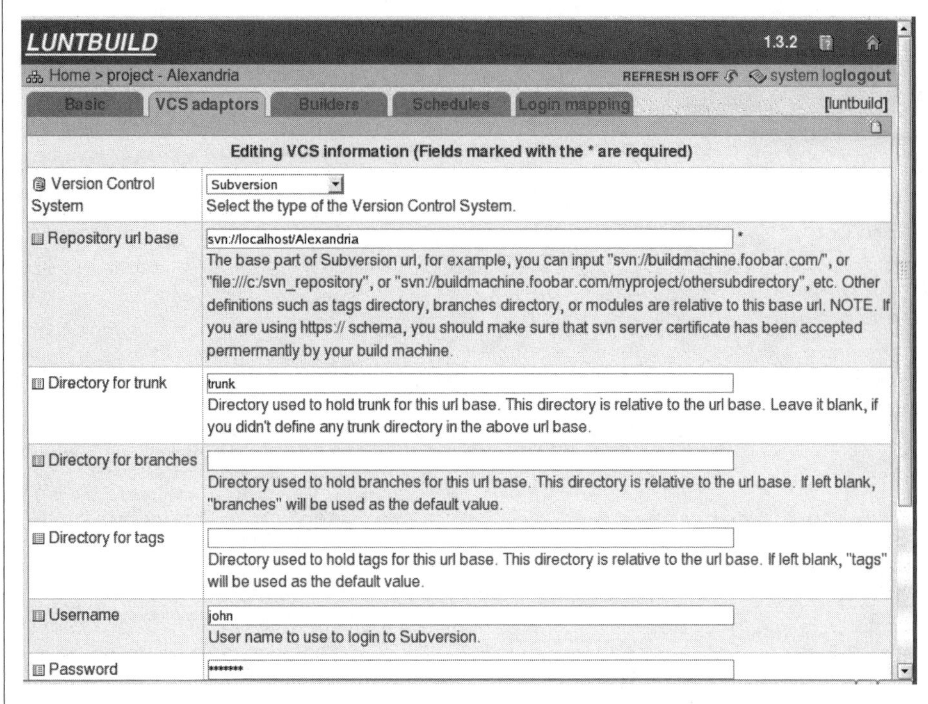

Figure 7-7. VCS Adaptors

repository is organized, this will be more or less useful. For example, if your project is stored on a dedicated Subversion repository, with no subprojects, modules will be of little use. By contrast, if you are using a Subversion repository that is shared among many projects, you will need to define a module corresponding to your project in the repository. If you are using CVS, the module will be your project directory on the repository server.

Although it is not a mandatory field, LuntBuild in fact expects you to define at least one. If you want to check out the entire project, just create a module with a dot (".") for the source path.

You can also define several VCS adaptors if you really need to; if different parts of your project come from different SCM repositories, for example.

Builders

One of the distinctive features of LuntBuild is the way that it distinguishes between configuring the builds and scheduling them. The Builders page (see Figure 7-8) lets you configure one or more build scripts for a project. LuntBuild handles several different

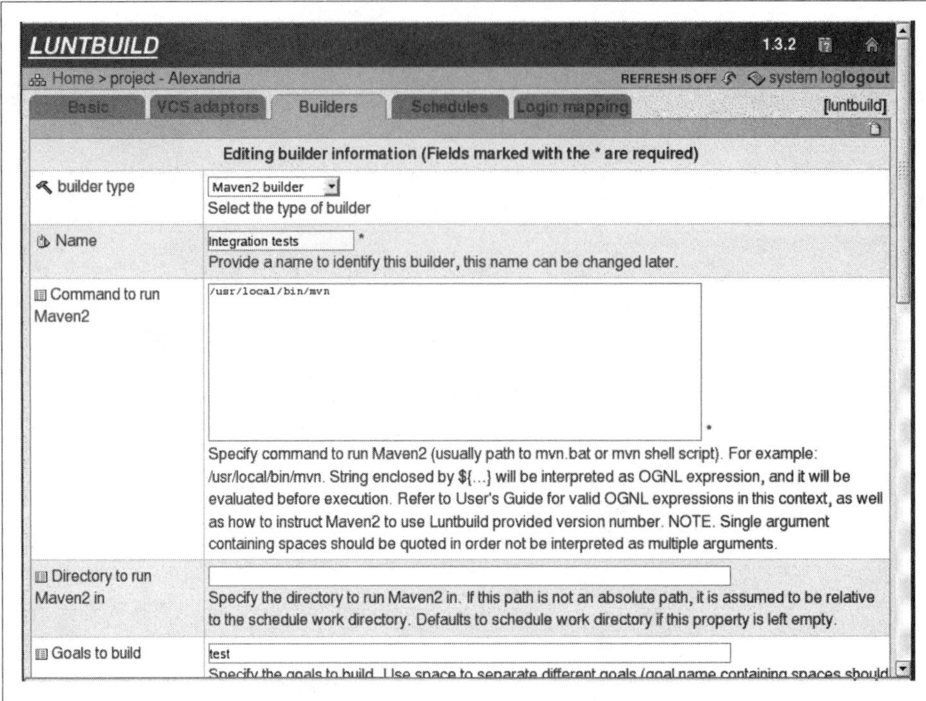

Figure 7-8. Builders

types of build scripts: Ant, Maven and Maven 2, command-line build scripts, and Rake (a build language similar to Ant for Ruby).

You should give your build a meaningful name (such as "Integration tests," "Nightly build," or "Maven site build"). LuntBuild lets you assign the same build to several different schedules, or several different builds may be assigned to the same schedule, so it is useful to be able to recognize your build configurations at a glance.

Configuring a build script is fairly intuitive. You need to provide the build script location, and (where appropriate) the goals or targets to be called. You can also provide build properties and environment variables, which can be used to customize the behavior of your build script.

Scheduling

Builders let you tell LuntBuild *how* to build your project; schedulers let you specify *when* the build scripts will be run (see Figure 7-9). By providing a clean separation of concerns, LuntBuild lets you configure modular build scripts that can be used and reused in different schedules.

Once you have provided a meaningful name and description, you define a naming strategy for the builds generated by this scheduler, using the "Next build version" field. This field displays the label of the next planned build. Each build has a unique, automatically-generated label, such as "myproject-1.14" or "library-core-1.0 (build 123)." By default, LuntBuild will simply increment the last number in the expression: "myproject-1.14" will become "myproject-1.15," and "library-core-1.0 (build 123)" will become "library-core-1.0 (build 124)." If you need a more sophisticated naming strategy, you can use project variables and OGNL expressions to build the version label programmatically (see Section 7.5).

The "Trigger Type" field lets you specify when and how a build is to be scheduled. You can schedule a build in one of three ways. "Manual" builds must be triggered by hand. "Simple" builds are run at regular intervals. And "cron" builds use a cron expression to determine when they should be run. LuntBuild does not support the polling approach.

By default, builds will be run only if an update is detected in the VCS. A build will also run if another build on which it depends has been rebuilt. This behavior suits most circumstances well. If it doesn't suit yours, you can use the "Build necessary condition" field to modify or fine-tune this behavior. Typical alternatives are "always" (always run the build), "never" (ignore this build), or "alwaysIfFailed" (keep trying to rebuild after a build has failed, even if there are no updates in the VCS).

LuntBuild is a flexible tool, and you can assign builds to a scheduler in several ways. The most common is to use the "Associated builders" field: The builders listed here will be executed in turn whenever this scheduler is run. You can also define "post-builders," which will be run after the main builds, if certain conditions are met. A typical use of a postbuild would be to deploy an application to a test server if and only if the nightly build succeeded.

LuntBuild also lets you configure a number of other scheduling options. You can configure builds to be clean (working directories are deleted and the whole project is rebuilt) or incremental. New labels may be generated after every build, or only if the build succeeds. The "Notify Strategy" lets you decide when notification messages should be sent: always, only if the build fails, whenever the build status changes (i.e., one message when a build breaks, then another when it is fixed), and so on.

You can also define dependencies between schedules. Suppose that your project depends on other libraries or components, which are also handled in LuntBuild. You may want to add dependencies to these projects so that any rebuilds in these dependent projects will automatically trigger a build in your project.

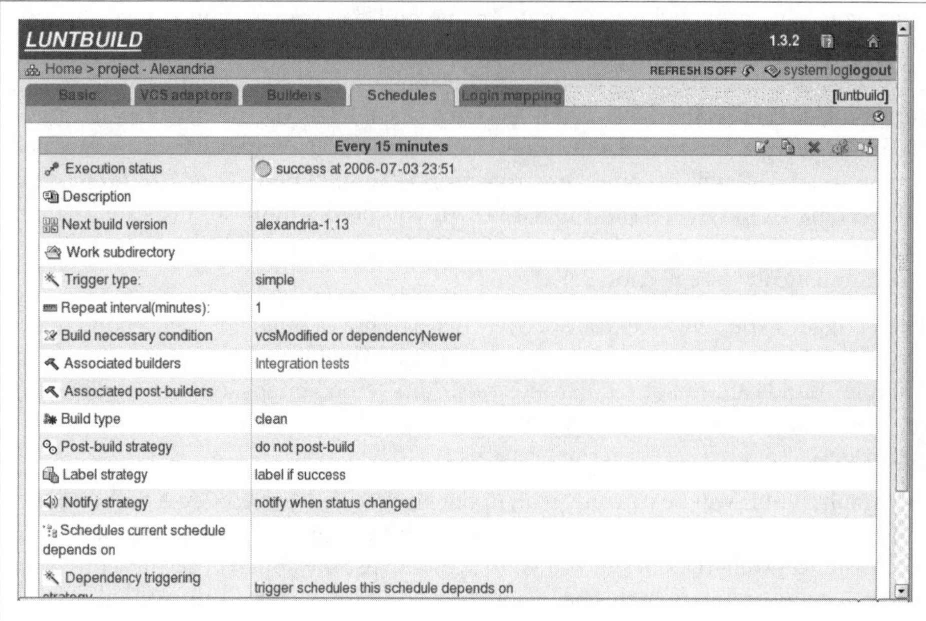

Figure 7-9. Schedules

Login Mapping

As a rule, it is better if your LuntBuild logins correspond to your VCS account names. This allows LuntBuild to know automatically who has made modifications in the source code repository, and send notifications as appropriate.

However, there are times when this is just not practical. Your VCS accounts may be a strange combination of letters and numbers that only a systems administrator can understand (yes, I've seen it done), and you may prefer more user-friendly logins for your LuntBuild system. This is where the Login Mapping screen (see Figure 7-10) comes in handy. This screen lets you map VCS logins to your LuntBuild user names. So, you can keep your user-friendly LuntBuild logins, and LuntBuild will still manage to notify the right users when changes are made in the repository.

7.5 Using Project Variables for Version Numbering

Managing version numbers is an important part of configuration management. LuntBuild provides several easy ways to do this, via the "Next build version" field in the "Schedules" tab.

If all you need is a basic counter, you simply provide the initial version text in the "Next build version" field. For example, if you place "my-project-1.0" in the "Next build

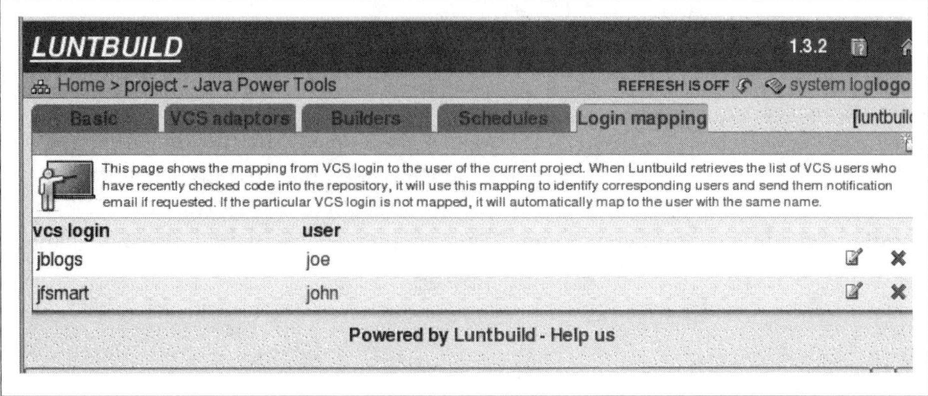

Figure 7-10. Login Mappings

version" field, the next build will be labeled "my-project-1.0," the following "my-project-1.1," and so on. This method simply takes the last number in the version label field and increments it, so "my-project-1.5.0_07-b10" would become "my-project-1.5.0_07-b11."

Now suppose you use a numbering system based on major and minor release numbers, followed by a build number; for example, "my-project-1.2.3." You can do this using project variables, which you define in the "Basic" tab (see "Configuring the Project Basics), and OGNL expressions.

OGNL, or Object-Graph Navigation Language, is an expression language for manipulating Java objects. It is often used in the open source Java world, in projects such as Tapestry and Webworks. It is similar but more expressive than the more well-known EL expression language used in JSTL, which only allows you to read object properties.

In LuntBuild, project variables are stored in a Map called *project.var*. So, to read a project variable called "versionNumber," you would use the following expression:

```
${project.var["versionNumber"]}
```

To define the "my-project-1.2.3" numbering strategy described above, you would define two variables in the project "Basic" tab called "majorVersionNumber" and "minorVersionNumber," and use a version label like this:

```
myproject-${project.var["majorVersionNumber"]}-${project.var["minorVersionNumber"]}-1
```

However, this won't work. When you introduce OGNL, the trick of incrementing the last number in the build label no longer works—you need to do this yourself. That's where OGNL expressions come in handy. Not only can you read object fields, but you can also modify them. Here, we need a third variable (say, "versionIterator") to keep track of the final build number. You use the *increaseAsInt()* method to do this, as shown here:

```
${project.var["versionIterator"].increaseAsInt()}
```

So, the final version label expression should look like this:

```
myproject-${project.var["majorVersionNumber"]}-${project.var["minorVersionNumber"]}
-${project.var["versionIterator"].increaseAsInt()}
```

Now suppose we want to keep track of nightly builds by using a date suffix, such as "project-1-2-nightly-2006-06-21." LuntBuild provides a helper object called "system" for this kind of situation. This object has a number of date-related fields such as year, month, dayOfMonth, numericMonth, hour, minute and so on. To obtain the above expression, we could use an expression like this:

```
${system.(year+"-"+numericMonth+"-"+dayOfMonth)}
```

So, the final expression would be:

```
myproject-${project.var["majorVersionNumber"]}-${project.var["minorVersionNumber"]}
-nightly-${system.(year+"-"+numericMonth+"-"+dayOfMonth)}
```

7.6 Build Results Diagnostics

On the home page of your LuntBuild site, you get a dashboard summary of the latest builds, with green lights for successful builds, and red lights for failed ones (see Figure 7-11). What can be a little confusing is the fact that both schedules and builds have status lights: Both can fail, apparently independently of each other.

If the schedule is marked with a red light (like the "Java Power Tools" schedule in Figure 7-11), the schedule is not (or is no longer) running correctly. The build, if any, is the last successful build on record.

If the build is marked with a red light (like the "alexandria-1.0" build in Figure 7-11), this tells you that your schedule may be running just fine, but your build script (or the configuration thereof) is broken.

In both cases, something probably needs to be fixed. Just click on the broken schedule or build to investigate further.

Finding out exactly what is wrong can be a little tricky, and sometimes needs some detective work. Let's look at the broken build first. If you want to see details about what is broken, just click on the broken build. This will open a page containing a detailed description of the build results (see Figure 7-12). You can do a few things here, such as displaying logfiles, and forcing a rebuild when you think you've fixed the problem (the "hammer" icon).

You can also attach this build script to a different scheduler using the green arrow icon (the operation is called "move" in LuntBuild jargon). This could be useful for example if you realise that the build you have scheduled to run every 10 minutes actually takes

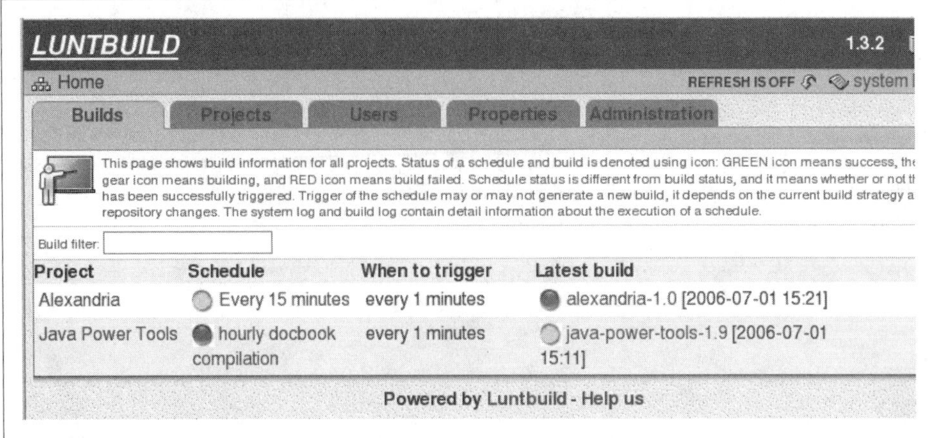

Figure 7-11. Displaying build results

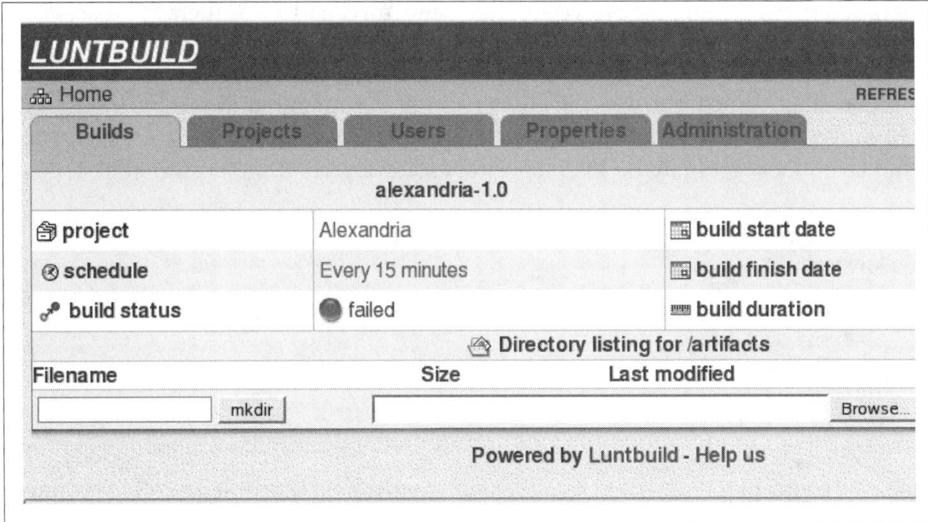

Figure 7-12. Build result details

30 minutes, to complete, which is an excellent way to overload your build server and to incur the wrath of your system administrator.

The revision log contains the list of changes recorded in the VCS since the last build. The build log (see Figure 7-13) gives a detailed record of the build's progress. Even if no error is explicitly mentioned here, you can generally figure out where the build got to. For example, in this case, we notice that the build stopped with the cryptic message "Seems that baseUrl 'svn://localhost/Alexandria/tags' does not exist, creating...."

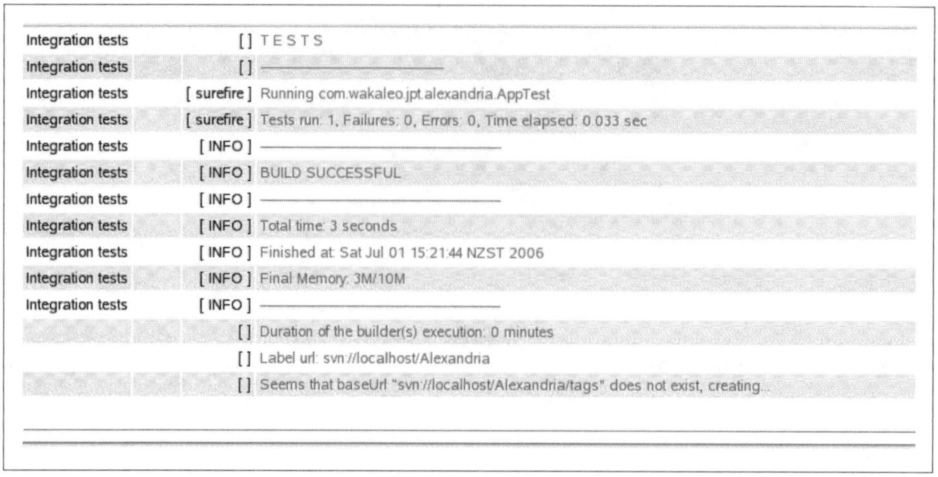

Integration tests	[ ]	T E S T S
Integration tests	[ ]	------------------------------
Integration tests	[surefire]	Running com.wakaleo.jpt.alexandria.AppTest
Integration tests	[surefire]	Tests run: 1, Failures: 0, Errors: 0, Time elapsed: 0.033 sec
Integration tests	[INFO]	------------------------------
Integration tests	[INFO]	BUILD SUCCESSFUL
Integration tests	[INFO]	------------------------------
Integration tests	[INFO]	Total time: 3 seconds
Integration tests	[INFO]	Finished at: Sat Jul 01 15:21:44 NZST 2006
Integration tests	[INFO]	Final Memory: 3M/10M
Integration tests	[INFO]	------------------------------
	[ ]	Duration of the builder(s) execution: 0 minutes
	[ ]	Label url: svn://localhost/Alexandria
	[ ]	Seems that baseUrl "svn://localhost/Alexandria/tags" does not exist, creating...

Figure 7-13. Build log

LuntBuild tries to create the Subversion tags directory, and stops there. This seems to indicate a problem with the Subversion connection.

In this case, it turned out that the Subversion user configured in the VCS entry had read-only access to the repository and so couldn't update the repository: Indeed, LuntBuild creates a new tag in the VCS repository for every build, as illustrated here:

```
> svn list svn://localhost/Alexandria/tags
alexandria-1_1/
alexandria-1_2/
alexandria-1_3/
alexandria-1_4/
alexandria-1_5/
alexandria-1_6/
alexandria-1_7/
alexandria-1_8/
...
```

Once the problem is fixed, you can either wait for the next scheduled build to go ahead or trigger a build manually from the build page.

Schedule errors are often harder to isolate, as there are no easily accessible logfiles available from the web site. Errors often come from incorrect VCS configurations or other configuration issues. One thing that can help is to look at the LuntBuild logfiles, which live in the *logs* directory. In the following example, I use *grep* to list errors logged in this file (with the *-C* option to get a bit of surrounding context:.

```
$ cd ~/LuntBuild
$ grep -C 1 ERROR logs/LuntBuild_log.txt
2006.07.01-21:22:11 [DefaultQuartzScheduler_Worker-7] INFO
com.luntsys.LuntBuild.BuildGenerator
- Getting revisions for url: svn://localhost/Alexandria/trunk
2006.07.01-21:22:11 [DefaultQuartzScheduler_Worker-5] ERROR
```

```
com.luntsys.LuntBuild.BuildGenerator
- Exception catched during job execution
java.lang.RuntimeException: Unable to evaluate expression
"vcsModified or dependencyNewer".
Please make sure that your VCS server's time is in sync with your LuntBuild machine!
--
...
```

7.7 Using LuntBuild with Eclipse

LuntBuild integrates well with the Eclipse IDE, via the Luntclipse plug-in. This plug-in is a neat little tool that gives you a full view of the status of your LuntBuild projects without having to leave your IDE or open a browser. Let's look at how to install and use the Luntclipse plug-in.

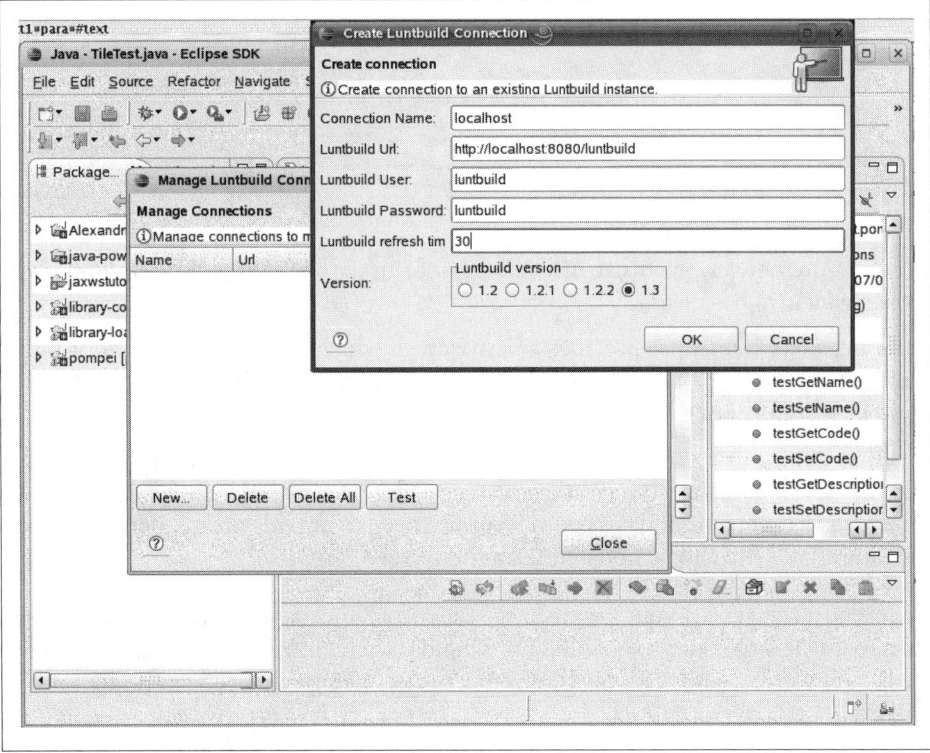

Figure 7-14. Setting up a Luntclipse connection

To install the plug-in, first download it from the LuntBuild web site (*http://LuntBuild.javaforge.com/*), unzip it into your Eclipse plug-ins directory, and then restart

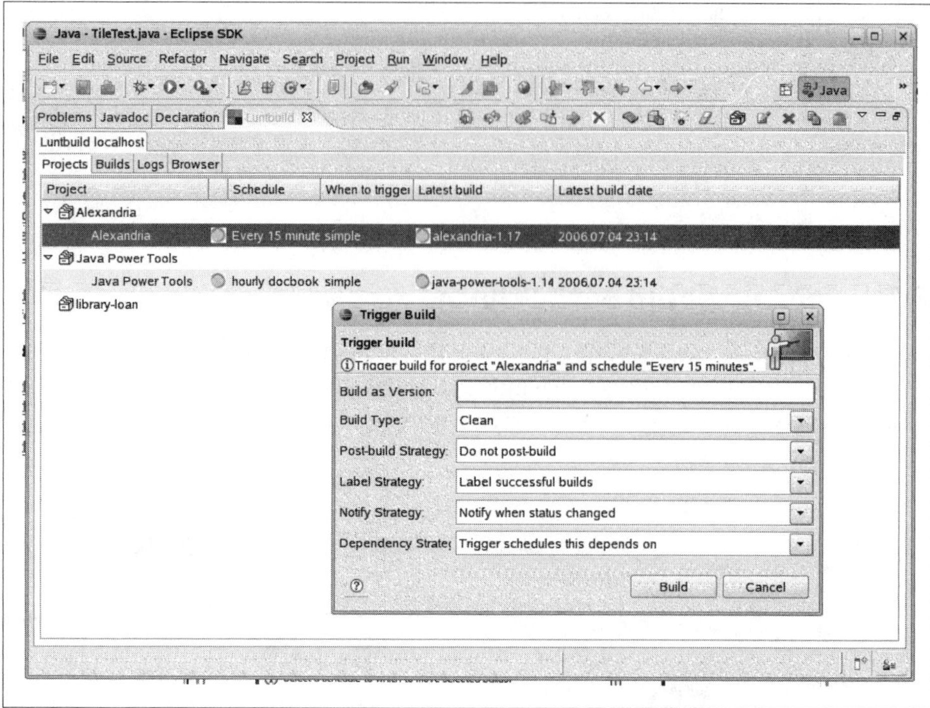

Figure 7-15. The Luntclipse plug-in

Eclipse. Alternatively, you can use the remote update site at *http://LuntBuild.javaforge.com/luntclipse-release*.

Once installed, Luntclipse provides a new view in which you can monitor your LuntBuild server. You can open this view by selecting "Window > Show View > Other... > Luntclipse > LuntBuild."

The first thing you need to do is to set up a connection to your LuntBuild server (see Figure 7-14). This is straightforward: you just need to specify the URL of your LuntBuild server, and a user name and password. You also need to provide the frequency at which the LuntBuild view will be updated from the server.

Once you have set up your connection, the LuntBuild view provides a convenient dashboard view of your projects and their builds (see Figure 7-15). Projects and builds are listed in a tree view, with the builds of a project being displayed as children of the project.

You can consult and manage virtually any aspect of your LuntBuild projects via this view. The contextual menu (see Figure 7-16) lets you perform a variety of tasks such as triggering, searching, moving or deleting builds, consulting logfiles, or even creating or modifying projects. The toolbar at the top of the view provides an alternative way

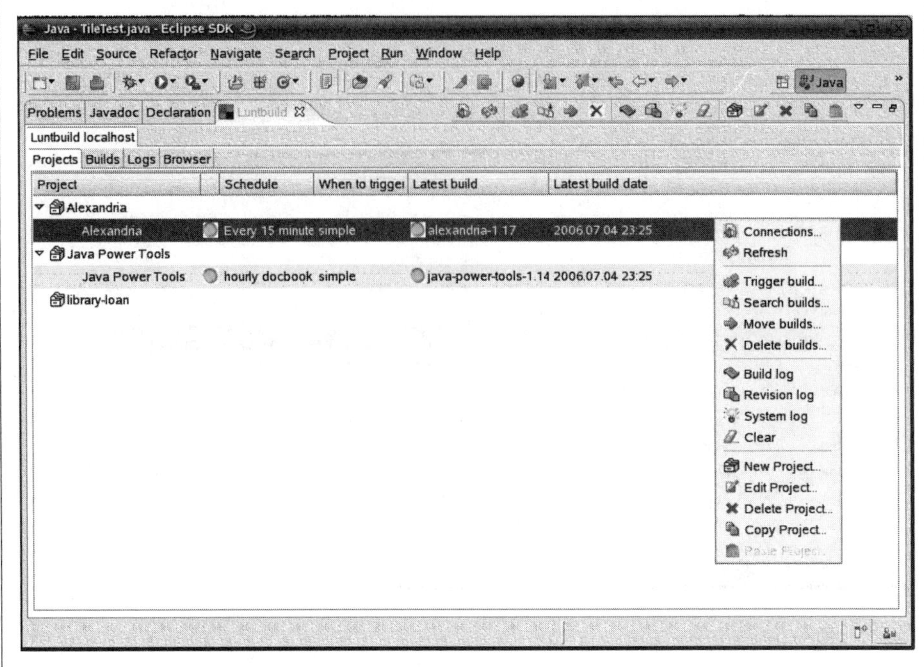

Figure 7-16. The Luntclipse contextual menu

of accessing these functionalities. You can also trigger a build by simply clicking on the build entry (see Figure 7-15).

The search function lets you view a set of past builds. This is useful if you want to visualise build history for a certain project over a certain period of time. The list of matching builds is displayed in the "Builds" tab (see Figure 7-17).

You can also create a new project, or modify any of the fields of an existing project (see Figure 7-18).

And, if all else fails, the Browser tab provides an embedded web browser connection to the Luntbuild server.

7.8 Reporting on Test Coverage in Luntbuild Using Cobertura

Contributed by: Jettro Conradie

Introduction

Luntbuild comes out-of-the-box with Junit integration; if your project build runs any JUnit tests, the build view will provide a convenient link to the corresponding JUnit

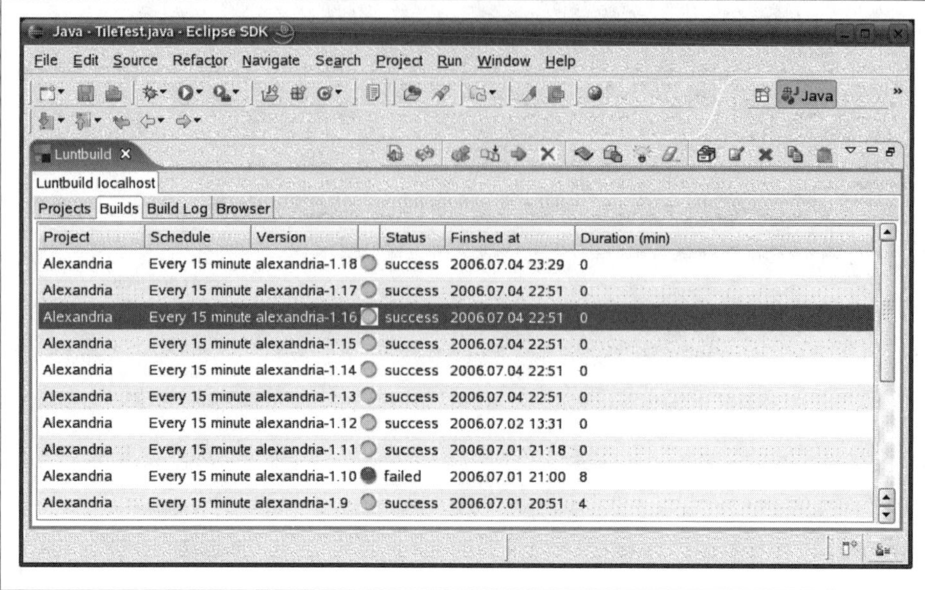

Figure 7-17. Builds in Luntclipse

reports. Test coverage reports (Chapter 12) can complement these unit test results nicely. Code coverage reports let you investigate how much of your code is actually being tested by your unit tests, and can be an excellent means of improving the quality of your unit tests. There are several code coverage tools available, both open source and commercial. One of the best open source code coverage tools is Cobertura (see Chapter 9). In this section, we will discuss how to produce and display Cobertura code coverage reports directly from within your Luntbuild build results, right alongside the standard unit test reports. We will also see how to extend Luntbuild functionalities using JavaBeans and Luntbuild extension points.

Extending Luntbuild with Extension Points

You can extend Luntbuild functionalities fairly easily using simple JavaBean classes. You encapsulate your new functionalities in a standard JavaBean class. You can access your bean from within Luntbuild using OGNL expressions. However, you need to give this file to Luntbuild in a form that it can cope with. Each Luntbuild extension is presented in the form of a JAR file containing the relevant classes along with a special properties file that tells Luntbuild how to integrate this extension. You bundle your bean, and any other classes it needs, into a JAR file containing the special property file named "luntbuild_extension.properties." This file must contain two property values:

luntbuild.extension.name
: The name of the extension, which you will use in Luntbuild to invoke the extension class.

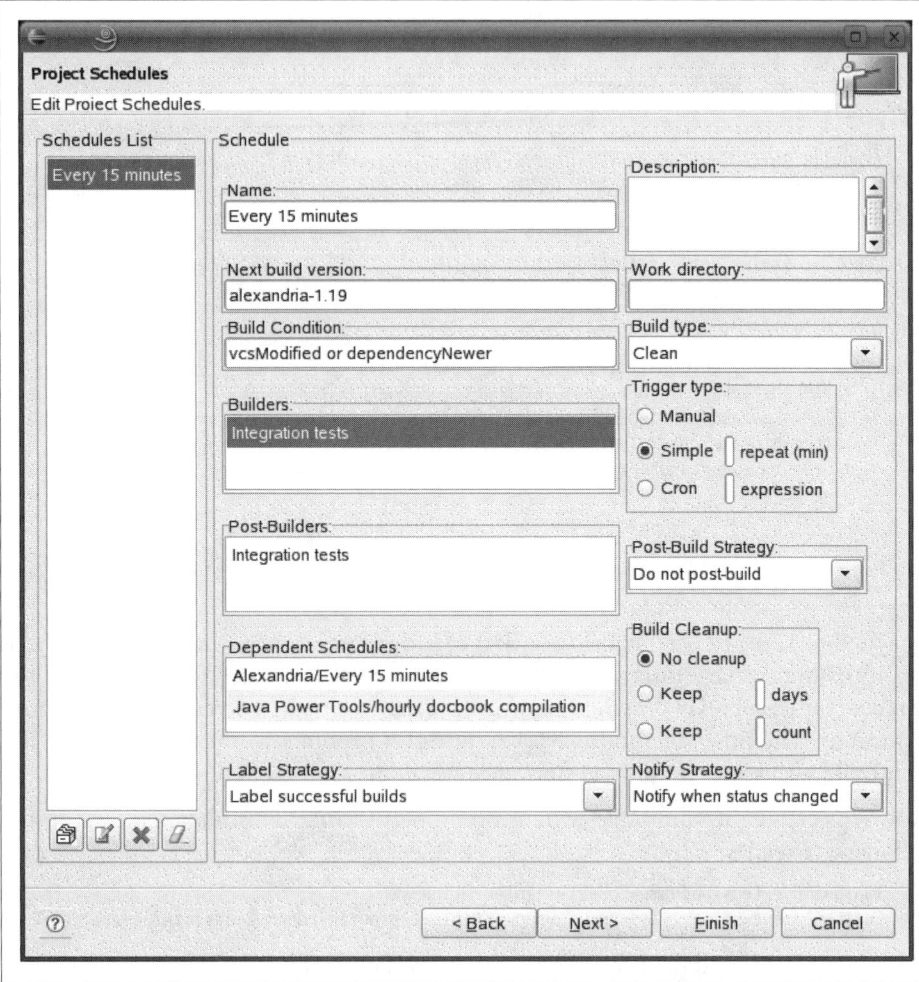

Figure 7-18. Editing a project in Luntclipse

luntbuild.extension.class
: The class that implements the extension.

Once you have bundled all this into a JAR file, you have your brand new Luntbuild extension! Note that you can only create one extension per JAR file.

Creating a Cobertura Luntbuild Extension

So creating a Luntbuild extension is quite an easy task. Now let's have a look at the bean we will be using to integrate Cobertura reports into LuntBuild. This JavaBean will basically tell Luntbuild where it can find the coverage report generated by Cobertura:

```
package com.javapowertools.luntbuild.addon;

import java.io.File;

public class CoberturaIntegration {
  private final String coberturaReportDir = "cobertura_report_dir";

  public String getCoberturaReportDir(String publishDir) {
    return publishDir + "\\\\" + coberturaReportDir;
  }

  public String getCoberturaReportDir() {
    return coberturaReportDir;
  }

  public String getCoberturaSite(String publishDir) {
    File pathToFile = (new File(getCoberturaReportDir(publishDir)+
    File.separator + "index.html"));
    if(pathToFile.exists()) {
      return coberturaReportDir + "/index.html";
    } else {
      return null;
    }
  }
}
```

The methods are pretty straightforward; the harder part is when to use which method. By providing the directory where all reports should be copied, the `getCoberturaReportDir()` method returns the exact path where to copy the Cobertura reports to. The other method, `getCoberturaSite()`, points to the path used by the Luntbuild web server to find the start page for all the Cobertura reports.

Now let's create the "luntbuild_extension.properties" file. This file must contain the following two lines:

```
luntbuild.extension.name=CoberturaIntegration
luntbuild.extension.class=com.javapowertools.luntbuild.addon.CoberturaIntegration
```

Now create a jar, with the bean and the property file. Luntbuild expects extension jars to be placed in the *$LUNTBUILD_HOME/web/WEB-INF/lib* directory. Copy your jar here and restart Luntbuild. Luntbuild will now be able to detect and use this extension. In the next section, we discuss how to use the new plug-in.

Using the Extension

The next step is to integrate the extension into the build process. In our case, we need to use this extension in the builder configuration screen of a project, and in the *BuildView.html* page which actually displays the build reports. You can however, use this bean in any OGNL expression throughout Luntbuild.

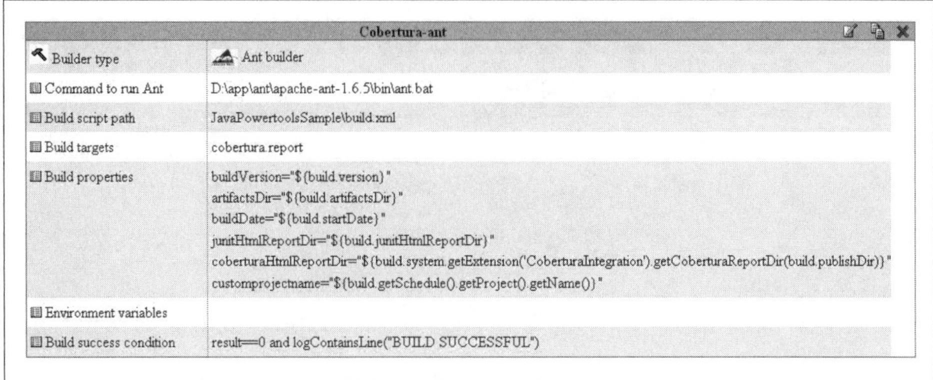

Figure 7-19. Ant builder configuration within the Luntbuild project wizard

Luntbuild needs to know into which directory the Cobertura reports needs to be copied. You need to expose this information in the parameter *coberturaHtmlReportDir*. Have a look at the following image that shows the ant builder configuration (see Figure 7-19).

Note the value for the *coberturaHtmlReportDir*. This OGNL expression uses the current build object. This object has a system member variable, which you use to access the Luntbuild extensions. Here, we obtain the reference to the CoberturaIntegration object, using the name that is defined in the *luntbuild_extension.properties* file. From there on, we can just manipulate methods of our bean. The next section will show you what you can do with this parameter from ant. Now let's have a look at the *BuildViewer.html* file that can be found in the WEB-INF folder.

The views use Tapestry. I am not giving you an introduction into Tapestry because you do not need it for this adjustment. Actually you can copy part of the junit example in this file. However, you need to know how to write the `ognl` expression. Search for this piece of code:

```
<td width="10%" align="center" class="buildTitleRight">
  <span jwcid="@Conditional" condition="ognl:junitHtmlReport!=null">
    <span jwcid="@GenericLink" href="ognl:'publish/'+build.schedule.project.name+'/'+
      build.schedule.name+'/'+build.version+ '/'+junitHtmlReport"
      title="junit report">junit report</span>
  </span>
</td>
```

Now add the following lines between the first "td" tag and the first "span":

```
<span jwcid="@Conditional"
    condition="ognl:build.system.getExtension('CoberturaIntegration')
    .getCoberturaSite(build.publishDir)!=null">
  <span jwcid="@GenericLink"
    href="ognl:'publish/'+build.schedule.project.name+'/'+build.schedule.name+'/'
      +build.version+ '/'+build.system.getExtension('CoberturaIntegration').
      getCoberturaSite(build.publishDir)" title="maven site">cobertura report</span>
</span>
```

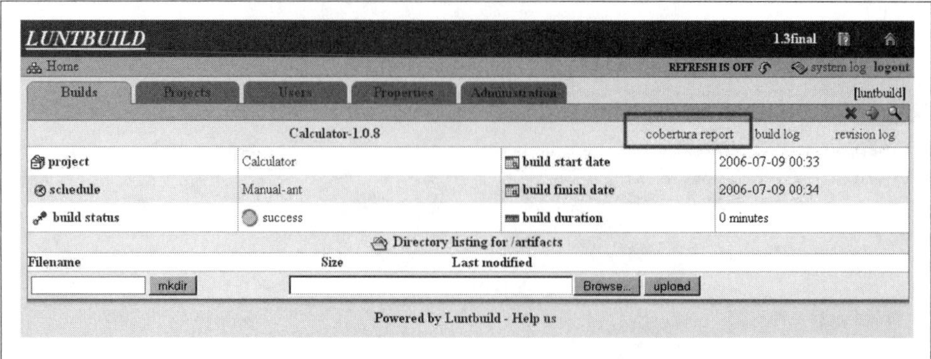

Figure 7-20. Build results screen showing the link to the Cobertura reports in the red box

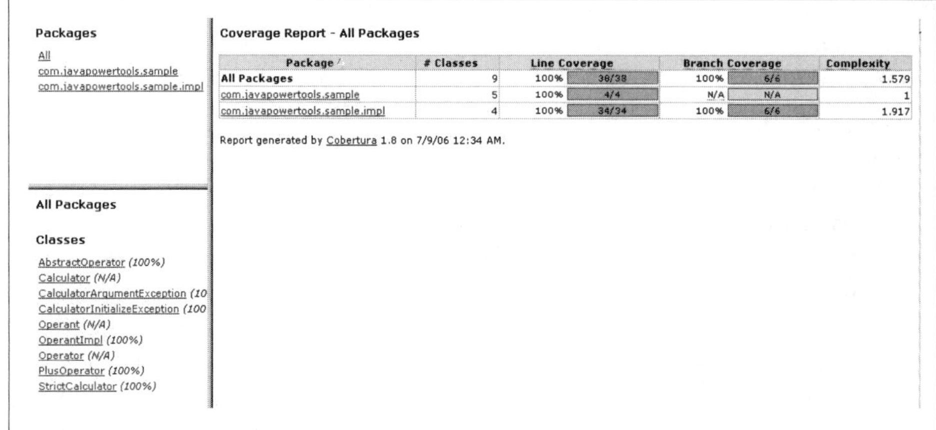

Figure 7-21. The sample Cobertura code coverage report

The construction of the path to the report resembles the method within the Luntbuild configuration screen. The second span that creates the href uses some other exposed properties to create the complete link. All these parameters are accessed through the BuildView object that contains a *getBuild()* method. From there on, you can find all the other objects as well. We have to use the ognl extension point as discussed before. Have a look at the following image (see Figure 7-20) to get the feeling how this all looks in a browser.

Clicking the link will show you the Cobertura screen (see Figure 7-21).

Running Cobertura with Ant

Until now, we did not show how to configure ant in order to create the Cobertura report. There are some steps to perform. This section will give you the different steps.

First, obtain the directories where to copy the junit and the Cobertura reports:

```
<property name="testdata"  location="${junitHtmlReportDir}"/>
<property name="coveragedata"  location="${coberturaHtmlReportDir}"/>
```

Then we must make Cobertura available to Ant:

```
<property name="cobertura.dir" value="D:/java/cobertura/cobertura-1.8"/>
<path id="cobertura.classpath">
    <fileset dir="${cobertura.dir}">
        <include name="cobertura.jar" />
        <include name="lib/**/*.jar" />
    </fileset>
</path>
<taskdef classpathref="cobertura.classpath" resource="tasks.properties" />
```

The next step is to instrument or post compile the classes. Cobertura adjusts the classes in a way that it can track which lines are called. This way it can calculate the code coverage and show you the nice reports. The instrumentation is shown in the next target:

```
<target name="cobertura.instrument" depends="compile"
    description="Create the isntrumented classes used by cobertura">
  <cobertura-instrument todir="${build.instrumented}">
    <ignore regex="org.apache.log4j.*" />
    <fileset dir="${build}">
      <include name="**/*.class" />
    </fileset>
  </cobertura-instrument>
</target>
```

Now we need to put the instrumented classes in front of the other classes while executing the junit test. This is done in the following part of the junit task. We also must tell junit where to find the Cobertura data file. This is done with a system property.

```
<target name="test" depends="compile,cobertura.instrument"
description="Runs JUnit tests">
  <junit printsummary="yes" fork="true" errorProperty="test.failed"
   failureProperty="test.failed">
    <sysproperty key="net.sourceforge.cobertura.datafile"
     file="${basedir}/cobertura.ser" />
    <classpath>

      <path location="${build.instrumented}"/>
      <path location="${build}"/>
      <path location="${buildtest}"/>
      <path location="lib/easymock-1.2_Java1.3.jar"/>
    </classpath>
    <classpath refid="cobertura.classpath" />
    <formatter type="xml"/>
    <batchtest todir="${testdata}">
      <fileset dir="${test}">
        <include name="**/*Test.java"/>
      </fileset>
    </batchtest>
  </junit>
```

```
    <fail if="test.failed">Unit tests failed.</fail>
  </target>
```

Finally, you want to create the reports based on the gathered data. This is done with the following target:

```
<target name="cobertura.report" depends="clean,test">
  <cobertura-report format="html" datafile="${basedir}/cobertura.ser"
    destdir="${coveragedata}" srcdir="${src}"/>
</target>
```

Now you are done. You can do the complete build, junit, and Cobertura reports by issuing the following command:

```
ant cobertura.report
```

Before doing this you need the complete Ant file, including the following targets: init, compile, dist, clean, and some extra properties. These are all presented in the following code listing:

```
<property name="src" location="src/main/java"/>
<property name="build" location="build"/>
<property name="proplocation" location="src/main/resources"/>
<property name="dist"  location="dist"/>
<property name="test"  location="src/test/java"/>
<property name="testdata"  location="${junitHtmlReportDir}"/>
<property name="coveragedata"  location="${coberturaHtmlReportDir}"/>
<property name="buildtest" location="buildtest"/>
<property name="build.instrumented" location="instrumented"/>

<target name="init">
  <tstamp/>
  <mkdir dir="${build}"/>
  <mkdir dir="${buildtest}"/>
  <mkdir dir="${testdata}"/>
  <mkdir dir="${build.instrumented}"/>
</target>

<target name="compile" depends="init" description="compile the source " >
  <javac srcdir="${src}" destdir="${build}" debug="true"/>
  <javac srcdir="${test}" destdir="${buildtest}">
    <classpath>
      <path location="${build}"/>
      <path location="lib/easymock-1.2_Java1.3.jar"/>
    </classpath>
  </javac>
</target>

<target name="dist" depends="compile" description="generate the distribution" >
  <mkdir dir="${dist}/lib"/>
  <copydir dest="${build}" src="${proplocation}"/>
  <jar jarfile="${dist}/lib/JavaPowerToolsSample-${DSTAMP}.jar" basedir="${build}"/>
</target>

<target name="clean" description="clean up" >
  <delete dir="${build}"/>
```

```
        <delete dir="${buildtest}"/>
        <delete dir="${dist}"/>
        <delete dir="${testdata}"/>
        <delete dir="${coveragedata}"/>
        <delete dir="${build.instrumented}"/>
        <delete file="cobertura.ser" />
    </target>
```

7.9 Integrating Luntbuild with Maven

Contributed by: Jettro Conradie

Introduction

Continuous Integration servers do a good job at, well, continuously building (and integrating) code. Another useful thing that you may want to do is to automatically generate and publish up-to-date project reports about different aspects of the project, such as javadoc, unit test reports, code coverage reports, and so on. You can use both Ant and Maven, both of which integrate well with Luntbuild (see "Builders) to generate this type of report.

You can also use Luntbuild to publish these reports for each build, which allows you to automatically generate and publish updated reports on a regular basis, and also to keep track of the reports generated for previous builds. In this section, we will see how to generate and publish a Maven-generated web site, which contains a wide range of quite useful reports. First, we write a Maven Mojo (plug-in class) that enables us to copy the generated Maven web site to the appropriate folder for Luntbuild to pick it up. Then we look at how to add the new Mojo to Maven. Finally, we configure Luntbuild to use our new Mojo to display the Maven web site on the Luntbuild build results pages.

Extending Maven to Support LuntBuild

The Maven core is actually very small: Maven uses plug-ins, or extensions, to implement most of the heavy-duty functionality. In Maven parlance, these plug-ins are called Mojos, and take the form of annotated Java classes.

Writing your Mojo in Java is a big advantage. This way, you can use the programming language you are used to. You can use the tools you are used to and, of course, do junit testing. Reuse of the Mojo over the different projects that you are into is also easy.

It is actually quite easy to build your own. In this section, we will go through the steps required to build a simple Mojo plug-in, which will publish your LuntBuild build results on your Maven web site. This Mojo will simply copy the build results from the LuntBuild web site to a designated directory on your Maven site.

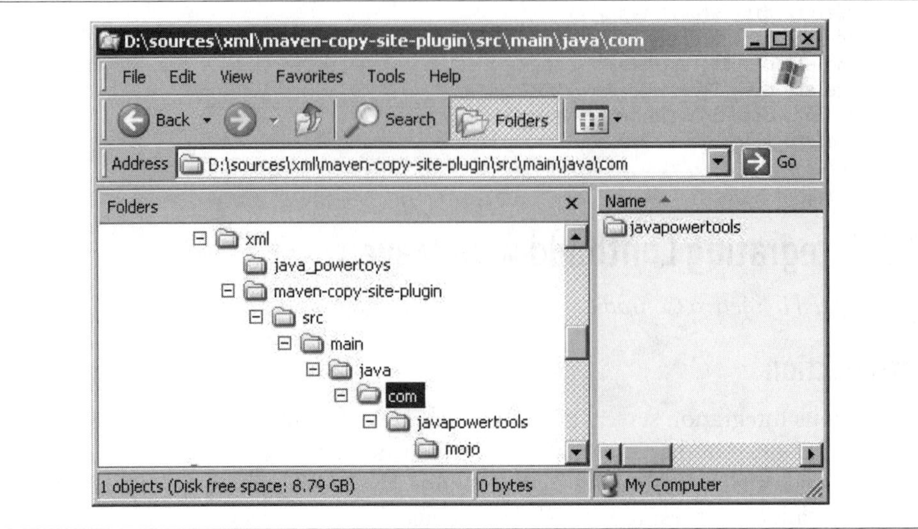

Figure 7-22. Directory structure after using the special maven archetype plug-in

Setting up your project

First, you need to set up a project for your Mojo plug-in. Maven provides a convenient plug-in called maven archetype that helps you set up a standard project directory structure (*http://maven.apache.org/plugins/maven-archetype-plugin*). There are multiple archetypes available, including web projects, standard Java projects, and Maven Mojos. Use the following command to set up your environment:

```
mvn archetype:create
      -DgroupId=com.javapowertools.mojo
      -DartifactId=maven-copy-site-plugin
      -DarchetypeArtifactId=maven-archetype-mojo
```

The directory contains the pom.xml file in the root of the folder and a sample mojo in the Mojo directory.

Creating the Mojo

A Mojo is basically just an annotated Java class. We create a class that extends `org.apache.maven.plugin.AbstractMojo`. Our class needs to implement the *execute()* method, as shown here:

```
/**
 * @author Jettro Coenradie
 *
 * @goal copydirectory
 *
 * @description Copies the provided directory to the other provided directory
 */
public class CopyFolderMojo extends AbstractMojo {
```

```
    public void execute() throws MojoExecutionException, MojoFailureException {

    }
}
```

This class illustrates the basic structure of a simple Mojo. As promised, it is a pretty straightforward Java class. One thing that should catch your attention is a special javadoc tag "@goal." This tells Maven to treat this class as a special maven plug-in. The value for goal ("copydirectory") is used later to identify this plug-in.

The aim of this Mojo is to copy the LuntBuild build results to the Maven web site. So we need to be able to specify the source and destination directories. In a Mojo class, you do this by using the "@parameter" annotation, as shown in the following example:

```
/**
 * Location of the directory to copy from.
 * @parameter expression="${project.build.directory}"
 * @required
 */
private File inputDirectory;

/**
 * Location of the directory to copy to.
 * @parameter expression="${project.copyto.directory}"
 * @required
 */
private File outputDirectory;

/**
 * Name of the current project
 * @parameter expression="${project.name}"
 * @required
 */
private String projectName;
```

The "@parameter" annotation lets you specify what parameters this Mojo is expecting. A number of parameters, like "project.name" and "project.build.directory," are automatically provided by Maven. Others (such as "project.copyto.directory") are specific to this Mojo, and you will need to provide them in some other way, such as by using the *-D* command-line option. In our case, the "project.copyto.directory" environment variable is set in the Luntbuild configuration (see "Luntbuild Configuration).

Finally, let's have a look at the implementation of the *execute()* method:

```
public void execute() throws MojoExecutionException, MojoFailureException {
  getLog().info("Input directory : "+inputDirectory.toString()+"\\site");
  getLog().info("Output directory : "+outputDirectory.toString());
  File in = new File(inputDirectory,"site");
  if (!in.exists()) {
    getLog().info("No site available to be copied");
    return;
  }
  File out = new File(outputDirectory,projectName);
  if (!out.exists()) {
```

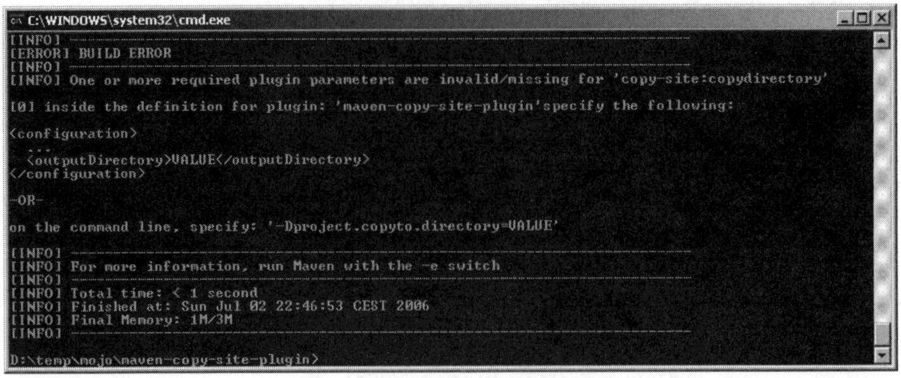

Figure 7-23. Shows the error indicating we are missing the parameter outputDirectory and a possible solution

```
            out.mkdirs();
        }
        in.renameTo(new File(out,in.getName()));
    }
```

This pretty straightforward Java code checks if the input and output directories exist, and, if so, copies the contents from the "inputDirectory" to the "outputDirectory." The *getLog()* method is provided by the super class.

Integrating the Mojo with Maven

Now that we have created the Mojo, it is time to package and install our new Mojo to the maven repository. We do this by issuing the command "mvn install." This places the plug-in into our repository so we can use it in other projects.

You can invoke the new Mojo from the command line as follows:

```
mvn com.javapowertools.mojo:maven-copy-site-plugin:1.0-SNAPSHOT:copydirectory
```

This should result in an error like the one in Figure 7-23, telling us that we are missing a required parameter outputDirectory:

In order to make it work, we provide the java environment variable like this:

```
mvn -Dproject.copyto.directory=D:/temp/output
        com.javapowertools.mojo:maven-copy-site-plugin:1.0-SNAPSHOT:copydirectory
```

This should get rid of the error, although the logfiles will tell you that there is no site available. That is OK for now. Move on to the Luntbuild configuration.

Luntbuild Configuration

Now that it is written, integrating this plug-in into Luntbuild is relatively easy, and is done in the build configuration page. Have a look at Figure 7-24.

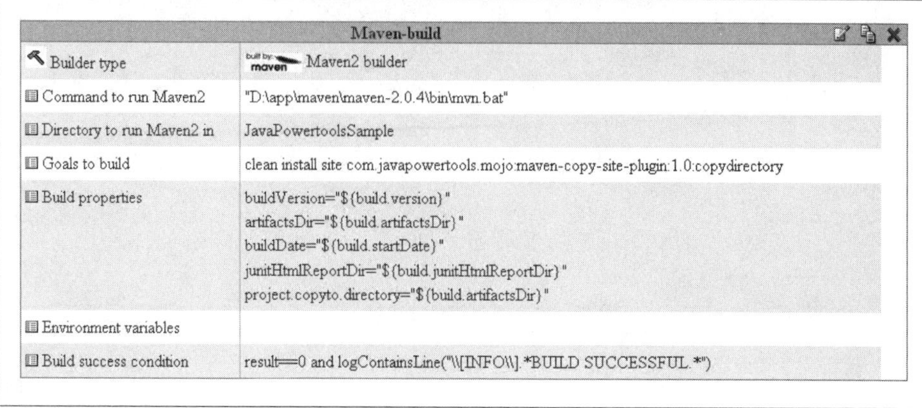

Maven-build
Builder type
Maven2 builder
Command to run Maven2
"D:\app\maven\maven-2.0.4\bin\mvn.bat"
Directory to run Maven2 in
JavaPowertoolsSample
Goals to build
clean install site com.javapowertools.mojo:maven-copy-site-plugin:1.0:copydirectory
Build properties
buildVersion="${build.version}"
artifactsDir="${build.artifactsDir}"
buildDate="${build.startDate}"
junitHtmlReportDir="${build.junitHtmlReportDir}"
project.copyto.directory="${build.artifactsDir}"
Environment variables
Build success condition
result==0 and logContainsLine("\\[INFO\\].*BUILD SUCCESSFUL.*")

Figure 7-24. The Builder tab of the project configuration in Luntbuild shows how to configure Maven as a builder

There are two things that you need to configure:

- Add a call to your Mojo plug-in as part of the build target. Typically, you will add this to a build configuration that already builds the Maven site, so it may look something like this:

```
clean install site
com.javapowertools.mojo:maven-copy=site=plugin:1.0:copydirectory
```

- Set up the build properties. The important thing here is to add the parameter "project.copyto.directory," which points to the artifacts directory of the current build:

```
project.copyto.directory=${builds.artifactsDir}
```

We'll let the build run from Luntbuild, it should be running fine. Then have a look at the results of the build in Figure 7-25, and you see an additional artifact called "Java Powertools Sample application—The Calculator." Click on the link and you can browse the uploaded reports. After the first artifacts link, click the link site and then index.html.

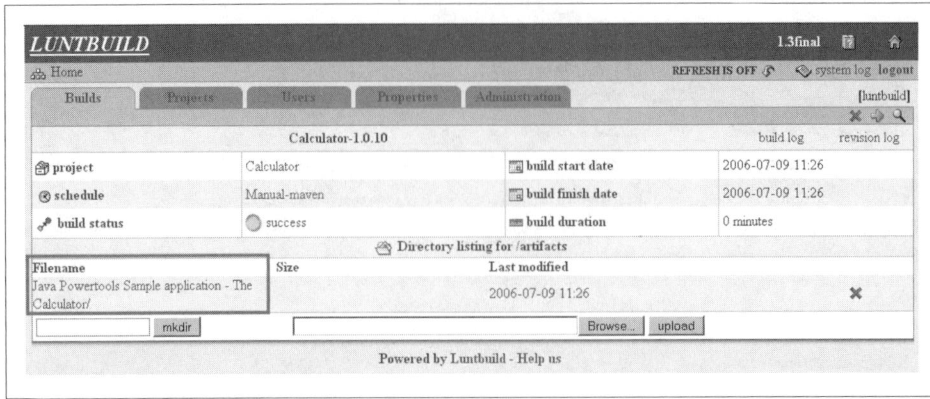

Figure 7-25. The build results view, where the red box shows you the uploaded artifact created with Maven and copied with the new plug-in

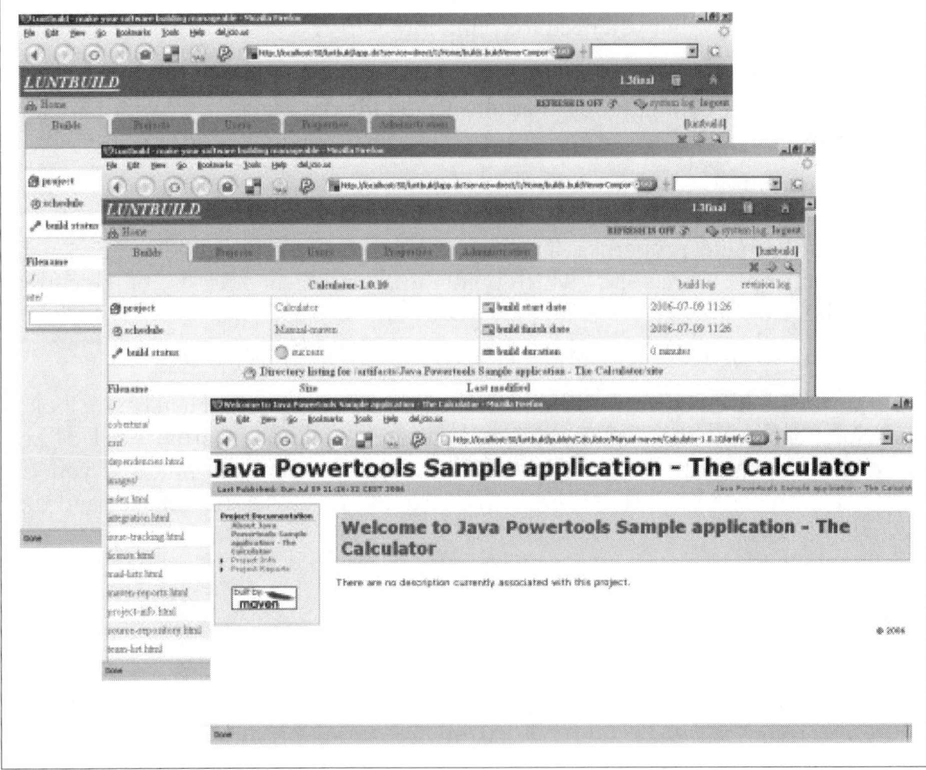

Figure 7-26. Displaying the Maven site from within the Luntbuild build page

Now you can browse an automatically generated, up-to-date version of the Maven project site for each build of your project (see Figure 7-26).

7.10 Conclusion

Overall, Luntbuild is a solid, feature-rich Continuous Integration tool with a clean (albeit slightly clunky) web interface, support for a wide range of SCM tools, and a reasonable range of notification techniques.

CHAPTER 8

Continuous Integration with Hudson

8.1 An Introduction to Hudson

Hudson is a relative newcomer to the Continuous Integration (CI) field. However, despite its relative youth, it is probably worth considering for any new CI projects you might be starting. Hosted by Java.net, Hudson is actively developed and maintained by Kohsuke Kawaguchi, who is working for Sun Microsystems at the time of this writing. This innovative product is widely used within Sun, and is starting to build up a sizeable user base because of its ease of use and slick user interface. It has also recently been adopted by JBoss (see *http://hudson.jboss.org/hudson/*).

In many regards, Hudson has considerably fewer features then the some of the other CI tools such as Continuum (see Chapter 5) and CruiseControl (see Chapter 6). It concentrates more on Subversion and CVS-based projects, and provides only a limited number of notification techniques. The product is still somewhat young, and a little immature, but the features it does have are extremely well thought-out, with some being quite innovative. Hudson is also extensible, and a growing collection of plug-ins are available on the Hudson web site.

8.2 Installing Hudson

Hudson is very easy to install and set up. It requires Java 5 or later. You can download the latest release from the Hudson web site (*https://hudson.dev.java.net*). Hudson comes bundled as a web archive (WAR) file that you can run directly using an embedded servlet container (Hudson uses the lightweight Winstone servlet engine). To run Hudson from the command line, just type the following:

```
$ java -jar hudson.war
```

This will run Hudson on the default 8080 port. If this doesn't suit you, you can also specify the port using the *--httpPort* option:

```
$ java -jar hudson.war --httpPort=8081
```

Running Hudson as a standalone product is a good option for evaluation purposes, but for production-quality deployment, you will probably want to deploy the Hudson WAR onto a more robust Java application server such as Tomcat. This is particularly true when you are installing Hudson on a build server, and you need Hudson to run as a service. You can deploy the Hudson WAR file as you would any other web application. For example, on a Tomcat server, you would deploy the `hudson.war` file to the `webapps` directory. You can then configure Tomcat to run as a service in the usual, OS-specific manner.

You can check out your new Hudson installation by connecting (e.g., *http://localhost:8080/hudson* if you are running it locally). The first time you run Hudson, you should get a screen like the one in Figure 8-1.

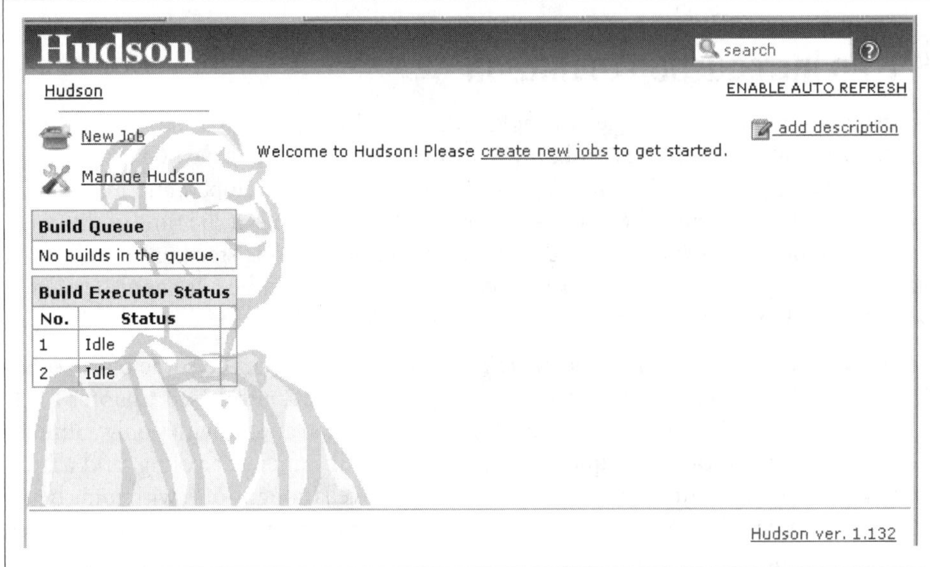

Figure 8-1. The Hudson web interface

8.3 Managing the Hudson Home Directory

Hudson stores its data in a special directory, known as the Hudson home directory. By default, the Hudson home directory is called ".hudson." placed in the user's home directory. This is not to be confused with the directory in which you place the downloaded hudson.war file, or the expanded Hudson web application on your local application server. Set the HUDSON_HOME environment variable before you start up Hudson to change the home directory.

Let's look at a practical example of this setup. Your boss wants you to install a Continuous Integration server for your new project. And he wants it to be done by lunchtime (it is now 11 a.m.). No sweat! Suppose we want to install Hudson onto a Linux box, and run it on a local Tomcat server. Let's see how you might configure your server.

First, a word about user accounts. It is often a good idea to run Hudson (as with other build infrastructure tools) in its own dedicated user account. This makes it easier to keep track of resource use on the server, and can be very handy when you have several Java tools running on the same server. For example, in the following listing, we connect to our build server as a special user called "cis" (for "Continuous Integration Server"). First we connect to the server using this user's account (I cheat a little by *su*-ing from root, but you get the idea):

```
# su - cis
$ pwd
/home/cis
$ ls .hudson/
config.xml                  hudson.triggers.SCMTrigger.xml
fingerprints                jobs
hudson.scm.CVSSCM.xml       plugins
hudson.tasks.Ant.xml        secret.key
hudson.tasks.Mailer.xml     users
hudson.tasks.Maven.xml      workspace-cleanup.log
hudson.tasks.Shell.xml
```

Here, we are in this user's home directory (`/home/cis`), using the default Hudson home directory of `.hudson` (`/home/cis/.hudson`). All of Hudson's application data and server configuration details are stored in the `.hudson` directory.

The Hudson web application is deployed onto a local instance of Tomcat, installed into a directory called `/usr/local/tomcat`. To deploy the application, we just copy the Hudson WAR file into the Tomcat `webapps` directory:

```
$cp hudson.war /usr/local/tomcat/webapps
```

Hudson will now be deployed and running on your Tomcat server.

8.4 Installing Upgrades

The Hudson project team is highly reactive, and new releases come out every few weeks, or even every few days! To upgrade Hudson to a new version, simply download and deploy the latest version to your web application server. As long as you don't delete your Hudson home directory, your application data won't be affected.

Before you upgrade the web application, you should stop any builds that are currently in progress. You can do this by selecting "Prepare for Shutdown" in the "Manage Hudson" screen.

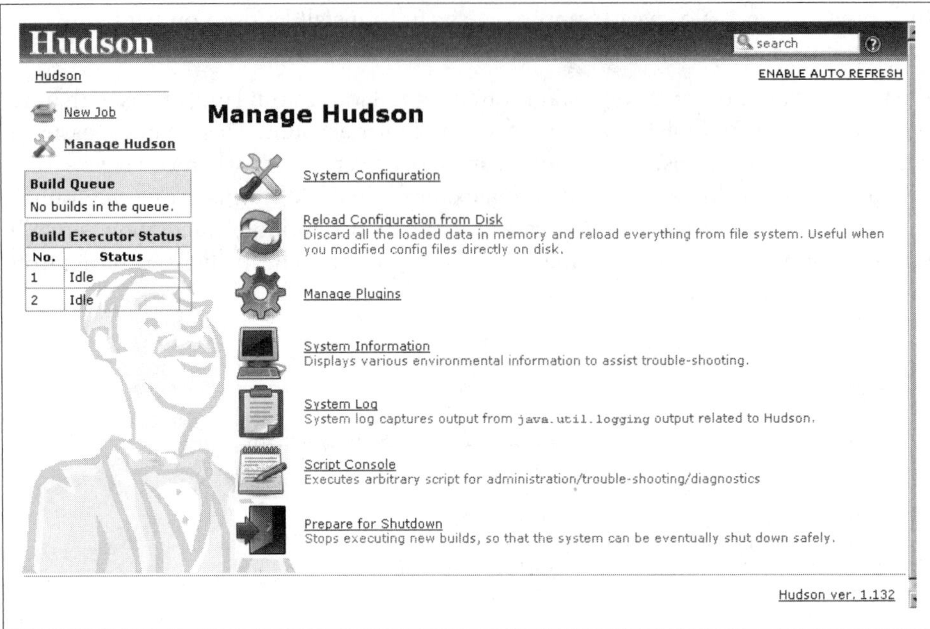

Figure 8-2. The Hudson administration screen

8.5 Configuring Hudson

In Hudson, you manage both system-wide parameters and individual projects directly via the Web interface. The "Manage Hudson" screen is the first port of call for all Hudson administrative tasks and serve configuration. From here, you can manage plug-ins, view the system logfile, and display system properties (see Figure 8-2).

The most important Hudson parameters are in the "System Configuration" screen (see Figure 8-3). This screen lets you configure the main server-wide parameters such as available Java Development Kits (JDKs) and build tools, security configuration and quiet period.

Let's look at some of these options. One nice feature in Hudson is that you can configure it to run builds in parallel. The "# of executors" field indicates the maximum number of parallel builds that Hudson will allow. Subsequent builds are queued. This can speed up the build process, to a point. However, builds can be CPU-intensive operations, so too many simultaneous builds can bring your build server to a grinding halt. The precise sweet point will depend on your particular environment, so start off the the default value (up to two builds in parallel) and experiment.

As with most other Continuous Integration servers, Hudson lets you define a "quiet period." This indicates the number of seconds that Hudson will wait after spotting a change in the source code repository, before starting a new build. This is mainly useful with CVS, which doesn't support atomic commits. This way, Hudson doesn't rush off

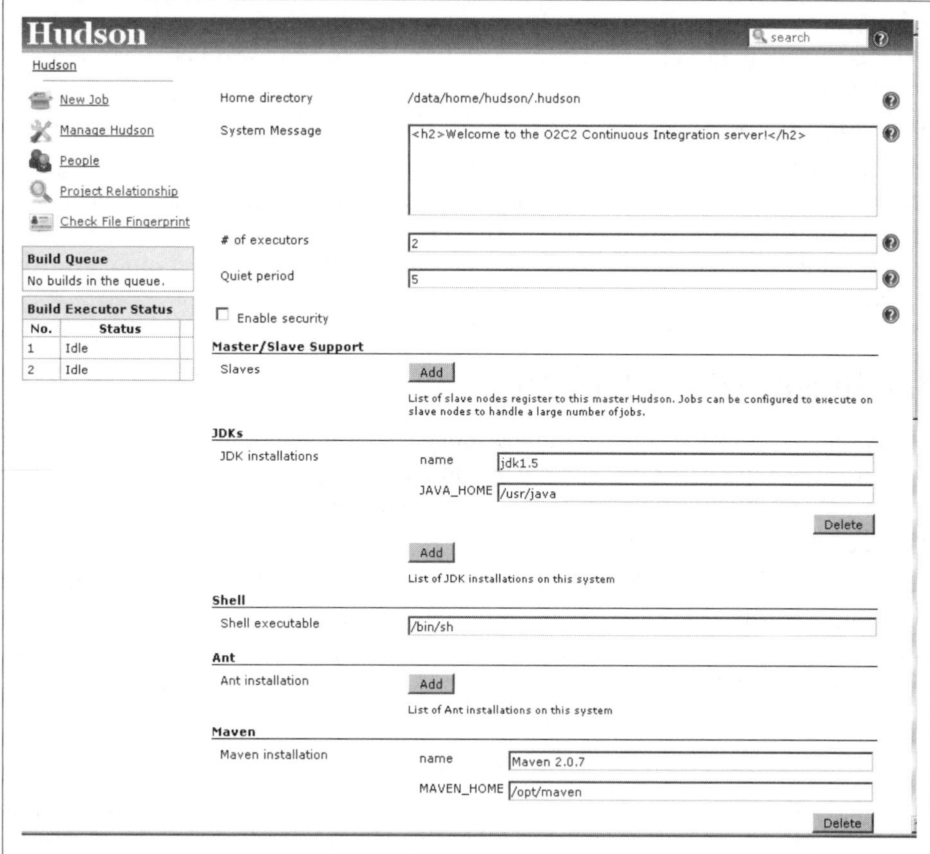

Figure 8-3. The Hudson administration screen

straight away to do a new build, but waits until it is sure that there are no more changes to be committed.

One of the areas in which Hudson is not particularly strong is in matters of security. By default, Hudson does not impose any security constraints on users. Any user can modify configuration details without needing to be authenticated. This is convenient for small teams, but may not be appropriate for larger organizations. You can however enable security by ticking the "Enable Security" checkbox. In this case, unauthenticated users can only view build results; They cannot launch builds or modify configuration parameters. Only authenticated users with the "admin" role can configure the server or schedule builds. We look at how to configure security in Section 8.11.

Sometimes you need to build different projects with different versions of Java. For example, one build might need to be run using Java 5, and another using Java 1.4. You can add as many JDK installations as required in the JDK section. These can be used later on to configure individual projects.

You also need to specify the path to the build tools you intend to use, whether you are using Ant, Maven or both. You can install multiple versions of each tool: for example, you might want to install both Ant 1.6.5 and Ant 1.7.0, and use different versions for different projects.

Both CVS and Subversion will work pretty much out of the box, as long as CVS is installed on the server. Hudson will look for a ".cvspass" file in the user home directory. This file is created when you log in to a CVS server, so you should do this manually from within the user account before asking Hudson to do it automatically. You also need to setup the SMTP server, if you are not using the local mail server running on the server.

8.6 Adding a New Build Job

In Hudson, you organize your Continuous Build environment by defining "build Jobs." A build job is simply a particular way of building your project. However, to make things simpler, the Hudson user interface also refers to "projects." In fact, for Hudson, the terms "project" and "job" are synonymous.

A software development project typically requires several build jobs, which are used in different circumstances. For example, you may have one build job to compile and run your unit tests, another to run the longer-running integration tests, and a third to perform more heavyweight analysis tasks such as static code analysis and test coverage.

To add a new build job, click on the "New Job" link. You can choose from several different types of projects. The most interesting are:

- A freestyle project, in which you can customize the whole build process by indicating exactly what you want the build to do. You need to configure pretty much everything. As you might imagine this is the most flexible way to set up a project, and the only way to set up an Ant project.
- A Maven 2 project, which uses the Maven POM file to glean as much information as possible about things such as version control systems and so forth.

You can also create a new project based on an existing one by copying it (quite handy at times), or create a few other types of projects.

This is illustrated in Figure 8-4. Let's go through the process of creating a build project.

Building a Freestyle Project

The first project we will build is a freestyle one. In this case, we will set up an Ant-based project stored in a Subversion repository. To get started, we click on "New Job" and choose "Build a freestyle software project" (see Figure 8-4). Here you give the project an appropriate name and click on OK. This will bring you to the screen shown in Figure 8-5.

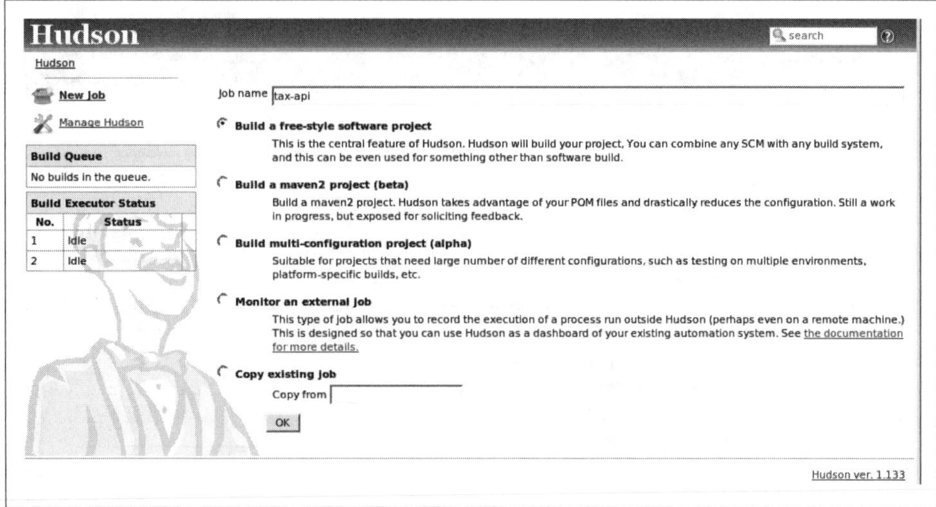

Figure 8-4. Creating a new project in Hudson

The first thing that you need to complete is the project name and description. You can also specify if you want Hudson to delete your old builds after a certain delay, or only keep a certain number of builds. This is useful to avoid cluttering your build environment too much. Come on, how long do you *really* need to keep last Thursday's snapshot build?

Of course, some builds have great sentimental value, and you wouldn't want to part with them for the world. This is not incompatible with deleting old builds. Indeed, you can tag a particular build to never be deleted.

This is also where you specify the source code repository. In this case, we are using Subversion. The Subversion configuration is simple: you only need to provide the repository URL. For a CVS configuration, you need to provide a bit more information, including CVSROOT and module details.

In both cases, you can tick the "Use Update" option. This will speed up builds by only performing an update rather than a full checkout. However, if CVS is being used, it can result in stale objects remaining in the repository and compromising the build.

Next, we define when the build should be executed, in the "Build Triggers" section (see Figure 8-6). Hudson proposes a number of options, each useful in certain circumstances. Probably the most common choice is "Poll SCM." This tells Hudson to poll the version control server at regular intervals in the hope of detecting any changes. This is the most reactive way to configure a Continuous Integration server: a build will start within minutes of anyone commiting a change to the version control server. This is also normally how a Continuous Integration server is supposed to work in normal circumstances. SCM Polling works well for Subversion, where commits are atomic, and a modification can be detected simply by monitoring the latest revision number. In

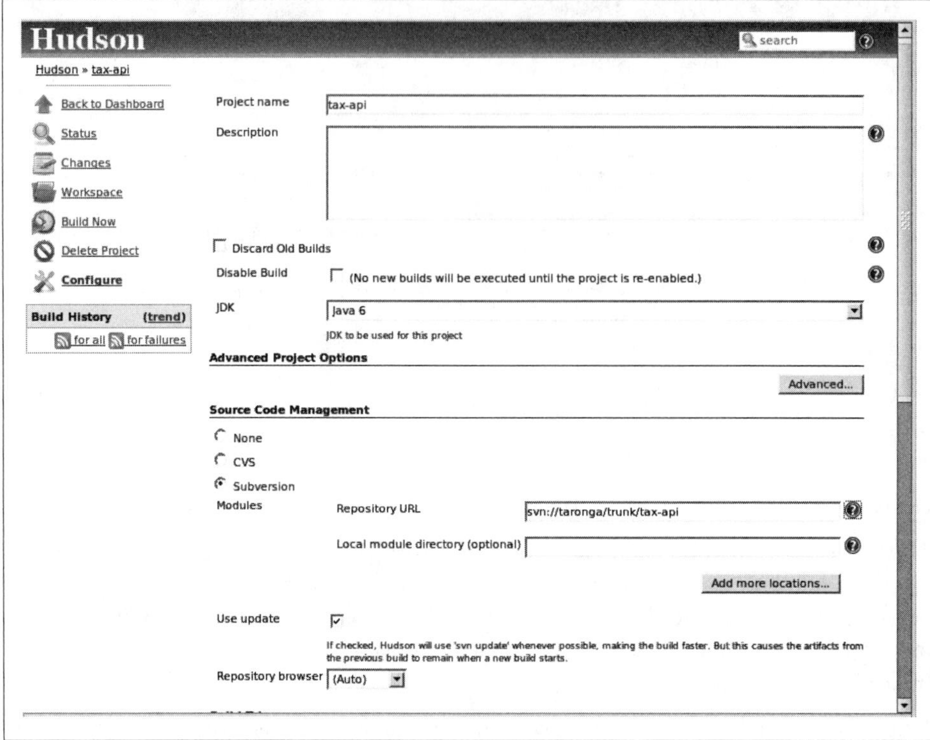

Figure 8-5. Creating a freestyle Hudson project

CVS, things are a bit more tricky because, to detect any updates, Hudson needs to scan the whole workspace for changes. This is obviously inefficient for any but the smallest of projects. For CVS, it is better to set up a trigger in CVS. The exact process for doing this is explained in the Hudson documentation.[*] When you choose to poll the SCM, you define a schedule indicating when the polling should happen. The schedule takes a cron-style expression, such as "* * * * *" for every minute, or "*/10 * * * *" for every 10 minutes. Normally, you make this as frequent as possible.

You can also opt to build periodically, again using a cron-style expression. If you choose this option, a build will be executed at regular intervals, independent of whether any changes have been made. This is not Continuous Integration with a capital C and a capital I. However, it can be useful for programming certain builds that take a long time to run. For example, in a large Maven project, building a full Maven site could take 10 to 15 minutes. A full set of integration and functional tests might also be time-consuming. A Continuous Integration server should be reactive, which means that

[*] *https://hudson.dev.java.net/build.html*

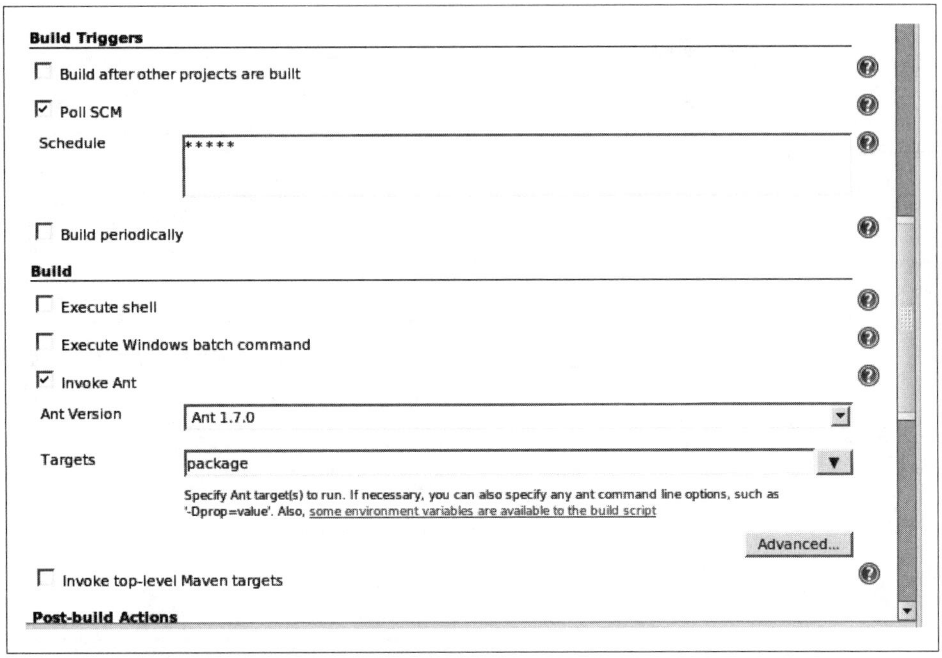

Figure 8-6. Configuring build triggers and build targets

the first-line builds should be fast. These heavyweight builds (sometimes called "staged builds" in the literature) can be scheduled at regular intervals.

A third option is to build your project only when certain other projects are built. This allows you to define dependencies between your project builds. For example, another way to keep your builds reactive without sacrificing your longer-running tests is to define a fast first-line build that runs only your unit tests, followed by a build that runs your longer integration and functional tests. If there are any failures in the unit tests, the first build will give rapid feedback. The second, longer build will be automatically scheduled to follow the first build.

You also need to tell Hudson what exactly you want it to do for this build. A build can be any number of things, including a Unix shell script, a Windows bat file, or, more commonly, an Ant or Maven target. In this case, we are invoking an Ant target.

Finally, you need to tell Hudson what to do if the build succeeds (see Figure 8-7). Hudson can store your build artifacts along with the build history if you ask it to. This is a convenient way of archiving your build results for future reference or deployment. You need to specify an Ant-style file expression indicating the files you want to archive. Hudson will store these files and list them in the build results page for each successful build.

You can also publish JUnit test reports and Javadoc documentation. We will look at these aspects in more detail later on.

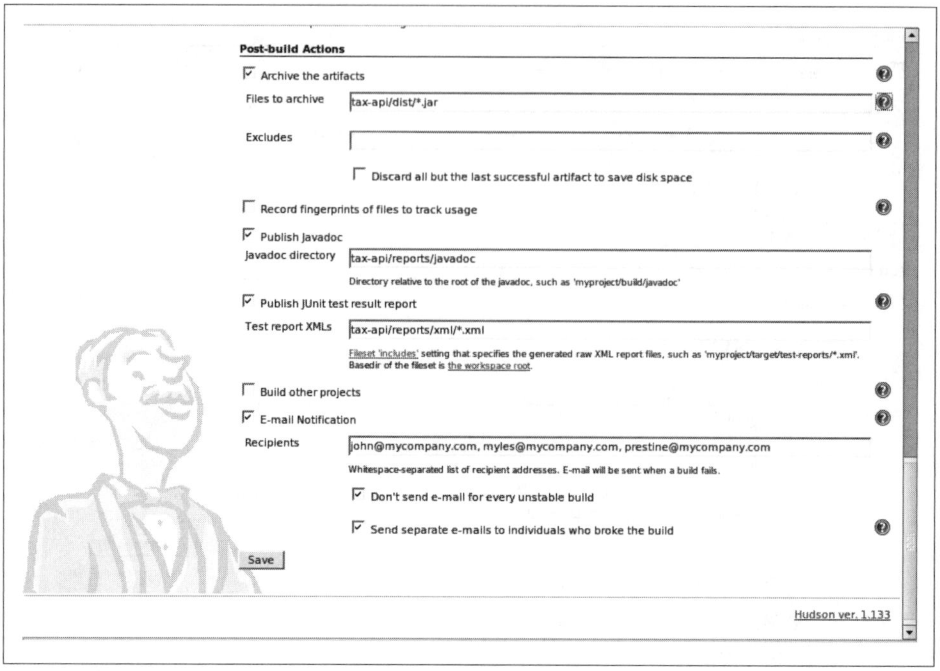

Figure 8-7. Configuring build triggers and build targets

Finally, you can set up email notifications. You need to list recipients that you want to receive systematic email notification. If you tick the "Send separate e-mails to individuals who broke the build." Hudson will try to identify the guilty party using the information entered in the People page, and notify them explicitly, no matter who is in the main recipients list. Of course, you need to provide email addresses for the users that Hudson lists in the People section.

That's it! Now save your new build job and run a build to get the workspace checked out of the version control system. Hudson needs you to do this before it can poll the version control server itself.

Building a Maven Project

Adding a Maven project to Hudson is theoretically much simpler than adding an Ant project, since a lot of the information Hudson needs can be gathered from the POM file. You need to provide information such as the JDK to use and the source code repository. Then you simply provide the POM file and the goals you want to execute. Hudson will work out what to do with the generated artifacts, javadoc, and test results automatically.

At the time of this writing, however, the Maven project was still in the beta stage, and the freestyle project provides a lot more power and flexibility, albeit at the cost of a bit more upfront configuration. To do this, you follow the same steps as discussed in the

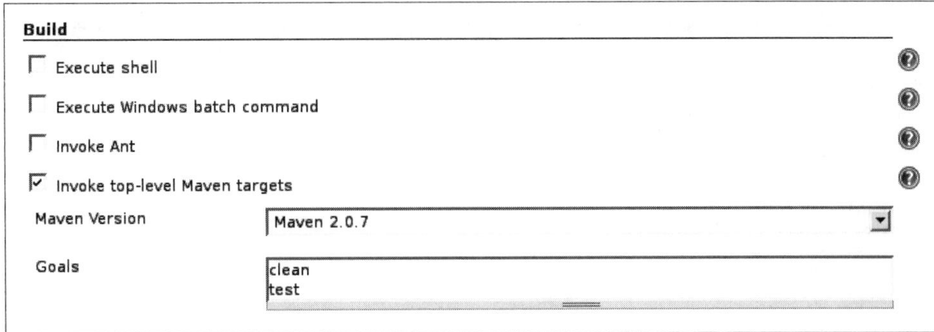

Figure 8-8. Configuring a Maven project using the freestyle project template

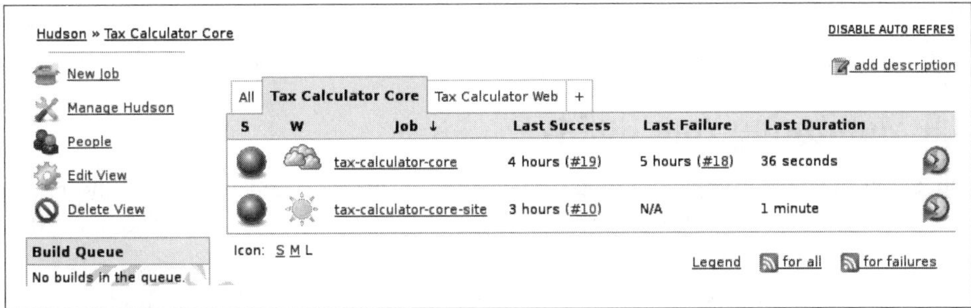

Figure 8-9. Hudson views

previous section. When you get to the build section, simply provide the Maven goals you wish to execute (see Figure 8-8).

8.7 Organizing Your Jobs

If your Hudson server is hosting several development projects, or even if your project has several modules, you can rapidly end up with an impressive number of projects appearing on the Hudson dashboard. Although Hudson does not have any formal notion of project groups, you can define views to make your dashboard a little clearer. These views appear as tabs on the main dashboard, as shown in Figure 8-9.

To create a new view, click on the "+" symbol to the right of the tabs on the Hudson home page. You will be able to give the view a meaningful name, and select the build projects that you want to include in this view. Don't worry if you forget some projects —you can always add more, or remove unwanted projects from the view, via the "Edit View" screen.

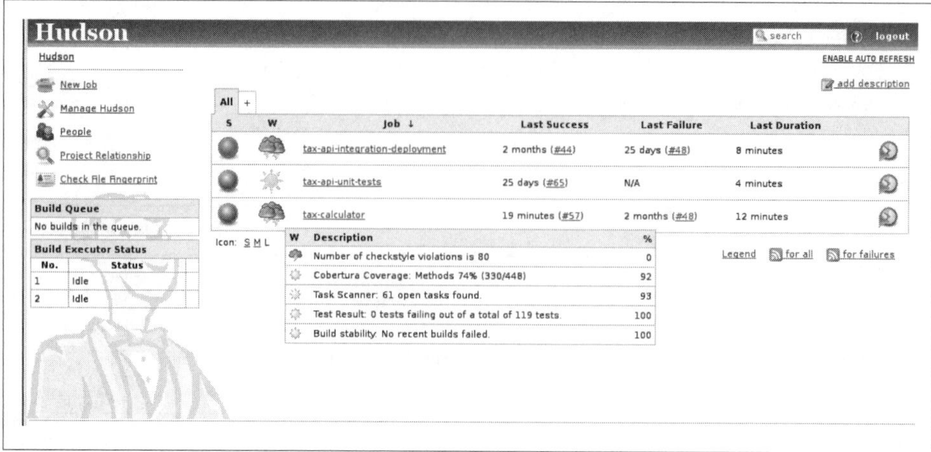

Figure 8-10. The dashboard on the Hudson home page.

8.8 Monitoring Your Builds

Once you have set up and organized your build projects, you can sit back and relax. The dashboard on the Hudson home page gives you an overview of the state of your projects, using some helpful graphical queues (see Figure 8-10).

The colored balls to the left give you an idea of the current state of your build. This is fairly intuitive: blue is good, red is bad, and yellow (not shown in the screen shot) is so-so. More precisely, blue means that your last build was sucessful, and red means that it failed in some spectacular manner. Yellow usually means that there were test failures.

The cute weather report icons aren't just for decoration—they give you a general picture of the overall health of your project, using data both from the current and from previous builds. This icon is also pretty intuitive—sunny weather is good, cloudy weather means that there are a few issues, and stormy weather means that your project health really needs some attention.

The project health indicator takes into account test results, but also code quality metrics such as test coverage, Checkstyle violations, and even the number of TODO tags in the code. The metrics used are primarily up to you, and many of them are provided by plug-ins (see Section 8.13). If you pass the mouse over the weather icon, you can visualize a more detailed explanation.

If you want to know more about the build history of a particular project, just click on the corresponding job name on the dashboard. This will display a summary of the build history for this project, including the latest build artifacts, Javadoc documentation, and test results (see Figure 8-11). You can learn a lot about a build and its history here.

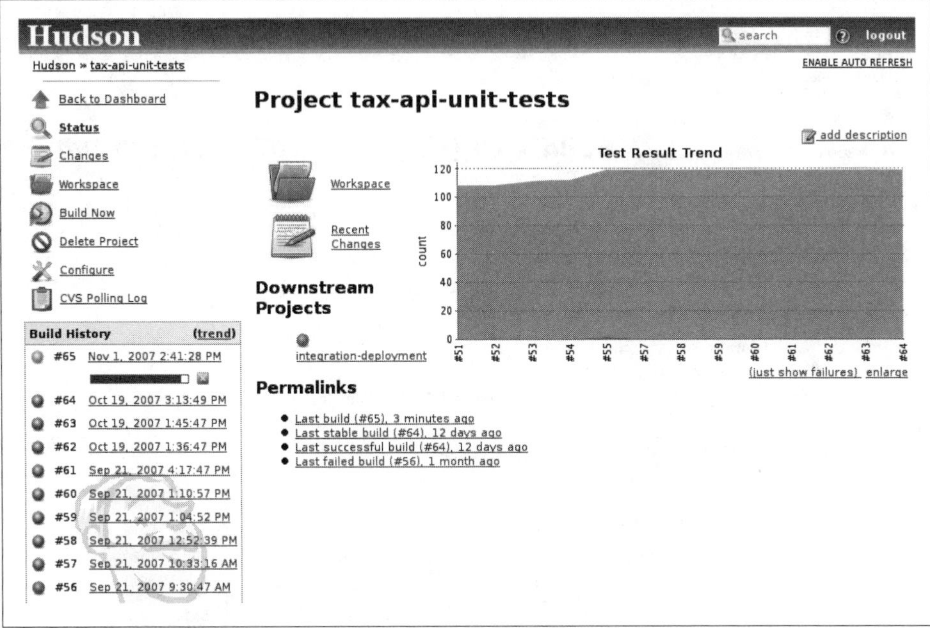

Figure 8-11. Displaying build results

The Changes link gives you a rundown of the messages logged in the version control system for each build, which can give you an idea of what changes lead to a particular build.

The Test Result Trend graph indicates the number of unit tests run per build. Normally, this should increase over time at a steady rate. If it remains flat too long, you should review the testing habits of your team!

8.9 Viewing and Promoting a Particular Build

Organizing releases is a crucial part of any development project. There are whole books on this subject, so we won't try to cover this in any detail here. Basically, you need to be able to identify and distribute versions of your software in a predictable, controlled way. You need to know what changes went into a given version, and why. Ideally, you should be able to deploy the same artifact to different platforms (test, user acceptance, production, and so on) without modification. This helps to ensure that the product you are delivering is the same one that has passed all your unit, integration, (please look out for missing serial commas) and functional tests. You also need to be able to know what changes were made to the source code, and what issues were addressed.

Although Hudson does not claim to be a SCM tool, it does provide some nice features to help keep track of builds and releases. If you click on any build number, Hudson will display a detailed description of that build (see Figure 8-12). From here, you can

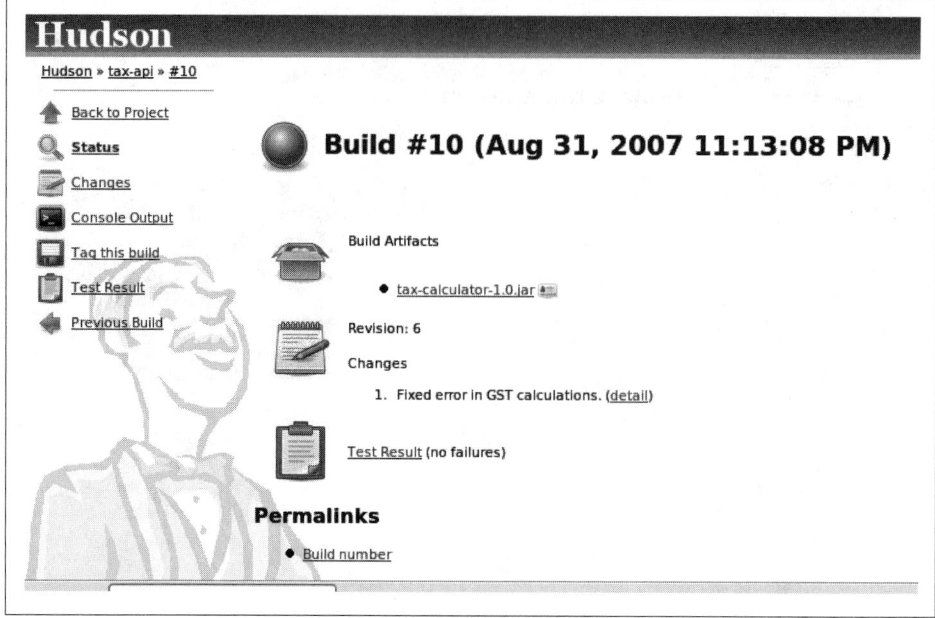

Figure 8-12. Displaying the details of a particular build

download the artifact produced by this build. You can also consult the changes made for this build, including log messages and modified files.

It is a good habit to tag significant builds in your version control system. However, if you are using CVS, this can be a long and CPU-intensive task, which can take literally hours on a large project. Hudson provides an interface to make this simpler. You can view tags that have already been placed on a build, and add new ones (see Figure 8-13). Using this approach, you have a good idea of what version you are tagging (which is not always so easy from the command line), and the grunt-work is done by Hudson—you just have to provide the tag.

8.10 Managing Users

One nice thing about Hudson is that it simplifies some of the boring administrative tasks you normally have to do when you maintain a CI server. For example, you don't need to explicitly identify team members for Hudson—Hudson will figure them out by seeing who's committing code to the source code repository. You can view these users in the "People" screen (see Figure 8-14).

This screen lets you do more than just see who is participating in the development effort, however. If you click on a user, Hudson will bring up a details screen where you

Figure 8-13. Tagging a build

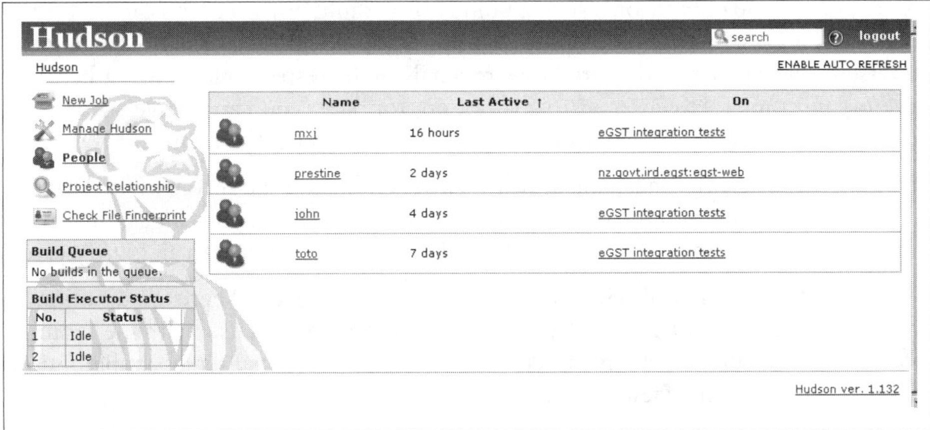

Figure 8-14. Managing users in Hudson

can configure the user's full name (for more readable screens and reports) and email address. This way, Hudson can directly notify individuals who break the build.

Hudson also lets you view the history of each developer's builds: when and how often they have committed changes, any broken builds, and even details of the build outputs (Figure 8-15).

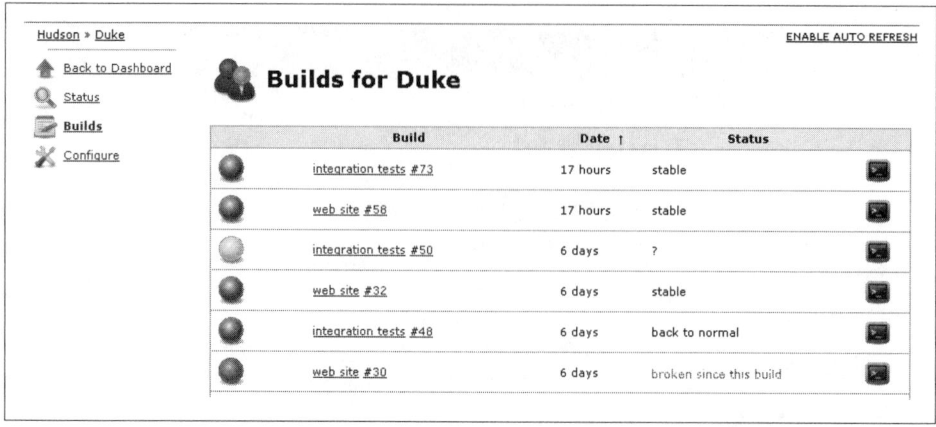

Figure 8-15. Hudson makes it easy to view each user's build history

8.11 Authentication and Security

Security is not one of Hudson's strong points. By default, any user who can access the Hudson web site can modify any project configuration, and even the server configuration itself. This is obviously geared toward small, agile, responsible teams rather than large organizations. However, if this is not appropriate, you can enable security by ticking the "Enable Security" checkbox in the Manage Hudson screen.

The underlying security mechanism will vary depending on the server where Hudson is running. If you are running Hudson on Tomcat, for example, you can use any of the Tomcat security realms, such as the Tomcat `JNDIRealm`, to connect to an LDAP server.

User-rights management in Hudson is not very sophisticated. There is no notion of project-specific roles or rights. When secure access is enabled, a user with the "admin" role can schedule builds for any project, and configure the global server configuration. All other users can only view build results.

If you really need to isolate projects, one (slightly clumsy) approach is to run a separate Hudson instance for each project or group of projects.

As an example, here is part of a simple tomcat-users.xml file. Only the "hudson-admin" user can modify the system configuration or schedule builds:

```
<verbatim>
<?xml version='1.0' encoding='utf-8'?>
<tomcat-users>
  ...
  <role rolename="admin"/>
  ...
  <user username="hudson-admin" password="secret" roles="admin"/>
</tomcat-users>
</verbatim>
```

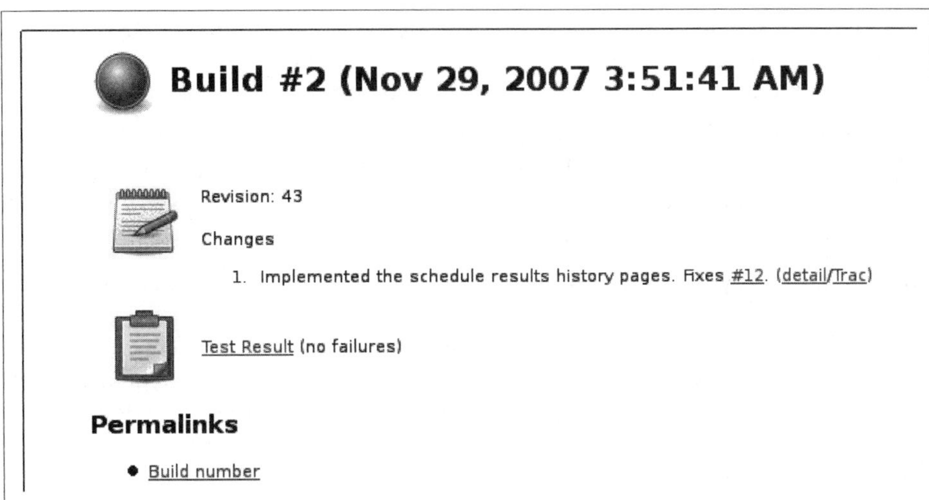

Figure 8-16. Viewing changes in Hudson

8.12 Viewing Changes

Hudson does a good job of keeping track of the changes. When you view the details of a particular build, you can see details of the log messages associated with this build (see Figure 8-16). You can also click on the "detail" link, which will display a list of all the files modified in this build.

Hudson also integrates with issue tracking management systems such as Trac and JIRA. In Figure 8-16, for example, the server has been configured with the Trac plug-in, which allows it to recognize Trac wiki syntax and add a hyperlink to the issue number referenced in the log message. In addition, the "Trac" link will open up the Trac changeset view corresponding to this build. This sort of integration is very useful for keeping tabs on exactly what has been changed in a particular build.

8.13 Hudson Plug-Ins

Hudson is particularly extensible, and integrates well with other products. It supports a flexible plug-in architecture, and a rapidly growing number of plug-ins are available on the Hudson web site to add extra functionality and integration with third-party tools. One of the most immediately useful extensions is to integrate Hudson with an issue tracking system such as Trac and JIRA. The Trac plug-in, for example, recognizes Trac wiki links in your log messages, creating links to the corresponding pages in Trac.

Other plug-ins provide more sophisticated reporting features. The "violations" plug-in, for example, reports on Checkstyle, PMD, CPD, and FindBugs violations, and the Cobertura plug-in integrates Cobertura coverage reports into Hudson.

Plug-ins are easy to install—you simply download the plug-in file from the Hudson web site, and install it onto your Hudson server in the "Manage plug-ins" screen. Alternatively, you can place the plug-in in the $HUDSON_HOME/plug-ins directory on your server. Restart the server and the plug-in will be active.

These plug-ins integrate seamlessly into the Hudson interface. They also provide high-quality reporting capabilities similar to those provided by the Maven site generation plugin. These reporting features are an excellent way to provide high-level visibility on your project. At the Maven site generation, these reports can be configured to work with both Ant and Maven projects (although there is still generally more configuration involved for an Ant project than for a Maven one). As such, they are an excellent way to provide consistent reporting on many different projects within an organization.

We will look at some of the things you can do with Hudson plug-ins in the following sections.

8.14 Keeping Track of Test Results

It makes sense to keep track of your unit test results, both in terms of how many tests are being executed, and of the test success rate. This is a useful way of keeping tabs on the number of tests in the project (it should increase over time), and on the number of test failures (which should remain fairly low on the build server).

Hudson comes with a useful built-in feature that allows you to record and publish test results in a graphical form. First of all, your project needs to generate JUnit XML test reports. If you are using Ant, you need to configure an XML formatter in your JUnit task (see Section 10.10). In Maven, XML test reports are generated automatically.

Next, you need to tell Hudson where it can find these reports. You do this in the project configuration screen, in the "Post-build Actions" section (see Figure 8-17). Here, you specify a regular expression, relative to your work directory, that will find the XML report files. In a normal Maven project, this will be `target/surefire-reports/*.xml`. For an Ant project, it will depend on how you have configured your Ant project.

Once you configure this, Hudson will automatically generate and keep track of JUnit test result statistics. The overall test result trends are displayed on the project home screen in Hudson (see Figure 8-11, earlier in this chapter). You can also click on the graph to display test results by package or by class (see Figure 8-18).

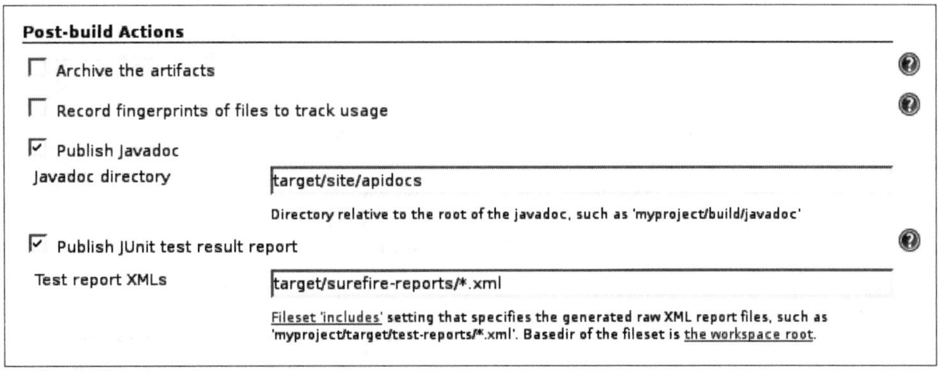

Figure 8-17. Keeping track of JUnit test results

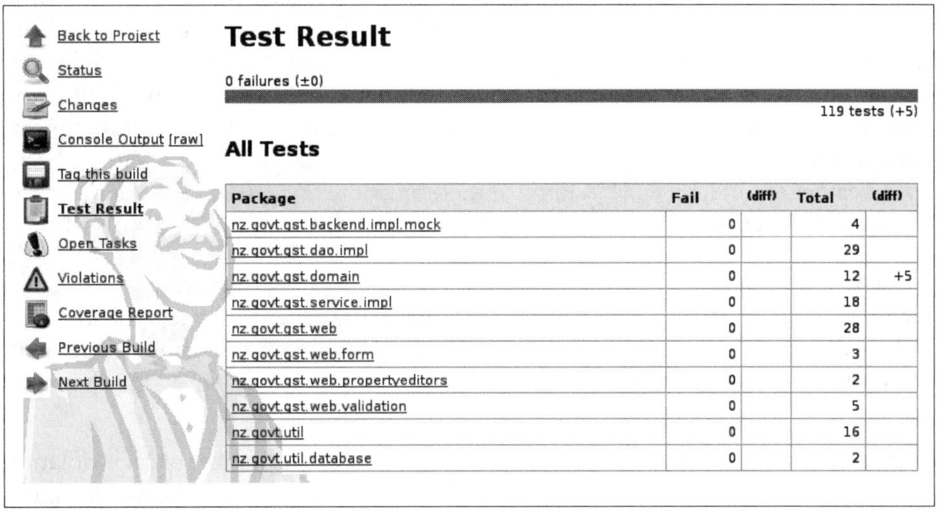

Package	Fail	(diff)	Total	(diff)
nz.govt.gst.backend.impl.mock	0		4	
nz.govt.gst.dao.impl	0		29	
nz.govt.gst.domain	0		12	+5
nz.govt.gst.service.impl	0		18	
nz.govt.gst.web	0		28	
nz.govt.gst.web.form	0		3	
nz.govt.gst.web.propertyeditors	0		2	
nz.govt.gst.web.validation	0		5	
nz.govt.util	0		16	
nz.govt.util.database	0		2	

Figure 8-18. Hudson displays interactive test result reports

8.15 Keeping Track of Code Metrics

Hudson also provides several useful plug-ins that allow you to keep track of code quality metrics. The most useful of these is probably the Violations plug-in. This plug-in lets you track and display statistics from a number of code analysis tools, including Checkstyle (Chapter 21), PMD and CPD (Chapter 22), and FindBugs (Chapter 23).

To activate the Violations plug-in, you need to tick the "Report Violations" checkbox in the "Post-build Actions" section of your project configuration screen (see Figure 8-19).

Then you need to tell Hudson where it can find the relevent report XML data. All of these tools can be configured to generate XML reports, and Hudson expects you to provide an Ant-style path pointing to these files.

Report Violations

Per file display limit: 100

This is the number of violations to display per file (per type)

type	(sun)	(storm)	XML filename pattern
checkstyle	10	200	target/checkstyle-result.xml
cpd	5	50	target/cpd.xml
findbugs	5	20	target/findbugs.xml
pmd	5	50	target/pmd.xml

Source Path Pattern (Optional): **/src/main/java

This is a file name pattern that can be used to resolve classes to sourcefiles (for example **/src/main/java).

Figure 8-19. Configuring the Hudson Violations plug-in

You can also provide two threshold values for each tool, which are used to control the weather report icons visible on the Hudson dashboard. The first, indicated by the sun icon, is the maximum number of violations allowed before the sunny weather report will be replaced by a cloudy one. The second, indicated by the storm icon, specifies the minimum number of violations that will cause the stormy weather report to appear. For example, in Figure 8-19, if there are 10 or fewer Checksyle violations, the Checkstyle weather report icon will be sunny. If there are more than 10 but less than 200, the weather will be cloudy. If there are 200 or more, a stormy icon will be displayed.

These weather icons aren't just used for the violation reports, they are also taken into account in the general weather report on the Hudson dashboard. This lets you integrate code quality metrics into the overall build result status—with too many code quality violations, the dashboard will display a bad-weather icon in the same way as too many successive build failures would do.

Once configured, Hudson will display a graphical view of the number of each violation type over time (see Figure 8-20). You can click on the graph to drill down to a more detailed view of the violations, with a report for each type of issue. From here, you can see the current number of violations that each tool has raised, a graph showing the trend over time, and the list of offending files. If you click on one of the files, you can then drill down to a detailed view of the issues raised for a particular file.

8.16 Reporting on Code Coverage

Code coverage (see Chapter 12) is a useful metric that tells you how much of your application code is being executed during your unit tests. This, in turn, gives you some idea of how well your application is being tested.

Hudson provides good reporting capabilities in this area. Plug-ins exist for several code coverage tools, including Clover, a popular commercial code coverage tool, Emma (see

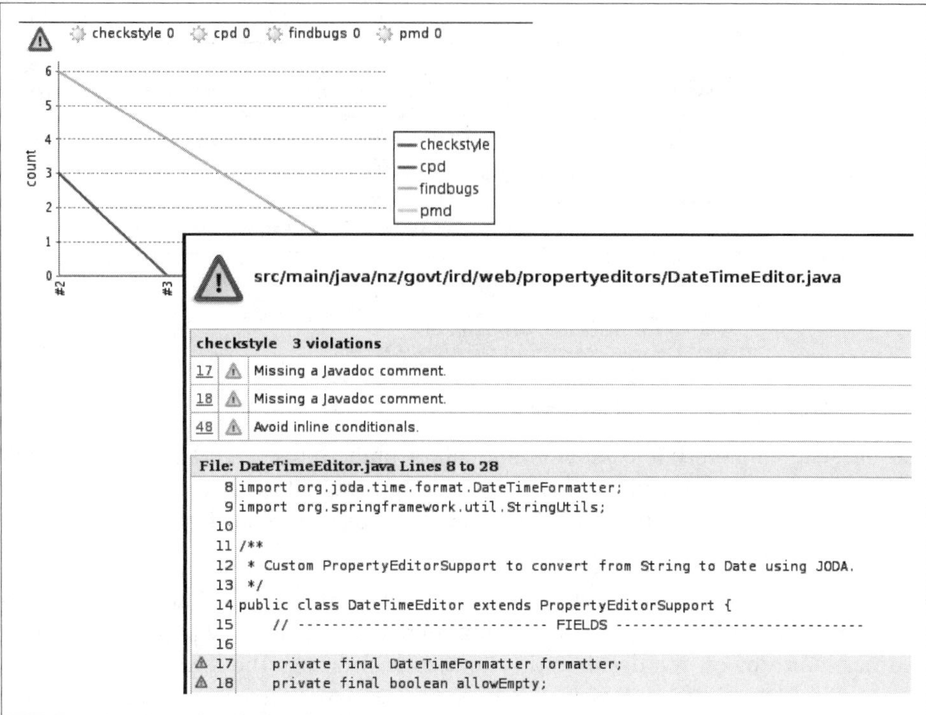

Figure 8-20. The Hudson Violations plugin in action

Section 12.8) and Cobertura (both in Chapter 12). In this section, we will look at how to use the Cobertura plug-in.

The Hudson Cobertura plug-in provides excellent reporting on test coverage, showing coverage statistics from the latest build as well as trends in test coverage throughout the life of the project. Like the other metrics tools, this plug-in relies on data generated during the build process, so you need to set up Cobertura in your project before you can go any further. In Ant, you need to generate XML reports explicitly (see Section 12.2). If you are using Cobertura in a Maven project, the XML reports will be generated automatically (see Section 12.6).

Once your project is correctly configured, you can tell Hudson where to find the Cobertura report data. You configure the Cobertura plug-in in the "Post-build Actions" section of your project configuratiom screen (see Figure 8-21). The most important field is the "Cobertura xml report pattern," where you need to provide an Ant-style file path that Hudson can use to find the Cobertura XML report. For Maven, this will usually be `**/target/site/cobertura/coverage.xml`. For Ant, it will depend on how you have configured the Cobertura task in your build file.

The other configuration parameters let you define various coverage metrics that you want to record. You can keep track of many different test coverage metrics, such as

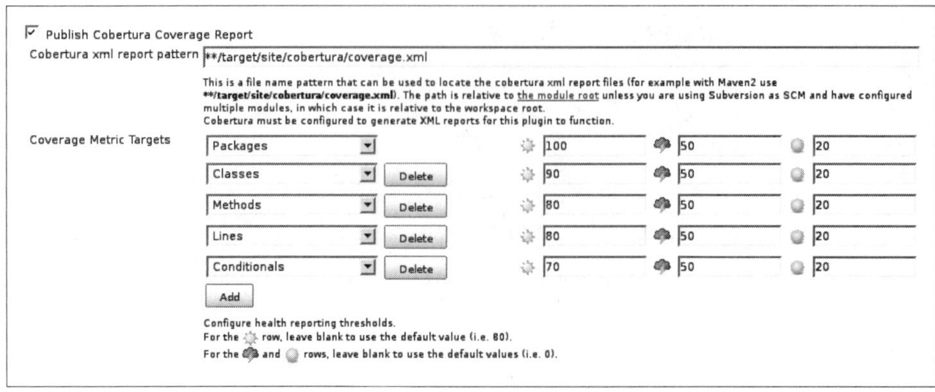

Figure 8-21. Configuring the Hudson Coverage Report

package, class, method, line and conditional (or branch) test coverage. This data will be recorded and displayed in the code coverage reports, allowing you to see how you are doing in your latest build, and also letting you observe trends in test coverage.

You can also different threshold values for each metric. These values determine how the coverage statistics will affect the project health indicators on the Hudson dashboard. The first column indicates the minimum coverage level required for a sunny weather indicator on the dashboard. The second indicates the level below which a stormy weather indicator will appear. Between these two extremes, Hudson will display differing degrees of cloudiness to indicate more or less satisfactory test coverage levels.

The third column lets you define a test coverage level that you consider unacceptable. If test coverage falls below this level, the build will be marked as unstable.

You may want to define more strict constraints on some values, and be more lenient on others. For example, you may require 100 percent coverage for packages and classes (all classes should be tested), but be more lenient on method and line coverage.

A summary of your project's code coverage statistics are displayed on the project home page. This is a great way to get an overview of how your project is doing in terms of code coverage. You can also display a more detailed report by clicking on the graph, or on the "Coverage Report" link (see Figure 8-22). Here, you can view coverage trends at a project, package, or class level, or see precisely what lines of code are being tested (and, more to the point, what aren't).

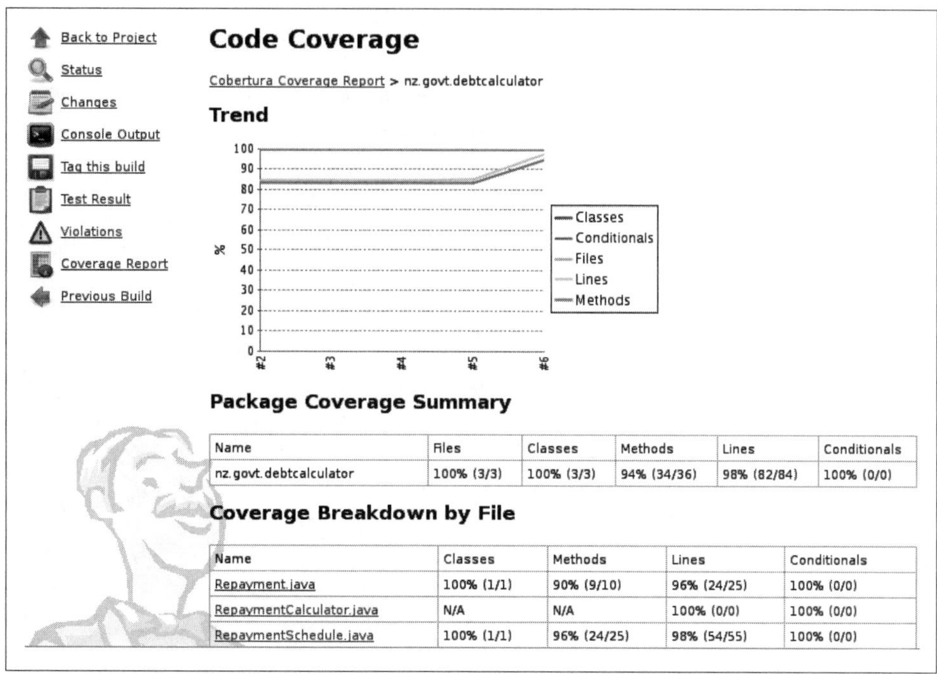

Name	Files	Classes	Methods	Lines	Conditionals
nz.govt.debtcalculator	100% (3/3)	100% (3/3)	94% (34/36)	98% (82/84)	100% (0/0)

Name	Classes	Methods	Lines	Conditionals
Repayment.java	100% (1/1)	90% (9/10)	96% (24/25)	100% (0/0)
RepaymentCalculator.java	N/A	N/A	100% (0/0)	100% (0/0)
RepaymentSchedule.java	100% (1/1)	96% (24/25)	98% (54/55)	100% (0/0)

Figure 8-22. Displaying coverage statistics in Hudson

CHAPTER 9

Setting Up an Instant Messaging Platform with Openfire

9.1 Instant Messaging in a Development Project

Today, communication by chat and instant messaging is almost ubiquitous. There is little need to introduce these technologies. However, they are often seen as purely recreational software tools, and their potential as a team communication tool is often ignored. Indeed, chat and instant messaging can be a useful complement to face-to-face meetings, telephones, and emails, without eliminating the need for any of these other communication techniques.

This is especially true when team members are scattered across different countries or continents because telephone communications are expensive, and IP telephone is not always feasible because of variable network quality.

One solution is to use one of the countless public messaging servers. There are many available, and they work well. However, this approach may be frowned upon by system administrators and/or management who do not wish to see potentially sensitive information circulating outside of the company.

The other solution is to install a private messaging server within your organization.

This is where Openfire can help. Openfire (formerly known as Wildfire) is a powerful open source Java chat and instant messaging server based on the XMPP (Jabber) protocol. It is simple to install and configure, administration is easy via a slick web console, and it offers an extremely rich range of features.

9.2 Installing Openfire

Installing Openfire is easy. Just download the installation package from the Openfire web site and decompress it in an appropriate place. Here we install it in */usr/local* on a Linux server:

```
# tar -xzvf Openfire_3_0_0.tar.gz
# mv Openfire /usr/local
```

If you prefer, it also comes bundled with a JRE in the form of a Windows installer or a Linux RPM.

Openfire comes with its own embedded HSQLDB database, which you can use to get up and running quickly. Openfire also lets you use an external database, which can potentially provide better performance. Openfire should work with any JDBC-enabled database, and comes bundled with drivers, scripts, and instructions for some of the more common databases such as MySQL, Oracle, PostgreSQL, and Microsoft SQLServer.

To start up Openfire, just use the Openfire script in the *bin* directory, as follows:

```
bin/Openfire start
```

To shutdown the Openfire server, use the same script with the *stop* option instead:

```
bin/Openfire stop
```

Finally, to finish your installation, open the administration web site by connecting to *http://127.0.0.1:9090/*. The administrator account is by default "admin," with a password of "admin." When you connect for the first time, you step through a series of screens in which you configure server settings such as language (there are nine to choose from), database configuration, and administrator email and password. When you've finished, you can connect to the Openfire Administration Console (see Figure 9-1).

9.3 Setting Up Users and Accounts on Openfire

All your users will need user accounts on the Openfire server. Openfire comes with a fairly intuitive screen where you can create and manage user accounts and user groups (see Figure 9-2).

You can also configure Openfire to connect to an LDAP directory (how to do this is well-documented in the Openfire documentation), an external database (see Section 9.4), or even a POP3 mail server (see Section 9.5).

Your users will, of course, need Jabber-compatible IM/Chat client software installed on their machines. There are hundreds to choose from. Jives Software, the editor behind Openfire, produces a Java-based open source IM client called Spark. Gaim and Kopete are other well-known clients.

9.4 Authenticating Users in an External Database

You may need to authenticate against users defined in an external database. Openfire provides a set of classes to authenticate users against a database via a JDBC connection.

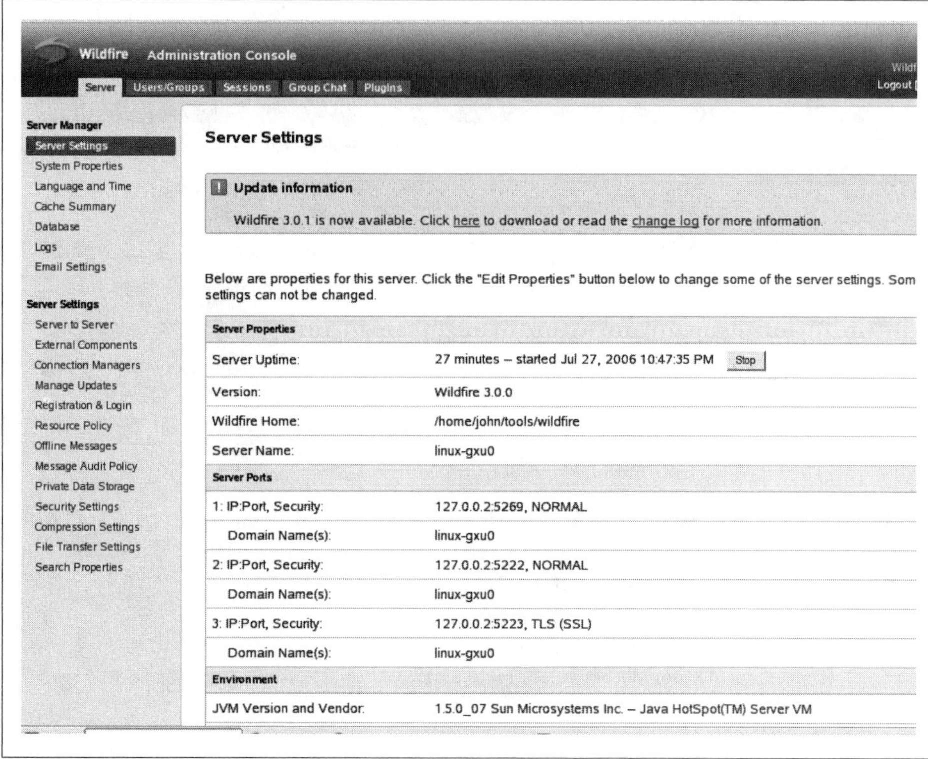

Figure 9-1. The Openfire Administration Console

As with most external authentication mechanisms, this is designed to provide read-only access—users and groups in the external database cannot be modified from within Openfire.

All configuration is done in the *Openfire.xml* configuration file, which you can find in the *conf* directory. You need to set up three "providers"—for users, groups, and for authentication, respectively:

```
<provider>
    <user>
        <className>org.jivesoftware.Openfire.user.JDBCUserProvider</className>
    </user>
    <group>
        <className>org.jivesoftware.Openfire.group.JDBCGroupProvider</className>
    </group>
    <auth>
        <className>org.jivesoftware.Openfire.auth.JDBCAuthProvider</className>
    </auth>
</provider>
```

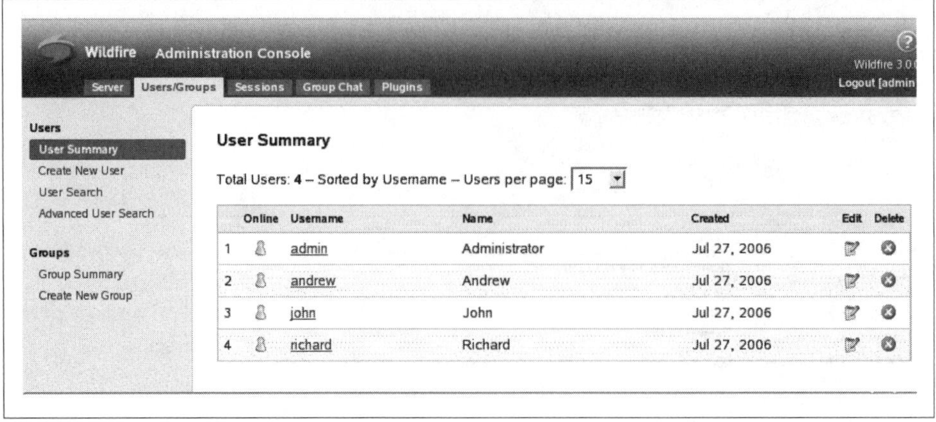

Figure 9-2. The Openfire User Management screen

Then, you need to describe the SQL queries Openfire will need to do to retrieve the users and groups, and to authenticate users. The *jdbcProvider* defines the JDBC connection to be used to access the external database:

```
<jdbcProvider>
    <driver>com.mysql.jdbc.Driver</driver>
    <connectionString>jdbc:mysql://localhost/mydatabase?user=scott&password=tiger
    </connectionString>
</jdbcProvider>
```

For this example, we will use an external database with three tables—user_account, group, and group_users:

```
CREATE TABLE user_account (
  username              VARCHAR(64)       NOT NULL,
  password              VARCHAR(32),
  name                  VARCHAR(100),
  email                 VARCHAR(100),
  PRIMARY KEY (username),
);

CREATE TABLE group (
  groupname             VARCHAR(50)       NOT NULL,
  description           VARCHAR(255),
  PRIMARY KEY (groupname)
);

CREATE TABLE group_users (
  groupname             VARCHAR(50)       NOT NULL,
  username              VARCHAR(100)      NOT NULL,
  administrator         CHAR              NOT NULL,
  PRIMARY KEY (groupName, username, administrator)
);
```

The *jdbcAuthProvider* element defines the SQL SELECT statement used to authenticate a user against the external database. You also need to specify how the password is stored —either as plain text ("plain"), or encoded as an MD5 ("md5") or SHA-1 ("sha1") hash code:

```
<jdbcAuthProvider>
     <passwordSQL>SELECT password FROM user_account WHERE username=?<passwordSQL>
     <passwordType>plain<passwordType>
</jdbcAuthProvider>
```

Finally, the *jdbcGroupProvider* and *jdbcUserProvider* elements define the various SQL queries needed to access users and groups in the database. The query names are fairly self-evident; *userCountSQL* counts the number of users, and *allUsersSQL* returns the list of primary key values for all users. The *loadUserSQL* query loads a user by primary key and expects to be provided with the name and email columns:

```
<jdbcUserProvider>
     <loadUserSQL>SELECT name, email FROM user_account WHERE username =
     ?</loadUserSQL>
     <userCountSQL>SELECT COUNT(*) FROM user_account</userCountSQL>
     <allUsersSQL>SELECT username FROM user_account</allUsersSQL>
     <searchSQL>SELECT username FROM user_account WHERE</searchSQL>
     <usernameField>username</usernameField>
     <nameField>name</nameField>
     <emailField>email</emailField>
</jdbcUserProvider>
```

The *jdbcGroupProvider* element is similar. Users may be administrators within a group, and two different queries (*loadMembersSQL* and *loadAdminsSQL*) need to be defined to distinguish between administrators and ordinary users:

```
<jdbcGroupProvider>
     <groupCountSQL>SELECT count(*) FROM user_group</groupCountSQL>
     <allGroupsSQL>SELECT groupname FROM user_group</allGroupsSQL>
     <userGroupsSQL>SELECT groupname FORM group_users WHERE username=?
     </userGroupsSQL>
     <descriptionSQL>SELECT description FROM user_group WHERE groupname=?
     </descriptionSQL>
     <loadMembersSQL>SELECT username FORM user_group WHERE groupname=?
      AND administrator='N'</loadMembersSQL>
     <loadAdminsSQL>SELECT username FORM user_group WHERE groupname=?
      AND administrator='Y'</loadAdminsSQL>
</jdbcGroupProvider>
```

Once all of this is defined, just restart the server.

9.5 Authenticating Users Against a POP3 Server

If you have a large number of users, it may not be convenient to manage them all by hand in Openfire. If your user mail accounts are stored on a POP3 mail server, Openfire provides the interesting possibility to authenticate users using this server. You need to specify the *POP3AuthProvider* and *POP3UserProvider* providers in the *Openfire.xml* configuration file. You also need to provide some details about the POP3 server:

<host>
: The name or IP address of your POP3 mail server

<port>
: The port of the POP3 mail server (110 by default, or 995 for SSL connections)

<domain>
: The mail domain

<authRequiresDomain>
: True if your POP3 server requires a full email address when authenticating, or just a username

<ssl>
: Should an SSL connection be used? (defaults to "false")

Here is a full example, providing POP3 authentication against a local mail server using an SSL connection:

```
<provider>
    <auth>
        <className>org.jivesoftware.Openfire.auth.POP3AuthProvider</className>
    </auth>
    <user>
        <className>org.jivesoftware.Openfire.user.POP3UserProvider</className>
    </user>
</provider>

<pop3>
    <host>pop.mycompany.com</host>
    <domain>mycompany.com</domain>
    <authRequiresDomain>true</authRequiresDomain>
    <ssl>true</ssl>
</pop3>
```

9.6 Virtual Team Meetings with the Group Chat

Group chat meetings can be particularly useful for dislocated development teams. Although they do not allow for the same types of reactions as a conference call, they require fewer resources and less planning (you don't need to reserve a meeting room equipped with conference call equipment, for example), and they can leave a convenient written trace of what was discussed, which avoids having to write meeting minutes.

Openfire provides some rich functionality in the way of group chat meetings. You create a chat room in the "Group Chat" tab (see Figure 9-3). Openfire lets you choose from a wide range of options. You can set up a moderated room, allow the occupants to invite other users or modify some of the chat room properties, and log the room's

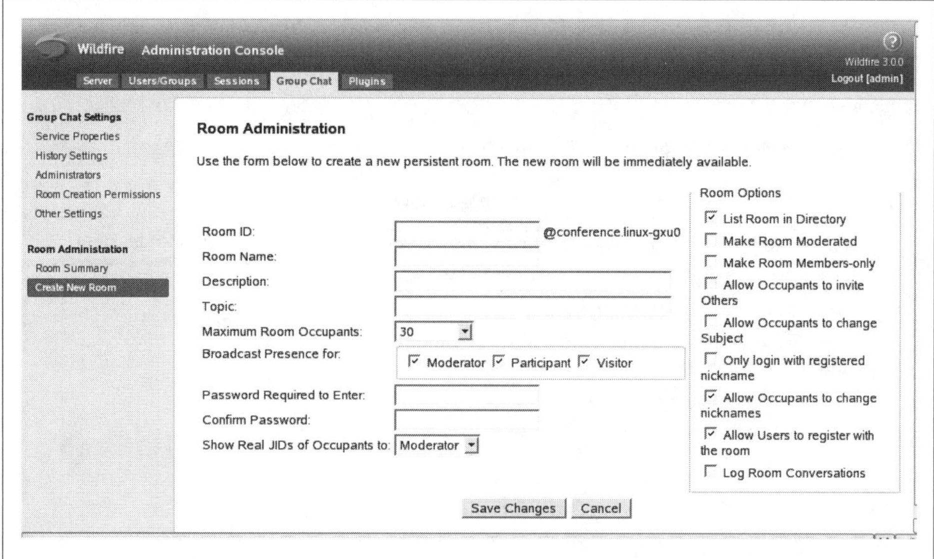

Figure 9-3. Creating a chat room in Openfire

conversations. This last option is probably the most useful in the context of team meetings.

Users connect to a chat room on the Openfire server in the same way that they would for a public chat, which largely depends on the IM client they are using. In Figure 9-4 you can see a typical group chat session, viewed from the Gaim IM client.

9.7 Extended Functionality with Openfire Plug-Ins

Openfire is highly extensible, and there is a growing number of external plug-ins available, which provides extra functionality. The *Broadcast* plug-in, for example, allows messages to be send to all users. The *User Import Export* plug-in lets you import and export users in an XML format. And the *User Service* plug-in allows the user database to be administrated from other applications via HTTP queries.

9.8 Using Openfire with Continuum

Instant messaging technology, in general, and Jabber-based IM, in particular, can be put to imaginative uses within a Java development project. In this section, we will discuss how to integrate Openfire with a continuous integration server. You can use this approach to send IM build failure notifications to developers, for example. Compared to email or RSS notifications, instant messages can provide a faster and more

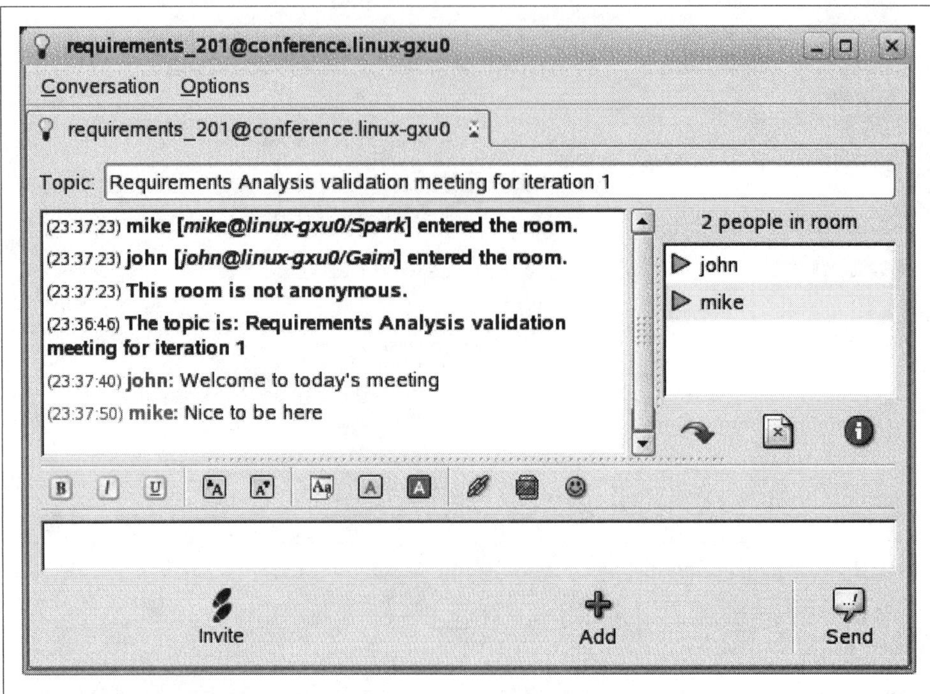

Figure 9-4. Participating in a chat room

dynamic way of informing developers of build failures, and contribute to shortening the development lifecycle.

First of all, you need to set up a dedicated user for your continuous integration server —this is the user who will send the messages, and shouldn't be one of the other user accounts. Here we will work with Continuum, so we'll call this user "continuum." Just create this user as you would any other user from the Openfire administration console (see Section 9.3).

Next, each developer should add this user to his or her list of Contacts. You will also have to open an IM client using the "continuum" account to approve the requests from users to add the "continuum" user to their contact lists.

Once this is done, you are ready to configure your Continuum project. If you are using a Maven 2 project, you can configure your Jabber notifiers either from the Continuum web site, or directly within the *pom.xml* file. Configuring notifications in the *pom.xml* file is more central, though some users may prefer the web console where all the possible fields are visible. A Jabber notification in a Maven 2 *pom.xml* file looks like this:

```
<ciManagement>
    <system>continuum</system>
```

```
    <notifiers>
      <notifier>
        <type>jabber</type>
        <configuration>
          <address>mike@mycompany.com</address>
          <from-address>continuum</from-address>
          <from-password>continuum</from-password>
          <host>localhost</host>
          <port>5222</port>
          <sslConnection>false</sslConnection>
          <isGroup>false</isGroup>
        </configuration>
        <sendOnError>true</sendOnError>
        <sendOnFailure>true</sendOnFailure>
        <sendOnSuccess>true</sendOnSuccess>
        <sendOnWarning>true</sendOnWarning>
      </notifier>
    </notifiers>
  </ciManagement>
```

From the web site, the process is a little more user-friendly, although the information you enter is essentially the same (see Figure 9-5).

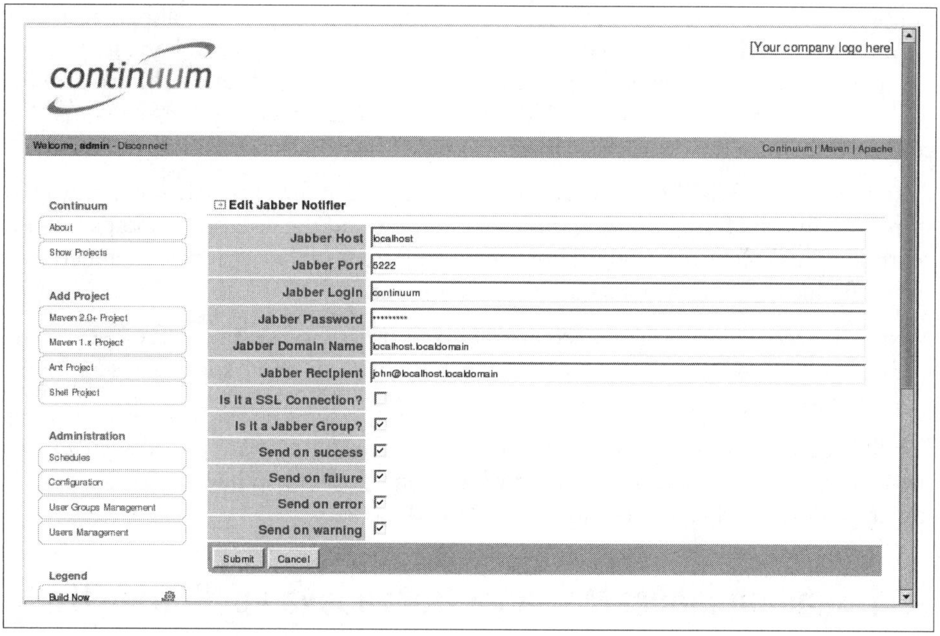

Figure 9-5. Using Jabber notification in Continuum

9.9 Using Openfire with CruiseControl

CruiseControl (discussed in Chapter 6) is a highly configurable Continuous Integration tool, and provides out-of-the-box support for Jabber IM notifications via the *jabber* element, which you add as a child of the *publishers* element in your CruiseControl configuration file (see Section 6.3). A typical Jabber notification looks like this:

```
<publishers>
    <jabber host="localhost"
            username="cruisecontrol"
            password="secret"
            recipient="john@localhost.localdomain"
            buildresultsurl="http://buildserver:8080/myproject/buildresults" />
</publishers>
```

Here, we use another dedicated Jabber message account, called "cruisecontrol," just to avoid mixing up the messages. Note that, as in Continuum, notification must be done on a user-by-user basis.

9.10 Using Openfire with Luntbuild

Luntbuild (discussed in Chapter 7) has well-thought-out support for Jabber, as it does for most of the other IM protocols. Indeed, of the three tools studied here, it arguably provides the most convenient support for IM messaging notification. Information is well centralized with no unnecessary duplication of data, and everything can be set up conveniently from the web console.

First, you set up the Jabber server configuration details in the Properties tab. Luntbuild stores this information, including the server address and the user name and password, centrally. This means that you cannot use two different Jabber servers simultaneously, although this is probably not a common occurrence.

Next, you need to assign Jabber accounts to your users. You do this in the Users page, in the "Jabber account" field. Once you define Jabber accounts for your users, Luntbuild will use them for all Jabber notifications, whatever the project.

Finally, you need to set up Jabber notification for the appropriate projects. Just go to the Project page, and select the Jabber notification method. While you're at it, don't forget to indicate which users should be notified.

9.11 Sending Jabber Messages from a Java Application Using the Smack API

The underlying technology behind Openfire is the Jabber/XMMP protocol. Jabber is an XML-based open standard for IM and presence services, allowing people or software to exchange messages over the Internet in real time. It is a free and open alternative to proprietary IM protocols such as AIM, MSN, and Yahoo!. There are hundreds of (mostly free) Jabber clients available, as well as many servers such as Openfire, OpenIM, ejabberd, and other open source and proprietary solutions.

Jabber uses a very simple XML protocol, supporting several different types of messages —the email-like "normal" messages, chat and groupchat messages used for instant messaging, and headline messages used for ticker-tape-style information such as stock quotes or news headlines. There is also a message type dedicated to error messages. The XML structure used to transmit these messages is clear and concise. Although the general form of the messages is common to all messages, each type of message is slightly different.

Despite the name, nomal messages are not what one normally imagines an IM message to be. A normal message is designed to transmit a message to a user who is not necessarily connected, and who is not expected to respond in real time. Many IM clients actually display normal messages in exactly the same way as IM (chat) messages. A typical normal message takes the following form:

```
<message from="john@myserver.com"
         to="mike@myserver.com"
         type="normal"
         id="message123">
  <subject>Greetings</subject>
  <body>Hi there!</body>
</message>
```

The form of this message is typical of all of the message types. The message is represented (appropriately enough) by the *<message>* element, which takes attributes such as *from*, *to*, and *id*, and provides routing information. The type attribute determines what sort of message is being transmitted. The actual text of the message is provided in the *<body>* element, which is present in all messages. Other elements, such as *<subject>* and *<thread>*, may also be included, depending on the type of message.

Chat messages are more lightweight messages used for real-time instant messaging. These are probably the most common type of messages used, and they are particularly simple. Chat messages generally don't need a *<subject>* element. A typical chat message looks like this:

```
<message to="mike@myserver.com"
         type="chat">
  <thread>thread01</thread>
  <body>Hi there!</body>
</message>
```

Another interesting type of message is the headline message. Headline messages are designed to be dispatched as one-off alerts or updates, such as ticker-tape stock quotes or news updates. Headline messages are fire-and-forget in nature—they usually don't have a *<thread>*, although they occasionally can have a *<subject>*. Here is an example:

```
<message to="mike@myserver.com"
         type="headline"
```

```
        id="message456">
  <body>Typhoon in China</body>
</message>
```

So, as we can see, there is nothing particularly complicated about the Jabber/XMMP XML message structure. It is quite possible to write a Jasper client that builds and transmits XMMP XML messages by hand. However, there is an easier way. The Smack API is a high-level Jabber client API written in Java, that encapsulates the XML layer beneath higher-level classes such as `Chat` and `GroupChat`. In the remainder of this section we will look at how to add Jabber messaging functionality to your Java applications, and how this can be used to enhance the build process.

The first thing you need to get started is to connect to the IM server. The principal class you use here is the `XMPPConnection` class. Establishing a connection is straightforward, as follows:

```
XMPPConnection connection = new XMPPConnection("myserver.com");
connection.login("user", "password");
```

One useful thing to know about Jabber connections is that many IM servers, including Openfire, seem to have trouble coping when they receive a lot of connections from the same user separated by extremely short time intervals, and can produce sporadic, albeit usually non-fatal, errors. Although this may be rare in the real world, this is typically what happens when you unit test your Jabber code. To get around this, just add a small delay after you create a new connection, as shown here:

```
XMPPConnection connection = new XMPPConnection("myserver.com");
try {
    Thread.sleep(100);
} catch (InterruptedException e) {
    e.printStackTrace();
}
connection.login("user", "password");
```

Chat messages are one of the principal uses of the Jabber protocol, and the Smack API provides some convenient features to make developing chat functionalities easier. For example, sending a chat message can be done as simply as this:

```
connection.createChat("mike@jabber.mycompany.com").sendMessage("Hi Mike!");
```

You can also use the `Message` class to manipulate messages on a lower level. This gives you access to all the optional attributes and elements, and lets you create some of the more exotic message types such as headlines, as shown here:

```
Message message = new Message();
message.setTo("mike@myserver.com");
message.setSubject("International News");
message.setBody("Typhoon in China");
message.setType(Message.Type.HEADLINE);
connection.sendPacket(message);
```

9.12 Detecting Presence Using the Smack API

The Smack API provides several other functionalities, which can be useful if you need to read and process IM messages from your Java code.

In the Smack world, a roster is the list of the other IM users you know and with whom you communicate. In IM client software, people in this list are often referred to as contacts, friends, or buddies. You can use this list to identify the users who are currently connected. To do this, you use the `getRoster()` method, as shown here:

```
Iterator iter = connection.getRoster().getEntries();
while (iter.hasNext()) {
    RosterEntry entry = (RosterEntry) iter.next();
    System.out.println(entry.getName() + " (" + entry.getUser() + ")");
}
```

This might produce something like the following:

```
mike (mike@myserver.com) (available)
john (john@myserver.com) (available)
chris (chris@myserver.com)
```

You can then use this list to send messages to all connected users, or to all connected users in a given domain, for example.

9.13 Receiving Messages Using the Smack API

The Smack API also provides a framework for receiving and analyzing Jabber messages. You can process incoming messages either synchronously by actively polling a queue of incoming messages, or asynchronously using a listener pattern, depending on your application's needs. In both cases, filter classes let you limit processing to the precise subset of messages in which you are interested.

The `org.jivesoftware.smack.PacketListener` class lets you set up listeners for incoming messages in order to process them asynchronously. You can use the `org.jivesoftware.smack.filter.PacketFilter` interface and its implementation classes to build message filters. The Smack API provides a rich set of classes that let you filter on message sender, type, thread, and so on. You can also build up quite complex filter conditions by combining the basic filters using the `AndFilter`, `OrFilter`, and `NotFilter` classes.

The actual listening is done with the `PacketListener` interface. This interface just has one method worthy of interest: the `processPacket()` method, which is called whenever a message corresponding to the given filter is received. You put it all together by adding the listener instance to your connection using the `addPacketListener()` method.

In the following example, we use the `PacketListener` interface to listen for Messages coming from the "continuum" user. Presumably, in a real application, we would do something sensible with the messages received; here we simply echo the message body to the standard output:

```
XMPPConnection connection = getConnection();
connection.login(getUsername(), getPassword());

PacketFilter filter
    = new AndFilter(new PacketTypeFilter(Message.class),
                    new FromContainsFilter("continuum@localhost.localdomain"));

PacketListener myListener = new PacketListener() {
    public void processPacket(Packet packet) {
            if (packet instanceof Message) {
                Message msg = (Message) packet;
                // Process message
                System.out.println("Message received, loud and clear:"
                + msg.getBody());

            }
    }
};
// Register the listener.
connection.addPacketListener(myListener, filter);
```

Using a `PacketListener` method is probably the most frequently used technique to process incoming messages. However, the Smack API also provides an alternative way, using the `PacketCollector` interface. A `PacketCollector` provides several methods of accessing the incoming message queue. The `nextResult()` method, shown here, blocks the application while it waits for a matching message to arrive:

```
XMPPConnection connection = getConnection();
connection.login(getUsername(), getPassword());

PacketFilter filter
    = new AndFilter(new PacketTypeFilter(Message.class),
                    new FromContainsFilter("continuum@localhost.localdomain"));

PacketCollector collector = connection.createPacketCollector(filter);
Message msg = (Message) collector.nextResult();
System.out.println("Message received:" + msg.getBody());
```

Alternatively, you can periodically poll the queue for new messages using the `pollResult()` method.

PART IV
Unit Testing

> The next moment the day became very bothering indeed, because Pooh was so busy not looking where he was going that he stepped on a piece of the Forest which had been left out by mistake.
>
> —"A Search is Organized, and Piglet Nearly Meets the Heffalump Again,"
> *The House at Pooh Corner*, A. A. Milne

Software development is very much a trial-and-error process, and it pays to proceed cautiously, little-by-little. This is why good testing is an essential part of the software development process. Although in practice it is often neglected, few developers today would deny the fundamental value of proper testing. Unit tests, especially when used in conjunction with modern agile development processes and techniques such as Test-Driven Development, have the potential to drastically increase the quality and reliability of your code.

Unit tests are also a very effective means of detecting regressions, especially when Continuous Integration techniques (Chapters 5, 6, 7) is being used. Whether you are adding functionality or refactoring existing code, a comprehensive set of unit tests provide a quick way of verifying that no existing functionality has been broken by recent changes.

Unit testing basically involves writing test cases to ensure that your classes function correctly. Unit tests are typically fairly low-level and modular—ideally, you should be able to execute a unit test in isolation, and not depend on any other test cases to be run beforehand. In other words, your tests should be able to be executed in any order, or individually, and still work correctly.

Another important best practice regarding unit tests is that unit test should leave the system in the same state as it was in before the test. For example, if you are testing a DAO class, your tests may well insert, update, and delete data in the database, but once the test has finished, the database should be in the same state as before the test was started. This is not always easy, as a failed test may well leave your environment in an unstable state. Developers often need to write special code (generally known as "fixture code") designed to set up a clean test environment before testing and to tidy up afterward.

Although it is possible to write unit tests entirely from scratch, unit testing frameworks make things at lot easier. By providing a simple, well-understood framework in which to write your tests, libraries such as JUnit and TestNG let developers concentrate on writing high quality unit tests. Testing frameworks also make it easier to organize your tests, to selectively run individual tests, to report on test results, and to write supporting fixture code.

Many books and articles have been written on unit testing, and on recommended testing practices in general. In this section, we will look at tools and techniques that can improve your productivity when it comes to testing your application.

We will also be looking at that vital complement to unit testing, code coverage, as well as at one of the leading open source code coverage tools, Cobertura. Code coverage tools help you verify what parts of your code are being tested by your unit tests, and, more important, what parts aren't. Although code coverage statistics offer little guarantee that your code is being tested *well*, they are certainly better than nothing and can give valuable tips on any shady areas of code that have been left untested. And it is well known that bugs like to accumulate in the shadows.

CHAPTER 10

Testing Your Code with JUnit

10.1 JUnit 3.8 and JUnit 4

JUnit was a groundbreaking piece of software in its day, and there are many, many useful JUnit extensions that help with unit testing in specialized areas and that still rely on the JUnit 3.x approach. We will look at a few of them later on in the book. This section is a brief refresher on JUnit 3.8, for future reference and to better understand the changes brought by newer frameworks such as JUnit 4 and TestNG (Chapter 20).

In JUnit 3, you write unit tests in special Java classes, called test cases. All JUnit 3 test cases must extend the `TestCase` class. You write unit tests as methods of these classes, following a special naming convention: test methods must return `void`, take no parameters, and start with the word "test." Your test classes usually also follow a particular naming convention, such as ending with the word `Test`.

Here is a simple Unit 3.8 test class that tests a class that calculates GST ("Goods and Services Tax," also known as a "Value Added Tax" in some countries). Suppose that the standard GST rate is 12.5 percent. Our unit test class might look like this:

```
public class PriceCalculatorTest extends TestCase {

    public void testCalculateGST() {
       calculator = new PriceCalculator();
       double amountWithGst = calculator.calculatePriceWithGST(100.00);
       assertEquals("Standard GST is 12.5%", 112.50, amountWithGst, 0.0);
    }
}
```

The TestCase base class comes with a large number of `assert` methods: `assertEquals()`, `assertTrue()`, `assertNotNull()`, and many more. These make up the core of your unit tests, since they are what you use to actually perform your tests. You use the assert methods to check your obtained results against the expected results. You can optionally provide a message as the first parameter of your asserts, which can help to make it easier to identify the error when you have a lot of unit tests to run.

You can override the `setUp()` and `tearDown()` methods (be careful of the capital letters!) to define initialization and housekeeping code that will be run, respectively, before and after each test. For example, if we have many test cases using the calculator object, we might want to create it only once in the `setUp()` method:

```
public class PriceCalculatorTest extends TestCase {

    PriceCalculator calculator;

    protected void setUp() throws Exception {
        calculator = new PriceCalculator();
    }

    public void testCalculateGST() {
        double amountWithGst = calculator.calculatePriceWithGST(100.00);
        assertEquals("Standard GST is 12.5%", 112.50, amountWithGst, 0.0);
    }
    // More tests with the calculator object
}
```

There is actually more to JUnit 3 than this, but you should now be familiar enough with the JUnit 3 architecture, to understand the innovations brought by the newer frameworks, and to use the JUnit 3 extensions that we discuss in other chapters. JUnit 4 is usually preferable, but 3.8 is still widely used, and many plug-ins still haven't been updated for JUnit 4. In the remainer of this chapter, we will refer exclusively to JUnit 4.

10.2 Unit Testing with JUnit 4

When it comes to unit testing frameworks, JUnit is the de facto standard. It is widely used and known, and has many useful extensions for more specialized testing. JUnit, originally written by Kent Beck and Erich Gamma, is widely recognized as a monumental piece of software that greatly contributed to the popularity (at least in theory) of decent unit testing practices in Java. However, over the last few years, the basic API has not evolved a great deal, and some other different and innovative testing frameworks such as TestNG (see Chapter 20) have emerged.

JUnit 3 imposes many constraints which are no longer justified in the world of Java 5, annotations and IOC programming. In JUnit 3, test classes need to extend a JUnit base class, and tests need to respect a special naming convention: you cannot use any old Java class as a test class. JUnit 3 test classes are initialised each time a test is executed, which makes it harder to refactorise and optimize test code. There is no support for data-driven testing (running your tests against externally provided data). It also lacks features such as dependencies between tests, and test groups.

JUnit 4 is a major rewrite of the JUnit API, which aims at taking advantage of the progress in Java technology over the pass few years. It is simpler, easier, and more flexible to use than its predecessor, with a few new features to boot! It introduces a lot of new features that can make writing your unit tests easier, such as the use of annotations and more flexible test class initialization. In JUnit 4, a test can be any old POJO class, and test methods don't need to respect any particular naming convention.

Let's see how our tax calculator tests (see Section 10.1) would look in JUnit 4:

```
import org.junit.Before;
import org.junit.Test;
import static org.junit.Assert.*;

public class PriceCalculatorTest {

   @Test
   public void calculateStandardGST() {
     PriceCalculator calculator = new PriceCalculator();
     double gst = calculator.calculatePriceWithGST(100.00);
     assertEquals(gst, 112.50 , 0.0);
   }

   @Test
   public void calculateReducedGST() {
     PriceCalculator calculator = new PriceCalculator();
     double gst = calculator.calculatePriceWithReducedGST(100.00);
     assertEquals(gst, 105.00 , 0.0);
   }

}
```

The first thing to notice is that, unlike test classes in JUnit 3, a JUnit 4 test case does not need to extend any particular class. JUnit 4, like TestNG, uses annotations to indicate which methods should be treated as unit tests. Any method marked by the *@Test* annotation is considered to be a unit test. There is no particular naming convention (tests no longer need to be called testThis or testThat), although the methods still do need to return `void` and take no parameters. In theory, you could even place your unit tests in the same class as the code you are testing, although in practice it is probably a good idea to keep them separate.

The `org.junit.Assert` class contains the old JUnit 3.x asserts we've all come to know and love. In JUnit 3, the assert methods were defined in the `TestCase` class, the base class of all JUnit test classes, and so could be used in any JUnit test. Not so in JUnit 4, where test classes no longer need to be derived from `TestCase`. To avoid much heartache and gnashing of teeth, you can do a static import on this class (as shown here) so that you can use these asserts (`assertEquals`, `assertNotNull`, and so on) in exactly the same way as in your old JUnit 3.x unit tests.

Alternatively, you can also use Java 5 assert statements:

```
assert (gst == 100*PriceCalculator.DEFAULT_GST_RATE);
```

This may look nicer, but there is a hitch: Java will blissfully ignore your asserts unless you use the *-ea* (enable assertions) command-line option.

10.3 Setting Up and Optimizing Your Unit Test Cases

As with as any other code, unit tests need to be coded efficiently and refactored where necessary. JUnit 4 provides a couple of annotations that can help you out here. The *@Before* annotation indicates a method that needs to be called before each test, effectively replacing the `setup()` method of JUnit 3.x. You can also use the *@After* annotation to indicate any cleanup methods that need to be run *after* each test. Here, the `initialize()` method will be called before, and `tidyup()` after, each unit test:

```
import org.junit.Before;
import org.junit.Test;
import static org.junit.Assert.*;

public class PriceCalculatorTest {

   private PriceCalculator calculator;

   @Before
   public void initialize() {
     calculator = new PriceCalculator();
   }

   @Test
   public void calculateStandardGST() {
     PriceCalculator calculator = new PriceCalculator();
     double gst = calculator.calculatePriceWithGST(100.00);
     assertEquals(gst, 112.50 , 0.0);
   }

   @Test
   public void calculateReducedGST() {
     PriceCalculator calculator = new PriceCalculator();
     double gst = calculator.calculatePriceWithReducedGST(100.00);
     assertEquals(gst, 105 , 0.0);
   }

   @After
   public void tidyup() {
     calculator.close();
     calculator = null;
   }
}
```

However, this may still not be optimal. JUnit also provides a few other annotations which you can use to improve things further. Sometimes, for the sake of efficiency, you would like to be able to be able to set up some resources before you run *any* of the unit tests in a given class, and then clean up afterward. You can do just that with the *@BeforeClass* and *@AfterClass* annotations. Methods annotated with *@BeforeClass* will be invoked just once, before any of the unit tests are executed. And, as you would expect, methods annotated with *@AfterClass* are executed only when all of the tests have been completed. In the above example, the calculator object should be created only once, at the start of the unit tests, and closed only after all of the tests have been completed. We might add a `reset()` method, called before each unit test, to reinitialize the calculator each time. Here is what our optimized unit test class might look like:

```
import org.junit.Before;
import org.junit.Test;
import static org.junit.Assert.*;

public class PriceCalculatorTest {

   private PriceCalculator calculator;

   @BeforeClass
   public void initialize() {
     calculator = new PriceCalculator();
   }

   @Before
   public void resetCalculator() {
     calculator.reset();
   }

   @Test
   public void calculateStandardGST() {
     PriceCalculator calculator = new PriceCalculator();
     double gst = calculator.calculatePriceWithGST(100.00);
     assertEquals(gst, 112.50 , 0.0);
   }

   @Test
   public void calculateReducedGST() {
     PriceCalculator calculator = new PriceCalculator();
     double gst = calculator.calculatePriceWithReducedGST(100.00);
     assertEquals(gst, 105 , 0.0);
   }

   @AfterClass
   public void tidyup() {
     calculator.close();
   }

}
```

10.4 Simple Performance Testing Using Timeouts

A very simple type of performance testing involves making sure that a particular test always executes within a certain timeframe. This can also be useful for database queries using O/R mapping tools such as Hibernate. Basic errors in Hibernate mapping files, for example, can result in very poor response times, even for relatively simple queries. Although a normal unit test wouldn't pick this up, a test with a timeout would.

This sort of check also works nicely for detecting infinite loops, although it is of course harder to know which parts of your code are likely to contain infinite loops....

This technique is directly integrated into the *@Test* annotation, which allows you to set an upper limit on the amount of time a test may run without failing. To do this, you specify the *timeout* parameter of the *@Test* annotation (in milliseconds), as shown here:

```
@Test(timeout=100)
public void lookupGST() {
   double gst = calculator.lookupRateForYear(2006);
   assertEquals(gst, GST_RATE_IN_2006 , 0.0);
}
```

Now, if the query takes more than 100 milliseconds, the test will fail:

```
Testsuite: com.wakaleo.jpt.alexandria.services.PriceCalculatorTest
Tests run: 3, Failures: 0, Errors: 1, Time elapsed: 0.136 sec

Testcase: calculateStandardGST took 0.009 sec
Testcase: lookupGST took 0.128 sec
        Caused an ERROR
test timed out after 100 milliseconds
java.lang.Exception: test timed out after 100 milliseconds
```

For some critial, high-performance methods, you might want to check that the classes perform with acceptable throughput. Of course, the lower the timeout value, the higher the chances are that some outside factor might slow down your tests and that your tests might timeout incorrectly. For example, in the following test case, we check that on average the `calculateInterest()` method never takes more than a millisecond to run:

```
@Test(timeout=50)
public void perfTestCalculateInterest() {
    InterestCalculator calc = new InterestCalculatorImpl();
    for(int i = 0 ; i < 50; i++) {
        calc.calculateInterest(principal, interestRate, startDate, periodInDays);
    }
}
```

This type of test is just a reality check to make sure your methods are not excessively slow, so don't be too demanding.

10.5 Checking for Exceptions the Easy Way

Sometimes you want to check that an exception is correctly thrown under certain circumstances. In JUnit 3.x, this is a fairly laborious task involving catching the exception and asserting success in this case and failure otherwise. In JUnit 4, you can use the *expected* parameter in the *@Test* annotation to the exception that should be thrown if all goes according to plan. In the following (somewhat contrived) example, we require the application to go through an `IllegalArgumentException` if the year is less than some arbitrary year. In JUnit 4, we can check this fairly easily as shown here:

```
@Test(expected = IllegalArgumentException.class)
public void lookupIllegalGSTYear() {
   double gst = calculator.lookupRateForYear(1066);
}
```

Now, if this method doesn't throw an `IllegalArgumentException`, the test will fail:

```
Testsuite: com.wakaleo.jpt.alexandria.services.PriceCalculatorTest
Tests run: 3, Failures: 1, Errors: 0, Time elapsed: 0.114 sec

Testcase: calculateStandardGST took 0.009 sec
Testcase: lookupGST took 0.01 sec
Testcase: lookupIllegalGSTYear took 0.003 sec
        FAILED
Expected exception: java.lang.IllegalArgumentException
junit.framework.AssertionFailedError: Expected exception:
java.lang.IllegalArgumentException
```

10.6 Using Parameterized Tests

Unit tests are dull things to write, and developers are prone to take shortcuts. However, there is no escaping that good unit tests need to test business functions with a wide range of different data, be it boundary cases, data classes, or whatever. The same test may well succeed with one set of data, but fail with another. But if a developer needs to write a separate test case for each value (which testing best practices would suggest), he will typically not test very many values. Wouldn't it be nice to be able to run the same unit test several times, using different data?

In fact, JUnit 4 does provide a neat feature that makes it easy to test using arbitrary sets of data. Basically, you can set up a collection of test data and feed it automatically into your unit test methods. Let's look at an example. Suppose that you need to write a class that calculates income tax for a given income in a certain year. The business class interface might look like this:

```
public interface TaxCalculator {
    public double calculateIncomeTax(int year, double taxableIncome);
}
```

Now working out income tax typically involves some pretty nontrivial calculations. Most countries use a progressive tax system of some sort, in which the tax rate increases with the taxable income, using a system of "tax brackets." In addition, the exact tax brackets sometimes vary from year to year. For this sort of application, it is important to test values within each tax bracket, as well as various boundary cases. So, we will set up a collection of test data containing the income, the year, and the expected income tax, over a wide range of values. Let's see how we could do this.

JUnit 4 lets us define sets of test data, which we can pass to our unit tests. In this case, we need to test various taxable incomes in the different tax brackets. In this example, we will only test against one year (2006), but, in a real-world application, we may want to test against several years. So, our test data sets will contain three values: taxable income, year, and the amount of payable income tax.

To use this test data, we need to set up a parameterized test class. This is basically a test class with a constructor that takes several parameters: precisely one parameter for each value in the test data sets. So, in our case, the constructor will take three parameters: taxable income, year and payable income tax. The parameterized test class will typically also have member variables corresponding to each of these fields. The constructor initialises these fields, and the unit test methods in the class use them to execute their tests.

JUnit will instantiate a new instance of your test class for each row in the test data and then execute the class's unit tests against this data. So, if you have 20 rows of test data, JUnit will instantiate your test class 20 times, each time running the unit tests against a different set of data.

Let's see how you would code this. The full test class is listed here:

```
@RunWith(Parameterized.class)
public class TaxCalculatorTest {

    @Parameters
    public static Collection data() {
        return Arrays.asList(new Object[][]{
                /* Income   Year     Tax  */
                {      0.00, 2006,     0.00},
                { 10000.00, 2006,  1950.00},
                { 20000.00, 2006,  3900.00},
                { 38000.00, 2006,  7410.00},
                { 38001.00, 2006,  7410.33},
                { 40000.00, 2006,  8070.00},
                { 60000.00, 2006, 14670.00},
                {100000.00, 2006, 30270.00},
        });
    }

    private double revenue;
    private int    year;
    private double expectedTax;

    public TaxCalculatorTest(double input, int year, double expectedTax) {
        this.revenue = revenue;
        this.year = year;
        this.expectedTax = expectedTax;
    }

    @Test public void calculateTax() {
        TaxCalculator calculator = getTaxCalculator();
        double calculatedTax = calculator.calculateIncomeTax(year, revenue);
        assertEquals(expectedTax, calculatedTax);
    }

    private TaxCalculator getTaxCalculator() {
```

```
        TaxCalculator calculator = new TaxCalculatorImpl();
        return calculator;
    }
}
```

Let's look at each part of this class in detail. First of all, you need to use the *@RunWith* annotation, specifying the `Parameterized` class, to let JUnit know that your test class contains parameterized test cases.

```
@RunWith(Parameterized.class)
public class TaxCalculatorTest {...
```

Next, you need to set up a collection of test data. You do this by defining a function, tagged with the *@Parameters* annotation, which returns the test data in the form of a collection. Behind the scenes, the test data is usually a list of arrays. In our case, we set up a list of arrays of values, with each array containing three values: the income, the year, and the expected tax for that income in that year:

```
    @Parameters
    public static Collection data() {
        return Arrays.asList(new Object[][]{
                /* Revenue  Year     Tax  */
                {      0.00, 2006,      0.00},
                { 10000.00, 2006,  1950.00},
                { 20000.00, 2006,  3900.00},
                { 38000.00, 2006,  7410.00},
                { 38001.00, 2006,  7410.33},
                { 40000.00, 2006,  8070.00},
                { 60000.00, 2006, 14670.00},
                {100000.00, 2006, 30270.00},
        });
    }
```

As we mentioned earlier, when JUnit 4 runs this class, it actually creates an instance of the class for each line in the test data collection. You need to provide member variables to store each of these values, and a public constructor to initialize them so that JUnit can set up each instance with the correct test data:

```
    private double revenue;
    private int    year;
    private double expectedTax;

    public TaxCalculatorTest(double revenue, int year, double expectedTax) {
        this.revenue = revenue;
        this.year = year;
        this.expectedTax = expectedTax;
    }
```

Now we just test against these values:

```
    @Test
    public void calculateTax() {
        TaxCalculator calculator = getTaxCalculator();
        double calculatedTax = calculator.calculateIncomeTax(year, revenue);
```

```
        assertEquals(expectedTax, calculatedTax);
    }
```

When you run these unit tests, the test will be run many times, once for each line in the data array:

```
Testsuite: com.wakaleo.jpt.alexandria.services.TaxCalculatorTest
Tests run: 8, Failures: 0, Errors: 0, Time elapsed: 0.119 sec

Testcase: calculateTax[0] took 0.012 sec
Testcase: calculateTax[1] took 0.001 sec
Testcase: calculateTax[2] took 0.002 sec
Testcase: calculateTax[3] took 0.001 sec
Testcase: calculateTax[4] took 0.001 sec
Testcase: calculateTax[5] took 0.001 sec
Testcase: calculateTax[6] took 0.002 sec
Testcase: calculateTax[7] took 0.003 sec
```

Note that you can put many unit tests in a parameterized unit test class, just as you would in a normal unit test class. Each individual unit test method will be run against each row of test data.

10.7 Using assertThat and the Hamcrest Library

JUnit 4.4 introduced a new notation for assert statements designed to make the intentions of the developer clearer and easier to read. This notation, originally developed by Joe Walnes,* uses the *assertThat* method, along with set of matcher statements (or constraints, or predicates, depending on your background), which can quite nicely improve the readability of your tests. For example, the following class tests that, in this situation, the calculated tax is zero:

```
import static org.junit.Assert.*;
import static org.hamcrest.CoreMatchers.*;

public class TaxCalculatorTest {

    @Test
    public void calculateTax() {
        TaxCalculator calculator = getTaxCalculator();
        double calculatedTax = calculator.calculateIncomeTax(2007, 0);
        assertThat(calculatedTax, is(0.0));
     }
}
```

Now *assertThat(calculatedTax, is(0.0))* is arguably more readable than *assertEquals (calculatedTax, 0.0, 0.0)*, although this may be a matter of personal preference. For me, it certainly reads more naturally. It's probably the fraction of a second that your brain takes to convert "assertsEquals" into a sentence structure along the lines of "yeah right,

* *http://joe.truemesh.com/blog/000511.html*

so calculated tax has to equal zero." With the first form, your brain goes "OK, we're asserting that calculated tax is zero." This requires less work.

More readable tests also mean more reliable and maintainable tests. If your tests are easy to read, it's easy to see that they are correct.

You can use the *equalTo* matcher (or *is*, in a shorthand form) as a more readable version of the *assertEquals* method:

```
String result = "red";
...
assertThat(result, equalTo("red"));
```

These statements can also be combined for more complex tests. For example, using the *anyOf* matcher statement, the following test checks that the color variable is red, green, or yellow:

```
assertThat(color, anyOf(is("red"),is("green"),is("yellow")));
```

If necessary, you can add a description of your test to make things even clearer:

```
String color = "noir";
assertThat("black is black", color, is("black"));
```

This will generate an error message with a bit more depth:

```
<<< FAILURE!
java.lang.AssertionError: black is black
Expected: "black"
     got: "noir"
...
```

You can also use the *not* matcher to negate any other matcher in a fairly intuitive way:

```
String color = "black";
assertThat(color, is(not(("white"))));
```

These new methods actually come from a third-party library called Hamcrest. The range of matchers that comes with JUnit 4.4 is actually relatively limited. For a more complete set, you should include the `hamcrest-all.jar` library in your project. You can download this API from the Hamcrest web site.* If you are using Maven, you can simply include a reference in your POM file, as shown here:

```
<dependency>
    <groupId>org.hamcrest</groupId>
    <artifactId>hamcrest-all</artifactId>
    <version>1.1</version>
    <scope>test</scope>
</dependency>
```

Then replace the static import of `org.hamcrest.CoreMatchers` to `org.hamcrest.Matchers`. This will give you access to a much richer set of matchers. Some of these additional features are discussed in the remainder of this section.

* *http://code.google.com/p/hamcrest/downloads/list*

Many of the more interesting matchers make it easy to work with collections. For example, the *hasItem* matcher can be used to search the contents of a list (*hasItemInArray* does the same thing for array structures):

```
List<String> colors = new ArrayList<String>();
colors.add("red");
colors.add("green");
colors.add("yellow");
...
assertThat(colors, hasItem("red"));
```

You can use the *hasItem* and *hasItemInArray* to build nontrivial tests about list values. Here, for example, we check that a list has no entry:

```
List<Integer> ages = new ArrayList<Integer>();
ages.add(20);
ages.add(30);
ages.add(40);
...
assertThat(ages, not(hasItem(lessThan(18))));
```

Conversely, the *isIn* matcher lets you check whether a particular object is contained in a list:

```
assertThat(20, isIn(ages));
```

Collection support is not limited to lists. The *hasKey* and *hasValue* matchers can be used to check whether a Map contains a certain key or value:

```
Map map = new HashMap();
map.put("color", "red");
...
assertThat(map, hasValue("red"));
```

You can even use the *hasProperty* matcher to perform tests on the properties of an object:

```
Client client = new Client();
client.setClientName("Jane");
...
assertThat(client, hasProperty("clientName", is("Jane")));
```

This is just a sample of what you can do with this type of expression. Check out the latest API documentation to see what else is available. The bottom line is that they can give your test cases more clarity and more expressiveness, which in turn allows you to code better, more reliable tests, more quickly and more easily.

10.8 JUnit 4 Theories

Another major new feature introduced in JUnit4.4, albeit with an experimental status, is the notion of *theories*. A theory expresses a general assertion that holds true across a, possibly infinite, number of data sets. Any constraints to the data sets to which the theory applies are specified as assumptions.

The developer first specifies a set of data points for testing the theory. A data point is a (generally constant) piece of test data, identified by the *@DataPoint* annotation. Alternatively, automated tools may analyze the code and automatically create data sets to reinforce or disprove the theory. For example, here we define the years 2007 and 2008 as valid test data:

```
@DataPoint public static int YEAR_2007 = 2007;
@DataPoint public static int YEAR_2008 = 2008;
```

Another set of data can be used to define test data used for possible revenue test data:

```
@DataPoint public static double INCOME_1 = 0.0;
@DataPoint public static double INCOME_2 = 0.01;
@DataPoint public static double INCOME_3 = 100.0;
@DataPoint public static double INCOME_4 = 13999.99;
@DataPoint public static double INCOME_5 = 14000.0;
```

To define a theory-enabled test, you use the *@Theory* annotation instead of the usual *@Test* annotation. A theory is an ordinary method that takes a certain number of parameters. JUnit will work out which data points to use for the various parameters in your test methods based on their respective types. Each data point will be passed to each parameter of the same type. This can be a little confusing if there are several parameters of the same type. As we will see, you use assumptions to limit the allowed values for each individual parameter.

The next step is to define your assumptions using the *@assumeThat* annotation. Indeed, by placing assumptions within a theory-enabled test case, you limit the test data that will be used to execute that test case. In the following example, we limit a test case to the year of 2007, for incomes greater than $0 and less than $14,000:

```
assumeThat(year, is(2007));
```

and

```
assumeThat(income, both(greaterThan(0.00)).and(lessThan(14000.00)));
```

The JUnitRunner runs the test with all possible combinations of the set of data points that pass the assumptions, in this case YEAR_2007 with INCOME_2, INCOME_3, and INCOME_4:

```
import static org.hamcrest.MatcherAssert.assertThat;
import static org.hamcrest.Matchers.*;
import static org.junit.Assume.assumeThat;

import java.math.BigDecimal;

import org.junit.experimental.theories.DataPoint;
import org.junit.experimental.theories.Theories;
import org.junit.experimental.theories.Theory;
import org.junit.runner.RunWith;

@RunWith(Theories.class)
public class TaxCalculatorTheoryTest {
```

```
    @DataPoint public static int YEAR_2007 = 2007;
    @DataPoint public static int YEAR_2008 = 2008;
    @DataPoint public static BigDecimal INCOME_1 = new BigDecimal(0.0);
    @DataPoint public static double INCOME_2 = 0.01;
    @DataPoint public static double INCOME_3 = 100.0;
    @DataPoint public static double INCOME_4 = 13999.99;
    @DataPoint public static double INCOME_5 = 14000.0;

    @SuppressWarnings("unchecked")
    @Theory
    public void lowTaxRateIsNineteenPercent(int year, double income) {
        assumeThat(year, is(2007));
        assumeThat(income, allOf(greaterThan(0.00),lessThan(14000.00)));

        TaxCalculator calculator = getTaxCalculator();
        double calculatedTax = calculator.calculateIncomeTax(year, income);
        double expectedIncome = calculatedTax * 1000/195;
        assertThat(expectedIncome, closeTo(income,0.001));
        System.out.println("Year: " + year + ", Income: " + income + ", Tax: "
        + calculatedTax);
    }

    private TaxCalculator getTaxCalculator() {
        return new TaxCalculatorImpl();
    }
}
```

Output from this test is:

```
Year: 2007, Income: 0.01, Tax: 0.0019500000000000001
Year: 2007, Income: 100.0, Tax: 19.5
Year: 2007, Income: 13999.99, Tax: 2729.99805
```

For simplicity, we are just using double values here. For a real business application, you would typically use a more precise type for the monetary values, such as `BigDecimal` or a dedicated `Money` class.

On failure of a test, a descriptive message includes details of the data points that caused the failure:

```
org.junit.experimental.theories.internal.ParameterizedAssertionError:
lowTaxRateIsNineteenPercent(2007, 0.01)
Caused by: java.lang.AssertionError:
    Expected: is <0.01>
    Got: is <0.0>
```

You can then add other theories to test other subsets of your test data. The applicable set of DataPoints, as constrained by the assumptions, will be applied to each Theory.

10.9 Using JUnit 4 with Maven 2

Maven 2 uses the Surefire plug-in to execute unit tests (see Section 2.13). The Surefire plug-in handles both JUnit 3 and JUnit 4 unit tests seamlessly: the test classes just need to be in the test directory and Maven will automatically detect and run them. You can even combine JUnit 3 and JUnit 4 tests in the same application. You run your unit tests in exactly the same way as you would any other tests in Maven, that is, by using the *mvn test* command:

```
$ mvn test
[INFO] Scanning for projects...
...
-------------------------------------------------------
 T E S T S
-------------------------------------------------------
...
Results :

Tests run: 68, Failures: 0, Errors: 0, Skipped: 0

[INFO] ------------------------------------------------------------------------
[INFO] BUILD SUCCESSFUL
[INFO] ------------------------------------------------------------------------
[INFO] Total time: 4 seconds
[INFO] Finished at: Tue Aug 14 22:28:51 GMT+12:00 2007
[INFO] Final Memory: 7M/67M
[INFO] ------------------------------------------------------------------------
```

This will run both your JUnit 3 and JUnit 4 tests, and generate the usual set of Surefire reports with the combined results of all your tests. This is very useful if you wish to use JUnit 4 features for your normal unit tests, but still benefit from the many excellent JUnit-3 based test libraries such as StrutsTestCase (see Chapter 19), the Spring MVC testing framework, or DBUnit.

10.10 Using JUnit 4 with Ant

JUnit 4 is poorly supported in any versions of Ant earlier than 1.7.0. From Ant 1.7.0 onward, however, JUnit 4 tests are fully supported and easy to configure. In this section, we will go through the steps of setting up, compiling, and running your JUnit 4 tests using Ant.

For completeness, we will go through the whole build file. Most of it will be straightforward to developers familiar with Ant (see Chapter 1). In the first part of the build file, we just define project directories and housekeeping tasks:

```
<project name="JUnit-Tests-Sample" default="runtests" basedir=".">
    <property name="junit.home"   value="/home/john/tools/junit4.1" />
    <property name="java.src"     value="src/main/java" />
    <property name="test.src"     value="src/test/java" />
    <property name="build.dir"    value="target" />
    <property name="java.classes" value="${build.dir}/classes" />
    <property name="test.classes" value="${build.dir}/test-classes" />
    <property name="test.reports" value="${build.dir}/test-reports" />

    <target name="init">
```

```
        <mkdir dir="${java.classes}"/>
        <mkdir dir="${test.classes}"/>
        <mkdir dir="${test.reports}"/>
    </target>

    <target name="clean">
        <delete dir="${build.dir}"/>
    </target>
```

Then, we define a task to compile our Java code:

```
    <target name="compile" depends="init" >
        <javac srcdir="${java.src}" destdir="${java.classes}" >
            <include name="**/*.java"/>
        </javac>
    </target>
```

Again, there is nothing special here: we are just compiling Java code using the standard Ant *<javac>* task. The next section, however, starts getting a little more interesting. Here, we set up a classpath that refers to the JUnit 4.1 JAR file and the application's compiled Java classes, and use it to compile the JUnit 4 unit tests. JUnit 4 is backward-compatible with JUnit 3, so unit tests written using the two APIs can comfortably live together in the same project without picking fights:

```
    <path id="test.classpath">
        <pathelement location="${junit.home}/junit-4.1.jar" />
        <pathelement location="${java.classes}" />
    </path>

    <target name="compiletests" depends="compile">
        <javac srcdir="${test.src}" destdir="${test.classes}">
            <classpath refid="test.classpath" />
            <include name="**/*.java"/>
        </javac>
    </target>
```

Now we are ready to actually run our unit tests. Ant 1.7.0 comes with a new and improved JUnit task that supports both JUnit 3 and JUnit 4 tests. A typical JUnit test task in Ant 1.7.0 looks like this:

```
    <target name="runtests" depends="compiletests">
        <junit printsummary="yes" haltonfailure="yes">
          <classpath>
              <path refid="test.classpath" />
              <pathelement location="${test.classes}"/>
          </classpath>

          <formatter type="plain"/>
          <formatter type="xml"/>

          <batchtest fork="yes" todir="${test.reports}">
            <fileset dir="${test.src}">
                <include name="**/*Test*.java"/>
```

```
            </fileset>
        </batchtest>
    </junit>
</target>
```

The first interesting item (for users of JUnit with previous versions of Ant) is the classpath entry. This is where you tell Ant where to find the JUnit 4 jar file. This is worth mentioning because, until Ant 1.6.5, you needed to place a copy of the *junit.jar* file in the Ant *lib* directory if you wanted the JUnit task to work. Although this quirk was documented in the Ant manual and officially declared "not a bug," it was messy at the best of times. However, as of Ant 1.7.0, you can simply declare your JUnit 4 JAR file in the nested classpath as shown here.

Next comes a list of formatter objects. Test results can be generated in several formats: *plain* generates simple text files, whereas *xml* results in more detailed test reports suitable for HTML report generation.

The actual tests are executed by the *<batchtest>* element, which runs all JUnit tests found in the specified fileset. No distinction is made between JUnit 3 and JUnit 4 unit tests.

When you invoke this target, you should get something like the following:

```
$ ant runtests
Buildfile: build.xml

init:

compile:
    [javac] Compiling 11 source files to
    /home/john/Documents/book/java-power-tools/src/sample-code/alexandria/target/classes

compiletests:
    [javac] Compiling 4 source files to
    /home/john/Documents/book/java-power-tools/src/sample-code/alexandria/target/
    test-classes

runtests:
    [junit] Running com.wakaleo.jpt.alexandria.domain.CatalogTest
    [junit] Tests run: 4, Failures: 0, Errors: 0, Time elapsed: 4.493 sec
    [junit] Running com.wakaleo.jpt.alexandria.domain.LegacyJUnit3CatalogTest
    [junit] Tests run: 4, Failures: 0, Errors: 0, Time elapsed: 0.041 sec
    [junit] Running com.wakaleo.jpt.alexandria.services.PriceCalculatorTest
    [junit] Tests run: 3, Failures: 0, Errors: 0, Time elapsed: 0.048 sec
    [junit] Running com.wakaleo.jpt.alexandria.services.TaxCalculatorTest
    [junit] Tests run: 8, Failures: 0, Errors: 0, Time elapsed: 0.054 sec

BUILD SUCCESSFUL
```

10.11 Selectively Running JUnit 4 Tests in Ant

The Ant JUnit task is a flexible tool, and you can use it to pick and choose which unit tests you want to run at a particular time. This section discusses various techniques you can use to do this.

Running Individual Tests

The usual way to run your unit tests is *en masse*, using the *<batchtest>* element. However, you can run individual tests, using the *<test>* element:

```
<target name="runtest" depends="compiletests">
    <junit printsummary="yes" haltonfailure="yes">
        ...
        <test name="com.wakaleo.jpt.alexandria.domain.CatalogTest"/>
    </junit>
</target>
```

Invoking this target runs only the unit tests found in this class:

```
$ ant runtest
Buildfile: build.xml

init:

compile:

compiletests:

runtest:
    [junit] Running com.wakaleo.jpt.alexandria.domain.CatalogTest
    [junit] Tests run: 4, Failures: 0, Errors: 0, Time elapsed: 9.02 sec

BUILD SUCCESSFUL
```

In this situation, you may well want to exclude this test from your main unit tests, using an *<exclude>* element as shown here:

```
<target name="runtests" depends="compiletests">
    <junit printsummary="yes" haltonfailure="yes">
      ...
      <batchtest fork="yes" todir="${test.reports}">
        <fileset dir="${test.src}">
            <include name="**/*Test*.java"/>
            <exclude name="**/CatalogTest.java"/>
        </fileset>
      </batchtest>
    </junit>
</target>
```

Running Tests Conditionally

In some cases, you may prefer *not* to run all of your test classes each time you run your normal unit tests. Some types of tests—such as load tests, integration tests and performance tests—can be time-consuming, and need not be run each time you recompile your application. Developer unit tests should be kept short and snappy, and the slower, more processor-intensive tests should only be run when needed. The latter tests are typically run only on request on the developer's machines but systematically on the integration server.

One way to do this is to use the *if* attribute of the *<batchtest>* element. This attribute specifies a property that must be set for the unit tests to run; otherwise, they are simply skipped.

The following target will be run only if the *perftests* property is set:

```
<target name="runperftests" depends="compiletests">
    <junit printsummary="yes" haltonfailure="yes">
      ...
      <batchtest fork="yes" todir="${test.reports}" if="perftests">
        <fileset dir="${test.src}">
            <include name="**/*PerfTest*.java"/>
        </fileset>
      </batchtest>
    </junit>
</target>
```

The performance tests will never be run unless this property is set, even if the target is called by name:

```
$ ant runperftests
Buildfile: build.xml

init:

compile:

compiletests:

runperftests:

BUILD SUCCESSFUL
Total time: 1 second
```

However, if you set the *perftests* property (to any value: it doesn't matter), the performance tests will be *correctly* executed. You can set properties in a number of ways: explicitly in the build file, in a properties file that is loaded into the build script using the *<property>* task, or simply from the command line:

```
$ ant runperftests -Dperftests=true
Buildfile: build.xml

init:
```

```
compile:

compiletests:

runperftests:
    [junit] Running com.wakaleo.jpt.alexandria.domain.CatalogPerfTest
    [junit] Tests run: 4, Failures: 0, Errors: 0, Time elapsed: 7.227 sec
    [junit] Running com.wakaleo.jpt.alexandria.services.PriceCalculatorPerfTest
    [junit] Tests run: 3, Failures: 0, Errors: 0, Time elapsed: 0.192 sec

BUILD SUCCESSFUL
```

One typically uses this command-line property uniquely on the integration server: performance and integration tests will only be run here, and not repeatedly on every developer's machine.

If you use this technique, don't forget to exclude these tests from the main unit test run using the *<exclude>* element discussed above.

10.12 Integration Tests

Unit tests should be short and snappy, and give a quick turnaround time. Unit tests shouldn't use external resources such as databases or web application frameworks. To do this, you often use interfaces, mock objects, and a variety of other techniques to ensure that you are testing each component in isolation.

However, you will need to see how the components fit together at some point. This point is called the "integration tests" phase. Here, you might test your Hibernate-based DAOs against a real database (as opposed to an embedded one), run queries that go all the way from the service layer to the database and back, or simulate a user's web browser using a tool like Selenium. You might also want to see how the application holds up under load, or with many simultaneous requests. These tests are vitally important, but they would slow things down far too much if they had to be run every time a developer runs through the ordinary unit tests. Slow unit tests discourage developers from testing, so you need a way to distinguish fast unit tests from the slower integration tests.

In Maven, you can configure the Surefire plug-in to determine what tests are run during the unit tests phase (when you run *mvn test*), and which ones are run during the integration tests (when you run *mvn integration-test*). In the following example, integration tests have names that end in "IntegrationTest." This is a simple, arbitrary convention: you can, of course, define your own. The following configuration excludes the integration tests from the ordinary unit tests (associated with the "test" phase), and attaches them to the "integration-test" phase instead:

```
<project>
  ...
  <build>
```

```
        <plugins>
          <plugin>
            <artifactId>maven-surefire-plugin</artifactId>
            <executions>
              <execution>
                <id>unit-tests</id>
                <phase>test</phase>
                <goals>
                  <goal>test</goal>
                </goals>
                <configuration>
                  <excludes>
                      <exclude>**/*IntegrationTest.java</exclude>
                  </excludes>
                </configuration>
              </execution>
              <execution>
                <id>integration-tests</id>
                <phase>integration-test</phase>
                <goals>
                  <goal>test</goal>
                </goals>
                <configuration>
                  <includes>
                      <include>**/*IntegrationTest.java</include>
                  </includes>
                </configuration>
              </execution>
            </executions>
          </plugin>
        </plugins>
      </build>
      ...
    </project>
```

Then, to run your performance tests, just invoke the integration test phase:

```
$ mvn integration-test
```

10.13 Using JUnit 4 in Eclipse

Working from within your IDE is probably the easiest and most productive way to run your unit tests. JUnit 4 integrates extremely smoothly with Eclipse: you run JUnit 4 tests in exactly the same way as for JUnit 3 tests, by using "Run As...JUnit Test." If you are using Java 5-style asserts, you will also need to place the *-ea* ("enable assertions") option in the Run configuration screen (see Figure 10-1). Otherwise, your asserts will simply be ignored.

Eclipse even handles JUnit 4-specific features such parameterized tests correctly (see Figure 10-2).

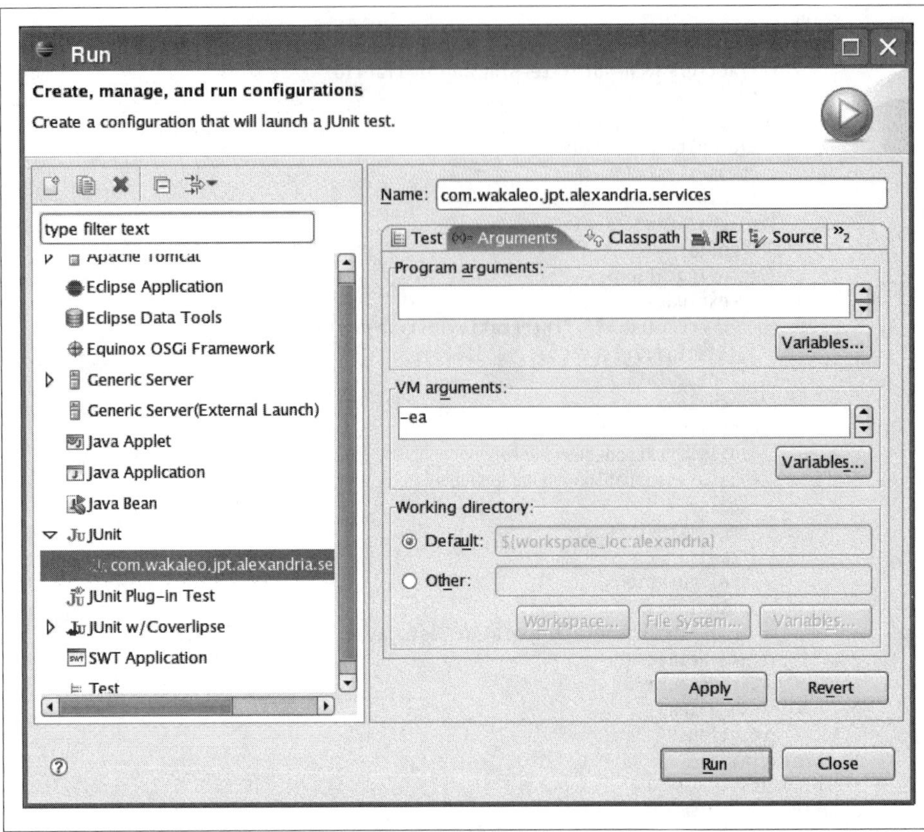

Figure 10-1. Configuring JUnit 4 test runs to use assert operations

You can also create new JUnit4 test cases easily in Eclipse by selecting "New...JUnit Unit Test" (see Figure 10-3). This dialog box lets you create either JUnit 3.8 or JUnit 4 test classes (you can uses both types of unit tests simultaneously in the same project).

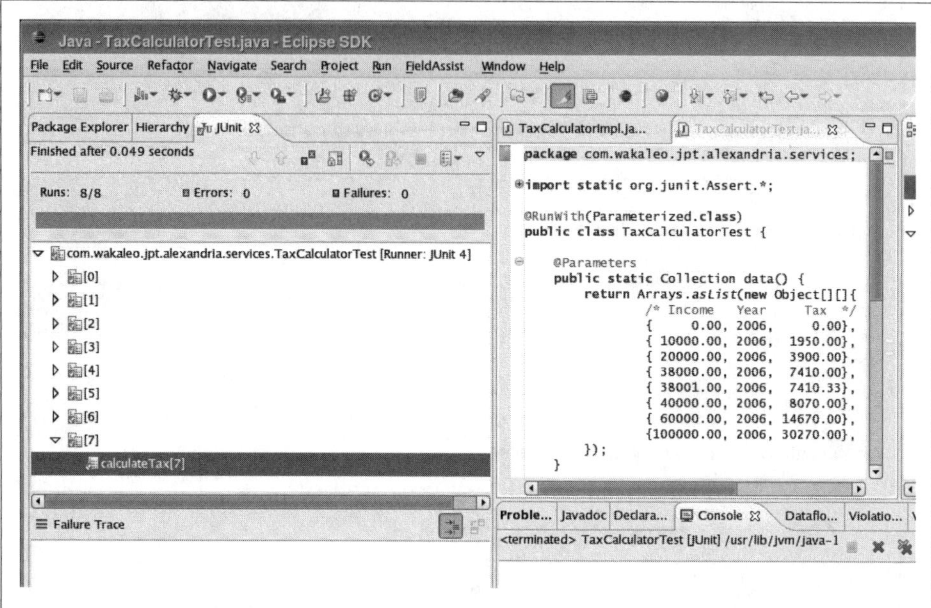

Figure 10-2. Running JUnit4 tests in Eclipse

Figure 10-3. Creating a new JUnit4 test in Eclipse

CHAPTER 11

Next-Generation Testing with TestNG

11.1 Introducing TestNG

TestNG is an innovative unit test framework, written by Cédric Beust and Alexandru Popescu, designed to overcome many of the perceived shortcomings of JUnit 3 (see Section 10.1). Like JUnit 4, TestNG improves on JUnit 3 in many ways, removing syntactical constraints and adding flexible, nonintrusive annotation-based testing. In addition, TestNG also supports many powerful features such as test groups, dependencies, and parallel testing—features that are not yet supported by JUnit 4 at the time of this writing. TestNG integrates well with IDEs such as Eclipse and build tools like Ant and Maven. All of these features make it easier to write better-designed, faster and more flexible unit tests.

11.2 Creating Simple Unit Tests with TestNG

Before discussing the more advanced features of TestNG, we will take a quick introductory tour. Let's look at how to get started with TestNG.

TestNG classes are ordinary Java classes with ordinary methods: They don't have to extend a particular class, nor do their methods have to follow any particular naming convention. You simply use the *@Test* annotation to flag unit test methods, and use Java 5 *asserts* to test calculated values against expected ones. Throughout this chapter, we will use the example of a class that calculates GST (goods and services tax, also known as a value added tax in some countries), which we introduced in Section 10.1. This class is supposed to calculate the net price of something, taking into account the current GST rate. Suppose that the standard GST rate is 12.5 percent. Our unit test class might look like this:

```
import org.testng.annotations.Test;

public class PriceCalculatorTests {

@Test
public void calculateGST() {
```

```
        PriceCalculator calculator = new PriceCalculator();
        double amountWithGst = calculator.calculateGST(100.00);
        assert (112.50 == amountWithGst) : "Standard GST should be 12.5%";
    }
}
```

You may prefer the old JUnit 3 assert methods (**assertEquals()**, and so on). TestNG via also supports these by using static imports. This approach is also used by JUnit 4 (see Section 10.2).

```
import org.testng.annotations.Test;
import static org.testng.Assert.assertEquals;

public class PriceCalculatorTests {

    @Test
    public void calculateGST() {
        PriceCalculator calculator = new PriceCalculator();
        double amountWithGst = calculator.calculateGST(100.00);
        assertEquals("Standard GST should be 12.5%", amountWithGst, 112.50 , 0.0);
    }
}
```

Test frameworks generally let you define code that needs to be run before every test. In JUnit 3.x, you override the `setUp()` and `tearDown()` methods. TestNG comes with a rich set of annotations for different types of fixture code (see Section 11.7). In the following example, we use the *@BeforeMethod* annotation to ensure that the `init()` method is called before each and every test case. Conversely, we use the *@AfterMethod* annotation to make sure the `tidyUp()` function is called after each test:

```
import org.testng.annotations.Test;
import static org.testng.Assert.assertEquals;

public class PriceCalculatorTests {

    PriceCalculator calculator = new PriceCalculator();

    @BeforeMethod
    public void init() {
        calculator = new PriceCalculator();
    }

    @Test
    public void calculateGST() {
        double amountWithGst = calculator.calculateGST(100.00);
        assertEquals("Standard GST should be 12.5%", amountWithGst, 112.50 , 0.0);
    }

    @AfterMethod
        public void tidyUp() {
        ...
    }
}
```

There are several ways to run TestNG tests. You can run it directly from the command line, but this option is not very practical for anything other than toy examples. You can also run TestNG tests directly from within Eclipse using the TestNG plug-in (see Section 11.4). Or you can integrate them into your build environment using Ant (see Section 11.5) or Maven (see Section 11.6). When you run a set of TestNG tests, it produces a report similar to the traditional JUnit reports, although, like JUnit 4 and unlike JUnit 3.x, no distinction is made between failed assertions and exceptions. The following listing is an example of running TestNG using the Ant task:

```
$ ant test
...
test:
[testng] [Parser] Running:
...
[testng] PASSED: findHotelsInCity
[testng] PASSED: calculateGST
[testng] PASSED: calculateReducedGST
[testng] PASSED: calculateStandardGST

[testng] ===============================================
[testng]     Ant test
[testng]     Tests run: 1037, Failures: 0, Skips: 0
[testng] ===============================================

[testng] ===============================================
[testng] Ant suite
[testng] Total tests run: 1037, Failures: 0, Skips: 0
[testng] ===============================================
```

This is just a quick overview of TestNG tests, which should let you get the feel of the API. There are many other annotations and features, such as groups and dependencies, which we will investigate later on in this chapter.

11.3 Defining TestNG Test Suites

Traditionally, TestNG unit tests are generally organized into test suites. In TestNG, a test suite is a logical set of tests that you expect to run together. You define TestNG test suites using a TestNG configuration file, an XML configuration file that tells TestNG how your tests are organized and where it needs to look for them. This is a little more complicated than a JUnit test configuration, where, if you are using Maven (see Section 11.6) or Ant (see Section 11.5), you can get away with just writing test classes and placing them in the test source code directory, without having to set up a TestNG configuration file. But it's sometimes worth the extra effort of using TestNG configuration files for the flexibility and readability it gives you.

Here is a simple test suite configuration file. Here, we simply list the test classes we want to test:

```
<!DOCTYPE suite SYSTEM "http://testng.org/testng-1.0.dtd" >
```

```
<suite name="Suite" verbose="2" >
    <test name="Domain tests" annotations="JDK">
      <classes>
        <class name="com.wakaleo.jpt.hotel.domain.PriceCalculatorTests"/>
        <class name="com.wakaleo.jpt.hotel.domain.HotelTests"/>
        <class name="com.wakaleo.jpt.hotel.domain.CityTest"/>
        <class name="com.wakaleo.jpt.hotel.domain.CountryTest"/>
      </classes>
    </test>
</suite>
```

TestNG supports both Java 5 annotations and the older Javadoc-style annotations for JDK 1-4. The annotations="JDK" attribute in the previous listing indicates that we are working with Java 5 annotations, which is what we will use throughout the rest of this chapter.

You can also specify a list of packages rather than a list of classes, which will run all the tests contained in the specified package:

```
<suite name="Suite" verbose="2" >
    <test name="Domain tests" annotations="JDK">
      <packages>
          <package name="com.wakaleo.jpt.hotel.domain" />
      </packages>
    </test>
</suite>
```

To make things even simpler, you can use wildcard characters in package and class names. The following test suite includes any classes in any packages directly or indirectly contained in the `com.wakaleo.jpt` package:

```
<suite name="Suite" verbose="2" >
    <test name="Application tests" annotations="JDK">
        <packages>
            <package name="com.wakaleo.jpt.*" />
        </packages>
    </test>
</suite>
```

Using configuration files in TestNG is not obligatory. In many cases, it is more convenient to run TestNG against a set of classes, using test groups if necessary to decide which tests should or should not be executed (see Section 11.8), which you can do fairly easily in Ant or directly from Eclipse (see Section 11.4). However, configuration files are sometimes useful to organize your tests in a clear and readable manner.

11.4 The TestNG Eclipse Plug-In

One of the most effective ways to run unit tests is from within an IDE such as Eclipse or NetBeans. This approach allows a more seamless development process and a tighter testing cycle. At the time of this writing, TestNG plug-ins exist for Eclipse and IntelliJ. In this section, we will look at how to install and use the Eclipse TestNG plug-in. This

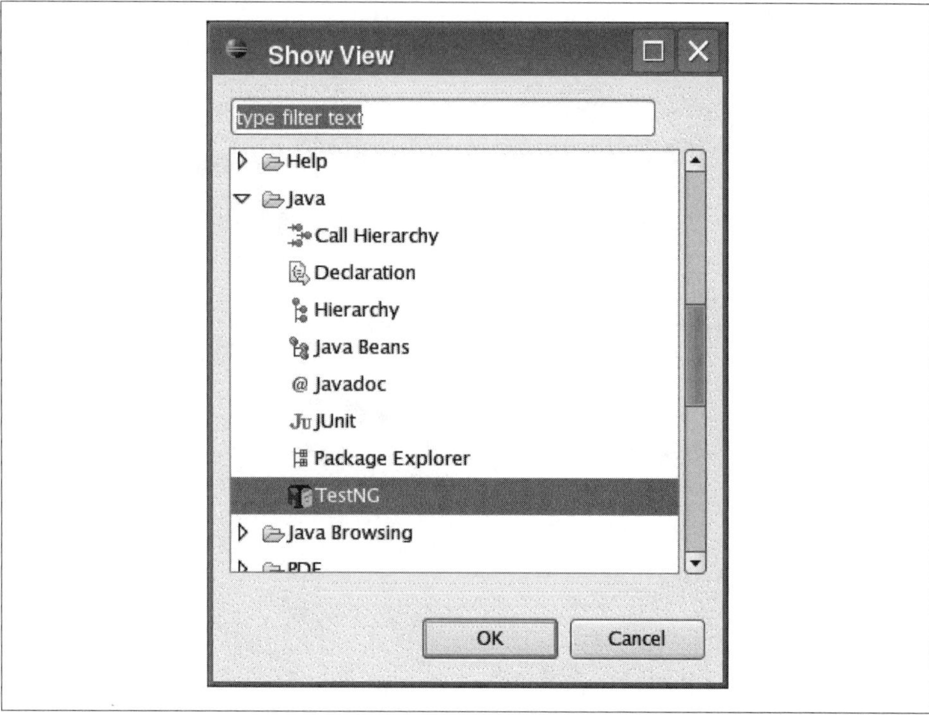

Figure 11-1. Opening the TestNG view in Eclipse

excellent piece of software provides invaluable tools for writing, maintaining, and running your TestNG test cases from within Eclipse.

Installing the TestNG Plug-In

You install the TestNG plug-in from the Remote Update site in the usual way:

1. Open the "Install/Update" window (Help→Software updates→Find and Install) and select "Search for new features to install."
2. Create a "New Remote Site."
3. Enter *http://beust.com/eclipse* for the URL and "TestNG Plugin" (or some other appropriate name) for the name.
4. Make sure the "TestNG Plugin" checkbox is checked in the site list, and click "Finish."
5. In the next window, check the "TestNG" box in the features to install, and step through the installation process.

Once you have finished, you may need to restart Eclipse. You can verify the installation by opening the TestNG view (Windows→Show View→Other...), as shown in Figure 11-1. This will open the TestNG dashboard at the bottom of the screen.

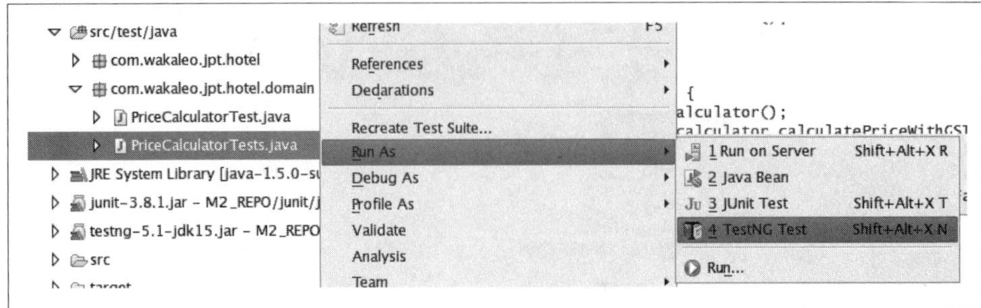

Figure 11-2. Running TestNG tests in Eclipse

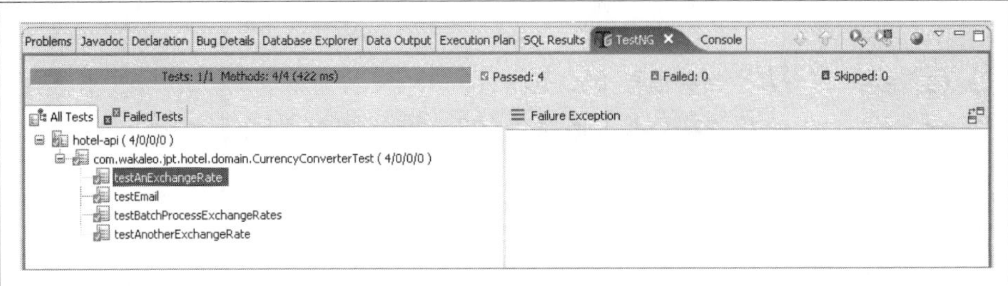

Figure 11-3. TestNG test results in Eclipse

Running TestNG Tests

Running a TestNG test class, or an individual TestNG-annotated unit test in Eclipse is intuitive and easy, and very similar to what you would do for a JUnit test case: just select the class or method in the Outline view and select "Run As→TestNG Test" in the contextual menu (see Figure 11-2). This will run the corresponding tests and display the results in the Console view and in the TestNG results view (see Figure 11-3). If you want to step through the code using the IDE debugging perspective, select "Debug As→TestNG Test" instead.

Running multiple tests is a bit more involved. One way is to use a test suite (see Section 11.3). First of all, you need a TestNG configuration file which defines the tests you want to run. Then, just select the configuration file in the Outline view, and select "Run As→TestNG Suite" in the contextual menu. This will run all of the tests defined in this test suite.

When you execute TestNG tests in Eclipse, either by running the tests in an individual class or by executing the tests defined in a test suite, TestNG will display the test results in the TestNG view at the bottom of the screen (see Figure 11-3).

Another way to run multiple tests is to use TestNG run configurations. You can set up run configurations to also configure TestNG in Eclipse to run a particular group (or groups) of tests. Test groups (see Section 11.8) are a particularly useful way of organ-

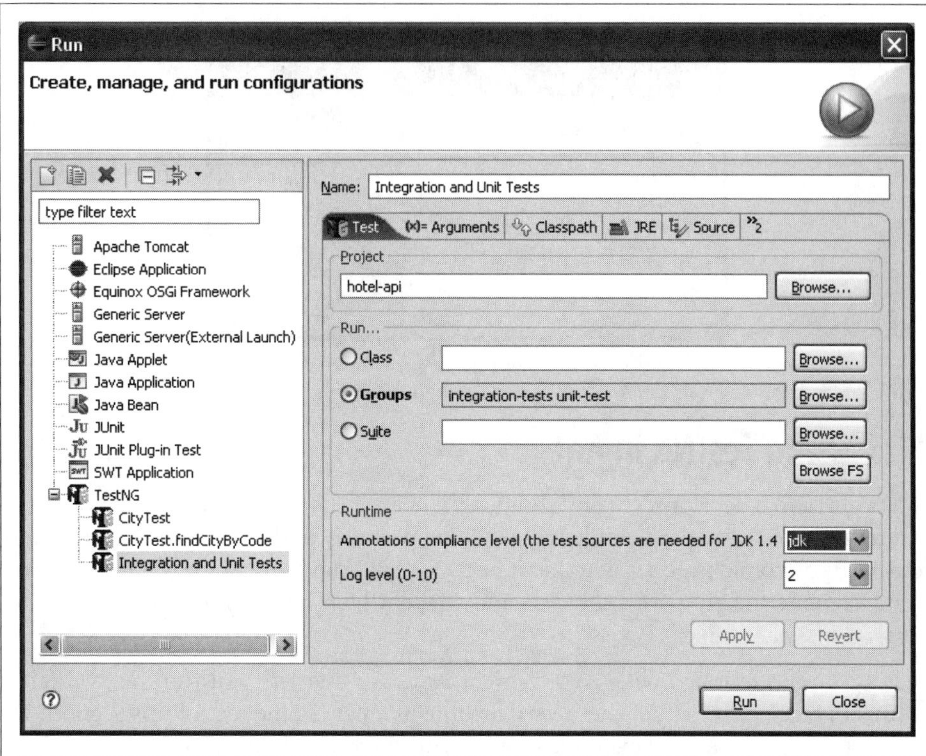

Figure 11-4. Setting up a TestNG Run Configuration

izing your unit tests into meaningful subsets, which can be run at different times or under different circumstances. To run all of the tests in a group, you need to set up a new Test Configuration. Open the Configuration Management window ("Run As→Run") and create a new TestNG configuration (see Figure 11-4). From here, you can set up a configuration to run a particular unit test class, group or groups, or test suite. The Browse buttons make it easy to select the various test objects. Browsing for classes will list all known TestNG classes (that is, all classes containing TestNG-annotated test methods). Browsing the groups lets you select from the known test groups defined within the project (see Figure 11-5). And browsing for Suites will list all the known test suite configuration files within the current projects.

Run configurations are a useful and reasonably flexible way to identify a given set of tests that you need to run repeatedly. This can be useful to separate quick-running unit tests from heavier integration tests, or to factor out performance tests, for example. Once you have finished setting up your run configuration, you can easily come back and run (or debug) it again at any time.

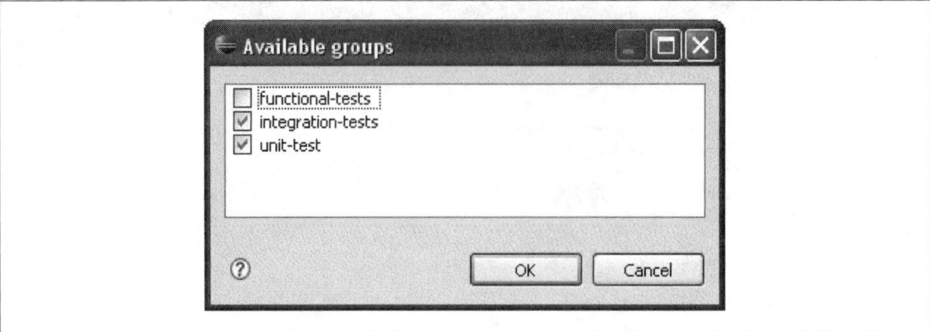

Figure 11-5. Selecting groups in a TestNG Run Configuration

11.5 Using TestNG in Ant

In a professional development environment, it is important to be able to run your tests in a reproducible and predictable manner. The best way to do this is to integrate your tests into your build process, whether it be using Ant, Maven, or some other build tool. TestNG works neatly with both Ant and Maven. Here we will look at how to use TestNG in Ant.

TestNG comes bundled with a convenient Ant task that lets you run TestNG tests, groups of tests, or test suites, in a very flexible manner. In the rest of this section, we will go through a practical example of what you can do with this task.

You define the TestNG task in a fairly standard manner, using the Ant *<taskdef>* task and indicating the location of the TestNG JAR file. In this example, I installed TestNG 5.3 in the */usr/local/testng* directory, and we are interested in the JDK 1.5 version of TestNG. So we could set up the Ant *<taskdef>* as follows:

```
<!-- TestNG resources  -->
<property name="testng.home"  value="/usr/local/testng" />
<property name="jdk15.testng.jar"  value="${testng.home}/testng-5.5-jdk15.jar" />

<taskdef resource="testngtasks"  classpath="${jdk15.testng.jar}"/>
```

The *<taskdef>* instruction defines the *<testng>* task, which you can use to run your unit tests in a number of ways. First, however, you need to compile your classes and test classes in the usual way. In a real-world Ant project, the way you would do this can vary quite a bit, particularly with regards to directory structures. For completeness, an example of these tasks is shown here. The directory structure is represented by Ant properties: *java.src* is the root directory containing the application source code; *test.src* is the root directory containing the unit test source code; *java.classes* and *test.classes* contain the compiled application classes and unit tests, respectively:

```
<target name="init" description="Create required work directories">
    <mkdir dir="${java.classes}"/>
    <mkdir dir="${test.classes}"/>
```

```
        <mkdir dir="${test.reports}"/>
    </target>

    <target name="compile" depends="init" description="Compile application classes">
        <javac srcdir="${java.src}" destdir="${java.classes}" includes="**/*.java" />
    </target>

    <path id="tests.classpath">
        <pathelement location="${jdk15.testng.jar}" />
        <pathelement location="${java.classes}" />
    </path>

    <target name="compiletests" depends="compile" description="Compile test classes">
        <javac srcdir="${test.src}" destdir="${test.classes}"
               classpathref="tests.classpath" includes="**/*.java" />
    </target>

    <path id="runtests.classpath">
        <path refid="tests.classpath"/>
        <pathelement location="${test.classes}" />
    </path>
```

This last classpath (*runtests.classpath*) is the one that we are going to use with the TestNG task. It contains, logically enough, all of the compiled application classes, test classes, dependencies, and the TestNG JAR file. Now we are ready to run our TestNG unit tests. The TestNG Ant task is flexible, and you can use it in many ways. The easiest way to get started is simply to run TestNG against a set of Java files. This is very easy to set up: all you need to define is the classpath that we set up earlier, and an output directory in which the test result reports will be generated (defined here by the *test.reports* property). Lots of other options are available: we also set the *verbose* attribute to see more details on the console, and we set the *haltonfailure* attribute to "true" to force the build to halt if there is a unit test failure:

```
<target name="runtests" depends="compiletests" description="Run TestNG unit tests">
    <testng classpathref="runtests.classpath" outputDir="${test.reports}"
            verbose="2" haltonfailure="true">
        <classfileset dir="${test.classes}" includes="**/*.class" />
    </testng>
</target>
```

Note that here you don't need to define a *TestNG* configuration file: TestNG will figure out which classes contain unit tests by itself just fine. Let's take it for a spin:

```
$ ant runtests
Buildfile: build.xml
...
runtests:
[testng] [Parser] Running:
[testng]   Ant suite

[testng] PASSED: findCityByCode
[testng] PASSED: loadCity
[testng] PASSED: saveCity
[testng] PASSED: findCityByName
```

```
[testng] PASSED: findCountryByCode
[testng] PASSED: loadCountry
[testng] PASSED: loadHotel
...
[testng] java.lang.AssertionError
[testng]     at com.wakaleo.jpt.hotel.domain.CountryTest.findCountryByName...
[testng] ... Removed 21 stack frames
[testng] FAILED: saveCountry
[testng] java.lang.AssertionError
[testng]     at com.wakaleo.jpt.hotel.domain.CountryTest.saveCountry...
[testng] ... Removed 21 stack frames

[testng] ===============================================
[testng]     Ant test
[testng]     Tests run: 22, Failures: 2, Skips: 0
[testng] ===============================================


[testng] ===============================================
[testng] Ant suite
[testng] Total tests run: 22, Failures: 2, Skips: 0
[testng] ===============================================


BUILD SUCCESSFUL
Total time: 1 second
```

This task runs every TestNG-compatible unit test in the test class directory, and sends JUnit-style output to the console. It also generates HTML reports that can be sent by email or displayed on a project web site (see Figure 11-6). Although not particularly pretty, these reports are pragmatic and to the point. For example, any failed tests are listed at the top, because presumably that's what the developer will be looking for first.

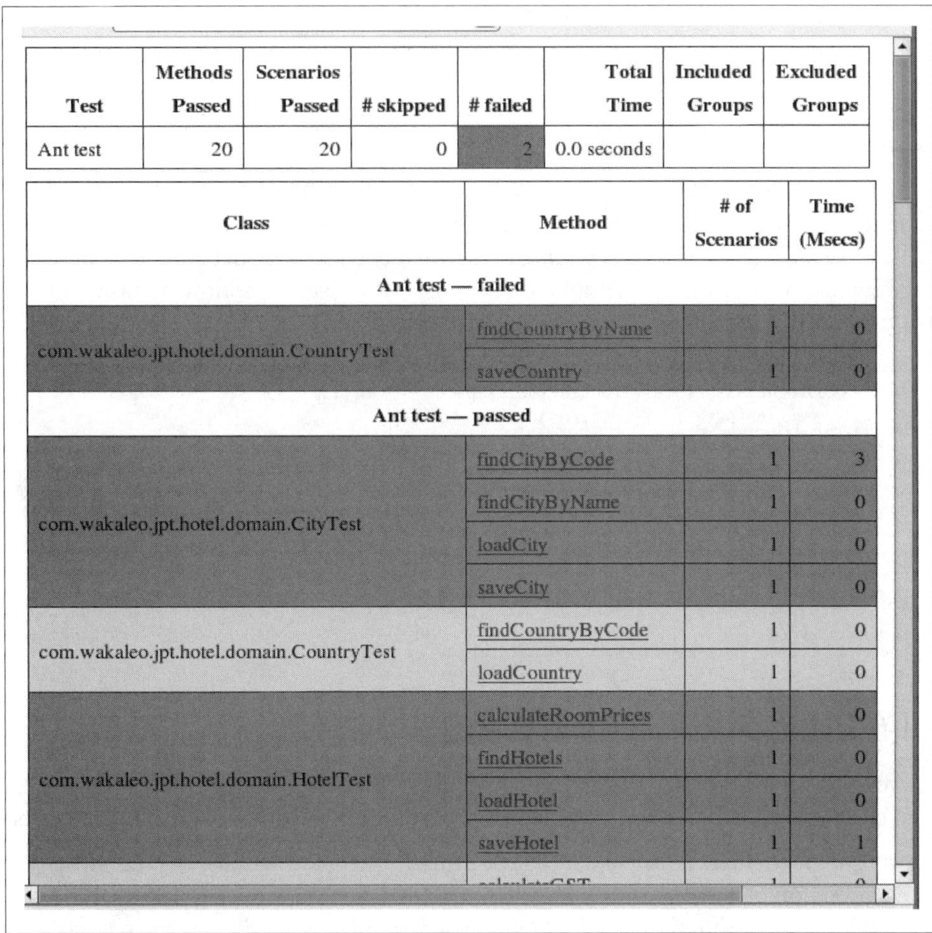

Test	Methods Passed	Scenarios Passed	# skipped	# failed	Total Time	Included Groups	Excluded Groups
Ant test	20	20	0	2	0.0 seconds		

Class	Method	# of Scenarios	Time (Msecs)
Ant test — failed			
com.wakaleo.jpt.hotel.domain.CountryTest	findCountryByName	1	0
	saveCountry	1	0
Ant test — passed			
com.wakaleo.jpt.hotel.domain.CityTest	findCityByCode	1	3
	findCityByName	1	0
	loadCity	1	0
	saveCity	1	0
com.wakaleo.jpt.hotel.domain.CountryTest	findCountryByCode	1	0
	loadCountry	1	0
com.wakaleo.jpt.hotel.domain.HotelTest	calculateRoomPrices	1	0
	findHotels	1	0
	loadHotel	1	0
	saveHotel	1	1

Figure 11-6. A TestNG report generated by the TestNG Ant plugin

If you prefer to use a TestNG configuration file (or even several!), you can do that, too. Just use the *<xmlfileset>* nested element to tell TestNG which configuration files you want to use, as shown here:

```
<target name="runtests" depends="compiletests" description="Run TestNG unit tests">
    <testng classpathref="runtests.classpath" outputDir="${test.reports}"
            verbose="2" haltonfailure="true">
        <xmlfileset dir="src/test/resources" includes="testng.xml"/>
    </testng>
</target>
```

The TestNG task is very flexible and you can choose which tests to run in a variety of ways. For example, you can also run all the TestNG tests in a particular group or set of groups (see Section 11.8), and/or exclude a group or set of groups, by using the *groups* or *excludedgroups* parameters:

```
<target name="unit-tests" depends="compiletests">
    <testng classpathref="runtests.classpath" outputDir="${test.reports}" verbose="2"
            haltonfailure="true" groups="unit">
        <classfileset dir="${test.classes}" includes="**/*.class"  />
    </testng>
</target>
```

Or you can run a set of tests simultaneously on several threads using the *parallel* parameter (see Section 11.10), in order to test thread-safety or simulate load. Methods will be executed in parallel on separate threads (except tests with dependencies between them, which will be run in the same thread). For example, the following task will run the unit tests of the group "web" in separate, parallel threads:

```
<target name="loadtests" depends="compiletests" description="Run TestNG unit tests">
    <testng classpathref="runtests.classpath"
            outputDir="${test.reports}"
            verbose="2"
            haltonfailure="true"
            parallel="methods"
            groups="web">
        <classfileset dir="${test.classes}" includes="**/*.class"  />
    </testng>
</target>
```

11.6 Using TestNG with Maven 2

Maven (or, more precisely, Surefire) recognizes TestNG test cases. In other words, Maven should pick up TestNG tests in exactly the same way as JUnit 3 and JUnit 4 tests.

TestNG dependencies in Maven are a little quirky. There are actually two distributions of each version of TestNG: one compiled for JDK 1.5, and one compiled for JDK 1.4. The APIs are quite different: the first uses Java 5 annotations, whereas the second uses the old javadoc-style annotations.

In the Maven repository, the TestNG 5.1 jars (the latest at the time of this writing) are called *testng-5.1-jdk15.jar* and *testng-5.1-jdk14.jar*, for JDK 1.5 and JDK 1.4, respectively. When you add a TestNG dependency to your Maven POM file, you need to specify which version you need, using the *<classifier>* element. In the following example, we are using TestNG 5.1, compiled for JDK 1.5:

```
<dependencies>
    ...
    <dependency>
    <groupId>org.testng</groupId>
    <artifactId>testng</artifactId>
    <version>5.1</version>
    <classifier>jdk15</classifier>
    <scope>test</scope>
    </dependency>
```

```
    ...
</dependencies>
```

11.7 Managing the Test Lifecycle

When you write unit tests for real-world applications, you often find yourself writing a lot of supporting code, which is generally designed to prepare a clean, predicable test environment for your tests to run in, and to tidy up afterward. This code is often referred to as "fixture" code. Writing this code well is crucial to successful, efficient testing, and it often represents a sizeable and time-consuming part of your test classes. TestNG provides a powerful set of annotations that let you write flexible fixture code that can be executed at various moments during the test lifecycle.

Unit testing frameworks such as TestNG or JUnit are designed to run your tests in an organized, predictable manner. The test lifecycle defines the way and the order in which your test classes are instantiated and your unit tests executed. Understanding the test lifecycle can help you write better, faster, and more maintainable unit tests.

TestNG gives you a great deal of control over the test lifecycle. You can define methods which are executed at virtually any point in the unit test lifecycle: before and after the unit tests themselves, but also before and after executing the tests in a particular class or in a test suite. You can also set up methods which must be run before and after tests in a given group (see Section 11.8) are executed. In this section, we will look at how to use these fixture annotations to improve the quality and speed of your unit tests.

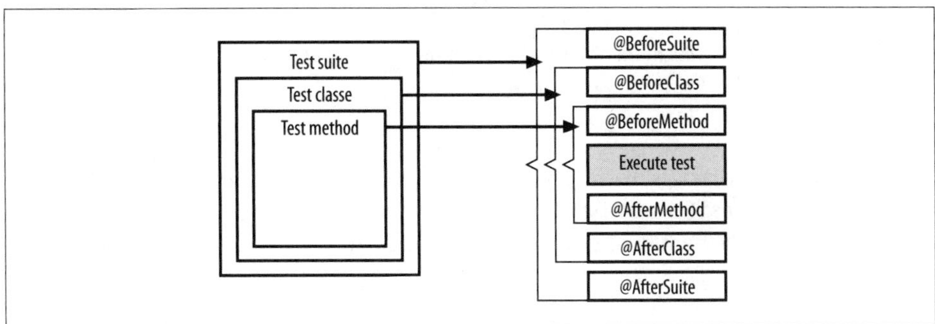

Figure 11-7. The TestNG test lifecycle and corresponding annotations

In TestNG, tests are organized into Test Suites. Each Test Suite is made up of test classes, which contain a number of unit tests, encoded within some test methods. TestNG provides annotations that let you insert fixture code before and after each of these components (see Figure 11-7).

Let's look at a some concrete examples.

One of the main uses of fixture code is to prepare a clean test environment for each unit test. In TestNG, methods tagged with the *@BeforeTest* and *@AfterTest* annotations will be executed before and after *each* unit test, respectively. This is the equivalent to the good old `setUp()` and `tearDown()` methods in JUnit 3.x, or the *@Before* annotation in JUnit 4. For example, suppose we need to set up some test data before doing each test. And, as good citizens, after each test we want to release any open database connections. We could do this using the *@BeforeMethod* and *@AfterMethod* annotations, as follows:

```
public class DataAccessTest {
    ...

    @BeforeMethod
    public void prepareTestData() {
        System.out.println("@BeforeMethod: prepareTestData");
        resetTestData();
    }

    @Test
    public void testSomething() {
        System.out.println("@Test: testSomething");
        ...
    }

    @Test
    public void testSomethingElse() {
        System.out.println("@Test: testSomethingElse");
        ...
    }

    @AfterMethod
    public void tidyUpAfterTest() {
        System.out.println("@AfterMethod: tidyUpAfterTest");
        releaseConnections();
    }
}
```

So, the `prepareTestData()` method will be run before every unit test, and in the same way, `tidyUpAfterTest()` will be run after each unit test. I've added a few messy `System.out.println`s here, just to illustrate the order in which the methods are called:

```
$ ant runtests
Buildfile: build.xml
...
runtests:
[testng] [Parser] Running:
[testng]   .../src/sample-code/hotel-api/src/test/resources/testng.xml

[testng] @BeforeMethod: prepareTestData
[testng] @Test: testSomethingElse
[testng] @AfterMethod: tidyUpAfterTest
[testng] @BeforeMethod: prepareTestData
[testng] @Test: testSomething
```

```
[testng] @AfterMethod: tidyUpAfterTest
[testng] PASSED: testSomethingElse
[testng] PASSED: testSomething

[testng] ===============================================
[testng]     GST tests
[testng]     Tests run: 2, Failures: 0, Skips: 0
[testng] ===============================================


[testng] ===============================================
[testng] Suite
[testng] Total tests run: 2, Failures: 0, Skips: 0
[testng] ===============================================


BUILD SUCCESSFUL
Total time: 1 second
```

One important detail is that within a lifecycle phase, methods are run in an arbitrary order. For example, `testSomethingElse()` is executed before `testSomething()`. This isn't usually an issue, as good unit tests should be independent. However, if you had several *@BeforeMethods* or *@AfterMethods*, you couldn't predict their execution order either. There is a solution. If you really need one method to be executed before another, you can do this declaratively using dependencies (see Section 11.9).

Sometimes you need to initialize data only once for the whole class, or do housekeeping functions once all of the tests have been executed. In JUnit 3.x, you would generally resort to static variables or lazy-loading to do this. TestNG provides a more elegant solution. The *@BeforeClass* and *@AfterClass* annotations are used for methods that are executed once before any of the tests in this class are run and once after they have all finished, respectively. For example, imagine creating a class that handles currency conversions. In a production environment, exchange rates are downloaded from an external web service. In a test environment, we need to use a predictable set of exchange rates for our tests. Setting this up is potentially a time- and resource-consuming operation. We would like to do it just once, before any tests are run. We also need to shut down the converter object cleanly once and for all at the end of the tests. And, as in the previous example, we need to set up some test data before each unit test, and tidy up afterward. Our test class might look like this:

```
public class CurrencyConverterTest {

    ...
    @BeforeClass public void setupExchangeRateTestData() {
        System.out.println("@BeforeClass: setupExchangeRateTestData");
        ...
    }

    @AfterClass public void tidyUpEnvironment() {
        System.out.println("@AfterClass : tidyUpEnvironment");
        ...
```

```
    }

    @BeforeMethod public void prepareTestData() {
        System.out.println("@BeforeMethod: prepareTestData");
        ...
    }

    @Test
    public void testAnExchangeRate() {
        System.out.println("@Test: testAnExchangeRate");
        ...
    }

    @Test
    public void testAnotherExchangeRate() {
        System.out.println("@Test: testAnotherExchangeRate");
        ...
    }

    @AfterMethod
    public void tidyUpTestData() {
        System.out.println("@AfterMethod: tidyUp");
        ...
    }
    ...
}
```

When we run this test class, as expected, our `setupExchangeRateTestData()` method is run before any of the unit tests are executed, and close `DownExchangeRateService()` is executed once all the tests in the class have been completed:

```
$ ant runtests
Buildfile: build.xml
...
runtests:
[testng] [Parser] Running:
[testng]   .../src/sample-code/hotel-api/src/test/resources/testng.xml

[testng] @BeforeClass: setupExchangeRateTestData
[testng] @BeforeMethod: prepareTestData
[testng] @Test: testAnExchangeRate
[testng] @AfterMethod: tidyUpTestData
[testng] @BeforeMethod: prepareTestData
[testng] @Test: testAnotherExchangeRate
[testng] @AfterMethod: tidyUpTestData
[testng] @AfterClass : tidyUpEnvironment
[testng] PASSED: testAnExchangeRate
[testng] PASSED: testAnotherExchangeRate

[testng] ===============================================
[testng]     GST tests
[testng]     Tests run: 2, Failures: 0, Skips: 0
[testng] ===============================================
```

```
[testng] ===============================================
[testng] Suite
[testng] Total tests run: 2, Failures: 0, Skips: 0
[testng] ===============================================

BUILD SUCCESSFUL
Total time: 1 second
```

This is all useful stuff. However, TestNG lets you take fixtures even further! Suppose you need to use the currency converter service, initialized with the test data, in several other test classes in the same test suite. It would be nice to be able to initialize the test currency converter service just once, and only when these tests are run. TestNG provides annotations for this type of situation. *@BeforeSuite* and *@AfterSuite* methods are executed at the beginning and end of a test suite:

```
public class CurrencyConverterTest {
    ...
    @BeforeSuite public void setupTestExchangeRateService() {
        System.out.println("@BeforeSuite setupTestExchangeRateService");
    }
    @AfterSuite public void closeDownExchangeRateService() {
        System.out.println("@AfterSuite closeDownExchangeRateService");
    }
}
```

In the following example, we have added a second test class (`PriceCalculatorTest`) to the test suite. This test class contains unit tests (`calculateDomesticPrice()` and `calculateForeignPrice()`) that use the currency converter which we set up in the `CurrencyConverterTest` test class. The *@BeforeSuite* annotation lets us guarantee that the service will be correctly created and initialized whenever these tests are executed. Conversely, the *@AfterSuite* annotation is run after all of the test classes have been executed. This example now illustrates the full TestNG lifecycle:

```
$ ant runtests
Buildfile: build.xml
...
runtests:
[testng] [Parser] Running:
[testng]   .../src/sample-code/hotel-api/src/test/resources/testng.xml

[testng] @BeforeSuite setupTestExchangeRateService
[testng] @BeforeClass: setupExchangeRateTestData
[testng] @BeforeMethod: prepareTestData
[testng] @Test: testAnExchangeRate
[testng] @AfterMethod: tidyUpTestData
[testng] @BeforeMethod: prepareTestData
[testng] @Test: testAnotherExchangeRate
[testng] @AfterMethod: tidyUpTestData
[testng] @AfterClass : tidyUpEnvironment
[testng] @BeforeClass (PriceCalculatorTest)
[testng] @BeforeMethod
[testng] @Test calculateDomesticPrice
[testng] @AfterMethod
```

```
[testng] @BeforeMethod
[testng] @Test calculateForeignPrice
[testng] @AfterMethod
[testng] @AfterClass (PriceCalculatorTest)
[testng] PASSED: testAnExchangeRate
[testng] PASSED: testAnotherExchangeRate
[testng] PASSED: calculateReducedGST
[testng] PASSED: calculateStandardGST


[testng] ===============================================
[testng]     GST tests
[testng]     Tests run: 4, Failures: 0, Skips: 0
[testng] ===============================================

[testng] @AfterSuite closeDownExchangeRateService

[testng] ===============================================
[testng] Suite
[testng] Total tests run: 4, Failures: 0, Skips: 0
[testng] ===============================================


BUILD SUCCESSFUL
Total time: 2 seconds
```

11.8 Using Test Groups

One of the more popular features of TestNG is its support for test groups. Test groups are useful in many situations, and they provide a degree of flexibility that opens the door to a whole new way of thinking about testing strategies. A typical example is when you need to distinguish between fast, lightweight tests (using mock-objects, for example) that are to be run regularly on the developer's machines, and longer, more complete integration and/or performance tests that need to be run on the server. You may need to distinguish between tests that must be run on a particular platform or environment. You may use groups to identify tests that run against certain parts of the system: database tests, user interface tests, and so on.

In TestNG, you can declare unit tests to belong to one or several groups. Then you can run certain groups of tests at different times or in different places. You add a method, or even an entire class, to a group by using the *groups* parameter in the *@Test* annotation. The syntax lets you add a class or method to one or several groups. Naming a group in a *@Test* annotation somewhere is all you need to do to bring it into existence —there is no "One File to Rule Them All"-style configuration file defining your groups:

```
@Test(groups = "unit-test, integration-test" )
public void testAnotherExchangeRate() {
    ...
}
```

```
    @Test(groups = { "integration-test" })
    public void testBatchProcessExchangeRates() {
        ...
    }
```

Adding an entire class to a group is a good way of defining a default group for all the unit tests within that class (it saves typing and fits in well with the DRY ["Don't Repeat Yourself"] principle). We could simplify the previous example by adding the class to the "integration-test" group, as shown here:

```
@Test(groups = { "integration-test" })
// All tests in this class should be considered as integration tests
public class CurrencyConverterTest {

    @Test(groups = "unit-test") // This one is a unit test too
    public void testAnotherExchangeRate() {
        ...
    }

    @Test
    public void testBatchProcessExchangeRates() {
        ...
    }
}
```

You can also set up test groups in your test suite, including or excluding particular groups. Using test groups lets you organize your testing strategy with a great deal of flexibility. For example, in the following test suite, we include all unit tests but exclude any unit tests that also belong to the integration test group:

```
<suite name="Suite" verbose="2" >
    <test name="Unit Tests" annotations="JDK">
        <groups>
            <run>
                <exclude name="integration-test"  />
                <include name="unit-test"  />
            </run>
        </groups>
        <packages>
            <package name="com.wakaleo.jpt.*" />
        </packages>
    </test>
</suite>
```

In TestNG, you can run all the tests in a group or set of groups, or alternatively, you can exclude tests in a particular group. For example, suppose you have written a class that sends email, but you can't test it on your development machine because an anti-virus software prevents your machine from acting as an email server. It would be unwise to abandon unit tests on this module for such a light excuse! Just declare an "email-test" group, as shown here, and exclude this group from unit tests on the development machine:

```
@Test(groups = "unit-test, email-test" )
 public void testEmailService() {
     ...
 }
```

Now it is an easy matter of excluding all tests in the "email-test" group. One way is to write a test suite entry that excludes this group, using the *<exclude>* element:

```
<suite name="Developer Unit Test Suite">
    <test verbose="2" name="Developer Unit Tests" annotations="JDK">
        <groups>
            <run>
                <include name="unit-test"/>
                <exclude name="email-test"/>
            </run>
        </groups>
        <classes>
            <class name="com.wakaleo.jpt.hotel.domain.CurrencyConverterTest"/>
            <class name="com.wakaleo.jpt.hotel.domain.PriceCalculatorTest"/>
        </classes>
    </test>
</suite>
```

This method will work fine. However, declaring test suites manually this way can be a bit long-winded. Luckily, there is an easier way to run (or exclude) groups of tests. If you are using Ant (see Section 11.5), you can run TestNG directly against a set of compiled unit test classes, without having to write an XML configuration file. You can use the *groups* attribute to indicate which groups you want to run. You can also use the *excludedgroups* to indicate test groups that are not to be executed:

```
<target name="unit-tests" depends="compiletests">
    <testng classpathref="runtests.classpath"
            outputDir="${test.reports}"
            verbose="2"
            haltonfailure="true"
            groups="unit-test"
            excludedgroups="email-tests">
        <classfileset dir="${test.classes}" includes="**/*.class"  />
    </testng>
</target>
```

11.9 Managing Dependencies

Test method dependencies are another area in which TestNG excels. Dependencies let you ensure that your test and fixture methods run in a particular order. This is clearly useful when you need to run your fixture methods in a certain order. For example, you may need to create an in-memory test database before filling it with test data. Another use is to create dependencies among tests. Sometimes, for example, if a particular key test in a test class fails, there is little point in running certain other tests. In this section, we look at how you can make the most out of test dependencies in TestNG.

One of the most common uses of TestNG dependencies is to coordinate test fixture code. Fixture code (see Section 11.7) is designed to set up and configure a predictable test environment before running your tests, and to clean up afterward. This sort of code plays an important role in any but the most trivial unit tests, and it is important that it be reliable and easily maintainable. For example, suppose that we need to run a series of tests against an in-memory database, with a predetermined set of test data. These tests are read-only, so we need to setup the database only once, at the start of the test class. One way of doing this would be to use the *@BeforeClass* annotation with some methods written to perform these two tasks. The code might look something like this:

```
...
@BeforeClass
public void createTestDatabase() {
    ...
}

@BeforeClass
public void prepareTestData() {
    ...
}
...
```

Now, it is fairly obvious that we need to create the database *before* we insert the test data. At first glance, the above code seems OK in this regard. However, there is actually no guarantee that the `createTestDatabase()` method will be called before the `prepareTestData()` method. In TestNG, methods will respect the lifecycle-related ordering discussed in Section 11.7, but, within a given phase (say, the *@BeforeClass* methods) the order of execution is not determined. And, in any case, it would be nicer to be able to define this sort of dependency declaratively.

In TestNG, you can do just that. All of the TestNG methods take the *dependsOnMethods* parameter, which you can use to list methods that must have been executed before a particular method. This is a convenient, elegant way of defining dependencies between test class methods. In the above example, we would simply indicate that the `prepareTestData()` method depends on the `createTestDatabase()` method, as shown here:

```
...
@BeforeClass
    public void createTestDatabase() {
    ...
}

@BeforeClass(dependsOnMethods = { "prepareTestData" })
public void prepareTestData() {
    ...
}
...
```

Dependencies have obvious uses for fixture code, but they can also be put to good use in test methods. In many cases, if a particular unit test fails, you can be sure that certain related subsequent tests will also fail. Running tests that are bound to fail is time-consuming, and pollutes your logfiles and reports without providing any useful information.

In TestNG, you can declare dependencies between test methods. Not only does this guarantee that your tests will run in a particular order, it will also skip a test if it depends on another test that has already failed. This lets you go straight to the root cause of the error, without having to sift through error messages generated by the failure of dependent tests. For example, in the following tests, we load a configuration file and run a series of tests on the data it contains. If the configuration file cannot be loaded correctly, than the following tests are irrelevant. To avoid unnecessary testing, we specify that the configuration data tests all depend on the initial **loadConfigurationFile()** test.

```
...
@Test
public void loadConfigurationFile() {
    ...
}

@Test (dependsOnMethods = { "loadConfigurationFile" })
public void testConfigurationData1() {
    ...
}

@Test (dependsOnMethods = { "loadConfigurationFile" })
public void testConfigurationData2() {
    ...
}
...
```

Now, if we run these tests, and the **loadConfigurationFile()** test fails, the subsequent tests on the configuration data will be skipped:

```
$ ant runtests
Buildfile: build.xml
...
runtests:
...
PASSED: testSomething
PASSED: testSomethingElse
FAILED: loadConfigurationFile
java.lang.AssertionError
at com.wakaleo.jpt.hotel.domain.DataAccessTest.loadConfigurationFile...
... Removed 21 stack frames
SKIPPED: testConfigurationData1
SKIPPED: testConfigurationData2

===============================================
com.wakaleo.jpt.hotel.domain.DataAccessTest
Tests run: 5, Failures: 1, Skips: 2
===============================================
```

You can also set up dependencies on class groups. This is a neat trick if some of your tests depend upon more than one method. For example, in the following tests, we load the configuration file and verify its structure before testing some access functions on this configuration data. The two initial methods (`loadConfigurationFile()` and `checkConfigurationFileStructure()`) need to have been successfully executed before we test the access functions (`fetchConfigurationData1()` and `fetchConfigurationData2()`). To enforce this, we place the first two methods in a group called "init," and then make the subsequent tests depend on this group:

```
...
@Test(groups = "init")
public void loadConfigurationFile() {
    ...
}

@Test(groups = "init", dependsOnMethods="loadConfigurationFile")
public void checkConfigurationFileStructure() {
    ...
}

@Test (dependsOnGroups = { "init" })
public void fetchConfigurationData1() {
    ...
}

@Test (dependsOnGroups = { "init" })
public void fetchConfigurationData2() {
    ...
}
...
```

11.10 Parallel Testing

Parallel testing is the ability to run unit tests simultaneously in several different threads. This fairly advanced testing technique can be useful in many situations. In web development, your application will typically be used by many concurrent users, and code may be required to run simultaneously on several threads. One of the best ways to check that your code supports this kind of simultaneous access is to run multithreaded unit tests against it. Multithreaded unit tests are also a good way to do low-level performance testing.

TestNG provides excellent built-in support for parallel testing. Multithreaded testing can be set up directly using the *@Test* annotation, using two main parameters: *threadPoolSize* and *invocationCount*. The *threadPoolSize* parameter lets you run unit tests from a number of threads running in parallel. The *invocationCount* parameter determines the number of times a test method will be executed in each thread. In the following example, TestNG will set up five threads (the *threadPoolSize* parameter).

Each thread will run (or "invoke") the `testConcurrentHotelSearch()` method 10 times (the *invocationCount* parameter):

```
@Test(threadPoolSize = 5, invocationCount = 10,  timeOut = 1000)
public void testConcurrentHotelSearch() {
    HotelSearchService hotelSearch = (HotelSearchService)
    beanFactory.getBean("hotelSearch");
    List<Hotel> hotels = hotelSearch.findByCity("Paris");
    ...
}
```

The *timeOut* parameter, which we see here, is useful for performance testing. It indicates the maximum time (in milliseconds) that a test method should take to run. If it takes any longer than this, the test will fail. You can use it with any test method, not just with multithreaded tests. However, when you are running multithreaded tests, you can use this parameter to guarantee that none of the threads will ever block the test run forever.

11.11 Test Parameters and Data-Driven Testing

Good testing involves more than simply exercising the code. You may also need to test your code against a wide range of input data. To make this easier, TestNG provides easy-to-use support for data-driven testing.

For example, suppose we want to test a business method that returns a list of hotels for a given city. We want to test this method using a number of different cities, making sure that the resulting list contains only hotels for that city. Let's see how we could do this using TestNG.

First of all, you need to set up a data provider. A data provider is simply a method which returns your test data, in the form of either a two-dimentional array of `Objects` (`Object[][]`) or an Iterator over a list of objects (`Iterator<Object[]>`). You set up a data provider by using (appropriately enough) the *@DataProvider* annotation, along with a unique name, as shown here:

```
@DataProvider(name = "test-cities")
public Object[][] fetchCityData() {
    return new Object[][] {
        new Object[] { "London" },
        new Object[] { "Paris" },
        new Object[] { "Madrid" },
        new Object[] { "Amsterdam" }
    };
}
```

Next, you can use this data provider to provide parameters for your test cases. TestNG tests can take parameters, so writing a test case that works with a data provider is easy. You simply create a test method with the correct number of parameters, and specify the data provider using the *dataProvider* parameter in the *@Test* annotation:

```
@Test(dataProvider="test-cities")
public void findHotelsInCity(String city) {
    List<Hotel> results = hotelFinder.findInCity(city);
    // Check that every hotel in this list belongs to the specified city.
    ...
}
```

Now, if we run this, TestNG will invoke this method as many times as necessary for each data entry returned by the data provider:

```
$ ant runtests
Buildfile: build.xml
...
runtests:
...
PASSED: findHotelsInCity("London")
PASSED: findHotelsInCity("Paris")
PASSED: findHotelsInCity("Madrid")
PASSED: findHotelsInCity("Amsterdam")
...
```

11.12 Checking for Exceptions

Testing proper error handling is another aspect of unit testing. Indeed, you sometimes need to check that a particular exception is correctly thrown under certain circumstances (see Section 10.5). In TestNG, you can do this easily by using the *expectedExceptions* annotation parameter. You just specify the Exception class which should be thrown by your test in this parameter, and TestNG does the rest. If the exception is thrown, the test passes; otherwise, it fails. In the following example, we test a method that searches for hotels in a given country. The country code comes from a pre-defined list, and if an illegal country code is provided, the method should throw an `UnknownCountryCodeException`. We could test this error handling process as follows:

```
@Test(expectedExceptions = UnknownCountryCodeException.class)
public void lookupHotelWithUnknownCountryCode() {
    HotelSearchService hotelSearch
        = (HotelSearchService) beanFactory.getBean("hotelSearch");
    List<Hotel> hotels = hotelSearch.findByCountryCode("XXX");
}
```

11.13 Handling Partial Failures

One tricky case to test is when you know that a certain (generally small) percentage of test runs *will* fail. This often occurs in integration or performance testing. For example, you may need to query a remote web service. The response time will be dependant on many factors: network traffic, the amount of data sent over the network, the execution time of the remote request, and so on. However, according to your performance requirements, you need to be able to perform this operation in less than 50 milliseconds, at least 99 percent of the time.

So, how do you test this in TestNG? It's actually pretty simple. TestNG provides a *successPercentage* parameter, which you use in conjunction with the *invocationCount* to verify that at least a given percentage of tests succeed. This is one way that we might test the performance requirements described above:

```
@Test(invocationCount=1000, successPercentage=99, timeOut=50)
public void loadTestWebserviceLookup() {
    ....
}
```

You obviously need the *invocationCount* parameter to be high enough to give statistically significant results. Ten tests are generally not enough, and even a hundred tests will still present a fair bit of statistical variation. Although it will depend on your application, you will usually need several hundred or thousand tests to be able to have any degree of statistical reliability.

It is also a good idea to place this sort of test in a special group reserved for long-running performance and load tests. And for more realistic testing, you can also toss in the *threadPoolSize* parameter (see Section 11.10) to run your tests in parallel and simulate a multiuser environment.

11.14 Rerunning Failed Tests

Large real-world applications will often contain hundreds or thousands of test cases. And it can be particularly frustrating when you have to rerun the entire test suite just because two or three tests have failed. Wouldn't it be nice if you could simply fix the code and only run the tests that failed? TestNG provides a neat little feature to do just this: You have the option of rerunning *only* the test methods that failed the last time round.

Whenever TestNG comes across a test failure, it creates (or appends to) a special test suite configuration file in the output directory called *testng-failed.xml*. Once all of the tests have been executed, this file will contain the complete list of the test methods which have failed. Then, once you have corrected your code, you just have to run TestNG using this configuration file and TestNG will rerun the failed tests. Needless to say, this can be an invaluable time-saver.

To run this from Ant (see Section 11.5), you could just add a simple target that runs TestNG against the *testng-failed.xml* configuration file, as shown here:

```
<target name="failed-tests" depends="compiletests" description="Run TestNG
unit tests">
    <testng classpathref="runtests.classpath" outputDir="${test.reports}"
     verbose="2"  haltonfailure="true">
       <xmlfileset dir="${test.reports}" includes="testng-failed.xml"/>
```

```
        </testng>
    </target>
```

The practice of rerunning failed tests is not of course designed to replace comprehensive unit and regression tests. It is always possible that a correction somewhere may have broken a test somewhere else, so you should still run the entire test suite at some point to ensure that everything is still working. However, if you need to fix just one or two errors out of hundreds of test cases, this is a big time-saver.

CHAPTER 12

Maximizing Test Coverage with Cobertura

12.1 Test Coverage

Unit testing is recognized as a crucial part of modern software development practices. Nevertheless, for a number of reasons discussed at length elsewhere, it is often done insufficiently and poorly. Basically, there are two main things that can make a unit test ineffective: it can execute the code but test the business logic poorly or not at all, or it can neglect to test parts of the code. The first case is fairly hard to detect automatically. In this chapter we will look at the second type of issue, which is the domain of test coverage tools.

It is fairly clear that if a part of your code isn't being executed during the unit tests, then it isn't being tested. And this is often a Bad Thing. This is where test coverage tools come it. Test coverage tools observe your code during unit tests, recording which lines have been executed (and therefore subject to at least some testing). And although the fact that a line of code is executed during unit tests offers absolutely no guarantee that it executes correctly (it is easy enough to write unit tests that exercise an entire class without testing any business logic at all!), in practice it is always preferable to minimize the amount of code that is not tested at all.

Cobertura* is a free, open source test coverage tool for Java. Cobertura works by instrumenting the compiled bytecode from your application, inserting code to detect and log which lines have and have not been executed during the unit tests. You run your unit tests normally, and the inserted bytecode logs the execution details. Finally, using these logs, Cobertura generates clear, readable test coverage reports in HTML. These reports provide a high-level overview of test coverage statistics across the entire project, and also let you drill down into individual packages and classes, and inspect which lines of code were and were not executed, allowing developers to correct or complete

* *http://cobertura.sf.net*

unit tests accordingly. Cobertura also measures complexity metrics such as McCabe cyclomatic code complexity.

Cobertura integrates well with both Ant and Maven. It can also be executed directly from the command line, though this is a pretty low-level stuff and should really only be done if you don't have any other choice. At the time of this writing, no IDE plug-ins (for Eclipse, NetBeans, or any other Java IDE) were available: IDE integration is an area where Cobertura lags behind the main commercial code coverage tools such as Clover and Cobertura's commercial cousin, JCoverage.

12.2 Running Cobertura from Ant

Cobertura integrates well with Ant: with a little configuration, you can have all the power and flexibility of the tool at your fingertips. Let's look at how to integrate Cobertura into an Ant project.

First of all, you need to install Cobertura. Just download the latest distribution from the Cobertura web site* and extract it into an appropriate directory. On my machine, I installed Cobertura into */usr/local/tools/cobertura-1.8*, and added a symbolic link called `/usr/local/tools/cobertura`.

Cobertura comes bundled with an Ant task. You just need to define this task in your *build.xml* file as follows:

```
<property name="cobertura.dir" value="/usr/local/tools/cobertura" />

<path id="cobertura.classpath">
  <fileset dir="${cobertura.dir}">
    <include name="cobertura.jar" />
    <include name="lib/**/*.jar" />
  </fileset>
</path>
<taskdef classpathref="cobertura.classpath" resource="tasks.properties" />
```

The next step is to instrument your files. You can do this using the *cobertura-instrument* task:

```
<property name="instrumented.dir" value="${build.dir}/instrumented-classes" />
<target name="instrument" depends="compile">
  <mkdir dir="${instrumented.dir}"/>
  <delete file="${basedir}/cobertura.ser" />
  <cobertura-instrument todir="${instrumented.dir}" datafile="${basedir}/cobertura.ser">
    <fileset dir="${build.classes.dir}">
      <include name="**/*.class" />
      <exclude name="**/*Test.class" />
    </fileset>
  </cobertura-instrument>
</target>
```

* *http://cobertura.sourceforge.net/download.html*

This task is fairly simple. It is good practice to place the instrumented classes into a different directory than the normal compiled classes. In this case, we generate them in the *instrumented-classes* directory, using the *todir* option.

Cobertura stores metadata about your classes in a special file, called by default *cobertura.ser*. Here, we use the *datafile* option to avoid any confusion (we will need to refer to *exactly* the same metadata file when we generate the reports). This file is updated with execution details during the test runs, and used then to generate the reports. To be sure that the results are reliable, we delete this file before instrumenting the files.

The actual classes to be instrumented are specified using a standard Ant fileset. Note that, for best results with Cobertura, you should activate line-level debugging when you compile your Java classes. In Ant, you can do this by using the *debug* and *debuglevel* attributes, as shown here:

```
<javac compiler="modern"
       srcdir="${java.src}"
       destdir="${java.classes}"
       includes="**/*.java"
       debug="true"
       debuglevel="lines,source">
   <classpath refid="java.classpath"/>
</javac>
```

Now call this target to make sure everything works so far. You should get something like this:

```
$ ant instrument
...
instrument:
    [mkdir] Created dir: /home/john/dev/commons-lang-2.2-src/target/
    instrumented-classes
   [delete] Deleting: /home/john/dev/commons-lang-2.2-src/cobertura.ser
[cobertura-instrument] Cobertura 1.8 - GNU GPL License (NO WARRANTY) -
See COPYRIGHT file
[cobertura-instrument] Instrumenting 123 files to
/home/john/dev/commons-lang-2.2-src/target/instrumented-classes
[cobertura-instrument] Cobertura: Saved information on 123 classes.
[cobertura-instrument] Instrument time: 1371ms
```

You should now run your unit tests (almost) normally. Well, not quite. In fact, you need to modify your JUnit tasks a fair bit to get things working properly. Because Cobertura tests take considerably longer to run than normal tests, it is actually a good idea to write a separate target exclusively for coverage tests. In this example, we define a target called "test.coverage" that instruments the code, and compiles and runs the unit tests against the instrumented code:

```
<target name="test.coverage" depends="instrument, compile.tests">
  <junit printsummary="true" showoutput="true" fork="true"
   haltonerror="${test.failonerror}">

    <sysproperty key="net.sourceforge.cobertura.datafile"
                 file="${basedir}/cobertura.ser" />
```

```
        <classpath location="${instrumented.dir}" />
        <classpath refid="test.classpath"/>
        <classpath refid="cobertura.classpath" />
        <batchtest todir="${reports.data.dir}" >
            <fileset dir="${test.classes.dir}" includes="**/*Test.class" />
        </batchtest>
      </junit>
    </target>
```

There are a few important things to note here. First, for technical reasons related to the way Cobertura generates its data files, the *fork* option in the JUnit task *must* be set to true. Second, you need to indicate the location of the *cobertura.ser* file in the *net.sourceforge.cobertura.datafile* system property, using the *sysproperty* task. Finally, you need to make sure that the classpath contains the instrumented classes (in first position) as well as the normal test classes, and also the Cobertura classes.

Running this target should produce something like the following:

```
$ ant test.coverage
...
test.coverage:
    [junit] Running org.apache.commons.lang.LangTestSuite

    [junit] Tests run: 635, Failures: 0, Errors: 0, Time elapsed: 4.664 sec
    [junit] Cobertura: Loaded information on 123 classes.
    [junit] Cobertura: Saved information on 123 classes.
```

Now we can get to the interesting stuff and generate the Cobertura report:

```
<property name="coveragereport.dir" value="${build.dir}/reports/cobertura" />
...
<target  name="cobertura.report" depends="instrument, test">
  <mkdir dir="${coveragereport.dir}"/>
  <cobertura-report format="html"
                    destdir="${coveragereport.dir}"
                    srcdir="src"
                    datafile="${basedir}/cobertura.ser" />
</target>
```

This will generate a set of reports in the *${build.dir}/reports/cobertura* directory, illustrated in Figure 12-1. Cobertura reports are fairly intuitive, especially if you have worked with other code coverage tools. We will look at some of the finer points of how to interpret a Cobertura report in Section 12.4.

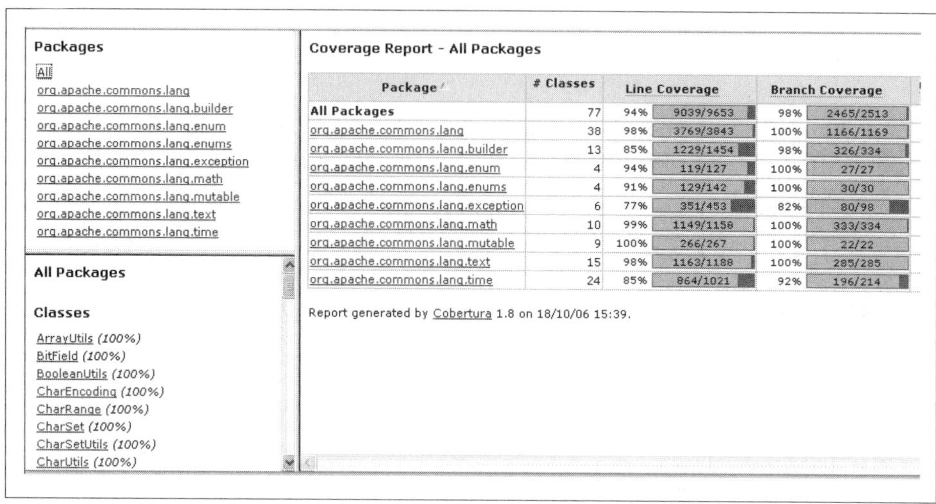

Figure 12-1. A Cobertura report

If your Cobertura reports are going to be used by another tool (such as the Hudson Continuous Integration server (see Section 8.16), you also will need to generate your reports in XML format. You do this as follows:

```
<property name="coveragereport.dir" value="${build.dir}/reports/cobertura" />
...
<target  name="cobertura.report" depends="instrument, test">
  <mkdir dir="${coveragereport.dir}"/>
  <cobertura-report format="xml"
                    destdir="${coveragereport.dir}"
                    srcdir="${source.home}"
                    datafile="${basedir}/cobertura.ser" />
</target>
```

12.3 Checking the Code Coverage of TestNG Tests

TestNG (see Chapter 11) is an innovative and flexible annotation-based testing framework that aims at overcoming many of the limitations of JUnit. Here, we look at how to use Cobertura to measure test coverage on TestNG tests. The technique presented here was initially described by Andy Glover.*

Cobertura is not limited to measuring test coverage on JUnit-based tests. Indeed, it can be used to measure test coverage even if you are using other unit testing frameworks such as TestNG. Running TestNG with Cobertura is a relatively simple task. First, you need to define the Cobertura task, and instrument your classes in the normal way, using

* *http://www-128.ibm.com/developerworks/forums/dw_thread.jsp?forum=812&thread=110765&cat=10*

the *cobertura-instrument* task (see Section 12.2). This code is listed here again for convenience:

```
...
<property name="cobertura.dir" value="/usr/local/tools/cobertura-1.8" />
<property name="instrumented.dir" value="${build.dir}/instrumented-classes" />

<path id="cobertura.classpath">
  <fileset dir="${cobertura.dir}">
    <include name="cobertura.jar" />
    <include name="lib/**/*.jar" />
  </fileset>
</path>

<!-- Define the Cobertura task -->
<taskdef classpathref="cobertura.classpath" resource="tasks.properties" />

<!-- Instrument classes -->
<target name="instrument" depends="compile">
  <mkdir dir="${instrumented.dir}"/>
  <delete file="${basedir}/cobertura.ser" />
  <cobertura-instrument todir="${instrumented.dir}"
   datafile="${basedir}/cobertura.ser">
    <fileset dir="${build.dir}/classes">
      <include name="**/*.class" />
      <exclude name="**/*Test.class" />
    </fileset>
  </cobertura-instrument>
</target>
```

Next, instead of running your tests using the JUnit task, you need to use the TestNG task instead. There are two things to remember here. First, you need to provide a *<classpath>* containing the instrumented classes, the test classes, and the Cobertura libraries. Second, you need to specify a *<sysproperty>* element that provides the path of the Cobertura data file (*cobertura.ser*). A typical example, which runs all the TestNG classes in the project, is shown here:

```
<target name="test.coverage" depends="instrument, compiletests">
    <testng outputDir="${test.reports}" verbose="2">
        <classpath>
             <pathelement location="${instrumented.dir}" />
             <pathelement location="${test.classes}" />
             <path refid="cobertura.classpath"/>
        </classpath>
        <sysproperty key="net.sourceforge.cobertura.datafile"
         file="${basedir}/cobertura.ser" />
        <classfileset dir="${test.classes}" includes="**/*.class" />
    </testng>
</target>
```

Of course, you can also use any of the other options in the TestNG Ant task (see Section 11.5), such as running specific test groups or running a test suite using a TestNG configuration file.

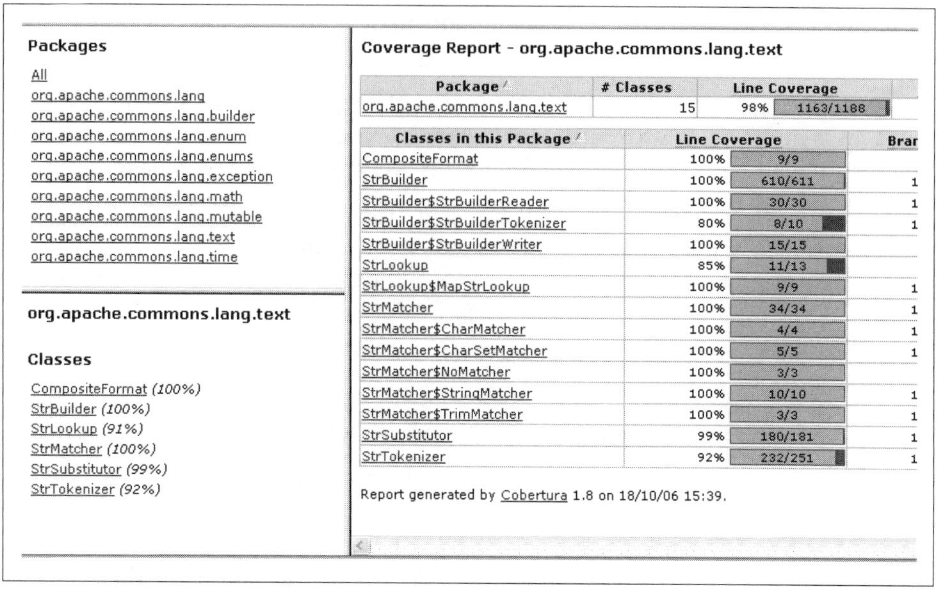

Packages

All
org.apache.commons.lang
org.apache.commons.lang.builder
org.apache.commons.lang.enum
org.apache.commons.lang.enums
org.apache.commons.lang.exception
org.apache.commons.lang.math
org.apache.commons.lang.mutable
org.apache.commons.lang.text
org.apache.commons.lang.time

org.apache.commons.lang.text

Classes

CompositeFormat *(100%)*
StrBuilder *(100%)*
StrLookup *(91%)*
StrMatcher *(100%)*
StrSubstitutor *(99%)*
StrTokenizer *(92%)*

Coverage Report - org.apache.commons.lang.text

Package	# Classes	Line Coverage
org.apache.commons.lang.text	15	98% 1163/1188

Classes in this Package	Line Coverage		Bran
CompositeFormat	100%	9/9	
StrBuilder	100%	610/611	1
StrBuilder$StrBuilderReader	100%	30/30	1
StrBuilder$StrBuilderTokenizer	80%	8/10	1
StrBuilder$StrBuilderWriter	100%	15/15	
StrLookup	85%	11/13	
StrLookup$MapStrLookup	100%	9/9	1
StrMatcher	100%	34/34	1
StrMatcher$CharMatcher	100%	4/4	1
StrMatcher$CharSetMatcher	100%	5/5	1
StrMatcher$NoMatcher	100%	3/3	
StrMatcher$StringMatcher	100%	10/10	1
StrMatcher$TrimMatcher	100%	3/3	1
StrSubstitutor	99%	180/181	1
StrTokenizer	92%	232/251	1

Report generated by Cobertura 1.8 on 18/10/06 15:39.

Figure 12-2. Drilling down to the package level

Finally, the Cobertura report generation is unchanged:

```
<property name="coveragereport.dir" value="${build.dir}/reports/cobertura" />
...
<target  name="cobertura.report" depends="test.coverage">
  <mkdir dir="${coveragereport.dir}"/>
  <cobertura-report format="html"
                    destdir="${coveragereport.dir}"
                    srcdir="${source.home}"
                    datafile="${basedir}/cobertura.ser" />
</target>
```

12.4 Interpreting the Cobertura Report

Interpreting a Cobertura report is a fine art. Well, actually it's not: in fact it's quite simple. As far as coverage reports go, Cobertura reports are quite clear and intuitive. A typical Cobertura report is illustrated in Figure 12-1. The report is generated in HTML, so you can drill down into individual packages (see Figure 12-2) and classes (see Figure 12-3), or just look at a high-level overview showing coverage across the whole project (see Figure 12-1).

The theory of code coverage can be a bit pedantic, and many of the more subtle details are really only of any interest to the authors of code coverage tools. However, the main coverage metrics are fairly simple, and can help in interpreting a code coverage report.

As we have seen, Cobertura covers line and branch coverage, and McCabe class complexity.

Line coverage represents the significant number of lines of code that have been executed. This is pretty straightforward: if a line of code hasn't been executed during your unit tests then it hasn't been tested. So, it is in everyone's interest to make sure your unit tests exercise as many lines as possible.

Branch coverage is a bit more fancy. Let's look at an example. In the following code, we call the `processExpensivePurchaseOrder()` method if the cost is greater or equal to 10,000:

```
public void processOrder(String productCode, int cost) {
  PurchaceOrder order = null;
  if (cost > 10000) {
    order = processExpensivePurchaseOrder(productCode, cost);
  }
  ...
  order.doSomething();
}
```

If your unit tests fail to cover this case, Line coverage will pick up the fact that `doSomething()` is never executed. That's fine. However, for a cost value of less than 10,000, `processExpensivePurchaseOrder()` will not be executed, which appears to be normal. However, if the order variable is never assigned elsewhere, the code will crash with a `NullPointerException` in the last line of the method.

Branch coverage will detect this case. It works by looking at conditional expressions and checking whether both possible outcomes of the condition were tested.

Branch coverage is a useful thing to have, and Cobertura gives a good indication of how many of the branches in your code are executed by your unit tests. The only problem is that Cobertura cannot actually tell you *which* branches are not correctly tested. (Admittedly, this is a tricky problem: none of the other code coverage tools that I know of can do this either).

McCabe cyclomatic complexity is not a measure of code coverage but a metric you can also measure with static code analysis tools such as Checkstyle (see Chapter 21) and PMD (see Chapter 22).

You measure the complexity of a method by counting the number of decision points (ifs, loops, case statements, and so on) it contains. The more decision points, the more the code is considered to be complex and difficult to understand and maintain. The McCabe cyclomatic complexity metric counts the number of distinct paths through the method, so you just take the number of decision points plus one. If there are no decision points at all, there is just one path through the code. (Each decision point adds an additional path.)

McCabe cyclomatic complexity is actually quite a good way of finding overly complex classes and methods. Long and complex sections of code tend to be fragile, hard to

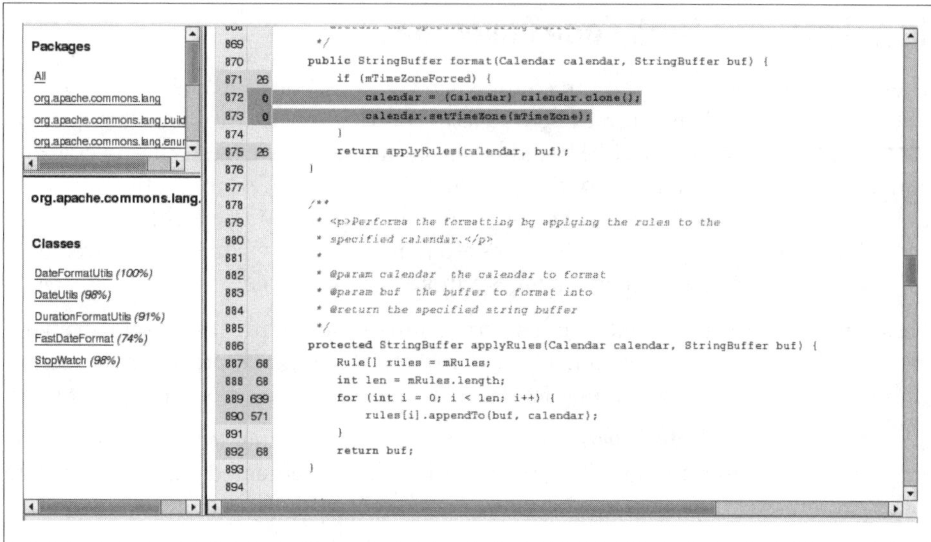

Figure 12-3. Code coverage at the class level

maintain, and prone to bugs. If a method is getting too long or too complex, it's probably a good candidate for refactoring. For Java code, most writers consider a value of 1–4 to indicate low, 5–7 moderate complexity, 8–10 highly complex, and over 10 excessively complex.

Cobertura gives only a general indication of the average complexity of a package or class. This is useful for a project manager or team leader, who can flag suspicious code for review and refactoring. However, to be really useful, you need to apply this metric directly to each method, which can be done using Checkstyle (see Section 21.5) or PMD (see Section 22.5).

One coverage metric is not currently handled by Cobertura. Method Coverage is available in some of the commercial code coverage products. Method Coverage is a high-level indicator of how many methods were called during the unit test executions.

At the class level (see Figure 12-3), Cobertura lets you see the line coverage for each individual line. In the margin, Cobertura displays which lines of code were and were not tested, and the number of times each line of code was executed. This lets you identify code that hasn't been tested and add new tests to check the untested code, or remove bits of redundant or unnecessary code.

Not all code can be feasibly tested. For example, you may have code that catches exceptions that will never be thrown, or implement methods in an interface that are never used. This is why 100 percent code coverage is not always possible. There's no need to be dogmatic about obtaining 100 percent coverage for each and every class: just remember, code coverage is a tool to improve the quality of your code, not an end in itself.

12.5 Enforcing High Code Coverage

There are two approaches you can adopt when you test code coverage with a tool like Cobertura. You can simply use Cobertura as a reporting tool to investigate areas where tests might be improved or code could be refactored. Users can read the coverage reports, and are free to take any corrective action they deem necessary. In this situation, Cobertura acts like a sort of advisory body. You can actively enforce high code coverage by building checks into your build process so that the build will fail if test coverage is insufficient. In this case, Cobertura takes a more legislative role.

These approaches can be used together: for example, you can run test coverage reports on a daily basis to help developers improve their tests in a development environment, and enforce minimum test coverage levels on the test or integration build environments.

Cobertura comes with the *cobertura-check* task, an Ant task that lets you enforce coverage levels. You insert this task just after you run your instrumented unit tests to ensure that a certain level of test coverage has been achieved, as shown here:

```
<target name="test.coverage" depends="instrument, compile.tests">
  <junit printsummary="true" showoutput="true" fork="true"
   haltonerror="${test.failonerror}">

    <sysproperty key="net.sourceforge.cobertura.datafile"
                 file="${basedir}/cobertura.ser" />
    <classpath location="${instrumented.dir}" />
    <classpath refid="test.classpath"/>
    <classpath refid="cobertura.classpath" />
    <test name="org.apache.commons.lang.LangTestSuite"/>
    </junit>
   <cobertura-check linerate="90" branchrate="90" totalbranchrate="90"
     totallinerate="90"/>
    </target>
```

You can define the required line and branch rates for each individual class (using the *linerate* and *branchrate* attributes), for each package (*packagelinerate* and *packagebranchrate*), or across the whole project (*totallinerate* and *totalbranchrate*). You can also define different levels of required coverage for specific packages, as shown here:

```
<cobertura-check linerate="80" branchrate="80" totalbranchrate="90"
totallinerate="90">
    <regex pattern="com.acme.myproject.highriskcode.*" branchrate="95"
     linerate="95"/>
</cobertura-check>
```

Now, if you run this task with insufficient test coverage, the build will fail:

```
$ ant test.coverage
...
[cobertura-check] org.apache.commons.lang.time.FastDateFormat failed check.
Branch coverage rate of 76.0% is below 90.0%
[cobertura-check] org.apache.commons.lang.NotImplementedException failed check.
Branch coverage rate of 83.3% is below 90.0%
[cobertura-check] org.apache.commons.lang.time.FastDateFormat$TimeZoneNameRule
```

```
failed check. Branch coverage rate of 83.3% is below 90.0%
[cobertura-check] org.apache.commons.lang.time.FastDateFormat$Pair
failed check. Branch coverage rate of 25.0% is below 90.0%
[cobertura-check] Project failed check. Total line coverage rate of 88.7%
is below 90.0%

BUILD FAILED
/home/john/dev/commons-lang-2.2-src/build.xml:228: Coverage check failed.
See messages above.
```

Systematically enforcing high code coverage in this way is debated in some circles. Developers may not appreciate build failures as a result of insufficient code coverage, on what they consider to be "work in progress," which is fair enough. However, it is a fact that tests should be written around the same time as the code being tested: they are easier to write and the tests are higher quality and generally more relevant. One good way to encourage regular, high quality testing is to integrate this type of check on the continuous integration server (see Chapters 5, 6, and 7), to ensure that code committed has been sufficiently tested.

It is worth pointing out that high test coverage does not assure correct testing (see the excellent article by Andrew Glover on this subject*). In fact, there is more to unit tests than just executing the lines of code. As Andrew Glover points out, test coverage is most useful to flag code that *hasn't* been tested, and it does do a very good job of this. And, in practice, Murphy's Law ensures that untested code will always contain more bugs than tested code!

12.6 Generating Cobertura Reports in Maven

Cobertura can also be used with Maven as well as Ant. The Mojo project† provides a Maven plug-in for Cobertura that lets you test code coverage, generate coverage reports, and enforce coverage levels. These functionalities are very similar to the Ant (see Section 12.2), although arguably (at the time of this writing, at least) less mature and less stable.

First, you need to set up the `cobertura-maven-plug-in` plug-in in the *<build>* section of your POM file. You can do this as follows:

```
<project>
  ...
  <build>
     ...
     <plugins>
     ...
        <plugin>
          <groupId>org.codehaus.mojo</groupId>
```

* "In pursuit of code quality: Don't be fooled by the coverage report," IBM Developer Works, January 31, 2006 (*http://www-128.ibm.com/developerworks/java/library/j-cq01316/index.html*)

† *http://mojo.codehaus.org/*

```
            <artifactId>cobertura-maven-plugin</artifactId>
            <version>2.2</version>*
          </plugin>
      ...
    </plugins>
    ...
  </build>
  ...
</project>
```

The plug-in comes with a few useful configuration options. In the following example, we increase the maximum memory allocated to the Cobertura task to 128M and indicate that all abstract classes and unit test classes should be excluded from the coverage calculations (otherwise, to have full test coverage, we would need to test the unit tests themselves as well):

```
<project>
    ...
    <build>
        ...
        <plugins>
        ...
          <plugin>
            <groupId>org.codehaus.mojo</groupId>
            <artifactId>cobertura-maven-plugin</artifactId>
            <version>2.2</version>
            <configuration>
              <maxmem>128m</maxmem>
              <instrumentation>
                <excludes>
                    <exclude>**/*Test.class</exclude>
                    <exclude>**/Abstract*.class</exclude>
                </excludes>
              </instrumentation>
            </configuration>
          </plugin>
      ...
    </plugins>
    ...
  </build>
  ...
</project>
```

You can run Cobertura by calling the *cobertura:cobertura* goal:

```
$mvn cobertura:cobertura
```

This will instrument your project's files, run the unit tests on the instrumented code, and generate a coverage report in the *target/site/cobertura* directory.

* At the time of this writing, you need to manually specify version 2.0 or 2.2 of the Maven Cobertura plug-in, as the most recent version does not work correctly.

This is nice for testing your configuration. In practice, however, you will need to integrate Cobertura more closely into your Maven build process. You can use Cobertura in two ways: simply to report on test coverage levels, or to actively enforce minimum required test coverage levels by refusing to build a product without sufficient test coverage (see Section 12.5 for more discussion on these two approaches). In a Maven project, you can integrate Cobertura reports into the standard Maven site reports by simply listing the *cobertura-maven-plugin* in the *<reporting>* section of your POM file, as shown here:

```
<project...>
  ...
  <reporting>
    <plugins>
      <plugin>
        <groupId>org.codehaus.mojo</groupId>
        <artifactId>cobertura-maven-plugin</artifactId>
        <version>2.2</version>
      </plugin>
    </plugins>
  </reporting>
</project>
```

Now, whenever the Maven site is generated using the *site:site* goal, Maven will also run code coverage tests and generate a coverage report, which will be neatly integrated into the Maven site:

```
$mvn site:site
```

12.7 Integrating Coverage Tests into the Maven Build Process

In some projects, you may want to enforce code coverage rules in a more proactive way than by simply reporting coverage details. In Maven, you can also enforce coverage levels using the *<check>* configuration element, which goes in the *<configuration>* section of your plug-in definition. Like the corresponding Ant task (see Section 12.5), the *<check>* element lets you define the minimum acceptable coverage levels for lines and branches, for each individual class (using the *<linerate>* and *<branchrate>* elements), for each package (using the *<packagelinerate>* and *<packagebranchrate>* elements), or for the whole project (using the *<totallinerate>* and *<totalbranchrate>* elements):

```
<project>
 ...
 <build>
  ...
  <plugins>
   ...
   <plugin>
      <groupId>org.codehaus.mojo</groupId>
      <artifactId>cobertura-maven-plugin</artifactId>
      <version>2.0</version>
```

```
        <configuration>
           <check>
              <branchRate>80</branchRate>
              <lineRate>70</lineRate>
              <totalBranchRate>70</totalBranchRate>
              <totalLineRate>60</totalLineRate>
            </check>
        </configuration>
        <executions>
          <execution>
            <goals>
              <goal>clean</goal>
              <goal>check</goal>
            </goals>
          </execution>
        </executions>
      </plugin>
      ...
    </plugins>
    ...
  </build>
  ...
</project>
```

You can run this test manually by running *mvn cobertura:check*:

```
$mvn cobertura:check
...
[INFO] [cobertura:check]
[INFO] Cobertura 1.7 - GNU GPL License (NO WARRANTY) - See COPYRIGHT file
Cobertura: Loaded information on 5 classes.

[ERROR] com.wakaleo.jpt.examples.library.domain.Library failed check.
Line coverage rate of 0.0% is below 70.0%
com.wakaleo.jpt.examples.library.App failed check. Line coverage rate of 0.0%
is below 70.0%
Project failed check. Total line coverage rate of 47.6% is below 60.0%

[INFO] ------------------------------------------------------------------------
[ERROR] BUILD ERROR
[INFO] ------------------------------------------------------------------------
[INFO] Coverage check failed. See messages above.
[INFO] ------------------------------------------------------------------------
[INFO] For more information, run Maven with the -e switch
[INFO] ------------------------------------------------------------------------
[INFO] Total time: 5 seconds
[INFO] Finished at: Tue Oct 24 00:38:05 NZDT 2006
[INFO] Final Memory: 5M/10M
[INFO] ------------------------------------------------------------------------
```

This is fine for testing purposes, but it is poorly integrated into the overall build process. This configuration will not stop a build from proceeding if you run *mvn package*, for example, no matter how poor your test coverage is! The check needs to be bound to a particular part of the Maven build lifecycle, such as the *package* lifecycle phase, which takes place just after the *test* phase, or the *verify* lifecycle phase, which is invoked just before the application is bundled up into its final form and installed into the local repository. To do this, just add another *<execution>* section to the plug-in definition, containing the target phase and the Cobertura goals you want to call (in our case, *clean* and *check*):

```
<plugin>
   <groupId>org.codehaus.mojo</groupId>
   <artifactId>cobertura-maven-plugin</artifactId>
   <configuration>
      <check>
         <branchRate>80</branchRate>
         <lineRate>70</lineRate>
         <totalBranchRate>70</totalBranchRate>
         <totalLineRate>60</totalLineRate>
       </check>
   </configuration>
   <executions>
     <execution>
       <goals>
         <goal>clean</goal>
         <goal>check</goal>
       </goals>
     </execution>
     <execution>
         <id>coverage-tests</id>
         <phase>verify</phase>
         <goals>
             <goal>clean</goal>
             <goal>check</goal>
         </goals>
     </execution>
   </executions>
 </plugin>
```

Now, whenever you try to build and install the application, Cobertura will be called to verify test coverage levels. If they are insufficient, the build will fail. You can check that this works by running *mvn install*:

```
$mvn install
...
[INFO] [cobertura:check]
[INFO] Cobertura 1.7 - GNU GPL License (NO WARRANTY) - See COPYRIGHT file
Cobertura: Loaded information on 5 classes.

[ERROR] com.wakaleo.jpt.examples.library.domain.Library failed check.
Line coverage rate of 0.0% is below 70.0%
com.wakaleo.jpt.examples.library.App failed check. Line coverage rate of 0.0%
is below 70.0%
Project failed check. Total line coverage rate of 47.6% is below 60.0%

[INFO] ------------------------------------------------------------------------
[ERROR] BUILD ERROR
[INFO] ------------------------------------------------------------------------
[INFO] Coverage check failed. See messages above.
[INFO] ------------------------------------------------------------------------
```

```
[INFO] For more information, run Maven with the -e switch
[INFO] ------------------------------------------------------------------------
[INFO] Total time: 5 seconds
[INFO] Finished at: Tue Oct 24 00:38:05 NZDT 2006
[INFO] Final Memory: 5M/10M
[INFO] ------------------------------------------------------------------------
```

12.8 Code Coverage in Eclipse

Another popular open source code coverage tool is Emma.* This tool has been around for a while and provides good quality coverage metrics including measures of class, method, and block and line coverage. Although it comes with an Ant plug-in, Emma provides no support for Maven 2, and space constraints prevent us from looking at it in any detail here.

One thing we will look at, however, is a nice test coverage plug-in for Eclipse that is based on Emma. This plug-in, called EclEmma,† lets you visualize test coverage measurements for your unit tests directly from within Eclipse.

The easiest way to install EclEmma is to use the update site. Select "Software Updates→Find and Install" in the help menu, and add a new remote update site. Set the URL to *http://update.eclemma.org*, and install the plug-ins from this site in the usual way. The installation is straightforward.

Once the plug-in is installed, you will be able to run your application in coverage mode. A new Coverage icon should appear alongside the other Run and Debug icons (see Figure 12-4). From here, you can run your unit tests with test coverage metrics activated. You can also use the contextual menu, by selecting "Coverage As" rather than "Run As" when you execute your unit tests.

You can run JUnit tests, TestNG tests, or even Java applications this way. EclEmma will automatically instrument your class files and keep track of coverage statistics while your code executes.

When you run your unit tests in the test coverage mode, EclEmma will automatically instrument your classes and record coverage statistics, which it will display in the "Coverage" view (see Figure 12-5). This view gives you a coverage graph with an overview of the coverage statistics for the code you just executed. You can drill down to package, class, and method level, and display a particular class in the source code editor. Executed code is displayed in green, partially executed lines are displayed in yellow, and unexecuted code is displayed in red.

* *http://emma.sourceforge.net/*

† *http://www.eclemma.org/*

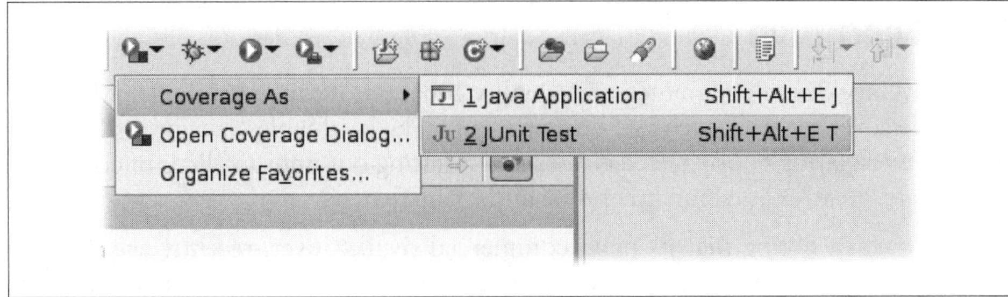

Figure 12-4. Running code coverage tests using EclEmma

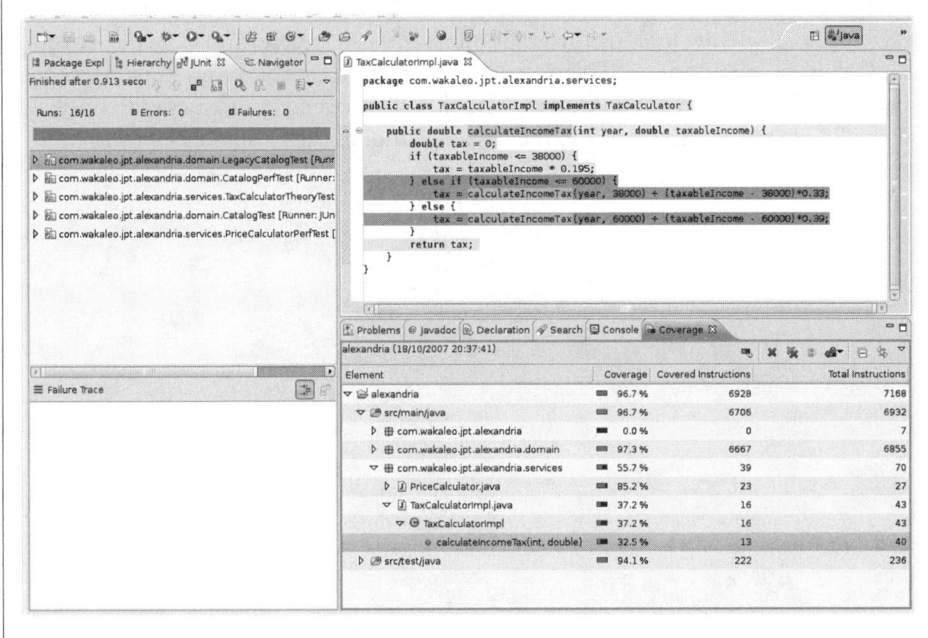

Figure 12-5. EclEmma displays test coverage statistics in Eclipse

By default, the view displays instruction-level coverage, but it also records other types of coverage statistics. You can use the view menu to display coverage statistics in terms of blocks (which corresponds to branches in Cobertura terminology), lines, methods, or types.

Another possibility is to use the test coverage tool integrated into the Eclipse TPTP toolset (see Section 19.8). This tool is a little less refined than EclEmma.

12.9 Conclusion

Code coverage doesn't guarantee high-quality code, but it can certainly help. In practice, code coverage tools such as Cobertura can make a valuable contribution to code quality. By isolating poorly tested classes and pointing out untested lines of code, Cobertura can greatly contribute to finding and fixing deficits.

It is also worth noting that its main commercial rival, Clover, recently acquired by Atlassian, is also an excellent product. Clover is used by many open source products, as Atlassian offers free licences for open source projects. Some of the principal extra features that Clover provides are method coverage statistics, more varied reporting formats (including PDF), and very good IDE integration.

Nevertheless, if you are looking for a high-quality, open source, and free code coverage tool, Cobertura should be sufficient for many projects, and it is certainly better than using no tool at all. And, if you want to visualize test coverage statistics in Eclipse, you can use EclEmma or, alternatively, the coverage tool in the EclipseTPTP toolset.

PART V

Integration, Functional, Load, and Performance Testing

When Eeyore saw the pot, he became quite excited. "Why!" he said. "I believe my Balloon will just go into that Pot!"

"Oh, no, Eeyore," said Pooh. "Balloons are much too big to go into Pots. What you do with a balloon is, you hold the balloon—"

"Not mine," said Eeyore proudly. "Look, Piglet!" And as Piglet looked sorrowfully round, Eeyore picked the balloon up with his teeth, and placed it carefully in the pot; picked it out and put it on the ground; and then picked it up again and put it carefully back.

"So it does!" said Pooh. "It goes in!"

"So it does!" said Piglet. "And it comes out!"

"Doesn't it?" said Eeyore. "It goes in and out like anything."

"I'm very glad," said Pooh happily, "that I thought of giving you a Useful Pot to put things in."

"I'm very glad," said Piglet happily, "that thought of giving you something to put in a Useful Pot."

But Eeyore wasn't listening. He was taking the balloon out, and putting it back again, as happy as could be....

—"Eeyore has a birthday," *Winnie the Pooh*, A. A. Milne

Today's software applications are composed of an increasingly large number of different components. In addition to the different layers and modules within your application, you often need to integrate with databases, external applications, mainframes, and more. It is essential that these parts fit together smoothly and correctly.

This is the realm of integration testing. Indeed, if unit tests are a vital part of the testing process, there is nevertheless much more to testing than just unit testing. Integration testing, performance testing, and load testing also have a critial role to play. And they, too, can benefit from being integrated into the SDLC.

Unit testing generally refers to the process of testing an individual class or module, as far as possible in isolation from the rest of the system. For example, this can involve using mock objects or stubs to simulate interactions with other parts of the system. By reducing the interactions with other components, you make it easier to write tests ensuring that your individual classes perform as expected. If you aren't sure that each component works precisely as expected, then you will have trouble guaranteeing the stability of the system as a whole.

However, unit tests are not the whole story. In the final system, the numerous classes and components interact with each other in often complex ways. The more interactions there are, the more complex the system becomes, and the more places there are for something to go wrong. Integration or system testing involves testing how the individual components of your application work together. For example, for a Struts application, you might use a tool like StrutsTestCase to test all the components from the controller layer, through the service and DAO layers, and right down to the database.

Functional testing involves using the system as an end-user would. In real terms, this involves testing the application via its user interface. Writing automatic tests for user interfaces has traditionnally been a thorny problem. We will be looking at two tools that you can use to integrate GUI tests into your automatic testing process. Selenium is a powerful, innovative tool originally developed by the people at ThoughtWorks that uses a web browser to run tests against your web application. And FEST is an equally innovative product that lets you integrate Swing testing into as part of your JUnit or TestNG tests.

If your application uses web services, these need to be tested, too. SoapUI is a powerful tool that can be used to perform functional and performance tests on web service–based applications.

Load Testing involves placing your application under continued stress over a long period of time, usually by simulating heavy use from many simultaneous users. The aim of the exercise is to predict the load capacity of your application (how many users can you handle?), and to identify performance issues, memory leaks, or other problems that would not otherwise surface until the application goes into production.

Performance Testing is done to ensure that your application meets the specified performance requirements, such as a minimum number of requests per second, maximum acceptable response time, and so on. We will be looking at how to use the popular JMeter tool to test both load and performance testing.

In many projects, performance issues are ignored until user acceptance tests make it obvious that some tuning is needed. Nevertheless, it is good practice to integrate routine performance tests into the standard development process. Regular performance tests in key areas can flush out performance-related design and architecture issues at early stages, when they are easier to rectify. Incorporating performance tests into unit test suites also helps with regression testing, and forces you to think about exactly how much performance you really need from your application: which parts of the code need to run fast, and how fast is fast? JUnitPerf is a JUnit library that lets you integrate simple performance tests directly into your unit test code.

With all this testing going on, you're bound to find *some* issues. You may need to use some profiling software. For a long time, graphical profiling tools were the domain of commercial tools, and expensive ones at that! Recently, however, a number of open-source tools have emerged that can help developers analyze the performance (or lack thereof) of their Java application. In the following chapters, you will learn about open source Java profiling tools that can help to identify and correct performance and memory problems: first, the standard Java monitoring toolset, built around JConsole, and, second, the Eclipse profiling tools.

CHAPTER 13

Testing a Struts Application with StrutsTestCase

13.0 Introduction

In this chapter, we will look at tools that can improve test quality and efficiency when you are working with Struts applications.

Struts is a popular, widely used and well-documented J2EE (Java 2 Platform, Enterprise Edition) application framework with a long history and an active user community. It is based on a Model-View-Controller (MVC) architecture, which separates an application into (at least) three distinct layers. The Model represents the application business layer, the View represents the presentation layer (in other words, the screens), and the Controller represents the navigational logic, that binds the screens to the business layer. In Struts, the Controller layer is primarily implemented by Action classes, which we will see a lot more of later in this chapter.

Testing user interfaces has always been one of the trickiest parts of testing a web application, and testing Struts user interfaces is no exception to this rule. If you are working on a Struts application, StrutsTestCase is a powerful and easy-to-use testing framework that can make your life a lot easier. Using Struts and then StrutsTestCase, in combination with traditional JUnit tests, will give you a very high level of test coverage and increase your product reliability accordingly.

Note that StrutsTestCase does not let you test the HTML or JSP parts of your user interface: you need a tool such as Selenium for that (see Section 20.1). StrutsTestCase allows you to test the Java part of your user interface, from the Struts actions down. StrutsTestCase is an open source testing framework based on JUnit for testing Struts actions. If you use Struts, it can provide an easy and efficient manner for testing the Struts action classes of your application.

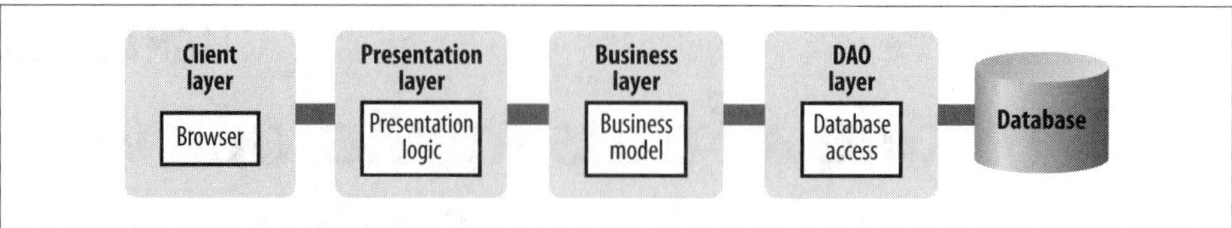

Figure 13-1. A typical J2EE architecture

13.1 Testing a Struts Application

Typical J2EE applications are built in layers (as illustrated in Figure 13-1):

- The DAO layer encapsulates database access. Hibernate mapping and object classes, Hibernate queries, JPA, entity EJBs, or some other entity-relation persistence technology may be found here.
- The business layer contains more high-level business services. Ideally, the business layer will be relatively independent of the database implementation. Session EJBs are often used in this layer.
- The presentation layer involves displaying application data for the user and interpreting the user requests. In a Struts application, this layer typically uses JSP/JSTL pages to display data and Struts actions to interpret the user queries.
- The client layer is basically the web browser running on the user's machine. Client-side logic (for example, JavaScript) is sometimes placed here, although it is hard to test efficiently.

The DAO and business layers can be tested either using classic JUnit tests or some of the various JUnit extensions, depending on the architectural details. DbUnit is a good choice for database unit testing (see Chapter 14).

Testing the presentation layer in a Struts application has always been difficult. Even when business logic is well confined to the business layer, Struts actions generally contain important data validation, conversion, and flow control code. By contrast, not testing the Struts actions leaves a nasty gap in your code coverage. StrutsTestCase lets you fill this gap.

Unit testing the action layer also provides other benefits:

- The view and control layers tend to be better-thought-out and often are simpler and clearer.
- Refactoring the action classes is easier.
- It helps to avoid redundant and unused action classes.
- The test cases help document the action code, which can help when writing the JSP screens.

These are typical benefits of test-driven development, and they are as applicable in the Struts action layer as anywhere else.

13.2 Introducing StrutsTestCase

The StrutsTestCase project provides a flexible and convenient way to test Struts actions from within the JUnit framework. It lets you do white-box testing on your Struts actions by setting up request parameters and checking the resulting Request or Session state after the action has been called.

StrutsTestCase allows either a mock-testing approach, where the framework simulates the web server container, or an in-container approach, where the Cactus framework is used to run the tests from within the server container (for example, Tomcat).

The mock-testing approach is more lightweight and runs faster than the Cactus approach, and thus allows a tighter development cycle. However, the mock-testing approach cannot reproduce all of the features of a full-blown servlet container. Some things are inevitably missing. It is much harder to access server resources or properties, or use JNDI functionality, for example.

The Cactus approach, also known as in-container testing, allows testing in a genuine running servlet container. This has the obvious advantage of simulating the production environment with more accuracy. It is, however, generally more complicated to set up and slower to run, especially if the servlet container has to restart each time you run your tests.

All StrutsTestCase unit test classes are derived from either `MockStrutsTestCase` for mock testing, or from `CactusStrutsTestCase` for in-container testing. Here, we will look at both techniques.

13.3 Mock Tests Using StrutsTestCase

Mock-testing in StrutsTestCase is fast and lightweight, as there is no need to start up a serlvet container before running the tests. The mock-testing approach simulates objects coming from the web container to give your Action objects the impression that they are in a real server environment.

To test an action using StrutsTestCase, you create a new test class that extends the `MockStrutsTestCase` class. The `MockStrutsTestCase` class provides methods to build a simulated HTTP request, to call the corresponding Struts action, and to verify the application state once the action has been completed.

Imagine you are asked to write an online accommodation database with a multicriteria search function. According to the specifications, the search function is to be implemented by the `/search.do` action. The action will perform a multicriteria search based on the specified criteria and places the result list in a request-scope attribute named *results* before forwarding it to the results list screen. For example, the following URL should display a list of all accommodation results in France:

```
/search.do?country=FR
```

To implement this function in Struts, we need to write the corresponding action class and update the Struts configuration file accordingly. Now, suppose that we want to implement this method using a test-driven approach. Using a strict test-driven approach, we would try to write the unit test first, and then write the Action afterward. In practice, the exact order may vary depending on the code to be tested. Here, in the first iteration, we just want to write an empty Action class and set up the configuration file correctly. StrutsTestCase mock tests can check this sort of code quickly and efficiently, which lets you keep the development loop tight and productivity high. The first test case is fairly simple, so we can start here. This initial test case might look like this:

```
public class SearchActionTest extends MockStrutsTestCase {
    public void testSearchByCountry() {
        setRequestPathInfo("/search.do");
        addRequestParameter("country", "FR");
        actionPerform();
    }
}
```

StrutsTestCase tests usually follow the same pattern. First, you need to set up the URL you want to test. Behind the scenes, you are actually determining which Struts action mapping, and which action, you are testing. StrutsTestCase is useful for this kind of testing because you can do end-to-end testing, pretty much from the HTTP request through the Struts configuration and mapping files, and down to the Action classes and underlying business logic.

You set the basic URL by using the `setRequestPathInfo()` method. You can add any request parameters using the `addRequestParameter()` method. The previous example sets up the URL "/search.do?country=FR" for testing.

When it is doing mock tests, StrutsTestCase does not try to test this URL on a real server: it simply studies the *struts-config.xml* file to check the mapping and invoke the underlying Action class. By convention, StrutsTestCase expects to find the *struts-config.xml* file in your WEB-INF directory. If, for some reason, you need to put it elsewhere, you will need to use the `setConfigFile()` method to let StrutsTestCase know where it is.

Once this is set up, you invoke the Action class by using the `actionPerform()` method. This creates mock `HttpServletRequest` and `HttpServletResponse` objects, and then lets Struts take control. Once Struts has finished running the appropriate Action methods, you should check the mock `HttpServletResponse` to make sure that the application is now in the state we where expecting. Are there any errors? Did Struts forward to the right page? Has the `HttpSession` been updated appropriately? And so on. In this simple case, we simply check that the action can be invoked correctly.

In our first iteration, we just want to write, configure, and invoke an empty Struts `Action` class. The main aim is to verify the Struts configuration. The `Action` class itself might look like this:

```
public class SearchAction extends Action {
  /**
   * Search by country
   */
  public ActionForward execute(ActionMapping mapping,
                               ActionForm form,
                               HttpServletRequest request,
                               HttpServletResponse response) {

    //
    // Invoke model layer to perform any necessary business logic
    //
    ...
    //
    // Success!
    //
    return mapping.findForward("success");
  }
}
```

We also update the Struts configuration file to use this class when the */search.do* URL is invoked. The relevant parts of the *struts-config.xml* file are shown here:

```
<struts-config>
  <form-beans>
    ...
    <form-bean name="searchForm" type="org.apache.struts.action.DynaActionForm">
      <form-property name="country" type="java.lang.String" />
    </form-bean>
    ...
  </form-beans>
  <action-mappings>
    ...
    <!--  Search -->
    <action path="/search" attribute="searchForm" name="searchForm"
            scope="request" type="com.wakaleo.jpt.struts.sample.actions.SearchAction"
            validate="false">
      <forward name="success" path="/pages/SearchResults.jsp" />
      <forward name="failure" path="/pages/Welcome.jsp" />
    </action>
    ...
  </action-mappings>
</struts-config>
```

This mapping is not particularly complex. We use a simple `DynaForm`, called "searchForm," to pass the query parameter to the action. The action itself is implemented by the `SearchAction` class shown above.

Now, without further ado, we can run our unit test and make sure that everything works. Our sample application uses Maven (see Chapter 2), so we just need to put the unit test class in the appropriate directory and run the tests as follows:

```
$ mvn test
.
-------------------------------------------------------
```

```
 T E S T S
-------------------------------------------------------
Running com.wakaleo.jpt.struts.sample.actions.SearchActionTest
...
INFO: Initialize action of type: com.wakaleo.jpt.struts.sample.actions.SearchAction
Tests run: 1, Failures: 0, Errors: 0, Skipped: 0, Time elapsed: 0.866 sec

Results :
Tests run: 1, Failures: 0, Errors: 0, Skipped: 0

[INFO] ------------------------------------------------------------------------
[INFO] BUILD SUCCESSFUL
[INFO] ------------------------------------------------------------------------
[INFO] Total time: 4 seconds
[INFO] Finished at: Tue Nov 14 23:16:44 NZDT 2006
[INFO] Final Memory: 4M/11M
[INFO] ------------------------------------------------------------------------
```

This test will verify the Struts configuration and call the corresponding Action class, which is certainly worth doing. As any Struts developer will confirm, a lot of time can be wasted because of silly errors in the *struts-config.xml* file. However, it will not check what the action actually does in any detail. To do that, we need to verify the action results.

StrutsTestCase provides many ways to check the outcome of your actions. Some of the principal techniques include the following: you also can inspect the state of the HTTP request and session objects, using `getRequest()`, `getResponse()`, and `getSession()`, respectively.

Error or informational messages
: It is often useful to test whether error conditions are being correctly returned to the presentation layer. You can check for the presence (or lack thereof) of action messages returned by the controller using methods such as `verifyNoActionErrors()` and `verifyActionErrors()`.

Navigation
: You can verify that the action has transferred control to a particular page, using either the logical forward name (`verifyForward()`) or the actual target path (`verifyForwardPath()`).

Application state
: You can also inspect the state of the HTTP request, response, and session objects, using `getRequest()`, `getResponse()`, and `getSession()`, respectively.

Some of these techniques are illustrated in the following test cases:

```
public class SearchActionTest extends MockStrutsTestCase {
    public void testSearchByCountry() {
        setRequestPathInfo("/search.do");
        addRequestParameter("country", "FR");
        actionPerform();
        verifyNoActionErrors();
        verifyForwardPath("/pages/SearchResults.jsp");
```

```
        assertNotNull(request.getAttribute("results"));
    }
}
```

Here, we check three things:

- There were no `ActionError` messages.
- Control was passed to the "/pages/SearchResults.jsp" page.
- The *results* attribute was placed in the request scope.

In this example, we are using simple JSP pages for the presentation layer. Many Struts projects use Tiles, which is a powerful templating system that ties in well with Struts. You can use StrutsTestCase to test your Tiles mappings as well. For example, you could check that the "success" forward actually points to the right tiles definition (in this case, "result.page"), using the *verifyTilesForward()* method, as follows:

```
verifyTilesForward("success", "result.page");
```

In practice, we will probably want to perform business-specific tests on the test results. For instance, suppose the results attribute is expected to be a list of exactly 100 Hotel domain objects, and that we want to be sure that all of the hotels in this list are in France. To do this type of test, the code will be very similar to standard JUnit testing:

```
public void testSearchByCountry() {
  setRequestPathInfo("/search.do");
  addRequestParameter("country", "FR");
  actionPerform();
  verifyNoActionErrors();
  verifyForwardPath("/pages/SearchResults.jsp");
  assertNotNull(request.getAttribute("results"));
  List<Hotel> results = (List<Hotel>) request.getAttribute("results");
  assertEquals(results.size(), 100);
  for (Hotel hotel : results) {
       assertEquals(hotel.getCountry(), "France");
  }
}
```

When you test more complex cases, you may want to test sequences of actions. For example, suppose we do a search on all hotels in France, and then click on an entry to display the details. Suppose we have a Struts action to display the details of a given hotel, which can be called as follows:

```
/displayDetails.do?id=123456
```

Using StrutsTestCase, we can easily simulate a sequence of actions in the same test case, where a user performs a search on all hotels in France, and then clicks on one to see the details:

```
public void testSearchAndDisplay() {
  setRequestPathInfo("/search.do");
  addRequestParameter("country", "FR");
  actionPerform();
  verifyNoActionErrors();
```

```
        verifyForward("success");
        assertNotNull(request.getAttribute("results"));
        List<Hotel> results = (List<Hotel>) request.getAttribute("results");
        Hotel hotel = (Hotel) results.get(0);

        setRequestPathInfo("/displayDetails.do");
        addRequestParameter("id", hotel.getId());
        actionPerform();
        verifyNoActionErrors();
        verifyForward("success");
        Hotel hotel = (Hotel) request.getAttribute("hotel");
        assertNotNull(hotel);
        ...
    }
```

13.4 Testing Struts Error Handling

Error handling is an important part of any web application and needs to be tested appropriately. In StrutsTestCase, you can test error handling principally by checking that your actions return the correct messages when something goes wrong. Suppose we want to check that the application behaves gracefully if an illegal country code is specified. We write a new test method and check the returned Struts ErrorMessages using `verifyActionErrors()`:

```
public void testSearchByInvalidCountry() {
  setRequestPathInfo("/search.do");
  addRequestParameter("country", "XX");
  actionPerform();
  verifyActionErrors(
      new String[] {"error.unknown,country"});
  verifyForward("failure");
}
```

Sometimes you want to verify data directly in the ActionForm object. You can do this using `getActionForm()`, as in the following example:

```
public void testSearchByInvalidCountry() {
  setRequestPathInfo("/search.do");
  addRequestParameter("country", "XX");
  actionPerform();
  verifyActionErrors(
      new String[] {"error.unknown,country"});
  verifyForward("failure");
  SearchForm form = (SearchForm) getActionForm();
  assertEquals("Scott", form.getCountry("XX"));
}
```

Here, we verify that the illegal country code is correctly kept in the ActionForm after an error.

13.5 Customizing the Test Environment

It is sometimes useful to override the `setUp()` method, which lets you specify non-default configuration options. In this example, we use a different *struts-config.xml* file and deactivate Extensible Markup Language (XML) configuration file validation:

```
public void setUp() {
  super.setUp();
  setConfigFile("/WEB-INF/my-struts-config.xml");
  setInitParameter("validating","false");
}
```

13.6 First-Level Performance Testing

Testing an action or a sequence of actions is an excellent way of testing that request response times are acceptable. Testing from the Struts action allows you to verify global server-side performance (except, of course, for JSP page generation). It is a very good idea to do some first-level performance testing at the unit-testing level to quickly isolate and remove performance problems, and also to integrate them into the build process to help avoid performance regressions. Here are some basic rules of thumb that I use for first-level Struts performance testing:

- Test multicriteria search queries with as many combinations as possible (to check that indexes are correctly defined).
- Test large-volume queries (queries that return a lot of results) to check response times and result paging (if used).
- Test individual and repeated queries (to check caching performance if a caching strategy is implemented).

Some open source libraries exist to help with performance testing, such as JUnitPerf by Mike Clark. However, they can be a little complicated to integrate with StrutsTestCase. In many instances, a simple timer can do the trick. Here is a very simple but efficient way of doing first-level performance testing:

```
public void testSearchByCountry() {
  setRequestPathInfo("/search.do");
  addRequestParameter("country", "FR");
  long t0 = System.currentTimeMillis();
  actionPerform();
  long t1 = System.currentTimeMillis() - t0;
  log.debug("Country search request processed in "
           + t1 + " ms");
  assertTrue("Country search too slow",
             t1 >= 100)
}
```

13.7 Conclusion

Unit testing is an essential part of agile programming, in general, and test-driven development, in particular. However, Struts actions have traditionally been a weak point in the unit testing process and tend to be poorly tested, thus introducing a high risk of bugs and unstable code. StrutsTestCase provides a good solution to this problem. StrutsTestCase is an easy and efficient way to unit test Struts actions, which are otherwise difficult to test using JUnit.

Mock testing is an excellent approach for developers to test their Struts actions, allowing quick testing and fast feedback. The more cumbersome in-container approach can be useful for integration testing.

CHAPTER 14

Integration Testing Databases with DbUnit

14.0 Introduction

The JUnit family provides the basic framework for unit testing for Java applications. On top of JUnit, there are many additional tools and frameworks for specialized areas of testing. In this chapter, we take a look at DbUnit,[*] an important tool for database integration testing.

We describe database testing as "integration testing" to distinguish it from ordinary "unit testing." Integration tests involve infrastructure beyond your own code. In the case of database integration testing, the additional infrastructure is a real database.

DbUnit is often referred to as a "JUnit extension." It is true that DbUnit provides TestCase subclasses, which you may extend in your own test classes. But DbUnit may be used in other ways independently of JUnit, too. For example, you can invoke DbUnit from within Ant to perform certain tasks.

In this chapter, we will describe the main purpose of DbUnit, give some simple examples of typical usage, and then proceed with several additional related topics.

14.1 Overview

Purpose of DbUnit

DbUnit has two main purposes:

To prime the database
: DbUnit can set up tables with known contents before each test method.

To verify the database
: DbUnit makes it easier to verify tables' contents after each test method.

[*] *http://dbunit.sourceforge.net*

If you were not using DbUnit, you would have several rather awkward alternatives to choose from. You could hand-code JDBC calls to prime and verify the database. This would usually be very awkward and a lot of work. Alternatively, if you are using object-relational mapping (ORM) in your main application, some people would advocate using that to populate your database with test data and to read values from the database for verification. This amounts to using your data access layer to test your data access layer, and may not be a good idea. ORM technology involves a fair amount of subtlety, such as caching for example, and we would prefer not to have this possibly confounding our tests.

DbUnit, by contrast, provides a relatively straighforward and flexible way to prime and verify the database independently of the code under test.

Setting Up DbUnit

The first thing you need to do to use DbUnit is to download the JAR file from *http://dbunit.sourceforge.net*. Place this JAR on the classpath of your IDE or your build script. You will also need the JDBC driver for your database on the classpath. There are no other dependencies for basic DbUnit usage.

You should also read the online documentation at *http://dbunit.sourceforge.net*. The documentation is not extensive, but it is short and relevant and definitely worth reading.

The next thing is to decide how you want to invoke DbUnit. For most testing scenarios, you will invoke DbUnit in your test classes, either directly or indirectly. You can also use DbUnit from Ant for some tasks, as we will see below.

Running with DbUnit

When you do database testing with DbUnit, you test against a real database. You need to have a connection to the real database at the time you run your tests.

Because DbUnit, and your code under test, will insert and modify data in this database, each developer needs to have more or less exclusive access to the database, or at least to a schema within it. Otherwise, if different developers run the tests at the same time, they may conflict with each other. The ideal setup is for each developer to have the database software installed on his machine. Machines these days are powerful enough to run virtually any database software with little overhead.

You don't have to have a copy of your entire production database on your machine. The nature of DbUnit tests is that they work best with relatively small amounts of data. DbUnit tests typically test the system for correct function, rather than for performance.

Some people suggest to use a lightweight embedded database (such as HSQLDB or Apache Derby) for running integration tests. This has the advantage of not requiring you to install special database software on your machine. Also, embedded databases typically run tests much faster than real databases because most of it can be done in memory and there is less overhead in general.

However, for a serious application this is usually misguided. Your application will often contain database-specific code or make use of database-specific features. These cannot be tested properly unless you use the same database when running your tests. Also, even if you are using an ORM layer such as Hibernate or JPA, which appears to make your code database-independent, the actual SQL generated by the ORM may well be different from one database to another. The JDBC drivers will certainly be different.

So, there are significant functional differences between an embedded database and your production database. To make your tests as useful and effective as possible, you should endeavor to make the database environments identical. Of course, if your production system itself uses an embedded database, then you are fortunate!

14.2 DbUnit Structure

The easiest way to use DbUnit when starting out is to extend one of its provided base classes. We will see some examples below where this is not necessary, or always advisable. For starting out, let's take a look at these base classes.

Like any good object-oriented framework or library, DbUnit contains a lot of interfaces. Most of the functionality of DbUnit is specified by interfaces. DbUnit adopts the convention that interfaces begin with a capital "I."

DbUnit often provides several concrete implementations of an interface. Typically, there is an abstract base implementation, with multiple specific concrete subclasses.

DatabaseTestCase

The main base class in DbUnit is `DatabaseTestCase`. Before DbUnit 2.2, you would extend `DatabaseTestCase` to create your test classes. As of DbUnit 2.2, there is a new subclass that you should extend instead, `DBTestCase`. The main difference with `DBTestCase` is that it provides a `getConnection()` method that delegates to the `IDatabaseTester`. You provide or override the default `IDatabaseTester` by overriding `newDatabaseTester()`.

The `IDatabaseTester` is responsible for providing several important features for testing:

- The database connection
- The setup test data set
- The setup operation (usually `CLEAN_INSERT`)
- The teardown operation (usually none)

DbUnit provides several standard `IDatabaseTester` implementations, and you can easily use one of these, extend one of them, or provide your own.

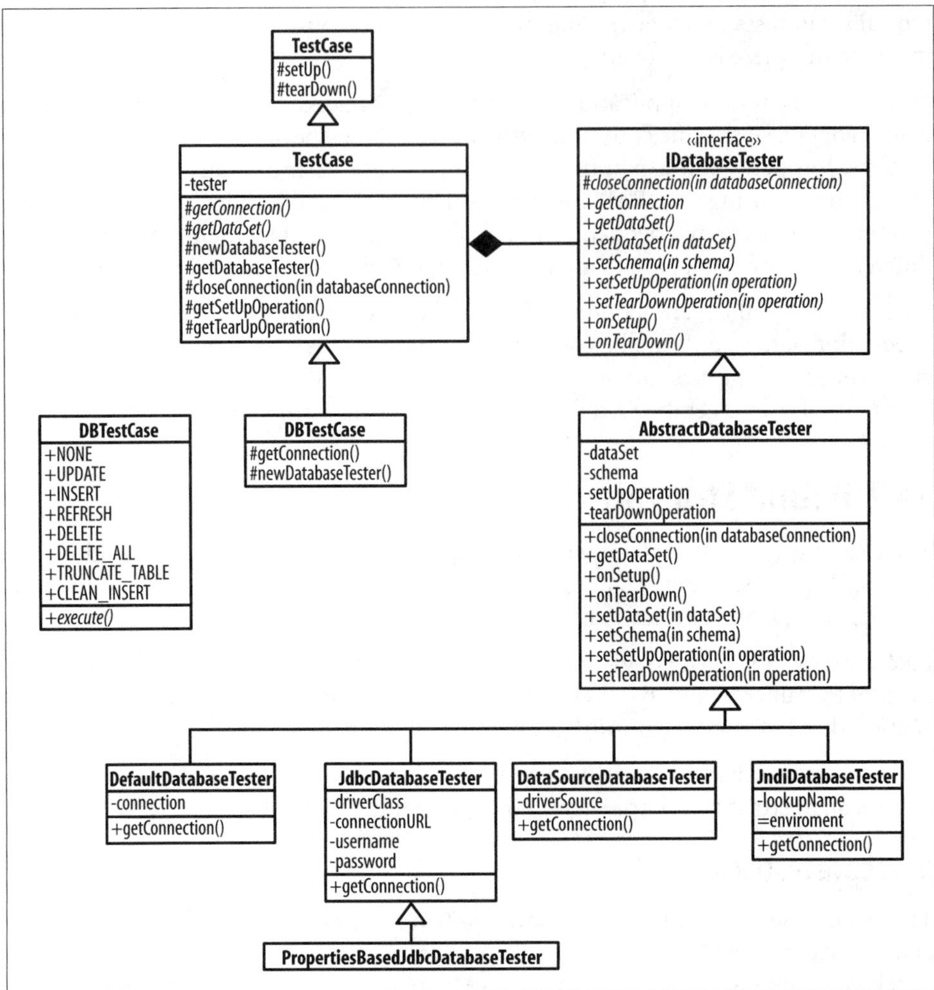

Figure 14-1. DatabaseTestCase, IDatabaseTester hierarchy

The `DatabaseTestCase` and `IDatabaseTester` hierarchies are shown in Figure 14-1.

We'll see how these classes work in some detail in our examples, and we will refer back to features from these diagrams as we explain them.

IDatabaseConnection

When a `DatabaseTestCase` or `IDatabaseTester` needs to access the actual database, it does so via an `IDatabaseConnection`. The `IDatabaseConnection` is basically a wrapper or adapter for a JDBC `Connection`. You can customize an `IDatabaseConnection` via its `DatabaseConfig`, which is a collection of name/value features and properties. These classes are shown in Figure 14-2.

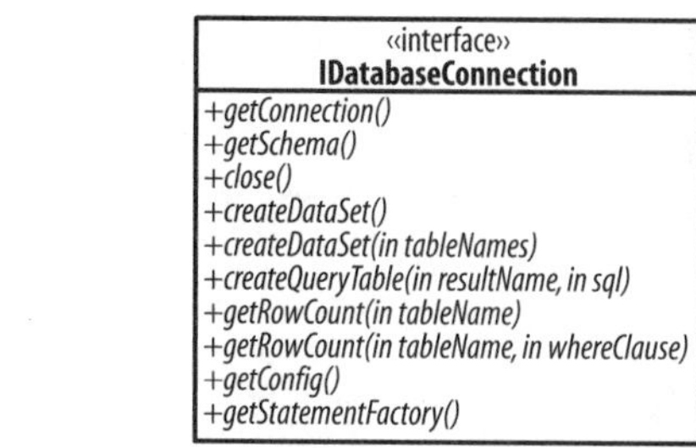

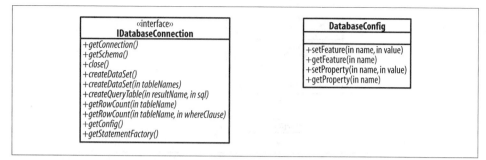

Figure 14-2. IDatabaseConnection and DatabaseConfig

IDataSet

DbUnit represents the actual data for tests as an `IDataSet`, which is an abstract representation of the data in a collection of tables.

DbUnit provides several concrete implementations of `IDataSet`, which you can use to obtain data sets from different sources, and to decorate them with additional functionality. Some of the implementations are shown in Figure 14-3. For example, `FlatXmlDataSet`, `CsvDataSet`, and `XlsDataSet` are different ways of representing data in files. We'll look at examples of these next. You can find others by examining the source code.

ITable

A table in turn is represented by an `ITable`, which is basically a set of rows and columns. Figure 14-4 shows `ITable`, along with some implementations.

ITableMetaData

Finally, DbUnit uses an `ITableMetaData` object to provide information about a table: its name and the characteristics of its columns. Figure 14-5 shows `ITableMetaData` and some implementations.

These interfaces represent the core functionality of DbUnit. Of course, DbUnit contains many more interfaces and classes than these. We will see some additional interfaces and classes in the examples that follow.

You don't need to understand all of these classes to start using DbUnit. Some of them, such as `ITableMetaData`, you will only use when customizing or extending DbUnit. The examples should give you a good idea of how the classes fit together, and how you can use them in your own projects.

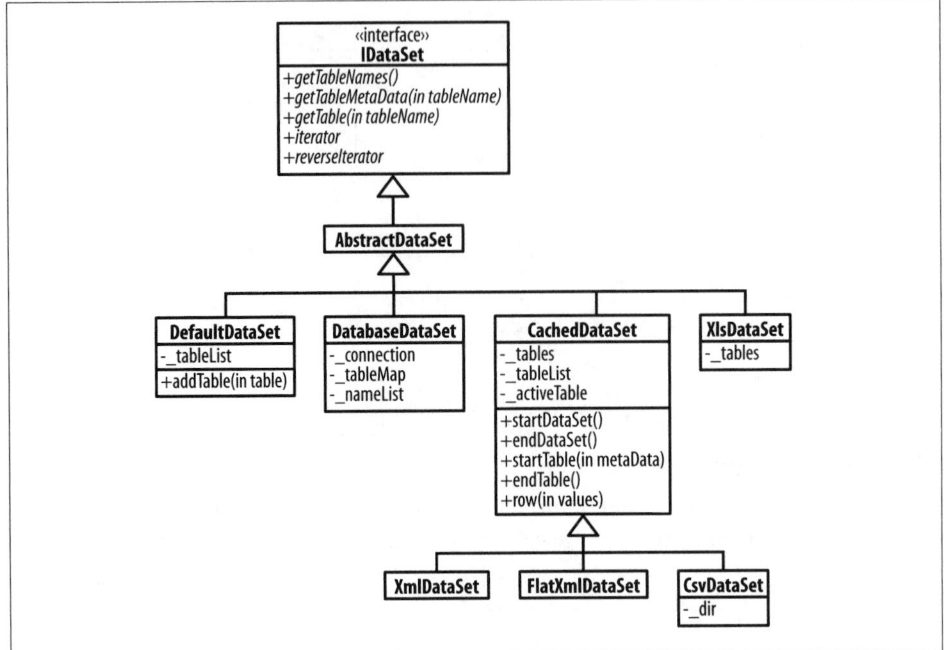

Figure 14-3. IDataSet and some implementations

14.3 Example Application

We'll explain various DbUnit features through a series of examples. The code for the examples is provided in the source code that accompanies this book. An Ant build script to set up and run the code is also provided.

For the examples, we'll use a database schema adapted from the PetClinic application provided with the Spring Framework.* This application is one of the samples provided with the Spring framework. It is an implementation of the classic (infamous) Pet Store J2EE demo application. Most of our examples do not depend on Spring—we're simply using this schema as a convenient sample application.

The PetClinic schema we'll use is shown in Figure 14-6. It is slightly modified from the original, in that we've added a couple of extra columns to use in demonstrating certain DbUnit features.

The Spring version of this application provides HSQLDB and MySQL variants of the database. For the examples in this book, I have adapted the schema to run on Oracle instead. (You can download Oracle Express Edition for free for Windows or GNU/Linux.) The Oracle SQL DDL to define this schema is provided in *create_tables.sql*.

* *http://www.springframework.org*

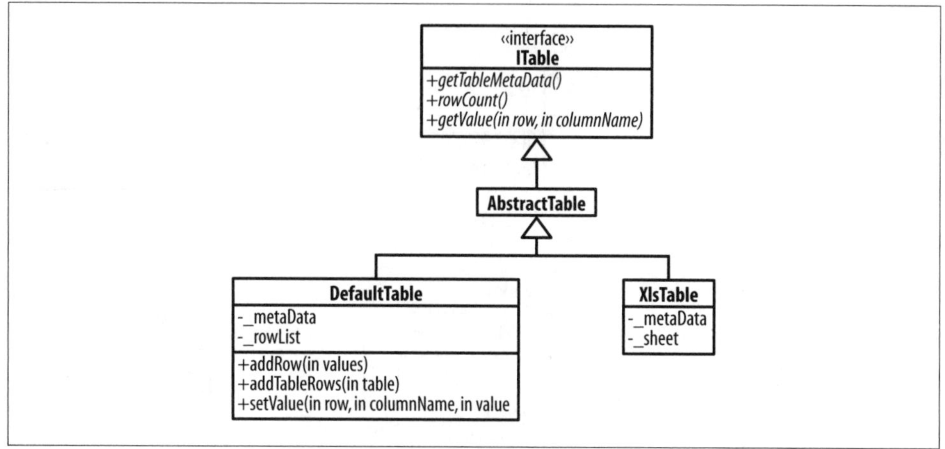

Figure 14-4. ITable and some implementations

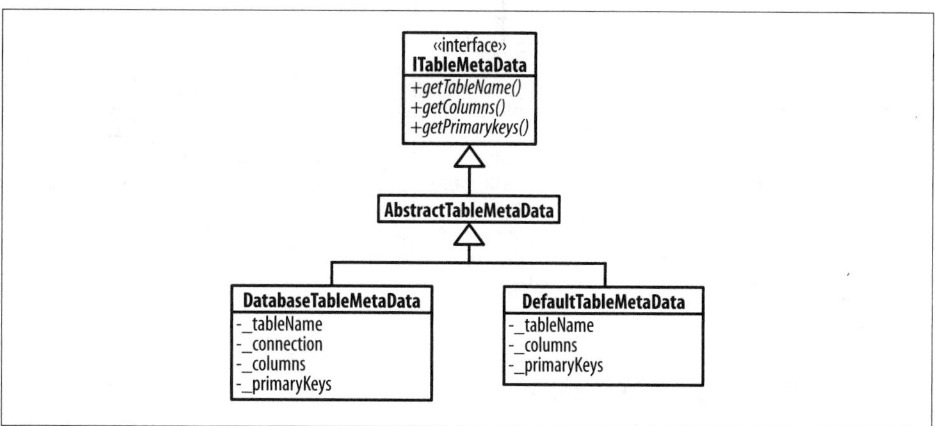

Figure 14-5. ITableMetaData and implementations

14.4 Priming the Database

For the first examples, I'll show how to use DbUnit to prime the database with known test data before a test. The standard way to do this is via the `setUp()` method of your test. Or rather, the `setUp()` method of `DatabaseTestCase`. The basic idea is that you provide an `IDataSet`, containing the data you want, and DbUnit loads the data.

In the first examples, we'll use the `FlatXmlDataSet`, which is probably the most commonly used implementation of `IDataSet`. Later, we'll show a couple of other alternatives.

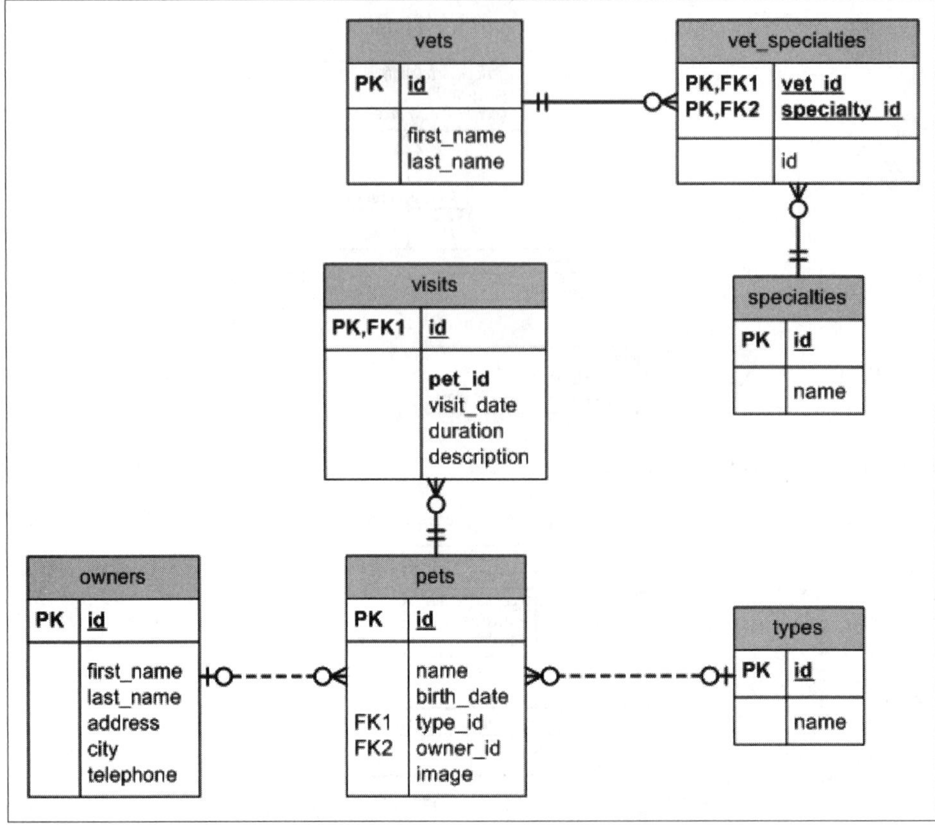

Figure 14-6. PetClinic schema

Verifying Querying a Single Row

The simplest kind of database test is to test some code that retrieves one single row from the database. Consider this interface for a Data Access Object (DAO) for the `owners` table:

```
public interface OwnerDao {
  Collection<Owner> findOwners(String lastName);
  Owner loadOwner(int id);
  void storeOwner(Owner owner);
  void deleteOwner(Owner owner);
}
```

The DAO includes a method, `loadOwner()`, for retrieving a single `Owner` by ID. The listing below shows a simple JDBC implementation of the `loadOwner()` method:

```
public class JdbcOwnerDao extends AbstractJdbcDao implements OwnerDao {

  // ...
```

```
public Owner loadOwner(int id) {
  Connection conn = null;
  PreparedStatement stmt = null;
  PreparedStatement stmt2 = null;
  ResultSet rs = null;
  try {
    conn = getConnection();
    stmt = conn.prepareStatement(
                "SELECT id, first_name, last_name, address, city, telephone "
              + "FROM owners WHERE id = ?");
    stmt.setInt(1, id);
    stmt2 = conn.prepareStatement(
                "SELECT p.id p_id, p.name p_name, p.birth_date, t.id t_id,
                 t.name t_name "
              + "FROM pets p JOIN types t ON t.id = p.type_id WHERE owner_id
              = ? ORDER BY 1");
    stmt2.setInt(1, id);
    rs = stmt.executeQuery();
    if (rs.next()) {
      Owner result = new Owner();
      result.setId(id);
      result.setFirstName(rs.getString("first_name"));
      result.setLastName(rs.getString("last_name"));
      result.setAddress(rs.getString("address"));
      result.setCity(rs.getString("city"));
      result.setTelephone(rs.getString("telephone"));
      Collection<Pet> pets = new ArrayList<Pet>();
      ResultSet rs2 = stmt2.executeQuery();
      while (rs2.next()) {
        Pet pet = new Pet();
        pet.setId(rs2.getInt("p_id"));
        pet.setName(rs2.getString("p_name"));
        pet.setBirthDate(DateUtils.localDate(rs2.getDate("birth_date")));
        Type type = new Type();
        type.setId(rs2.getInt("t_id"));
        type.setName(rs2.getString("t_name"));
        pet.setType(type);
        pets.add(pet);
      }
      result.setPets(pets);
      return result;
    }
    else {
      return null;
    }
  }
  catch (SQLException ex) {
    throw new RuntimeException(ex);
  }
  finally {
    closeResultSet(rs);
    closeStatement(stmt);
    closeStatement(stmt2);
    closeConnection(conn);
  }
```

```
    }

    // ...

}
```

This DAO implementation is intended only to illustrate how you would use DbUnit to test your own DAOs. We would not code a production DAO in a real system like this. There are many things wrong with it. For example:

- The JDBC code is verbose, repetitive, and does not handle exceptions properly.
- The code mixes low-level data access with connection management.
- The DAO is inflexible about when to fetch dependent relationships (i.e., the "pets" collection).
- The DAO has no capability for lazy-loading.
- There is no transaction management.

In a real system, we would use an ORM framework for DAOs, or a JDBC framework such as iBATIS or Spring JDBC DAO support. However, for the purposes of giving a DbUnit example, it will suffice.

We won't waste space including program listings of most of the DAO functions under test. The source code is included with the accompanying code, if you want to try running it for yourself. Remember that the DAO code is not to production standards—it is simply there to demonstrate DbUnit.

To test this DAO using DbUnit, we'll create a subclass of `DBTestCase`:

```
public class FlatXmlSelectOwnerTest extends DBTestCase {

  // ...

}
```

In this class, we override `newDatabaseTester()` to provide DbUnit with an `IDatabaseTester`:

```
  protected IDatabaseTester newDatabaseTester() throws Exception {
    return new DataSourceDatabaseTester(DataSourceUtils.getDataSource());
  }
```

In this case, we use a `DataSourceDatabaseTester`. This is a simple variant that uses a JDBC `DataSource` to obtain a connection to the database.

The several provided `IDatabaseTester` implementations obtain the connection to the database in different ways:

`DataSourceDatabaseTester`
: Gets connection from a `DataSource`

`DefaultDatabaseTester`
: Gets connection from one supplied in constructor

`JdbcDatabaseTester`
: Gets connection from JDBC via `DriverManager`

`JndiDatabaseTester`
: Gets connection from JNDI

We provide a `DataSource` obtained via a static utility method in our application: `DataSourceUtils.getDataSource()`. This method is hardcoded to return an appropriate data source for our application. Later in this chapter, we will see an alternative way to specify the data source without hard-coding it.

The current implementation of `DataSourceUtils` looks like this:

```
public class DataSourceUtils {

  private static final DataSource dataSource = createBasicDataSource();

  private static DataSource createBasicDataSource() {
    BasicDataSource result = new BasicDataSource();
    result.setDriverClassName("oracle.jdbc.OracleDriver");
    result.setUrl("jdbc:oracle:thin:@localhost:1521:XE");
    result.setUsername("jpt");
    result.setPassword("jpt");
    return result;
  }

  public static DataSource getDataSource() {
    return dataSource;
  }
}
```

Here, we are using `org.apache.commons.dbcp.BasicDataSource` to provide a *pooled data source*. If we use a more simplistic strategy for obtaining database connections, such as creating them from the JDBC `DriverManager`, we are likely to run into timing problems due to connection limits on the server. This is because `DriverManager` and similar approaches create a new physical connection to the server for every connection request. Because database tests request many connections in a short space of time, this can result in problems, even if you are running the server on your own machine.

Instead, the `BasicDataSource` uses a pool and in fact may create only one physical connection throughout the entire test suite. Not only does this eliminate resource and timing problems, it is also much faster.

The next thing we need to do is to provide an `IDataSet` containing the test data:

```
  protected IDataSet getDataSet() throws Exception {
    return new FlatXmlDataSet
    (getClass().getResourceAsStream("FlatXmlSelectOwnerTest.xml"));
  }
```

This method retrieves the file from an `InputStream` obtained on the classpath, but the constructor accepts any `InputStream`.

In this case, we're using a FlatXmlDataSet. This is an IDataSet that gets test data for tables from a single XML file. The XML for our data set looks like this:

```
<dataset>
  <owners id="1" first_name="Mandy" last_name="Smith" address="12 Oxford Street"
          city="Southfield" telephone="555-1234567"/>
  <owners id="2" first_name="Joe" last_name="Jeffries" address="25 Baywater Lane"
          city="Northbrook" telephone="555-2345678"/>
  <owners id="3" first_name="Herb" last_name="Dalton" address="2 Main St"
          city="Southfield" telephone="555-3456789"/>
  <owners id="4" first_name="Dave" last_name="Smith-Jones" address="12 Kent Way"
          city="Southfield" telephone="555-4567890"/>
  <pets/>
  <visits/>
</dataset>
```

The main document element is <dataset>. Within the document, there is an element for each table row. The element is named for the table the row belongs in, and there is an attribute for each column. You can also specify an empty table with an empty element, e.g., <pets/>.

DbUnit also provides the older XmlDataSet, which uses a more verbose and awkward XML format. We don't look at XmlDataSet in this book.

Providing this dataset via overriding the getDataSet() method is all we need to do to get DbUnit to prime the database. Before each test method in FlatXmlSelectOwnerTest, DbUnit will delete all rows in the tables in the data set, then repopulate them from the data in the XML file.

An important consideration when using CLEAN_INSERT, the default setup operation, is the order in which it processed the tables. The CLEAN_INSERT operation INSERTs data in the order it finds the tables in the data set. Prior to inserting them, it DELETEs from them, in the reverse order.

This sequence helps you to arrange the tables in your data set to avoid foreign key constraint violations when clearing and reloading tables. Generally, you put parent tables first and child tables after. Sometimes this isn't enough, such as when you have circular referential integrity rules. We'll consider how to deal with those later.

Now, on to the actual tests:

```
private OwnerDao getOwnerDao() {
  return new JdbcOwnerDao(DataSourceUtils.getDataSource());
}

private static void assertOwner(Owner owner, int id, String firstName,
                                String lastName, String address,
                                String city, String telephone) {
  assertEquals(id, owner.getId());
  assertEquals(firstName, owner.getFirstName());
  assertEquals(lastName, owner.getLastName());
  assertEquals(address, owner.getAddress());
  assertEquals(city, owner.getCity());
```

```
    assertEquals(telephone, owner.getTelephone());
  }

  public void testLoadOwner() {
    OwnerDao ownerDao = getOwnerDao();
    Owner joe = ownerDao.loadOwner(2);
    assertOwner(joe, 2, "Joe", "Jeffries", "25 Baywater Lane", "Northbrook",
    "555-2345678");
  }

  // ... more tests ...
```

In the `testLoadOwner()` method, we obtain an instance of the DAO. We use the DAO to retrieve the `Owner` with ID 2, and we verify the properties of the returned object.

If the returned object were different from what we expected, at least one of the assertions would fail, resulting in a failed test. These assertions have nothing to do with DbUnit, and can be anything you want them to be. We will now see how DbUnit can be used to make assertions about results in the database.

Verifying Querying Multiple Rows

We can easily extend the test case now to verify the `findOwners()` method, which returns a collection of `Owner` objects:

```
  public void testFindOwners() {
    OwnerDao ownerDao = getOwnerDao();
    Iterator<Owner> owners = ownerDao.findOwners("smith").iterator();
    assertOwner(owners.next(), 1, "Mandy", "Smith", "12 Oxford Street", "Southfield",
    "555-1234567");
    assertOwner(owners.next(), 4, "Dave", "Smith-Jones", "12 Kent Way", "Southfield",
    "555-4567890");
    assertFalse(owners.hasNext());
  }
```

This test works from the same data set as the previous one.

Specifying NULLs by Omission

So, what if we need to specify `NULL` for a data value? There are several ways to do this with DbUnit. Probably the simplest way is to omit the column's attribute in the row.

Here's an example of a `FlatXmlDataSet` with some `NULL` column values:

```
<dataset>
  <owners id="1" first_name="Mandy" last_name="Smith" address="12 Oxford Street"
          city="Southfield" telephone="555-1234567"/>
  <owners id="2" first_name="Joe" last_name="Jeffries" address="25 Baywater Lane"
          telephone="555-2345678"/>
  <owners id="3" first_name="Herb" last_name="Dalton" address="2 Main St"
          city="Southfield"/>
  <owners id="4" first_name="Dave" last_name="Smith-Jones" address="12 Kent Way"
          city="Southfield" telephone="555-4567890"/>
  <pets/>
```

```
  <visits/>
</dataset>
```

In this example, there is no value specified for the `city` column in the second row, or for the `telephone` column in the third row.

Here's a modified test method that verifies the null properties in the resulting objects:

```
public void testValues() {
  OwnerDao ownerDao = getOwnerDao();
  assertOwner(ownerDao.loadOwner(1), 1, "Mandy", "Smith", "12 Oxford Street",
                                     "Southfield", "555-1234567");
  assertOwner(ownerDao.loadOwner(2), 2, "Joe", "Jeffries", "25 Baywater Lane",
                                     null, "555-2345678");
  assertOwner(ownerDao.loadOwner(3), 3, "Herb", "Dalton", "2 Main St",
                                     "Southfield", null);
  assertOwner(ownerDao.loadOwner(4), 4, "Dave", "Smith-Jones", "12 Kent Way",
                                     "Southfield", "555-4567890");
}
```

It's important to note that the order of the rows for the `owners` table in the `FlatXmlDataSet` is important when using this method. The attributes found on the first row for each table in the XML file determine the columns that DbUnit will populate for that table. If you omit an attribute for the first row, that column will be omitted (will be `NULL`) for *all* rows, whether or not you include the attribute for later rows. So, generally you will need to include all columns of interest on the first row. This is not usually a problem. It would be a problem if, for example, you had a pair of columns such that one or the other of them could be nonnull but not both.

Specifying NULLs by DTD

Another way to specify null columns is to use the DTD feature `FlatXmlDataSet`. You can optionally associate a DTD with a `FlatXmlDataSet` to specify the columns for each table in it.

Here's an example DTD for our test data set:

```
<!ELEMENT dataset (owners*, pets*, visits*)>
<!ELEMENT owners EMPTY>
<!ATTLIST owners
  id CDATA #REQUIRED
  first_name CDATA #IMPLIED
  last_name CDATA #IMPLIED
  address CDATA #IMPLIED
  city CDATA #IMPLIED
  telephone CDATA #IMPLIED
>
<!ELEMENT pets EMPTY>
<!ATTLIST pets
  id CDATA #REQUIRED
  name CDATA #IMPLIED
  birth_date CDATA #IMPLIED
  type_id CDATA #IMPLIED
  owner_id CDATA #IMPLIED
```

```
>
<!ELEMENT visits EMPTY>
<!ATTLIST visits
  id CDATA #REQUIRED
  pet_id CDATA #REQUIRED
  visit_date CDATA #IMPLIED
  description CDATA #IMPLIED
>
```

With this DTD, we have specified the full set of columns for each table. We can now give an XML file where no row has every column included:

```
<!DOCTYPE dataset SYSTEM "FlatXmlSelectOwnerNullByDtdTest.dtd">
<dataset>
  <owners id="1" first_name="Mandy" last_name="Smith" address="12 Oxford Street"
                 city="Southfield"/>
  <owners id="2" first_name="Joe" last_name="Jeffries" address="25 Baywater Lane"
                 telephone="555-2345678"/>
  <owners id="3" first_name="Herb" last_name="Dalton" address="2 Main St"
                 city="Southfield"/>
  <owners id="4" first_name="Dave" last_name="Smith-Jones" address="12 Kent Way"
                 telephone="555-4567890"/>
  <pets/>
  <visits/>
</dataset>
```

To instruct DbUnit to use the DTD, we use this alternative `FlatXmlDataSet` constructor when creating the data set:

```
protected IDataSet getDataSet() throws Exception {
  return new FlatXmlDataSet(
    getClass().getResourceAsStream("FlatXmlSelectOwnerNullByDtdTest.xml"),
    getClass().getResourceAsStream("FlatXmlSelectOwnerNullByDtdTest.dtd")
  );
}
```

Again, note that both arguments to the constructor are `InputStreams`, in this case obtained from the classpath.

With this in place, we can verify the properties of the returned objects in a modified test:

```
public void testValues() {
  OwnerDao ownerDao = getOwnerDao();
  assertOwner(ownerDao.loadOwner(1), 1, "Mandy", "Smith", "12 Oxford Street",
                                        "Southfield", null);
  assertOwner(ownerDao.loadOwner(2), 2, "Joe", "Jeffries", "25 Baywater Lane",
                                        null, "555-2345678");
  assertOwner(ownerDao.loadOwner(3), 3, "Herb", "Dalton", "2 Main St", "Southfield",
                                        null);
  assertOwner(ownerDao.loadOwner(4), 4, "Dave", "Smith-Jones", "12 Kent Way", null,
                                        "555-4567890");
}
```

This gives you some basic tools for populating your database using `FlatXmlDataSet`. We'll look at some alternative data set formats shortly, and we'll also show how to specify more exotic data values. But first, let's see how we can use DbUnit to verify data in the database after a test case.

14.5 Verifying the Database

The second use you can put DbUnit to in your database tests is verifying the data in the database after (or during) a test case. In this section, we'll see how to do that, and take a look at some of the issues involved.

Verifying an UPDATE

Let's consider a test for the `storeOwner()` method of our DAO. The `storeOwner()` method adds a new `Owner` to the database, or updates an existing `Owner`. We'll start by testing updates to an existing `Owner`. Here is the test code:

```
public void testUpdateOwner() throws Exception {
  OwnerDao ownerDao = getOwnerDao();
  Owner owner = ownerDao.loadOwner(1);
  owner.setFirstName("Mandy-Jane");
  owner.setLastName("Brown");
  owner.setAddress("21 Ocean Parade");
  owner.setCity("Westport");
  owner.setTelephone("555-9876543");
  ownerDao.storeOwner(owner);
  IDataSet expectedDataSet
      = new FlatXmlDataSet(getClass().getResourceAsStream
       ("FlatXmlUpdateOwnerTest.xml"));
  ITable expectedTable = expectedDataSet.getTable("owners");
  ITable actualTable = getConnection().createDataSet().getTable("owners");
  Assertion.assertEquals(expectedTable, actualTable);
}
```

In this test, we obtain an `Owner` object, change it, then save the changed object back to the database with the `storeOwner()` method.

We specify the expected results in a new `FlatXmlDataSet`, obtained from file *FlatXmlUpdateOwnerTest.xml* in the classpath. The contents of the file look like this:

```
<dataset>
  <owners id="1" first_name="Mandy-Jane" last_name="Brown" address="21 Ocean Parade"
                 city="Westport" telephone="555-9876543"/>
  <owners id="2" first_name="Joe" last_name="Jeffries" address="25 Baywater Lane"
                 city="Northbrook" telephone="555-2345678"/>
  <owners id="3" first_name="Herb" last_name="Dalton" address="2 Main St"
                 city="Southfield" telephone="555-3456789"/>
  <owners id="4" first_name="Dave" last_name="Smith-Jones" address="12 Kent Way"
                 city="Southfield" telephone="555-4567890"/>
  <pets/>
  <visits/>
</dataset>
```

As you can see, the result data set contains the same data as we primed the database with, except that the first row of the `owners` table is changed.

To compare the actual database contents with the expected table data, we retrieve an `ITable` instance via the `createDataSet()` and `getTable()` calls on the `IDatabaseConnection`. Finally, we use the `assertEquals()` from DbUnit's `Assertion` class, overloaded for `ITable`.

This test passes. If the data was wrong, DbUnit would fail the test. For example, suppose we omit the call to `ownerDao.storeOwner()`, to simulate the DAO not saving the data. Then, when we run the test, we get an output such as:

```
junit.framework.AssertionFailedError: value (table=owners, row=0, col=address):
expected:<21 Ocean Parade>
but was:<12 Oxford Street>
    at org.dbunit.Assertion.assertEquals(Assertion.java:147)
    at com.ora.javapowertools.dao.test.FlatXmlUpdateOwnerTest.testUpdateOwner
    (FlatXmlUpdateOwnerTest.java:46)
    ...
```

Note that DbUnit counts rows from 0.

Verifying a DELETE

We can do a very similar test for the `deleteOwner()` method. In doing do, we notice that the work to compare the database table to an expected result is the same for both tests, so it's better if we move that out to a separate method like this:

```
private void assertTable(String dataSetFilename, String tableName)
throws Exception {
  IDataSet expectedDataSet = new FlatXmlDataSet(getClass().
  getResourceAsStream(dataSetFilename));
  ITable expectedTable = expectedDataSet.getTable(tableName);
  ITable actualTable = getConnection().createDataSet().getTable(tableName);
  Assertion.assertEquals(expectedTable, actualTable);
}
```

Now we can proceed to write the test for `deleteOwner()`:

```
public void testDeleteOwner() throws Exception {
  OwnerDao ownerDao = getOwnerDao();
  Owner owner = ownerDao.loadOwner(1);
  ownerDao.deleteOwner(owner);
  assertTable("FlatXmlDeleteOwnerTest.xml", "owners");
}
```

In this test, we compare the table to the expected data in another `FlatXmlDataSet`, stored in *FlatXmlDeleteOwnerTest.xml*:

```
<dataset>
  <owners id="2" first_name="Joe" last_name="Jeffries" address="25 Baywater Lane"
                 city="Northbrook" telephone="555-2345678"/>
  <owners id="3" first_name="Herb" last_name="Dalton" address="2 Main St"
                 city="Southfield" telephone="555-3456789"/>
```

```
  <owners id="4" first_name="Dave" last_name="Smith-Jones" address="12 Kent Way"
              city="Southfield" telephone="555-4567890"/>
  <pets/>
  <visits/>
</dataset>
```

This time, the first row of the table has been deleted.

If the `deleteOwner()` method did not work correctly, we would get a failed test with something like this:

```
junit.framework.AssertionFailedError: row count (table=owners) expected:<3> but was:<4>
    at org.dbunit.Assertion.assertEquals(Assertion.java:128)
    at com.ora.javapowertools.dao.test.FlatXmlDeleteOwnerTest.assertTable
    (FlatXmlDeleteOwnerTest.java:38)
    at com.ora.javapowertools.dao.test.FlatXmlDeleteOwnerTest.testDeleteOwner
    (FlatXmlDeleteOwnerTest.java:45)
    ...
```

This time DbUnit finds that the data set is short by a row.

Verifying an INSERT, Ignoring the Key

Verifying an `UPDATE` or `DELETE` is quite straightforward. `INSERT`s can be a little more tricky when using surrogate keys such as those obtained from database `SEQUENCE`s. In this scenario, the generated key depends on the current value of the sequence, and can be different from one run to the next. DbUnit's `setUp()` does not restore database `SEQUENCE`s.

One approach to this is simply to ignore the generated key. We can do so with some test code like this:

```
public void testInsertOwner() throws Exception {
  OwnerDao ownerDao = getOwnerDao();
  Owner owner = new Owner();
  owner.setFirstName("John");
  owner.setLastName("Hudson");
  owner.setAddress("15 Dorset Av");
  owner.setCity("Easton");
  owner.setTelephone("555-7654321");
  ownerDao.storeOwner(owner);
  assertTable("FlatXmlInsertOwnerIgnoreSequenceTest.xml", "owners");
}
```

This code adds a new object, then compares the result against an expected table in *FlatXmlInsertOwnerIgnoreSequenceTest.xml*. The expected data look like this:

```
<dataset>
  <owners first_name="Mandy" last_name="Smith" address="12 Oxford Street"
         city="Southfield" telephone="555-1234567"/>
  <owners first_name="Joe" last_name="Jeffries" address="25 Baywater Lane"
         city="Northbrook" telephone="555-2345678"/>
  <owners first_name="Herb" last_name="Dalton" address="2 Main St"
         city="Southfield" telephone="555-3456789"/>
```

```
  <owners first_name="Dave" last_name="Smith-Jones" address="12 Kent Way"
          city="Southfield" telephone="555-4567890"/>
  <owners first_name="John" last_name="Hudson" address="15 Dorset Av"
          city="Easton" telephone="555-7654321"/>
  <pets/>
  <visits/>
</dataset>
```

The id column has been left out of the data set. This test fails with this output:

```
junit.framework.AssertionFailedError: column count (table=owners)
expected:<5> but was:<6>
    at org.dbunit.Assertion.assertEquals(Assertion.java:112)
    at com.ora.javapowertools.dao.test.FlatXmlInsertOwnerIgnoreSequenceTest.
    assertTable
(FlatXmlInsertOwnerIgnoreSequenceTest.java:41)
    at com.ora.javapowertools.dao.test.FlatXmlInsertOwnerIgnoreSequenceTest.
    testInsertOwner
(FlatXmlInsertOwnerIgnoreSequenceTest.java:53)
  ...
```

This is because DbUnit by default compares all columns in the expected table to all columns in the actual table. Because the actual table contains the id column and the existing table does not, the test fails.

We can correct this by applying a decorator to the actual table to remove the columns that are not in the expected table. We do this with this code in our assertTable method:

```
private void assertTable(String dataSetFilename, String tableName) throws
Exception {
  IDataSet expectedDataSet =
  new FlatXmlDataSet(getClass().getResourceAsStream(dataSetFilename));
  ITable expectedTable = expectedDataSet.getTable(tableName);
  ITable actualTable = getConnection().createDataSet().getTable(tableName);
  ITable actualToCompare = DefaultColumnFilter
                           .includedColumnsTable(actualTable,
                                                 expectedTable.getTableMetaData().
                                                 getColumns());
  Assertion.assertEquals(expectedTable, actualToCompare);
}
```

This technique is often handy for "system" columns such as sequence numbers and timestamps.

Verifying an INSERT, with the Key

There are often times when you *do* want to check the value of a generated key. One way we can do this with our current test is to reset the sequence to a known value. We add a new method, setSequence>setSequence():

```
private void setSequence(String sequence, int startValue) {
  Connection conn = null;
  Statement stmt = null;
  try {
    conn = DataSourceUtils.getDataSource().getConnection();
```

```
      stmt = conn.createStatement();
      stmt.execute("DROP SEQUENCE " + sequence);
      stmt.execute("CREATE SEQUENCE " + sequence + " START WITH " + startValue);
    }
    catch (SQLException ex) {
      throw new RuntimeException(ex);
    }
    finally {
      JdbcUtils.closeStatement(stmt);
      JdbcUtils.closeConnection(conn);
    }
  }
```

Then, we change the test code to the following:

```
  public void testInsertOwner() throws Exception {
    setSequence("owners_seq", 5);
    OwnerDao ownerDao = getOwnerDao();
    Owner owner = new Owner();
    owner.setFirstName("John");
    owner.setLastName("Hudson");
    owner.setAddress("15 Dorset Av");
    owner.setCity("Easton");
    owner.setTelephone("555-7654321");
    ownerDao.storeOwner(owner);
    assertTable("FlatXmlInsertOwnerWithSequenceTest.xml", "owners");
  }
```

This method uses the Oracle-specific technique for resetting a sequence: dropping and recreating it. Obviously, you would need to substitute something else for this if you are using a different database.

Another point to note about this technique is that `DROP` and `CREATE` are DDL operations. This means that they cannot be contained within a transaction. Depending on how you are managing transactions in both your production and test code, this can have implications for the ways that you organize your code.

In the DbUnit tests that we've seen so far, the DbUnit `setUp()` and the code under test have been run in their own transactions. Thus, the data being primed into the database is `COMMIT`ted, and so are the data changed by the test. In this scenario, there is no problem with DDL running as part of the test.

Later, we'll look at an example in which we update the database but roll back the update at the end of the test. In that variation, we need to be careful not to use DDL within the transaction we wish to roll back.

As well as dropping and recreating sequences, you can use DDL at select points in your tests to achieve other things, too. For example, if you have circular dependencies in your foreign keys, you cannot arrange a sequence of tables such that they can be cleanly inserted or deleted. Instead, you could simply use DDL to `DROP DISABLE` the foreign key constraints before the clean insert, and restore them afterward. This requires hacking around in the set up operations, but it is a useful technique, nonetheless.

14.6 Replacing Values

We saw earlier a couple of ways of placing NULL into a FlatXmlDataSet. CsvDataSet also supports the literal null in a CSV file, and InlineDataSet can similarly support null values inline. It turns out that there are often times when you want to use custom replacement values in a data set.

DbUnit provides ReplacementDataSet, which can be used to replace values in a data set, either with null or other values. We can also write some code of our own for more advanced scenarios.

Using NULL with a ReplacementDataSet

DbUnit's ReplacementDataSet offers a simple replacement facility out of the box. Here's how we could use it to substitute NULLs into the database, in a similar way to our earlier examples:

```
protected IDataSet getDataSet() throws Exception {
  IDataSet result = dataSet(
    table("owners",
      col("id", "first_name", "last_name", "address", "city", "telephone"),
      row("1", "Mandy", "Smith", "12 Oxford Street", "Southfield", "(NULL)"),
      row("2", "Joe", "Jeffries", "25 Baywater Lane", "(NULL)", "555-2345678"),
      row("3", "Herb", "Dalton", "2 Main St", "Southfield", "(NULL)"),
      row("4", "Dave", "Smith-Jones", "12 Kent Way", "(NULL)", "555-4567890")
    ),
    table("pets", col("id")),
    table("visits", col("id"))
  );
  Map objectMap = new HashMap(1);
  objectMap.put("(NULL)", null);
  return new ReplacementDataSet(result, objectMap, null);
}
```

In this example, we've used ReplacementDataSet with an InlineDataSet. For this use it is rather pointless because, as mentioned, we can simply use a literal null with that data set anyway.

But ReplacementDataSet can be used in this way with *any* data set. ReplacementDataSet is a *decorator* and wraps an existing data set.

ReplacementDataSet works with a Map of replacement values. In our example, we placed a single entry in the Map: the string "(NULL)," with associated value null. You can place any number of key/value replacement pairs you like.

Using NULL with a ValueReplacer

DbUnit's own ReplacementDataSet is somewhat limited in that you can specify only literal values as replacements. Sometimes you need more flexibility. For example, it would be nice to have DbUnit call some arbitrary code to compute a replacement value.

We can add this functionality pretty easily. First, we define a `ValueReplacer` interface:

```
public interface ValueReplacer {
  Object replaceValue(Object value);
}
```

This defines a callback, or strategy, that we can get DbUnit to call.

To replace values in an `ITable`, we'll use a `ValueReplacerTable` decorator:

```
public class ValueReplacerTable implements ITable {
  private ITable target;
  private ValueReplacer valueReplacer;

  public ValueReplacerTable(ITable target, ValueReplacer valueReplacer) {
    this.target = target;
    this.valueReplacer = valueReplacer;
  }

  public ITableMetaData getTableMetaData() {
    return target.getTableMetaData();
  }

  public int getRowCount() {
    return target.getRowCount();
  }

  public Object getValue(int row, String column) throws DataSetException {
    Object value = target.getValue(row, column);
    return valueReplacer.replaceValue(value);
  }
}
```

This `ITable` decorates an existing `ITable`, replacing values in it according to the `ValueReplacer` strategy.

Let's define a trivial example of a `ValueReplacer` strategy, one that in effect does just the same as the existing `ReplacementDataSet`:

```
public class LiteralValueReplacer implements ValueReplacer {

  private String matchValue;
  private Object replacementValue;

  public LiteralValueReplacer() {
  }

  public LiteralValueReplacer(String matchValue, Object replacementValue) {
    this.matchValue = matchValue;
    this.replacementValue = replacementValue;
  }

  public void setMatchValue(String matchValue) {
    this.matchValue = matchValue;
  }
```

```
  public void setReplacementValue(Object replacementValue) {
    this.replacementValue = replacementValue;
  }

  public Object replaceValue(Object value) {
    if (value instanceof String) {
      String stringValue = (String) value;
      if (stringValue.equals(matchValue)) {
        return replacementValue;
      }
    }
    return value;
  }
}
```

We can use this `LiteralValueReplacer` to replace the string `"(NULL)"` with `null` as follows:

```
protected IDataSet getDataSet() throws Exception {
  return dataSet(
    new ValueReplacerTable(
      table("owners",
        col("id", "first_name", "last_name", "address", "city", "telephone"),
        row("1", "Mandy", "Smith", "12 Oxford Street", "Southfield", "(NULL)"),
        row("2", "Joe", "Jeffries", "25 Baywater Lane", "(NULL)", "555-2345678"),
        row("3", "Herb", "Dalton", "2 Main St", "Southfield", "(NULL)"),
        row("4", "Dave", "Smith-Jones", "12 Kent Way", "(NULL)", "555-4567890")
      ),
      new LiteralValueReplacer("(NULL)", null)
    ),
    table("pets", col("id")),
    table("visits", col("id"))
  );
}
```

Using an Image ValueReplacer

Let's now use `ValueReplacerTable` to do something that we can't do with the simplistic `ReplacementDataSet`. This time we'll use the `pets` table for our test, instead of the `owners` table. The `pets` table includes a BLOB column named `image` for the pet's photo. We'll specify a BLOB value in a dataset by giving a resource name from which to load the BLOB. We'll indicate that the value is a BLOB by prefixing the resource name with the string `"blob:,"` e.g., `"blob:fido.jpg."`

Because the idea of prefixing a value is quite general and distinct from actually using BLOBs, we'll start with a `PrefixValueReplacer`:

```
public abstract class PrefixValueReplacer implements ValueReplacer {

  private String prefix;

  protected PrefixValueReplacer(String prefix) {
    this.prefix = prefix;
```

```
    }

    public void setPrefix(String prefix) {
      this.prefix = prefix;
    }

    public Object replaceValue(Object value) {
      if (value instanceof String) {
        String stringValue = (String) value;
        if (stringValue.startsWith(prefix)) {
          String remainingString = stringValue.substring(prefix.length());
          return doReplaceValue(remainingString);
        }
      }
      return value;
    }

    protected abstract Object doReplaceValue(String remainingString);
  }
```

The `PrefixValueReplacer` class takes care of recognizing the prefix and deciding when it applies. We can now extend this class for the specific case of BLOBs:

```
  public class BlobValueReplacer extends PrefixValueReplacer {

    private static final String DEFAULT_PREFIX = "blob:";

    public BlobValueReplacer() {
      this(DEFAULT_PREFIX);
    }

    public BlobValueReplacer(String prefix) {
      super(prefix);
    }

    protected Object doReplaceValue(String remainingString) {
      InputStream inputStream = null;
      try {
        inputStream = getClass().getResourceAsStream(remainingString);
        return IOUtils.bytesFromStream(inputStream);
      }
      finally {
        IOUtils.closeInputStream(inputStream);
      }
    }
  }
```

The `BlobValueReplacer` loads the specified BLOB as a resource from the classpath, and uses it as the replacement value.

We can tie this together in a test case for the `PetDao` DAO. First, we apply our `ValueReplacerTable` in `getDataSet()`:

```
    protected IDataSet getDataSet() throws Exception {
      ITable typesTable = table("types",
        col("id", "name"),
```

```
    row("1", "Cat"),
    row("2", "Bird"),
    row("3", "Fish"),
    row("4", "Dog")
  );
  ITable ownersTable = table("owners",
    col("id", "first_name", "last_name", "address", "city", "telephone"),
    row("1", "Mandy", "Smith", "12 Oxford Street", "Southfield", "555-1234567"),
    row("2", "Joe", "Jeffries", "25 Baywater Lane", "Northbrook", "555-2345678"),
    row("3", "Herb", "Dalton", "2 Main St", "Southfield", "555-3456789"),
    row("4", "Dave", "Smith-Jones", "12 Kent Way", "Southfield", "555-4567890")
  );
  ITable petsTable = table("pets",
    col("id", "name", "birth_date", "type_id", "owner_id", "image"),
    row("1", "Fido", "1999-10-22", "4", "1", "blob:fido.jpg"),
    row("2", "Rex", "2001-01-20", "4", "4", "blob:rex.jpg"),
    row("3", "Guppers", "2006-12-25", "3", "2", "(NULL)"),
    row("4", "Bonnie", "2005-03-12", "1", "3", "(NULL)"),
    row("5", "Ditzy", "2004-07-08", "1", "3", "(NULL)")
  );
  petsTable = new ValueReplacerTable(petsTable,
              new LiteralValueReplacer("(NULL)", null));
  petsTable = new ValueReplacerTable(petsTable, new BlobValueReplacer());
  return dataSet(
    typesTable,
    ownersTable,
    petsTable
  );
}
```

We're actually using two `ValueReplacerTable`s: one for the BLOBs, and another for `NULL`s. We can wrap as many decorators as we wish around a given `ITable`.

The `pets` table has referential integrity constraints to both the `types` table and the `owners` table, so we need to provide data for them, too. The returned data set includes all three tables.

Now, we can write the test case, along with an assertion method for `Pet` objects:

```
private static void assertEquals(byte[] expected, byte[] actual) {
  if (expected == null) {
    assertNull(actual);
    return;
  }
  assertEquals(expected.length, actual.length);
  for (int i = 0; i < expected.length; i++) {
    assertEquals(expected[i], actual[i]);
  }
}

private byte[] image(String resource) {
  InputStream inputStream = null;
  try {
    inputStream = getClass().getResourceAsStream(resource);
    return IOUtils.bytesFromStream(inputStream);
```

```
    }
    finally {
      IOUtils.closeInputStream(inputStream);
    }
  }

  private static void assertPet(Pet pet, int id, String name, LocalDate birthDate,
                                String typeName, String ownerFirstName, byte[] image) {
    assertEquals(id, pet.getId());
    assertEquals(name, pet.getName());
    assertEquals(birthDate, pet.getBirthDate());
    assertEquals(typeName, pet.getType().getName());
    assertEquals(ownerFirstName, pet.getOwner().getFirstName());
    assertEquals(image, pet.getImage());
  }

  public void testValues() {
    PetDao petDao = getPetDao();
    assertPet(petDao.loadPet(1), 1, "Fido", ld(1999, 10, 22), "Dog", "Mandy",
    image("fido.jpg"));
    assertPet(petDao.loadPet(2), 2, "Rex", ld(2001, 1, 20), "Dog", "Dave",
    image("rex.jpg"));
    assertPet(petDao.loadPet(3), 3, "Guppers", ld(2006, 12, 25), "Fish",
    "Joe", null);
  }
```

In this test, as in our domain class, we're treating the image as a `byte[]` object. In a real domain model, you would probably use a higher level of abstraction. Either way, we need to verify that we got the correct set of bytes from the database.

Hopefully, this example has given you some idea of how you can extend DbUnit's data sets with decorators of your own to provide for quite flexible and elegant ways of loading data into your database, and verifying data.

14.7 Alternative Dataset Formats

The `FlatXmlDataSet` format for test data is the de facto "standard" format for DbUnit testing. It is quite flexible, and easy to use, and probably contains support for the most features. DbUnit does provide several additional options however. Let's take a look at a couple of them.

Using an XLS Dataset

One of the biggest drawbacks of the XML format is that it tends to lose the "tableness" of the data. The XML syntax, rather than highlighting the structure of the information, tends to obscure it. It would be nice if we could represent our test data in a format that looks more like a database table.

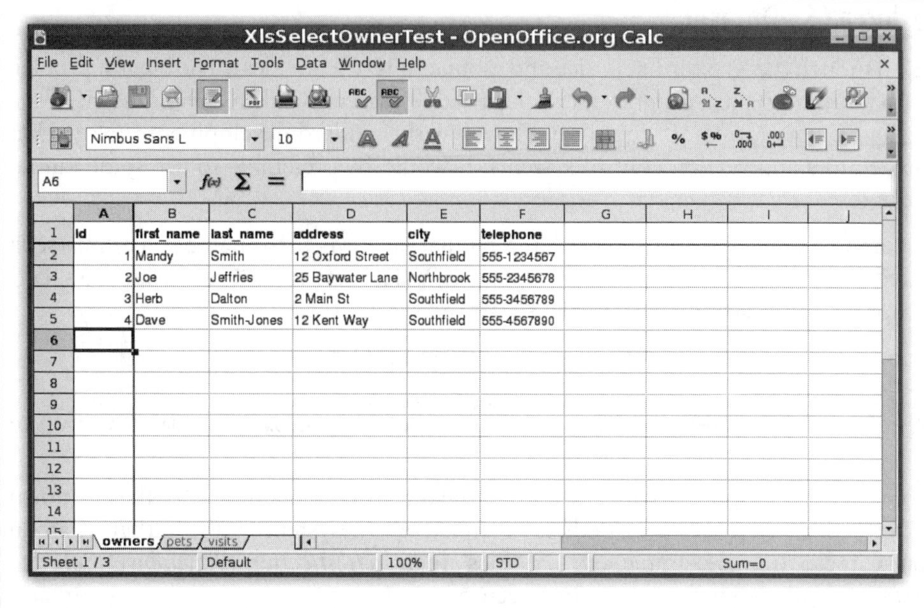

Figure 14-7. XLS data set

One commonly known tool that can represent data in a tabular form is a spreadsheet. Thanks to the Apache POI library,* DbUnit can offer support for data sets in Microsoft Excel (XLS) files via its `XlsDataSet` class. To use Excel files with DbUnit, you need to download the POI JAR and place it in your classpath.

Let's see how the data set looks using XLS files. We make each table a tab in the spreadsheet file, named for the table. The first row of tab contains the column names. The rest of the rows contain the data. For our `SELECT` test on the `owners` table, an example is shown in Figure 14-7.

To use this data set in our test, all we need to do is change the implementation of `getDataSet()` to use an `XlsDataSet`:

```
protected IDataSet getDataSet() throws Exception {
  return new XlsDataSet(getClass().getResourceAsStream("XlsSelectOwnerTest.xls"));
}
```

Notice that again the constructor accepts any `InputStream`, which is very convenient.

You can, of course, prepare your XLS files using Microsoft Excel. If you are using GNU/Linux, or even on Windows, you may prefer to use OpenOffice† instead. It's free, and it appears to create files that are more XLS-compatible than Excel itself. (You may have less trouble reading OpenOffice-saved XLS files with POI.)

* *http://poi.apache.org*

† *http://www.openoffice.org*

Using a CSV Dataset

Even though the XLS format is nice and tabular, it is still not ideal. The biggest problem with it, from a typical programmer's perspective, is that the file format is essentially an opaque binary format. It doesn't work well with standard development tools such as text editors and version control systems. It would be preferable to use some kind of plain text format.

A common plain text format that has a tabular layout is the venerable "comma-separated values" or CSV file. DbUnit supports CSV data sets via its `CsvDataSet` class. Let's adapt the `SelectOwner` test to use a `CsvDataSet`.

Again, the only change to our code is in **`getDataSet()`**:

```
protected IDataSet getDataSet() throws Exception {
  return new CsvDataSet(new File("src/test/com/ora/javapowertools/dao/test/csv/"));
}
```

For CSV data sets, we provide the path to the directory containing CSV files. Unfortunately, this must be provided as a (relative) filesystem path, rather than an `InputStream`. In our example, the CSV files are in *src/test/com/ora/javapowertools/dao/test/csv*, relative to the project root directory.

DbUnit's `CsvDataSet` first looks in this directory for a file named *table-ordering.txt*. This file names the data set's tables in the order in which DbUnit is to populate them. For our example, the file contains:

```
owners
pets
visits
```

Also in the directory, we place a CSV file for each table, with extension *.csv*. The *owners.csv* file contains these lines:

```
id,first_name,last_name,address,city,telephone
1,Mandy,Smith,12 Oxford Street,Southfield,555-1234567
2,Joe,Jeffries,25 Baywater Lane,Northbrook,555-2345678
3,Herb,Dalton,2 Main St,Southfield,555-3456789
4,Dave,Smith-Jones,12 Kent Way,Southfield,555-4567890
```

The `CsvDataSet` gives a nice text-based, tabular representation of the test data. It plays friendly with version control and other development tools. One disadvantage of `CsvDataSet` is that the test data is even more spread out and removed from the test code than before.

Using an InlineDataSet

A common problem with all of the data sets we've looked at so far is that the data is separated from the test code. Much of the time, this is not a problem; in fact it is desirable. It is a common practice with DbUnit to put common "reference" data into a data set to be loaded by a common base class for all tests. That way, a certain "baseline" set of data is always available.

In many tests, however, it would be nicer to place the data that relates specifically to the test closer to the test code. It would be nice to put the data *in* the test code. That's what we'll do now with an *inline* data set.

Our `InlineDataSet` is very simple, though it does make use of the varargs feature introduced in Java 5:

```
public class InlineDataSet {
  public static IDataSet dataSet(ITable... tables) {
    return new DefaultDataSet(tables);
  }

  public static ITable table(String name, String[] cols, String[]... data)
  throws DataSetException {
    Column[] columns = new Column[cols.length];
    for (int i = 0; i < cols.length; i++) {
      columns[i] = new Column(cols[i], DataType.UNKNOWN);
    }
    DefaultTable result = new DefaultTable(name, columns);
    for (String[] row : data) {
      result.addRow(row);
    }
    return result;
  }

  public static String[] col(String... columns) {
    return columns;
  }

  public static String[] row(String... data) {
    return data;
  }
}
```

The implementation is very brief, because it mostly uses preexisting functionality provided with DbUnit, such as `DefaultDataSet` and `DefaultTable`.

The static methods are intended to be imported and used by test classes, and the **`varargs`** argument lists allow test classes to represent data quite elegantly, as in the new version of our **`getDataSet()`** method:

```
  protected IDataSet getDataSet() throws Exception {
    return dataSet(
      table("owners",
        col("id", "first_name", "last_name", "address", "city", "telephone"),
        row("1", "Mandy", "Smith"      , "12 Oxford Street", "Southfield",
            "555-1234567"),
        row("2", "Joe"   , "Jeffries"   , "25 Baywater Lane", "Northbrook",
            "555-2345678"),
```

```
        row("3", "Herb" , "Dalton"     , "2 Main St"       , "Southfield",
            "555-3456789"),
        row("4", "Dave" , "Smith-Jones", "12 Kent Way"     , "Southfield",
            "555-4567890")
      ),
      table("pets", col("id")),
      table("visits", col("id"))
    );
  }
```

This time, there is no need to reference and `InputStream` or other external file for the data set. All of the data is included inline in the test code.

The rest of the code doesn't change. Now we have the test code and the data for it together, so it's easier to edit it and see what relates to what.

Again, we need to stress that this is appropriate only for data specific to each test case. If you have common data you want to use for a set of tests, or all your tests, you should load that data in a common `setUp()` routine, and you may find no advantage to placing the data inline.

14.8 Dealing with Custom Data Types

You may have noticed that in all of the data sets we've looked at, the data values are given simply as strings. How does DbUnit know what the type of a column is supposed to be? How does DbUnit distinguish among the treatment of a `VARCHAR` and a `NUMBER` and a `DATE`?

DbUnit uses `DataType`s to do this. A `DataType` is DbUnit's abstraction for a JDBC data type. DbUnit includes built-in `DataType`s for all of the standard JDBC data types.

Some databases treat certain `DataType`s differently. For example, although JDBC distinguishes among `DATE`, `TIME`, and `TIMESTAMP`, Oracle for a long time supported only a single `DATE` type, which served the purpose of all three.

DbUnit caters for variation of JDBC data types across databases using a `DataTypeFactory`. The `DataTypeFactory` determines the `DataType` for a column. DbUnit provides a basic `DataTypeFactory` for each of several popular databases out of the box.

For example, the `OracleDataTypeFactory` causes columns with JDBC type of either `DATE` or `TIMESTAMP` to be treated as `TIMESTAMP`s within DbUnit. To use the `OracleDataTypeFactory` in your test, you set a property in the `DatabaseConfig` on the `IDatabaseConnection`:

```
protected IDatabaseConnection getConnection() throws Exception {
  IDatabaseConnection result = super.getConnection();
  DatabaseConfig config = result.getConfig();
  config.setProperty(DatabaseConfig.PROPERTY_DATATYPE_FACTORY,
  new OracleDataTypeFactory());
  return result;
}
```

In this section, we'll see how you can extend DbUnit's `DataType` and `DataTypeFactory` framework and provide support for custom data types.

Specifying an INTERVALDS Data Type

Although the `INTERVAL` data types have been part of the SQL standard for a long time (since ANSI SQL-92), they have never been supported by JDBC. This is a pity, because they are often an appropriate choice for columns in a well-considered data model.

However, it is often possible to use `INTERVAL` types anyway, using vendor-specific JDBC extensions. Let's see how to use `INTERVAL`s with DbUnit, using an addition to the PetClinic schema.

I've added a `duration` column to the original `visits` table. The DDL is shown here:

```
CREATE TABLE visits (
  id INTEGER NOT NULL,
  pet_id INTEGER NOT NULL,
  visit_date DATE,
  duration INTERVAL DAY TO SECOND,
  description VARCHAR(255)
);
```

In the domain model, I've added a `duration` property, using the `Duration` class from the Joda-Time date/time library.*

As already mentioned, DbUnit's `OracleDataTypeFactory` handles standard JDBC date and time types. It also handles some variations of CLOBs and binary large object (BLOBs). There are several Oracle-specific data types that `OracleDataTypeFactory` does not handle, however. These include the `INTERVAL` types, and also Oracle's `XMLType` support, for example.

We'll define our own `DataType` for Oracle's `INTERAL DAY TO SECOND`. Before we do this, we need to know a few things about how the type works:

- What JDBC type does the driver return for an `INTERAL DAY TO SECOND` column?
- What Java class does the driver return for these objects?
- How should comparisons be done for this type?

One way to answer these questions is to write some simple exploratory code. We can define a simple test table like this:

```
CREATE TABLE t (
  c INTERVAL DAY TO SECOND
);

INSERT INTO t VALUES (INTERVAL '1' DAY);
INSERT INTO t VALUES (INTERVAL '1 2:03:04' DAY TO SECOND);
```

* *http://joda-time.sourceforge.net*

```
INSERT INTO t VALUES (INTERVAL '1' HOUR);
COMMIT WORK;
```

With this test table in place, we can investigate the JDBC properties of the column with some simple Java code:

```
public class PrintINTERVALDSMetaData {

  public static void main(String[] args) throws SQLException {
    Connection conn = DataSourceUtils.getDataSource().getConnection();
    ResultSet rs = conn.createStatement().executeQuery("SELECT * FROM t ORDER BY 1");
    ResultSetMetaData metaData = rs.getMetaData();
    System.out.println("metaData.getColumnType(1) = " + metaData.getColumnType(1));
    while (rs.next()) {
      Object c = rs.getObject(1);
      System.out.println("c.getClass() = " + c.getClass());
      System.out.println("c.toString() = " + c.toString());
    }
  }
}
```

This code prints the following output:

```
metaData.getColumnType(1) = -104
c.getClass() = class oracle.sql.INTERVALDS
c.toString() = 0 1:0:0.0
c.getClass() = class oracle.sql.INTERVALDS
c.toString() = 1 0:0:0.0
c.getClass() = class oracle.sql.INTERVALDS
c.toString() = 1 2:3:4.0
```

From this, we can determine the answers to our questions:

- The JDBC type for Oracle's `INTERVAL DAY TO SECOND` is –104. The constant `oracle.jdbc.OracleTypes.INTERVALDS` is defined to this value.
- The Java class is `oracle.sql.INTERVALDS`.
- For comparison purposes, as long as we only care about value equality, we can compare the `toString()` representation of the object.

With this information, we can define a `OracleINTERVALDSDataType` data type:

```
public class OracleINTERVALDSDataType extends AbstractDataType {
  public OracleINTERVALDSDataType() {
    super("INTERVALDS", OracleTypes.INTERVALDS, INTERVALDS.class, false);
  }

  public Object typeCast(Object value) throws TypeCastException {
    return value;
  }

  public int compare(Object o1, Object o2) throws TypeCastException {
    return o1.toString().equals(o2.toString()) ? 0 : 1;
  }
}
```

There is not much work to do because most of it can be done by the base class AbstractDataType, provided that we call its constructor and give it the appropriate values. In other cases, you may need to implement more methods of IDataType your self to get your custom data type to work. See the source code for more details.

In order to use this data type in our test, we need to create a DataTypeFactory that recognizes Oracle INTERVAL DAY TO SECOND columns and associates them with this data type:

```
public class OracleINTERVALDSDataTypeFactory extends DefaultDataTypeFactory {

  public static final DataType ORACLE_INTERVALDS = new OracleINTERVALDSDataType();

  public DataType createDataType(int sqlType, String sqlTypeName)
  throws DataTypeException {
    if (sqlType == OracleTypes.INTERVALDS || "INTERVALDS".equals(sqlTypeName)) {
      return ORACLE_INTERVALDS;
    }
    return super.createDataType(sqlType, sqlTypeName);
  }
}
```

Now we need to specify this data type factory on our IDatabaseConnection when the test runs:

```
protected IDatabaseConnection getConnection() throws Exception {
  IDatabaseConnection result = super.getConnection();
  DatabaseConfig config = result.getConfig();
  config.setProperty(DatabaseConfig.PROPERTY_DATATYPE_FACTORY,
  new OracleINTERVALDSDataTypeFactory());
  return result;
}
```

Finally, to specify INTERVAL DAY TO SECOND values in our test data set, we need a ValueReplacer that can create them. We'll use an extension of PrefixValueReplacer again, this time with default prefix "INTERVALDS:":

```
public class INTERVALDSValueReplacer extends PrefixValueReplacer {

  public static final String DEFAULT_PREFIX = "INTERVALDS:";

  public INTERVALDSValueReplacer() {
    this(DEFAULT_PREFIX);
  }

  public INTERVALDSValueReplacer(String prefix) {
    super(prefix);
  }

  protected INTERVALDS doReplaceValue(String remainingString) {
    return new INTERVALDS(remainingString);
  }
}
```

That is starting to seem like a lot of work, but we are almost done. We can now write a test method that specifies an expected `visits` table with an `INTERVAL DAY TO SECOND` column:

```
public void testValues() throws Exception {
  setSequence("visits_seq", 1);
  Pet fido = getPetDao().loadPet(1);
  Visit visit = new Visit();
  visit.setPet(fido);
  visit.setVisitDate(ld(2007, 11, 4));
  visit.setDuration(dur(1, 6, 30, 0));
  visit.setDescription("Upset tummy");
  VisitDao visitDao = getVisitDao();
  visitDao.storeVisit(visit);
  ITable expectedTable = table("visits",
    col("id", "pet_id", "visit_date", "duration", "description"),
    row("1", "1", "2007-11-04", "INTERVALDS:1 06:30:00.0", "Upset tummy")
  );
  expectedTable = new ValueReplacerTable(expectedTable,
  new INTERVALDSValueReplacer());
  assertTable(expectedTable, "visits");
}
```

Note again that although we've used the inline data set for the example, this value replacement technique can be used just as easily with any other DbUnit data set, including `FlatXmlDataSet`.

14.9 Other Applications

We have now looked in detail at many ways of specifying data sets and customizing their behavior. Let's look at some different aspects of DbUnit and database testing.

Injecting the Test Fixture

In our tests so far we've used the `DataSourceUtils.getDataSource()` utility method to obtain a `DataSource`. Real applications generally do not-hard code their data source configuration, although it may be perfectly acceptible for test code.

These days, it is popular to use *dependency injection* to obtain data sources and other external resources, and sometimes it may be an advantange to inject these dependencies into test code, too.

Probably the most popular dependency-injection framework today is Spring.* Spring provides a variety of useful services for JEE applications, and is very test-friendly. Spring even provides several base classes for integration testing, which can make set up much simpler for testing complex arrangements of components. Let's see how we can use Spring to inject the data source for our tests.

* *http://springframework.org*

Spring's basic support for dependency injection in tests is the base class AbstractDependencyInjectionSpringContextTests. By extending this base class, and telling it where to find your configuration data, you can get Spring to inject your test classes with resources such as DataSources.

Let's define a base class for our dependency-injected database tests:

```
public abstract class SpringDatabaseTestCase extends
AbstractDependencyInjectionSpringContextTests {

  private DataSource dataSource;
  private IDatabaseTester tester;

  public DataSource getDataSource() {
    return dataSource;
  }

  public void setDataSource(DataSource dataSource) {
    this.dataSource = dataSource;
  }

  protected String[] getConfigLocations() {
    return new String[] {
      "classpath:/applicationContext.xml"
    };
  }

  protected void onSetUp() throws Exception {
    super.onSetUp();
    tester = new DataSourceDatabaseTester(getDataSource());
    tester.setDataSet(getDataSet());
    tester.onSetup();
  }

  protected abstract IDataSet getDataSet() throws Exception;

  protected IDatabaseConnection getConnection() throws Exception {
    return tester.getConnection();
  }

  protected void closeConnection(IDatabaseConnection connection) throws Exception {
    tester.closeConnection(connection);
  }

}
```

This class does not extend DatabaseTestCase. It cannot because it extends Spring's AbstractDependencyInjectionSpringContextTests. Instead, it instantiates an IDatabaseTester of its own, and uses that to provide DbUnit functionality. The class provides getDataSet(), getConnection(), and closeConnection() methods as does IDatabaseTestCase, so the idea is it can be similarly extended by concrete test subclasses.

This base class instructs Spring to load the configuration from a single application context file, *applicationContext.xml*, located in the root of the classpath. We put this configuration in the file:

```
<!DOCTYPE beans PUBLIC "-//SPRING//DTD BEAN//EN"
"http://www.springframework.org/dtd/spring-beans.dtd">
<beans>
  <!-- DataSource -->
  <bean id="dataSource" class="org.apache.commons.dbcp.BasicDataSource">
    <!-- The first properties are standard required commons DBCP DataSource
     configuration. -->
    <property name="driverClassName" value="${db.driver}" />
    <property name="url" value="${db.url}" />
    <property name="username" value="${db.userid}" />
    <property name="password" value="${db.password}" />
  </bean>

  <bean class="org.springframework.beans.factory.config.PropertyPlaceholderConfigurer">
    <property name="location" value="classpath:/applicationContext.properties"/>
    <property name="systemPropertiesModeName" value="SYSTEM_PROPERTIES_MODE_OVERRIDE"/>
  </bean>

  <bean id="transactionManager"
  class="org.springframework.jdbc.datasource.DataSourceTransactionManager">
    <property name="dataSource" ref="dataSource"/>
  </bean>

</beans>
```

The configuration simply defines the `dataSource` bean as being a `org.apache.commons.dbcp.BasicDataSource` instance, as we had before. However, the class, URL, username, and password are now controlled by system properties. Also, there is a Spring `DataSourceTransactionManager` defined, which we would be using if we wrote our DAOs using Spring JDBC DAO support.

In a real application, you would also place configuration for your DAO themselves, your ORM configuration, and so forth, into the Spring application context file. To keep this example simple, we configure only the data source.

We can write a test class using this base class like this:

```
public class SpringInlineSelectOwnerTest extends SpringDatabaseTestCase {
  protected IDataSet getDataSet() throws Exception {
    return dataSet(
      table("owners",
        col("id", "first_name", "last_name", "address", "city", "telephone"),
        row("1", "Mandy", "Smith"      , "12 Oxford Street", "Southfield",
                 "555-1234567"),
        row("2", "Joe"  , "Jeffries"   , "25 Baywater Lane", "Northbrook",
                 "555-2345678"),
        row("3", "Herb" , "Dalton"     , "2 Main St"       , "Southfield",
                 "555-3456789"),
        row("4", "Dave" , "Smith-Jones", "12 Kent Way"     , "Southfield",
                 "555-4567890")
```

```
      ),
      table("pets", col("id")),
      table("visits", col("id"))
    );
  }

  private OwnerDao getOwnerDao() {
    return new SpringJdbcOwnerDao(getDataSource());
  }

  private static void assertOwner(Owner owner, int id, String firstName, String lastName,
                                  String address, String city, String telephone) {
    assertEquals(id, owner.getId());
    assertEquals(firstName, owner.getFirstName());
    assertEquals(lastName, owner.getLastName());
    assertEquals(address, owner.getAddress());
    assertEquals(city, owner.getCity());
    assertEquals(telephone, owner.getTelephone());
  }

  public void testValues() {
    OwnerDao ownerDao = getOwnerDao();
    assertOwner(ownerDao.loadOwner(1), 1, "Mandy", "Smith", "12 Oxford Street",
                                          "Southfield", "555-1234567");
    assertOwner(ownerDao.loadOwner(2), 2, "Joe", "Jeffries", "25 Baywater Lane",
                                          "Northbrook", "555-2345678");

    assertOwner(ownerDao.loadOwner(3), 3, "Herb", "Dalton", "2 Main St",
                                          "Southfield", "555-3456789");
    assertOwner(ownerDao.loadOwner(4), 4, "Dave", "Smith-Jones", "12 Kent Way",
                                          "Southfield", "555-4567890");
  }

}
```

Using Transaction Rollback Teardown

Another technique, or trick, that is often used in database integration tests is called *transaction rollback teardown*. This technique is to have the `tearDown()` method roll back changes made during the test. This avoids the need to prime the database with all data before every single test case. The sole advantage of this technique is in performance, but the benefit is sometimes considerable. Tests using this pattern can run much faster than tests without it.

Transaction rollback teardown requires careful management of database connections. It is necessary that priming the database, the code under test, and any verification code all use the same connection. It is also necessary that none of the code commits a transaction on the connection. And, finally, the `tearDown()` method needs to rollback the connection at some point.

In typical use, you would prime your database with standard reference data before running your test suite. Between tests, the database is always returned to its initial state. Individual tests can prime the database with any additional data they need that is peculiar to specific tests.

Spring provides a convenient base class for tests wanting to use transaction rollback teardown: `AbstractTransactionalSpringContextTests`. When using this base class, Spring manages all the transaction rollback for you. You need to ensure that all database access by your code is via Spring's transaction-aware utility classes such as `JdbcTemplate`. You also need to ensure that you don't inadvertently commit any changes at the wrong point. This means, for example, being careful where you execute any DDL.

Let's define a base class for our Spring transaction rollback teardown tests:

```
public abstract class SpringTransactionalDatabaseTestCase
                              extends AbstractTransactionalSpringContextTests {

  private DataSource dataSource;
  private IDatabaseTester tester;

  public DataSource getDataSource() {
    return dataSource;
  }

  public void setDataSource(DataSource dataSource) {
    this.dataSource = dataSource;
  }

  protected String[] getConfigLocations() {
    return new String[] {
      "classpath:/applicationContext.xml"
    };
  }

  protected void onSetUpInTransaction() throws Exception {
    super.onSetUpInTransaction();
    new JdbcTemplate(dataSource).execute(new ConnectionCallback() {
      public Object doInConnection(Connection con) throws DataAccessException {
        try {
          tester = new DefaultDatabaseTester(new DatabaseConnection(con));
          tester.setDataSet(getDataSet());
          tester.onSetup();
        }
        catch (Exception ex) {
          throw new RuntimeException(ex);
        }
        return null;
      }
    });
  }

  protected abstract IDataSet getDataSet() throws Exception;

  protected IDatabaseConnection getConnection() throws Exception {
```

```
        return tester.getConnection();
    }

    protected void closeConnection(IDatabaseConnection connection) throws Exception {
        tester.closeConnection(connection);
    }

}
```

This class is pretty similar to the `SpringDatabaseTestCase` class we defined earlier. The main difference is that we now prime the database with the initial data set inside a Spring `JdbcTemplate` method, which uses Spring's transaction-aware connection management.

Also, note that the setup method is now called `onSetUpInTransaction()`. Spring's `AbstractTransactionalSpringContextTests` provides both `onSetUpInTransaction()` and `onSetUpBeforeTransaction()`, so that you can place set up code inside or outside of the transaction as necessary. If we needed to run DDL, for example to reset a sequence, we could do it in `onSetUpBeforeTransaction()`.

With this base class written, our test is just the same as before, except that we extend the new base class. Note that the DAO implementation is `SpringJdbcOwnerDao`, which is a DAO class written using Spring's transaction-aware `JdbcDaoSupport`.

The transaction rollback teardown pattern does suffer from several potential pitfalls:

- You lose some test isolation. Each test assumes the database is in a certain starting condition *before* `setUp()` runs, and the rollback must revert it back to that condition. Each test is not responsible for priming the database with all the state that it needs.
- You can't see what's in the database when something goes wrong. If your test fails, you usually want to examine the database to see what happened. If you've rolled back the changes, it's harder to see the bug.
- You have to be careful not to inadvertently commit during your test. As mentioned already, any DDL must be run outside the transaction. However, it is easy to make a mistake with this, and the results can be very confusing.
- Some tests *do* need to commit changes, and you cannot easily mix these into the same suite. For example, you may wish to test PL/SQL stored procedures. These generally do explicit `COMMIT`s. You cannot mix these in the same JUnit suite with tests that assume that the database always remains in a certain state between tests.

The verdict on transaction rollback teardown is: make you own decision. Be aware of the consequences, and use it if the performance benefit outweighs the potential pitfalls. If you are careful in your test design, you may find that switching between the two approaches is not too hard.

Testing a Stored Procedure

So far we've talked about testing Java code such as DAOs. DbUnit can be used for any tests that involve a real database. Some of these tests might be end-to-end integration tests of components of your application. You might also find it easy to use DbUnit to test your database code itself, such as stored procedures.

There are, of course, unit testing frameworks for stored procedures for some databases. In many cases, they may be the most sensible tool to use for stored procedure tests. However, priming the database with known data, and verifying tables after a test—what DbUnit is specifically designed for—are both rather awkward in straight SQL or PL/SQL code. It is much the same problem as we'd faced when trying to do it with straight JDBC code. For these jobs, it is often better to use DbUnit. In addition, it integrates very neatly into your Java tests, which are used by your continuous integration system and IDE and all the other cool stuff you have for Java.

We'll use a rather contrived and simple example to test a stored procedure. Suppose we have a table `specialist_vets` in which we wish to store copies of all the `vets` rows that have more than one specialty in the `specialty` table. The `vet_specialties` table has the identical structure to `vets`. The stored procedure, in a PL/SQL package, looks like this:

```
CREATE OR REPLACE PACKAGE pkg_clinic AS
  PROCEDURE reload_specialist_vets;
END;
/

CREATE OR REPLACE PACKAGE BODY pkg_clinic AS
  PROCEDURE reload_specialist_vets IS
  BEGIN
    DELETE FROM specialist_vets;
    INSERT INTO specialist_vets
    SELECT id, first_name, last_name
    FROM   vets
    WHERE  EXISTS (
      SELECT vet_id, COUNT(*)
      FROM   vet_specialties
      WHERE  vet_id = vets.id
      GROUP BY vet_id
      HAVING COUNT(*) > 1
    );
    COMMIT WORK;
  END;
END;
/
```

It is surprisingly easy to use DbUnit to test this kind of code. We have a setup data set, just the same as before, which we won't repeat here. Then we have the test code:

```
  public void testReloadSpecialistVets() throws Exception {
    ITable expectedBefore = table("specialist_vets",
      col("id", "first_name", "last_name")
```

```
    );
    ITable expectedAfter = table("vw_specialist_vets",
      col("id", "first_name", "last_name"),
      row("1", "Harry", "Seuss"),
      row("2", "Mary", "Watson")
    );
    assertTable(expectedBefore, "specialist_vets");
    executeCallableStatement("{call pkg_clinic.reload_specialist_vets}");
    assertTable(expectedAfter, "specialist_vets");
  }

  private void executeCallableStatement(String sql) throws SQLException {
    Connection conn = null;
    CallableStatement stmt = null;
    try {
      conn = DataSourceUtils.getDataSource().getConnection();
      stmt = conn.prepareCall(sql);
      stmt.executeUpdate();
      conn.commit();
    }
    finally {
      JdbcUtils.closeStatement(stmt);
      JdbcUtils.closeConnection(conn);
    }
  }
```

The code first verifies that no data is in the `vet_specialties` table at the beginning of the test. Then it invokes the stored procedure. Finally, it verifies the `vet_specialties` table at the end.

Any time that you find yourself writing a nontrivial stored procedure, consider whether it would be worth adding a test for it to your test suite. Hopefully, this example shows that this is easy enough to do, once you have your DbUnit testing infrastructure set up.

Testing a View

Just as with stored procedures, we often find ourselves defining views that contain nontrivial logic. Again, these should be backed by tests, particularly the more complex ones. And again, DbUnit makes testing views remarkably easy.

Here is a view definition for `vw_vet_specialties`, a view that returns the `vets` rows having more than one specialty. This is a better solution to the requirement solved above by a stored procedure:

```
CREATE VIEW vw_specialist_vets AS
SELECT id, first_name, last_name
FROM   vets
WHERE  EXISTS (
  SELECT vet_id, COUNT(*)
  FROM   vet_specialties
  WHERE  vet_id = vets.id
  GROUP BY vet_id
  HAVING COUNT(*) > 1
);
```

```
private void assertView(ITable expectedView, String sql) throws Exception {
  ITable actualView = getConnection().createQueryTable("actual", sql);
  Assertion.assertEquals(expectedView, actualView);
}

public void testVwSpecialistVets() throws Exception {
  ITable expected = table("vw_specialist_vets",
    col("id", "first_name", "last_name"),
    row("1", "Harry", "Seuss"),
    row("2", "Mary", "Watson")
  );
  assertView(expected, "SELECT * FROM vw_specialist_vets ORDER BY 1");
}
```

This example shows how you can use DbUnit to verify the results of an arbitrary SQL query, just as easily as verifying a table. Sometimes this form is useful for tables, too, if you want to control the columns or the order of the rows returned.

Exporting a Dataset with Ant

Sometimes it is useful to be able to create a DbUnit `FlatXmlDataSet` file from data already existing in a database. You can use the DbUnit Ant targets for this.

To define the DbUnit Ant tasks in Ant, include this entry in your *build.xml* script:

```
<taskdef name="dbunit" classname="org.dbunit.ant.DbUnitTask">
  <classpath refid="classpath.lib"/>
</taskdef>
```

You need to specify the classpath where your *dbunit.jar* is.

To export data from your database, use the `<dbunit>` target with the `<export>` option, like this:

```
<target name="export"
        description="Export schema from database to ${dataset.export}">
  <dbunit driver="${db.driver}" url="${db.url}" userid="${db.userid}"
   password="${db.password}" schema="${db.schema}">
    <classpath refid="classpath.lib"/>
    <export dest="${dataset.export}"/>
  </dbunit>
</target>
```

You can also restrict the set of tables exported. See the DbUnit documentation online for more details.

Importing a Dataset with Ant

To import data from a `FlatXmlDataSet` file into the database using the Ant task, use the `<dbunit>` target with the `<operation>` option, like this:

```
<target name="import"
        description="Import schema from ${dataset.import} to database">
  <dbunit driver="${db.driver}" url="${db.url}" userid="${db.userid}"
   password="${db.password}" schema="${db.schema}">
```

```
    <classpath refid="classpath.lib"/>
    <operation type="CLEAN_INSERT" src="${dataset.import}"/>
  </dbunit>
</target>
```

This can be useful in combination with the transaction rollback teardown pattern, for setting the database into the initial state before running your test suite.

CHAPTER 15

Performance Testing with JUnitPerf

15.1 Introducing JUnitPerf

JUnitPerf is an extension of JUnit 3 (see Section 10.1) that adds the ability to time test cases and to do simple load and performance testing. Its features are similar to some of the TestNG annotations (see Section 11.10), but JUnitPerf uses a very different approach, integrating smoothly into the JUnit 3 architecture.

Using an elegant system of JUnit decorators, JUnitPerf lets you use existing unit tests to build simple but effective load and performance tests. First, you write your usual unit test cases to verify that the code is executing correctly and is behaving as expected. Then you can encapsulate some of your key unit tests using JUnitPerf decorators, effectively creating a suite of performance tests without having to modify your original unit tests. This also makes it easy to separate your performance tests from your ordinary unit tests, because you usually don't run them at the same time.

Incorporating some basic performance testing into your unit tests makes good sense. Without going overboard, it is a good way to detect major performance anomalies early on in the piece. You can also configure these tests to run separately from your ordinary unit tests, in order to avoid penalizing the fast feedback cycle that is one of the trademarks of good unit tests.

Note that we are talking about verifying performance, not optimizing code in an uncontrolled manner. Premature optimization has often been decried, and with some justification. Tony Hoare is frequently quoted as saying, "We should forget about small efficiencies, say about 97 percent of the time: premature optimization is the root of all evil." Optimization should indeed be a very focused task, with precise goals. It is a futile exercise to optimize code that is hardly ever used. However, making sure your application performs correctly where it needs to, right from the start, can be a huge timesaver. And, by formalizing the process and incorporating the tests into the application test suites, verifying your application's performance with JUnitPerf can help to encourage a more systematic approach to optimization. Rather than optimizing for the sake of optimizing, you measure the performance you have and check it against what you need. Only then do you decide if optimization is necessary.

15.2 Measuring Performance with TimedTests

The most basic performance test is to verify how long a test case takes to execute. JUnitPerf provides a simple JUnit decorator class called TimedTest, which lets you check that a unit test does not take more than a certain time to run. In this section, we will look at how to use this decorator. At the same time, we will go through many basic notions about JUnitPerf.

In this chapter, we are going to write some performance tests for a simple web application that manages a database of model planes. On the web application's home page, users can consult the list of known plane types, select a plane type, and then view the corresponding model planes. According to the performance requirements, this home page is expected to be heavily used, and needs to support a high load. More precisely, the specifications stipulate that "The home page must be displayed in less than 2 seconds (not counting network traffic) in the presence of 10 simultaneous users."

Note that we have numbers here. Performance requirements without numbers are pretty much useless. The aim of performance tests is to verify that your code will provide acceptable performance. If it does, there is no need to look further. If it doesn't, it is better to know about it sooner rather than later!

As it turns out, the main query in this page is the one that displays the list of plane types. In the application, plane types are represented by the `PlaneType` class. The DAO (Data Access Object) class for plane types implements the following interface:

```
public interface PlaneTypeDAO {
    PlaneType findById(long id);
    List<PlaneType> findAll();
    public void save(PlaneType planeType);
    public void delete(PlaneType planeType);
}
```

To list all available plane types, we need to invoke the `findAll()` method. The unit test class for this DAO is shown here:

```
public class PlaneTypeDaoTests extends TestCase {

    private PlaneTypeDAO dao;

    public PlaneTypeDaoTests(String value) {
        super(value);
    }

    public void setUp() throws SQLException {
        ApplicationContext ctx = SpringUtilsTestConfig.getApplicationContext();
        dao = (PlaneTypeDAO) ctx.getBean("planeTypeDAO");
    }
```

```
        public void testFindAll() {
            List<PlaneType> planes = dao.findAll();
            assertTrue(planes.size() > 0);
            ...
        }
        ...
    }
```

The `testFindAll()` unit test simply invokes the `findAll()` method, and checks that the results list is not empty. The `setUp()` method, executed before each test, obtains a DAO object using a Spring application context. Behind the scenes, this instantiates the DAO, along with the appropriate JDBC data source and Hibernate session, using an embedded Java database. It also populates the test database with test data.

Once we are sure that this test runs correctly, we can make sure it runs efficiently. Performance issues can come from many sources: is only the minimum data loaded, or are unnecessary associated objects loaded as well? Is the database correctly indexed?

The first thing to do is to create a test case containing the unit test we want to use, as shown here:

```
TestCase testCase = new PlaneTypeDaoTests("testFindAll");
```

Next, we create a TimedTest, specifying this test case along with the maximum allowable execution time in milliseconds. In the following example, the TimedTest waits until the test case finishes, and then fails if the `findAll()` method took more than 100 milliseconds to execute:

```
TimedTest timedTest = new TimedTest(testCase, 100);
```

If this test fails, the exception will indicate the maximum allowable time *and* the actual time that the method took to run:

```
junit.framework.AssertionFailedError: Maximum elapsed time exceeded! Expected 100ms,
but was 281ms.
...
```

The advantage of this approach is that if the test fails, you know by how much. Did it just scrape in over the limit, or did it take an order of magnitude longer to finish? This sort of information can be vital to know if you need to investigate further or just adjust your threshold values.

By contrast, you may prefer to let the test fail immediately once the time limit has expired. This helps to keep the length of your tests within reasonable limits—if your tests take too long to run, you will have a natural tendency to run them less often. To do this, you simply build the test as follows:

```
TimedTest timedTest = new TimedTest(testCase, 100, false);
```

This approach of encapsulating test methods is known as the decorator pattern. It is a very flexible way of extending existing unit tests. And it makes it very easy to reuse existing test cases. However, it means that you can't just write a JUnitPerf test case as you would an ordinary test case. You need to implement the `suite()` method, and create a `TestSuite` that contains your decorated unit tests. Tests defined in this method can be easily run in IDEs such as Eclipse and NetBeans, and can also be run automatically using Maven or Ant. The final test case looks like this:

```
import junit.framework.Test;
import junit.framework.TestCase;
import junit.framework.TestSuite;

import com.clarkware.junitperf.TimedTest;

public class PlaneTypeDaoPerfTests extends TestCase {

    public static Test suite() {
         TestSuite suite = new TestSuite();
         TestCase testCase = new PlaneTypeDaoTests("testFindAll");
         suite.addTest(testCase);

         TimedTest timedTest = new TimedTest(testCase, 500);
         suite.addTest(timedTest);
         return suite;
    }
}
```

There's a trick here: we actually add the plain (no pun intended!) test case before adding the decorated one. This is simply to ensure that the timed test does not measure one-off initialization tasks such as setting up the test database, initializing Spring and Hibernate, and so on. This is important to keep in mind, as you don't want initialization tasks to pollute your timing data. It is also useful to know that the time measured in a TimedTest test case includes the time spent in the `setUp()` and `tearDown()` methods. So, if you have essential and time-consuming code in these methods that you don't want to measure, be sure to factor it out of your timer thresholds.

15.3 SimulatingLoad with LoadTests

You can also do simple load tests with JUnitPerf. Load tests aim at verifying that an application will cope with multiple simultaneous users and still provide acceptable response times. A load test involves simulating a number of simultaneous users by running a series of unit tests on different threads. This is also useful to check that your code is thread-proof, which is an important aspect of web application development.

The following code will create a test with five simultaneous users:

```
TestCase testCase = new PlaneTypeDaoTests("testFindAll");
LoadTest loadTest = new LoadTest(testCase, 5);
```

This will start all five threads simultaneously. This is not always what you need for proper load testing. For more realistic testing, the tests on each thread should be spread out over time, and not all happen at exactly the same time. You can obtain a more even distribution by providing a Timer object. The following example will create 5 threads, 1 every 100 milliseconds:

```
TestCase testCase = new PlaneTypeDaoTests("testFindAll");
Timer timer = new ConstantTimer(100);
LoadTest loadTest = new LoadTest(testCase, 5, timer);
```

Alternatively, you can use the **RandomTimer** to create the new threads at random intervals.

The above code will start several simultaneous threads and run the test case once in each thread. If you want to do serious load testing, or even just make sure that your application performs correctly in a multiuser environment, you really need to run the test case several times in each thread. To run a test case repeatedly, you can use the RepeatedTest wrapper. In the following example, we create five threads randomly distributed over the space of one second. In each thread, we run the findAll() test case 10 times:

```
TestCase testCase = new PlaneTypeDaoTests("testFindAll");
Timer timer = new RandomTimer(100,500);
RepeatedTest repeatedTest = new RepeatedTest(testCase, 10);
LoadTest loadTest = new LoadTest(testCase, 5, timer);
```

This sort of test will check that your code works well in a multithreaded environment. However, you may also want to test the performance of the application under pressure. You can do this very nicely with JUnitPerf. In the following example, we check that 100 transactions, run simultaneously across 5 threads, can be executed within 25 seconds. That would round out to half a second per transaction with 10 users:

```
public class PlaneTypeDaoPerfTests extends TestCase {

    public static Test suite() {
        TestSuite suite = new TestSuite();
        TestCase testCase = new PlaneTypeDaoTests("testFindAll");
        suite.addTest(testCase);
        Timer timer = new RandomTimer(100,1000);
        RepeatedTest repeatedTest = new RepeatedTest(testCase, 10);
        LoadTest loadTest = new LoadTest(repeatedTest, 5, timer);
        TimedTest timedTest = new TimedTest(loadTest, 25000);
        suite.addTest(timedTest);
        return suite;
    }
}
```

Now, these numbers are not plucked out of the blue. Our original requirements specified that the application home page, which contains the list of all plane types, must be displayed in less than 2 seconds (not counting network traffic) 95 percent of the time, in the presence of 10 simultaneous users. If your main domain-layer query takes half a second, you should have no trouble displaying the page in less than two seconds. The exact numbers in this example don't matter. The point is you need to know what sort of performance you will require from your application before you can start to do sensible load tests, even at a unit-testing level. Note that this is not a reason not to do performance testing at an early stage: it is more of a reason to make sure you know what the performance requirements are before you start testing.

This code will check that the *average* transaction time is less than 500 milliseconds. Suppose that the client also stipulated the following (much) more demanding requirement: "No transaction must take over one second with 10 simultaneous users."

This may be hard to guarantee from a coding perspective, but at least it's easy to test. The JUnitPerf decorator-based approach is extremely flexible, and you can arrange the test wrappers in any way that suits you. To guarantee that no transaction takes over one second, you simply place a timed test first, directly encapsulating the unit test case. This way, the timed test will be executed every time the unit test is run, and not just at the end of the series as in the previous example. The following example will run 10 parallel threads and fail if any transaction takes more than 1 second:

```
TimedTest timedTest = new TimedTest(testCase, 1000);
RepeatedTest repeatedTest = new RepeatedTest(timedTest, 10);
Timer timer = new RandomTimer(100,1000);
LoadTest loadTest = new LoadTest(repeatedTest, 5, timer);
suite.addTest(loadTest);
```

Once you have this sort of test in place, you have a better idea of how your application stands up under pressure. If your tests are successful, that's great there is no further work to do. If not, you may need to tune your application, or in a worst case rethink your architecture, to get to the required performance level. To optimize your code, it is a good idea to use profiling tools such as jConsole (Chapter 18) or the TPTP profiling tools under Eclipse (Chapter 19) to identify where the tests are spending the most time.

One other important thing to remember about these numbers is not to ask too much: they are just estimates. Exact timings will vary from machine to machine, and will even vary on the same machine, and you need to take this into account to ensure that your tests are portable. As a rule, you should worry about orders of magnitude, not small percentages. If a test takes 5 or 10 times longer than what you expect, you have a serious problem. If it is a matter of 5 or 10 percent, it's probably not worth spending too much time on.

JUnitPerf does not claim to be a fully fledged load-testing framework. (Tools such as JMeter are better adapted for that.) What it does do is let you start to verify your application's performance at an early stage, which can avoid costly debugging sessions or architectural changes later on in the project.

Note that JUnit 4 now provides a somewhat similar feature to the JUnitPerf `TimedTest` class, allowing you to define timeouts for your tests (see Section 10.4). TestNG goes further, allowing you to define timeouts *and* run your tests in parallel (see Section 11.10).

15.4 Load-Testing Tests That Are Not Thread-Safe

Some test cases are atomic in nature: they run no risk of behaving strangely by modifying shared data in unpredictable ways. These tests can be safely invoked from several threads simultaneously. Other test classes set up a test environment using member variables in that class to simulate session state. Test cases within the test class manipulate these variables and they don't like other processes touching them. These tests are not thread-safe.

If you need to load-test a test class that uses member variables in this way or that is not thread-safe for some other reason, JUnitPerf has a solution. The `TestFactory` and `TestMethodFactory` classes let you create a factory object that will generate instances of your test class, one instance per thread. In the following example, we create a loadtest object that will start up 10 threads. We provide a factory that it will use to generate separate instances of the `PlaneTypeDaoTests` class. So, the 10 test cases can run safely in parallel, with no risk of interference:

```
Test factory = new TestMethodFactory(PlaneTypeDaoTests.class, "testFindAll");
LoadTest loadTest = new LoadTest(factory, 10);
```

15.5 Separating Performance Tests from Unit Tests in Ant

You typically run performance tests and ordinary unit tests at different points in the development lifecycle. Unit tests are (or should be) run very regularly. They need to be quick and snappy, and should avoid getting in the developer's way by taking too long to run. Performance tests are different. You run them less frequently, and they may take longer to run. It is a good idea to set up your build process to run them separately. One simple approach is to use a special naming convention to distinguish them. There is nothing very complicated about this. In the following extract from an Ant build file, for example, performance tests are identified by the suffix "PerfTests":

```
<target name="test" depends="compiletests">
    <junit printsummary="yes" haltonfailure="yes">
      <classpath>
          <path refid="test.classpath" />
          <pathelement location="${test.classes}"/>
      </classpath>

      <formatter type="plain"/>
      <formatter type="xml"/>

      <batchtest fork="yes" todir="${test.reports}">
        <fileset dir="${test.src}">
            <exclude name="**/*PerfTests.java"/>
        </fileset>
      </batchtest>
    </junit>
```

```
    </target>

    <target name="perftests" depends="tests, compiletests">
        <junit printsummary="yes" haltonfailure="yes">
          <classpath>
              <path refid="test.classpath" />
              <pathelement location="${test.classes}"/>
          </classpath>

          <formatter type="plain"/>
          <formatter type="xml"/>

          <batchtest fork="yes" todir="${test.reports}">
            <fileset dir="${test.src}">
                <include name="**/*PerfTests.java"/>
            </fileset>
          </batchtest>
        </junit>
    </target>
```

Now you can run your normal unit tests using "test" target and your performance tests by calling the "perftests" target.

15.6 Separating Performance Tests from Unit Tests in Maven

In Maven, the logical place to put performance tests is probably in the integration test phase. The following extract from a Maven POM file dissociates unit tests from performance tests using the same naming convention as above: performance tests have the suffix "PerfTests." With the following configuration, JUnitPerf performance tests will only be run during the integration test phase:

```
<project>
  ...
  <build>
    <plugins>
      <plugin>
        <artifactId>maven-surefire-plugin</artifactId>
        <executions>
          <execution>
            <id>unit-tests</id>
            <phase>test</phase>
            <goals>
              <goal>test</goal>
            </goals>
            <configuration>
              <excludes><exclude>**/*PerfTests.java</exclude></excludes>
            </configuration>
          </execution>
          <execution>
            <id>integration-tests</id>
            <phase>integration-test</phase>
            <goals>
              <goal>test</goal>
```

```
                </goals>
                <configuration>
                  <includes><include>**/*PerfTests.java</include></includes>
                </configuration>
              </execution>
            </executions>
          </plugin>
        </plugins>
      </build>
      ...
    </project>
```

Then, to run your performance tests, just invoke the integration test phase:

```
$ mvn integration-test
```

CHAPTER 16

Load and Performance Testing with JMeter

16.0 Introduction

JMeter is a powerful Java open source load and performance testing tool. With it, you can carry out performance tests on web application, databases, web services, and more.

Load testing (also known as stress testing) involves putting your application under continued stress over a long period of time, generally by simulating many concurrent users. This is a good way of ferreting out memory leaks or performance bottlenecks that otherwise would not appear until once the application is in production. Load testing can also be used to push an application to its limits, simulating expected peak loads, in order to study how it stands up under increasing pressure and to identify weak points in the application architecture.

Performance Testing is a little different. Performance testing involves making sure that your application performs as specified in the system requirements. For example, the requirements may include performance criteria such as the following: with 100 concurrent users, the home page must be displayed in fewer than 2 seconds on a broadband connection.

JMeter can be used very effectively to do both load and performance testing.

Before we start, a word on load testing: as with any other sort of performance testing and optimization, to load test your application well, you really need a plan. How many users is your application *supposed* to support? Are you writing a company application for limited internal use, or are you working on the new release of Amazon.com? What sort of response times are acceptable, and under what load?

Don't neglect environmental issues, either. Is the test server (you're not running your load tests on your production server, are you now?) similar in size and grunt power to the production server? What other applications will be running on the production server? How much memory will be available to your application in production?

These things should be thought through with everyone involved in the project (don't forget the system guys!), written down for all to see, and used to build at least a basic load-test plan.

16.1 Installing JMeter

Installing JMeter is straightforward. In the tradition of many open source tools, there are no fancy installers. Just download the latest version from the JMeter web site* (version 2.2 at the time of this writing), and extract the package into a directory of your choice. You will find startup scripts for Windows (*jmeter.bat*) and Unix (*jmeter*) to start JMeter in the *bin* subdirectory. You need to start JMeter in this directory. For example, if you had extracted the JMeter 2.3 distribution into the *D:\tools\jmete*r directory on a Windows machine, you could run JMeter as follows:

```
D:>cd D:\tools\jmeter\jakarta-jmeter-2.3\bin
D:\tools\jmeter\jakarta-jmeter-2.3\bin>jmeter.bat
```

Or, on a Unix box, with JMeter installed into the */usr/local/jmeter* directory, you would do the following:

```
$cd /usr/local/jmeter/jakarta-jmeter-2.3/bin
$jmeter
```

Running this command will start up the JMeter graphical console, which is were you write your test scripts (called "Test Plans" in JMeter parlance), run your tests, and view the results.

Depending on the type of tests you intend to do, you may need to provide JMeter with some additional JAR files. The simplest way to do this is to place them in the *lib* directory, where they will be detected automatically by the JMeter startup script. For example, if you intend to do any JDBC testing, you will need to supply the JDBC drivers, or if you are testing web services, you may need to add the *mail.jar* and *activation.jar* files.

16.2 Testing a Simple Web Application

Now, we will go though the steps involved in creating a typical test plan for a web application. The test plan will run a simple web application through its paces, simulating the expected load of 100 concurrent users. Our specifications stipulate that with 100 concurrent users, the average response time must be fewer than 2 seconds per page.

* *http://jakarta.apache.org/jmeter/*

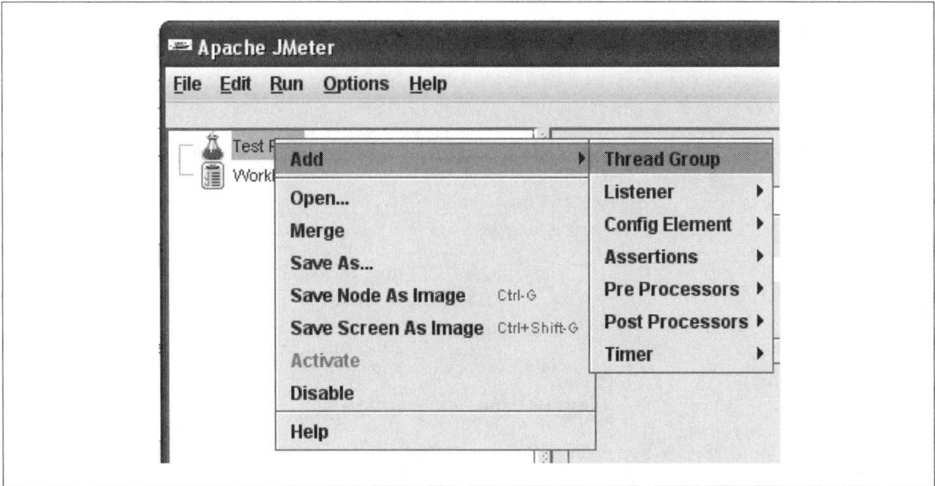

Figure 16-1. Creating a new thread group

Setting Up a Thread Group

JMeter works by simulating a set of concurrent users performing various tasks on your application. In JMeter, you use a thread group to manage this set of users. As the name suggests, a thread group defines a group of threads. Each simulated user is represented by a separate thread. So the number of threads represents the number of simulated simultaneous users generated by this Thread Group. To create a new thread group, just select *Edit→Add→Thread Group* in the main menu, or place the cursor on the Test Plan entry and use the contextual menu (see Figure 16-1).

The most important field in the Thread Group details screen (see Figure 16-2) is the number of users, which you define in the "Number of Threads" field.

To simulate load more realistically, the threads (think "users") are not started all at once—there is a short delay between starting each thread. This spreads the requests over time and makes for more realistic testing. The total time spent starting the threads is called the Ramp Up Period. So, if you have a thread group with 100 threads and a ramp up period of 3,000 seconds, a new thread will be started every 30 seconds.

Scheduling Your Tests

There are several ways to define how long you want your tests to run. The most simple, and arguably the least useful, is to define the number of times that the test case should be executed, or to simply leave the tests to run forever and stop the test process manually. In practice, it is difficult to estimate how long the test plan will take to run, especially in a concurrent environment. In addition, after running for a long period, JMeter can become sluggish, making it more difficult to stop the test process manually.

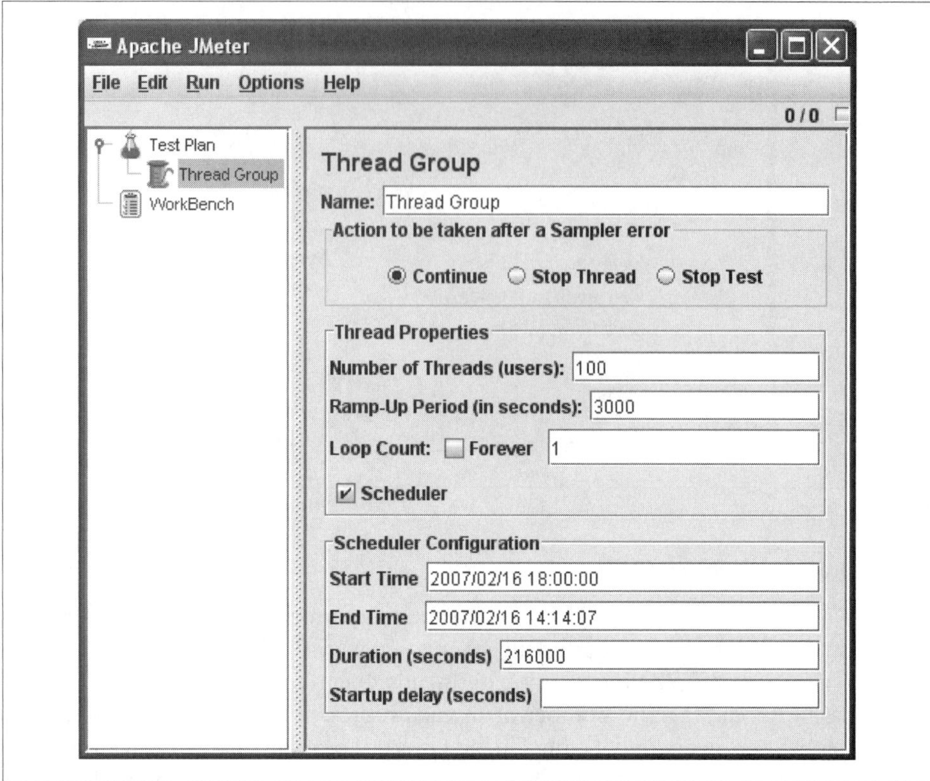

Figure 16-2. The Thread Group

The other possibility is to use the Scheduler, which allows you to schedule your load tests for some point in the future. You can specify a start and end time for your tests, useful if you want to run your tests outside working hours, for example. Alternatively, as shown in the illustration, you can specify a fixed duration (the End Time field is ignored in this case). You may also want to schedule the tests to start after a certain delay (say, in an hour's time), by providing a value in the Startup Delay field. In this case, the Start Time will be ignored.

Setting Up the HTTP Request Configuration Elements

Configuration tests scripts can be repetitive. When testing a web site, for example, all of the HTTP requests will typically be sent to the same server. In JMeter, you can use Configuration Elements to factorize a lot of this repeated data into one central location. If some pages are protected using Basic HTTP Authentication (other forms of authentication are not currently supported), user/password data can be shared. And if your web application uses cookies to manage sessions, JMeter can store these cookies when they are received and make them available to all subsequent requests.

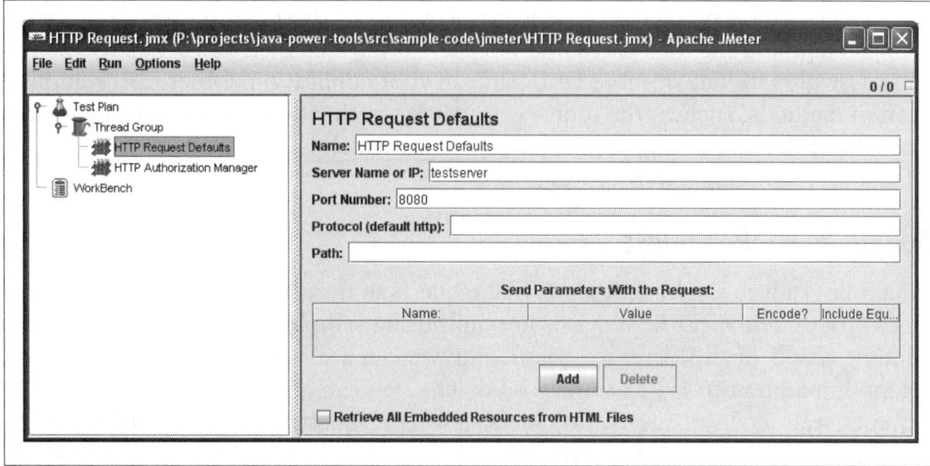

Figure 16-3. The HTTP Request Defaults

For web application testing, the most important configuration element is "HTTP Request Defaults." Add one to your test plan by clicking on Test Plan and selecting Add→Config Element→HTTP Request Defaults in the contextual menu. You can specify the name of your test server, the port your web application is running on, the protocol (HTTP or HTTPS), and the application context path. These values will be used by the HTTP Requests that you will set up later on.

Throughout the rest of this chapter, we will be performing some load testing on one of the open source implementations of the Java Pet Store. reference application.[*] In Figure 16-3, we set up the default data for our test platform, which is running on a local test server called *testserver*, on the 8080 port. This will be used by default for all the HTTP requests in this test plan.

If you check the "Retrieve All Embedded Resources from HTML Files" option, JMeter will download the images, Javacript files, CSS stylesheets, and so on associated with an HTTP request. However, JMeter does not cache images and downloaded files as a browser does, so it is generally not a good idea to activate this option in the request defaults and only activate it in selected HTTP requests.

Another very useful configuration element is the HTTP cookie manager. The cookie manager stores cookies and makes them available for subsequent requests to the same site, as an ordinary web browser would. Because each thread represents a different user, cookies are not shared among threads.

If some or all of your site is protected by basic HTTP authentication, you can provide usernames and passwords in the HTTP authorization manager. Basic HTTP authentication is the simplest of the standard HTTP authentication methods: when a user

[*] The `jpetstore` implementation, written by the IBATIS team

navigates to a page protected by basic HTTP authentication, the browser will open a dialog box prompting for a username and password. JMeter lets you set up usernames and passwords for one or more URL paths in your application. Other HTTP authentication methods, such as the more secure digest authentication, are not supported. Note that JMeter *does* support SSL connections, which is considered to be the most reliable way to secure a web application.

Adding an HTTP Request

JMeter tests a web site by sending HTTP requests to the server, simulating the action of real users. These HTTP requests are built using samplers. Samplers are the basic building blocks of all JMeter test plans, and come in a variety of different shapes and colors. In addition to HTTP request samplers, you can also build samplers for FTP requests, web service requests, JMS messages, JDBC queries, and many others. When you are testing a web site, however, the HTTP sampler is by far the most commonly used.

The web application we are testing is an open source implementation of the JPetstore demo application from iBatis (see Figure 16-4). If you want to follow along with the examples, you can download from the IBatis web site.* This is actually of little importance, as you can use JMeter to test just about any web site you like, and the techniques are similar for most sites. However, knowing what we are testing will make it easier to understand the examples.Creating a new HTTP Request sampler is straightforward, although it can be a little laborious if there are a lot of parameters. Typically, you would start off with a request for the home page. Although you don't need to understand all the nitty-gritty architectural details of the application you are testing, you do need to know what the request you want to send is supposed to look like. Usually, the most practical way to do this is to perform the action yourself in a web browser and look at the URL. In this case, the home page URL looks like *http://testserver:8080/jpetstore/shop/index.shtml*.

This is all we need to set up a JMeter HTTP sampler. Add an HTTP Request sampler to your test plan using *Add →Sampler→HTTP Request* (see Figure 16-5). Change the name to something meaningful, so that you will be able to identify this request easily in the test plan. You can leave the Web Server details empty; they will be retrieved from the HTTP default values we set up earlier. The only value we need to provide is the web page, independent of the application context. In this case, this would be "/index.shtml."

As discussed above, you can also choose to retrieve embedded resources such as images, javascript files, and css stylesheets. For a real user, the home page usually has a lot of images and resources that will be fetched here and cached by the browser, so it's often a good idea to retrieve these the first time you fetch the home page in your test plan.

* *http://ibatis.apache.org/javadownloads.cgi*

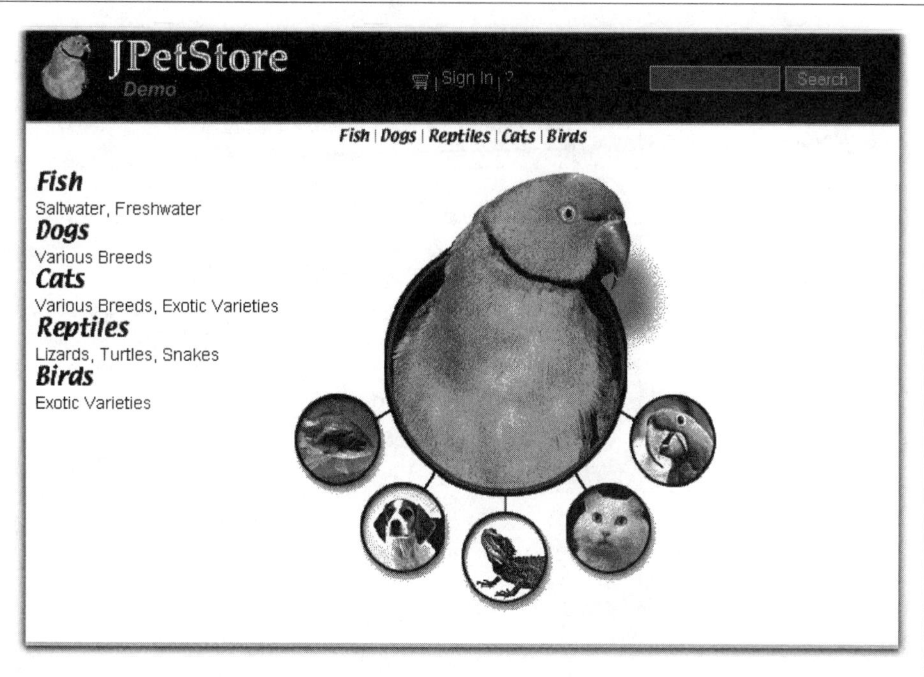

Figure 16-4. The JPetstore application

Next, we'll build an HTTP request to take us into the Reptiles section of the catalog. The URL for this page looks like *http://testserver:8080/jpetstore/shop/viewCategory.shtml?categoryId=REPTILES*.

Now we can set up a JMeter HTTP sampler for this query (see Figure 16-6). Add an HTTP Request sampler to your test plan using Add→Sampler→HTTP Request (see Figure 16-6), and give it some appropriate name ("Reptile catalog," for example). Then provide the Path value, which is the path to this page on the server, without any parameters. In this case, it is the following: */jpetstore/shop/viewCategory.shtml*.

Next, we need to add the unique query parameter for this request. Just enter the parameter name ("categoryId") and the corresponding value ("REPTILES") in the parameter table. You can add as many parameters as you like.

Using this approach, you can build up a test case query by query.

This approach works well when the queries are simple and the parameters easy to manipulate. Pages that contain large forms may require dozens of query parameters. If HTTP POSTs are being used, the parameter values will not appear in the URL, so you will need to find another way of discovering them. And this approach can be harder to use with some of the more recent frameworks such as JSF, which relies on javascripting to submit queries, and Tapestry, in which the URLs can be long, complex affairs.

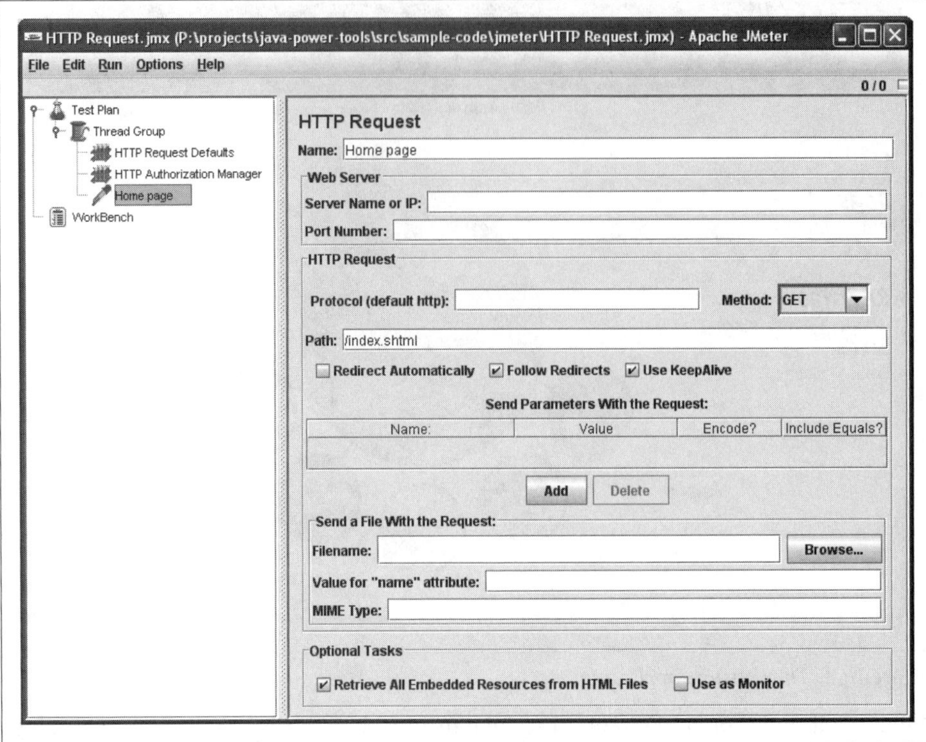

Figure 16-5. Querying the home page

Another approach is to use the JMeter proxy to record a test case for you, and then tailor it to your needs afterward. We look at this approach in detail in Section 16.5.

16.3 Structuring Your Test Case

JMeter lets you do a lot more than simply run your HTTP requests sequentially. In JMeter, you can use the various Logic Controller components to organize your samplers in sophisticated ways, which can help you to simulate user activity in a realistic manner. Some of the more useful controllers are described here (see Figure 16-7).

The Simple Controller lets you group samplers or other Logic Controllers together. This is a useful organization tool. In Figure 16-7, the "Browse Catalog" element is a Simple Controller that regroups a logical sequence of user actions.

The Loop Controller is another popular one. As the name would suggest, it lets you loop over any elements it contains a certain number of times. You can loop for a specified number of times, or just loop forever. In Figure 16-7, we loop through this sequence of actions 50 times each time the test case is performed.

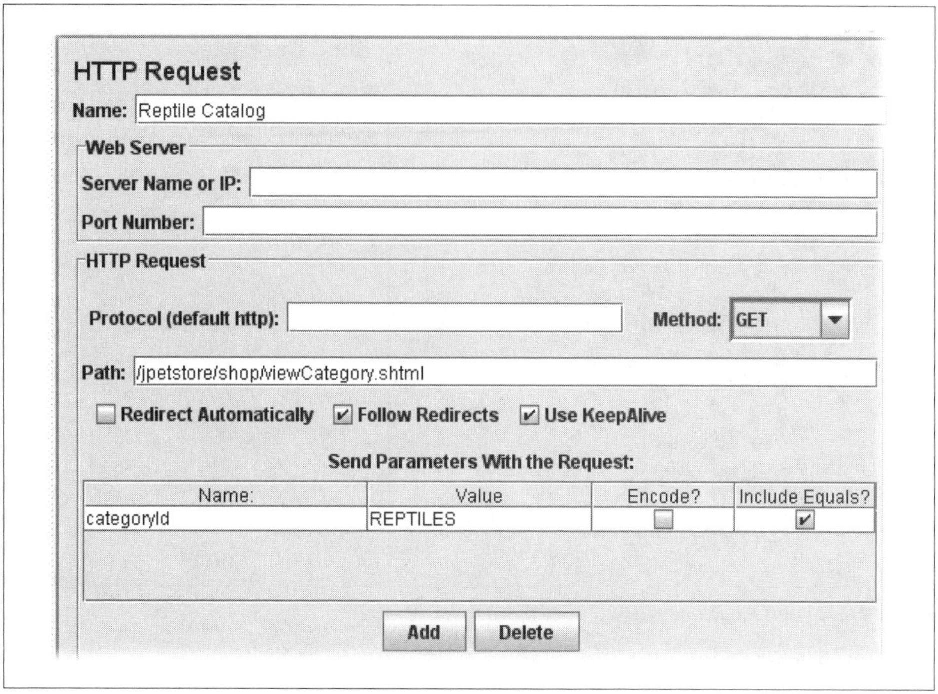

HTTP Request
Name: Reptile Catalog
Web Server
Server Name or IP:
Port Number:
HTTP Request
Protocol (default http):
Method: GET
Path: /jpetstore/shop/viewCategory.shtml
Redirect Automatically
Follow Redirects
Use KeepAlive
Send Parameters With the Request:

Name:	Value	Encode?	Include Equals?
categoryId	REPTILES	☐	☑

Add
Delete

Figure 16-6. Displaying the Reptile catalog

The Only Once Logic Controller can be used to define actions that should be run only once, no matter how many times the test case iterates over this element. This is useful for things like login screens, which need to be visited only once, regardless of how long the test case lasts for a particular user. In Figure 16-7, the user signs on to the site only once for each test case, despite the fact that this action is placed within a loop controller.

The Random Controller is useful when you want to simulate random or varied behavior on the part of your users. When you place a set of elements inside a Random Controller, JMeter will randomly select one of the elements each time the controller is invoked. You can use this to simulate a user browsing through different parts of a web site. In Figure 16-7, for example, the Random Controller is used to randomly pick a different details page (Iguana, Snake, Skink, or Turtle) in each iteration.

A useful alternative to the Random Controller is the Interleave Controller. As with the Random Controller, the InterLeave controller will successively choose different contained elements each time it is invoked. Unlike the Random Controller, however, it will invoke each element in the order in which they are listed.

The other vital part of any test case is the timers. Timer Controllers (see Figure 16-8) let you insert pauses at strategic places in your test case to simulate real user activity. A typical user will load a page, and then spend a second or two reading the resulting

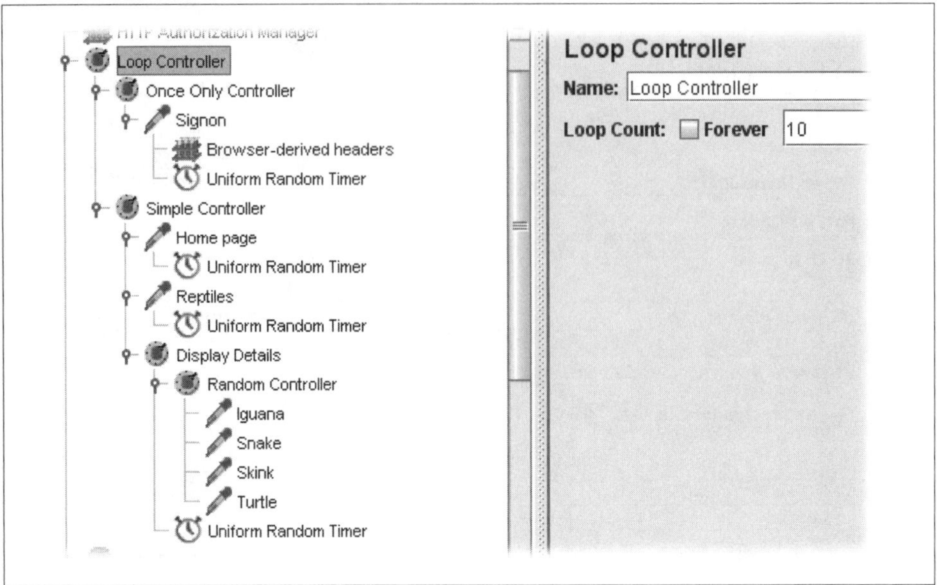

Figure 16-7. Logic Controllers

page, or at least waiting for it to be displayed. To simulate this, you typically place timers after your requests.

Timers come in different forms. Timers can be of fixed duration (the Constant Timer) or vary randomly within a specified range (the Uniform Random Timer or Gaussian Random Timer). You can also simulate high-load points using the Synchonizing Timer, which blocks threads until a certain number has been blocked and then releases them all at once. This simulates groups of users who pause and then (by intention or by bad luck) all start to work again at the same time.

Placing timers in your test case can be a bit tricky. Timers are executed before each sampler within a given scope. For example, in Figure 16-8, there is a constant timer before the signon action, which will be executed once, just before the signon. The second timer in this illustration is a Uniform Random Timer, which is placed at the start of the Simple Controller. This timer will be executed before every sampler within the Simple Controller. If several timers are present within a particular scope, the delay will be cumulated. For example, if we were to place an additional timer in the Display Details controller, there would be a supplementary delay before each details page (Iguana, Snake, Skink, and Turtle), in addition to the Uniform Random Timer at the top of this scope.

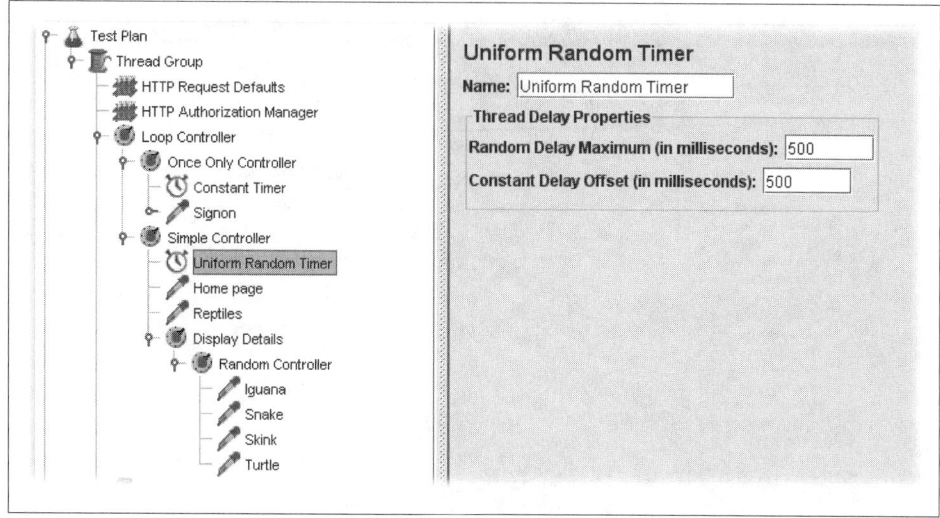

Figure 16-8. A typical Timer Controller

16.4 Recording and Displaying Test Results

When you run a series of load or performance tests, you generally need to be able to record and display test results. JMeter provides several useful tools allowing you to display your results in a useful form. In JMeter terms, these components are known as listeners. You simply add one or more listeners to your test plan, configuring them as necessary.

You should be aware that listeners can consume a lot of memory. Most listeners keep a copy of every recorded sample, which, over time, will use up all of your available memory. For long-running tests, you should stick to listeners such as "Summary Report" and "Monitor Results," which use a constant amount of memory.

When you run your load and performance tests, it is a good idea to use a monitoring tool such as jConsole (see Section 18.2) to keep tabs on your server's activity and performance. Indeed, intensive load tests are a good way to flush out memory leaks, synchronization issues, and deadlocks, as well as other hard-to-isolate problems.

Visualizing Performance with the Graph Listener

One of the most common requirements is to visualize performance results on a graph. You can set this up fairly easily with the Graph Results listener (see Figure 16-9). This graph plots server response times, and also displays average and median response times, standard deviation, and average throughput. Note that the recorded times include any delaying timers you may have added into your test plan to make it closer to the behavior of real users. This allows you to ramp up the number of users and measure throughput and response time under increasing loads in a realistic manner.

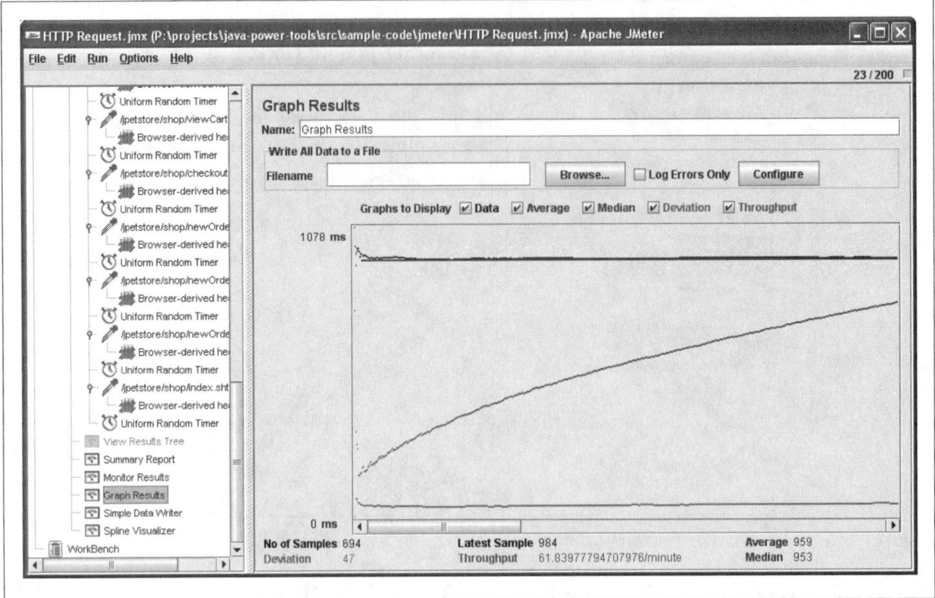

Figure 16-9. Performance graph using the JMeter Graph Listener

This graph gives a good, quick indication of how an application performs under strain. However, the JMeter graph listener is not particularly well adapted to displaying performance graphs over a prolonged period of time—after a time, the graph loops on itself and tends to become cluttered and difficult to read. A more efficient way of obtaining performance graphs over a long period is to use the Simple Data Writer listener (see Figure 16-10). This will record sampling data into a CSV or XML file. You can then load this data into your favorite spreadsheet and extract graphs to your heart's content.

Getting More Details with the View Results Tree Listener

Sometimes your application may fail unexpectedly during your test runs, or your test script may return a 100 percent error rate for no apparent reason, or maybe you just want to know what a typical web request returns. A good tool to do this is the View Results Tree listener (see Figure 16-11).

This listener gives you a detailed, behind-the-scenes look at what happened when the test case was run. It records the HTTP request sent for each of your requests, the HTML data it received in response, the time it took to receive a response, as well as response codes. You can view the HTML either as text or as rendered HTML form. The HTML rendering is usually pretty sloppy, but it can give you a rough idea of what the page is trying to display. For a better rendering, you can always click on "Download embedded resources," which will download associated stylesheets and images, although the results are still far from guaranteed.

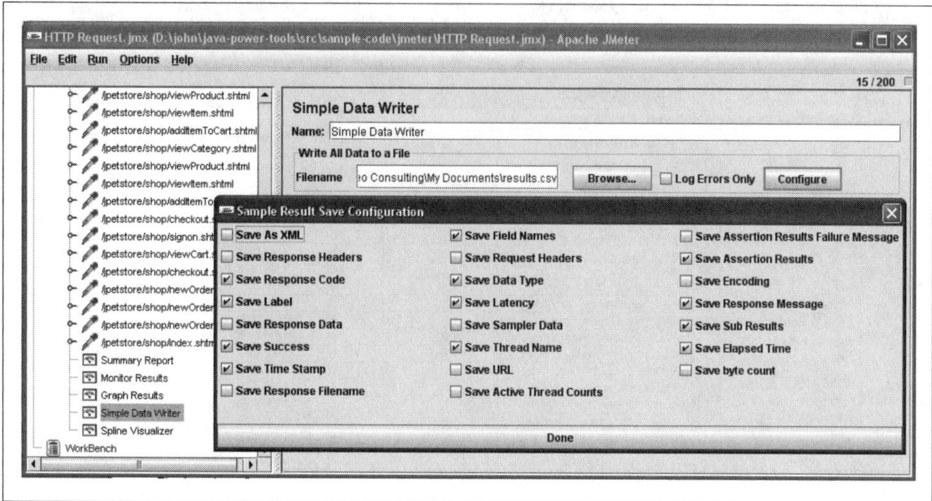

Figure 16-10. Configuring a Simple Data Writer

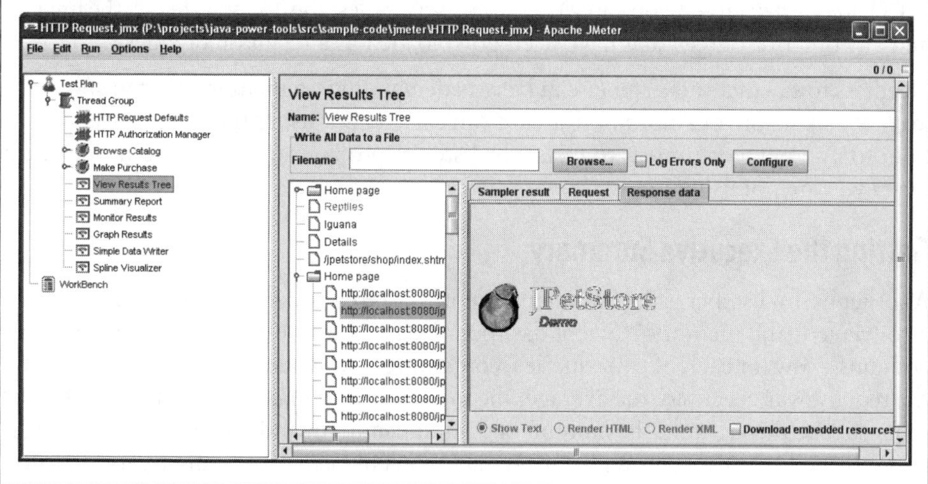

Figure 16-11. The View Results Tree listener in action

You can also use this listener as a debugging tool. Any requests that returned an error are displayed in red, and you can visualize both the returned HTML (generally an error page of some sort) and the HTTP error code (404 for a missing page, 500 for a server error, and so on). You can also choose to record only the results that contained an error (using the "Log Errors Only" option). This is a very useful option if you need to track down hard-to-reproduce errors, as it is not very demanding in terms of memory, and it can be left on during a long-running performance test.

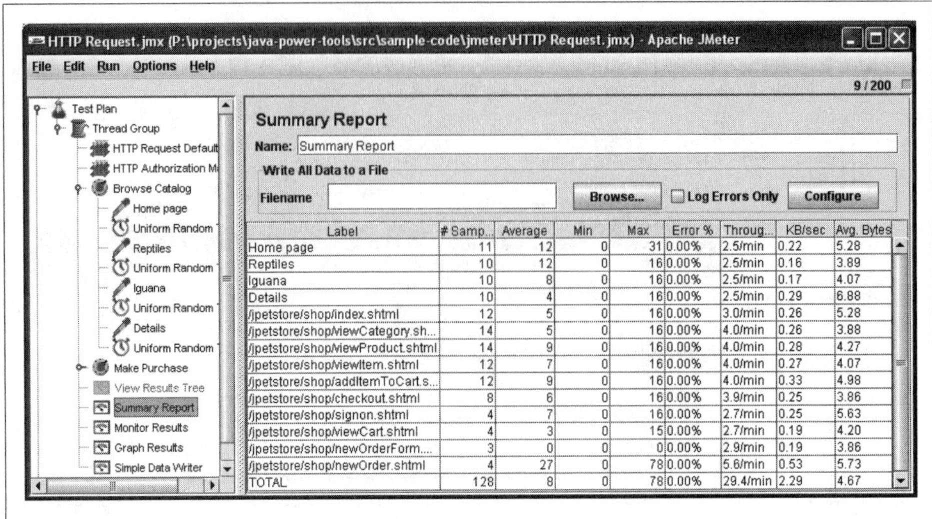

Figure 16-12. The Summary Report listener

In addition, if you have activated the "Retrieve All Embedded Resources" option in the HTTP Request sampler, you can view the javascript files, the css stylesheets, the images, and any other resources that have been downloaded as a result of a request.

Needless to say that this listener can be *very* demanding on memory, so you shouldn't leave it as part of your normal test case (unless you are using the "Log Errors Only" option). A good technique is to insert the listener into your test case, and deactivate it when you are not using it.

Getting the Executive Summary

Another useful listener is the Summary Report. This report (see Figure 16-12) provides a convenient and memory-efficient dashboard view of test results. The summary table contains a row for each of your queries, containing details such as the number of times the request was executed, the average, the minimum and maximum time taken for the requests, the throughput, the amount of data transmitted, and the percentage of pages that returned an error. This report makes an excellent executive summary for performance test results. It can also help isolate queries that take an abnormally long time to execute.

The *Aggregate Report* is similar, though with a more statistical orientation. In addition to the data provided by the Summary Report, this report also displays median result times and a "90% line" column. Statistically, 90 percent of requests took less time than this to complete.

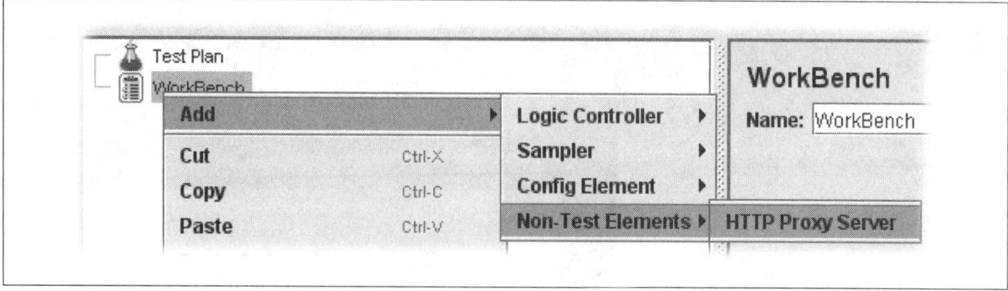

Figure 16-13. Adding an HTTP proxy server

16.5 Using the JMeter Proxy to Record a Test Case

Building a test case by hand gives you a very high degree of control over the requests you build, but it can be tiresome when complex queries are involved. Complex forms, HTTP POSTs, and javascripted submits can all make it hard to work out what parameters are being sent down the wire. Fortunately, JMeter provides an alternative approach. Using JMeter's HTTP proxy server, you can run through your test scenario using your habitual browser. JMeter will record the HTTP requests as they go to the server, and build corresponding HTTP samplers. Once you have recorded the HTTP requests you need, you can use them as building blocks to build a fully operational test case.

Using the proxy to record a test script has a number of advantages. For example, embedded resources, such as images, javascript files, and css stylesheets, are downloaded and cached by the browser. The test cases recorded in this way provide a very realistic picture of how a user's browser will behave.

You can add an HTTP Proxy Server from the WorkBench by selecting "Add→Non-Test Elements→HTTP Proxy Server" in the contextual menu (see Figure 16-13).

This will open the HTTP Proxy Server configuration window, which is where you set up your JMeter proxy. Make sure that the port is not already used on your local machine.

The "Target controller" field indicates the place in your test plan where the recorded elements will be stored. One useful trick is to configure an HTTP Request Defaults element with sensible default values in this element (see "Setting Up the HTTP Request Configuration Elements). If any of your default values match the recorded ones (for example, server name and port), they will be left blank in the recorded elements, letting your default values do their job. This makes your test case cleaner and easier to maintain.

By default, the JMeter HTTP Proxy will try to record everything, including HTML pages, javascript files, css stylesheets, images, and so on. This results in an overwhelming number of HTTP Request elements, most of which are not of much use for your test case. Remember: if you need to, you can instruct JMeter to fetch embedded

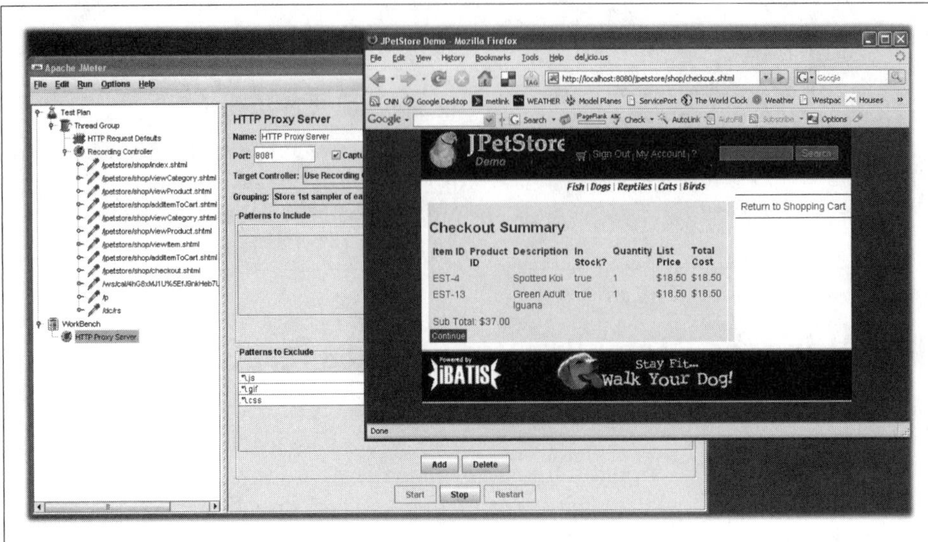

Figure 16-14. Recording a test scenario with JMeter

resources for particular HTTP requests. For any real application, you will need to be more selective in what you record.

There are several strategies that can help obtain only the HTTP Requests that you really want. Typically, you only need to include queries to the pages on your site. You can do this fairly easily by adding entries in the "Patterns to Include" list. These patterns take the form of regular expressions. For example, if your site uses JSP files, you could add ".*\.jsp" to the list of Patterns to Include. For frameworks like Struts, JSF, or Tapestry, you might need to add patterns such as ".*\.jsf" or ".*\.do."

Of course, if your site uses REST-style URLs, this approach may not work. Another possibility is to exclude the files you don't want to record. To do this, you need to add patterns to the "Patterns to Exclude" list. For example, you may want to exclude GIF images and css stylesheets from the recording process by adding ".*\.gif" and ".*\.css" to the excluded patterns list.

Now, to record your tests set up your favorite browser to use the JMeter proxy port. Then just connect to your test site and run through a few test scenarios (see Figure 16-14). When you have finished, press "Stop" to stop the recording.

You will now have an (almost) working, albeit not very flexible, test plan. You can use it as a starting point to build your own, more sophisticated test plan. One of the first things you should do is to add timers between the recorded queries: this will simulate user behavior in a more accurate way. Then you can add more sophisticated structures such as loops and random data selections.

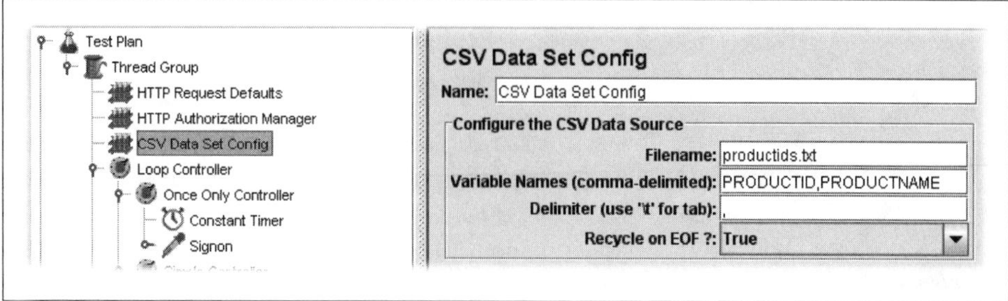

Figure 16-15. Setting up a CSV data set

16.6 Testing Using Variables

Sometimes it is useful to be able to use real data in your test scripts. For example, we might want to better simulate real user activity by displaying a wide range of different products from the database, with different users displaying different products. The easiest way to do this is to use a CSV-formatted file containing your test data. This file might look like this:

```
RP-LI-02,Iguana
RP-SN-01,Rattlesnake
K9-BD-01,Bulldog
K9-CW-01,Chihuahua
K9-DL-01,Dalmation
K9-PO-02,Poodle
...
```

You can import this data into your test plan using the CSV Data Set Configuration element (see Figure 16-15). You define variable names that you can use elsewhere to refer to the data read from this file. The data read from this file will be used to initialize these variables, one row at a time. Each new thread will get a new data row from the CSV file, so the data in the file will be dispatched evenly across all of your test threads. Within your test case elements, you can use these variable names to refer to this data. You can refer to these variables anywhere in your test case using the "*${...}*" notation. In Figure 16-16, for example, we use the *${PRODUCTID}* expression to insert a different product ID each time when displaying the viewProduct page.

In addition, we can use a *Response Assertion* element to make sure the server is sending back the right details page. This is more functional testing than performance testing, but it's always handy to know you are getting coherent responses from your application. In Figure 16-17, we use a Response Assertion to make sure that the returned HTML page contains the name (${PRODUCTNAME}) that we read from the CSV file.

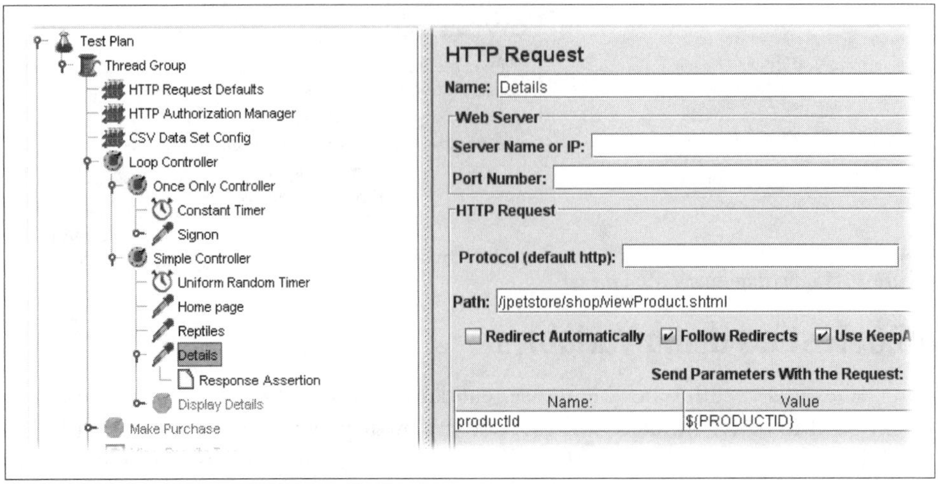

Figure 16-16. Using a variable from the CSV file

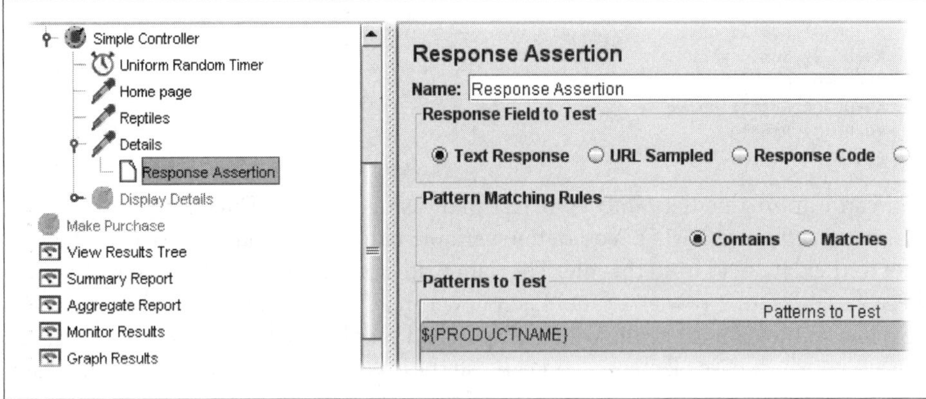

Figure 16-17. Using assertions to verify the response data

16.7 Testing on Multiple Machines

For very heavy load testing, involving thousands of simultaneous users or more, you may find that one machine is not enough. Indeed, you can only simulate so many users on the same machine before coming up against CPU and memory constraints. It is more efficient and more realistic to use several machines to simulate large numbers of users. In JMeter, you can do just this. Using JMeter, you can run test cases on a battery of remote test machines via a central JMeter client. The good thing about this approach is that the machines don't need to be high-powered workhorses—low-end desktops will do fine. Test results from the various machines are saved and displayed centrally.

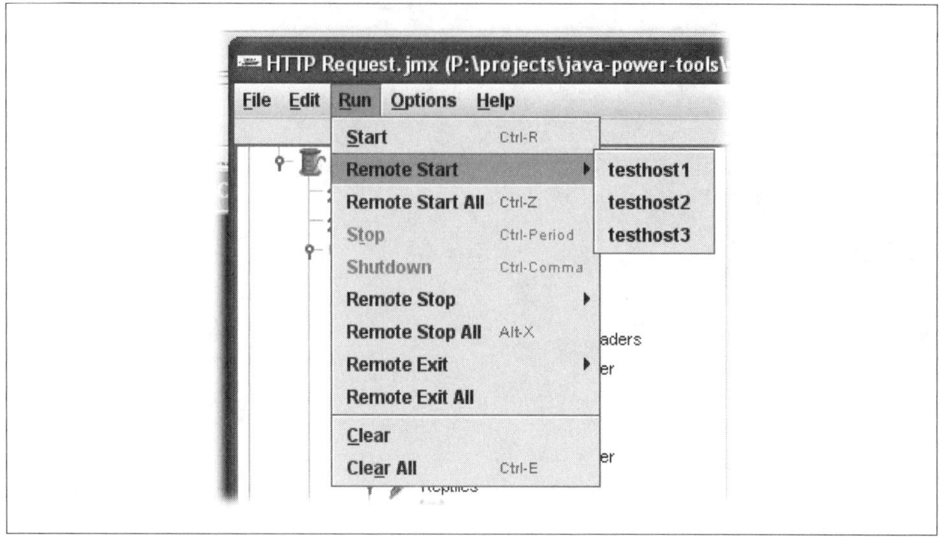

Figure 16-18. Managing remote test machines with JMeter

The first thing that you need to do is to start the JMeter engine on the remote machines manually. JMeter needs to be installed on each remote machine. You start the JMeter-Engine instance using the `jmeter-server` script, as follows:

```
D:>cd D:\tools\jmeter\jakarta-jmeter-2.3\bin
D:\tools\jmeter\jakarta-jmeter-2.3\bin>jmeter-server.bat
```

Or, in a Unix environment:

```
$cd /usr/local/jmeter/jakarta-jmeter-2.3/bin
$jmeter-server
```

Next you need to tell your main JMeter client which remote servers you will be controlling. You can do this in one of two ways. The first involves adding the hostnames of your remote machines to the *remote_hosts* variable in the `bin/jmeter.properties` file, as shown here:

```
# Remote Hosts - comma delimited
remote_hosts=testhost1,testhost2,testhost3
```

Alternatively, you can use the *-J* command-line option when you start JMeter, as shown here:

```
$jmeter -Jremote_hosts=testhost1,testhost2,testhost3
```

Now, when you run JMeter you can use the Run menu to manage your remote test machines (see Figure 16-18). You can start (and stop) remote machines either one by one, or all together using the *Remote Start All* option. The test results coming from the different servers will be aggregated and displayed on your JMeter client interface in the same way as for ordinary tests.

CHAPTER 17

Testing Web Services with SoapUI

17.0 Introduction

Web services are becoming more and more present in today's development projects. Indeed, they can prove to be an excellent choice for integrating loosely coupled systems.

Web services are often used to integrate different systems, possibly developed by different organizations. If you are on the receiving (client) end of a web service integration project, it is in your best interest to make sure that the web services you are calling return the data you expect them to return.

In this chapter, we look at SoapUI, a tool that can help you test your web services. SoapUI[*] is a powerful open source tool written by Eviware that helps you test your web services in a variety different scenarios. SoapUI supports a wide range of web service protocols, including Soap 1.1 and 1.2, MTOM, and SAAJ, making it suitable for testing a wide range of web services with different requirements. SoapUI also allows you to perform functional testing and put your web services under load and compliance tests along with some code generation capabilities that makes web service development easier.

17.1 An Introduction to SoapUI

Based on material contributed by: Masoud Kalali

SoapUI is a particularly rich tool. Its features fall into two main areas, which together cover a good part of the web service development lifecycle. These two areas are:

- Web service testing
- Web service development

Let's look at each of these in more detail.

[*] *http://www.soapui.org/*

Web Service Testing

SoapUI is first and foremost a test platform: it excels in letting you perform functional, load, and compliance tests on your web services.

You can perform functional testing by creating and executing complex test scripts (also known as test cases) against your web services. In addition to basic scripting features such as Conditional Goto and Delays, you can use Groovy to obtain a high level of control and flexibility over test execution flow.

You can also run load tests against a particular test case, using different load strategies and end criteria. Assertions can be used during testing to keep tabs on performance and functionality. And, as with most good load-testing tools, results can be displayed in both numerical and graphical form.

These tests can be done in several scenarios, for example:

- Data-driven tests, where you perform your tests using input data from external sources such as properties files or databases.
- Template-driven scenarios, which extend data-driven tests for reading test data for each test case execution sequentially.
- You can also use Groovy scripting to make interactive test cases, where you can use dialogs to get user input and to display results during test execution.
- Headless testing, where you can test your system without using the SoapUI GUI. This can help integrate SoapUI with your built system for continuous quality control.

Web Service Development

SoapUI is closely integrated with many of the tools commonly used in the Java web service trade, and it provides code generation features for several web services frameworks, WSDL generation using JBossWS, JAXB class binding generation, and more. You can access most of SoapUI features via the GUI frontend and through a command-line interface, allowing smooth integration with continuous build and integration systems. SoapUI can also perform validation on Soap requests and responses against their schema definitions.

When Is SoapUI Appropriate?

You should now have a basic idea about where SoapUI might come in handy. As we mentioned earlier, SoapUI's speciality is web service testing, although it can also help with web service development. Here are some situations where SoapUI should jump into the forefront of your mind:

- You have some web services that you need to performance test
- You have some web services and you need to verify how well they integrate

- You have some web services and you want to create mock objects for other web services to simplify your unit tests
- You are testing web services with custom SOAP messages such as MTOM and SAAJ, or you need to check a web service response message
- You want to do some basic code generation using one of the several supported web service frameworks

17.2 Installing SoapUI

SoapUI is written in Java, so it can run on any Java-compliant platform. Installing SoapUI is straightforward: you simply download and run the installer from the SoapUI web site.[*] Alternatively, you can install it using WebStart from the SoapUI web site.

SoapUI runs as a standalone Java client application with a rich user interface that looks and feels like a modern IDE. There are also plug-ins available for NetBeans, Eclipse, and IntelliJ.

17.3 Installing a Local Web Service

To illustrate the features of SoapUI, we will use a locally deployed web service. This is a simple web service that provides access to an imaginary customer database. The Java version of this service implements the following interface:

```
public interface CustomerService {
    public Customer findById(String id);
    public Customer[] findByName(String name);
    public Customer[] findByHomeCity(String city);
}
```

A basic understanding of the domain model will make it easier to follow the SOAP examples later on. The UML class diagram for this sample application (generated by DOxygen—see Section 30.2) is illustrated in Figure 17-1.

If you want to follow along at home, you will need to download and install Apache Axis 2,[†] which has been used to write a simple web service of our own. For detailed instructions on how to install and use Axis2, check out the web site. Here is the condensed version (with the corresponding Linux commands just for a bit of extra precision):

1. Download the Standard Binary Distribution of Apache Axis 2 and install it into a convenient directory. You will need this installation to properly build the sample code. You also need to set up an environment variable called AXIS2_HOME pointing to this directory:

[*] *http://www.soapui.org/*

[†] *http://ws.apache.org/axis2*

```
# cd /usr/local/tools
# wget http://ftp.wayne.edu/apache/ws/axis2/1_2/axis2-1.2.zip
# unzip axis2-1.2.zip
# export AXIS2_HOME = /usr/local/tools/axis2-1.2
```

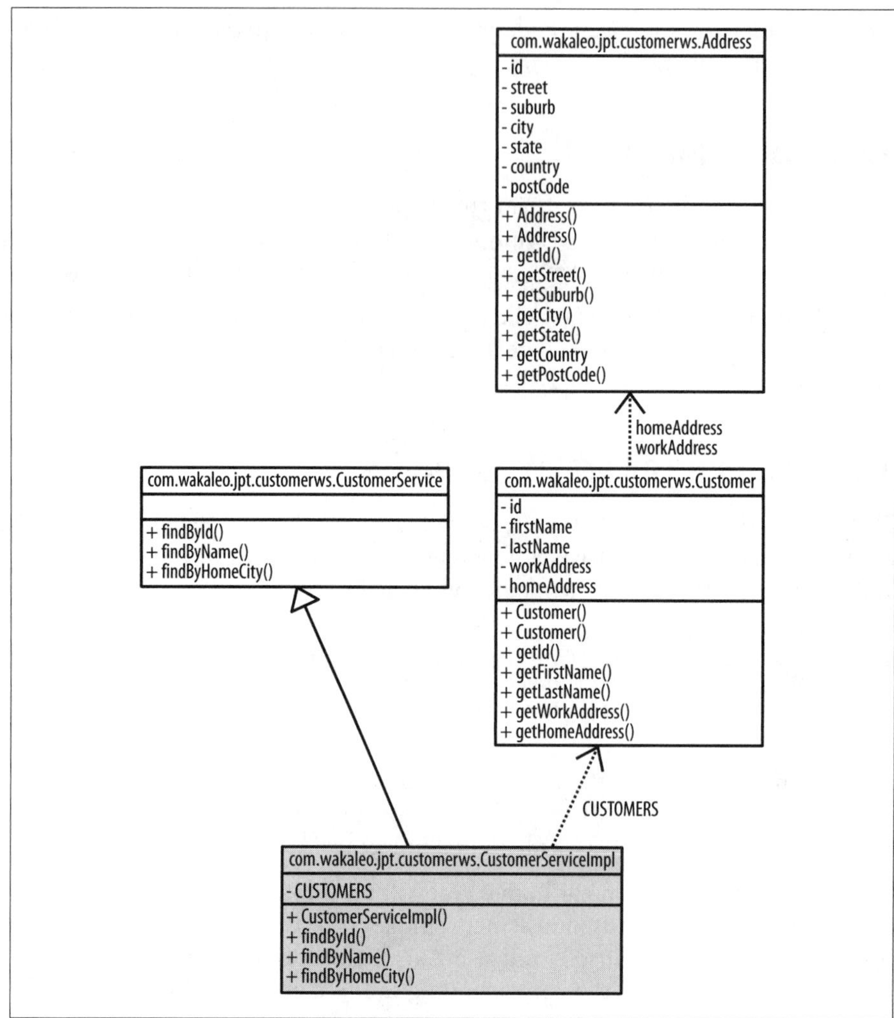

Figure 17-1. The UML class diagram for the CustomerService web service application

2. Start up the Axis2 server by running the $AXIS2_HOME\bin\axis2server.bat (for Windows) or $AXIS2_HOME/bin/axis2server.sh script (for *nix):

```
$ AXIS2_HOME/bin/axis2server.sh
 Using AXIS2_HOME:   /usr/local/tools/axis2-1.2
 Using JAVA_HOME:       /usr/local/java/jdk1.6.0/
26/05/2007 14:40:21 org.apache.axis2.transport.SimpleAxis2Server main
INFO: [SimpleAxisServer] Starting
```

```
...
INFO: [SimpleAxisServer] Started
26/05/2007 14:40:22 org.apache.axis2.transport.http.server.
DefaultConnectionListener run
INFO: Listening on port 8080
```

3. Check out the source code for the *customer-ws* sample application from the Java Power Tools book repository:

```
$ svn co https://wakaleo.devguard.com/svn/jpt-sample-code/customer-ws
/trunk customer-cs
A    customer-cs/.classpath
A    customer-cs/.project
A    customer-cs/src
...
A    customer-cs/build.xml
Checked out revision 5.
$ cd customer-cs
$ ant deploy.service
Buildfile: build.xml

compile.service:

generate.service:

deploy.service:
     [copy] Copying 1 file to /usr/local/tools/axis2-1.2/repository/services

BUILD SUCCESSFUL
Total time: 0 seconds
```

   This build script will deploy to a standalone Axis2 server installed in the $AXIS2_HOME directory. You can check that your web service was correctly deployed by opening a browser at *http://localhost:8080/axis2/services/*, where you should see CustomerService among the deployed web services.

Now that we have a local web service, we can do some testing.

17.4 Testing Web Services with SoapUI

Now let's see SoapUI in action. SoapUI has an initiative IDE-like GUI, which lets you easily create and execute your tests (see Figure 17-2). On the left side of the screen, you will find an overview of your project displayed in a tree-like structure.

In this section, we will go through the steps involved in setting up some simple unit tests for a web service. Start up SoapUI and create a new project using the "File→*New WSDL project*" menu (see Figure 17-3). The easiest way to get started is to provide a WSDL (Web Service Definition Language) file when you create the project. It is the cornerstone of any web service. In a real-world project, the WSDL may be defined from the outset as a contract between interoperating systems. Alternatively, it might be generated during the build process, based on the classes being deployed to the web service.

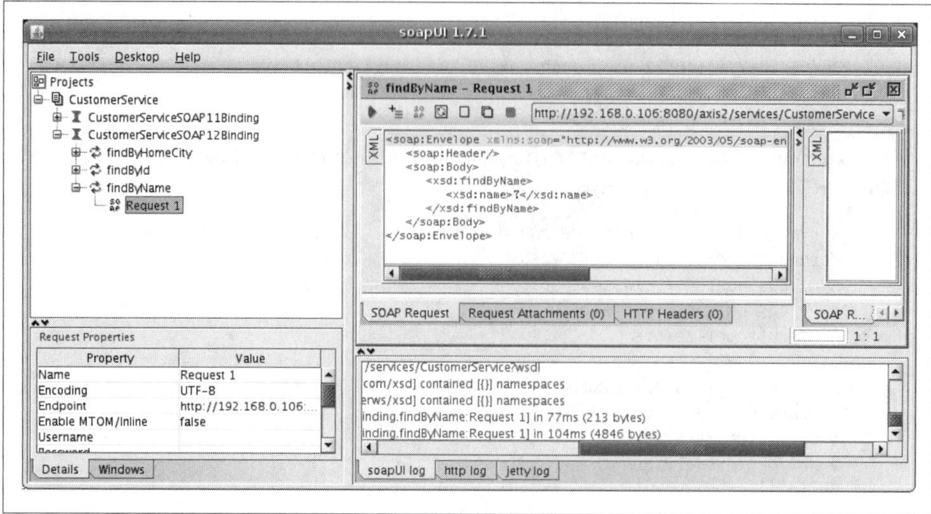

Figure 17-2. SoapUI has a rich and fairly intuitive user interface

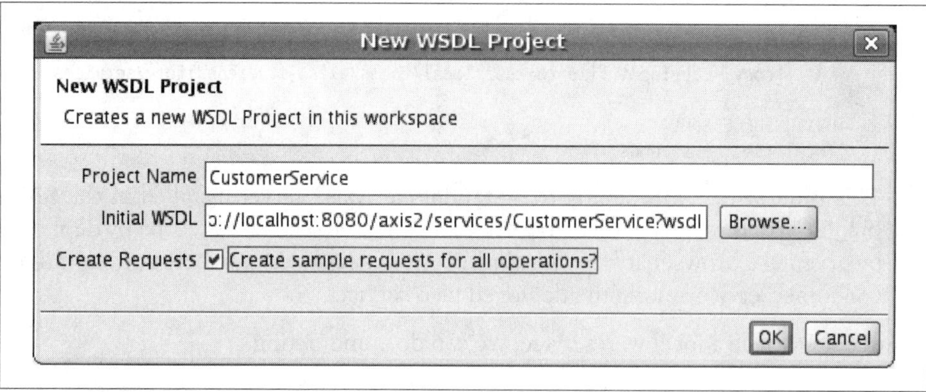

Figure 17-3. Creating a new WSDL project

Probably the easiest way to obtain a reliable, up-to-date WSDL file is to query the deployed web service itself. For example, the WSDL file for our locally deployed web service can be found at *http://localhost:8080/axis2/services/CustomerService?wsdl.*

This screen also lets you choose to create sample requests for all of your endpoint operations. These sample SOAP requests are a good starting point for your tests. You can use them as a convenient template for your own requests, which comes in handy if you don't remember the exact structure of a SOAP XML request off the top of your head.

Now just press OK, and let SoapUI create the new project for you.

Your new project will contain the list of operations available from this web service, as illustrated in Figure 17-2. From here, you can build SOAP requests for operations you want to test. Testing a web service using SoapUI basically involves creating SOAP requests for the operations to be tested and then organizing them into test cases and test suites. SoapUI is fairly flexible about how you create these requests; you can either create them directly within a test case, or you can create them from within an operation and then add them to a test case. Using this latter approach, you can create test requests, which can be reused in different test cases.

Let's create our first SOAP request, which will test the *findByName* operation. The *findByName* operation returns a list of customers with a given surname. It takes a single parameter called, appropriately enough, *name*. For our first test, we are going to look for all the clients named "Smart." Open the sample request (initially named "Request 1"). As illustrated in Figure 17-2, this request contains a full SOAP request with the operation parameters replaced by question marks:

```
<soap:Envelope xmlns:soap="http://www.w3.org/2003/05/soap-envelope"
 xmlns:xsd="http://com.wakaleo.jpt.customerws/xsd">
   <soap:Header/>
   <soap:Body>
      <xsd:findByName>
         <xsd:name>?</xsd:name>
      </xsd:findByName>
   </soap:Body>
</soap:Envelope>
```

So, all we need to do to tailor our request is fill in the gaps. Just replace the question mark in the *<xsd:name>* parameter with "Smart." The full SOAP request for this query looks like this:

```
<soap:Envelope xmlns:soap="http://www.w3.org/2003/05/soap-envelope"
 xmlns:xsd="http://com.wakaleo.jpt.customerws/xsd">
   <soap:Header/>
   <soap:Body>
      <xsd:findByName>
         <xsd:name>Smart</xsd:name>
      </xsd:findByName>
   </soap:Body>
</soap:Envelope>
```

Now, rename the request to something more appropriate (using the "Rename" option in the contextual menu) and run the request using the green arrow button in the request editor (see Figure 17-4). SoapUI will execute the request and display the SOAP response. Note that you are testing against a live server here: SoapUI does not verify the syntax or contents of your request before sending it off. So, you do need a fairly good understanding of SOAP and XML at this level, as well as a good idea of what your query is supposed to look like.

The next step involves creating a test suite. SoapUI, like many software testing products, lets you organize your individual test cases into test suites. Right-click on project node,

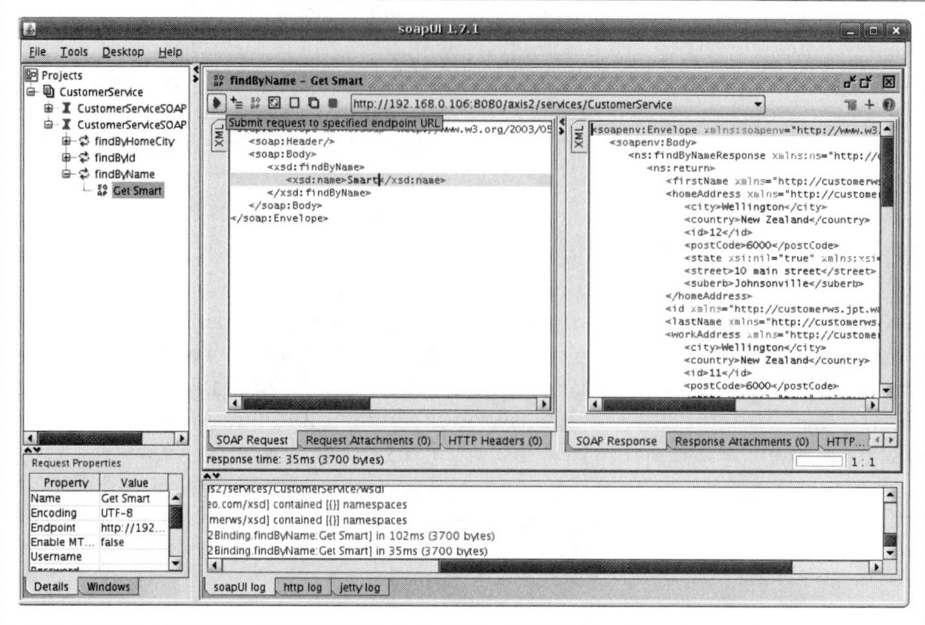

Figure 17-4. Executing a SOAP request in SoapUI

select *New TestSuite*, and enter an appropriate name. This Test Suite is simply a container designed to regroup a set of related test cases. As in unit tests, SoapUI test cases are where all the real testing gets done. So, without further ado, let's look at how to create a SoapUI test case.

Right-click on the test suite you created earlier, and select *New Test Case*. Name the test case something easy to remember, like "FindByName." Your new test case should appear nested in your test suite in the SoapUI project pane.

A *test case* is made up of a series of *test steps*, which are executed one after the other. A Test Step can come in a number of forms: sending a SOAP request, pausing for a certain period of time, reading data from an external source, running a Groovy script, and many more. For our simple unit test, we need to add a *Request* step, which sends a SOAP request to the web service and allows you to verify the response.

There are several ways to do this. You can insert a new request directly into the test steps by selecting the Test Steps node and choosing "New Step→Test Request" in the contextual menu. SoapUI will let you choose the operation you want to test, and create an empty SOAP message for this operation for you to fill in. This can be useful if you want to insert a one-off request that you do not intend to use elsewhere.

Alternatively, you can add an existing request to your test case, which is what we will be doing here. Go to the request we created earlier on, and select "Add to TestCase"

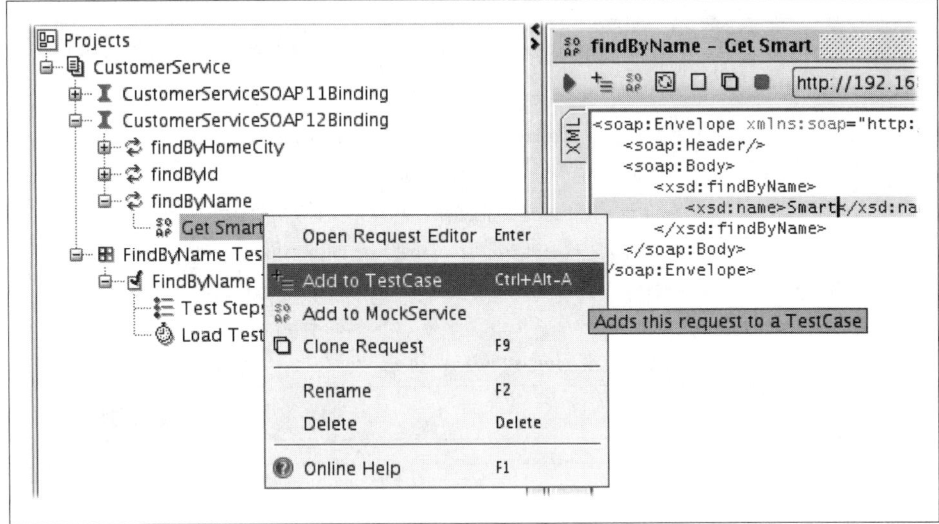

Figure 17-5. Inserting a new request in a test case

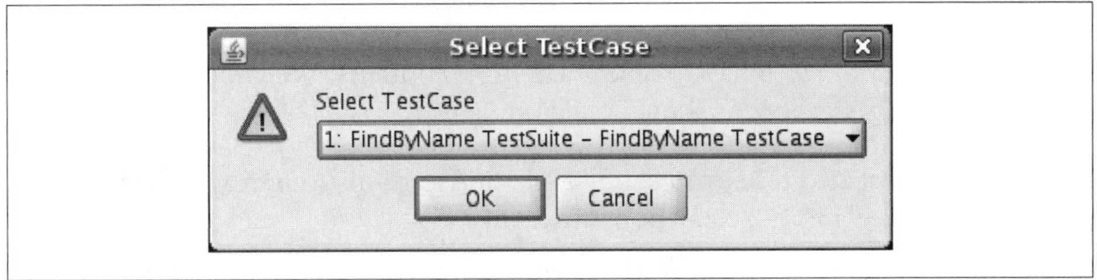

Figure 17-6. Selecting a test case

in the contextual menu (see Figure 17-5). SoapUI will propose a list of test cases where you can place your request (see Figure 17-6). Select the test case we created above.

A test case should not simply execute a piece of code; it should also verify the results. SoapUI lets you add different types of assertions to your test case to verify that the operation was successful. When you add a request to a test case, SoapUI proposes to add some basic assertions automatically (see Figure 17-7). These include optional tests that check that your request complies to the WSDL you specified, no server errors occurred, and the response is correctly formed.

When you are done, SoapUI will create a new SOAP request step within your test case. You can display and edit the SOAP request in the same way as we saw previously, with one addition: you can insert additional assertions (see Figure 17-8). Note that you are actually editing the original request that you created in the first operation, not a copy, so any changes you make will affect all the test cases that use this request.

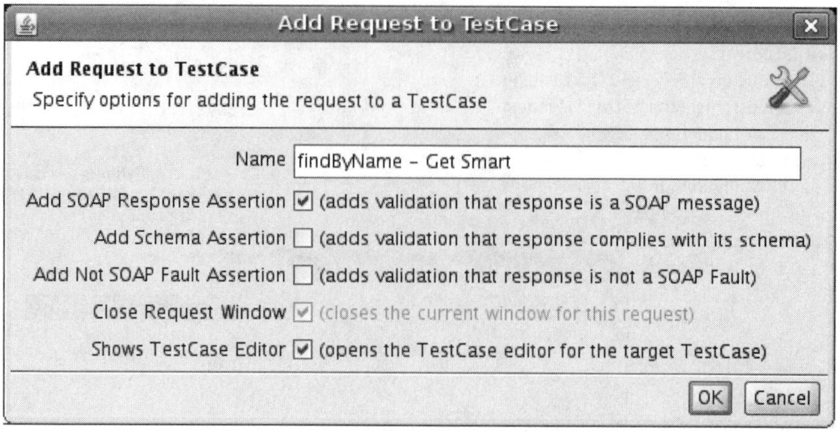

Add Request to TestCase

Add Request to TestCase
Specify options for adding the request to a TestCase

Name: findByName - Get Smart
Add SOAP Response Assertion ☑ (adds validation that response is a SOAP message)
Add Schema Assertion ☐ (adds validation that response complies with its schema)
Add Not SOAP Fault Assertion ☐ (adds validation that response is not a SOAP Fault)
Close Request Window ☑ (closes the current window for this request)
Shows TestCase Editor ☑ (opens the TestCase editor for the target TestCase)
OK Cancel

Figure 17-7. Adding a request to an existing test case

In addition to the basic assertions we saw earlier, SoapUI supports a number of other assertions, including "Contains," "Not Contains," and "XPath Match." You can use these to verify that the response contains the data that you expect. For example, we might want to make sure that every SOAP response in the findName query above at least contains the word "Smart" somewhere in its contents. We could do this with a Simple Contains Assertion, as shown in Figure 17-9.

For more sophisticated tests, you can use XPath Assertions to narrow down your assertion to a particular XML element or attribute.

In real-world situations, a typical test case may involve more than one request. For example, a unit test might involve simply invoking a web service once and making sure that the response contains the data you expect, or it could involve calling the web service several times with different data. Functional testing might involve invoking a series of requests to simulate a full business transaction.

Once you have a working SOAP request, it is easy to create other similar requests for the same operation using the "Clone Request" menu item. You can also clone Test Cases and Test Suites, so you can create a sizable battery of tests in very little time. As you would expect, you can either run test cases individually, or alternatively run all the test cases in a test suite simply by executing the test suite (see Figure 17-10). When you run a test suite, you can also choose to run the test cases sequentially (the default option) or in parallel.

This is a fairly trivial example. With a little practice you can build much more sophisticated test cases in SoapUI using properties, conditional expressions, or even the Groovy scripting language.

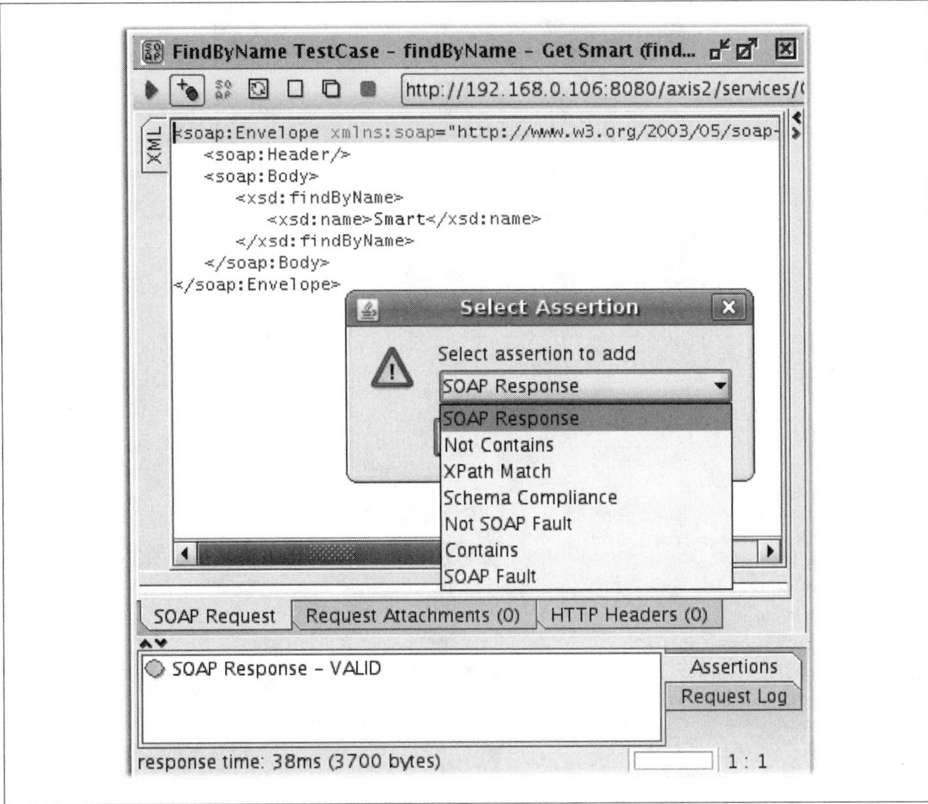

Figure 17-8. Adding an assertion to a test

17.5 Load-Testing with SoapUI

SoapUI comes with some convenient features for web service load-testing. Although these load-testing features are not as rich and flexible as those of tools like JMeter (see Chapter 16), they are sufficient to let you set up simple but effective load tests for your web services in a minimum of time. Load tests can be used to measure the performance of your web services under different loads, including assertions to ensure that performance always remains within acceptable limits.

In SoapUI, you create load tests for a given test case. We could use the test case we built in the previous chapter. SoapUI makes a clear distinction between load tests and functional tests, even when they are in the same test case. However, it is often useful to distinguish between functional tests and load tests, as you tend to run them at different times, and the test steps you run in a load test may not be the same as those of functional tests. So, here we will set up a test suite just for load testing. Create a new test suite and add a test case containing the requests that you want to include in your

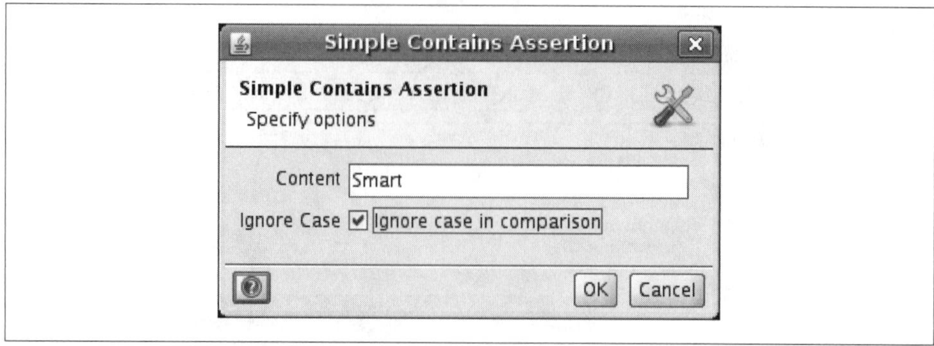

Figure 17-9. Adding an assertion to a test

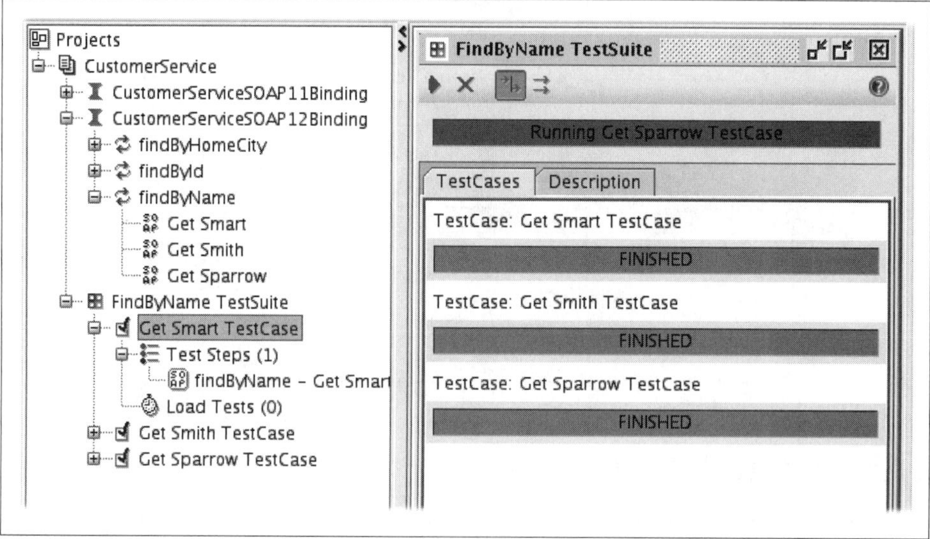

Figure 17-10. Running a TestSuite

load test. In Figure 17-11, the test case contains several requests, each separated by a one second delay.

Next, you need to create the actual load test. Select the "Load Tests" node in your new test case and choose "New LoadTest" in the contextual menu (see Figure 17-11). This will create a new load test ready to go.

The load test window (see Figure 17-12) gives you a central interface where you manage all load testing activities for a given test case. The interface is fairly intuitive. Like elsewhere in SoapUI, the green arrow starts the tests and the red cross stops them. So far so good. Running the load tests like this, using the default configuration, can yield some interesting initial results.

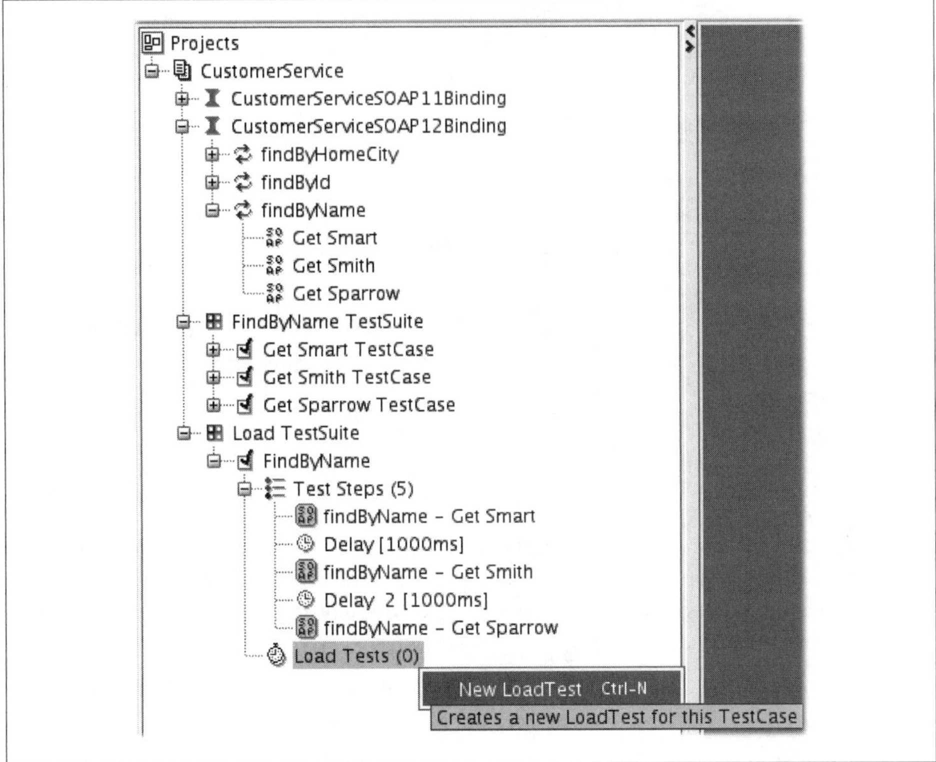

Figure 17-11. Creating a new load test

The *Threads* field lets you define the number of threads that will be run simultaneously, and therefore the number of users that are being simulated. The number of users that can be effectively simulated depends largely on your hardware configuration. You can also define a startup delay between each in the options window, which allows you to gradually build up user load. The total length of the load test is determined by the *Limit* field, in terms of either elapsed time (seconds) or the number of times the test case is executed in each thread (runs).

You can define load tests using several different strategies. In the *Simple* strategy, the test case will be invoked at (more or less) regular intervals in each thread. You can use the *Test Delay* and *Random* fields to define how long each thread should wait between calls, and how random this delay should be.

The *Variance* strategy lets you study a varying number of users over time. The number of active threads will decrease and increase periodically, simulating periods of more or less intensive load.

The *Burst* strategy simulates bursts of intensive use (the *Burst Duration*), followed by periods of inactivity (the *Burst Delay*).

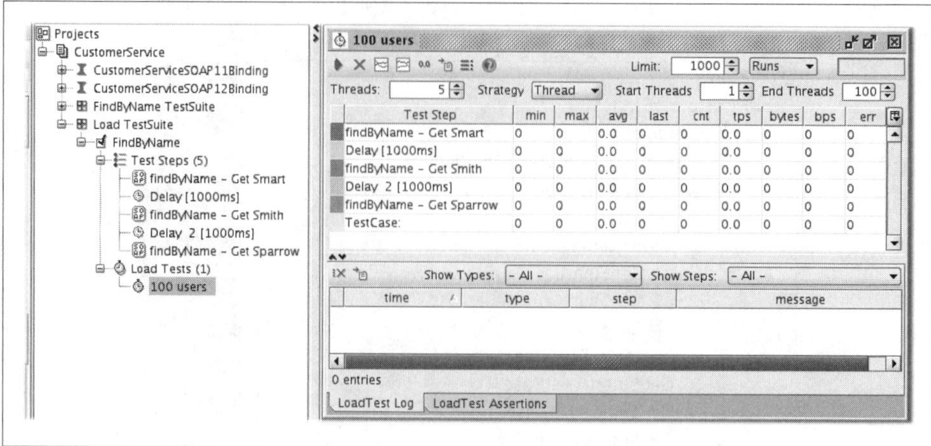

Figure 17-12. Configuring a load test

The *Threads* strategy lets you simulate a linearly increasing number of users over time.

When you execute the load test, SoapUI will display (and record) statistics about the web service calls: the shortest, longest and average time taken, the number of transactions per second, and so on. This data can also be displayed in graphical form. SoapUI supports two main types of graph:

- The *Statistics* graph, where you can view all of the recorded data in graphical form, for a given test case step
- The *Statistics History* graph, which tracks a particular statistic (average time per transaction, transactions per second, number of errors, or bytes per second) against the number of threads

In Figure 17-13, for example, you can see a statistical graph showing the number of errors increasing sharply as the thread count increases.

Assertions are another useful thing you can add to your load test (see Figure 17-14). Assertions let you make sure that the web service performs . You can define assertions in terms of the maximum number of permissible errors, the minimum number of transactions per second, the maximum total time required to run the load test, and more. Load-test assertions can be used alongside functional test assertions to perform sophisticated integration tests and to monitor your live web services.

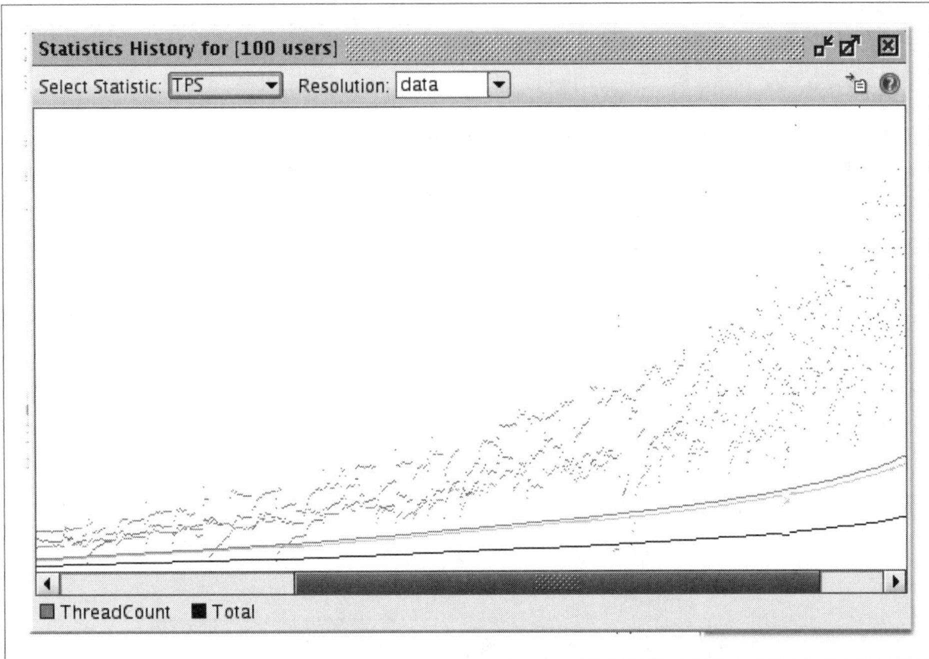

Figure 17-13. A statistical history graph of Transactions Per Second (TPS)

17.6 Running SoapUI from the Command Line

SoapUI can also be run from the command line, which can be useful for automated testing and web service monitoring. The *testrunner* script (*testrunner.bat* for Windows and *testrunner.sh* for Unix) will run all the functional tests in a given SoapUI project file:

```
$ $SOAPUI_HOME/bin/testrunner.sh -r CustomerService-soapui-project.xml
================================
=
= SOAPUI_HOME = /usr/local/tools/soapui-1.7.1/
=
================================
soapUI 1.7.1 TestCase Runner
Configuring log4j from [jar:file:/usr/local/tools/soapui-1.7.1/bin/soapui-1.7.1.jar!
/soapui-log4j.xml]
22:41:25,431 INFO  [SoapUITestCaseRunner] setting projectFile to
[test/CustomerService-soapui-project.xml]
22:41:25,432 INFO  [SoapUI] Missing folder [/home/john/projects/jpt-sample-code
/customer-cs/ext] for external libraries
22:41:25,998 WARN  [SoapUI] Failed to load settings [soapui-settings.xml (No such file
or directory)], creating new
22:41:26,098 INFO  [WsdlProject] Loaded project from [/home/john/projects/jpt-
sample-code/customer-cs/test/CustomerService-soapui-project.xml]
22:41:26,441 INFO  [SoapUITestCaseRunner] Running soapUI tests in project
[CustomerService]
```

```
22:41:26,444 INFO  [SoapUITestCaseRunner] Running soapUI suite [FindByName TestSuite],
runType = SEQUENTIAL
22:41:26,451 INFO  [SoapUITestCaseRunner] Running soapUI testcase
[Get Smart TestCase]
22:41:26,451 INFO  [SoapUITestCaseRunner] running step [findByName -
Get Smart]
...
22:41:29,958 INFO  [SoapUITestCaseRunner] Finished running soapUI testcase
[FindByName],
time taken: 2157ms, status: FINISHED
22:41:29,958 INFO  [SoapUITestCaseRunner] soapUI suite [Load TestSuite] finished
in 2190ms

SoapUI 1.7.1 TestCaseRunner Summary
-----------------------------
Time Taken: 3516ms
Total TestSuites: 2
Total TestCases: 4 (0 failed)
Total TestSteps: 8
Total Request Assertions: 5
Total Failed Assertions: 0
Total Exported Results: 0
```

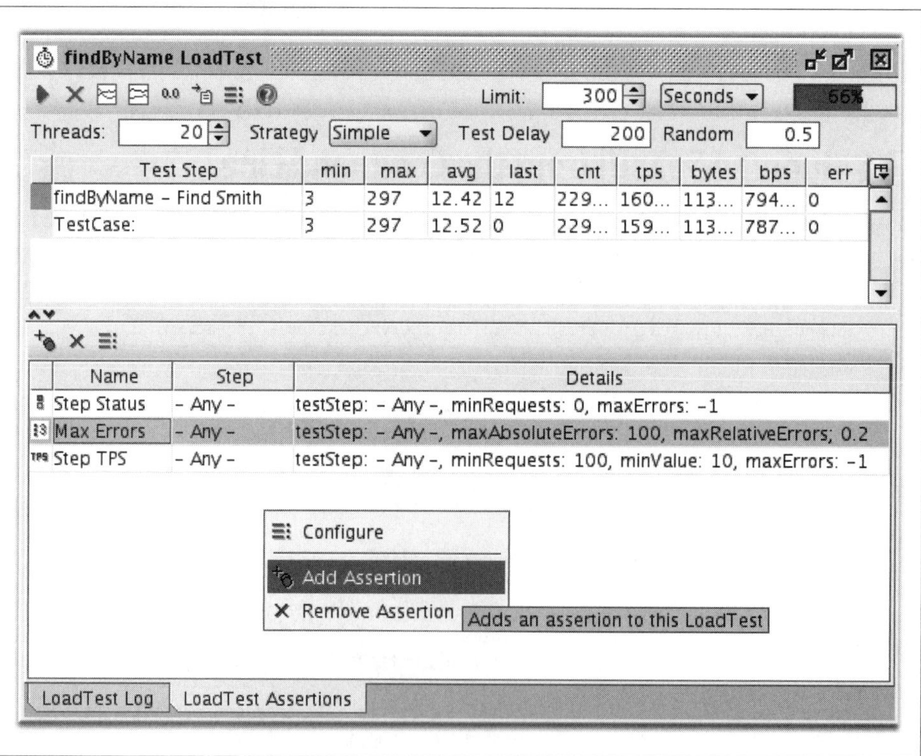

Figure 17-14. Assertions in a load test

The *-r* option used here displays a summary report at the end of the tests. You can also narrow down the scope of your tests using the *-s* (run only a specified test suite) or *-c* (run only a specified test case) options. At the time of this writing, this worked best if your test suite and test case names didn't have any spaces:

```
$ $SOAPUI_HOME/bin/testrunner.sh -r -sFindByName CustomerService-soapui-project.xml
```

In the same manner, you can use the *loadtestrunner* script to execute the load tests defined in a given SoapUI project:

```
$ $SOAPUI_HOME/bin/testrunner.sh CustomerService-soapui-project.xml -r
================================
=
= SOAPUI_HOME = /usr/local/tools/soapui-1.7.1/
=
================================
soapUI 1.7.1 LoadTest Runner
...
22:46:57,451 INFO  [SoapUILoadTestRunner] LoadTest [LoadTest 1] progress: 1.00565, 5
22:46:58,456 INFO  [SoapUILoadTestRunner] LoadTest [LoadTest 1] progress: 1.0224, 5
22:46:59,461 INFO  [SoapUILoadTestRunner] LoadTest [LoadTest 1] progress: 1.03915, 2
22:47:00,465 INFO  [SoapUILoadTestRunner] LoadTest [LoadTest 1] finished with status
FINISHED
22:47:00,465 INFO  [SoapUILoadTestRunner] Exporting log and statistics for LoadTest
[LoadTest 1]
22:47:00,469 INFO  [SoapUILoadTestRunner] Exported 2 log items to [LoadTest 1-log.txt]
22:47:00,469 INFO  [SoapUILoadTestRunner] Exported 0 error results
22:47:00,471 INFO  [SoapUILoadTestRunner] Exported 6 statistics to [LoadTest
1-statistics.txt]
22:47:00,471 INFO  [SoapUILoadTestRunner] soapUI suite [Load TestSuite] finished
in 63363ms
```

In addition to the options mentioned above, you can also use the *-l* option to narrow your tests down to a particular load test.

17.7 Running SoapUI from Ant

Integrating SoapUI tests into an Ant build isn't too difficult, although you do need to invoke the SoapUI scripts at the command line, which makes portability an issue. Indeed, to run the script correctly, you need an *<exec>* tag for each of your target operating systems.The *-j* command-line option tells SoapUI to generate Javadoc-style XML report data, so you can invoke *<junitreport>* to generate the results in HTML form.

```
<property environment="env"/>
<property name="AXIS2_HOME" value="${env.AXIS2_HOME}"/>
<property name="SOAPUI_HOME" value="${env.SOAPUI_HOME}"/>
<property name="soapui.home" value="${SOAPUI_HOME}" />

<property name="testrunner.sh" location="${soapui.home}/bin/testrunner.sh"/>
<property name="testrunner.bat" location="${soapui.home}/bin/testrunner.bat"/>
...
```

```
<target name="soapui-report">
  <mkdir dir="reports" />
  <exec executable="${testrunner.sh}" os="Linux" failonerror="true">
    <arg line="-j -freports CustomerService-soapui-project.xml"/>
  </exec>
  <exec executable="cmd.exe" os="Windows 2000" failonerror="true">
    <arg line="/c ${testrunner.bat} -j -freports CustomerService-soapui-
     project.xml"/>
  </exec>
  ...
  <junitreport todir="reports">
    <fileset dir="reports">
      <include name="TEST-*.xml"/>
    </fileset>
    <report format="frames" todir="reports/html"/>
  </junitreport>
</target>
```

Note that we are using the *SOAPUI_HOME* environment variable to find the SoapUI scripts. Indeed, this build script requires the *AXIS2_HOME* and *SOAPUI_HOME* environment variables to be correctly defined.

The *soapui-report* target will produce a JUnit-style report illustrated in Figure 17-15.

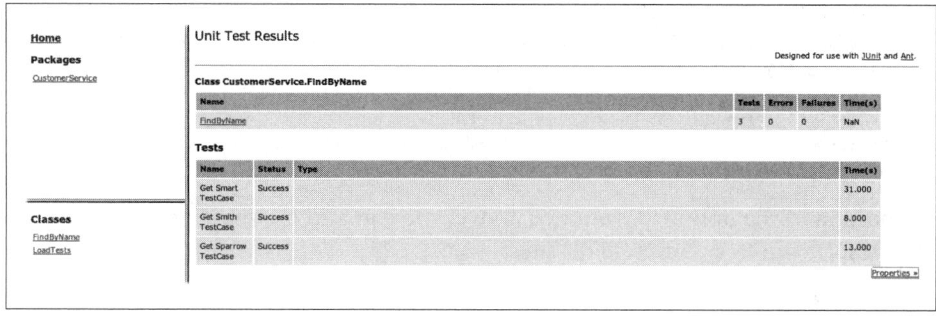

Figure 17-15. JUnit reports generated by SoapUI

17.8 Running SoapUI from Maven

SoapUI provides a Maven 2 plug-in, which is well documented on the SoapUI web site. The plug-in is not in the standard repositories, so you need to add the following to your plug-in repository list:

```
<pluginRepositories>
   <pluginRepository>
      <id>eviwarePluginRepository</id>
      <url>http://www.eviware.com/repository/maven2/</url>
   </pluginRepository>
</pluginRepositories>
```

Next, add the SoapUI plug-in to the *<build>* section of your *pom.xml* file:

```
<build>
    <plugins>
        ...
        <plugin>
            <groupId>eviware</groupId>
            <artifactId>maven-soapui-plugin</artifactId>
            <version>1.7</version>
            <configuration>
                <projectFile>CustomerService-soapui-project.xml
                </projectFile>
                <host>127.0.0.1:8080</host>
            </configuration>
            <executions>
                <execution>
                    <phase>integration-test</phase>
                    <goals>
                        <goal>test</goal>
                        <goal>loadtest</goal>
                    </goals>
                </execution>
            </executions>
        </plugin>
    </plugins>
</build>
```

This will execute both SoapUI functional and load tests during the integration test phase.

You can also run SoapUI functional tests directly using the *test* goal:

```
$ mvn eviware:maven-soapui-plugin:test
```

Load tests can be run using the *loadtest* goal:

```
$ mvn eviware:maven-soapui-plugin:loadtest
```

17.9 Continuous Testing

It is often useful to integrate web service functional and load tests into your Continuous Build process. Frequent functional tests serve the same purpose as periodic builds and unit tests; they let you detect errors as early as possible. Frequent load tests let you detect any performance problems that might have slipped into your application.

You can use SoapUI fairly easily to do this sort of continuous web service testing. Because SoapUI needs to work against a real server, you need to make sure you have the latest build of your application always running on a development server somewhere. You would typically build this into your standard Continuous Integration process, and reserve a deployment environment for this purpose. Then it is simply a matter of integrating the SoapUI tests into the build process.

If you are using Ant, just set the *failonerror* attribute to true when you invoke the SoapUI scripts. This will force the build to fail and notify the team if the web service tests fail. This is illustrated here:

```
<property name="soapui.home" value="/usr/local/tools/soapui-1.7.1" />
<property name="testrunner.sh" location="${soapui.home}/bin/
 testrunner.sh"/>
<property name="testrunner.bat" location="${soapui.home}/bin/
 testrunner.bat"/>
<property name="loadtestrunner.sh" location="${soapui.home}/bin/
 loadtestrunner.sh"/>
<property name="loadtestrunner.bat" location="${soapui.home}/bin/
 loadtestrunner.bat"/>
...
<target name="soapui-functional-tests">
    <echo>os.name = ${os.name}</echo>
    <mkdir dir="reports" />
    <exec executable="${testrunner.sh}" os="Linux" failonerror="true">
        <arg line="CustomerService-soapui-project.xml"/>
    </exec>
</target>

<target name="soapui-load-tests">
    <echo>os.name = ${os.name}</echo>
    <mkdir dir="reports" />
    <exec executable="${testrunner.sh}" os="Linux" failonerror="true">
        <arg line="CustomerService-soapui-project.xml"/>
    </exec>
</target>
```

Now you can just set up an Ant-based project in your favorite Continuous Integration tool and invoke these two targets. If the SoapUI tests fail, everyone will be automatically notified. Figure 17-16 illustrates how this could be done using Continuum.

For a Maven project, the process is even simpler. Set up the Maven project as described in Section 17.8 and then create a CI project that invokes the *integration-test* goal (see Figure 17-17).

17.10 Conclusion

This chapter gave a brief overview of how SoapUI can help you to test your web services. It is a powerful tool, with a fairly low learning curve, which can be a valuable asset in a project involving web services.

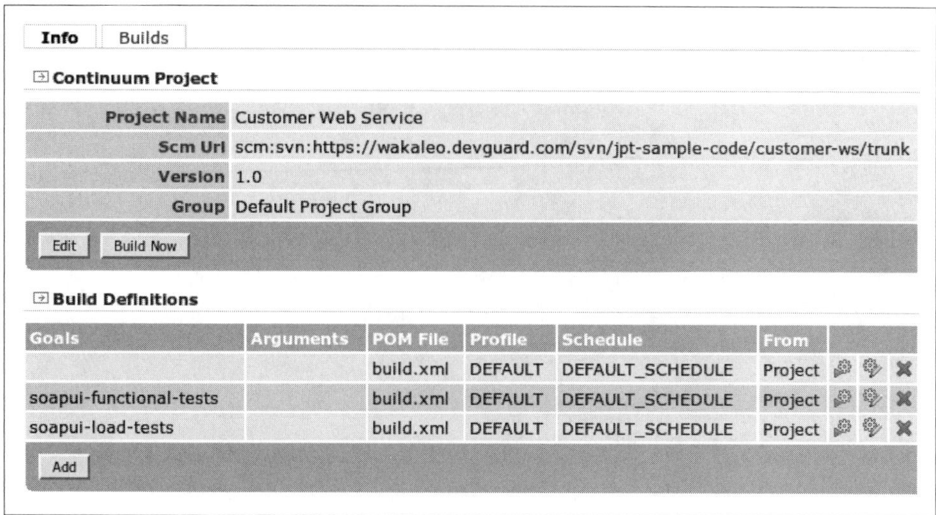

Figure 17-16. Continuous testing using SoapUI tests in an Ant file

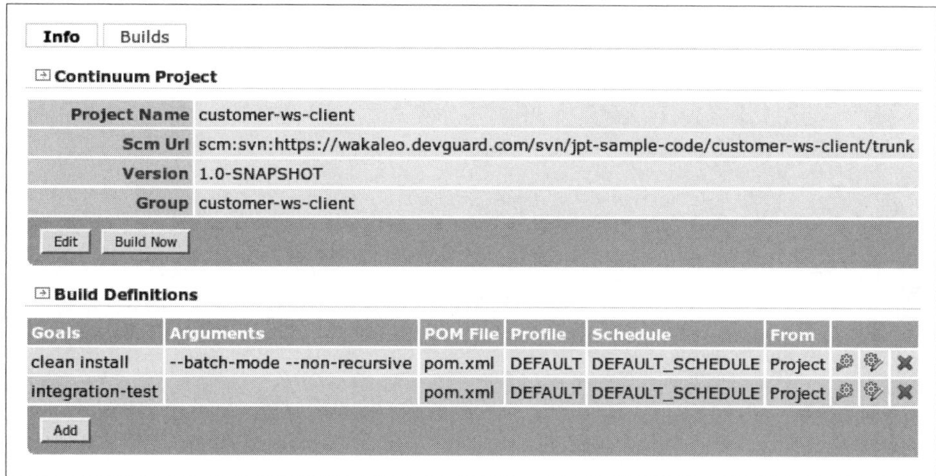

Figure 17-17. Continuous Testing using SoapUI tests in a Maven file

CHAPTER 18

Profiling and Monitoring Java Applications Using the Sun JDK Tools

18.1 The Sun JDK Profiling and Monitoring Tools

If you are using Java 5 or better, some of the most readily available profiling tools come bundled with your JDK. The Java Monitoring and Management Console tool, also known as jConsole, can be a valuable aide in monitoring your applications and identifying performance issues. The jConsole tool has a lot going for it as a first line performance profiling tool: it is readily available in any recent JDK distribution, you don't need to instrument or modify your code in any way, and you can run it with a minimum of configuration against local or remote Java applications. Heap analysis tools such as `jhat` help you identify and track down memory leaks.

Note that the tools we discuss here relate in particular to the Sun JDK. Although they may work with other JVMs, such as BEA's JRockit and the IBM virtual machines, these JVMs usually have their own more specific profiling tools.

The following articles discuss ways that you can use jConsole to monitor and analyze Java application performance on your own local machine and also on remote servers. When not otherwise stated, the tools used refer to the Java 6 versions.

18.2 Connecting To and Monitoring a Java Application with jConsole

Arguably one of the most useful of the JDK tools, JConsole is a graphical tool that uses JMX to monitor and report on the activities and resource use of Java applications. This section explains how to connect to and monitor a Java application running either locally or on another server.

JConsole works with applications running under Java 5 or Java 6. Java 5 comes bundled with JMX 1.2, but you do need to activate the JMX Agent at runtime when you start the application that you want to monitor. To monitor an application locally, you need to specify the (rather counterintuitively named) *com.sun.management.jmxremote* Java system property, as shown here:

```
$ java -Dcom.sun.management.jmxremote -jar myapp.jar
```

In Java 6, it is much easier to connect to local Java application with JConsole. The Java 6 version of jConsole can dynamically connect to and monitor any local application running in a Java 6 VM. JConsole dynamically activates the JMX management agent in the target VM, so you no longer need to start the monitored application in any particular way. This is very useful for analyzing performance issues in locally running applications with minimum effort.

Although this is the most convenient way to monitor an application, you should not use it to monitor applications running on a production server. JConsole can be demanding in terms of both memory and CPU, so you should run it on a separate machine (for example, your development workstation), connecting to the target VM over the network. JConsole can do this perfectly well, both in Java 5 and Java 6, but it requires some configuration of the target VM. You need to start the target JVM with (at least) the *com.sun.management.jmxremote.port* Java system property, which specifies the port to be used for JMX monitoring:

```
$ java -Dcom.sun.management.jmxremote.port=3000 -jar myAppInProduction.jar
```

This will enable you to monitor the application via JMX/RMI through the 3000 port.

In a real production environment, access will typically be secured and you will usually need to provide a username and password. This is fairly easy to set up and is well documented in the Sun documentation, so we won't be covering it here. Just be aware that you will probably need a user account and a cooperative system administrator to monitor a Java application on a production box.

You start jConsole from the command line as follows:

```
$ jconsole
```

This will open a window listing the JMX-compatible applications currently running on the local machine (see Figure 18-1). Alternatively, if you need to connect to an application running on a remote server, you can specify the address of a remote machine along with the JMX port for this application.

In some Windows environments, the Java process names are not very informative, and only the process IDs are displayed. In these cases, you may have trouble working out exactly what process you are supposed to be monitoring. Knowing the process ID you want can be a great help. In addition, if you know the process ID of the task you're after, you can save a bit of time using this process ID to connect directly to the application from the command line. On a Unix system, this is fairly easy to do using the *ps* command, as in the following example:

```
$ ps aux | grep java
```

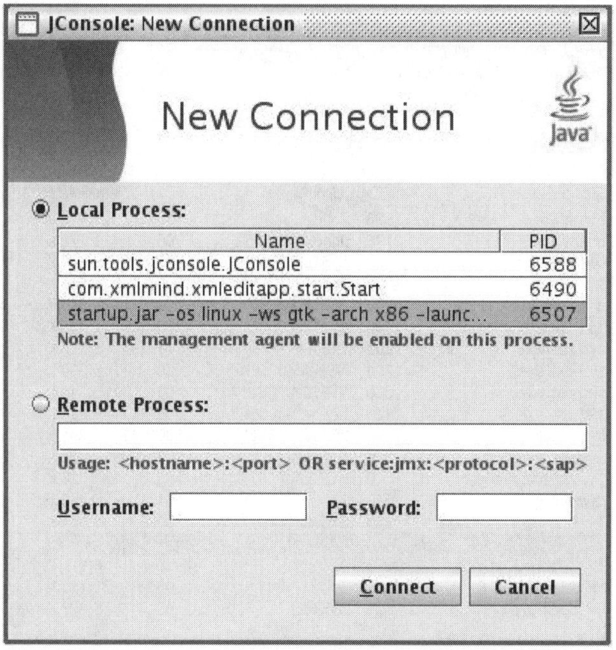

Figure 18-1. Starting JConsole

Another command-line tool for discovering Java process IDs is *jps*, which lists the current Java process (for the current user):

```
C:\> jps -l
984 com.xmlmind.xmleditapp.start.Start
3068 org.apache.catalina.startup.Bootstrap
3108 sun.tools.jps.Jps
$ jconsole 3068
```

The *jps* command-line tool is convenient, and it has the advantage of running on all platforms. However, it doesn't always display all the Java processes running on a Windows machine. It will not pick up a Tomcat instance run as a service on a Windows server, for example, if the service has been started under another account. In fact, in a Windows environment, a more reliable alternative is to identify the application instance using the Windows Task Manager.

It is fairly easy to use the Windows task manager to determine the process ID of the application you want to monitor. To do this, start up the Windows task manager, and open the "View→Select Columns..." menu. Then check the PID box so that process IDs are displayed as well as the application names. Now, in the Processes tab, you will be able to see the process id (PID) of each currently running application (see Figure 18-2).

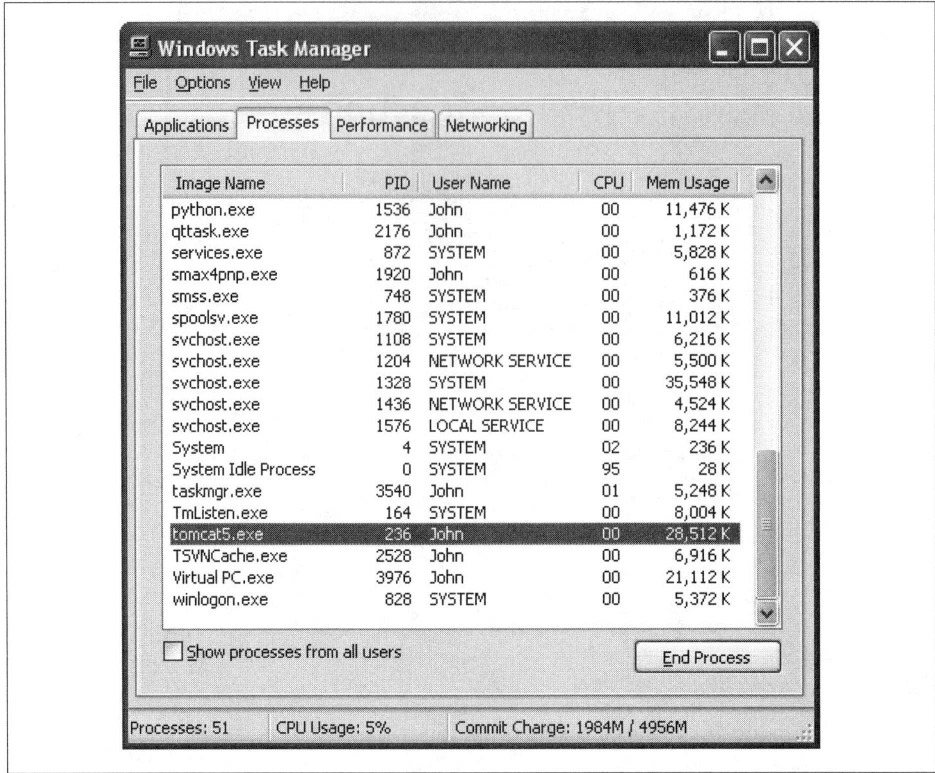

Figure 18-2. Starting JConsole processes tab

You can also start monitoring a remote application directly from the command line. Just give jConsole the server address and the JMX port, as shown here:

```
$ jconsole my.production.server:8086
```

Once connected, the jConsole application displays a summary of the current state of the target application (see Figure 18-3). Later in this chapter, we will see how to use these views to analyze the behavior of your application.

18.3 Monitoring a Remote Tomcat Application with jConsole

One common use of jConsole is to monitor an application deployed on a Java servlet container or application server such as Tomcat or JBoss. In this section, we will go through how to configure and monitor a Tomcat server using jConsole. The general approach—and, in particular, the script-based approach—is similar for other application servers.

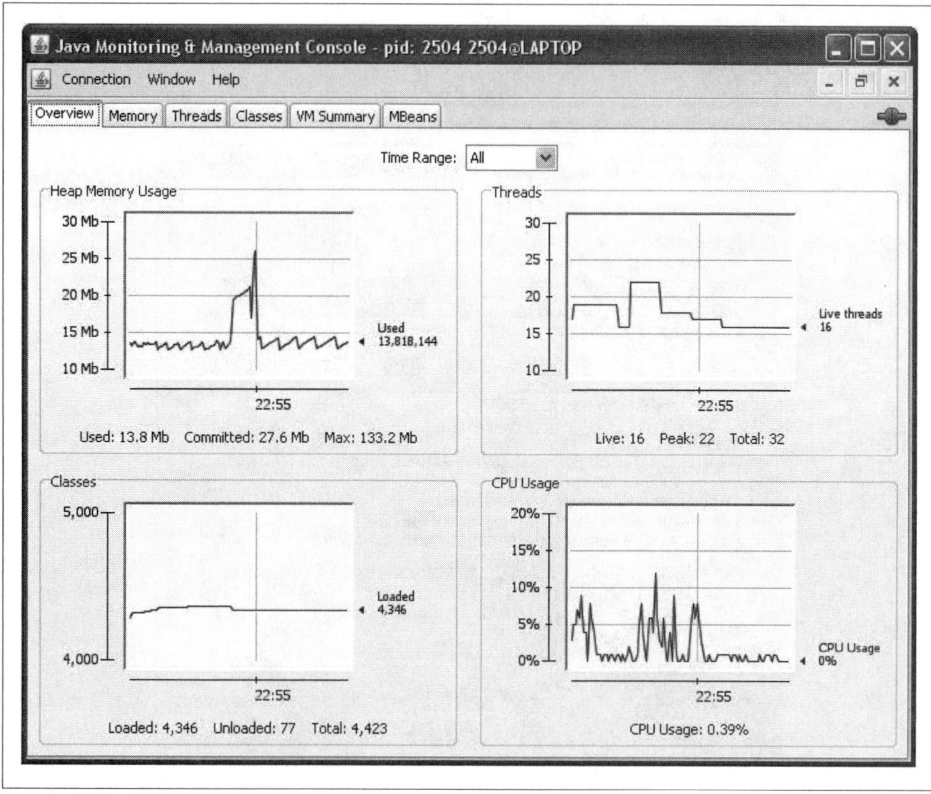

Figure 18-3. Monitoring a Java application with JConsole

As we noted earlier, for obvious security reasons, you can't just connect to any old Tomcat instance on a remote server; the server has to be configured correctly to allow remote monitoring of the Tomcat instance. In a Unix environment, you need to modify the Tomcat startup script to enable JMX monitoring. This simply involves integrating the appropriate JMX Java System properties into the Tomcat startup process. In Tomcat, you can either modify the JAVA_OPTS variable or the CATALINA_OPTS variable. Modifying the JAVA_OPTS variable will also work with most other Java application servers. In this example, we activate JMX on port 8086, and (for simplicity) deactivate SSL authentication, which would otherwise be activated by default:

```
JAVA_OPTS="$JAVA_OPTS "-Dcom.sun.management.jmxremote" \
                      "-Dcom.sun.management.jmxremote.port=8086" \
                      "-Dcom.sun.management.jmxremote.ssl=false" \
                      "-Dcom.sun.management.jmxremote.authenticate=false"
```

In a Windows environment where Tomcat has been installed as a service, open the "Apache Tomcat →Configure Tomcat" menu on the server, or run the *tomcat5w* application which can be found in the Tomcat *bin* directory. Go to the Java tab and add the following options at the end of the list of usual options (see Figure 18-4):

```
-Dcom.sun.management.jmxremote
-Dcom.sun.management.jmxremote.port=8086
-Dcom.sun.management.jmxremote.ssl=false
-Dcom.sun.management.jmxremote.authenticate=false
```

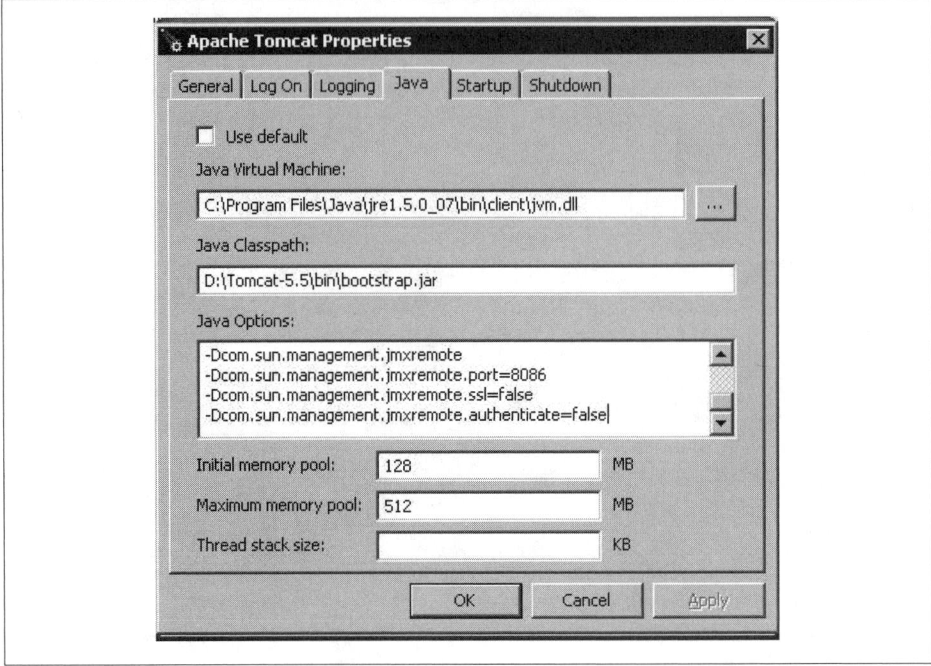

Figure 18-4. Configuring Tomcat to enable JMX monitoring

Back on your development machine, you can now connect to the Tomcat instance by choosing the "Remote Process" option in the "New Connection" dialog box (see Figure 18-5), specifying the remote server URL and port, as well as the username and password if needed for a secure connection. If no authentication is required, you can also run jConsole directly from the command line or by specifying the URL and port:

```
D:\> jconsole testserver:8086
```

18.4 Detecting and Identifying Memory Leaks with the JDK Tools

A common misconception about Java memory management is that, as a developer, you don't need to worry about it. The JVM takes care of everything, using a magical device called a garbage collector (or GC for short). Whenever you create a new object, the

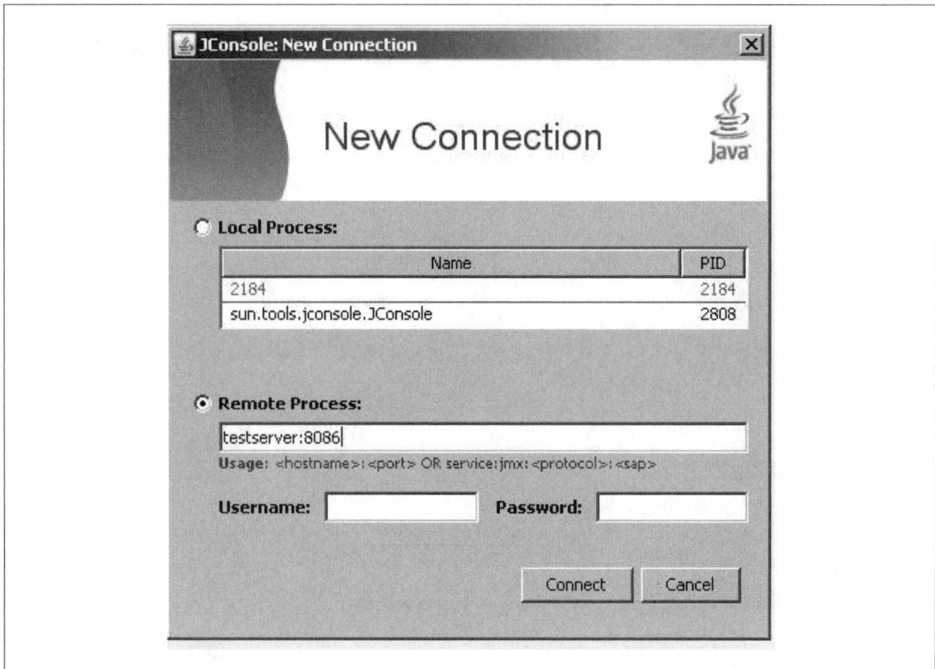

Figure 18-5. Configuring Tomcat to enable JMX monitoring

JVM automatically allocates the memory it needs, and recuperates it when you've finished using the object.

This is true up to a point. However, memory leaks can and do exist in Java applications. The Java JVM recycles any unreferenced objects it finds, but objects that are not released (such as objects in a cache) cannot be recuperated by the garbage collector, no matter how clever it is. Memory leaks are notoriously hard to isolate and track down and harder still to reproduce, often popping up only once your application has been deployed into production. They represent a major threat to application stability: if undetected or left unattended, a memory leak can lead to the application crashing with an `OutOfMemoryException`.

If you find yourself confronted by the dreaded `OutOfMemoryException` error, or if you just want to make sure it won't happen to your application, jConsole is a good starting point. jConsole is also a handy way to keep an eye on memory-consumption over a long period, such as during User Acceptance Testing. Because memory-related issues often appear for the first time when an application is left running over a long period of time, this can be a good way of catching memory leaks before the application goes into production.

The Memory tab (see Figure 18-6) is the first and most obvious port of call for memory-related issues. It gives you a graph of memory usage over time, either globally or for different types of objects. It also gives you an idea of how hard the garbage collector is

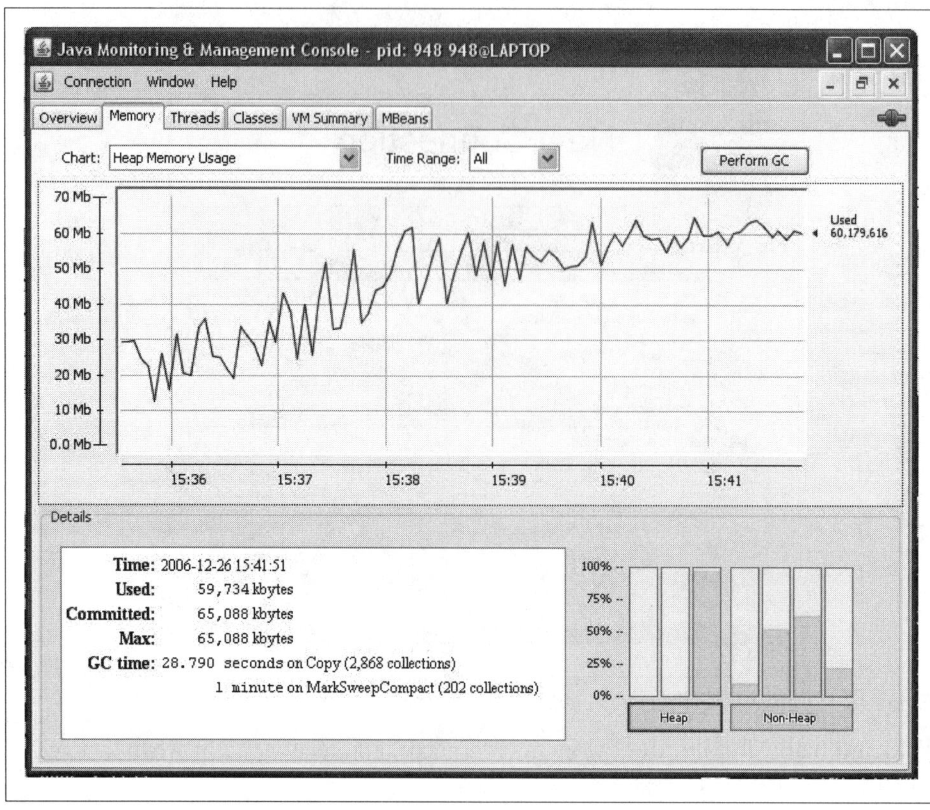

Figure 18-6. The Memory tab indicating a potential memory leak

working: a GC on overtime is often a sign of a poorly configured and poorly performing application.

The Overview tab (see Figure 18-3) can also be useful, since it gives you a quick summary of memory usage, active threads, loaded classes, and CPU usage. It also lets you make correlations between the different graphs: for example, a relationship between periods of heavy CPU usage and sustained increases in the number of loaded classes could indicate a memory leaking issue during data processing.

The JVM stores all class instances and arrays in what is known as heap memory, so this is the place you are likely to look for memory leaks. The obvious indicator that a memory leak is afoot is that heap memory is steadily increasing. You can observe this on the Overview tab, or on the Memory tab. In Figure 18-6, you can observe a potential memory leak. The heap memory is gradually, but steadily, increasing over time. The spikes in the graph show where the garbage collector is trying to do its job. However, despite the GC activity, memory usage keeps going up. In a real application, this may take hours, days, or weeks to appear. An excellent way to provoke this type of error is to perform load-testing using tools such as JMeter (see Chapter 16).

The JVM uses different types of memory to store different types of objects. The heap memory space, which is what you will usually be watching for memory leaks, contains two distinct areas: young generation and old generation. Non–heap memory is used by the JVM to store loaded classes and methods, and other low-level data. Memory leaks are usually only an issue in Heap memory. Without going into too much detail, it is useful to know how these zones are used when tracking down memory-related issues.

The young generation area is split into three distinct zones. The first zone, known as the Eden Space, is where the JVM places newly created objects (hence the name), and is mainly used for short-lived variables such as local variables within a method. When this space becomes too crowded, a fast, lightweight garbage collection process cleans it up and reclaims any unreferenced objects. Objects that are not freed by garbage collections in the Eden space are placed in a second zone, called the Survivor space. In fact, there are two, identically sized survivor spaces. When the first survivor space starts to fill up, a garbage collection frees dead objects and copies live ones into the second survivor space. Objects that stand the test of time and are not recycled from the second survivor space are placed in the old generation, also know as the Tenured Generation. This zone is usually reserved for long-lived objects such as static variables or frequently used cached objects. This space is usually much bigger than the others (by an order of magnitude or two), and memory can only be recycled here by a particularly expensive operation called a "mark and sweep" garbage collection.

When old generation space is running low, a longer, full-scale garbage collection process scans the entire heap space for recyclable objects. Again, this "mark and sweep" garbage collection is a particularly expensive operation and is the sort of thing that can bring your server to its knees if it happens too frequently.

You can see some of the typical symptoms of a memory leak in Figure 18-6. When you have a memory leak, recycled objects progressively fill up first the Survivor space and then the Tenured Generation space. As these larger spaces fill up, the application will slow down as heavy, full-scale garbage collection becomes a recurring activity. Excessive GC activity is also a typical sign of either memory leaks or a poorly configured JVM.

JConsole gives an indication of how full these different spaces are in the bar charts on the lower left of the memory tab. You can zoom in on any one of these zones by clicking on the corresponding bar, or by choosing the memory zone in the "Chart" drop-down list. The GC Time fields show the time spent and the number of operations in both young generation (Copy) and mark and sweep (MarkSweepCompact) garbage collection.

JConsole can also be configured to provide useful visual cues about potential memory leaks. This is a good way to keep tabs on memory consumption over a long period of time (such as during User Acceptance Testing), and can be useful for catching slow-to-appear memory leaks. JConsole lets you define usage thresholds for the various JVM memory pools in the MBeans tab (see Figure 18-7). Threshold values are defined in the

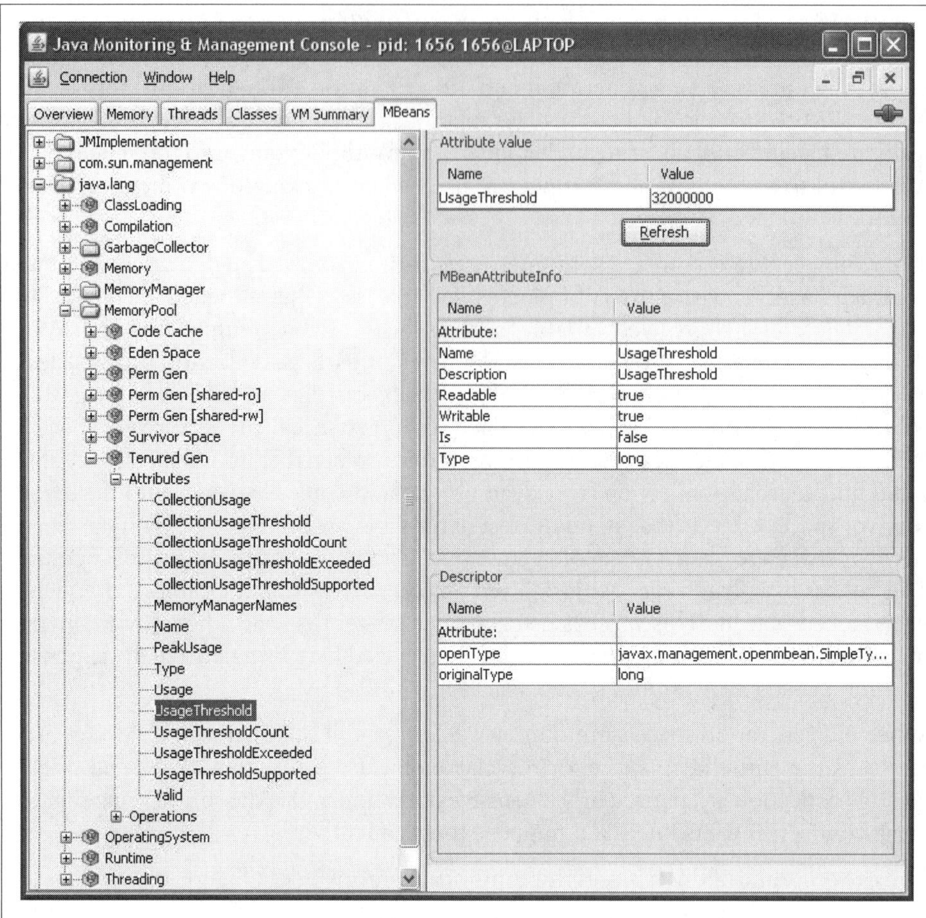

Figure 18-7. Setting up a threshold value using JMX

"Memory Pool" folder, which can be found in the "java.lang" package on the MBeans tab. The Memory Pool folder contains MBeans for all of the JVM memory pools, both Heap and Non-Heap. The main tool used to watch for memory leaks is the old generation Tenured Generation pool, so this is usually where you will define usage thresholds. Open the Attributes of the "Tenured Gen" and select the "UsageThreashold" attribute. This value is the maximum tolerable value of the old generation heap, in bytes. You can set this to whatever seems sensible for your application. If you set it to zero, the usage threshold will be deactivated.

Let's look at an example. In Figure 18-7, we define a usage threshold of 32000000 bytes (roughly 32 MB) for the Tenured Generation memory pool. In Figure 18-8, we can see this configuration in action. Heap memory is displayed in red, indicating a problem of some sort. The third bar, which represents the Tenured Generation memory pool, is

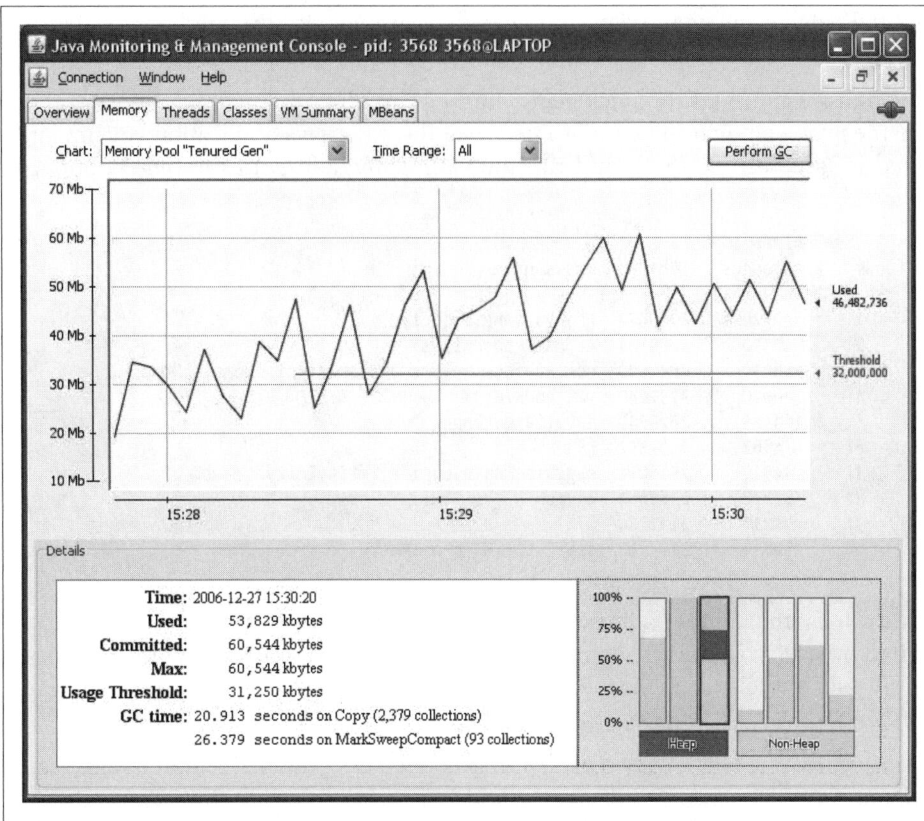

Figure 18-8. Monitoring the tenured generation

partially displayed in red, showing that Tenured Generation memory has exceeded the threshold we defined.

To get more details, select the Tenured Generation memory pool chart. Here, the usage threshold is shown as a red horizontal line, which makes it easier to see when and by how much the threshold has been exceeded.

18.5 Diagnosing Memory Leaks Using Heap Dumps, jmap, and jhat

JConsole is a great tool for detecting memory leaks. Once you have detected a memory leak, however, you need to look further to identify what classes and objects are being leaked, and jConsole is of limited use here. Profiling tools can be a good help here, but tend to be complicated to set up and use. We look at a few profiling tools in this chapter. If you need a quick diagnosis, one alternative is to use some of the tools bundled with the JDK such as *jmap* and *jhat*. In this section, we will go through how to use these tools to hunt down memory leaks by analyzing the JVM heap with these tools.

If you just want to take a quick glance at the heap of a running application, you can use the *jmap* command-line tool to find the PID of the Java application you are interested in (see Section 18.2), and run the *jmap* command with the *-histo* option, as follows:

```
$ jmap -histo 1060
num   #instances    #bytes  class name
--------------------------------------
  1:       97929    4769472  [Ljava.lang.Object;
  2:       40390    4685944  <constMethodKlass>
  3:      116050    4642000  com.equinox.jpt.modelplanes.core.domain.ModelPlane
  4:       40390    3232240  <methodKlass>
  5:      164315    2629040  java.lang.Long
  6:        4862    2597352  [B
  7:       44929    2516024  org.hibernate.engine.EntityEntry
  8:       53272    2369464  <symbolKlass>
  9:        4217    2182784  [I
 10:       89833    2155992  java.util.HashMap$Entry
...
```

This will list the number of instances and total size occupied by objects of each class, sorted by size. This can sometimes give you some good leads. For example, if you see any of your own classes in the top 10, it's probably a bad sign and should be investigated further.

Using *jmap* alone can be a good first approach, but it has its limits. A more sophisticated approach is to use *jhat*. The *jhat* command-line tool, new to Java 6, is a powerful way of investigating the JVM heap. The first thing you need is a heap dump to analyze. One way is to use the *jmap* command-line tool, which can obtain the heap dump of a running Java application. Find the PID of the Java application you are interested in (see Section 18.2), and run the *jmap* command with the *-dump* option, as follows:

```
$ jmap -dump:file=dump.bin 1060
Dumping heap to /home/john/dump.bin ...
Heap dump file created
```

This will generate a binary dump of the JVM heap in a file called *dump.bin*.

Another option if you suspect memory leaks on a production is to start your application with the *-XX:+HeapDumpOnOutOfMemoryError* command-line option. This won't prevent any memory leaks, but it will cause the VM to generate a heap dump, enabling you to analyze the heap afterward, using *jhat* or some other tool.

Now we need to be able to inspect the contents of the heap dump. This is where *jhat* comes into action. It analyzes a binary heap dump, and starts up a web server on a local port where you can interactively explore and query the Heap Dump. You run it as follows (the *-J-Xmx384m* allows a maximum heap space of 384 MB; this option is not mandatory, but *jhat* is fairly demanding in resources, so you should give it a fair bit of memory to work with):

```
$ jhat -J-Xmx384m dump.bin
Reading from dump.bin...
Dump file created Tue Dec 26 13:20:27 NZDT 2006
Snapshot read, resolving...
Resolving 949898 objects...
Chasing references, expect 189 dots.....................................
.......................................................................
.........................................................
Eliminating duplicate references........................................
.......................................................................
......................................................
Snapshot resolved.
Started HTTP server on port 7000
Server is ready.
```

You can now connect to this site with your favorite browser. The *jhat* web site won't win any prizes for its elegant design or usability, but it can provide some useful information. The first place to look is the heap histogram, which provides a list of the objects in the Heap (see Figure 18-9). This is similar to the *jmap* histogram, but with the additional possibility to sort by size, class, or object count, and to display the class details. In Figure 18-9, it is fairly easy to see that there may be an issue with the `ModelPlane`. (This is of course a simple example where a memory leak was inserted on purpose; memory leaks involving Strings or other commonly used classes are usually much harder to isolate.)

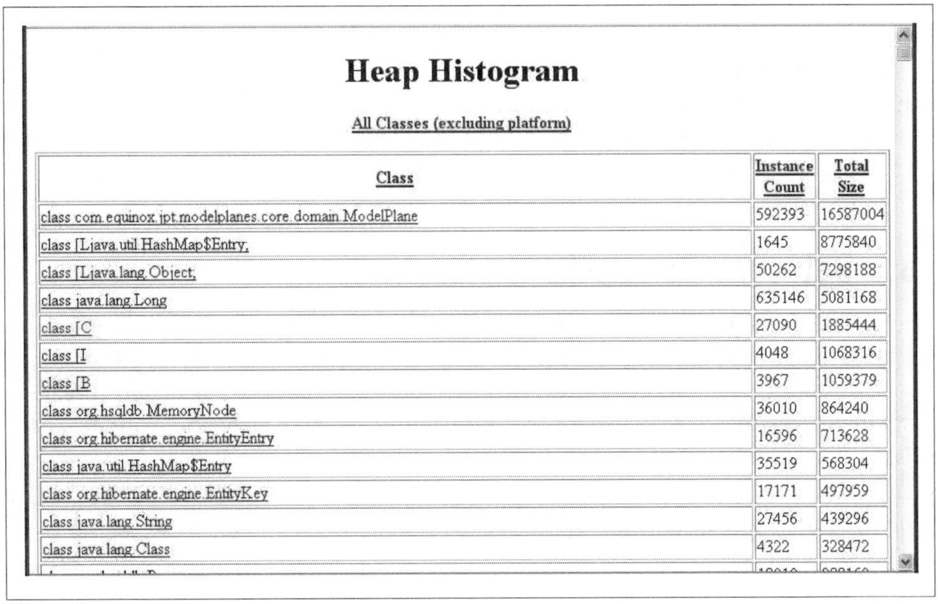

Heap Histogram

All Classes (excluding platform)

Class	Instance Count	Total Size
class com.equinox.jpt.modelplanes.core.domain.ModelPlane	592393	16587004
class [Ljava.util.HashMap$Entry;	1645	8775840
class [Ljava.lang.Object;	50262	7298188
class java.lang.Long	635146	5081168
class [C	27090	1885444
class [I	4048	1068316
class [B	3967	1059379
class org.hsqldb.MemoryNode	36010	864240
class org.hibernate.engine.EntityEntry	16596	713628
class java.util.HashMap$Entry	35519	568304
class org.hibernate.engine.EntityKey	17171	497959
class java.lang.String	27456	439296
class java.lang.Class	4322	328472

Figure 18-9. The jhat class histogram

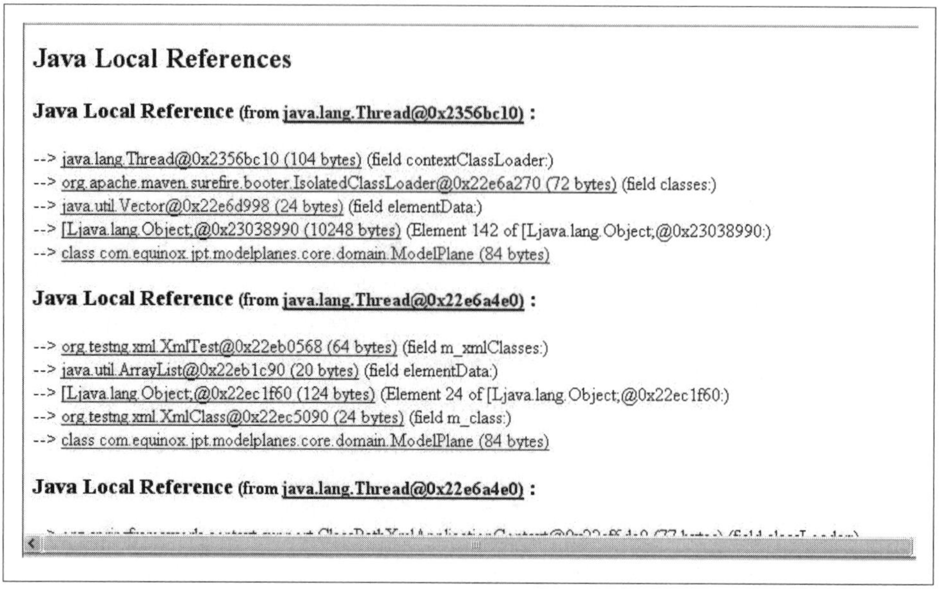

Java Local References

Java Local Reference (from java.lang.Thread@0x2356bc10) :

--> java.lang.Thread@0x2356bc10 (104 bytes) (field contextClassLoader:)
--> org.apache.maven.surefire.booter.IsolatedClassLoader@0x22e6a270 (72 bytes) (field classes:)
--> java.util.Vector@0x22e6d998 (24 bytes) (field elementData:)
--> [Ljava.lang.Object;@0x23038990 (10248 bytes) (Element 142 of [Ljava.lang.Object;@0x23038990:)
--> class com.equinox.jpt.modelplanes.core.domain.ModelPlane (84 bytes)

Java Local Reference (from java.lang.Thread@0x22e6a4e0) :

--> org.testng.xml.XmlTest@0x22eb0568 (64 bytes) (field m_xmlClasses:)
--> java.util.ArrayList@0x22eb1c90 (20 bytes) (field elementData:)
--> [Ljava.lang.Object;@0x22ec1f60 (124 bytes) (Element 24 of [Ljava.lang.Object;@0x22ec1f60:)
--> org.testng.xml.XmlClass@0x22ec5090 (24 bytes) (field m_class:)
--> class com.equinox.jpt.modelplanes.core.domain.ModelPlane (84 bytes)

Java Local Reference (from java.lang.Thread@0x22e6a4e0) :

Figure 18-10. A root reference query

If you click on one of the classes in this page, you will go to the class details page, which displays general information about the class (superclasses, subclasses, members, and so forth), as well as a list of classes that refer to this class. This page also lets you build root reference chains, which are arguably the most useful feature of *jhat*. You will find these under "Reference Chains from Rootset," in a section inconspicuously entitled "Other Queries" at the bottom of the screen. A reference chain lists the references to this object, going back up to the root thread (see Figure 18-10). The heap histogram can indicate which objects have been leaked. Using these chains, you can get a fairly good idea of where these leaked objects are being held.

18.6 Detecting Deadlocks

You can also use jConsole to easily identify deadlocked threads. If your application seems to hang, you may have a deadlock. In today's world of multithreaded programming, deadlocks are a common problem. A deadlock occurs when one thread is blocking access to a resource needed by another thread but is itself waiting on a resource held by this second thread.

Deadlocks are often hard to reproduce and, like memory leaks, sometimes won't appear until the application is in production. Also, like memory leaks, they can sometimes be provoked and detected using load-testing tools such as JMeter (see Chapter 16). However, when the deadlock does occur, it is notoriously hard to track down the source of the problem. This is where jConsole can help.

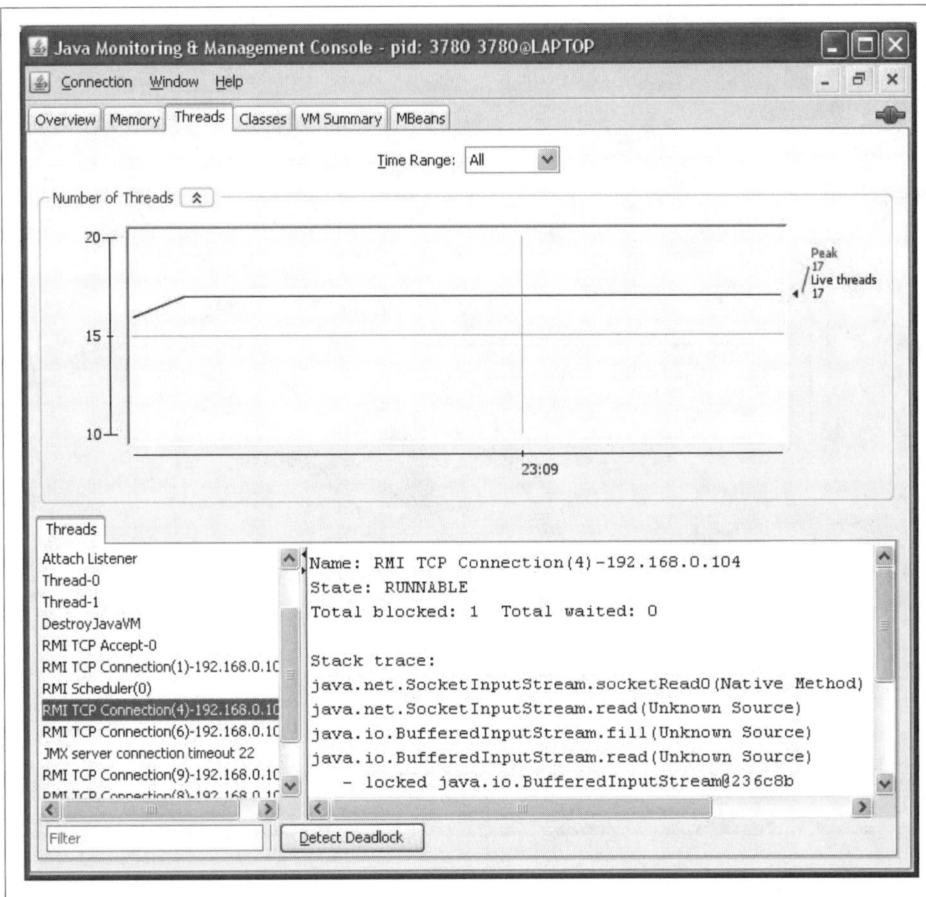

Figure 18-11. The Threads tab

The Threads tab (see Figure 18-11) displays information about threads running in your application, including a graph showing the number of active threads over time, and a list of application threads. Selecting a particular thread will show its the current stack trace. This is useful when you want to observe how your application handles multiple threads. However, the real power of the Threads tab is its ability to detect application deadlocks.

The "Detect Deadlocks" button at the bottom of the screen, new to Java 6, allows jConsole to check your application for deadlocks. Each detected deadlock is displayed in a new tab with a stack dump showing where the deadlock had occurred (see Figure 18-12).

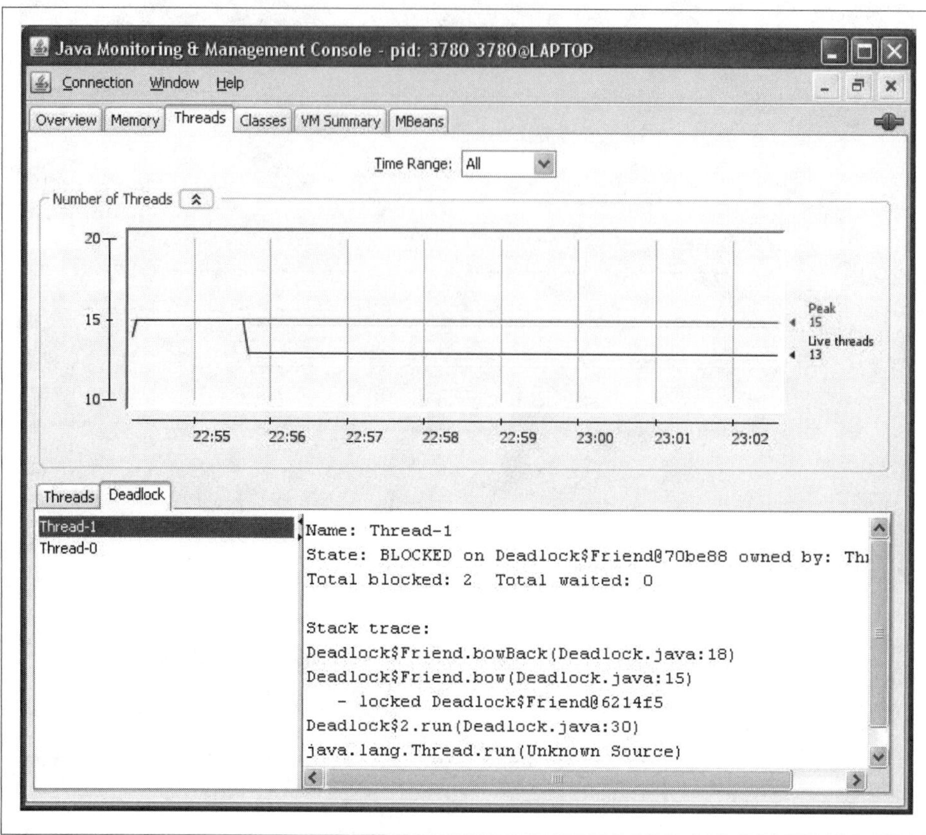

Figure 18-12. Detecting deadlocked threads

CHAPTER 19

Profiling Java Applications in Eclipse

19.1 Profiling Applications from Within an IDE

Recent years have seen an increasing awareness of the importance of development best practices such as unit testing and test-driven development. However, unit tests are not all there is to testing. High-quality software needs to perform well under stress, using system resources such as memory and processor time efficiently. Performance bottlenecks may need to be identified and removed and memory leaks detected and eliminated. Profiling and performance testing play a crucial part in this side of application development. And software profiling is an area in which it is virtually impossible to work effectively without a good toolset.

Most profiling tools, both in the open source and commercial domains, need to be run as standalone applications. You start them up when you detect a memory leak or performance issue in your application and run them against your application. However, when you are writing or debugging an application, there is a lot to be said for being able to run a profiler directly from within your development environment. This enables you to integrate performance testing and profiling directly into your day-to-day development environment using the tool with which you are familiar. In Eclipse, you can do just this with the Eclipse Test & Performance Tools Platform, or TPTP.

19.2 The Eclipse Test & Performance Tools Platform

The Eclipse IDE proposes a rich set of optional plug-ins designed to provide a coherent, integrated palette of extensions for the Eclipse development environment. This includes the convenient, although optional, profiling tool TPTP. TPTP provides a comprehensive suite of open source performance testing and profiling tools, including integrated application monitoring, testing, tracing, and profiling functionalities, as well as static code analysis tools. And in the Eclipse tradition, TPTP is more than simply a set of plug-ins; it is a platform that can be used to write test and performance tools integrated into the Eclipse development environment.

The Test & Performance Tools Platform contains an extensive set of profiling tools for Java applications. It is actually composed of four distinct but related components:

- The TPTP provides a shared underlying infrastructure on which the other testing tools are built.
- The monitoring tools let you collect data and provide statistics about the application's runtime behavior, both from application logfiles and from the JVM itself.
- The testing tools provide a framework for executing your tests, including support for JUnit and web application testing.
- The tracing and profiling tools allow you to collect and analyze performance-related data, such as CPU and memory use.

Profiling an application typically involves observing how the application copes under stress. A common way of doing this is to run a set of load tests on a deployed application and use profiling tools to record the application's behavior. You can then study the results to investigate any performance issues. This is often done at the end of the project, once the application is almost ready for production.

TPTP is well suited to this type of task. A typical use case would be to run load tests using a load-testing tool such as JMeter (see Chapter 16), and record and analyze the performance statistics using the TPTP tools.

However, this is not the only way you can profile an application with TPTP. As a rule, the earlier you test, the less problems you have later on. With TPTP, you can profile your code in a wide range of contexts, including JUnit test cases, Java applications, and web applications. And it is well integrated into the Eclipse IDE., so there is no reason not to start preliminary performance tests and profiling early on.

TPTP lets you test several aspects of your application's behavior, including memory usage (how many objects are being created, and how big they are), execution statistics (where did the application spend the most of it's time), and test coverage (how much of the code was actually executed during the tests). Each of these can provide invaluable information about your application's performance.

The sort of testing we are talking about here is not optimization as such. Optimization involves fine-tuning application performance using techniques such as caching. It is a highly technical activity, and it is best done at the very end of the project.

This type of preliminary performance testing and profiling discussed here simply involves making sure that the application performs correctly from the start, and that there are no coding errors or poor coding practices that will penalize performance later on. Indeed, fixing memory leaks and avoiding unnecessary object creation is not optimization: it is debugging and, as such, should be done as early as possible.

In this chapter, we will look at how you can use TPTP to guarantee high-quality and high-performance code, even during unit and integration testing.

19.3 Installing TPTP

The easiest way to install TPTP on an existing Eclipse installation is to use the Remote Update site (see Figure 19-1). Open the Remote Update window (Help→Software Updates→ Find and Install), and select the Discovery Site for your version of Eclipse. For the Europa edition, for example, this is called the "Europa Discovery Site." Here, Eclipse will propose the set of plug-ins. The TPTP tools are listed under "Testing and Performance." The easiest option, albeit the most time-consuming, is just to install all the proposed plug-ins. Even if you don't install the entire toolset, you will still need to install some other components needed by TPTP, such as "Charting and Reporting," "Enabling Features," and "Data Tool Performance."

19.4 TPTP and Java 6

An important thing to know about TPTP is that, at the time of this writing (using Eclipse 3.3 Europa), the TPTP profiling tools do not support Java 6. TPTP relies on JVMPI (JVM profiling interface), which it uses to capture data about applications running in the JVM. Now JVMPI was dropped in Java 6 in favor of the more modern and flexible JVMTI (JVM Tool Interface). If you try to run TPTP using a Java 6 VM, you will obtain an error along the lines of "FATAL ERROR: JVMPI, an experimental interface, is no longer supported." So if you are using Java 6, make sure that you are running Eclipse under Java 5 if you want to use TPTP.

You can run Eclipse using a different JVM using the *vm* command-line option. Here is how you might do this on a Windows machine:

```
D:\tools\eclipse\eclipse.exe -vm "C:\Program Files\Java\jdk1.5.0_10\jre\bin\javaw.exe"
-vmargs -Xmx512M
```

Or under Linux, you might do something like this:

```
$ /usr/local/eclipse/eclipse -vm  /usr/lib/jvm/java-1.5.0-sun/bin/java
 -vmargs -Xmx512M &
```

For the same reason, when you run your code from within Eclipse, you need to use a Java 5 JVM. If you have several JVMs configured in your Eclipse preferences, make sure you are compiling and executing your project in Java 5.

19.5 Basic Profiling with TPTP

One of the best ways to check that performance is (and remains) up to scratch is to write comprehensive performance-oriented unit (or "integration," if you prefer) tests for each of your use cases. In my experience, this is also one of the best ways of isolating and correcting performance issues. This involves writing simple performance-oriented unit tests for your key business functions. This approach has the additional advantage

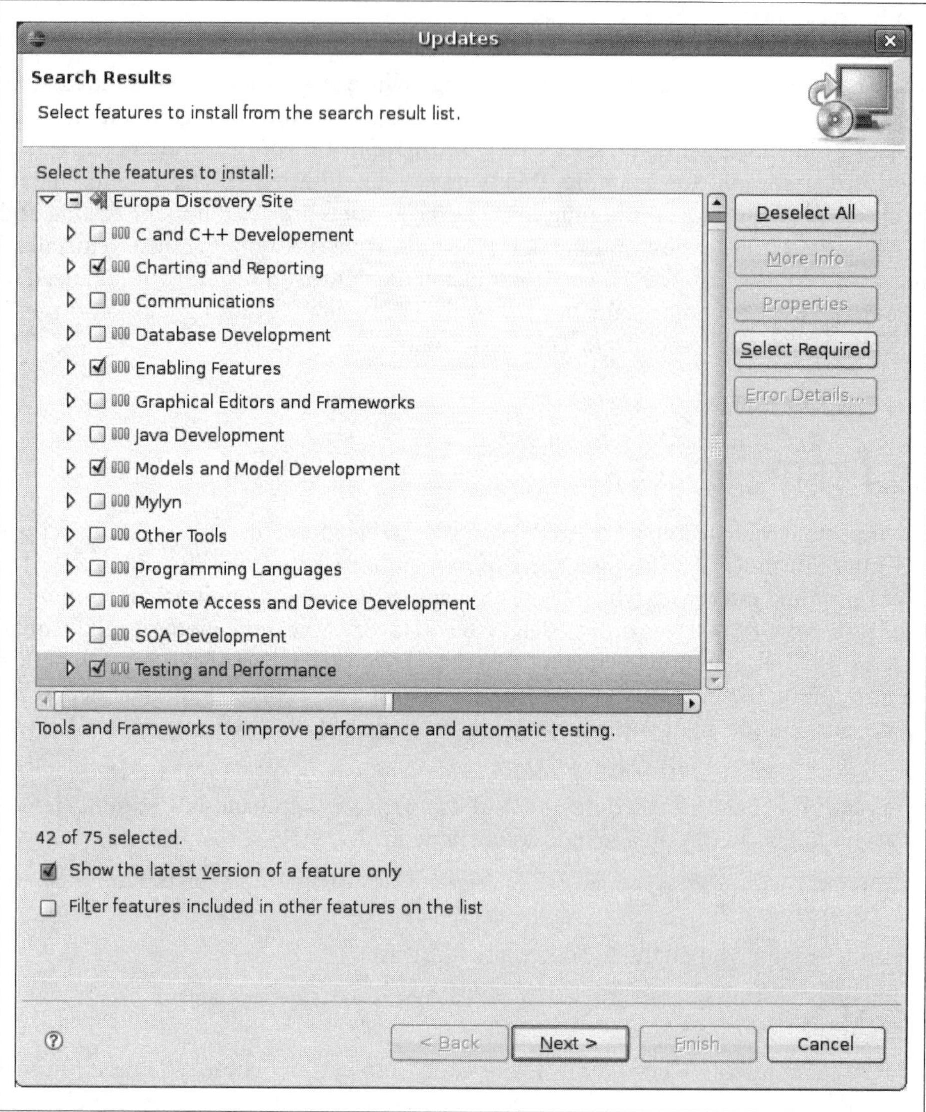

Figure 19-1. Installing TPTP from the Europa Discovery remote site

of progressively building a suite of regression tests for future development. Here, we go through the basics of profiling with TPTP, by looking at how to profile the behavior of an application using simple, performance-oriented unit tests.

As a rule, you should try to profile code that is as close as possible to the production code. Many people use mock objects to replace DAOs (Data Access Objects) for unit tests, and it can be a powerful technique to speed up the development lifecycle. If you use this type of approach, by all means, run your profiling with these tests: it can reveal useful information about memory usage and test coverage. However, the performance tests are of limited value, since performance in a database-related application is often dominated by database performance, so any serious performance testing should be done in this context. A good compromise is to run performance tests against an embedded Java database such as JavaDB/Derby or HSQLDB—this will give you an idea of how your application behaves against a real database, without incurring the overhead of network traffic or having to set up and maintain your own dedicated test database instance.

Throughout this chapter, we are going to test a simple web application that manages a database of model planes. In this web application, users can consult the list of known plane types, select a plane type, and then view the corresponding model planes.

For our first profiling exercise, we want to make sure that the application home page, which involves displaying the list of all available plane types, will not present any performance issues. This page will be heavily used, so it is important that it can support a high load. Let's see how we would do this using JUnit and TPTP in Eclipse.

In the application, plane types are represented by the `PlaneType` class. The DAO class for plane types implements the following interface:

```
public interface PlaneTypeDAO {
    PlaneType findById(long id);
    List<PlaneType> findAll();
    public void save(PlaneType planeType);
    public void delete(PlaneType planeType);
}
```

To list all available plane types, we need to invoke the `findAll()` method. It is important that this method always performs efficiently, with a minimum of SQL and in a minimum of time. Because we are using JUnit here, we will use Mike Clark's excellent performance unit testing library, JUnitPerf (see Chapter 28), to implement some simple performance tests on this method. The full unit test is shown here:

```
public class ModelPlaneDaoPerfTests extends TestCase {

    private PlaneTypeDAO dao;

    public ModelPlaneDaoPerfTests(String value) {
        super(value);
    }

    public void setUp() throws SQLException {
        ApplicationContext ctx = SpringUtilsTestConfig.getApplicationContext();
        dao = (PlaneTypeDAO) ctx.getBean("planeTypeDAO");
    }

    public void testFindAll() {
        List<PlaneType> planes = dao.findAll();
        assertTrue(planes.size() > 0);
    }
```

```
    public static Test suite() {
        TestSuite suite = new TestSuite();
        TestCase testCase = new ModelPlaneDaoPerfTests("testFindAll");
        suite.addTest(testCase);
        suite.addTest(new TimedTest(testCase, 1000));
        return suite;
    }
}
```

Our first unit test (`testFindAll()`) simply invokes the `findAll()` method, and checks that the results list is not empty. The `setUp()` method, executed before each test, obtains a DAO using a Spring application context. Behind the scenes, this instantiates the DAO, along with the appropriate JDBC data source and Hibernate session, using an embedded Java database. It also populates the test database with test data.

The performance testing is done in the `suite()` method, where we use the `TimedTest` decorator to ensure that this test case runs in less than a second. Note that, for fairness, we add the undecorated test case to the suite first. This ensures that the test database and application environment have been set up before we time the test.

You can run this test case easily in Eclipse in the usual way, using "Run As...JUnit Test." If you have JUnit 4 libraries on your build path, don't forget to run this class in Eclipse as a JUnit 3 test case. You can do this to make sure that the test runs correctly. Because profiling is a fairly time-consuming operation, this is usually a good idea. However, what we really want to do is profile the application's behavior when the tests are running. To do this, we need to use the TPTP profiling tools.

The first thing that you need to do is to set up a profile to run this particular test. Select "Profile As→Profile..." in the main Eclipse menu (see Figure 19-2).

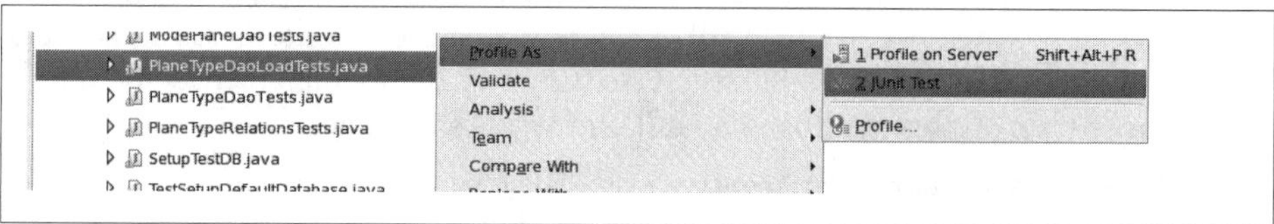

Figure 19-2. Profiling a JUnit test using the contextual menu

This opens a Wizard in which you can configure different sorts of testing profiles, shown in Figure 19-3. This is where you can set up configurations for profiling different sorts of applications such as web servers, Java applications, or JUnit tests. We are interested in the latter. Your unit test class should appear under the JUnit entry. If you've done it before, you can also create a JUnit test profile directly by selecting "Profile As...JUnit test" in the contextual menu.

TPTP is quite flexible, and this screen uses many of the same configuration options that you find when running, testing or debugging code in the Eclipse IDE. In the "Test" tab, you can either profile unit test classes individually, or group them by project or package. The "Arguments" tab lets you specify runtime arguments, and the

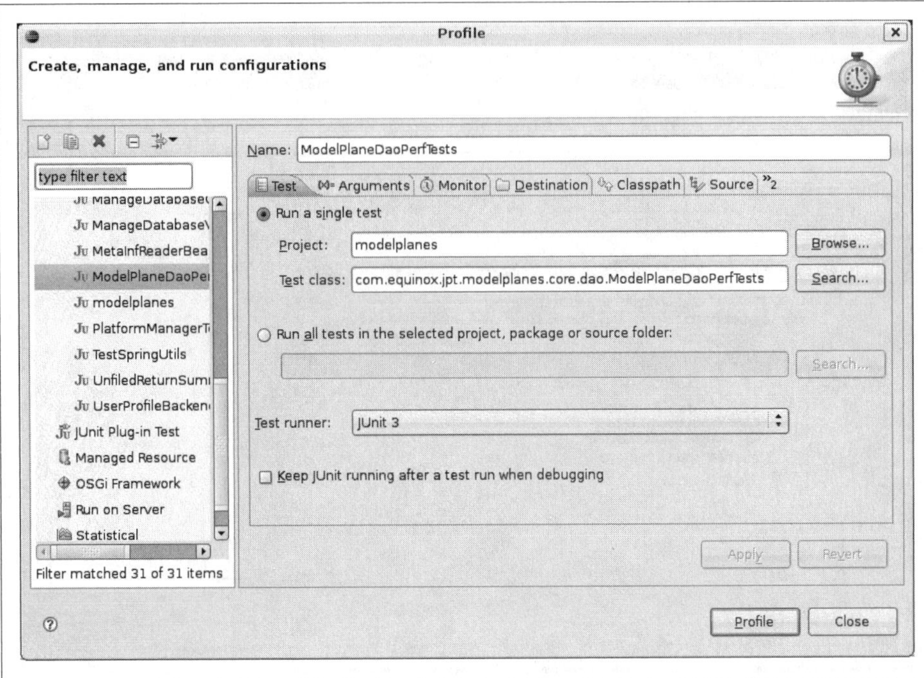

Figure 19-3. Creating a new TPTP profile configuration

"Environment" tab lets you define environment variables. There are also many options that are specific to the profiling tools. In the "Destination" tab, you can specify an external file where profiling data is to be saved for future use. But the most useful is the "Monitor" tab (see Figure 19-4), where you specify which performance-related data you want to record and study. The "Monitor" tab lets you define the type of profiling data you want to record. Profiling with Java 5.0 and higher uses a quite different library to the one used in previous versions. The most useful options here are the following:

Basic Memory Analysis
: This option records memory usage statistics, including the number of object instances created for each class and the overall memory used. This is handy for keeping track of memory consumption and identifying potential memory leaks.

Execution Time Analysis
: This option records performance data: how long the application spends in each method, and where did it spend most of its time. This sort of information makes it easier to identify and optimize execution hotspots.

Method Code Coverage
: This option notes which classes and methods were executed most frequently. When you profile against a running application this data can give you a good idea of which parts of your application are being used and how much. If you are profiling unit tests, this can give you a general idea of how well your tests actually test the

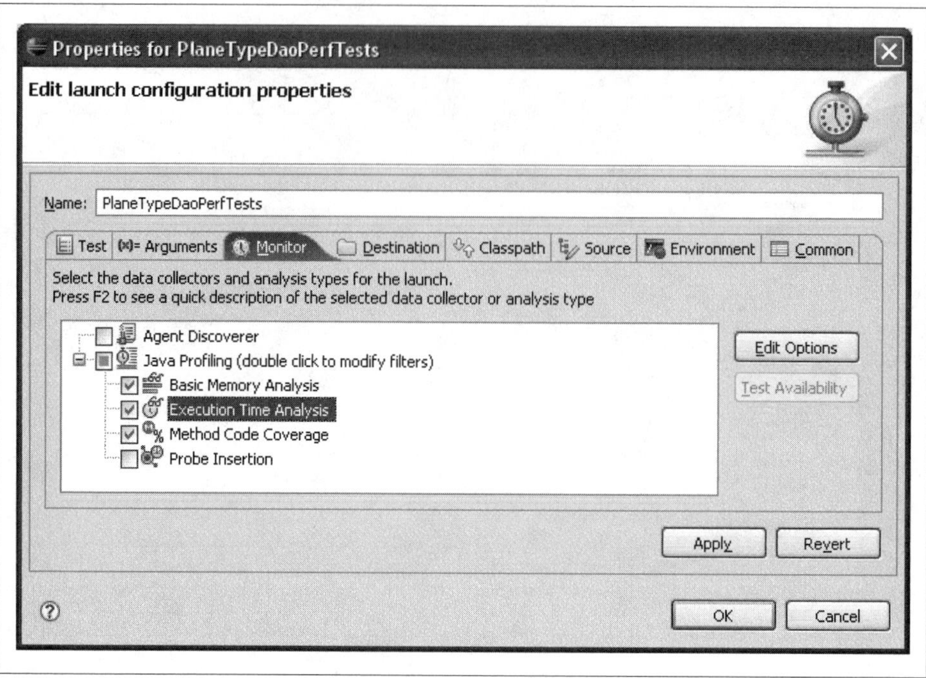

Figure 19-4. Launch configuration properties for a TPTP profile

code, although tools such as jCoverage (see Chapter 9) can do this as well, with more precision.

Double-clicking on "Basic Memory Analysis" or "Execution Time Analysis" enables you to specify some additional options.

You can either run the profiling tool directly from this window or, using the contextual menu positioned on the test class you want to profile, via the "Profile As" contextual menu entry. The profiling tool may take some time to run, depending on how big your test cases are. Once done, Eclipse will switch to the "Profiling and Logging" perspective from which you can display details of the results of each type of profiling (see Figure 19-5).

This perspective regroups a rich collection of views, which you can open using the contextual menu over the various profiling analysis results. The memory analysis view (see Section 19.6 and Figure 19-5) provides information about the number of instances of each class currently in memory, including how many have been collected by the garbage collector, and how many are in use. This can help in identifying and isolating memory leaks. The execution time analysis (see Section 19.7) helps you study the application's dynamic behavior.

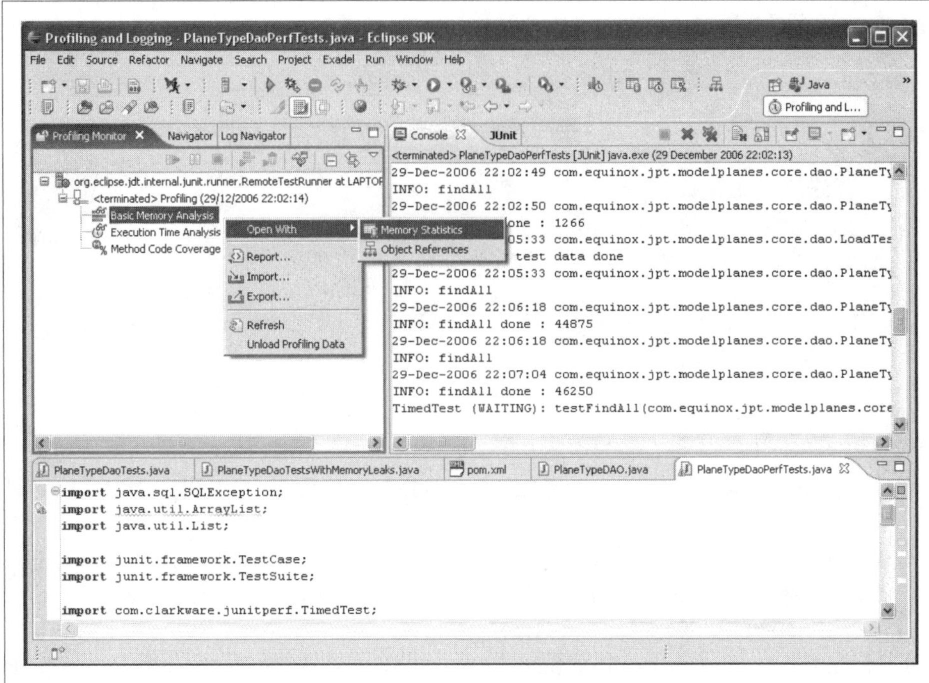

Figure 19-5. Visualizing TPTP memory analysis statistics

In the following sections of this chapter, we will take a closer look at how to use these views.

19.6 Studying Memory Use with the Basic Memory Analysis Results

The memory analysis provides useful information about which objects, and in what quantity, are created by the application. The "Memory Statistics" view (see Figure 19-6) displays the number of objects created by the application. The results can be organized by package (in the form of a tree view), or as a list of classes or instances.

This data can give you an idea of how many objects of each type are being created; unusually high numbers of created objects (especially high-level objects such as domain objects) should be treated with suspicion. This view displays information about:

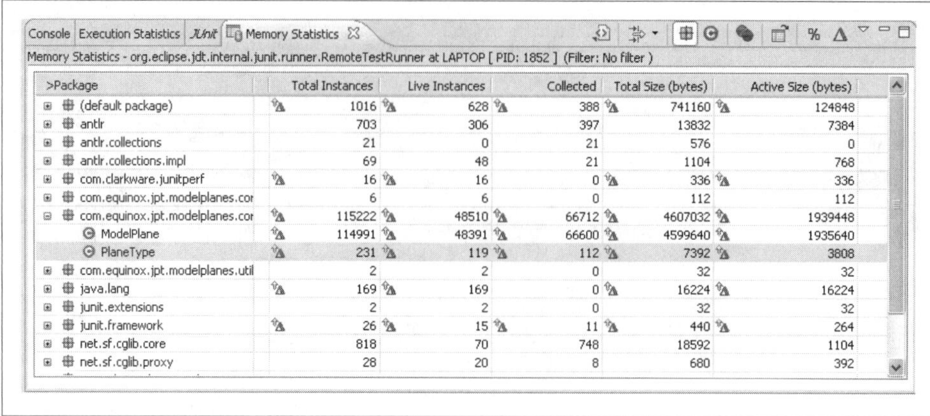

Figure 19-6. The Memory Statistics view

- The total number of instances ever created for each class, including both live and recycled instances.
- The number of live instances, or referenced objects that haven't been collected by the garbage collector. An unusually high number of live instances may be a symptom of a memory leak.
- The number of instances that have been recycled by the garbage collector. A high number of recycled instances may indicate that objects are being created unnecessarily at some point.
- The total memory taken by both the active instances and by all the instances ever created.

In many cases, the dynamics of object creation are just as important as the raw numbers at a given point in time. As the application runs, you can update the view using the "Refresh Views" in the contextual menu. The small triangles (actually, deltas) in Figure 19-6 indicate which values have changed since the last refresh. This helps you identify which objects were created during application initialization and which ones are being created as the application runs. The "Show Delta Columns" button (the delta symbol in the view's toolbar) adds an extra column for each field, showing how many instances were created since the last time the view was updated.

The "Show as percentage" button (the percentage symbol in the view's toolbar) shows the number of instances and size of each class as percentage values. This is a handy way of checking whether any particular classes take up a suspiciously high proportion of memory space or have an unusually high number of instances compared to the other classes. Again, this can be a symptom of a memory leak.

Another useful tool for detecting memory leaks is the "Collect Object References" view. To obtain this data, you need to activate reference collecting. After you start the profil-

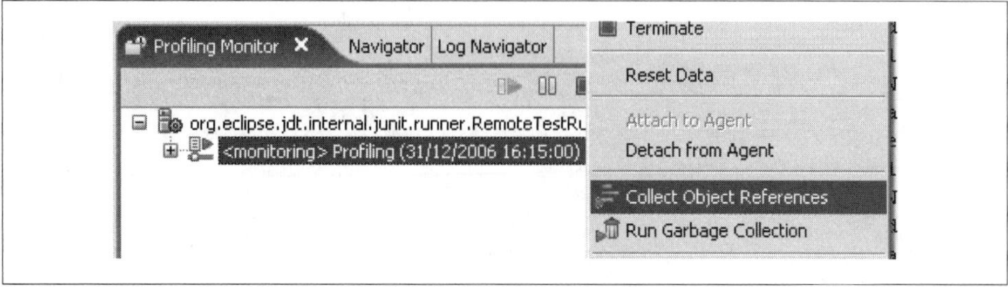

Figure 19-7. Activating reference collection

ing, click on the monitor entry and select "Collect Object References" in the contextual menu (see Figure 19-7).

Then open the "Collect Object References" view via the contextual menu ("Open with→Object References"). You will obtain a list of classes with the number of references to each class. This can give some clues concerning possible memory leaks.

You can also force the JVM to run a garbage collection, by selecting "Run Garbage Collection" in the contextual menu. This is a good way to flush out memory leaks (see Section 18.4). Indeed, a good way to check for potential memory leaks is to run the garbage collector and then to look at the remaining live instances.

19.7 Analyzing Execution Time

Execution time analysis provides useful information about the more dynamic aspects of the application, where the code spends the most time, and what is the flow between the objects.

The "Execution Statistics" view, shown in Figure 19-8, gives a good view of where your application is spending its time. The organization by package ("Package Level Information") lets you drill down to the classes ("Class Level Information") and methods ("Method Level Information") that are taking the most time to execute. Alternatively, you can display a list of classes or methods, which is useful for sorting by execution time.

Clicking on a method will open the "Method Invocation Details" view (Figure 19-9), which displays some finer details on the number of times that the method is being called, where it is being called from, and what other methods it invokes. You can also navigate through the methods listed in the view: clicking on a method will take you to the invocation details for that method. Although this view is not as well integrated into the source code views as some of the commercial tools (where it is possible to drill down into the source code itself), it can give some vital clues as to which methods may be performing badly.

Another interesting view that gives a useful description of the dynamics of the application is the "UML Trace Interactions" view (see Figure 19-10). This view is an annotated UML interactions diagram that displays an exhaustive view of every

Console | Object References | JUnit | Memory Statistics | Execution Statistics

Execution Statistics - org.eclipse.jdt.internal.junit.runner.RemoteTestRunner at LAPTOP [PID: :

>Package	Base Time (sec...	Average Base ...	Cumulative Tim...	Calls
antlr.collections.impl	0.021863	0.000012	0.021863	1886
com.clarkware.junitperf	0.001845	0.000231	46.362016	8
com.equinox.jpt.modelplanes.cor	248.401220	0.041228	287.755272	6025
DefaultDatabaseImpl	1.243620	0.177660	165.931622	7
LoadTestData	1.820016	0.303336	164.690320	6
-clinit-()	0.002287	0.002287	0.002287	1
getDataSource() javax.s	0.000000	0.000000	0.000000	0
getModelPlaneDAO() com	0.000000	0.000000	0.000000	0
getPlaneTypeDAO() com.	0.000000	0.000000	0.000000	0
loadData() void	1.817698	1.817698	164.688002	1
LoadTestData()	0.000014	0.000014	0.000014	1

Figure 19-8. Execution statistics

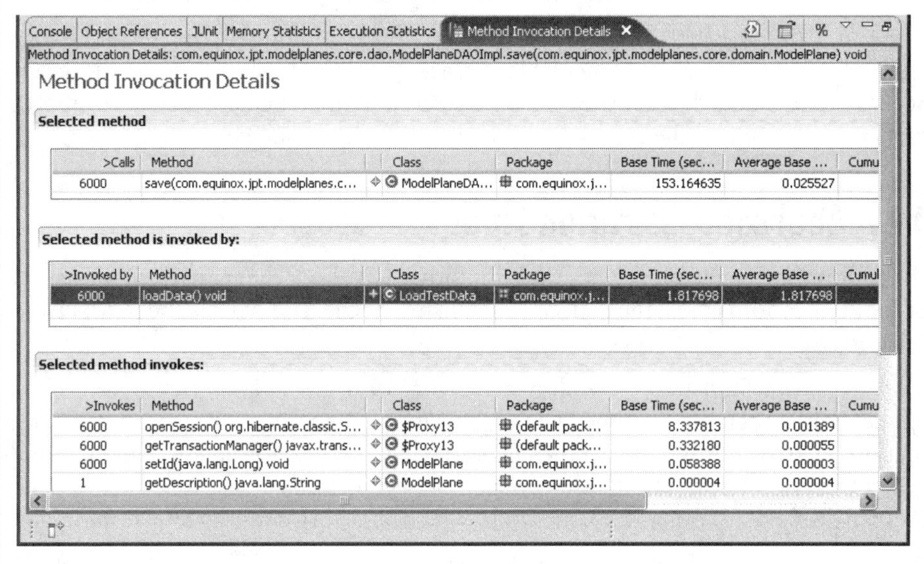

Figure 19-9. The Method Invocation Details view

interaction between every class during the course of the application execution. If you move the mouse over a particular interaction, Eclipse will display how long this interaction took. This information is enhanced by a colored bar in the lefthand margin, which gives an indication of the time spent in each phase: the redder the bar, the more time was spent in these interactions. In other words, this can give you a good high-level view of any application hotspots.

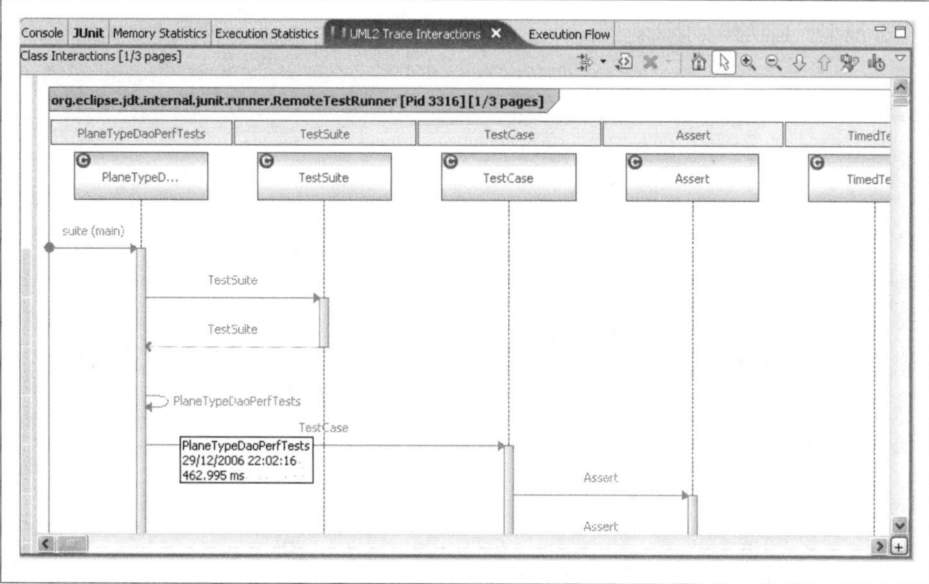

Figure 19-10. The UML Trace Interactions view

19.8 Displaying Coverage Statistics

The "Coverage Statistics" view (see Figure 19-11) provides information on which methods were used (and, therefore, tested, at least to some extent) by the test cases you just ran. The coverage statistics are a nice feature, although they don't provide the same level of detail as dedicated coverage tools such as Cobertura do (see Chapter 12), which provide line-precision coverage data as well as statistics on both line and branch coverage. Nevertheless, it does have the advantage of providing real-time coverage results, and, currently, only commercial code coverage tools such as Clover and jCoverage provide line-level coverage reporting and full IDE integration.

19.9 Using Filters to Refine Your Results

When you are profiling an application, there may be classes that you don't need or don't want to include in your analysis. For example, if you are testing a web application, you may want to exclude classes belonging to the web server. You can set this up when you set up your profiling configuration (using the "Profile As..." menu). Double-click on the "Java Profiling" entry to modify the profiling options. The first screen lets you select and customize a filter set for your profiling session (see Figure 19-12). Filter sets let you exclude certain classes or packages from data collection, which speeds up the profiling process and makes it easier to see relevant data.

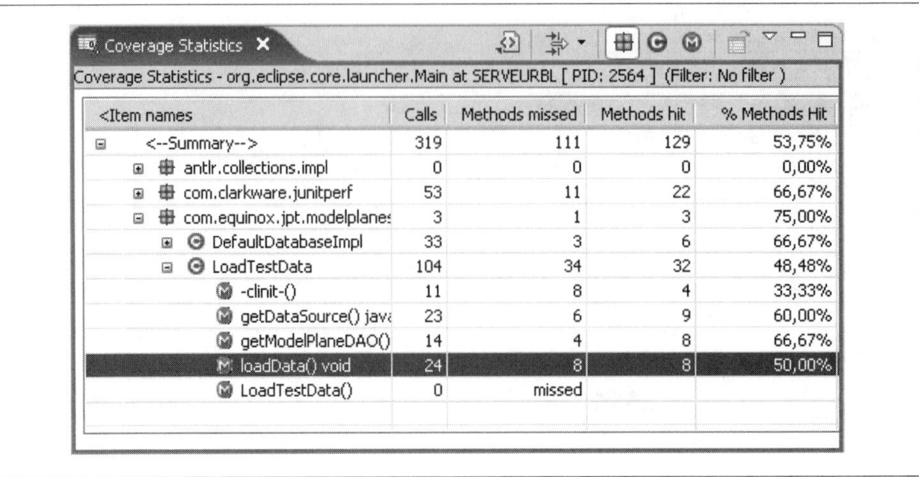

<Item names	Calls	Methods missed	Methods hit	% Methods Hit
<--Summary-->	319	111	129	53,75%
antlr.collections.impl	0	0	0	0,00%
com.clarkware.junitperf	53	11	22	66,67%
com.equinox.jpt.modelplanes	3	1	3	75,00%
DefaultDatabaseImpl	33	3	6	66,67%
LoadTestData	104	34	32	48,48%
-clinit-()	11	8	4	33,33%
getDataSource() java	23	6	9	60,00%
getModelPlaneDAO()	14	4	8	66,67%
loadData() void	24	8	8	50,00%
LoadTestData()	0	missed		

Figure 19-11. Coverage statistics view

TPTP comes with a few predefined filter sets that you can customize, or you can create a new one. A filter set is simply a list of rules that include or exclude classes or methods based on a regular expression. Although the most common use is to exclude entire packages, you can also exclude (or include) specific classes, or even a particular method in a particular class.

Filters are also used to refine and clarify the results of the profiling process.

Once you've started profiling and have displayed the profiling result views, you can narrow down the selection using the Filters menu (see Figure 19-13). You can choose from a few handy predefined filters such as "Highest 10 total size" (for Memory Statistics views) and "Highest 10 cumulative time" (for Execution Statistics views). Alternatively, you can create your own customized filter by selecting "Manage Filters...."

These filters are a powerful tool. TPTP lets you define sophisticated filter rules (see Figure 19-12). It is easy to filter the displayed data by package, class, or method names, using wildcard-based expressions. A common use is to filter results down to a particular package or group of packages, which makes it easier to focus your optimization efforts on certain classes or isolate memory leaks. In addition, using the "Advanced" tab, you can build more elaborate rules using the other collected fields, such as execution time or number of instances. For example, you can set up a filter to display only the methods whose average time is greater than half a second.

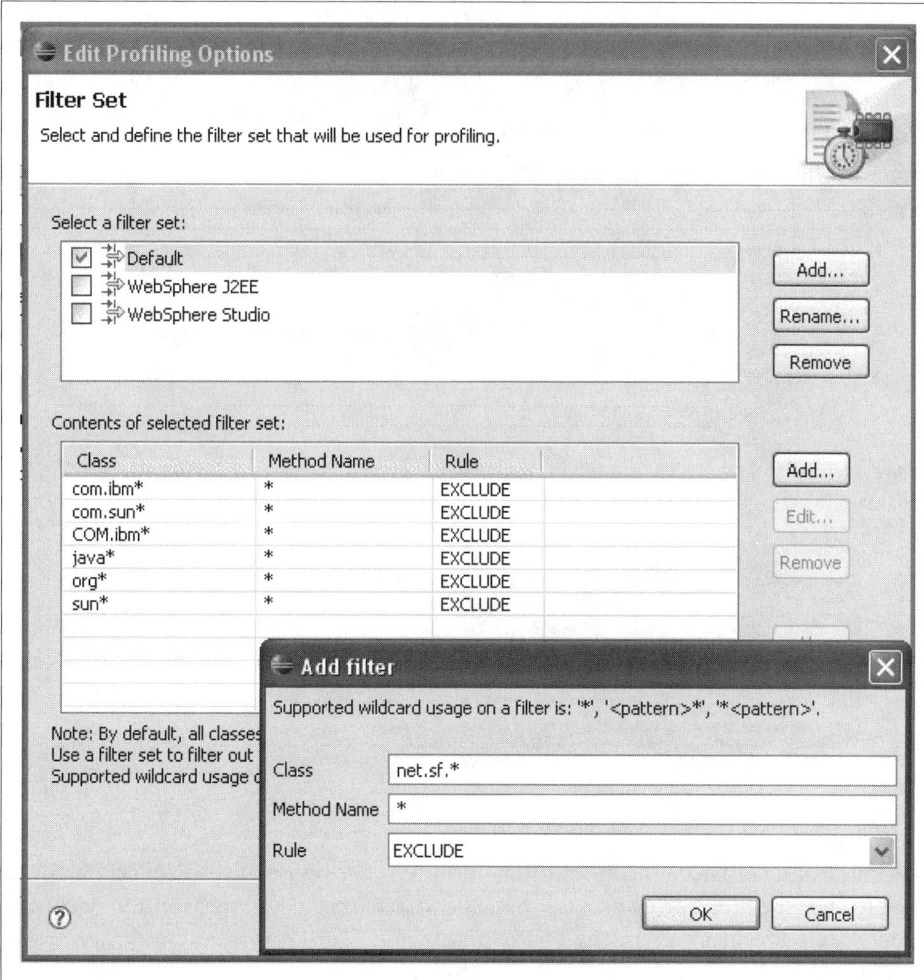

Figure 19-12. Refining results by applying a filter

19.10 Profiling a Web Application

TPTP can profile a wide range of tests and applications. If you are developing a web application in Eclipse, it is an easy matter to profile the application using the TPTP profiling features. This ties in well with a development environment in which an application is written, unit tested, and deployed for functional testing within the Eclipse workspace. Open the Server view, and right-click on the server you want to profile, and select "Profile" (see Figure 19-14).

This will open the "Profile on server" configuration screen (see Figure 19-15). Choose the Java Profiling Agent for the PID corresponding to your server (generally, there is

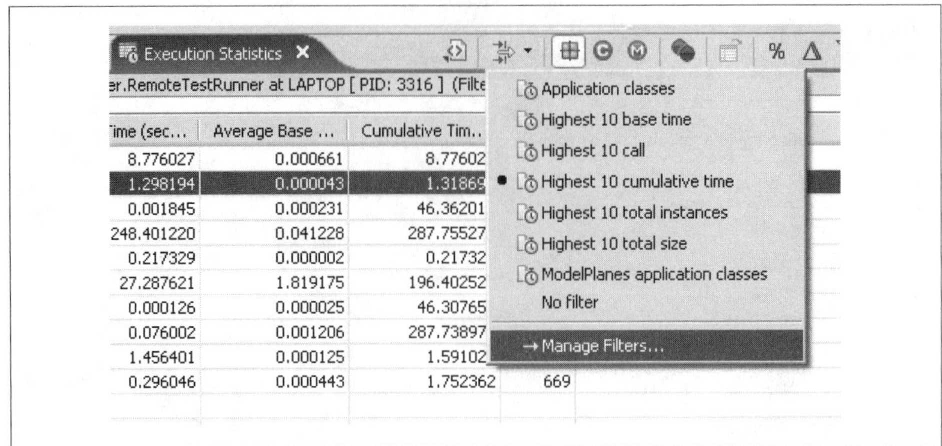

Figure 19-13. Refining results by applying a filter

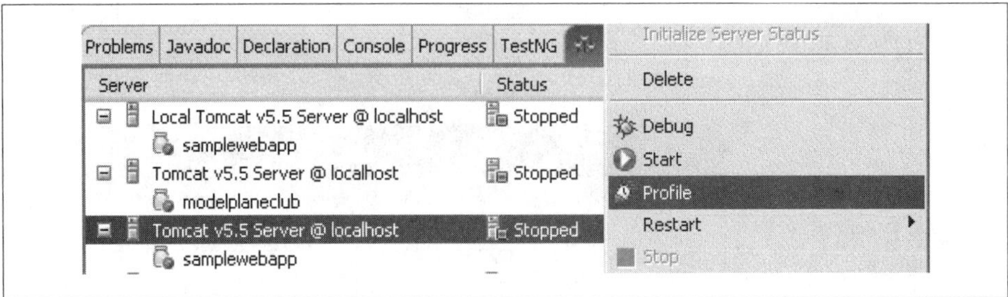

Figure 19-14. Profiling a web application

only one), and configure the monitoring options as above. Finally, to collect data, you need to start the monitoring process manually. Go to the "Profiling Monitor" view and select "Start Monitoring" in the contextual menu. Once you've done this, you can profile your web application just as you would an ordinary Java application.

19.11 Conclusion

The Eclipse Test & Performance Tools Platform is a valuable addition to the Eclipse IDE toolkit. The wide range of performance testing helps you to guarantee high-quality and high-performance code right from the first unit tests. TPTP is certainly not as developed as some of the commercial tools out there such as OptimizeIt and JProbe, which often have more sophisticated reporting and analysis functionalities and a more polished presentation. However, commercial profiling tools tend to be notoriously expensive, and it is often difficult justifying their use in all but the most dire of circumstances. Although it is still relatively young, TPTP is a powerful and capable

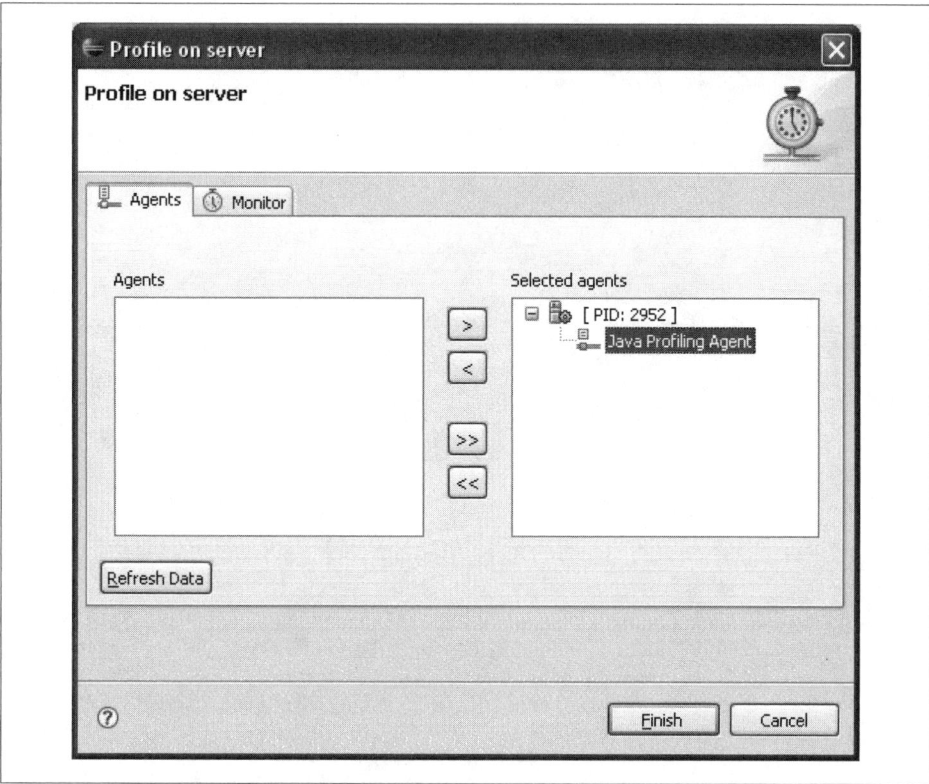

Figure 19-15. The Profile On Server configuration

product, and it can certainly provide valuable profiling data that many projects would otherwise have to do without.

It is worth noting that NetBeans also comes with an excellent, integrated profiling tool.

CHAPTER 20
Testing Your User Interfaces

20.0 Introduction

Automatically testing user interfaces has always been difficult. Indeed, for many projects, it has often been placed in the "too-hard" basket. In this chapter, we will look at two tools that can help with your automatic Graphical User Interface (GUI) testing: Selenium and Fixtures for Easy Software Testing (FEST). Selenium is an innovative tool that uses a web browser to run tests against your web application. And FEST is an equally innovative product that lets you integrate Swing testing as part of your JUnit or TestNG tests.

20.1 Testing Your Web Application with Selenium

Introduction

With a bit of practice and good tools, it isn't difficult to write good unit tests for a large part of most applications. Lightweight POJO-based frameworks such as Hibernate and Spring make it easier to design classes and components that can be unit-tested in isolation. Embedded Java databases such as Derby and HSQLDB, along with database testing frameworks such as DBUnit, make it a relatively simple task to test database access layers. EJB-based applications are an exception to this rule—you generally need to deploy your EJBs onto an application server before you can test them correctly, which makes unit testing unwieldy and difficult.

However, testing the user interface of a web application has always been problematic. Some libraries, such as `StrutsTestCase` (see Chapter 13) and the Spring MVC testing framework, make good use of mock objects approach to simulate interaction with the server. These tools fit smoothly into ordinary unit tests, and are excellent at testing (in MVC terminology) the Controller code. However, although they do a fine job of this, their limits lie in the fact that they only test the application code, and not the HTML screens themselves.

Other tools use different approaches. Some, like HttpUnit, allow you to write tests to run against a running web server, and then inspect the returned HTML code. Cactus lets you test applications by running the tests on the server itself. JMeter lets you do functional web testing to some extent, again by building HTTP requests. Frank Cohen's Test Maker is another interesting open source product in this field that lets you record web tests in Jython, edit them, and replay them as unit tests.

Selenium is a little different. Selenium is an open source testing tool, originally developed by ThoughtWorks and now hosted and maintained by OpenQA, which tests web applications by using them as a user would—via a browser. So, rather than building HTTP requests that a browser might send to the server and analyzing the results, Selenium drives a real browser, making it possible to test more sophisticated user interfaces. Selenium works on most platforms (Windows, Linux, and Mac OS X) and with most browsers (Firefox, Internet Explorer, Opera, Konqueror, Safari...), which makes Selenium a good choice when it comes to verifying cross-browser compatibility.

Using the Selenium IDE

Probably the easiest way to write Selenium test scripts is to use the Selenium IDE. The Selenium IDE is a Firefox plug-in, which you can download and install from the Selenium web site.* This tool allows you to create test scripts by using your web application just as a normal user would, through a browser.

Start up the IDE by selecting "Tools→Selenium IDE" in your Firefox menu bar. The Selenium IDE console will come up (see Figure 20-1). As soon as you open this Window, Selenium will automatically begin recording your every move. Now go to the site you want to test. If you haven't got a test server, try Selenium out on your favorite Internet site—Selenium will work against any site you can access from your browser.

To build a test script, just run through your application as if you were a normal user. Typically, this will involve navigating through your application, entering values into forms and submitting them to the server, and so on. On the way, you can insert different types of controls to make sure the web application is returning what you expect. At any point, you can use the contextual menu to insert the equivalent of assertions—for example, select a block of text that should always figure on this page, and then select "VerifyTextPresent" in the contextual menu (see Figure 20-2).

You can also check for other things on each page, such as the presence of a particular title (to check that you are on the right page, for example). The full range of options is available using the "Show All Available Commands" menu option.

Selenium is quite smart about how it identifies fields, and it will use unique field names or id values where possible. However, sometimes it will use less-than-optimal XPath expressions, which can be retouched by hand to make your script more robust. We will look at how to do this in "Writing Selenium Test Scripts," later in this section.

* *http://www.openqa.org/selenium-ide/download.action*

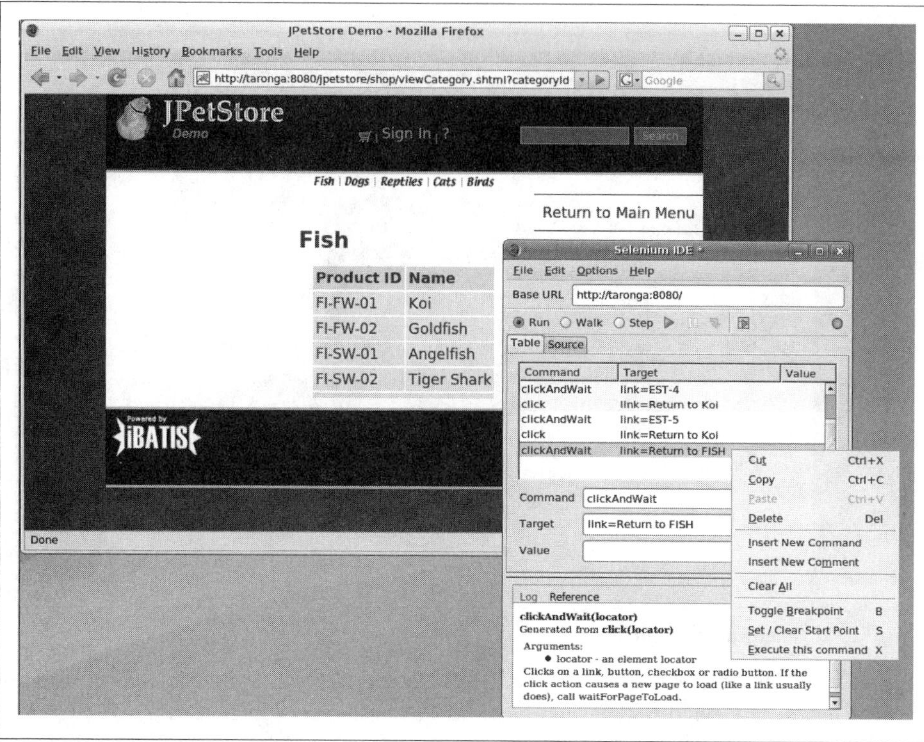

Figure 20-1. The Selenium IDE

Selenium does more than simply record your actions: it is also a scripting tool in its own right—a surprisingly powerful one. Once you have recorded your script, you can rerun the script completely or step through the commands one-by-one. You can also save the Selenium test script for future use. You can insert breakpoints, delete commands, and insert new ones. A useful technique when you are tailoring your test scripts is to insert a breakpoint at the command you want to modify, and then to let Selenium "walk" though the script (using the "Walk" checkbox) until it gets to the breakpoint. Then you can step through your modified commands one-by-one to make sure they work as expected.

The Command drop-down list also gives you instant access to all available Selenium commands. And just to make things even easier, whenever you select a command, the corresponding documentation will be displayed at the bottom of the Selenium window.

It is important to know that the Selenium recording process is not flawless. Sometimes, you may need to retouch your script to get it to work systematically. A common example is the *click* command. The *click* command, as you would expect, tells Selenium to click on an HTML element somewhere on your web page. Quite often, this will result in a new page being loaded. However, if you expect a new page to be loaded, you need to tell Selenium to wait until it is loaded before proceeding to the next instruction. The

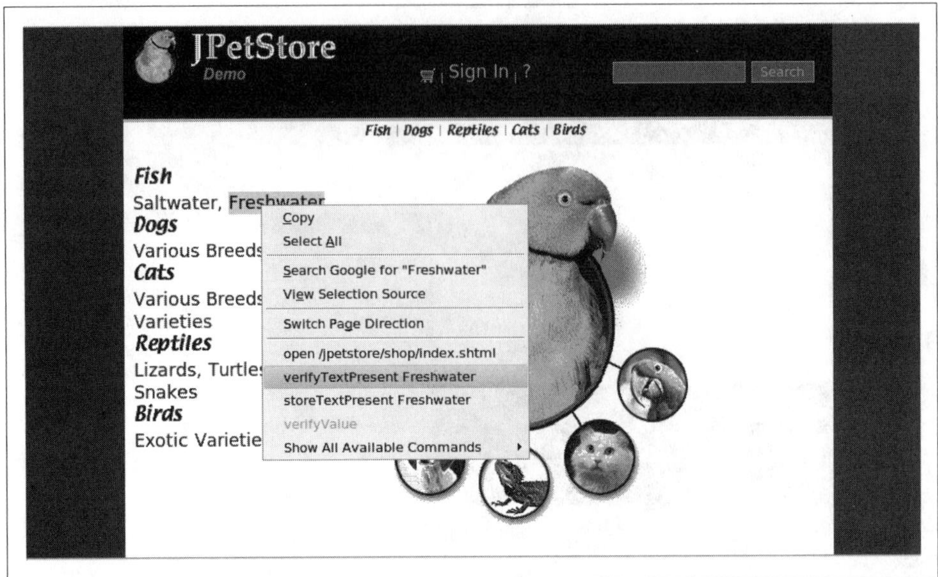

Figure 20-2. Adding a Selenium assertion

easiest way to do this is to use *clickAndWait* instead of *click*. Sometimes Selenium assumes that a new page will be loaded and correctly records *clickAndWait* when it should. But sometimes it doesn't. In those cases, you will need to go through your script and manually replace the *click* commands with *clickAndWait*.

Occasionally, the *clickAndWait* command does not wait long enough for the complete page to load. In this case, you may need to split the command into a *click*, followed by a separate *waitForPageToLoad*.

In addition, Selenium will, by design, record only the strict minimum of events that it thinks are necessary to reproduce the user actions. This can cause problems with more complex screens, especially ones that use Ajax-backed technologies. We will discuss the finer details of the Selenium scripting language in the next section.

Writing Selenium Test Scripts

The Selenium IDE is a great way to get started with Selenium testing—it is trivially easy to record and replay test scripts, and to study how Selenium records your interaction with a web site. However, Selenium also provides a powerful scripting language in its own right, known as "Selenese." To get the most out of Selenium, you will need to understand how this scripting language works. In this section, we will look at how to understand, and write your own, fully fledged Selenium test scripts using this language.

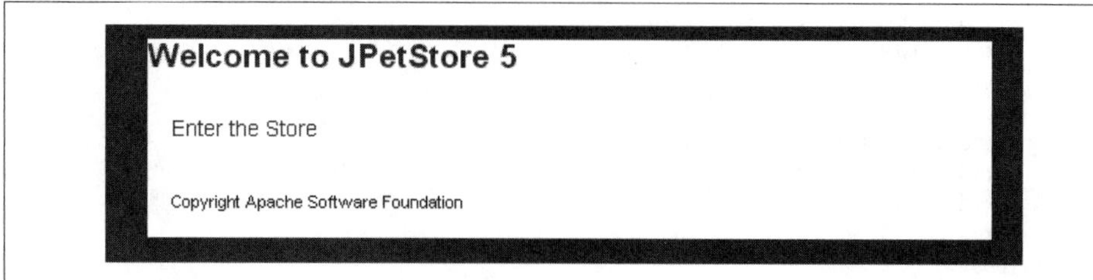

Figure 20-3. The JPetstore welcome page

An introduction to Selenese

A Selenium test script takes the form of an HTML table, made up of three columns. This makes it fairly easy to edit, either by hand or by using a visual HTML editor. However the easiest tool to use is probably the Selenium IDE itself. Using this tool, you can not only interactively run your test scripts but also delete commands and insert new ones, as well as have direct access to the documentation for each command.

For convenience, throughout this chapter we will be running our tests against Clinton Begin's JPetStore application, which you can obtain from the iBATIS web site.* This is an excellent lightweight version of Sun's PetStore demo application, built using Struts and iBATIS. To start off, we will simply go to the application URL, and click on the "Enter the Store" link (see Figure 20-3). This will take us to the application home page (see Figure 20-4), where we will verify the presence of the text "Saltwater" on the page.

Each row of the table contains a command in the first cell. A command takes one or two arguments, which appear in the following cells. A simple Selenium test script to do this might look like the following:

```
<html>
<head>
  <meta http-equiv="Content-Type" content="text/html; charset=UTF-8">
  <title>Petstore Tests</title>
</head>
<body>
<table border="1" cellpadding="1" cellspacing="1">
  <thead>
  <tr>
    <td rowspan="1" colspan="3">JPetStore tests</td>
  </tr>
  </thead>
  <tbody>
    <tr>
      <td>open</td>
      <td>http://testserver:8080/jpetstore/</td>
      <td></td>
    </tr>
    <tr>
      <td>clickAndWait</td>
```

* *http://ibatis.apache.org/javadownloads.cgi*

```
          <td>link=Enter the Store</td>
          <td></td>
        </tr>
        <tr>
          <td>verifyTextPresent</td>
          <td>Saltwater</td>
          <td></td>
        </tr>
      </tbody>
    </table>
    </body>
    </html>
```

In a more readable form, this table would look like the one shown here:

open	http://testserver:8080/jpetstore/
clickAndWait	link=Enter the Store
verifyTextPresent	Saltwater

The *open* command tells Selenium to open a particular URL in the browser. You can either use a full URL as shown here, or simply a relative path such as "/jpetstore/". The full URL is useful when you need to develop and/or run your test script using the Selenium IDE from any machine. The relative path is more portable, but can only be used on the same machine as the web server, using the approach described later on.

The second action shown here is the very useful *clickAndWait* command. The basic command here is actually *click*; the *AndWait* suffix tells Selenium to wait until the new page has been loaded before proceeding. This suffix also works with any of the other Selenium commands (*selectAndWait*, *typeAndWait*, and so on), with the exception of *open*, where the *AndWait* suffix is implicit. You should use this suffix wherever the command is expected to result in a new page being loaded.

The final action illustrated here is *verifyTextPresent*, which, as its name indicates, simply checks for the presence of a particular block of text on the HTML page. Despite its rather basic nature, this sort of test turns out to be useful for functional testing. We will look at other, more sophisticated ways of checking results further on.

Selenium test scripts are designed to be run either through the Selenium IDE, or directly on the target web server. In Figure 20-4, you can see this script being executed on a remote server using the Selenium IDE.

Referring to objects on the web page

Much of the power of Selenium comes from its ability to interact with a web site using a conventional browser. You can tell Selenium to interact with a web page in a number of ways, such as by clicking on a button or a link, ticking a checkbox, selecting an entry in a drop-down list, or entering a value in a field. In all of these cases, it is vital to be able to identify exactly which HTML element Selenium will be manipulating.

Figure 20-4. Running the JPetstore test script

Selenium provides a number of ways for you to identify objects on a screen using various sorts of *element locators*. Each sort of element locator uses a different strategy for finding target elements.

By far, the easiest way to identify an element is to simply refer to it by name or id. For example, in the JPetStore application, the "Update Cart" button is implemented as a "submit" button with the name attribute set to "update," as shown here:

```
<input type="submit" name="update" value="Update Cart"/>
```

In this case, you can simply refer to the *name* of the HTML element directly in the second column:

clickAndWait	update

This is in fact a shorthand notation that will work for any HTML element identified using either the *id* or the *name* attribute. More precisely, this strategy will find any element with the specified *id* attribute, or, failing that, the first element with the specified *name* attribute. The equivalent full notation would use the *identifier* locator, as shown here:

```
clickAndWait    identifier=update
```

This approach is convenient, but there are cases in which you may need to be more precise. If necessary, you can use the *id* or *name* locator values explicitly:

```
clickAndWait    name=update
```

Another commonly used element locator is the *link* locator, which identifies an HTML link. For example, suppose that we want to click on the following link:

```
<a href="/jpetstore/shop/index.shtml">Return to Main Menu</a>
```

In this case, all we need to do is identify the anchor element using the link locator and the enclosed text, as shown here:

```
click    link=Return to Main Menu
```

More complex or well-hidden objects can be located using XPath or DOM expressions. For example, the following HTML code displays the central image in Figure 20-4.

```
<div id="MainImageContent">
  <map name="estoremap">
    <area alt="Birds" coords="72,2,280,250" href="viewCategory.shtml
     ?categoryId=BIRDS".../>
    <area alt="Fish" coords="2,180,72,250" href="viewCategory.shtml
     ?categoryId=FISH".../>
    <area alt="Dogs" coords="60,250,130,320" href="viewCategory.shtml
     ?categoryId=DOGS".../>
    <area alt="Reptiles" coords="140,270,210,340" href="viewCategory.shtml
     ?categoryId=REPTILES".../>
    <area alt="Cats" coords="225,240,295,310" href="viewCategory.shtml
     ?categoryId=CATS".../>
    <area alt="Birds" coords="280,180,350,250" href="viewCategory.shtml
     ?categoryId=BIRDS".../>
  </map>
  <img height="355" src="../images/splash.gif" align="center"
   usemap="#estoremap" width="350"/>
</div>
```

Suppose that we want to click on the "Fish" area link. We can identify this link using the following simple XPath expression:

```
//area[2]
```

In Selenese, this becomes:

```
click    xpath=//area[2]
```

Selenium will recognize the form of an XPath expression so that the *xpath* locator is not strictly necessary. We can simplify the command to the following:

```
click   //area[2]
```

For more deeply nested elements, the XPath can get a bit more complicated. For example, the menu items on the home page (see Figure 20-4) are actually images. If you click on the small "Fish" menu item at the top of the screen, Selenium will record something like this:

```
click   //div[4]/a[1]/img
```

So, click on the image in the first anchor in the fourth div in the page. This is certainly precise but not particularly flexible. If the web designer modifies the page layout, this command could easily be broken. A better approach would be to use a more robust XPath expression that will find the image even if the structure of the page changes.

A useful tool for this sort of work is the excellent FireBug* plug-in for Firefox. This plug-in lets you inspect and interactively edit HTML, JavaScript, and CSS on your page (see Figure 20-5). If necessary, you can also copy the corresponding XPath into the clipboard.

In Figure 20-5, we can see the HTML code that implements the "Fish" menu option at the top of the screen:

```
<a href="/jpetstore/shop/viewCategory.shtml?categoryId=FISH">
  <img src="../images/sm_fish.gif"/>
</a>
```

The name of the image is unlikely to change very often. Assuming this, we can come up with an XPath expression that will find the first link containing this image:

```
//a/img[@src="../images/sm_fish.gif"]
```

So, in Selenese, our command becomes slightly longer, but much more robust:

```
click   //a/img[@src="../images/sm_fish.gif"]
```

Using variables

Testing navigation and static text is all very well, but for serious functional testing, you need to verify dynamic data as well. Selenium allows you to store data you find on a web page in variables for later use. For example, you might want to check that a

* *http://www.getfirebug.com/*

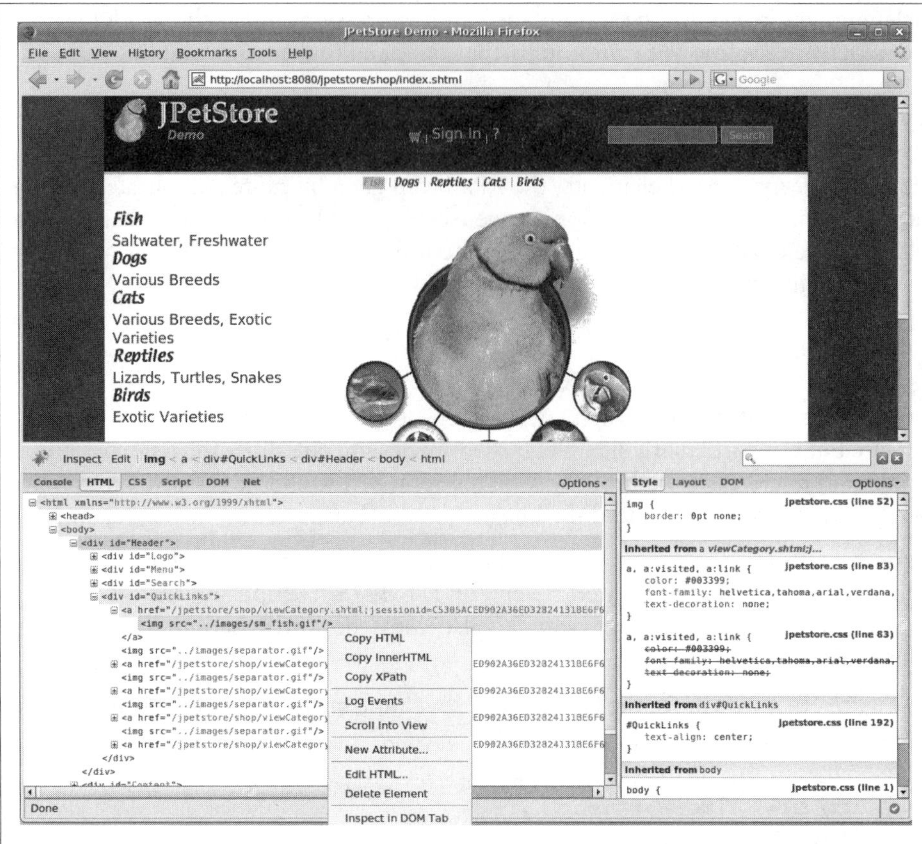

Figure 20-5. Using FireBug to obtain the XPath for a particular HTML element

purchased item is correctly placed in the user's shopping cart. Let's see how this is done using the Selenium IDE.

In the JPetstore application, users can add selected pets to their shopping carts using the "Add To Cart" button. Suppose that we need to check that the information going into the cart is correct. The first thing to do is to create a new Selenium test script and navigate to the details page of the pet you want to test. Alternatively, you can place a breakpoint in an existing test script at a details page, and step through the script to that point. In either case, you should end up displaying the details page of your favorite animal in the browser, along with a sequence of Selenium commands to get there (see Figure 20-6).

The next step is to locate and store the HTML elements that we need. In our case, we are going to make sure that, when we click on "Add to Cart," a line is added containing the animal product code ("EST-20"), title ("Adult Male Goldfish"), and price ($5.50). You can store data in a variable by using the *storeText* command. Just place the cursor on the field you want to save, and select "StoreText..." in the contextual menu. (If you

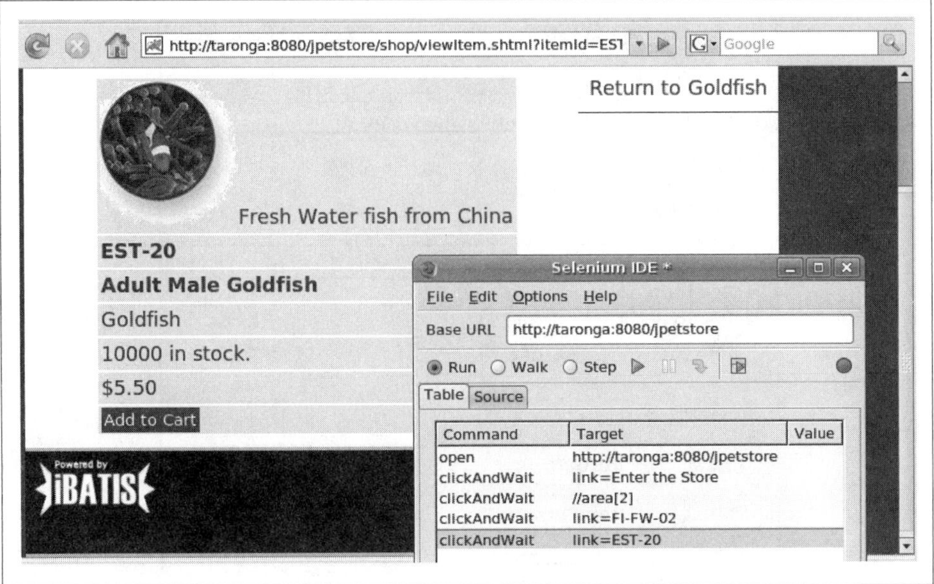

Figure 20-6. Navigating to a particular page in Selenium IDE

haven't used it before, you may need to look for this command in the "Show All Available Commands" submenu.) Selenium IDE will prompt you for a variable name, and then add the appropriate *storeText* command into your script. If you do this for the price field, the actual Selenium command will look something like this:

```
storeText    //tr[6]/td    itemPrice
```

You are telling Selenium to record the value in the first cell of the sixth row of the first table it finds on the page. In SeleniumIDE, it looks very similar (see Figure 20-7).

This is not too hard so far. However, the trick here is to correctly identify the right HTML element. For example, if you do the same thing for the item title ("Adult Male Goldfish"), Selenium will record something along the following lines:

```
storeText    //font    itemName
```

Selenium proposes to record the contents of the first *<font>* element it finds. This is accurate, but not particularly robust. If the web designer were to add a different *<font>* element before this one on the page, the test script would no longer work. So we may want to use an XPath expression with a little more context. Once again, the Firefox FireBug plug-in can come in handy here. Inspecting the item, we find that the title is actually the third line of a table (see Figure 20-8).

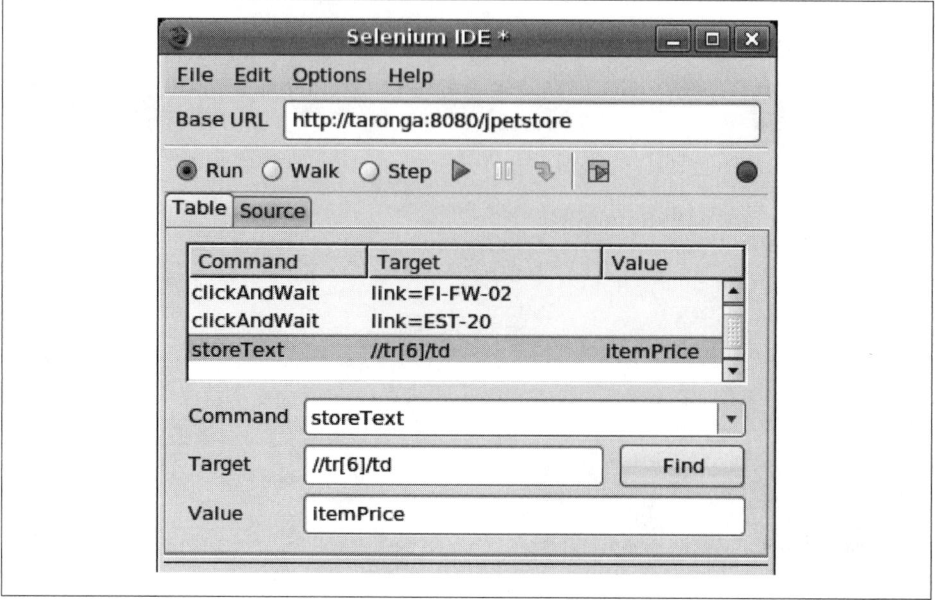

Figure 20-7. Storing a text variable in Selenium IDE

Knowing this, there are several ways we could make the XPath expression to this element more robust. For example, we could note that the title element is in the third row of the table nested in a *<div>* element. This *<div>* is uniquely identified by an *id* attribute value of "Catalog." Using this, we can localize all the fields we need to record in a fairly precise manner:

```
storeText    //div[@id="Catalog"]//tr[3]/td//font    itemName
storeText    //div[@id="Catalog"]//tr[2]/td          itemId
storeText    //div[@id="Catalog"]//tr[6]/td          itemPrice
```

Now that we have stored our variables, we can click on the "Add To Cart" button and proceed to the Shopping Cart screen. Before doing so, you may need to reactivate the Selenium IDE recording mode (if the round red button on the right of the screen is solid red, recording has been stopped and you will need to click on this button to start recording again).

Once you've clicked on the "Add To Cart" button, Selenium should record a command along the following lines:

```
clickAndWait    link=Add to Cart
```

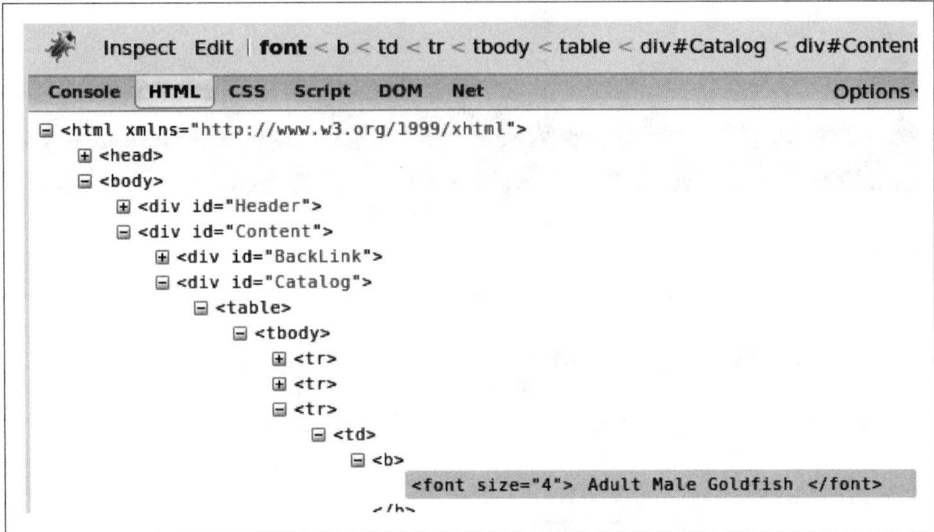

Figure 20-8. Inspecting the item title field

As we discussed above, Selenium IDE may record a *click* command rather than the more robust *clickAndWait*; in this case, just change it manually.

At this point, we should be on the Shopping Cart screen (see Figure 20-9). We can now check to make sure the displayed values are correct. Again, there are several ways of doing this. You can use the variables we have just created in any Selenium command, using the "${..}" notation. For example, we could opt to use the *verifyTextPresent* command to simply check for the presence of these values on the page, as shown here:

```
verifyTextPresent    ${itemId}
verifyTextPresent    ${itemTitle}
verifyTextPresent    ${itemPrice}
```

Or, we could opt for a more precise approach using XPath expressions, as shown here:

```
verifyText    //div[@id="Cart"]//tr[2]/td[1]    ${itemId}
verifyText    //div[@id="Cart"]//tr[2]/td[3]    ${itemTitle}
verifyText    //div[@id="Cart"]//tr[2]/td[6]    ${itemPrice}
```

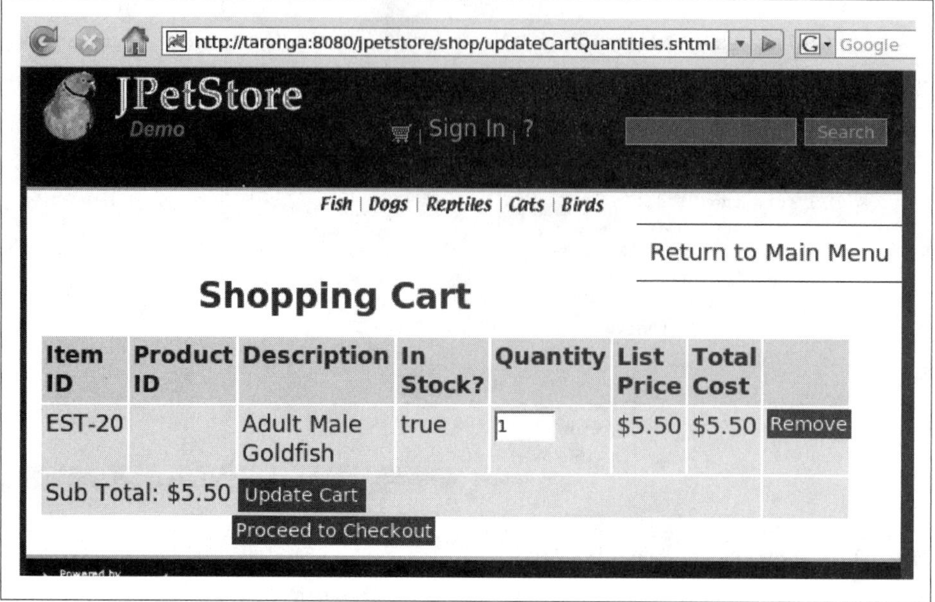

Figure 20-9. The Shopping Cart screen

Using assertions

Assertions are the bread-and-butter of any testing framework, and Selenium is no exception. Selenium comes with a rich set of assertions that allow you to verify the content of your web pages in great detail.

Selenium assertions come in three flavors: *Assert*s, *Verify*s, and *WaitFor*s. So, to test text fields, you can choose from *assertText*, *verifyText*, and *WaitForText*. If a *Verify* command fails, the failure will be logged, but the test script will continue, whereas if an *Assert* fails, all bets are off and the test script will abort immediately. *WaitFor* assertions will monitor a particular element, waiting for it to take a particular value. This has obvious applications if you are writing a site using Ajax.

You can also negate any assertion using *Not*: *assertNotText*, *verifyNotText*, and so on.

We have already seen the *verifyText* and *verifyTextPresent* commands in action earlier on. These assertions can be used to check text values displayed within HTML elements on the screen.

Another common use of assertions is to verify the values of form fields displayed on the screen. You can use *assertValue* (or *verifyValue* or *waitForValue*) to check the contents of ordinary *<input>* fields. For other field types, you need to use different types of assertions. The following list describes the most important commands you will need when working with forms:

assertSelectedValue
: Check the value of the selected entry in a drop-down list.

assertSelectedLabel
: Check the label of the selected entry in a drop-down list.

assertSelectedIndex
: Check the index of the selected entry in a drop-down list.

assertSelectedValues
: Check the values of selected entries in a multiple-choice drop-down list.

assertSelectedLabels
: Check the labels of selected entries in a multiple-choice drop-down list.

assertSelectedIndexs
: Check the indexes of selected entries in a multiple-choice drop-down list.

assertChecked
: Check whether a checkbox field has been checked.

For example, Figure 20-10 illustrates the payment order form page of the JPetStore application. On this screen, we might need to check that the credit card type drop-down list is set to "MasterCard," the credit card number is "999 9999 9999 9999," and the *shippingAddressRequired* checkbox is checked. We could do this as follows:

assertSelectedLabel	order.cardType	MasterCard
assertValue	order.creditCard	999 9999 9999 9999
assertChecked	shippingAddressRequired	

You can use assertions to check other aspects of the screen, as well. If your screen contains areas that are dynamically displayed or hidden using the CSS *visibility* property, you can check that this is working correctly with the *assertVisible* assertion:

assertVisible	order.cardType

In the same vein, you can check whether a field has been disabled using *assertEditable*:

assertEditable	order.billToFirstName

Or if your application uses JavaScript confirmation messages, you can test them using the *assertConfirmation* command, which lets you verify the text of the previously displayed JavaScript popup:

assertConfirmation	Deleting record - are you sure?

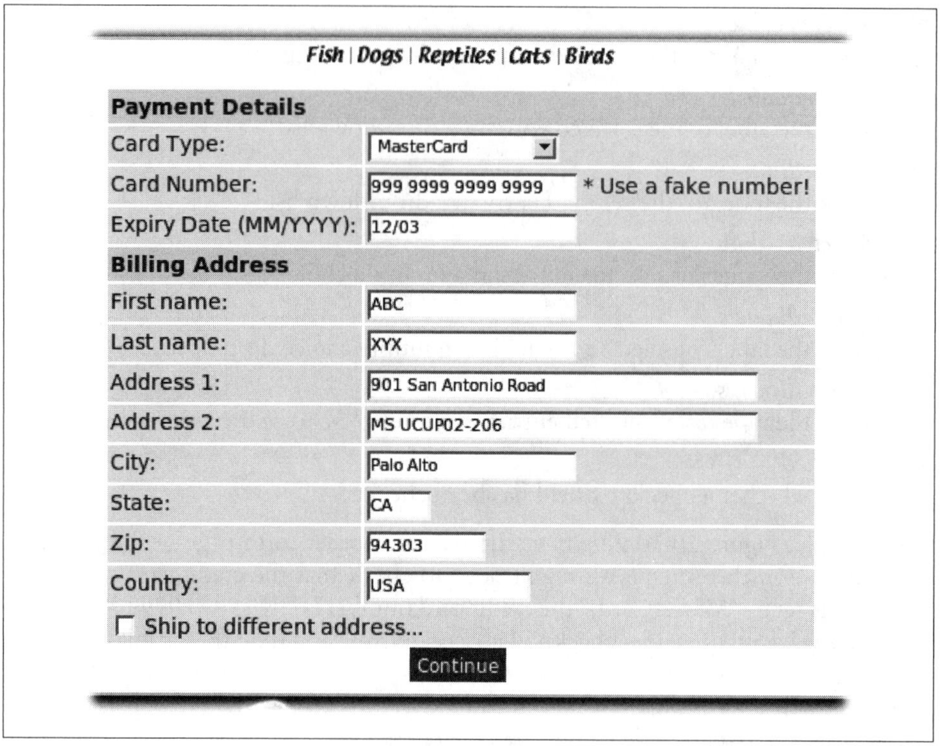

Fish | Dogs | Reptiles | Cats | Birds

Payment Details	
Card Type:	MasterCard
Card Number:	999 9999 9999 9999 * Use a fake number!
Expiry Date (MM/YYYY):	12/03
Billing Address	
First name:	ABC
Last name:	XYX
Address 1:	901 San Antonio Road
Address 2:	MS UCUP02-206
City:	Palo Alto
State:	CA
Zip:	94303
Country:	USA
Ship to different address...	

Continue

Figure 20-10. The Payment screen

Running a Selenium Test Suite with Selenium Core

The Selenium IDE is not the only way to execute a Selenium test script.

Selenium Core is a web-based testing platform in which you can run your Selenium test scripts on a central server. Because of JavaScript security constraints, you need to install Selenium Core on the same web server as the application to be tested. For a Java web server, this simply involves extracting the Selenium Core package into the `webapps` directory.

You can download the Selenium Core from the Selenium web site.[*] Unpack the ZIP file into the webapp directory of your test server (in the following example, the tests are being executed on a Tomcat server). A typical installation process might go like this:

```
$ cd $TOMCAT_BASE/webapps
$ wget http://release.openqa.org/selenium-core/1.0-beta-1/selenium-core-1.0-beta-1.zip
$ unzip selenium-core-1.0-beta-1.zip
$ mv selenium-core-1.0-beta-1 selenium-core
```

[*] *http://www.openqa.org/selenium-core/download.action*

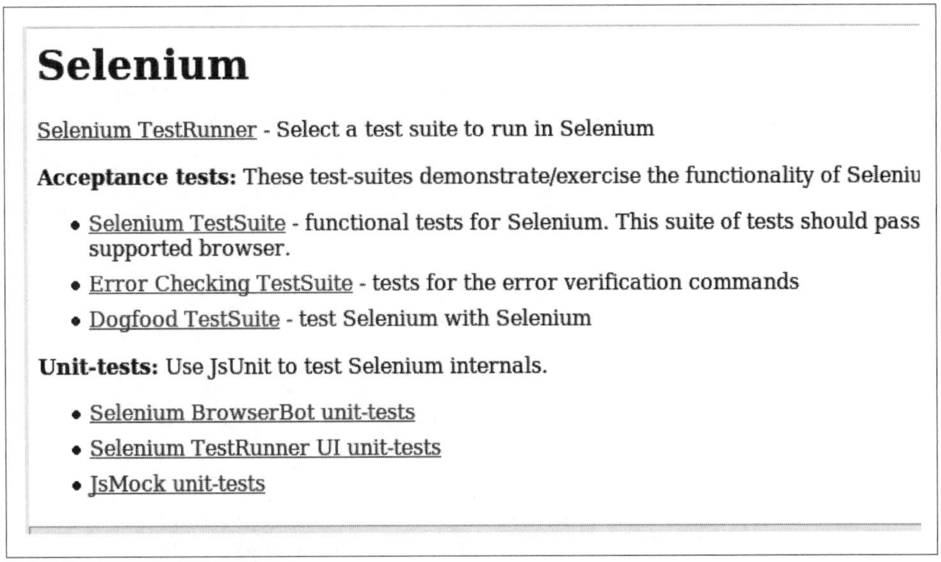

Selenium

Selenium TestRunner - Select a test suite to run in Selenium

Acceptance tests: These test-suites demonstrate/exercise the functionality of Seleniu

- Selenium TestSuite - functional tests for Selenium. This suite of tests should pass supported browser.
- Error Checking TestSuite - tests for the error verification commands
- Dogfood TestSuite - test Selenium with Selenium

Unit-tests: Use JsUnit to test Selenium internals.

- Selenium BrowserBot unit-tests
- Selenium TestRunner UI unit-tests
- JsMock unit-tests

Figure 20-11. The Selenium Core application home page

Now, if you open your browser to the selenium-core context on your web server, you should see a page like that shown in Figure 20-11. This page lets you experiment with Selenium's own test suites and, more important, provides you with access to the Selenium TestRunner, which is where all the interesting stuff happens.

It is good practice to create many smaller test scripts, rather than just one large one. This makes your test scripts easier to understand and to maintain, and makes selective testing easier. Typically, you would create a set of test scripts using the Selenium IDE, and then, once they are ready, place them on the Selenium Core server, where they can be used by the whole project team. Suppose that we have created a set of test scripts for the JPetStore application, as shown here:

```
$ cd ~/Documents/Selenium/jpetstore-*.html .
$ ls
jpetstore-cart.html     jpetstore-order.html     jpetstore-catalog.html
jpetstore-register.html
```

Also suppose that we want to deploy these scripts onto the Selenium Core server. To do this, you first need to create a directory where the test scripts will be stored. This can be anywhere, as long as it is within the Selenium Core web context. Create a directory called `jpetstore-tests` in the `webapps/selenium-core` directory, and place your test scripts there. In a Unix environment, for example, this process might look something like this:

```
$ mkdir $TOMCAT_BASE/webapps/selenium-core/jpetstore-tests
$ cd $TOMCAT_BASE/webapps/selenium-core/jpetstore-tests
$ cp ~/Documents/Selenium/jpetstore-*.html .
$ ls
```

```
jpetstore-cart.html     jpetstore-order.html     jpetstore-catalog.html
jpetstore-register.html
```

Next, we need a Selenium Test Suite. Selenium Core is designed to help you centralise your functional testing in one place, to do this, it organizes Selenium test scripts into test suites, defined in simple HTML files. A Selenium Test Suite is simply a single-column table, where each row in the table contains a link to a different test script. A typical test suite might look like this:

```
<html>
<head>
<meta content="text/html; charset=ISO-8859-1" http-equiv="content-type">
<title>JPetStore Test Suite</title>
</head>
<body>
    <table id="suiteTable" cellpadding="1" cellspacing="1" border="1">
        <tbody>
            <tr><td><b>Test Suite </b> </td> </tr>
            <tr><td><a href="jpetstore-cart.html">Shopping Cart</a></td></tr>
            <tr><td><a href="jpetstore-catalog.html">Catalog</a></td></tr>
            <tr><td><a href="jpetstore-order.html">Orders</a></td></tr>
            <tr><td><a href="jpetstore-register.html">User Registration</a></td></tr>
        </tbody>
    </table>
</body>
```

Save this file under the name of TestSuite.html, in the same directory as your test scripts.

Now we can load up this test suite into Selenium Core and try it out. Open a browser to the Selenium Core web application and click on the "Selenium Test Runner" link. This will open the Selenium Test Runner home page, where you will have to provide a test suite file path. This can be a relative path or an absolute path, within the selenium-core web context. To use the test suite file created previously, for example, enter "../jpetstore-tests/TestSuite.html" and click on Go. Alternatively, you can use the *test* parameter in the URL to directly specify your test script, as shown here (in this example, "taronga" is the hostname of the test server):

```
http://taronga:8080/selenium-core/core/TestRunner.html?test=../jpetstore-tests/
TestSuite.html
```

In both cases, Selenium will open your main workspace window, shown in Figure 20-12. From here, you can run any or all of your test scripts on the remote server. Clicking on the first of the green buttons in the "Execute Tests" zone will run through all of your test scripts, keeping track of how many test scripts, and how many commands have been executed, as well as any failures. As the test scripts are executed, the web site is displayed in the panel at the bottom of the screen, letting you visually keep track of what is happening.The second button does the same, but only for the currently displayed test script.

This can be a useful tool for testers to run automatic smoke or regression tests on a new release of the application.

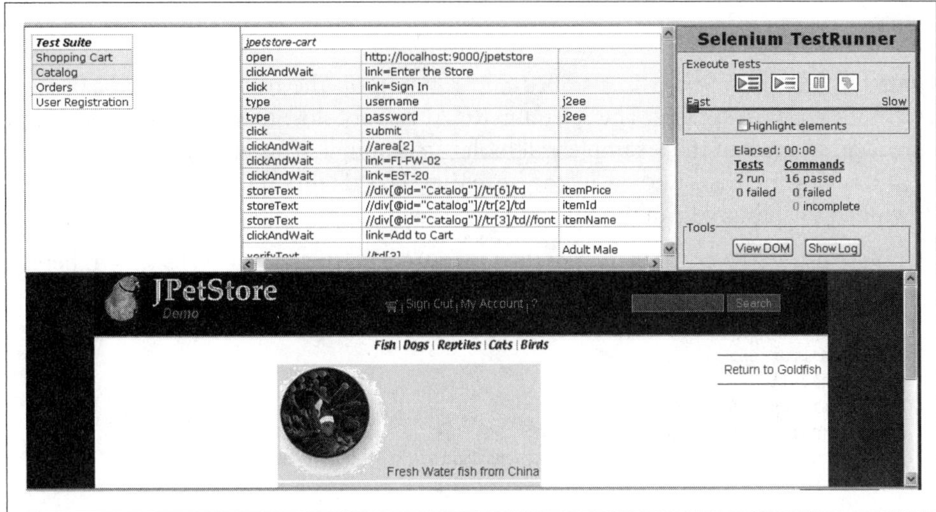

Figure 20-12. Loading a Test Suite

Writing JUnit Tests with Selenium

Although the Selenium IDE is convenient, many developers prefer to write integration tests directly in Java. With Selenium, it is quite easy to do this. Selenium Remote Control (or RC) allows you to write integration tests to run against a Selenium server. Selenium RC provides APIs for several programming languages, including Java, C#, Python, and Ruby. These APIs are designed to call a remote application that you install on your test server. This application, called the Selenium Server, receives commands from remote test clients and executes them on the local server, in much the same way Selenium IDE does.

You can download the Selenium RC package, which contains the Selenium Server from the Selenium RC web site.* Extract this package at a convenient place on your test server (on my machine, it lives at `/usr/local/selenium/selenium-remote-control`). Then start up the server as shown here:

```
$ cd /usr/local/selenium/selenium-remote-control/server/
$ java -jar selenium-server.jar
20/06/2007 20:23:10 org.mortbay.http.HttpServer doStart
INFO: Version Jetty/0.9.2-SNAPSHOT
20/06/2007 20:23:10 org.mortbay.util.Container start
INFO: Started HttpContext[/selenium-server/driver,/selenium-server/driver]
20/06/2007 20:23:10 org.mortbay.util.Container start
INFO: Started HttpContext[/selenium-server,/selenium-server]
20/06/2007 20:23:10 org.mortbay.util.Container start
INFO: Started HttpContext[/,/]
20/06/2007 20:23:10 org.mortbay.http.SocketListener start
INFO: Started SocketListener on 0.0.0.0:4444
```

* *http://www.openqa.org/selenium-rc/*

```
20/06/2007 20:23:10 org.mortbay.util.Container start
INFO: Started org.mortbay.jetty.Server@1632c2d
```

Once the Selenium Server is installed and running on the test server, you can start writing Selenium test cases. The Selenium RC API is very close to the Selenese command language, so most of this example will look very familiar. You will need the Selenium RC library, which is bundled in the `selenium-jar-client-driver.jar` file. You can download this library from the Selenium web site.*

If you are using Maven, you can use the OpenQA Maven repository, as shown here:

```
<project...>
  ...
  <repositories>
    <repository>
      <id>OpenQA</id>
      <name>OpenQA repository</name>
      <url>http://archiva.openqa.org/repository/releases</url>
    </repository>
    ...
  </repositories>
  ...
</project>
```

You also need to add some dependencies to your project:

```
<project...>
  ...
  <dependencies>
  ...
    <dependency>
      <dependency>
            <groupId>org.openqa.selenium.client-drivers</groupId>
            <artifactId>selenium-java-client-driver</artifactId>
            <version>1.0-beta-1</version>
       </dependency>
       <dependency>
            <groupId>org.openqa.selenium.server</groupId>
            <artifactId>selenium-server</artifactId>
            <version>1.0-beta-1</version>
        </dependency>
    ...
  </dependencies>
  ...
</project>
```

The Selenium RC API is easy to understand and to use, as the methods are very close to the Selenium commands we saw earlier. A good way to start a test case is to extend the `SeleneseTestCase` class. This is not obligatory, but it provides some basic housekeeping tasks and useful functions that you would otherwise have to write yourself.

* *http://www.openqa.org/selenium-rc/download.action*

This class also provides your test cases with a member variable called *selenium*. You use this variable to invoke the Selenium commands.

The first thing you need to do is to correctly initialise your test environment. You can do this in one of two ways. Providing the URL of your test server and, if necessary, the target browser, as shown below, is the simplest way to invoke the `SeleneseTestCase` `setup()` method:

```
public void setUp() throws Exception {
    super.setUp("http://taronga:8080", "*firefox");
}
```

Selenium supports a large number of browsers: Firefox, Internet Explorer, Opera, Konqueror, Safari, and so on. On Linux machines, you need to ensure that the corresponding executable (e.g., "firefox-bin" for Firefox) is on the system classpath, and that the application libraries are on the LD_LIBRARY_PATH. On Windows machines, standard browser installations seem to work well enough.

This will configure and start up the Selenium RC client for the specified address. The limitation of this approach is that it assumes you are running the tests directly on the test machine (which may be the case, say, for Continuous Integration testing), or that you are running the Selenium Server and web site to be tested locally (which is more typical if you are running integration or UI tests on your development machine). However, if you want to be able to run the tests on a separate test server from, say, a development machine, you need to create and start your own Selenium client object, as shown here:

```
public void setUp() throws Exception {
    selenium = new DefaultSelenium("taronga",
                                   SeleniumServer.getDefaultPort(),
                                   "*firefox",
                                   "http://taronga:8080");
    selenium.start();
}
```

Once you have set up the client object, things are fairly straightforward. Most of the commands are direct transcriptions of their Selenese equivalents:

```
selenium.open("/jpetstore");
...
selenium.click("link=Continue");
...
selenium.select("order.cardType", "label=MasterCard");
```

Commands like "clickAndWait" need to be expanded into the base command (e.g., "click()") and a "waitForPageToLoad()"), as shown here:

```
selenium.click("link=Enter the Store");
selenium.waitForPageToLoad("30000");
```

Using methods such as `getText()`, `getValue()`, `getSelectedValue()`, and so on, you can store variables:

```
String itemPrice = selenium.getText("//div[@id=\"Catalog\"]//tr[6]/td");
String creditCard = selenium.getValue("order.creditCard")
String cardType = selenium.getSelectedValue("order.cardType")
```

For your assertions, you can use both the ordinary JUnit *assert* instructions (`assertEquals()`...), as well as the special Selenese *verify* commands (`verifyEquals()`,...). The *verify* commands are implemented in the `SeleneseTestCase` class:

```
verifyEquals("999 9999 9999 9999", selenium.getValue("order.creditCard"));
assertEquals("MasterCard", selenium.getSelectedValue("order.cardType"));
```

The complete test class is listed here:

```
public class SeleniumTest extends SeleneseTestCase
{

      public SeleniumTest() {
        super();
    }

    public void setUp() throws Exception {
        super.setUp("http://taronga:8080", "*firefox");
    }

    public void tearDown() throws Exception {
        super.tearDown();
    }

    public void testSeleniumCart() throws Exception {
        selenium.open("/jpetstore");
        selenium.click("link=Enter the Store");
        selenium.waitForPageToLoad("30000");
        selenium.click("link=Sign In");
        selenium.waitForPageToLoad("30000");
        selenium.type("username", "j2ee");
        selenium.type("password", "j2ee");
        selenium.click("submit");
        selenium.waitForPageToLoad("30000");
        selenium.click("//area[2]");
        selenium.waitForPageToLoad("30000");
        selenium.click("link=FI-FW-02");
        selenium.waitForPageToLoad("30000");
        selenium.click("link=EST-20");
        selenium.waitForPageToLoad("30000");
        String itemPrice = selenium.getText("//div[@id=\"Catalog\"]//tr[6]/td");
        String itemId = selenium.getText("//div[@id=\"Catalog\"]//tr[2]/td");
        String itemName = selenium.getText("//div[@id=\"Catalog\"]//tr[3]/td//font");
        selenium.click("link=Add to Cart");
        selenium.waitForPageToLoad("30000");
        verifyEquals("Adult Male Goldfish", selenium.getText("//td[3]"));
        verifyEquals("$5.50", selenium.getText("//td[6]"));
        selenium.click("link=Proceed to Checkout");
        selenium.waitForPageToLoad("30000");
        selenium.click("link=Continue");
```

```
        selenium.waitForPageToLoad("30000");
        verifyEquals("999 9999 9999 9999", selenium.getValue("order.creditCard"));
        selenium.select("order.cardType", "label=MasterCard");
        assertEquals("MasterCard", selenium.getSelectedValue("order.cardType"));
        assertEquals("1", selenium.getSelectedIndex("order.cardType"));
        assertTrue(selenium.isVisible("order.cardType"));
        assertTrue(selenium.isEditable("order.cardType"));
        selenium.click("link=Sign Out");
    }
}
```

Another way to get a head start by first creating your script using the Selenium IDE, and then exporting it into a Java file. To do this, select "File→Export Test As...Java - Selenium RC" (see Figure 20-13).

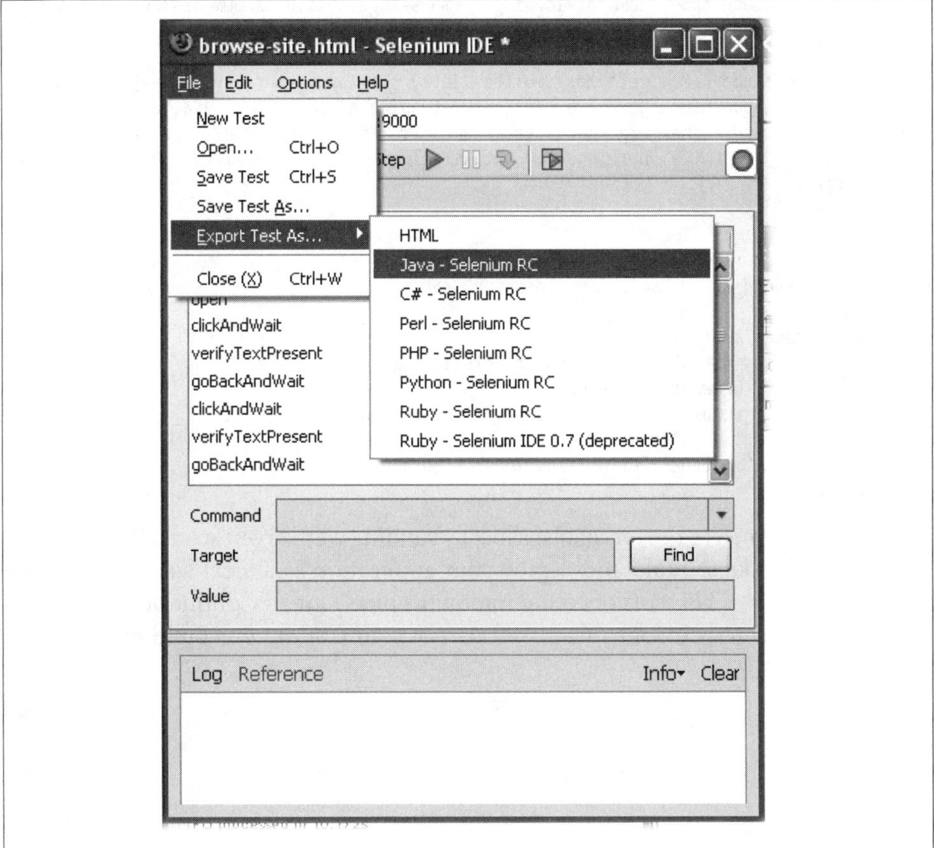

Figure 20-13. Exporting a test script as Java unit tests

Once you have Selenium tests written in the form of Java unit tests, it is fairly easy to integrate them into the build lifecycle at an appropriate place.

Using Selenium with Ant

Ideally, Selenium tests should be closely integrated with the normal build environment. If you are using Ant, Selenium comes bundled with the *<selenese>* Ant task, a convenient tool that allows you to run Selenium test suites from within Ant. Here is an extract from an Ant build file showing how to run a Selenium test suite using the *<selenese>* Ant task. The task starts up its own Selenium Server instance and then runs the test scripts through this instance against a remote test server. The test results are generated in the form of an HTML report, like the one illustrated in Figure 20-14.

```
    <path id="selenium.classpath">
      <fileset dir="${maven.repo.local}">
          <include name="org/openqa/selenium/server/selenium-server/1.0-beta-1/selenium-server-
                        1.0-beta-1.jar"/>
          <include name="commons-logging/commons-logging/1.0.4/commons-logging-1.0.4.jar"/>
          <include name="org/openqa/selenium/core/selenium-core/1.0-beta-1/selenium-core-1.0-
                        beta-1.jar"/>
          <include name="jetty/org.mortbay.jetty/5.1.10/org.mortbay.jetty-5.1.10.jar"/>
          <include name="javax/servlet/servlet-api/2.4/servlet-api-2.4.jar"/>
          <include name="org/openqa/selenium/server/selenium-server-coreless/selenium-server-
                        coreless-1.0-beta-1/selenium-server-coreless-1.0-beta-1.jar"/>
      </fileset>
  </path>
  ...
  <taskdef resource="selenium-ant.properties">
      <classpath refid="selenium.classpath" />
  </taskdef>
  <target name="test-web">
      <selenese suite="src/test/resources/selenium/TestSuite.html"
                browser="*firefox"
                results="target/test-reports/selenium-results.html"
                timeoutInSeconds="500"
                startURL="http://localhost:8080/jpetstore/" />
  </target>
```

This task is designed to be run against a locally running web server, so ideally you would probably add tasks to build and deploy your application to a local web server before running these tests. This sort of configuration fits nicely into a Continuous Integration environment—simply invoke this task at part of your Continuous Build process.

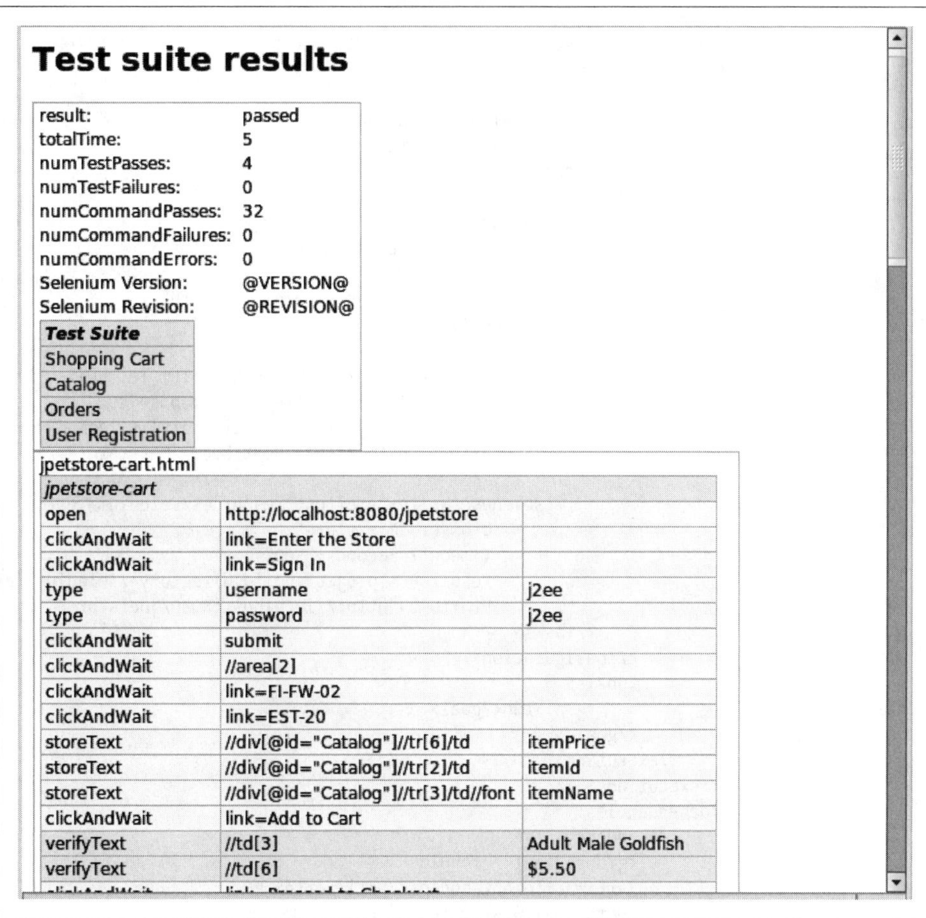

Test suite results

result:	passed
totalTime:	5
numTestPasses:	4
numTestFailures:	0
numCommandPasses:	32
numCommandFailures:	0
numCommandErrors:	0
Selenium Version:	@VERSION@
Selenium Revision:	@REVISION@

Test Suite
Shopping Cart
Catalog
Orders
User Registration

jpetstore-cart.html

jpetstore-cart		
open	http://localhost:8080/jpetstore	
clickAndWait	link=Enter the Store	
clickAndWait	link=Sign In	
type	username	j2ee
type	password	j2ee
clickAndWait	submit	
clickAndWait	//area[2]	
clickAndWait	link=FI-FW-02	
clickAndWait	link=EST-20	
storeText	//div[@id="Catalog"]//tr[6]/td	itemPrice
storeText	//div[@id="Catalog"]//tr[2]/td	itemId
storeText	//div[@id="Catalog"]//tr[3]/td//font	itemName
clickAndWait	link=Add to Cart	
verifyText	//td[3]	Adult Male Goldfish
verifyText	//td[6]	$5.50

Figure 20-14. The report generated by the <selenese> Ant task

Using Selenium with Maven

Integrating Selenium with Maven can be more or less complicated, depending on your situation. If you are only using HTML Selenium test scripts, one way to run your Selenium tests from Maven is simply to use the *<selenese>* Ant task we looked at in the previous section. As before, these tests are designed to run against an external test server. You can do this as follows:

```
<project...>
    ...
    <build>
        <plugins>
            ...
```

```
            <plugin>
                <artifactId>maven-antrun-plugin</artifactId>
                <executions>
                    <execution>
                        <id>launch-selenium</id>
                        <phase>integration-test</phase>
                        <configuration>
                            <tasks>
                                <taskdef
                                    resource="selenium-ant.properties">
                                    <classpath
                                        refid="maven.plugin.classpath" />
                                </taskdef>
                                <selenese
                                    suite="src/test/resources/selenium/TestSuite.html"
                                    browser="*firefox" timeoutInSeconds="500"
                                    results="${project.build.directory}/selenium-firefoxresults.ht
                                    startURL="http://localhost:8080/jpetstore/" />

                                <selenese suite="src/test/resources/selenium/TestSuite.html"
                                     browser="*iexplore"
                                     timeoutInSeconds="500"
                                     results="${project.build.directory}/selenium-iexploreresults
                                     startURL="http://localhost:8080/jpetstore/" />
                            </tasks>
                        </configuration>
                        <goals>
                            <goal>run</goal>
                        </goals>
                    </execution>
                </executions>
                <dependencies>
                    <dependency>
                        <groupId>ant</groupId>
                        <artifactId>ant-nodeps</artifactId>
                        <version>1.6.5</version>
                    </dependency>
                    <dependency>
                        <groupId>org.openqa.selenium.server</groupId>
                        <artifactId>selenium-server</artifactId>
                        <version>1.0-beta-1</version>
                    </dependency>
                </dependencies>
            </plugin>
        </plugins>
    </build>
    ...
</project>
```

In this example, we use the *<selenese>* Ant task to run the Selenium test scripts using Firefox and Internet Explorer.

The *<selenese>* task will start up an instance of the Selenium Server and run the specified Selenium test cases against this server. In the *<phase>* configuration element, we specify that these tasks are to be executed during the *integration-test* phase. To run these tests, use the *mvn integration-test goal*, as shown here:

```
$ mvn integration-test
[INFO] Scanning for projects...
...
Preparing Firefox profile...
Launching Firefox...
...*
Killing Firefox...
...
[INFO] ------------------------------------------------------------------------
[INFO] BUILD SUCCESSFUL
[INFO] ------------------------------------------------------------------------
[INFO] Total time: 1 minute
[INFO] Finished at: Thu Jun 21 16:05:45 NZST 2007
[INFO] Final Memory: 6M/13M
[INFO] ------------------------------------------------------------------------
```

Alternatively, you can use a more recent product, the *selenium-maven-plugin*, hosted at CodeHaus.* This plug-in allows you to execute Selenese test scripts directly from within Maven, without having to invoke the *<selenese>* Ant task. The configuration parameters are identical to those of the *<selenese>* Ant task. In the following example, we run the Selenium test suite using Firefox and Internet Explorer during the *integration-test* phase:

```
<project...>
  <build>
    ...
    <plugins>
      <plugin>
        <groupId>org.codehaus.mojo</groupId>
        <artifactId>selenium-maven-plugin</artifactId>
        <executions>
            <execution>
                <id>firefox-testscripts</id>
                <phase>integration-test</phase>
                <goals>
                    <goal>selenese</goal>
                </goals>
                <configuration>
                    <browser>*firefox</browser>
                    <startURL>http://localhost:8080</startURL>
                    <suite>src/test/resources/selenium/TestSuite.html</suite>
                    <results>${project.build.directory}/selenium-firefox-results.html
                    </results>
                </configuration>
            </execution>
            <execution>
                <id>iexplorer-testscripts</id>
                <phase>integration-test</phase>
```

* *http://mojo.codehaus.org/selenium-maven-plugin*

```
                <goals>
                    <goal>selenese</goal>
                </goals>
                <configuration>
                    <browser>*iexplorer</browser>
                    <startURL>http://localhost:8080</startURL>
                    <suite>src/test/resources/selenium/TestSuite.html</suite>
                    <results>${project.build.directory}/selenium-iexplorer-results.html
                    </results>
                </configuration>
            </execution>
        </executions>
      </plugin>
    </plugins>
  </build>
</project>
```

Both of these approaches work fine for HTML Selenium scripts, but, as we have seen, you can also write Selenium test cases in Java. Integrating these tests into the Maven build process requires a little more work. Unlike in the previous example, we need to start the Selenium Server ourselves. For this, we are going to use the *selenium-maven-plugin* again, this time to start and stop a Selenium Server process in the background just before the *integration-test* phase starts. This is quite easy to configure. Simply add the following plug-in configuration to your POM file:

```
<project...>
  <build>
    ...
    <plugins>
      <plugin>
        <groupId>org.codehaus.mojo</groupId>
        <artifactId>selenium-maven-plugin</artifactId>
        <executions>
            <execution>
                <phase>pre-integration-test</phase>
                <goals>
                    <goal>start-server</goal>
                </goals>
                <configuration>
                    <background>true</background>
                </configuration>
            </execution>
        </executions>
      </plugin>
    ...
    </plugins>
  </build>
</project>
```

Now, if you run your integration tests, a local Selenium Server instance will start automatically:

```
$ mvn integration-test
[INFO] Scanning for projects...
```

```
[INFO] ------------------------------------------------------------------------
[INFO] Building selenium-test-demo
[INFO]    task-segment: [integration-test]
[INFO] ------------------------------------------------------------------------
...
[INFO] [selenium:start-server {execution: default}]
[INFO] Starting Selenium server...
[INFO] User extensions: P:\projects\java-power-tools\src\sample-code\selenium
\selenium-test-demo\target\selenium\user-extensions.js
[INFO] 15:02:46,407 INFO  [org.mortbay.http.HttpServer] Version Jetty/0.8.1
[INFO] 15:02:46,423 INFO  [org.mortbay.util.Container] Started HttpContext
[/selenium-server/driver,/selenium-server/driver]
[INFO] 15:02:46,423 INFO  [org.mortbay.util.Container] Started HttpContext
[/selenium-server,/selenium-server]
[INFO] 15:02:46,423 INFO  [org.mortbay.util.Container] Started HttpContext[/,/]
[INFO] 15:02:46,438 INFO  [org.mortbay.http.SocketListener] Started SocketListener
on 0.0.0.0:4444
[INFO] 15:02:46,438 INFO  [org.mortbay.util.Container] Started org.mortbay.
jetty.Server@106082
[INFO] 15:02:46,657 INFO  [org.mortbay.util.Credential] Checking Resource aliases
[INFO] Selenium server started
...
```

So far so good.

Next, let's look into running some Selenium test cases written in Java. We need to ensure that these Selenium test cases will only be executed during the integration tests. To do this, we override the default configuration of the surefire plug-in, excluding the Selenium tests by default, but then including them during the *integration-test* phase. First of all, you need to define a convention identifying your Selenium unit tests. Here, they are all in a package called "selenium":

```
<plugin>
    <artifactId>maven-surefire-plugin</artifactId>
   <!-- Exclude Selenium tests from the usual unit tests -->
    <configuration>
        <excludes>
            <exclude>**/selenium/*Test.java</exclude>
        </excludes>
    </configuration>
<plugin>
```

Next, you need to add an *<execution>* element. This inverses the previous exclusion definition for this *integration-test* phase, ensuring that only the Selenium test cases will be executed during this phase:

```
<plugin>
    <artifactId>maven-surefire-plugin</artifactId>
    ...
    <executions>
        <execution>
            <id>surefire-integration-test</id>
            <phase>integration-test</phase>
            <goals>
                <goal>test</goal>
```

```
                    </goals>
                    <configuration>
                        <excludes>
                            <exclude>none</exclude>
                        </excludes>
                        <includes>
                            <include>**/selenium/*Test.java</include>
                        </includes>
                    </configuration>
                </execution>
            </executions>
        </plugin>
```

The full configuration is shown here:

```
<project...>
  <build>
    ...
      <plugin>
          <artifactId>maven-surefire-plugin</artifactId>
         <!-- Exclude Selenium tests from the usual unit tests -->
          <configuration>
              <excludes>
                  <exclude>**/selenium/*Test.java</exclude>
              </excludes>
          </configuration>

          <!-- Include Selenium tests during integration tests-->
          <executions>
              <execution>
                  <id>surefire-integration-test</id>
                  <phase>integration-test</phase>
                  <goals>
                      <goal>test</goal>
                  </goals>
                  <configuration>
                      <excludes>
                          <exclude>none</exclude>
                      </excludes>
                      <includes>
                          <include>**/selenium/*Test.java</include>
                      </includes>
                  </configuration>
              </execution>
          </executions>
      </plugin>
      ...
    </plugins>
  </build>
</project>
```

Note that if you are executing both Selenium HTML test scripts and Selenium integration tests written in Java, you will need a little extra configuration. In fact, each *<execution>* element uses its own Selenium Server instance, and therefore needs to use a separate port. You can do this by setting the *<port>* configuration parameter to some value other than the default value of 4444, as shown here:

```
<execution>
    <id>firefox-testscripts</id>
    <phase>integration-test</phase>
    <goals>
        <goal>selenese</goal>
    </goals>
    <configuration>
        <browser>*firefox</browser>
        <startURL>http://localhost:8080</startURL>
        <suite>src/test/resources/selenium/TestSuite.html</suite>
        <results>${project.build.directory}/selenium-firefox-results.html
        </results>
        <port>5555</port>
    </configuration>
</execution>
```

This way, your HTML and Java tests can run without getting in each other's way.

20.2 Testing Swing GUIs with FEST

*Contributed by: Alex Ruiz**

Introduction

Graphical User Interfaces (GUIs) have become a valuable way of interacting with computer programs. Testing GUIs is vital because it can improve the safety and fitness of the entire system. Any GUI, even the simplest one, is likely to enclose some level of complexity. Complexity in software needs to be tested because untested code is a potential source of bugs.

GUI testing is also important during application maintenance. During this stage, code might be refactored repeatedly to improve its design, and this code often includes great portions of the user interface. Having a solid test suite that covers the GUI code can give us assurance that we are not unintentionally introducing bugs.

This section introduces FEST, an open source library that facilitates functional GUI testing, and some practices that can simplify the creation and maintenance of thorough tests for Java Swing applications.

Testing GUIs Is Hard

Although essential, GUI testing can be difficult. Conventional unit testing, such as testing a class in isolation, normally is not appropriate for GUI testing: A GUI "unit"

* This section is based on material originally published in "Test-Driven GUI Development with TestNG and Abbot" by Alex Ruiz and Yvonne Wang Price, IEEE Software May/June 2007, and "Test-driven GUI development with FEST" by Alex Ruiz, JavaWorld.com, 07/17/07.

can be made up of more than one component, each of them enclosing more than one class. In many cases, functional testing is a more effective way to test GUIs.

The following factors are necessary to creating thorough functional GUI tests:

- Being able to simulate user events
- Having a reliable mechanism for finding GUI components
- Being able to tolerate changes in a component's position and/or layout

Introducing FEST

FEST (Fixtures for Easy Software Testing) is an open source library, licensed under Apache 2.0, which makes it easy to create and maintain large functional GUI tests. Although several open source projects have been devised for testing GUIs, FEST is distinguished by the following features:

- An easy-to-use Java API that exploits the concept of fluent interfaces to simplify coding.
- Assertion methods that detail the state of GUI components.
- Support for both JUnit 4 and TestNG.
- Screen shots of failing tests, which can be embedded in a HTML test report when using JUnit or TestNG. This configurable feature is useful when verifying that a test or group of tests failed because of an environment condition and not a programming error.
- A Groovy-based domain-specific language that simplifies GUI testing even further. (This feature is still under development and is considered experimental.)

Although FEST does provide some unique features, it does not reinvent the wheel. Instead of creating yet another mechanism for component lookup and even-user simulation, FEST builds on top of Abbot, a mature, open source project for GUI testing (see Figure 20-15). Many GUI testing libraries, including FEST and Abbot, depend on the AWT Robot to generate native input events as though they were generated by a user, instead of just sending events to the AWT event queue.

Tests created with FEST are strong because they are not affected by changes in layout or component size. In addition, FEST provides features not available in other GUI testing libraries—its simple but powerful API being the most important one. FEST can be downloaded at *http://code.google.com/p/fest*.

Testing GUIs with FEST

In the following sections, you will get to know FEST by walking through a testing example. Figure 20-16 is a sketch of the example GUI to be tested. It represents a login

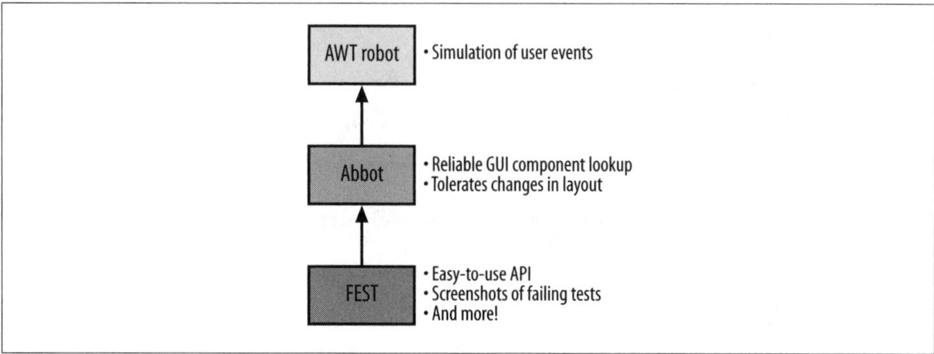

Figure 20-15. FEST's building blocks

dialog where the user enters her username, password, and domain name to log in to the system.

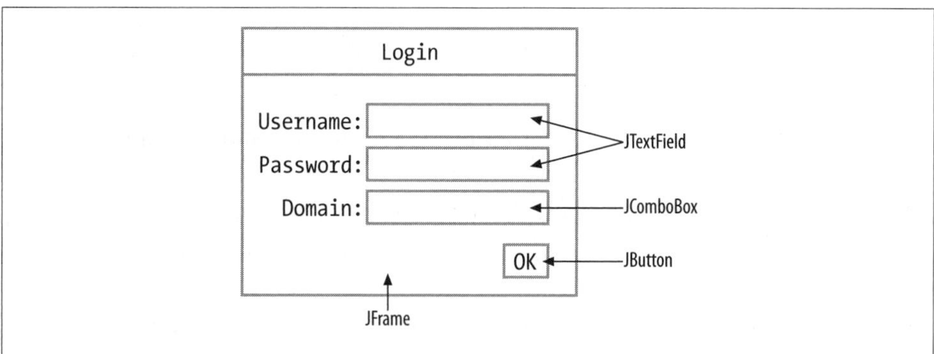

Figure 20-16. A Swing-based login GUI

The expected behavior of the dialog box is as follows:

- The user enters her username and password, both required.
- The user selects from the drop-down list the domain she wishes to connect to.
- If any field is left blank, a pop-up dialog box notifies the user that the missing information is required.

In Example 20-1, we are not going to cover implementation details of our login window. Nowadays, we can create this type of GUI in a few minutes with the help of a high-quality GUI builder (commercial or free). Instead, we are going to jump straight to our first test using TestNG:

Example 20-1. A FEST test that verifies an error message

```
// Omitted imports and package declaration

public class LoginWindowTest {
```

```
2
3     private FrameFixture login;
4
5     @BeforeMethod public void setUp() {
6       login = new FrameFixture(new LoginWindow());
7       login.show();
8     }
9
10    @Test public void shouldShowErrorIfUsernameIsMissing() {
11      login.textBox("username").deleteText();
12      login.textBox("password").enterText("secret");
13      login.comboBox("domain").selectItem("USERS");
14      login.button("ok").click();
15      login.optionPane().requireErrorMessage()
                          .requireMessage("Please enter your username");
16    }
17
18    @AfterMethod public void tearDown() {
19      login.cleanUp();
20    }
```

The test uses FEST to invoke the GUI being tested, simulate user events, and verify that the GUI works as expected. More specifically, the test does the following:

- Uses a `org.fest.swing.fixture.FrameFixture` to manage and launch the window to test (lines 6 and 7)
- Ensures that the text field where the user enters his username is empty (Line 11)
- Simulates a user entering the password "secret" in the appropriate text field (Line 12)
- Simulates a user selecting a domain from the drop-down list (Line 13)
- Simulates a user clicking the "OK" button
- Verifies that a pop-up window (a `JOptionPane`) is displayed showing an error message with the text "Please enter your username" (Line 15)

FEST performs *component lookup* using the component's unique name. In Example 20-2, we need to identify the components in the logging window with the same names that we use in the test:

Example 20-2. Specifying unique names for GUI components to guarantee reliable component lookup

```
// Omitted additional code generated by GUI builder.

  usernameField.setName("username");
  passwordField.setName("password");
  domainComboBox.setName("domain");
  okButton.setName("ok");
```

We perform component lookup using a unique name for these reasons:

- Finding GUI components by type is trivial as long as the GUI being tested has only one component of that type. If it has more than one component of the specified type, we must do some extra work to identify the one we are looking for.
- We cannot rely on a component's displayed text as a way to identify it. Displayed text tends to change, especially if the application supports multiple languages.
- Using a unique name for GUI components guarantees that we can always find them, regardless of any change in the GUI, as long as they haven't been removed from the GUI.

It is also important to note that is necessary to release resources used by FEST (such as the keyboard, mouse, and opened windows) following the execution of each test (as shown in Line 19). You can release used resources by calling the method `cleanUp` in `org.fest.swing.fixture.FrameFixture`, `org.fest.swing.fixture.DialogFixture`, or `org.fest.swing.RobotFixture`.

Following Windows with FEST

So far, we have created only one test. We're not quite finished with the login window, however. The requirements specify that we still need to implement the following behavior:

- An error message to be displayed if the user does not enter her password
- An error message to be displayed if the user does not choose the domain she wishes to connect to
- A successful login

The first two test cases are simple and involve testing a single window, similar to the test we just created. Testing a successful login is the "tricky" part. Authentication and authorization can take some time (depending on various factors such as network traffic) and we need to wait for the main window to appear to continue testing our application. With FEST it is pretty easy to test this case (see Example 20-3):

Example 20-3. Waiting for the main window to be displayed after a successful login

```
// correct user credentials
login.textBox("username").enterText("yvonne");
login.textBox("password").enterText("welcome1");
login.comboBox("domain").selectItem("USERS");
login.button("ok").click();

// we need to wait till login process is done
// and the main window is shown.
FrameFixture main = findFrame("main").using(login.robot);

// we can continue testing the main window.
```

The `findFrame` method (statically imported from `org.fest.swing.fixture.util.WindowFinder`) can look up a Frame (having "main" as its name in our example) with a default timeout of five seconds. In our case, if in five seconds the main window is not found, the test will fail. We can also specify a custom value for the timeout. For example, we can set the timeout to 10 seconds in 2 different ways, as shown in Example 20-4.

Example 20-4. Specifying a custom timeout for a window lookup

```
FrameFixture main = findFrame("main").withTimeout(10000)
                                     .using(login.robot);
// or
FrameFixture main = findFrame("main").withTimeout(10, SECONDS)
                                     .using(login.robot);
```

This feature is not limited to frame lookups by name. We can also use `WindowFinder` to look up frames and dialogs by name or by type.

Verifying Test Failures

On some occasions, a functional GUI test will run perfectly from within the IDE but will break when executed in a batch with other tests (such as when you are using Ant). This is because functional GUI tests are vulnerable to certain environment-related events, and FEST is no exception. For instance, it occasionally happens that antivirus software runs a scheduled scan while a GUI is under test. If the antivirus software pops up a dialog in front of the GUI, the FEST robot will not be able to access the GUI and will time out eventually, so the test will fail. In this case, the failure is not related to a programming error; it is just a case of bad timing. Fortunately, in such cases you can verify the cause of failure easily by rerunning your test suite.

As previously mentioned, one of the features of FEST is its ability to embed a screen shot of a failed test in its HTML test report. You then can use this screen shot to verify the cause of a failed test and discover whether it is program related or environmental. Configuring FEST to take screen shots of failed tests is pretty simple. The first step is to "mark" a GUI test with the annotation `org.fest.swing.GUITest`. We can place this annotation at either the class or method level.

The following code listing in Example 20-5 shows a class "marked" as a GUI test. Every test method in this class will be considered a GUI test, even the ones in subclasses.

Example 20-5. A class marked as a GUI test

```
import org.fest.swing.GUITest;
// rest of imports

@GUITest public class LoginWindowTest {

  @Test public void shouldShowErrorIfUsernameIsMissing() {
    // implementation of the test
  }
}
```

If you need more control, you can annotate only the methods that should be considered GUI tests. This is shown in the code listing in Example 20-6.

Example 20-6. A method marked as a GUI test

```
import org.fest.swing.GUITest;
// rest of imports

public class LoginWindowTest {

  @GUITest @Test public void shouldShowErrorIfUsernameIsMissing() {
    // implementation of the test
  }

  @Test public void someNonGUITest() {
    // implementation of the test
  }
}
```

If you override a method marked as a GUI test, the overriding method also will be considered a GUI test, even if it does not contain the `org.fest.swing.GUITest` annotation.

The second and final step is to alert your testing framework to notify FEST when a GUI test has failed. This way, FEST can take a screen shot of the failed test and embed it in the test report. It is quite easy to configure TestNG, thanks to its flexible architecture that supports extensions. The only change necessary is the declaration of the TestNG listener `org.fest.swing.testng.ScreenshotOnFailureListener`, which is provided by FEST. Example 20-7 shows configuration using TestNG and Ant.

Example 20-7. Configuring TestNG to notify FEST if a test fails

```
<target name="test" depends="compile">
  <testng listeners="org.fest.swing.testng.ScreenshotOnFailureListener"
      outputDir="${target.test.results.dir}">
    <classfileset dir="${target.test.classes.dir}"
      includes="**/*Test.class" />
    <classpath location="${target.test.classes.dir}" />
    <classpath location="${target.classes.dir}" />
    <classpath refid="test.classpath" />
  </testng>
</target>
```

Figure 20-17 shows an embedded screen shot of a TestNG test failure.

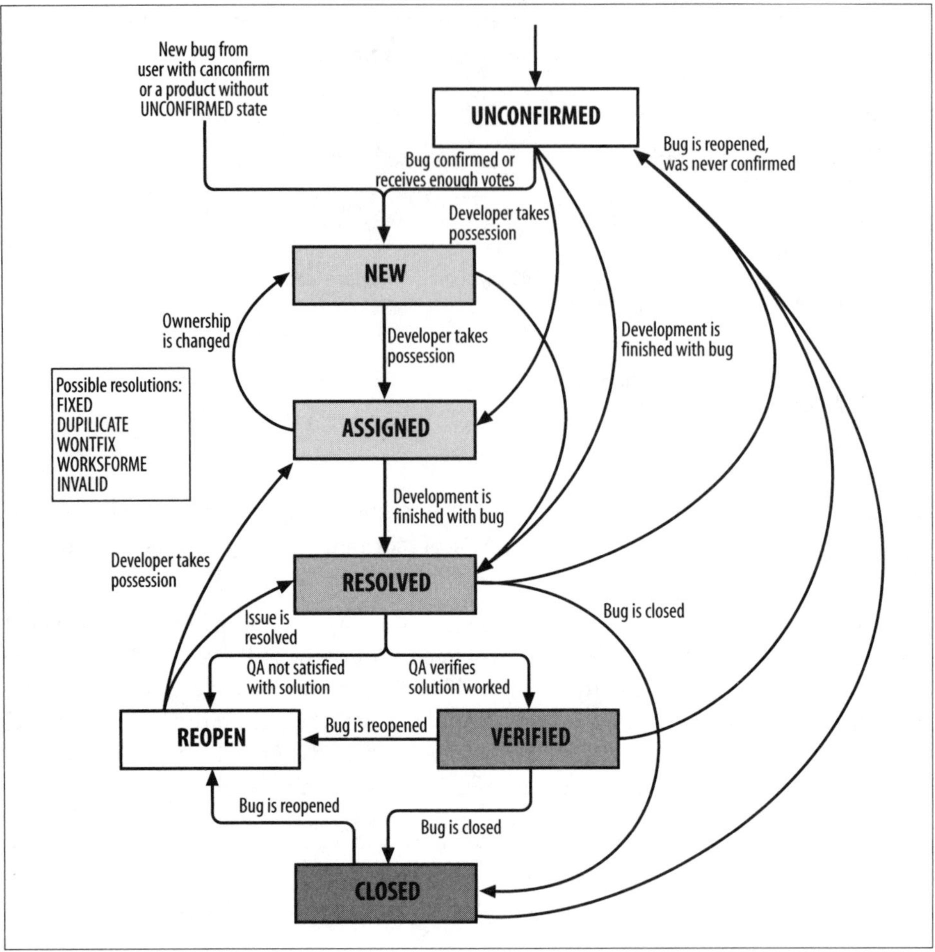

Figure 20-17. Embedded screen shot of a TestNG test failure

Configuring JUnit requires a little more work than TestNG. After marking tests with the `GUITest` annotation, we need to:

1. Add a definition of the Ant task `festreport`.
2. Use the formatter `org.fest.swing.junit.ScreenshotOnFailureResultFormatter` inside the Junit Ant task.
3. Use the Ant task `festreport` instead of `junitreport`, and specify in its classpath where the FEST jars file are.

It may look like a lot of work. The code listing in Example 20-8 shows that using FEST with Ant's JUnit task requires only a couple of extra lines.

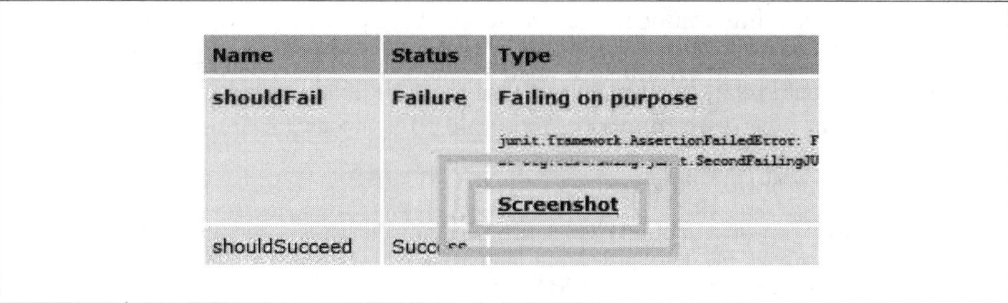

Figure 20-18. Embedded screen shot of a JUnit test failure

Example 20-8. Configuring JUnit to notify FEST if a test fails

```
<target name="test" depends="compile">
  <taskdef resource="festjunittasks" classpathref="lib.classpath" />
  <junit forkmode="perBatch" printsummary="yes">
    <classpath refid="lib.classpath" />
    <classpath location="${target.test.classes.dir}" />
    <classpath location="${target.classes.dir}" />
    <formatter extension=".xml"
        classname="org.fest.swing.junit.ScreenshotOnFailureResultFormatter" />
    <batchtest fork="yes" todir="${target.junit.results.dir}">
      <fileset dir="${target.test.classes.dir}" includes="**/*Test*.class" />
    </batchtest>
  </junit>
  <festreport todir="${target.junit.report.dir}">
    <classpath refid="lib.classpath" />
    <fileset dir="${target.junit.results.dir}">
      <include name="TEST-*.xml" />
    </fileset>
    <report format="frames" todir="${target.junit.report.dir}/html" />
  </festreport>
</target>
```

Figure 20-18 shows an embedded screen shot of a JUnit test failure.

Every testing methodology has its weakness and functional testing, with its vulnerability to environmental factors, is no exception. Although FEST doesn't overcome this weakness completely, it does let you account for it. Configuring FEST for failure notification makes it easy to determine whether a test has failed because of an environmental factor or because of a programming error.

Testing Legacy Applications

At this point, we have seen that FEST looks up GUI components by their name. We only need to be extra careful and provide a unique name to the components of the GUI we are creating. It is very likely that we already have a Swing application that we want to test, and unfortunately, its GUI components do not have any names at all. Instead of forcing us to go back and provide unique names to those components, FEST allows us to specify custom search criteria when them looking up.

Because we are not using unique names to identify GUI components, we need to specify a custom search criteria in a `org.fest.swing.GenericTypeMatcher` to find those components. `GenericTypeMatcher` in a abstract class that uses Java generics to specify the type of GUI component we want to match. Example 20-9 shows a matcher for a `JButton`:

Example 20-9. A matcher for a JButton

```
GenericTypeMatcher<JButton> matcher = new GenericTypeMatcher<JButton>() {
  protected boolean isMatching(JButton button) {
    return "OK".equals(button.getText);
  }
};
```

We need to implement the method `isMatching`, which provides a non `null` instance of a `JButton`. From this point, it is up to us to specify if the given component is the one we are looking for. In our example, we are looking for a `JButton` with the text "OK." If there are no components matching our search criteria, FEST will throw a `org.fest.swing.ComponentLookupException`, and our test will fail.

Tips for Writing Testable GUIs

Try the following suggestions for writing testable GUIs:

- Separate model and view, moving as much code as possible away from the GUI.
- Use a unique name for each GUI component to guarantee reliable component lookup.
- Do not test default component behavior; for example, do not test that a button reacts to a mouse click—that is the job of the Sun Microsystems Swing team!
- Concentrate on testing the expected behavior of your GUIs.

20.3 Conclusion

In spite of its importance, testing GUIs is difficult. FEST is an open source library that provides an easy-to-use API for GUI testing. FEST makes it easier to write and maintain robust GUI tests, which gives you more time to focus on what matters: specifying and verifying the behavior of your Swing GUIs.

FEST is a useful alternative to existing GUI-testing solutions. It's easy to learn and use, and it provides some unique features that can make GUI development more productive and fun.

Future improvements will cover support for third-party GUI components, such as the ones provided by SwingLabs' SwingX, and an easy-to-use Groovy and JRuby API for GUI tests.

PART VI

Quality Metrics Tools

"And I know it *seems* easy," said Piglet to himself, "but it isn't *every one* who could do it."

—"A House Is Built at Pooh Corner for Eeyore," *The House at Pooh Corner*, A. A. Milne

Despite all appearance to the contrary, writing good, reliable, flexible, maintainable, high-quality software is not an easy task. However, Java developers do not have to learn everything from scratch. Years of good programming habits have been codified in the form of coding standards and best practices.

Coding standards are a key part of many development processes, and for good reason. These standards codify (no pun intended) time-honored traditions and conventions, as well as best practices in the art of software writing. Some recommendations simply define a standard way to layout code or to name classes or variables, while others are designed to make code more reliable or better performing. However, as Andrew S. Tanenbaum, professor of Computer Science at Vrije Universiteit, Amsterdam, and author of the Minix operating system, said, "The nice thing about standards is that there are so many to choose from." Different companies, teams, and individual developers have developed different programming practices and habits over time. The problems start when developers who use different programming styles and conventions have to work together on a common code base. Indeed, many standards, such as indentation and naming conventions, are fairly arbitrary things. Should the curly brackets go directly after the instruction, as recommended by the Sun coding conventions?

```
while (i < 10) {
    i++;
}
```

Or should they be on a new line, as used by many C++ developers?

```
while (i < 10)
{
    i++;
}
```

There is no real objective reason to prefer one style over the other: the important thing is to have a well defined and accepted style within your project. Recognized coding standards help to harmonize the way a team or company works together. Once team members are familiar with an established set of coding standards, they will think less about details such as code layout and variable naming conventions and can concentrate better on the real work of coding. New project teams will lose less time at the start of a project making decisions of earth-shattering importance such as where to put the curly bracket after the if statement. The consistent use of standards also encourages a feeling of "esprit de corps" within a team or company. And code that is laid out consistently and that follows well-known conventions is easier to read, understand, and maintain. Sun has defined a set of coding conventions for the Java language that is widely accepted in the industry. Many companies and open source projects also publish their own set of coding conventions, often variations of the Sun conventions. A few typical coding standards are given here:

- Comments
  - —Write Javadoc comments for all classes, methods, and variables.
- Naming conventions
  - —Class names should be nouns, in mixed case with the first letter of each internal word capitalized (MyClass).
  - —Variable names should be nouns, in mixed case with a lowercase first letter, and with the first letter of each internal word in upper case (myVariable).
  - —Constants should be in all uppercase with words separated by underscore (MY_CONSTANT_VALUE).
- Indentation
  - —Spaces should be preferred to tabs for indenting purposes.
- Declarations
  - —One declaration per line, with comments, for example:

    ```
    int class; // The child's class, from 1 to 8
    int age;   // The child's age
    ```

    rather than:

    ```
    int class, age;
    ```
- Statements
  - —Opening braces in compound statements should be at the end of the line that begins the compound statement; the closing brace should begin a line and be indented to the beginning of the compound statement, for example:

    ```
    while (i < 10) {
        i++;
    }
    ```
- Best Practices
  - —Use the final keyword for variables and parameters that will not need to be modified.

—Don't declare variables within loops.

It is always a good idea to discuss the conventions to be applied within your company or project with all members of the development team. Each rule should be explained and justified. What is the underlying goal of the rule? Is the rule to be applied systematically, or can there be exceptions? As with many best practices, coding standards must be well understood by the whole team to be effective.

Indeed, like all technologies, software metrics can be used and abused. Coding standards and best practice rules should under no circumstances be applied blindly, nor should they be used as a way for management to evaluate team member performance. Rather, when issues are raised, they should be used as discussion topics, to point out potential coding errors or poor practices, or to tailor the rule set to correspond more closely to your team's programming style. When used well, software metrics can provide valuable feedback on the quality of the code being written, and allow the development team to learn and progress. To be successful, software metrics should be considered a team sport.

There are many static analysis tools around. In this section, we look at three of the most well-known: Checkstyle, PMD, and FindBugs.

Checkstyle is an open source tool that can help enforce coding standards and best practices, with a particular focus on coding conventions. It can be used as a standalone tool to generate reports on overall code quality, and can also be incorporated into the developer's work environment, providing real-time visual feedback about the code being written.

Static code analysis is another technique that can complement code reviews in preemptively finding potential errors or poor coding practices. It involves analyzing the structure of classes and detecting potentially dangerous patterns of code. By automatically detecting certain types of coding issues, static analysis tools can save time and energy in code reviews, and help encourage good coding practices. Although Checkstyle does cover some static code analysis features, we will also look at two other tools that are more specialized in this area: PMD and FindBugs. PMD can help to flush out a wide range of potential bugs and poor coding practice. FindBugs differs from the other two tools in concentrating exclusively on potential bugs, dangerous programming practices, and possible performance issues.

Code reviews are another highly effective way to improve code quality. Unfortunately, they are rarely practiced with any consistency. Using code analysis tools can reduce a lot of the drudgery involved with code reviews, by automatically checking coding standards and best practices. However, a human eye will always be able to see issues that a machine cannot. Another interesting tool that can help out with code reviews is Jupiter, an Eclipse plug-in that you can use to help set up an electronic code review process.

We will also look at Mylyn in this section. Although not directly related to code quality, this innovative eclipse plug-in does help users write better code by helping to manage their tasks more effectively, and to focus on the project resources relevent to the task at hand, filtering out the others.

Finally, tools such as QAlab and StatSCM keep track of various project metrics such as static code analysis results, test coverage, and the size and contents of your source code repository, and provide you with invaluable statistics about how your project evolves over time.

All these tools are highly configurable. The best coding standards and recommended practices are determined collaboratively, with active buy-in from the whole team.

CHAPTER 21

Detecting and Enforcing Coding Standards with Checkstyle

21.1 Using Checkstyle to Enforce Coding Standards

Checkstyle is an open source tool that enforces coding conventions and best practice rules for Java code. Although it was originally designed to enforce coding standards, it now lets you verify coding best practices as well, in much the same way as PMD (Chapter 22) and FindBugs (Chapter 23). It works by analyzing Java source code and reporting any breach of standards. It can be integrated into your favorite IDE via a plug-in so that developers can immediately see and correct any breaches of the official standards. It can also be used to generate project-wide reports that summarize the breaches found.

Checkstyle comes "out-of-the-box" with the standard Sun conventions, including more than 120 rules and standards, dealing with issues that range from code formatting and naming conventions to Enterprise JavaBean (EJB) best practices and code complexity metrics. Checkstyle supports standards related to the following:

- Javadoc comments
- Naming conventions
- File headers
- Import statements
- Whitespace
- Modifiers
- Blocks
- Coding problems
- Class design
- J2EE (Java 2 Platform, Enterprise Edition)
- And other miscellaneous issues

You can run Checkstyle from the command line, if you are so inclined. Download the Checkstyle distribution from the web site* and extract it in a convenient place. Then run the *checkstyle-all-4.3.jar* file as shown here:

```
$ java -jar checkstyle-all-4.3.jar -c sun_checks.xml -r src
```

This will analyze the code in the specified source directory and list any rule violations it finds. Here is an example, running the Sun Coding Standards provided with Checkstyle against one of the Java EE 5 sample applications provided by Sun:

```
$ java -jar checkstyle-all-4.3.jar -c sun_checks.xml -r javaee5/webservices/
hello-jaxws/src/
Starting audit...
/home/john/tools/checkstyle-4.3/javaee5/webservices/hello-jaxws/src/
endpoint/package.html:0:
Missing package documentation file.
/home/john/tools/checkstyle-4.3/javaee5/webservices/hello-jaxws/src/
client/package.html:0:
Missing package documentation file.
javaee5/webservices/hello-jaxws/src/endpoint/Hello.java:5:
Missing a Javadoc comment.
javaee5/webservices/hello-jaxws/src/endpoint/Hello.java:7:1:
'{' should be on the previous line.
javaee5/webservices/hello-jaxws/src/endpoint/Hello.java:8:5:
Method 'getHello' is not designed for extension - needs to
be abstract, final or empty.
javaee5/webservices/hello-jaxws/src/endpoint/Hello.java:8:5:
Missing a Javadoc comment.
javaee5/webservices/hello-jaxws/src/endpoint/Hello.java:8:28:
Parameter name should be final.
javaee5/webservices/hello-jaxws/src/endpoint/Hello.java:9:5:
'{' should be on the previous line.
javaee5/webservices/hello-jaxws/src/client/Client.java:13:
Missing a Javadoc comment.
javaee5/webservices/hello-jaxws/src/client/Client.java:14:1:
'{' should be on the previous line.
javaee5/webservices/hello-jaxws/src/client/Client.java:15:5:
Missing a Javadoc comment.
javaee5/webservices/hello-jaxws/src/client/Client.java:15:32:
'=' is not preceded with whitespace.
javaee5/webservices/hello-jaxws/src/client/Client.java:15:33:
'=' is not followed by whitespace.
javaee5/webservices/hello-jaxws/src/client/Client.java:16:25:
Variable 'service' must be private and have accessor methods.
javaee5/webservices/hello-jaxws/src/client/Client.java:17: L
ine has trailing spaces.
javaee5/webservices/hello-jaxws/src/client/Client.java:18:5:
 Missing a Javadoc comment.
javaee5/webservices/hello-jaxws/src/client/Client.java:18:29:
Parameter args should be final.
javaee5/webservices/hello-jaxws/src/client/Client.java:19:5:
'{' should be on the previous line.
```

* *http://eclipse-cs.sourceforge.net/*

```
javaee5/webservices/hello-jaxws/src/client/Client.java:23:
Line has trailing spaces.
javaee5/webservices/hello-jaxws/src/client/Client.java:24:5:
Method 'doHello' is not designed for extension - needs to be
abstract, final or empty.
javaee5/webservices/hello-jaxws/src/client/Client.java:24:5:
Missing a Javadoc comment.
javaee5/webservices/hello-jaxws/src/client/Client.java:25:5:
'{' should be on the previous line.
javaee5/webservices/hello-jaxws/src/client/Client.java:27:9:
'{' should be on the previous line.
javaee5/webservices/hello-jaxws/src/client/Client.java:31:9:
'}' should be on the same line.
javaee5/webservices/hello-jaxws/src/client/Client.java:32:14:
'catch' is not followed by whitespace.
javaee5/webservices/hello-jaxws/src/client/Client.java:33:9:
'{' should be on the previous line.
Audit done.
```

This does give some idea of the sort of tests Checkstyle does. However, for most users, this is actually about as useful as compiling from the command line: that is to say, in this day and age of IDEs and sophisticated build scripting, not very. We will see more useful ways of integrating Checkstyle in your daily work in the rest of this chapter, where we look at different ways you can use Checkstyle to improve your code quality and maintainability.

21.2 Using Checkstyle in Eclipse

Checkstyle can be used in a variety of ways, including from the command line or from within an Ant or Maven build script. However, from a developer's perspective, the most efficient way to use it is from within the IDE, as corrections can be made immediately and with little effort. Plug-ins exist for most of the major Java IDEs, including Eclipse, IntelliJ, NetBeans, JBuilder, and even JEdit. In this section, we go through how this is done using Eclipse 3.2 and Checkstyle 4.2.

The Eclipse Checkstyle plug-in is found at *http://eclipse-cs.sourceforge.net/*. The first thing you will need to do is to install the plug-in. Just use the plug-in's Remote Update site, which can be found at *http://eclipse-cs.sourceforge.net/update* (see Figure 21-1).

To install this plug-in, you follow the usual procedure for installing an Eclipse plug-in:

1. Open the Plug-in installation window by selecting the "Help→Software Updates→Find and Install" menu.
2. Select "Search for New Features."
3. Create a new remote site entry for the Checkstyle update server via the "New Remote Site" button.
4. Enter a name for the remote site (say "Checkstyle Plug-in") and the site URL (see Figure 21-1).

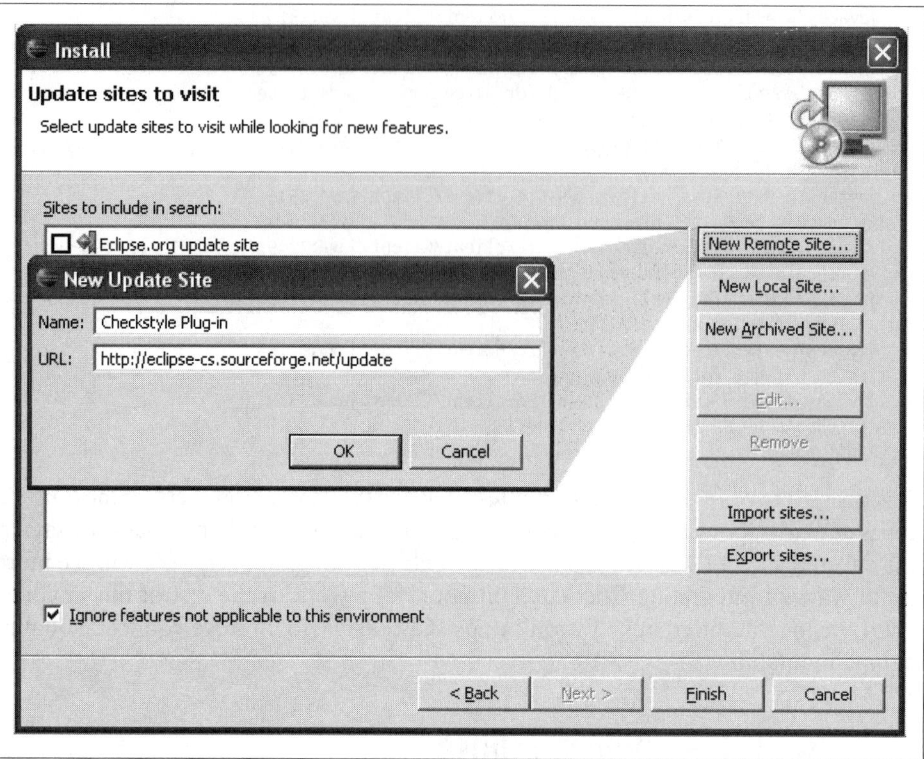

Figure 21-1. Installing Checkstyle on Eclipse

5. Step through the following installation screens.

Once the plug-in is installed, you need to activate Checkstyle checks for your particular project. By default, Checkstyle will not be activated for your projects: you need to set this up yourself. Open the project properties window (Project→Properties), and select the Checkstyle properties entry (see Figure 21-2). Make sure that the "Checkstyle active for this project" checkbox is selected.

You can also specify the set of rules you want to use for this project. The Eclipse Checkstyle plug-in comes out-of-the-box with two sets of rules: the Sun Java Coding Standards and a slightly modified version of these rules, better adapted to the standard Eclipse formatting conventions. You can use one of these to get started, although you will probably want to tailor the rules to your own needs later on (see Section 21.3).

A Checkstyle code audit can be time-consuming, especially if there are a lot of files to check. Too many errors can also make it harder to focus on the ones that really should be fixed. The "Exclude from checking..." option lets you filter out certain classes or packages that you don't need (or want) to be checked, which can save time and processing power.

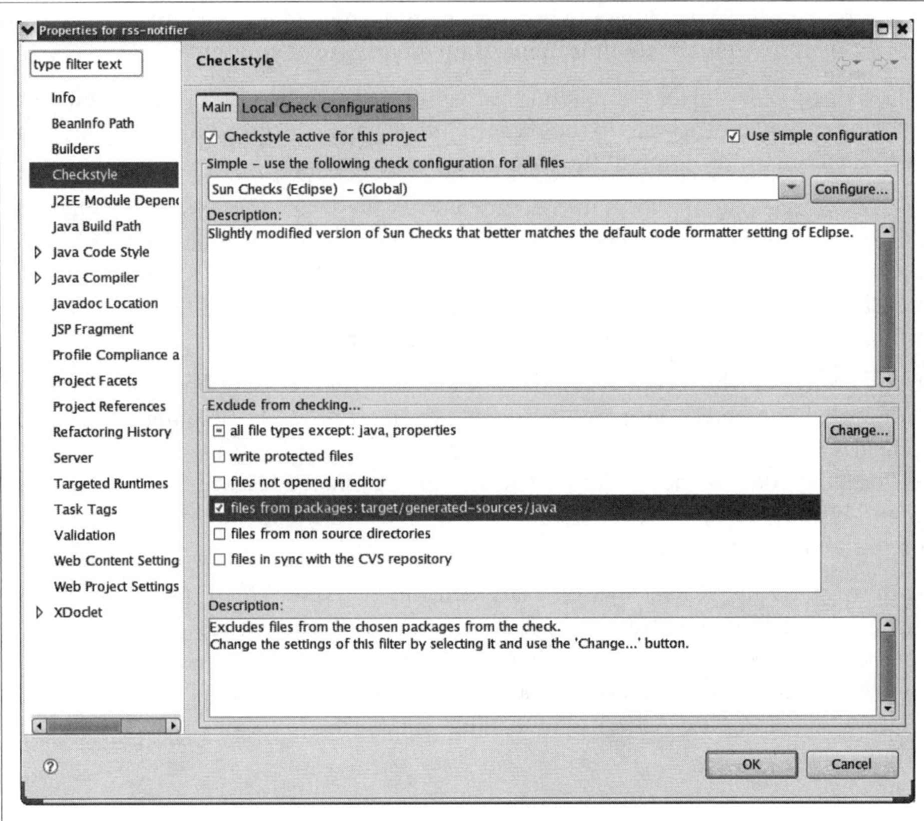

Figure 21-2. Activating Checkstyle for a project

For example, in modern Java development, code generation tools are often used to save time and effort for the developers. Examples include generating Hibernate classes from Hibernate schemas, or generating classes for EJB or web services using annotations. In general, you have little control over the coding conventions used in the generated code (and, if the code works correctly, you probably don't care).

Checkstyle lets you exclude this sort of code from its analysis. Your generated source code should be in a package of its own, preferably in a directory branch reserved for generated code (this is a common best practice that makes it easier to tidy up generated code when rebuilding the project). By convention, for example, Maven 2 places generated code in the *target/generated-sources* directory. Once you know where your generated source code is, just select the "files from packages" option in the "Exclude from checking..." list, and choose the packages you don't want analyzed (see Figure 21-2).

When you're happy with the configuration, press OK.

At this point, Checkstyle runs as a background task and audits the source code in your project. This may take some time, depending on the size of your project.

When Checkstyle finishes its audit, you will probably have a long list of standards violations, listed as warnings in the Problems view pane. Clicking on a problem in this list will automatically jump to the offending code segment.

The Checkstyle plug-in works in the same way as the Java compiler. Now, whenever you edit and save your Java classes in a Checkstyle-activated project, your code is automatically checked and any infringements are highlighted and explained (see Figure 21-3). They are rather hard to miss: the offending code is highlighted in yellow, with a corresponding marker in the margin for good measure.

In any project in which coding standards are to be enforced, developers need to work with an IDE correctly configured with Checkstyle. If properly encouraged, they will come to consider coding standard errors almost in the same way as syntax errors, correcting their code as they write it. And the project standards will be gradually and smoothly adopted by all team members. This is by far the most efficient way of enforcing coding standards.

By contrast, running Checkstyle on a large existing code base can be positively demoralizing, especially if no (or different) coding standards were previously enforced, as the number of errors can be overwhelming. This is an important factor when considering how to introduce coding standards into an organization. In Section 21.3, we will look at how to customize Checkstyle coding standards to your team's particular requirements.

21.3 Customizing Checkstyle Rules in Eclipse

The Sun coding standards—provided out-of-the-box via a configuration file—can be overwhelming at times. Checkstyle may well come up with hundreds of relatively minor rule violations (whitespace at the ends of lines, for example), especially if a lot of code has already been written without Checkstyle in place.

The more important standards may get lost in the mass of minor and relatively unimportant ones. This can result in two possible negative side effects:

- Developers will become discouraged and ignore all rule violations, which tends to defeat the purpose of installing Checkstyle in the first place.
- Developers will become overly zealous and pass hours removing spaces from the ends of lines. This will produce nice clean code, but will probably slow down developer productivity considerably.

To optimize the adoption of coding standards and the use of Checkstyle to enforce them, you often need to take a more flexible approach. The easiest way to do this is to

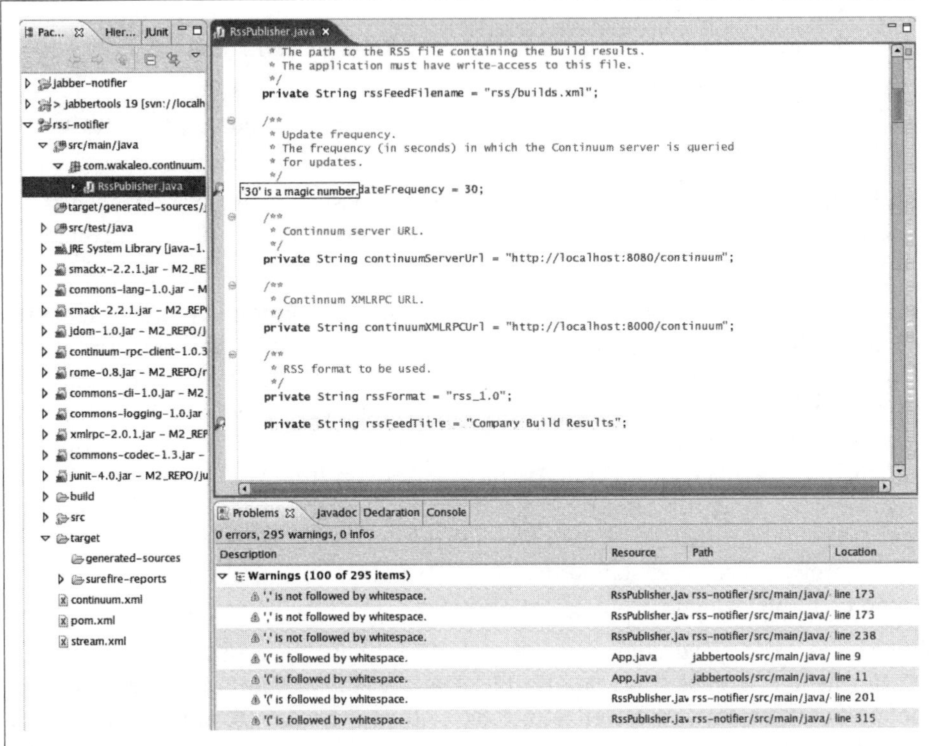

Figure 21-3. Checkstyle in Action

create a custom set of coding standards that is specifically designed either for your company or for a single project.

You can do this fairly easily from within Eclipse (see Figure 21-4). Go into the Preferences window, and select the Checkstyle preferences. You will see some built-in configuration files (the Sun coding standards and a slightly modified version of the Sun standards adapted to the default code formatting used by Eclipse).

To create a new Checkstyle configuration file, just click "New." Several types of configuration files are available, including:

Built-in configurations
: For example, the Sun coding standards, which are delivered with the Checkstyle plug-in, and which cannot be altered.

Internal configurations
: Stored within the Eclipse metadata. These are useful for experimenting locally with new configurations, but they cannot (easily) be shared with other team members.

External configurations
: Imported from an external source. External configurations may be imported from an external file on a local disk ("External Configuration") or from a web server

("Remote Configuration"), or be stored within the Eclipse project, under configuration management, for example, ("Project Relative Configuration").

Project Relative configurations
: Particularly useful when the corresponding Checkstyle configuration file is also used in the build process by other tools such as Ant or Maven.

Another less labor-intensive approach is to copy an existing configuration, such as the standard Sun conventions, or the modification version of these checks adapted for Eclipse.

Configuring the Checkstyle configuration file using the plug-in is straightforward. When you click on the new configuration, you open a window displaying the available Checkstyle modules, along with those that have been activated for this configuration file (see Figure 21-4). To add a module to your configuration file, simply click on the module and configure it to your particular needs. Each module has its own specific configuration parameters. It is important to get buy-in from your development team for any coding standards initiative. A good approach is to go through the list of standards with your team, discussing each one, and then to configure your module according to your project needs and standards. This helps developers understand the impetus behind each rule, which encourages adoption.

When you are happy with the results, you need to publish the configuration file so that all team members can use it. Export the file using the "Export" button in the Checkstyle configuration screen, and save it somewhere on your hard disk. Once you have the Extensible Markup Language (XML) configuration file, you need to publish it somewhere. One option, for project-specific rules, is to store it under source configuration management. In this way, it can be easily accessed by any users who obtain the project from the source code repository. To use such a file in Eclipse, just create a new Checkstyle "Project Relative Configuration," and choose the file you just created.

However, rules stored in this way are specific to each project, and you have to duplicate the rules for every new project. Another approach is to publish the configuration file on an internal web site or build server. This requires a little more work to set up and maintain, but the rules can be maintained centrally and shared across all projects. To use this type of configuration file, you need to create a new "External Configuration" (for a file on a shared directory) or "Remote Configuration" (for a file on a local web server).

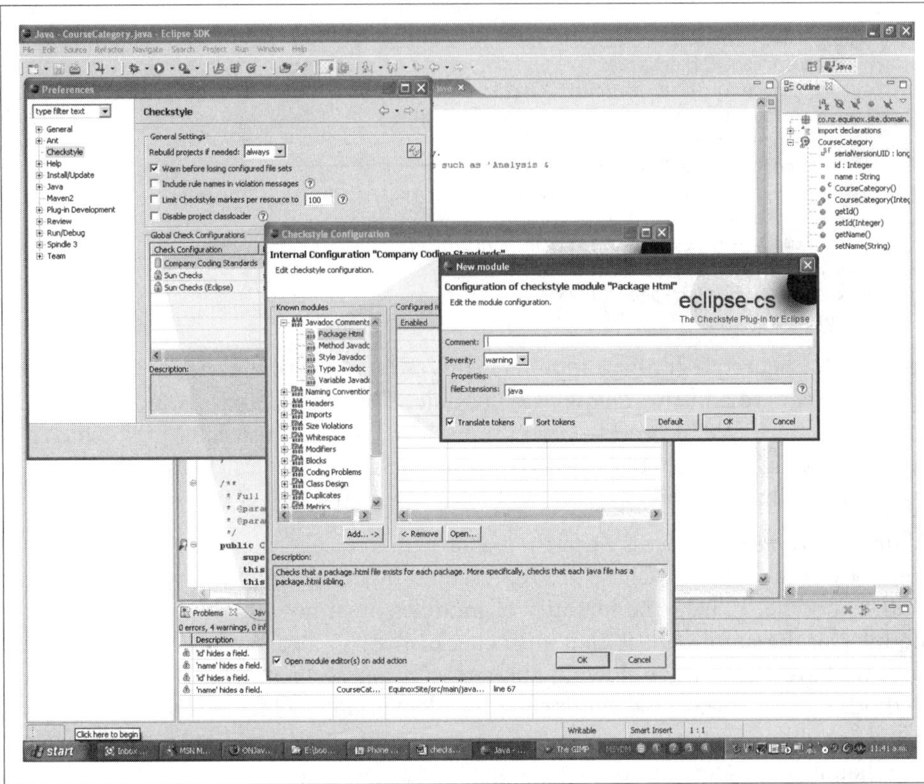

Figure 21-4. Customizing Checkstyle in Eclipse

21.4 Customizing Checkstyle Rules Using the XML Configuration Files

Under the hood, a Checkstyle configuration file is a standard XML file that defines a set of modules that are used to verify source code. Each module is specialized in one particular kind of coding standard or best practice.

The configuration file is basically an XML representation of a hierarchy of modules, starting from a special root module called the *Checker* module, which contains other modules. Some modules can also contain submodules. This is notably the case of the *TreeWalker* module, which parses a Java source file and then lets submodules verify different aspects of the parse tree. In fact, the majority of Checkstyle modules are submodules of the *TreeWalker* module.

A very simple Checkstyle configuration file might look like this:

```
<?xml version="1.0"?>
<!DOCTYPE module PUBLIC
    "-//Puppy Crawl//DTD Check Configuration 1.2//EN"
    "http://www.puppycrawl.com/dtds/configuration_1_2.dtd">
```

```
<module name="Checker">
    <module name="TreeWalker">
        <property name="tabWidth" value="4"/>
        <property name="charset" value="UTF-8"/>
        <module name="JavadocMethod"/>
        <module name="JavadocVariable"/>
            <property name="scope" value="protected"/>
        </module>
        <module name="AvoidStarImport"/>
    </module>
    <module name="PackageHtml"/>
</module>
```

As with all Checkstyle configuration files, this file starts with the special *Checker* root module. Next we add the *TreeWalker* module. This module parses individual Java source code files. We have added two properties to this module: *tabWidth*, which defines the number of spaces represented by a tab character when calculating line lengths, and *charset*, which (in this case) allows Checkstyle to handle UTF-8 source code files.

While we are in the process of parsing a Java source code file, we can also apply a number of other checks. These are represented by nested modules within the *TreeWalker* module. In fact, the majority of modules must be nested in the *TreeWalker* module, for the simple reason that most checks invovlve a particular Java class. In this case, we have added the following methods: *JavadocMethod*, which ensures that all methods have valid Javadoc comments; *JavadocVariable*, which ensures that all protected or public variables have Javadoc comments; and *AvoidStarImport*, which makes sure that import statements do not use the "*" notation.

Finally, the *PackageHtml* module checks, which ensures that all packages have a *package.html* file. The check is not included in the *TreeWalker* module as it does not apply to individual class files, but acts at a package level.

As seen here, module behavior can be customized using properties. Each module has a set of properties with default values. To override a property, you just add a property tag in the body of the module tag. For example, for the *LineLength* module the default maximum line length is 80 characters. If you want to check for lines longer than 70 characters instead, you would set the "max" property, as follows:

```
<module name="LineLength">
    <property name="max" value="70"/>
</module>
```

The severity property can be applied to any module and is used to determine the type of message that will be displayed. To deactivate a module, for example, set the severity to "ignore":

```
<module name="LineLength">
    <property name="severity" value="ignore"/>
    <property name="max" value="70"/>
</module>
```

Most modules perform well using the default configuration. The *JavadocType* module checks class and interface Javadoc comments. To activate this module with the default values, you just declare the module in the configuration file (it must be nested inside the "TreeWalker" module):

```
<module name="JavadocType"/>
```

By default, the @author tag is not required. For your project or company, you may decide to make it mandatory. If so, you would also define the "authorFormat" property for this module as follows (in this case, any nonnull string will do). This property is an example of how Checkstyle uses regular expressions. Regular expressions are widely used in Checkstyle for checks involving formatting or naming conventions. These regular expressions use the popular Jakarta *regexp*[*] library. The following example, for example, uses the "\S" regexp notation to indicate that a nonempty string is required (whitespaces are not acceptable):

```
<module name="JavadocType">
    <property name="authorFormat" value="\S"/>
</module>
```

These regular expressions can be useful for expressing more complex constraints. Here is a stricter version of the package naming convention, where only lowercase letters and digits are authorized in package names:

```
<module name="PackageName">
    <property name="format" value="^[a-z]+(\.[a-z][a-z0-9]*)*$"/>
</module>
```

There are many other modules that can be activated and configured. Check out the Checkstyle documentation for further details.

21.5 Customizing Checkstyle: Common Rules That You Can Do Without, and Some That You Could Use

The rules that Checkstyle provides out-of-the-box implement the Sun Coding Standards, but you may want to be a little more flexible, especially concerning arguably minor issues such as whitespaces. In Section 21.3 and Section 21.4, we discussed how you can create your own set of Checkstyle rules, adapted to your development practices. Here are a few pragmatic guidelines about which rules you may want to keep and which rules you may want to discard, based on the out-of-the-box Sun Checks:

Javadoc comments
: These rules are generally good to have, as they help to encourage better quality technical documentation. You can probably do without the *Package Html* rule,

[*] *http://jakarta.apache.org/regexp/*

which checks for the presence of a *package.html* file in each package, a recommendation that is rarely followed with any consistency in the real world.

Naming conventions
: Naming conventions play an important role in code readability—I generally stick to the Sun conventions here.

Headers
: The rules about headers are not included in the default Checkstyle configurations, as they tend to be company-specific. Don't bother with these unless you have some company-wide obligation to do so.

Imports
: The conventions around imports (no star (*) or redundant imports, imports in alphabetical order...) are beneficial for code readability, and are also supported by modern IDEs such as Eclipse and NetBeans with little extra effort. For example, in Eclipse, the "Source→Organize Imports" menu will automatically fix any import-related issues. I usually keep the default configuration here.

Size violations
: These limits on class and method size are designed to keep code short and simple, as recommended by many Java best practices and Agile methodologies. They are good to have.

Whitespace
: The Checkstyle whitespace rules contain an abundance of rules about where white space is (or isn't) required. Although many correspond to standard Java coding practices and make for more readable code, some are a little too pedantic for real-world use.

  One of the worst culprits is the *Tab Character* rule, which checks for the presence of tabs in the source code. There are good reasons to avoid tabs in source code, especially if the code needs to be read online. The problem is that many IDEs use tabs by default in their code templates and in generated code blocks. Keep this rule if you can, but make sure your IDEs are configured correctly.

  The "Whitespace Around" rule works poorly if you use generics. Using the standard configuration, for example, the following expression will generate errors

```
List<Integer> list = new ArrayList<Integer>();
```

  To avoid this, open up the details of this rule and disable the "Start of generic type arguments" and "End of the generic type arguments" entries.

Modifiers
: The *Modifier Order* rule makes sure modifiers are placed in the order recommended by Sun. For example, methods are *public static*, not *static public*. This is primarily a readability issue—having consistently ordered modifiers makes the code easier and smoother to read.

The *Redundant Modifier* rule enforces the Sun recommendation of not having *abstract* or *public* modifiers in interfaces. Interestingly, when you create an interface from a class in Eclipse, it does just that: by default, the generated interface has *public abstract* methods. If you include this rule, make sure you remember to uncheck these options if you create interfaces using Eclipse's "Refactoring→Extract Interface" function.

Blocks

Blocks are an important part of code conventions: I usually leave these rules as-is.

Coding problems

The coding problems are designed to avoid common coding errors by enforcing basic best practices. Most of these rules are sensible and reflect good programming practices.

One rule that can cause problems is the *Hidden Field* rule, which detects parameters with the same name as member variables. In most cases, this is a sensible rule, since it can cause considerable ambiguity in the code. However, there are situations where it is not appropriate. IDEs like Eclipse and NetBeans provide convenient functionalities for generating getters and setters, such as the one shown here:

```
public void setName(String name) {
    this.name = name;
}
```

Although this code is fine, Checkstyle will indicate a *Hidden Field* error here. To get around this, just open the configuration for this rule and check the "ignore-Setter" option.

There are a couple of additional rules that can be useful:

- The *Multiple String Literals* rule can be useful to detect duplicated string values that should be refactored into constants.
- The *String Literal Equality* rule detects cases in which strings are compared using "==" or "!=."

Class design

The *DesignForExtension* rule is a fairly obscure rule designed to limit the ability of subclasses to damage the behavior of a class by overriding its methods. This is a nice idea in theory, but it requires a lot of extra coding for little real benefit in most cases. I usually drop this rule.

Metrics

Metrics are not included in the standard rule set. Most metrics are not particularly easy to understand unless you are familiar with the theory of code metrics. However, there is one that's worth a look, even if you're not a specialist in code metrics: the *CyclomaticComplexity* rule.

The *CyclomaticComplexity* rule measures McCabe cyclomatic complexity, which is actually useful and fairly easy to understand. This metric measures the complexity of a method by counting the number of distinct paths through it. Each decision point (ifs, loops, case statements, and so on) adds a new path, and thus extra complexity. Overly complex methods with endless conditions and branches are harder to read and maintain, harder to test, and are prone to bugs. For Java code, most writers consider a cyclomatic complexity value of 1–4 to indicate low complexity, 5–7 to indicate moderate complexity, and 8–10 to indicate high complexity. A value over 10 indicates an excessively complex method that should probably be reviewed and refactored.

In Checkstyle, you can configure the maximum allowable complexity. By default, any method with a cyclomatic complexity of over 10 will be detected. In the following example, we lower the threshold to 7:

```
<module name="CyclomaticComplexity">
    <property name="max" value="7"/>
</module>
```

Miscellaneous

The default rules come with a rule called *Generic Illegal Regexp*, which is configured to detect trailing spaces at the end of lines in your code. You probably don't care about this, so this rule can be safely removed.

The *New Line At End Of File* rule integrates poorly with many IDEs such as Eclipse, as the new line character in question varies depending on the operating system and/or the IDE configuration. I usually drop this one for the sake of simplicity.

There are many other rules that are not activated by default in the Sun configuration, such as Metrics, EJB-specific rules, and code duplication detection. These should be added only on an as-needed basis, and when everyone in the team fully understands the rule. At the end of the day, don't forget that coding standards are designed to improve readability, reliability, and maintainability, and they should not add an excessive overhead to development efforts. If a rule does not fit in with your environment, don't use it.

21.6 Defining Rules for Source Code Headers with Checkstyle

Many companies and projects use a standard file header convention. Checkstyle offers many ways to enforce this. For simple cases, you can write a header template, where some lines are fixed and others may be modified by the developer. Suppose that your company standards impose a boxed-style comment with a copyright line at the bottom, as shown here:

```
////////////////////////////////////////////////////////////////////
// My Project Title
// A description of this file goes here.
//
// Copyright (C) 2006 My Company
////////////////////////////////////////////////////////////////////
```

One easy way to do this is to define a header template called java.header, which would contain the above text, and then indicate which lines may be modified:

```
<module name="Header">
    <property name="headerFile"
    value="java.header"/>
    <property name="ignoreLines" value="2, 3, 4"/>
</module>
```

Suppose that all you need to do is to put a copyright line at the top of each file:

```
// Copyright (C) 2006 MyCompany
// All rights reserved
```

At first sight, this looks like a static block of text. However, the year needs to change each year. To do this, you can define an inline regular expression using the RegexpHeader module, as shown here:

```
<module name="RegexpHeader">
    <property name="header"
    value="^// Copyright \(C\) \d\d\d\d My Company$\n^// All rights reserved$"/>
</module>
```

You can also define the header as a more complicated regular expression in an external file. Suppose your company or project standards require a file header containing dynamic elements coming from the source configuration system, as in the following example:

```
////////////////////////////////////////////////////////////////////
// My Project Title
// File: $Id$
// A short description goes here
//
// Last modified $Date$ by $Author $
// Copyright (C) 2006 My Company
////////////////////////////////////////////////////////////////////
```

This can be configured using the RegexpHeader module and an external file template (called "java.header" in this example):

```
<module name="RegexpHeader">
    <property name="headerFile" value="java.header"/>
</module>
```

The java.header file in this case would look like this:

```
^///////////////////////////////////////////////////////////////////
^// My Project Title
^// File: \$Id.*\$$
```

21.7 Suppressing Checkstyle Tests

There will be times when you come across a genuine reason for violating a coding standard for a particular section of code. For example, the following code extracts the list of students in each percentile:

```
for (int i = 1; i < 100; i++) {
    List<Student> students = extractCentile(i, examResults);
    ...
}
```

In this context, the use of the value 100, for example, is clear, and there is little added value in replacing it by a constant called ONE_HUNDRED. Checkstyle lets you get around this problem in several ways. The easiest way to deal with particular cases like this is to use the SuppressionCommentFilter module. This module lets you deactivate Checkstyle for a section of code:

```
// CHECKSTYLE:OFF - 100 is not a "magic number" in this case
for (int i = 1; i < 100; i++) {
// CHECKSTYLE:ON
    List<Student> students = extractCentile(i, examResults);
    ...
}
```

Another way to do this is to use the SuppressionFilter associated with an XML configuration file, where detailed suppressions can be specified. This approach is useful for deactivating rules for large blocks of code or across several classes:

```
<module name="SuppressionFilter">
    <property name="file" value="docs/suppressions.xml"/>
</module>
```

The code above calls a suppressions.xml file, a file that you need to write where you can deactivate particular checks for particular classes, or even for certain lines in a particular class. In the following example, all Javadoc checks are deactivated for the first 50 lines of the Catalog class, and the MagicNumberCheck is deactivated for all unit test classes:

```
<!DOCTYPE suppressions PUBLIC
    "-//Puppy Crawl//DTD Suppressions 1.0//EN"
    "http://www.puppycrawl.com/dtds/suppressions_1_0.dtd">
<suppressions>
    <suppress checks="Javadoc*" files="Catalog.java" lines="1-50"/>
    <suppress checks="MagicNumberCheck" files="*Test.java"/>
</suppressions>
```

This approach does require extra maintenance work to keep the *suppression.xml* file up-to-date. Developers also may be tempted to use wildcards a little excessively, which can reduce the efficiency of Checkstyle audits. In practice, this method should be used sparingly and only after other options have been considered and eliminated.

21.8 Using Checkstyle with Ant

Integrating Checkstyle into your standard build process is an important step in the road to improved code quality. We will look at how to integrate Checkstyle into a build process using Ant.

Checkstyle comes out-of-the-box with an Ant task that does just this. If you haven't already done so, download the Checkstyle installation file and unzip it into some convenient directory. Here, we have installed it into the "${user.home}/tools" directory:

```
$ cd ~/tools
$ unzip checkstyle-4.3.zip
```

The next thing you need to do is to add a task definition for the Checkstyle task. Something along the following lines should do:

```
<property name="checkstyle.home" location="${user.home}/tools/checkstyle-4.3" />
<taskdef resource="checkstyletask.properties"
classpath="${checkstyle.home}/checkstyle-all-4.3.jar"/>
```

Then, to run Checkstyle against your source code, just invoke the task as follows:

```
<checkstyle config="${checkstyle.home}/sun_checks.xml">
  <fileset dir="src" includes="**/*.java"/>
  <formatter type="plain"/>
  <formatter type="xml"/>
</checkstyle>
```

The only problem with this is that the results are not particularly readable. If the error messages are for human consumption, you should pass the generated XML through a stylesheet (several are provided with the Checkstyle distribution) to generate the results in a more readable HTML form:

```
<target name="checkstyle">
    <checkstyle config="${checkstyle.home}/sun_checks.xml"
     failOnViolation="false">
       <fileset dir="src" includes="**/*.java"/>
       <formatter type="plain"/>
       <formatter type="xml" tofile="checkstyle-report.xml"/>
    </checkstyle>
    <xslt in="checkstyle-report.xml"
              style="${checkstyle.home}/contrib/checkstyle-noframes.xsl"
              out="reports/checkstyle-report.html"/>
</target>
```

Don't forget the *failOnViolation* attribute. If this is not set to "false," the Checkstyle check will stop the build if it finds any violations, and never get to the report generation task.

Now you can run the task:

```
$ ant checkstyle

Buildfile: build.xml
```

```
checkstyle:
[checkstyle] Running Checkstyle 4.3 on 5 files
[checkstyle] /home/john/projects/.../taxcalculator/package.html:0:
Missing package documentation file.
...
[style] Processing
/home/john/projects/java-power-tools/src/code-listings/ch05/tax-calculator
/checkstyle-report.xml to
/home/john/projects/java-power-tools/src/code-listings/ch05/tax-calculator/reports/
checkstyle-report.html
[style] Loading stylesheet
/home/john/tools/checkstyle-4.3/contrib/checkstyle-noframes.xsl

BUILD SUCCESSFUL
```

This would produce an HTML report similar to the one shown in Figure 21-5.

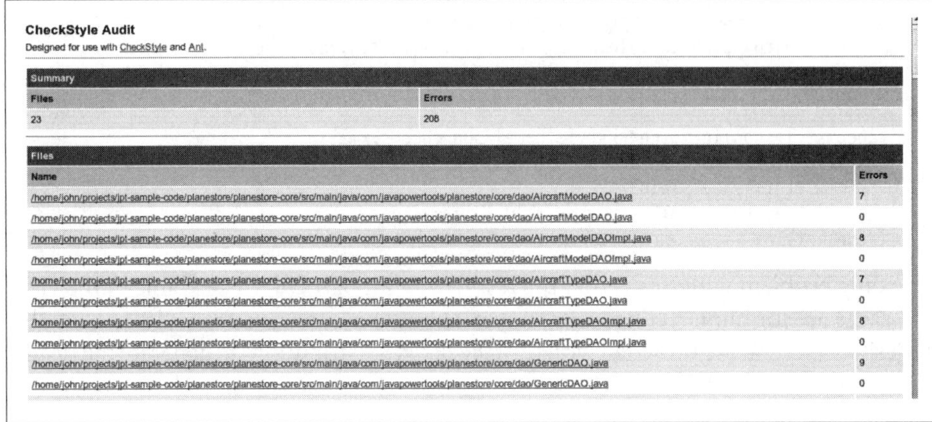

Figure 21-5. A Checkstyle report in Ant

21.9 Using Checkstyle with Maven

Checkstyle integrates extremely well with Maven, which comes with a Checkstyle report plug-in (see Figure 21-6). The Maven Checkstyle report contains summaries and more detailed information about the different detected issues in the code, with data presented using a convenient drill-down approach.

You set up the basic configuration in the *<reporting>* section of your *pom.xml* file, as shown here:

```
<reporting>
    <plugins>
        <plugin>
            <artifactId>maven-checkstyle-plugin</artifactId>
```

```
            <configuration>
                <configLocation>src/main/config/company_checks.xml</configLocation>
            </configuration>
        </plugin>
    </plugins>
</reporting>
```

The optional *<configuration>* tag lets you specify your own customized set of rules (in Section 21.3 and Section 21.4). By default, the standard Sun Java Coding Conventions will be used.

If you use a suppressions file (in Section 21.7), you can also specify this file in the *suppressionsLocation* configuration entry, as shown here:

```
<reporting>
    <plugins>
        <plugin>
            <artifactId>maven-checkstyle-plugin</artifactId>
            <configuration>
                <configLocation>src/main/config/company_checks.xml</configLocation>
                <suppressionsLocation>suppressions.xml</suppressionsLocation>
            </configuration>
        </plugin>
    </plugins>
</reporting>
```

In the same way, you can use *headerLocation* to specify a header template (Section 21.6).

You run the Checkstyle report by generating the maven site using the "*mvn site*" command (see Chapter 2), or directly from the command line, as shown here:

```
$ mvn checkstyle:checkstyle
```

A typical report is illustrated in Figure 21-6.

The Maven Checkstyle report is flexible and takes a large number of configuration options that you can use to fine-tune the layout and content of the report. For example, by default the Checkstyle report begins with a list of all the rules used. You can remove this by setting the *enableRulesSummary* configuration entry to *false*. If you want the build to stop if there are any Checkstyle errors, set the *failsOnError* configuration entry to true.

If you include the JXR report as well, the generated Checkstyle report will contain hyperlinks to the HTML version of the Java source code. You can include this file by adding the *maven-jxr-plugin* report plug-in, as shown here:

```
<reporting>
    <plugins>
        ...
        <plugin>
            <groupId>org.apache.maven.plugins</groupId>
            <artifactId>maven-jxr-plugin</artifactId>
        </plugin>
```

```
        </plugins>
    </reporting>
```

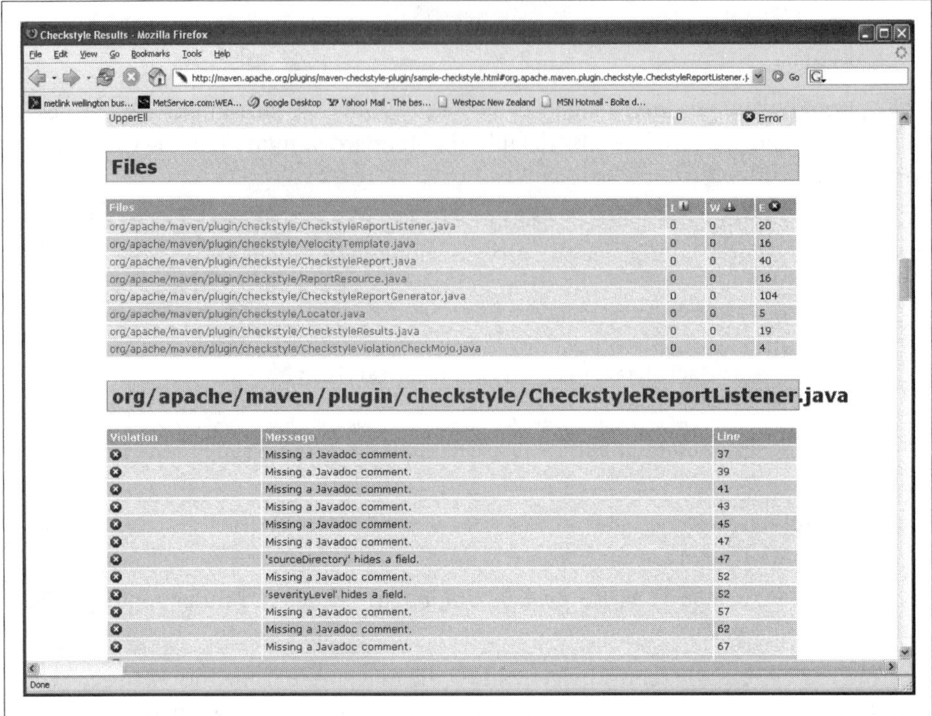

Figure 21-6. A Checkstyle report in Maven

CHAPTER 22

Preemptive Error Detection with PMD

22.1 PMD and Static Code Analysis

PMD is a static code analysis tool, capable of automatically detecting a wide range of potential defects and unsafe or nonoptimized code. Whereas other tools, such as Checkstyle (see Chapter 21), can verify that coding conventions and standards are respected, PMD focuses more on preemptive defect detection. It comes with a rich and highly configurable set of rules, and you can easily configure which particular rules should be used for a given project. PMD integrates well with IDEs such as Eclipse and NetBeans, and it also fits well into the build process thanks to its smooth integration with Ant and Maven.

22.2 Using PMD in Eclipse

PMD is designed to integrate well into a developer's work environment. Plug-ins exist for the principal IDEs, and they are the most productive and convenient way for a developer to use PMD. Plug-ins allow almost real-time code verification—they raise issues whenever you save the source code.

Installing the PMD Plug-In

The easiest way to install and use PMD under Eclipse is to use the remote update site, at *http://pmd.sf.net/eclipse*. You do this in the usual way:

1. Open the Help→Software Updates→Find and Install menu.
2. Click Next, and choose New Remote Site.
3. Now enter the URL of the remote site (*http://pmd.sf.net/eclipse*), and an appropriate name such as "PMD."
4. Make sure that you have the PMD site checked in the "Sites to include in search" window, and click Finish. Then just go through the installation screens to install the plug-in.

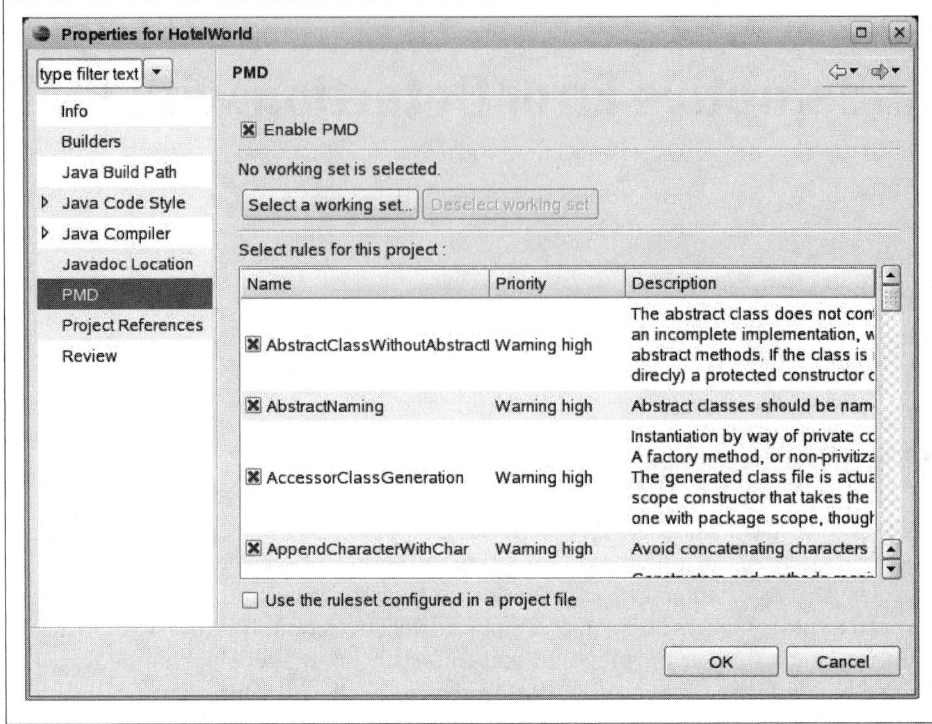

Figure 22-1. Configuring PMD for a project

Once you have installed the plug-in, you need to activate PMD for your project. Open the project properties window (Project→Properties). You will now have a PMD entry (see Figure 22-1). This window allows you to configure PMD in detail for your particular project, by selecting which rules you want to apply, and specifying their relative importance. For now, just check the "Enable PMD" box and leave the default set of rules.

Detecting and Displaying Errors

To run PMD, click on the project resource and select "PMD→Check code with PMD" in the contextual menu.

PMD rule violations are displayed as entries in the "Tasks" view (see Figure 22-2), with a priority (high, medium, or low) depending on the priority of the corresponding rule. As with any other task, clicking on the task will take you straight to the offending code. Some developers find this view convenient as a personal productivity tool: PMD issues are listed among other tasks (such as TODOs), and you can sort tasks by priority, manually reassign priorities, mark tasks as "done," and so on.

Problems | Tasks | Properties | Servers | Snippets

70 items

Description	Resource	Path	Location
Abstract classes should be named AbstractXXX	Search.java	HotelWorld/src/main/java/com/wakaleo/tutorials/hotelworld/tapestry	line 19
Avoid variables with short names like DE	HotelModel.java	HotelWorld/src/main/java/com/wakaleo/tutorials/hotelworld/model	line 146
Avoid variables with short names like EN	Language.java	HotelWorld/src/main/java/com/wakaleo/tutorials/hotelworld/businessobjects	line 22
Avoid variables with short names like ES	Country.java	HotelWorld/src/main/java/com/wakaleo/tutorials/hotelworld/businessobjects	line 30
Avoid variables with short names like ES	HotelModel.java	HotelWorld/src/main/java/com/wakaleo/tutorials/hotelworld/model	line 140
Avoid variables with short names like ES	Language.java	HotelWorld/src/main/java/com/wakaleo/tutorials/hotelworld/businessobjects	line 28
Avoid variables with short names like FR	Country.java	HotelWorld/src/main/java/com/wakaleo/tutorials/hotelworld/businessobjects	line 27
Avoid variables with short names like FR	HotelModel.java	HotelWorld/src/main/java/com/wakaleo/tutorials/hotelworld/model	line 137
Avoid variables with short names like FR	Language.java	HotelWorld/src/main/java/com/wakaleo/tutorials/hotelworld/businessobjects	line 25

Figure 22-2. PMD displays rule violations as tasks

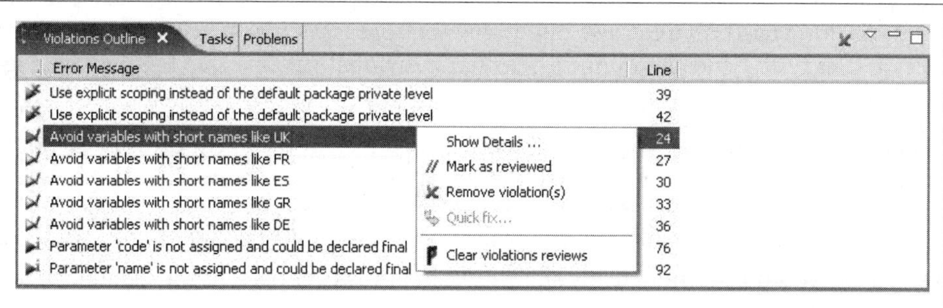

Figure 22-3. The "Violations Outline" view gives a more PMD displays rule violations as tasks

PMD also lets you visualize issues in other views that are more specifically tailored to PMD. The "Violation Outlines" view lists PMD issues by severity. To open this view, open the "Window→Show View →Other" menu, and choose the "PMD→Violations Outline" view (see Figure 22-3).

The short description of a PMD issue may not always be enough to know. You can use "Show Details" to display a (slightly) more verbose description of the rule, as well as an example of code illustrating the rule.

Once you have understood why PMD has raised the issue, you can decide how to deal with it. You may decide that the issue can be safely ignored. In this case, you can use the "Mark as reviewed" option. This will add a comment or annotation to the code indicating to PMD to ignore this issue here (see Section 22.7). You can also fix the issue manually and remove the violation directly from the list using "Remove violation." (Of course, if you didn't fix it to PMD's satisfaction, PMD will raise the issue again next time you analyze the code.)

PMD is quite smart. In some cases, it can propose fixes for the issues it raises. When this is possible, you can use the "Quick fix" menu option to correct the problem automatically.

22.3 Configuring PMD Rules in Eclipse

When you introduce coding standards and best practices into an organization, it is important to tailor the rules to your exact needs. This should be a team effort—get everyone who's going to be applying the rules involved. Each PMD rule has a detailed description and examples, available both on the web site and visible in the configuration screens. Review each rule and come to a joint decision on whether and when that rule should be applied in your organization. The most convenient place to configure the PMD ruleset is from within Eclipse, in the PMD entry of the "Windows→Preferences→PMD→Rules configuration" window (see Figure 22-1). This window contains a list of all the available PMD rules. From this list, you can go through the rules, adjust rule priorities, modify any of the other rule-specific properties, and also remove any rules you don't need. You can also build a ruleset from scratch: just delete all the current rules ("Clear All") and then import selected individual rulesets one by one (See Figure 22-4).

When you're happy with your new customized ruleset, you can export it in the form of an XML file ("Export Rule Set"). Other team members can now clear their existing ruleset and import the new ruleset into their environments. You can also activate or deactivate individual rules for a project in the project properties window (see Figure 11). And if you do anything really silly, you can always get back to the default ruleset using the "Restore Defaults" button.

22.4 More on the PMD Rulesets

PMD is a powerful and highly configurable tool. It delivers a rich set of more than 190 rules, and you can easily write additional ones if need be. PMD rules are divided into rulesets, each of which contains rules concerning a particular type of issue. We will run through the rulesets, and give some indication as to when each ruleset is or is not appropriate.

Basic rules (the "basic" ruleset)
: These rules verify some common, and useful, best practices, such as empty catch blocks or if statements, unnecessary temporary conversions when converting primitives to Strings, and so on.

JSF rules (the "basic-jsf" ruleset)
: This ruleset is designed to help improve the quality of JSF pages. At the time of writing, it relatively limited, containing only one rule. However, considering the current momentum of JSF, new rules will probably be added in future versions. It may be worthwhile including these rules if your project uses JSF with JSP/JSTL pages.

JSP rules (the "basic-jsp" ruleset)
: This ruleset contain some useful rules designed to help enforce quality coding in JSP pages. Examples of these rules include using tag libraries rather than scriptlets,

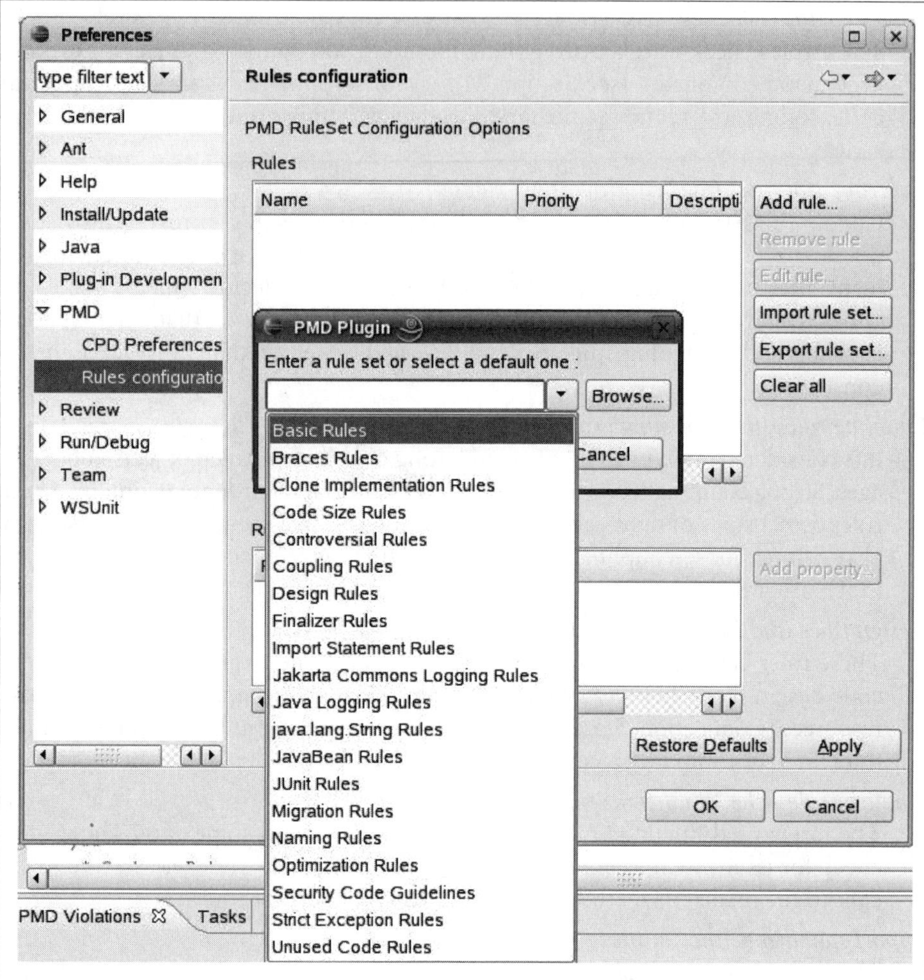

Figure 22-4. Configuring PMD rules from scratch

and placing all style information in CSS files rather than with the HTML tags in the JSP page. Include this ruleset if your project uses JSP.

Braces rules (the "braces" ruleset)
: These are coding standards that check that if, else, while, and for statements use curly braces. If you also are using Checkstyle to enforce coding conventions, these rules should be unnecessary.

Clone Implementation rules (the "clone" ruleset)
: These stipulate best practices that should be applied when implementing the `clone()` method: always invoke super.clone(); the class should implement `Cloneable`; and the `clone()` method should throw `CloneNotSupportedException`. This is handy if your project needs to use the `Cloneable` interface.

Code size (the "codesize" ruleset)
: These rules check for excessively long methods, too many parameters, excessive cyclomatic complexity (see Section 21.5), and so on, which can lead to unclear code, coding errors, and maintenance headaches. Similar rules also exist in Checkstyle.

Controversial rules (the "controversial" ruleset)
: Certain rules are subject to debate and may be considered controversial by some developers. For convenience, these rules are placed in a special ruleset, so that teams may easily examine and discuss them, and then decide which to take and which to leave. These rules check for issues such as having more than one exit point in a method, assigning null to variables, and ensuring that every class has a constructor.

Coupling rules (the "coupling" ruleset)
: It is considered good practice to avoid strong coupling between objects and packages. Strong coupling tends to make the code brittle and harder to maintain. These rules detect signs of tight coupling, such as an excessive number of imports. They also enforce loose-coupling best practices, such as exposing an interface (e.g., `List`) rather than an implementation class (e.g., `ArrayList`).

Design rules (the "design" ruleset)
: These rules check for potentially erroneous, inefficient, or just poorly conceived code design. For example, avoid deeply nested if...then statements; always close resources (Connection, Statement, ResultSet,...) after use; and use `equals()` rather than "==" to compare objects.

Finalizer rules (the "finalizers" ruleset)
: The rarely used finalize() method needs to be used with some care. These rules check for issues such as empty finalize() methods (which are useless), or explicit calls to the finalizer() method (that's the garbage collector's job).

Import statements (the "imports" ruleset)
: These check for duplicated or unused import statements. Checkstyle can do this quite well, too.

JavaBean rules (the "javabeans" ruleset)
: These rules help enforce the standard JavaBean conventions: JavaBeans must be serializable (all members must be transient, static, or have getters and setters); they must have a serialVersionUID field, and so on.

JUnit rules (the "junit" ruleset)
: Unit tests are a vital part of modern development processes. These rules help avoid common JUnit pitfalls and encourage testing best practices. If you are using the JUnit framework for your unit tests (as opposed to other unit testing frameworks such as TestNG), this is a good ruleset to have.

Jakarta logging rules (the "logging-jakarta" ruleset)
: These check for incorrect or dangerous use of the Jakarta Commons Logging framework.

Java logging rules (the "logging-java" ruleset)
: These verify the correct usage of the `java.util.logging.Logger` class: the logger variable should be static, final, and unique within a class; `System.out()` should be avoided, as should `printStackTrace()`.

Migration rules (the "migrating" ruleset)
: These rules help developers migrate code to a newer JDK. They suggest ways to modernize code, such as replacing vectors with the more recent java.util.List.

Naming rules (the "naming" ruleset)
: These rules check standard Java naming conventions, an area that is also well covered by Checkstyle. They can also pick up a few potential defects caused by naming errors, such as an equals(Object) method that doesn't return a boolean.

Optimization rules (the "optimizations" ruleset)
: Many best practices exist to optimize performance. PMD can detect a certain number of these, such as using the final statement where appropriate on fields, parameters, or methods (which allows for better compiler optimization) and avoiding instantiating objects in loops (which is very expensive in terms of object creation).

Strict Exception rules (the "strictexception" ruleset)
: These rules are guidelines about throwing and catching exceptions. For example, you should avoid catching Throwable, as it can mask more serious runtime errors.

String and StringBuffer rules (the "strings" ruleset)
: Many simple optimization techniques involve the proper use of Strings and StringBuffers. Examples include using `StringBuffer.length()` to see if a String is empty and avoiding duplicated String literals.

Sun Security Code guidelines (the "sunsecure" ruleset)
: These rules come from security recommendations published by Sun, such as never expose an internal array directly—it is safer to return a copy.

Unused code rules (the "unusedcode" ruleset)
: Unused fields or methods waste space and memory, and they complicate code unnecessarily. This ruleset detects unused private fields or methods, unused local variables, and unused parameters.

Some of these rules (often the ones focused on coding standards) are also covered by Checkstyle rules. Indeed, there is some overlap between the two tools, as both products have increasingly rich toolsets. It is a good idea to remove the extra rules from one tool or the other to simplify maintenance. I tend to let Checkstyle handle coding standards and leave the coding best-practice rules to PMD.

You can easily configure which rules you want to use for your project or organization (see Section 22.3 and Section 22.5).

22.5 Writing Your Own PMD Ruleset

For convenience, PMD rules are divided into rulesets (see Section 22.4). However, once you become familiar with the various rules, you may want to define a custom set of rules coming from different rulesets, in order to centralize maintenance and simplify project configuration. You can do this by writing your own PMD ruleset.

A PMD ruleset is simply an XML file that lists a set of rules that you wish to use. You can include entire rulesets, or selectively choose specific rules from within other rulesets. You can also provide extra parameters to certain rules in order to customize their behavior.

Suppose that we want to write our own company ruleset. To start off, our ruleset will contain the *basic*, *unusedcode*, *string*, and *junit* rulesets. We create a new *<ruleset>* XML file, containing references to these rulesets:

```
<?xml version="1.0" ?>
<ruleset name="CompanyRules" xmlns="http://pmd.sf.net/ruleset/1.0.0"
        xmlns:xsi="http://www.w3.org/2001/XMLSchema-instance"
        xsi:schemaLocation="http://pmd.sf.net/ruleset/1.0.0
        http://pmd.sf.net/ruleset_xml_schema.xsd"
        xsi:noNamespaceSchemaLocation="http://pmd.sf.net/ruleset_xml_schema.xsd">
  <description>CompanyRules</description>
  <rule ref="rulesets/basic.xml" />
  <rule ref="rulesets/junit.xml" />
  <rule ref="rulesets/strings.xml" />
  <rule ref="rulesets/unusedcode.xml" />
</ruleset>
```

In addition, we may want to include some, but not all, of the rules in the *design* ruleset. To do this, we add explicit references to the rules, rather than to the ruleset as a whole:

```
  <rule ref="rulesets/design.xml/UseSingleton" />
  <rule ref="rulesets/design.xml/SimplifyBooleanReturns" />
  <rule ref="rulesets/design.xml/EqualsNull" />
```

Some rules may need to be configured, to override the default property values. For example, we may want to be particularly strict on code complexity. So we will configure the McCabe Cyclometric Complexity rule (see Section 21.5) to allow at most moderately complex methods, with a cyclometric complexity of no more than 7:

```
  <rule ref="rulesets/codesize.xml/CyclomaticComplexity">
    <properties>
        <property name="reportLevel" value="7"/>
    </properties>
  </rule>
```

Earlier on, we included all the basic rules. In fact, we are particularly worried about empty statements in for loops. We want this sort of issue to be considered as a high-priority error, not just a warning. To do this, we customize the `EmptyStatementNotInLoop` rule, and override the *priority* property, as follows:

```
<rule ref="rulesets/basic.xml/EmptyStatementNotInLoop">
    <priority>1</priority>
</rule>
```

The final version of our company ruleset looks like this:

```
<?xml version="1.0" ?>
<ruleset name="CompanyRules" xmlns="http://pmd.sf.net/ruleset/1.0.0"
        xmlns:xsi="http://www.w3.org/2001/XMLSchema-instance"
        xsi:schemaLocation="http://pmd.sf.net/ruleset/1.0.0
        http://pmd.sf.net/ruleset_xml_schema.xsd"
        xsi:noNamespaceSchemaLocation="http://pmd.sf.net/ruleset_xml_schema.xsd">
  <description>CompanyRules</description>
  <!-- Include all rules from these rulesets -->
  <rule ref="rulesets/basic.xml" />
  <rule ref="rulesets/junit.xml" />
  <rule ref="rulesets/strings.xml" />
  <rule ref="rulesets/unusedcode.xml" />

  <!-- Include these rules explicitly -->
  <rule ref="rulesets/design.xml/UseSingleton" />
  <rule ref="rulesets/design.xml/SimplifyBooleanReturns" />
  <rule ref="rulesets/design.xml/EqualsNull" />

  <!-- Cyclomatic complexity customization -->
  <rule ref="rulesets/codesize.xml/CyclomaticComplexity">
    <properties>
        <property name="reportLevel" value="7"/>
    </properties>
  </rule>

  <!-- Give this rule a higher priority -->
  <rule ref="rulesets/basic.xml/EmptyStatementNotInLoop">
      <priority>1</priority>
  </rule>
</ruleset>
```

Of course, a real company ruleset generally is a lot bigger than this, but you get the idea.

To use your new ruleset in Eclipse, you will need to open the PMD Rules Configuration screen (in "Window→Preferences"), and remove all existing rules (using the "Clear All" button). Then load your ruleset using "Import Rule Set." When you close the window, Eclipse will rerun the PMD new checks on your project.

22.6 Generating a PMD Report in Eclipse

Many people are very attached to hard-copy outputs. If you are among them, you may appreciate the ability to generate PMD rule violation reports in CSV, HTML, TXT, and XML formats. Just go to the contextual menu on the project, and select "PMD→Generate Reports." The reports will be generated in the /report directory of the current project. Figure 22-5 shows an example of an HTML report.

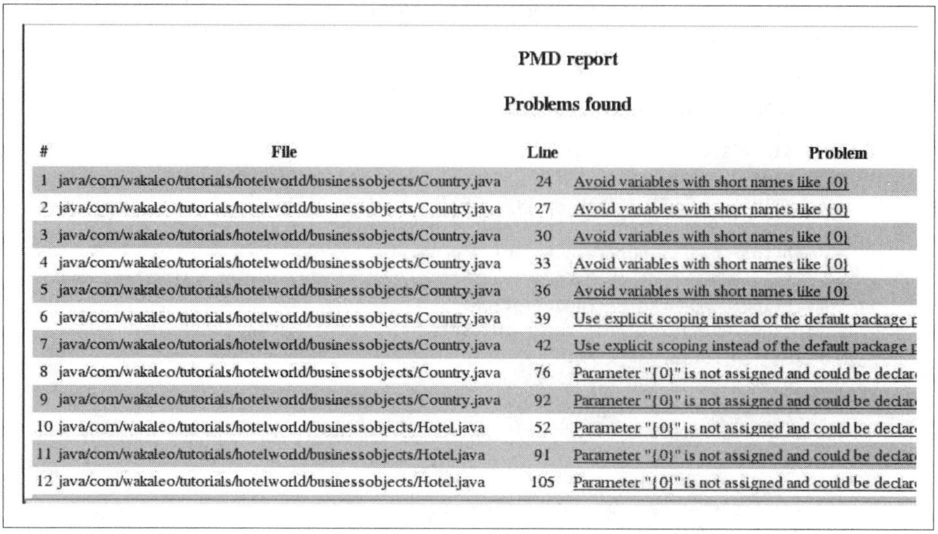

PMD report

Problems found

#	File	Line	Problem
1	java/com/wakaleo/tutorials/hotelworld/businessobjects/Country.java	24	Avoid variables with short names like {0}
2	java/com/wakaleo/tutorials/hotelworld/businessobjects/Country.java	27	Avoid variables with short names like {0}
3	java/com/wakaleo/tutorials/hotelworld/businessobjects/Country.java	30	Avoid variables with short names like {0}
4	java/com/wakaleo/tutorials/hotelworld/businessobjects/Country.java	33	Avoid variables with short names like {0}
5	java/com/wakaleo/tutorials/hotelworld/businessobjects/Country.java	36	Avoid variables with short names like {0}
6	java/com/wakaleo/tutorials/hotelworld/businessobjects/Country.java	39	Use explicit scoping instead of the default package p
7	java/com/wakaleo/tutorials/hotelworld/businessobjects/Country.java	42	Use explicit scoping instead of the default package p
8	java/com/wakaleo/tutorials/hotelworld/businessobjects/Country.java	76	Parameter "{0}" is not assigned and could be declar
9	java/com/wakaleo/tutorials/hotelworld/businessobjects/Country.java	92	Parameter "{0}" is not assigned and could be declar
10	java/com/wakaleo/tutorials/hotelworld/businessobjects/Hotel.java	52	Parameter "{0}" is not assigned and could be declar
11	java/com/wakaleo/tutorials/hotelworld/businessobjects/Hotel.java	91	Parameter "{0}" is not assigned and could be declar
12	java/com/wakaleo/tutorials/hotelworld/businessobjects/Hotel.java	105	Parameter "{0}" is not assigned and could be declar

Figure 22-5. Generating a report in PMD

22.7 Suppressing PMD Rules

All rules have exceptions. You will have occasions when PMD gets it wrong, and you have a legitimate reason for not respecting one of the PMD rules. For example, consider the following code:

```
/** Countries : USA */
public static final Country USA = new Country("us","United States");
```

Suppose that your company standards impose a minimum of four letters for variable names. In this case, PMD will incorrectly generate an error. To get around this, you can mark a violation as "Reviewed," which basically tells PMD that you've seen the issue and that it's fine by you. Click on the error and open the contextual menu, then select "Mark as reviewed." PMD will insert a special comment similar to the following:

```
/** Countries : USA */
// @PMD:REVIEWED:ShortVariable: by taronga on 4/13/06 7:25 AM
public static final Country USA = new Country("us","United States");
```

As long as you don't remove it, PMD will now ignore this violation for this particular case.

Another way of doing this while writing the code is to use the "NOPMD" marker, as follows:

```
// These are x and y coordinates, so short variable names are OK
int x = 0; // NOPMD
int y = 0; // NOPMD
```

The marker deactivates the ShortVariable rule for the variables.

If you are using JDK 1.5, you can also use the PMD SuppressWarnings annotation. This technique is particularly useful for generated classes or legacy code. In the following class, all PMD warnings are suppressed:

```
@SuppressWarnings("")
public class Country {
    ...
}
```

You may just want to suppress certain rules for a given class. In the following generated class, for example, private variables are prefixed with an underscore, which is not in line with PMD's rules concerning JavaBeans. To get around this, just suppress a specific PMD rule:

```
@SuppressWarnings("BeanMembersShouldSerialize")
public class Country {
    private String _code;
    ...
    public String getCode(){
        return _code;
    }
}
```

Sometimes, the rule may not be what you expect. In this case, for example, PMD expects a getter and setter for each nontransient and nonstatic class member variable. If a variable doesn't have a proper getter and setter, PMD will complain by saying that the variable is not serializable, and should be either transient or static, or have standardized getters and setters. So the naming conventions for accessor members are covered by this rule.

Thankfully, you don't have to know the nitty-gritty details of how each rule works, and which rule applies in a particular situation. From within Eclipse (using the "Violations Outline" view), you can easily display the full details of each raised issue, and mark the issue as "Reviewed" or remove the violation using the NOPMD comment.

22.8 Detecting Cut-and-Paste with CPD

Cutting and pasting code between classes is a bad habit. Areas of cut-and-pasted code increase maintenance costs unnecessarily, and indicate in the very least a good candidate for refactoring. In many cases, they are high-risk zones for potential errors.

PMD comes with a useful tool for detecting cut-and-pasted code called CPD (Cut-and-Paste Detector). You can run it from the contextual menu on the project, using the "PMD→Find Suspect Cut and Paste" menu option. Unfortunately, at the time of this writing, the results of this tool were not integrated into the IDE. The tool generates a text file called *cpd-report.txt* in the /report directory, which contains copy-and-paste suspects, as shown here:

```
=====================================================================
Found a 18 line (56 tokens) duplication in the following files:
Starting at line 69 of
    /home/taronga/Documents/articles/HotelWorld/src/main/java/com
    /wakaleo/tutorials/hotelworld
    /model/HotelModel.java
Starting at line 82 of
    /home/taronga/Documents/articles/HotelWorld/src/main/java/com
    /wakaleo/tutorials/hotelworld
    /model/HotelModel.java
        List hotelsFound = findHotelsByLanguage(language);
        Hotel hotel = null;
        for(int i = 0; i < hotels.length; i++) {
            hotel = (Hotel) hotels[i];
            if (hotel.getCity().equalsIgnoreCase(city)) {
                hotelsFound.add(hotel);
            }
        }

        return hotelsFound;
    }

    /**
     * Find hotels where a given language is spoken.
     * @param language
     * @return
     */
    public List findHotelsByLanguage(Language language) {
```

You can customize the minimum size of a copy-and-paste zone suspect in the workbench preferences under PMD→CPD Preferences. Just adjust the "Minimum tile size" field, and specify the minimum number of lines.

CPD is not limited to use within your IDE: you can also run CPD as a command-line tool, as an Ant task, or from within Maven. To run CPD as an Ant task, you first need to define a "cpd" task (using the `net.sourceforge.pmd.cpd.CPDTask` class, which is bundled with PMD). A typical usage might look like this:

```
<target name="cpd">
    <taskdef name="cpd" classname="net.sourceforge.pmd.cpd.CPDTask" />
    <cpd minimumTokenCount="100" outputFile="target/cpd.txt">
        <fileset dir="src">
            <include name="**/*.java"/>
        </fileset>
    </cpd>
</target>
```

22.9 Using PMD in Ant

Static analysis tools such as PMD can be used in two complementary ways, both of which have their place in the software development lifecycle. Developers use PMD most effectively from within the IDE, where they can quickly and interactively detect and fix issues. Lead developers, project managers, and quality assurance people, by contrast, prefer to see PMD integrated into the Continuous Build process, producing static reports, so that they can monitor code quality and potential issues over the whole project.

PMD comes with a flexible Ant task you can use to generate PMD reports. To get this to work, you need to copy the PMD jar to your Ant *lib* directory. Download the latest version of PMD from the web site* and decompress the package in a convenient place. On my Linux machine, for example, I placed it in the */usr/local/tools* directory and created a symbolic link (to make updating the library easier):

```
$ cd ~/tools
$ unzip pmd-bin-4.1.zip
$ ln -s pmd-4.1 pmd
```

Now you need to copy the PMD library to your Ant *lib* directory. You also need the other libraries required by PMD: there are two or three stored alongside the PMD library in the distributed bundle. On my installation, the Ant lib directory is in `/usr/share/ant/lib`, but this will obviously change depending on your exact environment. The easiest approach is to simply copy the whole lot into the Ant directory:

```
$ cd ~/pmd/
$ cp lib/*.jar /usr/share/ant/lib/
```

You can then declare the PMD task as follows:

```
<taskdef name="pmd" classname="net.sourceforge.pmd.ant.PMDTask"/>
```

A possibly more robust approach involves providing a classpath for the PMD task definition. You need to set up a classpath that points to the PMD jar files. Using this approach, you don't need to modify the Ant configuration on each machine, and the PMD JAR files can be stored in some central location. In the following code, we assume that PMD is installed as described above:

```
<property name="pmd.home" location="${user.home}/tools/pmd-4.1" />
<path id="pmd.classpath">
    <fileset dir="${pmd.home}/lib" includes="*.jar" />
</path>

<taskdef name="pmd" classname="net.sourceforge.pmd.ant.PMDTask"
 classpathref="pmd.classpath"/>
<taskdef name="cpd" classname="net.sourceforge.pmd.cpd.CPDTask"
 classpathref="pmd.classpath"/>
```

* *http://pmd.sourceforge.net/*

The PMD Ant task takes a number of parameters, the most important of which is the *rulesetfiles* attributes, where you specify the rulesets you want to use. You can use either the full filename (*rulesets/basic.xml*), or simply the name of the ruleset ("basic").

You will need to specify the *targetJdk* attribute to "1.5" if you are using Java 5. You can also use the *failonerror* attribute to force a build failure if errors are found. This can be useful for continuous integration environments.

Finally, you need to provide a formatter and a fileset specifying the classes to be analyzed.

A simple example is shown here:

```
<target name="pmd">
    <pmd rulesetfiles="basic,javabeans,junit,controversial" targetJdk="1.5"
     failonerror="true">
        <formatter type="html" toFile="reports/pmd-report.html"/>
        <fileset dir="src">
            <include name="**/*.java"/>
        </fileset>
    </pmd>
</target>
```

You can also specify the rulesets as nested elements, as shown here:

```
<target name="pmd">
    <pmd targetJdk="1.5">
        <ruleset>rulesets/controversial.xml</ruleset>
        <ruleset>rulesets/company-rules.xml</ruleset>
        <formatter type="html" toFile="reports/pmd-report.html"/>
        <fileset dir="src">
            <include name="**/*.java"/>
        </fileset>
    </pmd>
</target>
```

This will generate a report similar to the one in Figure 22-5. This is functional but not very pretty. PMD comes with a number of XSLT stylesheets that you can use to produce something a bit more presentable. Just produce an XML output and run it through one of the XSLT provided stylesheets, as shown here (see Figure 22-6):

```
<target name="pmd">
  <pmd rulesetfiles="basic,javabeans,junit,controversial" targetJdk="1.5"
   failonerror="true">
    <formatter type="xml" toFile="reports/pmd-report.xml"/>
    <fileset dir="src">
      <include name="**/*.java"/>
    </fileset>
  </pmd>

  <xslt in="reports/pmd-report.xml" style="${pmd.home}/etc/xslt/wz-pmd-report.xslt"
   out="reports/pmd-report.html" />
</target>
```

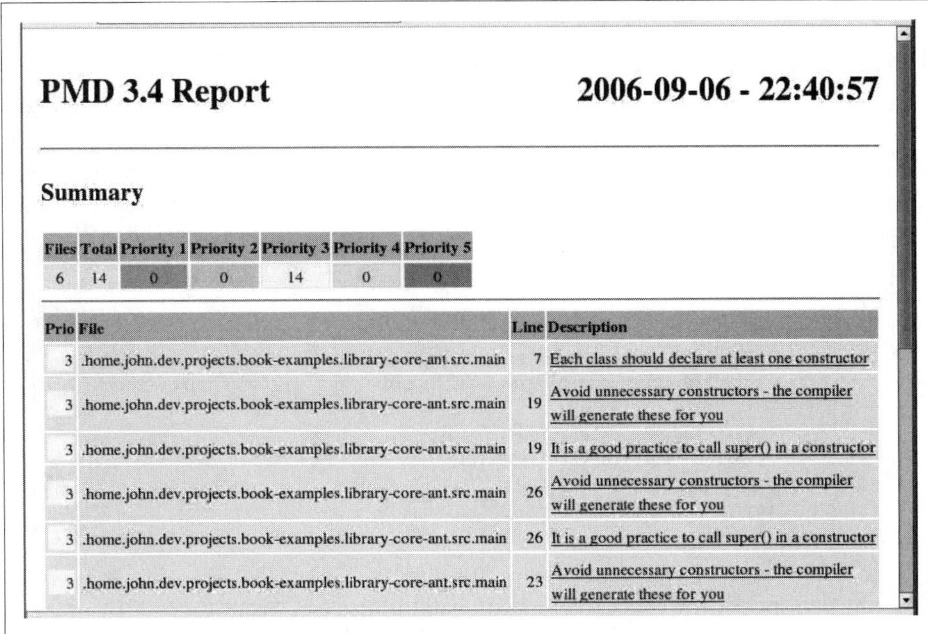

PMD 3.4 Report **2006-09-06 - 22:40:57**

Summary

Files	Total	Priority 1	Priority 2	Priority 3	Priority 4	Priority 5
6	14	0	0	14	0	0

Prio	File	Line	Description
3	.home.john.dev.projects.book-examples.library-core-ant.src.main	7	Each class should declare at least one constructor
3	.home.john.dev.projects.book-examples.library-core-ant.src.main	19	Avoid unnecessary constructors - the compiler will generate these for you
3	.home.john.dev.projects.book-examples.library-core-ant.src.main	19	It is a good practice to call super() in a constructor
3	.home.john.dev.projects.book-examples.library-core-ant.src.main	26	Avoid unnecessary constructors - the compiler will generate these for you
3	.home.john.dev.projects.book-examples.library-core-ant.src.main	26	It is a good practice to call super() in a constructor
3	.home.john.dev.projects.book-examples.library-core-ant.src.main	23	Avoid unnecessary constructors - the compiler will generate these for you

Figure 22-6. A PMD report generated by Ant

Alternatively, you can try out the corley-pmd-report.xslt or the pmd-report.xslt stylesheets, or write your own.

22.10 Using PMD in Maven

Like Checkstyle (see Section 21.9), PMD is well integrated with Maven, which is packaged with a PMD report plug-in. This plug-in will generate both the PMD and CPD reports, with cross-references to the HTML version of the source code generated by JXR (if the JXR report has been included—see Figure 22-7).

To set up basic PMD reporting in your Maven 2 project, just add a reference to the PMD plug-in in the reporting section of your *pom.xml* file:

```
<reporting>
  <plugins>
    <plugin>
      <groupId>org.apache.maven.plugins</groupId>
      <artifactId>maven-pmd-plugin</artifactId>
    </plugin>
  </plugins>
</reporting>
```

You can generate the report by either generating the entire Maven site (using the *mvn site* command), or by invoking the PMD report directly:

```
$ mvn pmd:pmd
```

This will generate the PMD and CPD reports in the `target/site` directory.

You will generally need to fine-tune the plug-in configuration by adding some extra parameters to the *<configuration>* element. For example, if your project uses JDK 1.5, you will need to specify this with the *<targetJdk>* configuration element. Another useful configuration element is *<failonerror>*, which forces build failure whenever errors are detected:

```
<reporting>
  <plugins>
      <plugin>
         <groupId>org.apache.maven.plugins</groupId>
         <artifactId>maven-pmd-plugin</artifactId>
         <configuration>
            <targetJdk>1.5</targetJdk>
            <failonerror>true</failonerror>
         </configuration>
      </plugin>
  </plugins>
</reporting>
```

You can also specify the exact rulesets you want to use (see Section 22.4). By default, the *basic*, *imports*, and *unusedcode* rulesets will be used. If you want to specify another set of rulesets, you list them in the *<ruleset>* element, as follows:

```
<reporting>
  <plugins>
      <plugin>
         <groupId>org.apache.maven.plugins</groupId>
         <artifactId>maven-pmd-plugin</artifactId>
         <configuration>
            <targetJdk>1.5</targetJdk>
            <rulesets>
               <ruleset>/rulesets/basic.xml</ruleset>
               <ruleset>/rulesets/javabeans.xml</ruleset>
               <ruleset>/rulesets/junit.xml</ruleset>
               <ruleset>/rulesets/controversial.xml</ruleset>
            </rulesets>
         </configuration>
      </plugin>
  </plugins>
</reporting>
```

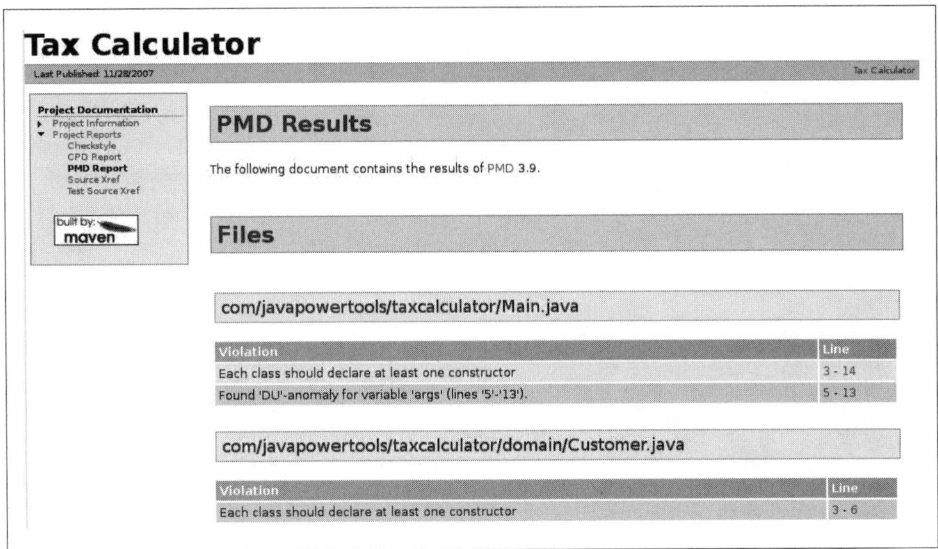
Tax Calculator
Last Published: 11/28/2007
Tax Calculator
Project Documentation
Project Information
Project Reports
Checkstyle
CPD Report
PMD Report
Source Xref
Test Source Xref
built by: maven
PMD Results
The following document contains the results of PMD 3.9.
Files
com/javapowertools/taxcalculator/Main.java
Violation
Line
Each class should declare at least one constructor
3 - 14
Found 'DU'-anomaly for variable 'args' (lines '5'-'13').
5 - 13
com/javapowertools/taxcalculator/domain/Customer.java
Violation
Line
Each class should declare at least one constructor
3 - 6

Figure 22-7. A PMD report generated by Maven

CHAPTER 23

Preemptive Error Detection with FindBugs

23.1 FindBugs: A Specialized Bug Killer

FindBugs is another static analysis tool for Java, similar in some ways to Checkstyle (see Chapter 21) and PMD (see Chapter 22), but with a quite different focus. FindBugs is not concerned by formatting or coding standards and only marginally interested in best practices: in fact, it concentrates on detecting potential bugs and performance issues. It does a very good job of finding these, and can detect many types of common, hard-to-find bugs. Indeed, FindBugs is capable of detecting quite a different set of issues than PMD or Checkstyle with a relatively high degree of precision. As such, it can be a useful addition to your static analysis toolbox.

FindBugs was written in response to the overwhelming number of issues raised by other tools such as Checkstyle and PMD. Many of the issues raised by these tools are actually false positives and both tools need to be fine-tuned to avoid real issues being hidden by too many false positives. FindBugs tries hard to concentrate on identifying only issues that involve genuine potential coding errors.

FindBugs is the result of a research project at the University of Maryland. It uses static code analysis to detect potential bugs using the notion of "bug patterns." Bug patterns are poor coding practices that are generally incorrect and may lead to application errors. For example, in the following code, if the address variable is null, the second line will generate a `NullPointerException`:

```
Address address = client.getAddress();
if ((address != null) || (address.getPostCode() != null)) {
    ...
}
```

Another example is shown here, in which the `items` member variable is accessed without having been initialized:

```
public class ShoppingCart {
    private List items;
```

```
        public addItem(Item item) {
            items.add(item);
        }
    }
```

Errors like these are often easy to identify simply by reading the code. However, although effective, code reviews are labor-intensive and time-consuming, and wherever possible it is easier to let the machine do the inspection for you! FindBugs is designed to do just that.

FindBugs uses the Apache BCEL library to analyze the classes in your application and detect potential bugs. FindBugs rules (or "detectors") use a variety of inspection techniques, from examining the structure of the class right through to studying the detailed dataflow through the class. In addition to the detectors provided by FindBugs, with a bit of work, you can write your own custom-built detectors.

FindBugs comes with over 200 rules divided into different categories:

Correctness
: These issues involve code that is probably incorrect in some way, for example, code that involves an infinite recursive loop or that reads a field that is never written. Issues in this category are almost certainly bugs.

Bad practice
: According to the FindBugs team, issues in this category involve "clear violation of recommended and standard coding practice." The bad practices that FindBugs is interested in generally have a direct correlation with potential defects, for example, code that drops exceptions or fails to close file or database resources. Some of these issues are also detected by PMD.

Performance
: These issues aim at detecting potential performance issues, such as code involving unnecessary object creation, or using string concatenation in a loop rather than using a StringBuffer.

Multithreaded correctness
: These is a special category of issues involving problems with synchronized and multithreaded code.

Dodgy
: This type of issue involves code which seems odd, or "smells bad," in XP terminology, such as unused local variables or unchecked casts. According to the FindBugs team, less than half of these issues involve actual bugs.

FindBugs can be used in three ways; as a standalone Swing application, in Eclipse using the Eclipse plug-in, or integrated into the build process as an Ant task or Maven report. In practice, the standalone application is rarely used: developers prefer to be able to invoke FindBugs directly from within their work environment, whereas project managers and quality assurance people appreciate being able to display project-wide bug reports using the reporting features.

In the rest of this chapter, we will look at how to use FindBugs in these different contexts.

23.2 Using FindBugs in Eclipse

FindBugs comes with an Eclipse plug-in that provides excellent integration with this IDE. Using FindBugs from within Eclipse has obvious advantages for a developer: potentially dangerous bugs can be identified and fixed even before code is committed to the repository, which allows for a much tighter development cycle.

Installing the FindBugs Plug-In

The easiest way to install the FindBugs Eclipse plug-in is to use the Eclipse Update site. You do this in the usual way:

1. Open the Help→Software Updates→Find and Install menu.
2. Click Next, and choose New Remote Site.
3. Enter the URL of the remote site (*http://findbugs.cs.umd.edu/eclipse/*) and an appropriate name such as "FindBugs."
4. Make sure you have the FindBugs site checked in the "Sites to include in search" window, and click Finish. Then just go through the installation screens to install the plug-in.

Alternatively, you can download it from the plug-in download site* and unzip the file into your Eclipse plug-in directory.

Once you have installed the plug-in, you need to activate FindBugs for your project. Open the project properties window (Project→Properties). You will now have a FindBugs entry (see Figure 23-1). This window allows you to configure FindBugs in detail for your particular project by selecting which rules you want to apply. If you check the "Run FindBugs automatically" checkbox, FindBugs will check for issues every time you modify a class.

You can also filter the types of issues you want reported, either by priority or by category. For example, if you want to ignore all low priority issues, just set the minimum priority to "Medium" (this is the recommended level).

Note that some FindBugs issues are quite slow, such as *FindTwoLockWait*, *FindNullDeref*, *FindOpenStream*, *FindInconsistentSync2*, and *FindSleepWithLockHeld*. On larger projects, you may want to disable these rules in the development environments and leave this sort of detection to the continuous integration environment.

* *http://findbugs.sourceforge.net/downloads.html*

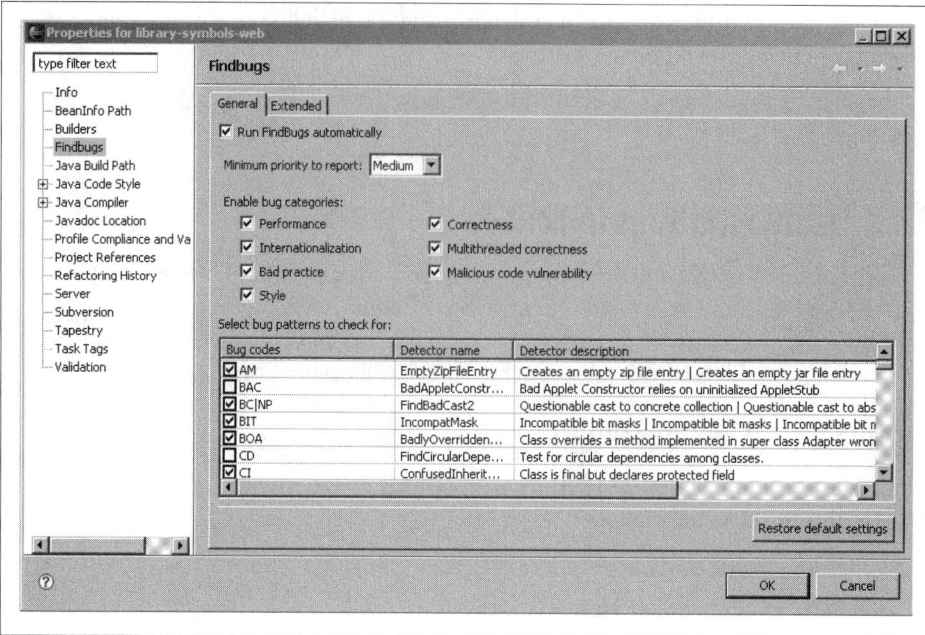

Figure 23-1. Configuring FindBugs for a project

Detecting and Displaying Errors

The FindBugs Eclipse plug-in is a simple, lightweight tool with few bells and whistles. If you have configured FindBugs to run automatically, it will check for bugs every time you modify a class. You can also run FindBugs using the "FindBugs" entry in the contextual menu. For large projects, this can take a while.

The simplest way to view the issues raised by FindBugs is in the Problems view, where they are listed with other errors and warnings (see Figure 23-2). FindBug issues are also indicated in the source code by a dedicated icon (an easily recognizable red bug). If you need more details, click on the bug icon in the margin or select the "Show Bug Details" entry in the contextual menu; this will display the "Bug Details" view, which contains a more detailed description of the issue.

One thing to remember about FindBugs is that it works on compiled bytecode, not on Java source files. So, if your project is not configured to build automatically after each modification (Project→Build Automatically), you won't see any changes in the errors displayed by FindBugs until you recompile manually.

23.3 Selectively Suppressing Rules with FindBug Filters

Like Checkstyle (see Section 21.7), FindBugs lets you define rules indicating which rules should be used or excluded in particular cases, such as in a particular class or

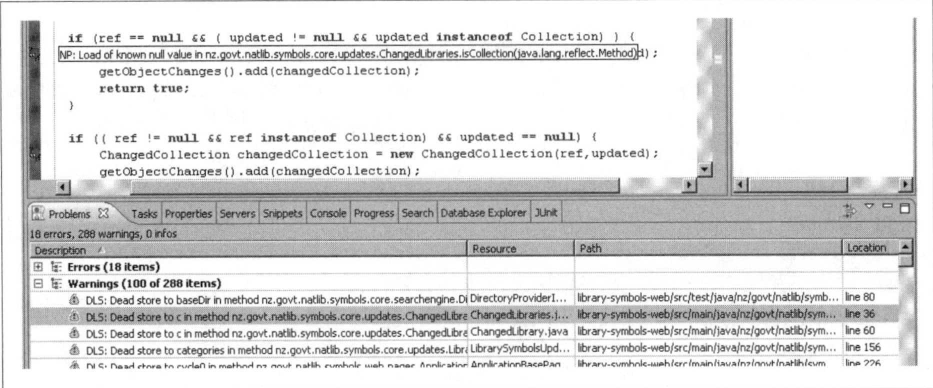

Figure 23-2. FindBug issues are listed in the Problems view

method. A FindBugs filter works by combining one or more filter clauses, such as *Class*, *BugCode*, *Method*, and *Priority*. Matching cases may be included or ignored, depending on how the filter file is used. In most cases, you use a filter file to ignore specific issues.

Let's look at some examples. The following filter will match DE (method might drop exception) and EI (method may expose internal representation) in the `com.mycompany.example.MyClass` class:

```
<FindBugsFilter>
     <Match>
       <Class name="com.mycompany.example.MyClass"/ >
       <BugCode name="DE, EI"/ >
     </Match>
</FindBugsFilter>
```

More precisely, we can go down to the method level. The following filter will match these issues, but only in the `processData()` method:

```
<FindBugsFilter>
     <Match>
       <Class name="com.mycompany.example.MyClass" />
       <Method name="processData" />
       <BugCode name="DE, EI" />
     </Match>
</FindBugsFilter>
```

Or, if there are several methods that need to match, you can use the *Or* clause:

```
<FindBugsFilter>
     <Match>
       <Class name="com.mycompany.example.MyClass" />
       <Or>
         <Method name="collectData" />
         <Method name="processData" />
       <Or/>
       <BugCode name="DE, EI" />
```

```
    </Match>
</FindBugsFilter>
```

You will often want to exclude certain rules for groups of classes, such as automatically-generated classes over which you have little control. To do this, you can use regular expressions in the class name expression. Regular expressions in FindBugs start with a “~”. The following deactivates the ICAST rule for all classes in the `com.wakaleo.continuum.jabber` package:

```
<FindBugsFilter>
    <Match>
        <Class name="~com.wakaleo.continuum.jabber.*" />
        <BugCode name="ICAST" />
    </Match>
</FindBugsFilter>
```

In Eclipse, you can use these files in the FindBugs properties page, in the “Extended” tab (see Figure 23-3). Simply add the filter files to the Include or Exclude list, as appropriate.

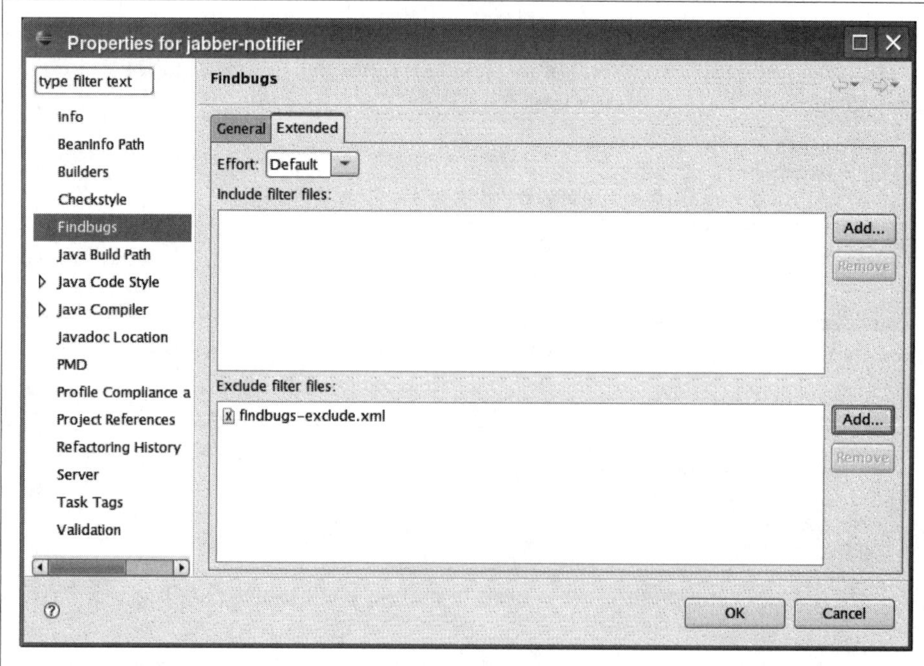

Figure 23-3. Using FindBugs filters in Eclipse

We will see further on other ways to invoke these filters.

23.4 Using FindBugs Annotations

Another interesting way to suppress FindBugs warnings is to use annotations. To use annotations, include the FindBugs *annotations.jar* file in your project classpath.

One of the most useful of the FindBugs annotations is *@SuppressWarnings*. You can use this at several levels. For example, if you use it at the class level, it will suppress all FindBugs warnings for this class:

```
import edu.umd.cs.findbugs.annotations.SuppressWarnings;

@SuppressWarnings
public class JabberPublisher {
...
}
```

Alternatively, you can use it at a method level, which limits the scope of the suppression to the method:

```
import edu.umd.cs.findbugs.annotations.SuppressWarnings;

public class JabberPublisher {

    @SuppressWarnings
    void doSomething() {
        ...
    }
}
```

Finally, you can specify the exact rule you want to deactivate. In the following example, we deactivate the *FindDeadLocalStores* rule for the `doSomething()` method:

```
import edu.umd.cs.findbugs.annotations.SuppressWarnings;

public class JabberPublisher {

    @SuppressWarnings("DLS")
    void doSomething() {
        ...
    }
}
```

Other annotations let you help FindBugs detect potentially incorrect uses of your code. For example, in the following code sample, the `getClientByAccountNumber()` method returns `null` if no matching client is found. Of course, you should mention this in the Javadoc, but you can also use the *@CheckForNull* annotation to ensure that anyone using this method checks to see if the method has returned `null`:

```
import edu.umd.cs.findbugs.annotations.CheckForNull;
...

    @CheckForNull
    void getClientByAccountNumber(String accNumber) throws HibernateException {
        ...
    }
```

23.5 Using FindBugs in Ant

FindBugs also integrates well into the project build lifecycle. Project managers and quality assurance staff appreciate the ability of tools such as FindBugs to monitor and report on code quality. In this section, we will look at how to use the FindBugs Ant task to run checks and generate reports using Ant.

To use FindBugs in Ant, you first need to download and install the FindBugs tool in a convenient directory. For example, you can install it into a directory called `tools` in your home directory, as shown here:

```
$ cd ~/tools
$ unzip findbugs-1.3.0.zip
$ ln -s findbugs-1.3.0 findbugs
```

The easiest way to use the FindBugs Ant task is to copy the *findbugs-ant.jar* file into your Ant *lib* directory, as shown in this example:

```
$ cd ~/tools/findbugs
$ cp lib/findbugs-ant.jar /usr/share/ant/lib/
```

If you can't (or don't want to) modify your Ant installation, you can install FindBugs into a local directory and refer to this directory using a *<classpath>* directive, as shown here:

```
<taskdef name="findbugs" classname="edu.umd.cs.findbugs.anttask.FindBugsTask" >
    <classpath>
        <fileset dir="${findbugs.home}/lib">
          <include name="**/*.jar"/>
        </fileset>
    </classpath>
</taskdef>
```

In both cases, you will need to specify your FindBugs installation directory. You typically do this by defining a property pointing to the `findbugs` directory:

```
<property name="findbugs.home" value="${user.home}/tools/findbugs" />
```

Now you can write your FindBugs task. The following target will generate an XML report listing the issues detected by FindBugs:

```
<target name="findbugs" depends="compile">
  <findbugs home="${findbugs.home}" output="xml" failOnError="true"
   outputFile="findbugs-report.xml">
    <class location="${build.classes.dir}" />
    <auxClasspath refId="compile.classpath" />
```

```
        <sourcePath path="src" />
      </findbugs>
    </target>
```

There are few mandatory attributes. You need to provide the path to your FindBugs installation in the *home* attribute. FindBugs operates on compiled bytecode, not on Java source code, so you also need to tell FindBugs where to find the compiled classes. The *class* attribute specifies the directory in which FindBugs can find the compiled classes to be analyzed. You can also specify a packaged file such as a JAR or ZIP file, for example.

The *auxClasspath* element is not mandatory, but it often comes in handy. You use it to list your dependencies, which FindBugs needs to be able to do a complete analysis of your code. You can define it in the same way as you would a normal Ant classpath element.

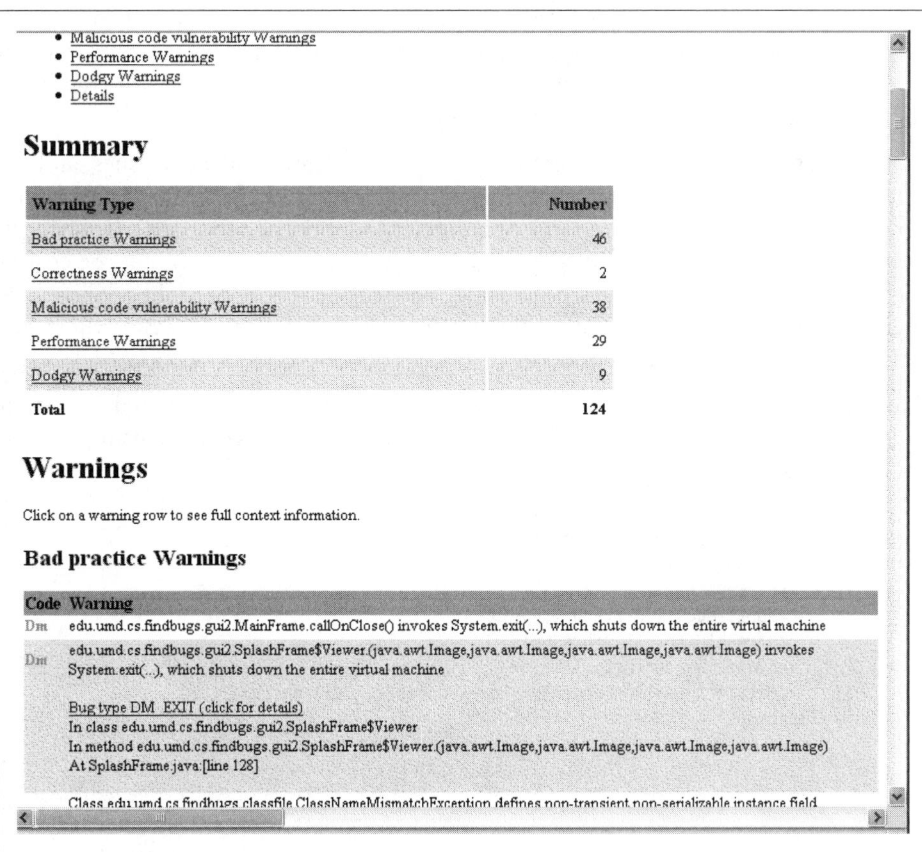

Malicious code vulnerability Warnings
Performance Warnings
Dodgy Warnings
Details
Summary
Warning Type
Number
Bad practice Warnings
46
Correctness Warnings
2
Malicious code vulnerability Warnings
38
Performance Warnings
29
Dodgy Warnings
9
Total
124
Warnings
Click on a warning row to see full context information.
Bad practice Warnings
Code
Warning
Dm
edu.umd.cs.findbugs.gui2.MainFrame.callOnClose() invokes System.exit(...), which shuts down the entire virtual machine
Dm
edu.umd.cs.findbugs.gui2.SplashFrame$Viewer.(java.awt.Image,java.awt.Image,java.awt.Image,java.awt.Image,java.awt.Image) invokes System.exit(...), which shuts down the entire virtual machine
Bug type DM_EXIT (click for details)
In class edu.umd.cs.findbugs.gui2.SplashFrame$Viewer
In method edu.umd.cs.findbugs.gui2.SplashFrame$Viewer.(java.awt.Image,java.awt.Image,java.awt.Image,java.awt.Image,java.awt.Image)
At SplashFrame.java:[line 128]

Figure 23-4. A FindBugs report generated by Ant"

By default, the output format is "xml," which produces a fairly laconic list of errors. The "xml:withMessages" output format will produce an XML file containing human-readable messages, which is useful if you want to use your own XSL stylesheet to generate a report. Otherwise, you can produce a more human-readable report using the "html" format. A typical report is shown in Figure 23-4.

On larger projects, FindBugs can be quite demanding in terms of memory and machine resources. If necessary, you can increase the memory available for the FindBugs analysis by using the *jvmArgs* option, as shown here:

```
<findbugs home="${findbugs.home}" output="html" failOnError="true"
 outputFile="findbugs-report.html" jvmArgs="-Xms256m -Xmx800m">
    <class location="${build.classes.dir}" />
    <sourcePath path="src" />
</findbugs>
```

The FindBugs task takes a lot of other optional parameters, such as *excludeFilter* and *includeFilter*, which let you specify filters describing which bugs to exclude or include respectively (see Section 23.3). It also takes *reportLevel*, which indicates the minimum priority of issues that will be raised, and *threshold*, which lets you limit the reporting to issues of at least the specified level of severity.

FindBugs uses some fairly complicated algorithms to identify potential issues, and the number and accuracy of bugs found will vary depending on how much computing power you use. You can use the *effort* parameter to influence FindBugs's behavior in this regard. Setting *effort* to "max" will allow you to increase precision at the cost of higher memory use and slower processing, whereas setting it to "min" will reduce memory use and increase speed, at the cost of lower precision. You can adjust this parameter in the Eclipse plug-in on the extended properties page (Section 23.3).

Another useful parameter is *omitVisitors*, which lets you list rules that you do not want to be applied anywhere in the project. Here is a more complete example using some of these options:

```
<findbugs home="${findbugs.home}" output="html" failOnError="true"
outputFile="findbugs-report.html" jvmArgs="-Xms256m -Xmx800m">
    <class location="${build.classes.dir}" />
    <sourcePath path="src" />
    <reportLevel>low</reportLevel>
    <threshold>normal</threshold>
    <effort>max</effort>
    <omitVisitors>FindDeadLocalStores,UnreadFields</omitVisitors>
</findbugs>
```

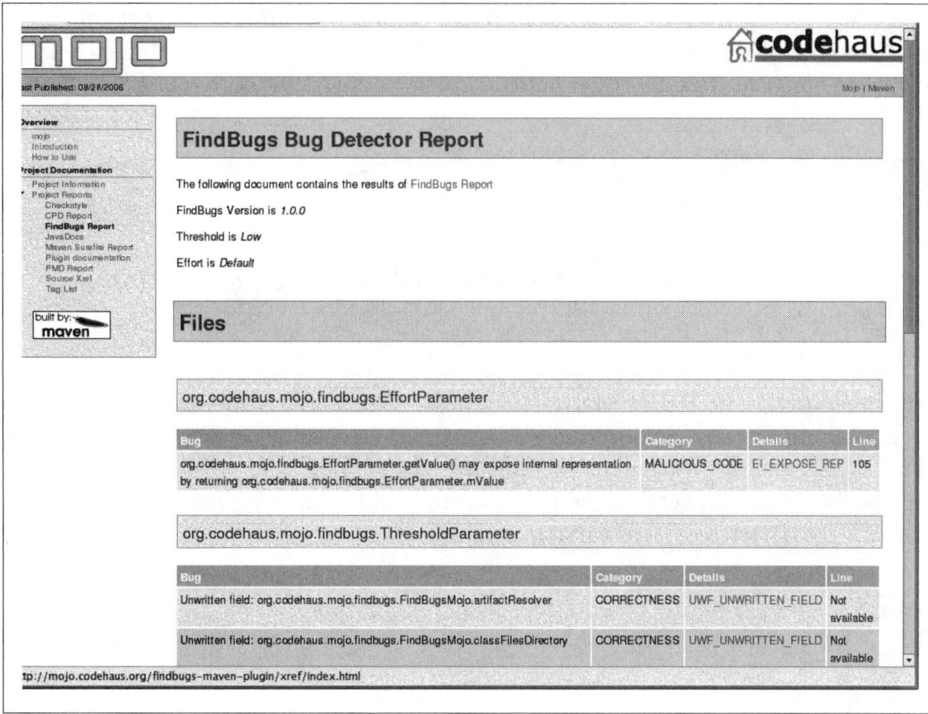

Figure 23-5. A FindBugs report generated by Maven

23.6 Using FindBugs in Maven

You can also use FindBugs to generate bug reports in your Maven build process, via the Maven 2 FindBugs report plug-in. Like many other innovative Maven tools, this plug-in is hosted by Codehaus under the Mojo project.* It is quite simple to use and integrates perfectly with the other reports in the Maven site.

Integrating a FindBugs report into your Maven site can be as simple as adding the following plug-in to the reports section in your *pom.xml* file:

```
<plugin>
  <groupId>org.codehaus.mojo</groupId>
  <artifactId>findbugs-maven-plugin</artifactId>
  <configuration>
    <threshold>Normal</threshold>
  </configuration>
</plugin>
```

You can create the report by generating the entire maven site, using the *mvn site* command. This will produce a report similar to the one in Figure 23-5.

* *http://mojo.codehaus.org/findbugs-maven-plugin/*

This plug-in takes most of the optional parameters as the Ant task (see Section 23.5), which you specify in the *<configuration>* section: *threshold*, *reportLevel*, *excludeFilterFile* and *includeFilterFile*, *effort*, and *omitVisitors* are all supported.

```
<plugin>
  <groupId>org.codehaus.mojo</groupId>
  <artifactId>findbugs-maven-plugin</artifactId>
  <configuration>
    <threshold>Normal</threshold>
    <effort>Max</effort>
    <excludeFilterFile>findbugs-exclude.xml</excludeFilterFile>
    <omitVisitors>FindDeadLocalStores,UnreadFields</omitVisitors>
  </configuration>
</plugin>
```

One notable exception is the *jvmArgs* parameter, which is not supported in the current version. FindBugs is a memory-hungry beast, and you will probably need to increase the available memory if your project is of any size. If you need to provide more memory for the FindBugs processing, you will need to do it at a higher level, using the *MAVEN_OPTS* environment variable, as shown here:

```
$ export MAVEN_OPTS=-Xmx512M
$ mvn site
```

23.7 Conclusion

FindBugs is a useful and innovative static analysis tool that concentrates on finding potential bugs rather than coding style. Issues related to coding style and best practices aim at making code more readable and easier to maintain, mostly affecting the developers working on the application, and, indirectly, the organization that is paying them. Bugs, by contrast, affect the end user.

Although there is some overlap with the rules of other static analysis tools such as Checkstyle and PMD in particular, FindBugs maintains a strong focus on only detecting potential bugs. As a result, FindBugs tends to raise fewer issues than these other tools; however, the issues raised should be taken seriously.

CHAPTER 24

Inspecting the Results—Semiautomated Code Review with Jupiter

24.1 Introducing Jupiter—A Code Review Tool for Eclipse

Code reviews are possibility the single most efficient way to reduce defects and improve code quality. Simply put, code reviews involve manually inspecting source code for defects, often using a checklist of common errors to help focus the search. In addition, they are an effective way of improving your team's development skills.

As Cédric Beust points out in his interesting blog entry on the topic,* there are two main approaches to code reviews, which he calls "blocking" code reviews and "nonblocking" code reviews. Blocking code reviews involve a more formal, rigid process in which code changes must be approved by a reviewer before they can be committed to the source code repository. Although this strategy should, theoretically at least, let less defects get into the code repository, it has the obvious disadvantage of potentially blocking a developer's work until her code changes are reviewed.

Nonblocking code reviews are less formal and more flexible. Developers submit their code changes to a reviewer, who will review them in due course. However, the developers don't need to wait for the review before submitting their changes to version control. This more agile approach avoids blocking developer work, without necessarily compromising quality. Indeed, knowing that your code will be examined is a strong motivation for writing clearer, well-commented code.

Whatever strategy you choose, you will need an underlying process that all team members must understand well and adopt. In general, if you want to introduce a new development process or best practice into an organization, it should be as simple as

* *http://beust.com/weblog/archives/000393.html*

possible. As Einstein once said, "Things should be made as simple as possible—but no simpler."

Heeding Einstein's advice, Jupiter, an open source collaborative Eclipse code review tool, uses a simple, lightweight code review process that is easy to learn and adopt. The result of a research project by the Collaborative Software Development Laboratory at the University of Hawaii, the Jupiter plug-in stores code reviews in an XML file format and maintains them in the project configuration management system alongside the source code.

This chapter will walk you through a Jupiter install and the stages of a Jupiter code review process.

24.2 Installing Jupiter in Eclipse

Jupiter is only available as an Eclipse plug-in. Like many Eclipse plug-ins, the easiest way to install Jupiter is to use the Remote Update site. Launch Eclipse and perform the following steps:

1. Open the Help→Software Updates→Find and Install menu.
2. Click Next, and choose New Remote Site.
3. Enter the remote site URL (*http://csdl.ics.hawaii.edu/Tools/Jupiter/Download*), and the site name (e.g., "Jupiter").
4. Make sure you have the Jupiter site checked in the "Sites to include in search" window, and click Finish. Then just go through the installation screens to install the plug-in.

The Jupiter plug-in adds a new perspective to your Eclipse workspace, called "Review," which is the workbench of the Jupiter code review process. You can open this perspective by selecting "Window →Open Perspective → Other... → Review" (see Figure 24-1). This perspective comes with views designed to help you visualize and manage review issues—such as the "Review Table" and "Review Editor" views—visualize existing review issues and add new ones in the source code, and switch between different review process phases.

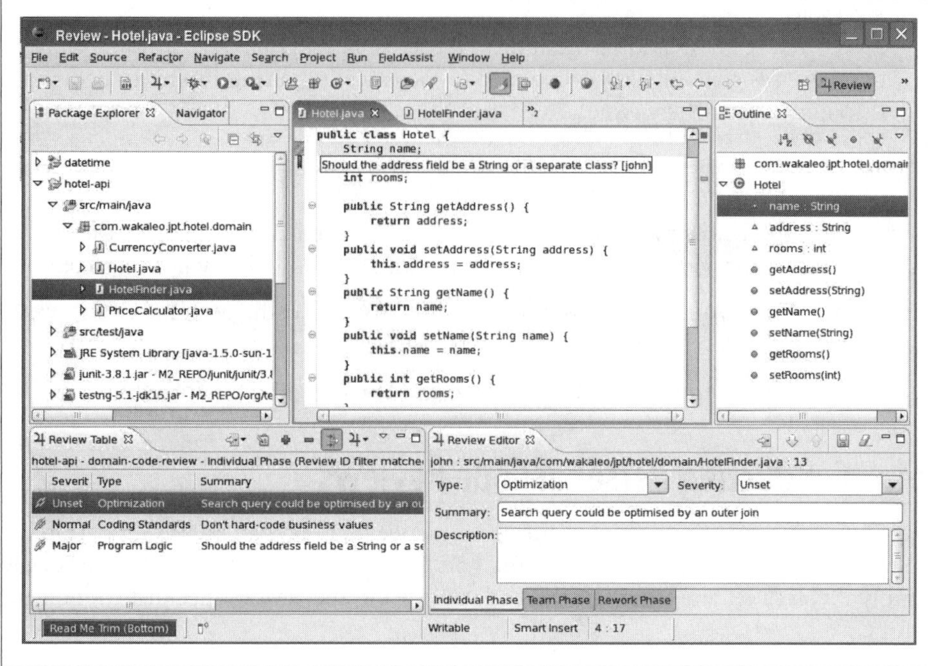

Figure 24-1. The Jupiter Review perspective

24.3 Understanding the Jupiter Code Review Process

The code review process implemented in Jupiter is relatively simple, and it should suffice for most projects. In Jupiter, you conduct a code review in the following four stages:

Configuration
: The review initiator sets up the review, defining a unique "Review ID" for this review, and specifying the files to be reviewed, who will review the code, and what issues can be raised. Depending on your organization, the review initiator could be the author, the team leader, or someone in QA.

Individual code review
: Each reviewer examines the code individually, using a review checklist and raising issues as they encounter them. To create a new issue, you just place the cursor on the suspicious code, right-click, and select "Add Jupiter Issue." Jupiter saves the issues you create in XML form directly in the project directory.

Team review

The review team (including the author) meet to discuss issues and decide on actions to take. This generally involves a face-to-face meeting, using Jupiter to help work through all the review issues.

Rework

The developer goes through the raised issues and fixes them.

Throughout the whole process, the review files are stored and updated in the source code repository, providing a history of raised issues and how they where corrected.

For completeness, you should also add a preliminary phase, the personal code review, during which the developer reviews his own code.

In the rest of this chapter, we will look at each of these stages in more detail.

24.4 Conducting Personal Code Reviews

Personal code reviews are a highly effective practice that plays an important part in the Software Engineering Institute's Personal Software Process. A personal code review simply involves reading through the code and using the review checklist to look for errors.

Using a review checklist is an important part of the review process. Reviews are much more efficient when you have precise goals in mind. With a review checklist, you actively hunt specific bugs, whereas, without one, you just wander through the code hoping to come across one.

A review checklist contains defects or categories of defects that are known to have caused problems in the past. If you are already using tools like Checkstyle (see Chapter 21) and PMD (see Chapter 22), you don't need to add any coding standards or duplicate any best practices that those other tools already have verified. Keep it short and simple to begin with, and then add new items as you come across them. And don't forget to get everyone involved.

One notable difference between the approach described here and the personal review process recommended in the Personal Software Process is that, in the latter, the individual review comes before compiling the code. One of the main arguments for this is that reviews conducted before compilation tend to be more thorough. Another reason is that if you let the tools find all the compilation errors, as well as the coding standards violations and other best practices errors, you will have a harder time tracking the number of issues raised.

However, knowing how hard it is to put any sort of rigorous software development process into place, I believe in getting the most leverage out of your available tools and reserving human involvement for work that only humans can do. Indeed, if you want to introduce a new process into an organization, you should put as few obstacles as possible in the way and make the process as painless as possible.

The following is a simple strategy for performing a personal code review:

1. Obtain the code review checklist and display the class to be reviewed.
2. Run through the defect categories in the checklist. For each category, go through the code and make sure it isn't an issue. If it is, either fix it (if it will take less than 30 seconds) or note it for later. Check off each item you finish.
3. When finished, fix any outstanding issues.

Once this is done, the peer review process can begin.

24.5 Configuration

Tools and processes are all well and good, but, in practice, someone has to get the ball rolling. That person is the review initiator. Many people can play this role. It could be the owner of the code, the team leader or project manager, the chief architect, or even a QA person. It's up to you to decide what suits your organization best.

Keep in mind that many developers will consider code reviews a bit of a chore at best, and they will not come forth and volunteer their code for a code review. Others will delay the process as long as possible, waiting for their code to be as perfect as possible (for example, after the delivery date when they have more time), or just hoping that people will forget about them. If this is the case, the team leader or architect should take responsibility for initiating code reviews.

A couple of other considerations may also weigh in favor of a centralized approach:

- Initiating a review involves assigning team members as reviewers.
- Initiating a review involves deciding which types of issues will be evaluated.

Many organizations will prefer to have these activities done centrally by one person (e.g., the project manager, the architect, or the lead developer).

By contrast, for some projects, it may be more appropriate to have individual developers commit their own code. The advantages of this approach include the following:

- When you notify reviewers that some code is ready to be reviewed, you should include a brief description of the purpose of the code (for new code) or the justification for the change (for changes to existing code). This is often best done by the developer.
- For any nontrivial classes, unit tests and unit test results should be submitted for review at the same time as the classes. Again, the developer is probably the best person to do this.

This approach works well if a single person is responsible for committing code to the next release version candidate. In open source projects, this person is often called the committer. In this sort of project organization, developers may commit their code to configuration management whenever necessary, but the committer is responsible for

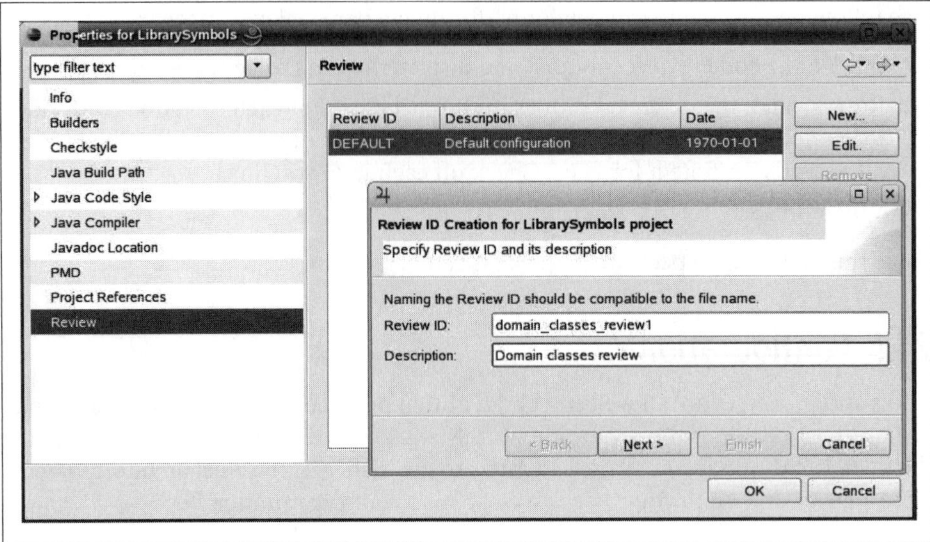

Figure 24-2. Creating a new review

committing reviewed code to the release candidate code (which is often a new branch in the configuration management system). This also gives developers a good reason to have their code reviewed; if it isn't reviewed, it won't make it into the release version!

In any case, whatever strategy you adopt, it is important to agree on who initiates code reviews and who participates. You need to put this down in writing and to make sure everyone knows and understands the process.

To initiate a review, open the project properties and go to the review entry. Click on "New..." to create a new review entry (see Figure 24-2).

Each review entry corresponds to a real physical code review. You need to specify an identifier (unique to this project) and a short description. The identifier becomes the name of the .jupiter file, which will end up in your source code repository, so remember to put something compatible with a filename structure. It is also worthwhile taking the time to come up with some sort off naming standard to make review files easier to identify later on.

Now, specify the source code files you want to review (see Figure 24-3). Typically, a code review will concentrate on one class, although it may include some other related or dependent classes as well.

The next thing you need to do is organize the review team. The following screens enable you to select the review team members and the code author (see Figure 24-4). Jupiter stores the comments of each team member in a separate file under configuration management, so you should use filename-compatible names (such as logins) for your team members. To make life easier, you should put the whole team into the DEFAULT review item (see Section 24.6); new reviews will then display this list by default.

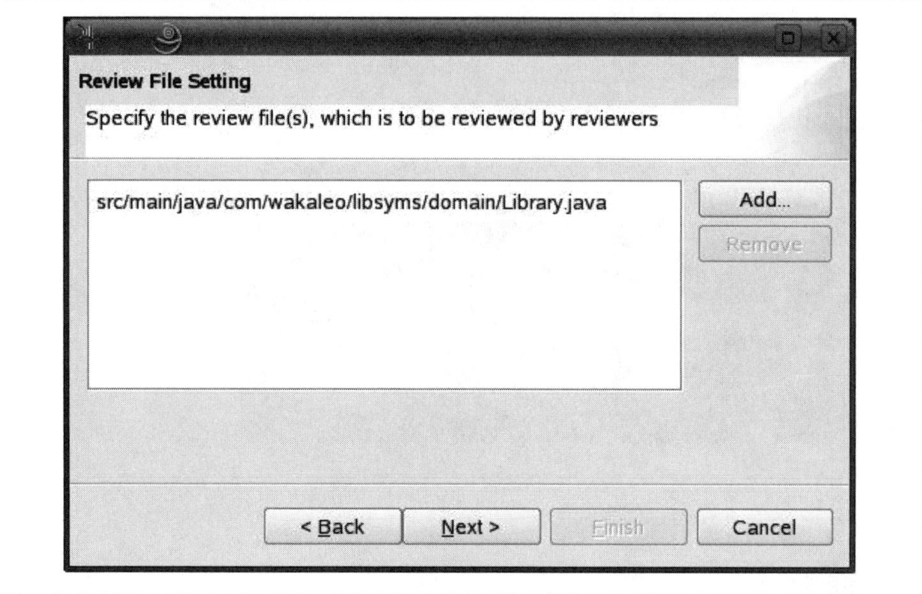

Figure 24-3. Specifying the source code files to be reviewed

In the following screens, you can specify issue types, severities, and so on. You usually leave these screens as-is: any modification of these lists should be done in the special DEFAULT review (see Section 24.6) so that other newly created reviews can adopt them by default.

Next, you have to define a place in your source code directories where the review XML files will be stored. This is a directory relative to your project root directory.

Finally, you can set up filters for different situations (see Figure 24-5). Jupiter uses filters to help guide issues through the review process workflow. Each phase has its own filter, which you can customize to let people concentrate better on the work to be done during that phase.

The filter feature is best illustrated by discussing the default filter for each review phase, which works quite well:

Individual phase
: The default filter for this phase is "Reviewer:automatic," which means that individual reviewers will see only their own review issues.

Team phase
: The default filter for this phase is "Resolution:unset," which simply means that during the team review, reviewers will see all the issues that have not been resolved. In Jupiter-speak, the "resolution" of an issue is when the review team decides on which action to take, either "Valid needs fixing" (the issue is a real issue, which

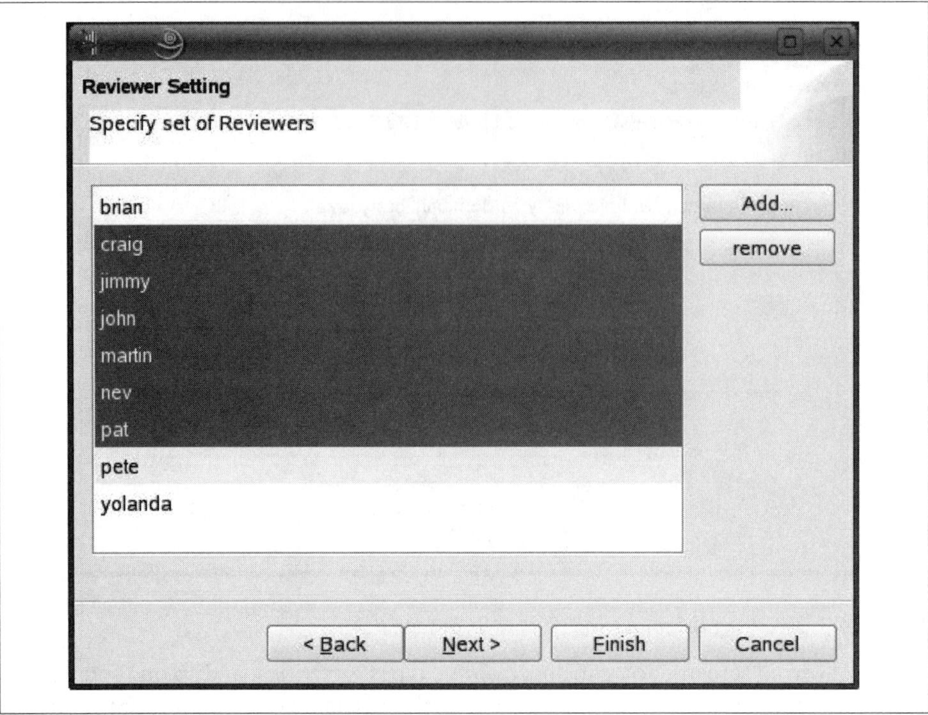

Figure 24-4. Naming the review team

needs to be fixed) or "Invalid won't fix" (the issue is not a valid issue, so no corrective action will be taken).

Rework phase
The default filters for this phase are "Assigned to:automatic" and "Status:open." When the reviewers decide on an action, the task is assigned to a team member (usually the author). These filters display only the issues that have been assigned to the current user and that are still open.

All of the fields described here take their default values from the special DEFAULT review item. So it is worthwhile to set up the DEFAULT review item with sensible project-wide values.

Once the review is set up, commit the ".jupiter" files to configuration management. Now you need to let all the reviewers know about it. A simple and efficient way to do this is to use a mailing list or a shared IMAP mailbox. You should define a suitable standard template for review notifications in your organization and project. A review notification format might include the following information:

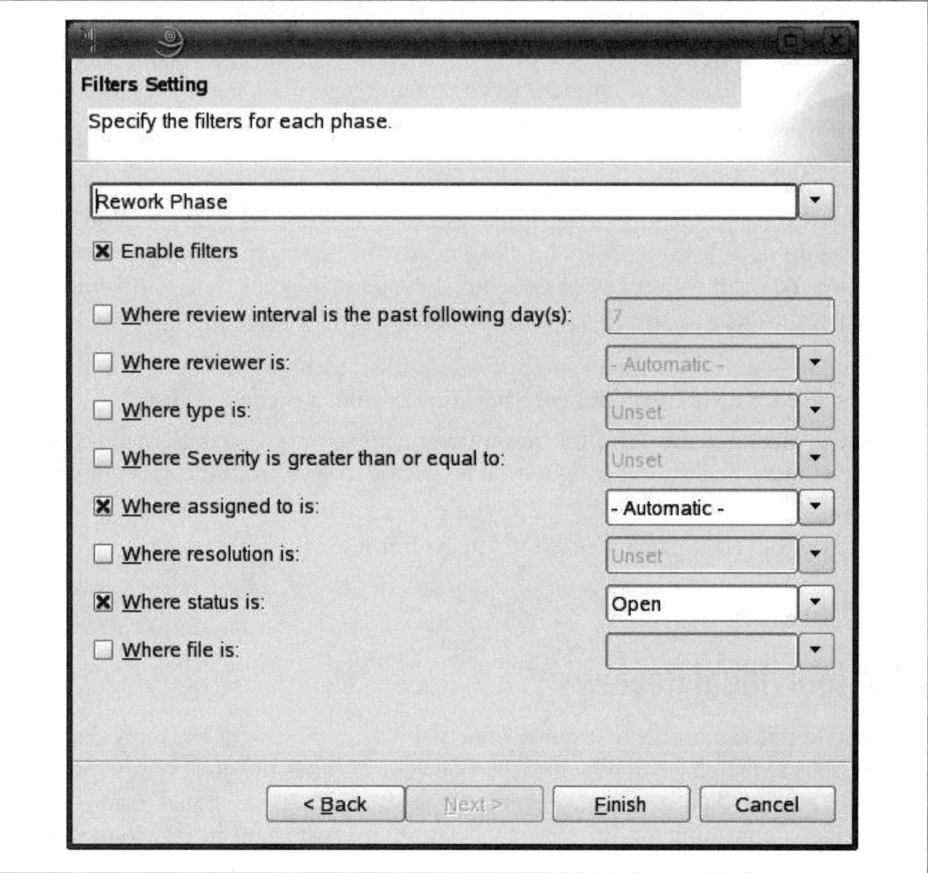

Figure 24-5. Setting up filters

- A standard subject field, including the project name, the designated reviewers, and possibly a component name.
- A description of the code to be, reviewed: what it does, what it fixes, and so on. (You may want to refer to requirements documents such as use cases.)
- A change log.
- New and deleted files, if any.
- Any affected components not included in the review.
- Unit test classes and unit test results.

Once everyone is notified, the actual review process can begin.

24.6 Setting Up Default Configuration Values

Setting up new reviews can be a repetitive process. Typically, for example, you will need to reenter the same team members again and again. To make life easier in this regard, Jupiter has a system-wide DEFAULT review configuration that can be used to set up default values for new review configurations. To modify this configuration, just open the Project Properties window, and select "Review." This will list all the reviews stored for this project, and also a special, system-wide DEFAULT review. You can use this to set up default values, which will be used whenever you create new reviews in the future. You can set up any of the configuration properties that you would in an ordinary review (see Figure 24-6). Useful default configurations are:

- Place all your team members in the Reviewer list, then you will be able to pick and choose your review team for each new review from a predefined list.
- Setup yourself as the default reviewer (unless it's always someone else, of course!). Remember, the default configuration is specific to your machine; it is not project- or organization-wide.
- Add custom issue categories in the "Items Entries" tab, if necessary.

24.7 Individual Reviews

The second phase, and the first phase of actual peer reviewing, is the individual code review. This is the phase in which each reviewer examines the code on their own, at their own pace, and at their own convenience. This aspect of individual reviews makes it particularly appealing for developers who suffer from an acute allergy to meetings.

The work involved in an individual code review is basically the same as that for a personal code review, except that the reviewer just raises the issues and does not fix the defects. Again, the use of a review checklist is very handy.

In Jupiter, raising issues is straightforward. Make sure you have checked out the latest code from the configuration management system. Then select the Jupiter Perspective, and then select individual phase (see Figure 24-7).

This will open a window allowing you to choose the project, review, and user that you want to use for this review phase (see Figure 24-8).

Now you can start the review. Go through the code looking for defects or issues. If you find something fishy, place the cursor on or simply select the suspicious-looking code, and select "Add Review Issue..." in the contextual menu. Next, specify the type and severity, and provide a summary and a description for this issue in the "Review Editor" window (see Figure 24-9). Don't worry too much about the type: it's just a tentative best guess for the moment, and you can change it during the team review phase.

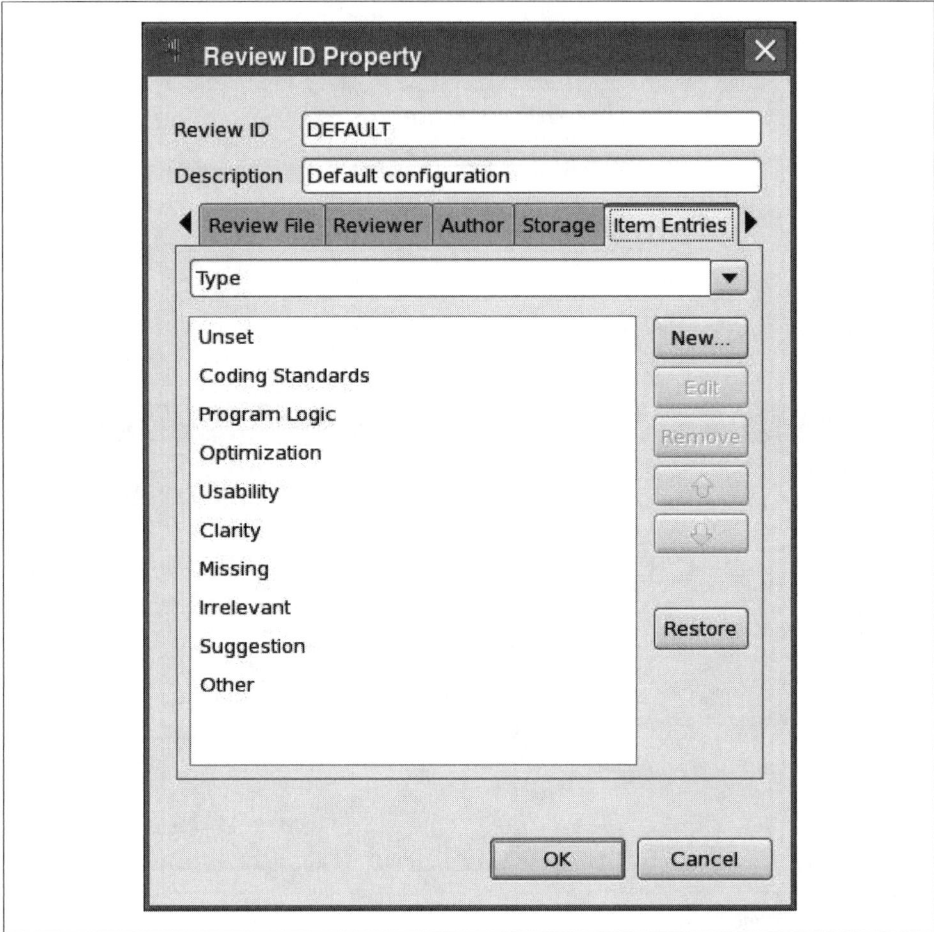

Figure 24-6. Setting default configuration values

The issue will also appear in the Review Table panel (see Figure 24-10), along with the other current issues. This table lets you add, delete, or edit issues; sort issues by severity or type; and jump directly to an issue in the source code.

In the source code window, recorded issues are marked by a purple marker (see Figure 24-11). If you move the cursor over them, the issue summary will appear.

The review issues are stored in XML format as review files in the review directory. To share your issues with other users, you have to commit these files to configuration management.

When each reviewer has finished their individual reviews, it's time for a little get-together: the team review.

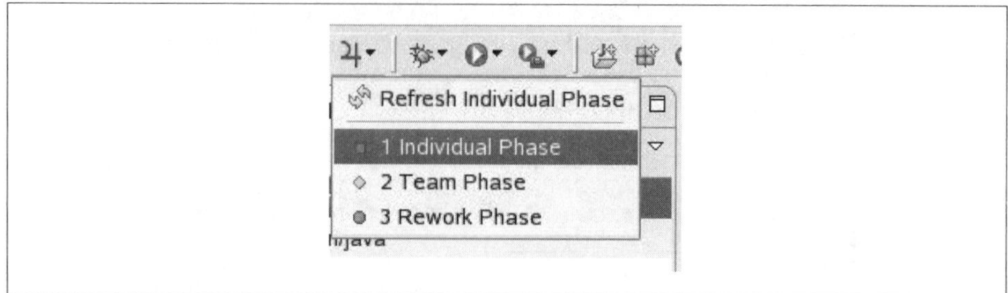

Figure 24-7. Starting the individual review

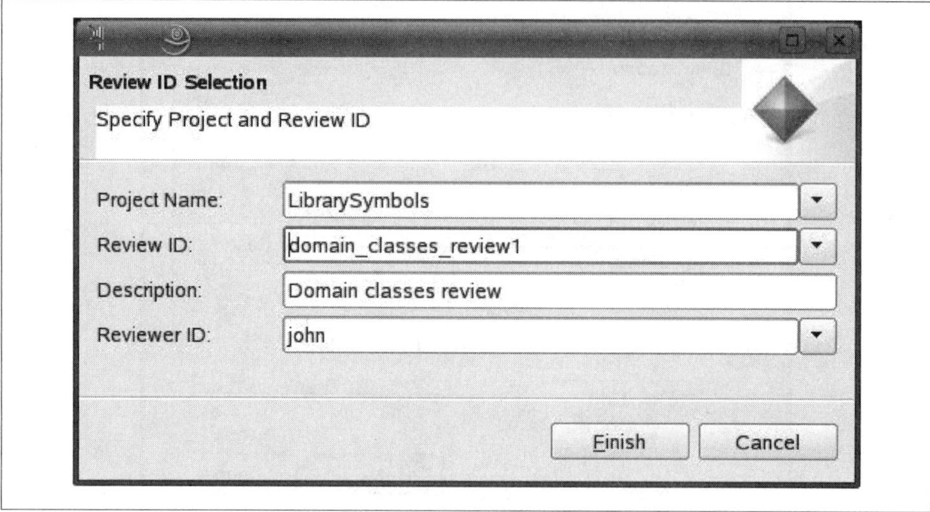

Figure 24-8. Selecting the review

24.8 Team Review

The team review phase involves getting the review team (including the author) together to discuss the issues raised during the individual reviews. Typically, the team will work on one workstation, using an overhead projector to display the screen in a meeting, for example, or just work around the same machine if the review team is small enough. The team review involves going through all the issues raised and making a collective decision on the action to take.

Team code reviews do have a lot going for them if not done to excess, and many organizations and projects report higher code quality and better team cohesion when using them.

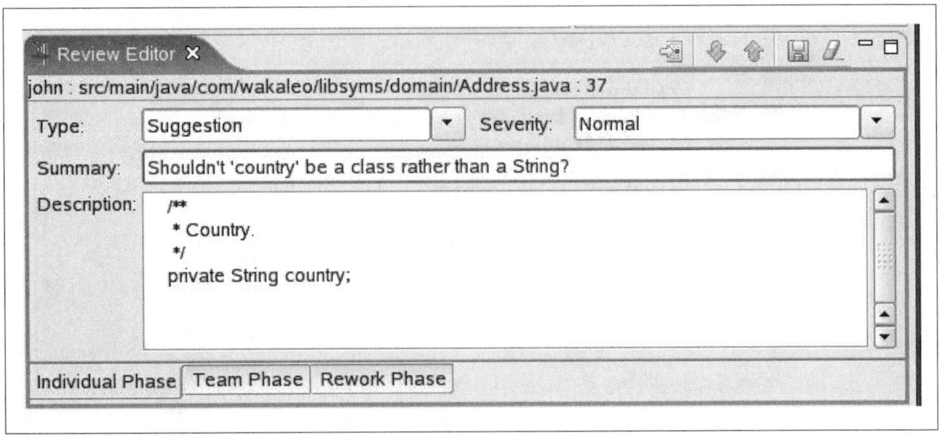

Figure 24-9. Describing an issue

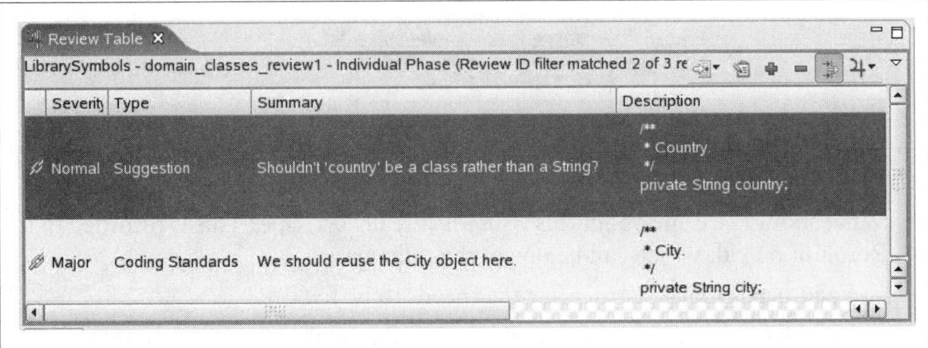

Figure 24-10. The Review Table

To start a team review, just select the team phase item in the Jupiter menu (see Figure 24-12). You then select the project, review, and reviewer ID in the Review ID Selection, as you did for the individual review phase (see Figure 24-8).

Now the Review Table will display all the issues raised by the individual reviewers (see Figure 24-13). The details of the selected issue are displayed in the Review Editor (see Figure 24-14).

You should go through each issue, discuss it with the review team members, and come to an agreement on the following:

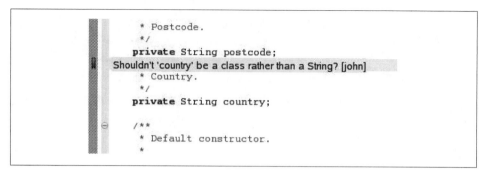

```
 * Postcode.
 */
private String postcode;
Shouldn't 'country' be a class rather than a String? [john]
 * Country.
 */
private String country;

/**
 * Default constructor.
 *
```

Figure 24-11. The issue in the source code

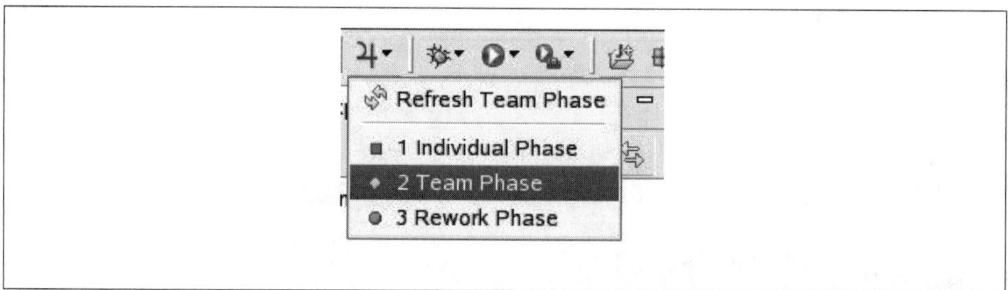

Figure 24-12. Initiating a team review

- What should be done about this issue? Is it really an issue? This is recorded in the Resolution field, which can be one of the following:
  - —Valid needs fixing (a real issue that needs to be fixed)
  - —Valid fix later (a real issue that you won't fix right away)
  - —Valid duplicate (such a real issue that it's already been mentioned)
  - —Valid won't fix (a real issue that you don't want to fix)
  - —Invalid won't fix ("it ain't broke, don't fix it!")
  - —Unsure validity (needs further investigation)
- Who should this issue be assigned to (the Assigned To field)? By default, it is the code author, but it can be changed if someone with specialist knowledge has to intervene, for example.
- What needs to go in the annotation field, which can be used to note any complementary information that came out of the review discussion?
- What is the type and severity of each issue? Check the type and severity fields in the individual phase tab, and make sure everyone agrees with them.

At the end of the team review, the updated review files are committed to the configuration management system so that all team members can recuperate the changes and get to work on the corrections. This is done in the next phase, rework.

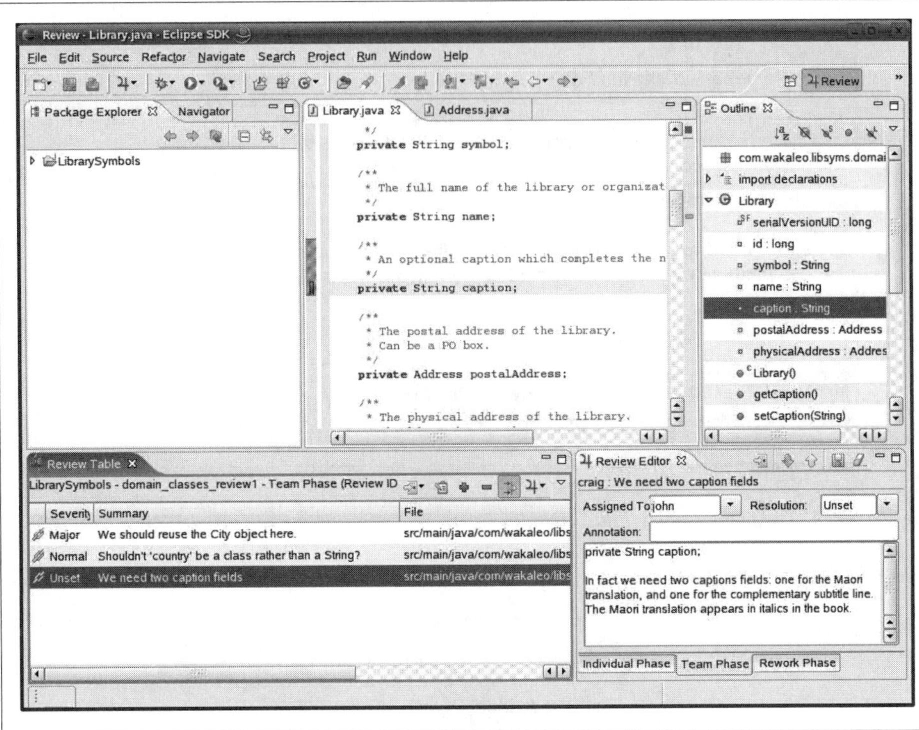

Figure 24-13. Conducting a team review

The team review phase may not suit all organizations. In practice, team review meetings may be difficult to organize for all but the most strategic classes. You'll often find the bulk of the added value during the individual review phase, and the team review phase may be harder to justify. And although it is not too difficult to convince developers to perform individual code reviews, team reviews can be much harder to put into place.

Indeed, open source projects manage quite well by skipping the team review phase and going directly to the rework phase. In open source projects, physical meetings are often impractical simply because team members tend to be distributed all over the world. In practice, they combine the individual and team reviews into one phase, with a single reviewer.

Another possibility is to maintain teams of several reviewers but combine the individual and team phases. In this approach, each reviewer fills in both the individual phase and team phase tabs in the Review Editor. This allows several reviewers to review the same code but avoids the overhead of organizing a review meeting for each and every code review.

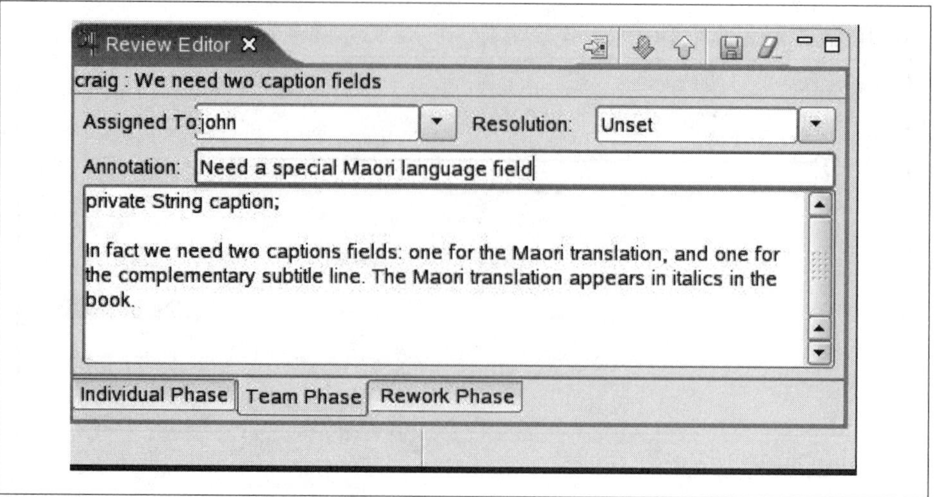

Figure 24-14. The team Review Editor window

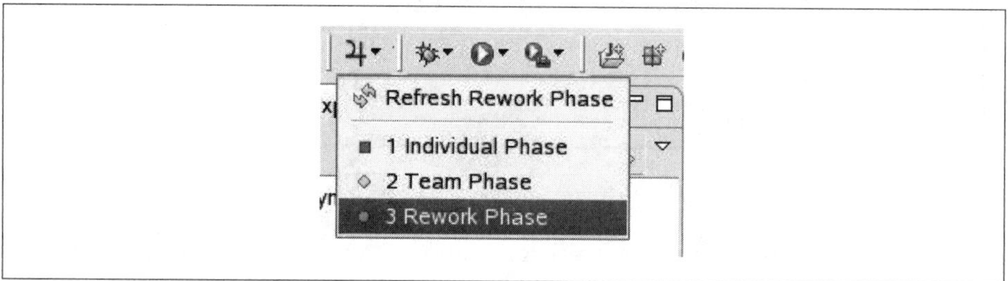

Figure 24-15. Initiating the rework phase

24.9 Rework Phase

The rework phase is the phase in which the developer goes through the raised issues and fixes the code accordingly. During the rework phase, Jupiter displays the list of issues that have been assigned to you so that you can go through them and correct them one-by-one.

To start the rework phase, select rework phase in the Jupiter menu (see Figure 24-15). As for the other phases, you have to select the project and review what you want to work on, and specify your user ID. The Review Table will contain a list of issues that have been assigned to you.

The details of the currently selected issue are displayed in the Review Editor (see Figure 24-16). When you fix a defect, you update the issue status field to Resolved. You may also want to add some details of your fix in the Revision field. When you've

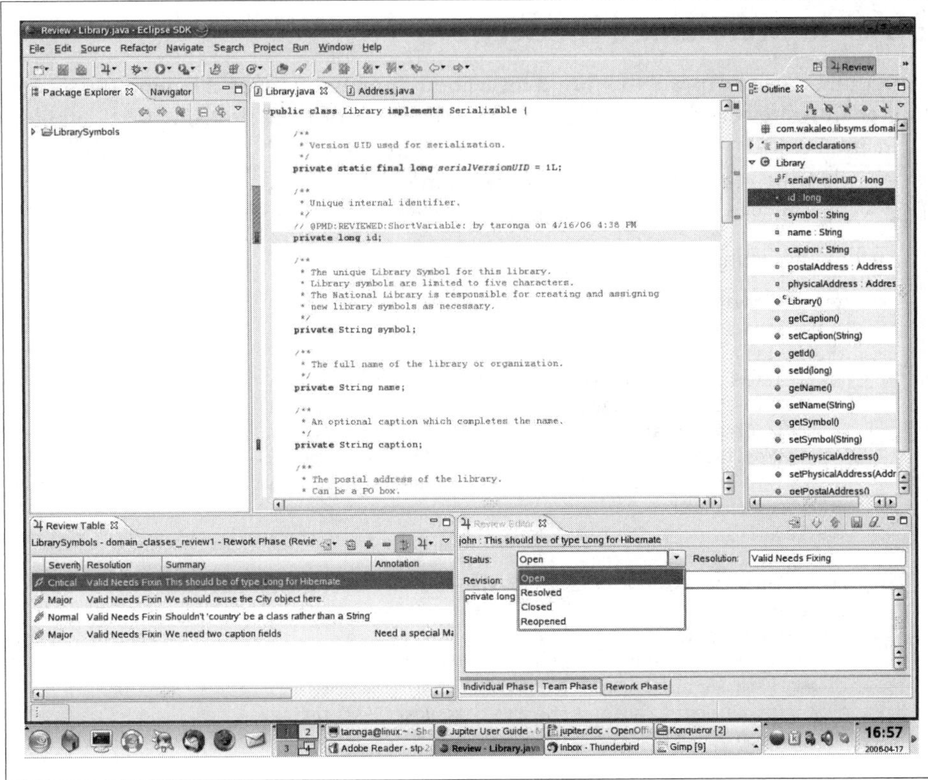

Figure 24-16. Reworking issues

Review Table

LibrarySymbols - domain_classes_review1 - Rework Phase (4 reviews)

Severity	Resolution	Summary	Annotation	Revision	Status	Assigned To
Critical	Valid Needs Fixin	This should be of type Long for Hibernate			Closed	john
Major	Valid Needs Fixin	We should reuse the City object here.			Resolved	john
Normal	Valid Needs Fixin	Shouldn't 'country' be a class rather than a String			Open	john
Major	Valid Needs Fixin	We need two caption fields	Need a special Maon la		Open	john

Figure 24-17. Deactivating the filter in the review table

finished, you can move on to the next issue. Resolved issues will automatically disappear from the Review Table.

Once the rework is finished, the reviewers should verify the corrections. If they are satisfied, they can approve a correction and close it (Closed status). If not, they can reopen it for further work (Reopened status). Jupiter makes it easy to see the state of all review issues by letting you turn off the filter on the Review Table (see Figure 24-17).

24.10 Jupiter Behind the Scenes

Sometimes it can be useful to know a little about how Jupiter works behind the scenes. Jupiter stores review data in XML files, in a directory of your choosing (the default is a directory called "review" in the project base directory. Each reviewer has their own review file which they share with other team members via the version control system. This way, reviewers don't get in each other's way during the review process.

The following listing shows a simple review file:

```
<Review id="review-1">
  <ReviewIssue id="F86M91IY">
    <ReviewIssueMeta>
      <CreationDate format="yyyy-MM-dd :: HH:mm:ss:SSS z">
       2007-10-25 :: 14:48:10:618
       NZDT</CreationDate>
      <LastModificationDate format="yyyy-MM-dd :: HH:mm:ss:SSS z">
       2007-10-25 :: 14:48:35:024 NZDT</LastModificationDate>
    </ReviewIssueMeta>
    <ReviewerId>george</ReviewerId>
    <AssignedTo>john</AssignedTo>
    <File line="28">src/main/java/com/equinox/jpt/modelplanes/core/domain
     /ModelPlane.java</File>
    <Type>item.type.label.optimization</Type>
    <Severity>item.severity.label.normal</Severity>
    <Summary>Sub-optimal query</Summary>
    <Description>Could cause performance issues</Description>
    <Annotation />
    <Revision />
    <Resolution>item.label.unset</Resolution>
    <Status>item.status.label.open</Status>
  </ReviewIssue>
</Review>
```

This review file contains a single raised issue. Note that the line number is recorded in the entry for the review issue. The Jupiter plug-in is smart enough to keep tabs on what Eclipse is doing: if any file under review is modified, the line numbers in the review file will automatically be updated to correspond. This also applies for other reviewers who update their local copies of both the source code and the review file; if any modifications are done within Eclipse, the review file will be updated accordingly.

However, if the file is changed outside of Eclipse, or if two file versions are merged, the review files may get out of synch with the source code files, and Jupiter may get a little confused about the line numbers. For this reason, it is wise to make your review comments clear enough not to rely absolutely on the line number."

24.11 Conclusion

Jupiter is an innovative and flexible tool that helps automate peer code reviews and track issues. Until recently, it was quite unique in this domain. Of late, however, it does have a commercial competitor, called Crucible, from Atlassian. Crucible is a new tool that also provides good support for online code reviews, and not surprisingly, integrates well with JIRA and the other Atlassian toolset.

Tools like Jupiter are never sufficient themselves to improve code quality; you also need a defined development process and, more importantly, team and management buy-in. Nevertheless, Jupiter is a valuable process streamliner. If you practice code reviews, or if you would like to, you should definitely try it out.

CHAPTER 25

Sharpen Your Focus with Mylyn

25.1 Introduction to Mylyn

Contributed by: Keith Coughtrey

Today's development projects, and the environments we use to build them, are increasingly rich and complex, and informative. However, in practical terms, there is a limit to the amount of information human beings can deal with simultaneously. Mylyn is an innovative Eclipse plug-in that enhances developer productivity by providing integrated task management and a contextual view of the tasks you are working on.

Mylyn benefits developers in two ways. The first provides a convenient integration with issue management systems such as Trac (see Chapter 28), Bugzilla (see Chapter 27), and JIRA, allowing you to view and manage tasks held in your issue tracker from within the IDE. This in itself is appreciable, but Mylyn goes much further than that. Mylyn also provides a way to hide much of the detail of your projects that is irrelevant to the task at hand. It is this second aspect, called context management, that provides a real increase in developer productivity because it cuts down on the amount of navigating, searching, and scanning through trees, lists, and code looking for the parts that are of interest when working on a particular task—whether that be a bug fix or the development of a new feature. Indeed, Mylyn is based on the observation that when you work on a particular development task, you actually need only to look at and manipulate a relatively small number of files. By masking out irrelevant information, Mylyn lets you focus exclusively on the files that need to be modified.

Also, because Mylyn maintains a separate context for each task, when you return to a task that was worked on previously, you are immediately presented with those parts of you project that were considered relevant at the time. Because the context can move with the task as it is assigned to different members of the team, it may be that when you open a task you see those parts of the code that a previous developer worked on when he or she looked at the task. This can be a real head start or a great memory jogger.

I'm sure you are wondering how Mylyn knows which parts of the project are relevant to a task. Essentially, that is determined by you and based on what you examine and

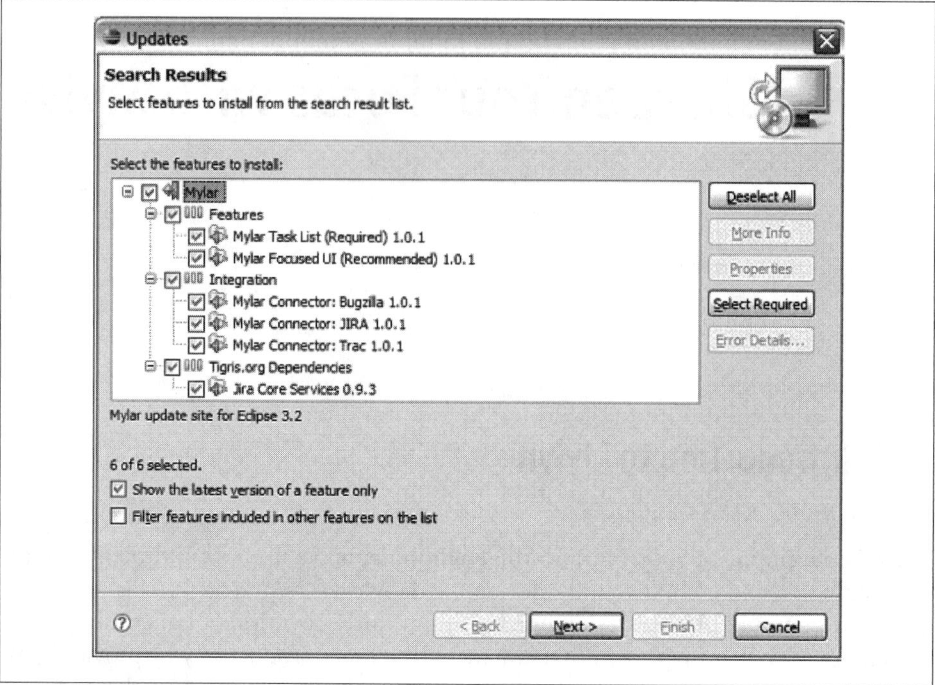

Figure 25-1. Installing the Mylyn plug-in

where you make changes as you work on a particular task. There will be more details regarding this later in this chapter.

25.2 Installing Mylyn

Mylyn comes bundled with Eclipse 3.3 and later versions. You can update the plug-in and install extra features using the Eclipse Remote Install feature. Open the "Find and Install" option from the Eclipse help menu, select the "Search for new features to install" and enter the URL of the update site. See Figure 25-1.*

Next you select the features you want to install. It's probably best to include everything, but you can leave out any connectors you don't intend to use.

Even if you do have a more recent version of Eclipse with Mylyn integrated, be sure to check out the optional connectors and the Mylyn Extras update site. Here you can get useful additional connectors to other Issue Management systems such as Trac and Jira, or experiment with integration with the XPlanner Agile project management tool (see Figure 25-2).

* You can find the latest live update sites at *http://www.eclipse.org/downloads/*.

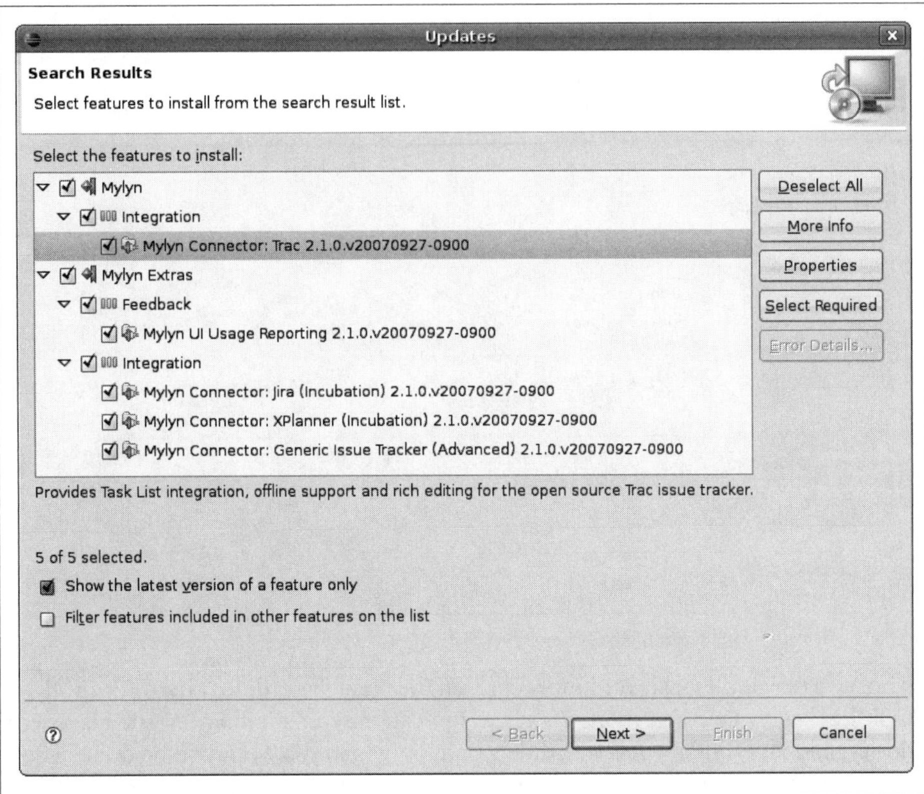

Figure 25-2. The Mylyn extras

25.3 Tracking Tasks and Issues

Tasks and issues can come from many sources. To-do lists are a well known and widely used technique for enhancing personal productivity. In a development project, developers can also define and record tasks as an effective way of organizing their work. QA staff will raise issues during testing: missing features, bugs to be fixed, and so on. Mylyn allows you to track the progress of tasks that can either be stored locally in your workspace or stored in the repository of your favorite issue tracker. Mylyn provides connectors for Bugzilla (see Chapter 27), Trac (see Chapter 28), and JIRA, among others.

Indeed, Mylyn is an excellent, lightweight task management system in its own right. It provides you with a convenient, centralized view of all your tasks, both the ones that you assign yourself (your own "to-do" list) and issues raised by other people. You can also keep an eye on tasks assigned to other people that you may need to follow up on. And you can do all this without having to leave your development environment!

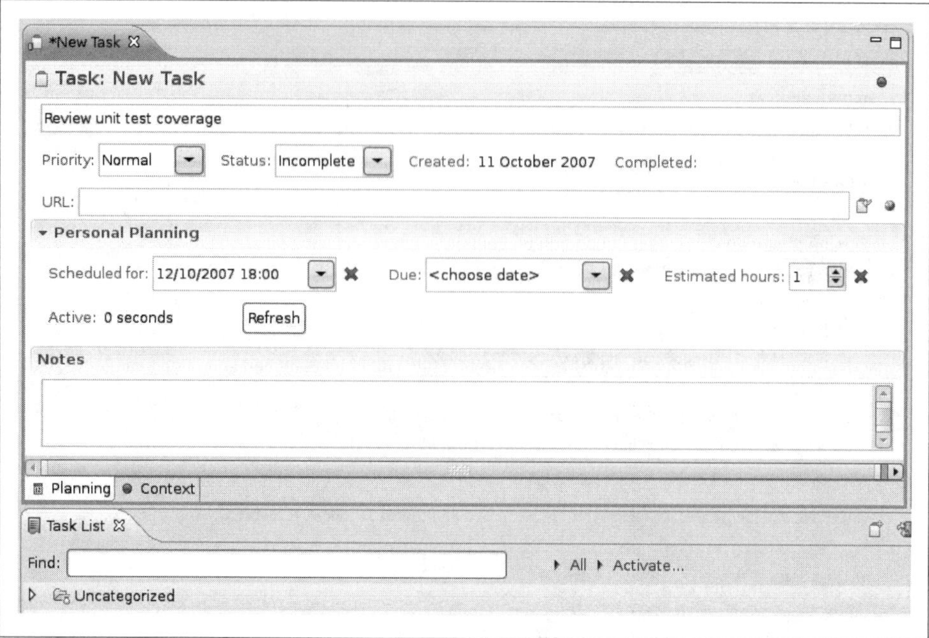

Figure 25-3. Adding a Mylyn task

To create a new local task, you simply click on the New Task toolbar button of Mylyn's "Task List" view (see Figure 25-3). Then you can enter a summary of the task, set a priority, add an estimate, and schedule a date on which the work will be done. These tasks are not visible to other users, so this is a good way to organize your work on a personal level.

The Mylyn "Task List" view provides a few nice features that help you stay focused on the most important jobs at hand. Completed tasks are barred, and the current active task (see Section 25.5) is shown in bold. If you have a lot of tasks (and you generally will!), a good trick is to focus on the tasks due in the current week. You can do this using the "Focus on Workweek" button on the Task List toolbar, or using the popdown menu (see Figure 25-4). You can also filter out completed tasks or tasks below a certain priority.

Mylyn also offers some simple but effective schedule management features. You can use the tasks to manage your time, rescheduling things if necessary as priorities change. When a task is overdue, it appears in red in the task list (see Figure 25-4), and a popup window appears on your desktop to remind you (just in case). If you do need to reschedule it, just use the "Schedule" option in the contextual menu (see Figure 25-5). With a simple right-click, you can indicate that a task is complete or defer it to a later date.

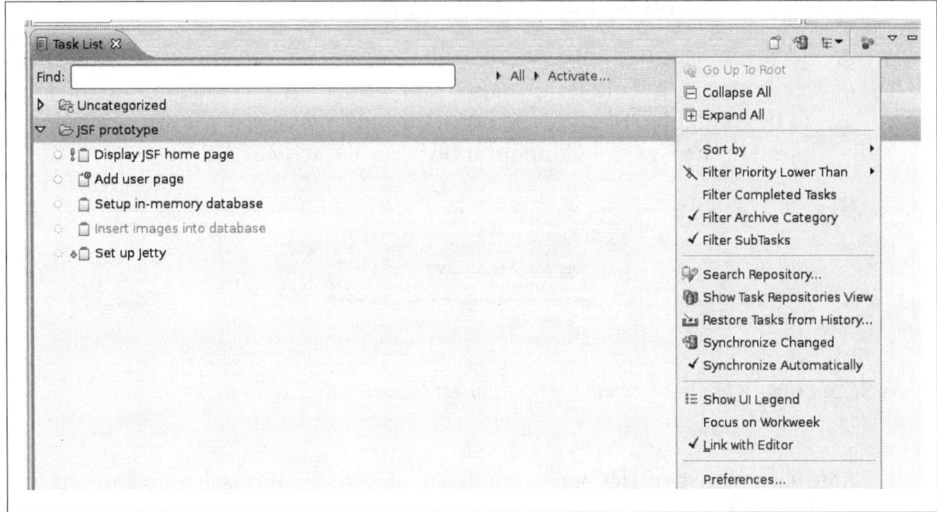

Figure 25-4. The Mylyn task list

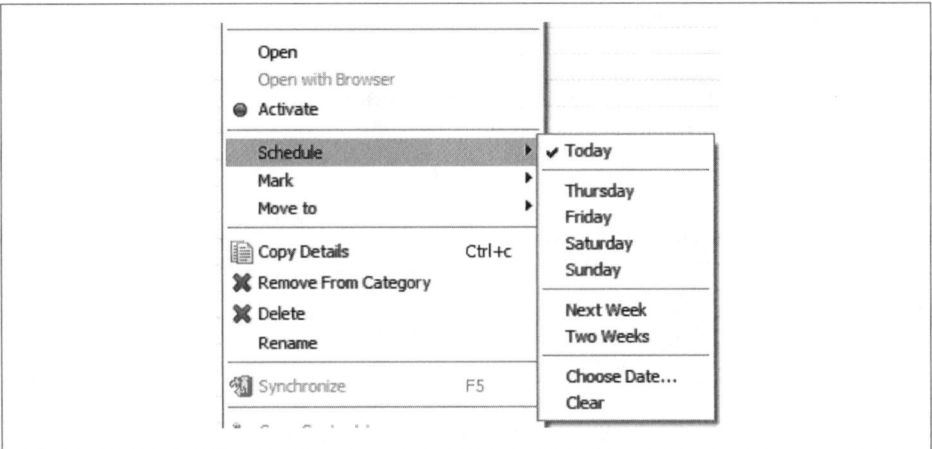

Figure 25-5. Scheduling a task in Mylyn

Tasks can also be grouped into categories and when displaying just those tasks scheduled for the current working week or hovering over a task category, you see a progress bar giving a visual indication of the proportion of tasks that have been completed (see Figure 25-6).

Turning to repository tasks, the plug-in gives the kind of facilities that have long been available for interacting with source repositories and synchronization with the repository works in much the same way.

25.4 Interacting with Task Repositories

Mylyn provides sophisticated integration with many issue tracking systems such as Bugzilla (see Chapter 27), Trac (see Chapter 28), and JIRA. To integrate with JIRA, JIRA needs to be configured to accept remote API calls (make sure the "Accept remote API calls" option in the General Configuration screen is activated).

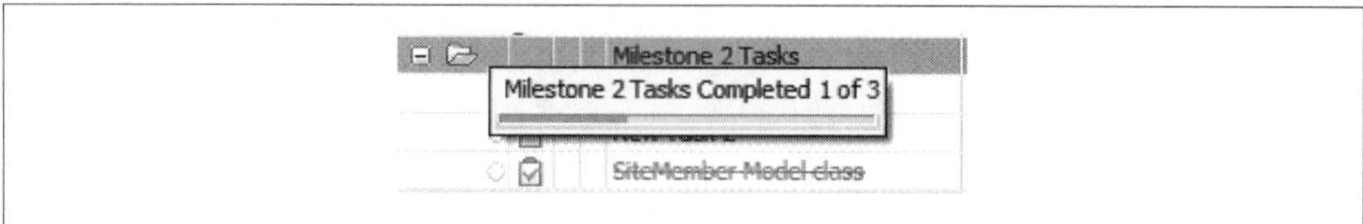

Figure 25-6. Progress bars give an idea of how much planned work has been completed

To integrate with your issue tracking system, you need to set up a task repository. Open the Mylyn Task repositories view and click on the toolbar button to create a new repository connection (see Figure 25-7). Select the repository type, click Next, then enter the server details. Choose Validate Settings and then Finish. You can set up as many task repositories as you want, which is useful if you are working on several projects that use different issue tracking systems.

At the time of this writing, the server drop-down has an example entry for both the Bugzilla and Trac repository types. It is worth exploring these repositories to get a feel for how the integration works.

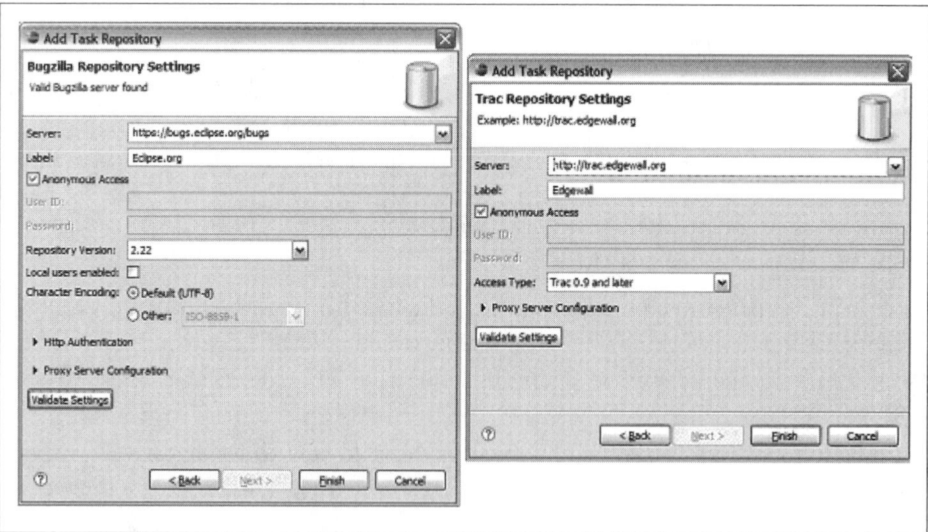

Figure 25-7. Adding a new task repository

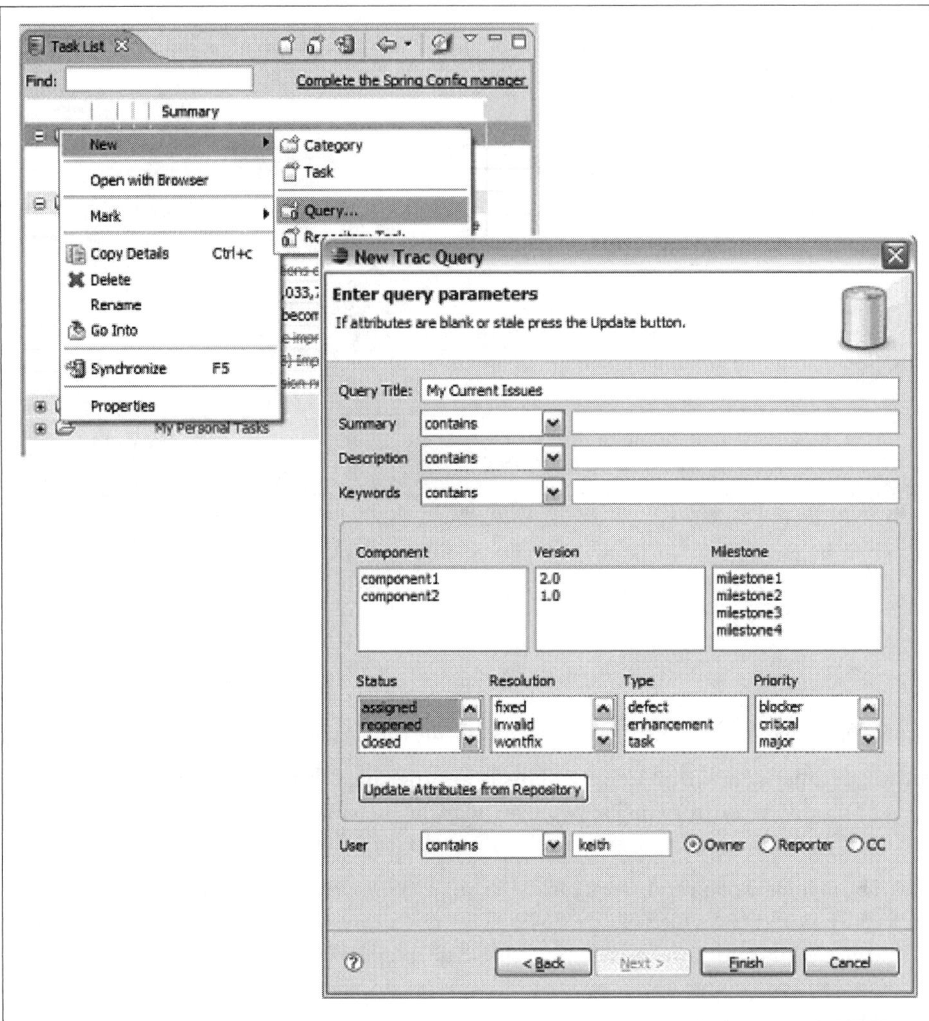

Figure 25-8. Querying the issue management system

Once you have set up a task repository, you can retrieve tasks and issues by querying the repository. For example, you might want to create a query to bring back all the issues assigned to you. You can create a new query from the "Task List" view using the "New→Query" menu option (see Figure 25-8).

The attributes displayed depend on the repository type but, as you can see, they give all the options you need to filter out a subset of the repository tasks that are of interest to you.

Once you have created the query, it will appear in your "Task List" view (see Figure 25-9). You can double-click on these tasks to view the details page in the web

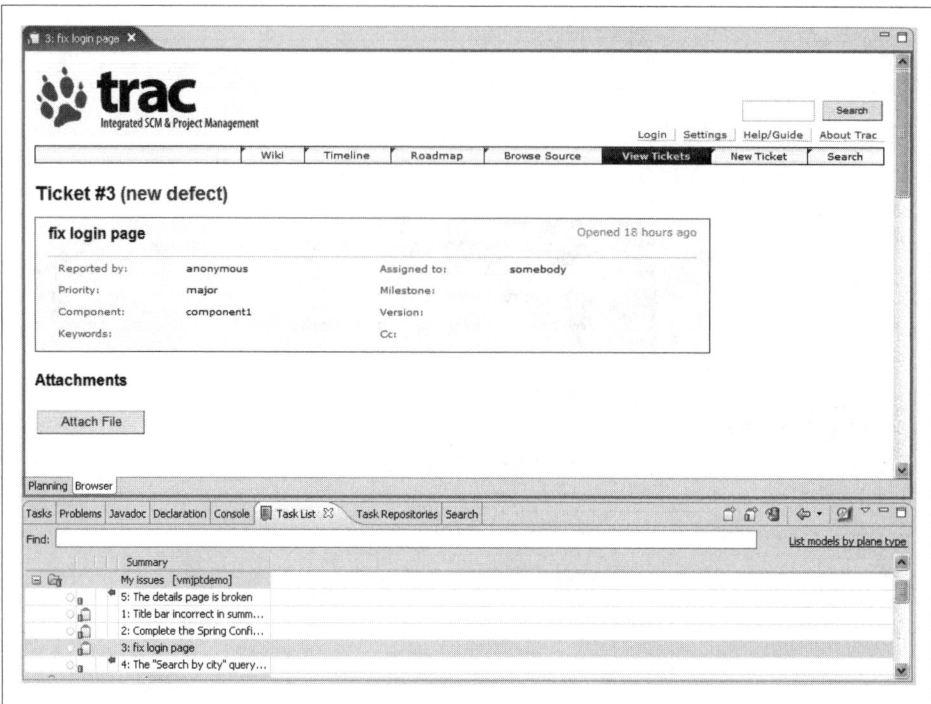

Figure 25-9. Repository tasks retrieved from queries appear in the task list

browser embedded within Eclipse. This is another nice thing about Mylyn: when you view or modify repository tasks, you use the same web interface as you would normally use with your issue tracking system. You just do it from within Eclipse.

The detailed view of a repository task also has a "Planning" tab, similar to the one used for locally stored tasks (see Figure 25-3). This tab allows you to add your own personal planning details and notes to a repository task in exactly the same way you would for a personal task, giving you a consistent way to manage planning all your tasks in a single place.

By default, Mylyn will automatically synchronize with your task repositories on a regular basis. This task is run as a discreet background process: your repository queries will be regularly updated to reflect the current repository content.

In addition, if another user creates an issue in the issue management system, or modifies an existing issue, Mylyn will automatically notify you of the change in a small pop-up (see Figure 25-10). The left-pointing arrow indicates a change coming down from the repository to your local system. This is a convenient way to keep tabs on any new issues. You don't need to monitor your email for incoming issues.

You can define how frequently you want Mylyn to synchronize with the repository in the *Windows →Preferences→Mylyn→Tasks* menu (the default is every 20 minutes).

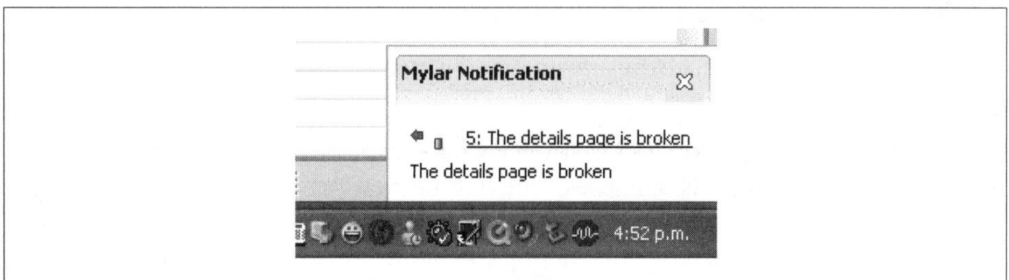

Figure 25-10. Mylyn will notify you of any new issues

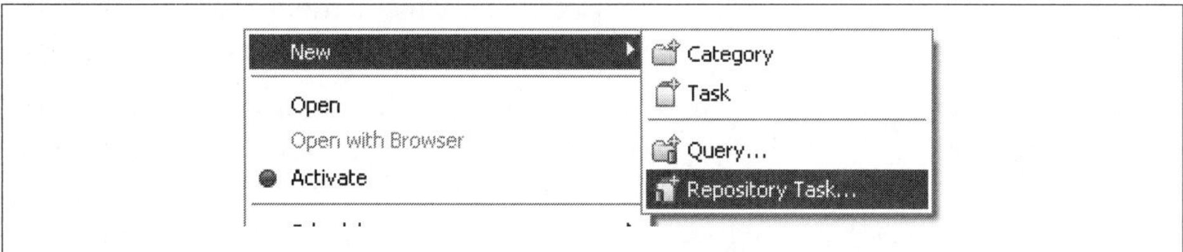

Figure 25-11. Adding a repository task

You can also place new tasks directly into this repository from within Eclipse. In the contextual menu in the "Task List" view, select "New→Repository Task" (see Figure 25-11). This will open a browser view in Eclipse, where you can add the new task into your issue management system using the usual web interface.

Both Bugzilla and Trac* integration support full off-line issue editing, meaning that you have a snapshot of the issues that you can amend locally. When you make a change to an issue and save, it assumes an outgoing mode (indicated by an arrow pointing to the right). This change can then be committed to the repository when appropriate.

Mylyn also lets you run "ad-hoc" search queries. Unlike queries made from the task list (Figure 25-8), the results of these searches are not stored in the "Task List" view. You can do this using the normal "Search" window, where you will find a special "Task Search" tab dedicated to task repository searches. This tab contains the same, repository-dependent search criteria as you find in the query window (see Figure 25-8).

Apart from avoiding the switching backward and forward between a browser and the IDE, the real benefit of having your issue tracker integrated into Eclipse comes in the links that can be made between the issue content and the project. For example, if the issue contains a stack trace, clicking on it will take you to the corresponding line of code in the same way it does when you click on a stack trace in the console.

* Supported from Trac version 0.10 onward using the XML-RPC access type.

25.5 Focusing on a Task with Context Management

The objective here is to reduce the information overload you typically get when working on projects in Eclipse.

Without Mylyn, you quickly find that the Package Explorer and Navigator have hundreds or perhaps thousands of entries. The outline view of a complex class may show dozens of properties and methods and you often end up with far too many code editors open to display. Also, when code assist pops up, it often contains a long list of possible selections.

Generally, only a small subset of all this information is relevant to the task in hand. For example, the class you are working on may contain many methods that are stable and not of interest in the particular context and of course the same goes for the Outline view.

With Mylyn all you need to do is to activate a task (by clicking a radio button in the task list) before you start working on it and from then on, your activity starts to build up the context. When you activate a task, the package explorer view will automatically be filtered to display only the objects deemed of interest for this particular task.

At the start, your context is empty and the various views such as the Package Explorer show what appears to be an empty project. The easiest way to add content is to use the Open Type dialog (*Ctrl+Shift+T*) to search for the object of interest. If you then select a class to open, that class is added to your context because you have shown an interest in it.

Initially, all of the methods in the class you have opened will be folded on the basis that none of them are of interest. However, as you click on methods they unfold and are added to your context, appearing in the Package Explorer and the Outline views.

The more that you work with elements, the more interesting they are presumed to be. Eventually they become landmarked, indicating that they are a key part of the context of this task. Mylyn adds a toggle button to the Package Explorer, Navigator, and Outline views that allows you to apply the task focus in two different ways. When the toggle is set to focus on the active task, these views show only those items that are of interest. However, when the task focus is toggled off, the views present everything that they would without Mylyn, but some decoration is added to make the items of interest stand out. By default, all uninteresting items are shown in gray, interesting items in black, and landmarks in bold.

This is illustrated in Figure 25-12. This screen shot illustrates a number of the key features of Mylyn context management. We can see the "Focus on Active Task" toogle button (1), which lets you switch context filtering on and off. Mylyn also applies filtering In the Java editor view, letting you concentrate on the specific code you want to work on. In this editor, when context filtering is activated, uninteresting code is automatically folded (2), making it easier to scan through the code quickly. If you select a folded element, it unfolds and is integrated into the task context.

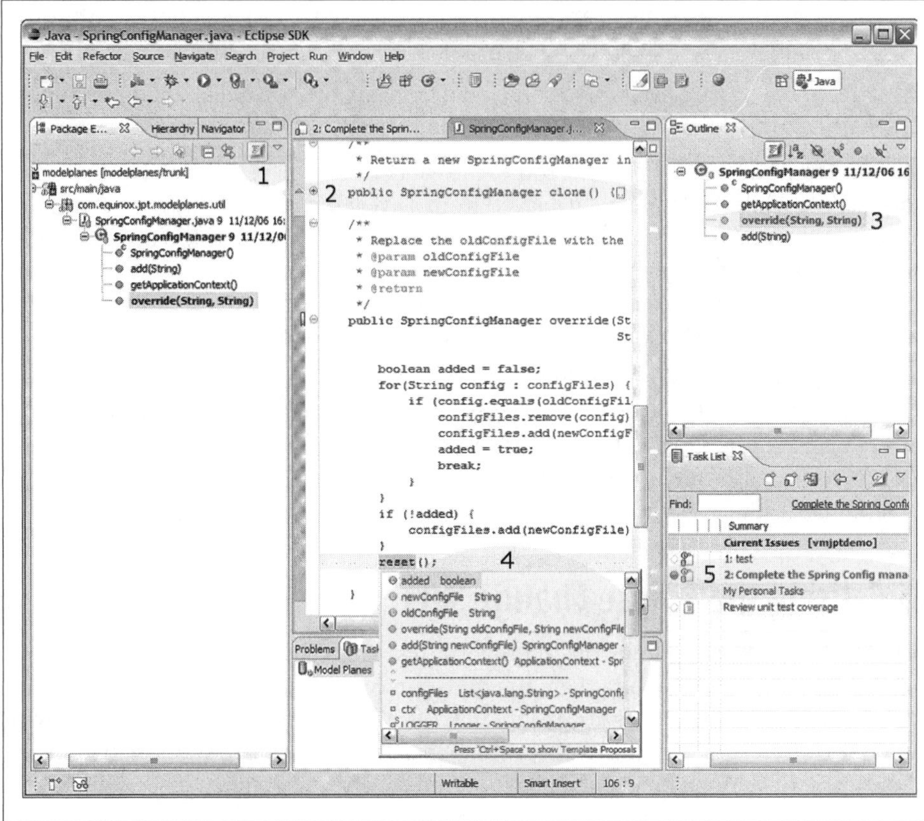

Figure 25-12. Using the Mylyn view in Eclipse

Context-sensitive filtering is also applied to the Java code-completion feature (4). Note how the code assist has been divided into two lists. Above the line are items that are in your context. In addition, these items are ranked by relevance for the active task. All in all, you have a pretty good chance that the item you want will be visible right away.

In the "Outline" view (3), landmarked items are shown in bold (for example, the `override()` method here), whereas uninteresting methods (such as the `clone()` method) are hidden.

When a task is activated, it appears in bold in the "Task List" view (5), making it easy to see at a glance.

The combination of all these features helps to mask irrelevant and unnecessary information from your view, and lets you concentrate on the task at hand. In a subtle but real way, this approach results in a surprising gain in developer productivity.

Clearly, if you work on a task for an extended period, your context would get bloated and you would start to lose the benefits of task focus. To avoid this happening, things that you haven't accessed much are progressively removed from your context. Any open editor associated with such an element will be closed automatically.

If you need to, you can give Mylyn some help by using the right-click menu options to "Mark as Landmark" or "Make Less Interesting" in the Package Explorer view.

The real beauty of the task context comes into play when you switch back to a task you worked on a while ago and you are saved from a great deal of searching around trying to recall and locate the objects of interest. When you deactivate a task, the corresponding editors are all closed. If you switch back to this task later on, they will all be opened again. To make things even easier a Back navigation button appears in the task list toolbar that will give you a list of the last 10 tasks you worked on.

Perhaps this is an obvious point but you should bear in mind that because whatever you touch gets added to your task context, it is important that you always have the correct task activated. This does require some discipline, but it's a good habit to get into. As Mylyn also tracks roughly how long you have spent on a task, this can help you compare estimates with actuals.

25.6 Using the Eclipse Change Sets

In Eclipse, *change sets* allow you to organize resources that you have modified into logical groups before updating them in your source code repository. Eclipse supports this mechanism for CVS and Subversion. In CVS, all of the changes are submitted with the same comment message. In Subversion, where change sets are supported natively, all of the modifications in the change set are submitted as a single transaction.

Change sets in Eclipse are good, but they are complicated to manage manually in any but the most trivial of cases. However, Mylyn can help you manage your change sets automatically. Whenever you activate a task, a new change set will be created for that task. Any files you modify while working on that task will be added to this change set automatically.

You can manage the Mylyn change set in the Eclipse Synchronize view ("Team→Synchronize"). To enable change set support, ensure the "Show Change Sets" button is set on the Synchronize view. Here, you can view the modified files that currently make up your change set, or commit or revert your changes. And, if you really need to, you can always manually add other modified files to the Mylyn change set using the contextual menu (see Figure 25-13).

Another advantage of using the Mylyn change sets is that the commit message is automatically initialized with a sensible message based on the title and status of your active task (see Figure 25-14). This makes it easier to relate source code modifications to issues in a consistent manner. If you are using Trac, it is also possible to configure Trac to automatically append this message to the issue whenever the changes are committed (see Section 28.11).

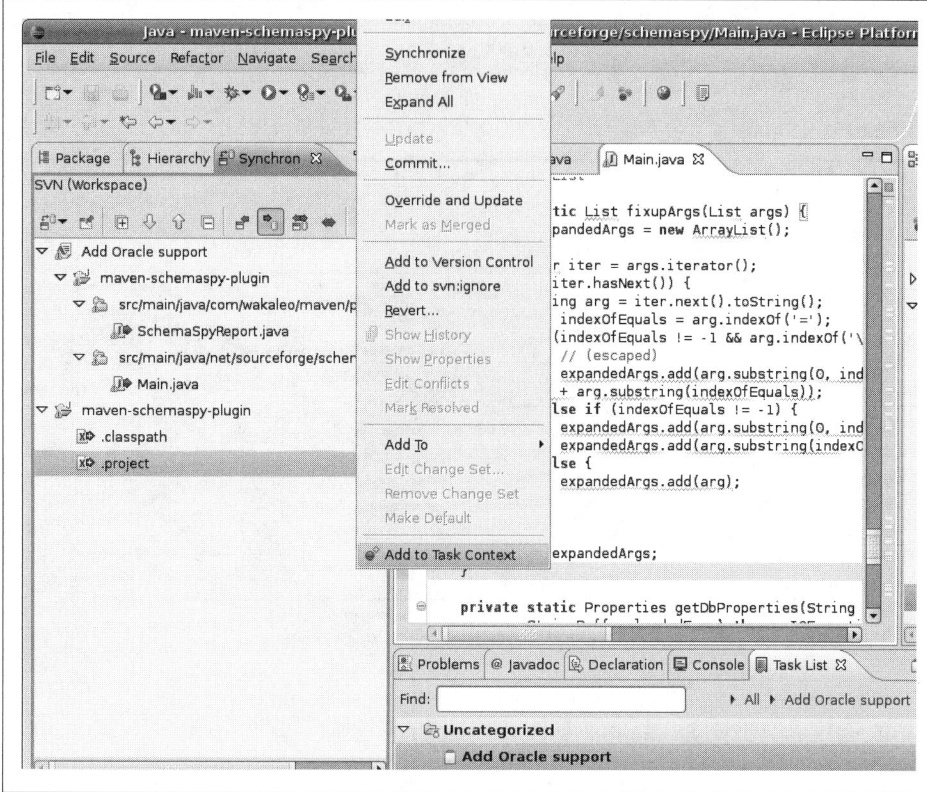

Figure 25-13. Eclipse change sets with Mylyn

It can be useful to customize the message format to suit your environment. For example, if you are using Subversion and Trac, you might want to configure Subversion to update the Trac issue based on the Subversion message (see Section 28.11). In this case, you can customize the message so that the Subversion hook will identify the Trac issue in the message, as shown in Figure 25-15.

This way, your Subversion message will be automatically added to the Trac issue.

Mylyn also integrates well with the History view (see Figure 25-16). In this view, you can see a history of the changes made to a particular file, including the messages associated with each commited change set. These messages also include a hyperlink to the corresponding task.

25.7 Sharing Context with Other Developers

The Mylyn context is a powerful tool that enables you to get up to speed very quickly when you reactivate a task. It also helps other developers who may have to pick up a

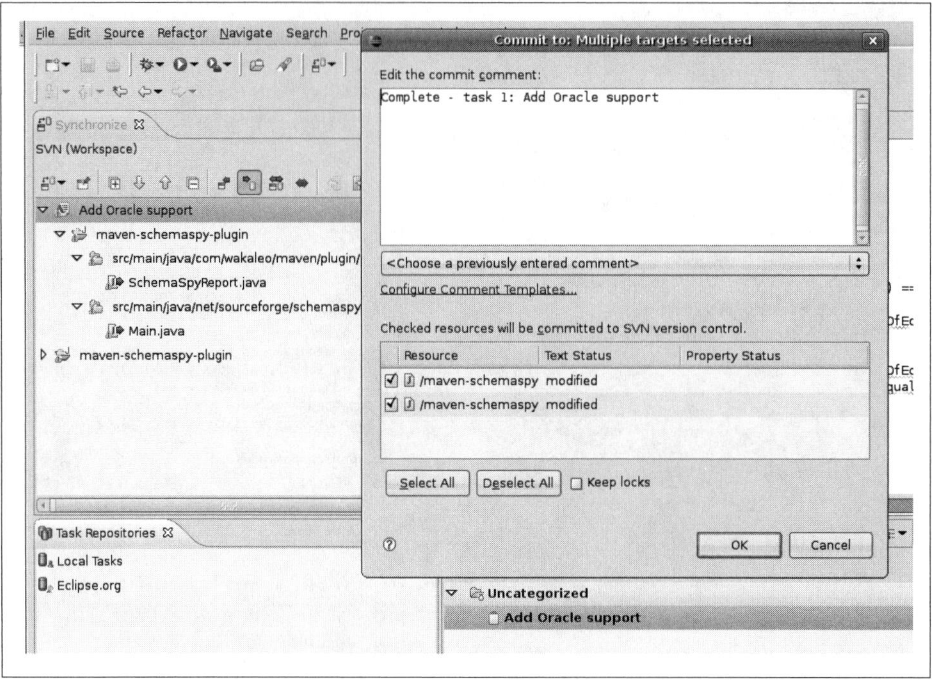

Figure 25-14. Committing a Mylyn change set

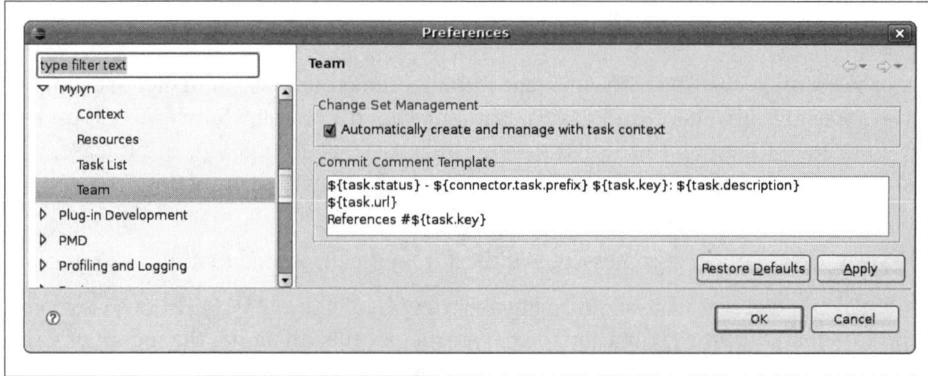

Figure 25-15. Committing a Mylyn change set

task from where you left off. Providing them with the context you so painstakingly created can be a valuable aid. The developer can immediately see what files you were modifying, what tests you where running, and so forth. This allows him to immediately focus on the correct trouble spots, rather than having to search for them himself.

In Mylyn, you can share your contexts with other developers. Mylyn lets you attach the current context to a task and record this context as an attachment to the

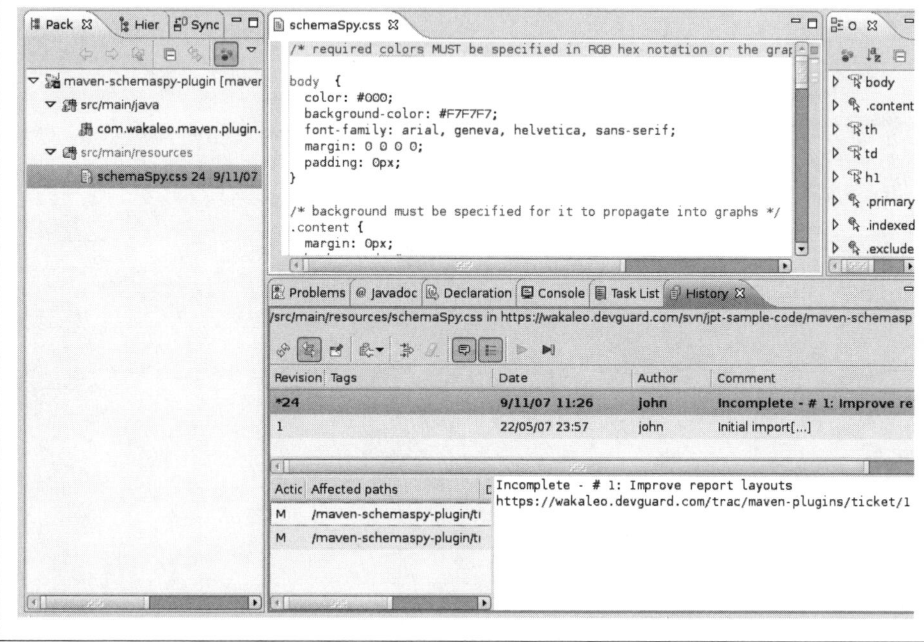

Figure 25-16. Viewing change history

corresponding ticket in the issue management system (at the time of this writing, this only worked for Bugzilla task repositories). You do this from the "Context" tab, using the "Attach context..." link. Subsequently, other developers can click on "Retrieve context..." to download and activate this context in their own Eclipse environment.

25.8 Conclusion

The task and context management features of Mylyn work together to help you focus your effort on the task at hand, making everything relevant easier to find and hiding the irrelevant. When you factor in the ability to share contexts with other teams members, these features make the plug-in a worthwhile addition to your Eclipse environment.

CHAPTER 26

Monitoring Build Statistics

26.0 Introduction

There are many open source reporting tools available that can give you useful information about your project. Checkstyle, PMD, and FindBugs analyze the project source code, looking for code that fails to respect coding conventions or contains errors. Cobertura reports on test coverage, giving you an idea of how well your code has been tested.

All of these tools can provide detailed information about one particular aspect of your project at a particular point in time. However, it can also be useful to see how these statistics evolve over the lifetime of a project. Does the average code coverage increase or decrease? How does the number of errors detected by PMD and FindBugs evolve over time. How much code has been added to the project over the last month? For this type of query, a snapshot analysis of your project will not be enough—you need to study the data over time.

There are many tools that can help you in this area. QALab collects data from these tools and reports on the evolution of these statistics over time. For example, you can visualize the evolution of code quality and test coverage statistics over the life of the project. In this chapter, we will look at some tools that you can use to collect and display this sort of time-related statistical data.

26.1 QALab

QALab collects data from tools such as static analysis results and code coverage, and reports on the evolution of these statistics over time. For example, you can visualize the evolution of code quality and test coverage statistics over the life of the project.

QALab works by extracting key information from the reports generated by the other tools, and storing this data in a single file called *qalab.xml*. Because QALab deals with statistical trends and not individual violations, only summary-level information is recorded. For QALab to work effectively, you need to generate data for QALab on a regular basis—such as during nightly builds or during the Continuous Build process.

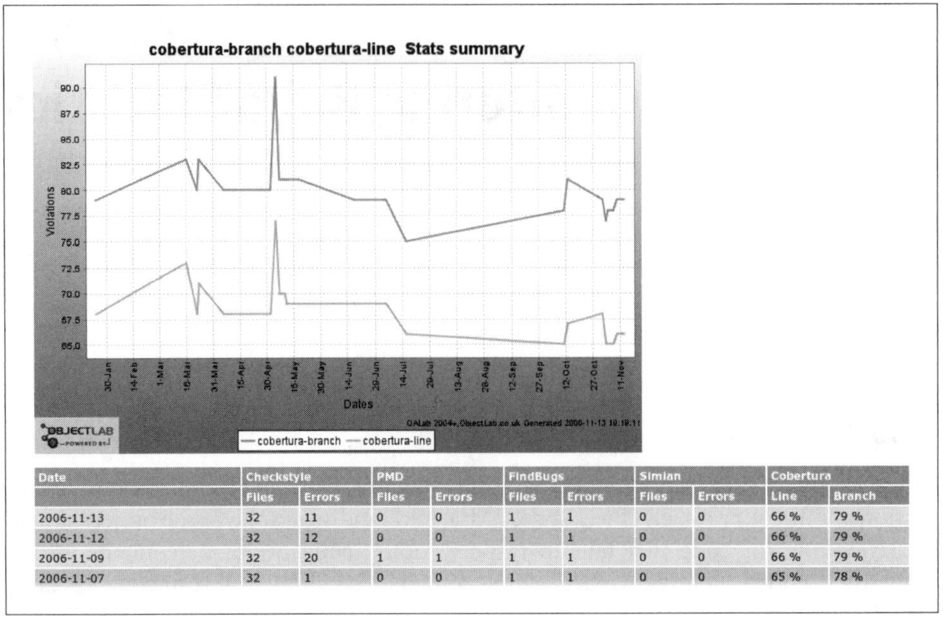

Date	Checkstyle		PMD		FindBugs		Simian		Cobertura	
	Files	Errors	Files	Errors	Files	Errors	Files	Errors	Line	Branch
2006-11-13	32	11	0	0	1	1	0	0	66 %	79 %
2006-11-12	32	12	0	0	1	1	0	0	66 %	79 %
2006-11-09	32	20	1	1	1	1	0	0	66 %	79 %
2006-11-07	32	1	0	0	1	1	0	0	65 %	78 %

Figure 26-1. QALab generates graphs of quality-related statistics such as Cobertura code coverage, and Checkstyle, PMD, and FindBugs violations over time

QALab generates two types of reports: Charts and Movers. The charts track the evolution of data since the start of the project (or since QALab was installed). You can see an example of a QALab chart in Figure 26-1. The movers allow you to see at a glance what has changed since the last QALab reports where generated. For example, rather than displaying Checkstyle results since the start of the project, movers focus on how many more (or less) violations there were today compared to yesterday.

The chart graph is quite powerful in a number of ways. If you click the graph, you will obtain a list of all the current files. Clicking any one of these files will display a graph containing the historical data just for this file. QALab integrates well with Ant and Maven.

Using QALab in Ant

Before you can use QALab in Ant, you need to download the latest QALab jar and the Maven QALab plug-in jar* —as well as its dependencies (jcommon, jfreechart, xerces, and xercesImpl). The dependencies are not provided in the QALab download, so you have to hunt them down yourself. The JCommon and JFreeChart libraries are available at the JFreeChart site (*http://www.jfree.org/jfreechart/*). If you have a lot of development machines to install, it may be easier to define a separate Ant build file (called, for

* Both are available at *http://qalab.sourceforge.net/*.

example, *bootstrap-qalab.xml*) containing a bootstrap task that downloads and installs the appropriate files, as shown here:

```
<project name="QALAB Bootstrap script" default="bootstrap" basedir="." >

  <!-- Define the environment-specific variable "qalab.home" in this file. -->
  <property file="${user.home}/ant-global.properties"/>
  <!-- This default value is used if no properties file is present -->
  <property name="qalab.home" value="${user.home}/.qalab"/>

  <property name="maven.repository"
            value="http://repo1.maven.org/maven2" />
  <property name="sourceforge.mirror"
            value="http://optusnet.dl.sourceforge.net/sourceforge" />

  <available file="${qalab.home}/lib/qalab-1.0.jar" property="qalab.installed"/>

  <target name="bootstrap" unless="qalab.installed">
    <echo>Installing QALib</echo>
    <mkdir dir="${qalab.home}/lib" />
    <!-- QALab -->
    <get src="${sourceforge.mirror}/qalab/qalab-1.0.jar"
         dest="${qalab.home}/lib/qalab-1.0.jar" usetimestamp="true"/>
    <get src="${sourceforge.mirror}/qalab/mvn-qalab-plugin-2.2.jar"
         dest="${qalab.home}/lib/mvn-qalab-plugin-2.2.jar" usetimestamp="true"/>
    <!-- Xerces -->
    <get src="${maven.repository}/xerces/xerces/2.4.0/xerces-2.4.0.jar"
         dest="${qalab.home}/lib/xerces-2.4.0.jar" usetimestamp="true"/>
    <!-- XercesImpl -->
    <get src="${maven.repository}/xerces/xercesImpl/2.6.2/xercesImpl-2.6.2.jar"
         dest="${qalab.home}/lib/xercesImpl-2.6.2.jar" usetimestamp="true"/>
    <!-- Freechart and JCommon -->
    <get src="${sourceforge.mirror}/jfreechart/jfreechart-1.0.5.zip"
         dest="${qalab.home}/lib/jfreechart-1.0.5.zip" usetimestamp="true"/>
    <unzip src="${qalab.home}/lib/jfreechart-1.0.5.zip"
          dest="${qalab.home}/lib"/>
  </target>

</project>
```

This will download and install the QALib library and its dependencies if (and only if) they have not already been locally installed. Then you can simply call this script at the start of your main Ant build file and define a classpath containing all of the QALab jars and dependencies:

```
<ant antfile="bootstrap-qalab.xml" target="bootstrap"/>

<path id="qalab.classpath">
    <fileset dir="${qalab.home}/lib">
      <include name="**/*.jar"/>
    </fileset>
</path>
```

Once the QALab files are installed, we can start to configure our Ant build file. As we have seen, QALab collects and aggregates quality-related data from a number of different data sources, and produces graphs tracking the evolution of this data over the life of a project. When you use QALab in Ant, you need to set up and configure each of these phases. This involves:

- Generating the statistical data from each tool in an appropriate form, as an XML document.
- Analyzing and aggregating this data into a consolidated QALab XML document.
- Generating one or more graphs using this consolidated data.

In this section, we will look at how to perform each of these activities.

As we mentioned previously, QALab is capable of handling data from a number of sources: Checkstyle (Chapter 21), PMD (Chapter 22), FindBugs (Chapter 23), Simian, or Cobertura (Chapter 20). Configuring QALab in Ant involves setting up each of these tools to produce the XML data that QALab needs to work with. All of these tools allow you to generate results in XML form, although the details vary for each tool. In Checkstyle, you do something like this:

```
<target name="checkstyle">
    <checkstyle config="config/company-checks.xml">
        <fileset dir="src/main/java" includes="**/*.java"/>
        <formatter type="xml" tofile="${build.dir}/reports/checkstyle-report.xml"/>
    </checkstyle>
</target>
```

In PMD, you use the XML formatter, as shown here:

```
<pmd rulesetfiles="basic,javabeans,junit,controversial" targetJdk="1.5"
failonerror="true">
        <formatter type="xml" toFile="${build.dir}/reports/pmd-
         report.xml"/>
        <fileset dir="${src}">
            <include name="**/*.java"/>
        </fileset>
</pmd>
```

In FindBugs, you use the *output* parameter to set the format to XML:

```
<findbugs home="${findbugs.home}" output="xml" outputFile="reports/
 findbugs-report.xml" >
  ...
</findbugs>
```

And, in Cobertura, you use the *<cobertura-report>* tag with the *format* attribute set to "xml." This will generate a file called `cobertura.xml` in the reports directory:

```
<cobertura-report format="xml"
                  destdir="${build.dir}/reports"
                  srcdir="${java.src}"
                  datafile="${basedir}/cobertura.ser" />
```

Once you are sure that your data is being generated (at least) in XML form, you need to tell QALab to integrate data from each file into the main QALab data file. To do this, you need to define and use the QALab *<mergestat>* task. The Ant type definition should look something like this:

```
<taskdef name="mergestat"
         classname="net.objectlab.qalab.ant.BuildStatMergeTask"
         classpathref="qalab.classpath" />
```

You need a *<mergestat>* task for each type of data that you want to integrate. QALab knows how to read the XML files generated by all of the above tools. There is a special handler class for each tool, which you specify in the *handler* attribute (`net.objectlab.qalab.parser.CheckstyleStatMerge`, `PMDStatMerge`, `FindBugsStatMerge`, and so on).

The form of each *<mergestat>* task is similar: you need to provide the generated XML data (using the *inputFile* attribute) and indicate where you want to store the QALab data file. Note that this file, typically called *qalab.xml*, is designed to remain in use throughout the project's lifespan, so it should be stored somewhere where it won't be erased whenever you do a clean build.

Here is a typical example of the *<mergestat>* task:

```
<mergestat inputFile="${build.dir}/checkstyle-report.xml"
           outputFile="${basedir}/qalab.xml"
           srcDir="${java.src}"
           handler="net.objectlab.qalab.parser.CheckstyleStatMerge" />
```

And here is a full example using output from all of the above tools. Because we are integrating data from several sources, we use the *mergerTimeStamp* attribute to ensure that all the data processed here is recorded with the same date and time. Recording the date and time (as opposed to just the date) allows you to record statistics several times a day, which is useful if you are running QALab during regular or Continuous Integration builds. If you don't use this attribute, the date (without the time) will be used:

```
<tstamp>
    <format property="TIMESTAMP" pattern="yyyy-MM-dd HH:mm:ss"/>
</tstamp>

<target name="qalab" depends="checkstyle, pmd, findbugs, cobertura.report" >

    <!-- Checkstyle -->
    <mergestat inputFile="${build.dir}/checkstyle-report.xml"
               outputFile="${basedir}/qalab.xml"
               srcDir="${java.src}"
               handler="net.objectlab.qalab.parser.CheckstyleStatMerge"
               mergerTimeStamp="${TIMESTAMP}"/>
    <!-- PMD -->
    <mergestat inputFile="${build.dir}/pmd-report.xml"
               outputFile="${basedir}/qalab.xml"
               srcDir="${java.src}"
               handler="net.objectlab.qalab.parser.PMDStatMerge"
               mergerTimeStamp="${TIMESTAMP}"/>
    <!-- FindBugs -->
    <mergestat inputFile="${build.dir}/findbugs-report.xml"
               outputFile="${basedir}/qalab.xml"
```

```
                    srcDir="${java.src}"
                    handler="net.objectlab.qalab.parser.FindBugsStatMerge"
                    mergerTimeStamp="${TIMESTAMP}"/>
        <!-- Cobertura -->
        <mergestat inputFile="${build.dir}/reports/coverage.xml"
                    outputFile="${basedir}/qalab.xml"
                    srcDir="${java.src}"
                    handler="net.objectlab.qalab.parser.CoberturaLineStatMerge"
                    mergerTimeStamp="${TIMESTAMP}"/>

        <mergestat inputFile="${build.dir}/reports/coverage.xml"
                    outputFile="${basedir}/qalab.xml"
                    srcDir="${java.src}"
                    handler="net.objectlab.qalab.parser.CoberturaBranchStatMerge"
                    mergerTimeStamp="${TIMESTAMP}"/>

    </target>
```

Once you can generate the *qalab.xml* file on a regular basis you are ready to build some charts. You generate charts using the *<buildchart>* task, which you need to define as follows:

```
<taskdef name="buildchart"
        classname="net.objectlab.qalab.ant.BuildStatChartTask"
        classpathref="qalab.classpath" />
```

You can use this task to generate a set of charts as follows:

```
    <buildchart inputFile="${basedir}/qalab.xml"
                toDir="${build.dir}/reports/charts/static-analysis"
                movingAverage="10"
                width="500" height="333"
                summaryOnly="false"
                summaryType="checkstyle,pmd,findbugs"
                type="checkstyle,pmd,findbugs"
                quiet="true"/>
```

This will generate a nice set of charts in JPG form and place them in the directory that you specified with the *toDir* attribute (see Figure 26-2). Other than this one, the most important attributes here are *summaryType* and *type*, which indicate what data should appear on the summary chart and on the main chart, respectively. You can put multiple values here: the graphs will contain a different colored line for each data type.

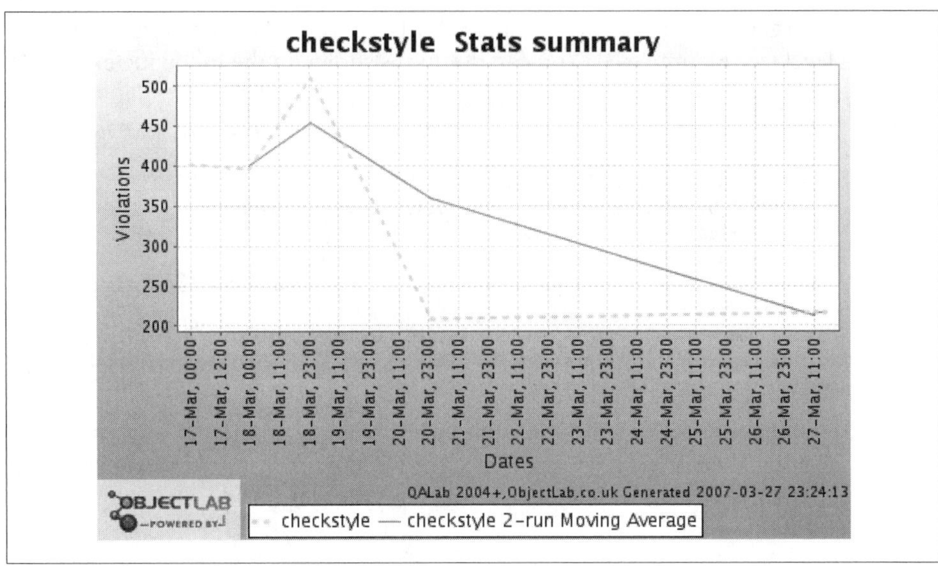

Figure 26-2. A typical QALab graph

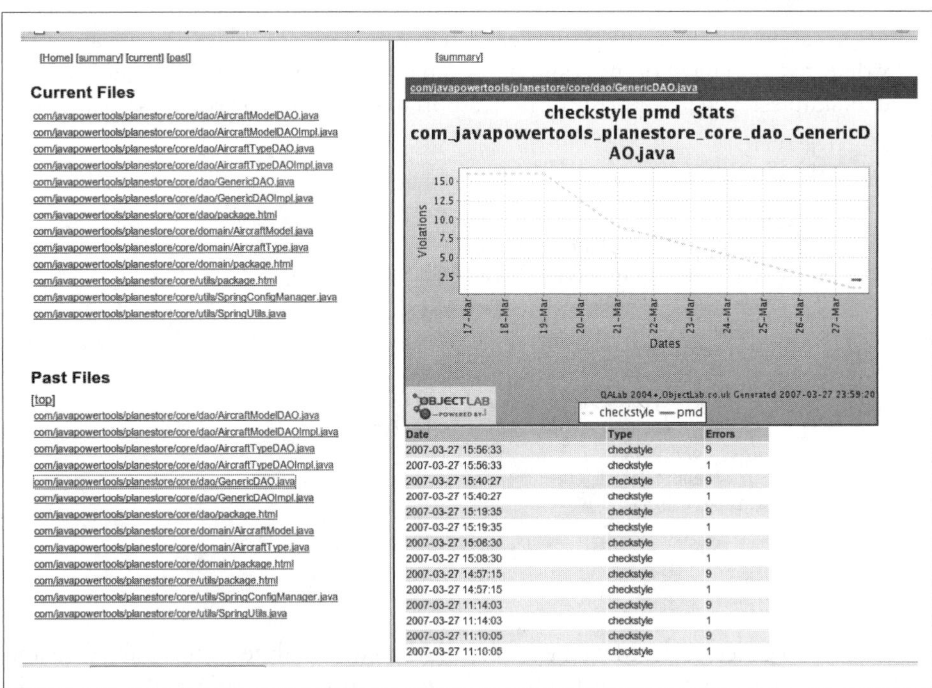

Figure 26-3. QALab can also produce HTML reports

Although this is certainly a useful function, it is probably not quite what you need for your project reporting. The Maven QALab plug-in comes with an XSL stylesheet that you can use to generate reasonable-looking HTML reports in which you can drill down to a class level (see Figure 26-3). You can do this as shown in the following example:

```
<tstamp>
  <format property="TIME" pattern="yyyy-MM-dd" offset="-48" unit="hour"/>
</tstamp>
<xslt in="${basedir}/qalab.xml"
      out="${build.dir}/reports/charts/static-analysis/hist.html"
      style="qalab-chart-html.xsl"
      classpathref="qalab.classpath">
  <param name="targetdir" expression="${build.dir}/reports/charts/static-
   analysis"/>
  <param name="type" expression="checkstyle,findbugs,pmd"/>
  <param name="offset" expression="${TIME}"/>
</xslt>
```

Note that you have to extract the XSL stylesheet manually and put it somewhere accessible. Another alternative, if you are using Ant 1.7, is to use a nested *<style>* element and to specify the stylesheet as a *<javaresource>* on the classpath.

Using QALab in Maven

Using QALab in Maven is much simpler than in Ant. The XML data files are automatically detected, and most of the configuration parameters have sensible default values. So, at its simplest, you just add the QALab report to your Maven reports, as shown here:

```
<reporting>
  <plugins>
     ...
     <plugin>
        <groupId>net.objectlab</groupId>
        <artifactId>mvn-qalab-plugin</artifactId>
        <version>2.2</version>
        <reportSets>
           <reportSet>
              <reports>
                 <report>report-merge-chart</report>
                 <report>report-movers-all</report>
              </reports>
           </reportSet>
        </reportSets>
     </plugin>
     ..
  </plugins>
</reporting>
```

Each time you generate the Maven web site, QALab will analyze your project data and update the `qalab.xml` file accordingly, and include historical reports like the one in Figure 26-1. QALab can find and incorporate XML data from Checkstyle (Chapter 21), PMD (Chapter 22), FindBugs (Chapter 23), or Cobertura (Chapter 20).

Because not all of these tools generate XML data by default, a little extra configuration is needed for some of them. The FindBugs report plug-in will generate XML data if you set the *xmlOutput* configuration variable to *true*:

```
<plugin>
  <groupId>org.codehaus.mojo</groupId>
  <artifactId>findbugs-maven-plugin</artifactId>
  <version>1.0.0</version>
  <configuration>
    <threshold>Normal</threshold>
    <xmlOutput>true</xmlOutput>
  </configuration>
</plugin>
```

The Cobertura report plug-in generates HTML reports by default. You can use the *format* configuration variable to force Cobertura to generate the XML data that QALab needs as follows:

```
<plugin>
    <groupId>org.codehaus.mojo</groupId>
    <artifactId>cobertura-maven-plugin</artifactId>
    <configuration>
      <formats>
          <format>html</format>
          <format>xml</format>
      </formats>
    </configuration>
</plugin>
```

Both the Checkstyle and PMD report plug-ins generates XML data by default, so no extra configuration is needed here.

26.2 Source Code Management Metrics with StatSCM

It is often useful (or merely satisfying) to know how much code has been added to a project over a certain period of time. In Maven 2, the *StatSCM* plug-in lets you do just that. Written by Doug Culnane, StatSCM is a wrapper on top of two other tools—*StatCVS* and *StatSVN*—which we will look at further on.

StatSCM is capable of generating an abundance of statistical information about your project, including:

- How fast the source code base has been growing
- Who is actively working on this project
- How much code each developer has been contributing, and how active they have been
- What release tags have been made
- Which files are being modified the most often

StatSVN also provides a graphical view of your repository structure.

StatSCM is easy to set up and to use. First, make sure the *<scm>* section (see "A Human-Readable Project Description" in Section 2.4) of your POM file is correct. StatSCM uses this information to find the source code repository and study the logfiles. For Subversion, it also counts the number of lines of code in each changeset, which can take quite a while for a big repository.

StatSCM is not in the standard Maven repository, so you need to add the following plug-in repositories to your POM file:

```
<pluginRepositories>
   <pluginRepository>
       <id>stat-scm-sourceforge</id>
       <url>http://stat-scm.sourceforge.net/maven2</url>
   </pluginRepository>
   <pluginRepository>
       <id>stat-scm-sourceforge-snapshot</id>
       <url>http://stat-scm.sourceforge.net/maven2-snapshots</url>
   </pluginRepository>
</pluginRepositories>
```

Then add the stat-scm report to your list of reports:

```
<reporting>
  <plugins>
    ...
    <plugin>
      <groupId>net.sf</groupId>
      <artifactId>stat-scm</artifactId>
    </plugin>
    ...
  </plugins>
</reporting>
```

Now, when you generate your Maven site, you will be able to browse through a very complete set of interactive reports containing statistical data about the evolution and activity of your project, from the point of view of its source code repository, during the life of the project (see Figure 26-4).

26.3 Statistics in Ant with StatSVN

The current version of StatSCM provides Maven 2 users with powerful statistical reporting functionalities about Subversion or CVS repository activity. If you are using Ant (see Chapter 1) and Subversion (see Chapter 4), you can obtain these detailed statistics by using the underlying StatSVN tool directly. StatSVN is a powerful tool designed to be run either directly from the command line, or using the built-in Ant Task. Here, we will concentrate on how to use StatSVN from within Ant.

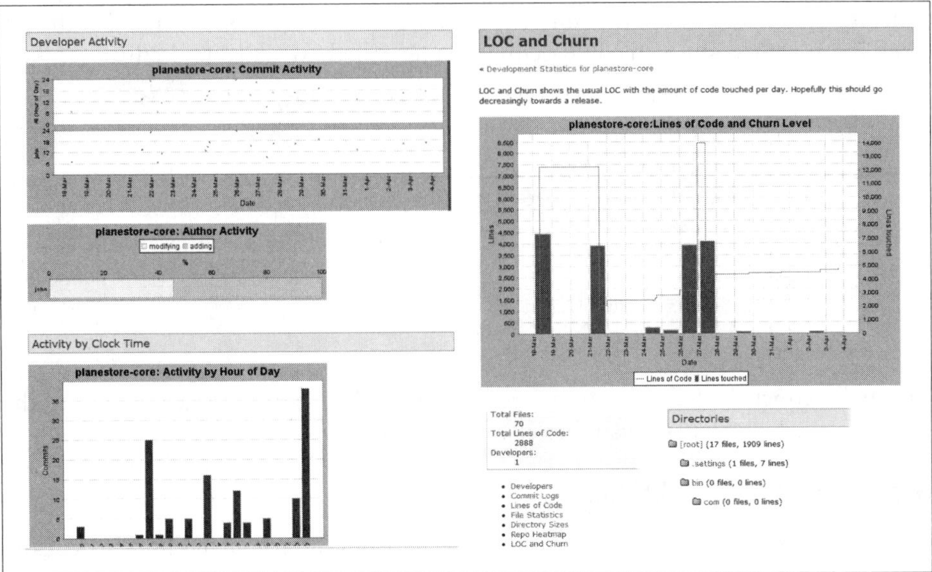

Figure 26-4. The Stat-SCM plug-in displays a range of statistical data describing the evolution of your project code base over time

Installing StatSVN

StatSVN is distributed as a simple JAR file. To install it, simply download the latest version from the StatSVN web site* and save this JAR file in an appropriate place on your disk. This JAR file also contains the StatSVN Ant task that we will be using. You can either copy the JAR file into your Ant `lib` directory, or, alternatively, refer to the JAR in your *<taskdef>* declaration, as shown here:

```
<taskdef name="statsvn"
         classname="net.sf.statsvn.ant.StatSvnTask"
         classpath="${statsvn.home}/statsvn.jar" />
```

Extracting the Subversion Logfiles

Although StatSVN is powerful, it is also fairly low level and involves working directly with your Subversion logfiles, which you must extract yourself. StatSVN works with the Subversion log messages in XML form. From the command line, you would need to execute the *svn log* command, as shown here:

```
$ svn log -v --xml http://svnserver.mycompany.com/svn/repos/myproject/trunk
```

In an ideal world, you would be able to use the SvnAnt library (see Section 4.30) to do this. However, at the time of this writing, the *svn log* command was not supported in

* *http://www.statsvn.org/downloads.html*

SvnAnt, so you need to use the Ant *<exec>* task to invoke the *svn* command at the OS level. From within Ant, you could define a target called "svn.log" to do this:

```
<property name="svnUrl" value="http://svnserver.mycompany.com/svn/repos
/myproject/trunk/" />

<target name="svn.log">
    <exec executable="svn" output="${basedir}/target/svn.log">
        <arg value="log"/>
        <arg value="-v"/>
        <arg value="--xml"/>
        <arg value="${svnUrl}"/>
    </exec>
 </target>
```

This will extract the Subversion log messages in XML form and place them into the `svn.`logfile, which StatSVN can then use to generate its reports.

Generating the StatSVN Reports

You can generate StatSVN reports either directly from the command line or by using the StatSVN Ant task. An example of how to use the *<statsvn>* task is shown here:

```
<target name="statsvn" depends="${basedir}/target/svn.log">
  <mkdir dir="${basedir}/target/statsvn"/>
  <statsvn
      path="P:\projects\java-power-tools\src"
      log="${basedir}/svn.log"
      outputDir="${basedir}/target/statsvn/stats"
      title="Java Power Tools" />
</target>
```

The path attribute refers to the root directory of the project being analyzed. This task will generate a very complete web site of statistical data and reports in the directory specified by the *output* attribute.

PART VII

Issue Management Tools

> And Eeyore whispered back: "I'm not saying there won't be an Accident *now*, mind you. They're funny things, Accidents. You never have them till you're having them."
>
> —"Tiggers Don't Climb Trees," *The House at Pooh Corner*, A. A. Milne

Despite all our best wishes and ardent efforts, bugs remain an inevitable part of the development process. Keeping track of defects, change requests, and tasks in general is a crucial best practice for any development project. All need to be tracked, prioritized, assigned, reviewed, and so on. A good tool facilitates interaction between project managers, testers, developers, and other team members, improves visibility on the current state of the project, and makes the development, testing, and debugging processes go more smoothly.

A good defect tracking system should also integrate smoothly with the version control system and make your life a little easier when it comes to organizing releases. For example, you should be able to indicate which issues were fixed when you commit changes to the version control system, and use this information to generate release notes listing the issues fixed in a particular release. When you commit code changes to your version control system, you should be able to refer to issues in your issue tracking system, and the issues should be updated accordingly. All of these little things make team communication just that much more efficient.

There are literally hundreds of bug tracking applications out there. There are a plenty of source solutions, of varying quality, as well as a wide range of commercial tools. It would be impossible even to list them all, let alone do them justice. Although we will not be discussing it in detail, JIRA—from Atlassian—is one commercial tool that deserves special mention, because it is both full-featured and highly usable.

In this part, we will limit ourselves to two open source products. Bugzilla is a well-known, robust, and feature-rich issue tracking system, well suited to large development teams and extended user communities. Trac, at the other end of the scale, is a lightweight issue-tracking tool that also offers some good project management and team communication features, as well as seamless integration with Subversion. Trac imposes little in the way of formal process and is well suited to small, agile teams using Subversion.

CHAPTER 27
Bugzilla

27.1 An Introduction to Bugzilla

Bugzilla[*] is probably the most well-known of the open source issue tracking solutions, and is used by many high-profile open source projects such as Mozilla, Apache, and Eclipse. It is a mature, high-performance, feature-rich open source issue management solution well adapted for use in very large projects. It has been adopted by a large number of organizations and projects, both in the open source world and for commercial products. On the downside, it has a fairly well-earned reputation of being hard to install and to maintain, and its default user interface—with its fast, lightweight, no-frills screens—is possibly one of the ugliest and most unfriendly around. In this chapter, we will look at how to install, use, and customize Bugzilla.

27.2 Installing Bugzilla

Bugzilla has an arguably justifiable reputation for being fairly hard to install.

Bugzilla is typically installed in a Unix or Linux environment, although the more recent versions work fine on Windows as well. Bugzilla runs on Perl, and uses either MySQL or PostgreSQL as a backing database. You also need a web server: Apache is the typical choice. Installation is done from the command line and basically involves installing all the necessary Perl modules, setting up the database, and scheduling external Perl scripts to collect data for bug graphs and to send notifications. Notifications are done by email, so you also need a mail server. The installation process is long and involved, often full of surprises, and only the bravest and most intrepid will come through a full Bugzilla installation unscathed. Here, I will go through the main steps, and try to point out some of the more common pitfalls.

[*] *http://www.bugzilla.org/*

This section concentrates on how to install Bugzilla into a Unix environment. On a Windows machine, the procedure is a little different; you can find a good tutorial on the Bugzilla web site.*

System Prerequisites

Bugzilla uses Perl as its scripting language, so you will need to have Perl installed on your machine. Most Unix/Linux distributions come with a recent version of Perl installed; if you have a doubt, run *perl --version* from the command line:

```
$ perl --version

This is perl, v5.8.8 built for i486-linux-gnu-thread-multi

Copyright 1987-2006, Larry Wall

Perl may be copied only under the terms of either the Artistic License or the
GNU General Public License, which may be found in the Perl 5 source kit.

Complete documentation for Perl, including FAQ lists, should be found on
this system using "man perl" or "perldoc perl".  If you have access to the
Internet, point your browser at http://www.perl.org/, the Perl Home Page.
```

If for some reason you don't have Perl on your machine (for example, if you happen to be running under Windows), you will need to download and install one of the binary distributions from the Perl web site.†

There are many distributions available. One of the most popular for Windows is ActivePerl,‡ from ActiveState.

You will also need a database: either MySQL (4.1.2 or higher) or PostgreSQL (8 or higher). These are the only databases currently supported by Bugzilla. Luckily, both are fairly easy to install on all platforms.

Finally, you will need a web server. In theory, any old web server capable of running CGIs will do, but by far the most common configuration is to install it with Apache.

Installing the Bugzilla Application

That was the easy bit. Now it is time to install Bugzilla itself. Download and uncompress the latest Bugzilla installation package from the Bugzilla site, as shown in the following example:

```
# wget http://ftp.mozilla.org/pub/mozilla.org/webtools/bugzilla-3.0.tar.gz
# tar vxfz bugzilla-3.0.tar.gz
# mv bugzilla-3.0 /usr/local/apache2/htdocs/bugzilla
```

* *http://www.bugzilla.org/docs/win32install.html*

† *http://www.perl.com*

‡ *http://www.activestate.com/Products/ActivePerl/*

This last line places Bugzilla in the typical Apache web directory. On this machine, Apache 2 was installed to the */usr/local/apache2* directory, so we put Bugzilla in the *htdocs* subdirectory, which is the web site root directory. Obviously, this will vary depending on your installation; */var/www/html* is another common option.

The unpacked Bugzilla directory must be accessible by the user that Apache runs under on your machine. This can be a pitfall if you run the installation scripts as root, and forget to change the permissions on the Bugzilla directory, for example. By default, Apache runs using the "nobody" user, but this is not considered to be a very secure practice. On many systems, the Apache server is run in a dedicated user account. This is configured in the Apache configuration (*httpd.conf*) file in the *User* directive:

```
# User/Group: The name (or #number) of the user/group to run httpd as.
# ...
User apache
```

Now go to this directory. The rest of the installation takes place there.

Installing the Perl Modules

One of the core parts of the Bugzilla installation process involves installing a long list of Perl modules that Bugzilla requires (and a few optional ones that Bugzilla would like to have). The main tool at your disposition for this task is the `checksetup.pl` script. This script analyzes your system and lists any Perl modules (and there will be) that are not present on your system, and that, therefore, you need to install. The first thing to do is to run this script as follows to determine exactly which modules you need to install. The script will provide OS-specific instructions on how to go about installing the missing modules:

```
# ./checksetup.pl --check-modules
* This is Bugzilla 3.0rc1 on perl 5.8.8
* Running on Linux 2.6.17-11-generic #2 SMP Thu Feb 1 19:52:28 UTC 2007

Checking perl modules...
Checking for       AppConfig (v1.52)    not found
Checking for             CGI (v2.93)   ok: found v3.20
Checking for    Data::Dumper (any)     ok: found v2.121_08
Checking for    Date::Format (v2.21)    not found
...
Checking available perl DBD modules...
Checking for          DBD-Pg (v1.45)    not found
Checking for       DBD-mysql (v2.9003) not found
...
**********************************************************************
COMMANDS TO INSTALL:

       DBD-mysql: /usr/bin/perl  -MCPAN -e 'install DBD::mysql'
       DBD-Pg: /usr/bin/perl  -MCPAN -e 'install DBD::Pg'
       ...
```

Depending on the state of your system, there can be quite a few modules to install. Each module can be installed using the appropriate (OS- and distribution-specific) Perl command. The Perl installation scripts will download, compile, and install any components you need for a each library. For example, on a Unix machine you would use the *perl -MCPAN* command to install the Perl PostgreSQL libraries:

```
# perl -MCPAN -e 'install DBD::Pg'
```

You need to do this for each of the missing modules. It is certainly long and tedious, but, in my experience, it is still the safest way to get things done. One simple but useful shortcut is to copy the commands listed by the checksetup script into a text file and massage them into a usable script, which you need to run only once.

Installing the Bugzilla Application

Once all of the Perl modules are installed, you can install Bugzilla itself. Again, you will be using the `checksetup.pl` script, but this time with no options, as shown here:

```
# ./checksetup.pl
```

This will generate a configuration file called localconfig, which you will need to tailor to your environment. There are several key properties in this configuration file that you may need to change:

$db_driver
: By default, this is set to MySQL. If you are using PostgreSQL, change this value to "Pg."

$db_name
: The name of the database Bugzilla will be using (you need to set this up yourself).

$db_user
: The database username.

$db_pass
: The database user password.

Next you need to set up an empty database and a corresponding user account in the database of your choice. The details of this will obviously depend on the database you are using. Here is how you might do it if you are using MySQL, for example:

```
mysql> GRANT ALL PRIVILEGES ON bugs.* TO bugs@localhost IDENTIFIED BY 'secret';
mysql> FLUSH PRIVILEGES;
```

When you are done, run `checkstyle.pl` again. It will detect your changes and populate the database with Bugzilla tables:

```
# ./checksetup.pl
...
Checking for       DBD-mysql (v2.9003) ok: found v4.003
Checking for           MySQL (v4.1.2)  ok: found v5.0.24a-Debian_9-log

Removing existing compiled templates ...
```

```
Precompiling templates...
Fixing file permissions...

Now that you have installed Bugzilla, you should visit the
'Parameters' page (linked in the footer of the Administrator
account) to ensure it is set up as you wish - this includes
setting the 'urlbase' option to the correct url.
```

At some point, the script will prompt you for an email address and password for your administrator account, as shown here:

```
Looks like we don't have an administrator set up yet.
Either this is your first time using Bugzilla, or your
administrator's privileges might have accidentally been deleted.

Enter the e-mail address of the administrator:
```

At the risk of stating the obvious, enter this address carefully; if you get it wrong or forget it, recovering or modifying it can be quite tricky.

Configuring the Web Server

Last, but not least, you need to set up the web server to process the Bugzilla pages correctly. In Apache, this simply involves activating CGI script handling for your Bugzilla directory. For the installation described above, we just need to add the following Directory directive to the Apache *httpd.conf* file (found in the */usr/local/apache2/conf* directory on my installation, although this file is often to be found in other places, such as */etc/httpd/conf*):

```
<Directory /usr/local/apache2/htdocs/bugzilla>
    AddHandler cgi-script .cgi
    Options +Indexes +ExecCGI
    DirectoryIndex index.cgi
    AllowOverride Limit
</Directory>
```

Now restart your web server, open your favorite browser, and go to the Bugzilla directory that you have just installed (*http://localhost/bugzilla*, if you have been following the examples given here). This should display the default Bugzilla main page, as shown in Figure 27-1.

27.3 Setting Up Your Bugzilla Environment

Once you get Bugzilla running, you will need to tailor it to your environment. Bugzilla asks you to define a few basic parameters the first time that you log in using your administration account (remember, the one we said not to forget at the start of the installation?). You need to set up things like the email address of the person responsible for maintaining the installation, the base URL of your Bugzilla installation, and whether some or all of the site should be protected by encrypted SSL access.

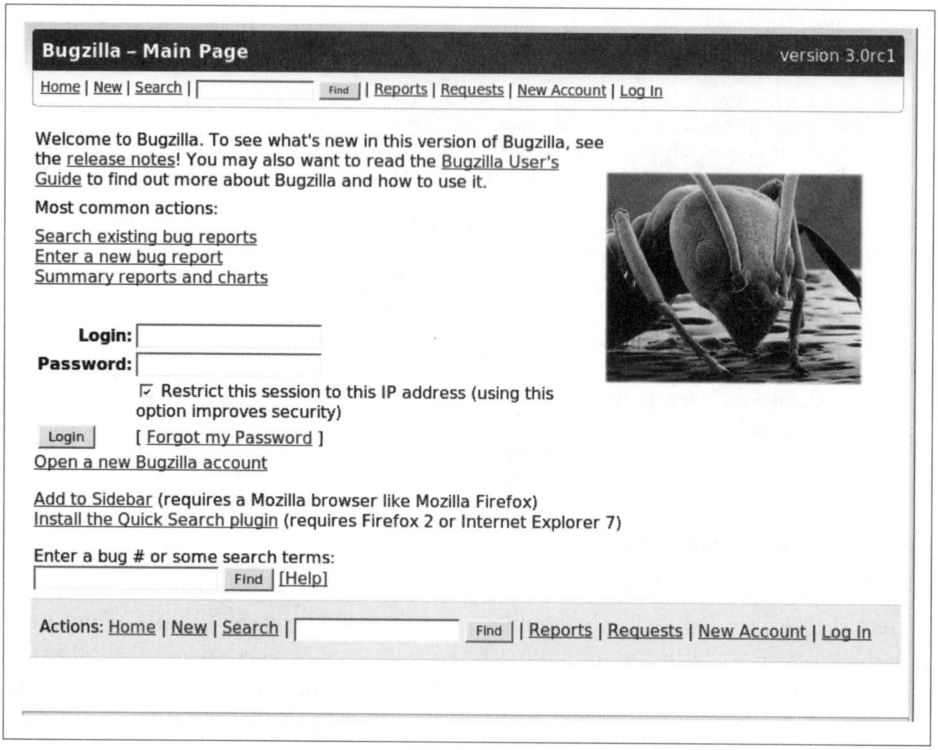

Figure 27-1. The default Bugzilla main page

27.4 Managing User Accounts

When it comes to user accounts, Bugzilla is very much based on an open source school of thought. By default, anyone can search and view bugs without needing to log in. You need to log in if you want to create or update bugs. Users can create their own accounts by clicking on the "New Account" link at the bottom of every screen. This is, in fact, the best and most convenient way to create new user accounts because users can manage their own email addresses and password details without having to bother the administrator. All a user needs to provide is a valid email address. New users created this way can freely search, create, and update bugs.This approach is fine for many projects, especially open source ones.

Bugzilla provides a useful web interface for creating and administrating user accounts. Administrators can manage user accounts in the "Users" screen (see Figure 27-2). This screen lets you search and list existing user accounts, modify user account details, and create new user accounts. Creating user accounts from the administration screens is usually only done for testing purposes, as users are not automatically notified when their account is created.

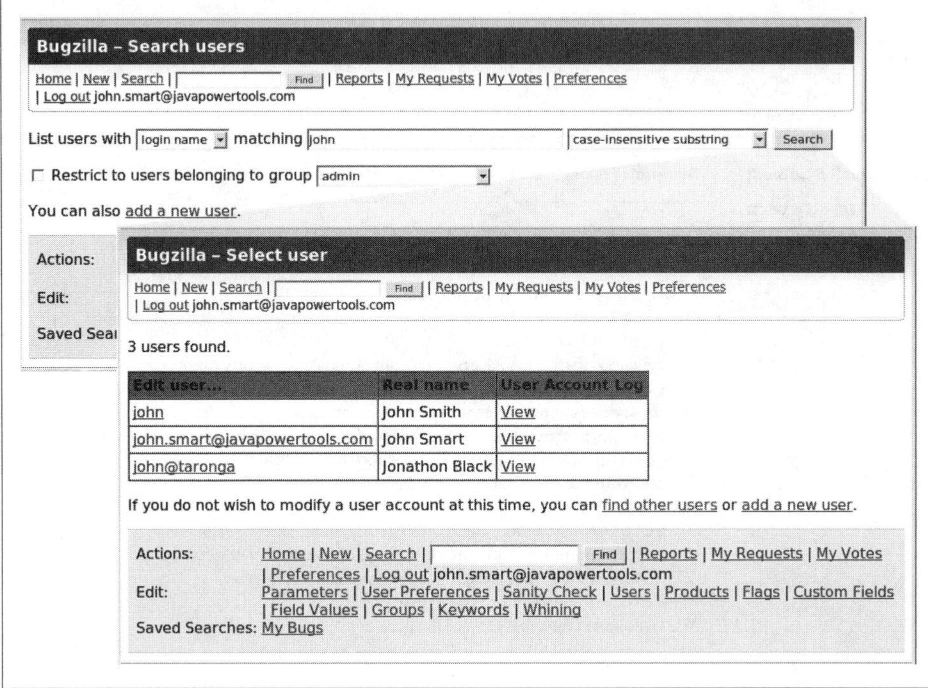

Figure 27-2. Managing Bugzilla user accounts

Default users can search, create, and update bugs, but they are not authorized to do very much else. Other functionalities, such as managing products and components, configuring periodic email notifications (known in Bugzilla terms as "whining"), and, indeed, managing users and user groups, are reserved for authorized users only. You can do this in the "Edit user" screen (see Figure 27-3). This screen lets you modify the user's login details and also authorize the user to access these other functionalities.

Bugzilla is fundamentally designed to be an open, public-facing issue management system, and any user can try to create his or her own account. By default, Bugzilla requires (and is happy with) a full, correctly formed email address (so it won't accept "jill" or "joe@myserver," for example). If your project requires more security, you can restrict access by modifying the *emailregexp*, in the "User Authentication" section of the "Parameters" screen. This field is a regular expression that user account email addresses must match. If you leave this field blank, Bugzilla will accept any email address (although it is likely to crash if the address isn't a real one). For example, you may want to limit user accounts to email addresses within your organization:

```
^[\w\.\+\-=]+@mycompany.com$
```

In this case, only email addresses with the domain "mycompany.com" will be accepted.

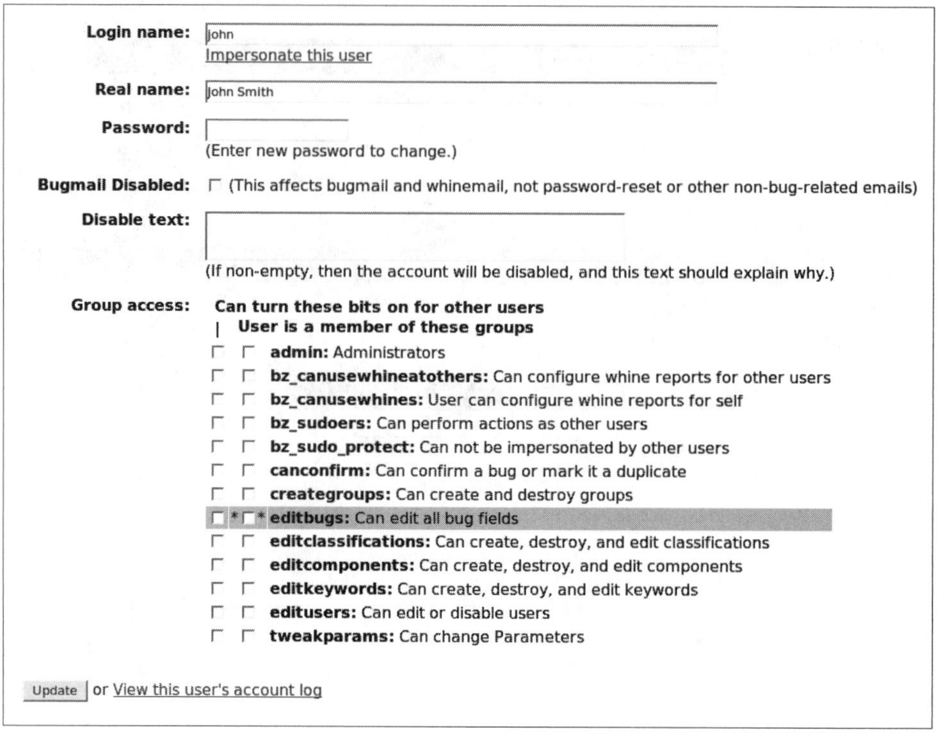

Login name: john
Impersonate this user
Real name: John Smith
Password:
(Enter new password to change.)
Bugmail Disabled: (This affects bugmail and whinemail, not password-reset or other non-bug-related emails)
Disable text:
(If non-empty, then the account will be disabled, and this text should explain why.)
Group access: **Can turn these bits on for other users**
| **User is a member of these groups**
admin: Administrators
bz_canusewhineatothers: Can configure whine reports for other users
bz_canusewhines: User can configure whine reports for self
bz_sudoers: Can perform actions as other users
bz_sudo_protect: Can not be impersonated by other users
canconfirm: Can confirm a bug or mark it a duplicate
creategroups: Can create and destroy groups
* * **editbugs:** Can edit all bug fields
editclassifications: Can create, destroy, and edit classifications
editcomponents: Can create, destroy, and edit components
editkeywords: Can create, destroy, and edit keywords
editusers: Can edit or disable users
tweakparams: Can change Parameters

Update or View this user's account log

Figure 27-3. Managing user account details in Bugzilla

Alternatively, you could allow only local usernames:

```
^[^@]+
```

In this case, you would also need to set the *emailsuffix* parameter to something like "*@mycompany.com*" so that Bugzilla can work out where to send notification emails.

If you need to restrict access to authentified users only, you can also activate the *requirelogin* parameter. If this is set to "true," users will be asked to log in before they can access Bugzilla at all.

27.5 Restricting Access Using User Groups

Bugs in Bugzilla are, by default, visible to any user. However, you can use groups to limit the visibility of certain bugs and products to certain users. For example, you may want to limit access to bugs in a particular project to members of the project team only. In this section, we will go through how to do this in Bugzilla using user groups.

The first thing you need to do is set up a new group. You do this in the "Groups" page (see Figure 27-4). This group will appear in the group lists alongside the special System groups such as *admin* and *editbugs*.

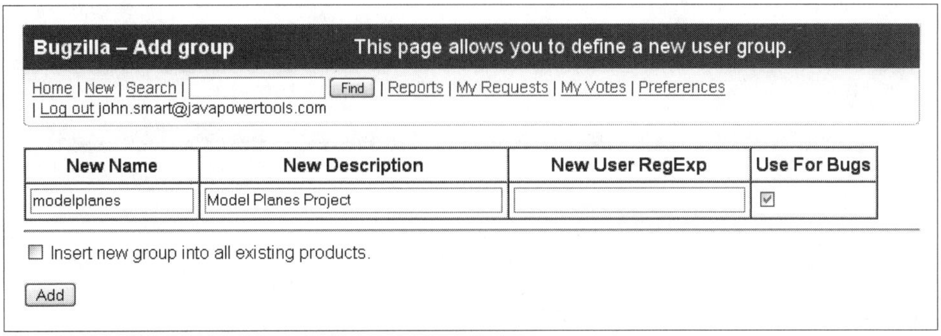

Bugzilla – Add group This page allows you to define a new user group.

Home | New | Search | [ ] Find | Reports | My Requests | My Votes | Preferences
| Log out john.smart@javapowertools.com

New Name	New Description	New User RegExp	Use For Bugs
modelplanes	Model Planes Project		☑

☐ Insert new group into all existing products.

Add

Figure 27-4. Adding a new user group in Bugzilla

Once you have added a group for your project, you need to place the team members in this group. Unfortunately, you have to do this individually for each user in the user details page (see Figure 27-3).

When you have assigned all of your team members to the new group, you can restrict access to a product in the "Edit Group Controls" page, which you can access by clicking the "Edit Group Access Controls" link in the product details page (see Figure 27-5). This screen contains a list of all the user-defined groups. Each column lets you restrict a different functionality to members of certain groups. The first two (*Entry* and *CanEdit*) *restrict* access to bugs for this project, whereas the final three (*editcomponents*, *canconfirm*, and *editbugs*) widen access, letting in users who otherwise wouldn't be able to view or edit the project bugs.

Entry
: If you check the "Entry" column for a particular group, only members of this group will be able to enter bugs against this product.

CanEdit
: Checking "CanEdit" will mean that only team members will be able to modify bugs for this project—other users will have read-only access.

editcomponents
: If you check this option, users who belong to a group with *editcomponents* privileges will be able to edit the product components, milestones, and versions, even if they don't belong to the project group.

canconfirm
: If you check this option, users who belong to a group with *canconfirm* privileges will be able to confirm UNCONFIRMED bugs, even if they don't belong to the project group.

editbugs
: If you activate this option, user who belong to a group with *editbugs* privileges (that is to say, pretty much any authenticated user) can modify bugs for this product.

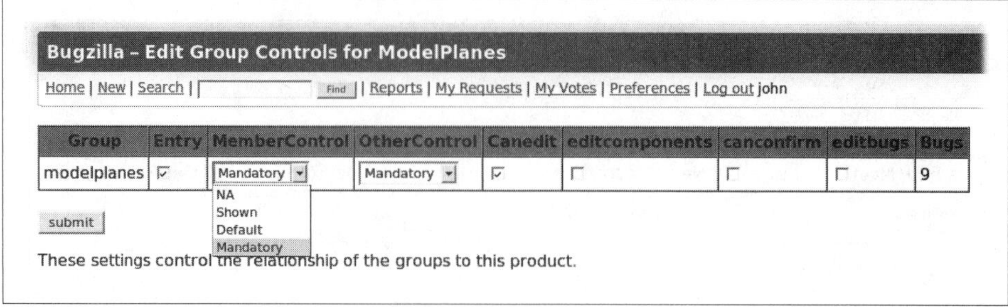

Figure 27-5. Limiting access to a product for a particular group

Figure 27-6. With the "Shown" and "Default" options, users can choose whether a bug should be given restricted access

The two other fields, *MemberControl* and *OtherControl*, determine whether or not bugs entered for this product are automatically placed in this group for members of this group (project team members) and for the rest of the world. If *NA* is chosen, bugs entered for this product by this type of user (team members for "MemberControl" and everyone else for "Other Control") are not placed in this group; therefore, there are no restrictions placed on them. *Shown* and *Default* are similar: the user is given the possibility to place the new bug in the restricted group (see Figure 27-6). With *Shown*, the option is not checked by default, whereas with Default, the option *is* checked by default. When *Mandatory* is chosen, bugs created for this project are automatically placed in this group.

The most intuitive option is to put both values to "Mandatory."

Note that the reporter, the assignee, and anyone copied (cc) on the bug will always be able to access the bug, no matter what group he or she belongs to.

27.6 Configuring a Product

It is fairly easy to set up a new project in Bugzilla. The main goal of a software development project is to create (or modify) a software application of some kind. In Bugzilla, a software application is known as a product. You manage products in the Bugzilla "Products" screen, which you can access via a link in any screen footer when logged in as an administrator (see Figure 27-7).

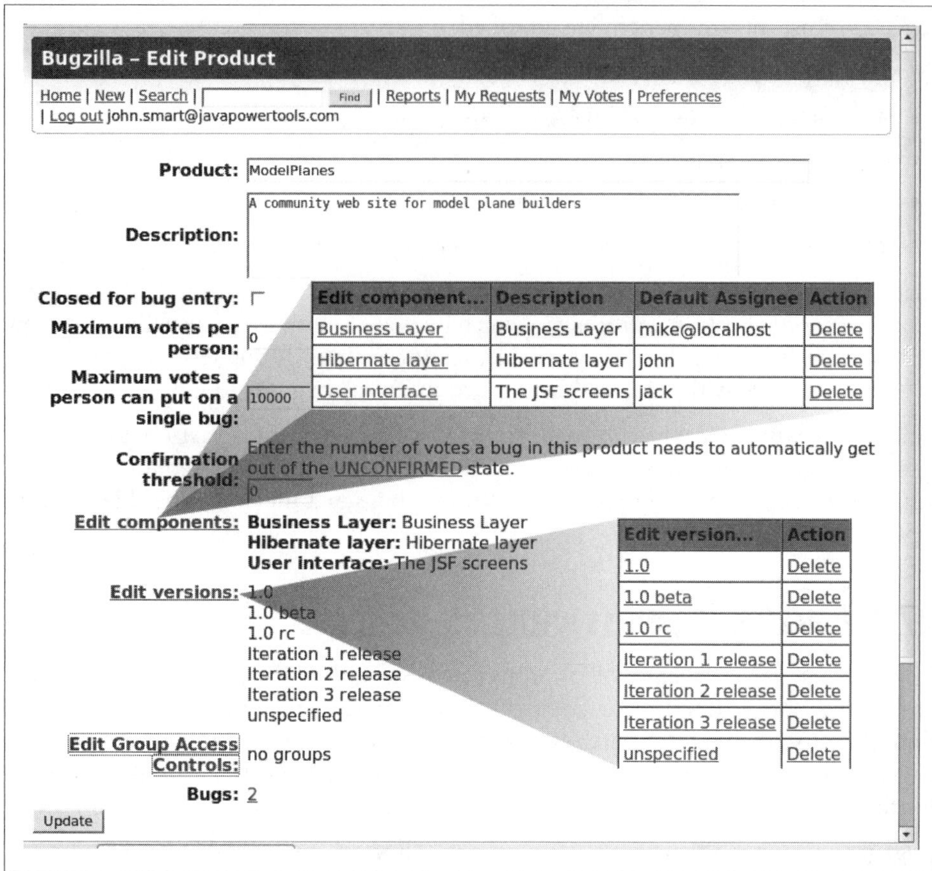

Figure 27-7. Managing products in Bugzilla

In Bugzilla, products are made up of components. You can define the components of a product by clicking on the "Edit components" link on the product details page. This will display a list of components for this product, letting you modify or delete existing components, or create new ones.

A product cannot exist by itself; you need to give it at least one component. While you're at it, however, you might as well add several. You use components to decompose your project into smaller chunks. Exactly how you do this will depend on your project and on your organization; Bugzilla doesn't really care. Typically, a component will be small enough to be the responsibility of a single developer, or have a readily identifiable development leader who coordinates work on the component. In Bugzilla, each component is the responsibility of a particular person, defined in the "Default Assignee" field. A component should be meaningful enough to an end user (or at least a QA person) to be able to log bugs against it with some degree of reliability. You can also use the "Default CC List" to define a list of users who will always be notified when bugs logged against this component are modified.

Some examples of what a component might be in your project are:

- A subproject within the main development project
- A software module
- A particular feature or functionality
- The implementation of a particular use case or user story

In a similar way, you can also define versions for your product using the "Edit versions" link. A version is a released product in which bugs are found, so you usually create new version entries in Bugzilla as they are released for testing. During testing, when a bug is found, you specify the version being tested when the bug was found.

Finally, once the project has finished, you may want to prevent users from logging any new bugs against this project. You can do this by checking the "Closed for bug entry" field. Users will still be able to search and consult bugs, but they won't be able to create new ones for this project.

27.7 Tracking Progress with Milestones

Milestones are an excellent tool for project tracking and prioritization. If you are using an iterative or agile development approach, you can set up a milestone for each iteration. Bugs can then be associated with a particular milestone, making it easier for the development team to know where to focus its development efforts, and making it easier for the testing team to know what it is meant to be testing.

Bugzilla has optional support for milestones. They are not available by default: you need to activate them by setting the "usetargetmilestone" option (in the "Bug Fields" section of the "Parameters" screen) to "On." When you do this, you can create milestones for a particular project (see Figure 27-8), define the target milestone for a particular bug, and view the list of bug corrections planned for a given milestone.

27.8 Managing Groups of Products with Classifications

Sometimes, it is useful to be able to associate several different but related products. You may want to regroup several distinct products that belong to the same program of work, a suite of software applications, or products that are related in some other way. Classifications let you group related products. By default, classifications are deactivated. To enable them, you need to activate the "useclassification" option (which is in the "Bug Fields" section of the "Parameters" screen). Once you have activated

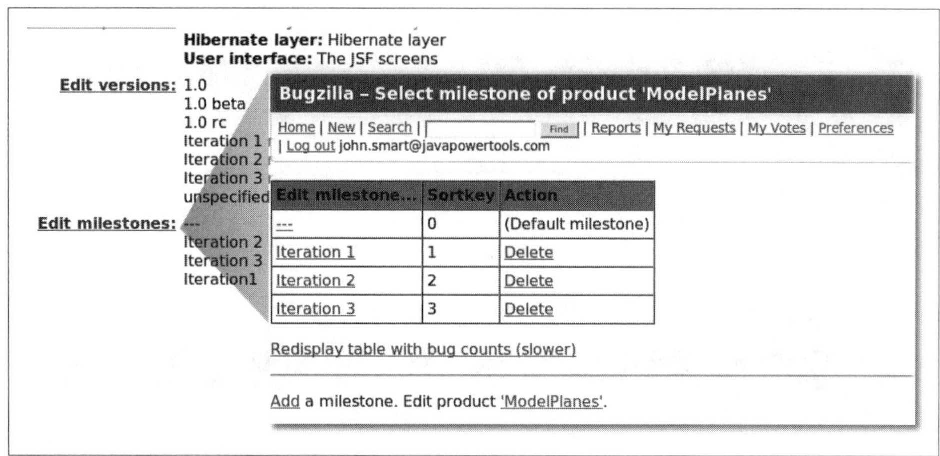

Figure 27-8. Managing milestones in Bugzilla

Bugzilla – Select classification

Home | New | Search | Find | Reports | My Requests | My Votes | Preferences | Log out joh

Edit Classification ...	Description	Sortkey	Products	Action
Hotels	Hotel Management software	0	reclassify (1)	delete
Modeling	Web applications about Modeling	0	reclassify (1)	delete
Unclassified	Not assigned to any classification	0	0	
Add a new classification				Add

Figure 27-9. Managing project classifications

classifications, an administrator will be able to manage them using the "Classifications" link in any screen footer (see Figure 27-9).

Setting up a classification simply involves giving it a name and associating some projects with it. Once you have at least two classifications set up with some projects in them, Bugzilla will ask you to choose a classification when you enter a bug (see Figure 27-10). You will also be able to use the classification field as a search criteria in the Advanced Search screen.

27.9 Searching for Bugs

Bugzilla is designed to be a robust, high-performance issue tracking system, capable of handling databases with hundreds of thousands of bugs. In a database with that many

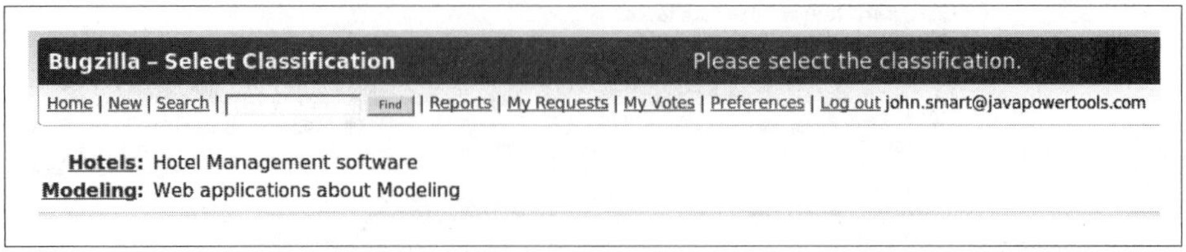

Figure 27-10. Selecting a classification during bug entry

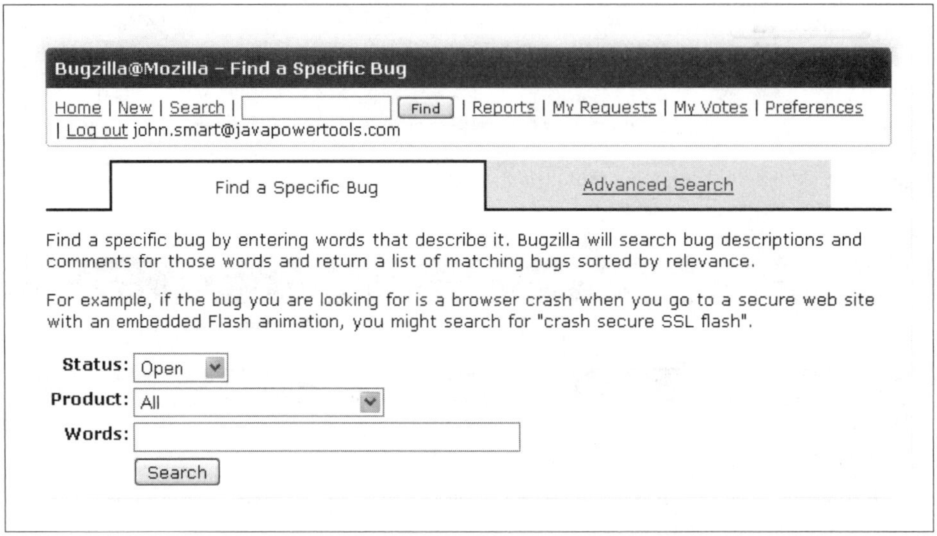

Figure 27-11. Selecting a classification during bug entry

bugs, you obviously need some good search functionality to find the ones you are looking for.

Bugzilla provides several ways to search the database, each appropriate in different situations. The simplest way to look for a bug is to use the search field in the page header. This provides a quick-and-easy full-text search across the entire database. You can also enter a numerical bug id, in which case Bugzilla will take you directly to the bug details.

You can do more elaborate searches in the Search screen (accessible using the "Search" link in the header of any page). From this screen, you can choose between two types of searches. Probably the most useful is the "Find a Specific Bug" tab. This tab provides a simple, full-text search (see Figure 27-11), possibly filtering by status or for a particular product.

The "Advanced Search" tab is a much more complicated beast that lets you search on virtually any field in the database.

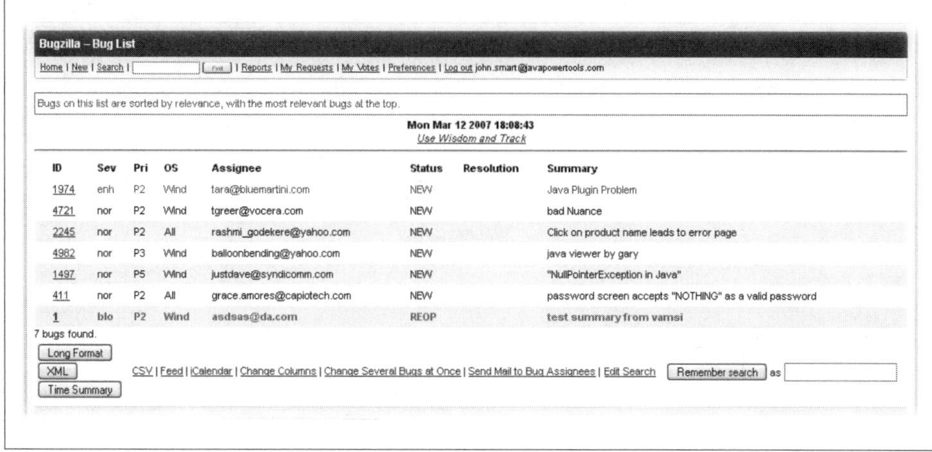

Figure 27-12. Search results are displayed as a simple list

Search results are displayed as a table (see Figure 27-12). Note that Bugzilla doesn't know about paging results, so if your query returns 4,000 bugs, you will get 4,000 entries on the one screen.

The results screen has a few nice additional features to it. The "Long Format" button displays a list of detailed information for each bug, including all the principal fields, the description, and any comments. This is especially useful for preparing those bug review meetings. You can also subscribe to a query in the form of an RSS feed, which is useful if you want to keep tabs on a certain category's issues (such as issues for the product you are working on) without having to continually open Bugzilla and run the search.

Another useful feature is the "iCalendar" button. It lets you download the list of bugs in iCalendar format so that you can import them as tasks in your agenda.

Finally, you can use the "Remember Search" button to give some meaningful name to your search and save it for later use. The saved search will appear in your page footer in the "My Searches" section.

27.10 Creating a New Bug

Although the interface is rudimentary and lacks many of the niceties of more recent Web sites, entering a new issue in Bugzilla is relatively straightforward. After selecting the buggy product, you arrive at the bug details screen (see Figure 27-13). Out of the numerous fields that you'll see, only the Summary and Component fields are actually mandatory. You will usually also provide other details, such as a version number (the version of the product in which the bug was found), severity of bug, platform, a target milestone, and so on. You can assign a bug directly to a developer if you know who

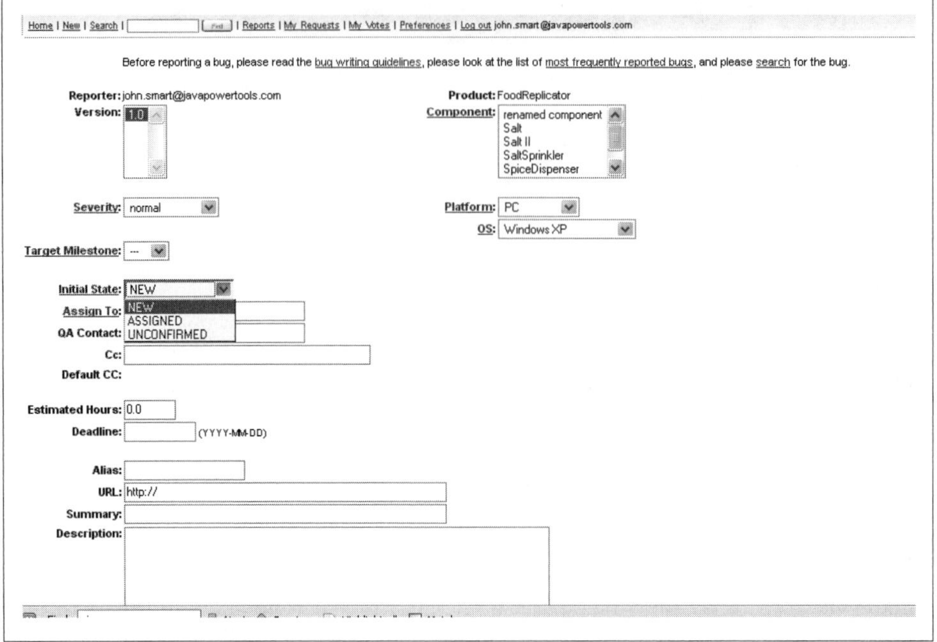

Figure 27-13. Entering a new issue

you are working with, or just wait for it to be picked up by some willing soul. If you can't remember the definitions of the various severity levels or how to use a particular field, convenient hyperlinks near each field let you display the appropriate help pages. You can also use attachments to add screen shots or the like.

27.11 The Lifecycle of a Bugzilla Bug

Bugzilla supports a fairly complete, albeit hardcoded, workflow model, illustrated in Figure 27-14.

Bugs begin life when a tester or user enters them in Bugzilla. Newly created bugs can be NEW, ASSIGNED, or UNCONFIRMED.

In simple terms, an UNCONFIRMED bug is one that needs to be reproduced by QA before it can be set to NEW and assigned to a developer. The UNCONFIRMED initial status is not available by default. If you want to allow UNCONFIRMED bugs, you need to activate the "usevotes" option in the "Bug Fields" section of the "Parameters" screen. Then you need to edit the product (see Section 27.6) to make sure that the "Number of votes a bug in this product needs to automatically get out of the UNCONFIRMED state" is greater than zero, and also that the Maximum votes per person is greater than zero. When this is done, you will be able to create new bugs in the UNCONFIRMED status.

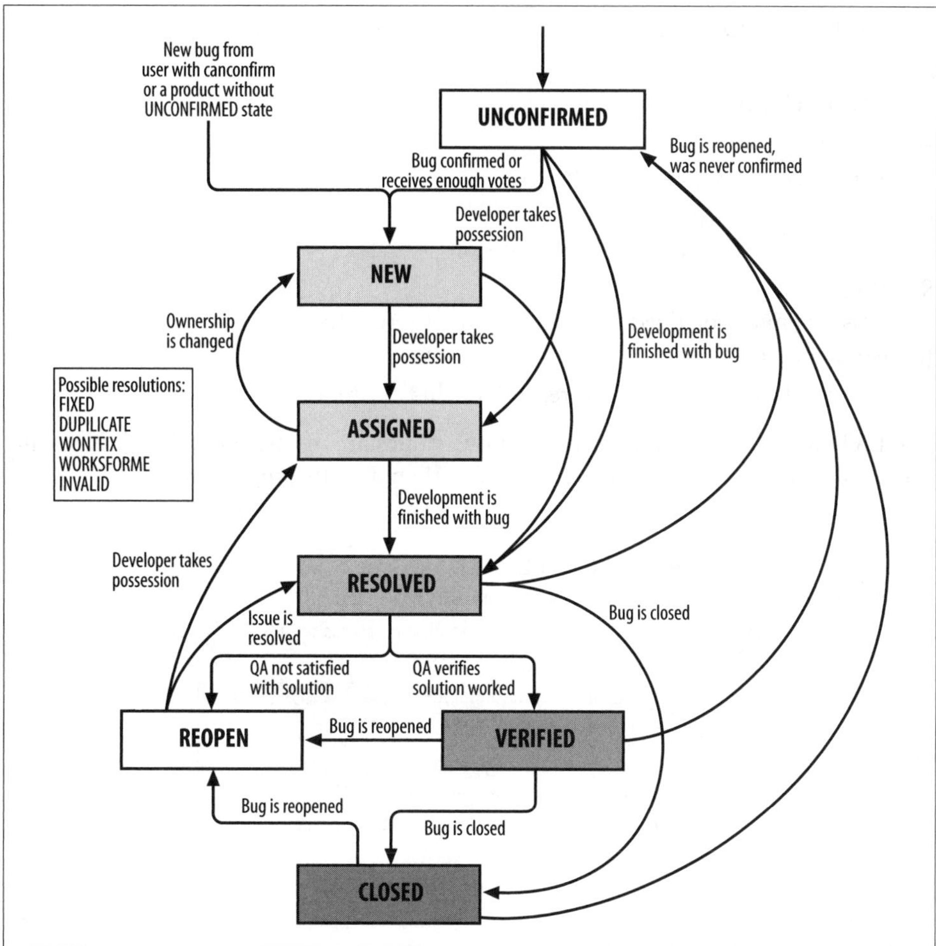

Figure 27-14. The lifecycle of a bug in Bugzilla

A bug can go from UNCONFIRMED to NEW either by having people vote for it, or when it is manually confirmed by a QA person (or any member of the *canconfirm* group). The QA person may assign the bug to a developer using the "Assigned To" field. Note that, even when a bug is "assigned to" a developer, it can still be in the NEW state. It will remain in this state until the developer reviews the issue and accepts it (in which case its state will go to ASSIGNED), or reassigns it to another developer. In fact, the ASSIGNED state actually means that a developer has accepted the bug and is actively (at least, in theory!) working on the problem.

Once the developer has finished working on an issue, he places it in the RESOLVED state. When he resolves a bug, he has to specify how it was resolved (see Figure 27-15). A bug can be resolved in several ways:

FIXED
: The bug was fixed and the correction submitted for testing by QA

INVALID
: The developer does not think this issue is really a bug

WONTFIX
: There is a bug, but it won't be fixed

LATER
: This bug will be fixed in a future version

REMIND
: This bug might be fixed for this version if there is time

WORKSFORME
: The developer was unable to reproduce this machine

The LATER and REMIND resolution status values are of dubious value; it is usually better to leave these issues open and reassign them to a future milestone.

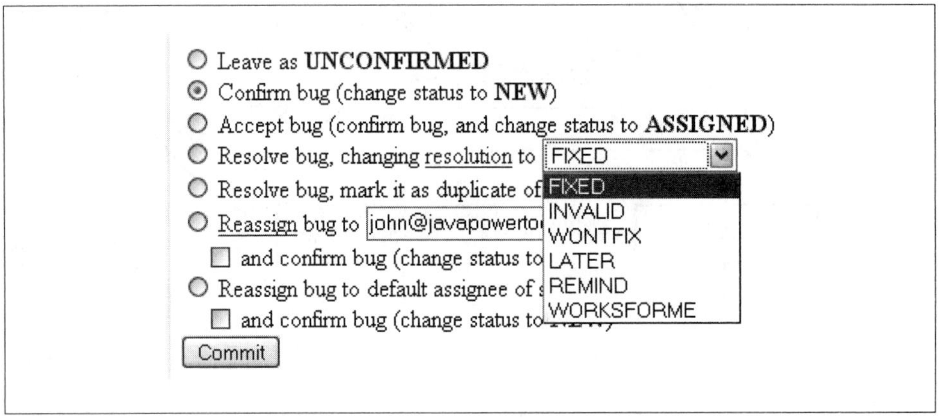

Figure 27-15. Updating a bug status

A RESOLVED bug needs to be verified by QA before the correction can be confirmed and released. QA staff typically review any allegedly FIXED bugs for the current milestone in order to make sure that the fixes work (see Figure 27-16). A bug is considered to be VERIFIED once the tester has confirmed that the fix works. When the version containing this fix is released, the bug can be CLOSED.

Although this workflow model cannot be customized in Bugzilla, it usually proves sufficient for most organizations.

27.12 Scheduling Notifications (Whining)

Bugzilla allows you to schedule notifications to be generated and sent to users on a regular basis. This process is known as whining. Whining basically involves scheduling

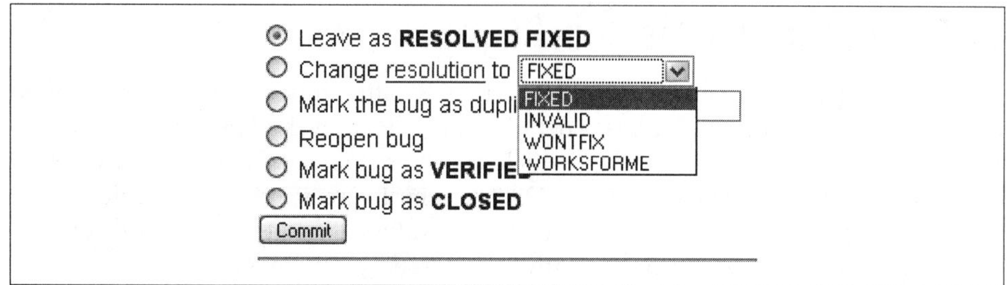

Figure 27-16. Verifying and closing a bug

Figure 27-17. Configuring Whining

predefined queries to be run at regular intervals or at specific times (for example, every Sunday). You can schedule any query you want; for example, you might want to send out the list of open bugs for a particular project to the project team every Sunday to remind them to prepare for the weekly status meeting.

The first thing to do is to build and run the query in the Search screen. Then save the query results using the "Remember Search" button. Once you have saved your query, go to the "Whining" configuration page (see Figure 27-17). Here, you simply specify when the notifications should be generated and sent out, what query should be used, and to whom they should be send. You can send notifications to individuals and to groups; both can be useful in some circumstances.

On the configuration side of things, the whining mechanism will only work if you run a PERL script called whine.pl at regular intervals (for example, every 15 minutes). You need to set this up outside of Bugzilla, for example, using cron.

27.13 Customizing Fields in Bugzilla

When you install an issue tracking system, there is often much debate about how to classify issues, particularly in terms of defining the various levels of priority and severity. Bugzilla lets you customize certain key fields such as Priority and Severity, as well as the environment-related fields such as "OS" and Hardware, via the "Field Values" link in the page footer. You can rename the existing values, add new ones, or delete unnecessary values (if they are not currently being used by any bugs).

It is important to note that if you do change these values, the corresponding contextual help screens will still refer to the default Bugzilla values. If you want to change these as well (which you probably should), you need to update the *fields.html.tmpl* file, which you will find somewhere under the *template* directory (the default English version of this page can be found at *template/en/default/pages/fields.html.tmpl*). Another alternative is to provide definitions of the terms in the label itself, such as "Critical: The software crashes, hangs, or causes you to loose data."

Although Bugzilla already has more than enough fields for many users, there may be times when you would like to have just one extra bit of information. For example, you may want to know on what test platform the error occurred, or you may need to know some other detail about how or where the application was deployed. Catering to this need, Bugzilla allows you to define custom fields via the (you guessed it!) "Custom Fields" link in the page footer. Custom fields are easy to create: you just need to provide an internal field name (which must start with "cf_"), a description (which will be used as the field label in the bug details page), and some other details such as whether the field should be visible when you create a new bug, and whether the field should be used in notification emails. Custom fields can currently be either plain text fields or drop-down lists.

When you create a custom field using a drop-down list, you can't set up the values immediately. You need to create the custom field, then edit the legal values for this field (see Figure 27-18).

Once a custom field has been created, you can't delete it; you can just declare it to be "Obsolete," in which case, it will no longer be displayed on new or existing bugs.

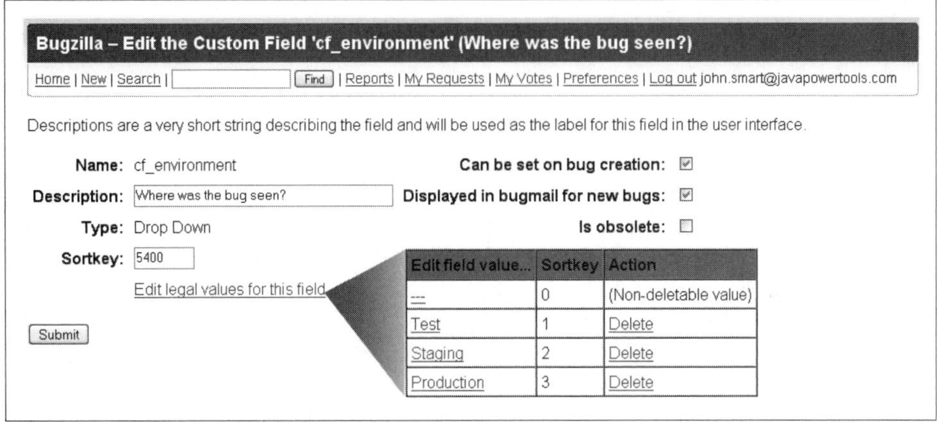

Figure 27-18. Defining a custom field

27.14 Conclusion

Bugzilla is a tried-and-true solution that will support very large projects and user bases. Its workflow features are more than sufficient for most organizations. On the downside, Bugzilla is particularly complicated to install and maintain, and the user interface won't win any prizes for design or usability. Its reporting features will do the job, although they are not particularly user-friendly.

CHAPTER 28

Trac—Lightweight Project Management

28.1 An Introduction to Trac

Trac[*] is a lightweight, open source issue tracking and project management tool that builds on Subversion (Chapter 4) by adding flexible web-based issue tracking, wiki, and reporting functionalities. Its second-to-none integration with Subversion makes it an excellent choice for development teams who use Subversion. It imposes no particular methodology, and so allows a great deal of flexibility in the way it is used. Although it does not provide as wide a range of features as products like Bugzilla, Trac is steadily gaining popularity in the Subversion community. Indeed, many commercial Subversion hosting companies now offer Trac as part of their package deals.

Trac provides a number of interesting features that make it a tool particularly well suited to small teams using lightweight, agile development processes. These include:

- A lightweight issue-tracking system, where issues can be entered and assigned to team members with a minimum of formality and effort
- An excellent web interface to your Subversion source code repository, allowing you to browse your source code and revisions, and keep tabs, via both the web site and RSS feeds, on what changes are happening in the repository
- A wiki-based project management tool, in which you can manage project milestones and iterations, assign tasks, and share documentation and ideas

But one of the nicest things about Trac is the way all of these features are integrated together. Using a wiki-style syntax, you can include references to Trac issues, tasks, or wiki pages in your Subversion commit messages, or refer to Subversion changesets from within Trac. These references are rendered as HTML links on the project web site. And a project timeline gives you an overall view of all activity on your project, making it

[*] *http://trac.edgewall.org/*

easy to keep track of changes made to issues, tasks, and within the source code repository.

In this chapter, we will discuss how to install and use Trac in your projects.

28.2 Installing Trac

Installing Trac is not a difficult task in itself, but the various dependencies can make things a little complicated, especially on a Windows machine. In addition, the Trac installation process tends to vary a great deal in its finer details from one system to another. In this chapter, we will cover the general steps and also a few tips to get you started. For more details, the best and most up-to-date reference remains the Trac web site itself (see *http://trac.edgewall.org/*).[*]

One thing that you should know from the start is that, at the time of this writing, Trac did not support network access to a Subversion repository. So, you need to either install Trac on the same machine as your Subversion repository, or mirror the Subversion repository to your Trac server.

Trac is written in Python,[†] so you will need to have Python installed on your machine. Python is bundled with many Linux distributions these days, and Windows installers and installation packages for other OSs are readily available on the Python web site. However, if you want to use the *mod_python* module for Trac (see Section 28.6), you may need to recompile Python yourself from the source code.

You will also need to install the Subversion Python Bindings. To do this on Windows, you can download and run the installer from the Subversion site, using version numbers corresponding to your local installation (e.g., svn-win32-1.4.5_py2.5.exe for Subversion 1.4.5 and Python 2.5). On a Linux box, this may well involve (re)building Subversion from the source code yourself with the correct configuration options. On Linux, another common error is to forget to update the library paths to include the newly compiled libraries (this usually involves defining or updating the LD_LIBRARY_PATH variable).

Trac also needs a relational database: you can use either SQLite,[‡] PostgreSQL,[‖] or MySQL,[§] all of which work well on both Windows and Linux machines.

* If you are installing Trac on an Ubuntu machine, in particular, the Trac web site contains a tutorial that may be able to save you a lot of time and effort. See *http://trac.edgewall.org/wiki/TracOnUbuntu*.

† *http://www.python.org/*

‡ *http://www.sqlite.org/*

‖ *http://www.postgresql.org/*

§ *http://www.mysql.com*

By default, Trac will use an embedded SQLite database written in C, which is easy to configure and quite sufficient for most projects. If you want to use this option, however, you still need to install SQLite onto your machine. There are precompiled packages (RPM or DEB) available for many Unix distributions, and this is generally the easiest option. Alternatively, you can build it from the source code, as shown here (you will need the TCL development libraries for this to work):

```
# wget http://www.sqlite.org/sqlite-3.5.1.tar.gz
# tar xvfz sqlite-3.5.1.tar.gz
# cd sqlite-3.5.1
# ./configure
# make install
```

If you use SQLite on Windows, you will also need to install PySQLLite,* the Python SQLLite API. Be sure to install a 1.x version (e.g., 1.1.7) rather than a 2.x version, as the latter will not work.

PostgreSQL is more appropriate for very large Trac projects, such as open source projects with public access. If you use a PostgreSQL database, you will need to install PostgreSQL, set up a user account, and install the appropriate scripts. This is well documented on the Trac web site.

In versions earlier than 0.11, Trac relies on an HTML templating language called Clearsilver.† If this is not already installed on your machine (which it probably isn't), you will need to install it as well. Binary installation packages exist for Windows, but for some *nix boxes, you might need to build it yourself from the source code. The basic process is shown here, although the exact details and requirements tend to vary from one system to another. Download the source code bundle from the Clearsilver web site, and extract it. You need to use the *--with-python* option when configuring the project, in which you provide the location of the *python* executable on your machine (usually something like */usr/bin/python*). You should also specify the *--disable-ruby* and *--disable-csharp* options. Finally, you build the library using the standard *make install*:

```
# wget http://www.clearsilver.net/downloads/clearsilver-0.10.4.tar.gz
# tar xvfz clearsilver-0.10.4.tar.gz
# cd clearsilver-0.10.4
# ./configure --enable-gettext --disable-ruby --disable-csharp
# make
# make install
```

As of version 0.11, Trac no longer requires ClearSilver, which simplifies the installation process somewhat, and means you can skip the previous step.

Once you have all the dependencies, you can install Trac itself. The Windows binaries come with a graphical installer. Just run this executable to install Trac in a Windows environment.

* *http://trac.edgewall.org/wiki/PySqlite*

† *http://www.clearsilver.net/*

Many Linux distributions have bundled binary packages. Otherwise, you have to run the installation script manually, as described here; once you're sure that you have everything you need, just unpack the downloaded package and run (as root) the *setup.py* python script as follows:

```
# tar xvfz trac-0.10.4.tar.gz
# cd trac-0.10.4
# python ./setup.py install
```

This should compile and install the Trac scripts and administration tools onto your machine.

The Trac web site* contains a useful rundown of the specificities involved when installing Trac in different environments.

Before starting Trac up for the first time, you need to set up a project environment. We discuss this in the next section.

28.3 Setting Up a Trac Project

In Trac, all project administration tasks are done at the command line using the *trac-admin* tool. Each Trac project has its own directory. To set up a new project, we use the *initenv* command, as shown here:

```
$ mkdir /data/trac
$ trac-admin /data/trac/myproject initenv
Creating a new Trac environment at /data/trac/myproject

Trac will first ask a few questions about your environment
in order to initalize and prepare the project database.

 Please enter the name of your project.
 This name will be used in page titles and descriptions.

Project Name [My Project]>
...
```

Note that the *trac-admin* utility will create the project directory (`myproject`), but not the parent directories (`/data/trac`), which you must have created beforehand.

On a Windows machine, you need to invoke *python* explicitly, as shown here:

```
C:\Python23\Scripts>mkdir D:\trac
C:\Python23\Scripts>python trac-admin D:\trac\myproject initenv
```

In both cases, this will run an interactive script prompting you for the configuration details Trac needs to set up your project, such as:

* *http://trac.edgewall.org/wiki/TracInstallPlatforms*

The name of the project
: This will be displayed at prominent places on your Trac web site, so make it meaningful.

The database connection
: By default, Trac will use an embedded SQLite database, which is sufficient for small projects. You can also configure Trac to use a PostgreSQL database. If you want to use PostgreSQL, create a database called "trac," and use a database connection string of the following form:

```
postgres://<user>:<password>@localhost/trac
```

The Subversion repository
: Trac needs the local path of your Subversion repository (*not* a Subversion-type URL), and also needs write-access to set up its own access.

: You can run Trac without a Subversion repository, in which it can work as an issue-tracking tool and project wiki, but without the integration with the source control management tool. To do this, simply do not provide a repository path

Once the script has finished asking questions, it will proceed to build the Trac database in the directory you provided. If all goes well, you should get something like this:

```
...
Creating and Initializing Project

 Installing default wiki pages
 /usr/share/trac/wiki-default/TracModPython => TracModPython
 /usr/share/trac/wiki-default/TracRss => TracRss
 ...

---------------------------------------------------------------------
Project environment for 'My Project' created.

You may now configure the environment by editing the file:

  /data/trac/myproject/conf/trac.ini

If you'd like to take this new project environment for a test drive,
try running the Trac standalone web server `tracd`:

  tracd --port 8000 /data/trac/myproject

Then point your browser to http://localhost:8000/myproject.
There you can also browse the documentation for your installed
version of Trac, including information on further setup (such as
deploying Trac to a real web server).

The latest documentation can also always be found on the project
web site:

  http://trac.edgewall.org/

Congratulations!
```

28.4 Running Trac on the Standalone Server

Trac comes with a small, very fast embedded web server called *tracd*. This configuration is easy to install and configure and can be quite sufficient for many enterprise projects.

To start the tracd server, run the *tracd* command as shown here:

```
$ tracd --port 8000 /data/trac/myproject
```

Your project will be available on *http://localhost:8000/myproject*.

For a Windows installation, the instruction is slightly different (because of the way Python works under Windows), and you need to explicitly invoke the *python* executable, as shown here:

```
C:\Python23\Scripts>python tracd --port 8000 D:\trac\myproject
```

If you have several trac environments on the same server, just list them as follows:

```
$ tracd --port 8000 /data/trac/project1 /data/trac/project2
```

Your projects will be available on separate URLs: *http://localhost:8000/myproject*1 and *http://localhost:8000/myproject*2.

However, this alone will not provide a very satisfying solution. Using this configuration, users will not be able to log on to the site. We need to set up user authentication.

Subversion can be configured to work with an Apache server, and to use an Apache-style basic or digest authentication file (see Section 4.21). If your Subversion server is set up to use such a file, you can tell Trac to use it, too. This has the obvious advantage of sharing user accounts directly between Subversion and Trac.

To do this, you use the *--basic-auth* or *--auth* options when starting *tracd* from the command line. You need to specify an *auth* command-line option for each of your Trac projects. The *auth* option takes the following form:

```
--auth project-name,/path/to/svn-digest-auth-file, realm-name
```

The realm name is the name specified in the AuthName parameter in your Apache configuration file (see Section 4.21). Here is a complete example:

```
python tracd -p 8000 \
   --auth project1,/data/svn/svn-digest-auth-file,"Subversion repository" \
   --auth project2,/data/svn/svn-digest-auth-file,"Subversion repository" \
   /data/trac/project1 /data/trac/project2
```

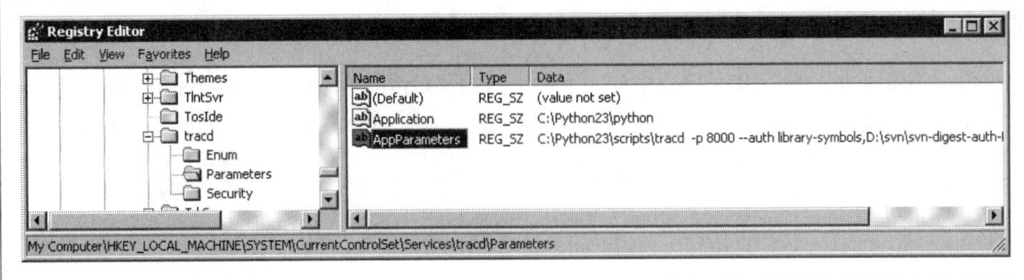

Figure 28-1. Configuring Trac as a Windows service

28.5 Setting Up Tracd As a Windows Service

It is quite easy to set up *tracd* as a Windows service using the techniques described in Section 4.24. Use InstSrv and Srvany to install a new service:

```
D:\trac>InstSrv tracd "C:\Program Files\Windows Resource Kits\Tools\srvany.exe"

The service was successfuly added!

Make sure that you go into the Control Panel and use
the Services applet to change the Account Name and
Password that this newly installed service will use
for its Security Context.
```

Next, you need to update the registry as shown for the Subversion service (see Section 4.24). Open the Windows Registry and open the *HKEY_LOCAL_MACHINE\System\CurrentControlSet\Services\tracd* entry (see Figure 28-1). Add a key called *Parameters*, and add two String values. The *Application* value should point to your python executable (typically something like "*C:\Python23\python*"). The AppParameters should contain the full path to the tracd script (for example,"*C:\Python23\scripts\tracd*"), followed by all the appropriate command-line options (see Section 28.4).

Once this is done, the service should be up and running. You can test by starting and stopping the script from the command line as follows:

```
D:\trac>net start tracd
The tracd service is starting.
The tracd service was started successfully.


D:\trac>net stop tracd

The tracd service was stopped successfully.
```

28.6 Installing Trac on an Apache Server

Trac is bundled with its own standalone server, which is fast and easy to install, but not as flexible as a full-blown web server such as Apache. You can also install Trac on an Apache server using either *FastCGI* or *mod_python* (CGI is also an option but not a recommended one).

There are several ways to do this. Here, we will install Trac onto an Apache server using the *mod_python* module.

This section refers to *Apache 2.0* and *mod_python 3.2.8*. Both can be downloaded from the Apache web site. The key aspect here is to correctly install the *mod_python* module, although installation details may vary from version to version and between platforms. Check out the mod_python web site* for details regarding how to install mod_python on your platform.

In all cases, you will need to load the *mod_python* module in the Apache configuration file. This usually takes the form of a line like the following one in your `httpd.conf` file:

```
LoadModule python_module modules/mod_python.so
```

The Apache configuration is quite similar to the Subversion equivalent (see Section 4.21). You can provide simple public access to your site for anonymous users by using the mod_python plug-in as follows:

```
<Location /trac/myproject1>
   SetHandler mod_python
   PythonHandler trac.web.modpython_frontend
   PythonOption TracEnv "D:/trac/myproject1"
   PythonOption TracUriRoot "/trac/myproject1"
</Location>
```

With this configuration, you could access your Trac site using a URL like *http://localhost/trac/myproject1*.

You can set up authentication to use the same Apache basic or digest authentication that you use for your Subversion installation: simply use the same authentication type (*AuthType*), realm name (*AuthName*), and authentication file (*AuthUserFile* or *AuthDigestFile*). Just associate the authentication file with the "/login" URL for your project, as follows:

```
<LocationMatch "/trac/myproject1/login">
   AuthType Digest
   AuthName "Subversion repository"
   AuthDigestDomain /trac/myproject1
   AuthDigestFile "/data/svn/svn-digest-auth-file"
   Require valid-user
</LocationMatch>
```

* *http://www.modpython.org/*

You can also configure several trac projects together by using the *TracEnvParentDir* field:

```
<Location /trac>
   SetHandler mod_python
   PythonHandler trac.web.modpython_frontend
   PythonOption TracEnvParentDir "/data/trac"
   PythonOption TracUriRoot "/trac"
</Location>
```

And if you want all your projects to share the same authentication file, you can configure this using a regular expression, as follows:

```
<LocationMatch "/trac/[^/]+/login">
   AuthType Digest
   AuthName "Subversion repository"
   AuthDigestDomain /trac/myproject1
   AuthDigestFile "/data/svn/svn-digest-auth-file"
   Require valid-user
</LocationMatch>
```

28.7 Administrating the Trac Site

By default, normal Trac users can do everything they need to do in their daily development activity. However, to perform more advanced tasks, such as creating milestones or reports or adding new ticket types, you need to use an account with extra rights.

In the standard installation of Trac, you manage user rights from the command line, using the *trac-admin* script. To list the current access rights, use the *permission list* command as follows:

```
$ trac-admin /data/trac/myproject permission list

User        Action
---------------------------
anonymous   BROWSER_VIEW
anonymous   CHANGESET_VIEW
anonymous   FILE_VIEW
anonymous   LOG_VIEW
anonymous   MILESTONE_VIEW
anonymous   REPORT_SQL_VIEW
anonymous   REPORT_VIEW
anonymous   ROADMAP_VIEW
anonymous   SEARCH_VIEW
anonymous   TICKET_CREATE
anonymous   TICKET_MODIFY
anonymous   TICKET_VIEW
anonymous   TIMELINE_VIEW
anonymous   WIKI_CREATE
anonymous   WIKI_MODIFY
anonymous   WIKI_VIEW
```

```
Available actions:
 BROWSER_VIEW, CHANGESET_VIEW, CONFIG_VIEW, FILE_VIEW, LOG_VIEW,
 MILESTONE_ADMIN, MILESTONE_CREATE, MILESTONE_DELETE, MILESTONE_MODIFY,
 MILESTONE_VIEW, REPORT_ADMIN, REPORT_CREATE, REPORT_DELETE, REPORT_MODIFY,
 REPORT_SQL_VIEW, REPORT_VIEW, ROADMAP_ADMIN, ROADMAP_VIEW, SEARCH_VIEW,
 TICKET_ADMIN, TICKET_APPEND, TICKET_CHGPROP, TICKET_CREATE, TICKET_MODIFY,
 TICKET_VIEW, TIMELINE_VIEW, TRAC_ADMIN, WIKI_ADMIN, WIKI_CREATE,
 WIKI_DELETE, WIKI_MODIFY, WIKI_VIEW
```

It is always useful to have an administrator account. Indeed, you need to create one to be able to do any serious customization work.

```
$ trac-admin /data/trac/myproject permission add mike TRAC_ADMIN
```

Mike is now administrator, and he can make any modifications that he wants to the site.

Trac also allows more fine-grained permissions, both for users and for user groups. For example, the following command lets Jill create new reports, a function that is not available for normal users:

```
$ trac-admin /data/trac/myproject permission add jill REPORT_CREATE
```

Another useful administration tool is the web administration console (see Figure 28-2). This module is integrated out-of-the-box into Trac 0.11, but for previous versions, you will need to download and install it yourself.

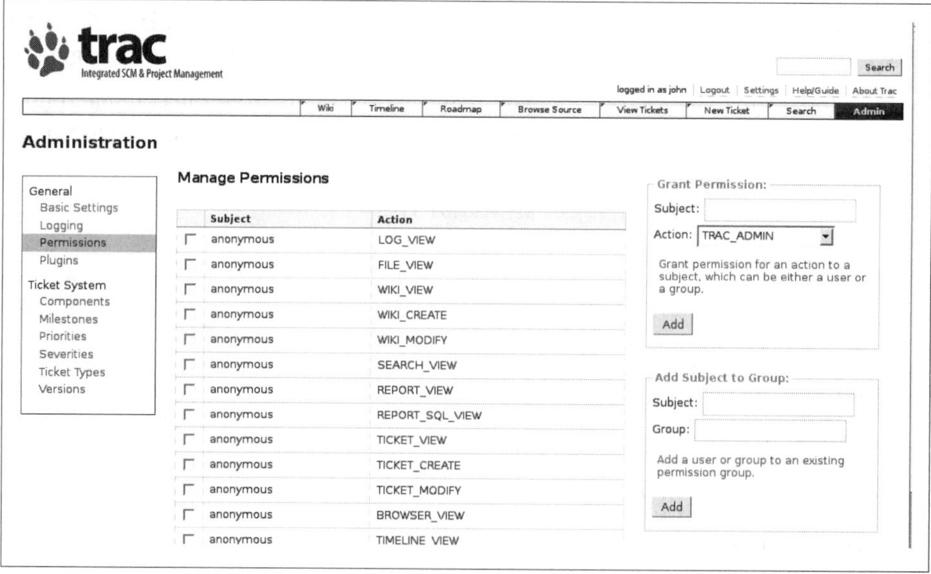

Figure 28-2. The Trac Web Administration console

Here is how to install it manually. Trac plug-ins need the EasyInstall python utility package.*

Download the *python ez_setup.py* file from this web site and install it as follows:

```
# python ez_setup.py
```

When this is done, download the latest packaged plug-in from the Trac web site,†remove the *zip* extension, and place the resulting .egg file in your project's *plug-ins* directory.

Alternatively, you can install the latest cut from the Subversion repository by doing something along the following lines:

```
$ svn export http://svn.edgewall.com/repos/trac/sandbox/webadmin/
$ cd webadmin
$ sudo python setup.py install
```

Next, you need to activate this component in your `trac.ini` file. Add the following lines at the end of this file:

```
[components]
webadmin.* = enabled
```

Trac should now load the plug-in and you should see (if you have TRAC_ADMIN priviledges, of course) the new "Admin" tab.

28.8 Managing User Accounts

In the default Trac installation, managing user accounts is a little cumbersome. Although the web administration console (see Section 28.7) does make it easier to manage user rights from the web interface, there is no way to create or delete users directly from the Web. You need to directly manipulate the Apache htpasswd or htdigest file from the command line.

However, there is a better way. Matthew Good has written a third-party plug-in for Trac called AccountManager, which makes managing user accounts a great deal simpler. This plug-in provides several nice features in this domain, such as:

- Viewing, creating, and deleting users stored in the Apache passwd or digest file
- Letting users register to create their own accounts
- Using HTML form-based login rather than HTTP authentication
- Letting existing users change their passwords or even delete their accounts
- Sending an email to users who have forgotten their passwords

* *http://peak.telecommunity.com/DevCenter/EasyInstall*

† *http://trac.edgewall.org/wiki/WebAdmin*

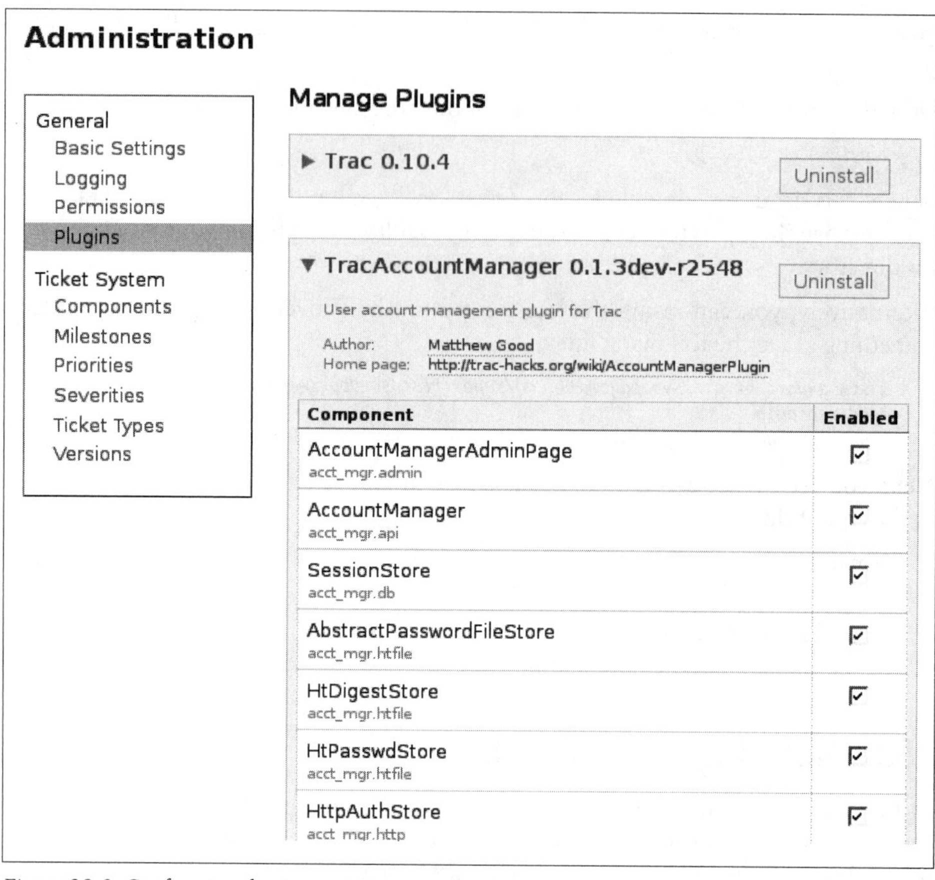

Figure 28-3. Configuring the AccountManager plug-in

In this section, we will go through how to install and use this plug-in. First of all, you need to install the plug-in. Before starting, you should install the web administration plug-in (see Section 28.7) if this is not already done. The exact installation instructions can be found on the plug-in web site.* Installation is straightforward, and it uses the easy_install python script. For Trac 0.10, you do something like this:

```
$ easy_install http://trac-hacks.org/svn/accountmanagerplug-in/0.10
```

Once you have installed the plug-in, go to the "Manage plug-ins" section on the Admin page. There should be a new entry for the AccountManager plug-in (see Figure 28-3), where you can activate the various modules that come with the plug-in.

The most common authentification setup in Trac is to use the same user logins and passwords that are used for the Subversion repository. If you are using Apache for your Subversion and Trac authentication, you will have either an HTDigest file or an

* *http://www.trac-hacks.org/wiki/AccountManagerplug-in*

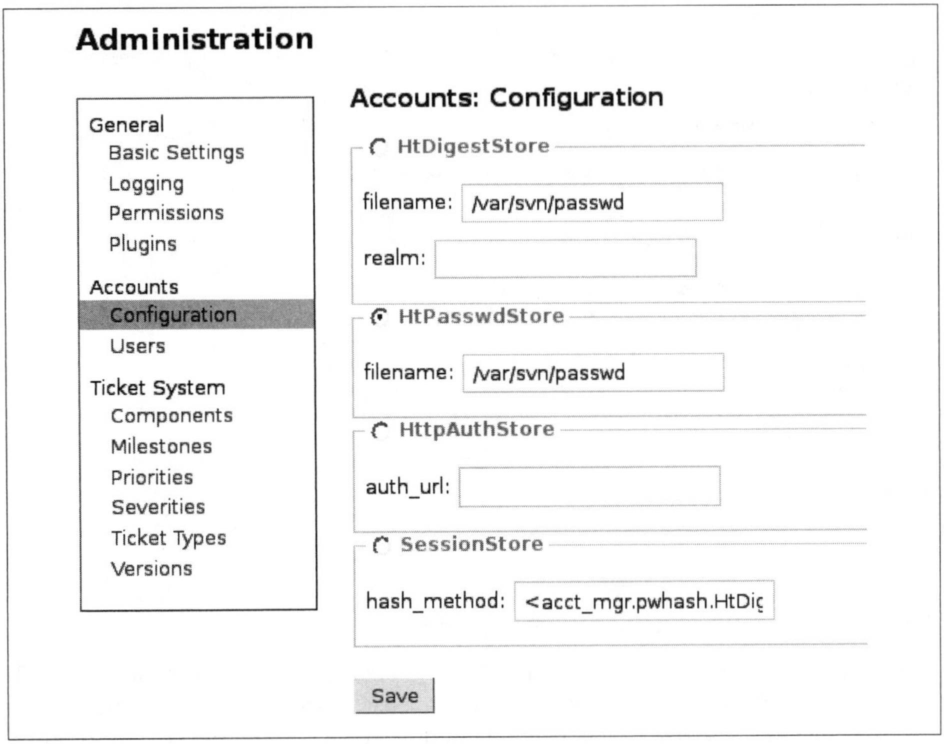

Figure 28-4. Configuring the AccountManager plug-in

HTPasswd file containing your users and encrypted passwords. You just need to tell the AccountManger plug-in which type of authentication you are using, and which file is being used, which you do in the Configuration screen (see Figure 28-4). The file and realm that you specify here need to correspond to the ones defined in your Apache configuration file for your normal Subversion authentication (see Section 4.21).

Once this is done, go to the "Users" screen (see Figure 28-5). This screen allows you to view the existing users, to delete a user, or to add a new one. Changes will be made automatically in the underlying authentication file, so any new users will also have access to the Subversion repository as well.

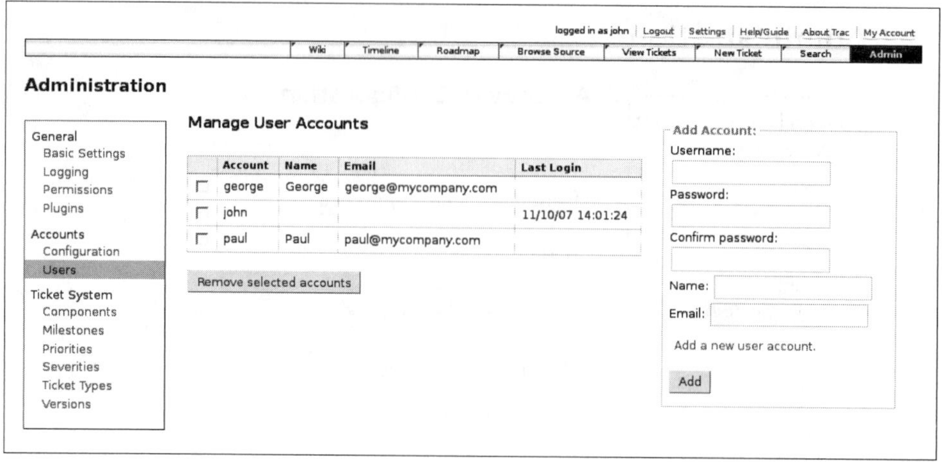

Figure 28-5. Managing users

In addition, users will now have access to a "My Account" link, where they can change their passwords or even delete their own accounts.

You can also set up the user login module to use an HTML form rather than the HTTP authentication. Note that if you are using Mylyn (see Chapter 25), the HTML authentification may confuse the Mylyn Trac integration, which, at the time of this writing, only understands the conventional HTTP authentication.

To activate HTML authentication, you need to remove (or comment out) any Apache authentication configurations related to the Trac login. They usually look like this:

```
<LocationMatch "/trac/login">
   AuthType Digest
   AuthName "Enterprise Subversion repository"
   AuthDigestDomain /trac
   AuthDigestFile "/var/svn/svn-digest-auth-file"
   Require valid-user
</LocationMatch>
```

You also need to disable the LoginModule in Trac either in the "Plugins" screen, under the Trac plug-ins entry, or directly in the *trac.ini* file, as shown here:

```
[components]
trac.web.auth.LoginModule = disabled
```

Now, users will be able to login using an ordinary HTML login form (see Figure 28-6). There is also the commonly seen "Forget your password?" link, which allows users to recover their lost passwords via email.

Finally, if you activate the RegistrationModule, users will even be able to create their own accounts, via a "Register" link that appears at the top of the screen.

Figure 28-6. The HTML login form

28.9 Tailoring the Trac Web Site: Using the Wiki Function

Trac is, first and foremost, a wiki-based application. Any page can be modified at will by any team member with the appropriate rights, and new pages can be created easily to describe specific aspects of your particular project.

Trac's online help describes the Trac wiki syntax in some detail. Most of the formatting language is very close to what you find on other wiki sites, and, in particular, that of the MoinMoin wiki engine. If you've never used a wiki before, here are some of the more useful markup codes:

Headings
: Headings and subheadings can be written using "=" and "==," as shown here:

```
= A heading =
...
== A sub-heading ==
...
```

Lists
: You can use "*" for unordered lists, as shown here:

```
 * Cats
   * Burmese
   * Siamese
 * Dogs
   * Bloodhound
   * Poodle
```

Trac expects you to respect some fairly strict formatting rules for lists: the first element must be indented by precisely one space and subsequent levels by exactly two spaces per level.

Formatting

Basic text formatting such as bold and italic can be done using single quotes, as shown here:

```
* '''bold'''
* ''italic''
```

Preformatted text can be displayed using {{{...}}}:

```
{{{
    public void foo(int bar) {
      ...
    }
}}}
```

For example, consider the following text:

```
= Feature: A clickable map =
== Description ==
We need to display a map on the home page. Users can click to display the list of
libraries in a region or city.
== Non-functional requirements ==
Here are the ''non-functional'' requirements:
 * The user interface must be '''fast'''
   * Zooming should be really fast and easy
   * No browser refreshing during map updates
 * The colours must be pretty

The server-side class must implement the following method:
{{{
    /**
     * The foo-bar function.
     */
    public void foo(int bar);
}}}
```

This text is rendered in Figure 28-7.

However, one of the most useful (and original) aspects of the Trac wiki is its ability to integrate with other Trac objects. Tickets, changesets, milestones, other wiki pages, and more can all be references using the special TracLink syntax. These hyperlinks can also be used both in commit messages and in object descriptions. Typical uses include listing corrected bugs when committing source code to the repository, referring to source code when describing work done to fix a bug, referring to a target milestone in a feature description, and so on. See Figure 28-8 for an example of a Trac ticket using the wiki formatting. Detailed documentation about available TracLink types is available in the Trac online documentation. Some of the more useful types are described here:

Trac tickets

Trac issue tickets can be referenced using either the "ticket" link type (*ticket:123*) or the # shorthand form (*#123*), as shown here:

```
This revision corrects the issues #123, #125 and #245
```

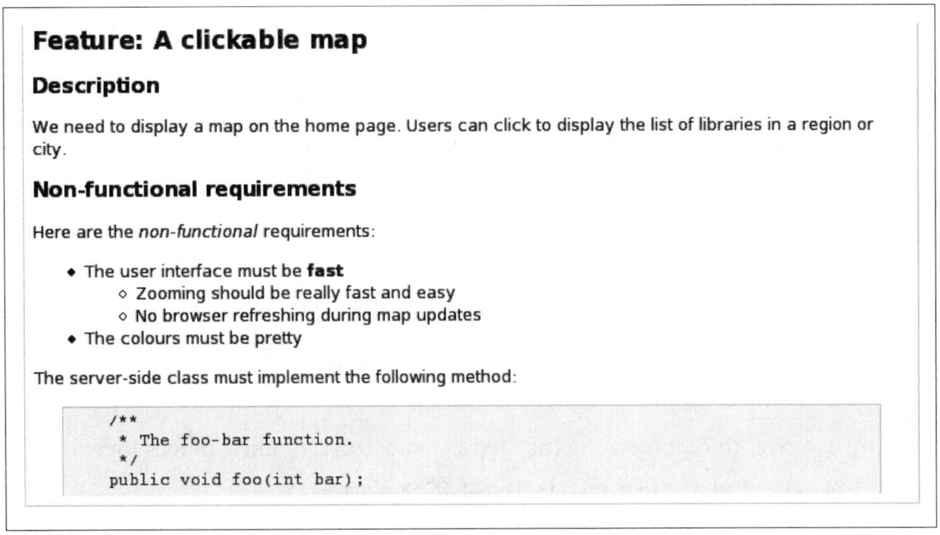

Feature: A clickable map

Description

We need to display a map on the home page. Users can click to display the list of libraries in a region or city.

Non-functional requirements

Here are the *non-functional* requirements:

- The user interface must be **fast**
    - Zooming should be really fast and easy
    - No browser refreshing during map updates
- The colours must be pretty

The server-side class must implement the following method:

```
/**
 * The foo-bar function.
 */
public void foo(int bar);
```

Figure 28-7. Formatted wiki text

Source code files

Trac provides many ways to set up links to your source code. At the simplest level, files in the source code repository can be referred to using the "source:" link type, followed by the full file path:

```
This bug was caused by an error in source:/trunk/src/main/java/com/wakaleo
/JavaLamp.java
```

You can also refer to a particular line within the file, using the "#L..." notation:

```
This bug was caused by an error in line 50:
see source:/trunk/src/main/java/com/wakaleo/JavaLamp.java#L50
```

Or to a particular version of the file, using the "@..." notation:

```
This bug was caused by an error in a previous version (version 10) of the file:
see source:/trunk/src/main/java/com/wakaleo/JavaLamp.java@10
```

It is even possible to combine these two notations to refer to a line number in a specific version:

```
This bug was caused by an error in a previous version (version 10) of the file
at line 50:
see source:/trunk/src/main/java/com/wakaleo/JavaLamp.java@10#L50
```

Changesets and logs

A changeset refers to a specific version of the code base committed by an individual developer. In Subversion, changesets are atomic (all the changes come from one developer, in one coherent unit), and, if correctly documented, can be very useful in understanding the changes done to the code base. When you click on a link to a changeset, you can conveniently visualize the set of modified files and the reason behind these modifications. Changsets can be referred to using the "changeset" type (*changeset:10*), or by the shortcut notations *r10* or *[10]*. An example is shown here:

```
The corrections for this bug were delivered in changeset:186
```

You can refer directly to the log messages for a set of changesets using the "log" notation (e.g., *log:@1:5*), or by using a shorthand form *r1:5*:

```
These changes are explained in r10:10
```

Milestones

You can refer to a milestone using the "milestone" link type:

```
This feature was originally planned for milestone:milestone1,
but was finally rescheduled to milestone:milestone2
```

Reports

You can refer to reports using the "report:" notation, or curly braces for short:

```
You will find all your tickets listed in this report:7
```

Diffs

It is sometimes useful to point out and document the differences between two files. For example, you might want to explain why you made certain changes, or explain why some particular changes where the cause of a bug. You can refer to the differences between versions of a paricular file:

```
To fix this bug, I had to change the class as shown
here: diff:/trunk/src/main/java/com/wakaleo/JavaLamp.java@10:11
```

Or display all the changes made to a particular set of files:

```
We did a lot of changes on the Java classes: diff:/trunk/src/main/java@10:11
```

Other wiki pages

Following a widely used convention, other wiki pages are identified using the "wiki" link type, or, more frequently, simply by writing a page name that respects CamelCase, the widely adopted naming convention for wiki pages. CamelCase involves writing the name of a page as a sequence of capitalized words joined together without spaces (JustLikeThis). To create a new wiki page, just include a term respecting this convention, as shown here:

```
Users are keen on this feature because it will help with CustomerBilling
```

A new page is not created immediately, the term will be displayed with a question mark ("CustomerBilling?"). When you click on the term, Trac lets you create a new page and edit it as you would any other page.

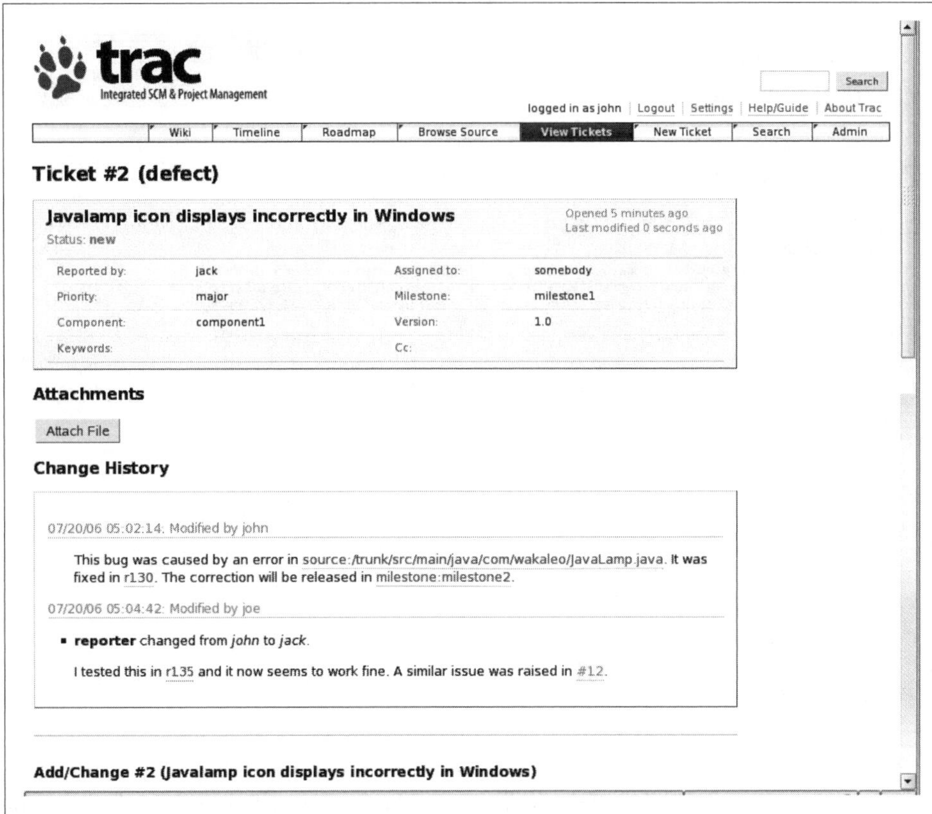

Figure 28-8. Trac tickets are one place you can put the wiki formatting to good use

Trac's linking capabilities are one of its most useful features. You can find more details about how to put them to good use on the Trac web site.*

28.10 Using the Trac Ticket Management System

Tickets are the bread-and-butter of the Trac issue management system. Tickets can be used to keep track of bugs and change requests, features, tasks, and just about anything else. The Trac ticket database is simple, flexible, and easy to customize. Trac is designed to be as lightweight and unobtrusive as possible. There are few constraints and virtually no mandatory fields, so users can put as little or as much information as they wish. (Of course, this may be a good thing or a bad thing depending on your particular environment.)

* *http://trac.edgewall.org/wiki/TracLinks*

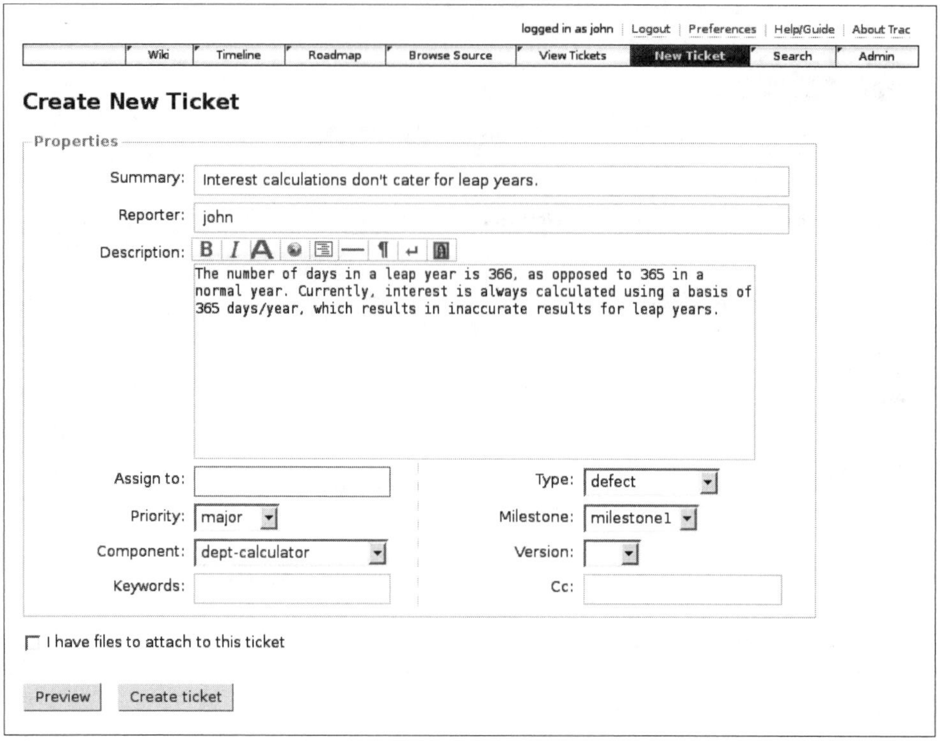

Figure 28-9. Creating a new Trac ticket

As a project management tool, Trac is more suited to the more lightweight, agile methodologies. It makes no claim to be a web equivalent of full-blown project management tools such as Microsoft Project. There is no support for defining dependencies between tasks or for producing Gantt chart reports, for example, although support for dependencies between tasks (defining tasks and subtasks) is planned for release 1.0 of the product. Of course, you can always use the wiki links (see Section 28.9) to list any dependencies in the ticket description. Another useful planning feature is to associate tasks, features, or bugs with milestones or versions (see Section 28.15).

In the rest of this section, we will look at how the Trac tickets can be used to improve your software development project.

Creating a New Ticket

Creating a new ticket in Trac is straightforward. You can create Trac tickets quickly and easily in the "New Ticket" screen (see Figure 28-9). Although there are no mandatory fields, you should enter at least the summary field (this is what is displayed in the reports), a type, and a description. You can use the usual wiki formatting in the description field, so a devoted developer can refer to the source code where the problem was fixed and the changeset in which this correction was delivered, for example.

The Ticket Type field lets you specify what sort of issue it is: a bug, an enhancement, a task, and so on. Ticket types are fairly arbitrary, and can be used to extend the ticket management system to far beyond simple issue tracking. Modifying the type of a ticket has no effect on any of the other fields: its main use is to identify different types of tickets and as a filter in reports and queries.

Priority and Severity are common fields in issue tracking systems. Severity refers to the impact a bug has on an application (in other words, how much damage it can do). Priority, by contrast, refers to the order in which bugs should be fixed.

By default, Trac displays only the Priority field, which, judging by the proposed values (blocker, critical, major, minor, trivial), is designed to reflect both priority *and* severity. Trac does support a "Severity" field, but you need to go to the "Administration" screen and specify a list of possible values before it will be displayed. Both these fields are fully customizable, so it is easy to tailor them to your own processes and preferences.

Milestones and Versions are useful for QA and project management tasks. The Version field lets you specify the version in which an issue was found, and the Milestone field lets you identify the target release in which this correction should be included.

The Component field can be used to associate tickets with different modules or subsystems of the project.

You assign a ticket to a particular person in the team, whose responsibility it is to see that this issue is addressed. This person is called The Owner. You can also provide a list of other people who may be interested in this issue in the CC field. By default, this field is a text field—you can enter any user name or email address you want. If you have a well-defined team, you can change this to a list (see Section 28.12).

The content of most of these fields can be customized in the Admin page (see Section 28.12).

The Lifecycle of a Trac Ticket

The lifecycle of a typical Trac ticket goes along the following lines. Joe is testing the company's new product when he comes across a bug. He creates a new ticket and assigns it to Sally, the project manager. Sally will be notified by email about the new bug. Sally sees the new bug on the Trac web site home page, and opens it. Here she has a choice (see Figure 28-10): basically, she can choose to accept the ticket herself or to reassign it to someone else. There is a third option; if the issue has already been resolved, or if it only takes a few minutes to fix, she can declare the issue to be resolved.

Normally, Sally would probably assign the ticket to another developer. In this case, the ticket would become "assigned." However, it turns out that this issue is in her domain, so she accepts the ticket and does the correction herself. The ticket now passes into the "accepted" state.

As a rule, when a developer commits code into the Subversion repository, he or she should include a descriptive message including, if applicable, references to the tickets

Figure 28-10. A user has several options when she receives a ticket

that have been addressed by this commit. In this case, Sally commits the corrections as follows:

```
$ svn commit \
  -m "Corrected the Catalog file loader. This fixes the bug raised in #123."
...
Transmitting file data.
Committed revision 172.
```

Now, when a Trac user displays this changeset (in the Timeline or Browse Source pages, for example), Trac will display the comment with a hyperlink to Ticket #123.

She also needs to update the ticket status in Trac. She adds some details on what she did and why in the Comments field. All added comments (in fact, all modifications of any sort) are recorded for posterity and can be consulted later on the Ticket page.

To close the ticket, Sally has to indicate why she considers the issue to be resolved. This is the same list we saw in Figure 28-10, and it includes values such as *fixed* (hopefully; the most frequently used), *invalid* ("it's a feature, not a bug"), *wontfix* ("it *is* a bug, but I don't want to fix it"), duplicate, and the oft-misused *worksforme*. In this case, Sally sets the value to *fixed*, and the issue is closed.

This workflow is a good, general-purpose one. However, there may be times when you want to tailor it to suit your own particular needs. In Trac 0.11 (in development at the time of this writing), you can customize this workflow to some extent.

28.11 Updating Trac Issues from Subversion

One nice trick is to get Subversion to update the relevant Trac tickets whenever someone commits changes to the repository. By using a postcommit hook (see Section 4.23), you can configure Subversion to update any Trac tickets referenced in the commit message. A sample script can be found on the Trac web site.* Just download this script and store it on your server in a convenient place (say, `/usr/share/trac/`

* *http://trac.edgewall.org/browser/trunk/contrib/trac-post-commit-hook* for the latest cutting-edge version, or *http://trac.edgewall.org/browser/branches/0.10-stable/contrib/trac-post-commit-hook* for Trac 0.10.x.

contrib/trac-post-commit-hook, or directly in the Subversion hooks directory). Make sure that the script matches your version of Trac, as the scripts don't tend to be compatible between versions.

Subversion hook scripts are stored in the hooks directory of your Subversion repository. For example, if your repository is stored in the /var/svn/repos directory, the hooks directory will be at /var/svn/repos/hooks:

```
# cd /var/svn/repos/hooks
# ls
post-commit         post-revprop-change.tmpl  pre-lock.tmpl             start-commit.tmpl
post-commit.tmpl    post-unlock.tmpl          pre-revprop-change.tmpl
post-lock.tmpl      pre-commit.tmpl           pre-unlock.tmpl
```

This directory contains mostly templates showing how to write Subversion hooks. The real hook scripts are the ones without the ".tmpl" suffix. In our case, we need a script called post-commit, which will call the script we just downloaded. You will find more detailed instructions in the trac-post-commit-hook script, but a typical implementation looks something like this (for Trac 0.10.4):

```
#!/bin/sh

# POST-COMMIT HOOK

REPOS="$1"
REV="$2"
LOG=`/usr/bin/svnlook log -r $REV $REPOS`
AUTHOR=`/usr/bin/svnlook author -r $REV $REPOS`
TRAC_ENV='/var/trac/myproject/'
TRAC_URL='http://buildserver/trac/myproject/'

/usr/local/bin/python /usr/local/src/trac/contrib/trac-post-commit-hook \
  -p "$TRAC_ENV"  \
  -r "$REV"       \
  -u "$AUTHOR"    \
  -m "$LOG"       \
  -s "$TRAC_URL"
```

Make sure both these scripts are executable, or Subversion will not be able to trigger them correctly. Subversion hooks are run with no environment variables initialized, so you may also need to define environment variables such as *LD_LIBRARY_PATH* or *PYTHON_EGG_CACHE* to get the Python scripts to work properly.

Once this is in place, whenever a developer commits a change, a new comment will be appended to the corresponding Trac tickets. The script works by recognizing certain key words associated with ticket numbers. When these keywords are detected, the commit message will be integrated into the corresponding track issues. In addition, certain key words can make Trac modify the state of the issue. The keywords take several variations (for example, "closes," "close," or "closed" all work). The main ones are shown here:

closes, fixes
: Closes the Trac issue, for example, "Close #1," or "This correction fixes #2 and # 3"

addresses, re, references, refs, see
: Leave the Trac issue in its current state, and just add the message to the issue, for example, "Addresses #1" or "see #1 and #2"

You can also prevent developers from committing code without a message that contains a reference to at least one Trac issue. You do this by setting up a precommit hook. A sample script for this can also be found on the Trac web site.*

This feature combines well with Mylyn and Eclipse changesets (see Section 25.6), allowing a very smooth integration between you IDE, the source code repository, and the issue management system. You work on a task or issue in Trac, and commit your changes from within Eclipse. Mylyn will automatically prepare a comment quoting the issue number.

28.12 Customizing Trac Ticket Fields

Trac lets you customize the ticket screen to some extent. All of the predefined lists can be customized in the Admin screens (see Figure 28-11). If you don't need a field, remove all its values and it won't be displayed on the "Ticket" screen.

By default, the "Assigned to" field is a text field. In many cases, it is more convenient to display a list of known Trac users. To do this, open the Trac configuration file, which you can find in *<projectenv>/conf/trac.ini*, and set the *restrict_owner* variable in the *ticket* group to *true*:

```
[ticket]
restrict_owner = true
```

This is actually only part of the picture. You also need user names to fill this list. At the time of this writing, Trac has no centralized interface where user accounts are managed. Users have to set up their own user accounts and email details in the "Settings" screens (see Section 28.13). Users who do this will automatically appear in the user list.

You can also add additional fields to the "Ticket" screens, although not via the web interface. If you want to add extra fields, you need to configure them in the Trac configuration file. You configure custom ticket fields in the [ticket-custom] block. Suppose that you want to add a simple text field for developers to record the time spent fixing a bug. This could be done as follows:†

* *http://trac.edgewall.org/browser/trunk/contrib/trac-pre-commit-hook*

† A more thorough way of tracking time spent would be to install the Timing and Estimating plug-in (see *http://trac.edgewall.org/wiki/TimeTracking*).

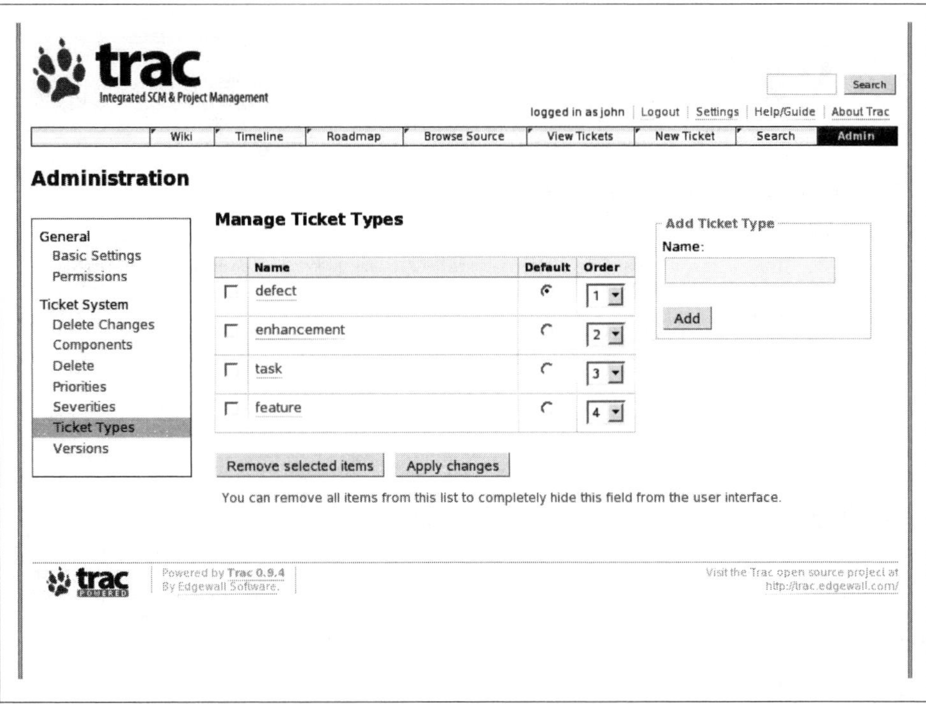

Figure 28-11. Customizing ticket fields in the Admin screens

```
[ticket-custom]
correctiontime = text
correctiontime.label = Time taken to correct
```

Now suppose that you need a list of operating systems:

```
[ticket-custom]
correctiontime = text
correctiontime.label = Time taken to correct

os = select
os.label = Operating System
os.options = All|Windows|Mac|Linux|Other
os.value = 1
```

Custom tickets can be of any of the HTML input types: *text*, *checkbox*, *select*, *radio*, or *textarea*.

28.13 Setting Up Email Notifications

To be efficient, users should be informed of any new or modified tickets as soon as possible. Trac notifies users by email. You can set this up in the Trac configuration file (*<projectenv>/conf/trac.ini*), in the *[notifications]* section. By default, email notification is deactivated. To activate it, set *smtp_enabled* to true, and provide sensible values for

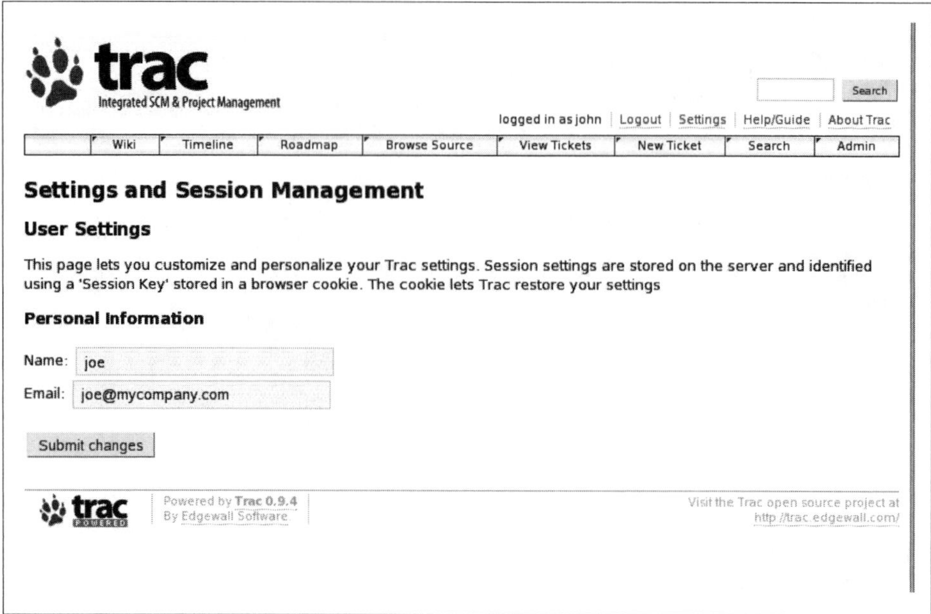

Figure 28-12. The Settings page

the other fields (which are mostly self-evident). The *always_notify_owner*, *always_notify_reporter*, and *always_notify_updater* fields let you specify who should be systematically informed of any changes made to a ticket:

```
[notification]
smtp_enabled = true
smtp_server = mail.mycompany.com
smtp_from = trac@mycompany.com
smtp_replyto = myproj@mycompany.com
smtp_always_cc = projectmanager@mycompany.com, qa@mycompany.com
always_notify_owner = true
always_notify_reported = true
always_notify_updater = true
```

This leaves just one minor detail: to send notifications to your users, Trac needs to know their email addresses. One approach is to use email addresses as usernames. This works, but it's not particularly elegant. In fact, there is an easier way.

The Settings page (see Figure 28-12) lets you associate an email address with your username. That way, you can have nice short usernames and still get your email notifications.

28.14 Reporting Using Trac Queries and Reports

For a long time, Trac users built reporting functions by using direct SQL queries on the Trac database. You can see an example in Figure 28-13. Although this approach is still in use, and currently offers the richest feature set, it is progressively being phased out in favor of a more intuitive query language, which can be configured via the web interface and also used directly within wiki pages (see Section 28.18).

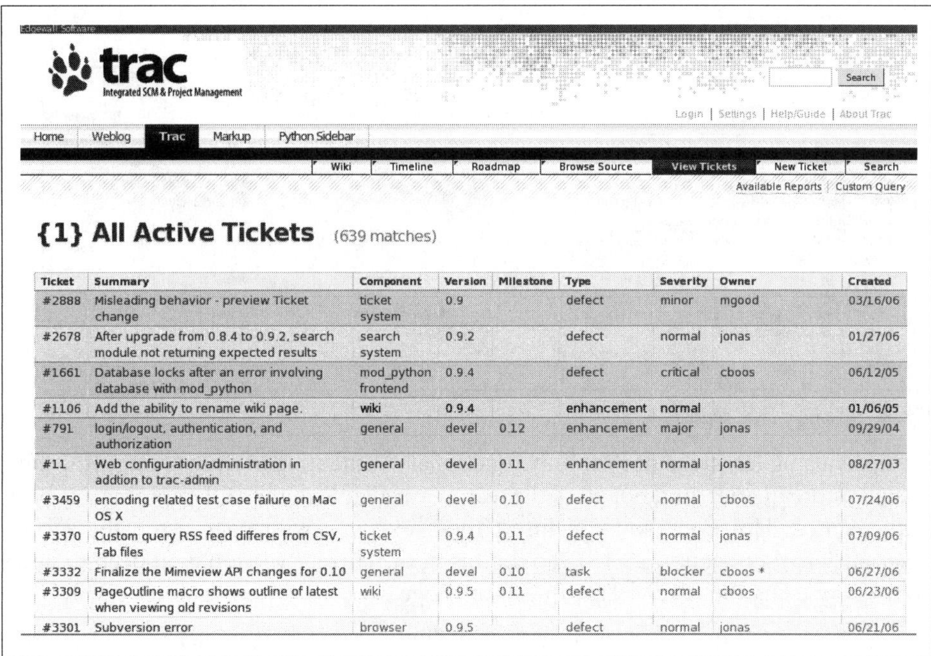

Ticket	Summary	Component	Version	Milestone	Type	Severity	Owner	Created
#2888	Misleading behavior - preview Ticket change	ticket system	0.9		defect	minor	mgood	03/16/06
#2678	After upgrade from 0.8.4 to 0.9.2, search module not returning expected results	search system	0.9.2		defect	normal	jonas	01/27/06
#1661	Database locks after an error involving database with mod_python	mod_python frontend	0.9.4		defect	critical	cboos	06/12/05
#1106	Add the ability to rename wiki page.	wiki	0.9.4		enhancement	normal		01/06/05
#791	login/logout, authentication, and authorization	general	devel	0.12	enhancement	major	jonas	09/29/04
#11	Web configuration/administration in addtion to trac-admin	general	devel	0.11	enhancement	normal	jonas	08/27/03
#3459	encoding related test case failure on Mac OS X	general	devel	0.10	defect	normal	cboos	07/24/06
#3370	Custom query RSS feed differes from CSV, Tab files	ticket system	0.9.4	0.11	defect	normal	jonas	07/09/06
#3332	Finalize the Mimeview API changes for 0.10	general	devel	0.10	task	blocker	cboos *	06/27/06
#3309	PageOutline macro shows outline of latest when viewing old revisions	wiki	0.9.5	0.11	defect	normal	cboos	06/23/06
#3301	Subversion error	browser	0.9.5		defect	normal	jonas	06/21/06

Figure 28-13. A Trac report

You configure Trac reports and queries in the "View Tickets" screen. Trac comes with a number of useful predefined reports such as "Active Tickets," "My Tickets," and "All Tickets by Milestone." If you need to define your own, you have to write your own custom SQL query. The following query, for example, lists all new, assigned, or reopened tickets for milestone1:

```
SELECT id AS ticket, status, severity, priority, owner, time as created, summary
FROM ticket
  WHERE status IN ('new', 'assigned', 'reopened') and milestone = 'milestone1'
  ORDER BY priority, time
```

This rather low-level approach is destined to be replaced by a more user-friendly one in which you dynamically build your query using a series of filters and group-by criteria (see Figure 28-13).

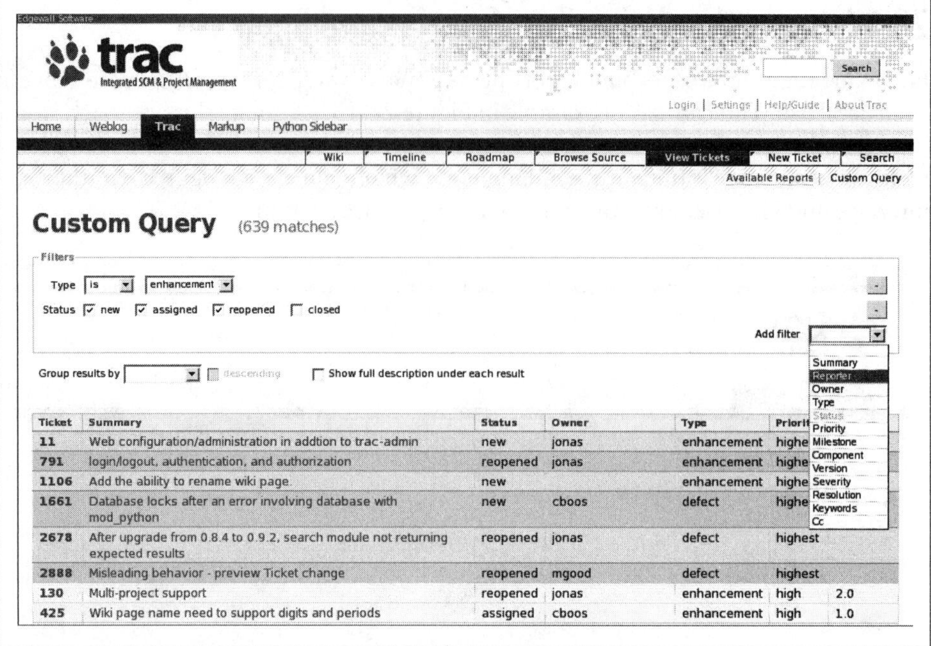

Figure 28-14. A Trac report

This promising feature is not yet fully functional. At the time of this writing, you can't actually store queries, and not all of the features available in the SQL reports have been implemented. However, you can insert them into any wiki page using the *TicketQuery* macro (see Section 28.18). To do this in the current version, you need to write your query using the special Trac query language.

Trac uses a simple query language in "query" links and in *TicketQuery* macro expressions, both of which can be placed directly in any wiki page. This language is simply a set of filter expressions separated by ampersands (&). Alternative values are separated by the pipe (|) character. For example, the following expression displays the list of all open (new, assigned, or reopened) tickets:

```
[query:status=new|assigned|reopened]
```

You can add a user-readable label by placing it after the query, as shown here:

```
[query:status=new|assigned|reopened Active tickets]
```

Filters can be combined using the "&" character. For example, the following query lists all open blocking or critical tickets:

```
[query:status=new|assigned|reopened&severity=blocker|critical Open Important Tickets]
```

Several other Boolean operators are supported. The "~=" operator indicates that the field contains one of a set of values. For example, the following query lists all tickets about cats and/or about dogs:

```
[query:summary~=cats|dogs Tickets about cats and dogs]
```

The "^=" operator indicates that the field starts with a given value, and the "$=" operator indicates that the field ends with a given value. For example, the following expression lists all the tickets of which the summary starts with the word "Test":

```
[query:summary^=Test Tickets with a summary starting with "Test"]
```

28.15 Managing Progress with Trac Roadmaps and Timelines

Trac provides convenient ways to plan, monitor, and publish information about project progress. In this section, we will look at how to plan, track and publish project progress using the "Milestone" screen, and how to keep tabs on detailed project activity using the "Timeline" screen.

Trac Milestones

The "Roadmap" screen (see Figure 28-15) gives an overview of current and future project milestones, including a description of each milestone and an indication of the progress made (based on the percentage of closed tickets associated with each milestone). Milestone descriptions use the Trac wiki formatting (see Section 28.9), so they can contain references to other Trac objects such as tickets or changesets.

To get the most out of this functionality, you need to integrate Trac into your daily project management. As part of the project planning activity, you create development tasks and associate them with different milestones. If an iterative approach is used, milestones may correspond to iterations, and tasks may be used to keep track of features or user stories.

From a project management point of view, the "Roadmap" view of project progress has a lot going for it:

- It gives a high-level overview of project progress useful for keeping management people happy.
- It requires very little extra overhead in terms of reporting or project management: progress is measured on the basis of the proportion of open tickets for a given milestone.
- The metrics used to measure progress are objective and Boolean: a ticket is closed or open, it is never 90 percent done.
- It can accurately reflect situations in which work may be progressing in parallel in several areas, toward different milestones.

If you need to know more about progress on a particular milestone, you can always click on the milestone to open a more detailed view (see Figure 28-16). In addition to the progress indicators visible in the "Roadmap" view, the "Milestone" view shows a

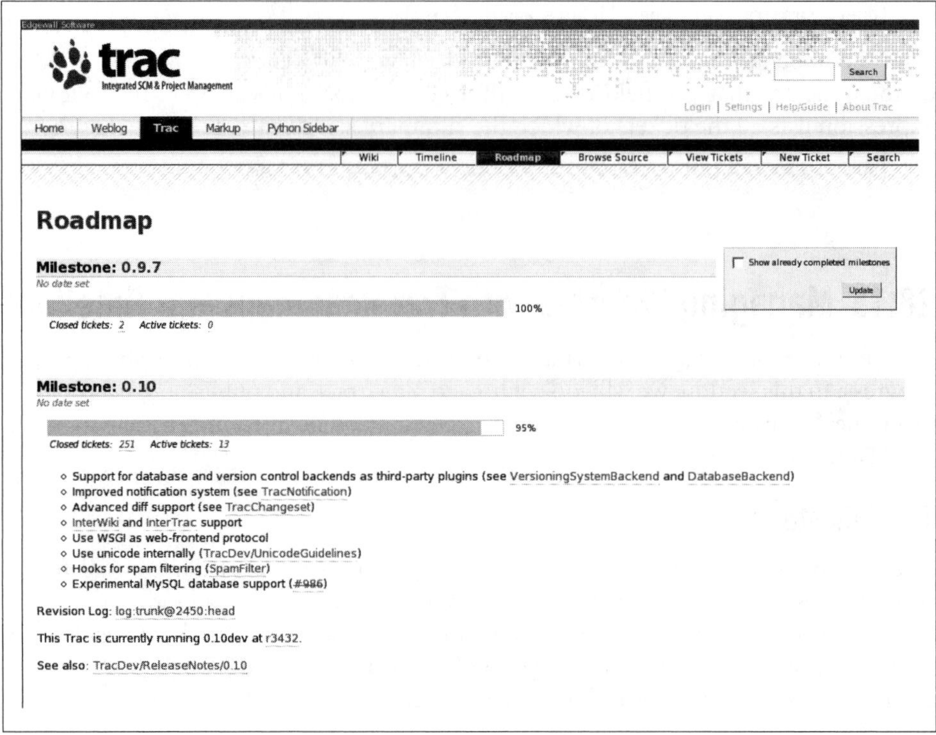

Figure 28-15. The Trac Roadmap view

graph of ticket status grouped by type, owner, component, severity, priority, and so on. Clicking on any of the graph lines will drill down further to the detailed list of all the corresponding tickets.

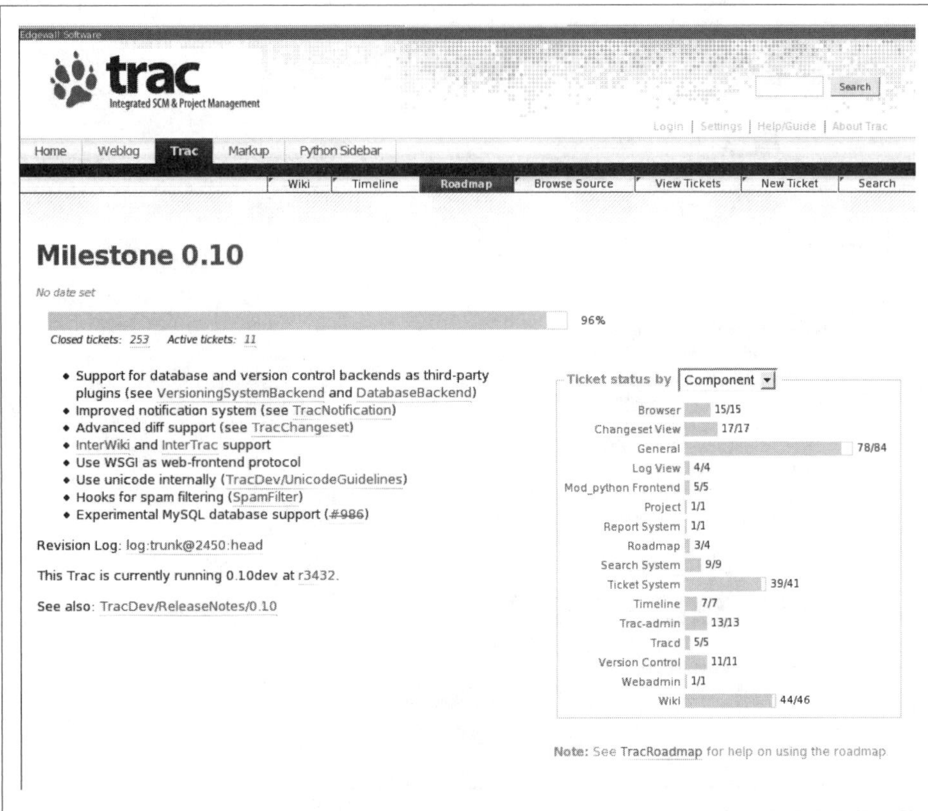

Figure 28-16. Drilling down to the milestone level

The Timeline View

The "Timeline" view is a useful way to keep track of the day-to-day activity on the project, both in terms of modifications to the code base and in terms of ticket activity (hopefully, there is some relation between the two!). See Figure 28-17.

28.16 Browsing the Source Code Repository

Trac provides full web access to the underlying Subversion repository (see Figure 28-18).

All directories and files are listed with their latest revision number. You can click on any revision number to display the corresponding change log. From here, you can view the changes between two revisions or the changes that were done in a particular file (see Figure 28-19).

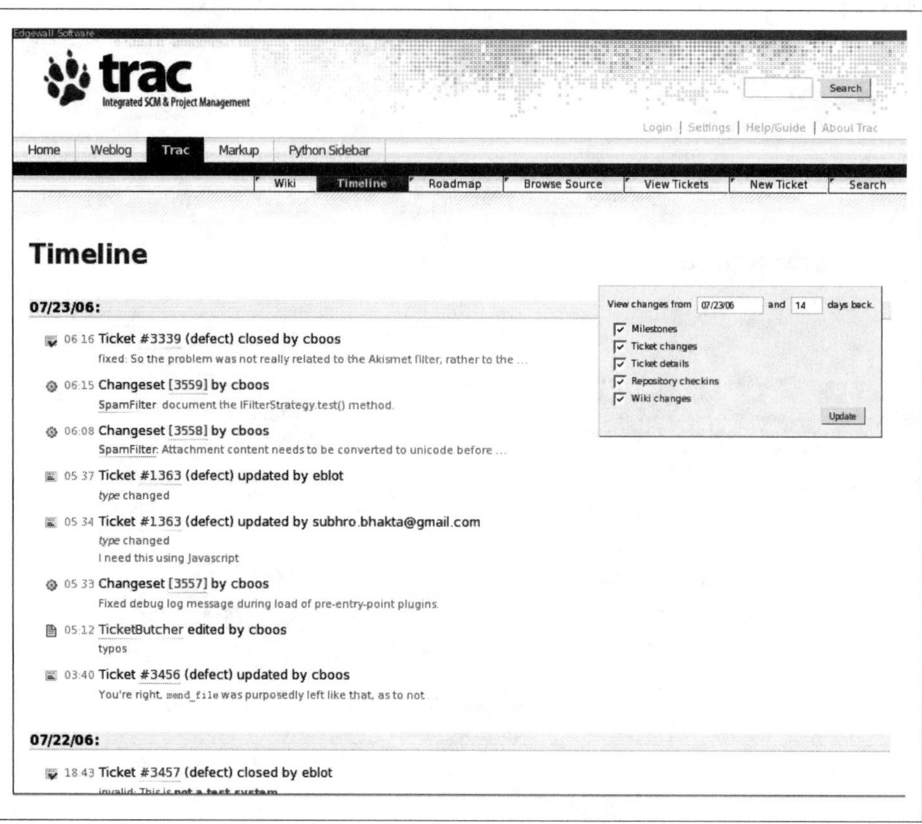

Figure 28-17. The Trac Timeline view

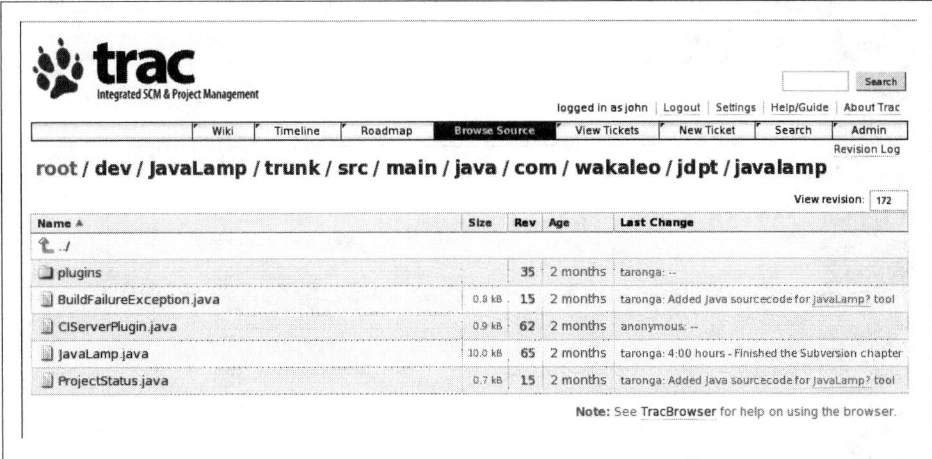

Figure 28-18. Browsing the source code repository

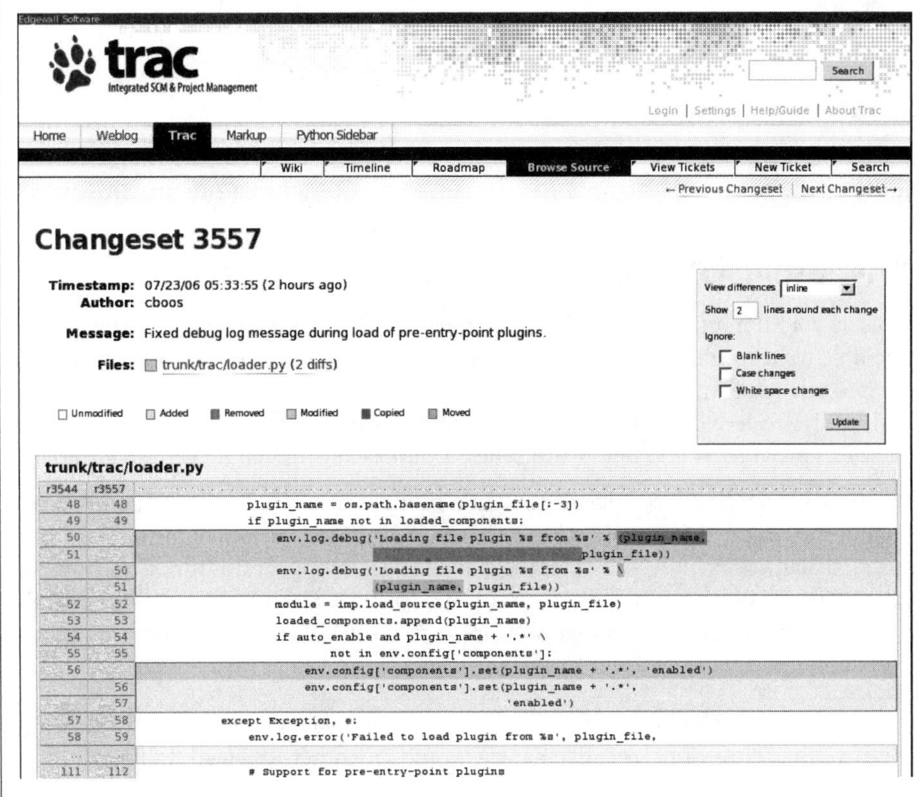

Figure 28-19. Viewing changes in the source code

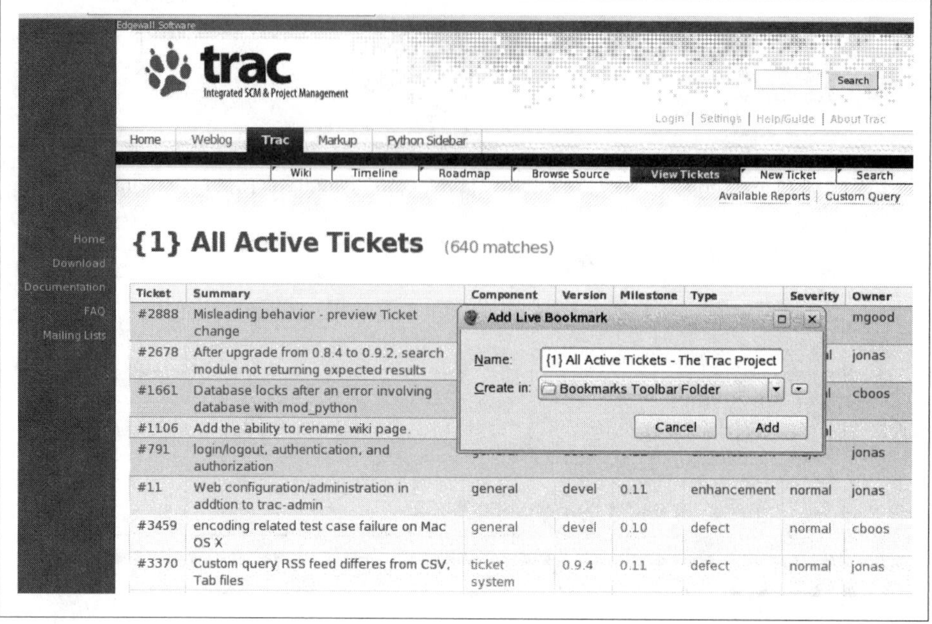

Figure 28-20. Subscribing to an RSS feed

You can also browse a previous version of the source code, using the "View Revision" field.

28.17 Using RSS and ICalendar

For users who don't consult the Trac web site several times a day, or who simply wish to be able to keep track of project progress without having to open a new web page, Trac provides RSS support for several types of project data. The "Timelines" screen provides an RSS feed concerning all project events, whereas each individual Report and Query can provide an RSS field listing the current tickets matching certain criteria.

Subscribing to an RSS feed can be done in a number of ways. Pages with an RSS feed available have the usual orange "XML RSS feed" icon at the bottom of the screen, which you can usually click on to subscribe. Not all browsers support this function, however. Recent versions of Firefox also provide support for Live Bookmarks; when you display a page with RSS support, an orange icon appears in the URL. You can click on this icon to subscribe (see Figure 28-20).

Once you've subscribed to the RSS feed, you can now keep tabs on the latest project activity or the status of tickets, just as you would any other RSS feed. In Figure 28-21, for example, you can see ticket status being displayed in Firefox using the Live Bookmark feature. There are, of course, many other tools and techniques to display RSS feeds: any tool that suits your work habits will do the job.

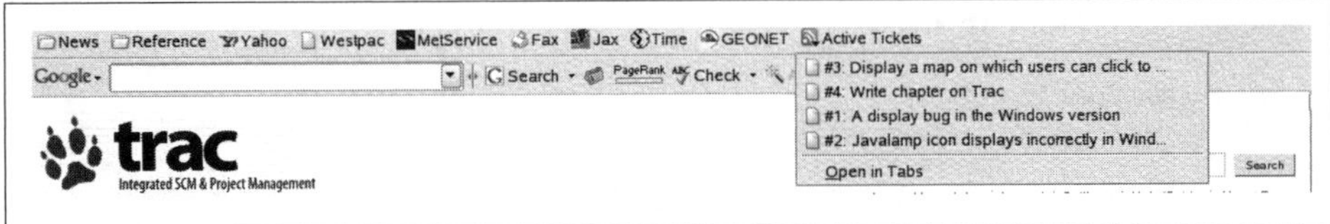

Figure 28-21. Monitoring a Trac report via an RSS feed

Trac also lets you download tasks from the Roadmap page in the standard iCalendar format. iCalendar is a standard data-exchange format designed to exchange meetings and tasks. It is supported by a number of products, including Lotus Notes, KOrganiser, Evolution, and Microsoft Outlook. From the RoadMap page, you can download data in iCalendar format and import the corresponding tasks into your calendar application. However, if your calendar tool lets you, it is more convenient to subscribe to the Trac site as a remote iCalendar calendar. This way tasks that are assigned to you are automatically updated in your local calendar.

28.18 Customizing a Wiki Page with Python

The Trac pages are extensible and easy to configure. In addition to modifying the text and layout of your wiki pages, you can also insert dynamic contents using macros.

Macros are enclosed in two square brackets and can take parameters provided between parentheses. Trac comes with a dozen or so standard macros, letting you do a few simple tasks. We'll look at some of the more interesting ones.

The *Image* macro inserts the image of your choice into the page. Images can come from a variety of places, including files attached directly to the current wiki page, as shown here:

```
[[Image(screenshot.gif)]]
```

Files can also come from other wiki pages or objects, or even from the repository, as shown here, from a ticket:

```
[[Image(ticket:16:screenshot.jpg)]]
```

and from the repository:

```
[[Image(source:/dev/JavaLamp/trunk/src/main/resources/images/green-lavalamp.gif)]]
```

The *RecentChanges* macro lists pages which have been recently modified. This can be handy on the home page, for example, in a "What's new" zone. You can specify the prefix of the pages you want to display and/or the maximum number of results. For example, the following macro lists the five most recently modified pages whose names begin with "Wiki":

```
[[RecentChanges(Wiki,5)]]
```

Finally, the *TicketQuery* macro lets you display the result of queries on the ticket database (see Section 28.14):

```
== Curren Open Tickets ==
[[TicketQuery(status=assigned)]]
```

28.19 Conclusion

Trac is, as the writers maintain, a lightweight issue tracking system with excellent Subversion integration. On the downside, it is not as feature-rich as many other issue-tracking solutions, and its reporting capabilities in the current version are somewhat limited. Nevertheless, for small, agile teams using Subversion, Trac is an excellent choice.

PART VIII

Technical Documentation Tools

> Eeyore was saying to himself, "This writing business. Pencils and what-not. Over-rated, if you ask me. Silly stuff. Nothing in it."
>
> —"A House Is Built at Pooh Corner for Eeyore," *The House at Pooh Corner*, A. A. Milne

A perfectly designed project is meaningless without good documentation to back it up. No matter how well it is designed, without a path to lead new developers up to your stride you may as well write spaghetti code. Without documentation to explain to users how one goes about using your project it will never gain popularity beyond a small group of people (often the developers themselves...and perhaps their moms).

Some proponents of agile develoment would have it that the source code itself should provide sufficient technical documentation for all purposes. There may be some merit in this statenent. After all, the source code is always up to date. However, looking at the code alone is a difficult way to understand an application. Comments are still essential to explain *why* a class does what it does: lines of code do a poor job of explaining business logic and design decisions. This is why it is still a good idea to document your classes in as much detail as reasonably possible.

Tools can help automate, complete, and enrich your documentation process. Tools such as Javadoc, SchemaSpy, and Doxygen can be used to produce decent, up-to-date, accurate, and reasonably usable online documentation, including (for the latter two) graphical database models and UML diagrams. With a few well-placed comments, and combined with a few strategic vision documents, this sort of automatically generated documentation might be just enough to help a new developer understand the architecture of your product. And by fully integrating the documentation generation process into the SDLC, you can guarantee permanently available and up-to-date technical documentation for the whole team.

In this part, we look at several tools that can help you automatically generate up-to-date documentation about your project. Maven 2 builds documentation generation as a cornerstone of a comprehensive software development management process. We will take a detailed look at how you can get the most out of your Maven-generated web site.

We will also look at three tools that can be used independently of Maven 2 to generate high-quality graphical representations of your project design and architecture: SchemaSpy for database models, and Doxygen and UmlGraph for UML-based source code documentation.

CHAPTER 29

Team Communication with the Maven 2 Project Web Site

29.1 The Maven 2 Project Web Site As a Communication Tool

Contributed by: Eric Redmond

Team communication is an essential part of any project. Wasting time looking for technical project information can be costly and frustrating. Clearly, any IT project will benefit from having its own dedicated technical web site. That's where the Maven2 site generator steps in. With little effort, you can have a professional-quality, low-maintenance project web site up and running in no time. Maven lets you generate a one-stop center of information about your project, including:

- General project information such as source repositories, defect tracking, and team members
- Unit test and test coverage reports
- Automatic code reviews with Checkstyle and PMD
- Configuration and versioning information
- Dependencies
- Javadocs
- Source code in indexed and cross-referenced HTML format
- And much more

Maven sites are frequently used on open source projects. A typical project site contains information about the project, largely derived from the *pom.xml* file, some generated reports (unit tests, Javadocs, Checkstyle code audits, etc.), as well as some project-specific content. In this chapter, we will look at how to generate different parts of the Maven web site.

29.2 Setting Up a Maven Site Project

Your Maven site will be one of the first places that newcomers will look to get to know your project, and the project information page is the place they will expect to find a summary of your project's organization. Much of this web site is built using information found in the *pom.xml* file. In this section, we will go through the basics of building an informative Maven web site.

The standard way to create a Maven site is to use the *mvn site* command, as shown here:

```
$ mvn site
[INFO] Scanning for projects...
[INFO] ------------------------------------------------------------------------
[INFO] Building Spitfire
[INFO]    task-segment: [site]
[INFO] ------------------------------------------------------------------------
...
[INFO] Generate "Dependencies" report.
[INFO] Generate "Issue Tracking" report.
[INFO] Generate "Project License" report.
[INFO] Generate "Mailing Lists" report.
[INFO] Generate "About" report.
[INFO] Generate "Project Summary" report.
[INFO] Generate "Source Repository" report.
[INFO] Generate "Project Team" report.
[INFO] ------------------------------------------------------------------------
[INFO] BUILD SUCCESSFUL
[INFO] ------------------------------------------------------------------------
[INFO] Total time: 5 seconds
[INFO] Finished at: Thu Jan 04 09:55:59 NZDT 2007
[INFO] Final Memory: 11M/22M
[INFO] ------------------------------------------------------------------------
```

This will create a simple Maven site, shown in Figure 29-1.

A site like this will be pretty sparse. You will probably want to add some details about your project. All zones are optional, but it is a good idea to put as much information as is relevant to your project. The rest of this section will discuss some useful items to add.

Describing the Project

The Maven site is above all a communication tool, so it is important to let people know what your project is all about. The POM file lets you provide plenty of details about your project, such as an appropriate project name, a short description, the project home page, and your organization's details. Here is a typical example:

```
<name>Spitfire</name>
<url>http://maven.mycompany.com/spitfire</url>
<description>A community website for model plane enthusiasts</description>
<organization>
  <name>Wakaleo Consulting Ltd</name>
```

```
    <url>http://www.wakaleo.com</url>
</organization>
```

Most projects have an internal name, used within the organization, which is different to the formal artifactId. You can specify this in the *<name>* field.

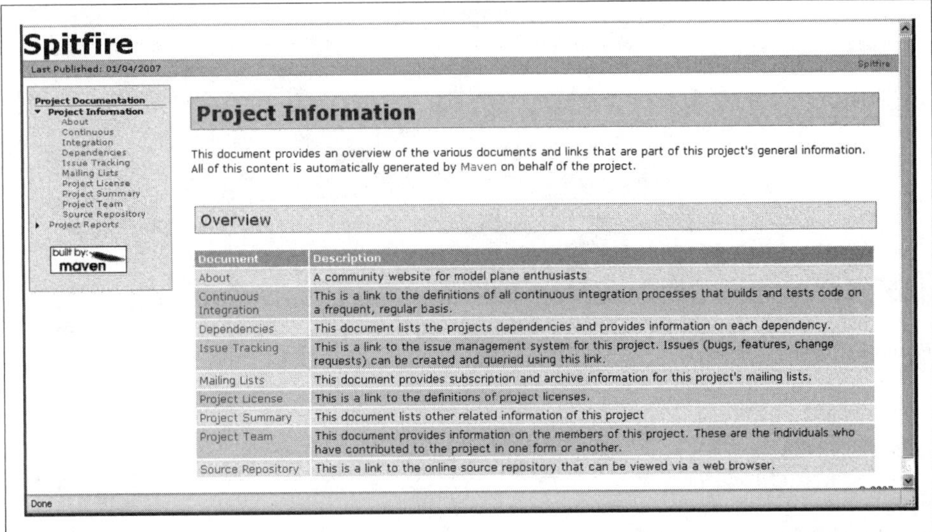

Figure 29-1. A simple Maven-generated web site

The URL is a handy link to the application home page. Of course, what you call the home page will vary depending on your project: for a public open source project, it might be the public URL to the project web site, whereas, for an internal site, it might point to the demonstration server. This URL appears on the Project Summary page, where it is called the "Homepage."

All this appears on your project's web site, in the "Project Summary" section (Figure 29-2).

Linking into the Issue Tracking System

It is handy to have a link to your issue tracking system available on your Maven site. This way, people will know where to look for it when they forget the URL (or haven't bothered asking...). Just put the name and URL of your project's issue management system (Bugzilla, JIRA, Scarab, or your own favorite issue tracking system) in your *pom.xml* file, using the *<issueManagement>*, as shown here:

```
<issueManagement>
    <system>trac</system>
    <url>http://buildserver.mycompany.com/trac/modelplanes</url>
</issueManagement>
```

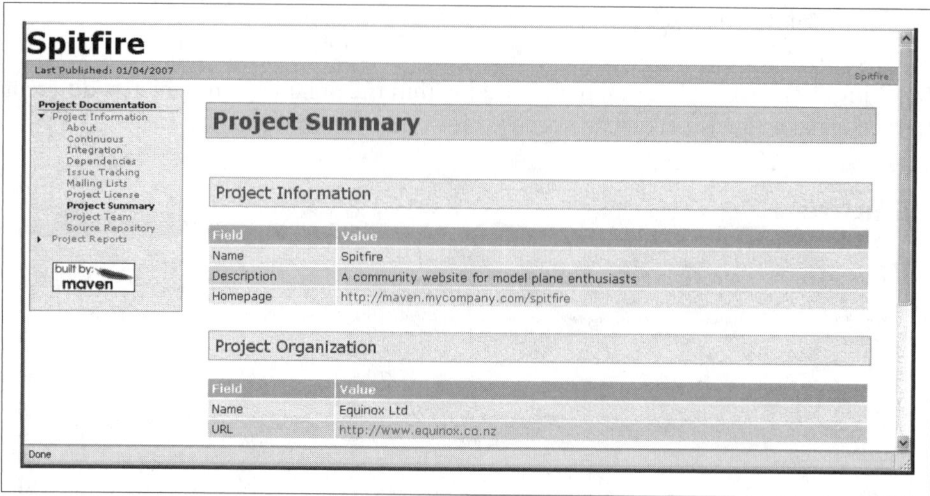

Figure 29-2. A project summary

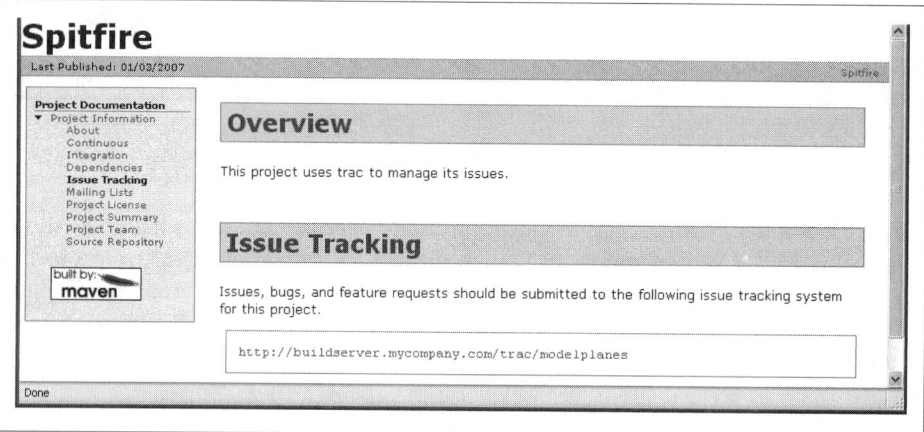

Figure 29-3. Integration with the issue tracking system

Maven's integration with the defect tracking system is largely informative: the Issue Tracking page will tell users what sort of issue tracking system is used (including a short blurb boasting its merits for systems such as Bugzilla and JIRA that Maven has heard of), and, more importantly, the URL that users need to connect to the issue tracking web site (see Figure 29-3).

The Continuous Integration System

Continuous Integration (or CI) is an increasingly popular development best practice that promotes regular automatic builds on a dedicated build server. If your project uses

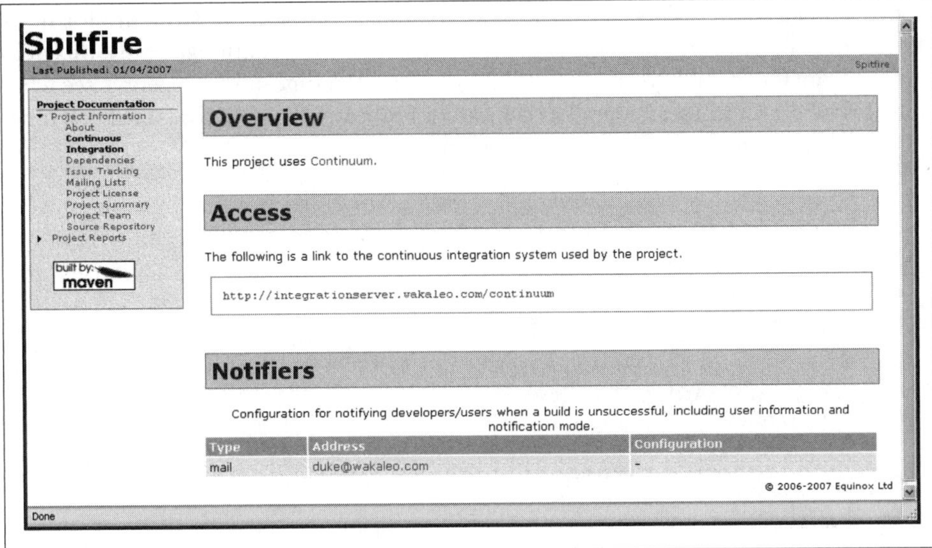

Figure 29-4. The Continuous Integration page

a continuous integration tool of some sort, such as Continuum (see Chapter 5), CruiseControl (see Chapter 6), or LuntBuild (see Chapter 7), you can provide details in the ciManagement tag, as shown in the code below. These details are published on the "Continuous Integration" page (see Figure 29-4), which, like the link to the issue tracking system, can be a handy reminder for forgetful users:

```
...
<ciManagement>
   <system>Continuum</system>
   <url>http://integrationserver.wakaleo.com/continuum</url>
   <notifiers>
      <notifier>
         <type>mail</type>
         <address>duke@wakaleo.com</address>
      </notifier>
   </notifiers>
</ciManagement>
```

Continuum (see Chapter 5) is a Continuous Integration system that integrates closely with Maven. Maven integration with Continuum is discussed in Section 5.7. If you use Continuum, you can centralize a lot of the CI configuration details, such as the server URL and even notification rules, in the POM file.

The Project Team

People like to know who they are working with, especially these days, when a project team can be spread across organizations and continents. In the developers section, list team member details. This can be a useful summary of the team structure for newcomers or stake holders. The timezone field is useful for international teams; this field is offset from Greenwich Mean Time (GMT), or London time, and lets people see what time it is wherever the team member is located. For example, –5 is for New York time, +1 is for Paris time, and +10 is for Sydney time:

```
...
<developers>
   <developer>
      <id>duke</id>
      <name>Duke Java</name>
      <email>duke@wakaleo.com</email>
      <roles>
         <role>Project Manager</role>
         <role>Architect</role>
      </roles>
      <organization>Acme.com</organization>
      <timezone>-5</timezone>
    </developer>
</developers>
```

For best results, the *<id>* field should be the user's software configuration management (SCM) login. The project team members defined here are automatically used in other screens reports, such as change reports (see "Change and Configuration Management).

Mailing Lists

If your project uses mailing lists, describe them in the mailingLists page. A typical mailing list configuration might look like this:

```
...
<mailingLists>
  <mailingList>
    <name>HotelDatabase project mailing list</name>
    <subscribe>dev-subscribe@wakaleo.com</subscribe>
    <unsubscribe>dev-unsubscribe@wakaleo.com</unsubscribe>
   <post>dev@wakaleo.com</post>
   <archive>http://mail-archives.wakaleo.com/modmbox/dev/</archive>
  </mailingList>
</mailingLists>
```

The Source Repository

Another vital part of any project is the source repository. The scm tag lets you document the configuration of your source repository, both for the Maven web site and for use by other plug-ins. If you are using CVS or Subversion, the source repository page will also give detailed, tool-dependent instructions on how to use the repository (see Figure 29-5). Here is an example of a typical SCM configuration:

```
...
<scm>
```

```
    <connection>scm:svn:http://svn.wakaleo.com/hoteldatabase/</connection>
    <developerConnection>scm:svn:http://svn.wakaleo.com/hoteldatabase/
    </developerConnection>
    <url>http://svn.wakaleo.com/viewcvs.cgi/hoteldatabase/</url>
</scm>
```

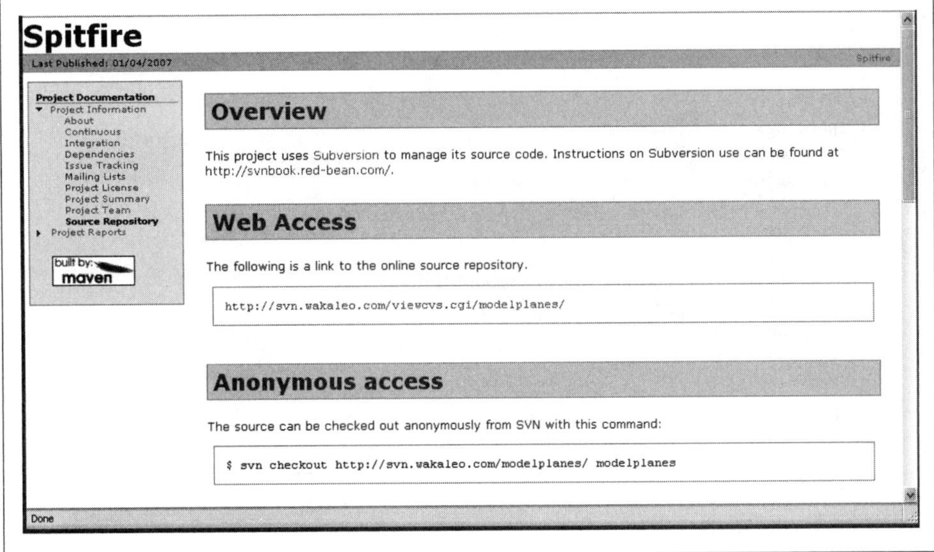

Figure 29-5. Integration with the issue tracking system

Generating the Site

Now you can try out your new Maven site! The command to generate the Maven site is:

```
$ mvn site
```

Your site will be generated in the *target/site* directory. Take a look at the project information link; you should find everything you just entered, and more!

29.3 Integrating Reports into Your Site

Maven also provides an extensive range of plug-ins for automatic report generation. Reports are a crucial part of the Maven web site, and can provide useful information on the state of the project from a technical point of view, as well as providing reference documentation such as Javadocs. Report generation in Maven 2 is easy: you just add the report plug-ins you need into the reporting section at the end of the *pom.xml* file.

Javadocs

Most likely, you will want to start by publishing your classes' Javadocs. This is as simple as adding Javadoc to the reporting section of your *pom.xml* file. While you're at it, add the jxr plug-in; this will generate an indexed and cross-referenced HTML version of your source code:

```
<project>
  <build>
    ...
  </build>
  <reporting>
    <plugins>
      <plugin>
        <artifactId>maven-javadoc-plugin</artifactId>
      </plugin>
      <plugin>
        <groupId>org.codehaus.mojo</groupId>
        <artifactId>jxr-maven-plugin</artifactId>
      </plugin>
    </plugins>
  </reporting>
  <dependencies>
    ...
  </dependencies>
</project>
```

Unit Test Reports

Writing unit tests for as much code as possible is highly recommended. Maven fully integrates unit testing into the build process—by default, all unit tests run at each build. Publishing test results for all to see is beneficial, since it tends to encourage developers to fix any broken unit tests. The Surefire plug-in runs all the unit tests and generates a detailed report:

```
<reporting>
  <plugins>
    ...
    <plugin>
      <groupId>org.apache.maven.plugins</groupId>
      <artifactId>maven-surefire-report-plugin</artifactId>
    </plugin>
  </plugins>
</reporting>
```

Test Coverage Reports

Test coverage can be a useful indication of the quality of your unit tests. Basically, it tells you how much of your code is actually run by your unit tests, which, in turn, can give you a good idea of the tests' quality. In some projects, requiring a certain percentage of test coverage in all classes is recommended. Tools such as Clover (a vigorous commercial test coverage tool) or Cobertura (see Chapter 30) generate useful test coverage reports. We discussed how to integrate Cobertura reports into Maven in Section 12.6.

Code Analysis Reports

Automatic code analysis is a useful way of improving code quality and encouraging good coding habits. Checkstyle (see Chapter 21) runs a wide range of tests aimed at enforcing coding standards and best practices. PMD (see Chapter 22) concentrates more on semantic errors and potential bugs. FindBugs (see Chapter 23) is another static analysis tool, which is more focused on detecting potential bugs and performance issues. All of these can provide useful information, although you may have to fine-tune them (especially Checkstyle) to obtain only the errors meaningful for your project.

We looked at how to integrate Checkstyle, PMD, and FindBugs into a Maven site in Section 21.9, Section 22.10, and Section 23.6, respectively.

Change and Configuration Management

Documenting changes is important in any project. Maven 2 provides a couple of useful features to make this task a little easier. The changes-maven-plugin plug-in uses a special XML file (*src/changes/changes.xml*) to track releases and changes in each release. This file looks something like this:

```
<?xml version="1.0" encoding="ISO-8859-1"?>
<document>
   <properties>
      <title>Spitfire model plane database application</title>
      <author email="duke@wakaleo.com">Duke Java</author>
   </properties>
   <body>
      <release version="current" description="Current work version">
           <action dev="duke" type="add">
               A new cool feature.
           </action>
           <action dev="richard" type="add">
               Another new cool feature.
           </action>
         </release>
      <release version="1.0.1" date="2005-11-18" description="Release fix">
           <action dev="duke" type="add">
               Added a cool feature.
           </action>
           <action dev="keith" type="fix" issue="1254">
               Fixed a nasty bug.
           </action>
           <action dev="jimmy" type="delete">
               Removed a feature that nobody liked.
           </action>
         </release>
```

```
    </body>
</document>
```

Here, you list your releases and describe the actions associated with each release: a new feature or evolution (add), a bug fix (fix), or something removed (delete). You should detail the modification, who made the change, and what issue was addressed. Using this file gives a clearer and more readable record of changes and release history.

Now add the changes plug-in to the Maven 2 reports. The issueLinkTemplate configuration parameter allows you to integrate with your issue management web site, using a template:

```
<reporting>
   <plugins>
     ...
     <plugin>
       <groupId>org.codehaus.mojo</groupId>
       <artifactId>changes-maven-plugin</artifactId>
     </plugin>
   </plugins>
 </reporting>
```

If you specify an issue number for the changes you describe in the change report, Maven can automatically generate a URL pointing to the issue in your issue management system. The default configuration works for JIRA. For all other systems, you need to tell Maven how to generate the URL pointing to the issue in the issue tracking system, using the *link_template*[*] configuration parameter. This template uses two variables:

%URL%
: The base URL specified in the *<issueManagement>* field, without the context path

%ISSUE%
: The issue identifier

If you are using Trac, issues can be displayed using a REST-style URL in the following form:

```
http://my.trac.server/myproject/tickets/123
```

This would display the Trac ticket # 123.

The plug-in configuration for our Trac issue management system would be the following:

```
<plugin>
  <groupId>org.codehaus.mojo</groupId>
  <artifactId>changes-maven-plugin</artifactId>
  <configuration>
    <link_template>%URL%/modelplanes/tickets/%ISSUE%</link_template>
  </configuration>
</plugin>
```

[*] This variable is to be renamed “issueLinkTemplate” in a future release.

Figure 29-6 shows an example of a the generated change report.

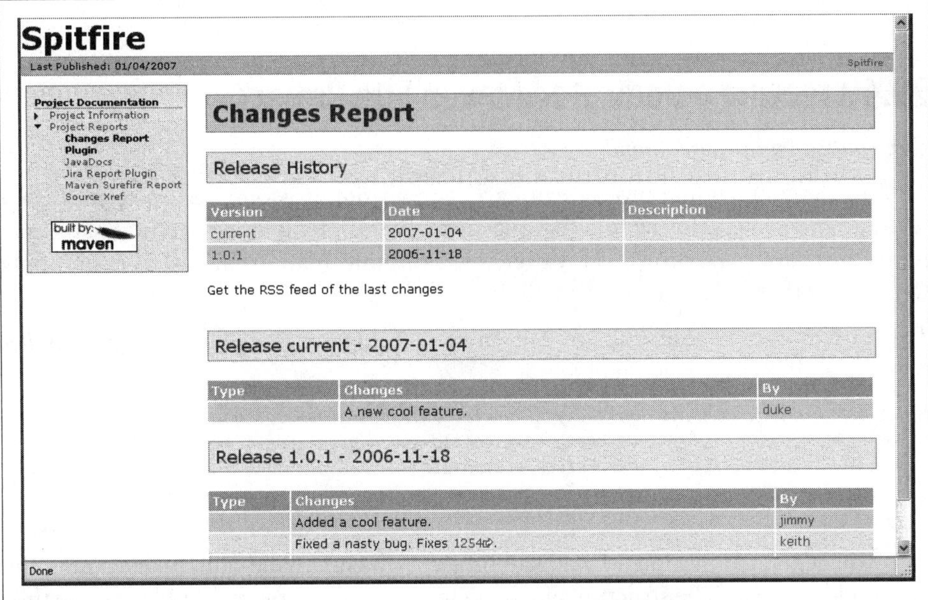

Figure 29-6. Example of a change report

Another more development-oriented option is to use your SCM repository to track changes. The changelog plug-in generates a nice report describing which files have been changed and by whom:

```
<reporting>
   <plugins>
     ...
     <plugin>
       <groupId>org.codehaus.mojo</groupId>
       <artifactId>changelog-maven-plugin</artifactId>
     </plugin>
   </plugins>
 </reporting>
```

Finally, if you use @todo tags to remind you of things to be done (which is a good coding practice), the taglist report will generate a list of all the items marked @todo or TODO:

```
<reporting>
   <plugins>
     ...
     <plugin>
       <groupId>org.codehaus.mojo</groupId>
       <artifactId>taglist-maven-plugin</artifactId>
     </plugin>
```

```
    </plugins>
  </reporting>
```

29.4 Creating a Dedicated Maven Site Project

Contributed by: Eric Redmond

Although any individual project can have its own site, it is often easier to manage a separate site project. In the following sections, we will look at how to build and customize a separate site project. However, all of this information can just as easily apply to a project that contains code as well.

The simplest way to bootstrap any Maven site development is to use the *maven-archetype-site* archetype, as shown here:

```
$ mvn archetype:create -DarchetypeGroupId=org.apache.maven.archetypes \
                       -DarchetypeArtifactId=maven-archetype-site \
                       -DarchetypeVersion=1.0 \
                       -DgroupId=com.mycompany \
                       -DartifactId=my-site
```

This will generate a sample Maven site project, which may be built by executing the `site` build lifecycle. The structure of your new Maven site project should look like this:

```
my-site
|-- pom.xml
`-- src
    `-- site
        |-- apt
        |   |-- format.apt
        |   `-- index.apt
        |-- fml
        |   `-- faq.fml
        |-- fr
        |   |-- apt
        |   |   |-- format.apt
        |   |   `-- index.apt
        |   |-- fml
        |   |   `-- faq.fml
        |   `-- xdoc
        |       `-- xdoc.xml
        |-- xdoc
        |   `-- xdoc.xml
        |-- site.xml
        `-- site_fr.xml
```

The items to note in the above structure are the `site.xml` file and the directories under `src/site`: `apt`, `fml` and `xdoc`; each representing a document notation type. You should have an index file somewhere (for example, a file called index.apt in the `site/apt` directory). This will be converted to a file called `index.html`, which will become the home page of your site. Without this file, Maven will generate a very boring home page.

Finally, the `site_fr.xml` and `src/site/fr` subdirectories contain a French language version of the documents, rounding out Maven's commitment to built-in internationalization. To activate this locale, you simply add the French language version to the site plug-in's configuration in the POM, as shown here:

```
<project>
  ...
  <build>
    <plugins>
      <plugin>
        <artifactId>maven-site-plugin</artifactId>
        <configuration>
          <locales>en,fr</locales>
        </configuration>
      </plugin>
    </plugins>
  </build>
</project>
```

29.5 Defining the Site Outline

Contributed by: Eric Redmond

The `site.xml` file is responsible for the structure of the site as a whole, defining the site's banners, the links (upper-right corner by default), and the left-hand side menu. A simple example is shown here:

```
<project name="Spitfire">
  <bannerLeft>
    <name>Spitfire</name>
    <src>/images/spitfire-logo.jpg</src>
    <href>http://spitfire.mycompany.com/</href>
  </bannerLeft>
  <bannerRight>
    <src>/images/hurricane-small.jpg</src>
  </bannerRight>
  <body>
    <links>
      <item name="Apache" href="http://www.apache.org/" />
      <item name="Maven 2" href="http://maven.apache.org/maven2/"/>
      <item name="Hibernate" href="http://www.hibernate.org/"/>
    </links>
     <menu name="The Spitfire project">
      <item name="Home" href="index.html"/>
      <item name="APT Format" href="format.html"/>
      <item name="FAQ" href="faq.html"/>
      <item name="Xdoc Example" href="xdoc.html"/>
    </menu>

    ${reports}

  </body>
</project>
```

Note that links in the menu defined below have similar names to the documents above, yet end with `.html`. This is because each of the document markups are converted to HTML by the site plug-in, more specifically, by Doxia.

A common initial requirement is to incorporate project and/or company logos. This is easy to do. The *<src>* tag in each banner points to an image to be displayed there. You can either use an absolute URL, or refer to a local resource within your web site project. To do the latter, just place any images you need to access in the *site/resources* directory. From here, you can access them using a local reference such as the "/images/spitfire-logo.jpg" shown above.

You may or may not want to include the standard Maven project reports in your custom site. If you do, you need to include the *${reports}* tag shown in the *site.xml* file above. This will be replaced by the "Project Information" and "Project Reports" menus that you have configured in your *pom.xml* file.

The resulting web site is illustrated in Figure 29-7.

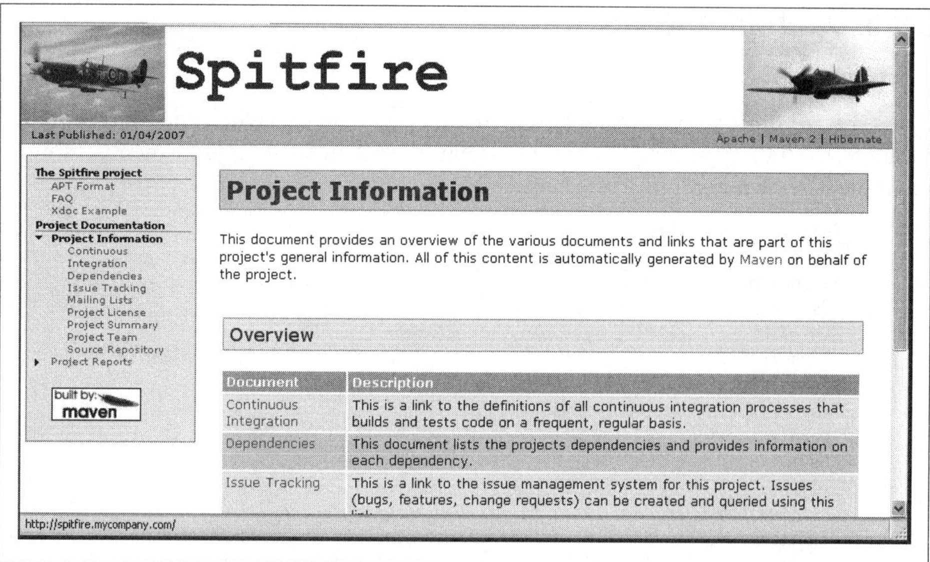

Figure 29-7. A simple customized web site

The `site` phase can easily generate sites of different languages. All you need to do is create a site descriptor file similar to the file above, yet suffix the filename with the language code of your choice. The archetype created a French language version for you, `site_fr.xml`. At this point, Maven will look for a matching language directory under `src/site` and generate that documentation for an audience of that particular language (usually by a web browser's language settings). If no matching language is found, the `site.xml`'s language is the default (presumed to be English).

29.6 The Maven Site Generation Architecture

Contributed by: Eric Redmond

You can use a number of different formats to build the content of your Maven 2 web site. This is largely a matter of taste. We will examine the basic architecture of the Maven 2 content generation system and run through the formats that you can use.

Doxia

The heart of the Maven site plug-in is the Doxia project, which is a self-contained subproject of Maven (*http://maven.apache.org/doxia*). Doxia is responsible for converting your chosen document markup to the html that can be deployed to a web site. Doxia also has the ability to convert a document from any supported markup to any other supported markup. It does this with *parsers* and *sinks*. A Doxia parser implements the `org.apache.maven.doxia.parser.Parser` Plexus role and is responsible for converting the implemented markup into a given sink. A Doxia sink implements the `org.apache.maven.doxia.sink.Sink` Plexus role and caters for a particular output format, for example XHTML or PDF. This is important to know if you ever decide to write your own modules for Doxia to support.

APT

Almost Plain Text, or APT, can be considered the default documentation method for Maven projects. It is a simple wiki-like syntax that is easily converted to a Doxia sink. If you built the site generated by maven-archetype-site, navigate to `target/site/format.html` and you will be treated to a comprehensive guide for using APT. A simple example is shown here:

```
    -----
    The Hotel Database Vision Statement
    -----
    The Wakaleo Team
    -----
    January 2006

 Introduction


    One of the nicer features of Maven is the ability to create an internal
    technical web site at very little cost. Maven 2 extends this functionality,
    and gives you powerful new ways to generate site content...


 * Sub-section title


    Team communication is an essential part of any project. And wasting time
    looking for technical project information can be costly and frustrating.
    Clearly, any IT project will benefit from having its own dedicated
```

```
technical web site...

* Item 1

* Item 2

  * Item 2.1

  * Item 2.2
```

The APT format is documented in excruciating detail on the Maven site, so we will just take you through the main things that you should know to get started.

Your APT document typically begins with a heading. The heading starts with a line of dashes, and contains three parts—the document title, the author, and the date—separated by lines of dashes:

```
-----
The Hotel Database Vision Statement
-----
The Wakaleo Team
-----
January 2006
```

Indentation and line spacing is important for APT. For example, section titles and subtitles cannot have any indenting, whereas normal text does need to be indented (more precisely, the first line of a normal paragraph needs to be indented). Subtitles are indicated with asterisks. You need a blank line between every element (paragraph, title, list item, and so on):

```
Main Title

  Say some stuff...


* Sub-title

  Some more detailed stuff...


** Sub-sub-title

   The heart of the matter...
```

You can see this in action in Figure 29-8.

You can also include lists, tables, and other formatting niceties (see Figure 29-9). For example, the following listing illustrates a definition list and an ordinary bullet-point list:

```
  The application is comprised of several main packages:
```

Main Title

Say some stuff...

Sub-title

Some more detailed stuff...

Sub-sub-title

The heart of the matter...

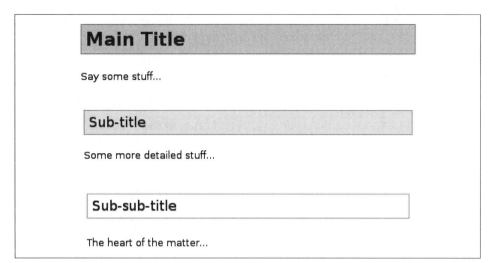

Figure 29-8. Some APT titles

```
    [com.mycompany.myapp.core] Core interface classes

    [com.mycompany.myapp.core.impl] Core implementation classes

    []

  These are cool packages for several reasons

    * The interfaces rock

    * The implementations are groovy

    * They are really well documented

    []
```

Note how lists need to be terminated by an empty list element ("[]").

The application is comprised of several main packages:

com.mycompany.myapp.core
    Core interface classes
com.mycompany.myapp.core.impl
    Core implementation classes

These are cool packages for several reasons

- The interfaces rock
- The implementations are groovy
- They are really well documented

Figure 29-9. APT lists

It is often useful to include snippets of code in your documentation, to show how to use or configure a class, for example. You can do this by surrounding the code listing with lines of dashes, as shown here:

```
You can configure this class in Spring as follows:

----------------------------------------
    <bean id="taxCalculator"
        class="com.mycompany.myapp.core.impl.TaxCalculatorImpl" >
        ...
    </bean>
----------------------------------------
```

If you want to include images in your APT files, you need to add them in the `resources` directory. For example, in the following directory structure, we have placed a PNG image in the `src/site/resources/images` directory:

```
my-site
|-- pom.xml
`-- src
    `-- site
        |-- ...
        |-- resources
            `-- images
                `-- domain-model.png
        |-- site.xml
        `-- site_fr.xml
```

You can also refer to these images in your document as follows:

```
  The domain model is illustrated in the following class diagram:

[images/domain-model.png] The application domain model
```

FML

FML is FAQ (frequently asked questions) markup language, and it specializes in the creation of the ubiquitous FAQ document. An example is as follows:

```
<faqs id="faqs1">
     <part id="part1">
       <faq id="faq1">
         <question>What is a good question?</question>
         <answer>
           <p>Any valid XHTML can be placed in the <code>answer</code> element</p>
         </answer>
       </faq>
     </part>
   </faqs>
```

The FML document can have any number of parts, and each part may have any number of FAQs, each with one question and one answer. When the document is generated, it will place all questions at the top of the page as links, which anchor to the answers later in the page (see Figure 29-10).

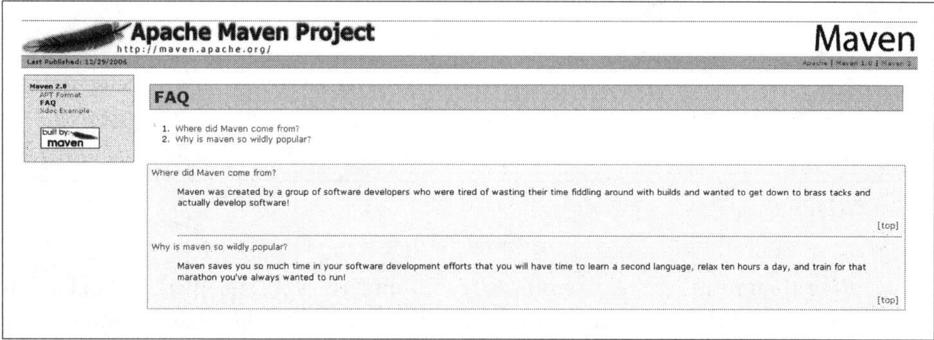

Figure 29-10. A simple Maven-generated FAQ screen

XDoc

XDoc is an XML markup for writing documents, and has been around since the early days of Maven 1 and Ant. It is similar to HTML, but it is document-centric with extra elements for sections and more constraints. All XDoc documents must be under the xdoc directory, with a `.xml` extension. Its support is mostly for historical reasons, and it is recommended that you write new documentation in APT format.

29.7 Using Snippets

Contributed by: Eric Redmond

A useful feature of Doxia are snippets. Snippets are macros that are given a file and an id. They can be a useful way of inserting or referencing key blocks of code from within your project in your technical documentation. You define a snippet as follows:

```
%{snippet|id=myID|file=some.file}
```

You define a snippet by encapsulating a block of code in specially formatted comments. The macro will search the file for the comment `START SNIPPET: myID` and ending comment `END SNIPPET: myID`. For example, add the following to your POM:

```
<project>
  ...
  <!-- START SNIPPET: props -->
  <properties>
    <my.prop>value</my.prop>
  </properties>
  <!-- END SNIPPET: props -->
</project>
```

Then add the following to your `format.apt` file:

```
%{snippet|id=props|url=file:pom.xml}
```

Now run the `site` phase, and be amazed! The block of code will now figure in the generated web page (see Figure 29-11).

```
<properties>
  <my.prop>value</my.prop>
</properties>
```

Figure 29-11. An example of a snippet

Hint: rather than running the `site` phase, try running the ***`site:run`*** goal. It will launch your documents under a web container accessible from port 8080 that will show your changes in real time.

29.8 Customizing the Look and Feel of Your Site

Contributed by: Eric Redmond

Whether it's just the company logo in the corner of the screen, or the whole site repainted using your company fonts and colors, adding that personal touch to your Maven site can do wonders for its appeal. You'd be surprised how many people pay more attention when the site matches the company colors! Maven provides a number of ways for you to customize the look and feel of your Maven web site. Here, we look at several ways to add your own personal touch.

Changing Skins

Like many sites, the look-and-feel of a Maven site is determined by what we call a "skin." A skin is, in fact, a collection of CSS stylesheets and graphical resources. Changing skins in Maven is easy. Just alter your POM, and voilà! Your entire site's look and feel has been altered. Better yet, it is all consistent. To switch the `my-site` project to use the Stylus theme, alter the `site.xml` file (*not* the POM):

```
<project>
   ...
   <skin>
     <groupId>org.apache.maven.skins</groupId>
     <artifactId>maven-stylus-skin</artifactId>
     <version>1.0</version>
   </skin>
</project>
```

This style is illustrated in Figure 29-12.

The list of default skins available from the Maven Central Repository can be found at *http://repo1.maven.org/maven2/org/apache/maven/skins/*. At the time of this writing, the list is:

- maven-classic-skin
- maven-default-skin
- maven-stylus-skin

As you probably guessed, maven-default-skin is the default.

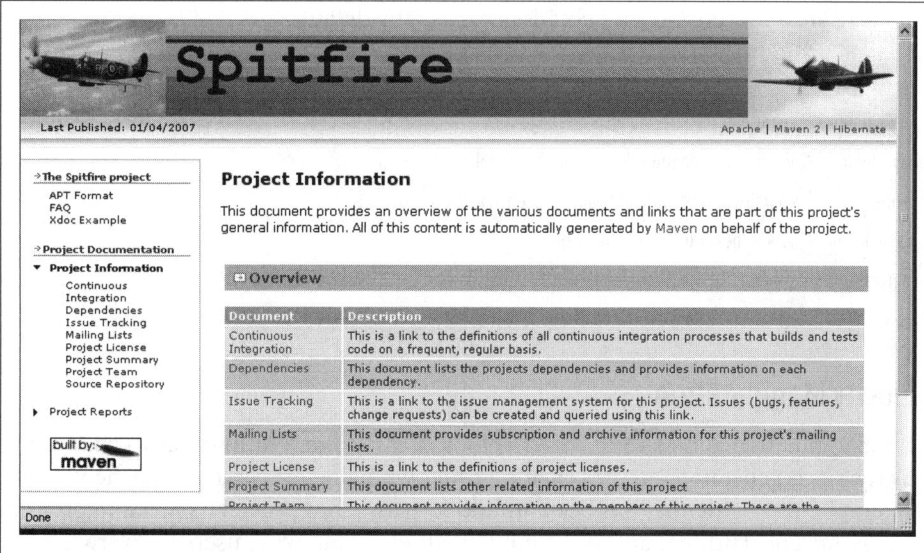

Figure 29-12. The Stylus skin

Creating Your Own Style

The predefined Maven skins give you some flexibility, and they can help you learn how to customize your site's look and feel. They are often just fine for internal sites with a limited, technically minded audience. However, there are times when the default skins just don't cut it. Let's see how to create your own personalized skin.

First, create a project with the following layout:

```
my-skin
 |-- pom.xml
 `-- src
     `-- main
         `-- resources
             |-- css
             |   `-- maven-theme.css
             `-- images
```

You will also need a simple `pom.xml`:

```
<project>
   <modelVersion>4.0.0</modelVersion>
   <groupId>com.mycompany</groupId>
```

```
    <artifactId>my-skin</artifactId>
    <version>1.0-SNAPSHOT</version>
</project>
```

The important file in a custom skin is the **maven-theme.css**. Also note the **src/main/resource/images** directory that allows you to add images into your CSS, accessible as "/images/my-image.ext." Most control of the CSS is via the basics such as **body** or **a**, but there are a few important CSS **ids** generated by default:

breadcrumbs	a sequence of data at the top of the page
leftColumn	represents the left column of the page
navcolumn	wraps the navigation elements in the left column
banner	contains the left and right banners defined in the `site.xml`
bodyColumn	wraps the contentBox of the page
contentBox	contains the main content of the page
footer	contains the data generated as a page footer

Velocity Manipulation

Skin manipulation is nice to change the look of your site, but in order to change the way the site is generated requires creating your own Velocity (`.vm`) file. Apache Velocity is a templating engine that has been around for years, has proven its metal in projects such as Apache Turbine, and is a simple method for allowing users to overwrite the default templates.

Rather than starting from scratch, it is far simpler to download the default **default-site.vm** file and manipulate it. The default renderer is available under the doxia-site-rendered project source code, available for download under the Doxia project. Doxia is available from the subversion repository at *http://svn.apache.org/repos/asf/maven/doxia/trunk/* (if not found there, check the Doxia web site at *http://maven.apache.org/doxia*. From there, the doxia-site renderer project's resource contains the template, at **doxia-site-renderer/src/main/resources/org/apache/maven/doxia/siterenderer/resources/default-site.vm**. Copy this file to your project at **src/site/my-site.vm**, and point your **my-site** project's **pom.xml** to utilize it:

```
<project>
  ...
  <build>
    <plugins>
      <plugin>
        <artifactId>maven-site-plugin</artifactId>
        <configuration>
          <templateFile>src/site/my-site.vm</templateFile>
        </configuration>
      </plugin>
    </plugins>
  </build>
```

If you look at the my-site.vm, you will notice the XHTML and CSS generated by it. This gives you the power to alter the structure of your generated Maven site, as well as allow your custom skins more control than merely the default (perhaps by adding more spans or more types of CSS classes).

Or, better yet, you can add the template to your skin to `src/main/resources/META-INF/maven/site.vm`. This way, when a project uses your skin, it automatically uses your template.

29.9 Distributing Your Site

Contributed by: Eric Redmond

The final step in site generation is publishing it to a location from which a public web server can access it. There is a special element in the `distributionManagement` element called `site`, which gives the location and method of distribution. In your `my-site` POM, you will notice the element has been added for you. Now you merely need to set it like any other Maven distribution. The example uses secure copy protocol (scp):

```
<project>
  ...
  <distributionManagement>
    <site>
      <id>website</id>
      <url>scp://webhost.company.com/www/website</url>
    </site>
  </distributionManagement>
</project>
```

If you need to supply a username and password when you copy to the remote site, you will also need to provide this information in your *settings.xml* file (see Section 2.7):

```
<settings>
  ...
  <servers>
    <server>
      <id>website</id>
      <username>scott</username>
      <password>tiger</password>
    </server>
  </servers>
</settings>
```

Setting up an enterprise repository was covered in Section 2.19.

With a suitable distribution setup, you merely run the `site-deploy` phase (which has bound to it the `site:site.deploy` goal):

```
mvn site-deploy
```

That's it! Maven will generate the documentation using your chosen template and skin, and copy those files to the specified location.

CHAPTER 30

Automatically Generating Technical Documentation

30.0 Introduction

Good-quality, reliable, and up-to-date technical documentation on a project is generally regarded as a Good Thing. Technical documentation is a great aid for the developers who are assigned to maintaining the product, once the original development team has been dispersed. Technical documentation can also help new developers come up to speed when they join a project.

However, good technical documentation comes at a cost—the more documentation you have, the more effort you need to put into maintaining this documentation. And the effort that goes into maintaining technical documentation is, of course, effort that could be spent on writing code. In this chapter, we look at three tools that you can use to reduce the time you spend on maintaining your technical documentation, without compromising too much on the quality: SchemaSpy, for database models, and Doxygen and UmlGraph for source code documentation.

30.1 Visualizing a Database Structure with SchemaSpy

Introduction

Relational databases play a key role in a majority of today's software applications, and database schemas are without doubt one of the most widely recognized and understood models in the IT field. Although they are relatively low-level, and lack some of the abstraction of an object-oriented class model, they can still be an extremely valuable asset when it comes to trying to understand the architecture of an application, both during the development phase and also during product maintenance once the application is in production.

However, the main problem with database schemas, like all other design models and documents, is keeping them up-to-date. As a rule, the chances of a design document being kept up to date are inversely proportional to the effort required to maintain them. That is to say, if human intervention is required to maintain a document, it will soon become out of date in all but the most rigorous of projects.

SchemaSpy can be a valuable asset in maintaining and publishing these models. Like Javadoc for Java source code, SchemaSpy provides an accurate, up-to-date view of the database structure, generated automatically from the actual database. As an automated tool, SchemaSpy incurs very little cost to set up and virtually no cost to maintain—the diagrams are automatically updated as the database schema evolves. This alone is a valuable time-saver for both development and maintenance teams.

An Overview of SchemaSpy

Based on material contributed by: Masoud Kalali

SchemaSpy* is a free, open source Java tool written by John Currier that can generate a rich interactive HTML view of your database, showing detailed information about the tables, views and relations that make up the database. SchemaSpy works by analyzing the metadata from a JDBC connection, and producing a set of detailed HTML reports describing the database. The HTML reports are richly annotated with hyperlinks letting you navigate between parents and children by simply clicking on the appropriate foreign key field. Primary keys, foreign keys, and indexes are visible at a glance.

Figure 30-1 shows a view of a typical SchemaSpy report. Information is categorized under a number of intuitively-titled tabs, such as "Tables," "Relationships," "Utility Tables," and so on. Hyperlinks make it easy to drill down to see details about particular tables.

SchemaSpy displays a wealth of useful information about your database, including:

- A list of all tables and views in the database, displayed appropriately enough in the Tables tab. This view also shows the number of rows in each table, as well as the number of parents and children for each table (see [4] in Figure 30-1).
- A graphical view of the relationships between tables in the database (see Figure 30-2). This view provides a powerful and succinct overview of the database structure, much appreciated by developers. This diagram is generated using Graphviz, and is enriched with HTML map and area tags that allow the user to click directly on a table in order to display the details for that table.
- Detailed information about any constraints present in the database (in the Constraints tab).
- A list of utility tables. Utility tables are tables that have no relation to any other tables. Utilities tables are typically used to store information such as counters. Any

* *http://schemaspy.sourceforge.net/*

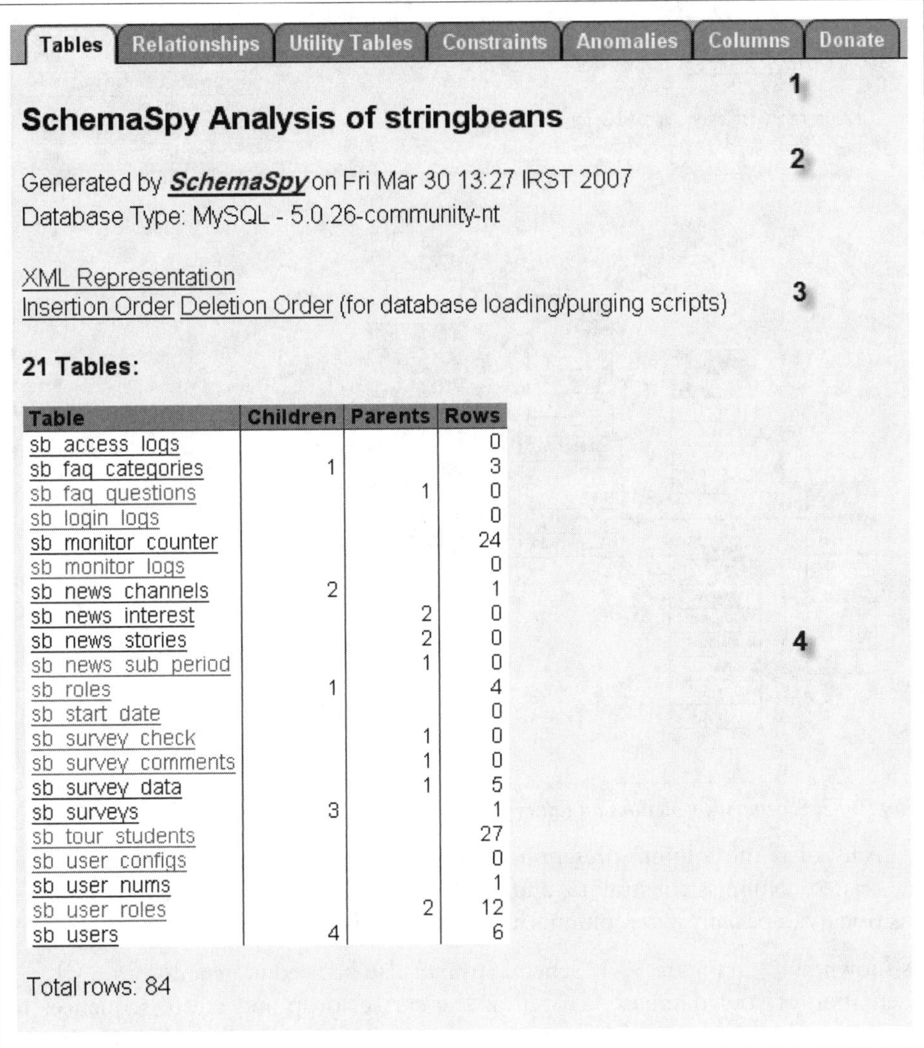

Table	Children	Parents	Rows
sb_access_logs			0
sb_faq_categories	1		3
sb_faq_questions		1	0
sb_login_logs			0
sb_monitor_counter			24
sb_monitor_logs			0
sb_news_channels	2		1
sb_news_interest		2	0
sb_news_stories		2	0
sb_news_sub_period		1	0
sb_roles	1		4
sb_start_date			0
sb_survey_check		1	0
sb_survey_comments		1	0
sb_survey_data		1	5
sb_surveys	3		1
sb_tour_students			27
sb_user_configs			0
sb_user_nums			1
sb_user_roles		2	12
sb_users	4		6

Figure 30-1. SchemaSpy provides a detailed view of your database structure

other tables appearing in this list should be considered suspect, and should be checked for possible missing foreign keys.

- Anomalies that are present in your database. This is another nice feature, where SchemaSpy checks your database for simple structural errors. SchemaSpy can detect several types of anomalies, such as columns that are flagged as both "nullable" and "must be unique," single column tables, tables without indexes, foreign keys that appear to be missing, and so on.

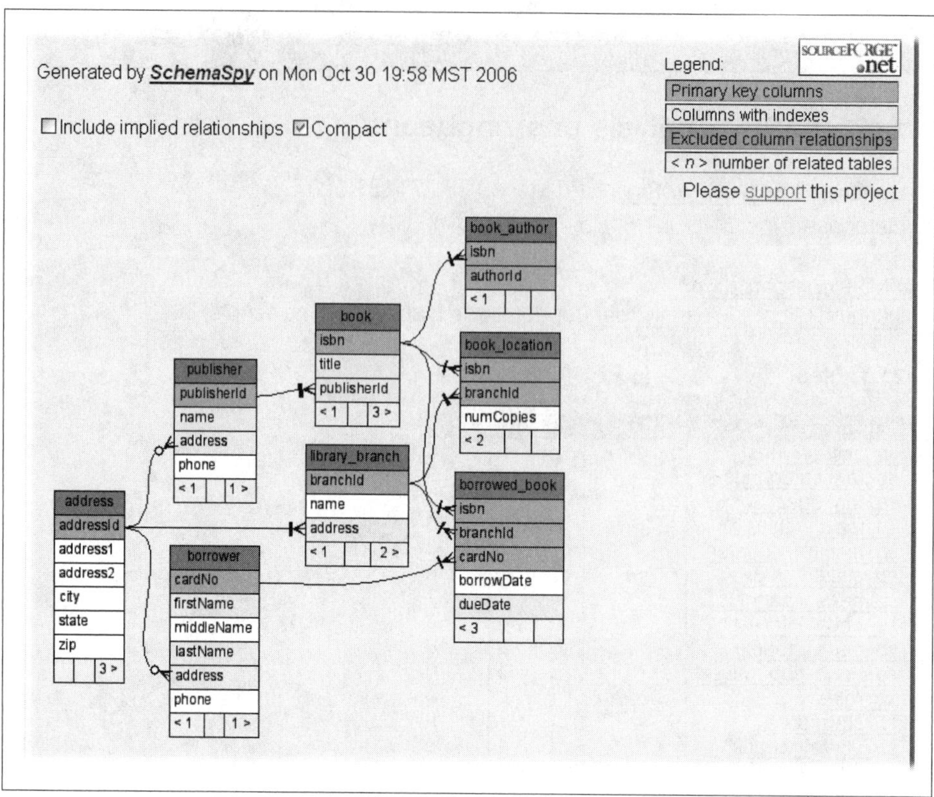

Figure 30-2. SchemaSpy generates an Entity-Relationship model of your database

- A list of all the columns present in the database with detailed information such as related columns, constraints, and comments. This can act as a handy data dictionary, especially if the columns have been commented in the SQL creation script.

As shown in (3) in Figure 30-1, SchemaSpy can also be used to generate an XML representation of your database, as well as the correct drop and create sequences for database tables. Drop and create sequences let you avoid those unresolved constraints during creation and dependency problems when you create or drop tables from the database.

The graphical view illustrated in Figure 30-2 is a great way of getting a global picture of your database structure. If you are interested in a particular table, it is easy to drill down into a table for more details. If you click on a table, either in the tables list or from one of the graphs, SchemaSpy will display detailed information about that table (see Figure 30-3). This view contains information such as:

- Column details—name, type, constraints, default value, related columns with table name, and so on
- Index-related information: index name, type, column(s) name

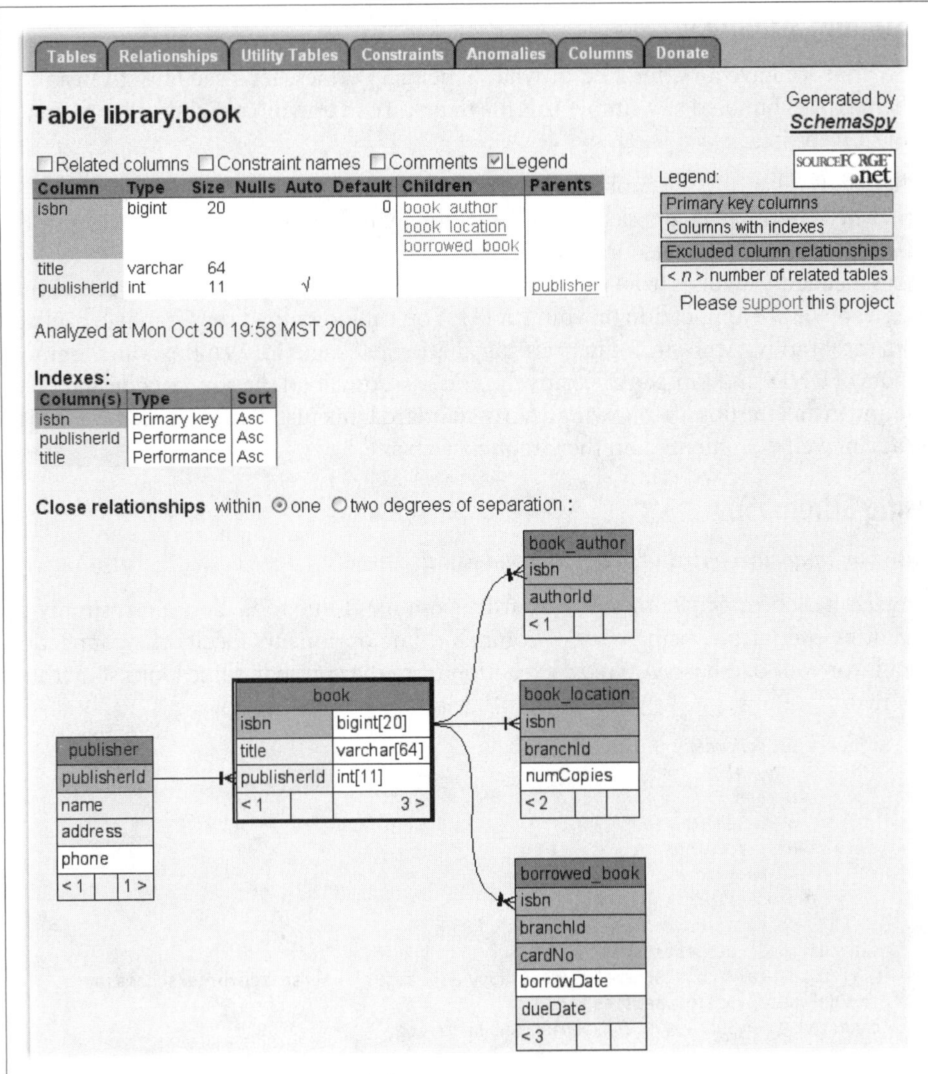

Column	Type	Size	Nulls	Auto	Default	Children	Parents
isbn	bigint	20			0	book_author book_location borrowed_book	
title	varchar	64					
publisherId	int	11	√				publisher

Column(s)	Type	Sort
isbn	Primary key	Asc
publisherId	Performance	Asc
title	Performance	Asc

Figure 30-3. Details about a given table

- A diagram showing relations with other tables

Once again, you can click on any of these tables to drill down to a more detailed view about that specific table. Each table also displays some numbers in the bottom left and right corners. These numbers represent, respectively, how many parent tables a given table is associated with (left corner), and how many children it has (right corner).

Installing SchemaSpy

Now that we have a better idea of what SchemaSpy does, let's see how to install it. SchemaSpy is bundled as a simple JAR file that you can download SchemaSpy from the project web site.*

SchemaSpy relies on the Graphviz library to generate the graphical views of the database structure. Graphviz is a collection of tools for manipulating and generating graphs, based on the *dot* language. Graphviz is not a Java tool but, rather, a native executable that SchemaSpy invokes from the command line. Therefore SchemaSpy expects to find the Graphviz *dot* application on your PATH. You can download the Graphviz package from the Graphviz web site.† There are installation packages for Windows and for most flavors of UNIX and Linux. Alternatively, you can download the source code and compile and install the library following a fairly standard Unix installation procedure, which is, again, well documented on the Graphviz web site.

Using SchemaSpy

Based on material contributed by: Masoud Kalali

By default, SchemaSpy comes as a no-frills, command-line tool. You run it simply by executing the Jar file, using a set of command-line options to specify the connection details for your database. A typical execution from the command line looks something like this:

```
$ java -jar schemaSpy_3.1.1.jar \
        -t mysql \
        -u root \
        -o db-schema-report \
        -host localhost \
        -db bookstore \
        -s bookstore \
        -cp mysql-connector-java-5.0.5.jar \
Using database properties:
    [/usr/local/tools/schemaSpy/schemaSpy_3.1.1.jar]/net/sourceforge/schemaspy
    /dbTypes/mysql.properties
Connected to MySQL - 5.0.24a-Debian_9ubuntu2-log

Gathering schema details.......................................................(0sec)
Writing/graphing summary........(12sec)
Writing/graphing results.......................................................(0sec)
Wrote relationship details of 55 tables/views to directory 'db-schema-report'
in 13 seconds.
Start with db-schema-report/index.html
```

You need to provide the JDBC driver yourself, either on the Java classpath or using the *-cp* option. The other options are described briefly here:

* *http://schemaspy.sourceforge.net/*

† *http://www.graphviz.org/*

-t databaseType
: This parameter lets you specify the database type you are working with. SchemaSpy provides built-in support for most of the major databases, including Oracle ("ora," which is the default value, or "orathin" for the 100% Java type-4 JDBC driver.), mysql, pgsql, db2, and mssql (Microsoft SQL Server). Database configurations are stored in properties files, which can be found in the `schemaSpy.jar` file, under the `net/sourceforge/schemaspy/dbTypes` directory. If your database is not supported, you can copy and adapt one of these properties files, and provide the path to your own customized properties file instead.

-db dbName
: The name of database that SchemaSpy will analyze.

-u user
: A valid database user with at least read access to the target database.

-p password
: The password for this user.

-o outputDirectory
: The generated HTML report will be placed in this directory.

Using SchemaSpy from the command line is a bit unwieldy. In the next two sections, we'll look at how to automate the process with Ant and Maven.

Using SchemaSpy in Ant

A tool like SchemaSpy really begins to excel when you can integrate it into your build process. At the time of writing, SchemaSpy did not come packaged with an Ant task, but it is possible to execute the SchemaSpy JAR file from within Ant using the *<java>* tag. SchemaSpy comes packaged as an executable JAR file, so you need to invoke the *<java>* tag using the *jar* attribute to specify the SchemaSpy JAR file. You also need to provide the JDBC driver using the *-cp* command line option. You provide the command-line options simply by using the *<arg>* parameter. Note that SchemaSpy does accept command-line options using a "property=value" syntax, which saves some space and reduces the number of *<arg>* lines.

This technique is illustrated here:

```
<!-- SchemaSpy property values -->
    <property name="schemaspy.report.dir" value="${build.dir}/schemaspy"/>
    <property name="schemaspy.jdbc.driver" value="${lib}/mysql-connector-
     java-5.0.5.jar"/>
    <property name="schemaspy.database" value="mydatabase" />
    <property name="schemaspy.driverClassName" value="com.mysql
    .jdbc.Driver" />
    <property name="schemaspy.database.host" value="localhost" />
    <property name="schemaspy.username" value="scott" />
    <property name="schemaspy.password" value="tiger" />

    // ...
```

```
<target name="schemaspy">
    <echo>Generating database schemas in ${schemaspy.report.dir}</echo>
    <java jar="${lib}/schemaSpy_3.1.1.jar"
        output="${schemaspy.report.dir}/schemaspy-out.log"
        error="${schemaspy.report.dir}/schemaspy-error.log"
        fork="true">
         <arg line="-t=mysql"/>
         <arg line="-db=${schemaspy.database}"/>
         <arg line="-u=${schemaspy.username}"/>
         <arg line="-p=${schemaspy.password}"/>
         <arg line="-cp=${schemaspy.jdbc.driver}"/>
         <arg line="-host=${schemaspy.database.host}"/>
         <arg line="-o=${schemaspy.report.dir}"/>
    </java>
</target>
```

This will generate the SchemaSpy web pages into the `target/schemaspy` directory.

Using SchemaSpy in Maven

If you are using Maven on your project, there are obvious advantages to incorporating SchemaSpy reports in the automatically generated Maven site. At the time of writing, however, there is no Maven 2 plug-in for SchemaSpy.

Integrating SchemaSpy with Maven is not a simple task. For one thing, SchemaSpy is bundled as an executable tool, not as an API, so you won't find it in any Maven repositories. You need to download and install it yourself (along with Graphvis), and make it available to Maven. In its simplest form, you can get Maven to generate the SchemaSpy reports during Maven site generation by incorporating a slightly adapted version of the Ant script listed above directly within your POM file:

```
</project>
  ...
  <build>
    <!-- SchemaSpy -->
    <plugin>
      <artifactId>maven-antrun-plugin</artifactId>
      <executions>
        <execution>
          <phase>site</phase>
          <configuration>
            <tasks>
              <echo>
                Generating database schemas in ${schemaspy.report.dir}
              </echo>
              <java
                jar="${schemaspy.home}/schemaSpy_${schemaspy.version}.jar"
                output="${schemaspy.report.dir}/schemaspy-out.log"
                error="${schemaspy.report.dir}/schemaspy-error.log"
                fork="true">
                <arg line="-t=mysql" />
                <arg line="-db=${schemaspy.database}" />
                <arg line="-u=${schemaspy.username}" />
```

```
              <arg line="-p=${schemaspy.password}" />
              <arg line="-cp=${schemaspy.jdbc.driver}" />
              <arg line="-host=${schemaspy.database.host}" />
              <arg line="-o=${schemaspy.report.dir}" />
            </java>
          </tasks>
        </configuration>
        <goals>
          <goal>run</goal>
        </goals>
      </execution>
    </executions>
  </plugin>
</plugins>
</build>
<dependencies>
  ...
  <dependency>
    <groupId>mysql</groupId>
    <artifactId>mysql-connector-java</artifactId>
    <version>5.0.5</version>
  </dependency>
  ...
</dependencies>
...
<properties>
  <schemaspy.home>${user.home}/.schemaspy</schemaspy.home>
  <schemaspy.version>3.1.1</schemaspy.version>
  <schemaspy.report.dir>${project.build.directory}/site/schemaspy</schemaspy.
   report.dir>
  <schemaspy.jdbc.driver>
    ${settings.localRepository}/mysql/mysql-connector-java/5.0.5/mysql-connector-
    java-5.0.5.jar
  </schemaspy.jdbc.driver>
  <schemaspy.database>planestore_test</schemaspy.database>
  <schemaspy.driverClassName>com.mysql.jdbc.Driver</schemaspy.driverClassName>
  <schemaspy.username>scott</schemaspy.username>
  <schemaspy.password>tiger</schemaspy.password>
  <schemaspy.database.host>localhost</schemaspy.database.host>
</properties>
</project>
```

We have placed the property values in a *<properties>* block at the end of the POM file. In a real-world application, these properties would probably find themselves placed in profiles (see "Defining Build Profiles" in Section 2.4) and/or in the local user's `settings.xml` file (see Section 2.7).

This will generate the SchemaSpy reports in a subdirectory of the `site` directory called `schemaspy`.

We need to pass a reference to the JDBC library we are using to SchemaSpy via the *-cp* command-line parameter. Because this JDBC library will certainly be listed in the project dependencies, one of the simpler approaches is to use the *${settings.localRepository}* property to refer to the copy of this library in our local repository.

Now we can generate the SchemaSpy report whenever the Maven site is built, we need to display it. Because SchemaSpy does not have a report plug-in, it is not easy to integrate a link to the SchemaSpy pages into the standard Maven report list. The simplest approach is to add a manual link to the page at an appropriate place on your site. (Chapter 29 discussed how to customize your Maven site in more detail.)

30.2 Generating Source Code Documentation with Doxygen

Introduction

Doxygen* is a tool for generating technical documentation from your Java source code written by Dimitri van Heesch. Doxygen is similar to the standard Javadoc tool: both tools analyze Java source code to produce interactive HTML documentation. However, Doxygen goes further than Javadoc: as well as documenting the classes, it also can generate a variety of diagrams, such as class diagrams, collaboration diagrams, and dependency graphs. Doxygen is not limited to Java source code. It also can document C, C++, and C# projects. It also can produce technical documentation in other formats, such as PDF, RTF, or LaTeX.

Another advantage of Doxygen is that it is much less obtrusive than Javadoc, making it easier to document your classes without having to think about formatting issues. For example, Doxygen will automatically recognize references to other classes (no need for *@link* commands), and uses a simple wiki-style notation for formatting, eliminating the need to add HTML code within your comments. This smooths the documentation process and makes for higher-quality, more relevent technical documentation.

The Doxygen Reports

Doxygen generates a rich set of browsable HTML documentation (see Figure 30-4). By way of comparison, Doxygen-generated documentation is similar to but more extensive than documentation generated by Javadoc. In addition to the lists of classes, packages, and files that you would expect, Doxygen can generate UML class diagrams and collaboration diagrams which can provide a better understanding of how the classes work together. Collaboration diagrams are based on structural relations (inheritance and member variables), but they do not include class usage within individual methods.

* *http:// www.doxygen.org*

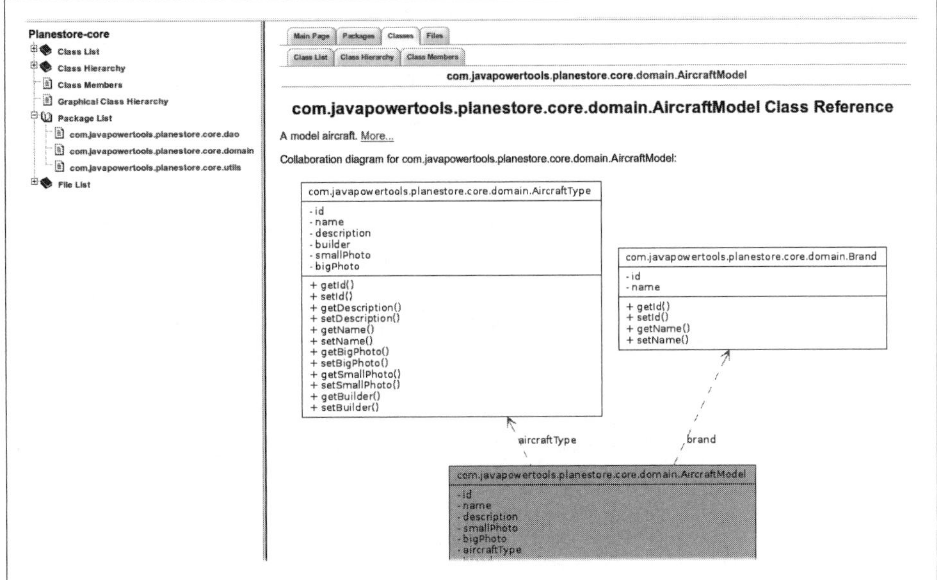

Figure 30-4. View of a class in the Doxygen report

The reports also include annotated and cross-referenced source code in HTML form.

Installing Doxygen

Doxygen is not a Java API: it is a command-line utility that you need to download and install on your machine. There are precompiled binary installations for many Linux platforms such as Red Hat, SuSE, and the Debian family. Otherwise, you will need to download, compile, and install the tool. This fairly straightforward procedure is described here. First, download and unpack the Doxygen source code:

```
$ tar xvfz doxygen-1.5.2.src.tar.gz
```

Next, configure and compile the source code:

```
$ ./configure
$ make
```

Finally, to install, just run the standard "*make install*":

```
# make install
```

If you run into any trouble, the Doxygen web site* has some useful tips for particular installation issues with certain platforms.

On Windows, you can use the packaged Windows installer to install Doxygen very easily.

* *http://www.stack.nl/~dimitri/doxygen/install.html*

Like SchemaSpy (see Section 30.1), Doxygen uses Graphviz to generate its graphs. So you will need to download and install this tool as well to get the best our of Doxygen. This is fairly straightforward and is explained in "Installing SchemaSpy," in Section 30.1.

Configuring Doxygen

Before you can run Doxygen, you need to set up a configuration file, which tells Doxygen what files to analyze and how to format the generated documentation. This configuration file is a simple text file with a Makefile-like format, containing a set of configuration options. You can generate a sample configuration file using the *-g* option, as shown here:

```
$ doxygen -g
```

A simple configuration file, suitable for a Java project, is illustrated here:

```
PROJECT_NAME           = Planestore-core
PROJECT_NUMBER         = 0.1
OUTPUT_DIRECTORY       = P:/projects/planestore-core/planestore-core/target/doxygen
JAVADOC_AUTOBRIEF      = YES
TAB_SIZE               = 4
OPTIMIZE_OUTPUT_JAVA   = YES
INPUT                  = P:/projects/planestore-core/planestore-core/src
RECURSIVE              = YES
HAVE_DOT               = YES
UML_LOOK               = YES
CLASS_GRAPH            = YES
COLLABORATION_GRAPH    = YES
GROUP_GRAPHS           = YES
GRAPHICAL_HIERARCHY    = YES
DIRECTORY_GRAPH        = YES
SHOW_DIRECTORIES       = YES
SOURCE_BROWSER         = YES
STRIP_CODE_COMMENTS    = NO
GENERATE_LATEX         = NO
GENERATE_TREEVIEW      = YES
```

This file is a not-quite-minimal configuration you would need for a Java project. As well as the strict minimum, there are a few useful extras added in along the way. You need the *HAVE_DOT* option to indicate that Graphviz *dot* tool is installed and available: in this case, Doxygen can generate a full range of graphs and diagrams, including class diagrams, collaboration diagrams and call graphs. The *UML_LOOK* option will instruct Doxygen to produce proper UML-style diagrams. The *GENERATE_TREEVIEW* option produces a JavaScript tree structure, which is displayed in a side panel (see Figure 30-4). The *SOURCE_BROWSER* option lets you generate a cross-referenced, browsable, HTML view of your application source code.

All the available configuration options are described in detail in the Doxygen documentation.[*] I will discuss some of the more useful ones later in the chapter.

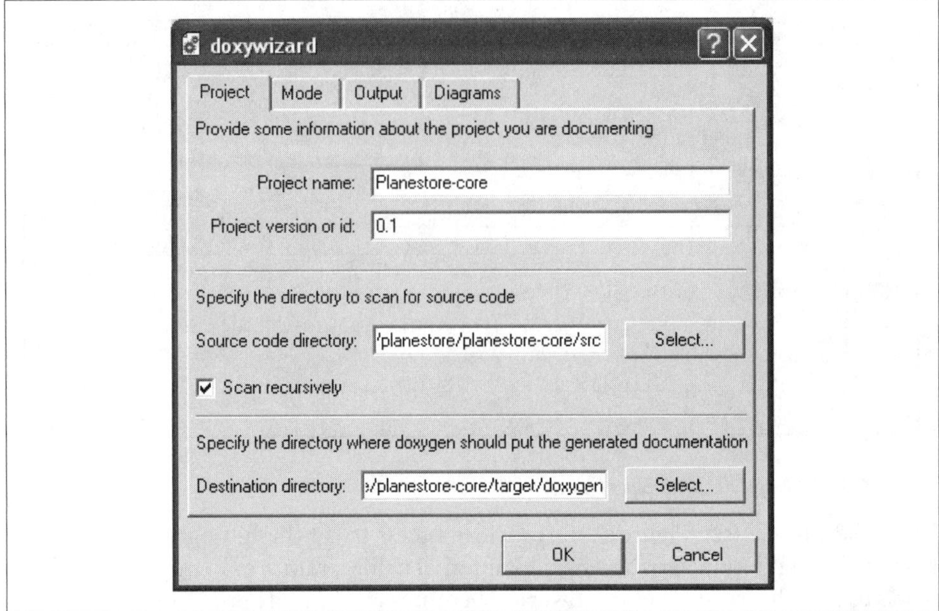

Figure 30-5. The graphical frontend for Doxygen

Rather than configuring this file by hand, you can also use the Doxygen graphical frontend tool, if it has been installed on your machine. (It comes bundled with the Windows installer, but for *NIX installations, you may need to configure and build Doxygen from the source code using the *--with-doxywizard* option.)

The graphical frontend (doxywizard) is useful for learning how to use Doxygen (see Figure 30-5), and is also a good way to obtain an initial Doxygen configuration file, which you may want to tailor afterward. The wizard mode (shown in Figure 30-5) lets you configure Doxygen quickly and intuitively, using just the most important configuration options, and sensible default values.

For a Java project, make sure that you tick the "Scan recursively" option on the Project page, and "Optimize for Java output" on the Mode page. It is also handy to include cross-referenced source code in the generated web site (this option is on the Mode page).

You should also configure the graphs and diagrams you would like to be generated. You do this on the Diagrams tab. By default, only simple class diagrams are generated. However, for the more sophisticated (and useful) diagrams, you need to use the Graphviz command-line tools. Just select the "Use dot tool from the Graphviz package" option, and choose the diagrams you want to produce.

* See *http://www.doxygen.org/config.html*.

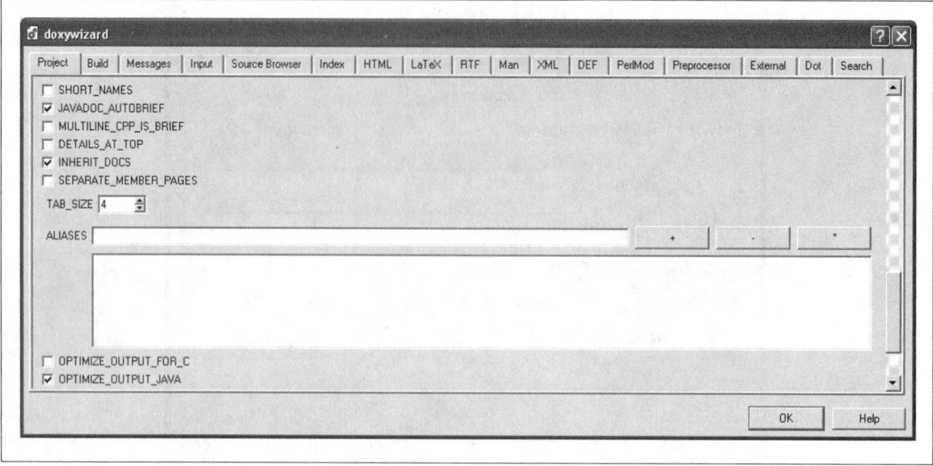

Figure 30-6. The doxywizard expert mode

The expert mode (see Figure 30-6) provides access to all the nitty-gritty details, and refers to configuration variables by their internal names, rather than the more readable labels used in the wizard mode. However, there are some useful options for Java projects which are *not* set by default, and which are only accessible from the Expert mode (or directly from the configuration file, of course). For example, the *JAVA-DOC_AUTOBRIEF* option, which I discuss below, is not set by default. By default, the *TAB_SIZE* option is set to the rather strange value of 6, rather than the more common values of 4 or possibly 8. And, if you want the more familiar UML-style class diagrams, you need to select the UML_LOOK option on the Dot tab.

When you are happy with your configuration file, save it into your project home directory.

Running Doxygen from the Command Line

Running Doxygen from the command line is easy. By default, Doxygen will look for a configuration file called `Doxyfile` in the current directory. If your configuration file is called `Doxyfile`, all you need to do is to run the Doxygen command:

```
$ doxygen
Searching for include files...
Searching for example files...
Searching for images...
Searching for dot files...
Searching for files to exclude
Searching for files to process...
Searching for files in directory P:/projects/planestore-core/planestore-core/src
...
Generating namespace member index...
Generating graph info page...
Generating file index...
```

```
Generating example index...
Generating file member index...
Generating page index...
```

Alternatively, you can provide the configuration file explicitly:

```
$ doxygen src/config/doxyfile.conf
```

This will analyze your project's source code and generate a web site in the designated output directory. Depending on the size of your project, this may take some time.

Using Doxygen with Ant

It is a straightforward task to use Doxygen with Ant. Karthik Kumar maintains an Ant plugin for Doxygen, which you can download from the project web site.* As you would expect, Doxygen and Graphviz need to be installed for this task to work.

Download and extract the binary distribution into an appropriate place on your local machine. Alternatively, you can use a bootstrap script along the following lines for more portability:

```
<project name="DOxygen Bootstrap script" default="bootstrap" basedir="." >

  <!-- Define the environment-specific "doxygen.ant.home" and "doxygen.ant.version"
       variables in this file if required.
    -->
  <property file="${user.home}/ant-global.properties"/>
  <!-- This default value is used if no properties file is present -->
  <property name="doxygen.ant.home" value="${user.home}/.doxygen-ant"/>
  <property name="doxygen.ant.version" value="1.4"/>

  <echo>Installing the DOxygen Ant task into ${doxygen.ant.home}</echo>
  <property name="sourceforge.mirror"
           value="http://optusnet.dl.sourceforge.net/sourceforge/ant-doxygen" />

  <available file="${doxygen.ant.home}/ant_doxygen-bin-${doxygen.ant.version}.tgz"
             property="doxygen.ant.installed"/>

  <echo>Bootstrap DOxygen</echo>
  <target name="bootstrap" unless="doxygen.ant.installed">
    <echo>Installing DOxygen task</echo>
    <mkdir dir="${doxygen.ant.home}" />
    <get src="${sourceforge.mirror}/ant_doxygen-bin-${doxygen.ant.version}.tgz"
         dest="${doxygen.ant.home}/ant_doxygen-bin-${doxygen.ant.version}.tgz"
         usetimestamp="true"/>

    <gunzip src="${doxygen.ant.home}/ant_doxygen-bin-${doxygen.ant.version}.tgz"
            dest="${doxygen.ant.home}/ant_doxygen-bin-${doxygen.ant.version}.tar"/>
    <untar src="${doxygen.ant.home}/ant_doxygen-bin-${doxygen.ant.version}.tar"
           dest="${doxygen.ant.home}/ant_doxygen-bin-${doxygen.ant.version}"/>

    <move todir="${doxygen.ant.home}">
```

* *http://ant-doxygen.sourceforge.net/*

```
        <fileset dir="${doxygen.ant.home}/ant_doxygen-bin-${doxygen.ant.version}">
          <include name="**/*"/>
        </fileset>
    </move>
    <delete dir="${doxygen.ant.home}/ant_doxygen-bin-${doxygen.ant.version}"/>
  </target>

</project>
```

Running Doxygen is now a simple matter: just declare the *doxygen* task using the JAR file we just downloaded, and invoke the task using the *configFilename* attribute to specify the configuration file:

```
<!-- This default value is used if no properties file is present -->
<property name="doxygen.ant.home" value="${user.home}/.doxygen-ant"/>
<property name="doxygen.ant.version" value="1.4"/>
...
<!-- Doxygen -->
<ant antfile="bootstrap-doxygen.xml"  />
<taskdef name="doxygen" classname="org.doxygen.tools.DoxygenTask"
         classpath="${doxygen.ant.home}/lib/ant_doxygen.jar" />

<target name="doxygen">
    <doxygen configFilename="src/config/doxyfile.conf" />
</target>
```

You can also explicitly specify configuration values, which allows more flexibility in the build parameters, as shown here:

```
<target name="doxygen">
    <mkdir dir="build/doxygen" />
    <doxygen>
        <property name="PROJECT_NAME" value="Planestore-core" />
        <property name="PROJECT_NUMBER" value="0.1" />
        <property name="OUTPUT_DIRECTORY" value="target/doxygen" />
        <property name="JAVADOC_AUTOBRIEF" value="YES" />
        <property name="TAB_SIZE" value="4" />
        <property name="OPTIMIZE_OUTPUT_JAVA" value="YES" />
        <property name="INPUT" value="src" />
        <property name="RECURSIVE" value="YES" />
        <property name="HAVE_DOT" value="YES" />
        <property name="UML_LOOK" value="YES" />
        <property name="CLASS_GRAPH" value="YES" />
        <property name="COLLABORATION_GRAPH" value="YES" />
        <property name="GROUP_GRAPHS" value="YES" />
        <property name="GRAPHICAL_HIERARCHY" value="YES" />
        <property name="DIRECTORY_GRAPH" value="YES" />
        <property name="SHOW_DIRECTORIES" value="YES" />
        <property name="SOURCE_BROWSER" value="YES" />
        <property name="STRIP_CODE_COMMENTS" value="NO" />
        <property name="GENERATE_LATEX" value="NO" />
        <property name="GENERATE_TREEVIEW" value="YES" />
    </doxygen>
</target>
```

How to Make Your Java Classes Doxygen-Friendly

Doxygen (and Javadoc, for that matter) will try their best to document your source code in a readable way, but there is always a limit to what a machine can do. Automatically-generated technical documentation of any quality requires a bit of effort when it comes to documenting your code. (Of course, writing well-documented code is a recommended best practice for any programming language, and not just where automatic documentation is to be used.) In this section, we look at a few tips for creating decent documentation when using Doxygen.

Using the brief descriptions

If you set the JAVADOC_AUTOBRIEF option to *true*, Doxygen will use the first sentence of a Javadoc comment as the brief description. The brief description is used in summary tables to give a—well—brief description of a class or method. There are other ways to do this, but this is by far the easiest and the most Java-friendly.

Lists

You can include lists in your documentation in a number of ways. If you are using both Javadoc and Doxygen, you should probably use standard HTML lists. However, if you are only using Doxygen, you can use the more convenient wiki-style lists such as the one shown here:

```
/**
 * This class handles three types of widget orders:
 *   - Orders received online
 *   - Orders received by phone:
 *       - By voice
 *       - By SMS
 *   - Orders received by carrier pigeon.
 */
```

This would generate something along the following lines:

This class handles three types of widget orders:

- Orders received online
- Orders received by phone:
  - — By Voice
  - — By SMS
- Orders received by carrier pigeon.

Links and references

Doxygen handles cross-references between classes particularly well. This means that, when you write your comments, you can add references to other classes with very little effort. Any qualified or unqualified class name that appears in your Javadoc comments will be automatically detected and rendered as a HTML link to the details page for the corresponding class. And you can refer to methods or variables using the "#" notation. Both techniques are shown here:

```
/**
 * A generic DAO interface.
 * All DAO interfaces derive from this one, and all DAO implementation classes
 * implement this interface.
 * A typical example is AircraftModelDAO and AircraftModelDAOImpl.
 * In particular, refer to the AircraftModelDAOImpl#findAll implementation for a
 * good example of how to implement this method.
 */
```

In the generated site, the class names and method name will be rendered as HTML links to the corresponding page. Similarly, any email addresses or URLs included in your documentation will be correctly rendered as HTML links.

You should note that Doxygen does not recognize the Javadoc-style *@link* or *@see* notations.

Documenting packages

Documenting packages is a much-neglected art. A little high-level documentation about your key packages can go a long way in making your application architecture easier to understand and more consistent. Take the time to sit down and write a few architectural notes for your key packages—what does this package do? How does it fit in to the overall application? How should the classes in this package be used? What patterns should be used when writing a new class in this package?

In Javadoc, you can use the "package.html" to do this. Unfortunately, at the time of writing, Doxygen didn't know much about this file, so if you want package-level documentation in your Doxygen reports, you need to do something a little more proprietary. In Doxygen, you can use the "*\package*" or "*@package*" notation, placed within a Java class, to document a package. The simplest approach is to place this block in one of the principal classes of a package, as shown here:

```
package com.javapowertools.planestore.core.dao;
/**
 * @package com.javapowertools.planestore.core.dao
 * Each DAO class provide basic database-related functions for a particular domain
 * object. Each DAO is written as an interface and an implementing class.
 * Implementation classes are derived from the GenericDAOImpl class, and
 * interfaces from the GenericDAO interface. The interface is used by other
 * classes in the application - the implementation class is referenced in the
 * Spring configuration file...
 *
 */

...

/**
 * A generic DAO interface.
 * All DAO interfaces should derive from this one...
```

```
 *
 * @param AnyType the domain object this DAO handles.
 * @param KeyType the type of the primary key of this domain object.
 */
public interface GenericDAO<AnyType, KeyType> {
  ...
}
```

Documenting the home page

You can customize the (by default empty) home page using the "*\homepage*" (or "*@homepage*") tag. You can also use the *@section*, *@subsection*, and *@subsubsection* tags to structure your text:

```
package com.javapowertools.planestore.core.domain;
/**
 * @mainpage The Planestore Core API package
 *
 * @section intro_sec Introduction
 *
 * This web site contains the technical documentation for the Planestore-Core API.
 * This page contains a high-level introduction to the application architecture.
 * etc...
 */
...
```

This block can be placed anywhere, but preferably you should place it in one of the main classes of your application, although, admittedly, this can be hard to find with a web application.

30.3 Embedding UML Diagrams in Your Javadoc with UmlGraph

Source-generated UML diagrams are an excellent way to communicate details of your application architecture and domain model. UML can provides a clear and (usually) readable representation of the state of your code. It can also highlight architectural flaws such as redundant dependencies or overly complex classes.

You can use generated diagrams both to learn about an API and also to verify that an application has been correctly implemented. For example, it is much easier to review and explain a domain model implementation using interactive UML diagrams than by just reading the source code. Typically, a modeling tool might be used to design a clean domain model. Round-trip UML tools are not particularly widespread, however, and in most organisation, most application coding ends up being done directly in the IDE. Generating UML diagrams directly from source code can let you make sure that the implemented classes correspond to the target model.

Diomidis D. Spinellis[*] has written, and maintains, another interesting tool in this domain, called UmlGraph.[‡] This quite brilliant tool lets you insert detailed UML class

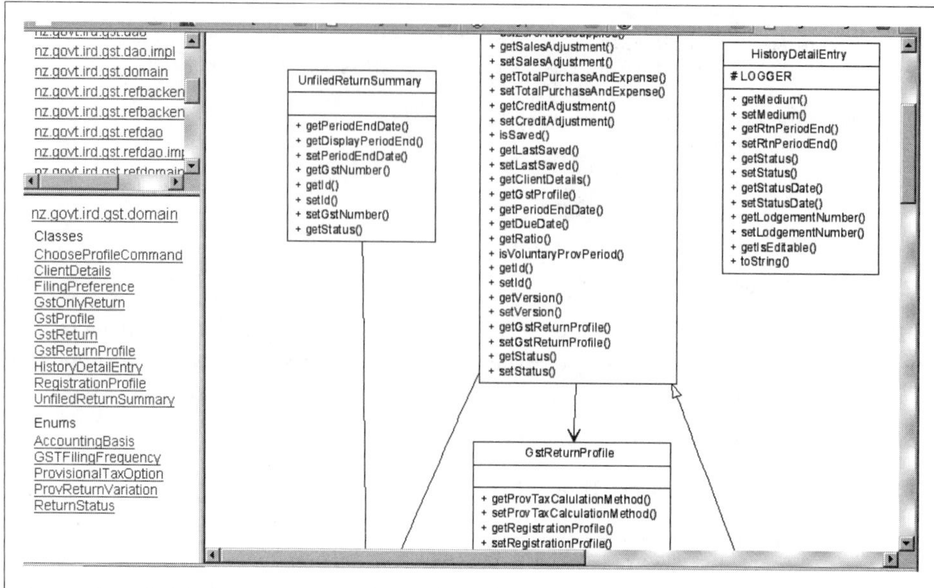

Figure 30-7. Javadoc embedded with UML class diagrams

diagrams seamlessly into your Javadoc. It does not go as far as Doxygen in the documentation that it generates—indeed, this tool is exclusively devoted to generating UML diagrams from your code. However, it does this very well.

Like Doxygen, UmlGraph relies on the Graphvis tool, so this needs to be installed on your system before you can use UmlGraph.

The most convenient way to use UmlGraph is via the UmlGraph doclet. This enables you to integrate UML class diagrams seamlessly in to your Javadoc (see Figure 30-7).

These graphs are interactive, so you can click on a class to go to the Javadoc page (and corresponding UML class diagram) of that class. This provides a clear, intuitive way of navigating though the application architecture.

UmlGraph is a command-line tool, but, in a real-world project, this is not necessarily the most convenient way to generate your graphs. It is far easier to integrate UmlGraph into your build process. To this end, UmlGraph also comes in the much more useful form of a Javadoc doclet, making it easy to integrate into your javadoc generation. This approach works perfectly with Ant and Maven.

UmlGraph is a flexible tool, with a large number of configuration options that you can use to fine-tune the layout of your diagrams. Some of the more interesting options are discussed here:

* *http://www.spinellis.gr/index.html.var*

‡ *http://www.spinellis.gr/sw/umlgraph/*

inferrel
: This option tells UmlGraph to derive relationships between classes from the fields of each class. For example, if a `Client` class has a member variable of type `Account`, UmlGraph will draw a relationship between these two classes in the class diagram. This option is deactivated by default.

inferdep
: Similar to *inferrel*, the *inferdep* option tells UmlGraph to draw any dependencies it can find within the class, based on method and parameter types. This is useful to give a real idea of what classes a particular class uses.

hide
: The hide option can be used to mask out certain classes from your diagrams. For example, you may not want the JDK classes to appear in your class diagrams.

collpackages
: This tells UmlGraph what classes it should consider to be collections. This is mainly used to depict cardinality in relationships.

attributes
: Show class attributes.

operations
: Show class operations.

enumerations
: Show enumerations as separate objects.

enumconstants
: List the constant values for enum types.

link
: You can use this parameter to provide the address of external Javadoc for classes that your application uses. This way, a user will be able to navigate directly to the external Javadoc. This is useful for the Java API itself, and key libraries such as Spring and Hibernate.

Using UmlGraph in Ant

UmlGraph integrates smoothly into Ant, using the *UmlGraphDoc* doclet wrapper. Simply embed a *<doclet>* tag in your *<javadoc>* task, as shown below. You can use the *<param>* tag to specify command-line options. The following configuration will produce a set of fairly complete and detailed UML diagrams embedded into your Javadoc:

```
<target name="javadoc" depends="compile,init" description="Generate JavaDocs.">

    <javadoc sourcepath="${src.dir}" destdir="${reports.javadoc}" access="private"
     classpathref="compile.classpath">
          <doclet name="org.umlgraph.doclet.UmlGraphDoc" path="lib/UmlGraph.jar">
                 <param name="-inferrel"/>
                 <param name="-inferdep"/>
                 <param name="-quiet"/>
```

```
                    <param name="-hide" value="java.*"/>
                    <param name="-collpackages" value="java.util.*"/>
                    <param name="-qualify"/>
                    <param name="-postfixpackage"/>
                    <param name="-nodefontsize" value="9"/>
                    <param name="-nodefontpackagesize" value="7"/>
                    <param name="-attributes"/>
                    <param name="-operations"/>
                    <param name="-enumerations"/>
                    <param name="-enumconstants"/>
                    <param name="-visibility"/>
                    <param name="-link" value="http://java.sun.com/j2se/1.5/docs
                     /api/"/>
                    <param name="-link" value="//static.springframework.org/spring/
                     docs/2.0.x/api/"/>
                    <param name="-link" value="http://www.hibernate.org/hib_docs/
                     v3/api"/>
                </doclet>
            </javadoc>
        </target>
```

Using UmlGraph in Maven

To integrate UmlGraph into Maven, you will need to configure the `maven-javadoc-plugin` in the *<reporting>* section of your POM file. You use the *<additionalparam>* tag to list the numerous UmlGraph options that you need to fine-tune your diagrams:

```
<project...>
    ...
    <reporting>
        <plugins>
            <!-- UML-enabled javadoc -->
            <plugin>
                <artifactId>maven-javadoc-plugin</artifactId>
                <configuration>
                    <source>1.5</source>
                    <doclet>
                        gr.spinellis.umlgraph.doclet.UmlGraphDoc
                    </doclet>
                    <docletArtifact>
                        <groupId>gr.spinellis</groupId>
                        <artifactId>UmlGraph</artifactId>
                        <version>4.4</version>
                    </docletArtifact>
                    <additionalparam>
                        -inferrel -inferdep -quiet -hide java.*
                        -collpackages java.util.* -qualify
                        -postfixpackage -nodefontsize 9
                        -nodefontpackagesize 7 -attributes -operations
                        -enumerations -enumconstants -visibility
                        -link "http://java.sun.com/j2se/1.5/docs/api/"
                        -link "http://static.springframework.org/spring/docs/2.0.x/api/"
                        -link "http://www.hibernate.org/hib_docs/v3/api/"
```

```
                </additionalparam>
            </configuration>
        </plugin>
    </plugins>
</reporting>
...
</project>
```

30.4 Conclusion

Good technical documentation is a valuable asset for any project. Now, *really good* technical documentation can only be produced by a combination of human-written text and automatically generated documentation. Some high-profile open source projects such as Hibernate* and the Spring framework† can be said to have high-quality documentation, combining well-crafted human-written documentation alongside automatically generated API documentation. It would be a mistake to think that the latter can replace the former.

However, for typical enterprise projects, budgetary constraints may not allow for such high-quality documentation, nor is it absolutely essential for all types of projects to have this level of technical documentation. Tools such as SchemaSpy, Doxygen, and UmlGraph—although not producing truly great documentation—can certainly go a long way to producing *adequate* documentation. Combined with good-quality and strategically placed comments, they can still provide valuable insight into the architecture and inner workings of an application, at a relatively small cost.

* *http://www.hibernate.org/5.html*

† *http://www.springframework.org/documentation*

Bibliography

Brown, Paul. *The 2nd most useful Java-Oracle Tool for 2006. http://www.oreillynet.com/onjava/blog/2006/04/the_2nd_most_useful_javaoracle.html*, April 2006.

A short blog entry in which SchemaSpy was named the second most useful Java/Oracle tool in 2006.

Casey John, Vincent Massol, Brett Porter, and Carlos Sanchez. *Better Builds with Maven*. DevZuz, March 2006.

Clark, Mike. *Pragmatic Project Automation*. Pragmatic Programmers, July 2004. 0-9745140-3-9.

Clark, Mike. *Continuous Performance Testing With JUnitPerf. http://www.javapronews.com*, July 2003.

Collins-Sussman Ben, Brian W. Fitzpatrick, and C. Michael Pilato. *Version Control with Subversion*. O'Reilly Media,

Duvall, Paul, Steve Matyas, and Andrew Glover. *Continuous Integration*. Addison-Wesley, June 2007. 0-3213363-8-0.

Edgewall Software. *The Trac Project Website: http://trac.edgewall.org/*.

Goodwin, Katherine and David. *Developing more effectively with Trac*. January, 2006.

Grindstaff, Chris. *FindBugs, Part 1: Improve the quality of your code*. IBM Developer-Works, May 2004.

Grindstaff, Chris. *FindBugs, Part 2: Writing custom detectors*. IBM DeveloperWorks, May 2004.

Glover, Andrew. *In pursuit of code quality: Performance testing with JUnitPerf*. IBM DeveloperWorks, November 2006.

Glover, Andrew. *The Disco Blog*.

Andy Glover's blog on code quality, testing, Groovy, and other related matters.

Holzner, Steven. *Ant: The Definitive Guide, 2nd Edition*. O'Reilly Media, April 2005. 978-0596006099.

Hovemeyer, David and, William Pugh. *Finding Bugs is Easy*. OOPSLA 2004 Companion, December 2004.

Hunt, Andy and Dave Thomas. *Pragmatic Unit Testing in Java with JUnit*. The Pragmatic Programmers, September 2003. 978-0974514017.

Loughran, Steve and Hatcher, Eric. *Ant int Action*. Manning Publications, 2007. 1-932394-80-X.

Mason, Mike. *Pragmatic Version Control: Using Subversion*. The Pragmatic Programmers, May 2006.

Redmond, Eric. *The Maven 2 POM demystified*. Javaworld, May 2006.

Schneider David and Koedderitzsch, Lars (project admins). *The Eclipse Checkstyle plug-in web site: http://eclipse-cs.sourceforge.net/basic_setup_project.html*.

Streicher, Martin. *Eclipse Test and Performance Tools Platform Tutorial (Parts 1, 2 and 3)*. IBM DeveloperWorks, February 2006.

Smart, John. *Test-Driven Development Using StrutsTestCase*. OnJava.com, October 2005.

Smart, John. *Get the most out of Maven site generation*. JavaWorld, February 2006.

Smart, John. *Maintain Better Coding Standards with Ease Using Checkstyle*. DevX, March 2006.

Smart, John. *PMD Squashes Code Bugs*. DevX, April 2006.

Smart, John. *Continuous Integration with Continuum*. Java.net, May 2006.

Smart, John. *Peer Code Reviews Made Easy with Eclipse Plug-In*. DevX, June 2006.

Smart, John. *Mastering Subversion in the Eclipse IDE*. InformIT, July 2006.

Smart, John. *Profiling Your Applications with Eclipse Callisto*. OnJava.com, August 2006.

Smart, John. *Which open source CI tool is best suited for your application's environment?*. JavaWorld, November 2006.

Thomas, Dave, and Andy Hunt. *Pragmatic Version Control Using CVS*. The Pragmatic Programmers, September 2003.

Tsoukalos, Mihalis. *An Introduction to GraphViz*. *Linux Journal*, September 2004.

van Wilgenburg, Jeroen. *Getting started with Cobertura—A Java Code Coverage Tool*. AMIS Technology blog, April 2006.

Zyl, Jason van, John Casey, and Eric Redmond. *Maven: The Definitive Guide*. Sonatype (*http://www.sonatype.com*), to be announced.

Index

We'd like to hear your suggestions for improving our indexes. Send email to *index@oreilly.com*.

B

D

E

F

G

H

I

J

K

L

M

N

O

P

Q

R

S

T

U

V

W

X

About the Author

John Ferguson Smart is a freelance consultant specializing in Enterprise Java, web development, and open source technologies. Renown in the Java community for his many published articles, John helps organizations optimize their Java development processes and infrastructures and provides training and mentoring in open source technologies, SDLC tools, and Agile Development processes. John is principal consultant at Wakaleo Consulting (*http://www.wakaleo.com/*), a company that provides consulting, training, and mentoring services in Enterprise Java and Agile Development. He is currently based in Wellington, New Zealand.

Colophon

The image on the cover of *Java Power Tools* is a drill press, a necessity in any workshop because of its high-precision drilling capabilities. A drill press consists of a base, column (or pillar), table, spindle (or quill), and drill head, which is usually driven by an induction motor. There are several advantages to working with a drill press rather than a handheld drill: less effort is required to apply the drill to the workpiece, and a lever working on a rack and pinion controls the movement of the chuck and spindle, giving the operator a considerable mechanical advantage; the drill can be mounted on a stand or secured to a workbench, making the operation more secure; and the angle of the spindle is fixed in relation to the table, allowing holes to be drilled accurately and repetitively.

The cover image is an original photograph by Frank Deras. The cover font is Adobe ITC Garamond. The text font is Linotype Birka; the heading font is Adobe Myriad Condensed; and the code font is LucasFont's TheSans Mono Condensed.